A CONCORDANCE TO THE COMPLETE WORKS OF ANNE BRADSTREET

A SPECIAL EDITION OF
STUDIES IN PURITAN AMERICAN SPIRITUALITY

Volume 1

Raymond A. Craig

The Edwin Mellen Press
Lewiston•Queenston•Lampeter

Library of Congress Cataloging-in-Publication Data

Craig, Raymond A.
A concordance to the complete works of Anne Bradstreet / Raymond A. Craig.
p. cm.
"Special edition of studies in Puritan American spirituality."
Includes indexes.
ISBN 0-7734-7812-4 (v. 1) -- ISBN 0-7734-7814-0 (v. 2)
1. Bradstreet, Anne, 1612?-1672--Concordances. 2. Christian poetry, American--Puritan authors--Concordances. I. Bradstreet, Anne, 1612?-1672. II. Title.

PS712.A2 C73 2000
811'.1--dc21

99-462312

A CIP catalog record for this book is available from the British Library.

The Edwin Mellen Press
Box 450
Lewiston, New York
USA 14092-0450

The Edwin Mellen Press
Box 67
Queenston, Ontario
CANADA L0S 1L0

The Edwin Mellen Press, Ltd.
Lampeter, Ceredigion, Wales
UNITED KINGDOM SA48 8LT

Printed in the United States of America

A Concordance to the Complete Works of Anne Bradstreet

STUDIES IN PURITAN AMERICAN SPIRITUALITY

ISSN 1048-8553 Special Volume VII ISBN 0-7734-7812-4

Contents

Volume One

Volume Two

Introduction

The Concordance to the Complete Works of Anne Bradstreet is a general-use concordance designed to meet the needs of Bradstreet scholars and students. To that end, the concordance is based on the scholarly edition of Anne Bradstreet's writing, *The Complete Works of Anne Bradstreet,* edited by Joseph R. McElrath Jr. and Allan P. Robb (Twayne, 1981), and on the 1650 *Tenth Muse Lately sprung up in America.* The concordance also includes all word and line variants that appear in the posthumous *Several Poems Compiled with great variety of Wit and Learning* of 1678, and, further, all words are identified by their location in the popular classroom edition, *The Works of Anne Bradstreet,* edited by Jeannine Hensley (Harvard UP, 1967). The concordance features extensive cross-referencing of orthographic variants, treatment of homographs as discrete words, and an index of nonsubstantive words and other words typically excluded from concordances. The intent is to be as accurate and consistent as possible in representing the poet's texts.

The ideal base text for a concordance is one that is both accurate and widely available. Anne Bradstreet's texts are currently available in a number of editions of varying quality, depending on one's view of what constitutes a "reliable" text. The John Harvard Ellis edition, *The Works of Anne Bradstreet in Prose and Verse* (1867), reproduces the first *Several Poems* edition and faithfully retains that text's variations and errors. Still available in an expensive reprint, the Ellis edition does not include line numbers but does reproduce the pagination (in brackets) of the copy texts. *The Tenth Muse* is still available in Josephine K. Piercy's 1965 facsimile edition, which includes the manuscript facsimiles as well. Inexpensive and widely available, Hensley's *The Works of Anne Bradstreet* is *the* classroom edition. This modernized version of *Several Poems* is not absolutely faithful to the copy texts, which is a consequence, perhaps, of the effort to modernize the work. Finally, the McElrath-Robb edition, produced using current editorial principles, is a careful and complete edition with useful scholarly apparatus. The editors used *The Tenth Muse* to avoid changes not introduced by Bradstreet herself, but, unfortunately, this decision also slights Bradstreet's own attempts to "trim" in "better dress" the poems in the second edition. Despite this difficulty, the McElrath-Robb edition is particularly useful because both *The Tenth Muse* and *Several Poems* are represented, the latter in the Apparatus. Soon after publication, however, this edition went out of print and is now available only in libraries (which seem themselves to be "going out of print").

Because an ideal Bradstreet base text does not exist, this concordance is based on hybrid text. The textual matter comes from McElrath-Robb, but this base text is emended by the addition of all *Several Poems* variants identified in the Apparatus. Thus, words and entire lines introduced into *Several Poems* are incorporated into this new, hybrid base text for the concordance. The concordance can serve the needs of those who use the scholarly edition of *The Tenth Muse* and the needs of students and other readers who prefer to use either the Hensley or Ellis *Several Poems* editions.

The typical poetry concordance is keyed to a single base text that has clearly marked line numbers. In this case, however, none of the base texts has a clear numbering scheme. The Hensley edition is the only edition to produce line numbers in the margins of the poems, and these are somewhat unusual. Whenever Bradstreet has provided a title to a poem, the Hensley edition assigns line numbers to the title as if they were lines of poetry (in such cases the first line of poetry is assigned a higher number, say 3 or 4). Whenever the poem title has emerged by convention, the Hensley edition does not assign line numbers to the title lines, and the first line of poetry is designated line 1 ("As Weary Pilgrim," for example, is a shortened first line standing as the title; it has no line number and the first line of poetry is line 1). The McElrath-Robb edition provides no line numbers in the margins of the text, but the Apparatus employs a page-specific line number, a somewhat unusual reference method for poetry. That is, each line of poetry is designated by page number and then a line number that is specific to that page. Line numbering begins with line 1 at the top of the page and begins again with line 1 at the top of the next page. When two poems appear on the same page, the line numbering does not begin again with the first line of the second poem—it is continuous through the end of the first poem, through the title of the second poem, on to the lines of poetry.

To make this concordance useful to users of both editions, the page-specific line numbering scheme of McElrath-Robb is used to create one type of reference code in the concordance, and the Hensley edition's poem-specific line numbering scheme (with its unusual treatment of titles) is used to create another reference code. An alternative might be to use another line numbering system—the traditional designation of the first line of the poetry as line 1 and so on—but to do so is to create another, mythical text and to force all users to renumber their favorite editions of the poetry. The Hensley reference codes can be used to determine approximate key word locations in Ellis, Piercy, and other editions—if users of those editions mark poem line numbers in their own copies.

Combining *The Tenth Muse* text with *Several Poems* variants and using line numbering from both McElrath-Robb and Hensley will make the concordance more useful to a greater number of users. It also makes the reference codes and line numbers within them more complex than usual; as a result, it is important that users take the time to review the User's Guide to become familiar with the reference codes.

Every effort was made to reproduce the base text and variants accurately. The McElrath-Robb edition was keyed into one file and then scanned using a Kurzweil scanner into a second file. These files were compared using PC-Case, a file comparison utility developed by Peter Shillingsburg. Because each method of producing the text produces different types of errors, the file comparison allows one to create a more accurate base text than either method alone. This text was then proofread a number of times against the original texts to produce as accurate a base text as possible. *Several Poems* variants were keyed into the text and proofread separately, and the final base text was proofread again. After concording, each variant spelling was verified against the original texts and the *Oxford English Dictionary* (2nd ed.) to ensure that the variant was not an error introduced to the base text.

Sid Reid allowed this work to be completed within the friendly environs of the Institute for Bibliography and Editing, which he directs. Michael Schuldiner, editor of *Studies in Puritan American Spirituality*, enthusiastically supported and William J. Scheick's readerly suggestions improved this project. Joanna Hildebrand Craig, my wife and friend, has lent her expertise to every page and made this concordance possible. My thanks for her love and support.

User's Guide

Words and Their Arrangement

This concordance indexes words alphabetically as they appear in the McElrath-Robb edition. Various inflected forms of single words are listed as discrete key words (*is* and *are*, forms of *be,* are listed separately), and all variants of the same word, whether produced by inconsistent spelling, punctuation, abbreviation, or contraction, are retained and listed as discrete key words. Hyphenated and unhyphenated word groups are listed as single words, but each element of the word group is cross-referenced (thus *pea cock* and *peacock* are listed together, but cross-references appear at *pea* and *cock*). Rather than deleting "nonsubstantives" and other words of less significance to the general scholar, I have placed these words in the appendix. A list of these conjunctions, prepositions, and pronouns appears at the beginning of the appendix and is then followed by a verbal index, in which the words appear alphabetically with reference codes but without context lines. Additionally, numbers that appear in the poems, excluding stanza numbers and meditation numbers, are also listed with reference codes at the end of the appendix.

Abbreviations typical of seventeenth-century script are alphabetized as they would appear if spelled out (*reme¯brances* appears with *remembrances,* and so on). Numerals designating the section of a poem or a meditation are excluded, such as those preceding every stanza of "Contemplations." No other exclusions were made.

Concordance Entries

Entries in the concordance consist of a key word and its frequency on one line, followed in subsequent lines by reference codes and the context lines (the lines of the poem or prose) in which the key words appear:

> **FOLLOWED (1)**
> TDUDLEY166:30 H72 His pious Footsteps followed by his race,

The key word entry and frequency number may be followed by information that distinguishes homographs or that refers to a related occurrence of the key word. Homographs are words with identical spelling but different meanings (e.g., the verb *will* and the noun *will* are homographs), as demonstrated by their appearance as distinct catch words in *The Oxford English Dictionary* (2nd ed.). In this concordance homographs are distinguished by an abbreviation indicating function: *adj.* for adjectives, *adv.* for adverbs, *n.* for nouns, and *v.* for verbs. When this distinction is insufficient, a synonym or other explanation appears in brackets.

BEHOLDING (2) [seeing]
DIALOG147:32 H256 That dazzled eyes beholding much shall wonder
MEDDM207:35 Hp289 by beholding their bed, the morning may mind them

Also in brackets, *pl.* and *poss.* distinguish plural nouns and possessive adjectives. In the case of orthographic variants, a bracketed clarifying reference word is properly inflected for the plural, possessive, and plural possessive key words (see *dayes*, possessive adjective, and *dayes*, plural possessive adjective, below). These distinctions are necessary due to the inconsistent use of the apostrophe in both seventeenth-century print editions of the poems and in the manuscripts. Unusual contractions and elisions are clarified by full forms within brackets; these should be treated as cross-references to the uncontracted or unelided forms.

DAYES (1) [day's]
MPERS89:10 H1444 Of this dayes cowardize, he feares the effects;
DAYES (1) [days']
MGREC107:36 H2211 On these, together ty'd, in six dayes space,
DAYLY (4) [daily]
ELEMEN~~9:18~~ H52 Your dainty {dayly} food, I wholsome make, I warme
DAY'S [poss.] See **DAYES**
DAYS (1) [pl.]
MPERS83:38 H1226 Where ninescore days, are spent in banquetting,

Reference Codes

Reference codes consist of three parts: a poem's or prose document's abbreviated title; a page:line number code referring to the McElrath-Robb edition; and an H:line number code referring to the Hensley edition. In this example, "Contemp" denotes the poem "Contemplations"; "168:27" indicates page 168, line 27 of McElrath-Robb; and "H34" indicates poem line 34 of "Contemplations" in the Hensley edition:

ANIMALS (1) [pl.]
CONTEM168:27 H34 Birds, insects, Animals with Vegative,

When using the McElrath-Robb edition, the user needs only page and line numbers to locate any key word within a passage. With the first reference code above, 168:27, the user turns to page 168 of McElrath-Robb and locates line 27. When using the Hensley (and any other edition), the user locates the poem with the title abbreviation CONTEM for "Comtemplations," and then locates the line by the poem line number. For prose passages, a page number, Hp259, or page 259, refers to the page in Hensley on which the key word appears. Lineation of the prose passages, of course, varies by edition and does not lend itself to concise referencing, except in the McElrath-Robb edition, for which the page:line number code still applies. The Key to Reference Codes, which follows this User's Guide, contains an alphabetized list of codes (abbreviations for poem titles) keyed to the full poem title and the initial page numbers for each poem in each edition. It also contains a second listing in which codes appear in the order in which the poems appear in McElrath-Robb and the order in which reference codes appear within individual key word entries in the concordance.

Cross-References

Retaining the variant spellings of the base texts makes cross-references a necessary feature. Cross-references direct the concordance user to the most common spelling of the key word (using the *Oxford English Dictionary*, 2nd ed.), to all variant spellings of the same word, and to hyphenated and unhyphenated word groups. At the variant, the most common spelling appears within brackets, directing the user to that location and clarifying the word or word form. At the most common spelling, "See" or "See also" appears after the frequency number. Cross-references only appear when two referenced key words are separated by one or more unrelated key words:

ASHAM'D (1) [ashamed]
MPERS78:8 H989 For truth's asham'd how many to expresse;
ASHAME (1)
MGREC115:12 H2521 This act (me thinks) his god-head should ashame;
ASHAMED (1) See also ASHAM'D
MEDDM208:26 Hp290 them, return with their empty pitchers ashamed,

When the most common spelling does not occur in the base texts, that word is placed in the concordance as a key word followed by cross-references to the variant spellings. The common-spelling key word is not inserted in the concordance if that key word and the variant(s) appear in the same location in the concordance.

Context Lines

The context is the line of poetry or prose in which the key word appears. The context line is reproduced as it appears in the McElrath-Robb edition of *The Tenth Muse. Several Poems* variants are also represented in two ways in the context lines. When a word or phrase has been changed, the new word or phrase is inserted, in braces, within the *Tenth Muse* context line immediately after the revised word or phrase. When a *Several Poems* variant is the key word in a line, the line number in the McElrath-Robb reference code appears with a strikeout line indicating that it is a variant not appearing in *The Tenth Muse*. In the first line below, *Arms* is a variant introduced in the later edition and does not appear in page 91, line 4:

MPERS~~91:4~~ H1512 With suit, their force, {Arms} against his {their} foes
MGREC~~131:1~~ H3190 With Arms and with provision stores them well,

When the *Several Poems* variant is an entire line, the McElrath-Robb reference code is struck out and no braces appear in the context line. In the example above, line 3190 in the Hensley edition is a line added to *Several Poems* that does not appear in *The Tenth Muse*. Likewise, when a line appears in *Tenth Muse* but was deleted from *Several Poems*, the Hensley reference code is struck out, but the code is there so that one can determine the approximate location of that change in the *Several Poems* version of the text:

MGREC101:34 ~~H1959~~ Both Armies meet, *Greeks* fight, the *Persians* run,

This is a more complex notation system than is found in the typical concordance. With some initial attention, however, the user will be able to decipher the reference codes, strikeouts and braces. Including variants also lengthens lines; excessively long context lines are shortened by editing the beginning or end of the line farthest from the location of the keyword. Prose lines are most frequently edited in this manner.

Key to Reference Codes

Title Code, Title, Page in McElrath-Robb (MR), Page in Hensley (H)
Codes are listed in alphanumeric order

Code	Title	MR	H
1HUSB	To my Dear and loving Husband	180	225
1LETTER	A Letter to her Husband	181	226
1SIMON	On . . . Simon Bradstreet	188	237
2LETTER	Another	181	227
2SIMON	For my deare Sonne Simon Bradstreet	195	271
2HUSB	Vpon my dear & loving husband	232	265
3LETTER	Another	182	229
11MAYA	May 11, 1657	226	256
11MAYB	May 11, 1661	228	259
13MAY	May 13, 1657	227	257
28AUG	August 28, 1656	225	254
30SEPT	September 30, 1657	227	257
ACK	In thankfull acknowledgmt	235	269
AGES	The Four Ages of Man	35	51
ANNEB	In memory of . . . Anne Bradstreet	187	236
AUTHOR	The Author to Her Book	177	221
BIRTH	Before the Birth of One of Her Children	179	224
BYNIGHT	By Night When Others Soundly Slept	220	247
CHILDRN	In reference to her Children	184	232
CONTEM	CONTEMPLATIONS	167	204
DAVID	Davids Lamentation for Saul and Jonathan	158	199
DDUDLEY	An EPITAPH on . . . Mrs. Dorothy Dudley	167	204
DIALOG	A Dialogue between Old England and New	141	179
DISTEMP	Vpon some distemper of body	179	223
DUBART	In honour of Du Bartas	152	192
ELEMEN	The Foure Elements	8	18
ELIZB	In memory of . . . Elizabeth Bradstreet	186	235
FAINTING	Delive[rc] from a fitt of Fainting	222	249
FATHER	To her most Honoured Father	5	13
FEVER	For Delive[rc] from a feaver	220	249
FLESH	The Flesh and the Spirit	175	215
HANNA	Vpon my Daughter Hanna Wiggin	230	263
HOURS	In my Solitary Houres	235	269

Code	Title	MR	H
HOUSE	[Upon the Burning of Our House]	236	292
HUMOUR	Of the foure humours in Mans constitution	20	33
JULY	July 8, 1656	223	251
MASSYR	The Assyrian being the first	53	73
MED	Meditations	223	250
MEDDM	Meditations Diuine and morall	195	272
MERCY	To the memory of . . . Mrs. Mercy Bradstreet	188	238
MGREC	The Third Monarchy, was the Grecian	93	121
MPERS	The Second Monarchy, being the Persian	68	92
MROMAN	The Roman Monarchy, being the Fourth	136	174
MYCHILD	My Dear Children	215	240
MYSOUL	My soul, rejoice thou in thy God	224	253
PILGRIM	[As weary pilgrim]	210	294
PROLOG	The Prologue	6	15
QELIZ	In honour of . . . Queen Elizabeth	155	195
REMB	In thankful Remb^{rc}	235	270
RESTOR	For the restoration of my dear Husband	229	261
SAMUEL	Vpon My Son Samuel	228	259
SEASONS	The Four Seasons of the Yeare	46	65
SICKNES	Upon a Fit of Sickness	178	222
SIDNEY	An Elegie upon . . . Sir Philip Sidney	149	189
SON	On my Sons Return	230	263
SOREFIT	From another sore fitt. etc.	221	248
TDUDLEY	To the Memory of Thomas Dudley Esq.	165	201
THEART	My thankfull heart wth glorying tongve	228	259
TOCHILD	To My Dear Children	215	240
VANITY	Of the vanity of all worldly creatures	159	219
VERSES	To Her Father with some verses	183	231
WHAT	What God is like to him I serve?	224	251

Title Code, Title, Page in McElrath-Robb (MR), Page in Hensley (H)
Codes are listed in the order poems appear in McElrath-Robb

Code	Title	MR	H
	The Tenth Muse		
FATHER	To her most Honoured Father	5	13
PROLOG	The Prologue	6	15
ELEMEN	The Foure Elements	8	18
HUMOUR	Of the foure humours in Mans constitution	20	33
AGES	The Four Ages of Man	35	51
SEASONS	The Four Seasons of the Yeare	46	65

Code	Title	MR	H
	The Foure Monarchies		
MASSYR	The Assyrian being the first	53	73
MPERS	The Second Monarchy, being the Persian	68	92
MGREC	The Third Monarchy, was the Grecian	93	121
MROMAN	The Roman Monarchy, being the Fourth	136	174
DIALOG	A Dialogue between Old England and New	141	179
SIDNEY	An Elegie upon . . . Sir Philip Sidney	149	189
DUBART	In honour of Du Bartas	152	192
QELIZ	In honour of . . . Queen Elizabeth	155	195
DAVID	Davids Lamentation for Saul and Jonathan	158	199
VANITY	Of the vanity of all worldly creatures	159	219
Several Poems			
TDUDLEY	To the Memory of Thomas Dudley Esq.	165	201
DDUDLEY	An EPITAPH on . . . Mrs. Dorothy Dudley	167	204
CONTEM	CONTEMPLATIONS	167	204
FLESH	The Flesh and the Spirit	175	215
AUTHOR	The Author to Her Book	177	221
SICKNES	Upon a Fit of Sickness	178	222
DISTEMP	Vpon some distemper of body	179	223
BIRTH	Before the Birth of One of Her Children	179	224
1HUSB	To my Dear and loving Husband	180	225
1LETTER	A Letter to her Husband	181	226
2LETTER	Another	181	227
3LETTER	Another	182	229
VERSES	To Her Father with some verses	183	231
CHILDRN	In reference to her Children	184	232
ELIZB	In memory of . . . Elizabeth Bradstreet	186	235
ANNEB	In memory of . . . Anne Bradstreet	187	236
1SIMON	On . . . Simon Bradstreet	188	237
MERCY	To the memory of . . . Mrs. Mercy Bradstreet	188	238
Manuscripts/Anne's Hand			
2SIMON	For my deare Sonne Simon Bradstreet	195	271
MEDDM	Meditations Diuine and morall	195	272
PILGRIM	[As weary pilgrim]	210	294
Andover Manuscripts/Simon's Hand			
TOCHILD	To My Dear Children	215	240
MYCHILD	My Dear Children	215	240
BYNIGHT	By Night When Others Soundly Slept	220	247
FEVER	For Delive^{rc} from a feaver	220	249
SOREFIT	From another sore fitt. etc.	221	248
FAINTING	Delive^{rc} from a fitt of Fainting	222	249
MED	Meditations	223	250
JULY	July 8, 1656	223	251
WHAT	What God is like to him I serve?	224	251

Code	Title	MR	H
MYSOUL	My soul, rejoice thou in thy God	224	253
28AUG	August 28, 1656	225	254
11MAYA	May 11, 1657	226	256
13MAY	May 13, 1657	227	257
30SEPT	September 30, 1657	227	257
SAMUEL	Vpon My Son Samuel	228	259
11MAYB	May 11, 1661	228	259
THEART	My thankfull heart wth glorying tongve	228	259
RESTOR	For the restoration of my dear Husband	229	261
HANNA	Vpon my Daughter Hanna Wiggin	230	263
SON	On my Sons Return	230	263
2HUSB	Vpon my dear & loving husband	232	265
HOURS	In my Solitary Houres	235	269
ACK	In thankfull acknowledgmt	235	269
REMB	In thankful Remb^{rc}	235	270
HOUSE	[Upon the Burning of Our House]	236	292

A CONCORDANCE TO THE COMPLETE WORKS OF ANNE BRADSTREET

VOLUME 1

A

A (15) [Anne]
PROLOG8:3 ~~H50~~ *A. B.*
SEASONS53:10 ~~H264~~ *A. B.*
SIDNEY149:6 ~~H5~~ By *A. B.* in the yeare, 1638.
DUBART152:32 H1 A. B.
BIRTH180:21 H31 *A. B.*
1LETTER181:29 H27 *A. B.*
3LETTER183:33 H35 *A. B.*
VERSES184:12 H16 *A.B.*
CHILDRN186:30 H97 *A. B.*
1SIMON188:16 H17 *A. B.*
MERCY189:17 H38 A. B.
2SIMON195:18 Hp271 mother A B
TOCHILD215:8 H8 A. B.
30SEPT227:33 Hp257 This is the desire of y^{r} Loving mother. A. B.
HOUSE~~237:28~~ H59 A. B.

ABANDONED (1)
MPERS87:20 ~~H1374~~ Ran back, and quite abandoned the same,

ABASE (1)
MEDDM197:23 Hp275 nothing will abase them more, then this What hast thou,

ABASED (1)
MGREC~~110:18~~ H2320 In looks or gesture not abased ought,

ABATE (4)
ELEMEN8:20 H18 Soone made the combatants abate their force;
HUMOUR30:3 H395 What is too hot, my coldnesse doth abate;
MASSYR58:30 H213 *Arbaces* courage he did sore {so} abate:
MPERS91:21 H1529 The two Queens, by his means, 'gin {seem} to abate

ABATED (2)
ELEMEN8:23 H21 But {Till gentle} Aire at length, contention so abated,
MEDDM201:12 Hp280 Fire hath its force abated by water not by wind,

ABATETH (1)
SEASONS50:12 H146 For yet {For much,} the South-ward Sun abateth not;

ABEL (2)
CONTEM170:14 H86 Here *Cain* and *Abel* come to sacrifice,
CONTEM170:22 H93 There *Abel* keeps his sheep, no ill he thinks,

ABELS (1) [poss.]
CONTEM170:16 H88 On *Abels* gift the fire descends from Skies,

ABHOR (1) See also ABHORRE
MASSYR58:27 H210 And though of wars, he did abhor the sight;

ABHOR'D (1) [abhorred]
SOREFIT221:18 H4 And when my Soul these things abhor'd

ABHORRE (1) [abhor]
HUMOUR25:2 H191 Yet do abhorre, such timerarious deeds,
ABIDE (21) See also **'BIDE, BIDE**
HUMOUR33:36 H550 The faculty of speech doth here abide,
MASSYR56:9 H115 That like a river, long it did abide.
MPERS90:17 ~~H1484~~ For these incursions he durst not abide;
MGREC95:20 H1699 For in that Peer, more valour did abide;
MGREC98:37 H1839 First, at *Euphrates,* what he's like to abide,
MGREC99:2 H1845 All those rich Kingdoms large, which {that} doe abide
MGREC99:18 H1861 For more repulse, the *Grecians* here abide,
MGREC101:24 H1949 Two Monarchies on Earth cannot abide,
MGREC110:8 H2308 Did here, and there, Isles full of trees abide;
MGREC110:38 H2342 Two Cities built, his fame {name} might there abide;
MGREC111:21 H2366 Upon those Flats they did not long abide;
MGREC117:20 H2627 His matchlesse force no Creature could abide;
MGREC121:35 H2817 But he alone now {most} faithfull did abide:
MGREC~~124:16~~ H2923 Firm (for his Fathers sake) to him abide.
MGREC124:20 H2927 But to the last {all in vain} he faithfull did abide;
MROMAN137:7 H3458 And this new gentle Government abide:
DIALOG146:10 H198 One battell, two or three I might abide,
CONTEM167:34 H10 If so much excellence abide below;
2LETTER182:7 H13 And if he love, how can he there abide?
MEDDM206:36 Hp288 they abide not in vnbeleif, god is able to grafte them in,
HOUSE237:12 H42 And did thy wealth on earth abide,
ABIDES (2)
MGREC104:24 H2076 Who wanting means t' resist, these wrongs abides.
MGREC124:16 ~~H2923~~ Firme to *Cassander* at this time abides:
ABIDUS (1)
MPERS79:18 H1044 And {Then} in *Abidus* Plaines, mustring his Forces,
ABILITIE (1) [ability]
MROMAN139:5 H3533 As wealth had made them of abilitie;
ABILITIES (3) [pl.] See also **ABILITYS**
MGREC112:7 H2393 It far exceeds my meane abilities,
MEDDM196:3 Hp272 that man whose head hath great abilities and his heart little
MEDDM197:15 Hp274 so a man of weak faith and mean abilities, may vndergo
ABILITY (2) See also **ABILITIE**
MGREC123:29 H2893 This *Polisperchons* great ability,
11MAYA226:15 Hp255 & some ability to p^{r}form ye Dutyes I owe to him, and the work
ABILITYS (1) [abilities]
MEDDM197:22 Hp275 Few men are so humble, as not to be proud of their abilitys,
ABJECT (2)
AGES44:27 H360 Sometime an abject, then again in place,
CONTEM169:22 H62 Shall Creatures abject, thus their voices raise?
ABLE (12)
PROLOG7:4 H19 And this to mend, alas, no Art is able,
MPERS80:16 H1083 {The Harbours} to receive, {contain} the Harbour was not able;
MPERS80:29 H1096 They no way able to withstand his force,
DUBART155:7 H92 *To rescue him from death, Art had been able:*
MEDDM196:33 Hp274 wch thousands of enemys wthout hath not been able to take
MEDDM198:32 Hp277 pleasant thing to behold the light, but sore eyes are not able to
MEDDM206:36 Hp288 they abide not in vnbeleif, god is able to grafte them in,

MEDDM208:35 Hp290 them as if Moses had been able by the hand of faith,
MYCHILD215:14 Hp240 I was able to compose some short matters, (for w^{t} else to call
MYCHILD219:2 Hp245 and y^{t} he is able to keep y^{t} I haue comitted to his charge.
MED223:16 Hp250 what he hath done for me, and then shall I bee able to praise
28AUG226:6 Hp254 gravnt y^{t} while I live I may doe y^{t} service I am able in this frail

ABODE (2)
MEDDM203:15 Hp283 must beware of desireing to make this the place of his abode,
HOURS233:28 H11 And thy Abode tho'st made wth me

ABOMINATION (1)
MGREC134:7 ~~H3339~~ By him was set up the abomination

ABOUE (2) [above]
MEDDM203:18 Hp283 may plainly declare that we seek a citty aboue and wait
MEDDM209:4 Hp291 all our seekings and gettings, let vs aboue all seek to obtain

ABOUND (5)
MGREC102:20 H1990 This City did abundantly abound;
MGREC103:5 H2016 None like to this in riches did abound.
DIALOG147:8 H234 And for my self, let miseries abound,
DUBART153:9 H13 Had caused flowers, and fruits, soone to abound;
QELIZ156:21 H48 Did ever wealth in *England* so {more} abound?

ABOUNDANT (1) [abundant] See also ABVNDANT
ELEMEN16:39 H362 And with aboundant wet, so coole the ground,

ABOUNDANTLY (1) [abundantly]
ELEMEN17:40 H404 Aboundantly more then my sisters three?

ABOUT (20) See also 'BOUT
AGES36:11 H35 Then prauncing on the Stage, about he wheels;
AGES36:24 H48 This {Thus} writ about: *This out, then I am done.*
SEASONS47:17 H33 Like Birds, now chirp, and hop about the field;
MASSYR54:20 H47 Four hundred forty Furlongs, wall'd about,
MASSYR56:8 H114 About the wall, a ditch so deep and wide,
MPERS68:36 H622 with him about two years.
MPERS70:6 H677 Now trebble wall'd, and moated so about,
MPERS80:1 H1068 How part, {some} might o're the Mountains goe about,
MPERS81:31 H1139 To adde unto his numbers, layes about,
MPERS87:27 H1379 The mazed King, was now {then} about to fly;
MPERS88:23 H1416 They {ready} were about to leave their King and fly,
MGREC100:31 H1915 About this time, *Darius* beauteous Queen,
MGREC120:3 H2734 Now dy'd (about the end of th' *Lamian* warre)
MGREC125:35 H2985 And throwes {threw} his bones about, to shew her spight.
MGREC~~132:20~~ H3259 With these he hopes to turn the world about:
MEDDM201:20 Hp280 from a thick ayre about them so may we sometime se,
MYCHILD215:24 Hp240 In my yovng years about 6. or 7. as I take it I began to make
MYCHILD216:1 Hp241 But as I grew vp to bee about 14. or 15. I fovnd my heart more
MYCHILD216:3 Hp241 About 16. The Lord layd his hand sore vpon me & smott me
RESTOR229:24 H7 Thou comforts me about.

ABOVE (24) See also ABOUE
ELEMEN14:32 H274 But thou art bound to me, above the rest;
ELEMEN14:37 H279 With springs below, and showers from above;
AGES39:29 H172 {elevate} my {high} thoughts above {beyond} the Pole.
SEASONS48:35 H86 Yet above all, this priviledge is thine,
MASSYR~~56:16~~ H122 Whose stately top, beyond {above} the clouds did rise;
MASSYR56:37 H143 Leaving the world, to *Venus,* soar'd above,

MASSYR66:32 ~~H538~~ For by the Heavens above it was decreed:
MASSYR67:37 H583 But he above, his doings did deride,
MGREC105:12 H2105 Yea, {But} above all, that neither eare, nor eye,
MGREC106:30 H2164 His fancied gods, above the firmament,
MGREC130:7 H3162 Choise above all, of *Ptolomy* she makes
DIALOG142:27 H56 Whence is this {the} storme, from Earth, or Heaven above?
SIDNEY151:18 ~~H69~~ Yet this preheminence thou hast above,
TDUDLEY166:1 H43 For truly his ambition lay above.
TDUDLEY166:13 H55 For he a Mansion had, prepar'd above,
CONTEM174:27 H225 Only above is found all with security.
FLESH176:8 H48 But my arise is from above,
FLESH176:21 H61 For my ambition lyes above.
CHILDRN185:6 H32 That he might chant above the rest,
MERCY189:5 H26 A Babe she left before, she soar'd above,
TOCHILD215:7 H7 And God shall blesse yov from above.
BYNIGHT220:9 H9 He bow'd his ear down from Above
HOUSE237:15 H45 Raise vp thy thovghts above the skye
HOUSE237:28 H58 My hope, and Treasure lyes Above.

ABRAHAMS (1) [poss.]
DIALOG148:21 H286 Oh *Abrahams* seed lift up your heads on high.

ABRAM (1)
MASSYR57:15 H162 'Gainst whom his trained Bands *Abram* did bring.

ABREST (1)
MASSYR54:23 H50 So broad, three Chariots run abrest there might,

ABROAD (3)
AGES38:39 H142 At home, abroad, my danger's manifold.
AUTHOR177:33 H5 Who thee abroad, expos'd to publick view,
3LETTER183:32 H34 *At home, abroad, and every where.*

ABROCOMES (1)
MPERS87:21 ~~H1374~~ *Abrocomes*, was this base cowards name,

ABRUPTEST (1)
2LETTER182:32 H38 Oppressed minds, abruptest tales do tell.

ABSENCE (8)
HUMOUR22:37 H106 My absence proves, it plain, her wit then flyes
MGREC94:7 H1641 That no combustion {rebellion in} in his absence be,
MGREC~~124:9~~ H2914 But in his absence *Polisperchon* takes
MGREC~~132:20~~ H3261 In his long absence to rule *Macedon.*
CONTEM168:35 H41 Thy presence makes it day, thy absence night,
3LETTER183:9 H11 The absence of her Love, and loving Mate,
MYCHILD217:31 Hp243 absence and presence of God y^{t} makes Heaven or Hell.
HOURS233:19 H1-2 In my Solitary houres in my dear husband his Absence.

ABSENT (5)
MGREC112:33 H2419 Enveighs against his Father, now absent,
MGREC124:9 ~~H2914~~ Those absent, banished, or else he slew
BIRTH180:18 H28 With some sad sighs honour my absent Herse;
1LETTER181:1 H0 *A Letter to her Husband, absent upon*
JULY223:24 Hp251 my God who never failed me, was not absent but helped me,

ABSENTS (1)
DIALOG145:38 H187 The King displeas'd, at *York* himself absents,

ABSOLUES (1) [absolves]
MEDDM205:15 Hp286 the evidence, so he absolues or condemnes, yea so Absolute

ABSOLUTE (1)
MEDDM205:15 Hp286 the evidence, so he absolues or condemnes, yea so Absolute
ABSOLVES See ABSOLUES
ABUNDANCE (1)
MYCHILD217:5 Hp242 abundance of Sweetnes and refreshment after affliction
ABUNDANT See ABOUNDANT, ABVNDANT
ABUNDANTLY (2) See also ABOUNDANTLY
SEASONS50:26 H160 His fruitful crop, abundantly requites.
MGREC102:20 H1990 This City did abundantly abound;
ABUS'D (1) [abused]
AGES39:36 H179 My gifts abus'd, my education lost,
ABUSED (2)
SEASONS51:4 H178 For nought's so good, but it may be abused,
MEDDM207:4 Hp288 that god, bestows on the sons of men, are not only abused
ABUSES (1)
MGREC104:40 H2092 Whom thus the execrable wretch abuses:
ABVNDANT (1) [abundant] See also ABOUNDANT
30SEPT227:20 Hp257 thankfully to submitt to him for I trvst it is out of his abvndant
ABYSSE (1)
ELEMEN14:1 H243 Because in the abysse of my darke wombe:
ACADEMY (1)
CHILDRN185:3 H29 One to the Academy flew
ACCAD (1)
MASSYR53:24 H14 *Erech, Accad,* and *Calneh* also made;
ACCENTS (1) [pl.]
2LETTER181:36 H6 The woful accents of my doleful sound,
ACCEPT (11)
FATHER6:11 H45 Accept my best, my worst vouchsafe a grave.
SEASONS53:6 H262 *Accept therefore of what is penn'd,*
MASSYR59:3 H227 T' accept of what they could, they him {all} beseech.
MASSYR63:27 H412 A Vice-roy from her foe, she's glad t' accept,
MGREC98:5 H1807 But they accept not this, in any wise,
MGREC99:11 H1854 But th'Kingdoms, and the Ladies, {Lady} soone accept;
MROMAN139:23 H3551 And people sweare, ne're to accept of King.
QELIZ155:27 H18 T' accept the tribute of a loyall Braine;
THEART229:15 H17 Accept O Lord my simple mite
2HUSB232:22 H23 O Lord accept of it.
ACCEPTANCE (1)
ELEMEN10:26 H101 I of acceptance was the holy signe.
ACCEPT^D (1) [accepted] See also ACCT^D
2SIMON195:9 Hp271 Such as they are I bequeath to you, Small legacys are accept^d
ACCEPTED (1) See also ACCT^D, ACCEPT^D
MEDDM205:19 Hp286 boldnes to go to the throne of grace to be accepted there,
ACCESSE (2)
13MAY227:7 H16 I haue accesse vnto his Throne,
REMB235:34 H15 My 'plaints haue had accesse.
ACCIDENT (1)
MPERS81:2 H1110 Which accident, the rest affrighted so,
ACCIDENTS (1) [pl.]
CHILDRN185:40 H66 Sore accidents on you may light.

ACCLAMATIONS (2) [pl.]
MPERS74:14 H837 But {And joyfull} acclamations ecchoes in the aire;
QELIZ155:29 H20 The acclamations of the poore, as rich;
ACCOMPANI'D (1) [accompanied]
MGREC102:2 H1972 Accompani'd with sorrow, fear, and shame;
ACCOMPANING (1)
MASSYR55:21 H87 Accompaning her husband *Menon* far,
ACCOMPLICES See ACCOMPLYCES
ACCOMPLISH (6) See also T'ACCOMPLISH
MASSYR65:7 H472 Before he could accomplish his intent;
MPERS89:32 H1466 Fit instruments t' accomplish what is ill;
MGREC123:35 H2899 Prest to accomplish what he would have done;
MGREC125:7 H2955 The better to accomplish these her ends;
MROMAN140:2 H3565 But 'fore I could accomplish my desire,
DUBART154:9 H54 But wishes cann't accomplish my desire,
ACCOMPLISHED (3)
MASSYR59:39 H263 But was accomplished now, in his {wicked} Son.
MPERS72:9 ~~H757~~ Accomplished this wicked Kings intent;
MPERS79:15 H1041 Firmly at length, {last} accomplished his wil;
ACCOMPLISHMENT (1)
MASSYR59:27 H251 By this accomplishment, their hearts were shaken:
ACCOMPLYCES (1) [accomplices]
MPERS73:24 ~~H809~~ And now with his accomplyces lye slaine.
ACCORD (3)
HUMOUR29:35 H386 Wise *Fabius* is her buckler: all accord.
MGREC103:1 H2012 For his receit with joy, they all accord;
MGREC109:15 H2274 Had to his mind, made all things now {to} accord:
ACCORDING (11)
PROLOG6:30 H14 But simple I, according to my skill.
AGES36:28 H52 Intend to speak, according to their age:
MPERS83:36 H1224 And payes them now, {both} according as he owes,
MGREC129:37 H3151 Who slew the prince according to desire:
ANNEB187:21 H11 To value things according to their price:
MEDDM196:31 Hp274 fit their nurture according to their Nature.
MEDDM198:2 Hp275 sutable comforts and supports for his children according to
MEDDM200:18 Hp279 god proportion his dispensations according to the stature
MEDDM200:36 Hp280 children as would crush them to the dust, but according to the
MYCHILD216:6 Hp241 But I rendered not to him according to ye benefitt rec.
11MAYB228:30 Hp259 But alas! I cannot render vnto ye Lord according to all his
ACCOUNT (11)
HUMOUR21:26 H54 In dangers to account himself more sure,
AGES43:22 H317 I hate {not} for to be had, {held} in small {high'st} account.
AGES44:33 H366 That but for shrubs they did themselves account;
MASSYR~~68:16~~ H602 Was held in more request, {account} then now he was,
MPERS73:18 H805 And kinsmen in account, to th'King they stood,
MGREC100:25 H1909 Two hundred fifty thousand by account,
MGREC103:15 H2026 To a {an} hundred thousand Tallents by account.
MROMAN139:6 H3534 A generall Muster takes, which by account,
QELIZ155:20 H11 That men account it no impiety,
VANITY160:29 H39 Who drinks thereof, the world doth naught account.
MEDDM197:24 Hp275 receiued? Come giue an account of thy stewardship.

ACCOUNTED (2)
MROMAN137:36 H3487 Accounted for some {a} god in after dayes.
MEDDM202:13 Hp281 accounted among the dead, and no other reason can be
ACCOUNTS (1)
MEDDM204:10 Hp284 the larger his accounts stands vpon gods score it therfore
ACCRUE (1)
MPERS77:34 H975 What infamy to's honour did accrue.
ACCT^{D}. (1) [accepted]
MYCHILD218:29 Hp244 and Sectaries, and some who hauest been acct^{d}. sincere
ACCUMULATE (1)
QELIZ155:23 H14 Thy world of honours to accumulate,
ACCURSED (1)
MEDDM209:14 Hp291 all their accursed inmates, but make a league with them,
ACCUS'D (4) [accused]
MPERS72:19 H767 Upon a Judge, for breach of Law {taking bribes} accus'd;
MPERS83:16 H1204 Accus'd *Darius, Xerxes* eldest son,
MPERS87:4 H1360 The one {last} accus'd the other, {first} for these {sad} wars:
MGREC112:21 H2407 Accus'd, because he did not certifie
ACCUSE (1)
MGREC113:11 H2438 For to {He might} accuse himself, as they had done;
ACCUSED See ACCUS'D
ACCUSER (2)
MGREC112:31 H2417 His Master is Accuser, Judge, and King,
MEDDM205:13 Hp286 alway kept by Conscience, who is both accuser excuser witnes
ACCUSERS (1) [pl.]
MGREC126:24 H3015 But made in Judgement her Accusers stand,
ACHAIA (1)
ELEMEN17:24 H388 As when *Achaia,* all under water stood,
ACHEMENES (2) [poss.]
MPERS69:5 H627 *Cambyses* was of *Achemenes* race,
MPERS73:17 H804 Descended all, of *Achemenes* blood,
ACHES (1) [pl.]
AGES~~41:9~~ H229 Of Marrow {aches} ful my bones, of Milk {woe} my breasts
ACHILLE'S (1) [poss.]
MGREC116:25 H2591 *Achille's* happinesse he did envy,
ACHILLES (2)
MGREC99:26 H1869 To imitate *Achilles* (in his shame)
SIDNEY150:19 H44 O brave *Achilles,* I wish some *Homer* would
ACHILLIS (1) [poss.]
MGREC94:22 H1660 And on *Achillis* Tombe, with wondrous joy,
ACHING See AKEING, AKING
ACKNOWLEDG (1)
MEDDM203:32 Hp284 are more ready to receiue mercys then we are to acknowledg
ACKNOWLEDG'D (1) [acknowledged]
MGREC111:11 H2356 Acknowledg'd for their Masters Soveraigne;
ACKNOWLEDGED (3)
HUMOUR21:4 H32 It is acknowledged, from whence I came,
MGREC~~120:20~~ H2757 Acknowledged for Chief that old Commander)
MGREC122:36 ~~H2857~~ Acknowledged for chief, this old Commander:
ACKNOWLEDGEMENT (1) [acknowledgment] See also ACKNOWLEDGMT
PROLOG7:33 H44 Yet grant some small acknowledgement of ours.

ACKNOWLEDGING (1)
MASSYR61:29 H334 Acknowledging th' *Assyrians* high desert,

ACKNOWLEDGMT (1) [acknowledgment] See also ACKNOWLEDGEMENT
ACK235:3 H1-3 In thankfull acknowledgmt for ye lrs rec'd. from my

ACQUAINTANCE (1)
1SIMON188:5 H6 Acquaintance short, yet parting caus'd us weep,

ACQUIRE (4)
HUMOUR31:35 H468 But I by vertue, do acquire the same.
MGREC127:17 H3047 Such as nor {no} threats, nor favour could acquire;
MGREC133:21 H3309 Whereby immortall honour they acquire.
FLESH175:26 H26 Dost honour like? acquire the same,

ACQUIRED (1)
MEDDM209:22 Hp291 let his parts naturall and acquired spirituall and morall,

ACQUITTED (1)
MGREC126:27 H3018 And so was he acquitted of his word,

ACRE (1)
MPERS79:36 H1062 This 'twixt the Mountains lyes (half Acre wide)

ACT (24)
HUMOUR23:36 H146 Again, ye know, how I act every part:
HUMOUR32:8 H482 I rarely feel to act his fierce indeavour.
AGES~~35:17~~ H3 Loe now! four other acts {act} upon the stage,
AGES36:19 H43 And last of al, to act upon this Stage;
AGES37:19 H81 Did act al folly, that it could expresse.
AGES38:20 H123 From thence I 'gan to sin, as soon as act.
AGES44:7 H340 And on this Stage am come to act my last:
AGES45:2 ~~H375~~ And silenc'd we, by Act of Parliament.
MPERS71:11 H727 But that the *Persian* King, may act his minde;
MPERS72:7 ~~H756~~ *Praraspes* now must act this tragedy;
MPERS~~72:9~~ H757 To act in secret, this his lewd intent:
MPERS82:22 H1169 Yet ceases not to act his villany:
MGREC104:30 H2082 To *Alexander* fly, {flyes} and told {tells} this act;
MGREC~~114:27~~ H2497 Of this unkingly deed, {act} doth *Seneca*
MGREC115:12 H2521 This act (me thinks) his god-head should ashame;
MGREC115:18 H2537 That he might next now act upon the Stage,
MGREC119:41 H2731 Act any thing of worth, as heretofore,
MGREC120:39 H2776 Great love did *Ptolomy* by this act gain.
MGREC123:22 H2886 Now {Then} *Polisperchon* 'gins to act in's place,
MGREC124:24 H2931 And act, as opportunity they finde:
MGREC124:26 H2933 More then he bidden was, could act no thing;
MGREC129:11 H3125 But for one act she did, just was her end,
DIALOG145:32 H181 This done, an Act they would have passed fain,
QELIZ155:36 H27 The World's the Theater where she did act;

ACTED (2)
AGES45:17 H399 Plotted and acted, so that none can tell,
SIDNEY149:21 H20 Are not his Tragick Comedies so acted,

ACTING (1)
HUMOUR26:9 H239 For acting these, I have nor wil, nor art,

ACTION (2)
MEDDM195:24 Hp272 There is no obiect that we see. no action that we doe, no good
MEDDM204:18 Hp285 action, as we see in Jehu, he is rewarded wth a kingdome to

ACTIONS (3) [pl.]

MPERS86:12	H1328	Judging all's {his} actions, tends to's injury.
MGREC123:30	H2894	Slights his commands, his actions he disclaimes,
TDUDLEY166:10	H52	His thoughts were more sublime, his actions wise,

ACTIUM (1)

MGREC135:1	H3371	At *Actium* slain, {where} his Navy {Navy's} put to flight.

ACTIVE (2)

ELEMEN~~8:28~~	H26	The noblest and most active Element.
HUMOUR29:3	H356	Had need be armed wel, and active too,

ACTS (2) v.

HUMOUR33:11	H525	But the spirits, by which it acts are thine;
CONTEM170:23	H94	His brother comes, then acts his fratricide,

ACTS (18) [pl.]

AGES35:17	H3	Loe now! four other acts {act} upon the stage,
MASSYR54:1	H28	Whose acts, and power, is not for certainty,
MASSYR57:31	H176	In deep oblivion, of acts bereft,
MASSYR57:35	H180	May feign as many acts, as he did names;
MASSYR~~63:28~~	H414	This King's less fam'd for all the acts he's done,
MASSYR~~63:30~~	H417	The famous Wars {acts}, of this Heroyick King,
MASSYR63:32	H419	Nor of his acts {Wars} have we the certainty,
MASSYR67:22	H568	Whose prophane acts, a sacred pen sets down.
MPERS91:39	~~H1553~~	Their Acts recorded not, as heretofore
MPERS92:9	H1567	What Acts he did, time hath not now left pend,
MGREC110:34	H2338	Whereon his acts, and travels, long appears;
MGREC116:11	H2577	Whose famous Acts {This Monarchs fame} must last, whilst
MGREC116:26	H2592	'Cause *Homer* kept his Acts to memory;
MGREC116:30	H2596	As oft his Acts throughout his reigne did {doth} shew:
MGREC118:34	H2683	To authorize his Acts in every thing.
MGREC120:24	H2761	The Acts of his Vice-royes, {Vice-Roy} now grown so high:
MGREC~~122:4~~	H2827	And much eclipse his {great Acts and} glory to rehearse
CONTEM169:32	H71	While of their persons & their acts his mind doth treat.

ADAM (6)

SEASONS51:19	H193	Great *Adam* {Our Grand-Sire} was of Paradice made King.
MGREC106:5	H2139	Yea, {And} thus must every Son of *Adam* lye,
CONTEM169:35	H73	Sees glorious *Adam* there made Lord of all,
CONTEM171:6	H111	How Adam sigh'd to see his Progeny,
FLESH176:7	H47	Thou by old Adam wast begot,
MEDDM202:5	Hp281	or sprung out of the loynes of one Adam, some set in y[e]

ADAMS (3) [poss.]

FATHER5:6	H7	(though made a pedestall for *Adams* Race) /world
AGES38:19	H122	From birth stayned, with Adams sinfull fact;
SICKNES178:24	H7	For Adams sake, this word God spake

ADDE (7)

ELEMEN14:19	H261	Ile say no more, yet {but} this thing adde I must,
ELEMEN20:7	H489	To adde to all I've said, was my intent,
MPERS81:31	H1139	To adde unto his numbers, layes about,
MGREC93:17	H1614	His Education, much to these {those} did adde.
MGREC134:33	H3364	To all these names we *Ptolomy* must adde,
MROMAN138:30	H3520	A hundred Senatours he more did adde;
MROMAN138:34	H3524	Much {Some} state, and glory, {splendor} did this *Priscus* adde:

ADDING (1)
ELEMEN16:40 H363 By adding cold to cold, no fruit proves sound;
ADDRESSE (3)
MPERS89:17 H1451 {Then} he sends {that} to's Tent, they straight addresse,
2HUSB233:2 H35 He shall make his Addresse.
ACK235:16 H16 In this his Buisnes and Addresse.
ADDREST (1)
MGREC~~96:6~~ H1726 As if they were, {if addrest} now all to run at {a} tilt:
ADDS (2)
SEASONS47:5 H19 Stil adds to th' last, til after pleasant *May;*
SIDNEY150:37 H64 Noble {Great} *Bartas,* this to thy praise adds more,
ADEIU (2) [adieu] See also ADUE
HOUSE237:10 H40 Adeiu, Adeiu, All's Vanity.
ADHERE (1)
DIALOG147:25 H249 And to this blessed {hopeful} Cause closely adhere
ADIEU (4) See also ADEIU, ADUE
MGREC100:33 H1917 Now bids the world adieu, her time {with pain} being spent,
CHILDRN184:37 H26 Hath also bid her Dam adieu:
CHILDRN186:7 H74 But former toyes (no joyes) adieu.
CHILDRN186:28 H95 Farewel my birds, farewel adieu,
ADJUDGED (1)
MASSYR55:11 H77 Adjudged to be drown'd, for what {th' crime} she'd done;
ADMIR'D (2) [admired]
MASSYR55:37 H103 Admir'd of all, but equaliz'd of none.
CONTEM169:8 H50 Admir'd, ador'd for ever, be that Majesty.
ADMIRABLE (1)
MEDDM208:28 Hp290 It is admirable to Consider the power of faith, by wch all things
ADMIRALL (1)
MPERS90:15 ~~H1484~~ Unto the *Spartan* Admirall did sue,
ADMIRATION (2)
DUBART154:34 H79 But monuments for {to} future admiration:
MEDDM202:2 Hp281 There is nothing admits of more admiration, then gods various
ADMIRE (8)
HUMOUR31:21 H454 Pray hear, admire, and learn instruction.
HUMOUR35:11 H607 But all admire our perfect amity;
MPERS72:17 H765 Thy cruelty will {all} Ages still admire.
SIDNEY151:25 ~~H73~~ Enough for me to look, and so admire.
DUBART154:10 H55 Pardon, if I adore, when I admire.
QELIZ157:31 H99 To read what others write, and then {so} admire.
CONTEM168:10 H19 Thy strength, and stature, more thy years admire,
MEDDM206:37 Hp288 make vs wth the Apostle to admire the iustice and mercy
ADMIRED (1) See also ADMIR'D
AGES~~45:4~~ H387 Admired for their magnanimity,
ADMIRES (4)
MASSYR56:21 H127 All eyes that saw, or ears that hears, {hear} admires.
MGREC102:9 H1979 The glory of the Castle he admires,
DUBART153:20 H24 The glittering Plate, and Jewels, he admires,
DUBART153:31 H35 Sits down in silence, deeply he admires:
ADMIT See ADMITT
ADMITS (2)
PROLOG7:12 H26 A weake or wounded braine admits no cure.

MEDDM202:2 Hp281 There is nothing admits of more admiration, then gods various

ADMITT (2) [admit]
MYCHILD218:18 Hp244 that admitt this bee ye true God whom wee worship,
MYCHILD218:24 Hp244 p^{r}secutions of the Saints, wch admitt were y^{y} as they terme

ADONIS (1)
AGES40:22 H203 Some young {new} *Adonis* I do strive to be,

ADOPTS (1)
MPERS69:12 H634 Adopts her Son for his, having no other:

ADOR'D (1) [adored]
CONTEM169:8 H50 Admir'd, ador'd for ever, be that Majesty.

ADORATION (1)
DIALOG143:30 H99 With foolish superstitious adoration;

ADORE (6)
MGREC96:34 H1754 The *Greekes* would all adore, and {but} would none fight.
MGREC106:32 H2166 Are strictly now commanded to adore;
MGREC114:22 H2492 Nor would adore him for a Deity:
DIALOG148:24 H289 And him you shall adore, who now despise,
DUBART154:10 H55 Pardon, if I adore, when I admire.
MEDDM206:30 Hp288 parents haue had pious children, it should make vs adore the

ADORED (1) See also ADOR'D
MPERS88:17 H1410 They straight adored *Cyrus* for their King,

ADORING (1)
MGREC131:20 H3212 But they adoring in prosperity,

ADORNE (1)
ELEMEN15:38 H320 Which *Cæsars, Consuls, Tribunes* all adorne;

ADORNINGS (1) [pl.]
MEDDM196:8 Hp273 so he that glorys in his gifts and adornings, should look

ADRIATIQUE (1)
ELEMEN16:5 H328 My sundry Seas, Black, White, and Adriatique

ADUANTAGE (1) [advantage]
MEDDM195:26 Hp272 aduantage of all and he that makes such improvment is wise

ADUE (1) [adieu] See also ADEIU
ELEMEN18:12 H416 To bid adue, to his dear Element.

ADUL'RATE (1) [adulterate]
SIDNEY151:19 ~~H69~~ That thine was true, but theirs adul'rate love.

ADULATION (1)
MGREC131:4 H3194 Most grossely base, was this {their} great adulation,

ADULTERATE See ADUL'RATE

ADULTERY (1)
DIALOG144:12 H122 For Bribery, Adultery, for Thefts, and Lyes,

ADUST (1)
HUMOUR~~31:5~~ H438 And so art call'd black Choler or adust,

ADUSTION (1)
HUMOUR23:19 H129 The excrement, adustion of me.

ADVANC'D (3) [advanced]
AGES45:9 H391 I've seen base {unworthy} men, advanc'd to great degree
MGREC123:32 H2896 Such as his father had advanc'd to place,
QELIZ156:25 H52 Her stately Troops advanc'd to *Lisbons* wall,

ADVANCE (4)
PROLOG7:18 H31 If what I doe prove well, it wo'nt advance,
MASSYR61:4 H309 What else he did, his Empire to advance,

MPERS84:20 H1256 Thinking his *Grecian* wars now to advance.
MPERS88:29 H1422 But treads down all, for to advance their Master;

ADVANCED (1) See also ADVANC'D
AGES39:19 H162 glistring {glitt'ring} Sword, {the Pistol} and wel advanced Pike;

ADVANTAGE (9) See also ADUANTAGE
AGES37:28 H90 Yet this advantage, had mine ignorance,
MASSYR57:21 ~~H168~~ Would now advantage take, their own to gain;
MASSYR61:23 H328 Gladly doth *Tiglath* this advantage take,
MASSYR63:6 H391 Of opportunity advantage takes,
MEDDM204:12 Hp284 call him to reckoning, he may receiue his owne wth advantage
MYCHILD215:17 Hp240 by y^{t} yov may gain some spirit: Advantage by my exper^{c}. I
MYCHILD216:29 Hp242 the times of my greatest Getting and Advantage, yea I haue
28AUG225:32 Hp254 but he doth it for my Advantage, and y^{t} I may bee a Gainer
11MAYA226:21 Hp255 espec: seing it is for my spirit^{l}. advantage, For I hope my soul

ADVERSE (4)
ELEMEN9:6 H40 The adverse wall's not shak'd, the Mine's not blowne,
ELEMEN13:22 H223 Now might {must} I shew my {mine} adverse quality,
CONTEM174:19 H218 Which 'gainst all adverse winds may serve for fort.
SON231:1 H13 And order'st so the adverse wind

ADVERSITIES (1) [pl.]
WHAT224:11 H11 Let them help in Adversities

ADVERSITY (8)
AGES44:25 H358 Sometimes {Sometime} again, rain'd all adversity;
MGREC131:21 H3213 Now shut their gates in his adversity,
BIRTH179:28 H4 Adversity doth still our joyes attend;
MEDDM196:22 Hp273 state makes a secure christian, but adversity makes
MEDDM197:12 Hp274 some times tast of adversity, prosperity would not be so
MEDDM201:32 Hp281 the most welcom so a faithfull friend in time of adversity,
28AUG225:31 Hp254 he hath no benefitt by my adversity, nor is he ye better for my
11MAYB228:30 Hp259 adversity, But alas! I cannot render vnto ye Lord according to

ADVICE (4)
AGES39:21 H164 Nor wait til good advice {success} our hopes do crown;
MPERS84:8 H1236 By *Memucan's* advice, this {so} was the doome.
MGREC104:7 H2059 With sage advice, he layes {sets} before his eyes,
MGREC113:18 H2445 This sound advice, at heart, pleas'd *Alexander,*

ADVISE (2)
HUMOUR22:10 H79 She'l first advise, if't be not best to stay.
MGREC109:37 H2296 But for the rest, his sword advise him should.

AEGEAN (1)
ELEMEN~~16:7~~ H330 The *Ponticke, {Aegean} Caspian,* Golden Rivers fine. {five,}

ÆGERIA (1)
MROMAN137:33 H3484 Goddesse *Ægeria* this to him told,

ÆGYPT (12) See also EGIPT, EGYPT
MASSYR64:23 H447 Then into *Ægypt, Necho* did retire,
MASSYR66:17 H523 A totall Conquest of rich *Ægypt* makes,
MASSYR67:14 H560 Faire *Ægypt* is, by his remissenesse lost;
MPERS83:29 H1217 He first, war with revolting *Ægypt* made.
MGREC100:1 H1885 From thence, to fruitfull *Ægypt* marcht with speed,
MGREC100:11 H1895 Now {Thence} back to *Ægypt* goes, and in few dayes,
MGREC100:14 H1898 In *Syria, Ægypt,* and *Phoenicia;*
MGREC101:10 H1935 With fertile *Ægypt,* and rich *Syria,*

MGREC120:35 H2772 At *Alexandria,* in *Ægypt* Land, {his tomb he plac'd}
MGREC121:6 H2784 And with his Army into {unto} *Ægypt* goes,
MGREC121:30 H2812 Thus *Ptolomy* rich *Ægypt* did retaine,
MGREC132:31 H3278 Rich *Ægypt* left, and what else he had won

ÆGYPTIAN (2) See also EGYPTIAN
MPERS71:34 H748 The Ægyptian *Apis* then he likewise slew,
QELIZ157:21 H89 But that she was a rich *Ægyptian* Queen;

ÆGYPTIANS (1) [pl.] See also EGYPTIANS
MPERS77:20 H961 Th' *Ægyptians* to reduce, and *Greece* to marre;

ÆGYPTS (3) [poss.] See also EGYPTS
ELEMEN15:35 H317 As *Ægypts* wanton *Cleopatra* drunke.
MASSYR62:7 H352 To *Ægypts* King, which did avail him nought;
MPERS71:15 H729 'Gainst *Ægypts* King, who there by him was slain,

ÆMULUS (1)
MROMAN136:26 H3440 But *Æmulus,* in Armour all disguis'd.

ÆTATIS (1)
SICKNES178:17 H0 *Ætatis suæ,* 19.

ÆTNA'S (1) [poss.]
ELEMEN10:28 H103 There's none more strange then *Ætna's* sulphery mount

AFAR (3)
ELEMEN18:18 H422 Which {That} tells afar, th' exployt which he {it} hath done.
SEASONS49:40 H133 Whose flaming breath doth melt us from afar,
2LETTER182:18 H24 Thy rayes afar, salute her from the south.

AFFABILITY (2)
MPERS74:30 H853 His affability, {courtesie} and milde aspect,
MGREC121:10 H2788 But *Ptolomy* by affability,

AFFABLE (1)
AGES39:25 H168 So affable that I do {can} suit each mind;

AFFAIRES (1) [affairs]
MPERS76:25 H923 Which husht, he straight so orders his affaires;

AFFECT'S (1) [affect is]
FLESH175:34 H34 Affect's thou pleasure? take thy fill,

AFFECTION (1)
AUTHOR178:2 H12 Yet being mine own, at length affection would

AFFECTIONATE (1)
2SIMON195:17 Hp271 your affectionate

AFFECTIONES (1) [affections]
MEDDM208:8 Hp290 of time (if there be no inter course) will coole the affectiones

AFFECTIONS (1) [pl.]
HUMOUR34:6 H561 Whence her affections, passions, speak so clear;

AFFINITIES (1) [pl.]
MGREC133:38 H3328 The affinities and warres *Daniel* set forth,

AFFINITY (1)
MGREC120:6 H2741 In love, and in affinity combine:

AFFIRME (1)
MROMAN137:23 H3474 Affirme, that by the Senate he was slaine.

AFFLICT (1)
28AUG225:30 Hp254 doth not afflict willingly, nor take delight in greiving ye children

AFFLICTED (3)
MGREC101:26 H1951 The afflicted King, finding him set to jar,
MYCHILD217:6 Hp242 circu̅spection in my walking after I haue been afflicted.

MYCHILD217:9 Hp242 Before I was afflicted I went astray, but now I keep thy

AFFLICTION (6) See also AFFLICT^{N}

CONTEM174:25 H223 But sad affliction comes & makes him see
MEDDM199:12 Hp277 some men into the furnace of affliction and then beats them
MEDDM200:12 Hp279 or lay affliction on their loynes that so they might shake hands
MYCHILD217:5 Hp242 of Sweetnes and refreshment after affliction and more
11MAYA226:19 Hp255 a contented thankfull h^{t} vnder my affliction & weaknes seing it
30SEPT227:25 Hp257 in ye furnace of affliction as some haue been, but haue rather

AFFLICTIONS (1) [pl.]

MEDDM200:35 Hp280 father (who knowes our mould) lay such afflictions vpon his

AFFLICT^{N} (3) [affliction]

MYCHILD215:34 Hp241 that afflict^{n}.
MYCHILD216:4 Hp241 When I was in my afflict^{n}. I besovght the Lord, and confessed
MYCHILD216:22 Hp241-2 but by one afflict^{n} or other hath made me look home,

AFFORD (4)

MGREC125:25 H2975 Bids chuse her death, such kindnesse she'l afford:
DIALOG143:22 H91 Destruction to a Land doth soone afford;
SIDNEY150:35 H62 Where is that envious tongue, but can afford,
MEDDM201:5 Hp280 more or lesse if god afford his help

AFFORDED (1)

MPERS69:17 H639 His nourishment afforded by a Bitch,

AFFORDS (1)

MEDDM202:25 Hp282 other time, yet he affords so much light as may direct our way,

AFFRICA (1) [africa]

ELEMEN17:10 H374 And but one land was *Affrica* and *Spayne,*

AFFRIGHTED (3)

ELEMEN13:40 H241 Ye affrighted wights, appall'd how do you shake
MASSYR68:11 H597 None answers the affrighted Kings intent.
MPERS81:2 H1110 Which accident, the rest affrighted so,

AFFRIGHTS (1) [pl.]

AGES40:41 H220 With sad affrights of death, doth menace me;

AFRAID (2)

MPERS90:14 ~~H1484~~ The King afraid what further they might doe,
MED223:18 Hp250 and let me bee no more afraid of Death, but even desire to

AFRESH (3)

SEASONS47:15 H31 And all that seem'd as dead, afresh do live.
MGREC119:13 H2703 Their ancient liberty, afresh now seeks,
MGREC131:6 H3196 These Kings fall now afresh to {their} warres again,

AFRICA (1) See also AFFRICA

MGREC121:32 H2814 Whilst *Perdicas* thus staid {encamp'd} in *Africa,*

AFTER (82) See also AFTER'S

ELEMEN9:35 H70 And trim thee gay {brave}, in green, after thy blacks?
ELEMEN12:31 H191 After three years, when men and meat is spent,
ELEMEN14:21 H263 And after death, whether inter'd, or burn'd;
ELEMEN17:30 H394 That after times, shall never feel like woe:
SEASONS47:5 H19 Stil adds to th' last, til after pleasant *May;*
SEASONS50:20 H154 Which after Manchet's made, {makes} for Kings to eat;
MASSYR53:14 H4 after the Floud.
MASSYR53:19 H9 This was the Golden Age, but after came
MASSYR53:34 H24 One hundred fourteen years, he after dyed.
MASSYR55:39 H105 That after ages, skil, by them were {was} taught.

MASSYR57:22	~~H169~~	So Province, after Province, rent away,
MASSYR~~57:23~~	H170	He many Ages liv'd after that day.
MASSYR60:32	H297	And from this heap did after Ages see,
MASSYR63:10	H395	After twelve years did *Essarhadon* dye,
MASSYR65:2	H467	Where after many assayes, they make {made} at last,
MASSYR65:36	H501	And after eighteen months he took them all,
MPERS70:21	H692	Had after {A} thousand yeares faire to be seen.
MPERS70:26	H697	Long after this, he 'gainst the *Sythians* goes,
MPERS~~70:37~~	H708	Where some long after fought in vain for prize
MPERS72:2	H754	He after this, saw in a Vision {upon suspition vain},
MPERS74:12	~~H836~~	And after *Persian* manner, kisse his feet.
MPERS76:23	H921	He after this, intends *Greece* to invade,
MPERS79:24	H1050	What after did ensue, had he fore-seen,
MPERS~~79:29~~	H1055	Which was not vaine, as it {after} soon appeared:
MPERS83:6	H1194	His wicked brother, {soon} after sent {him} a crew,
MPERS83:34	H1222	Then when the world, they after over-run:
MPERS85:18	H1294	A second trouble, after this succeeds.
MPERS88:34	H1427	After this trance, revenge, new spirits blew,
MPERS89:9	H1443	After a while his {hurri'd} thoughts he re-collects,
MPERS90:11	H1484	These {Who} after all, receiv'd them joyfully:
MPERS90:18	H1485	So after all {Thus finishing} their travell, danger, pain,
MPERS90:28	H1495	Town after town, with small resistance take,
MPERS92:1	~~H1555~~	In after wars were burnt, 'mongst other things?
MGREC94:8	H1642	In seeking after {Nor making Title unto} Soveraignity:
MGREC94:18	H1652	Then with alacrity he after goes:
MGREC95:25	H1704	Goes {Runs} after too {two}, and leaves all to disaster.
MGREC96:9	H1729	The Priests in their strange habit follow after;
MGREC103:13	H2024	Yet after all, as stories do expresse,
MGREC106:36	H2170	After that conquer'd, and luxurious Nation;
MGREC111:2	H2347	Some time he after spent upon that shore,
MGREC112:14	H2400	So after many dayes this {the} Banquet ends.
MGREC113:4	H2431	*Philotas* after him sends out this cry,
MGREC113:15	H2442	Look on *Parmenio,* after this disaster,
MGREC114:17	H2487	The next of worth, that suffered after these,
MGREC116:32	H2598	Vain thirsting after immortality:
MGREC117:39	H2646	After much tumult, they at last proclaim'd
MGREC118:23	H2670	After this {some} time, when stirs began to calme,
MGREC119:40	H2730	After this {which} time, the *Greeks* did never more
MGREC122:37	~~H2858~~	After a while, to *Macedon* he makes;
MGREC127:11	H3041	And rais'd *Cassandria* after his name,
MGREC132:3	H3236	This by *Lysimachus* soon {was} after slain,
MGREC132:25	H3270	After three years he dyed, left what he'd won
MGREC133:9	H3297	With *Ptolomy,* reign'd after *Alexander;*
MGREC~~134:2~~	H3334	Whose large Dominions after was made small,
MGREC134:28	H3359	After *Epiphanes,* sat on the Throne
MGREC~~134:30~~	H3361	And next to {after} him, did false *Lathurus* reigne,
MGREC~~135:1~~	H3373	Did by his Sword his life soon after send.
MGREC136:9	H3423	*After some dayes of rest, my restlesse heart,*
MROMAN137:36	H3487	Accounted for some {a} god in after dayes.
MROMAN138:6	H3496	Yet for {in} their compact, after false they play:
MROMAN138:29	H3519	He after *Martius* death the Kingdome had,

MROMAN138:36 H3526 And after all, by *Ancus* Sons was slaine.
DIALOG144:33 H141 This is fore-runner of my after clap,
DIALOG146:36 H222 After dark Popery the day did clear,
TDUDLEY165:18 H20 Who after death might make him falsly seem
TDUDLEY166:25 H67 Who after all his toyle, is now at rest:
AUTHOR177:31 H3 Who after birth did'st by my side remain,
CHILDRN184:22 H11 My mournful chirps I after send,
CHILDRN184:30 H19 Till after blown by *Southern* gales,
1SIMON188:13 H14 And smile again, after our bitter crosses.
MEDDM199:6 Hp277 do not often fall till after threat'ning.
MEDDM200:24 Hp279 is a liuely emblem of the resurrection, after a long winter
MEDDM200:27 Hp279 lost in the Autumn so shall it be at that great day after a long
MEDDM203:34 Hp284 shew great ingratitude after their successes, but he that
MYCHILD216:7 Hp241 After a short time I changed my Condition & was marryed,
MYCHILD216:9 Hp241 my heart rose, But after I was convinced it was ye way of God,
MYCHILD216:11 Hp241 After some time I fell into a lingering sicknes like a
MYCHILD216:16 Hp241 and after him gave me many more, of whom I now take y^{e}
MYCHILD217:5 Hp242 of Sweetnes and refreshment after affliction and more
MYCHILD217:6 Hp242 circu¯spection in my walking after I haue been afflicted.
28AUG225:26 Hp254 After mvch weaknes & sicknes when my spirits were worn out,
ACK235:10 H10 Nor payd me after my desert

AFTER'S (2) [after his]
MGREC126:41 H3030 Her Husbands Wife, {wives} and Children, after's death
MGREC133:10 H3298 *Cassanders* Sons, soone after's death were slaine,

AFTER-COMERS (1) [pl.]
TDUDLEY165:29 H31 That After-comers in them might have share.

AFTERWARD (1)
MGREC118:39 H2688 *Seleuchus* afterward held *Babylon*;

AFTERWARDS (1)
PROLOG7:8 H22 lisp'd at first, speake afterwards more {in future times} plaine

AGAIN (55) See also AGAINE, AGEN
ELEMEN13:36 H237 Again, when Delvers dare in hope of gold,
ELEMEN14:9 H251 Again, what veines of poyson in me lye;
ELEMEN19:32 H473 Again, what tempests,{furious storms} and what hericanoes
HUMOUR22:21 H90 Again, who sits, for learning, science, Arts?
HUMOUR23:36 H146 Again, ye know, how I act every part:
HUMOUR27:10 H281 Again, stomachs concoction thou dost claime,
HUMOUR~~30:9~~ H401 Thirdly, {Again} thou dost confine me to the spleen,
HUMOUR30:37 H429 Again, you often touch my swarthy hew,
HUMOUR34:31 H586 Again, none's fit for Kingly place but thou,
AGES~~42:17~~ H275 Sometimes {again,} mine age (in all) {mine Age} been worse
AGES44:25 H358 Sometimes {Sometime} again, rain'd all adversity;
AGES44:27 H360 Sometime an abject, then again in place,
AGES45:20 ~~H402~~ But yet may live, to see't made up again:
AGES~~45:22~~ H408 But ye may live to see't made up again.
SEASONS50:8 H142 Which makes the aged fields look young again,
SEASONS51:33 H209 His dead old stock, again shall mount on high.
MASSYR57:24 ~~H171~~ Again, the Country was left bare (there is no doubt)
MASSYR62:21 H366 And pleasant *Canaan* ne're see again:
MASSYR62:39 H384 With shame then turn'd to *Ninivie* again,
MASSYR65:25 H490 Then from his throne, he pull'd {pluck'd} him down again:

MASSYR67:11 H557 And native *Canaan,* never see again,
MPERS71:19 H733 Who grown a man, resum'd again his state)
MPERS75:25 H882 An Edict for the *Jews* publish'd again,
MPERS75:39 H896 Set up a Temple (though, a lesse) again.
MPERS79:26 H1052 Of *Artabanus* he again demands,
MPERS84:40 H1276 Again dispersed, his new levyed hoast.
MPERS85:31 H1307 And so each man again possest his owne.
MPERS89:2 H1436 The King upon the spur, runs back again;
MPERS89:21 H1455 The troubled King, his Herauld sends again,
MPERS89:40 H1474 Chose *Xenophon,* to lead them home again;
MPERS90:19 H1486 In peace they saw their Native soyl again.
MPERS~~92:19~~ H1577 But *Bogoas* falls to's practices again,
MGREC101:22 H1947 Thus to *Darius* he writes back again,
MGREC109:2 H2259 Those that submit, he doth restore {give them rule} again.
MGREC111:10 H2355 With rich rewards, he sent them home again,
MGREC120:19 H2754 But this again dislikes, and {he} would remain,
MGREC131:6 H3196 These Kings fall now afresh to {their} warres again,
MGREC134:29 H3360 *Philometer:* then *Evergetes* again.
SIDNEY152:20 H89 Which writ, she bad return't to them again.
QELIZ158:6 H115 *Eliza* shall rule *Albian* once again.
CONTEM169:16 H57 But Ah, and Ah, again, my imbecility!
CONTEM171:30 H132 Nor youth, nor strength, nor wisdom spring again
1SIMON188:13 H14 And smile again, after our bitter crosses.
MEDDM196:29 Hp273 but salt will keep from putrefaction, some again like tender
MEDDM202:6 Hp281 is capable of, and some again so base that they are Viler
MEDDM205:32 Hp286 is the breaking of their limbes, some again, are but meanly
MEDDM206:1 Hp287 to that fruitfullnes, altho they aime at perfection And again
MYCHILD216:5 Hp241 and Vanity and he was entreated of me, and again restored
MYCHILD216:18 Hp241 feares brovght yov to this, I now travail in birth again of yov till
MYCHILD218:27 Hp244 me to my own Relig^{n} again.
13MAY227:3 H12 But if they mvst eclipse again
SAMUEL228:7 H8 Hear me again, I giue him Thee.
SAMUEL228:15 H16 That I again may see his face,
RESTOR229:26 H9 Regau'st me him again
2HUSB233:11 H44 Lord let my Eyes see once Again

AGAINE (17) [again] See also **AGEN**

ELEMEN17:6 H370 And swallowes Countryes up, ne're seen againe:
MGREC97:35 H1796 And in short termes, sends this reply againe;
MGREC99:21 H1864 That *Greece* must {was forc'd to} yeeld a fresh supply againe;
MGREC106:11 H2145 Such as submits, he doth againe restore,
MGREC121:31 H2813 And *Pithon* turn'd to *Asia* againe.
MGREC128:29 H3102 *Demetrius* againe with *Ptolomy* did fight,
MGREC128:31 H3104 But bravely sends the Prisoners back againe,
MGREC133:17 H3305 And his againe, also {was nam'd} *Demetrius.*
MROMAN138:16 H3506 *Rome* he inlarg'd, new built againe the wall,
MROMAN138:31 H3521 Warres with the *Latins* he againe renewes,
DIALOG142:18 H47 Or is {is't} the fatall jarre againe begun,
DIALOG143:34 H103 That Pope, had hope, to find *Rome* here againe;
DUBART153:25 H29 At night turnes to his Mothers cot againe,
MEDDM202:8 Hp281 and some againe, so ignorant and sotish that they are more
MEDDM202:12 Hp281 and some againe so weak and feeble, that while they liue,

MEDDM202:23 Hp282 darknes till he arise againe, so god doth somtime vaile his face
MEDDM206:29 Hp288 good parents haue had bad children, and againe how many

AGAINST (28) See also AGST

MASSYR54:35 H62 Against the *Bactrians* (but that I doubt)
MASSYR58:18 H203 Against their monstrous King to bring {use} their might,
MASSYR64:10 H434 Against *Iehoiakim* marcht with his train;
MASSYR65:33 H498 But in the eighth, against his Prince rebels;
MPERS69:20 H642 Against great *Cressus,* then of *Lidia* head;
MPERS74:35 H858 But strength {men} against those walls was {were} of no use;
MPERS77:33 H974 Against the *Sythians,* and *Grecians* too,
MPERS81:25 H1133 Against the *Persians* they would use {bend} their force.
MPERS87:5 H1361 The wife, against the mother, still doth cry
MPERS87:29 H1381 Had not a Captain; {his Captains} sore against his will;
MPERS87:32 H1384 For his security, against his foes.
MPERS91:4 H1512 With suit, their force, {Arms} against his {their} foes be bent;
MGREC94:5 H1639 This done, against all {both} right, and natures laws,
MGREC101:27 H1952 Prepares against tomorrow for the war;
MGREC107:27 H2202 Then did {all} their wars, against the *Persian* King.
MGREC112:33 H2419 Enveighs against his Father, now absent,
MGREC114:6 H2474 Like this, against his deity to kick:
MGREC114:24 H2494 Against his Soveraigne, or against his Lawes,
MGREC114:24 H2494 Against his Soveraigne, or against his Lawes,
MGREC128:16 H3089 For {And} he declares against his {the others} injuries;
MGREC130:24 H3179 Then vengeance just, against the same {them} t' expresse;
MGREC~~132:6~~ H3239 Against *Lysimachus* who from him won.
MGREC~~132:20~~ H3263 As Heaven and Earth against him had been set:
MGREC134:6 H3339 Against {Amongst} the Jewes, we read in *Macchabees,*
DIALOG142:14 H43 Doe Barons rise, and side against their King?
MEDDM205:29 Hp286 will not sinne against him.
MYCHILD219:1 Hp244-5 neuer prevail against it, I know whom I haue trvsted, and
JULY223:33 Hp251 O never let Satan p^{r}vail against me, but strenghten

AGAST (1) [aghast]

DIALOG145:3 H152 My {Mine} heart obdurate, stood not yet agast.

AGE (52)

FATHER5:15 H16 Who for their age, their worth, and quality,
FATHER5:27 H28 Yours did contest, for Wealth, for Arts, for Age,
HUMOUR25:25 H214 Nor sparing Sex, nor age, nor fire, nor son.
HUMOUR30:16 H408 Yet time and age, shal soon declare it mine.
AGES36:2 H26 (As that fond age, doth most of al desire.)
AGES36:20 H44 Leaning upon his staffe, comes {came} up old age.
AGES36:28 H52 Intend to speak, according to their age:
AGES37:21 H83 In that which riper age did scorn, and slight:
AGES38:15 H118 Which sprouted forth, in my {mine} insuing age,
AGES41:14 H233 *Middle Age.*
AGES41:19 H238 Now age is more, more good ye do {may} expect;
AGES41:20 H239 But more my {mine} age, the more is my defect.
AGES42:16 H274 Thus hath mine age (in all) sometimes done wel.
AGES42:17 H275 Sometimes {again,} mine age (in all) {mine Age} been worse
AGES43:36 H331 Though some more incident to age, or youth:
AGES44:1 H334 *Old Age.*
AGES44:10 H343 In every Age i've found much vanitie,

AGES44:21 H354 Provides a staffe for {then} to support his age.
SEASONS50:31 H165 Like good Old Age, whose younger juycie roots,
SEASONS51:27 H203 Decrepit age must also have its time;
SEASONS51:30 H206 So doth Old Age stil tend unto his Grave,
SEASONS52:9 H224 Old cold, dry age, and earth, Autumne resembles,
MASSYR53:19 H9 This was the Golden Age, but after came
MPERS69:41 H671 Weighing the age, and greatnesse of the Prince,
MPERS78:39 H1020 To be to's age a comfort, and a stay,
MGREC93:15 H1612 The twenty first of's age, began to reign.
MGREC108:15 H2231 Nor sex, nor age, nor one, nor other spar'd,
MGREC109:4 ~~H2261~~ To age, nor sex, no pitty doth expresse,
MGREC115:19 H2538 And in a Tragedy there end his age.
MGREC115:39 H2558 His age, and journey long, he now {then} pretends;
MGREC116:9 H2569 The thirty third of's age doe all agree,
MGREC127:2 H3032 Now in her age she's forc't to taste that Cup,
MGREC128:41 H3114 Till *Alexander* unto age was grown,
MGREC130:34 ~~H3181~~ Yet in the flower of's age, he must lie dead,
DUBART152:33 H2 Amongst the happy wits this Age hath showne,
DUBART153:12 H16 If Summer, or my Autumne age, doe yeeld
VANITY160:10 H20 What, Is't in flowring youth, or manly age?
VANITY160:22 H32 If not in honour, beauty, age, nor treasure,
TDUDLEY165:3 H4-5 *Who deceased,* July 31, 1653. *and of his Age,* 77.
DDUDLEY167:8 H4-5 *Who deceased* Decemb. 27. 1643. *and of her age,* 61.
CONTEM171:21 H124 Nor age nor wrinkle on their front are seen;
FLESH177:23 H104 Nor withering age shall e're come there,
CHILDRN186:8 H75 My age I will not once lament,
MERCY188:19 H4-5 1669. *in the* 28. *year of her Age.*
MEDDM195:33 Hp272 Youth is the time of getting middle age of improuing, and old
MEDDM195:33 Hp272 is the time of getting middle age of improuing, and old age of
MEDDM195:35 Hp272 age, and both by an empty old age, he that hath nothing to
MEDDM199:23 Hp278 Dimne eyes, are the concomitants of old age, and short
PILGRIM210:21 H21 By age and paines brought to decay
13MAY227:11 H20 Blessd me in Youth, and elder Age

AGED (2)

SEASONS50:8 H142 Which makes the aged fields look young again,
CONTEM169:30 H69 It makes a man more aged in conceit,

AGEN (3) [again] See also AGAINE

MASSYR56:31 H137 (They say) but twenty, ere came back agen.
MPERS82:12 H1159 Three thousand scapes, for to {only can} run home agen;
DAVID159:8 H23 Did *Saul* with bloodlesse Sword turne back agen:

AGES (12) [pl.]

AGES35:16 H1-2 {Of} The Four Ages of Man.
AGES36:37 H61 With heed now stood, three ages of fraile man;
MASSYR55:39 H105 That after ages, skil, by them were {was} taught.
MASSYR~~57:23~~ H170 He many Ages liv'd after that day.
MASSYR60:32 H297 And from this heap did after Ages see,
MPERS72:17 H765 Thy cruelty will {all} Ages still admire.
MPERS73:6 H793 The Female {to} many ages did extend,
MROMAN140:9 H3572 Hath many Ages been upon his knees.
DUBART154:32 H77 All ages wondring at, shall never clime.
CONTEM169:26 H65 When present times look back to Ages past,

CONTEM171:2 H107 Who thinks not oft upon the Fathers ages.
MYCHILD218:12 Hp244 All Ages maugre all ye heathen Tyrants + all of the Enemyes

AGESILAUS (1)
MPERS91:7 H1515 *Agesilaus* is called home with speed,

AGESILUS (1)
MPERS90:31 H1498 {Their King} *Agesilus* himself doth over-goe {goe};

AGHAST See AGAST

AGGRAVATE (1)
MGREC112:32 H2418 Who to the height doth aggravate each thing;

AGREE (9) See also 'GREE, GREE
HUMOUR25:17 H206 The best of al the four, when they agree.
MASSYR55:16 H82 But all agree, that from no lawfull bed;
MASSYR58:21 H206 These all agree, and forty thousand make,
MPERS74:1 H826 But in conclusion they all agree,
MPERS81:14 H1122 The *Spartans,* fearing *Athens* would agree,
MGREC116:9 H2569 The thirty third of's age doe all agree,
MGREC117:26 H2633 A King they'l have, but who, none can agree:
MGREC120:9 H2744 Whilst they in *Macedon* doe thus agree,
SIDNEY149:11 H10 *Mars* and *Minerva* did in one agree,

AGREEMENT (1)
MGREC128:39 H3112 The terms of their agreement thus expresse,

AGRICOLTURE (1) [agriculture]
AGES42:24 H282 If to Agricolture, I was ordain'd:

AGST (1) [against]
MYCHILD217:21 Hp243 my self y^{t} agst svch a promis, svch tasts of sweetnes ye Gates

AGUE (4)
HUMOUR32:6 H480 Nor cold, nor hot, Ague, nor Plurisie;
AGES~~43:34~~ H329 The quartan Ague, dropsy, Lunacy:
DIALOG141:22 H21 Will bring Consumption, or an Ague quaking,
RESTOR229:20 H3 Ague. June 1661.

AGUES (1) [pl.]
AGES40:37 H216 Sometimes by {with} Agues all my body shaken;

AH (13)
AGES37:2 H64 Ah me! conceiv'd in sin, and born in {with} sorrow,
AGES~~38:13~~ H116 This was mine innocence, but oh {ah!} the seeds,
AGES44:37 H370 But ah, I saw at last those eyes to close:
MASSYR~~66:3~~ H509 A {Ah!} haplesse man, whose darksome contemplation,
MGREC94:35 H1673 Ah! fond vaine man, whose pen was taught ere while,
DIALOG141:13 H12 Ah, tell thy Daughter, she may simpathize.
SIDNEY150:25 H52 Ah, in his blooming prime, death pluckt this Rose,
TDUDLEY166:24 H66 Ah happy Soul, 'mongst Saints and Angels blest,
CONTEM169:16 H57 But Ah, and Ah, again, my imbecility!
CONTEM169:16 H57 But Ah, and Ah, again, my imbecility!
MERCY188:22 H8 Ah, woe is me, to write thy Funeral Song,
MERCY188:30 H16 But ah too soon those heavy tydings fly,
FAINT222:13 H3 But ah! it's not in me

AHAB (1)
MEDDM204:19 Hp285 for takeing veangence on the house of Ahab and yet a little

AHABS (1) [poss.]
MGREC132:13 H3248 *Jehu* in killing *Ahabs* house did well,

AHAZ (5)
MASSYR61:18 H323 To *Tiglath* then doth *Ahaz* send for ease.
MASSYR61:24 H329 And succours *Ahaz,* yet for *Tiglath's* sake,
MASSYR61:32 H337 Proves unto *Ahaz* but a feigned friend;
MASSYR61:36 H341 And *Ahaz* open, at his mercy lay,
MASSYR61:38 H343 (This was that *Ahaz,* which so much {high} transgrest.)

AID (4) See also AIDE, AYD, AYDE
MPERS~~78:24~~ H1005 In person {present} there, now for his help {aid} was seen;
MGREC127:31 H3061 But {And} he for aid to *Ptolomy* doth call.
DIALOG147:2 H228 Blest be thy Counties which do {who did} aid thee still
SIDNEY~~152:4~~ H76 The Muses aid I crav'd, they had no will

AIDE (6) [aid] See also AYD, AYDE
ELEMEN9:23 H57 A transmutation, it was through mine aide.
MASSYR58:15 H200 *Belosus,* promised *Arbaces* aide,
MASSYR60:10 H275 *Medes,* and *Persians,* {when he crav'd} their assisting aide;
MPERS83:30 H1218 To whom the perjur'd *Grecians* lent their aide,
MGREC124:5 H2910 Straight furnisht him with a sufficient aide,
MROMAN138:19 H3509 Of Boats, and Oares, no more they need the aide;

AILS See AYLES

AIM (1) See also AIME
MYCHILD215:16 Hp240 dayly in y^{r} rembrance, (Altho: y^{t} is the least in my aim in w^{t} I

AIM'D (1) [aimed]
HUMOUR29:25 H376 The blow that's aim'd thereat is latch'd by th'arm,

AIME (2) [aim]
MPERS77:8 H947 She lost her aime; her Husband, he lost more,
MEDDM206:1 Hp287 to that fruitfullnes, altho they aime at perfection And again

AIMED (1) See also AIM'D
MYCHILD219:8 Hp245 the mark wch I aimed at.

AIMES (1) [aims] See also AYMES
MEDDM199:20 Hp278 man aimes at profit by the one & content in the other, but often

AIMING (2) See also AYMING
MASSYR60:17 H282 Not so content, but aiming to be great,
MGREC~~128:3~~ H3076 And how he aymes {aiming now} to make himselfe a King,

AIMS See AIMES, AYMES

AIR (3) See also AIRE, AYRE
SEASONS47:29 H45 Of longer dayes, and a more temperate air;
SEASONS~~49:11~~ H102 Have throughly dry'd the earth, and heat the air.
CONTEM173:2 H170 Look how the wantons frisk to tast the air,

AIRE (26) [air] See also AYRE
FATHER5:32 H33 How Aire, and Earth, no correspondence hold,
ELEMEN8:5 H3 Fire, Aire, Earth, and Water, did all contest
ELEMEN8:14 H12 The Fire, the forced Aire, in sunder crack;
ELEMEN8:23 H21 But {Till gentle} Aire at length, contention so abated,
ELEMEN17:33 H397 And now give place unto our sister Aire.
ELEMEN17:34 H398 *Aire.*
ELEMEN17:35 H399 Content (quoth Aire) to speake the last of you,
ELEMEN18:2 H406 Yet Aire, beyond all these ye know t'excell.
ELEMEN18:8 H412 If my pure Aire, thy sonnes did not sustain.
ELEMEN18:16 H420 What is't? but forced Aire which must {doth} rebound,
ELEMEN18:29 H433 The ruddy sweet sanguine, is like to Aire,
ELEMEN19:12 H457 As my fresh Aire preserves, all things in life;

ELEMEN19:35 H476 But some fall down, and some flye up with aire.
ELEMEN19:39 H480 As battells pitcht ith' Aire (as Countries know;)
HUMOUR20:17 H9 Choler was own'd by Fire, and Blood by Aire,
HUMOUR31:33 H466 Now up, now down, transported like the Aire.
HUMOUR35:12 H608 Nor be discern'd, here's water, earth, aire, fire,
AGES35:22 H8 From blood and aire, for hot, and moist is he.
AGES36:8 H32 When blushing first, she 'gins to red {light} the Aire.
SEASONS49:1 H92 As Spring did aire, blood, youth in's equipage.
SEASONS49:11 ~~H102~~ Hath formerly much heat, the earth and aire.
MPERS74:14 H837 {And joyfull} acclamations ecchoes in the aire; {shrill they ring,}
MPERS76:13 H911 Possession of water, earth, and aire,
MGREC108:32 H2248 They flew so thick they seem'd to dark the aire:
DUBART154:36 H81 And whilst there's aire, or fire, or sea or land.
QELIZ158:10 H119 *Whose sweet perfume fills the all-filling aire,*

AIRY (1)
CONTEM173:32 H197 Where winter's never felt by that sweet airy legion.

AKEING (1) [aching] See also AKING
MEDDM198:25 Hp276 An akeing head requires a soft pillow, and a drooping heart a

AKING (1) [aching] See also AKEING
FEVER220:27 H7 My aking head did break,

AL (16) [all]
HUMOUR25:17 H206 The best of al the four, when they agree.
HUMOUR25:21 H210 A Souldier most compleat in al points makest.
HUMOUR26:1 H231 But such thou never art, when al alone;
HUMOUR26:2 H232 Yet such, when we al four are joyn'd in one.
HUMOUR30:14 H406 If I have not more part, then al ye three:
HUMOUR30:34 H426 The Spleen for al you three, was made a sinke,
HUMOUR30:35 H427 Of al the rest, thou'st nothing there to do;
HUMOUR31:9 H442 What officer thou art to al us three.
HUMOUR31:17 H450 And so {thence} with jaundise, Safferns al the skin.
HUMOUR31:20 H453 I now speake unto al, no more to one;
AGES35:26 H12 Solid, hating all lightnesse, and al folly.
AGES36:2 H26 (As that fond age, doth most of al desire.)
AGES36:19 H43 And last of al, to act upon this Stage;
AGES36:26 H50 And al gave eare, to what he had to say.
AGES37:19 H81 Did act al folly, that it could expresse.
AGES38:9 H112 I fear'd no stormes, nor al the windes that blows,

ALACRITY (2)
AGES37:12 H74 Who yet with love, and all alacrity,
MGREC94:18 H1652 Then with alacrity he after goes:

ALARMS (1) [pl.]
DIALOG141:9 H8 And sit i'th dust, to sigh these sad alarms?

ALAS (22)
PROLOG7:4 H19 And this to mend, alas, no Art is able,
ELEMEN9:5 H39 Without mine ayd, alas, what can they doe?
ELEMEN16:25 H348 Alas; thy ships and oares could do no good
HUMOUR~~22:41~~ H110 No, no, {Alas,} thou hast no spirits, thy company
HUMOUR28:32 H344 But why, alas, thus tedious should I be?
AGES39:32 H175 This is my best, but youth (is known) alas,
AGES40:30 ~~H210~~ Thus, thus alas! I have mispent my time,
MASSYR65:14 H479 But he (alas) whose fortunes {all were} now i'th ebbe,

MASSYR65:23 H488 For this was {is} he, for whom none said, Alas!
MPERS80:10 H1077 Alas, it is *Leonades* you want!
MPERS84:6 H1234 Alas, she from her Royalty's {Royalty} suspended.
DIALOG141:6 H5 Alas, deare Mother, fairest Queen, and best,
DIALOG141:30 H29 And thus, alas, your state you much deplore,
DIALOG144:24 ~~H133~~ These Prophets mouthes (alas the while) was stopt,
DAVID158:24 H4 Alas, slaine is the head of *Israel,*
CONTEM168:21 H29 Had I not better known, (alas) the same had I.
AUTHOR178:14 H24 And for thy Mother, she alas is poor,
1LETTER181:15 H13 In this dead time, alas, what can I more
3LETTER183:22 H24 I here, he there, alas, both kept by force:
CHILDRN185:26 H52 The net be spread, and caught, alas.
CHILDRN185:37 H63 Alas my birds, you wisdome want,
11MAYB228:30 Hp259 But alas! I cannot render vnto ye Lord according to all his

ALAYED (1) [allayed]
MEDDM201:13 Hp280 anger must be alayed, by cold words and not by blustering

ALBA (1)
MROMAN138:8 H3498 And from old *Alba* fetch the wealth away;

ALBANS (2) [pl.]
MROMAN138:1 H3491 War with the antient *Albans* he doth {did} wage,
MROMAN138:4 H3494 And *Curiatii,* three *Albans* provide;

ALBERTUS (1)
AGES44:35 H368 And *Philip,* and *Albertus,* half undone;

ALBIAN (1)
QELIZ158:6 H115 *Eliza* shall rule *Albian* once again.

ALBION (1)
ELEMEN17:8 H372 Thus *Albion* {*Britain* fair} (tis thought) was cut from *France,*

ALCIDES (1)
ELEMEN10:4 H79 The *Theban* stout *Alcides,* with his club:

ALCIES (1) [poss.]
DIALOG142:39 H68 Nor is it *Alcies* Son, and {nor} *Henries* Daughter,

ALEXANDER (77)
MPERS70:37 ~~H708~~ Where *Alexander* fought, in hope of prize,
MPERS~~70:40~~ H711 And *Alexander* coming to the same,
MPERS81:29 H1137 No lesse then Grand-sire to great *Alexander.*
MGREC93:8 H1605 under *Alexander* the Great,
MGREC6:10 H1607 Great *Alexander,* was wise *Phillips* son,
MGREC94:25 H1663 When newes of *Alexander,* came to th' Court,
MGREC94:37 H1675 To th' river *Granicke, Alexander* hyes,
MGREC95:4 H1683 This Victory did *Alexander* gain;
MGREC95:12 H1691 Next *Alexander* marcht, t'wards the black sea;
MGREC95:26 H1705 Now {Then} *Alexander* all *Cilicia* takes:
MGREC97:14 H1775 The Royall Captives, brought to *Alexander,*
MGREC97:20 H1781 And this to *Alexander* is more a fame,
MGREC97:29 H1790 Writes unto {To} *Alexander,* to {he would} restore
MGREC97:34 H1795 His {This} Letter *Alexander* doth disdaine,
MGREC97:38 H1799 Now {Next} *Alexander* unto *Tyre* doth goe,
MGREC98:32 H1834 And {now} must at *Gaza, Alexander* meet;
MGREC99:9 H1852 Was I as great, as is great *Alexander,*
MGREC99:12 H1855 To which, brave {proud} *Alexander* did {made} reply,
MGREC99:29 H1872 Can *Alexander* deale thus cruelly?

alexander

MGREC99:37	H1880	Whom with great reverence *Alexander* greets;
MGREC100:18	H1902	Great *Alexander* had been kept from Land;
MGREC100:35	H1919	Great *Alexander* mourns, as well as he,
MGREC101:1	H1926	Great *Alexander,* for this good regard;
MGREC101:16	H1941	To this, stout *Alexander,* gives no eare,
MGREC101:28	H1953	*Parmenio, Alexander* wisht, that night,
MGREC101:36	H1965	Forty five thousand *Alexander* had,
MGREC102:4	H1974	Which *Alexander* deals, as suits his pleasure.
MGREC103:14	H2025	The share of *Alexander* did amount,
MGREC104:1	H2053	But hearing, *Alexander* was so near;
MGREC104:6	H2058	Perswades him not to fight, with *Alexander.*
MGREC104:27	H2079	And thus to {t'ward} *Alexander,* on he goes,
MGREC104:30	H2082	To *Alexander* fly, {flyes} and told {tells} this act;
MGREC105:22	H2115	Prayes him, to *Alexander* to commend,
MGREC~~106:2~~	H2136	But *Alexander* will, for this regard
MGREC106:7	H2141	Now to the East great *Alexander* goes,
MGREC106:16	H2150	Her traine to *Alexander* (as 'tis thought)
MGREC106:21	H2155	As *Alexander* in his greatnesse growes,
MGREC108:13	H2229	But *Alexander* puts them to the sword,
MGREC109:18	H2277	Through his perswasion *Alexander* meets;
MGREC109:24	H2283	But *Alexander,* caus'd {made} him to behold;
MGREC109:30	H2289	To him doth *Alexander* thus declare,
MGREC109:38	H2297	Great *Alexander* vext at this reply,
MGREC110:5	H2305	Had *Alexander* such resistance seen,
MGREC110:9	H2309	His Army *Alexander* doth divide,
MGREC110:15	H2315	Yet work enough, here *Alexander* found,
MGREC110:18	H2318	When *Alexander* strives to win the field,
MGREC~~110:18~~	H2322	Did *Alexander* by his answers find:
MGREC110:21	H2325	East-ward, now *Alexander* would goe still,
MGREC113:5	H2432	Oh, *Alexander,* thy free clemency,
MGREC113:18	H2445	This sound advice, at heart, pleas'd *Alexander,*
MGREC114:2	H2470	*Alexander,* to rage, to kill, and sweare,
MGREC114:5	H2473	Nothing toucht *Alexander* to the quick
MGREC114:11	~~H2479~~	*Alexander* now no longer could containe,
MGREC114:29	H2499	Of *Alexander,* this th' eternall crime,
MGREC115:4	H2515	Now *Alexander* goes to *Media,*
MGREC117:17	H2624	Great *Alexander* dead, his Army's left,
MGREC117:29	H2636	Great *Alexander* has left {did leave} issue none,
MGREC117:37	H2644	A Sister *Alexander* had, but she
MGREC119:32	H2722	'Mongst all the Captains {princes} of great *Alexander,*
MGREC~~120:20~~	H2756	(For all the princes of great *Alexander*
MGREC122:14	H2839	If once young *Alexander* grow more strong,
MGREC122:21	~~H2834~~	Her mother *Cyna* sister to *Alexander,*
MGREC122:35	H2856	For all the Princes {nobles} of great {King} *Alexander*
MGREC122:39	H2860	Two Sons of *Alexander,* and the rest,
MGREC124:21	H2928	Nor could Mother, nor Sons of *Alexander,*
MGREC124:31	H2938	Hatefull the Name, and House of *Alexander,*
MGREC124:36	H2943	When *Alexander* knockt his head to th' wall:
MGREC128:41	H3114	Till *Alexander* unto age was grown,
MGREC129:12	H3126	No sooner was great *Alexander* dead,
MGREC129:33	H3147	And place their hopes o'th heire of *Alexander,*

MGREC129:38 H3152 Thus was the race, and house of *Alexander*
MGREC130:33 ~~H3181~~ If *Alexander* was not poysoned,
MGREC133:9 H3297 With *Ptolomy,* reign'd after *Alexander;*
MGREC133:20 H3308 And his son *Alexander* of *Epire,*
MGREC134:31 H3362 *Alexander,* then *Lathurus* in's stead,
SIDNEY151:8 ~~H69~~ O Princely *Philip,* rather *Alexander,*
SIDNEY152:25 H94 Philip *and* Alexander *both in one.*

ALEXANDER'S (1) [alexander is]
MGREC107:28 H2203 Here *Alexander's* almost at a stand,

ALEXANDERS (7) [poss.]
MPERS92:35 H1593 In *Alexanders* reign who did him quell,
MGREC95:19 H1698 To *Alexanders* heart's no little joy.
MGREC98:35 H1837 And layes before great *Alexanders* eyes,
MGREC104:34 H2086 Had *Alexanders* wrath incensed high;
MGREC112:15 H2401 Now, *Alexanders* conquests, all are done,
MGREC~~114:11~~ H2479 Which *Alexanders* wrath incens'd so high,
MGREC116:2 H2562 The thread of *Alexanders* life was spun;

ALEXANDRIA (5)
MGREC100:12 H1896 Faire *Alexandria* from the ground doth raise;
MGREC108:37 H2253 Which *Alexandria* he doth also {likewise} name,
MGREC120:35 H2772 At *Alexandria,* in *Ægypt* Land, {his tomb he plac'd}
MGREC134:21 H3352 The {At *Alexandria* a} Library at *Alexandria* built,
MGREC134:21 H3352 The {At *Alexandria* a} Library at *Alexandria* built,

ALGIRE (1)
ELEMEN19:25 H470 If nought was {were} known, but that before *Algire.*

ALIENATE (1)
MGREC121:9 H2787 Did alienate the Souldiers from his side;

ALIGHT (1) See also T'ALIGHT
MPERS74:11 H836 The Nobles all alight, {bow to} their King to greet,

ALIKE (1)
MGREC108:16 H2232 But in his cruelty alike they shar'd;

ALIMENT (1)
HUMOUR27:7 H278 If stil thou take along my Aliment,

ALIUE (1)
FAINT222:22 H12 And tho: as dead mad'st me aliue

ALIVE (11)
ELEMEN13:39 H240 Before they know, they are inter'd alive.
ELEMEN~~14:4~~ H248 Bur'ing himself alive for honours prize.
ELEMEN16:8 H331 *Asphaltis* Lake, where nought remains alive.
AGES44:41 H374 (For 'twas our hopes then kept our hearts alive)
MASSYR54:6 H33 Alive, and dead, a god they did him make;
MASSYR~~68:13~~ H599 As thus amort {dead, alive} he sits, as all {one} undone:
MPERS72:20 H768 Flayd him alive, hung up his stuffed skin
MGREC94:32 H1670 That he be tane alive, (for he intends)
MGREC117:2 H2609 A God alive him all must Idolize;
TDUDLEY165:13 H15 Or who alive then I, a greater debtor?
CONTEM171:13 H117 Living so little while we are alive;

ALL (557) See also AL
FATHER5:20 H21 These are of all, the life, the nurse, the grave,
FATHER6:2 H36 Some thing {something} of all (though mean) I did intend,
PROLOG6:21 H6 And {Or} how they all, or each, their dates have run:

PROLOG7:16	H29	A Poets Pen, all scorne, I should thus wrong;
PROLOG7:32	H43	Preheminence in each, and all is yours,
ELEMEN8:5	H3	Fire, Aire, Earth, and Water, did all contest
ELEMEN8:8	~~H6~~	For to declare, themselves they all ingage;
ELEMEN8:11	H9	All would be cheife, and all scorn'd to be under,
ELEMEN8:11	H9	All would be cheife, and all scorn'd to be under,
ELEMEN8:16	H14	All looked like a Chaos, or new birth;
ELEMEN8:26	H24	All stormes now laid, and they in perfect peace,
ELEMEN8:30	H28	What is my worth (both ye) and all things {men} know,
ELEMEN8:34	H32	The benefit all Beings, {living} by me finde;
ELEMEN~~8:35~~	H33	All sorts of Artists, here declare your mind,
ELEMEN9:39	H73	The Flye *Pyrausta* cal'd, all else expire.
ELEMEN10:27	H102	'Mong all my wonders which I might recount;
ELEMEN~~11:1~~	H120	But maugre all, that I, or foes could do
ELEMEN11:15	H135	And all therein at that great day of doome;
ELEMEN11:23	H143	In wealth and use I doe surpasse you all,
ELEMEN12:10	H170	But farewell all, for deare mount *Helicon,*
ELEMEN13:8	H209	And ye Artificers, all trades and sorts;
ELEMEN13:12	H213	And cholerick sister, thou (for all thine ire)
ELEMEN13:33	H234	But to all outrages their hunger runnes.
ELEMEN14:4	H246	*Korah* {*Dathan*} and all his Company well knew.
ELEMEN14:30	H272	Not one of us, all knowes, that's like to thee,
ELEMEN15:26	H308	There lives the oyly Whale, whom all men know,
ELEMEN15:38	H320	Which *Cæsars, Consuls, Tribunes* all adorne;
ELEMEN16:34	H357	All humours, Tumours, that {which} are bred of cold.
ELEMEN17:15	H379	My Ice and extream cold, which all men know.
ELEMEN17:22	H386	All know, what {that} innundations I have made;
ELEMEN17:24	H388	As when *Achaia,* all under water stood,
ELEMEN18:2	H406	Yet Aire, beyond all these ye know t'excell.
ELEMEN18:5	H409	And all the wealth, that ever earth did give,
ELEMEN18:7	H411	No world {earth}, thy witching trash, were all but vain.
ELEMEN19:1	H446	For all Philosophers make one of me.
ELEMEN19:12	H457	As my fresh Aire preserves, all things in life;
ELEMEN19:36	H477	Earth-quaks so hurtful and so fear'd of all,
ELEMEN20:7	H489	To adde to all I've said, was my intent,
HUMOUR20:19	H11	All having made obeysance to each Mother,
HUMOUR20:24	H16	Who had precedency of all the other.
HUMOUR20:26	H18	Pleading her selfe, was most of all desir'd;
HUMOUR20:29	H21	She was the silencest {silentest} of all the foure,
HUMOUR21:12	H40	Though under fire, we comprehend all heat,
HUMOUR21:35	H63	And there she wil out-bid us all, I think;
HUMOUR22:12	H81	So loving unto all, she scornes to fight.
HUMOUR22:19	H88	Here's three of you, all sees {see} now what you are,
HUMOUR23:12	H122	The sinke of all us three, the hatefull spleen;
HUMOUR24:1	H150	Nay, th' stomach, magazeen to all the rest,
HUMOUR24:6	H155	Of all that lives, I cause the propagation.
HUMOUR24:31	H180	And leave't to all, to judge where valour lyes.
HUMOUR24:39	H188	And scorn'st all Knightly sports, at turnament.
HUMOUR25:19	H208	Both them and all things else, she will {would} consume.
HUMOUR26:39	H269	Challenge not all, 'cause part we do allow,
HUMOUR27:2	H273	Which without all dispute, is Cholers owne;

HUMOUR27:26	H297	Of all your qualities, I do partake,
HUMOUR27:29	H300	I moderately am all, what need I more:
HUMOUR27:31	H302	If this {you} can't be disprov'd {disprove}, then all I hold:
HUMOUR27:36	H307	Nay, could I be from all your tangs but pure,
HUMOUR27:39	H310	So suddenly, the body all is fir'd:
HUMOUR28:11	H323	All to prevent, this curious care I take;
HUMOUR28:13	H325	Of all the perverse humours from mine owne,
HUMOUR28:19	H331	But yet for all my toyl, my care, my skil,
HUMOUR28:26	H338	And like the Liver, all benignious;
HUMOUR29:19	H370	Not past all reason, but in truth all shame:
HUMOUR29:19	H370	Not past all reason, but in truth all shame:
HUMOUR29:35	H386	Wise *Fabius* is her buckler: all accord.
HUMOUR30:8	H400	Then all the huge beasts of the fertile field.
HUMOUR30:21	H413	Then who's mans friend, when life and all forsakes?
HUMOUR31:11	H444	That casts out all that man or {e're} eates, or drinks.
HUMOUR33:3	H517	Sixty nine Princes, all stout *Hero* Knights,
HUMOUR33:18	H532	With all your flourishes, now Sisters three,
HUMOUR33:22	H536	The Brain's the noblest member all allow,
HUMOUR33:27	H541	Though it in all, and every part be whole:
HUMOUR34:1	H556	The optick nerve, coats, humours, all are mine,
HUMOUR34:9	H564	Of all the Sences, Sight shal be the Queen;
HUMOUR34:12	H567	Which runs through all the spondles of the rack,
HUMOUR34:14	H569	All nerves (except seven paire) to it retain;
HUMOUR35:3	H599	Unlesse we 'gree all fals into confusion.
HUMOUR35:11	H607	But all admire our perfect amity;
HUMOUR35:14	H610	This loving counsel pleas'd them all so wel,
AGES35:26	H12	Solid, hating all lightnesse, and al folly.
AGES35:36	H22	And when tis broke, then ends his life and all.
AGES36:29	H53	But wise Old-age, did with all gravity,
AGES37:12	H74	Who yet with love, and all alacrity,
AGES37:27	H89	Through ignorance, all troubles did surmount.
AGES38:14	H117	Lay raked up; of all the cursed weeds,
AGES38:38	H141	Strangely preserv'd, yet mind it not at all.
AGES39:24	H167	Though thus in field, at home, to all most kind,
AGES39:31	H174	Makes {Make} all to place their future hopes on me.
AGES39:37	H180	My woful Parents longing hopes all {are} crost,
AGES40:2	H183	My Lust doth hurry me, to all that's ill,
AGES40:7	H188	Of all at once, who not so wise, as fair,
AGES40:15	H196	To all obscenity, my {mine} eares I bend. {lend;}
AGES40:16	H197	All counsel hate, which tends to make me wise,
AGES40:29	H210	I want a {have no} heart {at} all this for to deplore.
AGES40:37	H216	Sometimes by {with} Agues all my body shaken;
AGES40:38	H217	Sometimes by Feavers, all my moisture drinking,
AGES41:41	H258	Yet all my powers, for self-ends are not spent,
AGES42:14	H272	Was I a laborer, I wrought all day,
AGES42:16	H274	Thus hath mine age (in all) sometimes done wel.
AGES42:17	H275	Sometimes {again,} mine age (in all) {mine Age} been worse
AGES43:5	H300	Opprest, and sunke, and sact, {stav'd} all in my way;
AGES43:20	H315	I judge, I should have room, in all mens hearts.
AGES43:35	H330	Subject to all Diseases, {distempers} that's the truth,
AGES44:3	H336	And all you say, say I, and something {somewhat} more;

AGES44:11	H344	An end of all perfection now I see.
AGES44:25	H358	Sometimes {Sometime} again, rain'd all adversity;
AGES44:36	H369	I saw all peace at home, terror to foes,
AGES~~45:40~~	H430	Now trembling, and {is all} fearful, sad, and cold;
AGES46:8	H439	From King to begger, all degrees shal finde
AGES46:10	H441	Yea knowing much, the pleasant'st {pleasants} life of all,
AGES46:14	H445	My studies, labours, readings, all are done,
AGES46:25	H456	And in that hope, I bid you all farewel.
SEASONS46:31	H7	In season all these Seasons I shal bring;
SEASONS46:37	H15	*March, April, May,* of all the rest most faire;
SEASONS47:1	H17	And bids defiance to all tedious Winters:
SEASONS47:15	H31	And all that seem'd as dead, afresh do live.
SEASONS47:37	H49	All Plants, and Flowers, {set and sown} for all delights, and
SEASONS47:37	H49	All Plants, and Flowers, {set and sown} for all delights, and
SEASONS48:15	H68	All flowers before the {with his} sun-beames now discloses,
SEASONS48:30	H83	But none in all that hath preheminence.
SEASONS48:35	H86	Yet above all, this priviledge is thine,
SEASONS49:3	H94	With haire all wet, she puffing thus began.
SEASONS49:22	~~H113~~	'Mongst all ye shepheards, never but one man,
SEASONS49:35	H128	Whose fragrant scent, {smel} all made-perfume surpasses;
SEASONS49:37	H130	And for all sorts of Pease this is the time.
SEASONS49:38	H131	*July* my next, the hot'st in all the year,
SEASONS50:5	H139	With weary stroaks, they take all in their way,
SEASONS50:23	H157	The Carter leads all home, with whistling voyce,
SEASONS51:11	H185	The season's now at hand, of all, and each;
SEASONS51:12	H186	Sure at this time, Time first of all began,
SEASONS51:16	H190	Or withered stocks, {which were} all dry, and dead,
SEASONS51:24	H200	The fruitful trees, all withered now do stand,
SEASONS52:3	~~H219~~	This month is timber for all uses fell'd,
SEASONS52:10	H225	And melancholy, which most of all dissembles.
SEASONS52:39	H254	Until by's heat he drives {drive} all cold away.
SEASONS53:7	H263	*And all the faults which {that} you shall spy,*
MASSYR53:25	H15	These were his first, all stood in *Shinar* land,
MASSYR54:28	H55	This Tyrant did his neighbours all oppresse,
MASSYR54:37	H64	And all the greater *Asia* did subdue;
MASSYR55:16	H82	But all agree, that from no lawfull bed;
MASSYR55:28	H94	That having no compeer, she might rule all,
MASSYR55:37	H103	Admir'd of all, but equaliz'd of none.
MASSYR56:12	H118	But {And} that which did, all cost, and art excell,
MASSYR56:21	H127	All eyes that saw, or ears that hears, {hear} admires.
MASSYR56:30	H136	But this is marvelous, of all those men,
MASSYR57:9	H156	This fraud, in war, nor peace, at all appears;
MASSYR57:16	~~H163~~	Some may object, his Parents ruling all,
MASSYR~~57:17~~	H164	Unto a Father that all Countryes won
MASSYR57:30	H175	For *Ninias,* and all his Race are left,
MASSYR57:36	H181	It is enough {may suffice}, if all be true that's past,
MASSYR57:40	H185	Who wallowed in all voluptuousnesse,
MASSYR58:21	H206	These all agree, and forty thousand make,
MASSYR58:36	H219	And with all terms of amity, he greets, {them greet.}
MASSYR58:38	H221	And their Taxations sore, all to revoake,
MASSYR~~59:3~~	H227	T' accept of what they could, they him {all} beseech.

MASSYR59:8	H232	But all {And now} surpris'd, by this unlookt for fright,
MASSYR59:10	H234	The King his Brother leaves, all to sustaine,
MASSYR59:16	H240	There with all store he was so wel provided,
MASSYR59:30	H254	But all his wealth, and friends, together gets,
MASSYR59:40	H264	*Arbaces* thus, of all becomming Lord,
MASSYR~~59:41~~	H265	Ingeniously with each {all} did keep his word;
MASSYR60:2	H267	With over-plus of all treasures {the wealth} therein,
MASSYR60:29	H294	*Arbaces* suffers all, and all he takes.
MASSYR60:29	H294	*Arbaces* suffers all, and all he takes.
MASSYR60:34	H299	When this was built, and all matters in peace,
MASSYR61:30	H335	To whom, he ought all loyalty of heart.
MASSYR61:33	H338	All *Israels* Land, {lands} beyond *Iordan,* he takes.
MASSYR63:13	H398	All yeelds to him, but *Ninivie* kept free,
MASSYR~~63:28~~	H414	This King's less fam'd for all the acts he's done,
MASSYR64:28	H452	As might not him, but all the world out-face;
MASSYR64:31	H455	How in all Merchandise she did excell,
MASSYR65:4	H469	And took the wealthy town, but all the gain
MASSYR~~65:14~~	H479	But he (alas) whose fortunes {all were} now i'th ebbe,
MASSYR65:15	H480	Had all his hopes like to a Spiders web;
MASSYR65:36	H501	And after eighteen months he took them all,
MASSYR65:41	H506	With Children, Wives, and Nobles, all they bring,
MASSYR66:1	H507	Where to the sword, all but himself was {were} put,
MASSYR66:11	H517	All now of worth, are captive led with tears,
MASSYR66:13	H519	With all these Conquests, *Babels* King rests not,
MASSYR66:16	H522	All Vassals, at his hands, for grace must sue;
MASSYR66:18	H524	All rule, he from the ancient *Pharoes* takes;
MASSYR66:23	H529	His sumptuous buildings passes all conceit,
MASSYR67:6	H552	Poor forlorn Prince, that {who} had all state forgot,
MASSYR67:15	H561	*Arabia,* and all the boardering coast.
MASSYR67:38	H584	And with a hand, soon dashed all his pride.
MASSYR68:13	H599	As thus amort {dead, alive} he sits, as all {one} undone:
MPERS69:26	H648	Where all that doe {dare} resist, are slaughter'd down;
MPERS69:35	H657	Then on a Pike being {wood-pile} set, where all might eye,
MPERS~~69:38~~	H664	And viewing all, at all nought mov'd was he:
MPERS~~69:38~~	H664	And viewing all, at all nought mov'd was he:
MPERS70:7	H678	That all the world they neither {need not} feare, nor doubt;
MPERS70:10	H681	That night *Belshazzar* feasted all his rout,
MPERS~~71:3~~	H715	Thirty two years in all this Prince
MPERS71:4	~~H716~~	Unto *Cambyses* then, all did remain.
MPERS71:12	~~H727~~	Which Law includes all Lawes, though lawlesse stil,
MPERS71:16	H730	And all of Royal bloud that came to hand,
MPERS71:36	H750	If all his {this} heat, had been for a good {pious} end,
MPERS~~72:17~~	H765	Thy cruelty will {all} Ages still admire.
MPERS72:26	~~H773~~	His cruell Master, for all service done,
MPERS72:32	H776	Fear'd of all, but lov'd of few, or none,
MPERS72:33	H777	All thought {wisht} his short reign long, till {past before} it was
MPERS73:17	H804	Descended all, of *Achemenes* blood,
MPERS73:29	H814	All things in peace, and Rebells throughly quel'd,
MPERS74:1	H826	But in conclusion they all agree,
MPERS74:3	H828	All envie to avoyd, this was thought on,
MPERS74:6	H831	Of all the Peers should have precedency.

MPERS74:7	H832	They all attend on the appointed houre,
MPERS74:11	H836	The Nobles all alight, {bow to} their King to greet,
MPERS~~74:17~~	H840	They then {all} attend him, to his royall roome,
MPERS74:18	H841	Thanks for all this to's crafty Stable-groome.
MPERS74:31	~~H854~~	Did win him loyalty, and all respect;
MPERS74:32	H855	Yet notwithstanding he did all so well,
MPERS75:8	H869	With all the Cities strength they him betrust,
MPERS75:11	H872	Delivers up the town, and all in it.
MPERS75:34	H891	And on all Kings he poures out execrations,
MPERS76:30	H928	Arm'd all they could, which elev'n thousand make;
MPERS77:6	H945	His Queen *Attossa,* caused all {author of} this stir,
MPERS77:13	H952	Unto {Then to} his eldest {second} Son, all did remain.
MPERS77:25	H966	Yet all his men, and instruments of slaughter,
MPERS~~77:36~~	H977	With certainty {conquest} of {all} *Europe* feeds his pride;
MPERS78:3	H984	His Army of all Nations, was compounded,
MPERS78:9	H990	The charge of all he severally commended,
MPERS78:11	H992	But the command of these Commanders all,
MPERS78:25	H1006	Whose Gallies all the rest in neatnesse passe,
MPERS78:31	H1012	At *Sardis,* in *Lidia,* these all doe meet,
MPERS78:33	H1014	Feasts all this multitude, of his own charge,
MPERS78:36	H1017	Which mighty sum, all wondred to behold.
MPERS~~79:31~~	H1057	His Hoast, who {all} *Lissus* drinks to quench their thirst,
MPERS79:32	H1058	And for his Cattell, all *Pissirus* Lake
MPERS79:40	H1066	And all that Army, then dismay'd, had fled,
MPERS81:4	H1112	He seeing {finding} all thus tend unto {to his} decay,
MPERS81:11	H1119	That all Hostility might {from} thence-forth cease;
MPERS81:13	H1121	So should all favour to their State be shown.
MPERS81:21	H1129	Their infamy would last till all things ends:
MPERS~~81:35~~	H1143	{In all} One hundred thousand, and ten thousand make.
MPERS81:38	~~H1143~~	But all their controversies to decide,
MPERS~~82:2~~	H1148	Then for one battel shortly all provide,
MPERS83:22	H1210	But all his family was likewise slain,
MPERS84:18	H1254	That in all {his} Loyalty his heart was bound;
MPERS84:31	H1267	But he all injury, had soon forgate,
MPERS85:9	H1285	Who now sole Monarch, doth of all remaine,
MPERS85:27	H1303	All Townes, held by his Ancestors before.
MPERS86:10	H1326	Yet doubts, {fears} all he injoyes, is not his own.
MPERS88:1	H1394	Arme, arme, the King {with all his host} is now approaching
MPERS88:13	H1406	And all good discipline to be neglected.
MPERS88:29	H1422	But treads down all, for to advance their Master;
MPERS89:6	H1440	Nor wound receiv'd, but one among them all:
MPERS89:18	H1452	And there all wait his mercy, weaponlesse;
MPERS89:25	H1459	The King great store of all provision sends,
MPERS89:35	H1469	And with all {the} Oathes, and deepest flattery,
MPERS~~89:38~~	H1472	And Villaine-like, there puts them {all} to the sword.
MPERS~~90:2~~	H1477	But when through difficulties still {all} they brake,
MPERS90:3	~~H1477~~	He sought all sustinance from them to take;
MPERS90:5	~~H1477~~	So to deprive them of all nourishment;
MPERS90:11	H1484	These {Who} after all, receiv'd them joyfully:
MPERS90:18	H1485	So after all {Thus finishing} their travell, danger, pain,
MPERS91:6	H1514	With broyls, and quarrels, sets all *Greece* on fire.

MPERS91:9 H1517 They now {Their winnings} lost all, and were a peace {their
MPERS91:16 H1524 All the peculiar vertues of a Prince:
MPERS91:19 H1527 The King from forraign foes, and all {parts now well} at ease,
MPERS91:27 ~~H1541~~ But yet for all his greatnesse, and long reign,
MPERS91:28 ~~H1542~~ He must leave all, and in the pit remain;
MPERS91:30 ~~H1544~~ As all the mighty ones, have done, and must:
MPERS~~92:23~~ H1581 Lost but his life for horrid treasons all.
MPERS92:39 H1597 One deluge came, and swept them all away;
MPERS93:2 H1599 Of all, did scarce his winding sheet retaine.
MGREC94:5 H1639 This done, against all {both} right, and natures laws,
MGREC~~94:9~~ H1643 And many more, {all} whom he suspects {or fears} will climbe,
MGREC95:3 H1682 Who in their backs did all their wounds receive.
MGREC95:15 H1694 Whose touch turn'd all to gold, yea even his meat:
MGREC95:17 H1696 Which who so did {doth}, must Lord of all remain,
MGREC95:25 H1704 Goes {Runs} after too {two}, and leaves all to disaster.
MGREC95:26 H1705 Now {Then} *Alexander* all *Cilicia* takes:
MGREC96:6 H1726 As if they were, {if addrest} now all to run at {a} tilt:
MGREC96:29 H1749 Now least this Gold, and all this goodly stuffe,
MGREC96:34 H1754 The *Greekes* would all adore, and {but} would none fight.
MGREC97:12 H1773 Yet all this grief, this losse, this over-throw,
MGREC97:25 H1786 But all *Phenicia* to his pleasures {pleasure} yeeld;
MGREC97:27 H1788 Unto *Parmenio,* of all, most fit;
MGREC98:16 H1818 The other by his men fetcht all by Land;
MGREC99:2 H1845 All those rich Kingdoms large, which {that} doe abide
MGREC99:7 H1850 For all he offered {offers} now, was but his owne:
MGREC100:13 H1897 Then setling all things in lesse *Asia,*
MGREC101:5 H1930 And offers all he did, and Kingdoms more;
MGREC101:7 H1932 (Nor was such match, in all the world beside)
MGREC101:8 H1933 And all those Countries, which (betwixt) did lye,
MGREC101:11 H1936 And all those Kingdoms in lesse *Asia;*
MGREC101:14 H1939 And till all this be wel perform'd, and sure,
MGREC101:29 H1954 To force his Camp, so put {vanquish} them all to {by} flight;
MGREC102:1 H1971 *Darius* stript of all, to *Media* came,
MGREC102:12 H1982 Which in few hours was carried all away;
MGREC102:19 H1989 With all pleasures that on earth was {are} found,
MGREC102:37 H2007 And furniture, the richest of {in} all Lands,
MGREC103:1 H2012 For his receit with joy, they all accord;
MGREC103:3 H2014 And all in it was at his high command;
MGREC103:4 H2015 Of all the Cities, that on Earth was found;
MGREC103:8 H2019 Here lay the bulk, of all those precious things;
MGREC103:13 H2024 Yet after all, as stories do expresse,
MGREC103:23 H2034 Now makes this King, his vertues all to drown.
MGREC103:24 H2035 He walloweth now, {That wallowing} in all licenciousnesse,
MGREC105:12 H2105 Yea, {But} above all, that neither eare, nor eye,
MGREC105:31 H2124 For all that {the} Kingly Grace he did expresse,
MGREC105:40 H2133 Of all good things (quoth he) once in my power,
MGREC106:13 H2147 On *Artabasus* more then all bestow'd,
MGREC~~106:35~~ H2169 His manners, habit, gestures, now doth {all did} fashion,
MGREC~~107:27~~ H2202 Then did {all} their wars, against the *Persian* King.
MGREC107:37 H2212 They all passe over, to the other place;
MGREC107:41 H2216 Hated of all, for's former treachery,

MGREC109:5 ~~H2262~~ But all fall by his sword, most mercilesse.
MGREC109:15 H2274 Had to his mind, made all things now {to} accord:
MGREC109:21 H2280 And tenders him the strength of all his lands, {land;}
MGREC109:26 H2285 His Presents all, with thanks he doth {did} restore;
MGREC109:28 H2287 Thus all the *Indian* Kings, to him submit;
MGREC111:6 H2351 These, all he feasts in state, on beds of gold,
MGREC111:27 H2372 That of them all, the fourth did scarce remaine.
MGREC112:6 H2392 Whose Sences all, were glutted with delights:
MGREC112:15 H2401 Now, *Alexanders* conquests, all are done,
MGREC112:17 H2403 His vertues dead, buried, and all {quite} forgot,
MGREC113:22 H2449 Wherefore at once all these to satisfie,
MGREC114:16 H2486 Then all the wrong to brave *Parmenio* done.
MGREC114:32 H2502 Nor all felicity, of his in war;
MGREC114:37 H2507 All Kingdoms, Countries, Provinces, he won, {wan}
MGREC114:39 H2509 All this he did, who knows not to be true,
MGREC115:2 H2513 All this he did, yea, and much more, 'tis true,
MGREC116:9 H2569 The thirty third of's age doe all agree,
MGREC~~116:10~~ H2575 All friends she shuns, yea, banished the light,
MGREC116:16 H2582 And so with black, be-clouded all his fame.
MGREC117:2 H2609 A God alive him all must Idolize;
MGREC117:4 H2611 Of all those kingdomes large which he had got,
MGREC117:10 H2617 Four of his Captains, all doe now divide,
MGREC~~117:22~~ H2629 Each man {All men} began for {streight} to contemn his might;
MGREC117:25 H2632 Now Court, and Camp, all in confusion be,
MGREC118:18 H2665 That he, who late, possest all earthly things,
MGREC118:26 H2675 But all his bowels, coloured well, and sound.
MGREC119:32 H2722 'Mongst all the Captains {princes} of great *Alexander,*
MGREC120:10 H2745 In *Asia* they all asunder be.
MGREC~~120:20~~ H2756 (For all the princes of great *Alexander*
MGREC120:30 H2767 And 'gainst *Perdicas,* all their strength combine.
MGREC~~120:41~~ H2778 *Perdicas* hears, his foes are now {all} combin'd,
MGREC121:21 H2803 And is of all received {most} joyfully;
MGREC121:36 H2818 The others all, had kingdomes in their eye,
MGREC122:9 H2834 For all that should be said, let this suffice,
MGREC122:30 H2849 Resign'd his place, and so let all alone;
MGREC122:35 H2856 For all the Princes {nobles} of great {King} *Alexander*
MGREC~~122:37~~ H2858 When to his pleasure all things they had done,
MGREC122:40 H2861 All to be order'd there as he thought best:
MGREC123:9 H2871 'Gainst him, that all deceits could scan, and try:
MGREC123:21 H2885 All *Syria,* and, *Phenicia* he wins;
MGREC123:40 H2904 By all the Bonds 'twixt him and's father past,
MGREC124:1 H2906 By these, and all, to grant him some supply,
MGREC124:6 ~~H2911~~ *Cassander* for return all speed now made:
MGREC124:10 ~~H2915~~ All such as he suspected to him true.
MGREC124:18 H2925 *Antigonus* doth all in *Asia* gaine;
MGREC~~124:20~~ H2927 But to the last {all in vain} he faithfull did abide;
MGREC124:40 H2947 As all her Husbands children by his Mates;
MGREC125:5 H2953 That under him she might rule all alone.
MGREC125:31 H2981 Till {'Gainst} all that lov'd *Cassander* was nigh spent; {she was
MGREC126:6 H2997 To give her for all cruelties {her cruelty} her dues:
MGREC127:14 H3044 True *Eumenes* endeavours by all skill,

MGREC127:24 H3054 Thus lost he all for his fidelity,
MGREC127:28 H3058 *Antigonus,* all *Persia* now gains {doth gain},
MGREC127:32 H3062 The Princes all begin now to envie
MGREC128:32 H3105 And {With} all the spoyle and booty they {he} had tane;
MGREC129:10 H3124 This *Roxane* for her beautie all commend,
MGREC129:22 H3136 *Cassander's* dead, the Princes {do} all detest,
MGREC129:40 H3154 *Antigonus* for all this doth not mourn,
MGREC129:41 H3155 He knows to's profit, all i'th end {this at last} will turn,
MGREC130:6 H3161 Where, by Embassage, all these Princes pray,
MGREC130:7 H3162 Choise above all, of *Ptolomy* she makes
MGREC130:19 H3174 And now he thinks {hopes}, he's ordered all so well,
MGREC131:1 H3187 To do as he, {by his Example all} the rest full soon presumes,
MGREC131:11 H3203 Near *Ephesus,* each bringing all their {his} might,
MGREC131:14 H3206 This day twixt these two foes {Kings} ends all the strife,
MGREC131:28 H3220 Falls so extreamly sick, all fear {fear'd} his life,
MGREC132:19 H3256 These to recover, musters all his might,
MGREC132:38 H3285 That now he had out-lived all the rest:
MGREC133:14 H3302 His Son *Demetrius,* all *Cassanders* gaines,
MGREC133:25 ~~H3315~~ Did take his rule, his sons, himself and all.
MGREC134:16 H3347 Vanquish'd in fight, and took those kingdomes all,
MGREC134:33 H3364 To all these names we *Ptolomy* must adde,
MGREC135:3 H3375 To take her life, and quit her from all harmes;
MGREC135:23 H3395 And last was Iron, which breaketh all with might.
MGREC135:26 H3398 Then gold, silver, brasse, iron, and all that {the} store,
MGREC135:35 H3407 All trembling stand, before that powerfull Lambe.
MGREC136:11 H3425 *And maugre all resolves, my fancy wrought*
MROMAN136:26 H3440 But *Æmulus,* in Armour all disguis'd.
MROMAN137:5 H3456 Great priviledges then, to all he grants,
MROMAN137:10 H3461 But all disdaine alliance then to make,
MROMAN137:13 H3464 To see these sports, the *Sabins* all are bent;
MROMAN138:36 H3526 And after all, by *Ancus* Sons was slaine.
MROMAN139:33 H3559 All thoughts of further progress laid aside,
DIALOG142:26 H55 Doth *Holland* quit you ill, for all your love?
DIALOG144:8 H118 'Mongst all the cruelties which I have {by great ones} done,
DIALOG145:2 H151 Such cruelty as all reports have past.
DIALOG145:7 H156 To all you've said, sad mother, I assent
DIALOG145:11 H160 But all you say, amounts to this effect,
DIALOG145:27 H176 Had they not held law fast, all had been gone,
DIALOG145:31 H180 All *Englands* Metropolitane that houre,
DIALOG145:34 H183 Here tugg'd they hard indeed, for all men saw,
DIALOG146:2 H190 Shews all was done, I'll therefore let it go.
DIALOG146:26 H212 recompence me {that} good, for all my ill {I've done to thee}.
DIALOG~~146:34~~ H221 Though now beclouded all with tears and blood:
DIALOG147:13 H239 Their Myters, Surplices, and all their tire,
DIALOG147:16 H242 Light Christendome, and all the world to see,
DIALOG147:17 H243 We hate *Romes* Whore, with all her trumperie.
DIALOG147:24 H248 And yee brave Nobles, chase away all fear,
DIALOG147:31 H255 Out of all mists, such glorious dayes will {shall} bring,
DIALOG147:35 H259 That all shall joy that thou display'dst thy banner,
DIALOG147:38 H262 Then Justice shall in all thy Courts take place,
DIALOG148:6 H271 To sack proud *Rome,* and all her vassalls rout:

DIALOG148:11	H276	Of all the woes thou canst let her be sped,
DIALOG148:16	H281	To th' 'stonishment of all that knew his state,
DIALOG148:32	H297	But if at all, thou didst not see't before.
SIDNEY149:27	~~H23~~	Yet doth thy shame (with all) purchase renown,
SIDNEY149:29	~~H23~~	In all records, thy Name I ever see,
SIDNEY~~150:12~~	H38	In all Records his name I ever see
SIDNEY152:8	H79	Since *Sydney* had exhausted all their store,
SIDNEY152:27	H96	*Learning, valour, beauty {Wisdome}, all in vertuous youth:*
DUBART153:19	H23	To comprehend the worth of all those knacks;
DUBART153:27	H31	Of all the glorious sights his eyes have had:
DUBART153:41	H45	In all the Arts make thee most liberall;
DUBART154:16	H61	In all the Zones, the temp'rate, hot and cold,
DUBART154:20	H65	Immortall bayes, all men to thee allows.
DUBART154:29	H74	Thou hast {hadst} thy part of all, but of the last,
DUBART154:32	H77	All ages wondring at, shall never clime.
QELIZ156:4	H31	From all the Kings on earth she won the prize;
QELIZ156:39	H66	Her Sea-men through all straights the world did round,
QELIZ157:11	H79	(Judging all valour, and all Majesty)
QELIZ157:11	H79	(Judging all valour, and all Majesty)
QELIZ157:23	H91	And of all these without compare the best;
DAVID159:20	H35	In mid'st of strength not succoured at all:
DAVID159:25	H40	Exceeding all the Love that's Feminine,
VANITY159:29	H1	*Of the vanity of all worldly creatures {things}.*
VANITY159:31	H3	O vanity, O vain all under skie,
VANITY160:5	H15	More vain then all, that's but to grasp the wind.
VANITY160:17	H27	He knows not all, that here is to be known,
VANITY~~161:6~~	H57	{And all} The rest's {rest} but vanity, and vain we find.
TDUDLEY166:6	H48	No ostentation seen in all his wayes,
TDUDLEY166:8	H50	Which all they have, and more still set to view,
TDUDLEY166:25	H67	Who after all his toyle, is now at rest:
DDUDLEY167:20	H17	*Religious in all her words and wayes,*
DDUDLEY167:22	H19	*Of all her Children, Children, liv'd to see,*
CONTEM167:27	H4	The trees all richly clad, yet void of pride,
CONTEM168:13	H22	If so, all these as nought, Eternity doth scorn.
CONTEM168:34	H40	All mortals here the feeling knowledg hath.
CONTEM169:35	H73	Sees glorious *Adam* there made Lord of all,
CONTEM171:7	H112	Cloath'd all in his black sinfull Livery,
CONTEM171:16	H120	And puts all pleasures vain unto eternal flight.
CONTEM171:26	H128	By birth more noble then those creatures all,
CONTEM172:25	H159	To *Thetis* house, where all imbrace and greet:
CONTEM174:9	H209	Nor all his losses, crosses and vexation,
CONTEM174:17	H216	But suddenly a storm spoiles all the sport,
CONTEM174:19	H218	Which 'gainst all adverse winds may serve for fort.
CONTEM174:27	H225	Only above is found all with security.
CONTEM174:33	H230	Their parts, their ports, their pomp's all laid in th' dust
CONTEM174:36	H233	Shall last and shine when all of these are gone.
FLESH175:19	H19	That all in th' world thou count'st but poor?
FLESH177:28	H109	Take thou the world, and all that will.
AUTHOR177:35	H7	Where errors were not lessened (all may judg).
SICKNES178:22	H5	All men must dye, and so must I
SICKNES178:28	H11	Where I shall have all I can crave,

DISTEMP179:18	H6	Till nature had exhausted all her store,
BIRTH179:27	H3	All things within this fading world hath end,
1HUSB180:28	H7	Or all the riches that the East doth hold.
2LETTER182:8	H14	My Interest's more then all the world beside.
2LETTER182:10	H16	Or all the grass that in the Meads do stand,
2LETTER182:14	H20	May count my sighs, and number all my drops:
2LETTER182:34	H40	By all our loves conjure him not to stay.
3LETTER183:7	H9	Or as the pensive Dove doth all alone
3LETTER183:21	H23	But worst of all, to him can't steer my course,
CHILDRN185:34	H60	And with my wings kept off all harm,
1SIMON188:12	H13	He will return, and make up all our losses,
MERCY189:4	H25	And then her sorrows all at once did go;
MERCY189:10	H31	All freed from grief (I trust) among the blest;
MERCY189:14	H35	In him alone, that caused all this smart;
2SIMON195:12	Hp271	though in value they fall short of all in this kinde yet I presume
MEDDM195:26	Hp272	aduantage of all and he that makes such improvment is wise
MEDDM196:14	Hp273	The hireling that labours all the day comforts himself, that
MEDDM196:34	Hp274	deliuered vp by one traytor wthin, and that man wch all the
MEDDM198:5	Hp276	if they stick in deepe mire and clay, and all his waues and
MEDDM198:11	Hp276	need ponder all his steps.
MEDDM198:17	Hp276	a hooke vnder all, Satan that great Angler hath his sundry
MEDDM198:18	Hp276	tempers of men, wch they all catch gre¯dily at but few
MEDDM199:17	Hp278	all, the most deiected
MEDDM200:8	Hp279	together so is it wth some Christians, let god imbitter all the
MEDDM201:7	Hp280	I haue seen an end of all perfection (sayd the royall prophet)
MEDDM201:8	Hp280	I haue seen an end of all Sinning, what he did say, may be
MEDDM201:32	Hp281	all seasons the most welcom so a faithfull friend in time of
MEDDM201:33	Hp281	is (of all other) most Comfortable
MEDDM202:13	Hp282	among the dead, and no other reason can be giuen of all this
MEDDM202:37	Hp282	whom all fullnes dwells
MEDDM203:2	Hp283	the wisest of men, taught vs this lesson, that all is vanity and
MEDDM203:4	Hp283	for what do we obtaine of all these things, but it is wth labour
MEDDM203:8	Hp283	vanity of vanityes, all is vanity
MEDDM203:11	Hp283	be all convenient and comfortable for him yet he hath no
MEDDM203:18	Hp283	may plainly declare that we seek a citty aboue and wait all the
MEDDM204:10	Hp284	wthall, the larger his accounts stands vpon gods score it
MEDDM204:35	Hp285	into tilth yet all must be ploughed and harrowed Some children
MEDDM206:8	Hp287	of bignes and brightnes, yet all receiue their light from that
MEDDM206:14	Hp287	and obscure, yet all receiue their luster (be it more or lesse)
MEDDM206:15	Hp287	from that glorious sun that inlightens all in all, and if some of
MEDDM206:27	Hp288	All the works and doings of god are wonderfull, but none more
MEDDM206:37	Hp288	all should make vs wth the Apostle to admire the iustice and
MEDDM207:13	Hp288	All the Comforts of this Life, may be compared to the gourd of
MEDDM207:21	Hp289	All men are truly sayd to be tenants at will, and it may as truly
MEDDM207:22	Hp289	sayd that all haue a lease of their liues, some longer some
MEDDM207:23	Hp289	pleases our great landlord to let: All haue their bounds set ouer
MEDDM207:31	Hp289	All weak and diseased bodys, haue hourly mementos of their
MEDDM208:1	Hp289	at whose comeing they shall all rise out of their beds, The
MEDDM208:3	Hp289	things must be what manner of persons ought we to be, in all
MEDDM208:28	Hp290	admirable to Consider the power of faith, by wch all things are
MEDDM208:32	Hp290	become firme footing, for peter to walk on, nay more then all

MEDDM209:4 Hp291 therfore wth all our seekings and gettings, let vs aboue all seek
MEDDM209:4 Hp291 wth all our seekings and gettings, let vs aboue all seek to
MEDDM209:14 Hp291 all their accursed inmates, but make a league with them, they
MEDDM209:18 Hp291 hath by his prouidence so ordered, that no one Covntry hath all
MEDDM209:22 Hp291 all excellences, let his parts naturall and acquired spirituall and
PILGRIM210:17 H17 All Cares and feares, he bids farwell
MYCHILD215:13 Hp240 opportvnity to speak to any of yov much lesse to All, thovght it
MYCHILD216:20 Hp241 Among all my experiences of gods gratious Dealings wth me I
MYCHILD217:37 Hp243 of ye Heaven + ye Earth, the order of all things night and day,
MYCHILD218:2 Hp243 vpon ye Earth, ye p^{r}serving + directing of All to its proper
MYCHILD218:12 Hp244 All Ages maugre all ye heathen Tyrants + all of the Enemyes
MYCHILD218:12 Hp244 All Ages maugre all ye heathen Tyrants + all of the Enemyes
MYCHILD218:36 Hp244 + if I perish, I perish, But I know all ye powers of Hell shall
SOREFIT221:29 H15 For all his Bovnty shew'd to me
SOREFIT221:31 H17 Where pitty most of all I see.
MED223:19 Hp250 bee dissolved and bee wth thee wch is best of All.
MYSOUL224:26 H2 Boast of him all ye Day,
MYSOUL225:9 H13 Thy teares shall All bee dryed vp
MYSOUL225:10 H14 Thy Sorrowes all shall flye.
11MAYA226:14 Hp255 lasted all this spring till this 11. May, yet hath my God given
13MAY226:28 H4 The earth all black is cloth'd in green
13MAY227:2 H11 And former clowdes seem now all fled
13MAY227:15 H24 All I can giue is but thine own
SAMUEL228:17 H18 And Blesse the for't even all my Dayes.
11MAYB228:30 Hp259 But alas! I cannot render vnto ye Lord according to all his
11MAYB228:32 Hp259 Lord Thou y^{t} knowest All things know'st that I desire to
HANNA230:18 H11 Shee loues thee all thy Dayes.
SON230:20 H3 All praise to him who hath now turn'd
SON231:12 H24 Without (all fraud) did'st sett him free
SON231:25 H37 That all thy favours great receivd
2HUSB232:3 H4 O thov most high who rulest All
2HUSB233:9 H42 That I and all thy servants may
2HUSB233:18 H51 All praises vnto Thee.
HOURS233:22 H5 My Troubles All are Thee before
HOURS234:19 H33 In Thee Alone is more then All;
HOURS234:28 H42 Of all thy Goodnes past.
ACK235:8 H8 Hast known my doubts and All my feares,
ACK235:19 H19 For All these mercyes I thee praise
ACK235:20 H20 And so desire Ev'n all my Dayes.
REMB235:32 H13 To Thee shall come all Flesh,
REMB236:3 H18 But Thankfullnes even all my dayes
HOUSE236:31 H23 He might of All iustly bereft,

ALL'S (1) [all his]

MPersian86:12 H1328 Judging all's {his} actions, tends to's injury.

ALL'S (4) [all is]

MPERS82:11 H1158 All's lost, and of three hundred thousand men,
MPERS92:32 H1590 And this 'mongst all's no controverted thing,
MGREC110:11 H2311 *Porus* encounters them, thinking {and thinks} all's there,
HOUSE237:10 H40 Adeiu, Adeiu, All's Vanity.

ALL-FILLING (1)

QELIZ158:10 H119 *Whose sweet perfume fills the all-filling aire,*

ALLAY (1)
MGREC105:39 H2132 To quench his thirst, and to allay his heat;
ALLAYED See ALAYED
ALLEADG'D (1) [alleged]
MGREC117:35 H2642 Alleadg'd by those, which {who} by their subtill plea
ALLEGATION (1)
AGES41:40 H257 I wanted not my ready allegation.
ALLIANCE (2)
AGES44:18 H351 Nor from alliance now can I have hope,
MROMAN137:10 H3461 But all disdaine alliance then to make,
ALLIED See ALLY'D
ALLOTTED (1)
SEASONS46:36 H14 Three months {(quoth she)} there are allotted to my share,
ALLOW (3)
HUMOUR26:39 H269 Challenge not all, 'cause part we do allow,
HUMOUR33:22 H536 The Brain's the noblest member all allow,
HUMOUR34:32 H587 If Tyrants be the best, i'le it allow;
ALLOWS (1)
DUBART154:20 H65 Immortall bayes, all men to thee allows.
ALLSEEING (1)
MEDDM205:25 Hp286 allseeing eye will be a bridle to restrain from evill, and a spur,
ALLURE See T'ALLURE
ALLUR'D (1) [allured]
CHILDRN185:25 H51 Or whilst allur'd with bell and glass,
ALLY'D (1) [allied]
AGES41:36 H251 But if none, then for kindred near ally'd.
ALLYE (1)
DIALOG142:24 H53 Doth your Allye, faire *France,* conspire your wrack?
ALMES (2) [pl.]
AGES45:8 ~~H390~~ A Royall one, by almes from Subjects hands,
THEART229:18 H20 For of thine Almes I liue.
ALMIGHTIES (1) [almighty's, poss.]
1SIMON188:7 H8 Cropt by th' Almighties hand; yet is he good,
ALMIGHTY (2)
MYCHILD217:4 Hp242 when ye Almighty hath hid his face from me, that yet I haue
MED223:7 Hp250 Almighty—Christ is my Brother, I ascend vnto my father, and
ALMOND-TREE (1)
AGES45:27 H417 My {Mine} Almond-tree (gray haires) doth flourish now,
ALMONDS (1) [pl.]
SEASONS~~51:10~~ H184 Of Medlar, Quince, of Warden, {Almonds, Quinces, Wardens}
ALMOST (11)
AGES36:23 H47 In's other hand a glasse, ev'n almost run,
AGES46:15 H446 And my last period now e'n almost run;
SEASONS51:23 H199 And his declining heat is almost done.
SEASONS51:38 H214 Almost at shortest is the shortned day,
MASSYR56:5 H111 Almost incredible, they were in breadth.
MPERS71:31 H745 A second Army there {he} had almost grav'd;
MPERS80:15 H1082 Of Vessels small almost innumerable,
MGREC95:35 H1714 (Both sexes there) was almost numberlesse.
MGREC104:35 H2087 Whose Army now, was almost within sight,
MGREC107:28 H2203 Here *Alexander's* almost at a stand,

MEDDM208:29 Hp290 (almost) possible to be done, it can remoue mountaines

ALONE (20)

HUMOUR21:15 H43 Where Monarch-like I play, and sway alone.
HUMOUR26:1 H231 But such thou never art, when al alone;
MASSYR55:35 H101 She for her potency, must go alone.
MPERS76:7 H905 By these alone his Hoast was pinch'd so sore,
MPERS78:28 H1009 For to command alone, she thought {judg'd} was best.
MPERS83:21 H1209 For which he dyed, and not he alone.
MGREC114:23 H2493 For this alone, and for no other cause,
MGREC121:35 H2817 But he alone now {most} faithfull did abide:
MGREC122:30 H2849 Resign'd his place, and so let all alone;
MGREC125:5 H2953 That under him she might rule all alone.
DIALOG141:28 H27 Let me lament alone, while thou art glad.
DIALOG146:9 H197 But could the field alone this cause {strife} decide,
CONTEM169:10 H51 Silent alone, where none or saw, or heard,
CONTEM172:22 H156 Nor is't enough, that thou alone may'st slide,
3LETTER183:7 H9 Or as the pensive Dove doth all alone
ELIZB187:11 H19 Is by his hand alone that guides nature and fate.
MERCY189:14 H35 In him alone, that caused all this smart;
MEDDM208:34 Hp290 intercedes for the people, god sath to him Let me alone, that I
PILGRIM210:38 H38 in power 'tis rais'd by Christ alone
HOURS234:19 H33 In Thee Alone is more then All;

ALONG (8)

HUMOUR27:7 H278 If stil thou take along my Aliment,
MGREC95:37 H1716 Along with him, the {greatest} Ladyes of the Court.
MGREC102:7 H1977 With showers of Flowers, the streets along are strown,
MGREC104:25 H2077 Then draws the Cart along, with chaines of gold;
MGREC122:38 H2859 The King, and Queen, along with him he takes. {to *Macedon*}
CONTEM172:24 H158 So hand in hand along with thee they glide
CHILDRN184:33 H22 Along the Beach among the treen,
MERCY189:2 H23 Because her Soul she'd sent along with thee.

ALOOF (1)

AGES39:23 H166 I fly to catch the Bullet that's {that} aloof;

ALPES (1)

ELEMEN12:4 H164 Whether Pyrenian, or the Alpes; both lyes

ALREADY (1)

MGREC116:40 H2606 To govern that he had already won:

ALSO (34)

HUMOUR31:30 H463 With me is noble patience also found,
AGES~~39:14~~ H157 The manners of the Court, I likewise {also} know,
AGES44:29 H362 In various times of state i've also been.
SEASONS51:8 H182 The Figge is {are} ripe, the Pomgranet also,
SEASONS51:27 H203 Decrepit age must also have its time;
SEASONS51:31 H207 Where also he, his Winter time must have;
MASSYR53:24 H14 *Erech, Accad,* and *Calneh* also made;
MASSYR54:32 H59 The *Median* country, he did also gain,
MASSYR60:21 H286 *Assyria* he also gain'd at length;
MASSYR61:13 H318 *Resin* their valiant King, he also slew,
MPERS84:5 H1233 Queen *Vashty* also feasts, but 'fore tis ended,
MPERS89:7 H1441 The King with his dispers'd also incampt,
MGREC97:7 H1768 And forty thousand Prisoners also tane;

MGREC98:4 H1806 And from whom also, lineally {he} descended:
MGREC98:20 H1822 Eight thousand by the sword now also dy'd,
MGREC101:41 H1970 And now {Together} with it, the town also obtain'd.
MGREC105:30 H2123 He also sends his humble thankfulnesse,
MGREC106:25 H2159 His past sobriety doth also hate,
MGREC108:37 H2253 Which *Alexandria* he doth also {likewise} name,
MGREC~~109:5~~ H2262 And also of the *Mallians* what is writ.
MGREC112:3 H2389 He fourscore *Persian* Ladies also gave;
MGREC~~115:15~~ H2529 Twelve thousand Talents also did intend,
MGREC133:17 H3305 And his againe, also {was nam'd} *Demetrius.*
DIALOG144:41 H149 Thousands of starved Christian there also.
CHILDRN184:37 H26 Hath also bid her Dam adieu:
MEDDM201:28 Hp281 only to bid them hold fast the form of sound Doctrin, but also,
MEDDM205:12 Hp286 fro continvally, here is also the great Court of iustice erected,
MEDDM205:17 Hp286 of heaven itself, for if our conscience condemn vs, he also
MEDDM206:7 Hp287 starres and those starres also, to differ much one from the
MEDDM206:35 Hp288 may also be a support to such as haue or had wicked parents,
MEDDM209:25 Hp291 below, as also that god will haue vs beholden one to another
MYCHILD215:28 Hp241 I was also troubled at ye neglect of private Dutyes tho:
MYCHILD215:29 Hp241 too often tardy y^{t} way. I also fovnd much comfort in reading y^{e}
HOURS234:14 H28 And freinds I haue also

ALSOE (1) [also]
MEDDM206:33 Hp288 it should alsoe teach the children of godly parents to walk wth

ALTARS (2) [pl.]
MGREC102:8 H1978 And Insence burnt, the silver Altars on;
MGREC110:33 H2337 Twelve Altars, he for Monuments then rears,

ALTHO (4) [although]
MEDDM206:1 Hp287 to that fruitfullnes, altho they aime at perfection And again
MEDDM208:6 Hp289 of a fire, if once severed, will of themselues goe out altho
MYCHILD215:16 Hp240 dayly in y^{r} rembrance, (Altho: y^{t} is the least in my aim in w^{t} I
MYCHILD217:26 Hp243 would but lift vp ye light of his Covnten^{c} vpon me, altho: he

ALTHOUGH (12)
HUMOUR32:2 H476 Although she beare the greatest obloquie.
HUMOUR32:27 H501 (Although my name do suffer detriment)
SEASONS50:22 H156 Although their Bread have not so white a face.
MASSYR66:26 H532 Although the Furnace be seven times more hot;
MPERS78:1 H982 Although he hasted, yet foure yeares was spent,
MPERS83:31 H1219 Although to *Xerxes,* they not long before,
MROMAN140:7 H3570 Although my Monarchies their legs do lack:
QELIZ155:14 H5 Although great Queen, thou now in silence lye,
MEDDM200:6 Hp279 Some children are hardly weaned although the teat be rub'd
MEDDM202:22 Hp282 although we may walk by his light, but when he is set, we are
MEDDM203:10 Hp283 He that is to saile into a farre country, although the ship,
MYCHILD217:17 Hp243 haue, although he hath not left me altogether wthout the

ALTITUDE (1)
DUBART153:6 H10 Reflection from their beaming altitude,

ALTOGETHER (2)
MYCHILD216:13 Hp241 & doe me Good: and it was not altogether ineffectuall.
MYCHILD217:17 Hp243 although he hath not left me altogether wthout the wittnes of

ALWAY (4)
MEDDM205:13 Hp286 wch is alway kept by Conscience, who is both accuser excuser

MEDDM205:24 Hp286 himself alway in the awefull presence of god, the consideration
MEDDM205:28 Hp286 we doe, but he that wth David, sets the lord alway in his sight
MYSOUL224:28 H4 Cleaue close to him alway.

ALWAYES (1) [always]
SICKNES178:35 H18 that alwayes art a breaking,

ALWISE (1)
MEDDM200:18 Hp279 will the alwise god proportion his dispensations according to

AM (51)
PROLOG7:14 H27 I am obnoxious to each carping tongue,
ELEMEN8:32 H30 But what I am, let learned *Grecians* say;
ELEMEN11:28 H148 I am th' originall of man and beast,
ELEMEN14:33 H275 Which {Who} am thy drink, thy blood, thy sap, and best.
ELEMEN15:1 H283 When I am gone, their fiercenesse none need {needs} doubt;
ELEMEN15:22 H304 But {And} such I am, in Rivers, showers and springs;
ELEMEN~~17:36~~ H400 Though {Yet am} not through ignorance, {ignorant} first was my
ELEMEN17:38 H402 I am the breath of every living soul.
ELEMEN18:35 H439 So when I am condens'd, I turne to water;
ELEMEN19:37 H478 Imprisoned I, am the original.
HUMOUR21:5 H33 It shal suffice, to tel {shew} you what I am:
HUMOUR23:8 H118 Tis true, when I am midwife to thy birth;
HUMOUR23:20 H130 But I am weary to dilate thy shame;
HUMOUR26:22 H252 I am as sure, the natural from me;
HUMOUR26:25 H255 I am the Fountaine which thy Cisterns fils,
HUMOUR27:29 H300 I moderately am all, what need I more:
HUMOUR29:21 H372 To play such furious pranks I am too wise;
HUMOUR30:38 H430 That black is black, and I am black, tis true;
HUMOUR~~31:6~~ H439 Thou witless think'st that I am thy excretion,
HUMOUR32:18 H492 Patient I am, patient i'd need to be,
HUMOUR32:30 H504 Valour {Valours} I want, no Souldier am, 'tis true,
HUMOUR33:21 H535 I am confounded, 'fore I speak of any:
AGES36:24 H48 This {Thus} writ about: *This out, then I am done.*
AGES38:18 H121 The sins, and dangers I am subject to.
AGES40:26 H207 And in a word, if what I am you'd heare,
AGES40:28 H209 Such wretch, such monster am I; but yet more,
AGES41:16 H235 And now am grown more staid, that {who} have been green,
AGES43:25 H320 Thus good, and bad, and what I am, you see,
AGES44:7 H340 And on this Stage am come to act my last:
MASSYR61:21 H326 I am thy Servant, and thy Son (quoth he)
DIALOG143:17 H86 What *Holland* is, I am in some suspence,
DIALOG144:4 H114 From crying bloods, yet cleansed am not I,
DIALOG146:8 H196 Am now destroy'd, and slaughter'd by mine own,
SIDNEY151:21 H71 But now into such Lab'rinths am I led
DAVID159:23 H38 Distrest I am, for thee, deare *Jonathan,*
FLESH176:23 H63 When I am victor over thee,
BIRTH180:4 H14 I may seem thine, who in effect am none.
CHILDRN186:29 H96 I happy am, if well with you.
2SIMON195:5 Hp271 their predecessors, but I am perswaded better things of y[o] you
MEDDM204:31 Hp285 Jacob, I am lesse then the least of thy mercys.
TOCHILD215:3 H3 I leaue for yov when I am dead,
MYCHILD215:15 Hp240 bequeath to yov, that when I am no more wth yov, yet I may
MED223:9 Hp250 thy maker is thy husband. Nay more, I am a member of his

MED223:13 Hp250 in me at y^{e} consideration $y^{r}$of, and I am confovnded to think
WHAT224:4 H4 For truly I am thine.
28AUG225:29 Hp254 stayes my Soul that this condition y^{t} I am in is y^{e} best for me,
28AUG226:6 Hp254 gravnt y^{t} while I live I may doe y^{t} service I am able in this frail
11MAYA226:20 Hp255 of God it should bee thus. Who am I y^{t} I should repine at his
13MAY227:13 H22 I studiovs am what I shall doe
2HUSB232:17 H18 Thou see'st how weak + frail I am,
REMB235:30 H11 And I am filld wth shame,

AMAIN (5)
SEASONS50:7 H141 The Forks, and Rakes do follow them amain,
MASSYR59:11 H235 And speeds himself to *Ninivie* amain;
MPERS86:19 H1335 These and like motives, hurry him amain,
MPERS89:1 H1435 But was deceiv'd; to it they make amain,
MGREC104:31 H2083 Who doubling of his march, posts on amain,

AMAZ'D (2) [amazed] See also 'MAZED, MAZED
ELEMEN11:7 H127 Which Kings, and mighty ones; amaz'd with wonder,
CONTEM168:17 H25 The more I look'd, the more I grew amaz'd,

AMAZED (1) See also AMAZ'D, 'MAZED, MAZED
MASSYR68:10 H596 Amazed at the writing, and the hand.

AMAZEMENT (1)
MYCHILD218:3 Hp243 consideration of these things would wth amazement certainly

AMAZIA (1)
MASSYR59:35 H259 That *Amazia* was King of *Israel;*

AMAZING (1)
MERCY188:31 H17 To strike thee with amazing misery;

AMAZON (1)
QELIZ157:10 H78 Our *Amazon* i'th' Campe at {of} *Tilberry:*

AMAZONS (1) [pl.]
MGREC106:15 H2149 *Thalestris,* Queen of th' *Amazons,* now brought

AMBASSADOR (2)
MPERS81:17 H1125 By their Ambassador they thus complain;
MPERS81:26 H1134 Nor could the brave Ambassador be {he} sent,

AMBER-GREECE (1)
ELEMEN15:40 H322 Thy gallant rich perfuming Amber-greece:

AMBIGUOUS (1)
MPERS69:23 H645 And the ambiguous Oracle did trust,

AMBITION (8)
ELEMEN13:3 H204 That you ambition laid, ought but my bones?
MASSYR55:27 H93 Till her ambition, caus'd him to be slaine:
MASSYR66:24 H530 Which wealth, and strong ambition made so great;
MGREC106:10 H2144 Could bound his boundlesse, fond ambition)
MGREC116:31 ~~H2597~~ More boundles in ambition then the skie,
TDUDLEY166:1 H43 For truly his ambition lay above.
FLESH176:21 H61 For my ambition lyes above.
CHILDRN185:5 H31 Ambition moves still in his breast

AMBITIOUS (7)
AGES37:23 H85 My then ambitious thoughts, were low enough.
AGES43:3 H298 But {And} by ambitious sailes, I was so carryed;
MPERS77:38 H979 That his ambitious humour best can fit;
MGREC~~116:31~~ H2597 Ambitious so, that nought could satisfie,
MGREC~~127:41~~ H3073 Shews his ambitious practises as well.

SIDNEY151:24 ~~H73~~ Calls me ambitious fool, that durst aspire,
MEDDM199:15 Hp278 Ambitious men are like hops that neuer rest climbing soe long

AMEN (1)
MYCHILD219:5 Hp245 Amen.

AMEND (1)
AUTHOR178:3 H13 Thy blemishes amend, if so I could:

AMENDED (1)
MPERS86:31 H1347 The King finding, revenues now amended;

AMENDMENT (1)
30SEPT227:24 Hp257 amendment, and then thy stroakes shall bee welcome,

AMERGES (1)
MPERS85:20 H1296 *Amerges,* whom their {for} Vice-roy he ordain'd

AMERICANS (1) [pl.]
ELEMEN16:2 H325 Which *Spaines Americans,* do gladly hold.

AMESTRIS (1)
MPERS82:29 H1176 When jealous Queen *Amestris,* of this knew,

AMIDST (3)
MPERS69:31 H653 Amidst {Among} the tumult, bloud-shed, and the strife,
MGREC119:31 H2721 The valiant Chief, amidst his foes was slain,
CHILDRN184:25 H14 Fly back and sing amidst this Quire.

AMINTAS (1)
MGREC93:11 H1608 He, to *Amintas,* Kings of *Macedon;*

AMISSE (7)
HUMOUR22:17 H86 She dare, {dares} not challenge if I speake amisse;
HUMOUR22:34 H103 She thinks I never shot so farre amisse;
HUMOUR24:18 H167 Do'st know thy selfe so well, us so amisse?
MGREC117:23 H2630 For ayming still amisse, his dreadfull blowes
MGREC129:20 H3134 *Perdicas* had before, for his amisse,
MGREC136:17 H3431 *What e're is found amisse, take in best {good} part,*
MYCHILD216:23 Hp242 w^{t} was amisse. So vsually thvs it hath been wth me

AMITY (4)
ELEMEN8:10 H8 But enmity, this amity did breake:
HUMOUR35:11 H607 But all admire our perfect amity;
MASSYR58:36 H219 And with all terms of amity, he greets, {them greet.}
MPERS83:32 H1220 A league of amity, had sworn before. {firmly swore,}

AMONG (29) See also **'MONG**
ELEMEN11:27 H147 Among my praises this I count not least,
ELEMEN14:26 H268 Among your boastings to have praised me;
HUMOUR26:38 H268 Thy fiery yellow froth, is mixt among.
AGES41:22 ~~H239~~ And then a world of drosse among my gold.
SEASONS47:41 H53 Among the verduous Grasse hath Nature set,
MASSYR66:38 H544 This King among the righteous had a part:
MASSYR67:8 H554 Among the Conquered Kings, that there did lye,
MPERS~~69:31~~ H653 Amidst {Among} the tumult, bloud-shed, and the strife,
MPERS89:6 H1440 Nor wound receiv'd, but one among them all:
MGREC~~94:18~~ H1654 His little wealth among his Souldiers gave.
MGREC109:1 H2258 He enters now {then} the *Indian* Kings among;
MGREC~~115:15~~ H2534 Among the Demy Gods they might inthrone.
MGREC125:6 H2954 For ayde {she} goes to *Epire,* among her friends,
MGREC127:8 H3038 Among their Ancestors by him there {they're} laid,
DIALOG143:41 H110 And thou, poore soule, wast {wert} jeer'd among the rest,

CHILDRN184:33 H22 Along the Beach among the treen,

CHILDRN185:4 H30 To chat among that learned crew:

CHILDRN186:17 H84 Among your young ones take your rest,

1SIMON188:15 H16 Among the blest in endless joyes remain.

MERCY189:10 H31 All freed from grief (I trust) among the blest;

MEDDM198:9 Hp276 He that walks among briars and thorns will be very carefull,

MEDDM202:3 Hp281 dispensation of his gifts among the sons of men, betwixt whom

MEDDM202:8 Hp281 among men, and some againe, so ignorant and sotish that they

MEDDM202:13 Hp282 accounted among the dead, and no other reason can be giuen

MEDDM205:34 Hp286 among them are dry stocks so is it in the church wch is gods

MEDDM206:6 Hp287 in the firmament there is but one Sun, among a multitude of

MEDDM208:13 Hp290 to haue a good repute among good men, yet it is not that, wch

PILGRIM210:24 H24 And soare on high among the blest.

MYCHILD216:20 Hp241 Among all my experiences of gods gratious Dealings wth me I

AMONGST (8) See also 'MONGST

AGES46:11 H442 Hath yet amongst that sweet, some bitter gall.

MPERS80:12 H1079 Amongst the rest, two brothers he lost there;

MPERS83:27 H1215 Amongst the Monarchs next, this Prince had place

MGREC121:41 H2823 And brave *Craterus* slew, amongst the rest,

MGREC127:5 H3035 And *Pellas* faine to yeeld amongst the rest;

MGREC~~134:6~~ H3339 Against {Amongst} the Jewes, we read in *Macchabees,*

DUBART152:33 H2 Amongst the happy wits this Age hath showne,

CHILDRN186:26 H93 Thus gone, amongst you I may live,

AMOROUS (2)

MASSYR55:23 H89 That *Ninus* of her, amorous soon did grow;

MGREC124:37 H2944 These, with his love, unto the amorous Queen

AMORT (1)

MASSYR68:13 H599 As thus amort {dead, alive} he sits, as all {one} undone:

AMOUNT (4)

ELEMEN10:16 H91 My story to a Volume would amount:

MGREC100:26 H1910 Of Horse, and Foot, this {his} Army did amount;

MGREC103:14 H2025 The share of *Alexander* did amount,

MROMAN139:7 H3535 To eighty thousand soules then did amount:

AMOUNTS (2)

DIALOG145:11 H160 But all you say, amounts to this effect,

VERSES184:3 H7 Yet handled ill, amounts but to this crum;

AMPHIONS (1) [poss.]

DUBART154:3 H48 More sencelesse then the Stones to *Amphions* Lute,

AMPHIPOLIS (2)

MGREC125:20 H2968 Then {The} King, and Queen, to *Amphipolis* doe fly, {seeing

MGREC~~125:21~~ H2969 To save their lives t' *Amphipolis* do fly;

AMPLE (1)

MEDDM200:26 Hp279 their former vigor and beavty in a more ample manner then

AMRAPHEL (1)

MASSYR57:13 H160 But is suppos'd to be that *Amraphel,*

ANALYZE See ANNALISE

ANATOMIST (1)

HUMOUR26:8 H238 Nor yet Phisitian, nor Anatomist.

ANATOMY (1)

DUBART153:37 H41 And curious in-sight in Anatomy;

ANCESTOR (1)
MGREC94:24 H1662 To him, his mothers Ancestor (men say.)
ANCESTORS (4) [pl.]
MPERS69:14 H636 Whose Ancestors, were royal in degree;
MPERS85:27 H1303 All Townes, held by his Ancestors before.
MGREC120:22 H2759 Which of his Ancestors was once the throne,
MGREC127:8 H3038 Among their Ancestors by him there {they're} laid,
ANCESTOURS (1) [ancestors]
DIALOG148:8 H273 As did thine Ancestours in *Palestine,*
ANCHOR (2)
ELEMEN12:39 H199 Your Tackling, Anchor, Compasse too, is mine;
DISTEMP179:23 H11 My Anchor cast i'th' vale with safety.
ANCIENT (6) See also ANTIENT
MASSYR61:11 H316 *Damascus,* ancient seat of famous Kings,
MASSYR63:24 H409 The ancient {famous} *Niniveh* by him was won;
MASSYR66:18 H524 All rule, he from the ancient *Pharoes* takes;
MGREC119:13 H2703 Their ancient liberty, afresh now seeks,
MGREC125:16 H2964 But when her Souldiers saw their ancient Queen,
MGREC133:31 H3321 To whom Ancient {the old} *Berosus* (so much fam'd)
ANCUS (3)
MROMAN138:13 H3503 *Ancus Martius.*
MROMAN138:14 H3504 Next, *Ancus Martius* sits upon the Throne,
MROMAN138:36 H3526 And after all, by *Ancus* Sons was slaine.
ANEW (3)
MASSYR57:33 H178 Save a few names anew, *Berosus* writ.
MASSYR60:14 H279 Who did this Monarchy begin anew.
CONTEM173:29 H194 And warbling out the old, begin anew,
ANGELL (1)
MEDDM209:1 Hp291 wth god face to face in penvel Let me go, sath that Angell, I
ANGELLS (1) [angels]
MEDDM202:7 Hp281 earth some so wise and learned, that they seeme like Angells
ANGELS (3) [pl.]
TDUDLEY166:24 H66 Ah happy Soul, 'mongst Saints and Angels blest,
FLESH177:10 H91 And Angels are for Porters there;
MEDDM206:11 Hp287 Company of Saints, and Angels those Saintes haue their
ANGELS (1) [poss.]
DUBART154:8 H53 Had I an Angels voice, or *Barta's* pen,
ANGELS (1) [pl., poss.]
FLESH177:4 H85 But such as Angels heads infold.
ANGELS-WINGS (1) [pl.]
MYSOUL225:5 H9 Wth Angels-wings thy Soul shall movnt
ANGER (2)
HUMOUR32:20 H494 Though wit I want, and anger I have lesse,
MEDDM201:12 Hp280 hath its force abated by water not by wind, and anger must be
ANGLER (1)
MEDDM198:17 Hp276 Satan that great Angler hath his sundry baits for
ANGRY (4)
ELEMEN14:24 H266 Scarce Earth had done, but th' angry waters {water} mov'd;
AGES45:2 H378 In prime of youth seiz'd by heavens angry hand,
MPERS69:38 H665 That *Cressus* angry, urg'd him to express,
MPERS77:2 H941 Go *Persians,* carry home that angry peece,

ANGUISH (1)
DISTEMP179:14 H2 In anguish of my heart repleat with woes,
ANIMAL (4)
HUMOUR22:31 H100 The Animal I claime, as wel as these,
HUMOUR26:6 H236 Which natural, vital, animal we name.
HUMOUR26:16 H246 His life now animal, from vegative?
HUMOUR33:37 H551 The spirits animal, from whence doth {hence do} slide,
ANIMALS (1) [pl.]
CONTEM168:27 H34 Birds, insects, Animals with Vegative,
ANIMATING (1)
MGREC~~120:4~~ H2737 For animating the *Athenian* strife:
ANNALISE (1) [analyze]
HUMOUR24:24 H173 I will annalise, {this} thy so proud relation;
ANNE (2)
FATHER6:14 H48 ANNE BRADSTREET.
ANNEB187:13 H2 Anne Bradstreet.
ANNO (4)
MROMAN136:21 H3435 beginning, *Anno Mundi,*
DIALOG141:4 H3 Anno 1642.
SIDNEY149:5 H5 Anno 1586.
SICKNES178:16 H0 Upon a Fit of Sickness, *Anno,* 1632.
ANNUAL (1)
CONTEM168:31 H37 Thy swift Annual, and diurnal Course,
ANOINTED (1)
AGES~~45:4~~ H384 And Land & Nobels sav'd with their anointed.
ANON (1)
MASSYR67:27 H573 Who with his own, and Uncles power anon;
ANOTHER (22)
ELEMEN9:29 H63 Our Sages new, another tale have told:
ELEMEN18:37 H441 Thus I another body can assume,
HUMOUR33:15 ~~H529~~ Beholding unto me another way.
HUMOUR~~33:15~~ H529 I do as much for thee another way:
AGES41:28 H245 Thus out of one extreame, into another.
AGES45:13 H395 I've seen one stab'd, another {and some to} loose his head
AGES~~45:22~~ H412 Men may more freely speak another day.
SEASONS46:28 H4 Another Four i've {left} yet for to bring on,
MPERS92:12 H1570 But now's divolved, to another Stem.
MGREC98:30 H1832 And therefore {So} gives this {his little} Lord-ship to another.
MGREC100:21 H1905 Yet he (poore Prince) another Hoast doth muster,
MGREC123:26 H2890 This new Protector's of another minde,
DIALOG148:34 H299 And in a while you'l tell another tale.
QELIZ158:14 H123 Another.
2LETTER181:30 H0 *Another.*
3LETTER182:35 H0 *Another.*
MEDDM209:19 Hp291 wthin it self, but what it wants, another shall supply, that
MEDDM209:23 Hp291 so large, yet he stands in need of something wch another man
MEDDM209:25 Hp291 below, as also that god will haue vs beholden one to another
MYCHILD218:17 Hp244 I haue gott over this Block y^{n} have I another pvtt in my way, &
MYCHILD218:21 Hp244 way wee another.
SOREFIT221:15 H1 From another sore fitt. etc.

ANSWER (8)

MASSYR57:18 ~~H165~~ This answer may suffice, whom it wil please,
MPERS79:28 H1054 His answer was, both Land and Sea he feared,
MPERS81:30 H1138 *Mardonius* proud, hearing this answer stout,
MGREC109:34 H2293 But Kingly *Porus* this brave answer sent,
MGREC116:1 H2561 Before his answer came to *Babylon,*
MGREC120:26 H2763 And summons him, to answer these {his} complaints;
DIALOG143:25 H94 But yet, I answer not what you demand,
3LETTER183:2 H4 Her dearest Deer, might answer ear or eye;

ANSWERED (2)

SON231:28 H39 Particular, and how gratiovsly thov hast answered my Desires.
REMB235:33 H14 Thou hast me heard + answered,

ANSWERS (2) v.

MASSYR68:11 H597 None answers the affrighted Kings intent.
MYCHILD217:11 Hp242 comfortable Answers to me, either in granting ye Thing I

ANSWERS (1) [pl.]

MGREC~~110:18~~ H2322 Did *Alexander* by his answers find:

ANTHONY (1)

QELIZ156:26 H53 *Don Anthony* in's right for {there} to install;

ANTICK (1) [antique]

PROLOG7:21 H33 But sure the antick *Greeks* were far more milde,

ANTIDOTE (1)

ELEMEN12:20 H180 Poysons sure antidote lyes in his horne.

ANTIENT (2) [ancient]

MPERS80:8 H1075 Where is the valour, of your antient State?
MROMAN138:1 H3491 War with the antient *Albans* he doth {did} wage,

ANTIGONUS (29) [sg.]

MGREC118:37 H2686 *Antigonus,* for his share *Asia* takes,
MGREC120:25 H2762 *Antigonus* of Treason first attaints,
MGREC121:33 H2815 *Antigonus* did enter *Asia,*
MGREC122:41 H2862 The Army with *Antigonus* did {doth} leave,
MGREC123:3 H2865 On which *Antigonus* his height doth raise:
MGREC123:18 H2882 *Antigonus* hearing of his decease,
MGREC123:39 H2903 Goes to *Antigonus,* and both implore,
MGREC124:3 H2908 For this *Antigonus* needed {did need} no spurs,
MGREC124:18 H2925 *Antigonus* doth all in *Asia* gaine;
MGREC127:15 H3045 To keep *Antigonus* from *Susha* still,
MGREC127:19 H3049 *Antigonus* came off still honourlesse,
MGREC127:22 H3052 *Antigonus,* then takes {who took} his life unjust,
MGREC127:28 H3058 *Antigonus,* all *Persia* now gains {doth gain},
MGREC127:33 H3063 *Antigonus,* his growing up so hye,
MGREC127:38 H3068 *Antigonus,* desirous of the *Greeks,*
MGREC128:23 H3096 *Antigonus* {These princes} at {the} Sea soone had a fight,
MGREC~~128:24~~ H3097 Where {great Antigonus} *Ptolomy,* and the rest {was} put him
MGREC128:35 H3108 *Antigonus* did much rejoyce his son,
MGREC129:40 H3154 *Antigonus* for all this doth not mourn,
MGREC130:12 H3167 *Antigonus* thus had a wolf by th' ears,
MGREC~~131:1~~ H3188 *Antigonus* himself to ingratiate,
MGREC131:10 H3202 *Antigonus* and *Seleuchus,* now {then his} fight
MGREC131:15 H3207 For here *Antigonus* lost rule, and life,
MGREC~~132:20~~ H3260 Leaving *Antigonus* his eldest Son,

MGREC132:26 H3271 In *Greece*, unto *Antigonus*, his son,
MGREC133:8 H3296 *Antigonus, Seleuchus,* and *Cassander,*
MGREC133:12 H3300 *Antigonus* his Kingdoms lost, and's life,
MGREC133:16 H3304 *Demetrius* Son was call'd *Antigonus,*
MGREC133:26 H3316 This of *Antigonus,* his seed's the fate,

ANTIGONUS' (1) [poss.]
MGREC130:9 H3164 *Antigonus'* Lieutenant stayes her still,

ANTIOCHUS (6)
MGREC131:26 H3218 *Antiochus, Seleuchus* dear lov'd son,
MGREC133:30 H3320 *Antiochus Soter* his son was nam'd,
MGREC133:36 H3326 *Antiochus Theos* was *Soters* son,
MGREC134:2 H3333 And then *Antiochus* surnam'd the great,
MGREC134:3 H3336 {Fourth} *Seleuchus* next *Antiochus* succeeds,
MGREC134:9 H3340 *Antiochus Eupator* was the next,

ANTIPATER (20)
MGREC94:15 H1649 Leaves sage *Antipater* at home to sway,
MGREC102:26 H1996 *Antipater,* from *Greece,* sends great {fresh} supplyes;
MGREC108:39 H2255 His {A} third supply, *Antipater* now sent,
MGREC115:17 H2536 To meet him there, t' *Antipater* had {he'd} sent,
MGREC115:26 H2545 But now, *Antipater* had liv'd thus {so} long,
MGREC116:5 H2565 Sons of *Antipater,* {and} bearers of his Cup,
MGREC118:40 H2689 *Antipater*, had long rul'd *Macedon,*
MGREC119:16 H2706 The *Athenians,* force *Antipater* to fly
MGREC119:22 H2712 For to *Antipater* he now might go,
MGREC119:27 H2717 He joyn not with *Antipater,* that {their} foe.
MGREC119:34 H2724 Now to *Antipater, Craterus* goes,
MGREC119:39 H2729 *Antipater* releas'd from's prisonment,
MGREC~~120:4~~ H2736 Who fear'd *Antipater* would take his life
MGREC120:5 H2740 *Craterus,* and *Antipater* now joyn
MGREC120:17 H2752 With *Antipater* t' joyn, sometimes he thought,
MGREC120:28 H2765 Goes to *Antipater,* and tels what's done;
MGREC122:31 H2850 In's stead, {room} the Souldiers chose *Antipater,*
MGREC123:2 H2864 And thus *Antipater* the ground-work layes,
MGREC123:14 H2878 Now {When} great *Antipater,* the world doth {must} leave
MGREC123:24 H2888 *Antipater* had banisht her from thence,

ANTIPATER'S (1) [antipater is]
MGREC115:34 H2553 So to be caught, *Antipater's* too wise,

ANTIPHILUS (1)
MGREC119:24 H2714 *Antiphilus* the *Athenian* Generall,

ANTIQUE See ANTICK

ANTONY (1)
MGREC134:39 H3368 She with her Paramour *Mark Antony,*

ANUILE (1) [anvil]
MEDDM199:13 Hp277 on his anuile into what frame he pleases

ANXIETIES (1) [pl.]
AGES44:6 H339 Sicknesse, dangers, and anxieties have past,

ANXIOUS (2)
VANITY160:1 H11 No, that's but labour anxious, care and pain.
3LETTER183:3 H5 So doth my anxious soul, which now doth miss,

ANY (44)
ELEMEN15:36 H318 Or hast thou any colour can come nigh;

ELEMEN19:7 H452 The Phoenix too (if any be) are mine;
HUMOUR22:13 H82 If any threaten her, she'l in a trice,
HUMOUR31:14 H445 If any doubt this {the} truth, whence this should come;
HUMOUR33:21 H535 I am confounded, 'fore I speak of any:
AGES40:18 H199 If any care I take, 'tis to be fine,
AGES40:20 H201 If any time from company {leud Companions} I {can} spare,
AGES43:21 H316 And envy gnawes, if any do surmount.
MASSYR54:2 H29 Left to the world, by any History;
MASSYR63:19 H404 Of whom is little said in any thing; [22 years.
MPERS75:32 H889 Shall let the work, or keep back any thing,
MPERS89:5 H1439 Nor lackt they any of their number small,
MGREC96:28 H1748 And as much good she did, as any other.
MGREC98:5 H1807 But they accept not this, in any wise,
MGREC106:8 H2142 To see if any dare his might oppose;
MGREC106:9 H2143 (For scarce the world, or any bounds thereon,
MGREC107:30 H2205 For Boats here's none, nor neare it any wood,
MGREC~~116:10~~ H2572 She laid it more to heart, then any other,
MGREC119:41 H2731 Act any thing of worth, as heretofore,
MGREC123:33 H2897 Or by his favour {favours} any way did grace, {had grac'd}
MGREC124:22 H2929 Put trust in any, but in this Commander;
DIALOG146:23 H209 If any pity in thy heart remain,
DIALOG146:24 H210 Or any child-like love thou dost retain,
SIDNEY152:6 H77 To give to their detractor any quill.
DUBART154:25 H70 If e'r this golden gift was showr'd on any,
DAVID158:35 H15 Nor any pleasant thing e're may you show;
BIRTH180:9 H19 If any worth or virtue were in me,
MEDDM199:16 Hp278 haue any thing to stay vpon, but take away their props and
MEDDM201:10 Hp280 by any.
MEDDM201:19 Hp280 often se stones hang wth drops not from any innate moisture,
MEDDM201:21 Hp281 full of contrition, but it is not from any dew of grace wthin,
MEDDM204:9 Hp284 call for great returnes, the more that any man is intrusted
MEDDM204:22 Hp285 wch should warn him, that doth any speciall seruice for god, to
MEDDM209:21 Hp291 so it is with men, there was neuer yet any one man that had
TOCHILD215:2 H2 This Book by Any yet vnread,
MYCHILD215:13 Hp240 opportvnity to speak to any of yov much lesse to All, thovght it
MYCHILD215:26 Hp240 et^{c}. I avoided it. If at any time I was overtaken wth ye evills,
MYCHILD217:1 Hp242 If at any time yov are chastened of God take it as Thankfully
MYCHILD217:34 Hp243 God, I never saw any miracles to confirm me,
MYCHILD218:13 Hp244 Is there any story but that wch showes the beginnings of
MYCHILD218:15 Hp244 in it fullfilled wch could not haue been so long foretold by any
MYCHILD219:7 Hp245 but if yov can pick any Benefitt out of it, It is
MED223:3 Hp250 Lord why should I doubt any more w^{n} thov hast given me such
REMB236:8 H23 Or any way expresse.

APACE (4)

AGES45:28 H418 And back, once straight, begins apace to bow.
MPERS82:4 H1151 *Mardonius* finding victuals wast apace,
MPERS91:2 H1510 {*Spartan* State} which now apace doth {so fast did} rise;
MEDDM196:17 Hp273 drought of the day, when he perceiues his sun apace to decline

APAID See APAID

APIS (1)

MPERS71:34 H748 The Ægyptian *Apis* then he likewise slew,

APISH (1)
MASSYR58:26 H209 *Sardanapalus* leaves his Apish play.
APOLLO (5)
MPERS69:22 H644 For information to *Apollo* went:
MPERS80:39 H1106 To rob the wealthy Temple of *Apollo,*
MGREC126:38 H3027 His sword unto *Apollo* consecrates:
SIDNEY151:39 ~~H75~~ I leave't in brief, *Apollo* do't at large.
SIDNEY151:40 ~~H75~~ *Apollo* laught to patch up what's begun,
APOLOGIE (1)
MGREC136:5 H3418 To frame Apologie for some offence,
APOLOGY (1)
MROMAN139:26 H3552 *An Apology.*
APOSTATE (1)
SEASONS51:13 H187 And in this month was made apostate man;
APOSTATES (1) [pl.]
TDUDLEY165:33 H35 Which caus'd Apostates to maligne so.
APOSTLE (2)
MEDDM206:37 Hp288 make vs wth the Apostle to admire the iustice and mercy
MEDDM208:18 Hp290 Well doth the Apostle call riches deceitfull riches, and they
APPAID (1) [apaid]
MGREC~~124:6~~ H2911 And so he quick returns thus well appaid,
APPAL (1) [appall]
HUMOUR21:24 H52 What makes him face his foe, without appal?
APPALL'D (2) [appalled]
ELEMEN13:40 H241 Ye affrighted wights, appall'd how do you shake
MASSYR68:3 H589 With quaking knees, and heart appall'd, he crys,
APPEALE (2) [appeal]
HUMOUR28:38 H350 No braggs i've us'd, t' your selves {to you} I dare appeale,
MEDDM205:16 Hp286 is this Court of Judicature, that there is no appeale from it,
APPEAR (10) See also APPEARE
FATHER5:26 H27 Their discord may {doth} appear, by these harsh rimes.
FATHER6:9 H43 These ragged lines, will do't, when they appear.
ELEMEN19:24 H469 What woeful wracks I've made, may wel appear,
HUMOUR23:23 H133 As objects best appear, by contraries.
MGREC96:24 H1744 Then such a world of Wagons did appear,
MGREC~~118:24~~ H2672 His countenance so lively did appear,
DIALOG146:37 H223 But now the Sun in's brightnesse shall appear,
SIDNEY152:16 ~~H85~~ But I had blemish'd theirs, to make 't appear;
VERSES183:36 H3 If worth in me, or ought I do appear,
MEDDM200:28 Hp279 when the Sun of righteoussnes shall appear those dry bones
APPEAR'D (1) [appeared]
MGREC111:23 H2368 To th' coast which by *Euphrates* mouth appear'd;
APPEARE (1) [appear]
MGREC114:20 H2490 As did appeare, in flattering him the least:
APPEARED (1) See also APPEAR'D
MPERS79:29 H1055 Which was not vaine, as it {after} soon appeared:
APPEARES (1) [appears]
ELEMEN19:41 H482 That earth appeares in heaven, oh wonder great!
APPEARING (2)
2SIMON195:15 Hp271 reioyceing at that great day of appearing, wch is the continuall
MEDDM207:36 Hp289 and the sun approaching, of the appearing of the Sun of

APPEARS (4) See also APPEARES
SEASONS50:34 H168 Yet then appears the worthy deeds he 'ath done:
MASSYR57:9 H156 This fraud, in war, nor peace, at all appears;
MGREC110:34 H2338 Whereon his acts, and travels, long appears;
CHILDRN185:1 H27 And where *Aurora* first appears,
APPEAS'D (1) [appeased]
MPERS85:7 ~~H1283~~ That nought appeas'd him, but his brothers life.
APPEASE (4)
AGES37:15 H77 Who sought stil to appease me, with her {the} brest,
MPERS85:25 H1301 So that he might, these tumults {those troubles} soon appease.
MPERS91:20 H1528 His home-bred troubles seeketh {sought how} to appease;
VANITY160:7 H17 Mean while the conscience rage, who shall appease?
APPEASED See APPEAS'D
APPETITE (3)
HUMOUR30:30 H422 The first it draines, o'th' last quicks appetite,
MGREC135:32 H3404 And when he had no appetite to eate,
MEDDM201:15 Hp280 A sharp appetite and a through Concoction, is a signe of an
APPLE (2)
AGES38:2 H105 But for an Apple, Plumbe, or some such prize,
CONTEM169:36 H74 Fancyes the Apple, dangle on the Tree,
APPLE-TREE (1)
SEASONS47:38 H50 The Pear, the Plumbe, and Apple-tree now flourish,
APPLES (2) [pl.]
SEASONS51:9 H183 And Apples now their yellow sides do show;
ELIZB187:6 H14 And Plumbs and Apples throughly ripe do fall,
APPLY (1)
MEDDM207:27 Hp289 should make vs so to number our dayes as to apply our hearts
APPOINTED (4)
MPERS74:7 H832 They all attend on the appointed houre,
MGREC130:15 H3170 Her women are appointed to this deed,
MEDDM202:29 Hp282 when ye morning (wch is the appointed time) is come the Sun
MEDDM203:19 Hp283 dayes of our appointed time till our chang shall come,
APPOINTS (1)
MGREC122:28 H2847 What he appoints, She purposely withstands.
APPREHENDED (1)
MGREC112:23 H2409 Upon suspicion being apprehended,
APPROACH (6)
ELEMEN9:36 H70 Both man and beast, rejoyce at his approach,
MPERS86:4 H1320 But in his slow approach, ere he came there;
MGREC102:41 H2011 In his approach, the Governour sends word,
CONTEM169:5 H47 As to approach it, can no earthly mould.
MEDDM200:25 Hp279 the leavlesse trees and dry stocks (at the approach of the Sun)
HANNA230:13 H6 When death did seem ev'n to approach
APPROACHES (1)
SEASONS52:35 H250 And North-ward stil approaches to the Line;
APPROACHING (3)
MPERS88:1 H1394 arme, the King {with all his host} is now approaching nigh;
MGREC93:22 H1619 An Omen, to their near approaching woe;
MEDDM207:36 Hp289 and the sun approaching, of the appearing of the Sun of
APRICOCK (1) [apricot]
SEASONS50:27 H161 Now's ripe the Pear, Pear-plumbe, and Apricock,

APRIL (2)
SEASONS46:37 H15 *March, April, May,* of all the rest most faire;
SEASONS47:28 H44 My second month is *April,* green, and fair,
APT (1)
MYCHILD217:8 Hp242 but I haue been apt to forgett him and my Self
APULIA'S (1) [poss.]
ELEMEN10:32 H107 *Apulia's* jacent parts were covered;
AQUARIAS (1)
SEASONS52:26 H241 In *Aquarias,* now keeps the loved {long wisht} Sun,
ARABIA (1)
MASSYR67:15 H561 *Arabia,* and all the boardering coast.
ARABIAN (1)
ELEMEN14:15 H257 Much might I say, of the *Arabian* sands; {hot *Libian* sand}
ARABIANS (2) [pl.]
MASSYR58:20 H205 And the *Arabians,* to further his desire.
MASSYR66:15 H521 *Kedar,* {and} *Hazer,* the *Arabians* too,
ARAXIS (1)
MGREC98:38 H1840 And then at *Tigris,* and *Araxis* side:
ARAY (1) [array]
SEASONS48:10 H63 Wherein the earth, is clad in rich aray:
ARAYES (1) [arrays]
MPERS88:3 H1396 Gets on his armes, arayes himselfe for fight;
ARBACES (10) [sg.]
MASSYR58:7 H192 At last {It chanc'd} *Arbaces* brave, unwarily,
MASSYR58:15 H200 *Belosus,* promised *Arbaces* aide,
MASSYR58:16 H201 *Arbaces* him, fully to be repaid.
MASSYR58:24 ~~H207~~ *Arbaces* must be master of their lands.
MASSYR58:35 H218 These with celerity, *Arbaces* meets {meet},
MASSYR59:17 H241 That what *Arbaces* did, was but derided;
MASSYR59:22 H246 *Arbaces* marches in, the town did {he} take {takes},
MASSYR59:40 H264 *Arbaces* thus, of all becomming Lord,
MASSYR60:29 H294 *Arbaces* suffers all, and all he takes.
MPERS69:4 H626 He in descent the seventh from *Arbaces.*
ARBACES (1) [poss.]
MASSYR58:30 H213 *Arbaces* courage he did sore {so} abate:
ARBELA (2)
MGREC101:40 H1969 At *Arbela,* this victory gain'd,
MGREC102:3 H1973 At *Arbela* left, his ornaments, and treasure,
ARBITRATED (1)
ELEMEN8:24 H22 That betwixt hot and cold, she arbitrated
ARCADIA (1)
SIDNEY149:20 H19 (Witnesse *Arcadia,* penn'd in his youth)
ARCHADIAN (1)
SEASONS49:23 ~~H114~~ Was like that noble, brave *Archadian.*
ARCHER (1)
ELEMEN10:11 H86 The Crown, the Whale, the Archer, Bernice Hare,
ARCHES (1) [pl.]
MASSYR56:20 H126 Her gardens, bridges, arches, mounts, and spires;
ARCHITECT (1)
HOUSE237:18 H48 Fram'd by that mighty Architect,

ARDENT (1)

2LETTER182:29	H35	Nought but the fervor of his ardent beams

ARE (207)

FATHER5:18	H19	They are your bounden handmaids to attend.
FATHER5:19	H20	These same are they, of {from} whom we being have,
FATHER5:20	H21	These are of all, the life, the nurse, the grave,
FATHER5:21	H22	These are, the hot, the cold, the moist, the dry,
FATHER6:5	H39	My goods are true (though poor) I love no stealth,
FATHER6:10	H44	On what they are, your mild aspect I crave,
PROLOG6:20	H5	For my mean Pen, are too superiour things,
PROLOG7:28	H39	Let *Greeks* be *Greeks,* and Women what they are,
ELEMEN10:13	H88	Nay more then these, Rivers 'mongst stars are found,
ELEMEN11:38	H158	Whose numbers now are growne innumerous;
ELEMEN13:39	H240	Before they know, they are inter'd alive.
ELEMEN15:19	H301	That she can spare, when Nations round are poore.
ELEMEN16:12	~~H335~~	Then Seas are deep, Mountains are never high.
ELEMEN16:34	H357	All humours, Tumours, that {which} are bred of cold.
ELEMEN17:19	H383	That *Caucasus* high mounts, are seldom free.
ELEMEN17:27	H391	But these are trifles to the Flood of *Noe.*
ELEMEN18:13	H417	Nay, what are words, which doe reveale the mind?
ELEMEN18:14	H418	Speak, who, or what they will, they are but wind.
ELEMEN18:17	H421	And such are Ecchoes, and report o'th gun
ELEMEN18:19	H423	Your songs and pleasant tunes, they are the same,
ELEMEN19:4	H449	Next, of my Fowles such multitudes there are;
ELEMEN19:7	H452	The Phoenix too (if any be) are mine;
HUMOUR21:17	H45	One of your selves are my compeers, in place:
HUMOUR22:19	H88	Here's three of you, all sees {see} now what you are,
HUMOUR23:5	H115	But a good head from these are disonant;
HUMOUR23:7	H117	Thou sayst, thy wits are stai'd, subtle and fine:
HUMOUR23:27	H137	They're held for Oracles, they are so wise.
HUMOUR23:28	H138	Their wrathfull looks are death, their words are laws;
HUMOUR23:28	H138	Their wrathfull looks are death, their words are laws;
HUMOUR23:33	H143	Forsooth you are to blame, he grave reply'd.
HUMOUR24:14	H163	Your selves may plead, your wrongs are no whit lesse,
HUMOUR26:2	H232	Yet such, when we al four are joyn'd in one.
HUMOUR26:3	H233	And when such thou art, even such are we.
HUMOUR26:12	H242	For there are {is} none, thou say'st, if some, not best.
HUMOUR26:13	H243	That there are some, and best, I dare averre;
HUMOUR26:33	H263	The spirits through thy heat, are made perfect there,
HUMOUR27:27	H298	And what you singly {single} are, the whole I make.
HUMOUR27:28	H299	Your hot, dry, moyst, cold, natures are {but} foure,
HUMOUR28:24	H336	Of such as to the Sanguine are inclin'd,
HUMOUR28:27	H339	For Arts, and Sciences, they are the fittest,
HUMOUR28:28	H340	And maugre (Choler) stil they are the wittest,
HUMOUR31:37	H470	But these with you, are seldome resident.
HUMOUR32:1	H475	Nor are ye free, from this inormity,
HUMOUR32:11	H485	Strange Chymera's are in my phantasie,
HUMOUR33:11	H525	But the spirits, by which it acts are thine;
HUMOUR33:20	H534	My excellencies are so great, so many,
HUMOUR34:1	H556	The optick nerve, coats, humours, all are mine,
AGES~~38:27~~	H130	As many was {are} my sins, so dangers too:

AGES39:5 H148 Declare some greater riches are within;
AGES~~39:37~~ H180 My woful Parents longing hopes all {are} crost,
AGES40:39 H218 My heart lyes frying, and my {mine} eyes are sinking;
AGES~~41:13~~ H232 Child-hood and youth is {are} vaine, yea {ye} vanity.
AGES41:41 H258 Yet all my powers, for self-ends are not spent,
AGES~~45:22~~ H411 What are my thoughts, this is no time to say.
AGES45:23 H413 These are no old wives tales, but this is truth;
AGES45:29 H419 My grinders now are few, my sight doth faile
AGES45:30 H420 My skin is wrinkled, and my cheeks are pale.
AGES46:14 H445 My studies, labours, readings, all are done,
SEASONS46:36 H14 Three months {(quoth she)} there are allotted to my share,
SEASONS49:4 H95 Bright *June, July,* and *August,* hot are mine,
SEASONS49:34 H127 This Month the Roses are distill'd in Glasses,
SEASONS~~49:36~~ H129 The Cherry, Goos-berry, is {are} now i'th prime,
SEASONS50:39 H173 Now day and night are equal in each clime;
SEASONS51:2 H176 The Vintage now is ripe, the Grapes are prest,
SEASONS~~51:8~~ H182 The Figge is {are} ripe, the Pomgranet also,
SEASONS51:25 H201 Whose yellow saplesse leaves by winds are fann'd:
SEASONS52:5 H220 Beef, Brawn, and Pork, are now in great'st {great} request,
SEASONS52:37 H252 And some warm glances from the Sun {his face} are felt,
SEASONS53:1 H257 *My Subjects bare, my Brains are {Brain is} bad,*
MASSYR54:8 H35 Whose Preists, in Stories, oft are mentioned;
MASSYR55:1 H67 Fifty two years he reign'd (as we are told)
MASSYR56:41 H147 But by what means, we are not certifi'd.
MASSYR57:30 H175 For *Ninias,* and all his Race are left,
MASSYR62:22 H367 Where now those ten Tribes are, can no man tel,
MASSYR62:28 H373 But what, or where they are, yet know we this;
MASSYR66:11 H517 All now of worth, are captive led with tears,
MPERS69:18 H640 Are fit for such, whose eares for fables itch;
MPERS69:26 H648 Where all that doe {dare} resist, are slaughter'd down;
MPERS83:38 H1226 Where ninescore days, are spent in banquetting,
MPERS85:10 H1286 These two lewd {first} sons, are by hystorians thought,
MPERS89:12 H1446 What dastards in the field the *Persians* are;
MPERS91:10 H1518 The Kings {on such} conditions they are forc't to take; {as King
MPERS91:26 ~~H1540~~ Who sooths him up, his owne desires are Lawes:
MGREC~~100:20~~ H1904 And now of valour both were {are} destitute;
MGREC102:7 H1977 With showers of Flowers, the streets along are strown,
MGREC~~102:19~~ H1989 With all pleasures that on earth was {are} found,
MGREC106:32 H2166 Are strictly now commanded to adore;
MGREC109:3 H2260 that {Such as} doe not, both they, {them} and theirs, are slain;
MGREC109:7 H2266 Whose feasts are celebrated by this Prince;
MGREC112:15 H2401 Now, *Alexanders* conquests, all are done,
MGREC113:10 H2437 Are {Were} now inflicted on *Parmenio's* Son,
MGREC~~115:15~~ H2525 The Mules and Horses are for sorrow shorne,
MGREC~~115:15~~ H2526 The battlements from off the walls are torne.
MGREC116:41 H2607 His thoughts are perish'd he aspires no more,
MGREC120:41 H2778 *Perdicas* hears, his foes are now {all} combin'd,
MGREC123:34 H2898 Are now at the devotion of the Son,
MGREC125:21 ~~H2969~~ But soone are brought into captivity;
MGREC129:25 H3139 And now they are, {were} free Lords, of what they had,
MGREC130:15 H3170 Her women are appointed to this deed,

MROMAN137:13	H3464	To see these sports, the *Sabins* all are bent;
DIALOG143:28	H97	Which are my Sins, the breach of sacred Lawes;
DIALOG~~143:31~~	H100	And {Are} lik'd, and countenanc'd by men of might,
DIALOG143:33	H102	Church Offices are {were} sold, and bought, for gaine,
DIALOG145:5	H154	The bottome dregs reserved are for me.
DIALOG146:30	H216	You are my mother, nurse, {and} I once your flesh,
DIALOG147:10	H236	These are the dayes, the Churches foes to crush,
DIALOG147:27	H251	When they are gone, then drown your self in teares.
DIALOG147:30	H254	These, these, are they (I trust) with *Charles* our King,
SIDNEY149:21	H20	Are not his Tragick Comedies so acted,
SIDNEY151:30	~~H75~~	Which are in worth, as far short of his due,
DUBART154:4	H49	Mine eyes are sightlesse, and my tongue is mute;
DUBART154:27	H72	Unto each man his riches are {is} assign'd,
DUBART154:33	H78	Thy sacred works are not for imitation,
DAVID159:27	H42	How are the mighty falne into decay,
VANITY160:20	H30	Such stoicks are but stocks, such teaching vain:
VANITY160:41	H51	Nor death shall see, but are immortal made,
CONTEM169:27	H66	And men in being fancy those are dead,
CONTEM171:13	H117	Living so little while we are alive;
CONTEM171:21	H124	Nor age nor wrinkle on their front are seen;
CONTEM174:32	H229	Their names without a Record are forgot,
CONTEM174:36	H233	Shall last and shine when all of these are gone.
FLESH175:5	H5	Things that are past, and things to come;
FLESH175:21	H21	To catch at shadowes which are not?
FLESH176:4	H44	Sisters we are, yea twins we be,
FLESH176:6	H46	For from one father are we not,
FLESH176:19	H59	Thy riches are to me no bait,
FLESH176:32	H72	Nor are they shadows which I catch,
FLESH176:34	H74	But reach at things that are so high,
FLESH176:40	H80	My garments are not silk nor gold,
FLESH177:8	H89	Are made of pretious *Jasper* stone;
FLESH177:10	H91	And Angels are for Porters there;
FLESH177:15	H96	Of Life, there are the waters sure,
BIRTH180:1	H11	We both are ignorant, yet love bids me
3LETTER183:26	H28	The substance gone, O me, these are but dreams.
CHILDRN185:18	H44	Let others know what are my fears
CHILDRN185:35	H61	My cares are more, and fears then ever,
CHILDRN185:38	H64	Of perils you are ignorant,
CHILDRN186:6	H73	Once young and pleasant, as are you,
ELIZB187:5	H13	By nature Trees do rot when they are grown.
ELIZB187:7	H15	And Corn and grass are in their season mown,
2SIMON195:9	Hp271	Such as they are I bequeath to you, Small legacys are acceptd
2SIMON195:9	Hp271	as they are I bequeath to you, Small legacys are acceptd by
MEDDM195:29	Hp272	speak well, but few can do well. We are better scholars in the
MEDDM196:25	Hp273	Sweet words are like hony, a little may refresh, but too much
MEDDM196:28	Hp273	children, haue their different natures, some are like flesh wch
MEDDM196:30	Hp273	fruits that are best preserued wth sugar, those parents are wise
MEDDM197:7	Hp274	The reason why christians are so loth to exchang this world for
MEDDM197:22	Hp275	Few men are so humble, as not to be proud of their abilitys,
MEDDM197:33	Hp275	pain till they turn to dust, and then are they fine manchet for
MEDDM198:32	Hp277	pleasant thing to behold the light, but sore eyes are not able to

MEDDM199:9 Hp277 dry and sapless performances are simptoms of little spiritull
MEDDM199:15 Hp278 Ambitious men are like hops that neuer rest climbing soe long
MEDDM199:16 Hp278 thing to stay vpon, but take away their props and they are of
MEDDM199:23 Hp278 Dimne eyes, are the concomitants of old age, and short
MEDDM199:24 Hp278 those that are eyes of a Republique, foretels a declineing
MEDDM200:6 Hp279 Some children are hardly weaned although the teat be rub'd
MEDDM200:10 Hp279 yet they are so childishly sottish that they are still huging and
MEDDM201:2 Hp280 his strong men, such as are come to a full stature in Christ,
MEDDM201:25 Hp281 The words of the wise (sath Solom) are as nailes, and as
MEDDM201:31 Hp281 in the parching sun, & a shelter in a blustering storme are of
MEDDM202:6 Hp281 is capable of, and some again so base that they are Viler
MEDDM202:8 Hp281 and some againe, so ignorant and sotish that they are more
MEDDM202:11 Hp281 healthfull y^{t} their bones are full of marrow & their breasts of
MEDDM202:12 Hp281 some againe so weak and feeble, that while they liue, they are
MEDDM202:22 Hp282 we may walk by his light, but when he is set, we are in
MEDDM202:32 Hp282 The eyes and the eares are the inlets or doores of the soule,
MEDDM203:6 Hp283 loose them then they are lesse then vanity & more then
MEDDM203:32 Hp284 we are more ready to receiue mercys then we are to
MEDDM203:32 Hp284 are more ready to receiue mercys then we are to acknowledg
MEDDM203:33 Hp284 men can vse great importunity when they are in distresses and
MEDDM204:6 Hp284 yesterday, to day ȧnd for euer, we are the same that stand
MEDDM205:1 Hp285 (like sowre land) are of so tough and morose a dispotion that
MEDDM205:5 Hp285 nurture they are brought into a fit capacity, let the seed of good
MEDDM205:10 Hp286 Commonwealth, his more fixed and resolued thoughts, are like
MEDDM205:11 Hp286 inhabitants his slight and flitting thoughts are like passengers,
MEDDM205:32 Hp286 is the breaking of their limbes, some again, are but meanly
MEDDM205:34 Hp286 among them are dry stocks so is it in the church wch is gods
MEDDM205:35 Hp286 there are some eminent Christians, that are soe frequent in
MEDDM205:35 Hp287 some eminent Christians, that are soe frequent in good dutys,
MEDDM205:37 Hp287 and ther are some (and they sincere ones too) who haue not
MEDDM206:2 Hp287 there are others that haue nothing to commend them, but only
MEDDM206:3 Hp287 profession, and these are but leavie Christians, wch are in as
MEDDM206:3 Hp287 and these are but leavie Christians, wch are in as much
MEDDM206:12 Hp287 euen in this life, some are Stars of the first magnitude,
MEDDM206:17 Hp287 shall they be, when they are fixt in their heauenly spheres
MEDDM206:27 Hp288 All the works and doings of god are wonderfull, but none more
MEDDM207:1 Hp288 god and say how vnsearchable are his wayes and his footsteps
MEDDM207:4 Hp288 that god, bestows on the sons of men, are not only abused
MEDDM207:8 Hp288 driuen them the further from him, that they are ready to say,
MEDDM207:9 Hp288 we are lords we will come no more at thee If outward
MEDDM207:21 Hp289 All men are truly sayd to be tenants at will, and it may as truly
MEDDM207:28 Hp289 that when wee are put out of these houses of Clay, we
MEDDM208:28 Hp290 admirable to Consider the power of faith, by wch all things are
MEDDM209:12 Hp291 slauery, so it is most certain that those that are disobedient
MYCHILD215:11 Hp240 leaue to speak, and those espec. sink deepest wch are spoke
MYCHILD216:32 Hp242 me and try me, see what wayes of wickednes are in me, and
MYCHILD217:1 Hp242 If at any time yov are chastened of God take it as Thankfully
MYCHILD218:23 Hp244 that are in their Relign: together wth their lying miracles, and
MED223:12 Hp250 to haue thought it? So wonderfull are these thoughts that my
13MAY227:1 H10 My winters past my stormes are gone
SAMUEL228:11 H12 For mortall helpes are brittle Dvst.

11MAYB228:34 Hp259 Conversation may speak that thy vowes are vpon me.
HOURS233:22 H5 My Troubles All are Thee before
HOURS234:16 H30 They are no Joy, but woe.

ARGUE (2)
HUMOUR~~27:19~~ H290 Nor what you've said, doth argue my disgrace,
MEDDM199:8 Hp277 Yellow leaues argue want of sap and gray haires want of

ARGUED See ARGVED

ARGUES (2)
HUMOUR32:14 H488 Nor multitude of words, argues our strength;
MEDDM201:16 Hp280 a quick reception, and a deliberate cogitation argues a sound

ARGUMENT (2)
HUMOUR24:23 H172 But to evince the truth, by argument.
QELIZ156:14 H41 She's argument enough to make you mute;

ARGUMENTS (1) [pl.]
MPERS73:39 H824 What arguments they us'd, I know not well,

ARGVED (1) [argued]
MYCHILD218:7 Hp244 I haue argved thvs wth my self, That there is a God I

ARID (7)
MGREC117:16 H2623 *Arid æus.*
MGREC117:40 H2647 His base born Brother, *Arid æus* nam'd,
MGREC118:27 H2676 *Perdicas,* seeing *Arid æus* must be King,
MGREC122:13 H2838 Perceives {Sees} *Arid æus* must not king it long,
MGREC124:25 H2932 *Arid æus* the scorn'd, and simple King,
MGREC124:39 H2946 *Olimpias, Arid æus* deadly hates,
MGREC127:7 H3037 Of *Arid æus,* and his Queen, with state;

ARIDAEUS (1)
MGREC130:30 ~~H3181~~ *Aridaeus* and his Queen by slaughters ta'ne;

ARIES (1)
SEASONS46:38 H16 The tenth o'th' first *Sol* into *Aries* enters,

ARIGHT (1)
MEDDM203:35 Hp284 conuersation aright will glorifie him that heard him in the day of

ARIONS (1) [poss.]
ELEMEN15:28 H310 The Dolphin (loving musique) *Arions* friend.

ARISE (7)
HUMOUR34:15 H570 And the strong ligaments, from hence arise,
DIALOG146:29 H215 Shake off your dust, chear up, and now arise,
FLESH176:8 H48 But my arise is from above,
2LETTER182:21 H27 Which day by day long wait for thy arise,
MEDDM200:29 Hp279 shall arise in far more glory, then that wch they lost at their
MEDDM202:23 Hp282 darknes till he arise againe, so god doth somtime vaile his face
MEDDM202:30 Hp282 of righteousnes will arise wth healing in his wings.

ARISES (1)
MED223:5 Hp250 I thy servant, But hence arises not my comfort, Thou art

ARISTOCRACY (1)
MPERS73:36 H821 If governed by an Aristocracy.

ARISTOTLE (1)
MGREC116:17 H2583 Wise *Aristotle,* tutour to his youth,

ARISTOTLES (1) [poss.]
ELEMEN16:18 H341 Which wondring *Aristotles* wit, ne'r knowes.

ARM (1) n. [limb] See also ARME, TH'ARM
HOUSE237:14 H44 The arm of flesh didst make thy trvst?

ARM'D (2) [armed]
ELEMEN10:3 H78 With {There's} *Orion* arm'd, attended by his dog,
MPERS76:30 H928 Arm'd all they could, which elev'n thousand make;
ARMADO (1)
DIALOG142:23 H52 Pray, doe not {you} feare *Spaines* bragging Armado?
ARMADOE (1)
QELIZ156:24 H51 She ract, she sackt, she sunk his Armadoe;
ARME (2) n. [arm, limb] See also TH'ARM
AGES36:17 H41 Of Autumne {Autumns} fruits a basket on his arme.
AGES36:21 H45 Under his arme a Sheafe of wheat he bore,
ARME (1) n. [arm, troops]
MPERS81:40 H1144 The *Athenians* could but forty thousand arme,
ARME (2) v. [arm]
MPERS88:1 H1394 Arme, arme, the King {with all his host} is now approaching
ARMED (1) See also ARM'D
HUMOUR29:3 H356 Had need be armed wel, and active too,
ARMENIA (1)
ELEMEN12:8 H168 Dividing great *Armenia* from the least,
ARMENIAN (2)
MASSYR54:30 H57 *Barzanes,* the great *Armenian* King,
MGREC134:13 H3344 That {Then} *Tygranes* the great *Armenian* King,
ARMES (10) [arms, limbs]
AGES37:16 H78 With weary armes, she danc'd, and *By, By,* sung,
AGES45:35 H425 My hands and armes, once strong, have lost their might,
AGES88:37 H1430 Their armes grew weake, through {by their} slaughters that
MGREC135:2 H3374 {His brave *Virago*} Aspes she sets unto {to} her Armes,
MGREC135:21 H3393 Next, armes and breast, of silver to behold;
DIALOG141:8 H7 What ayles thee hang thy head, and crosse thine armes?
DIALOG142:31 H60 Though Armes, nor Purse she hath, for your releif:
DIALOG143:14 H83 Her Lillies in mine Armes avouch the same.
MEDDM208:36 Hp291 lasting armes of the mighty god of Jacob yea Jacob himself
2HUSB232:7 H8 Into thy Everlasting Armes
ARMES (6) [arms, weapons]
ELEMEN12:1 H161 For Learning, Armes, and Arts, I love it well:
HUMOUR24:34 H183 Whose glorious deeds in armes, the world can tel,
MPERS87:40 H1392 And here, and there, in carts their Armes they throw,
MPERS88:3 H1396 Gets on his armes, arayes himselfe for fight;
MGREC128:13 H3086 Requires them therefore to take up their Armes,
SIDNEY149:12 H11 Of Armes, and Arts, thou {he} should'st a patterne be.
ARMIE (1) [army]
ELEMEN~~14:17~~ H259 whole Armies {*Cambyses* Armie} I have {was} overthrown;
ARMIES (7) [pl.] See also ARMYES
ELEMEN14:17 H259 whole Armies {*Cambyses* Armie} I have {was} overthrown;
MPERS82:3 H1150 Ten dayes these Armies did each other face,
MGREC96:35 H1755 But when both Armies met, he might behold,
MGREC101:34 ~~H1959~~ Both Armies meet, *Greeks* fight, the *Persians* run,
MGREC119:3 H2693 But held command o'th' Armies {Army} which was best;
DIALOG144:38 H146 I saw (unmov'd) her Armies foil'd and fled,
DIALOG148:5 H270 When thus in Peace: thine Armies brave send out,
ARMOUR (2)
MROMAN136:26 H3440 But *Æmulus,* in Armour all disguis'd.

CONTEM173:8 H176 Whose armour is their scales, their spreading fins their shield.

ARMS (2) [limbs] See also ARMES

MGREC135:25 H3397 And smote those feet, those legs, those arms and thighs;
BIRTH180:12 H22 Yet love thy dead, who long lay in thine arms:

ARMS (5) [weapons] See also ARMES

HUMOUR23:24 H134 Thus {But} arms, and arts I claim, and higher things;
MPERS90:40 H1507 *Tythraustes* trusts more to his wit then Arms,
MPERS~~91:4~~ H1512 With suit, their force, {Arms} against his {their} foes be bent;
MGREC~~131:1~~ H3190 With Arms and with provision stores them well,
DIALOG147:7 H233 That help thee not with prayers, arms, and purse,

ARMY (39)

ELEMEN11:1 H117 The Army through my helpe victorious rose;
MASSYR54:34 H61 An army of three Millions he led out,
MASSYR56:26 H132 Her Army of four Millions did consist,
MASSYR58:33 H216 From *Bactaria* an Army was at hand,
MASSYR59:12 H236 But *Salmeneus* slaine, his {the} Army fals,
MASSYR61:25 H330 When *Rezin's* slain, his Army over-thrown,
MASSYR62:38 H383 Which made his Army into nothing melt;
MASSYR64:21 H445 By great *Euphrates* did his Army fall,
MASSYR64:25 H449 A mighty Army next, he doth prepare,
MASSYR65:3 H468 The Sea firm Land, whereon the Army past,
MASSYR65:8 H473 And though a Victor home his Army leads,
MASSYR67:18 H564 His Army routed, and himselfe there slain,
MPERS69:19 H641 He in his younger dayes an Army led,
MPERS70:27 H698 And *Tomris* Son, an Army over-throwes;
MPERS71:31 H745 A second Army there {he} had almost grav'd;
MPERS76:5 H903 His Army fought with Hunger, and with Cold,
MPERS76:26 H924 For *Attica* an Army he prepares;
MPERS78:3 H984 His Army of all Nations, was compounded,
MPERS79:40 H1066 And all that Army, then dismay'd, had fled,
MPERS82:20 H1167 That Army, which did fright the Universe;
MPERS90:33 ~~H1500~~ But *Tyssaphernes* with his Army fled;
MGREC~~100:16~~ H1900 to resist {man's there} his valour showes {Army to oppose};
MGREC100:26 H1910 Of Horse, and Foot, this {his} Army did amount;
MGREC103:39 H2050 Had now his fourth, and last Army compounded,
MGREC104:35 H2087 Whose Army now, was almost within sight,
MGREC107:20 H2195 Now with his Army, doth he hast {post} away,
MGREC~~108:28~~ H2244 Where *Scithians* rude, his valour {army} doth oppose,
MGREC108:40 H2256 Which did his former Army {forces} much augment,
MGREC110:3 H2303 A potent Army with him, like a King,
MGREC110:9 H2309 His Army *Alexander* doth divide,
MGREC~~119:3~~ H2693 But held command o'th' Armies {Army} which was best;
MGREC~~119:25~~ H2715 With speed his forces {Army} doth together call,
MGREC119:28 H2718 The *Athenian* Army was the greater far,
MGREC121:6 H2784 And with his Army into {unto} *Ægypt* goes,
MGREC122:22 ~~H2845~~ Who had an Army, like a great Commander.
MGREC122:41 H2862 The Army with *Antigonus* did {doth} leave,
MGREC~~124:7~~ H2912 With ships at Sea, an Army for the Land,
MGREC126:3 H2994 His Army he divides, sends part away,
MGREC~~132:20~~ H3258 A mighty Navy rig'd, an Army stout,

ARMY'S (1) [army has]
MGREC117:17 H2624 Great *Alexander* dead, his Army's left,
ARMYES (1) [armies]
MGREC~~101:34~~ H1961 The Armyes joyn'd a while, the Persians fight,
ARPAD (1)
MASSYR62:34 H379 On *Henah, Arpad,* and on *Ivdah* least {*Juahs* coast};
ARRAY (4) See also ARAY
MASSYR58:25 H208 These Forces mustered, and in array,
MPERS~~79:3~~ H1025 'Twixt which his souldiers marcht in good array.
DAVID159:17 H32 On your array put ornaments of gold,
AUTHOR178:10 H20 In this array, 'mongst Vulgars mayst thou roam,
ARREST (1)
SICKNES179:3 H23 Then deaths arrest I shall count best,
ARRESTS (1) [pl.]
AGES41:11 ~~H230~~ Ceas'd by the gripes of Serjeant Death's Arrests:
ARRIV'D (1) [arrived]
MGREC121:28 H2810 Had it but in *Perdicas* life arriv'd,
ARRIVALL (1)
REMB235:21 H1-3 In thankfull Rembrc for my dear husbands safe Arrivall.
ARRIVE (4) See also ARRIV'D
AGES37:10 H72 With tears into this {the} world I did arrive;
CONTEM171:11 H115 Who to the tenth of theirs doth now arrive?
CONTEM172:19 H154 Till thou arrive at thy beloved place,
MERCY189:7 H28 E're nature would, it hither did arrive,
ARRIVES (1)
MPERS87:1 H1357 But fame more quick, arrives ere he came {comes} there,
ARROGANCE (2)
HUMOUR~~24:19~~ H168 Is't ignorance, {arrogance} or folly causeth this?
AGES37:29 H91 Freedome from Envy, and from Arrogance.
ARROW (4)
MPERS76:11 H909 A Frog, a Mouse, a Bird, an Arrow sent,
MEDDM199:26 Hp278 in Scripture of three sorts of Arrows the arrow of an enemy
MEDDM199:27 Hp278 the arrow of pestilence, and the arrow of a slanderous tongue,
MEDDM199:27 Hp278 the arrow of pestilence, and the arrow of a slanderous tongue,
ARROWES (4) [arrows]
MGREC96:40 H1760 Let fly their Arrowes, in the *Persians* face;
MGREC108:24 H2240 Imprinted deep in's legg, by Arrowes shot;
MGREC108:31 H2247 Of Darts, and Arrowes, made so little spare,
MGREC125:19 H2967 Nor Darts, nor Arrowes now, none shoots, nor flings;
ARROWS (2) [pl.]
MPERS76:18 H916 Or *Sythian* arrows in our sides must stick.
MEDDM199:26 Hp278 in Scripture of three sorts of Arrows the arrow of an enemy
ARSAMES (5)
MPERS92:4 H1558 *Arsames,* or *Arses.*
MPERS92:5 ~~H1559~~ Why *Arsames* his brother should succeed,
MPERS~~92:5~~ H1559 *Arsames* plac'd now in his fathers stead,
MPERS~~92:5~~ H1561 Some write that *Arsames* was *Ochus* brother,
MPERS92:22 ~~H1580~~ That *Ochus* unto *Arsames* was father,
ARSEMES (1)
MGREC95:22 H1701 There {In's stead} *Arsemes* {*Arses*} was plac'd, yet {but} durst

RSES (3)
MPERS92:4 H1558 *Arsames,* or *Arses.*
MPERS92:20 ~~H1578~~ Some writers say, that he was *Arses* son,
MGREC95:22 H1701 There {In's stead} *Arsemes* {*Arses*} was plac'd, yet {but} durst

ART (21) n.
PROLOG7:4 H19 And this to mend, alas, no Art is able,
PROLOG7:9 H23 By Art, he gladly found what he did seeke,
PROLOG7:11 H25 Art can doe much, but this maxime's most sure,
ELEMEN16:19 H342 Nor will I speake of waters made by Art,
HUMOUR26:9 H239 For acting these, I have nor wil, nor art,
HUMOUR28:5 H317 And Flegme likewise can shew, her cruel art,
HUMOUR29:28 H379 To use thy sword, thy courage, and thy Art,
HUMOUR~~31:7~~ H440 So mean thou art in art as in discretion:
MASSYR56:12 H118 But {And} that which did, all cost, and art excell,
MPERS87:23 H1375 This place was {so} made, by nature, and by art;
MGREC93:18 H1615 By Art, and Nature both, he was made fit,
MGREC95:40 H1719 Sure its {much} beyond my time, and little Art;
MGREC122:25 ~~H2845~~ Her Daughter she instructed in that Art,
MGREC153:5 H9 Where Art, and more then Art in Nature shines;
MGREC153:34 H38 Thy Art, in Naturall Philosophy:
MGREC153:40 H44 Sure liberall Nature, did with Art not small,
MGREC155:4 H89 *Art and Nature joyn'd, by heavens high decree,*
MGREC155:7 H92 *To rescue him from death, Art had been able:*
MGREC155:8 H93 *But Nature vanquish'd Art, so* Bartas *dy'd,*
CONTEM169:21 H61 Seeming to glory in their little Art.

ART (31) v. See also THOU'RT
ELEMEN14:32 H274 But thou art bound to me, above the rest;
ELEMEN14:34 H276 If I withhold, what art thou, dead, dry lump
HUMOUR23:18 H128 So base thou art, that baser cannot be;
HUMOUR25:11 H200 But now Ile shew, what Souldier thou art.
HUMOUR25:23 H212 Thou art a fury, or infernal Fiend.
HUMOUR26:1 H231 But such thou never art, when al alone;
HUMOUR26:3 H233 And when such thou art, even such are we.
HUMOUR~~31:5~~ H438 And so art call'd black Choler or adust,
HUMOUR~~31:7~~ H440 So mean thou art in art as in discretion:
HUMOUR31:9 H442 What officer thou art to al us three.
HUMOUR33:14 ~~H528~~ But yet thou art as much, I truly say,
HUMOUR33:16 H530 And though I grant, thou art my helper here,
DIALOG141:15 H14 Art ignorant indeed, of these my woes?
DIALOG141:28 H27 Let me lament alone, while thou art glad.
DIALOG147:18 H244 on brave *Essex,* shew whose son thou art {with a loyal heart},
SIDNEY151:4 ~~H69~~ But thou art gone, such Meteors never last,
DUBART152:34 H3 Great, deare, sweet *Bartas,* thou art matchlesse knowne;
CONTEM169:2 H44 Art thou so full of glory, that no Eye
FLESH175:20 H20 Art fancy sick, or turn'd a Sot
AUTHOR178:12 H22 And take thy way where yet thou art not known,
SICKNES178:35 H18 that alwayes art a breaking,
1LETTER181:19 H17 O strange effect! now thou art *Southward* gone,
ELIZB187:3 H12 Sith thou art setled in an Everlasting state.
ANNEB187:33 H23 Thou with thy Saviour art in endless bliss.
FAINT222:12 H2 Worthy art Thou o Ld of praise,

MED223:4 Hp250 pledges of thy Loue. First thov art my Creator, I thy creature,
MED223:5 Hp250 I thy servant, But hence arises not my comfort, Thou art my
MED223:18 Hp250 art pure, and let me bee no more afraid of Death,
JULY223:31 Hp251 for thov art my God, Thou hast said and shall not I beleiue it?
28AUG226:10 Hp254 O let me ever see Thee that Art invisible, and I shall not bee
2HUSB232:16 H17 Thou art my strenght and stay;

ARTABANUS (3)
MPERS77:27 H968 Sage *Artabanus* counsell, had he taken,
MPERS79:26 H1052 Of *Artabanus* he again demands,
MPERS83:14 H1202 The {Then} *Artabanus* hirer of this deed,

ARTABASSUS (1)
MGREC104:17 H2069 Bidding his {Then bids} servant *Artabassus* true;

ARTABASUS (2)
MGREC106:13 H2147 On *Artabasus* more then all bestow'd,
MGREC117:30 H2637 Except by *Artabasus* daughter one;

ARTAXERXES (5)
MPERS83:26 H1214 *Artaxerxes Longimanus.*
MPERS85:4 H1280 Three sons great *Artaxerxes* left behind;
MPERS86:8 H1324 *Artaxerxes Mnemon.*
MPERS90:29 H1496 Which rumor makes great *Artaxerxes* quake;
MPERS91:34 ~~H1548~~ Great *Artaxerxes* dead, *Ochus* succeeds,

ARTEMESIA (1)
MPERS78:23 H1004 *Artemesia, Halicarna's* Queene,

ARTERIES (1) [pl.]
HUMOUR22:28 H97 And through the arteries sends {it} o're the frame,

ARTIFICER (1)
SEASONS48:6 H59 A natural Artificer compleate.

ARTIFICERS (1) [pl.]
ELEMEN13:8 H209 And ye Artificers, all trades and sorts;

ARTISTS (3) [pl.]
ELEMEN8:35 ~~H33~~ Come first ye Artists, and declare your minde.
ELEMEN~~8:35~~ H33 All sorts of Artists, here declare your mind,
MGREC116:22 H2588 And curious Artists evermore rewarded.

ARTS (11) [pl.]
FATHER5:27 H28 Yours did contest, for Wealth, for Arts, for Age,
PROLOG7:24 H36 So 'mongst the rest, they plac'd the Arts divine:
ELEMEN12:1 H161 For Learning, Armes, and Arts, I love it well:
HUMOUR22:21 H90 Again, who sits, for learning, science, Arts?
HUMOUR23:24 H134 Thus {But} arms, and arts I claim, and higher things;
HUMOUR28:27 H339 For Arts, and Sciences, they are the fittest,
AGES39:13 H156 Of Science, Arts, and Tongues, I know the rules,
MASSYR62:26 H371 Or else those *Chinoes* rare, whose wealth, and Arts,
SIDNEY149:12 H11 Of Armes, and Arts, thou {he} should'st a patterne be.
DUBART153:41 H45 In all the Arts make thee most liberall;
VANITY160:12 H22 Where is it then? in wisdome, learning, arts?

AS (399)
ELEMEN11:19 H139 As I: impart your usefulnesse, and force.
ELEMEN13:14 H215 As I ingenuously (with thanks) confesse
ELEMEN~~13:29~~ H230 And buds from fruitfull trees, before they'r {as soon as} blowne:
ELEMEN13:29 H230 And buds from fruitfull trees, before they'r {as soon as} blowne:
ELEMEN14:10 ~~H252~~ As *Stibium* and unfixt *Mercury:*

ELEMEN14:22 H264 As earth at first, so into earth return'd.
ELEMEN14:27 H269 Cause of your fruitfulnesse, as you shall see:
ELEMEN15:15 H297 If not, soon ends his life, as did his voyce.
ELEMEN15:33 H315 Not thou, but shell-fish yeelds, as *Pliny* clears.
ELEMEN15:35 H317 As *Ægypts* wanton *Cleopatra* drunke.
ELEMEN15:41 H323 I lightly cast ashoare as frothy fleece.
ELEMEN~~16:12~~ H335 I soon can match them with my seas as deep.
ELEMEN16:37 H360 As I with showers oft time {times} refresh the earth;
ELEMEN17:24 H388 As when *Achaia,* all under water stood,
ELEMEN18:33 H437 I grow more pure and pure, as I mount higher,
ELEMEN19:12 H457 As my fresh Aire preserves, all things in life;
ELEMEN19:19 H464 That birds have not scap'd death, as they have flown,
ELEMEN19:39 H480 As battells pitcht ith' Aire (as Countries know;)
ELEMEN19:39 H480 As battells pitcht ith' Aire (as Countries know;)
HUMOUR21:6 H34 My self, and Mother, one as you shal see,
HUMOUR21:38 H66 She'l ride a Horse as bravely, as the best,
HUMOUR21:38 H66 She'l ride a Horse as bravely, as the best,
HUMOUR22:31 H100 The Animal I claime, as wel as these,
HUMOUR22:31 H100 The Animal I claime, as wel as these,
HUMOUR23:9 H119 Thy self's as dul, as is thy mother Earth.
HUMOUR23:9 H119 Thy self's as dul, as is thy mother Earth.
HUMOUR23:23 H133 As objects best appear, by contraries.
HUMOUR24:12 H161 Good sisters give me leave (as is my place)
HUMOUR24:37 H186 And how to strike ful sweet, as wel as sharpe.
HUMOUR24:37 H186 And how to strike ful sweet, as wel as sharpe.
HUMOUR25:3 H192 As thy unbridled, barb'rous Choler yeelds. {breeds:}
HUMOUR25:9 H198 Shal vanish as of no validity.
HUMOUR25:16 H205 As with thy mother Fire, so 'tis with thee,
HUMOUR26:20 H250 As plants, trees, and small Embryon know'th,
HUMOUR26:22 H252 I am as sure, the natural from me;
HUMOUR26:40 H270 Thou know'st I've there to do, as wel as thou;
HUMOUR26:40 H270 Thou know'st I've there to do, as wel as thou;
HUMOUR~~27:12~~ H283 Unless as heat, it be thy faculty,
HUMOUR27:24 H295 Shal firstly {chiefly} take her {the} place, as is her {my} due,
HUMOUR27:30 H301 As thus, if hot, then dry; if moist, then cold;
HUMOUR28:8 H320 As if she'd leave no flesh to turn to clay,
HUMOUR28:24 H336 Of such as to the Sanguine are inclin'd,
HUMOUR28:41 H353 As I to you, to me, do ye the same.
HUMOUR29:11 H364 I'le flatter for a time, as thou did'st me,
HUMOUR29:17 ~~H368~~ If not as yet, by me, thou shalt be quell'd:
HUMOUR30:10 H402 As of that only part I was {were} the Queen:
HUMOUR30:28 H420 Yet is a bowel cal'd wel as the rest.
HUMOUR~~31:7~~ H440 So mean thou art in art as in discretion:
HUMOUR32:5 H479 Unto diseases not inclin'd as ye:
HUMOUR33:6 H520 But 'twere as vain, to prove the {this} truth of mine,
HUMOUR33:7 H521 As at noon day to tel, the Sun doth shine.
HUMOUR33:14 ~~H528~~ But yet thou art as much, I truly say,
HUMOUR~~33:15~~ H529 I do as much for thee another way:
HUMOUR34:33 H588 But if love be, as requisite as feare,
HUMOUR34:33 H588 But if love be, as requisite as feare,
AGES35:31 H17 Such cold mean flowers (as these) blossome {the spring puts

AGES36:2 H26 (As that fond age, doth most of al desire.)
AGES36:7 H31 His face as fresh, as is *Aurora* faire,
AGES36:7 H31 His face as fresh, as is *Aurora* faire,
AGES36:12 H36 But as he went, death waited at his heeles.
AGES36:14 H38 As one that cared, for a good report.
AGES36:16 H40 But neither us'd (as yet) for he was wise.
AGES36:33 H57 To do as he, the rest {each one} ful soon assents,
AGES37:11 H73 My mother stil did waste, as I did thrive:
AGES38:4 H107 My little wrath did cease {end} soon as my wars.
AGES38:16 H119 As he can tell, that next comes on the stage.
AGES38:20 H123 From thence I 'gan to sin, as soon as act.
AGES38:20 H123 From thence I 'gan to sin, as soon as act.
AGES38:23 H126 A lying tongue as soon as it could speak,
AGES38:23 H126 A lying tongue as soon as it could speak,
AGES38:27 H130 As many was {are} my sins, so dangers too:
AGES39:11 H154 As might my self, and others, profit much:
AGES39:33 H176 To be as wilde as is the snuffing Asse,
AGES39:33 H176 To be as wilde as is the snuffing Asse,
AGES39:34 H177 As vain as froth, as {or} vanity can be,
AGES39:34 H177 As vain as froth, as {or} vanity can be,
AGES39:34 H177 As vain as froth, as {or} vanity can be,
AGES40:7 H188 Of all at once, who not so wise, as fair,
AGES41:18 H237 As was their praise, or shame, so mine must be.
AGES42:9 H267 And gently lead the lambes, as they had need,
AGES42:13 H271 As readily as could my Leader say:
AGES42:13 H271 As readily as could my Leader say:
AGES42:15 H273 As chearfully as ere I took my pay.
AGES42:15 H273 As chearfully as ere I took my pay.
AGES42:20 H278 Was I as poor, as poverty could be,
AGES42:20 H278 Was I as poor, as poverty could be,
AGES42:22 H280 Such scum, as Hedges, and High-wayes do yeeld,
AGES42:23 H281 As neither sow, nor reape, nor plant, nor build.
AGES43:14 H307 such as might my son, {Competitors} or his {as might in time}
AGES43:15 ~~H307~~ Then heapt up gold, and riches as the clay;
AGES44:8 H341 I have bin young, and strong, and wise as you,
AGES45:37 H427 My comely legs, as nimble as the Roe,
AGES45:37 H427 My comely legs, as nimble as the Roe,
AGES45:39 H429 My heart sometimes as fierce, as Lions bold,
AGES45:39 H429 My heart sometimes as fierce, as Lions bold,
SEASONS47:15 H31 And all that seem'd as dead, afresh do live.
SEASONS48:2 H55 These might as Lace, set out her Garments fine;
SEASONS49:1 H92 As Spring did aire, blood, youth in's equipage.
SEASONS49:12 H103 Like as an oven, that long time hath been heat.
SEASONS49:15 H106 She's {Tis} for a time as fervent as before.
SEASONS49:15 H106 She's {Tis} for a time as fervent as before.
SEASONS~~50:28~~ H162 The Prince of Plumbs, whose stone is {as} hard as Rock.
SEASONS50:28 H162 The Prince of Plumbs, whose stone is {as} hard as Rock.
SEASONS~~51:19~~ H195 If scited as the most Judicious take.
MASSYR54:13 H40 His reign was short, for as I calculate,
MASSYR55:1 H67 Fifty two years he reign'd (as we are told)
MASSYR55:31 H97 As of {on} her life, licentious, and unchast.

MASSYR55:33 H99 As {By} their aspersions, cast upon the same.
MASSYR56:27 H133 (Each man beleive it, as his fancy list)
MASSYR56:29 H135 As puzzells best hystorians to remember:
MASSYR57:34 H179 And such as care not, what befals their fames,
MASSYR57:35 H180 May feign as many acts, as he did names;
MASSYR57:35 H180 May feign as many acts, as he did names;
MASSYR59:34 H258 Twenty he reign'd, same time, as Stories tel,
MASSYR59:36 H260 His Father was then King (as we suppose)
MASSYR60:33 H298 As fair a Town, as the first *Ninivie.*
MASSYR60:33 H298 As fair a Town, as the first *Ninivie.*
MASSYR62:25 H370 Or wild *Tartarians,* as yet ne're blest,
MASSYR~~63:8~~ H393 And {As} *Belosus,* first, his {Soveraign} did unthrone,
MASSYR64:28 H452 As might not him, but all the world out-face;
MASSYR65:30 H495 But he, as perjur'd as *Iehoiakim,*
MASSYR65:30 H495 But he, as perjur'd as *Iehoiakim,*
MASSYR66:6 H512 Yet as was told, ne're saw it with his eyes;
MASSYR66:34 H540 {But} Resumes his Government, as heretofore,
MASSYR67:3 H549 His son possesses wealth, and rule, as just;
MASSYR68:13 H599 As thus amort {dead, alive} he sits, as all {one} undone:
MASSYR68:13 H599 As thus amort {dead, alive} he sits, as all {one} undone:
MPERS69:8 H630 And from that time, had held it as his own;
MPERS69:24 H646 So over-thrown of *Cyrus,* as was just;
MPERS69:29 H651 But as he past, his Son, who was born dumbe,
MPERS69:40 H670 Now up, now {and} down, as fortune turnes her hand,
MPERS70:33 H704 Using such taunting words as she thought good.
MPERS71:28 H742 But as they marched o're those desart sands,
MPERS72:37 H781 Ruling as they thought good, {best} under his head.
MPERS~~72:37~~ H783 Obedience yielded as to *Cyrus* son.
MPERS72:40 H786 Unsheathes, as he his horse mounted on high,
MPERS73:16 H803 (Who like to Kings, rul'd Kingdomes as they please,)
MPERS76:27 H925 But as before, so now with ill successe,
MPERS77:3 H942 As the best trophe that {which} ye won in *Greece.*
MPERS77:18 H959 As is {was} the Son, of pride, and cruelty;
MPERS77:24 H965 As if to dust he meant to grinde that Nation;
MPERS79:29 H1055 Which was not vaine, as it {after} soon appeared:
MPERS80:9 H1076 When as one thousand, could some Millions {a million} daunt;
MPERS80:13 H1080 And as at Land, so he at Sea was crost,
MPERS80:19 H1086 But they as valiant by {fortunate at} Sea, as Land,
MPERS80:19 H1086 But they as valiant by {fortunate at} Sea, as Land,
MPERS80:20 H1087 In this Streight, as the other, firmly stand.
MPERS80:33 H1100 And as a friend, warns him, what e're he doe,
MPERS81:15 H1123 As had *Macedon, Thebes,* and *Thessalie,*
MPERS81:19 H1127 And they had helpt them, as confederate;
MPERS82:28 H1175 But she was stil, as when it {he} first begun.
MPERS83:1 H1189 Tels as he could, his unexpressed woes,
MPERS83:36 H1224 And payes them now, {both} according as he owes,
MPERS87:9 H1365 But as he goes, his Forces still augments,
MPERS88:2 H1395 In this confusion, each man as he might,
MPERS88:9 H1402 And black and blacker grew, as they drew nigh.
MPERS89:30 H1464 And feares as much to let them march away;
MPERS89:31 H1465 But Kings ne're want such as can serve their will,

MPERS89:33 H1467 As *Tyssaphern,* knowing his Masters minde,
MPERS89:34 H1468 Invites their chief Commander, as most {Commanders feasts
MPERS90:4 ~~H1478~~ Before them burnt the country as they went,
MPERS90:7 H1480 O're mountains, rocks, and hils, as Lions bold;
MPERS90:20 H1487 The *Greeks* now (as the *Persian* King suspects)
MPERS~~91:10~~ H1518 {on such} conditions they are forc't to take; {as King will make}
MPERS91:15 H1523 Who had (as noble *Raleigh* doth evince)
MPERS91:18 H1526 And turne to *Persia,* as is pertinent;
MPERS~~91:27~~ H1541 Such as would know at large his warrs and reign,
MPERS91:30 ~~H1544~~ As all the mighty ones, have done, and must:
MPERS91:39 ~~H1553~~ Their Acts recorded not, as heretofore
MPERS~~92:7~~ H1565 His brother, as tis said, long since was slain,
MPERS92:10 H1568 But as 'tis thought, {most suppose} in him had {did} *Cyrus* end:
MPERS92:13 H1571 Three years he reign'd, as Chronicles expresse, {then drank
MPERS92:18 ~~H1576~~ If not (as is before) of *Cyrus* race,
MPERS92:25 ~~H1583~~ By one *Bagoas,* an Eunuch (as is sed.)
MPERS92:27 ~~H1585~~ But as before doth (well read) *Raleigh* write,
MGREC93:34 H1631 (For as worlds Monarch, now we speak not on,
MGREC6:35 H1632 But as the King of little *Macedon.)*
MGREC95:24 H1703 His substitute, as fearfull as his master,
MGREC95:24 H1703 His substitute, as fearfull as his master,
MGREC96:6 H1726 As if they were, {if addrest} now all to run at {a} tilt:
MGREC96:10 H1730 An object not so much of fear, as laughter.
MGREC96:26 H1746 As if she'd drawne, whole *Sushan* at her heeles.
MGREC96:28 H1748 And as much good she did, as any other.
MGREC96:28 H1748 And as much good she did, as any other.
MGREC97:23 H1784 By too much heat, not wounds (as Authors write.)
MGREC97:37 H1798 But of *Darius* King, as he should know.
MGREC98:11 H1813 And now, as *Babels* King did once before,
MGREC98:27 H1829 For that which easily comes, as freely goes;
MGREC99:9 H1852 Was I as great, as is great *Alexander,*
MGREC99:9 H1852 Was I as great, as is great *Alexander,*
MGREC99:35 H1878 But in no hostile way (as I suppose)
MGREC100:19 H1903 But as the King is, so's the multitude,
MGREC100:35 H1919 Great *Alexander* mourns, as well as he,
MGREC100:35 H1919 Great *Alexander* mourns, as well as he,
MGREC101:4 H1929 And now for peace he sues, as once before,
MGREC101:35 H1964 So make {made} an end, before they {as soon as} well begun;
MGREC101:39 H1968 But *Quintus Curtius,* as was said before.
MGREC102:4 H1974 Which *Alexander* deals, as suits his pleasure.
MGREC103:13 H2024 Yet after all, as stories do expresse,
MGREC103:17 H2028 (As first at *Sushan,* and at *Babylon*)
MGREC103:20 H2031 Their charge, {place} gave to his Captains (as most {was} just)
MGREC~~103:37~~ H2048 Who was retir'd, and gone to {as far as} *Media.*
MGREC103:37 H2048 Who was retir'd, and gone to {as far as} *Media.*
MGREC105:36 H2129 And that his rule as farre extended be,
MGREC105:37 H2130 As men, the rising, setting Sun shall see.
MGREC106:11 H2145 Such as submits, he doth againe restore,
MGREC106:16 H2150 Her traine to *Alexander* (as 'tis thought)
MGREC106:21 H2155 As *Alexander* in his greatnesse growes,
MGREC106:26 H2160 As most incompatible to his state;

MGREC106:31	H2165	And such as shew'd but reverence before,
MGREC~~109:3~~	H2260	Those that {Such as} doe not, both they, {them} and theirs, are
MGREC109:19	H2278	And as his Sovereign Lord, him humbly greets.
MGREC109:29	H2288	But *Porus* stout, who will not yeeld as yet;
MGREC109:32	H2291	Unto his Kingdoms borders, and as due,
MGREC109:33	H2292	His Homage unto him {to himself} as Soveraigne doe.
MGREC109:36	H2295	And come as well provided as he could,
MGREC109:36	H2295	And come as well provided as he could,
MGREC110:30	H2334	As never Horse his Provender could eye;
MGREC111:13	H2358	These {Those} obscure Nations yeelded as before;
MGREC111:32	H2377	Now through these goodly countries as he past,
MGREC113:8	H2435	Such torments great, as wit could first {worst} invent,
MGREC113:11	H2438	For to {He might} accuse himself, as they had done;
MGREC113:17	H2444	Was to dispatch the Father, as the Son.
MGREC113:20	H2447	As he would ne're confesse, nor could {yet} reward,
MGREC114:20	H2490	As did appeare, in flattering him the least:
MGREC~~116:28~~	H2594	For those that {such as} pleas'd him: had both wealth and
MGREC116:30	H2596	As oft his Acts throughout his reigne did {doth} shew:
MGREC117:1	H2608	Nor can he kill, or save as heretofore,
MGREC117:8	H2615	And {But} as he took delight, much bloud to spill,
MGREC117:11	H2618	As *Daniel,* before had Prophesied;
MGREC117:28	H2635	Yet {But} none so hardy found as so durst say.
MGREC119:41	H2731	Act any thing of worth, as heretofore,
MGREC120:15	H2750	To suffer them goe on, as they begun,
MGREC~~122:27~~	H2846	*Pithons* commands, {as oft} She ever countermands
MGREC122:33	H2854	He plac'd, displac'd, controld, rul'd, as he list,
MGREC~~122:36~~	H2857	Their bonnets vail'd to him as chief Commander.
MGREC122:40	H2861	All to be order'd there as he thought best:
MGREC123:32	H2896	Such as his father had advanc'd to place,
MGREC124:10	~~H2915~~	All such as he suspected to him true.
MGREC~~124:10~~	H2915	Such friends away as for his Interest makes
MGREC124:13	H2920	the worst {beaten was} at Sea, as well as {and foil'd at} Land,
MGREC124:24	H2931	And act, as opportunity they finde:
MGREC124:40	H2947	As all her Husbands children by his Mates;
MGREC~~125:21~~	H2971	And needs will have their lives as well as State:
MGREC127:17	H3047	Such as nor {no} threats, nor favour could acquire;
MGREC127:26	H3056	But as that to a period did haste,
MGREC~~127:41~~	H3073	Shews his ambitious practises as well.
MGREC128:33	H3106	Curtious, as noble *Ptolomy,* or more,
MGREC129:7	H3121	To render up such kingdomes as he had
MGREC130:18	H3173	As vile conspiratours that took {stopt} her breath,
MGREC131:1	H3187	To do as he, {by his Example all} the rest full soon presumes,
MGREC132:16	H3251	And now as King, in *Macedon* he reigns;
MGREC~~132:20~~	H3263	As Heaven and Earth against him had been set:
MGREC133:4	H3292	*Seleuchus* was as {a} Father, and a friend,
MGREC~~133:25~~	H3315	Such riches too As Rome did never see:
MGREC133:35	H3325	Which we oft wish were {was} extant as before.
MGREC136:18	H3432	*As faults proceeding from my head, not heart.*
MROMAN136:25	H3439	His Father was not *Mars,* as some devis'd,
MROMAN137:17	H3468	And *Sabins,* as one people, dwelt in *Rome.*
MROMAN138:33	H3523	To such rude triumphs, as young *Rome* then had,

MROMAN139:5 H3533 As wealth had made them of abilitie;
MROMAN139:34 H3560 Though oft perswaded, I as oft deny'd,
DIALOG142:33 H62 A supplyant for your help, as she is bound.
DIALOG145:2 H151 Such cruelty as all reports have past.
DIALOG145:25 H174 As puts me to a stand what I should say,
DIALOG~~147:21~~ H247 By force {As Duty binds,} expell, destroy, and tread them
DIALOG148:8 H273 As did thine Ancestours in *Palestine,*
DIALOG148:20 H285 And do to *Gog,* as thou hast done to *Rome.*
SIDNEY~~149:9~~ H8 No lesse {As well} an Honour to our *British* Land,
SIDNEY~~149:10~~ H9 Then {As} she that sway'd the Scepter with her hand:
SIDNEY149:22 H21 As if your nine-fold wit had been compacted;
SIDNEY149:32 ~~H23~~ The love thy Country ought thee, was as much.
SIDNEY149:36 ~~H23~~ But leaves the rest, as most unprofitable:
SIDNEY~~150:12~~ H41 The love his Country ought him, was as much.
SIDNEY150:17 ~~H49~~ Then let such Crowes as I, thy praises sing,
SIDNEY151:1 ~~H69~~ Such prince as he, his race should shortly end:
SIDNEY151:2 ~~H69~~ If such Stars as these, sad presages be,
SIDNEY151:5 ~~H69~~ And as thy beauty, so thy name would wast,
SIDNEY151:30 ~~H75~~ Which are in worth, as far short of his due,
SIDNEY151:31 ~~H75~~ As *Vulcan* is, of *Venus* native hue.
DUBART154:15 H60 Thy fame is spread as farre, I dare be bold,
QELIZ155:28 H19 Thy clemency did yerst esteeme as much
QELIZ155:29 H20 The acclamations of the poore, as rich;
QELIZ156:35 H62 Had ever Prince such Counsellors as she?
QELIZ156:38 H65 As were the subjects of our *(Pallas)* Queen:
QELIZ157:36 H104 Let such, as say our sex is void of reason,
QELIZ158:19 H128 If many worlds, as that fantastick framed,
DAVID159:4 H19 As if his head ne're felt the sacred Oyle:
VANITY159:30 H2 As he said vanity, so vain say I,
VANITY160:18 H28 What is it then? to do as Stoicks tell,
TDUDLEY165:19 H21 Such as in life, no man could justly deem.
TDUDLEY165:37 H39 But as a Pilgrim what he had, possest.
TDUDLEY166:7 H49 As in the mean ones, of our foolish dayes,
TDUDLEY166:18 H60 Now fully ripe, as shock of wheat that's grown,
TDUDLEY166:19 H61 Death as a Sickle hath him timely mown,
TDUDLEY166:27 H69 As joy in heaven, on earth let praise resound.
DDUDLEY167:15 H12 *And as they did, so they reward did find:*
CONTEM168:13 H22 If so, all these as nought, Eternity doth scorn.
CONTEM168:23 H30 Thou as a Bridegroom from thy Chamber rushes,
CONTEM168:24 H31 And as a strong man, joyes to run a race,
CONTEM169:5 H47 As to approach it, can no earthly mould.
CONTEM169:24 H64 Whilst I as mute, can warble forth no higher layes.
CONTEM171:18 H121 When I behold the heavens as in their prime,
CONTEM174:15 H214 As if he had command of wind and tide,
FLESH175:27 H27 As some to their immortal fame:
FLESH176:1 H41 Thee as a foe, still to pursue.
FLESH177:4 H85 But such as Angels heads infold.
FLESH177:12 H93 Such as no Eye did e're behold,
AUTHOR177:38 H10 I cast thee by as one unfit for light,
SICKNES178:37 H20 ev'n as a word that's speaking.
BIRTH180:11 H21 And when thou feel'st no grief, as I no harms,

1LETTER181:5	H3	If two be one, as surely thou and I,
3LETTER182:36	H1	As loving Hind that (Hartless) wants her Deer,
3LETTER183:7	H9	Or as the pensive Dove doth all alone
3LETTER183:15	H17	Or as the loving Mullet, that true Fish,
VERSES183:35	H2	Most truly honoured, and as truly dear,
VERSES184:9	H13	But as I can, I'le pay it while I live:
CHILDRN185:11	H37	And as his wings increase in strength,
CHILDRN185:14	H40	Untill they'r grown, then as the rest,
CHILDRN185:16	H42	As is ordain'd, so shall they light.
CHILDRN185:36	H62	My throbs such now, as 'fore were never:
CHILDRN186:6	H73	Once young and pleasant, as are you,
ANNEB187:24	H14	I knew she was but as a withering flour,
ANNEB187:26	H16	Like as a bubble, or the brittle glass,
ANNEB187:27	H17	Or like a shadow turning as it was.
ANNEB187:29	H19	As if mine own, when thus impermanent.
1SIMON188:11	H12	Let's say he's merciful, as well as just,
1SIMON188:11	H12	Let's say he's merciful, as well as just,
2SIMON195:9	Hp271	Such as they are I bequeath to you, Small legacys are accept[d]
MEDDM195:26	Hp272	of all and he that makes such improvment is wise as well as
MEDDM197:22	Hp275	Few men are so humble, as not to be proud of their abilitys,
MEDDM198:13	Hp276	Want of prudence as well as piety hath brought men into great
MEDDM198:13	Hp276	Want of prudence as well as piety hath brought men into great
MEDDM199:15	Hp278	men are like hops that neuer rest climbing soe long as they
MEDDM200:36	Hp280	weak children as would crush them to the dust, but according
MEDDM201:1	Hp280	he will proportion the load, as god hath his little Children so
MEDDM201:2	Hp280	his strong men, such as are come to a full stature in Christ,
MEDDM201:25	Hp281	words of the wise (sath Solom) are as nailes, and as goads,
MEDDM202:24	Hp282	that we cannot behold the light of his Countenance, as at
MEDDM202:25	Hp282	other time, yet he affords so much light as may direct our way,
MEDDM203:17	Hp283	sees land we must therfore be heer as strangers and pilgrims,
MEDDM204:7	Hp284	in need of him, to day as well as yesterday, and so shall for
MEDDM204:18	Hp285	action, as we see in Jehu, he is rewarded wth a kingdome to
MEDDM204:33	Hp285	produced wth much labour (as the husbandman well knowes)
MEDDM205:9	Hp286	As man is called the little world so his heart may be cal'd the
MEDDM205:15	Hp286	as he finds the evidence, so he absolues or condemnes, yea
MEDDM205:28	Hp286	life as we doe, but he that wth David, sets the lord alway in his
MEDDM206:3	Hp287	and these are but leavie Christians, w[ch] are in as much
MEDDM206:4	Hp287	of being cut down, as the dry stock, for both cumber the
MEDDM206:35	Hp288	may also be a support to such as haue or had wicked parents,
MEDDM207:6	Hp288	they were giuen for, as health wealth and honour, w[ch] might be
MEDDM207:10	Hp288	as wings to help vs mount vpwards, they will Certainly proue
MEDDM207:21	Hp289	men are truly sayd to be tenants at will, and it may as truly be
MEDDM207:22	Hp289	all haue a lease of their liues, some longer some shorter, as it
MEDDM207:27	Hp289	should make vs so to number our dayes as to apply our hearts
MEDDM208:6	Hp289	As the brands of a fire, if once severed, will of themselues goe
MEDDM208:12	Hp290	A good name, is as a precious oyntment, and it is a great
MEDDM208:15	Hp290	Judgment we must be tryed and as he passes the sentence, so
MEDDM208:33	Hp290	it hath ouer come the omnipotent himself, as when Moses
MEDDM208:35	Hp291	them as if Moses had been able by the hand of faith, to hold
MEDDM209:7	Hp291	christians do by their lusts and corruptions as the Isralits did
MEDDM209:9	Hp291	they could do (as they thought) wth lesse hazard and more

MEDDM209:20 Hp291 there may be a mutuall commerce through ye world As it is wth
MEDDM209:25 Hp291 below, as also that god will haue vs beholden one to another
PILGRIM210:1 H1 As weary pilgrim, now at rest
PILGRIM211:1 H42 as eare ner' heard nor tongue ere told
MYCHILD215:24 Hp240 In my yovng years about 6. or 7. as I take it I began to make
MYCHILD215:25 Hp240 & what I knew was sinfull as lying, disobedc. to parents.
MYCHILD215:31 Hp241 as I grew to haue more vnderstanding, so ye more solace I
MYCHILD216:1 Hp241 But as I grew vp to bee about 14. or 15. I fovnd my heart more
MYCHILD216:16 Hp241 him gave me many more, of whom I now take ye care, yt as
MYCHILD217:1 Hp242 at any time yov are chastened of God take it as Thankfully and
MYCHILD217:2 Hp242 Joyfully as in greatest mercyes, For if yee bee his yee shall
MYCHILD218:5 Hp243 a God as I worship in Trinity, + such a Savr as I rely upon,
MYCHILD218:14 Hp244 + how ye world came to bee as wee see, Do wee not know ye
MYCHILD218:24 Hp244 of the Saints, wch admitt were yy as they terme ym yet
FAINT222:16 H6 My life as Spiders webb's cutt off
FAINT222:22 H12 And tho: as dead mad'st me aliue
MED223:17 Hp250 him as I ovght. Lord haueing this hope let me purefye my self
MED223:17 Hp250 I ovght. Lord haueing this hope let me purefye my self as thou
MYSOUL225:15 H19 And praise thee shall ev'n as I ovght
13MAY226:26 H2 As spring the winter doth succeed
30SEPT227:25 Hp257 in ye furnace of affliction as some haue been, but haue rather
11MAYB228:31 Hp259 kindnes, nor take ye cup of salvation wth Thanksgiving as I
RESTOR230:6 H21 My Soul as destitute
SON230:24 H7 Thou di'st prserve him as he went,
SON231:6 H18 From such as 'fore nere saw his face.
HOURS234:22 H36 As thou before ha'st done
HOURS234:24 H38 As thou didst once my Sonne.
REMB236:11 H26 And walk before thee as they ought,
HOUSE237:23 H53 A prise so vast as is vnknown

ASCALON (1)
MASSYR55:8 H74 Her birth-place was *Philistrius Ascalon,*

ASCEND (2)
MROMAN137:21 H3472 Some faining say, to heav'n {to the Gods} he did ascend;
MED223:7 Hp250 —Christ is my Brother, I ascend vnto my father, and your

ASCENDED (1)
SEASONS50:32 H166 Hath stil ascended up in {to bear} goodly Fruits,

ASCENDS (1)
MROMAN139:1 H3529 Ascends not up, by merits of his owne,

ASHAM'D (1) [ashamed]
MPERS78:8 H989 For truth's asham'd how many to expresse;

ASHAME (1)
MGREC115:12 H2521 This act (me thinks) his god-head should ashame;

ASHAMED (1) See also ASHAM'D
MEDDM208:26 Hp290 them, return with their empty pitchers ashamed,

ASHES (6) [pl.]
ELEMEN10:31 H106 And with the ashes, that it sometimes shed
ELEMEN10:38 H113 In confus'd heaps of ashes may ye see.
MASSYR60:26 H291 But {For} though his Palace, did in ashes lye,
MPERS69:34 H656 (A hard decree) to ashes he consume;
QELIZ157:27 H95 Her ashes not reviv'd more Phoenix she;
HOUSE237:1 H31 My pleasant things in ashes lye

ASHOARE (1)
ELEMEN15:41 H323 I lightly cast ashoare as frothy fleece.

ASIA (24)
HUMOUR33:2 H516 Country with Country, *Greece* with *Asia* fights,
MASSYR54:37 H64 And all the greater *Asia* did subdue;
MPERS76:24 H922 But troubles in lesse *Asia* him stay'd;
MPERS82:16 H1163 The *Grecians* at *Mycale* in Asia meet,
MPERS85:19 H1295 Which from remissenesse, in *{Less}* *Asia* proceeds {breeds.}
MPERS85:26 H1302 But they in *Asia,* must first restore
MPERS86:28 H1344 Some Townes commodious in lesse *Asia,*
MPERS90:27 H1494 Who with his {the} *Spartans* on the *Asia* coast;
MGREC94:14 H1648 His course to *Asia,* next Spring he steers.
MGREC94:31 H1669 Then to his Lieutenant, {he} in *Asia* sends,
MGREC100:13 H1897 Then setling all things in lesse *Asia,*
MGREC101:11 H1936 And all those Kingdoms in lesse *Asia;*
MGREC118:37 H2686 *Antigonus,* for his share *Asia* takes,
MGREC120:10 H2745 In *Asia* they all asunder be.
MGREC121:31 H2813 And *Pithon* turn'd to *Asia* againe.
MGREC121:33 H2815 *Antigonus* did enter *Asia,*
MGREC~~122:32~~ H2852 From *Macedonia* to Asia he came,
MGREC123:1 H2863 And government of *Asia* to him gave;
MGREC~~123:13~~ H2876 But while these Chieftains doe in Asia fight,
MGREC124:18 H2925 *Antigonus* doth all in *Asia* gaine;
MGREC127:13 H3043 And {now} for a while, let's into *Asia* turn,
MGREC131:13 H3205 Of *Asia* the Lordship shall retain.
MGREC132:17 H3254 *Seleuchus, Asia* holds, that grieves him sore,
MGREC132:28 H3273 Did ne'r regain one foot in *Asia.*

ASIAN (1)
MGREC121:4 H2782 Leaves *Eumenes,* the *Asian* coast to free,

ASIATIQUES (1) [pl.]
MPERS90:21 H1488 The *Asiatiques,* cowardize detects; {victoryes}

ASIDE (6)
AGES37:35 H97 Make strong my selfe, and turne aside weak right.
SEASONS48:13 H66 Our Winter {thicker} rayment, makes us lay aside,
MASSYR60:11 H276 A while he, and his race, aside must stand,
MGREC128:38 H3111 Sought for a peace, and laid aside their jarres:
MROMAN139:33 H3559 All thoughts of further progress laid aside,
HOUSE236:34 H26 My sorrowing eyes aside did cast

ASK (1) See also ASKE
REMB236:1 H16 What did I ask but thov gav'st?

ASK'D (1) [asked]
MGREC~~94:18~~ H1655 And being ask'd what for himself was left,

ASKE (3) [ask]
PROLOG7:38 H48 Give wholsome {Thyme or} Parsley wreath, I aske no Bayes:
ELEMEN18:3 H407 I aske the man condemn'd, that's near his death:
MGREC96:22 H1742 Would aske more time, then were {was} their bodys worth.

ASKED See ASK'D

ASKELON (1)
DAVID158:29 H9 Nor published in streets of *Askelon,*

ASKES (1) [asks]
MEDDM204:34 Hp285 and some land askes much more paines, then some other doth

ASKING (1)
MPERS89:20 H1454 Asking no favour, where they fear'd no bands.

ASKT (1)
AUTHOR178:13 H23 If for thy Father askt, say, thou hadst none:

ASLEEP (1)
1SIMON188:4 H5 No sooner come, but gone, and fal'n asleep,

ASPECT (5)
FATHER6:10 H44 On what they are, your mild aspect I crave,
ELEMEN9:30 H64 But be he what they list {will}, yet his aspect,
AGES36:25 H49 His hoary haires, and grave aspect made way;
MPERS74:30 H853 His affability, {courtesie} and milde aspect,
SIDNEY150:40 ~~H68~~ If thine aspect was milde to *Astrophell;*

ASPERSION (1)
QELIZ156:7 H34 She hath wip'd off th' aspersion of her Sex,

ASPERSIONS (1) [pl.]
MASSYR55:33 H99 As {By} their aspersions, cast upon the same.

ASPES (1) [asps]
MGREC135:2 H3374 {His brave *Virago*} Aspes she sets unto {to} her Armes,

ASPHALTIS (1)
ELEMEN16:8 H331 *Asphaltis* Lake, where nought remains alive.

ASPIRE (4)
AGES42:36 H292 To greater things, I never did aspire,
SIDNEY151:24 ~~H73~~ Calls me ambitious fool, that durst aspire,
QELIZ157:30 H98 Which I may not, my pride doth but aspire,
CONTEM168:8 H17 Whose ruffling top the Clouds seem'd to aspire;

ASPIRES (2)
ELEMEN9:26 H60 But let me leave these things, my flame aspires
MGREC116:41 H2607 His thoughts are perish'd he aspires no more,

ASPS See ASPES

ASS See ASSE

ASSAILANTS See ASSAYLENTS

ASSAIL'D (1) [assailed] See also ASSAYL'D
HOURS233:26 H9 Tho: losse and sicknes me assail'd,

ASSAILE (2) [assail]
MPERS76:6 H904 Which two then to assaile, his {royal} Camp was bold:
PILGRIM210:27 H27 No fainting fits shall me assaile

ASSAULT (2)
HUMOUR29:7 H360 The tongue's no weapon to assault a foe,
HUMOUR29:33 H384 Then by assault to gain one, not our own.

ASSAULTED (1)
HUMOUR22:16 H85 And 'fore she be assaulted, quits the place,

ASSAYES (1) [assays]
MASSYR65:2 H467 Where after many assayes, they make {made} at last,

ASSAYL'D (1) [assailed] See also ASSAIL'D
MGREC110:13 H2313 But {And} whilst the first he valiantly assayl'd,

ASSAYLENTS (1) [assailants]
HUMOUR29:2 H355 He that with two assaylents hath to do,

ASSE (2)
AGES39:33 H176 To be as wilde as is the snuffing Asse,
MASSYR65:22 H487 Thus {Then} cast him out, like to a naked Asse,

ASSE-EARD (1)
MGREC95:14 H1693 (Of Asse-eard) *Midas,* once the regall seat,
ASSEMBLE (1)
AGES39:8 H151 For thus to do, we on this Stage assemble,
ASSEMBLYS (1) [assemblies]
MEDDM201:27 Hp281 precepts of the wise masters of assemblys to their heareres,
ASSENT (3)
HUMOUR27:6 H277 That this is true, I easily can assent,
HUMOUR32:26 H500 To what is truth, I freely wil assent,
DIALOG145:7 H156 To all you've said, sad mother, I assent
ASSENTS (1)
AGES36:33 H57 To do as he, the rest {each one} ful soon assents,
ASSIGN'D (2) [assigned]
HUMOUR23:11 H121 Yet hast thy {the} seat assign'd, a goodly part,
DUBART154:27 H72 Unto each man his riches are {is} assign'd,
ASSIST (1)
HOURS235:1 H53 If thou assist me Lord I shall
ASSISTING (1)
MASSYR60:10 H275 *Medes,* and *Persians,* {when he crav'd} their assisting aide;
ASSOCIATES (1)
HUMOUR25:20 H209 Whil'st us, for thine associates thou takest,
ASSUM'D (1) [assumed] See also ASUM'D
AGES46:21 H452 This body, by this soul, shal be assum'd;
ASSUME (3)
ELEMEN18:37 H441 Thus I another body can assume,
HUMOUR31:5 ~~H438~~ Thou do'st assume my name, wel be it just;
MASSYR63:11 H396 And *Merodach* assume the Monarchy.
ASSUMED See ASSUM'D, ASUM'D
ASSUMES (1)
MGREC130:41 H3186 *Demetrius* is first, that so assumes, {the royal stile asum'd,}
ASSURED (1)
MED223:3 Hp250 should I doubt any more w^n thov hast given me such assured
ASSURS (1) [poss.]
MGREC133:32 H3322 His book of *Assurs* Monarchs dedicates,
ASSYRIA (3)
MASSYR53:26 H16 From thence he went *Assyria* to command;
MASSYR60:21 H286 *Assyria* he also gain'd at length;
MGREC123:19 H2883 On most part of *Assyria* doth seize,
ASSYRIA'S (1) [poss.]
MASSYR61:20 H325 And to *Assyria's* King a Present sends.
ASSYRIAN (4)
MASSYR53:12 H2 the *Assyrian* being the first,
MASSYR54:17 H44 Transfers his Seat, to the *Assyrian* plain,
MASSYR68:31 H617 *The end of the* Assyrian *Monarchy.*
MGREC135:12 H3384 The *Assyrian* Monarchy long time did stand,
ASSYRIANS (3) [pl.]
MASSYR56:38 H144 Which made the *Assyrians* many a day,
MASSYR61:29 H334 Acknowledging th' *Assyrians* high desert,
MASSYR64:24 H448 Which in few years proves the *Assyrians* hire;
A STATE (1) [estate]
MASSYR~~62:12~~ H357 Those that from *Ioshua's* time had been Estate {a state},

ASTHMA See ASTMA

ASTIAGES (1)

MPERS69:3 H625 She Daughter unto great *Astiages,*

ASTMA (1) [asthma]

AGES~~43:33~~ H328 The Astma, Megrim, Palsy, Lethargie,

ASTONISH (1)

MGREC118:17 H2664 A contemplation to astonish Kings,

ASTONISH'D (1) [astonished]

DUBART154:5 H50 My full astonish'd heart doth pant to break,

ASTONISHMENT (1) See also 'STONISHMENT

ELEMEN17:5 H369 And with astonishment, the world confounds.

ASTRAY (1)

MYCHILD217:9 Hp242 Before I was afflicted I went astray, but now I keep thy

ASTROLOGERS (2) [pl.]

MASSYR56:17 H123 From whence, Astrologers, oft view'd the skies.
MASSYR68:9 H595 But dumb the gazing Astrologers stand,

ASTRONOMERS (1) [pl.]

ELEMEN9:40 H74 Yet men and beasts, {beast} Astronomers can tell,

ASTRONOMY (1)

DUBART153:36 H40 Thy peircing skill in high Astronomy,

ASTROPHEL (1)

SIDNEY~~150:41~~ H69 For the sad loss of her dear *Astrophel.*

ASTROPHELL (1)

SIDNEY150:40 ~~H68~~ If thine aspect was milde to *Astrophell;*

ASUM'D (1) [assumed] See also ASSUM'D

MGREC130:41 H3186 *Demetrius* is first, that so assumes, {the royal stile asum'd,}

ASUNDER (1)

MGREC120:10 H2745 In *Asia* they all asunder be.

'ATH (1) [hath]

SEASONS50:34 H168 Yet then appears the worthy deeds he 'ath done:

ATHEISME (1) [astheism]

MYCHILD217:33 Hp243 many times by Atheisme how I could know whether there was

ATHENIAN (4)

MPERS76:36 H934 Where an *Athenian* shew'd a valiant deed,
MGREC119:24 H2714 *Antiphilus* the *Athenian* Generall,
MGREC119:28 H2718 The *Athenian* Army was the greater far,
MGREC~~120:4~~ H2737 For animating the *Athenian* strife:

ATHENIANS (3) [pl.]

MPERS81:22 H1130 But the *Athenians,* this peace detest,
MPERS81:40 H1144 The *Athenians* could but forty thousand arme,
MGREC119:16 H2706 The *Athenians,* force *Antipater* to fly

ATHENS (10)

MPERS76:29 H927 *Athens* perceiving now their desperate state,
MPERS81:10 H1118 He instantly to *Athens* sends for peace,
MPERS81:14 H1122 The *Spartans,* fearing *Athens* would agree,
MPERS81:18 H1126 That *Xerxes* quarrel was 'gainst *Athens* State,
MPERS84:15 H1251 For such ingratitude, did *Athens* show
MGREC94:3 H1637 *Thebes,* and old {stiff} *Athens,* both 'gainst him rebell,
MGREC124:15 H2922 *Athens,* with many Townes in *Greece* besides, {beside}
MGREC~~131:1~~ H3189 Doth promise liberty to *Athens* State;
MGREC131:2 H3192 To *Athens* then he {*Demetrius* thether} goes, is entertain'd,

MGREC131:18 H3210 *Demetrius* with his troops to *Athens* flies,

ATHOS (1)

MPERS79:9 H1031 A Sea passage cuts, behind *Orthos* {*Athos*} Mount.

ATLANTICKE (1)

ELEMEN17:13 H377 A mighty Country ith' *Atlanticke* Ocean.

ATLANTIQUE (1)

ELEMEN16:6 H329 *Ionian, Balticke,* and the vast *Atlantique;*

ATROPOS (1)

SIDNEY150:26 H53 E're he was ripe; his thred cut *Atropos.*

ATTAIN (3)

MPERS92:16 ~~H1574~~ How this *Darius* did attain the Crown,
MGREC118:2 H2649 Their ends they might the better still attain.
JULY223:34 Hp251 my faith in Thee, 'till I shall attain ye End of my hopes, Even

ATTAINED (1)

MEDDM206:1 Hp287 attained to that fruitfullnes, altho they aime at perfection And

ATTAINS (1)

MPERS~~69:38~~ H668 Whose happy life attains an happy end.

ATTAINTS (1)

MGREC120:25 H2762 *Antigonus* of Treason first attaints,

ATTEMPTS (1) [pl.]

AGES39:16 H159 The brave attempts of valiant Knights I prize,

ATTEND (8)

FATHER5:18 H19 They are your bounden handmaids to attend.
HUMOUR24:9 H158 To what you now shal say, I wil attend,
AGES40:34 H213 Though dangers do attend me every houre,
MPERS74:7 H832 They all attend on the appointed houre,
MPERS74:17 H840 They then {all} attend him, to his royall roome,
MGREC109:35 H2294 That to attend him there, was his intent;
BIRTH179:28 H4 Adversity doth still our joyes attend;
BIRTH179:33 H9 How soon, my Dear, death may my steps attend,

ATTENDANTS (2) [pl.]

MGREC95:34 H1713 The rest attendants, which made up no lesse;
MGREC111:8 H2353 The meat, and drink, attendants, every thing,

ATTENDED (2)

ELEMEN10:3 H78 With {There's} *Orion* arm'd, attended by his dog,
MEDDM195:34 Hp272 a negligent youth is vsually attended by an ignorant middle

ATTICA (2)

MPERS76:26 H924 For *Attica* an Army he prepares;
MPERS84:22 H1258 Fair *Attica,* a third time to invade.

ATTIRE (2) See also TIRE

AGES36:1 H25 Next, youth came up, in gorgeous attire;
MROMAN137:31 H3482 Their Augurs strange, their habit, and attire,

ATTIRES See TIRES

ATTOSSA (1)

MPERS77:6 H945 His Queen *Attossa,* caused all {author of} this stir,

ATTOSSA'S (1) [poss.]

MPERS77:15 H954 *Xerxes, Darius,* and *Attossa's* Son,

AUDACIOUS (1)

ELEMEN13:37 H238 To ope those veines of Mine, audacious bold:

AUDACITY (1)

MGREC94:29 H1667 Reproves him, for his proud audacity;

AUDITOURS (1) [pl.]
ELEMEN13:35 H236 But to such auditours 'twere of no use.
AUG (1) [August]
PILGRIM211:4 H45 Aug: 31 69
AUGMENT (7)
ELEMEN10:22 H97 Augment his heat, which was too hot before:
SEASONS49:9 H100 Yet doth his parching heat the {but} more augment,
MGREC102:40 H2010 Which newes doth still augment *Darius* woes;
MGREC103:41 H2052 Was straight in *Bactria* these {soon} to augment,
MGREC108:40 H2256 Which did his former Army {forces} much augment,
MGREC115:31 H2550 His honours, and his riches, to augment
CONTEM172:17 H152 Could hinder ought, but still augment its force:
AUGMENTED (1)
SEASONS52:29 H244 The cold not lessened, but augmented more.
AUGMENTS (1)
MPERS87:9 H1365 But as he goes, his Forces still augments,
AUGURS (1) [pl.]
MROMAN137:31 H3482 Their Augurs strange, their habit, and attire,
AUGUST (5) See also AUG
SEASONS49:4 H95 Bright *June, July,* and *August,* hot are mine,
SEASONS50:11 H145 My next, and last, is *August,* fiery hot,
SEASONS50:15 H149 *August,* of great *Augustus* took its name,
ELIZB186:32 H3-4 *Bradstreet, who deceased August, 1665*
28AUG225:25 Hp254 August. 28. 1656.
AUGUSTUS (4)
SEASONS50:15 H149 *August,* of great *Augustus* took its name,
MGREC116:37 H2603 This folly great *Augustus* did deride,
MGREC134:41 H3370 Till great *Augustus* had with him a fight,
SIDNEY150:15 ~~H49~~ Yet great *Augustus* was content (we know)
AULETES (1)
MGREC134:32 H3363 Next *Auletes,* who cut off *Pompey's* head:
AURELIUS (1)
QELIZ157:24 H92 (Whom none but great *Aurelius* could quell)
AURORA (2)
AGES36:7 H31 His face as fresh, as is *Aurora* faire,
CHILDRN185:1 H27 And where *Aurora* first appears,
AUTHENTICK (1)
ELEMEN19:3 H448 Is more authentick then their {our} moderne wit.
AUTHOR (4) See also AUTHOUR
MPERS~~77:6~~ H945 His Queen *Attossa,* caused all {author of} this stir,
MPERS87:6 H1362 To be the Author of conspiracy.
MGREC133:13 H3301 Unto *Seleuchus,* author of that strife.
AUTHOR177:29 H1 *The Author to her Book.*
AUTHORITY (1)
MEDDM197:4 Hp274 Authority wthout wisedome is like a heavy axe, wthout an edg
AUTHORIZE (1)
MGREC118:34 H2683 To authorize his Acts in every thing.
AUTHORS (2) [pl.]
MGREC97:23 H1784 By too much heat, not wounds (as Authors write.)
AUTHORS (1) [poss.] See also AUTHOURS
2SIMON195:13 Hp271 they will be better pris'd by you, for the Authors sake. the lord

AUTHOUR (1) [author]
MPERS83:17 H1205 To be the Authour of the deed {crime} was done,
AUTHOURS (1) [poss.]
MGREC126:36 H3025 The Authours death she did so much lament,
AUTUMN (1) See also AUTUMNE, AUTVMNE
MEDDM200:27 Hp279 what they lost in the Autumn so shall it be at that great day
AUTUMNAL (2)
ELEMEN13:18 H219 How the Autumnal season I do sway;
CONTEM167:25 H2 Sometime now past in the Autumnal Tide,
AUTUMNE (7) [autumn] See also AUTVMNE
AGES36:17 H41 Of Autumne {Autumns} fruits a basket on his arme.
SEASONS46:30 H6 The Winter, Summer, Autumne, and the Spring,
SEASONS50:29 H163 {Summer seems but} short, the beauteous Autumne hastes,
SEASONS50:37 H171 *Autumne.*
SEASONS50:38 H172 Of Autumne months, *September* is the prime,
SEASONS52:9 H224 Old cold, dry age, and earth, Autumne resembles,
DUBART153:12 H16 If Summer, or my Autumne age, doe yeeld
AUTUMNS (1) [poss.]
AGES~~36:17~~ H41 Of Autumne {Autumns} fruits a basket on his arme.
AUTVMNE (1)
MYCHILD218:1 Hp243 & Winter, Spring and Autvmne, the dayly providing for this
AVAIL (1)
MASSYR62:7 H352 To *Ægypts* King, which did avail him nought;
AVENG'D (1) [avenged]
MGREC132:14 H3249 Yet be aveng'd, must th' blood of *Jesreel.*
AVENGE (1)
MEDDM204:20 Hp285 (sath god) and I will avenge the blood of Jezerel vpon the
AVER (1)
HUMOUR30:6 H398 The melancholy Snake shal it aver.
AVERRE (1)
HUMOUR26:13 H243 That there are some, and best, I dare averre;
AVOID See AVOYD
AVOIDED (1) See also AVOYDED
MYCHILD215:26 Hp240 etc. I avoided it. If at any time I was overtaken wth ye evills, it
AVOIDS See AVOYDS
AVOUCH (1)
DIALOG143:14 H83 Her Lillies in mine Armes avouch the same.
AVOW (2)
HUMOUR30:39 H431 But yet more comely far, I dare avow,
HUMOUR33:23 H537 The scituation, and {Its} form wil it avow,
AVOYD (1) [avoid]
MPERS74:3 H828 All envie to avoyd, this was thought on,
AVOYDED (1) [avoided]
2SIMON195:10 Hp271 much more by duty full children, I haue avoyded incroaching
AVOYDS (1) [avoids]
MGREC120:27 H2764 This he avoyds, and ships himself, and's Son,
AWAKE (1)
AGES45:32 H422 But do awake, {waking glad to hear} at the cocks clanging {shrill}
AWAY (57)
HUMOUR22:9 H78 But be she beaten, she'l not run away,

HUMOUR28:7 H319 The Lungs, she rots, the body weares away,
HUMOUR29:20 H371 Thy fiery spirit shal bear away this prize,
HUMOUR33:4 H518 Under *Troys* wals, ten years wil wast {wear} away,
SEASONS50:9 H143 The groaning Carts to bear away this prise,
SEASONS52:39 H254 Until by's heat he drives {drive} all cold away.
MASSYR56:32 H138 The River *Indus* swept them half away,
MASSYR57:22 ~~H169~~ So Province, after Province, rent away,
MASSYR59:6 H230 Who revelling in Cups, sung care away,
MASSYR66:7 H513 The Temple's burnt, the Vessels had away,
MASSYR66:30 H536 Which for seven years his reason took away;
MPERS73:27 H812 Some write that sorely hurt, they 'scap'd away;
MPERS74:37 ~~H858~~ And fear'd, he now with scorn must march away:
MPERS78:40 H1021 The other four he freely gave away:
MPERS86:27 H1343 From the Lieutenant first, he takes away,
MPERS86:34 H1350 (One *Greeke* could make ten *Persians* run away)
MPERS88:15 H1408 For at first charge the *Persians* ran away.
MPERS89:30 H1464 And feares as much to let them march away;
MPERS92:39 H1597 One deluge came, and swept them all away;
MGREC95:23 H1702 But sets {Yet set} one in his roome, and ran away.
MGREC97:3 H1764 And cast away his Crown, for swifter flight;
MGREC97:5 H1766 Now finds both leggs, and Horse, to run away;
MGREC102:12 H1982 Which in few hours was carried all away;
MGREC105:6 H2099 This done, they with their Hoast, soon speed away,
MGREC106:3 H2137 This said, his fainting breath did fleet away,
MGREC107:20 H2195 Now with his Army, doth he hast {post} away,
MGREC108:8 H2224 Whom *Xerxes* from their country led away;
MGREC110:36 H2340 And so his memory might {would} fade away,
MGREC117:27 H2634 Each Captain wisht this prize to beare away,
MGREC117:36 H2643 Had hope themselves, to beare the Crown away;
MGREC~~118:30~~ H2679 Was stiffe *Meleager,* whom he would take down {away},
MGREC~~124:10~~ H2915 Such friends away as for his Interest makes
MGREC125:39 H2989 Where hearing of this newes he speeds away,
MGREC126:3 H2994 His Army he divides, sends part away,
MGREC~~126:21~~ H3012 But his occasions calling him away,
MGREC130:36 ~~H3181~~ And's kingdomes rent away by each Commander:
MGREC132:6 ~~H3239~~ Who took away his now pretended right:
MROMAN138:8 H3498 And from old *Alba* fetch the wealth away;
DIALOG144:21 H131 I mock'd the Preachers, put it farre away;
DIALOG147:24 H248 And yee brave Nobles, chase away all fear,
DAVID159:2 H17 The Shield of *Saul* was vilely cast away;
DAVID159:28 H43 And war-like weapons perished away.
VANITY160:37 H47 It steeres {stores} with wealth, which time cann't wear away.
DISTEMP179:22 H10 He chac'd away those clouds, and let me see
ELIZB186:37 H9 Then ta'en away unto Eternity.
MEDDM199:16 Hp278 thing to stay vpon, but take away their props and they are of
MEDDM206:24 Hp287 for it, shall meet with miserable disapointment, going away
MEDDM207:29 Hp289 may be sure of an euer lasting habitation that fades not away.
MEDDM208:2 Hp289 long night shall fly away, and the day of eternity shall never
PILGRIM210:22 H22 and my Clay house mouldring away
PILGRIM211:3 H44 then Come deare bridgrome Come away
MYCHILD218:30 Hp244 Xtians haue been carryed away wth them, that somt: I haue

RESTOR229:27 H10 Distempers thou didst chase away.
RESTOR230:7 H22 Nor turnd his ear away from me
2HUSB232:18 H19 Hide not thy face Away.
2HUSB233:6 H39 Bee sold away for Novght.
HOUSE237:16 H46 That dunghill mists away may flie.

AWE (2)
MPERS88:11 H1404 That, more then multitudes, their hearts did awe:
1SIMON188:8 H9 With dreadful awe before him let's be mute,

AWEFUL (1) [awful] See also AWEFULL, AWFULL
DDUDLEY167:14 H11 *To Servants wisely aweful, but yet kind,*

AWEFULL (1) [awful] See also AWEFUL, AWFULL
MEDDM205:24 Hp286 himself alway in the awefull presence of god, the consideration

AWES (1)
HUMOUR23:29 H139 Their courage, {Courage it} friend, and foe, and subject awes,

AWFULL (1) [awful] See also AWEFUL, AWEFULL
MEDDM206:27 Hp288 works and doings of god are wonderfull, but none more awfull

AWRY (1)
AGES45:25 H415 But I returne, from whence I stept awry,

AXE (1)
MEDDM197:4 Hp274 Authority w[th]out wisedome is like a heavy axe, w[th]out an edg

AYD (2) [aid] See also AIDE, AYDE
ELEMEN9:5 H39 Without mine ayd, alas, what can they doe?
DIALOG142:20 H49 Must *Richmonds* ayd, the Nobles now implore,

AYDE (3) [aid] See also AIDE, AYD
MPERS78:30 H1011 But pitty 'twas, thine ayde that {thou} here did'st lend,
MGREC125:6 H2954 For ayde {she} goes to *Epire,* among her friends,
DIALOG142:15 H44 And call in Forreign ayde, to help the thing?

AYE (4)
FEVER221:14 H29 Praises to him for Aye.
SOREFIT222:8 H27 O Lord for aye is my request
WHAT224:20 H20 And I shall liue for aye.
WHAT224:23 H23 The first and last y[t] liues for aye,

AYLES (1)
DIALOG141:8 H7 What ayles thee hang thy head, and crosse thine armes?

AYMES (2) [aimes]
MGREC123:31 H2895 And to be great {chief} himselfe now bends his aymes;
MGREC128:3 H3076 And how he aymes {aiming now} to make himselfe a King,

AYMING (1) [aiming]
MGREC117:23 H2630 For ayming still amisse, his dreadfull blowes

AYRE (2) [air] See also AIRE
HUMOUR26:35 H265 Their wondrous mixture, is of blood, and ayre,
MEDDM201:20 Hp280 from a thick ayre about them so may we sometime se, marble

AZURE (1)
SEASONS47:40 H52 The Primrose pale, and azure Violet,

B

B (15)
PROLOG8:3 ~~H50~~ *A. B.*
SEASONS53:10 ~~H264~~ *A. B.*
SIDNEY149:6 ~~H5~~ By *A. B.* in the yeare, 1638.
DUBART152:32 H1 A. B.
BIRTH180:21 H31 *A. B.*
1LETTER181:29 H27 *A. B.*
3LETTER183:33 H35 *A. B.*
VERSES184:12 H16 *A.B.*
CHILDRN186:30 H97 *A. B.*
1SIMON188:16 H17 *A. B.*
MERCY189:17 H38 A. B.
2SIMON195:18 Hp271 mother A B
TOCHILD215:8 H8 A. B.
30SEPT227:33 Hp257 him then before, This is the desire of y^{r} Loving mother. A. B.
HOUSE~~237:28~~ H59 A. B.

BAAL (1)
MASSYR~~54:9~~ H36 This is that *Bell,{Baal}* to whom the *Israelites*

BAALS (1) [poss.]
DIALOG147:12 H238 Let's bring *Baals* vestments out, {forth} to make a fire,

BABE (6)
MGREC118:4 H2651 And th' unborn babe of *Roxan* be proclaim'd;
ELIZB186:34 H6 Farewel dear babe, my hearts too much content,
ELIZB186:35 H7 Farewel sweet babe, the pleasure of mine eye,
ELIZB187:1 H10 Blest babe why should I once bewail thy fate,
1SIMON188:14 H15 Go pretty babe, go rest with Sisters twain
MERCY189:5 H26 A Babe she left before, she soar'd above,

BABEL (4) See also BABELL
MASSYR53:23 H13 The strong foundation of proud *Babel* laid,
MASSYR65:20 H485 Fast bound, intends at {to} *Babel* he shal stay {him to send},
MASSYR65:26 H491 Whom with his Mother, he to *Babel* led,
MASSYR66:5 H511 In mid'st of *Babel* now, til death he lyes,

BABELL (2) [babel]
MASSYR56:23 H129 This wonder of the world, this *Babell* stood.
MASSYR67:10 H556 But yet in *Babell,* he must still remain:

BABEL'S (1) [poss.]
MASSYR64:16 H440 By the victorious King to *Babel's* prest;

BABELS (7) [poss.]
MASSYR64:34 H458 Can *Babels* tired Souldiers tell with pain;
MASSYR65:13 H478 While *Babels* King thus deep ingaged stands;
MASSYR65:40 H505 But being caught, to *Babels* wrathful King,

MASSYR66:13 H519 With all these Conquests, *Babels* King rests not,
MASSYR67:2 H548 *Babels* great Monarch, now laid in the dust,
MGREC98:11 H1813 And now, as *Babels* King did once before,
QELIZ157:6 H74 She plac'd {built} her glory but on *Babels* walls,

BABES (3) [pl.]
DIALOG144:9 H119 Oh, *Edwards* Babes {youths}, and *Clarence* haplesse Son,
DIALOG144:39 H147 Wives forc'd, babes toss'd, her houses calcined,
BIRTH180:14 H24 Look to my little babes my dear remains.

BABES (1) [pl., poss.]
AGES44:4 H337 Babes innocence, Youths wildnes I have seen,

BABILON (1) [babylon]
MPERS~~91:22~~ H1534 From Court exile her unto *Babilon*:

BABLES (1) [baubles]
AGES37:22 H84 In Rattles, Bables, and such toyish stuffe.

BABYLON (20) See also BABILON
MASSYR55:36 H102 Her wealth she shew'd, in building *Babylon;*
MASSYR58:13 H198 These two rul'd *Media* and *Babylon,*
MASSYR60:1 H266 Of *Babylon, Belosus* he made King,
MASSYR60:24 H289 Who own'd the treasures of proud *Babylon,*
MASSYR63:5 H390 In *Babylon,* Leiutenant to this man,
MASSYR63:9 H394 So he's now stil'd, the King of *Babylon;*
MASSYR67:28 H574 Layes siedge to's regall seat, proud *Babylon,*
MASSYR67:36 H582 Protectors of his {this} Crown, and *Babylon,*
MPERS70:5 H676 Was conquest of the stately *Babylon,*
MPERS~~71:4~~ H716 But eight whilst *Babylon*, he did retain:
MPERS73:7 H794 A *Babylon* in *Egypt* did he make.
MGREC102:5 H1975 This Conquerour now {then} goes to *Babylon,*
MGREC102:25 H1995 Whilst revelling at *Babylon,* he lyes,
MGREC103:6 H2017 Though *Babylon* was rich, and *Sushan* too;
MGREC103:17 H2028 (As first at *Sushan,* and at *Babylon*)
MGREC111:38 H2383 From hence to *Babylon,* some time there spent,
MGREC115:16 H2535 From *Media* to *Babylon* he went,
MGREC116:1 H2561 Before his answer came to *Babylon,*
MGREC118:39 H2688 *Seleuchus* afterward held *Babylon*;
MGREC128:27 H3100 And *Seleuchus* recovers *Babylon,*

BABYLONIANS (1) [pl.]
MPERS74:33 H856 The *Babylonians* 'gainst their Prince rebell;

BABYLONS (1) [poss.]
MASSYR66:20 H526 To *Babylons* proud King, now yeelds the day.

BACA (2)
11MAYA226:18 Hp255 this valley of Baca many pools of water, That wch now I cheifly
13MAY227:12 H21 My Baca made a springing flood?

BACCHUS (1)
MGREC109:6 H2265 He t' *Nisa* goes, by *Bacchus* built long since,

BACK (24)
ELEMEN~~9:34~~ H68 How doth his warmth refresh thy frozen backs, {back}
HUMOUR34:11 H566 Mine likewise is the marrow of the back,
AGES45:28 H418 And back, once straight, begins apace to bow.
MASSYR56:31 H137 (They say) but twenty, ere came back agen.
MPERS75:32 H889 Shall let the work, or keep back any thing,
MPERS87:20 ~~H1374~~ Ran back, and quite abandoned the same,

MPERS89:2 H1436 The King upon the spur, runs back again;
MGREC100:11 H1895 Now {Thence} back to *Ægypt* goes, and in few dayes,
MGREC101:22 H1947 Thus to *Darius* he writes back again,
MGREC110:14 H2314 The last set on his back, and so prevail'd:
MGREC128:31 H3104 But bravely sends the Prisoners back againe,
DIALOG142:25 H54 Or, doth {do} the *Scots* play false behind your back?
DAVID159:8 H23 Did *Saul* with bloodlesse Sword turne back agen:
CONTEM169:26 H65 When present times look back to Ages past,
CONTEM169:29 H68 And calls back moneths and years that long since fled
CHILDRN184:25 H14 Fly back and sing amidst this Quire.
MEDDM197:27 Hp275 on his back, will finde it a wearysome if not an impossible task
MEDDM205:2 Hp285 correction must make long furrows on their back and the
MYCHILD217:7 Hp242 child, that no longer then the rod has been on my back
SAMUEL228:13 H14 Protect him there & bring him back.
2HUSB232:12 H13 Nor novght could keep him back
2HUSB233:8 H41 Wth Joy lend back my Dear
HOURS234:23 H37 Bring back my husband I beseech
ACK235:17 H17 And y^{t} thov wilt return him back

BACKS (5) [pl.]
ELEMEN9:34 H68 How doth his warmth refresh thy frozen backs, {back}
AGES~~42:2~~ H260 Whose loynes {backs} I've cloth'd, and bellies I have fed;
MPERS80:2 H1069 And wound the backs of those bold {brave} Warriours stout.
MGREC95:3 H1682 Who in their backs did all their wounds receive.
DIALOG144:25 ~~H134~~ Unworthily, some backs whipt, and eares cropt;

BACKSLIDING (1)
CONTEM170:4 H78 A penalty impos'd on his backsliding Race.

BACKT (1)
MPERS75:36 H893 They thus backt of {by} the King, in spight of foes,

BACTARIA (1)
MASSYR58:33 H216 From *Bactaria* an Army was at hand,

BACTR'A (1) [bactria]
MPERS87:28 H1380 To th' utmost parts of *Bactr'a,* and {for a time} there lye.

BACTRIA (6)
MPERS83:5 H1193 To *Bactria* his houshold did remove.
MGREC103:41 H2052 Was straight in *Bactria* these {soon} to augment,
MGREC105:7 H2100 To hide themselves, remote, in *Bactria;*
MGREC107:21 H2196 False *Bessus* to finde out, in *Bactria;*
MGREC108:7 H2223 Here was of *Greeks,* a town in *Bactria,*
MGREC108:19 H2235 Whilst thus he spent some time in *Bactria,*

BACTRIAN (1)
MASSYR55:20 H86 This gallant dame, unto the *Bactrian* war;

BACTRIANS (3) [pl.]
MASSYR54:35 H62 Against the *Bactrians* (but that I doubt)
MASSYR60:3 H268 To *Bactrians,* he gave their liberty,
MGREC108:25 H2241 And now the *Bactrians* 'gainst him {now} rebel,

BAD (14)
HUMOUR34:7 H562 O! good, O bad, O true, O traiterous eyes!
AGES36:36 H60 Both good and bad, but yet no more then's true.
AGES41:25 H242 My reason, then bad judge, how little hope,
AGES43:25 H320 Thus good, and bad, and what I am, you see,
AGES~~45:26~~ H416 My memory is short {bad}, and braine is dry.

SEASONS53:1 H257 *My Subjects bare, my Brains are {Brain is} bad,*
SEASONS53:5 H261 *The last, though bad, I could not mend,*
MASSYR61:15 H320 *Iuda's* bad King occasioned this War,
MPERS72:29 ~~H773~~ Who said but what, the King bad him expresse.
SIDNEY151:41 ~~H75~~ He bad me drive, and he would hold the Sun;
SIDNEY152:20 H89 Which writ, she bad return't to them again.
TDUDLEY167:2 H84 *The Good him lov'd, the bad did fear,*
MEDDM206:29 Hp288 how many good parents haue had bad children, and againe
MEDDM206:30 Hp288 bad parents haue had pious children, it should make vs adore

BAD'ST (1) [baddest]
FLESH176:15 H55 Then when I did what thou bad'st doe.

BADGE (1)
HUMOUR27:34 H305 This scarlet die's a badge of what's within,

BAGOAS (2)
MPERS~~92:3~~ H1557 Was by his *Eunuch* the proud *Bagoas* slain.
MPERS92:25 ~~H1583~~ By one *Bagoas,* an Eunuch (as is sed.)

BAIT (3)
AGES43:17 H312 Sometimes vaine-glory is the only bait,
MPERS89:23 H1457 The smiling *Greeks* reply, they first must bait,
FLESH176:19 H59 Thy riches are to me no bait,

BAITS (4) [pl.]
MGREC96:37 H1757 And how {that} his wealth serv'd but for baits t'allure,
MGREC115:37 H2556 Nor by his baits could be ensnared so:
MEDDM198:16 Hp276 The skillfull fisher hath his severall baits, for severall fish, but
MEDDM198:17 Hp276 vnder all, Satan that great Angler hath his sundry baits for

BAJAZET (1)
SEASONS49:28 H117 Which made great *Bajazet* cry out in's woes,

BAK'D (2) [baked]
HUMOUR31:4 H437 When by thy heat, thou'st bak'd thy selfe to crust,
MPERS70:32 H703 The which she bak'd {bath'd} within a But of bloud,

BAL-PEOR (1)
MASSYR54:12 H39 Likewise *Bal-peor,* of the *Moabites:*

BALADAN (2) See also BALLADAN
MASSYR63:12 H397 *Merodach Baladan.*
MASSYR68:29 H615 With him did end the race of *Baladan,*

BALANCE See ballance

BALDED (1)
MASSYR65:9 H474 With peeled shoulders, and with balded heads,

BALLADAN (1) See also BALADAN
MASSYR63:4 H389 Brave *Merodach,* the Son of *Balladan,*

BALLANCE (2)
ELEMEN10:8 H83 The maid with ballance, wayn with horses three;
MEDDM208:14 Hp290 Commends vs to god, for by his ballance we must be weighed,

BALLAST (1)
MEDDM196:2 Hp272 A ship that beares much saile & little or no ballast, is easily

BALS (1) [balls]
HUMOUR34:8 H563 What wonderments, within your bals there lyes?

BALTICKE (1) [baltic]
ELEMEN16:6 H329 *Ionian, Balticke,* and the vast *Atlantique;*

BANCK (1) [bank]
MGREC108:35 H2251 Upon this River banck in seventeen dayes,

BAND (4)
AGES42:10 H268 A Captain I, with skil I train'd my band;
MASSYR64:20 H444 Quite vanquish'd *Pharaoh Necho,* and {with} his Band;
MGREC100:17 H1901 Had *Betis* now been there, but with his Band,
SIDNEY151:9 ~~H69~~ Who wert of honours band, the chief Commander.

BANDS (2) [bond]
MASSYR65:12 H477 Thinks this the fittest time to break his bands,
MPERS89:20 H1454 Asking no favour, where they fear'd no bands.

BANDS (4) [companies]
MASSYR57:15 H162 'Gainst whom his trained Bands *Abram* did bring.
MASSYR59:4 H228 Both sides their hearts, their hands, their {&} bands unite,
MPERS71:29 H743 The stormed dust o'r-whelm'd his daring bands;
MGREC102:27 H1997 He then to *Sushan* goes, with his fresh {new} bands,

BANDS (2) [ties]
MPERS~~79:12~~ H1034 But winds, and waves those iron bands did break;
MGREC104:22 H2074 Lays hold on's Lord, and binding him with bands.

BANISHED (2)
MGREC~~116:10~~ H2575 All friends she shuns, yea, banished the light,
MGREC124:9 ~~H2914~~ Those absent, banished, or else he slew

BANISHMENT (2)
MGREC~~124:10~~ H2916 By death by prison, or by banishment,
MROMAN139:21 H3549 In banishment perpetuall, to dwell;

BANISHT (2)
MGREC123:24 H2888 *Antipater* had banisht her from thence,
BYNIGHT220:15 H14 And banisht thence my Doubts + feares.

BANK See BANCK

BANKRUPTS (1) [pl.]
HUMOUR30:18 H410 When you poor bankrupts prove, then have I most.

BANKS (5)
MASSYR54:24 H51 Upon the pleasant banks of *Tigris* flood,
MPERS70:11 H682 He cuts those banks, and let the river out;
MGREC94:41 H1679 Those banks so steep, the *Greeks,* now {yet} scramble up
MGREC110:1 H2301 But on the banks doth {stout} *Porus* ready stand,
FLESH175:3 H3 Close by the Banks of *Lacrim* flood

BANNER (1)
DIALOG147:35 H259 That all shall joy that thou display'dst thy banner,

BANQUET (1)
MGREC112:14 H2400 So after many dayes this {the} Banquet ends.

BANQUETING (1)
MGREC102:22 H1992 And gives {gave} himself to banqueting, and play:

BANQUETTING (2)
MASSYR67:30 H576 To banquetting, and revelling now falls,
MPERS83:38 H1226 Where ninescore days, are spent in banquetting,

BAR See BARR

BARBADOES (1)
ELEMEN19:33 H474 Knowes {Know} Western Isles, *Christophers, Barbadoes;*

BARBAROUS (1) See also BARB'ROUS
MPERS76:3 H901 But in that Desart, 'mongst his barbarous foes,

BARBAROUSLY (1)
MPERS83:7 H1195 Which {With} him, and his, most barbarously there slew,

BARBELL (1)
ELEMEN15:29 H311 The crafty {witty} Barbell, whose wit {craft} doth her commend;
BARB'ROUS (2) [barbarous]
HUMOUR25:3 H192 As thy unbridled, barb'rous Choler yeelds. {breeds:}
MPERS79:3 ~~H1025~~ Nay, more then monstrous barb'rous cruelty!
BARD (1)
MGREC117:34 H2641 But meannesse of their Mothers bard the same:
BARE (4)
AGES37:36 H98 No malice bare, to this, or that great Peer,
SEASONS53:1 H257 *My Subjects bare, my Brains are {Brain is} bad,*
MASSYR57:24 ~~H171~~ Again, the Country was left bare (there is no doubt)
28AUG226:1 Hp254 me a vessell fitt for his vse why should I not bare it not only
BARGE (1)
MPERS76:1 H899 A bridge he made, which serv'd for boat, and barge,
BARLEY (1)
SEASONS50:21 H155 The Barley, and the Rye, should first had place,
BARN (2)
TDUDLEY166:20 H62 And in celestial Barn hath hous'd him high,
CONTEM173:19 H185 That neither toyles nor hoards up in thy barn,
BARNS (1) [pl.]
SEASONS50:10 H144 To Barns, and Stacks, where it for Fodder lyes.
BARON (1)
AGES37:31 H93 A Baron or a Duke, ne'r made my mark.
BARONS (1) [pl.]
DIALOG142:14 H43 Doe Barons rise, and side against their King?
BARQUE (1)
CONTEM174:14 H213 Sings merrily, and steers his Barque with ease,
BARR (1) [bar]
CONTEM170:30 H100 Who fancyes not his looks now at the Barr,
BARR'D (2) [barred]
ELEMEN9:9 H43 Set ope those gates, that 'fore so strong was {were} barr'd.
AGES43:12 ~~H305~~ When to a Monarchy, my way they barr'd.
BARREN (5)
SEASONS48:32 ~~H83~~ Sometime a theame that's large, proves barren fields.
MPERS75:41 H898 Entring that large and barren country far;
DIALOG144:37 H145 Her fruitfull land, a barren heath remain.
DUBART153:10 H14 But barren I, my Daysey here doe bring,
DAVID158:33 H13 Nor fruitfull showers your barren tops bestrew,
BARTA'S (1) [poss.]
DUBART154:8 H53 Had I an Angels voice, or *Barta's* pen,
BARTAS (3) [poss.]
PROLOG6:26 H10 Great *Bartas* sugar'd lines doe but read o're;
DUBART153:15 H19 And prostrate off'red at great *Bartas* Herse.
DUBART154:35 H80 Thus *Bartas* fame shall last while starres do stand,
BARTAS (7) [pl.]
FATHER6:3 H37 But fear'd you'ld judge, one *Bartas* was my friend,
PROLOG6:29 H13 A *Bartas* can, doe what a *Bartas* wil,
PROLOG6:29 H13 A *Bartas* can, doe what a *Bartas* wil,
SIDNEY150:37 H64 Noble {Great} *Bartas,* this to thy praise adds more,
DUBART152:30 H1 In honour of *Du Bartas.*
DUBART152:34 H3 Great, deare, sweet *Bartas,* thou art matchlesse knowne;

DUBART155:8 H93 *But Nature vanquish'd Art, so* Bartas *dy'd,*

BARTER (1)

MEDDM206:24 Hp287 barter for it, shall meet with miserable disapointment, going

BARZANES (1)

MASSYR54:30 H57 *Barzanes,* the great *Armenian* King,

BASE (12)

HUMOUR23:18 H128 So base thou art, that baser cannot be;
HUMOUR25:5 H194 And real complements, base flattery.
AGES37:33 H95 With costly presents, {presence} or base flattery.
AGES45:9 H391 I've seen base {unworthy} men, advanc'd to great degree
MASSYR67:25 H571 His life so base, and dissolute, invites
MPERS87:21 ~~H1374~~ *Abrocomes,* was this base cowards name,
MGREC103:28 H2039 He at a bold, base {proud} Strumpets, lewd desire;
MGREC105:25 H2118 Of Treason, murther, and base cruelty,
MGREC117:40 H2647 His base born Brother, *Aridæus* nam'd,
MGREC131:4 H3194 Most grossely base, was this {their} great adulation,
MEDDM202:6 Hp281 is capable of, and some again so base that they are Viler
MYSOUL225:17 H21 Base World I trample on thy face,

BASELY (1)

MGREC97:1 H1762 Most basely run {ran}, and left their King at large,

BASENESSE (3)

AGES42:21 H279 Then basenesse was companion unto me.
MASSYR58:5 H190 Knowing his basenesse, and the peoples hate,
MGREC106:23 H2157 He basenesse counts his former clemency,

BASER (1)

HUMOUR23:18 H128 So base thou art, that baser cannot be;

BASKET (1)

AGES36:17 H41 Of Autumne {Autumns} fruits a basket on his arme.

BATH'D (2) [bathed]

MPERS~~70:32~~ H703 The which she bak'd {bath'd} within a But of bloud,
MGREC105:8 H2101 *Darius* bath'd in bloud, sends out his groanes,

BATHES (1) [pl.]

ELEMEN16:15 H338 My wholesome Bathes, together with their cures.

BATTALIA (1)

HUMOUR29:26 H377 When in Battalia my foes I face,

BATTEL (1)

MPERS~~82:2~~ H1148 Then for one battel shortly all provide,

BATTELL (4)

MPERS81:39 ~~H1143~~ For one maine Battell shortly, both provide;
MGREC122:24 ~~H2845~~ And in a Battell slew her hand to hand;
DIALOG146:10 H198 One battell, two or three I might abide,
DAVID159:19 H34 O! how in battell did the mighty fall,

BATTELLS (3) [pl.]

ELEMEN19:39 H480 As battells pitcht ith' Aire (as Countries know;)
MGREC121:40 H2822 Two battells now he fought, and had {of both} the best,
MGREC131:9 H3199 Their severall battells, and their severall fate,

BATTELS (3) [pl.]

MGREC123:6 H2868 With *Eumenes* he divers Battels fought,
MGREC127:18 H3048 In divers battels, he had good successe,
MGREC133:18 H3306 I must let passe those many battels fought,

BATTER'D (1) [battered]
MPERS80:21 H1088 And *Xerxes* mighty Gallies batter'd so,
BATTLEMENTS (2) [pl.]
AGES39:17 H160 That dare climbe Battlements, {scale walls and forts} rear'd to
MGREC~~115:15~~ H2526 The battlements from off the walls are torne.
BAUBLES See BABLES
BAY (2)
AGES43:6 H301 That did oppose me, to my longed bay:
MPERS79:17 H1043 Was marching o're this interrupting Bay; {new devised way.}
BAYES (3) [pl.]
PROLOG7:38 H48 Give wholsome {Thyme or} Parsley wreath, I aske no Bayes:
SIDNEY149:8 H7 Her noble *Sidney* wore the Crown of Bayes;
DUBART154:20 H65 Immortall bayes, all men to thee allows.
BE (332) See also BEE
PROLOG7:28 H39 Let *Greeks* be *Greeks,* and Women what they are,
ELEMEN8:11 H9 All would be cheife, and all scorn'd to be under,
ELEMEN8:11 H9 All would be cheife, and all scorn'd to be under,
ELEMEN9:30 H64 But be he what they list {will}, yet his aspect,
ELEMEN10:33 H108 And though I be a servant to each man;
ELEMEN10:41 H116 Which when they could not be o're come by foes
ELEMEN11:21 H141 The next in place, Earth judg'd to be her due,
ELEMEN~~16:11~~ H334 And be thy mountains n'er so high and steep,
ELEMEN16:31 H354 These be my benefits which may suffice:
ELEMEN17:18 H382 And of my chilling colds, such plenty be;
ELEMEN18:36 H440 Which may be done, by holding down my vapour.
ELEMEN18:41 H445 Let such suspend their thoughts, and silent be;
ELEMEN19:7 H452 The Phoenix too (if any be) are mine;
HUMOUR20:33 H25 Wel, thus they parle, and chide, but to be briefe,
HUMOUR20:34 H26 Or wil they nil they, Choler wil be cheife;
HUMOUR21:22 H50 Be he a Souldier, I more fence his heart
HUMOUR21:39 H67 And break a staffe, provided't be in jest,
HUMOUR22:8 H77 Then by a quick encounter, to be slaine;
HUMOUR22:9 H78 But be she beaten, she'l not run away,
HUMOUR22:10 H79 She'l first advise, if't be not best to stay.
HUMOUR22:16 H85 And 'fore she be assaulted, quits the place,
HUMOUR22:40 H109 To be distill'd a drop on every line!
HUMOUR23:18 H128 So base thou art, that baser cannot be;
HUMOUR25:36 H225 If murthers be thy glory, tis no lesse.
HUMOUR25:40 H229 Be dangers neer so high, and courage great,
HUMOUR26:28 H258 If thou'rt the taker, I must be the giver:
HUMOUR26:31 H261 But why the heart, should be usurpt by thee,
HUMOUR27:4 H275 Can be imputed unto none, but Fire;
HUMOUR~~27:12~~ H283 Unless as heat, it be thy faculty,
HUMOUR27:16 H287 To meddle further, I shal be but shent,
HUMOUR27:31 H302 If this {you} can't be disprov'd {disprove}, then all I hold:
HUMOUR27:36 H307 Nay, could I be from all your tangs but pure,
HUMOUR28:32 H344 But why, alas, thus tedious should I be?
HUMOUR28:35 H347 Yet could not be more breif, without much wrong.
HUMOUR29:3 H356 Had need be armed wel, and active too,
HUMOUR29:8 H361 But sith we fight with words, we might be kind,
HUMOUR29:13 H366 Thy soothing girds shal fully be repaid;

HUMOUR29:14 H367 But Choler, be thou cool'd, or chaf'd, i'le venter,
HUMOUR29:17 ~~H368~~ If not as yet, by me, thou shalt be quell'd:
HUMOUR29:22 H373 If in a Souldier rashnesse be so precious,
HUMOUR29:34 H385 And if *Marcellus* bold, be call'd *Romes* sword,
HUMOUR30:5 H397 If I be partial judg'd, or thought to erre,
HUMOUR31:1 H434 In {Is} charging me, to be thy excrement.
HUMOUR31:5 ~~H438~~ Thou do'st assume my name, wel be it just;
HUMOUR32:18 H492 Patient I am, patient i'd need to be,
HUMOUR32:29 H503 And when i've nothing left to say, be mute;
HUMOUR33:27 H541 Though it in all, and every part be whole:
HUMOUR34:9 H564 Of all the Sences, Sight shal be the Queen;
HUMOUR34:32 H587 If Tyrants be the best, i'le it allow;
HUMOUR34:33 H588 But if love be, as requisite as feare,
HUMOUR34:35 H590 Wel, to be breif, Choler I hope now's laid,
HUMOUR34:41 H596 Let's now be freinds, 'tis {its} time our spight was {were} spent,
HUMOUR35:5 H601 To take her moyst, my moistnesse {moisture} wil be bold;
HUMOUR35:8 H604 Two hot, two moist, two cold, two dry here be,
HUMOUR35:12 H608 Nor be discern'd, here's water, earth, aire, fire,
AGES37:9 H71 To tel that paine, which cann't be told by tongue;
AGES37:13 H75 Spending was willing, to be spent for me;
AGES37:30 H92 How to be rich, or great, I did not carke;
AGES39:33 H176 To be as wilde as is the snuffing Asse,
AGES39:34 H177 As vain as froth, as {or} vanity can be,
AGES40:11 H192 Until mine own be gone, my wit, and wealth;
AGES40:18 H199 If any care I take, 'tis to be fine,
AGES40:22 H203 Some young {new} *Adonis* I do strive to be,
AGES41:18 H237 As was their praise, or shame, so mine must be.
AGES41:31 H248 Be my condition mean, I then take paines;
AGES42:20 H278 Was I as poor, as poverty could be,
AGES42:38 H294 If to be rich, or great, it was my fate;
AGES~~43:8~~ H304 Then Kings must be depos'd or put to flight,
AGES43:19 H314 Be I of worth {wit}, of learning, or {and} of parts;
AGES43:22 H317 I hate {not} for to be had, {held} in small {high'st} account.
AGES43:26 H321 Now in a word, what my diseases be.
AGES43:37 H332 And to conclude, I may not tedious be,
AGES46:1 H432 Shal both be broke, by wracking death so strong;
AGES46:19 H450 There, {Where} I shal rest, til heavens shal be no more;
AGES46:20 H451 And when this flesh shal rot, and be consum'd,
AGES46:21 H452 This body, by this soul, shal be assum'd;
SEASONS48:14 H67 Least by his fervor, we be terrifi'd,
SEASONS~~49:7~~ H98 And {Then} retrograde, now is {must be} my burning Sun.
SEASONS50:33 H167 Until his head be gray, and strength be gone,
SEASONS50:33 H167 Until his head be gray, and strength be gone,
SEASONS51:4 H178 For nought's so good, but it may be abused,
SEASONS51:6 H180 The Raisins now in clusters dryed be,
SEASONS52:11 H226 I must be short, and short's, the shortned day,
MASSYR54:33 H60 *Pharmus, {Thermus}* their King, he caused to be slain;
MASSYR55:11 H77 Adjudged to be drown'd, for what {th' crime} she'd done;
MASSYR55:27 H93 Till her ambition, caus'd him to be slaine:
MASSYR57:13 H160 But is suppos'd to be that *Amraphel,*
MASSYR57:17 ~~H164~~ How he thus suddenly should be thus small?

MASSYR57:36 H181 It is enough {may suffice}, if all be true that's past,
MASSYR58:16 H201 *Arbaces* him, fully to be repaid.
MASSYR58:24 ~~H207~~ *Arbaces* must be master of their lands.
MASSYR59:26 H250 Their strong wall'd town should suddenly be taken;
MASSYR60:17 H282 Not so content, but aiming to be great,
MASSYR60:37 H302 Who to be rid of such a guest, was glad;
MASSYR60:40 H305 That he, and *Belochus,* one could not be,
MASSYR66:26 H532 Although the Furnace be seven times more hot;
MPERS70:21 H692 Had after {A} thousand yeares faire to be seen.
MPERS70:23 H694 An Edict makes {made}, the Temple builded be,
MPERS70:38 H709 But in this {his} Tombe was only to be found
MPERS71:25 H739 But {For} he would be profest god of their Weal;
MPERS71:30 H744 But scorning thus by *Jove* to be out-brav'd,
MPERS~~72:3~~ H755 Unjustly caus'd his brother to be slain.
MPERS72:30 H774 'T would be no pleasant {pleasure}, but a tedious thing,
MPERS73:35 H820 And thought the people, would more happy be,
MPERS74:2 H827 That {Out} of the seven a Monarch chosen be;
MPERS78:38 H1019 One of his five Sons there, might be releast;
MPERS78:39 H1020 To be to's age a comfort, and a stay,
MPERS81:12 H1120 And that with *Xerxes* they would be at one,
MPERS81:13 H1121 So should all favour to their State be shown.
MPERS81:26 H1134 Nor could the brave Ambassador be {he} sent,
MPERS83:15 H1203 That from suspition he might be freed,
MPERS83:17 H1205 To be the Authour of the deed {crime} was done,
MPERS83:40 H1228 To be partakers in {of} these festivalls.
MPERS85:11 H1287 To be by *Hester,* {fair Queen Ester} to her husband brought.
MPERS85:23 H1299 Before to quietnesse things could be brought,
MPERS86:17 H1333 His brothers little love, like to be gone,
MPERS87:6 H1362 To be the Author of conspiracy.
MPERS87:11 H1367 And others to be warm'd by this new sun,
MPERS87:22 ~~H1374~~ Not worthy to be known, but for his shame:
MPERS88:13 H1406 And all good discipline to be neglected.
MPERS89:15 ~~H1449~~ That their return be stopt, he judg'd was best,
MPERS90:35 H1502 That *Tyssapherne* must be Vice-roy no more;
MPERS91:4 H1512 With suit, their force, {Arms} against his {their} foes be bent;
MPERS~~91:30~~ H1544 His life may read in *Plutarch* to be seen.
MPERS~~91:39~~ H1553 Of brethren and of kindred to be slain.
MPERS92:7 ~~H1565~~ It may be thought, surely he had no Son,
MPERS~~92:30~~ H1588 Yet in these {such} differences, we may behold; {be bold,}
MGREC93:24 H1621 His rule to *Greece,* he scorn'd should be confin'd:
MGREC94:7 H1641 That no combustion {rebellion in} in his absence be,
MGREC94:32 H1670 That he be tane alive, (for he intends)
MGREC95:32 H1711 Though some there be, and that {(perhaps)} more likely, write;
MGREC97:9 H1770 If *Curtius* be true, in his report.
MGREC99:23 H1866 (For 'twas decreed, that Empire should be shaken)
MGREC99:31 H1874 Though in an enemy it should be found;
MGREC100:6 H1890 For to be call'd {install'd} a god, was his intent;
MGREC101:12 H1937 With thirty thousand Tallents, to be paid
MGREC101:14 H1939 And till all this be wel perform'd, and sure,
MGREC101:33 H1958 The Sun should witnesse of his valour be:
MGREC104:10 H2062 Then with so few, how likely to be crost.

MGREC105:33	H2126	Which made their long restraint, seeme to be none;
MGREC105:35	H2128	Might be subjected to his royall hand;
MGREC105:36	H2129	And that his rule as farre extended be,
MGREC107:8	H2183	Now that his Hoast from luggage might be free,
MGREC107:9	H2184	And no man with his burden, burdened be,
MGREC108:12	H2228	From bondage, long to be infranchised;
MGREC110:24	H2328	Could by no means be further {farther} drawn, or led:
MGREC110:26	H2330	Be had in everlasting memory,
MGREC110:32	H2336	Which might be found, and so for {great} wonders kept:
MGREC112:2	H2388	That by this match he might be yet more neare.
MGREC113:16	H2443	They knew not; wherefore, best now to be done,
MGREC114:12	~~H2480~~	But instantly commands him to be slaine;
MGREC114:21	H2491	In his esteem, a God he could not be,
MGREC114:30	H2500	Which shall not be obliterate by time,
MGREC114:39	H2509	All this he did, who knows not to be true,
MGREC115:34	H2553	So to be caught, *Antipater's* too wise,
MGREC115:37	H2556	Nor by his baits could be ensnared so:
MGREC116:12	H2578	And Conquests be talkt of, whilst there is Land;
MGREC116:20	H2586	Might to the last (when sober) be discern'd.
MGREC116:36	H2602	There was {were} no worlds, more, to be conquered:
MGREC116:39	H2605	He would have found enough for {there} to be done,
MGREC117:25	H2632	Now Court, and Camp, all in confusion be,
MGREC117:32	H2639	Was neare her time to be delivered;
MGREC117:38	H2645	Claim'd not, perhaps her Sex might hindrance be.
MGREC118:4	H2651	And th' unborn babe of *Roxan* be proclaim'd;
MGREC118:10	H2657	Hoping to be elect more generally;
MGREC118:20	H2667	Might be esteemed for a Deity;
MGREC118:25	H2674	On which, no signe of poyson could be {in his intrails} found,
MGREC118:27	H2676	*Perdicas,* seeing *Aridæus* must be King,
MGREC120:8	H2743	Their friendship may {might} the more be strengthened:
MGREC120:10	H2745	In *Asia* they all asunder be.
MGREC120:16	H2751	Was to give way, himself might be undone;
MGREC120:18	H2753	That by his help, the rest might low be brought:
MGREC122:9	H2834	For all that should be said, let this suffice,
MGREC122:29	H2848	He wearied out, at last, would needs be gone,
MGREC122:40	H2861	All to be order'd there as he thought best:
MGREC123:31	H2895	And to be great {chief} himselfe now bends his aymes;
MGREC~~124:10~~	H2917	That no supply by these here might be lent,
MGREC124:38	H2945	Did make him vow her servant to be seen.
MGREC126:26	H3017	Desiring Justice might be done for guilt;
MGREC129:1	H3115	Who then shall {should} be installed in the throne:
MGREC129:6	H3120	That in few years he must be forc'd or glad
MGREC130:13	H3168	Resolves at last the Princesse should be slain,
MGREC131:8	H3198	'Twould be an endlesse story to relate
MGREC132:8	H3243	And so falls out to be extinct in one,
MGREC132:10	H3245	His seed to be extirpt, was destined,
MGREC132:14	H3249	Yet be aveng'd, must th' blood of *Jesreel.*
MGREC135:5	H3377	But some disgrace, in triumph to be led.
MGREC136:12	H3426	*This fourth to th' other three, now might be brought.*
DIALOG141:27	H26	Then weigh our case, if't be not justly sad,
DIALOG142:16	H45	Must *Edward* be depos'd, or is't the houre

DIALOG142:17	H46	That second *Richard* must be clapt i'th' Tower?
DIALOG142:32	H61	Such is her poverty, yet shall be found
DIALOG144:15	H125	These be the *Hydra's* of my stout transgression;
DIALOG144:16	H126	These be the bitter fountains, heads, and roots,
DIALOG145:4	H153	Nor sip I of that cup, and just 't may be,
DIALOG145:35	H184	This must be done by Gospel, not by law.
DIALOG146:11	H199	But these may be beginnings of more woe,
DIALOG~~146:12~~	H200	Who knows, the worst, the best {this} may {be my} overthrow;
DIALOG~~146:32~~	H219	Out of your troubles much good fruit to be;
DIALOG146:35	~~H221~~	That Right may have its right, though't be with blood;
DIALOG146:38	H224	Blest be the Nobles of thy Noble Land,
DIALOG146:40	H226	Blest be thy Commons, who for Common good,
DIALOG147:2	H228	Blest be thy Counties which do {who did} aid thee still
DIALOG147:4	H230	Blest be thy Preachers, who do chear thee on,
DIALOG147:9	H235	If mindlesse of thy state I e'r be found.
DIALOG147:22	~~H247~~	Let Gaoles be fill'd with th' remnant of that pack,
DIALOG148:9	H274	And let her spoils, full pay, with int'rest be,
DIALOG148:11	H276	Of all the woes thou canst let her be sped,
DIALOG148:29	H294	No Canaanite shall then be found ith' land,
SIDNEY149:12	H11	Of Armes, and Arts, thou {he} should'st a patterne be.
SIDNEY150:16	~~H49~~	To be saluted by a silly Crow;
SIDNEY151:2	~~H69~~	If such Stars as these, sad presages be,
SIDNEY151:13	~~H69~~	To be within the bounds of one world kept,
SIDNEY151:35	~~H75~~	He left that charge by *Phoebus* to be man'd:
SIDNEY152:12	H81	I to be eas'd of such a task was glad.
DUBART153:14	H18	They shall be consecrated in my Verse,
DUBART154:15	H60	Thy fame is spread as farre, I dare be bold,
QELIZ156:36	H63	Her selfe *Minerva,* caus'd them so to be;
QELIZ157:20	H88	Of her what worth in Story's to be seen,
QELIZ157:26	H94	She was a Phoenix Queen, so shall she be,
QELIZ158:20	H129	*In every one, be her great glory famed.*
DAVID158:28	H8	In *Gath,* let not this thing {things} be spoken on,
VANITY159:34	H6	What is't in honour, to be set on high?
VANITY160:13	H23	Sure if on earth, it must be in those parts;
VANITY160:17	H27	He knows not all, that here is to be known,
VANITY160:31	H41	With pearl and gold it shall not valued be:
TDUDLEY165:25	H27	While others tell his worth, I'le not be dumb:
TDUDLEY165:35	H37	My Fathers God, be God of me and mine.
TDUDLEY166:9	H51	Their greatness may be judg'd by what they shew.
TDUDLEY166:15	H57	He might be cloath'd upon, for evermore.
TDUDLEY166:28	H70	Forgotten never be his memory,
TDUDLEY166:33	H75	And parted more by death shal never be.
CONTEM169:6	H48	How full of glory then must thy Creator be?
CONTEM169:8	H50	Admir'd, ador'd for ever, be that Majesty.
CONTEM169:34	H72	Sometimes in *Eden* fair, he seems to be,
CONTEM170:11	H84	And how she lost her bliss, to be more wise,
FLESH175:38	H38	*Spir.* Be still thou unregenerate part,
FLESH176:4	H44	Sisters we are, yea twins we be,
FLESH176:22	H62	My greatest honour it shall be
FLESH176:25	H65	When thou my Captive shalt be led,
FLESH176:37	H77	With which inriched I would be:

FLESH177:20 H101 For there shall be no darksome night.
FLESH177:22 H103 For evermore they shall be free,
FLESH177:24 H105 But beauty shall be bright and clear;
FLESH177:26 H107 For things unclean there shall not be:
SICKNES178:23 H6 this cannot be revok'd.
SICKNES179:2 H22 I doing good may be.
BIRTH179:34 H10 How soon't may be thy Lot to lose thy friend,
BIRTH180:8 H18 Let be interr'd in my oblivious grave;
BIRTH180:13 H23 And when thy loss shall be repaid with gains
1LETTER181:5 H3 If two be one, as surely thou and I,
1LETTER181:8 H6 If but a neck, soon should we be together:
2LETTER181:31 H1 *Phoebus* make haste, the day's too long, be gone,
VERSES184:7 H11 Where nothing's to be had Kings loose their right
CHILDRN185:20 H46 And be surpriz'd for want of watch,
CHILDRN185:26 H52 The net be spread, and caught, alas.
CHILDRN185:27 H53 Or least by Lime-twigs they be foyl'd,
CHILDRN185:28 H54 Or by some greedy hawks be spoyl'd.
CHILDRN186:20 H87 That did what could be done for young,
ELIZB187:9 H17 But plants new set to be eradicate,
1SIMON188:8 H9 With dreadful awe before him let's be mute,
MERCY189:1 H22 Thou being gone, she longer could not be,
MERCY189:12 H33 The Heavens vouchsafe she may so ever be.
MERCY189:15 H36 What though, thy strokes full sad & grievous be,
2SIMON195:13 Hp271 they will be better pris'd by you, for the Authors sake. the lord
MEDDM196:18 Hp273 shadowes of his euening to be stretched out, lifts vp his head
MEDDM197:11 Hp274 If we had no winter the spring would not be so pleasant, if we
MEDDM197:12 Hp274 times tast of adversity, prosperity would not be so welcome
MEDDM197:22 Hp275 Few men are so humble, as not to be proud of their abilitys,
MEDDM198:9 Hp276 He that walks among briars and thorns will be very carefull,
MEDDM198:19 Hp276 the hook till it be to late.
MEDDM198:21 Hp276 is no new thing vnder ye Sun there is nothing that can be sayd
MEDDM198:34 Hp277 shall rather choose to be buried vnder rocks and mountains
MEDDM199:11 Hp277 Iron till it be throughly heat is vncapable to be wrought, so god
MEDDM200:6 Hp279 children are hardly weaned although the teat be rub'd w^th^
MEDDM200:27 Hp279 they lost in the Autumn so shall it be at that great day after
MEDDM201:4 Hp280 go vpright vnder them, but it matters not whether the load be
MEDDM201:8 Hp280 I haue seen an end of all Sinning, what he did say, may be
MEDDM201:9 Hp280 by many, but what he did not say, cannot (truly) be vttered
MEDDM201:12 Hp280 hath its force abated by water not by wind, and anger must be
MEDDM201:27 Hp281 should be the precepts of the wise masters of assemblys to
MEDDM202:13 Hp282 among the dead, and no other reason can be giuen of all this
MEDDM202:16 Hp282 The treasures of this world may well be compared to huskes,
MEDDM202:18 Hp282 but cannot fill their bellys, they may be choaked by them,
MEDDM202:19 Hp282 but cannot be satisfied wth them.
MEDDM202:27 Hp282 set and be quite gone out of sight then must we needs walk in
MEDDM202:36 Hp282 it self, and sees an impossibility, euer to be filled, but by him,
MEDDM203:11 Hp283 prouision, be all convenient and comfortable for him yet he
MEDDM203:17 Hp283 sees land we must therfore be heer as strangers and pilgrims,
MEDDM203:21 Hp283 He that neuer felt, what it was to be sick or wounded, doth not
MEDDM204:14 Hp284 shame euer goe together He that would be freed from the last,
MEDDM204:15 Hp284 must be sure to shun the company of the first.

MEDDM204:26 Hp285 He that would be content, wth a mean condition, must not cast
MEDDM204:34 Hp285 land askes much more paines, then some other doth to be
MEDDM204:35 Hp285 into tilth yet all must be ploughed and harrowed Some children
MEDDM205:6 Hp285 instruction and exhortation be sown, in the spring of their
MEDDM205:7 Hp285 plentifull crop may be expected in the haruest of their yeares.
MEDDM205:9 Hp286 man is called the little world so his heart may be cal'd the little
MEDDM205:19 Hp286 boldnes to go to the throne of grace to be accepted there,
MEDDM205:20 Hp286 must be sure to carry a certificate from the Court of
MEDDM205:25 Hp286 allseeing eye will be a bridle to restrain from evill, and a spur,
MEDDM206:14 Hp287 and obscure, yet all receiue their luster (be it more or lesse)
MEDDM206:17 Hp287 shall they be, when they are fixt in their heauenly spheres
MEDDM206:31 Hp288 Souerainty of god, who will not be tyed to time nor place, nor
MEDDM206:35 Hp288 may also be a support to such as haue or had wicked parents,
MEDDM207:6 Hp288 giuen for, as health wealth and honour, wch might be so many
MEDDM207:9 Hp288 lords we will come no more at thee If outward blessings, be not
MEDDM207:13 Hp288 All the Comforts of this Life, may be compared to the gourd of
MEDDM207:21 Hp289 men are truly sayd to be tenants at will, and it may as truly be
MEDDM207:29 Hp289 may be sure of an euer lasting habitation that fades not away.
MEDDM208:3 Hp289 these things must be what manner of persons ought we to be,
MEDDM208:8 Hp290 of time (if there be no inter course) will coole the affectiones
MEDDM208:9 Hp290 friends, though there should be no displeasence betweene
MEDDM208:14 Hp290 Commends vs to god, for by his ballance we must be weighed,
MEDDM208:15 Hp290 Judgment we must be tryed and as he passes the sentence, so
MEDDM208:19 Hp290 be compared to deceitfull friends who speak faire and promise
MEDDM208:29 Hp290 (almost) possible to be done, it can remoue mountaines (if
MEDDM209:20 Hp291 so there may be a mutuall commerce through ye world As it is
MEDDM209:23 Hp291 be neuer so large, yet he stands in need of something w^{ch}
PILGRIM210:23 H23 Oh how I long to be at rest
PILGRIM210:29 H29 Wth cares and fears ner' cumbred be
PILGRIM210:33 H33 And when a few yeares shall be gone
PILGRIM210:34 H34 this mortall shall be cloth'd vpon
MYCHILD215:21 Hp240 last is the best, let it be best pleasing to yov.
MYCHILD215:27 Hp240 Trouble, & I could not be at rest 'till by prayer I had confest
MYCHILD216:19 Hp241 Christ be formed in yov.
MED223:6 Hp250 I thy child, yee shall be my Sons and Daughters saith ye Lord
HOUSE236:30 H22 Far be it y^{t} I should repine,
HOUSE237:5 H35 No pleasant tale shall 'ere be told

BE'T (1) [be it]
DIALOG145:30 H179 And to their *Laud* be't spoke, they held i'th' Tower,

BEACH (1)
CHILDRN184:33 H22 Along the Beach among the treen,

BEAGLE (1)
ELEMEN10:9 H84 The Ram, the Bull, the Lyon, and the Beagle;

BEAK (1)
SEASONS48:8 H61 With wings, and beak, defends them from the gleads.

BEAMING (1)
DUBART153:6 H10 Reflection from their beaming altitude,

BEAMS (4) [pl.]
SEASONS~~47:32~~ H47 And with his warmer beams glanceth from thence
CONTEM168:16 H24 Whose beams was shaded by the leavie Tree,
2LETTER182:24 H30 Restrain'd the beams of thy beloved shine,

2LETTER182:29 H35 Nought but the fervor of his ardent beams

BEAR (3) n.
ELEMEN10:10 H85 The Bear, the Goate, the Raven, and the Eagle,
ELEMEN14:40 H282 Thy Bear, thy Tyger, and thy Lyon stout,
MGREC135:34 H3406 But yet this Lion, Bear, this Leopard, Ram,

BEAR (13) v.
ELEMEN10:12 H87 The Hidra, Dolphin, Boys, that waters {water} bear.
ELEMEN16:35 H358 O're childehood, and {ore} Winter, I bear the sway;
HUMOUR29:20 H371 Thy fiery spirit shal bear away this prize,
HUMOUR32:19 H493 To bear {with} the injurious taunts of three;
AGES41:34 H253 To bear me out i'th' world, and feed the poor,
SEASONS50:9 H143 The groaning Carts to bear away this prise,
SEASONS~~50:32~~ H166 Hath stil ascended up in {to bear} goodly Fruits,
MPERS84:32 H1268 And to his Country-men {native land} could bear no hate.
MPERS~~90:39~~ H1506 Whom the old Queen did bear a mortal hate.
MGREC113:9 H2436 Or flesh, or {and} life, could bear, till both were spent
MGREC113:21 H2448 Nor could his Captaines bear so great regard;
CONTEM169:19 H59 The black clad Cricket, bear a second part,
MERCY188:33 H19 And in thy griefs still bear a second part:

BEARE (1) n. See also BEAR n.
MEDDM204:4 Hp284 the paw of the Beare will deliuer mee from this vncircumscised

BEARE (6) v. See also BEAR v.
HUMOUR32:2 H476 Although she beare the greatest obloquie.
MGREC117:27 H2634 Each Captain wisht this prize to beare away,
MGREC117:36 H2643 Had hope themselves, to beare the Crown away;
MGREC123:17 H2881 Too young {rash} to beare that charge, if on him lay'd;
MGREC135:28 H3400 The first a Lion, second was a Beare,
DIALOG144:26 ~~H135~~ Their reverent cheeks, did beare the glorious markes

BEAREING (1) [bearing]
MEDDM206:25 Hp287 empty beareing the reproch of his pride and folly.

BEARERS (1) [pl.]
MGREC116:5 H2565 Sons of *Antipater,* {and} bearers of his Cup,

BEARES (4) v. [bears]
MPERS75:29 H886 Out of his owne revenues beares the charge;
MGREC135:19 H3391 Their Crownes, their Titles, riches beares by force.
MEDDM196:2 Hp272 A ship that beares much saile & little or no ballast, is easily
MEDDM204:28 Hp285 that is lower then he is and if he se, that such a one beares

BEARING (2) See also BEAREING
AGES37:8 H70 To shew her bearing pangs {pains}, I should do wrong,
SEASONS50:6 H140 Bearing the burning heat of the long day;

BEARS (1) v. See also BEARES
MGREC115:20 H2539 The Queen *Olimpias,* bears him deadly hate,

BEAR'ST (1) [bearest]
ELEMEN14:35 H277 Thou bear'st no {nor} grasse, nor {or} plant, nor tree, nor

BEAST (12)
ELEMEN9:36 H70 Both man and beast, rejoyce at his approach,
ELEMEN~~9:40~~ H74 Yet men and beasts, {beast} Astronomers can tell,
ELEMEN11:28 H148 I am th' originall of man and beast,
ELEMEN14:13 H255 Thus I occasion death to man and beast,
ELEMEN16:27 H350 The wary Merchant, on his weary beast
AGES42:30 H286 My weary beast, rest from his toile can find;

SEASONS~~47:39~~ H51 growes long, the tender Lambs {hungry beast} to nourish;
MASSYR58:10 H195 Longer to serve this Metamorphos'd beast;
MASSYR64:8 H432 Was turned {changed} from a King, unto {into} a Beast;
MASSYR66:33 H539 The time expir'd, remains a Beast no more,
MGREC135:31 H3403 Whose Iron teeth devoured every beast;
DIALOG148:13 H278 Bring forth the beast that rul'd the world with's beck,

BEASTLY (1)
AGES39:39 H182 My valour, in some beastly quarrel's spent;

BEASTS (12) [pl.]
ELEMEN9:40 H74 Yet men and beasts, {beast} Astronomers can tell,
ELEMEN15:5 H287 The Woolves and savage Beasts, forsake their Dens.
ELEMEN15:31 H313 Thy silence of thy beasts, doth cause the same.
ELEMEN19:5 H450 Earths Beasts, and Waters Fish, scarce can compare.
HUMOUR23:35 H145 Then a dead Lyon? by beasts triumpht ore.
HUMOUR30:8 H400 Then all the huge beasts of the fertile field.
MASSYR53:22 H12 Both Beasts and Men subjected to his spoyls.
MASSYR64:4 H428 Under whose shadow, birds, and beasts, had birth;
MPERS78:7 H988 His Camels, beasts, for carriage numberlesse,
MGREC105:2 H2095 Yea, wounds the beasts (that drew him) unto death,
VANITY159:35 H7 No, they like beasts, and sonnes of men shall die,
MEDDM202:9 Hp281 like beasts then men, some pious saints, some incarnate

BEAT (3)
HUMOUR29:9 H362 To spare our selves, and beat the whistling winde.
MGREC95:1 H1680 And beat the coward *Persians* from the top,
PILGRIM210:8 H8 Nor stormy raines, on him shall beat

BEATEN (3)
HUMOUR22:9 H78 But be she beaten, she'l not run away,
MPERS80:27 H1094 Twice beaten thus by {at} Sea, he warr'd no more:
MGREC~~124:13~~ H2920 But had the worst {beaten was} at Sea, as well as {and foil'd

BEATEOUS (1) [beauteous] See also BEAUTIOUS
HUMOUR33:5 H519 Rather then loose, one beateous *Hellena;*

BEATS (1)
MEDDM199:12 Hp277 some men into the furnace of affliction and then beats them

BEAUTEOUS (7) See also BEATEOUS, BEAUTIOUS
AGES39:4 H147 My goodly cloathing, and my beauteous skin,
SEASONS50:29 H163 {Summer seems but} short, the beauteous Autumne hastes,
MGREC100:31 H1915 About this time, *Darius* beauteous Queen,
MGREC131:33 H3225 But willingly resign'd the beauteous dame:
DIALOG142:36 H65 My beauteous Body at this present maime;
DAVID159:13 H28 O *Israels* Dames, o're-flow your beauteous eyes,
DAVID159:18 H33 Which made you yet more beauteous to behold.

BEAUTIE (1) [beauty] See also BEAVTY
MGREC129:10 H3124 This *Roxane* for her beautie all commend,

BEAUTIES (1) [pl.]
MGREC97:16 H1777 For though their beauties were unparalled

BEAUTIFIES (2)
HUMOUR27:35 H306 One touch thereof so beautifies the skin;
VANITY160:39 H49 And truly beautifies without deceit.

BEAUTIFULL (1)
MROMAN138:17 H3507 Much stronger, and more beautifull withall;

BEAUTIOUS (4) [beauteous] See also BEATEOUS
ELEMEN17:29 H393 And to this day, impaires her beautious face.
MASSYR55:13 H79 Her beautious face (they feign) retaining still.
MPERS82:24 H1171 The chaste, and beautious Dame, refuses still.
MGREC95:38 H1717 His mother old, {his} beautious wife, {Queen} and daughters,

BEAUTY (11) See also BEAUTIE, BEAVTY
PROLOG7:2 H17 Nor perfect beauty, where's a maine defect,
SIDNEY151:5 ~~H69~~ And as thy beauty, so thy name would wast,
SIDNEY152:27 H96 *Learning, valour, beauty {Wisdome}, all in vertuous youth:*
DAVID158:25 H5 Illustrious *Saul,* whose beauty did excell
VANITY160:8 H18 What is't in beauty? no, that's but a snare,
VANITY160:22 H32 If not in honour, beauty, age, nor treasure,
CONTEM168:2 H12 Whose power and beauty by his works we know.
CONTEM168:37 H43 Hail Creature, full of sweetness, beauty & delight.
CONTEM171:35 H136 Because their beauty and their strength last longer
FLESH177:24 H105 But beauty shall be bright and clear;
MEDDM202:10 Hp281 exceeding beauty full, and some extreamly deformed some so

BEAVTY (1) [beauty] See also BEAUTIE
MEDDM200:26 Hp279 resume their former vigor and beavty in a more ample manner

BECAME (2)
MGREC135:27 H3399 Became like chaffe upon the threshing-floor;
MEDDM209:10 Hp291 what was y^{c} Issue, they became a snare vnto them, pricks in

BECAUSE (28)
ELEMEN11:17 H137 And then, because no matter more for fire:
ELEMEN14:1 H243 Because in the abysse of my darke wombe:
HUMOUR21:41 H69 She loves her sword, only because its gilt;
HUMOUR24:40 H189 Thou sayst I love my sword, because tis {it's} guilt. {gilt,}
HUMOUR31:34 H467 Flegm's patient, because her nature's tame:
HUMOUR33:17 H531 No debtor I, because 'tis {it's} paid else where;
SEASONS49:10 H101 reason why {Though he decline}, because his flames so faire,
MPERS73:4 H791 And more, because he dyed issulesse.
MPERS~~77:16~~ H957 Because this was, first born of *Cyrus* race.)
MPERS~~79:13~~ H1039 Because they wanted skill the same to've staid.
MPERS91:36 ~~H1550~~ Was it because the *Grecians* now at war,
MGREC~~100:36~~ H1920 The more because not set at liberty;
MGREC105:26 H2119 If not, because *Darius* thus did pray,
MGREC112:21 H2407 Accus'd, because he did not certifie
MGREC113:27 H2454 Thinking {Fearing} no harme, because he none did owe {doe},
MGREC115:11 H2520 Because he let {He suffer, his friend} *Ephestion* to dye.
MGREC118:6 H2653 Because his Master gave to him his Ring,
MGREC127:23 H3053 Because he never would let go {forgoe} his trust:
DIALOG144:11 H121 Because of Royall Stem, that was thy crime;
DIALOG146:20 H206 Because he knows not, who shall inn his crop:
SIDNEY152:15 ~~H85~~ Not because, sweet *Sydney's* fame was not dear,
CONTEM171:35 H136 Because their beauty and their strength last longer
CONTEM172:1 H138 Because they're bigger, & their bodyes stronger?
SICKNES179:4 H24 because it's thy decree;
MERCY189:2 H23 Because her Soul she'd sent along with thee.
2SIMON195:11 Hp271 others conceptions because I would leaue you nothing but
MEDDM197:8 Hp274 better, is because they haue more sence then faith they se
JULY223:22 Hp251 it took me, and so mvch the sorer it was to me because my

BECAVSE (1) [because]
MYCHILD217:13 Hp242 him, becavse I have fovnd my heart through his goodnes
BECK (1)
DIALOG148:13 H278 Bring forth the beast that rul'd the world with's beck,
BE-CLOUDED (1)
MGREC116:16 H2582 And so with black, be-clouded all his fame.
BECLOUDED (2)
DIALOG~~146:34~~ H221 Though now beclouded all with tears and blood:
FEVER220:30 H10 Beclouded was my Soul wth fear
BECOME (1)
MEDDM208:32 Hp290 the water become firme footing, for peter to walk on, nay more
BECOMES (1)
CONTEM174:16 H215 And now becomes great Master of the seas;
BECOMMING (2) [becoming]
MASSYR59:40 H264 *Arbaces* thus, of all becomming Lord,
MGREC106:28 H2162 No ways becomming such a mighty King;
BED (19)
ELEMEN~~11:1~~ H121 That *Phaenix* from her Bed, is risen New.
ELEMEN11:9 H129 Foolish *Caligula,* creep under's bed
AGES41:7 H227 That yet my bed in darknesse is not made,
AGES44:16 H349 It's not my goodly house {state}, nor bed of down,
MASSYR55:16 H82 But all agree, that from no lawfull bed;
MPERS70:34 H705 But *Zenophon* reports, he dy'd in's bed,
MPERS74:23 H846 Two of his Neeces takes to nuptiall bed;
MPERS83:12 H1200 Which wretch, {Who} him privately smother'd in's bed,
MGREC~~101:34~~ H1959 And careless in his bed, next morne he lyes,
MGREC132:9 H3244 Yea {And} though *Cassander* died in his bed,
QELIZ158:8 H117 *Here sleeps THE Queen, this is the royall bed.*
CONTEM167:26 H3 When *Phœbus* wanted but one hour to bed,
CONTEM173:23 H189 Thy bed a bough, thy drink the water cleer,
DISTEMP179:16 H4 In tossing slumbers on my wakeful bed,
MEDDM195:36 Hp272 vanity and lyes must needs lye down in the Bed of sorrow.
MEDDM207:35 Hp289 eyes, by beholding their bed, the morning may mind them of
PILGRIM210:32 H32 it is the bed Christ did perfume
MYCHILD215:12 Hp240 latest, + being ignorant whether on my death bed I shall haue
MYCHILD215:32 Hp241 In a long fitt of sicknes wch I had on my bed I often comvned
BEDEW'D (1) [bedewed]
AGES36:6 H30 Seemed to grow on's head (bedew'd with showers:)
BEDEWS (1)
DIALOG142:11 H40 With *English* blood bedews thy conquered Land?
BEDLAM (1)
AGES41:4 H224 That oft for it, in *Bedlam* I remain.
BEDRENCHT (1)
DISTEMP179:17 H5 Bedrencht with tears that flow'd from mournful head.
BEDS (5)
MPERS84:2 H1230 With gold and silver beds, most gorgiously.
MGREC102:36 H2006 Those beds of gold, and couches of delight,
MGREC111:6 H2351 These, all he feasts in state, on beds of gold,
MEDDM196:21 Hp273 Downny beds make drosey persons but hard lodging, keeps
MEDDM208:1 Hp289 at whose comeing they shall all rise out of their beds, The

BEE (1) n.
SEASONS48:17 H70 Now swarmes the busie buzzing {witty,} hony Bee.
BEE (54) v. [be]
MEDDM205:3 Hp285 goe often ouer them, before they bee fit soile, to sow the
MYCHILD215:16 Hp240 bee dayly in y^{r} rembrance, (Altho: y^{t} is the least in my aim in
MYCHILD215:22 Hp240 The method I will observe shall bee this—I will begin wth Gods
MYCHILD216:1 Hp241 But as I grew vp to bee about 14. or 15. I fovnd my heart more
MYCHILD217:2 Hp242 mercyes, For if yee bee his yee shall reap the greatest
MYCHILD217:19 Hp243 shall bee well with me. I haue somt. tasted of y^{t} hidden Manna
MYCHILD217:27 Hp243 grovnd me to powder it would bee but Light to me, yea oft
MYCHILD217:29 Hp243 me, it would bee a Heaven And could I haue been in Heaven
MYCHILD218:8 Hp244 If ever this God hath revealed himself it mvst bee in his word,
MYCHILD218:9 Hp244 this mvst bee it or none. Haue I not fovnd y^{t} operation by it
MYCHILD218:14 Hp244 Times, + how ye world came to bee as wee see, Do wee not
MYCHILD218:18 Hp244 that admitt this bee ye true God whom wee worship, and y^{t} bee
MYCHILD218:18 Hp244 admitt this bee ye true God whom wee worship, and y^{t} bee his
MYCHILD218:19 Hp244 yet why may not ye popish Relign. bee ye right, They haue the
MYCHILD218:25 Hp244 so to bee dealt withall.
MYCHILD218:32 Hp244 I haue remēbred the words of Christ that so it must bee, and
MYCHILD218:33 Hp244 it were possible ye very elect should bee deceived. Behold
MYCHILD219:3 Hp245 to ye King Imortall, Eternall invisible, the only wise God, bee
FEVER221:5 H20 What tho: in dust it shall bee lay'd
FEVER221:6 H21 To Glory t' shall bee brovght.
SOREFIT222:1 H20 My life shall dedicated bee
FAINT222:19 H9 But bee in silence layd.
FAINT222:26 H16 O Lord, no longer bee my Dayes
FAINT222:27 H17 Then I may frvitfull bee.
MED223:8 Hp250 vnto my God and your God—But least this should not bee
MED223:16 Hp250 what he hath done for me, and then shall I bee able to praise
MED223:18 Hp250 art pure, and let me bee no more afraid of Death, but even
MED223:19 Hp250 bee dissolved and bee wth thee wch is best of All.
MED223:19 Hp250 bee dissolved and bee wth thee wch is best of All.
JULY223:26 Hp251 Remēbrance, y^{t} it may bee a support to me when I shall haue
JULY223:28 Hp251 that I now hope for, y^{t} so they may bee encourag^{d} to trust in
WHAT224:14 H14 Your selves shall Judges bee;
MYSOUL225:3 H7 Thy body vile it shall bee chang'd,
MYSOUL225:9 H13 Thy teares shall All bee dryed vp
MYSOUL225:11 H15 Thy Sinns shall ne'r bee sumon'd vp
MYSOUL225:24 H28 'Till I dissolved bee.
28AUG225:32 Hp254 but he doth it for my Advantage, and y^{t} I may bee a Gainer
28AUG226:3 Hp254 somt. I haue had, least my heart should bee drawn from him,
28AUG226:7 Hp254 Body, and bee in continuall xpectat^{n} of my change, and let me
28AUG226:10 Hp254 O let me ever see Thee that Art invisible, and I shall not bee
11MAYA226:20 Hp255 ye will of God it should bee thus. Who am I y^{t} I should repine
11MAYA226:23 Hp255 man shall bee a meanes to strenghten my inner-man
30SEPT227:24 Hp257 then thy stroakes shall bee welcome, I haue not been refined
SAMUEL228:19 H20 Thy Will bee done, for that is best
HANNA230:11 H4 Bles't bee thy Name who did'st restore
SON231:20 H32 That ever I may thankfull bee
2HUSB232:14 H15 O help and bee not slack.
2HUSB232:27 H28 Lord bee thov pilott to ye ship

2HUSB233:6	H39	Bee sold away for Novght.
2HUSB233:16	H49	Shall consecrated bee
HOURS234:1	H15	Tho: husband dear bee from me gone
HOURS234:34	H48	Then better shall I bee,
HOUSE237:8	H38	Nor bridegroom's voice ere heard shall bee.
HOUSE237:20	H50	Stands permanent tho: this bee fled.

BEEF (1)

SEASONS52:5	H220	Beef, Brawn, and Pork, are now in great'st {great} request,

BEELZEBUB (1)

DIALOG143:36	H105	From *Beelzebub* himself, such language heare?

BEEN (75) See also BIN

ELEMEN18:39	H443	Some for this cause (of late) have been so bold,
HUMOUR24:7	H156	I have been sparing, what I might have said,
HUMOUR28:34	H346	If time I have transgrest, and been too long,
HUMOUR29:16	~~H368~~	Thy boasted valour stoutly's been repell'd,
AGES~~41:12~~	H231	Thus I have said, and what i've said {been,} you see,
AGES41:16	H235	And now am grown more staid, that {who} have been green,
AGES42:17	H275	{again,} mine age (in all) {mine Age} been worse then hell.
AGES43:10	~~H305~~	Have been curst furtherers of mine intents.
AGES44:2	H335	What you have been, ev'n such have I before,
AGES44:29	H362	In various times of state i've also been.
SEASONS~~46:35~~	H11	She trim'd her locks, which late had frosted been,
SEASONS~~47:5~~	H21	Who for some months have been but starry lights.
SEASONS49:12	H103	Like as an oven, that long time hath been heat.
SEASONS49:21	H112	With robes thereof, Kings have been dignifi'd.
MASSYR53:33	H23	When thus with rule he had been dignified,
MASSYR62:12	H357	Those that from *Ioshua's* time had been Estate {a state},
MASSYR63:25	H410	For fifty years, or more, it had been free,
MPERS71:36	H750	If all his {this} heat, had been for a good {pious} end,
MPERS79:25	H1051	Of so long time, his thoughts had never been.
MPERS88:18	H1411	So had he been, and got the victory,
MGREC96:30	H1750	Had not been spoile, and booty rich enough,
MGREC100:17	H1901	Had *Betis* now been there, but with his Band,
MGREC100:18	H1902	Great *Alexander* had been kept from Land;
MGREC110:6	H2306	On *Tygris* side, here now he had not been;
MGREC121:29	H2811	With greater joy it would have been receiv'd;
MGREC125:17	H2965	Remembring {Calling to mind} what sometime she had been,
MGREC125:37	H2987	Wisht in *Epire* she still had been confin'd;
MGREC126:30	H3021	Whose fury yet unparalleld {scarcely parallel'd} hath been;
MGREC127:20	H3050	When victor oft had {he'd} been, and so might still,
MGREC~~132:20~~	H3263	As Heaven and Earth against him had been set:
MROMAN140:9	H3572	Hath many Ages been upon his knees.
DIALOG145:27	H176	Had they not held law fast, all had been gone,
SIDNEY149:22	H21	As if your nine-fold wit had been compacted;
DUBART155:6	H91	*And Natures Law; had it been revocable,*
DUBART155:7	H92	*To rescue him from death, Art had been able:*
QELIZ156:11	H38	The *Salique* Law had not in force now been,
QELIZ157:39	H107	O {Yea} happy, happy, had those dayes still been,
DAVID159:26	H41	So pleasant hast thou been, deare brother mine:
VANITY160:27	H37	Where lions fierce, nor lions whelps hath {have} been,
CONTEM170:25	H96	But since that time she often hath been cloy'd;

MEDDM196:33 Hp274 wch thousands of enemys wthout hath not been able to take

MEDDM196:34 Hp274 hath been deliuered vp by one traytor wthin, and that man w^{ch}

MEDDM197:1 Hp274 of Sathan without could not hurt, hath, been foild by one

MEDDM197:31 Hp275 till it haue past through the Mill and been ground to powder,

MEDDM198:22 Hp276 but either that or something like it, hath been both done and

MEDDM208:35 Hp290 them as if Moses had been able by the hand of faith, to hold

MYCHILD215:20 Hp240 ye former it had been perhaps better pleasing to yov, but seing

MYCHILD216:23 Hp242 So vsually thvs it hath been wth me that I haue no sooner

MYCHILD216:25 Hp242 comonly hath been vpon my own person, in sicknesse

MYCHILD216:29 Hp242 haue been the times of my greatest Getting and Advantage,

MYCHILD217:3 Hp242 benefitt by it: It hath been no small support to me in times of

MYCHILD217:6 Hp242 circ̄spection in my walking after I haue been afflicted. I haue

MYCHILD217:6 Hp242 walking after I haue been afflicted. I haue been wth God like

MYCHILD217:7 Hp242 child, that no longer then the rod has been on my back

MYCHILD217:8 Hp242 at least in sight) but I haue been apt to forgett him and my Self

MYCHILD217:12 Hp242 my mind wthout it, and I haue been confident it hath been

MYCHILD217:15 Hp243 I haue often been p^{r}plexed y^{t} I haue not fovnd that constant

MYCHILD217:23 Hp243 that felicity that somt. I haue done, But when I haue been

MYCHILD217:25 Hp243 ye Lord, and when I haue been in sicknes + pain, I haue

MYCHILD217:29 Hp243 would bee a Heaven And could I haue been in Heaven without

MYCHILD217:30 Hp243 Love of God, it would haue been a Hell to me for in Truth it is

MYCHILD218:6 Hp243-4 this hath thovsands of Times been svggested to me, yet God

MYCHILD218:11 Hp244 who haue scornd + contemd it, hath it not been p^{r}served thro:

MYCHILD218:15 Hp244 in it fullfilled wch could not haue been so long foretold

MYCHILD218:28 Hp244 some new Troubles I haue had since ye world has been filled

MYCHILD218:29 Hp244 Blasphemy, and Sectaries, and some who hauest been acct^{d}.

MYCHILD218:30 Hp244 Xtians haue been carryed away wth them, that somt: I haue

MED223:1 Hp250 Meditations when my Soul hath been refreshed wth the

30SEPT227:24 Hp257 then thy stroakes shall bee welcome, I haue not been refined

30SEPT227:25 Hp257 furnace of affliction as some haue been, but haue rather been

11MAYB228:25 Hp259 of January 'till May I haue been by fitts very ill & weak. The

HOURS233:24 H7 Thou hetherto hast been my God

REMB236:5 H20 Thy mercyes Lord haue been so great

BEETLE (1)

SIDNEY150:5 H30 Yet, {But} he's a beetle head, that cann't discry

BEFALL (1)

MGREC93:33 H1630 Which honour to his son, now did befall.

BEFALLEN (1)

MYCHILD218:10 Hp244 Invention can work vpon ye Soul, hath no Judgments befallen

BEFALS (1)

MASSYR57:34 H179 And such as care not, what befals their fames,

BEFELL (1)

MGREC122:5 H2828 {To shew} The difficulties {dangers} *Eumenes* befell,

BEFITS (1)

MGREC135:41 H3413 This taske befits not women, like to men:

BEFITTING (1)

HUMOUR23:25 H135 The Princely quality, {qualities} befitting Kings.

BEFORE (88) See also **'FORE**

ELEMEN10:22 H97 Augment his heat, which was too hot before:

ELEMEN11:16 H136 Not before then, shal cease my raging ire,

ELEMEN13:28 H229 The Corne, and Hay, both fall before they'r mowne;

ELEMEN13:29	H230	And buds from fruitfull trees, before they'r {as soon as} blowne:
ELEMEN13:39	H240	Before they know, they are inter'd alive.
ELEMEN19:25	H470	If nought was {were} known, but that before *Algire.*
AGES35:32	H18	Before the Sun hath throughly warm'd {heat} the clime.
AGES36:32	H56	That he was young, before he grew so old.
AGES38:17	H120	But yet let me relate, before I go,
AGES39:20	H163	I cannot lye in trench, {intrench'd} before a Town,
AGES44:2	H335	What you have been, ev'n such have I before,
SEASONS47:21	H37	Now {Do} jump, and play, before their feeding Dams,
SEASONS48:15	H68	All flowers before the {with his} sun-beames now discloses,
SEASONS49:15	H106	She's {Tis} for a time as fervent as before.
SEASONS52:28	H243	The day much longer then it was before,
MASSYR65:7	H472	Before he could accomplish his intent;
MASSYR68:17	H603	*Daniel* in haste, is brought before the King,
MPERS~~72:33~~	H777	{wisht} his short reign long, till {past before} it was done.
MPERS73:1	H788	Which ends before begun, the *Persian* {his home-bred} Warre,
MPERS74:5	H830	And he whose Horse before the rest should neigh,
MPERS74:36	~~H858~~	For twice ten months before the town he lay,
MPERS76:27	H925	But as before, so now with ill successe,
MPERS76:32	H930	*Darius* multitude before them fled;
MPERS77:31	H972	The first deports, {dehorts} and layes before his eyes,
MPERS83:31	H1219	Although to *Xerxes,* they not long before,
MPERS83:32	H1220	A league of amity, had sworn before. {firmly swore,}
MPERS84:36	H1272	To wrong himselfe by death, he chose before:
MPERS85:23	H1299	Before to quietnesse things could be brought,
MPERS85:27	H1303	All Townes, held by his Ancestors before.
MPERS90:4	~~H1478~~	Before them burnt the country as they went,
MPERS92:18	~~H1576~~	If not (as is before) of *Cyrus* race,
MPERS92:27	~~H1585~~	But as before doth (well read) *Raleigh* write,
MGREC93:19	H1616	T'accomplish that, which long before was writ.
MGREC94:34	H1672	That boy so mallepart, before the King.
MGREC96:7	H1727	The Holy fire, was borne before the Host:
MGREC97:28	H1789	*Darius* now, more humble {less lofty} then before,
MGREC98:11	H1813	And now, as *Babels* King did once before,
MGREC98:35	H1837	And layes before great *Alexanders* eyes,
MGREC101:4	H1929	And now for peace he sues, as once before,
MGREC~~101:34~~	H1960	By Captains twice is call'd before hee'l rise,
MGREC~~101:34~~	H1962	And spilt the Greeks some bloud before their flight
MGREC101:35	H1964	So make {made} an end, before they {as soon as} well begun;
MGREC101:39	H1968	But *Quintus Curtius,* as was said before.
MGREC103:31	H2042	And layes before his eyes, if he persist
MGREC104:7	H2059	With sage advice, he layes {sets} before his eyes,
MGREC106:31	H2165	And such as shew'd but reverence before,
MGREC107:11	H2186	Into the Market-place, before the King;
MGREC108:4	H2220	This Malefactor vild, {vile} before the King,
MGREC109:14	H2273	Who comming thither, long before his Lord;
MGREC111:13	H2358	These {Those} obscure Nations yeelded as before;
MGREC115:35	H2554	*Parmenio's* death's too fresh before his eyes;
MGREC116:1	H2561	Before his answer came to *Babylon,*
MGREC117:11	H2618	As *Daniel,* before had Prophesied;
MGREC119:14	H2704	would} Shakes {shake} off the yoke, sometimes before laid on

MGREC128:22 H3095 Before he weare the universall Crown;
MGREC128:34 H3107 Who at *Gaza* did th' like to him before.
MGREC129:20 H3134 *Perdicas* had before, for his amisse,
MGREC132:4 H3237 (Whose daughter unto wife, he'd newly {not long before} ta'n)
MGREC132:18 H3255 Those Countries large, his father got before,
MGREC133:35 H3325 Which we oft wish were {was} extant as before.
MGREC135:35 H3407 All trembling stand, before that powerfull Lambe.
DIALOG143:27 H96 Before I tell the effect, ile shew the cause,
DIALOG148:32 H297 But if at all, thou didst not see't before.
SIDNEY149:23 H22 To shew the world, they never saw before,
DUBART153:3 H7 Gave o're the work, before begun withall:
QELIZ155:25 H16 Mine bleating stands before thy royall Herse:
QELIZ156:34 H61 And {the proud} *Tiron* bound, before her picture fell.
QELIZ158:12 H121 *On neither tree did grow such Rose before,*
CONTEM173:7 H175 And take the trembling prey before it yield,
BIRTH179:26 H1-2 *Before the Birth of one of her Children.*
1SIMON188:8 H9 With dreadful awe before him let's be mute,
MERCY189:5 H26 A Babe she left before, she soar'd above,
MEDDM198:23 Hp276 both done and sayd before—
MEDDM200:13 Hp279 world before it bid them farwell
MEDDM203:17 Hp283 before he sees land we must therfore be heer as strangers and
MEDDM203:24 Hp283 whom he slighted before, so he that neuer felt the sicknes of
MEDDM205:3 Hp285 discipline goe often ouer them, before they bee fit soile, to sow
MEDDM207:34 Hp289 their death, but their graue, is liuely represented before their
MYCHILD216:15 Hp241 to me, and cost me many prayers + tears before I obtaind one,
MYCHILD217:9 Hp242 Before I was afflicted I went astray, but now I keep thy
MYCHILD218:34 Hp244 Sav^{r}. I have told yov before. That hath stayed my heart, and I
FEVER220:33 H13 W^{ch} oft I read before.
30SEPT227:33 Hp257 closely with him then before, This is the desire of y^{r} Loving
SON231:2 H14 That he before them gott to Land.
HOURS233:22 H5 My Troubles All are Thee before
HOURS234:22 H36 As thou before ha'st done
HOURS234:31 H45 And serve thee better then before
REMB236:11 H26 And walk before thee as they ought,

BEG (2)

DIALOG145:39 H188 They humbly beg return, shew their intents,
MEDDM206:21 Hp287 wayes rather, then to beg forgiuenes for their sinnes, nature

BEGAN (14) See also 'GAN

AGES36:38 H62 To hear the child, who crying, thus began.
SEASONS46:35 ~~H11~~ She gently thus began, like some fair Queen;
SEASONS49:3 H94 With haire all wet, she puffing thus began.
SEASONS51:12 H186 Sure at this time, Time first of all began,
MASSYR55:14 H80 Sure from this fiction, *Dagon* first began,
MASSYR68:30 H616 And now the *Persian* Monarchy began.
MPERS~~68:33~~ H619 being the *Persian,* begun {began} under
MPERS76:20 H918 His {This} fruitlesse war, began late to repent;
MGREC93:15 H1612 The twenty first of's age, began to reign.
MGREC117:22 H2629 Each man {All men} began for {streight} to contemn his might;
MGREC118:23 H2670 After this {some} time, when stirs began to calme,
MGREC~~118:28~~ H2677 Under his name begins {began} to rule each thing.
MGREC129:31 H3145 This {Orphan} Prince began for to compassionate.

MYCHILD215:24 Hp240 years about 6. or 7. as I take it I began to make cons^{c}. of

BEGGER (1)
AGES46:8 H439 From King to begger, all degrees shal finde

BEGIN (13) See also **'GIN**
ELEMEN8:27 H25 That Fire should first begin, the rest consent,
SEASONS48:38 H89 When Spring had done, then {the} Summer must {did} begin,
SEASONS51:21 H197 The Northern Winter blasts begin to hisse;
SEASONS~~52:39~~ H256 Where first it did begin, in th' end its found.
MASSYR60:14 H279 Who did this Monarchy begin anew.
MGREC94:11 H1645 Nor wonder is't, if he in blood begin,
MGREC121:2 ~~H2780~~ With *Ptolomy* for to begin was best,
MGREC122:26 ~~H2845~~ Which made her now begin to play her part;
MGREC124:23 H2930 The great ones now begin to shew their minde,
MGREC127:32 H3062 The Princes all begin now to envie
MGREC129:32 H3146 Begin to mutter much 'gainst proud *Cassander,*
CONTEM173:29 H194 And warbling out the old, begin anew,
MYCHILD215:22 Hp240 I will observe shall bee this—I will begin wth Gods dealing

BEGINNING (5)
AGES37:4 H66 Whose mean beginning, blushing cann't reveale,
MASSYR53:13 H3 beginning under *Nimrod,* 131. yeares
MGREC93:7 H1604 {being} the *Grecian,* beginning
MGREC97:13 H1774 Was but beginning of his future woe;
MROMAN136:21 H3435 beginning, *Anno Mundi,*

BEGINNINGS (3) [pl.]
MGREC135:38 H3410 And how from small beginnings it did grow,
DIALOG146:11 H199 But these may be beginnings of more woe,
MYCHILD218:13 Hp244 it? Is there any story but that wch showes the beginnings of

BEGINS (7) See also **'GINS**
AGES45:28 H418 And back, once straight, begins apace to bow.
MASSYR54:16 H43 His father dead, *Ninus* begins his reign,
MPERS71:8 H724 His reign with Bloud, and Incest, first begins,
MGREC102:24 H1994 And former Discipline begins to hate;
MGREC118:28 H2677 Under his name begins {began} to rule each thing.
MGREC122:12 H2837 His rule Queen *Euridice* begins to hate,
MGREC123:20 H2884 And *Ptolomy,* now {next} to encroach begins,

BEGIRT See **BEGYRT**

BEGOT (1)
FLESH176:7 H47 Thou by old Adam wast begot,

BEGUN (17)
PROLOG6:19 H4 Of Cities founded, Common-wealths begun,
AGES35:34 H20 And in his hand an hour-glasse new begun,
MASSYR53:27 H17 And mighty *Ninivie,* he there begun,
MASSYR53:37 H27 Confirmes the rule his Father had begun,
MPERS68:33 H619 being the *Persian,* begun {began} under
MPERS73:1 H788 Which ends before begun, the *Persian* {his home-bred} Warre,
MPERS77:21 H962 The first begun, and finish'd in such hast,
MPERS82:28 H1175 But she was stil, as when it {he} first begun.
MGREC101:35 H1964 So make {made} an end, before they {as soon as} well begun;
MGREC120:15 H2750 To suffer them goe on, as they begun,
MGREC133:37 H3327 Who a long warre with *Egypts* King begun.
MGREC136:10 H3424 *To finish what {what's} begun, new thoughts impart*

MROMAN137:1 H3452 A forme of Government he next begun;
MROMAN139:27 H3553 To finish what's begun, was my intent,
DIALOG142:18 H47 Or is {is't} the fatall jarre againe begun,
SIDNEY151:40 ~~H75~~ *Apollo* laught to patch up what's begun,
DUBART153:3 H7 Gave o're the work, before begun withall:

BEGYRT (1) [begirt]
FEVER220:22 H2 When Sorrowes had begyrt me rovnd,

BEHALFE (1)
ELEMEN12:26 H186 In his behalfe to speak a word the more;

BEHELD (1)
HOUSE236:23 H15 Then coming out beheld a space

BEHEMM'D (1) [behemmed]
MPERS80:3 H1070 They thus behemm'd with multitude of foes,

BEHEMOTH (1)
ELEMEN12:19 H179 The Behemoth, and rare found Unicorne,

BEHIND (5)
MPERS71:1 H713 Three Daughters, and two Sons, he left behind,
MPERS79:9 H1031 A Sea passage cuts, behind *Orthos* {*Athos*} Mount.
MPERS81:6 H1114 Three hundred thousand yet he left behind,
MPERS85:4 H1280 Three sons great *Artaxerxes* left behind;
DIALOG142:25 H54 Or, doth {do} the *Scots* play false behind your back?

BEHOLD (26)
ELEMEN17:31 H395 Her confirm'd sonnes, behold my colour'd bow.
AGES41:6 H226 That wonder 'tis I yet behold the light,
AGES41:21 ~~H239~~ But what's of worth, your eyes shal first behold,
MASSYR64:2 H426 The richest, and the dreadfull'st to behold;
MPERS78:36 H1017 Which mighty sum, all wondred to behold.
MPERS82:35 H1182 He dying to behold, that wounding sight;
MPERS92:30 H1588 Yet in these {such} differences, we may behold; {be bold,}
MGREC96:3 H1723 Oh {Sure} 'twas a goodly sight, there to behold;
MGREC96:12 H1732 With Robes and Crowne, most glorious to behold.
MGREC96:35 H1755 But when both Armies met, he might behold,
MGREC109:24 H2283 But *Alexander,* caus'd {made} him to behold;
MGREC111:7 H2352 His furniture most sumptuous to behold;
MGREC135:21 H3393 Next, armes and breast, of silver to behold;
DAVID159:18 H33 Which made you yet more beauteous to behold.
CONTEM169:3 H45 Hath strength, thy shining Rayes once to behold?
CONTEM171:18 H121 When I behold the heavens as in their prime,
FLESH175:31 H31 Behold enough of precious store.
FLESH177:12 H93 Such as no Eye did e're behold,
2LETTER182:26 H32 Behold a Chaos blacker then the first.
MEDDM198:32 Hp277 It is a pleasant thing to behold the light, but sore eyes are not
MEDDM198:35 Hp277 behold the presence of the lamb
MEDDM202:24 Hp282 a moment that we cannot behold the light of his Countenance,
PILGRIM210:41 H41 Such lasting ioyes, shall there behold
MYCHILD218:33 Hp244 possible ye very elect should bee deceived. Behold saith o^{r}
SON231:18 H30 That I thy Mercyes might behold.
HOUSE237:2 H32 And them behold no more shall I.

BEHOLDEN (1)
MEDDM209:25 Hp291 below, as also that god will haue vs beholden one to another

BEHOLDETH (1)
SEASONS51:39 H215 The Northern Pole beholdeth not one ray.
BEHOLDING (1) [beholden]
HUMOUR33:15 ~~H529~~ Beholding unto me another way.
BEHOLDING (2) [seeing]
DIALOG147:32 H256 That dazzled eyes beholding much shall wonder
MEDDM207:35 Hp289 eyes, by beholding their bed, the morning may mind them of
BEHOUES (1) [behoves]
MEDDM204:11 Hp284 behoues euery man so to improue his talents, that when his
BEHOV'D (1) [behoved]
ELEMEN14:25 H267 Sister (quoth she) it had full well behov'd
BEING (1) n.
MYCHILD218:4 Hp243 resolve me that there is an Eternall Being. But how should I
BEING (46) v.
FATHER5:19 H20 These same are they, of {from} whom we being have,
ELEMEN8:25 H23 The others enmity: {difference,} being lesse, did cease
ELEMEN8:28 ~~H26~~ Being the most impatient Element.
AGES36:27 H51 These being met, each in his equipage,
MASSYR53:12 H2 the *Assyrian* being the first,
MASSYR57:10 H157 It is more like, being {his lust} with pleasures fed,
MASSYR~~57:16~~ H163 But this is farre unlike, he being Son
MASSYR~~63:28~~ H415 Then being Father to so great a Son.
MASSYR65:40 H505 But being caught, to *Babels* wrathful King,
MASSYR66:39 H545 Forty four years he reign'd, which being run,
MPERS68:33 H619 being the *Persian,* begun {began} under
MPERS68:34 H620 *Cyrus, Darius* (being his Vnckle,
MPERS69:35 H657 Then on a Pike being {wood-pile} set, where all might eye,
MPERS76:31 H929 By brave *Miltiades* (their chief) being led,
MPERS78:41 H1022 The Kings cals for the Youth, who being brought,
MPERS84:29 H1265 Provisions, {then} and season now being fit,
MPERS89:4 H1438 Being Victors oft, now to their Camp they came;
MPERS~~91:35~~ H1549 Succeeds in th' throne his father being gone.
MPERS~~91:38~~ H1552 And being king commands those that remain,
MGREC~~93:7~~ H1604 {being} the *Grecian,* beginning
MGREC~~94:18~~ H1655 And being ask'd what for himself was left,
MGREC100:33 H1917 Now bids the world adieu, her time {with pain} being spent,
MGREC103:26 H2037 Being inflam'd with wine upon a season,
MGREC104:36 H2088 His hopes being dasht, prepares himself for flight:
MGREC108:41 H2257 And being an {one} hundred twenty thousand strong,
MGREC112:23 H2409 Upon suspicion being apprehended,
MGREC121:15 ~~H2793~~ Being entreated by him scornfully,
MGREC126:1 H2992 But being stopt, at Straight *Tharmipoley*
MGREC126:28 H3019 For Justice sake she being put to th' sword.
MGREC134:19 H3350 First *Ptolomy* being dead, his famous son,
MROMAN136:20 H3434 being the Fourth, and last,
MROMAN139:19 H3547 With *Junius Brutus* rose, and being strong,
MROMAN139:25 ~~H3551~~ *being the fourth and last.*
SIDNEY150:34 H61 Thus being over-come, he over-came.
SIDNEY152:10 ~~H79~~ In being done by one of their own sex;
CONTEM169:27 H66 And men in being fancy those are dead,
AUTHOR178:2 H12 Yet being mine own, at length affection would

3LETTER183:19 H21 Mine being gone, I lead a joyless life,
ELIZB186:33 H4-5 *being a year and half old.*
ANNEB187:14 H3-4 *Who deceased* June 20. 1669. *being three years and*
1SIMON188:2 H2-3 *Who dyed on* 16. Novemb. 1669. *being but*
MERCY189:1 H22 Thou being gone, she longer could not be,
MEDDM206:4 Hp287 danger of being cut down, as the dry stock, for both cumber
TOCHILD215:4 H4 That being gone, here yov may find
MYCHILD215:12 Hp240 latest, + being ignorant whether on my death bed I shall haue
11MAYB228:27 Hp259 y^{t} ever I had lasting 4 dayes, and ye weather being very hott

BEINGS (1) [pl.]
ELEMEN8:34 H32 The benefit all Beings, {living} by me finde;

BELEAGUERED (1)
MASSYR~~57:25~~ H172 When famous *Troy* was so beleaguered:

BELEEFE (1) [belief]
MASSYR62:27 H372 Hath bred more wonder, then beleefe in hearts;

BELEEV'D (1) [believed] See also BELEIVED, BELIEV'D
MPERS75:7 H868 For they beleev'd his nose, more then his tongue;

BELEIUE (1) [believe] See also BELEIVE
JULY223:31 Hp251 for thov art my God, Thou hast said and shall not I beleiue it?

BELEIVE (1) [believe] See also BELEIUE
MASSYR56:27 H133 (Each man beleive it, as his fancy list)

BELEIVED (1) [believed] See also BELEEV'D, BELIEV'D
MYCHILD219:2 Hp245 beleived and y^{t} he is able to keep y^{t} I haue comitted to his

BELGIA (1)
SIDNEY150:22 H47 Of which, {at} this day, faire *Belgia* doth {may} boast.

BELIEF See beleefe

BELIEV'D (2) [believed] See also BELEEV'D, BELEIVED
DIALOG~~144:25~~ H134 I then believ'd not, now I feel and see,
FLESH176:13 H53 When I believ'd, what thou hast said,

BELIEVE (1) See also BELEIVE
MGREC130:20 H3175 The world must needs believe what he doth tell:

BELIEVED See BELEEV'D, BELEIVED, BELIEV'D

BELIEVING (1)
CONTEM170:12 H85 Believing him that was, and is, Father of lyes.

BELL (4)
MASSYR54:7 H34 This is that *Bell,* the *Chaldees* worshipped,
MASSYR54:9 H36 This is that *Bell,{ Baal}* to whom the *Israelites*
MASSYR56:13 H119 The wondrous Temple was, she rear'd to *Bell;*
CHILDRN185:25 H51 Or whilst allur'd with bell and glass,

BELLEROPHON (1)
ELEMEN10:6 H81 The Horse that kill'd *Bellerophon,* then flew.

BELLIES (1) [pl.] See also BELLYS
AGES42:2 H260 Whose loynes {backs} I've cloth'd, and bellies I have fed;

BELLOWES (1)
ELEMEN18:21 H425 Ye forging Smiths, if Bellowes once were gone;

BELLS (1) [pl.]
DIALOG148:30 H295 And holinesse, on horses bells shall stand,

BELLUS (2)
MASSYR53:35 H25 *Bellus.*
MASSYR53:36 H26 Great *Nimrod* dead, *Bellus* the next, his Son,

BELLY (1)
MGREC135:22 H3394 The third, belly and thighs of brasse in sight,
BELLYS (1) [bellies]
MEDDM202:18 Hp282 their throats, but cannot fill their bellys, they may be choaked
BELOCHUS (3)
MASSYR60:13 H278 But *Belochus* in's progeny pursue,
MASSYR60:15 H280 *Belosus,* or *Belochus.*
MASSYR60:40 H305 That he, and *Belochus,* one could not be,
BELONG (1)
MPERS78:6 H987 Eight hundred thousand Horse to them {these} belong;
BELONGS (1) See also LONGS
SICKNES179:12 H32 the foyle belongs to thee.
BELOSUS (9)
MASSYR58:11 H196 Unto *Belosus,* then he brake his minde,
MASSYR58:15 H200 *Belosus,* promised *Arbaces* aide,
MASSYR58:19 H204 *Belosus* the *Chaldeans* doth require,
MASSYR58:32 H215 But with fresh hopes *Belosus* succoured.
MASSYR60:1 H266 Of *Babylon, Belosus* he made King,
MASSYR60:15 H280 *Belosus,* or *Belochus.*
MASSYR60:16 H281 *Belosus* setled, in his new, old seat,
MASSYR61:9 H314 *Belosus* dead, *Tiglath* his warlike Son
MASSYR63:8 H393 And {As} *Belosus,* first, his {Soveraign} did unthrone,
BELOSUS (2) [poss.]
MASSYR58:23 ~~H207~~ By prophesie, *Belosus* strength's their hands,
MASSYR63:3 H388 The fifth, and last, of great *Belosus* race;
BELOUED (2)
HOURS234:3 H17 I haue a more beloued one
HOURS234:27 H41 And talk to my Beloued one
BELOV'D (1) [beloved]
MGREC113:40 H2467 *Clitus,* belov'd next to *Ephestion,*
BELOVED (4)
MPERS72:27 ~~H773~~ Shot through the heart of his beloved son:
MGREC122:2 H2825 And his beloved foe, full sore laments.
CONTEM172:19 H154 Till thou arrive at thy beloved place,
2LETTER182:24 H30 Restrain'd the beams of thy beloved shine,
BELOW (5)
ELEMEN14:37 H279 With springs below, and showers from above;
CONTEM167:34 H10 If so much excellence abide below;
ANNEB187:22 H12 Was ever stable joy yet found below?
MEDDM209:25 Hp291 below, as also that god will haue vs beholden one to another
MYSOUL225:19 H23 No gain I find in ovght below
BELSHAZZAR (4)
MASSYR67:19 H565 His Kingdome to *Belshazzar* did remain.
MASSYR67:20 H566 *Belshazzar.*
MASSYR67:21 H567 Unworthy *Belshazzar* next weares the Crown,
MPERS70:10 H681 That night *Belshazzar* feasted all his rout,
BELZEBUB (1)
MASSYR54:11 H38 This is *Belzebub,* god of *Ekronites,*
BE-MARS (1)
AGES41:1 H221 the loathsome {two fold} Pox, my face {me sore} be-mars,

BEMOAN (3)
MGREC114:15 H2485 This pot companion he did more bemoan,
VANITY160:16 H26 And he that knows the most doth still bemoan,
3LETTER183:8 H10 (On withered bough) most uncouthly bemoan

BEMOAN'D (1) [bemoaned]
MGREC126:37 H3026 With Garlands crown'd his head, bemoan'd his Fates,

BEMOANE (1)
MPERS72:12 H760 His woful fate with tears did so bemoane,

BEN (2)
MASSYR63:17 H402 *Ben. Merodach.*
MASSYR63:18 H403 *Ben. Merodach,* Successor to this King,

BEND (4)
HUMOUR32:39 H513 The Monarchs bend, and sue, but for my grace;
AGES40:15 H196 To all obscenity, my {mine} eares I bend. {lend;}
MPERS~~81:25~~ H1133 Against the *Persians* they would use {bend} their force.
CHILDRN184:28 H17 *Southward* they both their course did bend,

BENDED (2)
MPERS71:22 H736 Made *Evelthon* their King, with bended knee,
MPERS80:35 H1102 He hearing this, his thoughts, and course home bended,

BENDING (1)
SEASONS~~50:17~~ H151 With Sickles now, the painful {bending} Reapers go,

BENDS (2)
MGREC109:12 H2271 To th' river *Indus* next, his course he bends,
MGREC123:31 H2895 And to be great {chief} himselfe now bends his aymes;

BENEFIT (2) See also BENEFITT
ELEMEN8:34 H32 The benefit all Beings, {living} by me finde;
HUMOUR27:15 H286 Who th' benefit o'th' whole ever intends:

BENEFITS (1) [pl.]
ELEMEN16:31 H354 These be my benefits which may suffice:

BENEFITT (4) [benefit]
MYCHILD216:6 Hp241 me. But I rendered not to him according to ye benefitt rec.
MYCHILD217:3 Hp242 benefitt by it: It hath been no small support to me in times of
MYCHILD219:7 Hp245 & imperfectly done, but if yov can pick any Benefitt out of it, It
28AUG225:31 Hp254 men, he hath no benefitt by my adversity, nor is he ye better

BENIGNIOUS (1) [benignness]
HUMOUR28:26 H338 And like the Liver, all benignious;

BENT (8)
HUMOUR30:41 H433 But that which shewes how high thy spight is bent,
SEASONS49:8 H99 Who to his Southward tropick still is bent,
MPERS91:4 H1512 With suit, their force, {Arms} against his {their} foes be bent;
MPERS91:17 H1525 But let us leave these *Greeks,* to discord bent,
MGREC103:34 H2045 But deafe to reason, (bent to have his will;)
MGREC125:31 H2981 all that lov'd *Cassander* was nigh spent; {she was bent}
MROMAN137:13 H3464 To see these sports, the *Sabins* all are bent;
MROMAN139:28 H3554 My thoughts and my endeavours thereto bent;

BENUMS (1)
ELEMEN14:12 ~~H254~~ In hot, and cold, and some benums with sleeps,

BEOTIAN (1)
MPERS81:36 ~~H1143~~ The *Beotian* Fields, of war, the seats,

BEQUEATH (4)
MGREC~~123:15~~ H2879 To *Polisperchon,* then his place he gave, {did bequeath}

2SIMON195:9 Hp271 Such as they are I bequeath to you, Small legacys are accept[d]
MYCHILD215:15 Hp240 not) and bequeath to yov, that when I am no more wth yov, yet
28AUG226:9 Hp254 lye down & bequeath my Soul to thee and Death seem'd no

BEREAVE (3)
HUMOUR26:30 H260 For of such glory I shal thee bereave;
HUMOUR29:40 H391 Of Learning, and of Policie, thou would'st bereave me,
MGREC95:2 H1681 And twenty thousand, of their lives bereave,

BEREFT (7)
HUMOUR27:40 H311 And of the sweet, calme temper, quite bereft,
MASSYR57:31 H176 In deep oblivion, of acts bereft,
MASSYR59:9 H233 Bereft of wits, were slaughtered down right.
MPERS76:40 H938 Renews his hold; but {and} when of that bereft,
MGREC104:19 H2071 Who was of hopes, and comfort quite bereft;
MGREC117:18 H2625 Like to that Giant, of his eye bereft;
HOUSE236:31 H23 He might of All iustly bereft,

BERNICE (1)
ELEMEN10:11 H86 The Crown, the Whale, the Archer, Bernice Hare,

BEROSUS (2)
MASSYR57:33 H178 Save a few names anew, *Berosus* writ.
MGREC133:31 H3321 To whom Ancient {the old} *Berosus* (so much fam'd)

BESEECH (2)
MASSYR59:3 H227 T' accept of what they could, they him {all} beseech.
HOURS234:23 H37 Bring back my husband I beseech

BESEEM'D (1) [beseemed]
MGREC132:23 H3268 Injoy'd what so {ere} beseem'd his Royalty,

BESEEMING (1)
MGREC106:24 H2158 And not beseeming such a dignity;

BESET (1) See also BESETT
MGREC~~108:30~~ H2246 Besets {Beset} his Camp, or Military Court;

BESETS (1)
MGREC108:30 H2246 Besets {Beset} his Camp, or Military Court;

BESETT (1) [beset]
RESTOR229:21 H4 When feares and sorrowes me besett

BESIDE (6)
MPERS~~77:16~~ H956 (His eldest brother put beside the place,
MGREC95:21 H1700 Then in *Darius* multitudes {multitude} beside:
MGREC99:19 H1862 Then in the *Persian* Monarchy beside;
MGREC101:7 H1932 (Nor was such match, in all the world beside)
MGREC~~124:15~~ H2922 *Athens,* with many Townes in *Greece* besides, {beside}
2LETTER182:8 H14 My Interest's more then all the world beside.

BESIDES (8)
ELEMEN12:35 H195 Besides the use you have {of roots}, of Hearbs and Plants,
HUMOUR27:3 H274 Besides the vehement heat, only there known,
MPERS78:21 H1002 Besides, the Vessels for this transportation,
MGREC97:8 H1769 Besides, the Queens, and Ladies of the Court,
MGREC98:15 H1817 Besides, {Moreover} he had a Navie at command,
MGREC123:36 H2900 Besides, he was the young Queens favourite,
MGREC124:15 H2922 *Athens,* with many Townes in *Greece* besides, {beside}
MEDDM198:4 Hp276 them lye down in green pastures and leades them besides

BESIEG'D (3) [besieged]
MASSYR62:9 H354 Besieg'd his regal town, and spoyl'd his Coast,

MASSYR64:11 H435 *Iudah's* poor King besieg'd, who {and} succourlesse,
MASSYR65:35 H500 Besieg'd his City, Temple, *Zions* Tower;

BESMEAR'D (1) [besmeared]
MPERS82:32 H1179 And leaves her thus, besmear'd with {in} blood, and tears.

BESOUGHT (1)
MPERS79:1 H1023 Cuts him in twain, for whom his Sire besought.

BESOVGHT (2)
MYCHILD216:4 Hp241 When I was in my afflict^{n}. I besovght the Lord, and confessed
ACK235:12 H12 For whom I thee so oft besovght

BESSUS (8)
MPERS93:4 H1601 Him, to the grave, did Traytor *Bessus* send.
MGREC104:5 H2057 But *Bessus* false, who was his cheife Commander;
MGREC104:21 H2073 Straight *Bessus* comes, and with his traiterous hands,
MGREC104:33 H2085 *Bessus* gets knowledge, his disloyalty,
MGREC105:4 H2097 *(Bessus,* his Partner in this Tragedy,
MGREC107:6 H2181 Then {And} hearing, *Bessus* makes himselfe a King,
MGREC107:21 H2196 False *Bessus* to finde out, in *Bactria;*
MGREC107:38 H2213 Had *Bessus* had but valour to his wil,

BEST (61)
FATHER6:11 H45 Accept my best, my worst vouchsafe a grave.
PROLOG7:31 H42 Men can doe best, and Women know it well;
ELEMEN8:6 H4 Which was the strongest, noblest, & the best,
ELEMEN11:11 H131 But to leave those to'th' wise, I judge is {it} best,
ELEMEN14:33 H275 Which {Who} am thy drink, thy blood, thy sap, and best.
HUMOUR21:38 H66 She'l ride a Horse as bravely, as the best,
HUMOUR22:10 H79 She'l first advise, if't be not best to stay.
HUMOUR23:23 H133 As objects best appear, by contraries.
HUMOUR25:6 H195 For drink, which of us twain, like it the best,
HUMOUR25:17 H206 The best of al the four, when they agree.
HUMOUR26:12 H242 For there are {is} none, thou say'st, if some, not best.
HUMOUR26:13 H243 That there are some, and best, I dare averre;
HUMOUR30:27 H419 Likewise the useful spleen, though not the best,
HUMOUR34:32 H587 If Tyrants be the best, i'le it allow;
AGES36:22 H46 A {An} Harvest of the best, what needs he more.
AGES39:6 H149 But what is best i'le first present to view,
AGES39:32 H175 This is my best, but youth (is known) alas,
AGES40:31 ~~H210~~ My youth, my best, my strength, my bud, and prime:
AGES43:38 H333 Man at his best estate is vanity.
MASSYR56:29 H135 As puzzells best hystorians to remember:
MASSYR62:18 H363 {He} Plac'd *Israel* in's Land {there}, where he thought best,
MPERS~~72:37~~ H781 Ruling as they thought good, {best} under his head.
MPERS73:32 H817 The old, or new, which best, in what respect,
MPERS77:3 H942 As the best trophe that {which} ye won in *Greece.*
MPERS77:38 H979 That his ambitious humour best can fit;
MPERS78:22 H1003 {Which to} Three thousand (or more) {came} by best relation,
MPERS78:28 H1009 For to command alone, she thought {judg'd} was best.
MPERS81:5 H1113 Thought it {Fearing} his best {bridge}, no longer for to {there
MPERS83:28 H1216 The best that ever sprang {sprung} of *Cyrus* race.
MPERS86:21 H1337 And thought it best, now in his mothers time,
MPERS89:15 ~~H1449~~ That their return be stopt, he judg'd was best,
MGREC96:20 H1740 For so to fright the *Greekes* he judg'd was best,

MGREC106:17 H2151 Though some {most} of reading best, and soundest minde,
MGREC113:16 H2443 They knew not; wherefore, best now to be done,
MGREC119:3 H2693 But held command o'th' Armies {Army} which was best;
MGREC121:2 ~~H2780~~ With *Ptolomy* for to begin was best,
MGREC121:40 H2822 Two battells now he fought, and had {of both} the best,
MGREC122:40 H2861 All to be order'd there as he thought best:
MGREC129:23 H3137 But 'twas in shew, in heart it pleas'd them best.
MGREC136:17 H3431 *What e're is found amisse, take in best {good} part,*
DIALOG141:6 H5 Alas, deare Mother, fairest Queen, and best,
DIALOG146:12 H200 Who knows, the worst, the best {this} may {be my} overthrow;
QELIZ157:23 H91 And of all these without compare the best;
CONTEM172:26 H160 Thou Emblem true, of what I count the best,
CONTEM172:32 H165 Now salt, now fresh where you think best to glide
CONTEM173:34 H198 Man at the best a creature frail and vain,
SICKNES179:3 H23 Then deaths arrest I shall count best,
DISTEMP179:15 H3 And wasting pains, which best my body knows,
MERCY189:16 H37 He knows it is the best for thee and me.
MEDDM196:30 Hp273 fruits that are best preserued wth sugar, those parents are wise
MEDDM200:17 Hp279 the best, but falls and bruises, or perhaps somewhat worse,
MYCHILD215:13 Hp240 speak to any of yov much lesse to All, thovght it ye best whilst
MYCHILD215:21 Hp240 last is the best, let it be best pleasing to yov.
MYCHILD215:21 Hp240 last is the best, let it be best pleasing to yov.
BYNIGHT220:5 H6 And so to lye I fovnd it best.
SOREFIT222:10 H29 And then wth thee which is the Best
MED223:19 Hp250 bee dissolved and bee wth thee wch is best of All.
28AUG225:29 Hp254 my Soul that this condition y^{t} I am in is ye best for me, for god
28AUG225:33 Hp254 it——And if he knowes that weaknes, & a frail body is ye best
SAMUEL228:19 H20 Thy Will bee done, for that is best
HOUSE236:38 H30 There lay that store I covnted best

BESTOW (3)
MGREC101:3 H1928 Let them on him, that {this} dignity bestow:
SICKNES179:5 H25 Bestow much cost there's nothing lost,
JULY223:33 Hp251 bestow upon me. O never let Satan p^{r}vail against me, but

BESTOW'D (2) [bestowed]
MASSYR56:11 H117 Bestow'd their labour, and receiv'd their pay,
MGREC106:13 H2147 On *Artabasus* more then all bestow'd,

BESTOWES (2)
MGREC98:28 H1830 *Zidon* he on *Ephestion* bestowes:
MEDDM200:19 Hp279 strength of the person he bestowes them on, larg indowments

BESTOWS (1)
MEDDM207:4 Hp288 The gifts that god, bestows on the sons of men, are not only

BESTOW'ST (1)
THEART229:17 H19 What thou bestow'st I shall restore

BESTREW (1)
DAVID158:33 H13 Nor fruitfull showers your barren tops bestrew,

BETHINK (1)
MEDDM206:19 Hp287 Men that haue walked very extrauagantly, and at last bethink

BETHINKS (1)
ELEMEN15:21 H303 To meet with want, each woefull man bethinks.

BETIME (1)
AGES35:31 H17 flowers (as these) blossome {the spring puts forth} betime,

BETIS (3)

MGREC99:16 H1859 Where valiant *Betis,* doth defend {stoutly keeps} the town,
MGREC~~99:24~~ H1867 The Captaine {Thus *Betis*} tane, had holes bor'd through his
MGREC100:17 H1901 Had *Betis* now been there, but with his Band,

BETRAY (1)

MGREC127:21 H3051 *Pencestas* did betray him by a wile,

BETRUST (1)

MPERS75:8 H869 With all the Cities strength they him betrust,

BETTER (44)

PROLOG7:15 H28 Who sayes, my hand a needle better fits,
ELEMEN12:14 H174 Unlesse thou prove a better friend to me;
HUMOUR21:36 H64 She loves a Fiddle, better then a Drum,
HUMOUR29:29 H380 For {There} to defend my self, thy better part;
AGES41:26 H243 Such {My} empty seed should yeeld a better crop.
AGES~~45:10~~ H392 And worthy {better} ones, put to {suffer} extremity:
SEASONS48:34 ~~H85~~ In this harsh strain, I find no melody,
SEASONS53:2 H258 *Or better Lines you should have had;*
MASSYR~~57:22~~ H169 We may with learned *Vsher* better say,
MASSYR62:33 H378 His Wars none better then himself can boast,
MPERS73:38 H823 But {That} better one, then many Tyrants reigne.
MPERS81:27 H1135 With Rhetorick, t' gain better complement:
MPERS92:34 H1592 Whose warres and losses we may better tell;
MGREC94:28 H1666 Stiles him disloyall servant, and no better;
MGREC106:19 H2153 Then tell her errand, we had better spare
MGREC118:2 H2649 Their ends they might the better still attain.
MGREC125:7 H2955 The better to accomplish these her ends;
MGREC130:16 H3171 They for their great reward no better speed,
MGREC~~131:1~~ H3191 The better 'gainst *Cassander* to rebel.
MGREC135:40 H3412 My tired braine, leaves to a {some} better pen,
MROMAN140:4 H3567 And thus my pains (with better things) I lost,
DIALOG145:20 H169 {'Tis said,} My better part in Court of Parliament,
DIALOG147:19 H245 Not false to King, nor Countrey in thy heart, {to the better part;}
SIDNEY152:1 ~~H75~~ Better my hap, then was his darlings fate,
SIDNEY~~152:14~~ H84 Then wonder not if I no better sped,
QELIZ156:10 H37 She taught them better manners to their cost.
QELIZ156:19 H46 Was ever people better rul'd then hers?
TDUDLEY165:12 H14 Who heard or saw, observ'd or knew him better?
CONTEM168:21 H29 Had I not better known, (alas) the same had I.
CONTEM173:15 H182 I judg'd my hearing better then my sight,
CONTEM173:31 H196 Then follow thee into a better Region,
AUTHOR178:8 H18 In better dress to trim thee was my mind,
VERSES183:37 H4 Who can of right better demand the same?
2SIMON195:5 Hp271 their predecessors, but I am perswaded better things of y^{o} you
2SIMON195:13 Hp271 they will be better pris'd by you, for the Authors sake. the lord
MEDDM195:29 Hp272 speak well, but few can do well. We are better scholars in the
MEDDM197:8 Hp274 better, is because they haue more sence then faith they se
MEDDM199:3 Hp277 inheritance, is better, then an inheritance wthout wisedome
MEDDM204:27 Hp285 vpon one that is in a far better estate then himself, but let him
MYCHILD215:20 Hp240 ye former it had been perhaps better pleasing to yov, but seing
28AUG225:31 Hp254 he hath no benefitt by my adversity, nor is he ye better for my
HOURS234:31 H45 And serve thee better then before

HOURS234:33 H47 But give me Lord a better heart
HOURS234:34 H48 Then better shall I bee,

BETWEEN (3)
MPERS73:11 H798 *The inter-Regnum between* Cambyses,
MGREC133:19 H3307 Between those Kings, and noble *Pyrrus* stout,
DIALOG141:1 H1 A dialogue between Old

BETWEENE (1)
MEDDM208:9 Hp290 friends, though there should be no displeasence betweene

BETWIXT (6) See also 'TWIXT
ELEMEN8:24 H22 That betwixt hot and cold, she arbitrated
HUMOUR33:8 H522 Next difference {that} betwixt us twain doth lye,
MGREC99:3 H1846 Betwixt the *Hellespont,* and *Hallis* side;
MGREC101:8 H1933 And all those Countries, which (betwixt) did lye,
MEDDM202:3 Hp281 his gifts among the sons of men, betwixt whom he hath put so
MEDDM205:26 Hp286 to good dutys, we certainly dream of some remotnes betwixt

BEWAIL (2)
3LETTER183:12 H14 Bewail my turtle true, who now is gone,
ELIZB187:1 H10 Blest babe why should I once bewail thy fate,

BEWAILING (1)
MASSYR66:12 H518 There {And} sit bewailing *Zion* seventy years,

BEWAILS (1)
CONTEM170:9 H82 Bewails his unknown hap, and fate forlorn;

BEWARE (2)
AUTHOR178:11 H21 In Criticks hands, beware thou dost not come;
MEDDM203:15 Hp283 but he must beware of desireing to make this the place of his

BEYOND (13)
ELEMEN16:9 H332 But I should go beyond thee in thy {my} boasts,
ELEMEN18:2 H406 Yet Aire, beyond all these ye know t'excell.
ELEMEN20:8 H490 But dare not go, beyond my Element.
AGES~~39:29~~ H172 {elevate} my {high} thoughts above {beyond} the Pole.
MASSYR56:16 H122 Whose stately top, beyond {above} the clouds did rise;
MASSYR61:33 H338 All *Israels* Land, {lands} beyond *Iordan,* he takes.
MGREC95:40 H1719 Sure its {much} beyond my time, and little Art;
MGREC136:4 H3417 The Subject was too high, beyond my straine;
SIDNEY150:14 H49 Thy fame, and praise, is farre beyond my straine;
VANITY160:38 H48 It yeeldeth pleasures, farre beyond conceit,
FLESH175:16 H16 Dost dream of things beyond the Moon
FLESH176:35 H75 Beyond thy dull Capacity;
CHILDRN186:11 H78 Into a country beyond sight,

BIAS (1)
AGES43:23 H318 If *Bias* like, I'm stript unto my skin,

BIBLE (1)
MGREC134:24 H3355 They might translate the Bible into *Greek,*

BID (6)
ELEMEN18:12 H416 To bid adue, to his dear Element.
AGES46:25 H456 And in that hope, I bid you all farewel.
CHILDRN184:37 H26 Hath also bid her Dam adieu:
MEDDM200:13 Hp279 world before it bid them farwell
MEDDM201:28 Hp281 not only to bid them hold fast the form of sound Doctrin, but
MEDDM203:28 Hp284 bid him welcome, that brings a plaister for his sore, or a

BIDDEN (2)
MPERS84:4 H1232 To drink more then he list, none bidden was:
MGREC124:26 H2933 More then he bidden was, could act no thing;
BIDDING (1)
MGREC104:17 H2069 Bidding his {Then bids} servant *Artabassus* true;
'BIDE (3) [abide]
HUMOUR28:16 H328 The Melancholly to the Spleen to 'bide;
CONTEM172:30 H163 Ye Fish which in this liquid Region 'bide,
FAINT222:23 H13 I here a while might 'bide.
BIDE (2) [abide]
MPERS80:24 H1091 If that smal number his great force could bide;
MPERS88:5 H1398 The brunt of that huge multitude to bide.
BIDS (7)
SEASONS47:1 H17 And bids defiance to all tedious Winters:
MGREC100:33 H1917 Now bids the world adieu, her time {with pain} being spent,
MGREC~~104:17~~ H2069 Bidding his {Then bids} servant *Artabassus* true;
MGREC104:38 H2090 And bids him, save himself, by speedy course:
MGREC125:25 H2975 Bids chuse her death, such kindnesse she'l afford:
BIRTH180:1 H11 We both are ignorant, yet love bids me
PILGRIM210:17 H17 All Cares and feares, he bids farwell
BIGGER (1)
CONTEM172:1 H138 Because they're bigger, & their bodyes stronger?
BIGNES (1)
MEDDM206:8 Hp287 regard of bignes and brightnes, yet all receiue their light from
BIG'ST (1) [biggest]
ELEMEN17:20 H384 Mine Ice doth glaze *Europs* big'st Rivers o're,
BILLOWES (1) [billows]
ELEMEN14:16 H258 Which rise like mighty {tumbling} billowes on the lands: {Land}
BILLOWS (1) [pl.]
MEDDM198:6 Hp276 billows goe ouer their heads he then leads them to the Rock
BIN (3) [been]
AGES44:5 H338 And in perplexed Middle-age have bin,
AGES44:8 H341 I have bin young, and strong, and wise as you,
DIALOG143:16 H85 Though she hath bin injurious heretofore.
BINDE (1) [bind]
MPERS74:28 H851 Yet more the peoples hearts firmly to binde,
BINDING (2)
SEASONS47:24 H40 For though the Frost hath lost his binding power,
MGREC104:22 H2074 Lays hold on's Lord, and binding him with bands.
BINDS (1)
DIALOG147:21 H247 By force {As Duty binds,} expell, destroy, and tread them
BIRD (5)
SEASONS48:3 H56 The fearful Bird, his little house now builds,
MPERS76:11 H909 A Frog, a Mouse, a Bird, an Arrow sent,
CONTEM173:18 H184 O merry Bird (said I) that fears no snares,
CHILDRN184:26 H15 My second bird did take her flight,
CHILDRN184:32 H21 A prettier bird was no where seen,
BIRDS (11) [pl.]
ELEMEN9:37 H71 And birds do sing, to see his glittering Coach.
ELEMEN19:19 H464 That birds have not scap'd death, as they have flown,
SEASONS47:17 H33 Like Birds, now chirp, and hop about the field;

MASSYR55:19 H85 Whence rose that fable, she by birds was fed.
MASSYR64:4 H428 Under whose shadow, birds, and beasts, had birth;
MPERS76:17 H915 Or fly like birds, in unknown wayes full quick;
CONTEM168:27 H34 Birds, insects, Animals with Vegative,
CHILDRN184:14 H3 I had eight birds hatcht in one nest,
CHILDRN185:17 H43 If birds could weep, then would my tears
CHILDRN185:37 H63 Alas my birds, you wisdome want,
CHILDRN186:28 H95 Farewel my birds, farewel adieu,

BIRTH (12)
ELEMEN8:16 H14 All looked like a Chaos, or new birth;
HUMOUR23:8 H118 Tis true, when I am midwife to thy birth;
AGES38:19 H122 From birth stayned, with Adams sinfull fact;
SEASONS51:29 H205 There rests, untill the Sun give it a birth:
MASSYR64:4 H428 Under whose shadow, birds, and beasts, had birth;
MPERS71:2 H714 Innobled more by birth, then by their mind;
DUBART155:3 H88 *The world rejoyc'd at's birth, at's death was sorry;*
CONTEM171:26 H128 By birth more noble then those creatures all,
CONTEM171:36 H137 Shall I wish there, or never to had birth,
AUTHOR177:31 H3 Who after birth did'st by my side remain,
BIRTH179:26 H1-2 *Before the Birth of one of her Children.*
MYCHILD216:18 Hp241 feares brovght yov to this, I now travail in birth again of yov till

BIRTH-PLACE (1)
MASSYR55:8 H74 Her birth-place was *Philistrius Ascalon,*

BIRTHRIGHT (1)
MGREC122:17 H2842 She knew her birthright gave her *Macedon,*

BIRTH-RIGHTS (1)
MPERS85:39 H1315 Prefers his brother, for his birth-rights sake.

BIS (1)
AGES44:9 H342 But now, *Bis pueri senes,* is too true;

BISHOPRICK (1)
DIALOG145:33 H182 No prelate should his Bishoprick retain;

BIT (1) v.
CONTEM174:22 H220 Feeding on sweets, that never bit of th' sowre,

BIT n. See BITT

BITCH (1)
MPERS69:17 H639 His nourishment afforded by a Bitch,

BITE (1)
TDUDLEY165:14 H16 Let malice bite, and envy knaw its fill,

BITHYNIA (1)
MPERS90:13 ~~H1484~~ Into *Bithynia* often in-rodes made;

BITING (1)
HUMOUR~~31:15~~ H447 Thy biting quality still irritates,

BITS (1)
MGREC~~122:3~~ H2826 I should but snip a story into verse, {bits}

BITT (1) n. [small piece]
HOUSE237:4 H34 Nor at thy Table eat a bitt.

BITTER (8)
HUMOUR28:14 H326 The bitter choler, most malignant knowne
HUMOUR32:22 H496 I've not forgot how bitter Choler spake,
AGES46:11 H442 Hath yet amongst that sweet, some bitter gall.
MPERS87:3 H1359 The young Queen, and old, at bitter jars:

MGREC125:26 H2976 The Queen with many a curse, and bitter check,
DIALOG144:16 H126 These be the bitter fountains, heads, and roots,
1SIMON188:13 H14 And smile again, after our bitter crosses.
MEDDM200:8 Hp279 bitter together so is it wth some Christians, let god imbitter all

BITTERING (1)
HUMOUR31:12 ~~H444~~ Thy bittering quality, stil irretates,

BITTERNESSE (1)
HUMOUR28:40 H352 I've us'd no bitternesse, nor taxt your name,

BLAB (1)
HUMOUR25:28 H217 Nay should I tel, thou wouldst count me no blab,

BLACK (21)
FATHER5:4 H5 Of your four sisters, deckt {cloth'd} in black & white /four parts
ELEMEN8:13 H11 The quaking Earth did groan, the skie look't black,
ELEMEN16:5 H328 My sundry Seas, Black, White, and Adriatique
HUMOUR20:18 H10 Earth knew her black swarth childe, Water her faire;
HUMOUR22:1 H70 Then here's our sad black Sister, worse then you,
HUMOUR23:13 H123 Of that black region, Nature made thee Queen;
HUMOUR25:10 H199 Of thy black calumnies, this is but part:
HUMOUR30:38 H430 That black is black, and I am black, tis true;
HUMOUR30:38 H430 That black is black, and I am black, tis true;
HUMOUR30:38 H430 That black is black, and I am black, tis true;
HUMOUR~~31:5~~ H438 And so art call'd black Choler or adust,
AGES41:8 H228 And I in black oblivions den long {now} laid;
MPERS88:9 H1402 And black and blacker grew, as they drew nigh.
MGREC95:12 H1691 Next *Alexander* marcht, t'wards the black sea;
MGREC116:16 H2582 And so with black, be-clouded all his fame.
CONTEM169:19 H59 The black clad Cricket, bear a second part,
CONTEM171:7 H112 Cloath'd all in his black sinfull Livery,
1LETTER181:9 H7 I like the earth this season, mourn in black,
MEDDM196:7 Hp272 ruffles them vp, but spying his black feet, he soon lets fall his
MEDDM201:22 Hp281 but from some black Clouds that impends them, wch produces
13MAY226:28 H4 The earth all black is cloth'd in green

BLACK-BIRD (1)
SEASONS47:18 H34 The Nitingale, the Black-bird, and the Thrush,

BLACKER (2)
MPERS88:9 H1402 And black and blacker grew, as they drew nigh.
2LETTER182:26 H32 Behold a Chaos blacker then the first.

BLACKS (1) [pl.]
ELEMEN9:35 H70 And trim thee gay {brave}, in green, after thy blacks?

BLADDER (2)
HUMOUR30:12 H404 To {So} prison thee within that bladder smal.
AGES43:27 H322 The vexing Stone, in bladder and in reines,

BLADE (1)
HUMOUR25:1 H190 But know, I love the blade, more then the hilt. {Hill;}

BLADES (1) [pl.]
DIALOG148:18 H283 (For then what is't, but English blades dare do)

BLAME (3)
HUMOUR23:33 H143 Forsooth you are to blame, he grave reply'd.
MASSYR55:32 ~~H98~~ And that her worth, deserved no such blame,
MGREC115:13 H2522 To punish, where himself deserved blame:

BLAMLESSE (1)
MEDDM205:23 Hp286 He that would keep a pure heart and lead a blamlesse life,
BLASPHEMIES (1) [pl.]
DIALOG143:35 H104 For Oathes, and Blasphemies did ever eare
BLASPHEMY (1)
MYCHILD218:29 Hp244 Blasphemy, and Sectaries, and some who hauest been acct^{d}.
BLAST (3)
HUMOUR28:37 H349 Such venome lyes in words, though but a blast,
AGES~~43:16~~ H309 But in a trice 'tis ruin'd by a blast,
SICKNES178:34 H17 O Bubble blast, how long can'st last?
BLASTS (1) [pl.]
SEASONS51:21 H197 The Northern Winter blasts begin to hisse;
BLAZE (1)
QELIZ158:16 H125 So blaze it fame, here's feathers for thy wings,
BLAZERS (1) [pl.]
SIDNEY151:3 ~~H69~~ I wish no more such Blazers we may see;
BLAZING (1)
ELEMEN20:1 H483 Sometimes strange {red} flaming swords, and blazing stars,
BLEATING (1)
QELIZ155:25 H16 Mine bleating stands before thy royall Herse:
BLEEDING (2)
DIALOG145:1 H150 I saw poore *Ireland* bleeding out her last,
MERCY189:13 H34 Chear up (dear Son) thy fainting bleeding heart,
BLEEDS (1)
DIALOG146:6 H194 That thousands lay on heaps, here bleeds my woes.
BLEMISH'D (2) [blemished]
PROLOG7:3 H18 My foolish, broken, blemish'd Muse so sings;
SIDNEY152:16 ~~H85~~ But I had blemish'd theirs, to make 't appear;
BLEMISHES (1)
AUTHOR178:3 H13 Thy blemishes amend, if so I could:
BLESSD (1) [blessed]
13MAY227:11 H20 Blessd me in Youth, and elder Age
BLESSE (5) [bless]
AGES42:1 H259 For hundreds blesse me, for my bounty sent {lent}.
2SIMON195:13 Hp271 better pris'd by you, for the Authors sake. the lord blesse you
MEDDM209:2 Hp291 will not let thee go replys Jacob till thou blesse me, faith is not
TOCHILD215:7 H7 And God shall blesse yov from above.
SAMUEL228:17 H18 And Blesse the for't even all my Dayes.
BLESSED (4) See also BLESSD
DIALOG147:25 H249 And to this blessed {hopeful} Cause closely adhere
DDUDLEY167:23 H20 *Then dying, left a blessed memory.*
MYSOUL225:21 H25 Come Jesvs qvickly, Blessed Lord
HOURS234:17 H31 O shine vpon me blessed Lord
BLESSES (1)
PILGRIM210:5 H5 Blesses himself, to think vpon
BLESSING (1)
TDUDLEY166:29 H71 His blessing rest on his posterity:
BLESSINGS (2) [pl.]
MEDDM207:9 Hp288 are lords we will come no more at thee If outward blessings,
HOURS234:32 H46 Whose Blessings thvs surmovnt.

BLES'T (1) [blesst]
HANNA230:11 H4 Bles't bee thy Name who did'st restore
BLEST (18) [blesst]
AGES~~45:2~~ H376 We joy'd in many blest and prosperous dayes.
SEASONS~~49:22~~ H113 Blest rustick Swains, your pleasant quiet life,
SEASONS51:3 H177 Whose lively liquor oft is curst, and blest;
SEASONS52:23 H238 Now's held, a Guest, {(but ghest)} (but blest) Nativity.
MASSYR62:25 H370 Or wild *Tartarians,* as yet ne're blest,
DIALOG141:7 H6 With honour, wealth, and peace, happy and blest;
DIALOG146:38 H224 Blest be the Nobles of thy Noble Land,
DIALOG146:40 H226 Blest be thy Commons, who for Common good,
DIALOG147:2 H228 Blest be thy Counties which do {who did} aid thee still
DIALOG147:4 H230 Blest be thy Preachers, who do chear thee on,
DIALOG148:28 H293 Whose lot doth fall to live therein is blest:
TDUDLEY166:24 H66 Ah happy Soul, 'mongst Saints and Angels blest,
CONTEM172:28 H162 So may we press to that vast mansion, ever blest.
ELIZB187:1 H10 Blest babe why should I once bewail thy fate,
1SIMON188:15 H16 Among the blest in endless joyes remain.
MERCY189:10 H31 All freed from grief (I trust) among the blest;
PILGRIM210:24 H24 And soare on high among the blest.
HOUSE236:26 H18 I blest his Name y^{t} gave + took,
BLEW (3)
HUMOUR21:31 H59 Nay milk-sops, at such brunts you look but blew,
HUMOUR26:26 H256 Through th' warme, blew conduits of my veinal rils;
MPERS88:34 H1427 After this trance, revenge, new spirits blew,
BLINDED (2)
SEASONS47:2 ~~H17~~ And now makes glad those blinded Northern wights,
DIALOG148:23 H288 The scales shall fall from your long blinded eyes,
BLISS (4)
CONTEM170:11 H84 And how she lost her bliss, to be more wise,
SICKNES178:27 H10 in place of highest bliss,
ANNEB187:23 H13 Or perfect bliss without mixture of woe.
ANNEB187:33 H23 Thou with thy Saviour art in endless bliss.
BLISSE (4)
MASSYR59:1 H225 And win the Crown, which was the way to blisse,
MASSYR62:29 H374 They shal return, and *Zion* see, with blisse.
MGREC102:15 H1985 And to possesse, he counts no little blisse,
MYSOUL225:6 H10 To Blisse vnseen by Eye,
BLOATED (1)
HUMOUR~~23:4~~ H114 Of greasie paunch, and palled {bloated} cheeks, go vaunt,
BLOCK (1)
MYCHILD218:17 Hp244 When I haue gott over this Block y^{n} have I another pvtt in my
BLOCK'D (1) [blocked]
MGREC126:9 H3000 There by *Cassander* she's block'd up, so long,
BLOCKS (1) [pl.]
DIALOG144:6 H116 How many Princely heads on blocks laid down,
BLOCKT (1)
MGREC119:35 H2725 Blockt up in *Lamia,* still by his foes;
BLOOD (40) See also BLOUD
ELEMEN14:33 H275 Which {Who} am thy drink, thy blood, thy sap, and best.
HUMOUR20:17 H9 Choler was own'd by Fire, and Blood by Aire,

HUMOUR23:40 ~~H149~~ The spongy Lungs, I feed with frothy blood.
HUMOUR24:11 H160 *Blood.*
HUMOUR25:31 H220 That naught but blood, {death} the same may expiate.
HUMOUR~~25:33~~ H222 So spils {shed'st} that life {blood}, thou'rt bounden to preserve.
HUMOUR26:35 H265 Their wondrous mixture, is of blood, and ayre,
AGES35:22 H8 From blood and aire, for hot, and moist is he.
AGES~~38:3~~ H106 My stroks did cause no death {blood}, nor wounds, nor {or}
AGES45:21 ~~H403~~ I've seen it shaken, rent, and soak'd in blood,
AGES~~45:22~~ H404 To see them swill in blood untill they burst.
SEASONS49:1 H92 As Spring did aire, blood, youth in's equipage.
SEASONS52:25 H240 Chilling the blood, and shrinking up the skin.
MPERS73:17 H804 Descended all, of *Achemenes* blood,
MPERS73:25 H810 But yet, 'fore this was done, much blood was shed,
MPERS82:32 H1179 And leaves her thus, besmear'd with {in} blood, and tears.
MPERS82:38 H1185 O're-flown with torrent of her ruby {guiltless} blood.
MPERS85:35 H1311 No match was high enough, but their own blood,)
MGREC94:11 H1645 Nor wonder is't, if he in blood begin,
MGREC126:25 H3016 And plead the blood of their deare Kindred {friends and
MGREC130:25 H3180 Now blood was paid with blood, for what was done
MGREC130:25 H3180 Now blood was paid with blood, for what was done
MGREC130:28 ~~H3181~~ And wronging innocents whose blood they spilt,
MGREC130:32 ~~H3181~~ And *Cleopatra's* blood, now likewise spill'd,
MGREC132:11 H3246 For blood which was decreed, that he should spill,
MGREC132:14 H3249 Yet be aveng'd, must th' blood of *Jesreel.*
MGREC134:12 H3343 The Royall blood was quite {nigh} extinguished.
MROMAN139:17 H3545 And shed her guiltlesse blood, with guilty knife,
DIALOG142:11 H40 With *English* blood bedews thy conquered Land?
DIALOG143:8 H75 Their hands in Kindreds blood, whom they did foyle:
DIALOG~~146:34~~ H221 Though now beclouded all with tears and blood:
DIALOG146:35 ~~H221~~ That Right may have its right, though't be with blood;
SIDNEY149:34 ~~H23~~ Which have the self-same blood yet in my veines;
SIDNEY~~150:12~~ H43 Whilst English blood yet runs within my veins.
QELIZ156:31 H58 Her Nobles sacrific'd their noble blood,
DAVID159:5 H20 Sometimes from crimson blood of gastly slaine,
CONTEM170:20 H92 Upon whose blood his future good he hopes to raise.
CONTEM170:24 H95 The Virgin Earth, of blood her first draught drinks
MEDDM204:20 Hp285 (sath god) and I will avenge the blood of Jezerel vpon the
BYNIGHT220:14 H13 My smarting wounds washt in his blood,

BLOODLESSE (1)
DAVID159:8 H23 Did *Saul* with bloodlesse Sword turne back agen:

BLOODS (1) [pl.]
DIALOG144:4 H114 From crying bloods, yet cleansed am not I,

BLOODY (3) [bloudy]
HUMOUR32:32 H506 I love no thundering Drums {guns}, nor bloody Wars,
MPERS72:31 H775 To tell the facts, of this most bloody King.
CONTEM170:7 H80 And in her lap, her bloody *Cain* new born,

BLOOMING (1)
SIDNEY150:25 H52 Ah, in his blooming prime, death pluckt this Rose,

BLOSSOME (1)
AGES35:31 H17 Such cold mean flowers (as these) blossome {the spring puts

BLOT (3)
MASSYR54:3 H30 But yet this blot for ever on him lyes,
MGREC112:18 H2404 But vice remaines, to his eternall blot.
MGREC129:14 H3128 Both thrown into a well to hide her blot,
BLOUD (18) [blood]
HUMOUR21:40 H68 But shuns to look on wounds, and bloud that's spilt,
AGES~~43:16~~ H310 Though cemented with more the noble bloud,
AGES~~45:22~~ H409 I've seen it plunder'd, taxt and soak'd in bloud,
MASSYR64:14 H438 Children of Royal bloud, unblemish'd youth;
MPERS70:32 H703 The which she bak'd {bath'd} within a But of bloud,
MPERS71:8 H724 His reign with Bloud, and Incest, first begins,
MPERS71:16 H730 And all of Royal bloud that came to hand,
MPERS74:26 H849 And now a King, by marriage, choyce, and bloud,
MPERS74:39 H860 His manly face dis-figures, spares no bloud,
MPERS77:1 H940 Off flyes his head, down showres his frolick bloud.
MPERS78:10 H991 To Princes of the *Persian* bloud descended,
MGREC~~101:34~~ H1962 And spilt the Greeks some bloud before their flight
MGREC105:8 H2101 *Darius* bath'd in bloud, sends out his groanes,
MGREC117:6 H2613 For by that hand, which still revengeth bloud,
MGREC117:8 H2615 And {But} as he took delight, much bloud to spill,
MROMAN136:35 H3449 The Stones at first was cimented with bloud,
MROMAN137:28 H3479 Kept shut in peace, but {set} ope when bloud was spilt;
DUBART154:14 H59 Who tam'd his foes, in bloud, in skarres {warrs,} and sweat,
BLOUD-SHED (1)
MPERS69:31 H653 Amidst {Among} the tumult, bloud-shed, and the strife,
BLOUDY (5) [bloody]
AGES~~45:20~~ H402 By bloudy Popish, hellish miscreants:
MPERS71:20 H734 He next to *Cyprus* sends his bloudy Hoast,
MPERS76:33 H931 At *Marathon* this bloudy field was fought,
MGREC105:16 H2109 So chanc'd these bloudy Horses to espy,
MROMAN136:36 H3450 And bloudy hath it prov'd, since first it stood:
BLOW (3) n.
HUMOUR29:25 H376 The blow that's aim'd thereat is latch'd by th'arm,
MPERS70:31 H702 And at one blow, worlds head, she headlesse makes;
BIRTH179:30 H6 But with deaths parting blow is sure to meet.
BLOW (4) v.
AGES45:4 H382 A plot to blow up Nobles, and their King;
BLOW'S (1) [blow is]
HUMOUR29:5 H358 That blow's most deadly, where it is intended;
BLOWES (2) [blows] n.
MPERS80:4 H1071 Laid on more fiercely, their deep mortall blowes;
MGREC117:23 H2630 For ayming still amisse, his dreadfull blowes
BLOWN (5) [air]
ELEMEN14:18 H260 But windy sister, 'twas when you have blown.
CHILDRN184:30 H19 Till after blown by *Southern* gales,
BLOWN (3) [bloom] See also BLOWNE
SICKNES178:36 H19 No sooner blown, but dead and gone,
ELIZB187:10 H18 And buds new blown, to have so short a date,
1SIMON188:6 H7 Three flours, two scarcely blown, the last i'th' bud,
BLOWNE (1) [destruction]
ELEMEN9:6 H40 The adverse wall's not shak'd, the Mine's not blowne,

BLOWNE (1) [blown; bloom]
ELEMEN13:29 H230 And buds from fruitfull trees, before they'r {as soon as} blowne:
BLOWS (2) n. See also BLOWES
ELEMEN40:12 H193 From pipe to pot, from pot to words, and blows,
DIALOG146:5 H193 They worded it so long, they fell to blows,
BLOWS (1) v.
AGES38:9 H112 I fear'd no stormes, nor al the windes that blows,
BLUNT (1)
MGREC100:24 H1908 Fit for to blunt the swords of *Macedon;*
BLUR (1)
HUMOUR23:21 H131 Nor is't my pleasure, thus to blur thy name:
BLUR'D (1) [blurred]
MASSYR~~55:32~~ H98 That undeserv'd, they blur'd her name and fame
BLUSH (4)
HUMOUR22:18 H87 Nor hath she wit, or heat, to blush at this.
HUMOUR31:41 H474 Then cause her blush, while I dilate {relate} the same.
MGREC136:1 H3414 For what is past I blush, excuse to make,
SIDNEY150:4 ~~H29~~ And modest Maids, and Wives, blush at thy glory;
BLUSHES (1) [pl.]
CONTEM168:25 H32 The morn doth usher thee, with smiles & blushes,
BLUSHING (4)
HUMOUR27:19 ~~H290~~ Though cast upon my guiltlesse blushing face;
AGES36:8 H32 When blushing first, she 'gins to red {light} the Aire.
AGES37:4 H66 Whose mean beginning, blushing cann't reveale,
AUTHOR177:36 H8 At thy return my blushing was not small,
BLUSTERING (2)
MEDDM201:13 Hp280 alayed, by cold words and not by blustering threats.
MEDDM201:31 Hp281 in the parching sun, & a shelter in a blustering storme are of
BOAR (1)
DIALOG142:21 H50 To come, and break the tushes of the Boar?
BOARDERING (1) See also BORD'RING
MASSYR67:15 H561 *Arabia,* and all the boardering coast.
BOAST (7)
HUMOUR26:29 H259 Then never boast of what thou do'st receive,
MASSYR62:33 H378 His Wars none better then himself can boast,
MASSYR64:29 H453 That in her pride, she knew not which to boast,
MROMAN140:5 H3568 Which none had cause to wail, nor I to boast.
SIDNEY150:22 H47 Of which, {at} this day, faire *Belgia* doth {may} boast.
TDUDLEY165:11 H13 For who more cause to boast his worth then I?
MYSOUL224:26 H2 Boast of him all ye Day,
BOASTED (1)
HUMOUR29:16 ~~H368~~ Thy boasted valour stoutly's been repell'd,
BOASTING (2)
HUMOUR24:8 H157 I love no boasting, that's but childrens trade:
HUMOUR24:25 H174 So ful of boasting, and prevarication.
BOASTINGS (1) [pl.]
ELEMEN14:26 H268 Among your boastings to have praised me;
BOASTS (1) [pl.]
ELEMEN16:9 H332 But I should go beyond thee in thy {my} boasts,
BOAT (1)
MPERS76:1 H899 A bridge he made, which serv'd for boat, and barge,

BOATS (4) [pl.]
MPERS79:11 H1033 Of Boats, together coupled, and there laid;
MGREC107:30 H2205 For Boats here's none, nor neare it any wood,
MGREC109:13 H2272 Boats to prepare, *Ephestion* first he sends,
MROMAN138:19 H3509 Of Boats, and Oares, no more they need the aide;
BODIES (2) [pl.] See also BODYES, BODYS
HUMOUR23:17 H127 But bodies wasting, and destruction.
MGREC107:23 H2198 drought, and heat, their bodies much doth {sore did} parch;
BODY (36)
ELEMEN18:37 H441 Thus I another body can assume,
HUMOUR27:39 H310 So suddenly, the body all is fir'd:
HUMOUR28:3 H315 The body dryes, the minde sublime doth smother,
HUMOUR28:7 H319 The Lungs, she rots, the body weares away,
HUMOUR34:16 H571 With {Which} joynt to joynt, the entire body tyes;
HUMOUR35:13 H609 But here's a {so} compact body, whole, entire:
AGES40:37 H216 Sometimes by {with} Agues all my body shaken;
AGES46:21 H452 This body, by this soul, shal be assum'd;
MGREC~~114:12~~ H2482 And in a rage him through the body ran,
MGREC118:24 H2671 The *Egyptians,* his body did enbalme;
MGREC125:1 H2949 Which damage both to minde and body brought:
MGREC~~132:28~~ H3274 His body *Seleucus* sends to his Son,
MROMAN139:31 H3557 The subject large my mind and body weak,
DIALOG141:20 H19 My weakned fainting body now to reele?
DIALOG142:36 H65 My beauteous Body at this present maime;
DUBART154:28 H73 Of names {Name}, of state, of body, or {and} of mind,
CONTEM173:37 H201 Each storm his state, his mind, his body break,
DISTEMP179:13 H1 *Vpon some distemper of body.*
DISTEMP179:15 H3 And wasting pains, which best my body knows,
MEDDM198:28 Hp277 A sore finger may disquiet the whole body, but an vlcer wthin
MEDDM199:19 Hp278 Much Labour wearys the body, and many thoughts oppresse
MEDDM199:28 Hp278 first kill the body, the last the good name the two former leaue
MEDDM200:20 Hp279 honour, wealth, or a helthfull body, would quite ouer throw,
MEDDM201:16 Hp280 body, so a quick reception, and a deliberate cogitation argues
PILGRIM210:25 H25 This body shall in silence sleep,
PILGRIM210:28 H28 nor grinding paines, my body fraile.
PILGRIM210:36 H36 a glorious body it shall rise
PILGRIM210:39 H39 Then soule and body shall vnite
FEVER221:8 H23 And spar'd by Body frail,
MED223:10 Hp250 Body he my head. Such priviledges had not ye word of Truth
MYSOUL225:3 H7 Thy body vile it shall bee chang'd,
28AUG225:33 Hp254 by it—And if he knowes that weaknes, & a frail body is ye best
28AUG226:7 Hp254 Body, and bee in continuall xpectat^{n} of my change, and let me
11MAYA226:22 Hp255 shall flourish while my body decayes, and ye weaknes of this
13MAY226:31 H7 My Soul and Body doth rejoice,
HOURS234:10 H24 Of Body and of mind
BODYES (2) [bodies] See also BODYS
FATHER5:23 H24 Of these consists, our bodyes, cloathes, and food,
CONTEM172:1 H138 Because they're bigger, & their bodyes stronger?
BODYS (1) [bodies] See also BODYES
MEDDM205:36 Hp287 that many times, the waight thereof impares both their bodys
MEDDM207:31 Hp289 All weak and diseased bodys, haue hourly mementos of their

BODYS (1) [bodies']
MGREC96:22 H1742 Would aske more time, then were {was} their bodys worth.
BOGOAS (3)
MPERS~~92:5~~ H1562 Inthron'd by *Bogoas* in the room of th' other:
MPERS~~92:16~~ H1574 *Darius* by this *Bogoas* set in throne,
MPERS~~92:19~~ H1577 But *Bogoas* falls to's practices again,
BOIL See BOYLE
BOILING (1)
HUMOUR24:2 H151 Without my boiling heat cannot digest.
BOISTEROUS See BOYSTEROUS
BOLD (17)
ELEMEN13:37 H238 To ope those veines of Mine, audacious bold:
ELEMEN18:39 H443 Some for this cause (of late) have been so bold,
HUMOUR29:34 H385 And if *Marcellus* bold, be call'd *Romes* sword,
HUMOUR35:5 H601 To take her moyst, my moistnesse {moisture} wil be bold;
AGES45:39 H429 My heart sometimes as fierce, as Lions bold,
AGES46:7 H438 To mean, to noble, fearful, or to bold:
MPERS71:33 H747 So left his sacrilegious bold intents:
MPERS76:6 H904 Which two then to assaile, his {royal} Camp was bold:
MPERS80:2 H1069 And wound the backs of those bold {brave} Warriours stout.
MPERS82:1 H1146 But that which helpt defects, and made them bold,
MPERS90:7 H1480 O're mountains, rocks, and hils, as Lions bold;
MPERS~~92:30~~ H1588 Yet in these {such} differences, we may behold; {be bold,}
MGREC103:28 H2039 He at a bold, base {proud} Strumpets, lewd desire;
MGREC114:9 H2477 From jeast, to earnest, and at last so bold,
MGREC120:11 H2746 *Perdicas* griev'd, to see the Princes bold,
MROMAN137:34 H3485 So to delude the people he was bold:
DUBART154:15 H60 Thy fame is spread as farre, I dare be bold,
BOLDLY (1)
DIALOG147:1 H227 And thine {thy} infringed Lawes have boldly stood.
BOLDNES (1)
MEDDM205:19 Hp286 would haue boldnes to go to the throne of grace to be
BOLDNESSE (1)
MGREC136:6 H3419 Converts our boldnesse, into impudence.
BOND (2)
VERSES184:5 H9 My Bond remains in force unto this day;
VERSES184:10 H14 Such is my bond, none can discharge but I,
BONDAGE (2)
MGREC108:12 H2228 From bondage, long to be infranchised;
MEDDM209:15 Hp291 last fall in to perpetuall bondage vnder them vnlesse the great
BONDS (2) [pl.]
MGREC123:40 H2904 By all the Bonds 'twixt him and's father past,
MYCHILD216:36 Hp242 and Bonds vpon my Soul to p^{r}form his righteovs comands.
BONE (2)
1LETTER181:27 H25 Flesh of thy flesh, bone of thy bone,
1LETTER181:27 H25 Flesh of thy flesh, bone of thy bone,
BONES (8) [pl.]
ELEMEN13:3 H204 That you ambition laid, ought but my bones?
HUMOUR30:25 H417 And first, the firme dry bones, I justly claim:
AGES41:9 H229 Of Marrow {aches} ful my bones, of Milk {woe} my breasts
AGES43:34 ~~H329~~ And the Consumption, to the bones doth wast me;

MGREC125:35 H2985 And throwes {threw} his bones about, to shew her spight.
SIDNEY152:22 H91 His bones do lie interr'd in stately *Pauls.*
MEDDM200:28 Hp279 when the Sun of righteoussnes shall appear those dry bones
MEDDM202:11 Hp281 and healthfull y^t their bones are full of marrow & their breasts

BONNETS (1) [pl.]
MGREC~~122:36~~ H2857 Their bonnets vail'd to him as chief Commander.

BONUM (1)
VANITY160:25 H35 That *summum Bonum* which may stay my mind?

BOOK (6)
MASSYR63:34 H421 Nor's Metamorphosis from *Ovids* Book,
MGREC~~121:15~~ H2794 Who could not book so great indignity,
MGREC133:32 H3322 His book of *Assurs* Monarchs dedicates,
SIDNEY150:11 H36 Yea, and Divinity within thy {his} Book,
AUTHOR177:29 H1 *The Author to her Book.*
TOCHILD215:2 H2 This Book by Any yet vnread,

BOOKS (1) [pl.]
MASSYR67:23 H569 His lust, and cruelty, {crueltyes} in books {storyes} we find,

BOON (1)
2LETTER182:2 H8 I crave this boon, this Errand by the way,

BOONE (1)
SIDNEY150:31 H58 But yet impartiall Death {Fates} this Boone did give,

BOOTLESSE (1)
ELEMEN9:4 H38 Your Cannon's bootlesse, and your powder too

BOOTY (2)
MGREC96:30 H1750 Had not been spoile, and booty rich enough,
MGREC128:32 H3105 And {With} all the spoyle and booty they {he} had tane;

BOR'D (1) [bored]
MGREC99:24 H1867 The Captaine {Thus *Betis*} tane, had holes bor'd through his

BORDERS (2)
MASSYR61:16 H321 When *Resins* force his borders sore did mar.
MGREC109:32 H2291 Unto his Kingdoms borders, and as due,

BORD'RING (1) [boardering]
MASSYR60:18 H283 Incroached {Incroaching} stil upon the bord'ring Lands,

BORE (3)
AGES36:21 H45 Under his arme a Sheafe of wheat he bore,
MPERS85:36 H1312 Two sons she bore, the youngest *Cyrus* nam'd,
1LETTER181:16 H14 Then view those fruits which through thy heat I bore?

BORED See BOR'D

BORN (13)
HUMOUR30:20 H412 You high born (from that lump) then take your flight
AGES37:2 H64 Ah me! conceiv'd in sin, and born in {with} sorrow,
MASSYR66:19 H525 Who had for sixteen hundred years born sway,
MPERS69:29 H651 But as he past, his Son, who was born dumbe,
MPERS72:15 H763 Who would have born a Nephew, and a Son.
MPERS~~77:16~~ H957 Because this was, first born of *Cyrus* race.)
MPERS~~81:28~~ H1136 A *Macedonian* born, and great Commander,
MGREC117:40 H2647 His base born Brother, *Aridæus* nam'd,
MGREC131:36 H3228 Two sons he left, born of King *Philips* daughter,
CONTEM168:11 H20 Hath hundred winters past since thou wast born?
CONTEM170:7 H80 And in her lap, her bloody *Cain* new born,
CONTEM171:28 H130 No sooner born, but grief and care makes fall

MEDDM196:16 Hp273 that hath wrought hard in gods vine yard and hath born the

BORNE (5)

MPERS81:28 ~~H1136~~ Though of this Nation borne a great Commander,
MGREC96:7 H1727 The Holy fire, was borne before the Host:
MROMAN138:25 H3515 *Tarquin,* a *Greek,* at *Corinth* borne, and bred,
MROMAN138:35 H3525 Thirty eight yeares (this Stranger borne) did reigne,
SIDNEY150:27 H54 Thus man is borne to dye, and dead is he,

BOSTON (1)

MYCHILD216:10 Hp241 submitted to it & joined to ye chh., at Boston.

BOTH (94)

ELEMEN8:18 H16 Both by their darings; Water so provoked,
ELEMEN8:30 H28 What is my worth (both ye) and all things {men} know,
ELEMEN9:36 H70 Both man and beast, rejoyce at his approach,
ELEMEN10:1 H76 My Planets, of both Sexes, whose degree
ELEMEN12:4 H164 Whether Pyrenian, or the Alpes; both lyes
ELEMEN12:23 H183 Thousands in woods, and planes, both wild, and tame,
ELEMEN12:38 H198 And Oares to row, when both my sisters failes?
ELEMEN13:28 H229 The Corne, and Hay, both fall before they'r mowne;
ELEMEN16:24 H347 Both when we list, to water we convert.
ELEMEN16:41 H364 The Farmer, and the Plowman both {Grasier do} complain
HUMOUR21:8 H36 We both once Masculines, the world doth know,
HUMOUR25:19 H208 Both them and all things else, she will {would} consume.
HUMOUR32:21 H495 Enough of both, my wrongs for {now} to expresse;
HUMOUR34:2 H557 Both {The} watry, glassie, and the christaline.
HUMOUR34:39 H594 And too much talk; both which, I do {here} confesse,
AGES36:36 H60 Both good and bad, but yet no more then's true.
AGES41:27 H244 I then with both hands, graspt the world together,
AGES45:14 H396 fly their Country, through their {struck both with gilt and} dread.
AGES46:1 H432 Shal both be broke, by wracking death so strong;
AGES46:17 H448 Mother, and sisters both; the worms, that crawl,
SEASONS48:23 H76 But both rejoyce, at th'heavens clear smiling face,
MASSYR53:22 H12 Both Beasts and Men subjected to his spoyls.
MASSYR55:7 H73 And was both shame, and glory of her sex;
MASSYR58:14 H199 Both, for their King, held their dominion,
MASSYR59:4 H228 Both sides their hearts, their hands, their {&} bands unite,
MASSYR61:2 H307 And times of both computed, so fall out,
MPERS72:14 H762 She with her fruit was {were} both at once undone,
MPERS~~79:2~~ H1024 Then laid his parts on both sides of the way,
MPERS79:28 H1054 His answer was, both Land and Sea he feared,
MPERS81:37 ~~H1143~~ Where both sides exercis'd their manly feats;
MPERS81:39 ~~H1143~~ For one maine Battell shortly, both provide;
MPERS~~82:2~~ H1149 Where both their Controversies they'l decide;
MPERS83:35 H1223 *Greeks* and *Egyptians* both, he overthrows,
MPERS~~83:36~~ H1224 And payes them now, {both} according as he owes,
MPERS89:14 H1448 And rob him both of Scepter, and of Crown;
MPERS91:12 H1520 Til many a Captain fel, both wise, and strong,
MPERS92:24 ~~H1582~~ That son, and father, both were murthered
MGREC93:18 H1615 By Art, and Nature both, he was made fit,
MGREC6:36 H1633 Restlesse both day and night, his heart now {then} was,
MGREC94:3 H1637 *Thebes,* and old {stiff} *Athens,* both 'gainst him rebell,
MGREC~~94:5~~ H1639 This done, against all {both} right, and natures laws,

MGREC95:35 H1714 (Both sexes there) was almost numberlesse.
MGREC96:35 H1755 But when both Armies met, he might behold,
MGREC97:5 H1766 Now finds both leggs, and Horse, to run away;
MGREC100:20 H1904 And now of valour both were {are} destitute;
MGREC101:34 ~~H1959~~ Both Armies meet, *Greeks* fight, the *Persians* run,
MGREC106:41 H2175 The certainty of both comes to his eares,
MGREC109:3 H2260 Those that {Such as} doe not, both they, {them} and theirs, are
MGREC113:9 H2436 Or flesh, or {and} life, could bear, till both were spent
MGREC114:1 H2469 When both were drunk, *Clitus* was wont to jeere;
MGREC114:7 ~~H2475~~ Upon a time, when both had drunken well,
MGREC~~114:7~~ H2475 Both at a Feast when they had tippled well
MGREC116:28 H2594 those that {such as} pleas'd him: had both wealth and heart:
MGREC120:29 H2766 He, and *Craterus,* both with him now {do} joyn,
MGREC~~121:40~~ H2822 Two battells now he fought, and had {of both} the best,
MGREC122:10 H2835 He was both valiant, faithfull, patient, wise.
MGREC123:39 H2903 Goes to *Antigonus,* and both implore,
MGREC125:1 H2949 Which damage both to minde and body brought:
MGREC129:3 H3117 Imprisoning both the mother, and her {the} son,
MGREC129:14 H3128 Both thrown into a well to hide her blot,
MGREC130:29 ~~H3181~~ *Philip* and *Olympias* both were slain,
MGREC~~132:7~~ H3242 Thus *Philips,* and *Cassander's* race is {both} gone,
MGREC~~132:16~~ H3252 Though men and mony both he hath at will,
DIALOG146:33 ~~H219~~ To weep for that we both have pray'd for long,
SIDNEY152:25 H94 Philip *and* Alexander *both in one.*
DUBART155:9 H94 *But Fame, out-living both, he is reviv'd.*
DAVID159:9 H24 Pleasant and lovely were they both in life,
TDUDLEY165:21 H23 Both in his native, and in foreign coast,
TDUDLEY166:36 H78 *That was both pious, just and wise,*
FLESH177:7 H88 The stately Walls both high and strong,
FLESH177:9 H90 The Gates of Pearl, both rich and clear,
BIRTH180:1 H11 We both are ignorant, yet love bids me
1LETTER181:28 H26 I here, thou there, yet both but one.
3LETTER183:22 H24 I here, he there, alas, both kept by force:
CHILDRN184:28 H17 *Southward* they both their course did bend,
ELIZB187:8 H16 And time brings down what is both strong and tall.
MERCY188:27 H13 That thou dear Son has lost both Tree and fruit:
MEDDM195:31 Hp272 proficient in both.
MEDDM195:35 Hp272 age, and both by an empty old age, he that hath nothing to
MEDDM196:15 Hp273 comes he shall both take his rest and receiue his reward, the
MEDDM197:16 Hp274 more patiently then he that excells him, both in gifts & graces
MEDDM198:14 Hp276 but he that is well stored wth both, seldom is so insnared
MEDDM198:22 Hp276 but either that or something like it, hath been both done and
MEDDM199:21 Hp278 of both, and findes nothing but vanity and vexation of spirit
MEDDM201:25 Hp281 of the wise (sath Solom) are as nailes, and as goads, both
MEDDM204:17 Hp285 god doth many times, both reward and punish for one and y^{e}
MEDDM205:13 Hp286 alway kept by Conscience, who is both accuser excuser witnes
MEDDM205:36 Hp287 many times, the waight thereof impares both their bodys and
MEDDM206:4 Hp287 being cut down, as the dry stock, for both cumber the ground
MEDDM206:9 Hp287 one Sun, so is it in the Church both militant and triumphant,
BYNIGHT220:3 H4 And hath at once both ease and Rest,
RESTOR230:2 H17 That thou by both may'st learn

SON231:23 H35 In both o[r] hearts erect a frame
HOURS234:29 H43 So both of vs thy Kindnes Lord

BOTTLE (1)
BYNIGHT220:13 H12 He in his Bottle putt my teares,

BOTTOM (1)
AGES~~43:16~~ H311 The bottom nought, and so no longer stood.

BOTTOME (2)
DIALOG145:5 H154 The bottome dregs reserved are for me.
CONTEM173:3 H171 Then to the colder bottome streight they dive,

BOUGH (3)
CONTEM173:23 H189 Thy bed a bough, thy drink the water cleer,
3LETTER183:8 H10 (On withered bough) most uncouthly bemoan
CHILDRN186:10 H77 And from the top bough take my flight,

BOUGHES (1) [boughs]
SEASONS50:35 H169 To feed his boughes, exhausted hath his sap,

BOUGHS (3) [pl.]
SEASONS51:15 H189 Boughs full of leaves, or fruits, but raw, and {unripe or} green,
DIALOG144:17 H127 Whence flow'd the source, the sprigs, the boughs, and fruits;
CHILDRN185:12 H38 On higher boughs he'l perch at length.

BOUGHT (1)
DIALOG143:33 H102 Church Offices are {were} sold, and bought, for gaine,

BOUND (9) [bind]
ELEMEN14:32 H274 But thou art bound to me, above the rest;
SEASONS52:16 H231 Bound up with Frosts, and furr'd with Hails, and Snows,
MASSYR60:9 H274 {Such} was the {his} promise bound, since first {which} he
MASSYR65:20 H485 Fast bound, intends at {to} *Babel* he shal stay {him to send},
MPERS84:18 H1254 That in all {his} Loyalty his heart was bound;
MGREC108:1 H2217 Is by his owne, now bound in Iron chaines,
DIALOG142:33 H62 A supplyant for your help, as she is bound.
QELIZ156:34 H61 And {the proud} *Tiron* bound, before her picture fell.
TDUDLEY165:4 H6 By duty bound, and not by custome led

BOUND (2) [boundary]
MGREC~~93:25~~ H1622 universe, scarce bounds {bound} his large {proud} vast minde;
MGREC106:10 H2144 Could bound his boundlesse, fond ambition)

BOUNDEN (2)
FATHER5:18 H19 They are your bounden handmaids to attend.
HUMOUR25:33 H222 So spils {shed'st} that life {blood}, thou'rt bounden to preserve.

BOUNDLES (1) [boundless]
MGREC116:31 ~~H2597~~ More boundles in ambition then the skie,

BOUNDLESSE (5)
FATHER6:13 H47 Then waters, {water} in the boundlesse Ocean flowes.
HUMOUR27:37 H308 Mans life to boundlesse time might stil endure;
MGREC101:21 H1946 Him boundlesse made, in vice, and cruelty;
MGREC106:10 H2144 Could bound his boundlesse, fond ambition)
MGREC126:33 ~~H3023~~ So boundlesse was her pride, and cruelty,

BOUNDS (8) n. [boundary]
ELEMEN17:4 H368 Nay many times, my Ocean breaks his bounds:
HUMOUR25:27 H216 Thou oft hast broke bounds of humanity.
MGREC93:25 H1622 universe, scarce bounds {bound} his large {proud} vast minde;
MGREC106:9 H2143 (For scarce the world, or any bounds thereon,
MGREC110:20 H2324 Restores him, and his bounds further {farther} extends;

MGREC115:1 H2512 Unto the furthest {farthest} bounds of th' orient;
MGREC126:34 ~~H3023~~ She oft forgot bounds of Humanity.
SIDNEY151:13 ~~H69~~ To be within the bounds of one world kept,
BOUNDS (2) n. [destinies]
MGREC135:9 H3381 Their standings, over-turnings, bounds and fates;
MEDDM207:23 Hp289 great landlord to let: All haue their bounds set ouer wch they
BOUNT'OUS (1) [bounteous]
MGREC~~94:18~~ H1653 And with a bount'ous heart and courage brave,
BOUNTEOUSLY (1)
MGREC~~97:18~~ H1779 Preserv'd their honour, us'd them courteously {bounteously},
BOUNTIFULL (1)
MGREC116:27 H2593 Profusely bountifull, without desert,
BOUNTY (8) See also BOVNTY
ELEMEN13:9 H210 My bounty calls you forth to make reports,
AGES39:30 H173 My wit, my bounty, and my courtesie,
AGES42:1 H259 For hundreds blesse me, for my bounty sent {lent}.
MPERS~~84:12~~ H1244 His bounty did *Darius* far exceed.
MPERS~~84:17~~ H1253 Such entertainment {royal bounty} with this {his} Prince he
MPERS~~84:34~~ H1270 To {By} whom oblig'd, by favour {bounty}, and by love;
MGREC132:30 H3277 Renown'd for bounty, valour, clemency,
MEDDM207:7 Hp288 draw men to god in consideration of his bounty towards them,
'BOUT (1) [about]
MPERS~~86:6~~ H1322 {this} *Nothus* reign'd {'bout} nineteen years, which run,
BOVNTY (1) [bounty]
SOREFIT221:29 H15 For all his Bovnty shew'd to me
BOW (3) n.
ELEMEN17:31 H395 Her confirm'd sonnes, behold my colour'd bow.
MPERS74:27 H850 Three strings to's bow, the least of which is good;
DAVID159:6 H21 The bow of *Jonathan* ne're turn'd in vaine,
BOW (3) v.
AGES45:28 H418 And back, once straight, begins apace to bow.
MASSYR63:14 H399 Until his Grand-childe made her bow the knee;
MPERS~~74:11~~ H836 The Nobles all alight, {bow to} their King to greet,
BOW'D (1) [bowed]
BYNIGHT220:9 H9 He bow'd his ear down from Above
BOWEL (1)
HUMOUR30:28 H420 Yet is a bowel cal'd wel as the rest.
BOWELS (5) [pl.]
ELEMEN13:7 H208 But you will see what in my bowels lyes?
AGES38:6 H109 My foe should weltering, with {in} his bowels reek.
AGES43:29 H324 The windy Cholick oft my bowels rend,
MGREC118:26 H2675 But all his bowels, coloured well, and sound.
DIALOG146:31 H217 Your sunken bowels gladly would refresh:
BOWER (1)
CONTEM174:24 H222 Fond fool, he takes this earth ev'n for heav'ns bower.
BOWERS (1) [pl.]
MGREC102:16 H1986 The Towers, and Bowers, of proud *Semiramis:*
BOWES (1) [pl.]
MPERS70:39 H710 Two *Sythian* bowes, a sword, and target round;
BOWL (1)
AGES45:41 H431 My golden Bowl, and silver Cord, e're long,

BOWS See BOWES

BOY (2)

MGREC94:34 H1672 That boy so mallepart, before the King.
CHILDRN185:24 H50 Some untoward boy at them do fling.

BOYISH (1)

HUMOUR21:19 H47 The man proves boyish, sottish, ignorant,

BOYLE (1) [boil]

FEVER220:26 H6 My burning flesh in sweat did boyle

BOYS (1)

ELEMEN10:12 H87 The Hidra, Dolphin, Boys, that waters {water} bear.

BOYSTEROUS (1)

MASSYR53:20 H10 The boysterous Sons of *Cush, {Chus,}* Grand-child to *Ham,*

BRADSTREET (6)

FATHER6:14 H48 ANNE BRADSTREET.
ELIZB186:32 H3-4 *Bradstreet, who deceased August, 1665*
ANNEB187:13 H2 Anne Bradstreet.
1SIMON188:1 H1-2 *On my dear Grand-child* Simon Bradstreet,
MERCY188:18 H2-4 *Mrs. Mercy Bradstreet, who deceased* Sept. 6.
2SIMON195:2 Hp271 Simon Bradstreet

BRAGGING (1)

DIALOG142:23 H52 Pray, doe not {you} feare *Spaines* bragging Armado?

BRAGGS (1) [pl.]

HUMOUR28:38 H350 No braggs i've us'd, t' your selves {to you} I dare appeale,

BRAIN (16) See also BRAINE, BRAIN'S

HUMOUR22:35 H104 The Brain she challenges, the Head's her seat,
HUMOUR22:36 H105 But know'ts a foolish brain, that wanteth heat;
HUMOUR30:2 H394 Then he whose brain a touch my humour gives.
HUMOUR33:9 H523 Who doth possesse the Brain, or thou, or I;
HUMOUR33:32 H546 The conjugations {Conjugation} of the parts toth' brain
HUMOUR34:13 H568 It is the substitute o'th royal Brain,
HUMOUR34:17 H572 Some other parts there issue from the Brain,
HUMOUR34:23 H578 A foolish Brain (saith {quoth} Choler) wanting heat,
HUMOUR~~34:27~~ H582 Then, my head {brain} for learning is not the fittest,
AGES41:3 H223 Sometimes the Phrensie, strangely madds my Brain,
SEASONS~~53:1~~ H257 *My Subjects bare, my Brains are {Brain is} bad,*
MGREC109:10 H2269 When thus, ten dayes, his brain with wine he'd soak'd,
DUBART154:18 H63 Thine the quintessence of an Heroick brain.
DUBART154:30 H75 Oh pregnant brain, Oh comprehension vast:
CONTEM173:11 H178 And thousand fancies buzzing in my brain,
AUTHOR177:30 H2 Thou ill-form'd offspring of my feeble brain,

BRAIN'D (2) [brained]

ELEMEN17:17 H381 That *Israels* enemies, therewith was {were} brain'd.
DUBART153:32 H36 Thus weake brain'd I, reading the lofty stile,

BRAINE (5)

PROLOG7:12 H26 A weake or wounded braine admits no cure.
AGES45:26 H416 My memory is short {bad}, and braine is dry.
MPERS73:37 H822 But others thought (none of the dullest braine,)
MGREC135:40 H3412 My tired braine, leaves to a {some} better pen,
QELIZ155:27 H18 T' accept the tribute of a loyall Braine;

BRAINED See BRAIN'D

BRAINES (2) [pl.]
SEASONS48:31 ~~H83~~ Some subject, shallow braines, much matter yeelds,
MGREC121:17 H2799 Knocks out his braines, to *Ptolomy* then went,
BRAIN'S (1) [brain is]
HUMOUR33:22 H536 The Brain's the noblest member all allow,
BRAINS (2) [pl.]
HUMOUR34:22 H577 For what's the Brains, is mine, by consequence;
SEASONS53:1 H257 *My Subjects bare, my Brains are {Brain is} bad,*
BRAKE (6)
HUMOUR32:23 H497 Nor how her Gaul on me she causeless brake;
MASSYR58:11 H196 Unto *Belosus,* then he brake his minde,
MPERS69:32 H654 Brake his long silence, cry'd, spare *Cressus* life:
MPERS80:41 H1108 Two mighty Rocks, brake from *Parnassus* Hil,
MPERS90:2 H1477 But when through difficulties still {all} they brake,
MGREC~~93:28~~ H1625 That broke {brake} his hornes, that threw him on the ground,
BRAKEST (1)
CONTEM168:12 H21 Or thousand since thou brakest thy shell of horn,
BRAKISH (1)
2LETTER182:5 H11 My dumpish thoughts, my groans, my brakish tears
BRAN (1)
MEDDM196:11 Hp273 The finest bread hath the least bran the purest hony the least
BRANCES (1) [branches]
MASSYR64:3 H427 This was that tree, whose brances fill'd the earth,
BRANCH (1)
DIALOG147:11 H237 To root out Prelates, {Popelings} head, tail, branch, and rush.
BRANCHES (2) [pl.] See also BRANCES
SEASONS47:10 H26 The Gardner, now superfluous branches lops,
MERCY188:24 H10 I saw the branches lopt the Tree now fall,
BRANDED (1)
CONTEM170:34 H104 Branded with guilt, and crusht with treble woes,
BRANDISH'D (1) [brandished]
DIALOG148:17 H282 This done, with brandish'd swords, to *Turky* go,
BRANDS (1) [pl.]
MEDDM208:6 Hp289 As the brands of a fire, if once severed, will of themselues goe
BRASEN (1)
HUMOUR30:40 H432 Then is thy torrid nose, or brasen brow.
BRASSE (2)
MGREC135:22 H3394 The third, belly and thighs of brasse in sight,
MGREC135:26 H3398 Then gold, silver, brasse, iron, and all that {the} store,
BRAT (1)
AUTHOR177:37 H9 My rambling brat (in print) should mother call,
BRAULES (1) [brawls]
ELEMEN12:6 H166 Strong forts from *Spanish* and *Italian* braules,
BRAVE (38)
ELEMEN~~9:35~~ H70 And trim thee gay {brave}, in green, after thy blacks?
AGES39:16 H159 The brave attempts of valiant Knights I prize,
AGES~~39:28~~ H171 Sweet Musick rapteth {raps} my {brave} harmonious Soul,
SEASONS49:23 ~~H114~~ Was like that noble, brave *Archadian.*
MASSYR55:6 H72 She like a brave Virago, play'd the rex,
MASSYR56:14 H120 Which is the midst, of this brave Town was plac'd,
MASSYR58:7 H192 At last {It chanc'd} *Arbaces* brave, unwarily,

MASSYR63:4 H389 Brave *Merodach,* the Son of *Balladan,*

MASSYR63:23 H408 Brave *Nebulassar* to this King was Sonne,

MPERS74:38 H859 Then brave *Zopirus,* for his Masters good,

MPERS76:31 H929 By brave *Miltiades* (their chief) being led,

MPERS79:35 H1061 The *Spartan* meets him, brave *Leonade,*

MPERS~~80:2~~ H1069 And wound the backs of those bold {brave} Warriours stout.

MPERS80:30 H1097 That brave *Thymistocles* takes this wise course,

MPERS81:26 H1134 Nor could the brave Ambassador be {he} sent,

MGREC~~94:18~~ H1653 And with a bount'ous heart and courage brave,

MGREC96:27 H1747 This brave Virago, to the King was mother;

MGREC98:24 H1826 Who was the son of that *Parmenio* brave;

MGREC99:8 H1851 But, quoth *Parmenio,* (that brave Commander)

MGREC99:12 H1855 To which, brave {proud} *Alexander* did {made} reply,

MGREC109:34 H2293 But Kingly *Porus* this brave answer sent,

MGREC112:4 H2390 At the {this} same time, unto his Captains brave;

MGREC114:16 H2486 Then all the wrong to brave *Parmenio* done.

MGREC119:18 H2708 To brave *Craterus,* then, he sends with speed,

MGREC120:31 H2768 Brave *Ptolomy,* to make a fourth now {then} sent,

MGREC121:7 H2785 Brave *Ptolomy* to th' utmost to oppose.

MGREC121:41 H2823 And brave *Craterus* slew, amongst the rest,

MGREC132:29 H3276 Now {Next} dyed the brave and noble *Ptolomy,*

MGREC135:2 H3374 Then poysonous {His brave *Virago*} Aspes she sets unto {to}

DIALOG142:8 H37 Or hath *Canutus,* that brave valiant *Dane,*

DIALOG147:18 H244 Go on brave *Essex,* shew whose son thou art {with a loyal

DIALOG147:24 H248 And yee brave Nobles, chase away all fear,

DIALOG148:5 H270 When thus in Peace: thine Armies brave send out,

SIDNEY150:8 H33 (O brave Refiner of our *Brittish* Tongue;)

SIDNEY150:19 H44 O brave *Achilles,* I wish some *Homer* would

SIDNEY150:28 H55 Brave *Hector* by the walls of *Troy,* we see:

DUBART153:23 H27 Some part, at least, of that brave wealth was his;

QELIZ156:27 H54 She frankly help'd *Franks* (brave) distressed King,

BRAVELY (5)

ELEMEN14:8 ~~H250~~ Who bravely rode into my yawning chinke.

HUMOUR21:38 H66 She'l ride a Horse as bravely, as the best,

MPERS~~82:5~~ H1152 No longer dar'd, but fiercely {bravely} on-set gave,

MGREC125:15 H2963 The Queen to meet her, bravely marched {marches} on;

MGREC128:31 H3104 But bravely sends the Prisoners back againe,

BRAVING (1)

DIALOG143:11 H80 *Spaines* braving Fleet a second time is sunke,

BRAWLS See BRAULES

BRAWN (1)

SEASONS52:5 H220 Beef, Brawn, and Pork, are now in great'st {great} request,

BRAWNIE (1)

MEDDM199:31 Hp278 Sore labourers haue hard hands and old sinners haue brawnie

BRAZEN See BRASEN

BREACH (4)

HUMOUR21:25 H53 To storme a Breach, or scale a City wal?

MPERS72:19 H767 Upon a Judge, for breach of Law {taking bribes} accus'd;

MPERS84:25 H1261 For punishment, their breach of oath did call,

DIALOG143:28 H97 Which are my Sins, the breach of sacred Lawes;

BREACHES (1) [pl.]
AGES38:35 H138 What breaches, knocks, and falls I daily have?
BREAD (8)
ELEMEN15:10 H292 Man wants his bread, and wine, and pleasant fruits;
AGES42:3 H261 With mine owne fleece, and with my houshold bread.
SEASONS50:22 H156 Although their Bread have not so white a face.
DIALOG146:21 H207 The poore they want their pay, their children bread,
CONTEM170:3 H77 To get his bread with pain, and sweat of face:
MEDDM196:11 Hp273 The finest bread hath the least bran the purest hony the least
MEDDM197:32 Hp275 is not fit for bread, god so deales wth his servants, he grindes
PILGRIM210:12 H12 Nor wild fruits eate, in stead of bread
BREADTH (2)
MASSYR56:5 H111 Almost incredible, they were in breadth.
MPERS87:34 H1386 Some fifty, or else sixty foote in breadth.
BREAK (12)
HUMOUR21:39 H67 And break a staffe, provided't be in jest,
HUMOUR24:17 H166 Or honestie such ties, unfriendly break?
AGES38:24 H127 And fift Commandement do daily break.
AGES43:30 H325 To break the darksome prison, where it's pend;
MASSYR65:12 H477 Thinks this the fittest time to break his bands,
MPERS~~79:12~~ H1034 But winds, and waves those iron bands did break;
MPERS80:32 H1099 That *Greeks* to break his bridge shortly intends;
MPERS~~85:29~~ H1305 Re-gaines his own, and then {doth} the Rebell breaks: {break,}
DIALOG142:21 H50 To come, and break the tushes of the Boar?
DUBART154:5 H50 My full astonish'd heart doth pant to break,
CONTEM173:37 H201 Each storm his state, his mind, his body break,
FEVER220:27 H7 My aking head did break,
BREAKE (1)
ELEMEN8:10 H8 But enmity, this amity did breake:
BREAKETH (1)
MGREC135:23 H3395 And last was Iron, which breaketh all with might.
BREAKING (2)
SICKNES178:35 H18 that alwayes art a breaking,
MEDDM205:32 Hp286 Burden, is the breaking of their limbes, some again, are but
BREAKS (2)
ELEMEN17:4 H368 Nay many times, my Ocean breaks his bounds:
MPERS85:29 H1305 Re-gaines his own, and then {doth} the Rebell breaks: {break,}
BREAST (5) See also BREST
MGREC132:37 H3284 'Twas no small joy, unto *Seleuchus* breast,
MGREC135:21 H3393 Next, armes and breast, of silver to behold;
1LETTER181:23 H21 Within the Cancer of my glowing breast,
CHILDRN185:5 H31 Ambition moves still in his breast
CHILDRN185:29 H55 O would my young, ye saw my breast,
BREASTS (4) See also BRESTS
AGES41:9 H229 Marrow {aches} ful my bones, of Milk {woe} my breasts {heart},
MPERS82:31 H1178 Cut off her lilly breasts, her nose, and ears;
MPERS82:39 H1186 To see those breasts, where chastity did dwel,
MEDDM202:11 Hp281 y^{t} their bones are full of marrow & their breasts of milk,
BREATH (11)
ELEMEN17:38 H402 I am the breath of every living soul.
ELEMEN18:4 H408 How gladly should his gold purchase his breath,

SEASONS~~46:35~~ H12 Nor hot nor cold, she spake, but with a breath,
SEASONS49:40 H133 Whose flaming breath doth melt us from afar,
MPERS88:32 H1425 Sencelesse and mute they stand, yet breath out groans,
MGREC104:4 H2056 Then still with infamy, to draw his breath.
MGREC105:3 H2096 And leaves him thus, to gaspe out his last breath.
MGREC106:3 H2137 This said, his fainting breath did fleet away,
MGREC127:1 H3031 Some slew, some fry'd, of others, stopt the breath;
MGREC130:18 H3173 As vile conspiratours that took {stopt} her breath,
SICKNES178:19 H2 Since nature gave me breath,

BRED (6)
ELEMEN16:34 H357 All humours, Tumours, that {which} are bred of cold.
AGES38:33 H136 What crudities my cold stomach hath bred?
SEASONS~~49:23~~ H114 Hath envy bred in Kings that were at strife,
MASSYR62:27 H372 Hath bred more wonder, then beleefe in hearts;
MROMAN138:25 H3515 *Tarquin,* a *Greek,* at *Corinth* borne, and bred,
CHILDRN185:31 H57 Great was my pain when I you bred,

BREEDING (2)
AGES37:6 H68 My mothers breeding sicknes, I will spare;
AGES38:32 H135 What tortures I, in breeding teeth sustain?

BREEDS (3)
HUMOUR22:26 H95 Poor spirits the Liver breeds, which is thy seat,
HUMOUR~~25:3~~ H192 As thy unbridled, barb'rous Choler yeelds. {breeds:}
MPERS~~85:19~~ H1295 Which from remissenesse, in *{Less} Asia* proceeds {breeds.}

BREIF (2) [brief] See also BRIEFE
HUMOUR28:35 H347 Yet could not be more breif, without much wrong.
HUMOUR34:35 H590 Wel, to be breif, Choler I hope now's laid,

BREST (2) [breast]
AGES37:15 H77 Who sought stil to appease me, with her {the} brest,
AGES39:26 H169 I can insinuate into the brest,

BRESTS (1) [breasts]
MEDDM200:11 Hp279 these empty brests, that god is forced to hedg vp their way wth

BRETHERN (1)
MGREC125:32 H2982 His Brethern, Kinsfolk, and his chiefest friends,

BRETHREN (2)
MPERS~~91:39~~ H1553 Of brethren and of kindred to be slain.
MGREC112:34 H2420 And's Brethren, whom {who} for him their lives had spent;

BREVITY (1)
MGREC136:14 H3428 *Will force me to a confus'd brevity;*

BRIARS (1) [pl.]
MEDDM198:9 Hp276 He that walks among briars and thorns will be very carefull,

BRIBERY (1)
DIALOG144:12 H122 For Bribery, Adultery, for Thefts, and Lyes,

BRIBES (3) [pl.]
MPERS~~72:19~~ H767 Upon a Judge, for breach of Law {taking bribes} accus'd;
DIALOG147:40 H264 Then bribes shall cease, and suits shall not stick long,
MEDDM205:14 Hp286 Judg, whom no bribes can pervert, nor flattery cause to favour

BRIDE (1)
MGREC101:6 H1931 His eldest Daughter, for his Princely Bride,

BRIDEGROOM (1) See also BRIDGROME
CONTEM168:23 H30 Thou as a Bridegroom from thy Chamber rushes,

BRIDEGROOM'S (1) [poss.]
HOUSE237:8 H38 Nor bridegroom's voice ere heard shall bee.
BRIDGE (6)
MPERS76:1 H899 A bridge he made, which serv'd for boat, and barge,
MPERS79:10 H1032 Next, o're the *Hellispont* a bridge he made,
MPERS~~79:13~~ H1038 The work-men put to death the bridge that made,
MPERS80:32 H1099 That *Greeks* to break his bridge shortly intends;
MPERS~~81:5~~ H1113 Thought it {Fearing} his best {bridge}, no longer for to {there
MROMAN138:18 H3508 A stately Bridge he over *Tyber* made,
BRIDGES (1) [pl.]
MASSYR56:20 H126 Her gardens, bridges, arches, mounts, and spires;
BRIDGROME (1) [bridegroom]
PILGRIM211:3 H44 then Come deare bridgrome Come away
BRIDLE (1)
MEDDM205:25 Hp286 allseeing eye will be a bridle to restrain from evill, and a spur,
BRIDLES (1) [pl.]
MGREC110:31 H2335 Huge Bridles made, which here, and there, he left,
BRIEF (1) See also BREIF, BRIEFE
SIDNEY151:39 ~~H75~~ I leave't in brief, *Apollo* do't at large.
BRIEFE (1) [brief] See also BREIF
HUMOUR20:33 H25 Wel, thus they parle, and chide, but to be briefe,
BRIGHT (5)
SEASONS47:26 H42 Doth darken *Sols* bright face, makes us remember
SEASONS49:4 H95 Bright *June, July,* and *August,* hot are mine,
CONTEM169:7 H49 Who gave this bright light luster unto thee:
FLESH177:24 H105 But beauty shall be bright and clear;
MEDDM206:16 Hp287 shine so bright while they moue on earth, how transcendently
BRIGHTNES (1)
MEDDM206:8 Hp287 regard of bignes and brightnes, yet all receiue their light from
BRIGHTNESSE (1)
DIALOG146:37 H223 But now the Sun in's brightnesse shall appear,
BRINE (1)
30SEPT227:26 Hp257 p^{r}served wth sugar then brine, yet will he p^{r}serve me to his
BRING (41)
FATHER5:13 H14 I bring my four times {and} four, now meanly clad,
HUMOUR24:32 H181 No pattern, nor no Patron will I bring,
SEASONS46:28 H4 Another Four i've {left} yet for to bring on,
SEASONS46:31 H7 In season all these Seasons I shal bring;
MASSYR54:31 H58 By force, {and fraud} his tributary, he did {under Tribute} bring.
MASSYR57:15 H162 'Gainst whom his trained Bands *Abram* did bring.
MASSYR58:18 H203 Against their monstrous King to bring {use} their might,
MASSYR61:28 H333 His humble thankfulnesse (with {in} hast) to bring,
MASSYR62:11 H356 Into perpetual thraldome that time bring;
MASSYR65:41 H506 With Children, Wives, and Nobles, all they bring,
MPERS69:2 H624 Whom Lady *Mandana* did to him bring;
MPERS88:16 H1409 Which did such courage to the *Grecians* bring,
MGREC93:37 H1634 His high resolves which way to bring to passe:
MGREC94:33 H1671 To whip him well with rods, and then {so} to bring,
MGREC97:32 H1793 But down his haughty stomach could not bring,
MGREC107:7 H2182 Intends with speed, that Traitor down {to his end} to bring;
MGREC107:10 H2185 Commands forth-with, each man his fardle bring,

MGREC107:18 H2193 Nor wonder lesse, to Readers may it bring,

MGREC107:26 H2201 This {Which} more mortality to them did bring,

MGREC108:3 H2219 And in this sort, they rather drag, then bring,

MGREC110:4 H2304 And ninety Elephants for war did bring;

MGREC128:4 H3077 And that some title he might seeme to bring,

MROMAN136:24 H3438 Whom vestall *Rhea,* into {to} th' world did bring

MROMAN137:39 H3490 Who Martiall Discipline in use did bring;

MROMAN139:22 H3550 The Government they change, a new one bring,

DIALOG141:22 H21 Will bring Consumption, or an Ague quaking,

DIALOG143:2 H71 French *Lewis* {Jews} unjustly to the Crown to bring;

DIALOG147:12 H238 Let's bring *Baals* vestments out, {forth} to make a fire,

DIALOG147:31 H255 Out of all mists, such glorious dayes will {shall} bring,

DIALOG148:13 H278 Bring forth the beast that rul'd the world with's beck,

DUBART153:10 H14 But barren I, my Daysey here doe bring,

DUBART154:40 H85 Good will, not skill, did cause me bring my mite.

QELIZ155:22 H13 Thousands bring off'rings, (though out of date)

TDUDLEY166:31 H73 At last will bring us to that happy place

CONTEM170:15 H87 Fruits of the Earth, and Fatlings each do bring,

BIRTH180:17 H27 And if chance to thine eyes shall bring this verse,

CHILDRN186:5 H72 And things that past, to mind I'le bring.

MEDDM206:23 Hp287 for mercy wthout mony & wthout price but bring his filthy raggs

SAMUEL228:13 H14 Protect him there & bring him back.

SON230:26 H9 Did'st that ship bring to quiet port,

HOURS234:23 H37 Bring back my husband I beseech

BRINGING (2)

MGREC111:5 H2350 Bringing their Presents, rare, and precious things:

MGREC131:11 H3203 Near *Ephesus,* each bringing all their {his} might,

BRINGS (11)

ELEMEN15:23 H305 But what's the wealth that my rich Ocean brings?

AGES38:28 H131 For sin brings sorrow, sicknesse, death, and woe.

AGES46:13 H444 Yet studying much, brings wearinesse to th' flesh;

MASSYR61:12 H317 Under subjection by his sword he brings;

MGREC104:37 H2089 Unto *Darius,* first he brings a Horse,

MGREC109:20 H2279 Fifty six Elephants he brings to's hands: {hand,}

MGREC126:32 H3023 But Royalty no good conditions brings;

MGREC129:27 H3141 *Polisperchon* brings up the other son,

VANITY160:36 H46 It brings to honour, which shall not {ne're} decay,

ELIZB187:8 H16 And time brings down what is both strong and tall.

MEDDM203:28 Hp284 bid him welcome, that brings a plaister for his sore, or a

BRINK (1)

MGREC107:24 H2199 At length, they came to th' River *Oxus* brink,

BRINKS (1) [pl.]

ELEMEN15:20 H302 When I run low, and not o'reflow her brinks;

BRINY (1)

DIALOG147:29 H253 The briny Ocean will o'rflow your shore,

BRITAIN (1)

ELEMEN17:8 H372 Thus *Albion* {*Britain* fair} (tis thought) was cut from *France,*

BRITAIN'S (1) [poss.]

ELEMEN~~11:1~~ H118 And stately *London,* (our great *Britain's* glory)

BRITISH (1)

SIDNEY149:9 H8 No lesse {As well} an Honour to our *British* Land,

BRITTISH (2)
AGES40:27 H208 Seek out a Brittish, bruitish Cavaleer;
SIDNEY150:8 H33 (O brave Refiner of our *Brittish* Tongue;)

BRITTLE (4)
HUMOUR34:30 H585 For memory, the sand is not more brittle.
VANITY159:33 H5 On brittle earth, a consolation sound?
ANNEB187:26 H16 Like as a bubble, or the brittle glass,
SAMUEL228:11 H12 For mortall helpes are brittle Dvst.

BROAD (1)
MASSYR54:23 H50 So broad, three Chariots run abrest there might,

BROILE (1)
AGES42:19 H277 Did toile, did broile, oppress'd, did steal and lye.

BROILED See BROY'D, BROYLED

BROILES (1) [pl.] See also BROYLS
MASSYR67:17 H563 (Within which broiles, rich *Crœsus* was engaged,)

BROKE (6)
HUMOUR25:27 H216 Thou oft hast broke bounds of humanity.
AGES35:36 H22 And when tis broke, then ends his life and all.
AGES46:1 H432 Shal both be broke, by wracking death so strong;
MPERS69:37 ~~H659~~ Upon demand, his minde to *Cyrus* broke,
MGREC93:28 H1625 That broke {brake} his hornes, that threw him on the ground,
MGREC117:13 H2620 The great Horn broke, the lesse did tytannize;

BROKEN (2)
PROLOG7:1 H16 Nor yet a sweet Consort, from broken strings,
PROLOG7:3 H18 My foolish, broken, blemish'd Muse so sings;

BROOD (4)
SEASONS48:7 H60 clocking hen, her chipping brood now {chirping chickins} leads,
MASSYR62:14 H359 This was that strange degenerated brood,
CHILDRN184:20 H9 Chief of the Brood then took his flight,
CHILDRN185:19 H45 Lest this my brood some harm should catch,

BROOKS (2) [pl.]
SEASONS~~49:33~~ H124 By purling Brooks looking how fishes swims.
CONTEM172:23 H157 But hundred brooks in thy cleer waves do meet,

BROTHER (28)
MASSYR59:10 H234 The King his Brother leaves, all to sustaine,
MPERS69:11 H633 *Darius* was unto *Mandana* brother,
MPERS72:3 ~~H755~~ His brother *Smerdis* sit upon his throne;
MPERS~~72:3~~ H755 Unjustly caus'd his brother to be slain.
MPERS72:11 H759 Hearing her harmlesse brother thus was dead,
MPERS72:16 H764 O hellish Husband, Brother, Vnckle, Sire,
MPERS~~77:16~~ H956 (His eldest brother put beside the place,
MPERS83:6 H1194 His wicked brother, {soon} after sent {him} a crew,
MPERS85:6 H1282 But he, with his next {second} brother {him} fell at strife,
MPERS85:39 H1315 Prefers his brother, for his birth-rights sake.
MPERS86:11 H1327 Still on his brother, casts a jealous eye,
MPERS86:16 H1332 More deare to's mother, then his brother far.
MPERS87:12 H1368 In numbers from his brother daily run.
MPERS87:16 ~~H1370~~ To look his manly brother in the face.
MPERS92:5 ~~H1559~~ Why *Arsames* his brother should succeed,
MPERS~~92:5~~ H1561 Some write that *Arsames* was *Ochus* brother,
MPERS~~92:5~~ H1563 But why brother 'fore his son succeeds

MPERS~~92:7~~ H1565 His brother, as tis said, long since was slain,
MGREC108:5 H2221 Who to *Darius* Brother gives the wretch,
MGREC117:40 H2647 His base born Brother, *Aridæus* nam'd,
MGREC122:19 H2844 Who was *Perdicas, Philips* elder {eldest} brother,
MGREC125:34 H2984 Digg'd up his brother dead, 'gainst natures right,
MGREC129:28 H3142 Call'd *Hercules,* and elder then his brother,
MGREC134:37 ~~H3367~~ Her brother by him, lost his trayterous head
MROMAN136:33 H3447 His Brother *Remus* there, by him was slaine,
DAVID159:26 H41 So pleasant hast thou been, deare brother mine:
CONTEM170:23 H94 His brother comes, then acts his fratricide,
MED223:7 Hp250 Almighty—Christ is my Brother, I ascend vnto my father, and

BROTHERS (4) [pl.]
AGES43:11 ~~H305~~ Nor Brothers, Nephewes, Sons, nor Sires I've spar'd.
MPERS80:12 H1079 Amongst the rest, two brothers he lost there;
MPERS~~91:36~~ H1550 Two of his brothers in his Fathers dayes
MROMAN138:2 H3492 The strife to end, six Brothers doe ingage;

BROTHERS (8) [poss.]
MPERS73:3 H790 Griefe for his brothers death, he did expresse,
MPERS82:23 H1170 His brothers wife, sollicites to his will;
MPERS83:3 H1191 His brothers recompence was naught but jears:
MPERS85:7 ~~H1283~~ That nought appeas'd him, but his brothers life.
MPERS85:40 H1316 But *Cyrus* scornes, his brothers feeble wit;
MPERS86:17 H1333 His brothers little love, like to be gone,
MPERS87:35 H1387 Yet for his brothers comming, durst not stay,
CONTEM170:19 H91 Hath thousand thoughts to end his brothers dayes,

BROUGHT (26) See also BROVGHT
MASSYR66:8 H514 The Towers, and Palaces, brought to decay;
MASSYR67:33 H579 The holy vessells, thither brought long since,
MASSYR68:17 H603 *Daniel* in haste, is brought before the King,
MPERS78:41 H1022 The Kings cals for the Youth, who being brought,
MPERS85:11 H1287 To be by *Hester,* {fair Queen Ester} to her husband brought.
MPERS85:23 H1299 Before to quietnesse things could be brought,
MPERS88:22 H1415 And brought his Souldiers on so gallantly,
MGREC95:36 H1715 For this wise King, had brought to see the sport;
MGREC96:23 H1743 Great *Sisigambis,* she brought up the Reare;
MGREC97:14 H1775 The Royall Captives, brought to *Alexander,*
MGREC98:18 H1820 Whose glory, now {then} a second time's brought down;
MGREC100:4 H1888 For in few dayes he brought that Kingdom under.
MGREC106:15 H2149 *Thalestris,* Queen of th' *Amazons,* now brought
MGREC~~110:18~~ H2319 The kingly Captive 'fore the Victor's brought,
MGREC112:29 H2415 Yet is *Philotas* unto Judgement brought,
MGREC116:4 H2564 By *Philip,* and *Cassander,* to him brought,
MGREC120:18 H2753 That by his help, the rest might low be brought:
MGREC125:1 H2949 Which damage both to minde and body brought:
MGREC125:21 ~~H2969~~ But soone are brought into captivity;
MGREC135:10 H3382 Now up, now down, now chief, and then brought under;
MGREC136:12 H3426 *This fourth to th' other three, now might be brought.*
DISTEMP179:25 H13 And brought me to the shore from troubled Main.
MEDDM198:13 Hp276 Want of prudence as well as piety hath brought men into great
MEDDM204:35 Hp285 brought into tilth yet all must be ploughed and harrowed Some
MEDDM205:5 Hp285 nurture they are brought into a fit capacity, let the seed of good

PILGRIM210:21 H21 By age and paines brought to decay

BROUZE (1) [browse]

3LETTER183:27 H29 Together at one Tree, oh let us brouze,

BROVGHT (6) [brought]

MYCHILD216:17 Hp241 I have brovght yov into ye world, and wth great paines,

MYCHILD216:18 Hp241 + feares brovght yov to this, I now travail in birth again of yov

FEVER221:6 H21 To Glory t' shall bee brovght.

SON231:15 H27 On Eagles wings him hether brovght

2HUSB233:4 H37 To Wildernesse ha'st brovght

ACK235:11 H11 Thou hast to shore him safely brovght

BROW (2)

HUMOUR30:40 H432 Then is thy torrid nose, or brasen brow.

SEASONS49:2 H93 Wiping her {the} sweat from off {of} her brow, that ran,

BROWES (1) [brows]

DUBART154:19 H64 The Oaken garland ought to deck their browes,

BROWSE See BROUZE

BROY'D (1) [broiled] See also BROYLED

AGES42:39 H295 How was I broy'd with envy, and with hate?

BROYLED (1) [broiled] See also BROY'D

ELEMEN8:17 H15 Fire broyled Earth, and scorched Earth it choaked,

BROYLS (1) [broils] See also BROILES

MPERS91:6 H1514 With broyls, and quarrels, sets all *Greece* on fire.

BRUISE (1)

MEDDM197:5 Hp274 bruise, then polish

BRUISED (1)

MERCY188:26 H12 My bruised heart lies sobbing at the Root,

BRUISES (1)

MEDDM200:17 Hp279 the best, but falls and bruises, or perhaps somewhat worse,

BRUITISH (3) [brutish]

ELEMEN11:4 H124 And more then bruitish *Sodome* for her lust,

AGES40:27 H208 Seek out a Brittish, bruitish Cavaleer;

MASSYR67:24 H570 A Royall State, rul'd by a bruitish mind.

BRUNT (1)

MPERS88:5 H1398 The brunt of that huge multitude to bide.

BRUNTS (1) [pl.]

HUMOUR21:31 H59 Nay milk-sops, at such brunts you look but blew,

BRUTISH See BRUITISH

BRUTUS (1)

MROMAN139:19 H3547 With *Junius Brutus* rose, and being strong,

BRYARS (1) [pl.]

PILGRIM210:9 H9 The bryars and thornes no more shall scrat

BUBBLE (2)

SICKNES178:34 H17 O Bubble blast, how long can'st last?

ANNEB187:26 H16 Like as a bubble, or the brittle glass,

BUCEPHALON (1)

MGREC110:39 H2343 The first *Nicea,* the next *Bucephalon,*

BUCKLER (1)

HUMOUR29:35 H386 Wise *Fabius* is her buckler: all accord.

BUD (2)

AGES40:31 ~~H210~~ My youth, my best, my strength, my bud, and prime:

1SIMON188:6 H7 Three flours, two scarcely blown, the last i'th' bud,

BUDDING (1)
SEASONS47:22 H38 The tender tops of budding Grasse they crop,
BUDS (2) [pl.]
ELEMEN13:29 H230 And buds from fruitfull trees, before they'r {as soon as} blowne:
ELIZB187:10 H18 And buds new blown, to have so short a date,
BUILD (3)
AGES42:23 H281 As neither sow, nor reape, nor plant, nor build.
TDUDLEY165:36 H38 Upon the earth he did not build his nest,
MYCHILD218:35 Hp244 o my Soul to thy Rest, vpon this Rock Xt Jesus will I build
BUILDED (1)
MPERS70:23 H694 An Edict makes {made}, the Temple builded be,
BUILDING (2)
MASSYR55:36 H102 Her wealth she shew'd, in building *Babylon;*
MGREC127:12 H3042 But leave him building, other in their urn,
BUILDINGS (2) [pl.]
MASSYR66:23 H529 His sumptuous buildings passes all conceit,
CONTEM174:34 H231 Nor wit nor gold, nor buildings scape times rust;
BUILDS (2)
SEASONS48:3 H56 The fearful Bird, his little house now builds,
CONTEM170:36 H106 A City builds, that wals might him secure from foes.
BUILT (16)
ELEMEN13:1 H202 Built Cities, Monuments call'd by your names;
HUMOUR33:34 H548 Within this high built Cittadel doth lye,
MASSYR60:34 H299 When this was built, and all matters in peace,
MPERS73:8 H795 And built fair *Meroe,* for his sisters sake.
MPERS75:37 H894 Built on, and prosper'd, till their walls did {house they} close;
MGREC109:6 H2265 He t' *Nisa* goes, by *Bacchus* built long since,
MGREC110:38 H2342 Two Cities built, his fame {name} might there abide;
MGREC111:14 H2359 A City here he built, cal'd by his name,
MGREC128:7 H3080 Had built, and call'd a City by his name,
MGREC134:21 H3352 The {At *Alexandria* a} Library at *Alexandria* built,
MROMAN136:37 H3451 This City built, and Sacrifices done,
MROMAN137:6 H3457 That wil within these strong built walls reside,
MROMAN137:27 H3478 To *Janus,* he that famous Temple built,
MROMAN138:16 H3506 *Rome* he inlarg'd, new built againe the wall,
MROMAN138:20 H3510 Faire *Ostia* he built, this Town, it stood,
QELIZ~~157:6~~ H74 She plac'd {built} her glory but on *Babels* walls,
BUISNES (1) [business] See also BUSSINES
ACK235:16 H16 In this his Buisnes and Addresse.
BULK (2)
MGREC103:8 H2019 Here lay the bulk, of all those precious things;
MGREC117:19 H2626 When of his monstrous bulk it was the guide,
BULL (2)
ELEMEN10:9 H84 The Ram, the Bull, the Lyon, and the Beagle;
ELEMEN15:2 H284 The Camell hath no strength, thy Bull no force;
BULLET (1)
AGES39:23 H166 I fly to catch the Bullet that's {that} aloof;
BULWARKS (1)
MASSYR55:40 H106 With Towers, and Bulwarks made of costly stone
BUNDLES (1) n.
MGREC107:35 H2210 And stuffing them with straw, he bundles makes;

BUNDLES (2) v.
SEASONS50:19 H153 And bundles up in sheaves the weighty Wheat,
BURDEN (7)
AGES37:7 H69 Her nine months weary burden not declare.
SEASONS50:4 H138 The Medows of their burden {riches} to dispoyl;
MASSYR65:1 H466 And in the channell throw {threw} each burden down;
MGREC107:9 H2184 And no man with his burden, burdened be,
MEDDM197:26 Hp275 will vntertake to climb vp a steep mountain wth a great burden
MEDDM200:33 Hp280 A wise father will not lay a burden on a child of seven yeares
MEDDM205:32 Hp286 Burden, is the breaking of their limbes, some again, are but
BURDENED (1)
MGREC107:9 H2184 And no man with his burden, burdened be,
BURDENS (1) [pl.]
MEDDM201:3 Hp280 many times he imposes waighty burdens on their shoulders,
BURIED (2)
MGREC112:17 H2403 His vertues dead, buried, and all {quite} forgot,
MEDDM198:34 Hp277 shall rather choose to be buried vnder rocks and mountains
BUR'ING (1) [burying]
ELEMEN~~14:4~~ H248 Bur'ing himself alive for honours prize.
BURN (1)
1LETTER181:22 H20 I wish my Sun may never set, but burn
BURN'D (2) [burned]
ELEMEN10:36 H111 What lasting Forts my kindled wrath hath burn'd?
ELEMEN14:21 H263 And after death, whether inter'd, or burn'd;
BURNES (1) [burns]
MPERS77:5 H944 And for revenge his heart still restlesse burnes;
BURNING (9)
ELEMEN9:31 H65 A burning fiery heat we find reflect;
ELEMEN18:25 H429 When burning heat, doth cause you faint, I coole,
HUMOUR32:7 H481 Nor Cough, nor Quinsie, nor the burning Feavor.
SEASONS49:7 H98 And {Then} retrograde, now is {must be} my burning Sun.
SEASONS49:14 H105 That if you do, remove {withdtaw} her burning store,
SEASONS50:6 H140 Bearing the burning heat of the long day;
PILGRIM210:7 H7 The burning sun no more shall heat
FEVER220:26 H6 My burning flesh in sweat did boyle
RESTOR229:19 H1-2 For the restoration of my dear Husband from a burning
BURNINGS (1) [pl.]
FEVER220:35 H15 From Burnings keep my Soul.
BURNS See BURNES
BURNT (7)
MASSYR66:7 H513 The Temple's burnt, the Vessels had away,
MPERS90:4 ~~H1478~~ Before them burnt the country as they went,
MPERS~~90:4~~ H1478 The Country burnt, they no relief might take.
MPERS92:1 ~~H1555~~ In after wars were burnt, 'mongst other things?
MGREC93:21 H1618 To th' ground was burnt, *Diana's* Temple high,
MGREC102:8 H1978 And Insence burnt, the silver Altars on;
MGREC131:5 H3195 Who incense burnt, and offered oblation.
BURST (1)
AGES~~45:22~~ H404 To see them swill in blood untill they burst.
BURY (1)
ELEMEN19:17 H462 The living, scarce had power, to bury dead.

BURYING See BUR'ING
BUSH (2)
SEASONS47:19 H35 Now tune their layes, on sprays of every bush;
3LETTER183:1 H3 Perplext, in every bush & nook doth pry,
BUSHES (1)
CHILDRN185:10 H36 Is 'mongst the shrubs and bushes flown,
BUSIE (1)
SEASONS48:17 H70 Now swarmes the busie buzzing {witty,} hony Bee.
BUSSINES (1) [business] See also BUISNES
MEDDM203:13 Hp283 wher his bussines lyes, a christian is sailing through this world
BUT'S (1) [but is]
HUMOUR29:41 H392 But's not thy {thine} ignorance shal thus deceive me.
BUY (2)
ELEMEN15:25 H307 Shouldst thou but buy, it would exhaust thy gold.
AGES37:32 H94 Nor studious was, Kings favours how to buy,
BUZZING (3)
AGES37:37 H99 Nor unto buzzing whisperors, gave ear.
SEASONS48:17 H70 Now swarmes the busie buzzing {witty,} hony Bee.
CONTEM173:11 H178 And thousand fancies buzzing in my brain,

C

CABBIN (1)
MEDDM203:10 Hp283 that is to saile into a farre country, although the ship, cabbin
CABINS (1) [pl.]
MGREC110:28 H2332 And for his Souldiers larger Cabins make;
CADES (2)
AGES45:5 H389 I've seen designes at {for} *Ree,* and *Cades* {*Rochel*} crost,
QELIZ157:1 H69 Her *Essex* took *Cades,* their *Herculean* hold:
CÆSAR (17)
ELEMEN11:8 H128 Which made a *Cæsar,* (Romes) the worlds proud head,
SEASONS50:1 H135 This month from *Julius Cæsar* took the {its} name,
MGREC134:36 H3367 Whom *Julius Cæsar* set in Royall place,
SIDNEY150:18 ~~H49~~ A Crow's a Crow, and *Cæsar* is a King.
CÆSARS (1)
ELEMEN15:38 H320 Which *Cæsars, Consuls, Tribunes* all adorne;
CAIN (2)
CONTEM170:7 H80 And in her lap, her bloody *Cain* new born,
CONTEM170:14 H86 Here *Cain* and *Abel* come to sacrifice,
CAIN'S (1) [poss.]
CONTEM170:17 H89 But no such sign on false *Cain's* offering;
CAL (1) [call]
HUMOUR25:34 H223 Wilt thou this valour, manhood, courage cal:

CAL'D (5) [called] See also CALL'D, CALLD
ELEMEN9:39 H73 The Flye *Pyrausta* cal'd, all else expire.
HUMOUR30:28 H420 Yet is a bowel cal'd wel as the rest.
MGREC111:14 H2359 A City here he built, cal'd by his name,
MGREC134:20 H3351 Cal'd *Philadelphus,* next sat on {did possess} the throne,
MEDDM205:9 Hp286 man is called the little world so his heart may be cal'd the little
CALCINED (1)
DIALOG144:39 H147 Wives forc'd, babes toss'd, her houses calcined,
CALCULATE (1)
MASSYR54:13 H40 His reign was short, for as I calculate,
CALDES (1)
MPERS70:18 H689 This head of Kingdoms, *Caldes* excellence,
CALEH (1)
MASSYR53:29 H19 *Resen, Caleh,* and *Rehoboth* likewise,
CALES (1)
AGES44:34 H367 Then saw I *France,* and *Holland* sav'd, *Cales* won,
CALIGULA (1)
ELEMEN11:9 H129 Foolish *Caligula,* creep under's bed
CALISTHINES (5)
MGREC114:18 H2488 Was vertuous, learned wise *Calisthines,*
MGREC114:34 H2504 Yea, and *Calisthines* to death he drew,
MGREC114:36 H2506 Yea, and he kild *Calisthines* by name; {of fame.}
MGREC114:40 H2510 But yet withall, *Calisthines* he slew;
MGREC115:3 H2514 But yet withall, *Calisthines* he slew.
CALL (16) See also CAL
ELEMEN11:24 H144 And Mother Earth, of old, men did me call,
ELEMEN15:17 H299 I call thine *Egypt,* this to verifie;
AGES46:16 H447 Corruption, my Father, I do call,
MASSYR53:32 H22 Whom succeeding times a god did call:
MPERS84:25 H1261 For punishment, their breach of oath did call,
MPERS89:28 H1462 They quak'd, to heare them, to each other call.
MGREC119:25 H2715 With speed his forces {Army} doth together call,
MGREC127:31 H3061 But {And} he for aid to *Ptolomy* doth call.
DIALOG142:15 H44 And call in Forreign ayde, to help the thing?
AUTHOR177:37 H9 My rambling brat (in print) should mother call,
1LETTER181:26 H24 Till natures sad decree shall call thee hence;
MEDDM204:9 Hp284 great receipts, call for great returnes, the more that any man is
MEDDM204:12 Hp284 shall call him to reckoning, he may receiue his owne wth
MEDDM208:18 Hp290 Well doth the Apostle call riches deceitfull riches, and they
MYCHILD215:14 Hp240 to compose some short matters, (for w^{t} else to call y^{m} I know
28AUG226:5 Hp254 I can wait, looking every day when my Sav^{r} shall call for me.
CALL'D (14) [called] See also CAL'D, CALLD
ELEMEN12:12 H172 That heaven it selfe was oft call'd by that name;
ELEMEN13:1 H202 Built Cities, Monuments call'd by your names;
HUMOUR22:29 H98 The vitall spirits they're call'd, and wel they may,
HUMOUR29:34 H385 And if *Marcellus* bold, be call'd *Romes* sword,
HUMOUR~~31:5~~ H438 And so art call'd black Choler or adust,
MPERS73:15 H802 Of which the cheife were {was} seven, call'd *Satrapes,*
MGREC100:6 H1890 For to be call'd {install'd} a god, was his intent;
MGREC~~101:34~~ H1960 By Captains twice is call'd before hee'l rise,
MGREC128:7 H3080 Had built, and call'd a City by his name,

MGREC129:28 H3142 Call'd *Hercules,* and elder then his brother,
MGREC~~132:5~~ H3238 *Demetrius* is call'd in by th' youngest Son,
MGREC133:16 H3304 *Demetrius* Son was call'd *Antigonus,*
MROMAN138:3 H3493 Three call'd *Horatii,* on *Romans* side,
FLESH175:6 H6 One flesh was call'd, who had her eye
CALLD (1) [called] See also CAL'D, CALL'D
MEDDM207:33 Hp289 of death, wch is their sleep (for so is death often calld)
CALLED (4) See also CAL'D, CALL'D, CALLD
MPERS91:7 H1515 *Agesilaus* is called home with speed,
MGREC134:14 H3345 To take the government was called in,
MROMAN139:12 H3540 *Tarquin* the proud, from manners called so,
MEDDM205:9 Hp286 As man is called the little world so his heart may be cal'd the
CALLING (2)
MGREC~~125:17~~ H2965 Remembring {Calling to mind} what sometime she had been,
MGREC~~126:21~~ H3012 But his occasions calling him away,
CALLIOPE (1)
SIDNEY149:13 H12 *Calliope* with *Terpsechor* did sing,
CALLIOPE'S (1) [poss.]
PROLOG7:23 H35 And poesy made, *Calliope's* owne childe,
CALLS (6) See also CALS
ELEMEN13:9 H210 My bounty calls you forth to make reports,
MPERS83:39 H1227 His Princes, Nobles, and his Captaines calls,
MPERS~~91:22~~ H1535 But shortly calls her home, her counsells prize,
MGREC133:39 H3329 And calls them there, the Kings of South, and North;
SIDNEY151:24 ~~H73~~ Calls me ambitious fool, that durst aspire,
CONTEM169:29 H68 And calls back moneths and years that long since fled
CALME (2)
HUMOUR27:40 H311 And of the sweet, calme temper, quite bereft,
MGREC118:23 H2670 After this {some} time, when stirs began to calme,
CALNEH (1)
MASSYR53:24 H14 *Erech, Accad,* and *Calneh* also made;
CALS (1) [calls]
MPERS78:41 H1022 The Kings cals for the Youth, who being brought,
CALUMNIES (1) [pl.]
HUMOUR25:10 H199 Of thy black calumnies, this is but part:
CALVES (1) [pl.]
ELEMEN15:4 H286 Hindes leave their Calves, the Elephant the Fens;
CALVISH (1)
MPERS71:35 H749 Laughing to scorn that calvish, sottish crew.
CAMBYSES (13)
ELEMEN14:17 H259 Wherein whole Armies {*Cambyses* Armie} I have {was}
MPERS69:1 H623 *Cyrus Cambyses,* Son of *Persia's* {Persia} King,
MPERS69:5 H627 *Cambyses* was of *Achemenes* race,
MPERS71:4 ~~H716~~ Unto *Cambyses* then, all did remain.
MPERS71:5 H721 *Cambyses.*
MPERS71:6 H722 *Cambyses,* no wayes like, his noble Sire,
MPERS71:37 H751 *Cambyses* to the clouds, we might commend;
MPERS72:24 ~~H772~~ *Praraspes,* to *Cambyses* favourite,
MPERS73:11 H798 *The inter-Regnum between* Cambyses,
MPERS73:13 H800 Childlesse *Cambyses,* on the sudden dead,
MPERS74:16 H839 Let tyranny now with {dead} *Cambyses* dye.

MPERS75:27 H884 Since *Cyrus* time, *Cambyses* did molest;
MPERS85:32 H1308 The {This} King, his sister, like *Cambyses,* wed;

CAME (38)

ELEMEN8:19 H17 That roaring in it came, and with its source
HUMOUR21:4 H32 It is acknowledged, from whence I came,
AGES36:1 H25 Next, youth came up, in gorgeous attire;
AGES36:13 H37 The next came up, in a more {much} graver sort,
AGES~~36:20~~ H44 Leaning upon his staffe, comes {came} up old age.
MASSYR53:19 H9 This was the Golden Age, but after came
MASSYR56:31 H137 (They say) but twenty, ere came back agen.
MASSYR59:14 H238 But he once in, pursuers came too late,
MASSYR65:34 H499 The ninth, came *Nebuchadnezar* with power,
MPERS71:16 H730 And all of Royal bloud that came to hand,
MPERS~~78:22~~ H1003 {Which to} Three thousand (or more) {came} by best relation,
MPERS86:4 H1320 But in his slow approach, ere he came there;
MPERS87:1 H1357 But fame more quick, arrives ere he came {comes} there,
MPERS89:4 H1438 Being Victors oft, now to their Camp they came;
MPERS92:39 H1597 One deluge came, and swept them all away;
MGREC93:26 H1623 This is the hee-goat, which from *Grecia* came,
MGREC94:25 H1663 When newes of *Alexander,* came to th' Court,
MGREC95:31 H1710 Who came with thousand thousands at his feet,
MGREC~~96:39~~ H1759 The *Greeks* come {came} on, and with a gallant grace,
MGREC102:1 H1971 *Darius* stript of all, to *Media* came,
MGREC107:24 H2199 At length, they came to th' River *Oxus* brink,
MGREC108:21 H2237 Down from the mountains twenty thousand came,
MGREC111:4 H2349 Came with submission, from the *Indian* Kings
MGREC116:1 H2561 Before his answer came to *Babylon,*
MGREC~~116:10~~ H2571 When this sad news came to *Darius* Mother,
MGREC119:11 H2701 That if he came, good welcome he should find:
MGREC~~121:20~~ H2802 Next day into the Camp comes {came} *Ptolomy,*
MGREC~~122:32~~ H2852 From *Macedonia* to Asia he came,
MGREC125:33 H2983 That were {fell} within her reach, came to their ends;
MGREC127:19 H3049 *Antigonus* came off still honourlesse,
MGREC129:17 H3131 But yet at {the} last the hand of vengeance came,
MGREC135:17 H3389 Then came the *Romane,* like a raging flood,
DIALOG~~145:24~~ H173 So many obstacles comes {came} in their way,
QELIZ156:41 H68 Her *Drake* came laded home with *Spanish* gold,
SICKNES178:31 H14 since first we came from womb,
VERSES184:1 H5 Then may your worthy self from whom it came.
MYCHILD216:7 Hp241 short time I changed my Condition & was marryed, and came
MYCHILD218:14 Hp244 Times, + how ye world came to bee as wee see, Do wee not

CAMELL (1)

ELEMEN15:2 H284 The Camell hath no strength, thy Bull no force;

CAMELLS (2) [camels]

MASSYR56:28 H134 Her Camells, Chariots, Gallyes in such number,
MGREC96:31 H1751 A thousand Mules, and Camells ready wait.

CAMELS (1) [pl.]

MPERS78:7 H988 His Camels, beasts, for carriage numberlesse,

CAMP (9)

MASSYR59:5 H229 And set upon their Princes Camp that night;
MPERS76:6 H904 Which two then to assaile, his {royal} Camp was bold:

MPERS89:4	H1438	Being Victors oft, now to their Camp they came;
MGREC101:29	H1954	To force his Camp, so put {vanquish} them all to {by} flight;
MGREC108:20	H2236	And in his Camp strong, and securely lay,
MGREC108:30	H2246	Besets {Beset} his Camp, or Military Court;
MGREC110:27	H2331	Doth for his Camp a greater circuit take,
MGREC117:25	H2632	Now Court, and Camp, all in confusion be,
MGREC121:20	H2802	Next day into the Camp comes {came} *Ptolomy,*
CAMPE (2)		
MPERS87:37	H1389	*Cyrus* finding his campe, and no man there;
QELIZ157:10	H78	Our *Amazon* i'th' Campe at {of} *Tilberry:*
CAN (110)		
PROLOG6:29	H13	A *Bartas* can, doe what a *Bartas* wil,
PROLOG7:7	H21	Nor can I, like that fluent sweet tongu'd *Greek*
PROLOG7:11	H25	Art can doe much, but this maxime's most sure,
PROLOG7:31	H42	Men can doe best, and Women know it well;
ELEMEN8:31	H29	Where {In} little is, {time} I can but little show,
ELEMEN8:33	H31	What I can doe, well skill'd Mechanicks may,
ELEMEN9:5	H39	Without mine ayd, alas, what can they doe?
ELEMEN9:40	H74	Yet men and beasts, {beast} Astronomers can tell,
ELEMEN10:34	H109	Yet by my force, master my master can.
ELEMEN11:13	H133	Not sparing life when I can take the same;
ELEMEN11:34	H154	Of these so common things, can make report:
ELEMEN15:19	H301	That she can spare, when Nations round are poore.
ELEMEN15:36	H318	Or hast thou any colour can come nigh;
ELEMEN~~16:12~~	H335	I soon can match them with my seas as deep.
ELEMEN16:20	H343	Which can to life, restore a fainting heart:
ELEMEN17:21	H385	Till Sun release, their ships can saile no more.
ELEMEN18:37	H441	Thus I another body can assume,
ELEMEN19:5	H450	Earths Beasts, and Waters Fish, scarce can compare.
HUMOUR24:34	H183	Whose glorious deeds in armes, the world can tel,
HUMOUR25:15	H204	But useful, when a mixture can indure.
HUMOUR26:19	H249	But I, without thy help can give a growth,
HUMOUR27:4	H275	Can be imputed unto none, but Fire;
HUMOUR27:6	H277	That this is true, I easily can assent,
HUMOUR28:5	H317	And Flegme likewise can shew, her cruel art,
HUMOUR33:12	H526	Thou speakest truth, and I can speak {say} no lesse,
HUMOUR33:19	H533	Who is't or {that} dare, or can compare with me;
HUMOUR34:4	H559	Thy perfect temperament, who can expresse?
AGES38:16	H119	As he can tell, that next comes on the stage.
AGES38:26	H129	Then nought can please, and yet I know not why.
AGES39:2	H145	For 'tis but little, that a childe can say.
AGES~~39:25~~	H168	So affable that I do {can} suit each mind;
AGES39:26	H169	I can insinuate into the brest,
AGES39:27	H170	And by my mirth can raise the heart deprest;
AGES39:34	H177	As vain as froth, as {or} vanity can be,
AGES~~40:20~~	H201	If any time from company {leud Companions} I {can} spare,
AGES41:38	H255	If not, yet wealth, {riches} Nobility can gain.
AGES42:30	H286	My weary beast, rest from his toile can find;
AGES44:13	H346	My ruin'd house, now falling can uphold;
AGES44:17	H350	That can refresh, or ease, if Conscience frown;
AGES44:18	H351	Nor from alliance now can I have hope,

AGES45:17 H399 Plotted and acted, so that none can tell,
AGES~~45:36~~ H426 I cannot labour, nor {much less} I cannot {can} fight:
AGES45:38 H428 Now stiffe and numb, can hardly creep or go.
AGES46:5 H436 That earth can give no consolation sound.
SEASONS~~48:34~~ H85 Let some describe thee better then can I.
SEASONS52:6 H221 And solid'st meats, our stomachs can digest;
MASSYR57:12 H159 What then he did, of worth, can no man tel,
MASSYR~~57:20~~ H167 Nor can those Reasons which wise *Raleigh* finds,
MASSYR62:22 H367 Where now those ten Tribes are, can no man tel,
MASSYR62:33 H378 His Wars none better then himself can boast,
MASSYR64:34 H458 Can *Babels* tired Souldiers tell with pain;
MPERS75:16 H877 Nor can *Darius* in his Monarchy,
MPERS77:38 H979 That his ambitious humour best can fit;
MPERS~~82:12~~ H1159 Three thousand scapes, for to {only can} run home agen;
MPERS89:31 H1465 But Kings ne're want such as can serve their will,
MPERS92:6 H1564 I can no reason give, cause none I read;
MGREC99:29 H1872 Can *Alexander* deale thus cruelly?
MGREC~~103:21~~ H2032 For such revolters false, what Prince will {King can} trust:
MGREC113:7 H2434 Thy Kingly word can easily terminate;
MGREC114:31 H2501 Which vertues fame can ne're redeem by farre,
MGREC117:1 H2608 Nor can he kill, or save as heretofore,
MGREC117:26 H2633 A King they'l have, but who, none can agree:
MGREC127:16 H3046 Having Command o'th treasure he can hire,
MGREC130:40 H3185 For to their Crowns, there's none can title make.
DIALOG147:26 H250 O mother, can you weep, and have such Peeres.
SIDNEY150:35 H62 Where is that envious tongue, but can afford,
SIDNEY151:27 H75 But *Sydney's* Muse, can sing his worthinesse.
QELIZ155:35 H26 *Eliza's* works, wars, praise, can e're compact,
QELIZ156:1 H28 No memories, nor volumes can containe,
QELIZ156:13 H40 But can you Doctors now this point dispute,
QELIZ156:18 H45 Come shew me such a Phoenix if you can;
VANITY159:32 H4 Where is the man can say, lo, I have found
TDUDLEY165:31 H33 Who is't can tax thee ought, but for thy zeal?
TDUDLEY166:21 H63 Where storms, nor showrs, nor ought can damnifie.
CONTEM169:5 H47 As to approach it, can no earthly mould.
CONTEM169:24 H64 Whilst I as mute, can warble forth no higher layes.
CONTEM172:20 H155 Nor is it rocks or shoals that can obstruct thy pace.
CONTEM174:11 H211 Can make him deeply groan for that divine Translation.
FLESH175:14 H14 Can Speculation satisfy
FLESH175:33 H33 Then eyes can see, or hands can hold.
FLESH175:33 H33 Then eyes can see, or hands can hold.
FLESH176:31 H71 Then can thy hours in pleasure spent.
FLESH177:6 H87 There's none on Earth can parallel;
SICKNES178:28 H11 Where I shall have all I can crave,
1HUSB180:26 H5 Compare with me ye women if you can.
1HUSB180:31 H10 Thy love is such I can no way repay,
1LETTER181:15 H13 In this dead time, alas, what can I more
2LETTER182:7 H13 And if he love, how can he there abide?
2LETTER182:9 H15 He that can tell the starrs or Ocean sand,
VERSES183:37 H4 Who can of right better demand the same?
VERSES184:9 H13 But as I can, I'le pay it while I live:

VERSES184:10 H14 Such is my bond, none can discharge but I,
MEDDM195:29 Hp272 Many can speak well, but few can do well. We are better
MEDDM196:30 Hp274 are best preserued wth sugar, those parents are wise that can
MEDDM197:14 Hp274 A low man, can goe vpright, vnder that door, wher a taller is
MEDDM198:21 Hp276 is no new thing vnder ye Sun there is nothing that can be sayd
MEDDM202:13 Hp282 among the dead, and no other reason can be giuen of all this
MEDDM203:33 Hp284 men can vse great importunity when they are in distresses and
MEDDM205:14 Hp286 Judg, whom no bribes can pervert, nor flattery cause to favour
MEDDM208:29 Hp290 possible to be done, it can remoue mountaines (if need were)
MYCHILD218:10 Hp244 humane Invention can work vpon ye Soul, hath no Judgments
MYCHILD218:34 Hp244 told yov before. That hath stayed my heart, and I can now
MYCHILD219:7 Hp245 & imperfectly done, but if yov can pick any Benefitt out of it, It
28AUG226:5 Hp254 Now I can wait, looking every day when my Sav^{r} shall call for
13MAY227:15 H24 All I can giue is but thine own
30SEPT227:22 Hp257 I haue fovnd by Exper^{c}. I can no more liue wthout correction
HOURS233:29 H12 Wth Thee my soul can talk
HOURS234:37 H51 Vnlesse thou help w^{t} can I doe
REMB235:27 H8 I ow so mvch so little can

CANAAN (2)
MASSYR62:21 H366 And pleasant *Canaan* ne're see again:
MASSYR67:11 H557 And native *Canaan,* never see again,

CANAANITE (1)
DIALOG148:29 H294 No Canaanite shall then be found ith' land,

CANAANITES (1) [pl.]
MEDDM209:8 Hp291 the Canaanites, not destroy them, but put them vnder tribute,

CANCER (2)
SEASONS49:5 H96 Ith' first, *Sol* doth in crabed *Cancer* shine.
1LETTER181:23 H21 Within the Cancer of my glowing breast,

CANDIDLY (1)
HUMOUR33:13 H527 Thy heat doth much, I candidly confesse,

CANDLE (2)
FLESH177:19 H100 No Candle there, nor yet Torch light,
HOUSE237:7 H37 No Candle 'ere shall shine in Thee

CANICULAR (1)
SEASONS49:41 H134 Increased by the Star *Canicular;*

CANKERED (1)
AGES42:29 ~~H285~~ By cankered care, who centinel doth keep.

CANN'T (6) [can't] See also CANNOT
AGES37:4 H66 Whose mean beginning, blushing cann't reveale,
AGES37:9 H71 To tel that paine, which cann't be told by tongue;
DIALOG144:13 H123 Where is the Nation, I cann't paralize;
SIDNEY150:5 H30 Yet, {But} he's a beetle head, that cann't discry
DUBART154:9 H54 But wishes cann't accomplish my desire,
VANITY160:37 H47 It steeres {stores} with wealth, which time cann't wear away.

CANNON'S (1) [cannon is]
ELEMEN9:4 H38 Your Cannon's bootlesse, and your powder too

CANNOT (23) See also CANN'T, CAN'T
HUMOUR23:18 H128 So base thou art, that baser cannot be;
HUMOUR24:2 H151 Without my boiling heat cannot digest.
HUMOUR26:15 H245 What is there living, which cannot derive
HUMOUR30:32 H424 These two in one cannot have residence.

AGES39:20 H163 I cannot lye in trench, {intrench'd} before a Town,
AGES45:33 H423 I cannot scent, savours of pleasant meat,
AGES45:36 H426 I cannot labour, nor {much less} I cannot {can} fight:
AGES45:36 H426 I cannot labour, nor {much less} I cannot {can} fight:
MASSYR57:29 H174 We may suggest our thoughts, but cannot tel;
MPERS~~92:28~~ H1586 If so, or not, we cannot tell, but find
MGREC101:23 H1948 The Firmament two Suns cannot contain;
MGREC101:24 H1949 Two Monarchies on Earth cannot abide,
SICKNES178:23 H6 this cannot be revok'd.
1HUSB180:29 H8 My love is such that Rivers cannot quench,
2LETTER182:31 H37 Tell him I would say more, but cannot well,
MEDDM201:9 Hp280 by many, but what he did not say, cannot (truly) be vttered
MEDDM202:18 Hp282 throats, but cannot fill their bellys, they may be choaked by
MEDDM202:19 Hp282 but cannot be satisfied wth them.
MEDDM202:21 Hp282 the sun is only shadowed by a cloud, that wee cannot se his
MEDDM202:24 Hp282 a moment that we cannot behold the light of his Countenance,
MEDDM207:24 Hp289 cannot passe, and till the expiratnon of that time, no dangers
11MAYB228:30 Hp259 adversity, But alas! I cannot render vnto ye Lord according to
THEART229:16 H18 For more I cannot giue

CANONIZ'D (1) [canonized]
MASSYR54:26 H53 This *Ninus* for a god, his father canoniz'd,

CANOPY (1)
MGREC96:14 H1734 Support a party coloured canopy.

CAN'ST (1)
SICKNES178:34 H17 O Bubble blast, how long can'st last?

CANST (10)
ELEMEN15:16 H298 That this is true, earth thou canst not deny;
HUMOUR23:10 H120 Thou canst not claime, the Liver, Head nor Heart;
HUMOUR27:11 H282 But by what right, nor do'st, nor canst thou name;
DIALOG144:18 H128 Of more then thou canst heare, or I relate,
DIALOG148:11 H276 Of all the woes thou canst let her be sped,
QELIZ155:26 H17 Thou never didst, nor canst thou now disdaine,
VANITY160:4 H14 What then? content in pleasures canst thou find?
FLESH175:24 H24 What canst desire, but thou maist see
2LETTER182:1 H7 If in thy swift Carrier thou canst make stay,
2LETTER182:17 H23 And when thou canst not treat by loving mouth,

CAN'T (3)
ELEMEN14:7 ~~H250~~ And *Rome,* her *Curtius,* can't forget I think;
HUMOUR27:31 H302 If this {you} can't be disprov'd {disprove}, then all I hold:
3LETTER183:21 H23 But worst of all, to him can't steer my course,

CANUTUS (1)
DIALOG142:8 H37 Or hath *Canutus,* that brave valiant *Dane,*

CAPABLE (1)
MEDDM202:6 Hp281 that Mortality is capable of, and some again so base that they

CAPACITY (2)
FLESH176:35 H75 Beyond thy dull Capacity;
MEDDM205:5 Hp285 nurture they are brought into a fit capacity, let the seed of good

CAPITULATE (2)
MPERS89:24 H1458 They were too hungry to capitulate;
MGREC126:15 H3006 would she come now to {this wretched Queen} capitulate,

CAPRICORN (2)
SEASONS52:20 H235 This month he's hous'd in horned *Capricorn,*
1LETTER181:14 H12 Return, return sweet *Sol* from *Capricorn;*

CAPTAIN (8)
AGES42:10 H268 A Captain I, with skil I train'd my band;
MPERS78:12 H993 To *Mardonius,* Captain {made their} Generall;
MPERS87:19 H1373 Their Captain hearing, but of *Cyrus* name.
MPERS87:29 H1381 Had not a Captain; {his Captains} sore against his will;
MPERS91:12 H1520 Til many a Captain fel, both wise, and strong,
MGREC93:32 H1629 The *Greeks* had chose him Captain Generall,
MGREC117:27 H2634 Each Captain wisht this prize to beare away,
MGREC~~121:16~~ H2797 Who vow to make this captain recompence,

CAPTAINE (5)
MPERS84:39 H1275 The King this noble Captaine having lost,
MGREC97:24 H1785 No sooner had this Captaine {Victor} won the field,
MGREC99:24 H1867 The Captaine {Thus *Betis*} tane, had holes bor'd through his
MGREC113:29 H2456 (The most renowned Captaine of his time)
MGREC121:14 ~~H2792~~ *Pithon,* next *Perdicas,* a Captaine high,

CAPTAINES (8) [pl.]
PROLOG6:18 H3 To sing of Wars, of Captaines, and of Kings,
MPERS83:39 H1227 His Princes, Nobles, and his Captaines calls,
MPERS89:39 H1473 The *Greeks,* having {seeing} their valiant Captaines slaine,
MGREC109:23 H2282 And {Then} eighty Tallents to his Captaines down.
MGREC113:14 H2441 But how these Captaines should, or yet their Master,
MGREC113:21 H2448 Nor could his Captaines bear so great regard;
MGREC133:6 H3294 Thus with these Kingly Captaines have we done,
QELIZ156:37 H64 Such Souldiers, and such Captaines never seen,

CAPTAINS (11) [pl.]
HUMOUR33:1 H515 Princes hath slav'd, and Captains captived:
MPERS~~87:29~~ H1381 Had not a Captain; {his Captains} sore against his will;
MGREC98:26 H1828 For now's the time, Captains like Kings may live;
MGREC~~101:34~~ H1960 By Captains twice is call'd before hee'l rise,
MGREC103:20 H2031 Their charge, {place} gave to his Captains (as most {was} just)
MGREC106:37 H2171 His Captains, that were vertuously enclin'd,
MGREC112:4 H2390 At the {this} same time, unto his Captains brave;
MGREC117:10 H2617 Four of his Captains, all doe now divide,
MGREC119:32 H2722 'Mongst all the Captains {princes} of great *Alexander,*
MGREC120:14 H2749 For's Souldiers 'gainst those Captains would not goe;
MGREC130:39 H3184 These Captains now, the stile of Kings do take,

CAPTIVE (5)
MASSYR66:11 H517 All now of worth, are captive led with tears,
MGREC~~110:18~~ H2319 The kingly Captive 'fore the Victor's brought,
VANITY~~159:37~~ H9 He's now a slave {captive}, that was a Prince {King} of late.
FLESH176:25 H65 When thou my Captive shalt be led,
3LETTER183:18 H20 Where she her captive husband doth espy.

CAPTIVED (1)
HUMOUR33:1 H515 Princes hath slav'd, and Captains captived:

CAPTIVES (3) [pl.]
MASSYR66:25 H531 His Image, *Iudahs* Captives worship not,
MPERS70:22 H693 *Cyrus* doth now the *Jewish* captives free,
MGREC97:14 H1775 The Royall Captives, brought to *Alexander,*

CAPTIVITY (6)
MASSYR63:21 H406 Led King *Manasseh,* to captivity.
MASSYR63:26 H411 Now yeelds her neck unto captivity: [12 *years.*
MASSYR67:5 H551 Easeth *Jehoiakims* captivity.
MGREC97:30 H1791 Those mournfull Ladies, from captivity,
MGREC100:36 ~~H1920~~ For this lost Queen (though in captivity).
MGREC125:21 ~~H2969~~ But soone are brought into captivity;
CARCASSE (1)
PILGRIM210:35 H35 A Corrupt Carcasse downe it lyes
CARDS (1) [pl.]
AGES40:24 H205 Cards, Dice, and Oaths, concomitant, I love;
CARE (19)
HUMOUR28:11 H323 All to prevent, this curious care I take;
HUMOUR28:19 H331 But yet for all my toyl, my care, my skil,
HUMOUR31:32 H465 What Sanguine is, she doth not heed, nor care.
AGES40:18 H199 If any care I take, 'tis to be fine,
AGES42:29 ~~H285~~ By cankered care, who centinel doth keep.
SEASONS52:33 H248 I care not how the Winter time doth haste;
MASSYR57:34 H179 And such as care not, what befals their fames,
MASSYR59:6 H230 Who revelling in Cups, sung care away,
MPERS86:35 H1351 Great care was his pretence, those Souldiers stout,
MGREC113:36 H2463 Who for his prudence, valour, care, and trust,
VANITY160:1 H11 No, that's but labour anxious, care and pain.
TDUDLEY165:28 H30 Who spent his state, his strength, & years with care
CONTEM171:28 H130 No sooner born, but grief and care makes fall
SICKNES178:30 H13 For what's this life, but care and strife?
CHILDRN184:16 H5 I nurst them up with pain and care,
CHILDRN185:21 H47 Whilst pecking corn, and void of care
CHILDRN185:32 H58 Great was my care, when I you fed,
MEDDM203:22 Hp283 care for the company of the phisitian or chirurgian, but if he
MYCHILD216:16 Hp241 him gave me many more, of whom I now take ye care, y^t as
CARED (1)
AGES36:14 H38 As one that cared, for a good report.
CAREER (1) See also CARREAR
MPERS88:25 H1418 And with a full career, at him he ran.
CAREFUL (1)
SEASONS50:25 H159 His sweat, his toyl, his careful, wakeful nights,
CAREFULL (1)
MEDDM198:9 Hp276 He that walks among briars and thorns will be very carefull,
CAREFULLY (1)
SEASONS47:13 H29 And carefully manures his trees of fruits.
CARELESS (1)
MGREC~~101:34~~ H1959 And careless in his bed, next morne he lyes,
CARELESSE (2)
SEASONS49:26 H115 Carelesse of worldly wealth, you sit {sing} and pipe,
MPERS87:39 H1391 On this, he and his Souldiers carelesse grow,
CARES (10) [pl.]
MGREC103:38 H2049 (And there with sorrows, fears, and cares surrounded)
VANITY161:3 H54 Nor change of state, nor cares shall ever see,
CONTEM173:20 H186 Feels no sad thoughts, nor cruciating cares
CHILDRN185:35 H61 My cares are more, and fears then ever,

MEDDM197:28 Hp275 to mount to heaven clog'd wth the Cares and riches of this Life,
MEDDM203:25 Hp283 of a guilty Conscience, cares not how far he keeps from him
PILGRIM210:17 H17 All Cares and feares, he bids farwell
PILGRIM210:20 H20 Wth sinns wth cares and sorrows vext
PILGRIM210:29 H29 Wth cares and fears ner' cumbred be
MYCHILD216:17 Hp241 yov into ye world, and wth great paines, weaknes, cares

CARIANS (1)
MPERS78:19 H1000 *Lycians, Carians,* and *Ionians,*

CARKE (1)
AGES37:30 H92 How to be rich, or great, I did not carke;

CARMANIA (1)
MGREC111:30 H2375 And thence he marcht into *Carmania,*

CARNALL (1)
MYCHILD216:1 Hp241 grew vp to bee about 14. or 15. I fovnd my heart more carnall,

CAROUS'D (1) [caroused]
MASSYR67:34 H580 Carous'd they in; and sacrilegious Prince,

CAROUSING (1)
AGES40:10 H191 Sometimes I sit carousing others health,

CARPING (1)
PROLOG7:14 H27 I am obnoxious to each carping tongue,

CARREAR (1) [career]
SEASONS49:39 H132 The Sun in {thro} Leo now hath {takes} his carrear,

CARRIAGE (2)
MPERS78:7 H988 His Camels, beasts, for carriage numberlesse,
MGREC121:8 H2786 *Perdicas* surly carriage, and his pride,

CARRIAGES (1) [pl.]
MGREC107:34 H2209 So {Then} from his carriages the Hides he takes,

CARRIED (2) See also CARRYED
MASSYR57:25 ~~H172~~ Of men, and wealth, his mother carried out;
MGREC102:12 H1982 Which in few hours was carried all away;

CARRIER (1)
2LETTER182:1 H7 If in thy swift Carrier thou canst make stay,

CARRY (5)
AGES38:36 H139 And some perhaps, I carry to my grave.
MPERS77:2 H941 Go *Persians,* carry home that angry peece,
MPERS82:18 H1165 Scarce one was left, to carry home the fame;
MPERS86:38 H1354 He meant {Prepares} himselfe to carry the report.
MEDDM205:20 Hp286 be sure to carry a certificate from the Court of conscience

CARRYED (2) [carried]
AGES43:3 H298 But {And} by ambitious sailes, I was so carryed;
MYCHILD218:30 Hp244 Xtians haue been carryed away wth them, that somt: I haue

CART (3)
MGREC104:23 H2075 Into a cart him throwes, covered with hides;
MGREC104:25 H2077 Then draws the Cart along, with chaines of gold;
MGREC105:18 H2111 To them he goes, and {repairs then} looking in the Cart,

CARTER (1)
SEASONS50:23 H157 The Carter leads all home, with whistling voyce,

CARTHAGE (2)
ELEMEN10:40 H115 *Carthage,* and hundred moe, in stories told,
QELIZ157:14 H82 *Dido* first Foundresse of proud *Carthage* walls,

CARTS (2) [pl.]
SEASONS50:9 H143 The groaning Carts to bear away this prise,
MPERS87:40 H1392 And here, and there, in carts their Armes they throw,
CASE (2)
DIALOG141:27 H26 Then weigh our case, if't be not justly sad,
DIALOG147:39 H263 Without respect of persons {person}, or of case,
CASPIAN (1)
ELEMEN16:7 H330 The *Ponticke, {Aegean} Caspian,* Golden Rivers fine. {five,}
CASSANDER (27)
MGREC116:4 H2564 By *Philip,* and *Cassander,* to him brought,
MGREC123:16 H2880 Fearing his Son *Cassander* was unstay'd,
MGREC123:28 H2892 *Cassander* could not (like his father) see
MGREC124:6 ~~H2911~~ *Cassander* for return all speed now made:
MGREC124:11 H2918 *Cassander* with his Hoast to *Grecia* goes,
MGREC124:16 ~~H2923~~ Firme to *Cassander* at this time abides:
MGREC124:30 H2937 And to *Cassander* of this wrong complaines;
MGREC124:32 H2939 Was to this proud, vindicative *Cassander,*
MGREC125:9 H2957 In hast {haste} unto her deare *Cassander* sends,
MGREC125:31 H2981 Till {'Gainst} all that lov'd *Cassander* was nigh spent; {she was
MGREC125:38 H2988 In *Pelloponesus* then *Cassander* lay,
MGREC126:9 H3000 There by *Cassander* she's block'd up, so long,
MGREC126:13 H3004 *Cassander* is resolv'd, there to remaine,
MGREC126:16 H3007 Cassander will not heare {Her foe would give no Ear}, such is
MGREC126:18 H3009 By stealth unto *Cassander* daily fly;
MGREC127:36 H3066 *Seleuchus, Ptolomy, Cassander* joynes,
MGREC127:39 H3069 To make *Cassander* odious to them, seeks,
MGREC129:2 H3116 This touch'd *Cassander* sore, for what he'd done,
MGREC129:32 H3146 Begin to mutter much 'gainst proud *Cassander,*
MGREC129:34 H3148 *Cassander* fear'd what might of this insue,
MGREC129:39 H3153 Extinct, by this inhumane wretch *Cassander;*
MGREC130:4 H3159 And vile {lewd} *Cassander* too, sticks not for shame;
MGREC130:35 ~~H3181~~ His wife and sons then slain by this *Cassander,*
MGREC~~131:1~~ H3191 The better 'gainst *Cassander* to rebel.
MGREC131:34 H3226 *Cassander* now must die, his race is run,
MGREC132:9 H3244 Yea {And} though *Cassander* died in his bed,
MGREC133:8 H3296 *Antigonus, Seleuchus,* and *Cassander,*
CASSANDER'S (1) [cassander is]
MGREC129:22 H3136 *Cassander's* dead, the Princes {do} all detest,
CASSANDER'S (1) [poss.]
MGREC132:7 H3242 Thus *Philips,* and *Cassander's* race is {both} gone,
CASSANDERS (6) [poss.]
MGREC124:14 H2921 And his opponent still got {*Cassanders* forces had the} upper
MGREC~~127:41~~ H3072 *Cassanders* outrages at large doth tell,
MGREC130:22 H3177 Except *Cassanders* wife, who yet not dead,
MGREC132:15 H3250 *Demetrius,* {thus} *Cassanders* Kingdomes gains,
MGREC133:10 H3298 *Cassanders* Sons, soone after's death were slaine,
MGREC133:14 H3302 His Son *Demetrius,* all *Cassanders* gaines,
CASSANDRA (1)
MGREC127:6 H3036 The Funeralls *Cassandra* celebrates,
CASSANDRIA (1)
MGREC127:11 H3041 And rais'd *Cassandria* after his name,

CAST (18)
PROLOG7:17 H30 For such despight they cast on female wits:
ELEMEN15:41 H323 I lightly cast ashoare as frothy fleece.
HUMOUR27:19 ~~H290~~ Though cast upon my guiltlesse blushing face;
HUMOUR28:36 H348 I've scarce wip'd off the spots, proud Choler cast,
MASSYR55:30 H96 Some think the *Greeks,* this slander on her cast,
MASSYR55:33 H99 As {By} their aspersions, cast upon the same.
MASSYR65:22 H487 Thus {Then} cast him out, like to a naked Asse,
MPERS75:20 H879 Yet o're thy glory we must cast this vaile,
MPERS~~79:13~~ H1037 He fetters cast therein the same to chain.
MGREC97:3 H1764 And cast away his Crown, for swifter flight;
DAVID159:2 H17 The Shield of *Saul* was vilely cast away;
CONTEM168:7 H16 Then on a stately Oak I cast mine Eye,
AUTHOR177:38 H10 I cast thee by as one unfit for light,
DISTEMP179:23 H11 My Anchor cast i'th' vale with safety.
MEDDM199:12 Hp277 good to cast some men into the furnace of affliction and then
MEDDM204:26 Hp285 would be content, wth a mean condition, must not cast his eye
MEDDM208:30 Hp290 stayd the Course of the Sun raised the dead, cast out divels,
HOUSE236:34 H26 My sorrowing eyes aside did cast

CASTING (1)
MASSYR67:39 H585 The King, upon the wall casting his eye,

CASTLE (1)
MGREC102:9 H1979 The glory of the Castle he admires,

CASTLES (1) [pl.]
HUMOUR21:27 H55 Then timerous Hares, whom Castles doe immure?

CASTS (3)
HUMOUR31:11 H444 That casts out all that man or {e're} eates, or drinks.
SEASONS47:9 H25 In hope, the more he casts, the more to gain;
MPERS86:11 H1327 Still on his brother, casts a jealous eye,

CATASTROPHE (1)
MPERS93:3 H1600 And last; a sad catastrophe to end,

CATCH (7)
PROLOG7:36 H46 And ever with your prey, still catch your praise,
AGES39:23 H166 I fly to catch the Bullet that's {that} aloof;
FLESH175:21 H21 To catch at shadowes which are not?
FLESH176:32 H72 Nor are they shadows which I catch,
CHILDRN185:19 H45 Lest this my brood some harm should catch,
MEDDM198:18 Hp276 of men, wch they all catch gre¯dily at but few perceiues
PILGRIM210:10 H10 nor hungry wolues at him shall catch

CATCHPOLES (1) [pl.]
DIALOG148:2 H267 And Pursevants and Catchpoles want their pay,

CATTELL (1)
MPERS79:32 H1058 And for his Cattell, all *Pissirus* Lake

CATTLE (3)
ELEMEN17:3 H367 Their Cattle, Hay, and Corne, I sweep down current,
ELEMEN19:20 H465 Of murrain, Cattle numberlesse did fall.
AGES~~42:34~~ H290 My fatted Oxe {thriving Cattle}, and my exuberous {new-milch-

CAUCASUS (1)
ELEMEN17:19 H383 That *Caucasus* high mounts, are seldom free.

CAUGHT (7)
AGES43:18 H313 Whereby my empty soule, is lur'd and caught.

MASSYR65:40 H505 But being caught, to *Babels* wrathful King,
MPERS72:13 H761 That by her Husbands charge, she caught her owne;
MGREC115:34 H2553 So to be caught, *Antipater's* too wise,
MROMAN137:14 H3465 Their Daughters by the *Romans* then were caught,
SIDNEY150:1 H26 But some infatuate fooles soone caught therein,
CHILDRN185:26 H52 The net be spread, and caught, alas.

CAUS'D (11) [caused]

MASSYR55:27 H93 Till her ambition, caus'd him to be slaine:
MASSYR59:21 H245 Part of the {that stately} wal it level caus'd to lye; {was
MASSYR65:21 H486 minde, and slew him by the way; {& caus'd his life there end,}
MPERS70:25 H696 And caus'd his foes in Lions den to dye.
MPERS~~72:3~~ H755 Unjustly caus'd his brother to be slain.
MPERS~~91:22~~ H1532 By poyson caus'd, the young one to lose her life.
MGREC109:24 H2283 But *Alexander,* caus'd {made} him to behold;
QELIZ156:36 H63 Her selfe *Minerva,* caus'd them so to be;
TDUDLEY165:33 H35 Which caus'd Apostates to maligne so.
AUTHOR178:15 H25 Which caus'd her thus to send thee out of door.
1SIMON188:5 H6 Acquaintance short, yet parting caus'd us weep,

CAUSE (44)

FATHER5:11 H12 Yet view thereof, did cause my thoughts to soare,
PROLOG7:5 H20 'Cause Nature made it so irreparable.
ELEMEN9:25 H59 What mingled lay with earth, I cause to shine.
ELEMEN10:19 H94 Ile here let passe, my Choler cause of warres,
ELEMEN12:2 H162 But chiefly, 'cause the Muses there did dwell;
ELEMEN14:27 H269 Cause of your fruitfulnesse, as you shall see:
ELEMEN15:31 H313 Thy silence of thy beasts, doth cause the same.
ELEMEN16:17 H340 Th' uncertain cause, of certain ebbs and flowes;
ELEMEN16:38 H361 So oft in my excesse, I cause a dearth:
ELEMEN18:25 H429 When burning heat, doth cause you faint, I coole,
ELEMEN18:39 H443 Some for this cause (of late) have been so bold,
HUMOUR22:5 H74 If great perswasions, cause her meet her foe;
HUMOUR24:6 H155 Of all that lives, I cause the propagation.
HUMOUR26:39 H269 Challenge not all, 'cause part we do allow,
HUMOUR31:41 H474 Then cause her blush, while I dilate {relate} the same.
AGES38:3 H106 My stroks did cause no death {blood}, nor wounds, nor {or}
AGES39:40 ~~H182~~ Martial deeds I love not, 'cause they're vertuous,
MASSYR55:25 H91 Which was the cause, poor *Menon* lost his life,
MPERS91:25 ~~H1539~~ His Mothers wicked counsell was the cause,
MPERS92:6 H1564 I can no reason give, cause none I read;
MGREC94:6 H1640 kinsmen puts {put} to death without least {who gave no} cause;
MGREC101:30 H1955 For tumult in the dark {night} doth cause most dread,
MGREC108:14 H2230 Without {least} cause, given by {from} them, in deed, or word:
MGREC114:23 H2493 For this alone, and for no other cause,
MGREC116:26 H2592 'Cause *Homer* kept his Acts to memory;
MGREC121:12 H2790 Did make his owne firme to his cause remaine,
MGREC126:40 H3029 How for no cause, but her inverterate hate;
MGREC127:41 H3071 And shews {clear} what cause they {he} had to take up {make
MROMAN140:5 H3568 Which none had cause to wail, nor I to boast.
DIALOG142:40 H69 Whose proud contention cause this slaughter;
DIALOG143:27 H96 Before I tell the effect, ile shew the cause,
DIALOG144:31 H139 Who heard {saw} their cause, and wrongs {hath} judg'd

DIALOG145:8 H157 Your fearfull sinnes, great cause there's to lament,
DIALOG146:9 H197 But could the field alone this cause {strife} decide,
DIALOG147:25 H249 And to this blessed {hopeful} Cause closely adhere
DIALOG~~148:33~~ H298 Farewell dear mother, Parliament, {rightest cause} prevail,
DUBART154:40 H85 Good will, not skill, did cause me bring my mite.
TDUDLEY165:11 H13 For who more cause to boast his worth then I?
FLESH176:14 H54 And never had more cause of woe
1LETTER181:12 H10 His warmth such frigid colds did cause to melt.
MEDDM203:7 Hp283 he haue good cause often to repeat that sentence, vanity of
MEDDM203:16 Hp283 meet wth such tossings that may cause him to long for shore,
MEDDM205:14 Hp286 whom no bribes can pervert, nor flattery cause to favour but
PILGRIM210:16 H16 nor stumps nor rocks cause him to fall

CAUSED (7) See also CAUS'D
MASSYR54:33 H60 *Pharmus, {Thermus}* their King, he caused to be slain;
MASSYR60:4 H269 Of *Ninivites,* he caused none to dye,
MPERS77:6 H945 His Queen *Attossa,* caused all {author of} this stir,
MGREC134:8 ~~H3339~~ I'th' holy place, which caused desolation;
DUBART153:9 H13 Had caused flowers, and fruits, soone to abound;
CONTEM168:36 H42 Quaternal Seasons caused by thy might:
MERCY189:14 H35 In him alone, that caused all this smart;

CAUSELESLY (1) [causelessly]
DIALOG144:5 H115 Martyrs, and others, dying causelesly:

CAUSELESS (1) See also CAUSLESSE
HUMOUR32:23 H497 Nor how her Gaul on me she causeless brake;

CAUSES (1) [pl.]
MASSYR66:31 H537 Which from no natural causes did proceed,

CAUSETH (1)
HUMOUR24:19 H168 Is't ignorance, {arrogance} or folly causeth this?

CAUSLESSE (1) [causeless]
MPERS72:4 ~~H755~~ He strait to rid himself of causlesse fears,

CAVALEER (1)
AGES40:27 H208 Seek out a Brittish, bruitish Cavaleer;

CEAS'D (1) [ceased]
AGES41:11 ~~H230~~ Ceas'd by the gripes of Serjeant Death's Arrests:

CEASE (8)
ELEMEN8:25 H23 The others enmity: {difference,} being lesse, did cease
ELEMEN11:16 H136 Not before then, shal cease my raging ire,
ELEMEN15:9 H291 Do cease to flourish in this misery.
AGES38:4 H107 My little wrath did cease {end} soon as my wars.
MPERS81:11 H1119 That all Hostility might {from} thence-forth cease;
DIALOG146:28 H214 Dear mother cease complaints, and wipe your eyes,
DIALOG147:40 H264 Then bribes shall cease, and suits shall not stick long,
TDUDLEY166:22 H64 His Generation serv'd his labours cease;

CEASED See CEAS'D

CEASES (2)
HUMOUR28:1 H313 So Melancholly ceases {seizes} on a man;
MPERS82:22 H1169 Yet ceases not to act his villany:

CEASING (1)
HUMOUR20:12 H4 Ceasing to vaunt, their good, or threat their force.

CEDAR (1)
AGES44:32 H365 And like a Cedar, others so surmount,

CEDARS (1) [pl.]
ELEMEN15:8 H290 The Pine, the Cedars, yea and *Daph'nes* tree;
CEL (1) [cell]
HUMOUR28:15 H327 I turn into his cel, close by my side,
CELEBRATE (9)
MPERS~~70:41~~ H712 With honours great, did celebrate his fame.
MGREC120:34 H2771 His Masters Funerals doth celebrate;
DUBART154:38 H83 To celebrate thy merits in my Song,
TDUDLEY165:5 H7 To celebrate the praises of the dead,
SOREFIT222:7 H26 Thy Name & praise to celebrate
SAMUEL228:16 H17 Then shall I celebrate thy praise
THEART228:36 H2 Shall celebrate thy Name.
HANNA230:16 H9 And celebrate thy praise
HOURS234:25 H39 So shall I celebrate thy praise.
CELEBRATED (2)
SEASONS50:2 H136 By *Romans* celebrated to his fame.
MGREC109:7 H2266 Whose feasts are celebrated by this Prince;
CELEBRATES (2)
MGREC115:7 H2518 He celebrates his mournfull obsequies;
MGREC127:6 H3036 The Funeralls *Cassandra* celebrates,
CELERITY (1)
MASSYR58:35 H218 These with celerity, *Arbaces* meets {meet},
CELESTIAL (2)
AGES44:31 H364 When it was rul'd by that Celestial she;
TDUDLEY166:20 H62 And in celestial Barn hath hous'd him high,
CELESTIALL (1)
ELEMEN9:27 H61 To match on high with the Celestiall fires.
CELL See CEL
CELLS (1) [pl.]
SEASONS~~49:33~~ H125 If pride within your lowly Cells ere haunt,
CEMENTED (1) See also CIMENTED
AGES~~43:16~~ H310 Though cemented with more the noble bloud,
CENSURE (1)
MGREC114:28 H2498 This censure passe, and not unwisely, say,
CENTINEL (1)
AGES42:29 ~~H285~~ By cankered care, who centinel doth keep.
CERANNUS (1)
MGREC133:1 H3289 He was by *Ptolomy Cerannus* slaine.
CERIA (1)
MGREC122:23 ~~H2845~~ *Ceria* the *Phrigian* Queen for to withstand,
CERTAIN (2)
ELEMEN16:17 H340 Th' uncertain cause, of certain ebbs and flowes;
MEDDM209:12 Hp291 slauery, so it is most certain that those that are disobedient
CERTAINLY (3)
MEDDM205:26 Hp286 to good dutys, we certainly dream of some remotnes betwixt
MEDDM207:10 Hp288 to help vs mount vpwards, they will Certainly proue Clogs
MYCHILD218:3 Hp243 consideration of these things would wth amazement certainly
CERTAINTY (5)
MASSYR54:1 H28 Whose acts, and power, is not for certainty,
MASSYR63:32 H419 Nor of his acts {Wars} have we the certainty,
MPERS77:36 H977 With certainty {conquest} of {all} *Europe* feeds his pride;

MGREC106:41 H2175 The certainty of both comes to his eares,
MEDDM207:25 Hp289 nor troubles, shall put a period to our dayes, the certainty
CERTIFI'D (1) [certified]
MASSYR56:41 H147 But by what means, we are not certifi'd.
CERTIFICATE (1)
MEDDM205:20 Hp286 be sure to carry a certificate from the Court of conscience
CERTIFIE (3) [certify]
MPERS82:14 H1161 To certifie this finall over-throw.
MGREC112:21 H2407 Accus'd, because he did not certifie
MGREC~~121:16~~ H2795 But of his wrongs his friends doth certifie;
CERTIFIED See CERTIFI'D
CERTIFY See CERTIFIE
CESSATION (1)
CONTEM174:1 H202 From some of these he never finds cessation,
CHAC'D (1) [chased]
DISTEMP179:22 H10 He chac'd away those clouds, and let me see
CHAF'D (1) [chafed]
HUMOUR29:14 H367 But Choler, be thou cool'd, or chaf'd, i'le venter,
CHAFFE (1)
MGREC135:27 H3399 Became like chaffe upon the threshing-floor;
CHAIN (2)
MASSYR~~68:6~~ H592 With guifts of Scarlet robe, and Chaines {Chain} of gold,
MPERS~~79:13~~ H1037 He fetters cast therein the same to chain.
CHAIN'D (1) [chained]
MPERS79:14 H1040 Seven thousand Gallies chain'd, by *Tyrians* skil,
CHAINED (1)
DUBART154:22 H67 Leadst millions chained by eyes, by eares, by tongues,
CHAINES (3) [pl.]
MASSYR68:6 H592 With guifts of Scarlet robe, and Chaines {Chain} of gold,
MGREC104:25 H2077 Then draws the Cart along, with chaines of gold;
MGREC108:1 H2217 Is by his owne, now bound in Iron chaines,
CHALDEANS (2) [pl.]
MASSYR58:19 H204 *Belosus* the *Chaldeans* doth require,
MASSYR64:39 H463 But the *Chaldeans* had nor ships, nor skill,
CHALDEES (1) [pl.]
MASSYR54:7 H34 This is that *Bell,* the *Chaldees* worshipped,
CHALLENGE (4)
HUMOUR22:17 H86 She dare, {dares} not challenge if I speake amisse;
HUMOUR25:32 H221 To crosse thy wil, a challenge doth deserve.
HUMOUR26:39 H269 Challenge not all, 'cause part we do allow,
AGES38:5 H108 My duel was no challenge, nor did seek.
CHALLENGES (1)
HUMOUR22:35 H104 The Brain she challenges, the Head's her seat,
CHALLENGEST (1)
HUMOUR~~27:13~~ H284 And so thou challengest her property.
CHAMBER (3)
HUMOUR21:37 H65 A Chamber wel, in field she dares not come;
MPERS~~92:25~~ H1583 Was to his Predecessors Chamber page.
CONTEM168:23 H30 Thou as a Bridegroom from thy Chamber rushes,
CHAMDENS (1) [pl.]
QELIZ155:34 H25 No *Speeds,* nor *Chamdens* learned History;

CHANC'D (3) [chanced]
MASSYR~~58:7~~ H192 At last {It chanc'd} *Arbaces* brave, unwarily,
MASSYR58:8 H193 His master like a Strumpet chanc'd to {clad did} spy,
MGREC105:16 H2109 So chanc'd these bloudy Horses to espy,
CHANCE (6)
PROLOG7:19 H32 They'l say its stolne, or else, it was by chance.
ELEMEN17:9 H373 *Cicily* from *Italy,* by th'like chance.
MPERS84:19 H1255 The King not little joyfull of this chance,
MPERS88:31 H1424 Who knowes the sudden change made by this chance;
MGREC116:6 H2566 Least {Lest} of such like, their Father chance to sup:
BIRTH180:17 H27 And if chance to thine eyes shall bring this verse,
CHANCED See CHANC'D
CHANG (1) [change]
MEDDM203:19 Hp283 dayes of our appointed time till our chang shall come,
CHANG'D (4) [changed]
AGES~~45:2~~ H375 We chang'd our queen for king under whose rayes
MASSYR65:21 H486 But chang'd his minde, and slew him by the way; {& caus'd his
ANNEB187:17 H7 The Heavens have chang'd to sorrow my delight.
MYSOUL225:3 H7 Thy body vile it shall bee chang'd,
CHANGE (7) See also CHANG
MASSYR66:28 H534 And his unhappy change with grief fore-tel;
MPERS88:31 H1424 Who knowes the sudden change made by this chance;
MGREC106:38 H2172 Griev'd at this change of manners, and of minde:
MROMAN139:22 H3550 The Government they change, a new one bring,
VANITY160:32 H42 For *Saphyre, Onix, Topas,* who will {would} change,
VANITY161:3 H54 Nor change of state, nor cares shall ever see,
28AUG226:7 Hp254 and bee in continuall xpectat^{n} of my change, and let me never
CHANGED (2) See also CHANG'D
MASSYR~~64:8~~ H432 Was turned {changed} from a King, unto {into} a Beast;
MYCHILD216:7 Hp241 After a short time I changed my Condition & was marryed, and
CHANGES (1) [pl.]
AGES44:28 H361 Such private changes oft mine eyes have seen,
CHANGING (1)
MASSYR55:15 H81 Changing his {the} womans face, into a man.
CHANNEL (1)
MASSYR64:36 H460 Divided from the maine, by channel great;
CHANNELL (1)
MASSYR65:1 H466 And in the channell throw {threw} each burden down;
CHANT (1)
CHILDRN185:6 H32 That he might chant above the rest,
CHANTED (1)
CONTEM173:13 H180 And chanted forth a most melodious strain
CHAOS (3)
ELEMEN8:16 H14 All looked like a Chaos, or new birth;
MGREC136:15 H3429 *Yet in this Chaos, one shall easily spy,*
2LETTER182:26 H32 Behold a Chaos blacker then the first.
CHAPPS (1) [pl.]
ELEMEN14:38 H280 Or else thy sun-burnt face, and gaping chapps;
CHARACTERS (1) [pl.]
SIDNEY150:20 H45 Engrave on Marble, in characters of Gold,

CHARG'D (1) [charged]
HUMOUR34:20 H575 But modesty hath charg'd me to conceal;
CHARGE (14)
MPERS72:13 H761 That by her Husbands charge, she caught her owne;
MPERS75:29 H886 Out of his owne revenues beares the charge;
MPERS76:2 H900 Over fair *Ister,* at a {with labour and with} mighty charge;
MPERS78:9 H990 The charge of all he severally commended,
MPERS78:33 H1014 Feasts all this multitude, of his own charge,
MPERS~~87:20~~ H1374 Forsook his charge to his eternal shame:
MPERS88:15 H1408 For at first charge the *Persians* ran away.
MGREC96:41 H1761 The cowards feeling this sharp stinging charge,
MGREC103:20 H2031 Their charge, {place} gave to his Captains (as most {was} just)
MGREC123:17 H2881 Too young {rash} to beare that charge, if on him lay'd;
SIDNEY151:35 ~~H75~~ He left that charge by *Phoebus* to be man'd:
SIDNEY151:38 ~~H75~~ Till terrour-struck for my too weighty charge.
TDUDLEY166:5 H47 Gave his in charge, that Jewel rich to prize.
MYCHILD219:2 Hp245 and y^t he is able to keep y^t I haue comitted to his charge.
CHARGED See CHARG'D
CHARGING (2)
HUMOUR31:1 H434 In {Is} charging me, to be thy excrement.
MGREC106:34 H2168 Charging the same on his Nobility;
CHARIOT (2)
MGREC96:11 H1731 The King sat in a chariot made of gold,
SIDNEY151:37 ~~H75~~ Fame's flaming Chariot for to drive.
CHARIOTS (3) [pl.]
MASSYR54:23 H50 So broad, three Chariots run abrest there might,
MASSYR56:6 H112 Most {Some} writers say, six chariots might a front,
MASSYR56:28 H134 Her Camells, Chariots, Gallyes in such number,
CHARIOTS () [poss.]
MGREC96:16 H1736 Least he should need them, in his chariots stead.
CHARLEMAIN (1)
DUBART154:12 H57 Then in thy *Pippin, Martell, Charlemain.*
CHARLES (2)
ELEMEN19:26 H471 Where famous *Charles* the fift, more losse sustain'd,
DIALOG147:30 H254 These, these, are they (I trust) with *Charles* our King,
CHARM (1)
AGES36:18 H42 His golden god in's purse, which was his charm.
CHARM'D (1) [charmed]
DUBART154:2 H47 Movelesse, stand charm'd by thy sweet influences,
CHARMS (1) [pl.]
FLESH176:16 H56 Ile stop mine ears at these thy charms,
CHARTER (1)
MPERS75:28 H885 He like a King, now grants a Charter large,
CHASE (3)
MPERS88:28 H1421 His Host in chase, knowes not of his {this} disaster,
DIALOG147:24 H248 And yee brave Nobles, chase away all fear,
RESTOR229:27 H10 Distempers thou didst chase away.
CHASED See CHAC'D
CHASTE (1)
MPERS82:24 H1171 The chaste, and beautious Dame, refuses still.

CHASTENED (2)
MYCHILD216:28 Hp242 chastened by losses in estate, and these Times (thro: his great
MYCHILD217:1 Hp242 If at any time yov are chastened of God take it as Thankfully
CHASTETY (1)
MROMAN139:15 H3543 *Lucretia* force, mirrour of chastety;
CHASTISE (1)
MPERS86:3 H1319 Meaning to chastise him, in sharpest sort,
CHASTISED (1)
MASSYR65:19 H484 Whom he chastised {thus} for his proud offence;
CHASTITY (2)
HUMOUR31:36 H469 My temperance, chastity, is eminent,
MPERS82:39 H1186 To see those breasts, where chastity did dwel,
CHAT (1)
CHILDRN185:4 H30 To chat among that learned crew:
CHATTER (1)
HUMOUR22:15 H84 Her teeth wil chatter, dead and wan's her face,
CHEAR (8) [cheer]
AGES42:5 H263 To chear the good, and wicked to deface.
MASSYR67:32 H578 To chear his friends, and scorn his foes the more.
MASSYR68:14 H600 In comes the Queen, to chear her heartlesse son.
DIALOG146:29 H215 Shake off your dust, chear up, and now arise,
DIALOG147:4 H230 Blest be thy Preachers, who do chear thee on,
TDUDLEY166:16 H58 Oft spake of death, and with a smiling chear,
MERCY189:13 H34 Chear up (dear Son) thy fainting bleeding heart,
2HUSB233:10 H43 Rejoice wth heavenly chear—
CHEAR'D (2) [cheered]
MGREC105:20 H2113 Who not a little chear'd, to have some eye,
ANNEB187:32 H22 Mean time my throbbing heart's chear'd up with this
CHEARFULLY (1) [cheerfully]
AGES42:15 H273 As chearfully as ere I took my pay.
CHEAT (1)
AGES40:6 H187 Sometimes I cheat (unkind) a female Heir,
CHECK (1)
MGREC125:26 H2976 The Queen with many a curse, and bitter check,
CHEEK (1)
HUMOUR~~24:35~~ H184 A rosie cheek'd {cheek} musitian, thou know'st wel.
CHEEK'D (1) [cheeked]
HUMOUR24:35 H184 A rosie cheek'd {cheek} musitian, thou know'st wel.
CHEEKS (3) [pl.]
HUMOUR23:4 H114 Of greasie paunch, and palled {bloated} cheeks, go vaunt,
AGES45:30 H420 My skin is wrinkled, and my cheeks are pale.
DIALOG144:26 ~~H135~~ Their reverent cheeks, did beare the glorious markes
CHEER See CHEAR
CHEERD (1) [cheered]
SON231:10 H22 Thou heal'dst his flesh + cheerd his heart.
CHEERFULLY See CHEARFULLY
CHEIF (2) [chief] See also CHEIFE
MGREC98:19 H1821 Two thousand of the cheif he crucifi'd,
MGREC115:6 H2517 Here his cheif favourite *Ephestion* dyes,
CHEIFE (4) [chief] See also CHEIF
ELEMEN8:11 H9 All would be cheife, and all scorn'd to be under,

HUMOUR20:34 H26 Or wil they nil they, Choler wil be cheife;
MPERS73:15 H802 Of which the cheife were {was} seven, call'd *Satrapes,*
MGREC104:5 H2057 But *Bessus* false, who was his cheife Commander;

CHEIFEST (1) [chiefest]
JULY223:23 Hp251 was from home (who is my cheifest comforter on Earth)

CHEIFLY (2) [chidfly
HUMOUR32:9 H483 My sicknesse cheifly in conceit doth lye,
11MAYA226:18 Hp255 of Baca many pools of water, That wch now I cheifly labour

CHEMISTRY See CHYMESTRY

CHERRY (2)
SEASONS48:25 H78 For fruits, my season yeelds, the early Cherry,
SEASONS49:36 H129 The Cherry, Goos-berry, is {are} now i'th prime,

CHEST (1)
HOUSE236:37 H29 Here stood that Trunk, and there y^t^ chest

CHH (1) [church]
MYCHILD216:10 Hp241 submitted to it & joined to ye chh., at Boston.

CHICKINS (1) [chickens]
SEASONS~~48:7~~ H60 clocking hen, her chipping brood now {chirping chickins} leads,

CHIDE (3)
HUMOUR20:33 H25 Wel, thus they parle, and chide, but to be briefe,
FAINT222:21 H11 My Doubting thou didst chide
HOUSE237:11 H41 Then streight I 'gin my heart to chide,

CHIDREN (1) [children]
MERCY189:9 H30 So with her Chidren four, she's now at rest,

CHIEF (18) See also CHEIF, CHEIFE
MPERS~~70:3~~ H674 Did to him still his chief designs commend.
MPERS76:31 H929 By brave *Miltiades* (their chief) being led,
MPERS81:9 H1117 (Chief instigater of this hopelesse {hapless} War;)
MPERS89:34 H1468 Invites their chief Commander, as most {Commanders feasts
MGREC~~98:31~~ H1833 *Ephestion* now, hath the {having chief} command o' th' Fleet,
MGREC113:41 H2468 And in his cups, his chief Companion;
MGREC118:29 H2678 His chief opponents who kept off the Crown, {Control'd his
MGREC119:31 H2721 The valiant Chief, amidst his foes was slain,
MGREC~~120:20~~ H2757 Acknowledged for Chief that old Commander)
MGREC122:36 ~~H2857~~ Acknowledged for chief, this old Commander:
MGREC~~122:36~~ H2857 Their bonnets vail'd to him as chief Commander.
MGREC~~123:31~~ H2895 And to be great {chief} himselfe now bends his aymes;
MGREC123:37 H2901 On whom ('twas thought) she set her chief delight;
MGREC~~126:7~~ H2998 She with the flow'r {chief} o'th Court to *Pidna* flyes,
MGREC135:10 H3382 Now up, now down, now chief, and then brought under;
DIALOG145:18 H167 Which is the chief, the law, or else the King,
SIDNEY151:9 ~~H69~~ Who wert of honours band, the chief Commander.
CHILDRN184:20 H9 Chief of the Brood then took his flight,

CHIEFEST (2) See also CHEIFEST
HUMOUR~~20:31~~ H23 Cold {Mild} flegme, did not contest for highest {chiefest} place,
MGREC125:32 H2982 His Brethern, Kinsfolk, and his chiefest friends,

CHIEFLY (2) See also CHEIFLY
ELEMEN12:2 H162 But chiefly, 'cause the Muses there did dwell;
HUMOUR~~27:24~~ H295 Shal firstly {chiefly} take her {the} place, as is her {my} due,

CHIEFTAINS (1) [pl.]
MGREC~~123:13~~ H2876 But while these Chieftains doe in Asia fight,

CHILD (10)
AGES36:38 H62 To hear the child, who crying, thus began.
MGREC132:1 H3234 (Rather then *Philips* child must {race should} longer live
DIALOG146:14 ~~H200~~ Pray now dear child, for sacred *Zion's* sake,
ANNEB187:30 H20 Farewel dear child, thou ne're shall come to me,
MEDDM200:33 Hp280 A wise father will not lay a burden on a child of seven yeares
MYCHILD216:14 Hp241 God to keep me a long time wthout a child wch was a great
MYCHILD216:27 Hp242 towards him. Somt. he hath smott a child wth sicknes, somt.
MYCHILD217:7 Hp242 an vntoward child, that no longer then the rod has been on my
MED223:6 Hp250 father I thy child, yee shall be my Sons and Daughters saith y^{e}
SAMUEL228:5 H6 The child I stay'd for many yeares.
CHILDE (8) [child]
PROLOG7:23 H35 And poesy made, *Calliope's* owne childe,
HUMOUR20:18 H10 Earth knew her black swarth childe, Water her faire;
AGES39:2 H145 For 'tis but little, that a childe can say.
MASSYR57:20 ~~H167~~ Each wronged Prince, or childe that did remain,
DIALOG141:19 H18 And thou a childe, a Limbe, and dost not feele
DIALOG142:30 H59 Your humble Childe intreats you, shew your grief,
DUBART153:16 H20 My Muse unto a Childe, I fitly may compare,
MEDDM200:15 Hp279 A prudent mother will not cloth her little childe wth a long and
CHILDEHOOD (2) [childhood]
ELEMEN16:35 H358 O're childehood, and {ore} Winter, I bear the sway;
AGES41:15 H234 Childehood and youth, forgot, sometimes I've seen,
CHILD-HOOD (1) [childhood]
AGES41:13 H232 Child-hood and youth is {are} vaine, yea {ye} vanity.
CHILDHOOD (5)
AGES35:18 H4 Childhood, and Youth, the Manly, and Old-age.
AGES35:27 H13 Childhood was cloath'd in white, and given {green} to show,
AGES36:30 H54 To childish childhood, give precedency.
AGES37:1 H63 *Childhood.*
MYCHILD215:23 Hp240 wth me fr my childhood to this Day.
CHILDISH (2)
HUMOUR24:26 H175 Thy childish {foolish} incongruities, Ile show:
AGES36:30 H54 To childish childhood, give precedency.
CHILDISHLY (1)
MEDDM200:10 Hp279 yet they are so childishly sottish that they are still huging and
CHILDISHNESSE (1)
AGES37:18 H80 When Infancy was past, my Childishnesse,
CHILDLESSE (1)
MPERS73:13 H800 Childlesse *Cambyses,* on the sudden dead,
CHILD-LIKE (1)
DIALOG146:24 H210 Or any child-like love thou dost retain,
CHILDREN (29) See also CHIDREN
AGES41:35 H250 If a father {I}, then for children must provide:
MASSYR64:14 H438 Children of Royal bloud, unblemish'd youth;
MASSYR65:41 H506 With Children, Wives, and Nobles, all they bring,
MGREC105:32 H2125 To's Mother, Children deare, and Wife now gone,
MGREC124:40 H2947 As all her Husbands children by his Mates;
MGREC126:41 H3030 Her Husbands Wife, {wives} and Children, after's death
MGREC130:31 ~~H3181~~ Two other children by *Olympias* kill'd,
MGREC132:12 H3247 Yet must his children pay for fathers ill.

DIALOG146:21 H207 The poore they want their pay, their children bread,
DDUDLEY167:22H19 *Of all her Children, Children, liv'd to see,*
DDUDLEY167:22H19 *Of all her Children, Children, liv'd to see,*
BIRTH179:26 H1-2 *Before the Birth of one of her Children.*
CHILDRN184:13 H1-2 *In reference to her Children, 23. June, 1659.*
2SIMON195:4 Hp271 their imitation Children do natureally, rather follow the failings
2SIMON195:10 Hp271 true friends much more by duty full children, I haue avoyded
MEDDM196:28 Hp273 Diuerse children, haue their different natures, some are like
MEDDM198:2 Hp275 hath sutable comforts and supports for his children according
MEDDM200:6 Hp279 Some children are hardly weaned although the teat be rub'd
MEDDM200:36 Hp280 weak children as would crush them to the dust, but according
MEDDM201:1 Hp280 he will proportion the load, as god hath his little Children so
MEDDM204:35 Hp285 into tilth yet all must be ploughed and harrowed Some children
MEDDM206:29 Hp288 how many good parents haue had bad children, and againe
MEDDM206:30 Hp288 bad parents haue had pious children, it should make vs adore
MEDDM206:33 Hp288 it should alsoe teach the children of godly parents to walk wth
TOCHILD215:1 H1 To my dear children.
MYCHILD215:9 Hp240 My dear children.
28AUG225:30 Hp254 not afflict willingly, nor take delight in greiving ye children of
30SEPT227:28 Hp257 Thus (dear children) haue yee seen ye many sicknesses and
HOURS234:13 H27 Tho: children thou hast given me

CHILDRENS (1) [poss.]
HUMOUR24:8 H157 I love no boasting, that's but childrens trade:

CHILLED (1)
1LETTER181:13 H11 My chilled limbs now nummed lye forlorn;

CHILLING (2)
ELEMEN17:18 H382 And of my chilling colds, such plenty be;
SEASONS52:25 H240 Chilling the blood, and shrinking up the skin.

CHINKE (1)
ELEMEN14:8 ~~H250~~ Who bravely rode into my yawning chinke.

CHINOES (1) [pl.]
MASSYR62:26 H371 Or else those *Chinoes* rare, whose wealth, and Arts,

CHIPPING (1)
SEASONS48:7 H60 The clocking hen, her chipping brood now {chirping chickins}

CHIRP (1)
SEASONS47:17 H33 Like Birds, now chirp, and hop about the field;

CHIRPING (2)
SEASONS~~48:7~~ H60 clocking hen, her chipping brood now {chirping chickins} leads,
CHILDRN186:18 H85 In chirping languages, oft them tell,

CHIRPS (1) [pl.]
CHILDRN184:22 H11 My mournful chirps I after send,

CHIRURGIAN (1)
MEDDM203:22 Hp283 care for the company of the phisitian or chirurgian, but if he

CHOAK'D (1) [choked]
MGREC109:11 H2270 And with delicious meats, his Pallat choak'd,

CHOAKED (2) [choked]
ELEMEN8:17 H15 Fire broyled Earth, and scorched Earth it choaked,
MEDDM202:18 Hp282 but cannot fill their bellys, they may be choaked by them,

CHOAKING (1) [choking]
ELEMEN10:29 H104 The choaking flames, that from *Vesuvius* flew

CHOICE See CHOISE, CHOYCE, CHOYSE

CHOIR See QUIRE
CHOISE (1) [choice] See also CHOYCE, CHOYSE
MGREC130:7 H3162 Choise above all, of *Ptolomy* she makes
CHOKE See CHOAKE
CHOKED See CHOAK'D, CHOAKED
CHOKING See CHOAKING
CHOLER (27)
ELEMEN10:19 H94 Ile here let passe, my Choler cause of warres,
HUMOUR20:17 H9 Choler was own'd by Fire, and Blood by Aire,
HUMOUR20:23 H15 Choler {first} hotly claim'd, right by her mother,
HUMOUR20:34 H26 Or wil they nil they, Choler wil be cheife;
HUMOUR21:1 H29 *Choler.*
HUMOUR21:13 H41 Yet man for Choler, is the proper seat.
HUMOUR23:34 H144 Take choler from a Prince, what is he more,
HUMOUR25:3 H192 As thy unbridled, barb'rous Choler yeelds. {breeds:}
HUMOUR25:14 H203 Thy Choler is but rage, when tis most pure.
HUMOUR25:41 H230 Ile praise that fury, {prowess} valour, choler, heat.
HUMOUR28:14 H326 The bitter choler, most malignant knowne
HUMOUR28:28 H340 And maugre (Choler) stil they are the wittest,
HUMOUR28:36 H348 I've scarce wip'd off the spots, proud Choler cast,
HUMOUR29:6 H359 Though Choler rage, and raile, i'le not do so,
HUMOUR29:14 H367 But Choler, be thou cool'd, or chaf'd, i'le venter,
HUMOUR29:27 H378 I then command, proud Choler stand thy place,
HUMOUR~~31:5~~ H438 And so art call'd black Choler or adust,
HUMOUR31:31 H464 Impatient Choler loveth not the sound.
HUMOUR32:22 H496 I've not forgot how bitter Choler spake,
HUMOUR34:23 H578 A foolish Brain (saith {quoth} Choler) wanting heat,
HUMOUR34:28 H583 Ne're did {Nor will} I heare {yield} that Choler was the witt'est;
HUMOUR34:35 H590 Wel, to be breif, Choler I hope now's laid,
HUMOUR35:4 H600 Let Sanguine, Choler, with her hot hand hold,
AGES35:23 H9 The third, of fire, and choler is compos'd,
AGES36:15 H39 His Sword by's side, and choler in his eyes;
SEASONS48:40 H91 Resembling choler, fire and middle-age;
MGREC~~93:27~~ H1624 Who {That} ran in fury, {Choler} on the *Persian* Ram,
CHOLERICK (1)
ELEMEN13:12 H213 And cholerick sister, thou (for all thine ire)
CHOLER'S (1) [choler is]
HUMOUR31:24 H457 Choler's too rash, this golden gift to hold.
CHOLERS (2) [poss.]
HUMOUR27:2 H273 Which without all dispute, is Cholers owne;
HUMOUR35:7 H603 Her dry, dry Cholers other hand shal grasp;
CHOLICK (1)
AGES43:29 H324 The windy Cholick oft my bowels rend,
CHOOSE (1) See also CHUSE
MEDDM198:34 Hp277 shall rather choose to be buried vnder rocks and mountains
CHOOSES See CHUSES
CHOOSING See CHUSING
CHOSE (10)
MPERS84:36 H1272 To wrong himselfe by death, he chose before:
MPERS86:39 H1355 And for that end, five hundred Horse he chose,
MPERS89:40 H1474 Chose *Xenophon,* to lead them home again;

MGREC93:32 H1629 The *Greeks* had chose him Captain Generall,
MGREC~~104:3~~ H2055 Chusing {And} rather {chose} an honorable death:
MGREC~~120:4~~ H2738 To end his dayes by poison, rather chose
MGREC122:11 H2836 *Python* now chose protector of the State,
MGREC122:31 H2850 In's stead, {room} the Souldiers chose *Antipater,*
MROMAN137:2 H3453 A hundred Senators he likewise chose,
MROMAN~~137:25~~ H3476 *Nvma Pompilius,* is next chosen {chose they} King,

CHOSEN (2)
MPERS74:2 H827 That {Out} of the seven a Monarch chosen be;
MROMAN137:25 H3476 *Nvma Pompilius,* is next chosen {chose they} King,

CHOYCE (3) [choice] See also CHOYSE
ELEMEN12:22 H182 Out of huge {great} numbers, I might pick my choyce,
MPERS74:26 H849 And now a King, by marriage, choyce, and bloud,
MPERS77:39 H980 And by this choyce, unwarily posts on,

CHOYSE (2) [choice] See also CHOYCE
MGREC118:3 H2650 This choyse *Perdicas,* vehemently disclaim'd,
DAVID159:16 H31 And choyse delights, full of variety.

CHRIST (9) See also XT
MEDDM201:2 Hp280 his strong men, such as are come to a full stature in Christ,
MEDDM206:10 Hp287 but one Christ, who is the Sun of righteousnes, in the midest of
MEDDM209:16 Hp291 Christ Jesus come to their rescue.
PILGRIM210:32 H32 it is the bed Christ did perfume
PILGRIM210:38 H38 in power 'tis rais'd by Christ alone
MYCHILD216:19 Hp241 Christ be formed in yov.
MYCHILD218:20 Hp244 same God, the same Christ, ye same word, They only
MYCHILD218:32 Hp244 I haue remēbred the words of Christ that so it must bee, and
MED223:7 Hp250 Almighty—Christ is my Brother, I ascend vnto my father, and

CHRISTALINE (1)
HUMOUR34:2 H557 Both {The} watry, glassie, and the christaline.

CHRISTALL (1) See also CHRYSTAL
VANITY160:28 H38 Which leads unto that living Christall fount,

CHRISTENDOME (3)
SEASONS52:22 H237 Through Christendome, with great festivity
DIALOG141:18 H17 Which 'mazed Christendome stands wondring at?
DIALOG147:16 H242 Light Christendome, and all the world to see,

CHRISTIAN (7)
DIALOG144:41 H149 Thousands of starved Christian there also.
MEDDM195:30 Hp272 then the practique part, but he is a true Christian that is a
MEDDM196:12 Hp273 the sincerest christian the least self loue
MEDDM196:16 Hp273 christian that hath wrought hard in gods vine yard and hath
MEDDM196:22 Hp273 a prosperous state makes a secure christian, but adversity
MEDDM200:21 Hp279 Christian, therfore god cuts their garments short, to keep them
MEDDM203:13 Hp283 wher his bussines lyes, a christian is sailing through this world

CHRISTIANS (5) [pl.] See also XTIANS
MEDDM197:7 Hp274 The reason why christians are so loth to exchang this world for
MEDDM200:8 Hp279 bitter together so is it wth some Christians, let god imbitter all
MEDDM205:35 Hp287 there are some eminent Christians, that are soe frequent in
MEDDM206:3 Hp287 and these are but leavie Christians, wch are in as much
MEDDM209:7 Hp291 Some christians do by their lusts and corruptions as the Isralits

CHRISTOPHERS (1) [pl.]
ELEMEN19:33 H474 Knowes {Know} Western Isles, *Christophers, Barbadoes;*

CHRONICLES (1) [pl.]
MPERS92:13 H1571 Three years he reign'd, as Chronicles expresse, {then drank

CHRYSTAL (1) See also CHRISTALL
FLESH177:13 H94 A Chrystal River there doth run,

CHURCH (5) See also CHH
DIALOG143:33 H102 Church Offices are {were} sold, and bought, for gaine,
DIALOG145:23 H172 To help the Church, and stay the Common-Weal,
DIALOG147:34 H258 Thy Church and Weal, establish'd in such manner,
MEDDM205:34 Hp286 them are dry stocks so is it in the church wch is gods orchard,
MEDDM206:9 Hp287 one Sun, so is it in the Church both militant and triumphant,

CHURCHES (1) [poss.]
DIALOG147:10 H236 These are the dayes, the Churches foes to crush,

CHUS (1)
MASSYR~~53:20~~ H10 The boysterous Sons of *Cush, {Chus,}* Grand-child to *Ham,*

CHUSE (3) [choose]
MPERS73:14 H801 The Princes meet to chuse one in his stead,
MPERS84:27 H1263 Who for his wrong, he could not chuse but deem,
MGREC125:25 H2975 Bids chuse her death, such kindnesse she'l afford:

CHUSES (1) [chooses]
MEDDM206:32 Hp288 persons, but takes and chuses, when and where and whom he

CHUSING (1) [choosing]
MGREC104:3 H2055 Chusing {And} rather {chose} an honorable death:

CHYMERA'S (1) [pl.]
HUMOUR32:11 H485 Strange Chymera's are in my phantasie,

CHYMESTRY (1) [chemistry]
ELEMEN9:21 H55 In chymestry, unlesse I help you Stil,

CICILY (1)
ELEMEN17:9 H373 *Cicily* from *Italy,* by th'like chance.

CILCIA (1)
MGREC98:25 H1827 *Cilcia* he to *Socrates* doth give,

CILICIA (2)
MGREC95:26 H1705 Now {Then} *Alexander* all *Cilicia* takes:
MGREC119:36 H2726 Long marches through *Cilicia* he makes,

CILICIANS (1) [pl.]
MPERS78:18 H999 *Cipriots, Dorians,* and *Cilicians,*

CIMENTED (1) [cemented]
MROMAN136:35 H3449 The Stones at first was cimented with bloud,

CINDERS (1) [pl.]
ELEMEN10:35 H110 What famous Townes to cinders have I turn'd?

CIPRIOTS (1) [pl.]
MPERS78:18 H999 *Cipriots, Dorians,* and *Cilicians,*

CIRCLE (1)
SEASONS~~52:39~~ H255 And thus the year in circle runneth round:

CIRCUIT (1)
MGREC110:27 H2331 Doth for his Camp a greater circuit take,

CIRC̄SPECTION (1) [circumspection]
MYCHILD217:6 Hp242 circ̄spection in my walking after I haue been afflicted. I haue

CIRCUMSTANCE (1)
MASSYR61:1 H306 But circumstance, doth prove the verity;

CIRCUMVENT (1)
MGREC123:7 H2869 And by his sleights to circumvent him sought;

CIRUS (1)
QELIZ157:8 H76 Feirce *Tomris* (*Cirus* Heads-man, *Sythians* Queen)
CISTERNS (1)
HUMOUR26:25 H255 I am the Fountaine which thy Cisterns fils,
CITADEL See CITTADEL
CITED See SCITED
CITIES (10) [PL.]
PROLOG6:19 H4 Of Cities founded, Common-wealths begun,
ELEMEN11:37 H157 My cities famous, rich, and populous,
ELEMEN13:1 H202 Built Cities, Monuments call'd by your names;
ELEMEN14:2 H244 Your Cities and your selves I oft intombe.
SEASONS48:4 H57 In trees, and wals, in cities, and in fields;
MASSYR53:30 H20 By him, to Cities eminent did rise;
MASSYR61:17 H322 And divers Cities, by strong hand did seize,
MGREC103:4 H2015 Of all the Cities, that on Earth was found;
MGREC107:15 H2190 The wealth of many Cities doth {Kindomes did} consume:
MGREC110:38 H2342 Two Cities built, his fame {name} might there abide;
CITIES (1) [city's]
MPERS75:8 H869 With all the Cities strength they him betrust,
CITTADEL (1)
HUMOUR33:34 H548 Within this high built Cittadel doth lye,
CITTY (3)
MROMAN136:31 H3445 A Citty faire did *Romulus* erect:
MEDDM202:26 Hp282 we may go forwards to the Citty of habitation, but when he
MEDDM203:18 Hp283 we may plainly declare that we seek a citty aboue and wait all
CITY (21)
ELEMEN9:7 H41 And in despight the City keeps her owne,
HUMOUR21:25 H53 To storme a Breach, or scale a City wal?
MASSYR59:13 H237 The King pursu'd unto the City wals;
MASSYR60:7 H272 For he demonished that City great,
MASSYR64:35 H459 Within an Island had this City seat,
MASSYR65:35 H500 Besieg'd his City, Temple, *Zions* Tower;
MPERS70:17 H688 Forty five mile {miles} this City scarce could round;
MPERS74:34 H857 An Hoast he rais'd, the City to reduce,
MPERS~~84:12~~ H1246 Went to *Jerusalem* his city dear,
MGREC102:13 H1983 With greedy eyes, he views this City round,
MGREC102:20 H1990 This City did abundantly abound;
MGREC108:36 H2252 A goodly City doth compleatly raise;
MGREC111:14 H2359 A City here he built, cal'd by his name,
MGREC128:7 H3080 Had built, and call'd a City by his name,
MGREC128:20 H3093 And Lord o'th' City {royal} *Susha* did remain.
MROMAN136:37 H3451 This City built, and Sacrifices done,
MROMAN137:4 H3455 His City to replenish, men he wants,
SIDNEY150:23 H50 O *Zutphon, Zutphon,* that most fatall City,
CONTEM170:36 H106 A City builds, that wals might him secure from foes.
FLESH177:5 H86 The City where I hope to dwell,
FLESH177:25 H106 This City pure is not for thee,
CLAD (7)
FATHER5:13 H14 I bring my four times {and} four, now meanly clad,
SEASONS48:10 H63 Wherein the earth, is clad in rich aray:
MASSYR~~58:8~~ H193 His master like a Strumpet chanc'd to {clad did} spy,

MGREC96:4 H1724 The *Persians* clad in silk, and glitt'ring {glistering} gold;
CONTEM167:27 H4 The trees all richly clad, yet void of pride,
CONTEM169:19 H59 The black clad Cricket, bear a second part,
CONTEM171:19 H122 And then the earth (though old) stil clad in green,

CLAIM (2) See also CLAIME
HUMOUR23:24 H134 Thus {But} arms, and arts I claim, and higher things;
HUMOUR30:25 H417 And first, the firme dry bones, I justly claim:

CLAIM'D (3) [claimed]
HUMOUR20:23 H15 Choler {first} hotly claim'd, right by her mother,
SEASONS46:33 H9 At present claim'd, and had priority,
MGREC117:38 H2645 Claim'd not, perhaps her Sex might hindrance be.

CLAIME (10) [claim]
FATHER5:16 H17 Might seem of yours to claime precedency;
ELEMEN10:23 H98 The Summer ripening season I do claime;
ELEMEN11:26 H146 Which none ere gave, nor {or} you could claime of right,
HUMOUR22:31 H100 The Animal I claime, as wel as these,
HUMOUR23:10 H120 Thou canst not claime, the Liver, Head nor Heart;
HUMOUR26:5 H235 Nextly, the spirits thou do'st wholly claime,
HUMOUR26:24 H254 Shal justly claime priority of thine;
HUMOUR27:10 H281 Again, stomachs concoction thou dost claime,
HUMOUR27:13 ~~H284~~ Thou do'st unjustly claime, her property,
MGREC117:33 H2640 By Natures right, these had enough to claime,

CLAIMED See CLAIM'D

CLAIMES (1) [claims]
AGES35:21 H7 The second, frolick, claimes his pedigree,

CLAMBERING (1)
SEASONS47:11 H27 And Poles erects, for his green {young} clambering Hops;

CLANGING (1)
AGES45:32 H422 {waking glad to hear} at the cocks clanging {shrill} voyce.

CLAP (1)
DIALOG144:33 H141 This is fore-runner of my after clap,

CLAPS (1) [pl.]
MPERS~~76:41~~ H939 His whetted teeth he sticks {claps} in the firm wood,

CLAPT (2)
AGES41:10 H230 Clapt in that prison, never thence to start.
DIALOG142:17 H46 That second *Richard* must be clapt i'th' Tower?

CLARENCE (1)
DIALOG144:9 H119 Oh, *Edwards* Babes {youths}, and *Clarence* haplesse Son,

CLASP (1)
HUMOUR35:6 H602 My cold, cold Melanchollies {melancholy} hand shal clasp,

CLAW (1)
HUMOUR21:34 H62 Unlesse to court, and claw, and {to} dice, and drink,

CLAY (7)
HUMOUR22:30 H99 For when they faile, man turnes unto his clay:
HUMOUR28:8 H320 As if she'd leave no flesh to turn to clay,
AGES43:15 ~~H307~~ Then heapt up gold, and riches as the clay;
MGREC106:4 H2138 And though a Monarch once {late}, now lyes like clay;
MEDDM198:5 Hp276 waters, if they stick in deepe mire and clay, and all his waues
MEDDM207:28 Hp289 that when wee are put out of these houses of Clay, we
PILGRIM210:22 H22 and my Clay house mouldring away

CLEAN (2)

MASSYR65:11 H476 *Jehoiakim* his Oath had clean forgot;

MEDDM207:5 Hp288 but most Commonly imployed for a Clean Contrary end, then

CLEANLY (2)

SEASONS48:19 H72 The cleanly huswives Dary, now's ith' prime,

MEDDM197:18 Hp275 house wch is not often swept makes the cleanly inhabitant

CLEANSED (2)

DIALOG144:4 H114 From crying bloods, yet cleansed am not I,

MEDDM203:31 Hp284 We read of ten lepers that were Cleansed, but of one that

CLEANSER (1)

HUMOUR31:10 H443 The Kitchin Drudge, the cleanser of the sinks,

CLEAR (9) See also CLEARE, CLEER

FATHER6:8 H42 I shall not need my {mine} innocence to clear,

HUMOUR34:6 H561 Whence her affections, passions, speak so clear;

SEASONS48:23 H76 But both rejoyce, at th'heavens clear smiling face,

MASSYR68:8 H594 To him that could interpret clear this thing:

MGREC~~127:41~~ H3071 And shews {clear} what cause they {he} had to take up {make

DIALOG146:36 H222 After dark Popery the day did clear,

FLESH177:9 H90 The Gates of Pearl, both rich and clear,

FLESH177:24 H105 But beauty shall be bright and clear;

BIRTH179:29 H5 No tyes so strong, no friends so clear and sweet,

CLEAR'D (1) [cleared]

HUMOUR31:19 H452 I trust I've clear'd your slandrous imputations {inputation}.

CLEARE (1) [clear] See also CLEER

HUMOUR26:34 H264 But the materials none of thine, that's cleare,

CLEARED See CLEAR'D

CLEARS (1)

ELEMEN15:33 H315 Not thou, but shell-fish yeelds, as *Pliny* clears.

CLEAUE (1) [cleave]

MYSOUL224:28 H4 Cleaue close to him alway.

CLEER (2) [clear] See also CLEARE

CONTEM172:23 H157 But hundred brooks in thy cleer waves do meet,

CONTEM173:23 H189 Thy bed a bough, thy drink the water cleer,

CLEMENCY (4)

MGREC106:23 H2157 He basenesse counts his former clemency,

MGREC113:5 H2432 Oh, *Alexander,* thy free clemency,

MGREC132:30 H3277 Renown'd for bounty, valour, clemency,

QELIZ155:28 H19 Thy clemency did yerst esteeme as much

CLEOPATRA (6)

ELEMEN15:35 H317 As *Ægypts* wanton *Cleopatra* drunke.

MGREC119:8 H2698 But *Cleopatra,* this suitour did deny,

MGREC119:29 H2719 (Which did his match with *Cleopatra* mar)

MGREC130:2 H3157 For marriage to *Cleopatra,* doth send

MGREC134:35 H3366 Fair *Cleopatra* next, last of that race,

QELIZ157:18 H86 Proud profuse *Cleopatra,* whose wrong name,

CLEOPATRA'S (1) [poss.]

MGREC130:32 ~~H3181~~ And *Cleopatra's* blood, now likewise spill'd,

CLERKE (1)

HUMOUR30:1 H393 What greater Clerke, or polititian lives?

CLERKES (1) [pl.]

DIALOG144:27 ~~H135~~ Of stinking, stigmatizing, Romish Clerkes;

CLIENTS (1) [pl.]
DIALOG147:41 H265 Patience, and purse of Clients for {oft} to wrong:
CLIMB (1) See also CLIMBE, CLIME
MEDDM197:26 Hp275 He that will vntertake to climb vp a steep mountain wth a great
CLIMBE (6) [climb] See also CLIME
FATHER5:9 H10 To climbe their Climes, I have nor strength, nor skill,
AGES39:17 H160 That dare climbe Battlements, {scale walls and forts} rear'd to
MPERS86:22 H1338 By lesser {lower} steps, towards the top to climbe;
MGREC94:9 H1643 And many more, {all} whom he suspects {or fears} will climbe,
MROMAN138:28 H3518 By wealth, and favour, doth to honour climbe;
VANITY160:24 H34 Where shall I climbe, sound, seek, search or find,
CLIMBES (2) [climbs]
AGES41:30 H247 Who climbes without hold, climbes dangerously.
AGES41:30 H247 Who climbes without hold, climbes dangerously.
CLIMBING (1)
MEDDM199:15 Hp278 men are like hops that neuer rest climbing soe long as they
CLIMBS (1) See also CLIMBES
MPERS74:25 H848 That by such steps to Kingdoms often climbs {clime}.
CLIME (5) [climate]
AGES35:32 H18 Before the Sun hath throughly warm'd {heat} the clime.
SEASONS48:28 H81 Each season, hath his fruit, so hath each clime.
SEASONS50:39 H173 Now day and night are equal in each clime;
SEASONS~~51:19~~ H194 Nor could that temp'rate Clime such difference make,
QELIZ155:16 H7 Thy wondrous worth proclaime, in every clime,
CLIME (2) [climb]
MPERS~~74:25~~ H848 That by such steps to Kingdoms often climbs {clime}.
DUBART154:32 H77 All ages wondring at, shall never clime.
CLIMES (1) [pl.]
FATHER5:9 H10 To climbe their Climes, I have nor strength, nor skill,
CLIO (1)
SIDNEY149:18 H17 More worth was thine, {his} then *Clio* could set down.
CLITUS (4)
MGREC113:40 H2467 *Clitus,* belov'd next to *Ephestion,*
MGREC114:1 H2469 When both were drunk, *Clitus* was wont to jeere;
MGREC114:8 H2476 Upon this dangerous theam fond *Clitus* fell;
MGREC114:14 H2484 And would have slaine himself, for *Clitus* gone,
CLITUS (1) [poss.]
MGREC114:3 H2471 Nothing more pleasing to mad *Clitus* tongue,
CLOAKE (1)
MASSYR68:18 H604 Who doth not flatter, nor once cloake the thing.
CLOATH (1) [cloth]
DAVID159:15 H30 Who cloathed you in cloath of richest dye,
CLOATH'D (4) [clothed] See also CLOATHED, CLOTH'D
AGES35:27 H13 Childhood was cloath'd in white, and given {green} to show,
SEASONS49:17 H108 To wash their {the} thick cloath'd flocks, with pipes ful glad.
TDUDLEY166:15 H57 He might be cloath'd upon, for evermore.
CONTEM171:7 H112 Cloath'd all in his black sinfull Livery,
CLOATHED (1) [clothed] See also CLOATH'D, CLOTH'D
DAVID159:15 H30 Who cloathed you in cloath of richest dye,
CLOATHES (1) [clothes]
FATHER5:23 H24 Of these consists, our bodyes, cloathes, and food,

CLOATHING (1)
AGES39:4 H147 My goodly cloathing, and my beauteous skin,
CLOATHS (2) [cloths]
SEASONS52:7 H222 This time warm cloaths, ful diet, and good fires,
CONTEM173:22 H188 Thy cloaths ne're wear, thy meat is every where,
CLOCKING (1)
SEASONS48:7 H60 The clocking hen, her chipping brood now {chirping chickins}
CLOG'D (1) [clogged]
MEDDM197:28 Hp275 thinkes to mount to heaven clog'd wth the Cares and riches of
CLOGS (1)
MEDDM207:10 Hp288 to help vs mount vpwards, they will Certainly proue Clogs
CLOSE (6) [near]
HUMOUR28:15 H327 I turn into his cel, close by my side,
MASSYR58:6 H191 Kept ever close, fearing some dismal {his well deserved} fate;
MROMAN138:21 H3511 Close by the mouth of famous *Tyber* flood:
CONTEM172:7 H143 Close sate I by a goodly Rivers side,
FLESH175:3 H3 Close by the Banks of *Lacrim* flood
MYSOUL224:28 H4 Cleaue close to him alway.
CLOSE (1) [enclosed]
MGREC128:2 H3075 His Wife, and Son, in prison close had shut;
CLOSE (5) v.
HUMOUR24:5 H154 And one thing more to close with {up} my narration.
AGES44:37 H370 But ah, I saw at last those eyes to close:
MASSYR66:2 H508 And with that woful sight his eyes close shut.
MPERS75:37 H894 Built on, and prosper'd, till their walls did {house they} close;
MPERS82:34 H1181 The sorrow of his heart, did close his eye:
CLOSELY (2)
DIALOG147:25 H249 And to this blessed {hopeful} Cause closely adhere
30SEPT227:33 Hp257 closely with him then before, This is the desire of y^r^ Loving
CLOSET (1)
DDUDLEY167:19 H16 *And in her Closet constant hours she spent;*
CLOTH (2) See also CLOATH
AUTHOR178:9 H19 But nought save home-spun Cloth, i' th' house I find.
MEDDM200:15 Hp279 A prudent mother will not cloth her little childe wth a long and
CLOTH'D (4) [clothed] See also CLOATH'D, CLOATHED
FATHER~~5:4~~ H5 Of your four sisters, deckt {cloth'd} in black & white /four parts
AGES42:2 H260 Whose loynes {backs} I've cloth'd, and bellies I have fed;
PILGRIM210:34 H34 this mortall shall be cloth'd vpon
13MAY226:28 H4 The earth all black is cloth'd in green
CLOTHED (1) See also CLOATH'D, CLOATHED, CLOTH'D
DDUDLEY167:13 H10 *Whom oft she fed, and clothed with her store;*
CLOTHES See CLOATHES, CLOATHS
CLOTHING See CLOATHING
CLOUD (2)
MPERS88:8 H1401 Which like a mighty cloud darkned the skye;
MEDDM202:21 Hp282 Sometimes the sun is only shadowed by a cloud, that wee
CLOUDS (5) [pl.] See also CLOWDES
MASSYR56:16 H122 Whose stately top, beyond {above} the clouds did rise;
MPERS71:37 H751 *Cambyses* to the clouds, we might commend;
CONTEM168:8 H17 Whose ruffling top the Clouds seem'd to aspire;
DISTEMP179:22 H10 He chac'd away those clouds, and let me see

MEDDM201:22 Hp281 but from some black Clouds that impends them, wch produces

CLOUTS (1) [pl.]
SEASONS52:15 H230 In Swadling clouts, like new-born infancy,

CLOWDES (1)
13MAY227:2 H11 And former clowdes seem now all fled

CLOY'D (1) [cloyed]
CONTEM170:25 H96 But since that time she often hath been cloy'd;

CLUB (1)
ELEMEN10:4 H79 The *Theban* stout *Alcides,* with his club:

CLUSTER (1)
MGREC100:22 H1906 Of *Persians, Scithians, Indians,* in a cluster;

CLUSTERS (1) [pl.]
SEASONS51:6 H180 The Raisins now in clusters dryed be,

COACH (2)
ELEMEN9:37 H71 And birds do sing, to see his glittering Coach.
MGREC97:2 H1763 Who from his golden Coach is glad t'alight,

COADJUTORS (1) [pl.]
HUMOUR26:4 H234 The friendly coadjutors, stil to {of} thee.

COAST (10)
MASSYR62:9 H354 Besieg'd his regal town, and spoyl'd his Coast,
MASSYR~~62:34~~ H379 On *Henah, Arpad,* and on *Ivdah* least {*Juahs* coast};
MASSYR67:15 H561 *Arabia,* and all the boardering coast.
MPERS71:21 H735 Who landed {landing} soon upon that fruitful coast,
MPERS90:27 H1494 Who with his {the} *Spartans* on the *Asia* coast;
MGREC111:23 H2368 To th' coast which by *Euphrates* mouth appear'd;
MGREC121:4 H2782 Leaves *Eumenes,* the *Asian* coast to free,
SIDNEY150:21 H46 What famous feats thou didst, on *Flanders* coast,
TDUDLEY165:21 H23 Both in his native, and in foreign coast,
MERCY188:28 H14 Thou then on Seas sailing to forreign Coast;

COASTS (3) [pl.]
ELEMEN16:10 H333 If I should shew,{name} more Seas, then thou hast Coasts.
QELIZ156:22 H49 Her Victories in forraigne Coasts resound?
CONTEM172:33 H166 To unknown coasts to give a visitation,

COATES (1) [coats]
SEASONS49:19 H110 Rubbing their dirty coates, till they look white.

COATS (2) [pl.]
HUMOUR34:1 H556 The optick nerve, coats, humours, all are mine,
MROMAN136:29 H3443 Where Shepheards once had Coats, and Sheep their Folds,

COCK (1) See also PEA COCK
AGES42:26 H284 The early Cock, did summon but in vaine,

COCKS (1) [pl.]
CHILDRN184:15 H4 Four Cocks there were, and Hens the rest,

COCKS (1) [poss.]
AGES45:32 H422 {waking glad to hear} at the cocks clanging {shrill} voyce.

CODOMANUS (2)
MPERS92:15 H1573 *Darius Codomanus.*
MPERS~~92:24~~ H1582 This *Codomanus* now upon the stage

COGITATION (1)
MEDDM201:16 Hp280 a quick reception, and a deliberate cogitation argues a sound

COIN See COYN, COYNE

COLD (42)

FATHER5:21	H22	These are, the hot, the cold, the moist, the dry,
FATHER5:31	H32	How hot, and dry, contend with moist, and cold,
ELEMEN8:24	H22	That betwixt hot and cold, she arbitrated
ELEMEN9:19	H53	Your shrinking limbs, which winters cold doth harme;
ELEMEN~~9:33~~	H67	Good {Cold} sister Earth, no witnesse needs but thine;
ELEMEN13:15	H216	My cold, thy (fruitfull) heat, doth crave no lesse:
ELEMEN13:16	H217	But how my cold, dry temper, works upon
ELEMEN14:12	~~H254~~	In hot, and cold, and some benums with sleeps,
ELEMEN16:34	H357	All humours, Tumours, that {which} are bred of cold.
ELEMEN16:40	H363	By adding cold to cold, no fruit proves sound;
ELEMEN16:40	H363	By adding cold to cold, no fruit proves sound;
ELEMEN17:15	H379	My Ice and extream cold, which all men know.
HUMOUR20:31	H23	Cold {Mild} flegme, did not contest for highest {chiefest} place,
HUMOUR22:11	H80	But {Now} let's give, cold, white, Sister Flegme her right.
HUMOUR24:27	H176	So walke thee til thou'rt cold, then let thee go.
HUMOUR27:28	H299	Your hot, dry, moyst, cold, natures are {but} foure,
HUMOUR27:30	H301	As thus, if hot, then dry; if moist, then cold;
HUMOUR28:6	H318	With cold distempers, to pain every part;
HUMOUR30:7	H399	Those {Whose} cold dry heads, {head} more subtilly doth yeild,
HUMOUR32:6	H480	Nor cold, nor hot, Ague, nor Plurisie;
HUMOUR35:6	H602	My cold, cold Melanchollies {melancholy} hand shal clasp,
HUMOUR35:6	H602	My cold, cold Melanchollies {melancholy} hand shal clasp,
HUMOUR35:8	H604	Two hot, two moist, two cold, two dry here be,
AGES35:31	H17	Such cold mean flowers (as these) blossome {the spring puts
AGES38:33	H136	What crudities my cold stomach hath bred?
AGES45:40	H430	Now trembling, and {is all} fearful, sad, and cold;
SEASONS~~46:35~~	H12	Nor hot nor cold, she spake, but with a breath,
SEASONS47:27	H43	The pinching Nor-west {North-west} cold, {wind} of fierce
SEASONS49:31	H120	But whist'leth to thy Flock in cold, and heat,
SEASONS52:4	~~H219~~	When cold, the sap to th' roots hath low'st repell'd;
SEASONS52:9	H224	Old cold, dry age, and earth, Autumne resembles,
SEASONS52:14	H229	Cold, moist, young, flegmy Winter now doth lye
SEASONS52:24	H239	Cold frozen *January* next comes in,
SEASONS52:29	H244	The cold not lessened, but augmented more.
SEASONS52:39	H254	Until by's heat he drives {drive} all cold away.
MPERS76:5	H903	His Army fought with Hunger, and with Cold,
MPERS90:6	H1479	But on they march, through hunger, and through cold,
MGREC111:26	H2371	By hunger, and by cold, so many slaine,
DUBART154:16	H61	In all the Zones, the temp'rate, hot and cold,
CHILDRN186:14	H81	No seasons cold, nor storms they see;
MEDDM201:13	Hp280	alayed, by cold words and not by blustering threats.
PILGRIM210:13	H13	for waters cold he doth not long

COLDER (1)

CONTEM173:3	H171	Then to the colder bottome streight they dive,

COLDLY (1)

ELEMEN18:22	H426	Your red hot work, more coldly would go on.

COLDNESSE (1)

HUMOUR30:3	H395	What is too hot, my coldnesse doth abate;

COLD'S (1) [cold is]

AGES35:20	H6	Unstable, supple, moist, and cold's his Naure.

COLDS (3) [pl.]
ELEMEN~~14:12~~ H254 In heats & colds & gripes & drowsy sleeps:
ELEMEN17:18 H382 And of my chilling colds, such plenty be;
1LETTER181:12 H10 His warmth such frigid colds did cause to melt.
COLLER (1)
MGREC108:2 H2218 (A coller of the same his neck containes)
COLONIES (1) [pl.]
MASSYR62:19 H364 Then sent his Colonies, theirs to invest;
COLONY (1)
MPERS90:10 H1483 There was of *Greeks,* setled a Colony,
COLOUR (4)
ELEMEN15:36 H318 Or hast thou any colour can come nigh;
HUMOUR34:3 H558 O! mixture strange, oh {O} colour, colourlesse,
MASSYR68:23 H609 The guilty King, with colour pale, and dead,
CHILDRN184:34 H23 I have a third of colour white,
COLOUR'D (1) [coloured]
ELEMEN17:31 H395 Her confirm'd sonnes, behold my colour'd bow.
COLOURED (2)
MGREC96:14 H1734 Support a party coloured canopy.
MGREC118:26 H2675 But all his bowels, coloured well, and sound.
COLOURLESSE (1)
HUMOUR34:3 H558 O! mixture strange, oh {O} colour, colourlesse,
COLOURS (1) [pl.]
ELEMEN11:31 H151 Their kinds, their tasts, their colours, and their smels,
COMAND (1) [command]
2HUSB232:11 H12 At thy comand O Lord he went
COMANDS (1) n. [commands]
MYCHILD216:36 Hp242 and Bonds vpon my Soul to p^{r}form his righteovs comands.
COMBAT See COMBATE
COMBATANTS (1) [pl.]
ELEMEN8:20 H18 Soone made the combatants abate their force;
COMBATE (1) [combat]
FLESH176:2 H42 And combate with thee will and must,
COMBATES (1) [combats]
AGES40:36 H215 Sometimes by wounds in idle combates taken,
COMBIN'D (1) [combined]
MGREC120:41 H2778 *Perdicas* hears, his foes are now {all} combin'd,
COMBINATION (1)
MGREC127:35 H3065 Enter {Enters} into a combination strong:
COMBINE (3)
MGREC120:6 H2741 In love, and in affinity combine:
MGREC120:30 H2767 And 'gainst *Perdicas,* all their strength combine.
MGREC125:2 H2950 She now with *Polisperchon* doth combine,
COMBINED See COMBIN'D
COMBINES (1)
MGREC127:37 H3067 *Lysimachus* to make a fourth combines:
COMBUSTION (1)
MGREC94:7 H1641 That no combustion {rebellion in} in his absence be,
COME (59)
ELEMEN8:35 ~~H33~~ Come first ye Artists, and declare your minde.
ELEMEN10:41 H116 Which when they could not be o're come by foes

ELEMEN11:22	H142	Sister, in worth {quoth shee} I come not short of you;
ELEMEN12:33	H193	Ye *Galenists,* my Drugs that come from thence
ELEMEN15:36	H318	Or hast thou any colour can come nigh;
HUMOUR21:37	H65	A Chamber wel, in field she dares not come;
HUMOUR29:39	H390	I'le come to that which wounds me somewhat more:
HUMOUR31:14	H445	If any doubt this {the} truth, whence this should come;
AGES40:33	H212	Nor yet that heavy reckoning for {soon} to come;
AGES44:7	H340	And on this Stage am come to act my last:
AGES46:2	H433	I then shal go, whence I shal come no more,
MPERS~~72:24~~	H772	His cruelty was come unto that height,
MPERS87:41	H1393	When suddenly their Scouts come in and cry,
MPERS89:13	H1447	They soone may come, and {in short time might} place one in
MGREC96:39	H1759	The *Greeks* come {came} on, and with a gallant grace,
MGREC109:36	H2295	And come as well provided as he could,
MGREC~~118:24~~	H2673	That for a while they durst not come so near:
MGREC119:19	H2709	To come and {For succours} to release {relieve} him in his
MGREC125:11	H2959	To come and succour {To save the King} her, in this great
MGREC126:15	H3006	Faine would she come now to {this wretched Queen}
MROMAN137:16	H3467	But in the end, to finall peace they come,
DIALOG142:21	H50	To come, and break the tushes of the Boar?
DIALOG146:3	H191	But now I come to speak of my disaster,
DIALOG146:19	H205	The seed time's come, but Ploughman hath no hope,
DIALOG147:37	H261	That nursing Kings, shall come and lick thy dust:
QELIZ156:18	H45	Come shew me such a Phoenix if you can;
CONTEM170:14	H86	Here *Cain* and *Abel* come to sacrifice,
CONTEM171:22	H125	If winter come, and greeness then do fade,
CONTEM173:24	H190	Reminds not what is past, nor whats to come dost fear.
FLESH175:5	H5	Things that are past, and things to come;
FLESH175:22	H22	Come, come, Ile shew unto thy sence,
FLESH175:22	H22	Come, come, Ile shew unto thy sence,
FLESH177:23	H104	Nor withering age shall e're come there,
AUTHOR178:11	H21	In Criticks hands, beware thou dost not come;
ANNEB187:30	H20	Farewel dear child, thou ne're shall come to me,
1SIMON188:4	H5	No sooner come, but gone, and fal'n asleep,
MEDDM197:9	Hp274	they do but hope for that wch is to Come
MEDDM197:24	Hp275	receiued? Come giue an account of thy stewardship.
MEDDM201:2	Hp280	his strong men, such as are come to a full stature in Christ,
MEDDM202:29	Hp282	when ye morning (wch is the appointed time) is come the Sun
MEDDM203:19	Hp283	dayes of our appointed time till our chang shall come,
MEDDM206:22	Hp287	at a Compensation then at a pardon, but he that will not Come
MEDDM207:9	Hp288	are lords we will come no more at thee If outward blessings,
MEDDM207:26	Hp289	that time will come, together, wth the vncertainty, how where,
MEDDM208:33	Hp290	these, it hath ouer come the omnipotent himself, as when
MEDDM209:16	Hp291	Christ Jesus come to their rescue.
PILGRIM211:3	H44	then Come deare bridgrome Come away
PILGRIM211:3	H44	then Come deare bridgrome Come away
MED223:15	Hp250	is my comfort, When I come into Heaven, I shall vnderstand
JULY223:36	Hp251	Come Lord Jesus, come quickly.
JULY223:36	Hp251	Come Lord Jesus, come quickly.
MYSOUL225:12	H16	Nor come in memory.
MYSOUL225:21	H25	Come Jesvs qvickly, Blessed Lord

28AUG226:11 Hp254 vnwilling to come tho: by so rovgh a Messenger.
11MAYA226:24 Hp255 a little while and he that shall come will come and will not tarry.
11MAYA226:24 Hp255 a little while and he that shall come will come and will not tarry.
SON230:23 H6 He's come for whom I waited long.
SON231:13 H25 That wthout scandall he might come
REMB235:32 H13 To Thee shall come all Flesh,

COMEDIES (1) [pl.]
SIDNEY149:21 H20 Are not his Tragick Comedies so acted,

COMEING (1) [coming] See also COMMING
MEDDM208:1 Hp289 at whose comeing they shall all rise out of their beds, The

COMELY (2)
HUMOUR30:39 H431 But yet more comely far, I dare avow,
AGES45:37 H427 My comely legs, as nimble as the Roe,

COMES (25)
HUMOUR21:30 H58 But valour, when comes that? from none of you;
HUMOUR22:27 H96 What comes from thence, my heat refines the same,
HUMOUR30:36 H428 But if thou hast, that malice comes {is} from you.
AGES36:20 H44 Leaning upon his staffe, comes {came} up old age.
AGES38:16 H119 As he can tell, that next comes on the stage.
SEASONS52:24 H239 Cold frozen *January* next comes in,
MASSYR61:27 H332 Unto *Damascus* then, comes *Iudah's* King,
MASSYR68:14 H600 In comes the Queen, to chear her heartlesse son.
MPERS78:32 H1013 Whither rich *Pithyus* comes, *Xerxes* to greet;
MPERS82:33 H1180 Straight comes her Lord, and finds his wife thus lie,
MPERS~~87:1~~ H1357 But fame more quick, arrives ere he came {comes} there,
MGREC98:27 H1829 For that which easily comes, as freely goes;
MGREC104:21 H2073 Straight *Bessus* comes, and with his traiterous hands,
MGREC106:41 H2175 The certainty of both comes to his eares,
MGREC110:2 H2302 For to receive {To give} him, {welcome} when he comes to
MGREC121:20 H2802 Next day into the Camp comes {came} *Ptolomy,*
MGREC121:26 H2808 Now comes the newes of a great victory,
MROMAN137:20 H3471 But *Romulus* then comes unto his end,
DIALOG145:24 H173 So many obstacles comes {came} in their way,
CONTEM170:23 H94 His brother comes, then acts his fratricide,
CONTEM171:15 H119 So unawares comes on perpetual night,
CONTEM174:25 H223 But sad affliction comes & makes him see
SICKNES179:8 H28 comes by profession pure.
MEDDM196:15 Hp273 comes he shall both take his rest and receiue his reward, the
MEDDM200:2 Hp278 Wickednes comes to its height by degrees, He that dares say

COMET See COMMET

COMFORT (8)
MPERS78:39 H1020 To be to's age a comfort, and a stay,
MGREC104:19 H2071 Who was of hopes, and comfort quite bereft;
MGREC~~116:10~~ H2573 Nor meat, nor drink, nor comfort would she take,
MYCHILD215:29 Hp241 too often tardy y^{t} way. I also fovnd much comfort in reading y^{e}
SOREFIT221:17 H3 When novght on Earth could comfort giue
MED223:5 Hp250 I thy servant, But hence arises not my comfort, Thou art my
MED223:15 Hp250 But this is my comfort, When I come into Heaven, I shall
HOURS234:11 H25 I in this world no comfort haue,

COMFORTABLE (4)
MEDDM201:33 Hp281 is (of all other) most Comfortable

MEDDM203:11 Hp283 be all convenient and comfortable for him yet he hath no
MEDDM207:15 Hp288 find their shadow very comfortable, yet there is some worm or
MYCHILD217:11 Hp242 comfortable Answers to me, either in granting ye Thing I

COMFORTABLY (1)

MEDDM204:29 Hp285 pouerty comfortably it will help to quiet him, but if that will not

COMFORTER (1)

JULY223:23 Hp251 was from home (who is my cheifest comforter on Earth)

COMFORTS (2) v.

MEDDM196:14 Hp273 The hireling that labours all the day comforts himself, that
RESTOR229:24 H7 Thou comforts me about.

COMFORTS (5) n.

MEDDM198:2 Hp275 God hath sutable comforts and supports for his children
MEDDM203:14 Hp283 country, and heere he hath many conueniences and comforts
MEDDM207:13 Hp288 All the Comforts of this Life, may be compared to the gourd of
MEDDM207:18 Hp289 perceiue a decay, in their greennes for were earthly comforts
HOURS234:4 H18 Whose comforts far excell.

COMING (2) See also COMEING, COMMING

MPERS~~70:40~~ H711 And *Alexander* coming to the same,
HOUSE236:23 H15 Then coming out beheld a space

COMITTED (1) [committed]

MYCHILD219:2 Hp245 and y^{t} he is able to keep y^{t} I haue comitted to his charge.

COMMAND (20) See also COMAND

HUMOUR29:27 H378 I then command, proud Choler stand thy place,
SEASONS47:35 ~~H47~~ But only once at *Joshua's* strange command;
MASSYR53:26 H16 From thence he went *Assyria* to command;
MASSYR58:34 H217 Prest for this service, by the Kings command;
MPERS75:9 H870 If he command, obey the greatest must:
MPERS78:11 H992 But the command of these Commanders all,
MPERS78:28 H1009 For to command alone, she thought {judg'd} was best.
MPERS90:37 H1504 And {Commission} hath command, to take the others head,
MGREC98:15 H1817 Besides, {Moreover} he had a Navie at command,
MGREC98:31 H1833 *Ephestion* now, hath the {having chief} command o' th' Fleet,
MGREC99:25 H1868 And by command was drawn through every street,
MGREC103:3 H2014 And all in it was at his high command;
MGREC109:16 H2275 The Vessells ready were, at his command;
MGREC118:33 H2682 Using the name, and the command o'th' King
MGREC119:3 H2693 But held command o'th' Armies {Army} which was best;
MGREC127:16 H3046 Having Command o'th treasure he can hire,
MGREC130:17 H3172 For straight way by command they'r put to death,
CONTEM174:15 H214 As if he had command of wind and tide,
MEDDM204:23 Hp285 fixe his eye on the command, and not on his own ends, lest he
MEDDM209:13 Hp291 to the Command of god, and endeavour not to the vtmost to

COMMANDED (1)

MGREC106:32 H2166 Are strictly now commanded to adore;

COMMANDEMENT (1) [commandment]

AGES38:24 H127 And fift Commandement do daily break.

COMMANDER (15)

MPERS81:28 ~~H1136~~ Though of this Nation borne a great Commander,
MPERS~~81:28~~ H1136 A *Macedonian* born, and great Commander,
MPERS89:34 H1468 Invites their chief Commander, as most {Commanders feasts
MGREC97:15 H1776 T'ward them, demean'd himself like a Commander;

MGREC99:8 H1851 But, quoth *Parmenio,* (that brave Commander)
MGREC104:5 H2057 But *Bessus* false, who was his cheife Commander;
MGREC113:19 H2446 Who was so much engag'd, to this Commander,
MGREC119:33 H2723 For personage, none was like {to} this Commander:
MGREC~~120:20~~ H2757 Acknowledged for Chief that old Commander)
MGREC122:22 ~~H2845~~ Who had an Army, like a great Commander.
MGREC122:36 ~~H2857~~ Acknowledged for chief, this old Commander:
MGREC~~122:36~~ H2857 Their bonnets vail'd to him as chief Commander.
MGREC124:22 H2929 Put trust in any, but in this Commander;
MGREC130:36 ~~H3181~~ And's kingdomes rent away by each Commander:
SIDNEY151:9 ~~H69~~ Who wert of honours band, the chief Commander.

COMMANDERS (2) [pl.]
MPERS78:11 H992 But the command of these Commanders all,
MPERS~~89:34~~ H1468 Commander, as most {Commanders feasts and yet more}

COMMANDMENT (1) See also COMMANDEMENT
MEDDM200:22 Hp279 a trim that they might run the wayes of his Commandment

COMMANDS (2) [pl.] See also COMANDS
MPERS89:19 H1453 The *Greeks* with scorn reject his proud commands;
MGREC123:30 H2894 Slights his commands, his actions he disclaimes,

COMMANDS (6) v.
MPERS~~91:38~~ H1552 And being king commands those that remain,
MGREC97:19 H1780 Commands, no man should doe them injury,
MGREC103:29 H2040 Commands to set this goodly town on fire.
MGREC107:10 H2185 Commands forth-with, each man his fardle bring,
MGREC114:12 ~~H2480~~ But instantly commands him to be slaine;
MGREC122:27 H2846 *Pithons* commands, {as oft} She ever countermands

COMMEND (12)
ELEMEN12:27 H187 Whose trust, and valour I might here commend:
ELEMEN15:29 H311 The crafty {witty} Barbell, whose wit {craft} doth her commend;
HUMOUR27:21 H292 My worth in humble manner, to commend.
MPERS~~69:38~~ H667 (Quoth he) that man for happy we commend,
MPERS~~70:3~~ H674 Did to him still his chief designs commend.
MPERS71:37 H751 *Cambyses* to the clouds, we might commend;
MPERS78:29 H1010 O noble Queen, thy valour I commend,
MGREC105:22 H2115 Prayes him, to *Alexander* to commend,
MGREC129:10 H3124 This *Roxane* for her beautie all commend,
2LETTER182:3 H9 Commend me to the man more lov'd then life,
MEDDM206:2 Hp287 there are others that haue nothing to commend them, but only
2HUSB232:8 H9 Of mercy I commend

COMMENDED (1)
MPERS78:9 H990 The charge of all he severally commended,

COMMENDS (2)
MGREC110:19 H2323 His fortitude his Kingly {royal} foe commends;
MEDDM208:14 Hp290 Commends vs to god, for by his ballance we must be weighed,

COMMERCE (1)
MEDDM209:20 Hp291 so there may be a mutuall commerce through y[e] world As it is

COMMET (1) [comet]
SIDNEY150:41 ~~H69~~ I feare thou wert a Commet, did portend

COMMING (6) [coming] See also COMEING
AGES46:23 H454 My strong Redeemer, comming in the skies;
MPERS87:35 H1387 Yet for his brothers comming, durst not stay,

MGREC94:17 H1651 Comming to land, his dart on shoar he throwes,
MGREC109:14 H2273 Who comming thither, long before his Lord;
MGREC111:12 H2357 Then sayling South, and comming to the {that} shore,
MGREC128:30 H3103 And comming unawares put him to flight;

COMMISSION (3)
MPERS72:8 H756 Who into *Persia* with Commission sent,
MPERS~~84:12~~ H1242 Did for the Jews commission large obtain,
MPERS~~90:37~~ H1504 And {Commission} hath command, to take the others head,

COMMISSIONS (1) [pl.]
DIALOG148:1 H266 Then High Commissions shall fall to decay,

COMMIT (2)
MPERS84:30 H1266 T'*Thymistocles* he doth his {this} war commit,
MGREC97:26 H1787 Of which, the Government he doth commit

COMMITTED See COMITTED

COMMODIOUS (1)
MPERS86:28 H1344 Some Townes commodious in lesse *Asia,*

COMMODITIES (1) [pl.]
ELEMEN12:32 H192 My rich commodities payes double rent.

COMMODITYS (1) [commodities]
MEDDM209:19 Hp291 Commoditys wthin it self, but what it wants, another shall

COMMON (3)
ELEMEN11:34 H154 Of these so common things, can make report:
DIALOG146:40 H226 Blest be thy Commons, who for Common good,
BIRTH179:32 H8 A common thing, yet oh inevitable;

COMMONLY (1) See also COMONLY
MEDDM207:5 Hp288 but most Commonly imployed for a Clean Contrary end, then

COMMONS (1) [pl.]
DIALOG146:40 H226 Blest be thy Commons, who for Common good,

COMMON-WEAL (1)
DIALOG145:23 H172 To help the Church, and stay the Common-Weal,

COMMONWEAL (1)
TDUDLEY165:30 H32 True Patriot of this little Commonweal,

COMMONWEALTH (2)
MEDDM198:29 Hp277 enemy wthout may disturb a Commonwealth, but dissentions
MEDDM205:10 Hp286 Commonwealth, his more fixed and resolued thoughts, are like

COMMON-WEALTHS (1)
PROLOG6:19 H4 Of Cities founded, Common-wealths begun,

COMMUNED See COMVNED

COMONLY (1) [commonly]
MYCHILD216:25 Hp242 comonly hath been vpon my own person, in sicknesse

COMPACT (2) adj.
HUMOUR35:13 H609 But here's a {so} compact body, whole, entire:
QELIZ155:35 H26 *Eliza's* works, wars, praise, can e're compact,

COMPACT (1) n.
MROMAN138:6 H3496 Yet for {in} their compact, after false they play:

COMPACTED (1)
SIDNEY149:22 H21 As if your nine-fold wit had been compacted;

COMPANION (3)
AGES42:21 H279 Then basenesse was companion unto me.
MGREC113:41 H2468 And in his cups, his chief Companion;
MGREC114:15 H2485 This pot companion he did more bemoan,

COMPANIONS (2) [pl.]
HUMOUR23:15 H125 Where envy, malice, thy companions lurke.
AGES~~40:20~~ H201 If any time from company {leud Companions} I {can} spare,

COMPANY (7)
ELEMEN14:4 H246 *Korah* {*Dathan*} and all his Company well knew.
HUMOUR22:41 H110 No, no, {Alas,} thou hast no spirits, thy company
AGES40:20 H201 If any time from company {leud Companions} I {can} spare,
TDUDLEY166:40 H82 *A Prizer of good Company*
MEDDM203:22 Hp283 care for the company of the phisitian or chirurgian, but if he
MEDDM204:15 Hp284 must be sure to shun the company of the first.
MEDDM206:11 Hp287 innumerable Company of Saints, and Angels those Saintes

COMPAR'D (1) [compared]
QELIZ157:16 H84 A great *Eliza,* but compar'd with ours,

COMPARE (9)
ELEMEN18:30 H434 And youth, and spring, sages to me compare.
ELEMEN19:5 H450 Earths Beasts, and Waters Fish, scarce can compare.
HUMOUR31:22 H455 My vertues yours surpasse, without compare:
HUMOUR33:19 H533 Who is't or {that} dare, or can compare with me;
MGREC103:7 H2018 Yet to compare with this, they might not do.
DUBART153:16 H20 My Muse unto a Childe, I fitly may compare,
QELIZ157:23 H91 And of all these without compare the best;
CONTEM171:10 H114 Our life compare we with their length of dayes
1HUSB180:26 H5 Compare with me ye women if you can.

COMPARED (3) See also COMPAR'D
MEDDM202:16 Hp282 The treasures of this world may well be compared to huskes,
MEDDM207:13 Hp288 Comforts of this Life, may be compared to the gourd of Jonah,
MEDDM208:19 Hp290 be compared to deceitfull friends who speak faire and promise

COMPASSE (1)
ELEMEN12:39 H199 Your Tackling, Anchor, Compasse too, is mine;

COMPASSION (1)
MGREC106:1 H2135 Thy pitty, and compassion to reward,

COMPASSIONATE (2)
MGREC129:31 H3145 This {Orphan} Prince began for to compassionate.
MGREC131:23 H3215 Tries foes, since friends will not compassionate,

COMPEER (1)
MASSYR55:28 H94 That having no compeer, she might rule all,

COMPEERS (1) [pl.]
HUMOUR21:17 H45 One of your selves are my compeers, in place:

COMPENSATION (1)
MEDDM206:22 Hp287 more at a Compensation then at a pardon, but he that will not

COMPETITORS (1) [pl.]
AGES~~43:14~~ H307 Of such as might my son, {Competitors} or his {as might in

COMPILED (1)
ELEMEN13:2 H203 Was {Were} those compiled heapes of massy stones?

COMPLAIN (2)
ELEMEN16:41 H364 The Farmer, and the Plowman both {Grasier do} complain
MPERS81:17 H1125 By their Ambassador they thus complain;

COMPLAINES (2) [complains]
ELEMEN14:39 H281 Complaines to th'heaven, when {if} I withhold my drops:
MGREC124:30 H2937 And to *Cassander* of this wrong complaines;

COMPLAINTS (4) [pl.] See also PLAINTS, 'PLAINTS
MPERS83:2 H1190 But for his deep complaints; and showres of tears,
MGREC120:26 H2763 And summons him, to answer these {his} complaints;
MGREC122:1 H2824 For this great {sad} strife, he pours out his complaints,
DIALOG146:28 H214 Dear mother cease complaints, and wipe your eyes,
COMPLEAT (1)
HUMOUR25:21 H210 A Souldier most compleat in al points makest.
COMPLEATE (1)
SEASONS48:6 H59 A natural Artificer compleate.
COMPLEATLY (1)
MGREC108:36 H2252 A goodly City doth compleatly raise;
COMPLEMENT (2)
MASSYR63:16 H401 His health congratulates with complement.
MPERS81:27 H1135 With Rhetorick, t' gain better complement:
COMPLEMENTS (1) [pl.]
HUMOUR25:5 H194 And real complements, base flattery.
COMPLEXION (1)
HUMOUR27:33 H304 My sweet complexion, proves the verity,
COMPLOTS (1)
MPERS72:5 ~~H755~~ Complots the Princes death, in his green years,
COMPLOTTER (1)
MPERS~~92:17~~ H1575 (Complotter with him in the murther done)
COMPOS'D (1) [composed]
AGES35:23 H9 The third, of fire, and choler is compos'd,
COMPOSE (1)
MYCHILD215:14 Hp240 I was able to compose some short matters, (for w^{t} else to call
COMPOSED See COMPOS'D
COMPOUND (1)
MASSYR60:20 H285 And either by compound, or else by strength,
COMPOUNDED (2)
MPERS78:3 H984 His Army of all Nations, was compounded,
MGREC103:39 H2050 Had now his fourth, and last Army compounded,
COMPREHEND (2)
HUMOUR21:12 H40 Though under fire, we comprehend all heat,
DUBART153:19 H23 To comprehend the worth of all those knacks;
COMPREHENSION (1)
DUBART154:30 H75 Oh pregnant brain, Oh comprehension vast:
COMPUTED (1)
MASSYR61:2 H307 And times of both computed, so fall out,
COMVNED (1) [communed]
MYCHILD215:32 Hp241 fitt of sicknes wch I had on my bed I often comvned wth my
CONCEAL (2)
HUMOUR34:20 H575 But modesty hath charg'd me to conceal;
AGES37:5 H67 But night and darkenesse, must with shame conceal.
CONCEALE (2)
HUMOUR28:39 H351 If modesty my worth do not conceale.
HUMOUR32:4 H478 But wisdome 'tis, my wisdom to conceale.
CONCEIT (4)
HUMOUR32:9 H483 My sicknesse cheifly in conceit doth lye,
MASSYR66:23 H529 His sumptuous buildings passes all conceit,
VANITY160:38 H48 It yeeldeth pleasures, farre beyond conceit,

CONTEM169:30 H69 It makes a man more aged in conceit,

CONCEIV'D (1) [conceived]

AGES37:2 H64 Ah me! conceiv'd in sin, and born in {with} sorrow,

CONCEPTIONS (1) [pl.]

2SIMON195:11 Hp271 vpon others conceptions because I would leaue you nothing

CONCERNED (1)

MYCHILD215:30 Hp241 espec: those places I thought most concerned my Condition,

CONCERNING (2)

DIALOG141:2 H2 *England* and New, concerning

MYCHILD217:32 Hp243 Many times hath Satan troubled me concerning ye verity of y^e

CONCLUDE (2)

AGES43:37 H332 And to conclude, I may not tedious be,

SIDNEY152:19 H88 For to conclude my poem two lines they daigne,

CONCLUSION (2)

HUMOUR35:2 H598 Such premises wil force a sad conclusion,

MPERS74:1 H826 But in conclusion they all agree,

CONCOCTION (3)

HUMOUR27:10 H281 Again, stomachs concoction thou dost claime,

HUMOUR28:12 H324 Ith' last concoction, segregation make.

MEDDM201:15 Hp280 A sharp appetite and a through Concoction, is a signe of an

CONCOMITANT (1)

AGES40:24 H205 Cards, Dice, and Oaths, concomitant, I love;

CONCOMITANTS (1) [pl.]

MEDDM199:23 Hp278 Dimne eyes, are the concomitants of old age, and short

CONDEMN (1)

MEDDM205:17 Hp286 Court of heaven itself, for if our conscience condemn vs, he

CONDEMN'D (2) [condemned]

ELEMEN18:3 H407 I aske the man condemn'd, that's near his death:

SIDNEY149:37 H24 Thy {His} wiser dayes, condemn'd thy {his} witty works,

CONDEMNES (1)

MEDDM205:15 Hp286 the evidence, so he absolues or condemnes, yea so Absolute

CONDENS'D (1) [condensed]

ELEMEN18:35 H439 So when I am condens'd, I turne to water;

CONDESCEND (1)

HUMOUR24:10 H159 And to your weaknesse, gently condescend.

CONDITION (5)

AGES41:31 H248 Be my condition mean, I then take paines;

MEDDM204:26 Hp285 He that would be content, wth a mean condition, must not cast

MYCHILD215:30 Hp241 espec: those places I thought most concerned my Condition,

MYCHILD216:7 Hp241 After a short time I changed my Condition & was marryed, and

28AUG225:29 Hp254 stayes my Soul that this condition y^t I am in is ye best for me,

CONDITIONS (3) [pl.]

MPERS91:10 H1518 The Kings {on such} conditions they are forc't to take; {as King

MGREC126:32 H3023 But Royalty no good conditions brings;

MEDDM198:3 Hp275 their seuerall conditions, if he will make his face to shine vpon

CONDUITS (2) [pl.]

HUMOUR26:26 H256 Through th' warme, blew conduits of my veinal rils;

SIDNEY~~150:40~~ H68 *Stella* the fair, whose streams from Conduits fell

CONFEDERATE (3)

MASSYR~~57:19~~ H166 With petty Kings to joyne Confederate.

MPERS81:19 H1127 And they had helpt them, as confederate;

MPERS81:34 H1142 The other *Greeks,* which were confederate,
CONFERS (1)
MGREC121:23 H2805 Confers {Yields} them {to} *Pithon* on, for's courtesie;
CONFESSE (8)
ELEMEN13:14 H215 As I ingenuously (with thanks) confesse
HUMOUR24:15 H164 Your patience more then mine, I must confesse.
HUMOUR26:32 H262 I must confesse, is somewhat strange to me,
HUMOUR33:13 H527 Thy heat doth much, I candidly confesse,
HUMOUR34:39 H594 And too much talk; both which, I do {here} confesse,
MGREC113:20 H2447 As he would ne're confesse, nor could {yet} reward,
DIALOG142:35 H64 I must confesse, some of those Sores you name,
SIDNEY151:26 H74 And {Which} makes me now with *Sylvester* confesse,
CONFESSED (1)
MYCHILD216:4 Hp241 When I was in my afflict^{n}. I besovght the Lord, and confessed
CONFEST (1)
MYCHILD215:27 Hp240 Trouble, & I could not be at rest 'till by prayer I had confest
CONFIDENCE (1)
MEDDM208:22 Hp290 miserably delude men and make them put great Confidence in
CONFIDENT (1)
MYCHILD217:12 Hp242 my mind wthout it, and I haue been confident it hath been
CONFIN'D (3) [confined]
AGES37:24 H86 My high-borne soule, so straitly was confin'd:
MGREC93:24 H1621 His rule to *Greece,* he scorn'd should be confin'd:
MGREC125:37 H2987 Wisht in *Epire* she still had been confin'd;
CONFINE (2)
HUMOUR30:9 H401 Thirdly, {Again} thou dost confine me to the spleen,
SIDNEY151:10 ~~H69~~ How could that *Stella,* so confine thy will?
CONFINED See CONFIN'D
CONFIRM (1)
MYCHILD217:34 Hp243 God, I never saw any miracles to confirm me, and those wch I
CONFIRM'D (1) [confirmed]
ELEMEN17:31 H395 Her confirm'd sonnes, behold my colour'd bow.
CONFIRMES (1)
MASSYR53:37 H27 Confirmes the rule his Father had begun,
CONFLICT (1)
MPERS84:37 H1273 In this sad conflict, marching on his ways,
CONFOUNDED (1) See also CONFOVNDED
HUMOUR33:21 H535 I am confounded, 'fore I speak of any:
CONFOUNDS (1)
ELEMEN17:5 H369 And with astonishment, the world confounds.
CONFOVNDED (1) [confounded]
MED223:13 Hp250 in me at ye consideration y^{r}of, and I am confovnded to think
CONFUS'D (2) [confused]
ELEMEN10:38 H113 In confus'd heaps of ashes may ye see.
MGREC136:14 H3428 *Will force me to a confus'd brevity;*
CONFUSED (1)
2LETTER182:27 H33 Tell him here's worse then a confused matter,
CONFUSION (6)
ELEMEN8:22 H20 The worlds confusion it did seeme to threat;
HUMOUR35:3 H599 Unlesse we 'gree all fals into confusion.
MPERS88:2 H1395 In this confusion, each man as he might,

MPERS88:12 H1405 For tumult and confusion they expected,
MGREC117:25 H2632 Now Court, and Camp, all in confusion be,
REMB235:29 H10 Confusion seases on my Soul

CONFUTATION (1)
HUMOUR~~31:18~~ H451 No further time ile spend, in confutations, {confutation}

CONFUTATIONS (1) [pl.]
HUMOUR31:18 H451 No further time ile spend, in confutations, {confutation}

CONGEALED See CONJEALED

CONGRATULATES (1)
MASSYR63:16 H401 His health congratulates with complement.

CONJEALED (1) [congealed]
HUMOUR22:14 H83 Convert from water, to conjealed Ice;

CONJECTURE (2)
MASSYR63:20 H405 But by conjecture this, and none but he,
MPERS92:3 ~~H1557~~ The rest is but conjecture of my minde.

CONJUGATION (1)
HUMOUR~~33:32~~ H546 The conjugations {Conjugation} of the parts toth' brain

CONJUGATIONS (1) [pl.]
HUMOUR33:32 H546 The conjugations {Conjugation} of the parts toth' brain

CONJUNCTION (1)
ELEMEN10:21 H96 When in conjunction with the sun, yet {do} more,

CONJURE (1)
2LETTER182:34 H40 By all our loves conjure him not to stay.

CONQUER'D (2) [conquered]
MGREC97:17 H1778 Conquer'd himself (now he had conquered)
MGREC106:36 H2170 After that conquer'd, and luxurious Nation;

CONQUERED (5)
HUMOUR32:35 H509 At home, the Conquerours, have conquered:
MASSYR67:8 H554 Among the Conquered Kings, that there did lye,
MGREC97:17 H1778 Conquer'd himself (now he had conquered)
MGREC116:36 H2602 There was {were} no worlds, more, to be conquered:
DIALOG142:11 H40 With *English* blood bedews thy conquered Land?

CONQUERER (1) [conquerour]
MPERS73:2 H789 Yeelding {So yields} to death, that dreadfull Conquerer.

CONQUERETH (1)
MROMAN138:5 H3495 The *Romans* Conquereth, others {other} yeeld the day,

CONQUERING (1)
MGREC119:15 H2705 {Sometimes} By warlike *Philip,* and his conquering son.

CONQUEROUR (6) See also CONQUERER
MPERS70:40 ~~H711~~ Where that proud Conquerour could doe no lesse,
MGREC97:33 H1794 To give his Conquerour, the stile of King;
MGREC102:5 H1975 This Conquerour now {then} goes to *Babylon,*
MGREC116:10 H2570 This Conquerour did yeeld to destiny;
MGREC116:35 H2601 This conquerour did oft lament ('tis sed)
MGREC131:12 H3204 And he that conquerour shall now remain,

CONQUEROURS (1) [pl.]
HUMOUR32:35 H509 At home, the Conquerours, have conquered:

CONQUERS (2)
MASSYR66:22 H528 Where e're he goes, he Conquers every Land;
MPERS~~91:40~~ H1554 Then raises forces, conquers *Egypt* land,

CONQUEST (5)
MASSYR66:17 H523 A totall Conquest of rich *Ægypt* makes,
MASSYR66:40 H546 He left his Wealth, and Conquest, to his Son.
MPERS70:5 H676 Was conquest of the stately *Babylon,*
MPERS~~77:36~~ H977 With certainty {conquest} of {all} *Europe* feeds his pride;
MGREC93:30 H1627 *Phillip,* on this great conquest had an eye;
CONQUESTS (4) [pl.]
MASSYR66:13 H519 With all these Conquests, *Babels* King rests not,
MPERS~~71:4~~ H717 And though his conquests made the earth to groan,
MGREC112:15 H2401 Now, *Alexanders* conquests, all are done,
MGREC116:12 H2578 And Conquests be talkt of, whilst there is Land;
CONS (1)
MYCHILD215:24 Hp240 years about 6. or 7. as I take it I began to make cons^{c}. of
CONSCIENCE (8)
AGES44:17 H350 That can refresh, or ease, if Conscience frown;
VANITY160:7 H17 Mean while the conscience rage, who shall appease?
MEDDM198:33 Hp277 it, the pure in heart shall se god, but the defiled in conscience
MEDDM203:25 Hp283 the wounds of a guilty Conscience, cares not how far he keeps
MEDDM205:13 Hp286 wch is alway kept by Conscience, who is both accuser excuser
MEDDM205:17 Hp286 Court of heaven itself, for if our conscience condemn vs, he
MEDDM205:18 Hp286 who is greater then our Conscience will do it much more, but
MEDDM205:20 Hp286 sure to carry a certificate from the Court of conscience that he
CONSCIENCES (1)
MEDDM199:32 Hp278 Consciences.
CONSECRATED (2)
DUBART153:14 H18 They shall be consecrated in my Verse,
2HUSB233:16 H49 Shall consecrated bee
CONSECRATES (1)
MGREC126:38 H3027 His sword unto *Apollo* consecrates:
CONSENT (2)
ELEMEN8:27 H25 That Fire should first begin, the rest consent,
MGREC126:35 H3024 To Husbands death ('twas {'tis} thought) she gave consent,
CONSEQUENCE (4)
ELEMEN19:15 H460 With divers moe, worke deadly consequence.
HUMOUR34:22 H577 For what's the Brains, is mine, by consequence;
MGREC112:25 H2411 His silence, guilt was, of such consequence,
DIALOG142:29 H58 Dost feele the smart, or feare the consequence?
CONSIDER (3)
MEDDM196:23 Hp273 him consider
MEDDM206:28 Hp288 his great worke of election and Reprobation, when we consider
MEDDM208:28 Hp290 It is admirable to Consider the power of faith, by wch all things
CONSIDERATE (1)
MASSYR~~57:21~~ H168 Well satisfie the most considerate minds:
CONSIDERATION (5)
MEDDM205:24 Hp286 alway in the awefull presence of god, the consideration of his
MEDDM207:7 Hp288 draw men to god in consideration of his bounty towards them,
MYCHILD218:3 Hp243 End, The consideration of these things would wth amazement
MYCHILD218:26 Hp244 The consideration of these things and many ye like would soon
MED223:13 Hp250 spirit failes in me at ye consideration y^{r}of, and I am
CONSIST (1)
MASSYR56:26 H132 Her Army of four Millions did consist,

CONSISTS (1)
FATHER5:23 H24 Of these consists, our bodyes, cloathes, and food,
CONSOLATION (2)
AGES46:5 H436 That earth can give no consolation sound.
VANITY159:33 H5 On brittle earth, a consolation sound?
CONSOLATIONS (1) [pl.]
MED223:2 Hp250 Consolations wch the world knowes not.
CONSOLIDATE (1)
HUMOUR30:4 H396 What's diffluent, I do consolidate.
CONSORT (1)
PROLOG7:1 H16 Nor yet a sweet Consort, from broken strings,
CONSPIRACY (2)
MPERS87:6 H1362 To be the Author of conspiracy.
MGREC112:22 H2408 The King of treason, and conspiracy;
CONSPIRATORS (1) [pl.]
MPERS73:22 H809 This King, with {his} conspirators so stout,
CONSPIRATOURS (1) [conspirators]
MGREC130:18 H3173 As vile conspiratours that took {stopt} her breath,
CONSPIRE (2)
MPERS83:10 H1198 At last his Uncle, did his death conspire,
DIALOG142:24 H53 Doth your Allye, faire *France,* conspire your wrack?
CONSTANCY (1)
HUMOUR31:23 H456 The first, my constancy, that jewel rare.
CONSTANT (3)
HUMOUR31:27 H460 Constant in nothing, but inconstancy {unconstancy},
DDUDLEY167:19 H16 *And in her Closet constant hours she spent;*
MYCHILD217:15 Hp243 been p^rplexed y^t I haue not fovnd that constant Joy in my
CONSTANTLY (1)
MYCHILD216:21 Hp241 constantly observed this y^t he hath never suffered me long to
CONSTELLATIONS (1) [pl.]
ELEMEN9:41 H75 Fixed in heavenly constellations dwell,
CONSTITUTION (3)
ELEMEN13:17 H218 The melancholy constitution.
ELEMEN16:33 H356 The flegmy constitution I uphold;
HUMOUR20:10 H2 Mans constitution.
CONSULS (1) [pl.]
ELEMEN15:38 H320 Which *Cæsars, Consuls, Tribunes* all adorne;
CONSULTATION (1)
MPERS73:30 H815 A Consultation by the {those} States was held.
CONSUM'D (1) [consumed]
AGES46:20 H451 And when this flesh shal rot, and be consum'd,
CONSUME (9) See also CONSVME
ELEMEN11:5 H125 With neighbouring Townes I did consume to dust,
ELEMEN11:14 H134 And in a word, the World I shal consume,
HUMOUR25:19 H208 Both them and all things else, she will {would} consume.
MPERS69:34 H656 (A hard decree) to ashes he consume;
MPERS82:19 H1166 Thus did the *Greeks* destroy, consume, disperce,
MGREC107:15 H2190 The wealth of many Cities doth {Kindomes did} consume:
DIALOG147:15 H241 And let their names consume, but let the flash
PILGRIM210:31 H31 What tho my flesh shall there consume
FEVER221:4 H19 Tho: flesh consume to novght,

CONSUMED See CONSUM'D

CONSUMMATES (1)
QELIZ157:15 H83 (Who living consummates her Funerals)

CONSUMPTION (2) See also CONSVMPTION
AGES43:34 ~~H329~~ And the Consumption, to the bones doth wast me;
DIALOG141:22 H21 Will bring Consumption, or an Ague quaking,

CONSVME (1) [consume]
HOUSE236:24 H16 The flame consvme my dwelling place,

CONSVMPTION (1) [consumption]
MYCHILD216:11 Hp241 some time I fell into a lingering sicknes like a consvmption

CONTAGIOUS (1)
ELEMEN19:18 H463 Yea so contagious, Countries have me {we} known;

CONTAIN (2)
MPERS~~80:16~~ H1083 {The Harbours} to receive, {contain} the Harbour was not able;
MGREC101:23 H1948 The Firmament two Suns cannot contain;

CONTAINE (2) [contain]
MGREC114:11 ~~H2479~~ *Alexander* now no longer could containe,
QELIZ156:1 H28 No memories, nor volumes can containe,

CONTAINES (1)
MGREC108:2 H2218 (A coller of the same his neck containes)

CONTEMD (1) [contemned]
MYCHILD218:11 Hp244 Diverse who haue scornd + contemd it, hath it not been

CONTEMN (2)
MPERS72:1 ~~H753~~ And contemn them, woful is his doome.
MGREC117:22 H2629 Each man {All men} began for {streight} to contemn his might;

CONTEMNED See CONTEMD

CONTEMPLATING (1)
MASSYR66:36 H542 Contemplating those times he lost his wits;

CONTEMPLATION (4)
MASSYR66:3 H509 A {Ah!} haplesse man, whose darksome contemplation,
MGREC118:17 H2664 A contemplation to astonish Kings,
CONTEM173:10 H177 While musing thus with contemplation fed,
FLESH175:12 H12 Doth Contemplation feed thee so

CONTEMPLATIONS (1) [pl.]
CONTEM167:24 H1 *CONTEMPLATIONS.*

CONTEMPT (1)
SIDNEY152:9 ~~H79~~ That this contempt it did the more perplex,

CONTEMPTUOUS (1)
MGREC94:27 H1665 Sends him a frothy, and contemptuous letter,

CONTEND (2)
FATHER5:31 H32 How hot, and dry, contend with moist, and cold,
DIALOG142:13 H42 Doe *Maud,* and *Stephen* for the Crown contend?

CONTENT (17)
ELEMEN17:35 H399 Content (quoth Aire) to speake the last of you,
MASSYR60:17 H282 Not so content, but aiming to be great,
MASSYR61:5 H310 To rest content we must, in ignorance.
MPERS82:26 H1173 words {Nor prayers}, nor guifts, could win him least content:
MGREC111:25 H2370 Unto his starved Souldiers small content;
MGREC~~115:15~~ H2531 What e're he did, or thought not so content,
MGREC118:19 H2666 And yet not so content, unlesse that he
MGREC121:24 H2806 With what he held, he now was well {more} content,

MGREC125:30 H2980 This done, the cruell Queen rests not content,
MGREC~~132:16~~ H3253 In neither finds content if he sits still:
SIDNEY150:15 ~~H49~~ Yet great *Augustus* was content (we know)
VANITY160:4 H14 What then? content in pleasures canst thou find?
FLESH176:30 H70 My thoughts do yield me more content
ELIZB186:34 H6 Farewel dear babe, my hearts too much content,
MEDDM199:20 Hp278 man aimes at profit by the one & content in the other, but often
MEDDM204:26 Hp285 He that would be content, wth a mean condition, must not cast
HOURS234:20 H34 And there content I'll take

CONTENTED (1)
11MAYA226:19 Hp255 for is a contented thankfull h^{t} vnder my affliction & weaknes

CONTENTION (3)
ELEMEN8:23 H21 But {Till gentle} Aire at length, contention so abated,
DIALOG142:40 H69 Whose proud contention cause this slaughter;
DIALOG~~146:4~~ H192 Contention's {Contention} grown 'twixt Subjects and their

CONTENTION'S (1) [contention is]
DIALOG146:4 H192 Contention's {Contention} grown 'twixt Subjects and their

CONTENTIONS (2) [pl.]
MGREC117:14 H2621 What troubles, and contentions did ensue,
MGREC118:13 H2660 'Mongst these contentions, tumults, jealousies,

CONTENTIONS (1) [poss.]
HUMOUR29:15 H368 And in contentions lists, now justly enter.

CONTENTMENT (1)
1LETTER181:17 H15 Which sweet contentment yield me for a space,

CONTEST (4)
FATHER5:27 H28 Yours did contest, for Wealth, for Arts, for Age,
ELEMEN8:5 H3 Fire, Aire, Earth, and Water, did all contest
HUMOUR20:31 H23 Cold {Mild} flegme, did not contest for highest {chiefest} place,
HUMOUR26:11 H241 For th' natural, thou dost not much contest,

CONTINUALL (2) [continual]
2SIMON195:15 Hp271 reioyceing at that great day of appearing, wch is the continuall
28AUG226:7 Hp254 and bee in continuall xpectat^{n} of my change, and let me never

CONTINUALLY (1) See also CONTINVALLY
MEDDM197:19 Hp275 it, and that heart wch is not continually purifieing it self is no fit

CONTINUED (1)
MPERS91:11 H1519 Dissention in *Greece* continued {so} long,

CONTINUING (1)
MASSYR56:15 H121 (Continuing, till *Xerxes* it defac'd)

CONTINVALLY (1) [continually]
MEDDM205:12 Hp286 to and fro continvally, here is also the great Court of iustice ,

CONTRARIES (1) [pl.]
HUMOUR23:23 H133 As objects best appear, by contraries.

CONTRARY (2)
MEDDM201:26 Hp281 vsed for Contrary ends, the one holds fast, the other puts
MEDDM207:5 Hp288 but most Commonly imployed for a Clean Contrary end, then

CONTRITION (1)
MEDDM201:21 Hp281 sinners, seem full of contrition, but it is not from any dew of

CONTROL See CONTROLE

CONTROL'D (1) [controlled]
MGREC~~118:29~~ H2678 chief opponents who kept off the Crown, {Control'd his sway,}

CONTROLD (1) [controlled]
MGREC122:33 H2854 He plac'd, displac'd, controld, rul'd, as he list,
CONTROLE (1) [control]
ELEMEN17:37 H401 I doe suppose, you'l yeeld without controle;
CONTROVERSIES (2)
MPERS81:38 ~~H1143~~ But all their controversies to decide,
MPERS~~82:2~~ H1149 Where both their Controversies they'l decide;
CONTROVERTED (1)
MPERS92:32 H1590 And this 'mongst all's no controverted thing,
CONUENIENCES (1) [conveniences]
MEDDM203:14 Hp283 country, and heere he hath many conueniences and comforts
CONUERSATION (1) [conversation]
MEDDM203:35 Hp284 conuersation aright will glorifie him that heard him in the day of
CONVENIENCES See CONUENIENCES
CONVENIENT (2)
MPERS70:9 H680 But till convenient time their heads kept shut;
MEDDM203:11 Hp283 be all convenient and comfortable for him yet he hath
CONVERSATION (3) See also CONUERSATION
MEDDM208:4 Hp290 good conversation
11MAYB228:34 Hp259 Conversation may speak that thy vowes are vpon me.
HANNA230:17 H10 And let her Conversation say
CONVERSE (1)
HUMOUR34:26 H581 With a tame foole converse, then with a mad.
CONVERT (2)
ELEMEN16:24 H347 Both when we list, to water we convert.
HUMOUR22:14 H83 Convert from water, to conjealed Ice;
CONVERTS (1)
MGREC136:6 H3419 Converts our boldnesse, into impudence.
CONVINCED (1)
MYCHILD216:9 Hp241 my heart rose, But after I was convinced it was ye way of God,
COOES (1) [pl.]
3LETTER183:14 H16 With thousand doleful sighs & mournfull Cooes.
COOKS (1) [pl.]
ELEMEN9:16 H50 Ye Cooks, your kitchin implements I fram'd, {frame}
COOL (1) See also COOLE
SEASONS~~48:26~~ H79 The hasty Pease, and wholesome red {cool} Strawberry,
COOL'D (1) [cooled]
HUMOUR29:14 H367 But Choler, be thou cool'd, or chaf'd, i'le venter,
COOLE (5) [cool]
ELEMEN16:39 H362 And with aboundant wet, so coole the ground,
ELEMEN18:25 H429 When burning heat, doth cause you faint, I coole,
HUMOUR23:41 ~~H149~~ They coole my heat, and so repay my good.
SEASONS49:18 H109 In the coole streames they labour with delight,
MEDDM208:8 Hp290 of time (if there be no inter course) will coole the affectiones
COOLED See COOL'D
COOLING (1)
CONTEM172:6 H142 Under the cooling shadow of a stately Elm
COOS See COOES
COPES (1) [pl.]
DIALOG147:14 H240 Copes, Rochets, Crossiers, and such {empty} trash,

CORD (1)
AGES45:41 H431 My golden Bowl, and silver Cord, e're long,
CORDIAL (1)
DIALOG141:23 H22 Unlesse some Cordial thou fetch from high,
CORDIALL (1)
MEDDM203:28 Hp284 welcome, that brings a plaister for his sore, or a cordiall for his
CORINTH (1)
MROMAN138:25 H3515 *Tarquin,* a *Greek,* at *Corinth* borne, and bred,
CORN (2)
CHILDRN185:21 H47 Whilst pecking corn, and void of care
ELIZB187:7 H15 And Corn and grass are in their season mown,
CORNE (6)
ELEMEN11:30 H150 In vine-yards, orchards, gardens, and corne fields,
ELEMEN13:28 H229 The Corne, and Hay, both fall before they'r mowne;
ELEMEN17:3 H367 Their Cattle, Hay, and Corne, I sweep down current,
ELEMEN18:27 H431 I {help to} ripe the corne, I turne the grinding mill;
MEDDM197:31 Hp275 Corne till it haue past through the Mill and been ground to
MEDDM204:33 Hp285 Corne is produced wth much labour (as the husbandman well
CORN-FIELD (1)
2LETTER182:12 H18 Or in a corn-field number every grain,
CORPS (1)
MGREC118:14 H2661 Seven dayes the Corps of their great Master lyes
CORRECT^N^ (1) [correction]
MYCHILD216:24 Hp242 felt my heart out of order, but I haue expected correct^n^ for it,
CORRECTION (4)
MEDDM205:2 Hp285 of correction must make long furrows on their back and the
MYCHILD216:12 Hp241 wth a lamenesse wch correction I saw the Lord sent to hu¯ble
30SEPT227:22 Hp257 I haue fovnd by Exper^c^. I can no more liue w^th^out correction
30SEPT227:23 Hp257 then without food. Lord wth y^y^ correction giue Instrvction and
CORRESPONDENCE (1)
FATHER5:32 H33 How Aire, and Earth, no correspondence hold,
CORRUPT (2)
ELEMEN19:13 H458 So when's corrupt, mortality is rife.
PILGRIM210:35 H35 A Corrupt Carcasse downe it lyes
CORRUPTION (2)
HUMOUR28:22 H334 That mortal man, might turn to his corruption.
AGES46:16 H447 Corruption, my Father, I do call,
CORRUPTIONS (2) [pl.]
MEDDM196:9 Hp273 Corruptions, and y^t^ will damp his high thoughts
MEDDM209:7 Hp291 christians do by their lusts and corruptions as the Isralits did
CORSLET (2)
HUMOUR21:23 H51 Then Iron Corslet, 'gainst a sword or dart;
AGES39:22 H165 I scorn the heavy Corslet, Musket-proof,
COST (11)
ELEMEN12:36 H196 That with lesse cost, neare home, supplyes {supply} your
MASSYR56:12 H118 But {And} that which did, all cost, and art excell,
MASSYR65:5 H470 Requited not the cost {loss}, the toyle, and pain.
MPERS80:11 H1078 This shamefull Victory cost *Xerxes* deare,
MGREC98:13 H1815 But far lesse cost, and time, he doth {did} expend,
MGREC123:13 H2875 He to his cost was righteously repaid.
SIDNEY151:34 ~~H75~~ Till taught to's cost, for his too hasty hand,

QELIZ156:10 H37 She taught them better manners to their cost.
SICKNES179:5 H25 Bestow much cost there's nothing lost,
CHILDRN184:17 H6 Nor cost, nor labour did I spare,
MYCHILD216:15 Hp241 greif to me, and cost me many prayers + tears before I obtaind

COSTLY (5)

AGES37:33 H95 With costly presents, {presence} or base flattery.
MASSYR55:40 H106 With Towers, and Bulwarks made of costly stone
MASSYR60:23 H288 A costly work, which none could doe but he,
MASSYR64:37 H461 Of costly Ships, and Gallies, she had store,
MGREC107:12 H2187 Which done, sets fire upon those costly {goodly} spoyls

COT (1)

DUBART153:25 H29 At night turnes to his Mothers cot againe,

COUCHES (1) [pl.]

MGREC102:36 H2006 Those beds of gold, and couches of delight,

COUGH (2)

HUMOUR32:7 H481 Nor Cough, nor Quinsie, nor the burning Feavor.
AGES40:40 H219 Sometimes the Cough, Stitch, {the Quinsey} painful Plurisie,

COULD (114)

ELEMEN8:7 ~~H5~~ Who the most good could shew, & who most rage
ELEMEN10:41 H116 Which when they could not be o're come by foes
ELEMEN~~11:1~~ H120 But maugre all, that I, or foes could do
ELEMEN11:26 H146 Which none ere gave, nor {or} you could claime of right,
ELEMEN11:32 H152 Would so passe time, I could say nothing else;
ELEMEN16:25 H348 Alas; thy ships and oares could do no good
ELEMEN19:23 H468 Which neither ships nor houses could withstand.
HUMOUR20:28 H20 The second, third, or last could not digest;
HUMOUR27:36 H307 Nay, could I be from all your tangs but pure,
HUMOUR28:35 H347 Yet could not be more breif, without much wrong.
HUMOUR31:38 H471 Now could I stain my ruddy sisters face,
HUMOUR32:36 H510 Nay, I could tel you (what's more true then meet)
AGES37:19 H81 Did act al folly, that it could expresse.
AGES38:23 H126 A lying tongue as soon as it could speak,
AGES42:13 H271 As readily as could my Leader say:
AGES42:20 H278 Was I as poor, as poverty could be,
AGES42:37 H293 My dunghil thoughts, or hopes, could reach no higher.
AGES45:12 ~~H394~~ Could once reverse, their shamefull destiny.
AGES~~45:12~~ H394 Could length their dayes or once reverse their fate
SEASONS~~51:19~~ H194 Nor could that temp'rate Clime such difference make,
SEASONS53:4 H260 *I could {knew} not tell how to passe't by:*
SEASONS53:5 H261 *The last, though bad, I could not mend,*
MASSYR58:39 H222 T'infranchise them, to grant what they could crave,
MASSYR59:3 H227 T' accept of what they could, they him {all} beseech.
MASSYR60:23 H288 A costly work, which none could doe but he,
MASSYR60:27 H292 The fire, those Mettals could not damnifie;
MASSYR60:40 H305 That he, and *Belochus,* one could not be,
MASSYR62:15 H360 On whom, nor threats, nor mercies could do good;
MASSYR65:7 H472 Before he could accomplish his intent;
MASSYR65:38 H503 The cursed King, by flight could no wise flee {fly}
MASSYR68:8 H594 To him that could interpret clear this thing:
MPERS70:17 H688 Forty five mile {miles} this City scarce could round;
MPERS70:40 ~~H711~~ Where that proud Conquerour could doe no lesse,

MPERS76:30 H928 Arm'd all they could, which elev'n thousand make;
MPERS~~79:23~~ H1049 none of these should {those could} live a {an} hundred yeares:
MPERS80:9 H1076 When as one thousand, could some Millions {a million} daunt;
MPERS80:24 H1091 If that smal number his great force could bide;
MPERS81:26 H1134 Nor could the brave Ambassador be {he} sent,
MPERS81:40 H1144 The *Athenians* could but forty thousand arme,
MPERS82:26 H1173 Yet words {Nor prayers}, nor guifts, could win him least
MPERS83:1 H1189 Tels as he could, his unexpressed woes,
MPERS84:27 H1263 Who for his wrong, he could not chuse but deem,
MPERS84:32 H1268 And to his Country-men {native land} could bear no hate.
MPERS85:23 H1299 Before to quietnesse things could be brought,
MPERS86:20 H1336 To win by force, what right could not obtain.
MPERS86:25 H1341 He hop'd, if fraud, nor force the Crown could {would} gaine;
MPERS86:34 H1350 (One *Greeke* could make ten *Persians* run away)
MPERS89:41 H1475 But *Tyssaphern* did what he could devise,
MPERS90:8 H1481 Nor rivers course, nor *Persians* force could stay,
MPERS91:13 H1521 Whose courage nought but death could ever tame,
MGREC97:32 H1793 But down his haughty stomach could not bring,
MGREC106:10 H2144 Could bound his boundlesse, fond ambition)
MGREC107:40 H2215 But coward, durst not fight, nor could he fly,
MGREC108:17 H2233 Nor could he reason give, for this great wrong,
MGREC108:34 H2250 Whose {Their} nakednesse could not endure their might;
MGREC108:38 H2254 And furlongs sixty could not {but} round the same.
MGREC109:36 H2295 And come as well provided as he could,
MGREC110:24 H2328 Could by no means be further {farther} drawn, or led:
MGREC110:30 H2334 As never Horse his Provender could eye;
MGREC111:15 H2360 Which could not sound too oft, with too much fame;
MGREC112:9 H2395 Spectators here, could scarce relate the story,
MGREC112:36 H2422 Which no merit could obliterate, or time:
MGREC113:8 H2435 Such torments great, as wit could first {worst} invent,
MGREC113:9 H2436 Or flesh, or {and} life, could bear, till both were spent
MGREC113:20 H2447 As he would ne're confesse, nor could {yet} reward,
MGREC113:21 H2448 Nor could his Captaines bear so great regard;
MGREC114:11 ~~H2479~~ *Alexander* now no longer could containe,
MGREC~~114:12~~ H2480 Nought but his life for this could satisfie;
MGREC114:21 H2491 In his esteem, a God he could not be,
MGREC115:37 H2556 Nor by his baits could be ensnared so:
MGREC~~116:31~~ H2597 Ambitious so, that nought could satisfie,
MGREC117:20 H2627 His matchlesse force no Creature could abide;
MGREC118:25 H2674 On which, no signe of poyson could be {in his intrails} found,
MGREC~~121:15~~ H2794 Who could not book so great indignity,
MGREC121:38 H2820 Nor could *Craterus* (whom he much did love)
MGREC123:9 H2871 'Gainst him, that all deceits could scan, and try:
MGREC123:28 H2892 *Cassander* could not (like his father) see
MGREC124:21 H2928 Nor could Mother, nor Sons of *Alexander,*
MGREC124:26 H2933 More then he bidden was, could act no thing;
MGREC127:17 H3047 Such as nor {no} threats, nor favour could acquire;
MGREC130:14 H3169 So hinders him of her, he could not gain.
MROMAN140:2 H3565 But 'fore I could accomplish my desire,
DIALOG146:9 H197 But could the field alone this cause {strife} decide,
SIDNEY149:18 H17 More worth was thine, {his} then *Clio* could set down.

SIDNEY151:10 ~~H69~~ How could that *Stella,* so confine thy will?
DUBART154:7 H52 Vollies of praises could I eccho then,
QELIZ157:3 H71 To tell of halfe she did, or she could doe;
QELIZ157:24 H92 (Whom none but great *Aurelius* could quell)
TDUDLEY165:9 H11 To whom I ought whatever I could doe:
TDUDLEY165:19 H21 Such as in life, no man could justly deem.
TDUDLEY165:22 H24 These to the world his merits could make known,
CONTEM170:28 H99 Though none on Earth but kindred near then could he find.
CONTEM171:8 H113 Who neither guilt, nor yet the punishment could fly.
CONTEM172:17 H152 Could hinder ought, but still augment its force:
CONTEM172:27 H161 O could I lead my Rivolets to rest,
AUTHOR178:3 H13 Thy blemishes amend, if so I could:
CHILDRN185:17 H43 If birds could weep, then would my tears
CHILDRN186:20 H87 That did what could be done for young,
MERCY189:1 H22 Thou being gone, she longer could not be,
2SIMON195:7 Hp271 you should see me no more, I could think of nothing more
MEDDM197:1 Hp274 temptations of Sathan without could not hurt, hath, been foild
MEDDM209:9 Hp291 that they could do (as they thought) wth lesse hazard and more
MYCHILD215:27 Hp240 Trouble, & I could not be at rest 'till by prayer I had confest
MYCHILD217:28 Hp243 thovght were it hell it self and could there find ye Love of God
MYCHILD217:29 Hp243 it would bee a Heaven And could I haue been in Heaven
MYCHILD217:33 Hp243 many times by Atheisme how I could know whether there was
MYCHILD218:15 Hp244 in it fullfilled wch could not haue been so long foretold by any
FEVER220:29 H9 So faint I could not speak.
FEVER220:32 H12 Nor could I read my Evidence
SOREFIT221:17 H3 When novght on Earth could comfort giue
28AUG226:8 Hp254 thy great Love to my soul so lately expressed, when I could
2HUSB232:12 H13 Nor novght could keep him back
REMB236:2 H17 What could I more desire?
HOUSE236:25 H17 And when I could no longer look

COULD'ST (1)
2LETTER182:25 H31 At thy return, if so thou could'st or durst

COULTER'S (1) [coulter is]
ELEMEN9:10 H44 Ye Husband-men, your coulter's made by me,

COUNSEL (4)
HUMOUR35:14 H610 This loving counsel pleas'd them all so wel,
AGES40:16 H197 All counsel hate, which tends to make me wise,
AGES45:18 H400 Who gave the counsel, but the Prince of hell.
CHILDRN186:27 H94 And dead, yet speak, and counsel give:

COUNSELL (6)
MPERS77:27 H968 Sage *Artabanus* counsell, had he taken,
MPERS77:37 H978 Vaine *Xerxes* thinks his counsell hath most wit,
MPERS91:25 ~~H1539~~ His Mothers wicked counsell was the cause,
MGREC104:11 H2063 This counsell, for his safety, he pretended,
MGREC115:33 H2552 And for his Counsell, ne're the King to live.
MGREC129:35 H3149 So *Polisperchon* to his Counsell drew,

COUNSELLORS (1) [pl.]
QELIZ156:35 H62 Had ever Prince such Counsellors as she?

COUNSELLS (1) [poss.]
MPERS~~91:22~~ H1535 But shortly calls her home, her counsells prize,

COUNT (10) See also COVNT
ELEMEN11:27 H147 Among my praises this I count not least,
HUMOUR25:28 H217 Nay should I tel, thou wouldst count me no blab,
HUMOUR29:30 H381 This warinesse count not for cowardise,
AGES37:26 H88 This little house of flesh, did spacious count:
AGES40:17 H198 And dearest freinds count for mine enemies;
VANITY160:33 H43 Its hid from eyes of men, they count it strange,
CONTEM172:26 H160 Thou Emblem true, of what I count the best,
FLESH176:17 H57 And count them for my deadly harms.
SICKNES179:3 H23 Then deaths arrest I shall count best,
2LETTER182:14 H20 May count my sighs, and number all my drops:
COUNTED See COVNTED
COUNTENANC'D (1) [countenanced]
DIALOG143:31 H100 And {Are} lik'd, and countenanc'd by men of might,
COUNTENANCE (3) See also COVNTEN^c
AGES36:4 H28 In's countenance, his pride quickly was seen.
MGREC~~118:24~~ H2672 His countenance so lively did appear,
MEDDM202:24 Hp282 a moment that we cannot behold the light of his Countenance,
CONTENANCED See CONTENANC'D
COUNTERMANDS (1)
MGREC122:27 H2846 *Pithons* commands, {as oft} She ever countermands
COUNTIES (1) [pl.]
DIALOG147:2 H228 Blest be thy Counties which do {who did} aid thee still
COUNTLESS (1)
2LETTER182:15 H21 Tell him, the countless steps that thou dost trace,
COUNTREY (1) [country] See also COVNTRY
DIALOG147:19 H245 Not false to King, nor Countrey in thy heart, {to the better part;}
COUNTRIES (10) [pl.] See also COVNTRYS
ELEMEN11:35 H155 To tell you of my Countries, and my regions
ELEMEN19:18 H463 Yea so contagious, Countries have me {we} known;
ELEMEN19:39 H480 As battells pitcht ith' Aire (as Countries know;)
MGREC101:8 H1933 And all those Countries, which (betwixt) did lye,
MGREC111:32 H2377 Now through these goodly countries as he past,
MGREC114:37 H2507 All Kingdoms, Countries, Provinces, he won, {wan}
MGREC128:28 H3101 Still gaining Countries East-ward goes he on.
MGREC132:18 H3255 Those Countries large, his father got before,
COUNTRIES (1) [poss.]
QELIZ157:19 H87 Instead of glory prov'd her Countries shame:
COUNTRIES (1) [pl., poss.]
HUMOUR25:39 H228 For Countries good, thy life thou darst expose:
COUNTRY (26) See also COUNTREY, COVNTRY
ELEMEN12:5 H165 On either side the country of the *Gaules,*
ELEMEN17:13 H377 A mighty Country ith' *Atlanticke* Ocean.
HUMOUR33:2 H516 Country with Country, *Greece* with *Asia* fights,
HUMOUR33:2 H516 Country with Country, *Greece* with *Asia* fights,
AGES39:15 H158 Nor ignorant {And so likewise} what they in Country do;
AGES45:14 H396 And others fly their Country, through their {struck both with gilt
MASSYR54:32 H59 The *Median* country, he did also gain,
MASSYR~~56:25~~ H131 Great King *Staurobates,* for {his Country} to invade.
MASSYR56:35 H141 Who in her Country never more was seen.
MASSYR57:24 ~~H171~~ Again, the Country was left bare (there is no doubt)

MPERS75:41 H898 Entring that large and barren country far;
MPERS~~80:28~~ H1095 But {the} *Phocians* Land, {Country} he then wasted sore:
MPERS84:28 H1264 His Country, nor his Kindred {Friends} would {much} esteem,
MPERS85:22 H1298 Invades {Plunders} the Country, and much trouble {mischief}
MPERS88:38 H1431 The King unto a country Village flyes,
MPERS89:11 H1445 If *Greeks* unto their Country-men {own Country should}
MPERS90:4 ~~H1478~~ Before them burnt the country as they went,
MPERS~~90:4~~ H1478 The Country burnt, they no relief might take.
MGREC106:18 H2152 Such country there, nor yet such people finde.
MGREC108:8 H2224 Whom *Xerxes* from their country led away;
MROMAN138:26 H3516 Who for sedition from his Country fled;
SIDNEY149:32 ~~H23~~ The love thy Country ought thee, was as much.
SIDNEY~~150:12~~ H41 The love his Country ought him, was as much.
CHILDRN186:11 H78 Into a country beyond sight,
MEDDM203:10 Hp283 He that is to saile into a farre country, although the ship,
MEDDM203:14 Hp283 heauenly country, and heere he hath many conueniences and

COUNTRY-MEN (3)
MPERS84:10 H1238 And how her Country-men from spoile she freed.
MPERS84:32 H1268 And to his Country-men {native land} could bear no hate.
MPERS89:11 H1445 If *Greeks* unto their Country-men {own Country should}

COUNTRYES (2) [countries] See also COUNTRYS, COVNTRYS
ELEMEN17:6 H370 And swallowes Countryes up, ne're seen againe:
MASSYR~~57:17~~ H164 Unto a Father that all Countryes won

COUNTRYS (1) [countries] See also COUNTRYES, COVNTRYS
ELEMEN16:3 H326 Earth, thou hast not more Countrys, Vales and Mounds,

COUNTS (5)
HUMOUR25:4 H193 Thy rudenesse counts, good manners vanity,
MPERS87:14 H1370 And counts nine hundred thousand foot and horses:
MGREC102:15 H1985 And to possesse, he counts no little blisse,
MGREC106:23 H2157 He basenesse counts his former clemency,
MGREC124:35 H2942 Nor counts {thought} he that indignity but {was} small,

COUNT'ST (1) [countest]
FLESH175:19 H19 That all in th' world thou count'st but poor?

COUPLED (2)
MPERS79:11 H1033 Of Boats, together coupled, and there laid;
CHILDRN184:36 H25 Coupled with mate loving and true,

COUPLES (1) [pl.]
MPERS79:12 ~~H1034~~ But winds, and waves, these couples soon dissever'd,

COURAGE (10)
HUMOUR23:29 H139 Their courage, {Courage it} friend, and foe, and subject awes,
HUMOUR~~23:29~~ H139 Their courage, {Courage it} friend, and foe, and subject awes,
HUMOUR25:34 H223 Wilt thou this valour, manhood, courage cal:
HUMOUR25:40 H229 Be dangers neer so high, and courage great,
HUMOUR29:28 H379 To use thy sword, thy courage, and thy Art,
MASSYR58:30 H213 *Arbaces* courage he did sore {so} abate:
MPERS88:16 H1409 Which did such courage to the *Grecians* bring,
MPERS91:13 H1521 Whose courage nought but death could ever tame,
MGREC~~94:18~~ H1653 And with a bount'ous heart and courage brave,
MGREC~~121:15~~ H2793 *Python* of haughty mind, and courage great.

COURAGIOUS (1)
ELEMEN15:3 H285 Nor mettl's found in the couragious Horse:

COURSE (22)

ELEMEN11:18 H138 Now Sisters, pray proceed, each in her {your} course,
HUMOUR32:15 H489 I've done, pray Sister Flegme proceed in course,
SEASONS~~52:27~~ H242 And North-ward his unwearied race {Course} doth run;
MASSYR59:15 H239 The wals, and gates, their course {hast} did terminate;
MASSYR65:17 H482 To *Judah* marches with a speedy course,
MPERS80:30 H1097 That brave *Thymistocles* takes this wise course,
MPERS80:35 H1102 He hearing this, his thoughts, and course home bended,
MPERS81:24 H1132 That whilst the Sun did run his endlesse course,
MPERS~~89:16~~ H1450 He judg'd his wisest and his safest Course.
MPERS90:8 H1481 Nor rivers course, nor *Persians* force could stay,
MGREC94:14 H1648 His course to *Asia,* next Spring he steers.
MGREC104:38 H2090 And bids him, save himself, by speedy course:
MGREC109:12 H2271 To th' river *Indus* next, his course he bends,
MGREC111:22 H2367 Passing faire *Indus* mouth, his course he stear'd,
MGREC135:18 H3390 And with the torrent of his rapid course,
MROMAN137:11 H3462 So *Romulus* was forc'd this course to take.
CONTEM168:31 H37 Thy swift Annual, and diurnal Course,
CONTEM172:15 H150 Which to the long'd for Ocean held its course,
3LETTER183:21 H23 But worst of all, to him can't steer my course,
CHILDRN184:28 H17 *Southward* they both their course did bend,
MEDDM205:27 Hp286 vs, or else we should not so often faile in our whole Course of
MEDDM208:30 Hp290 it hath stayd the Course of the Sun raised the dead, cast out

COURSERS (1)

MPERS74:9 H834 Then mounting on their snorting coursers proud,

COURT (20)

HUMOUR21:34 H62 Unlesse to court, and claw, and {to} dice, and drink,
AGES39:14 H157 The manners of the Court, I likewise {also} know,
MPERS~~69:38~~ H662 That *Solon* sometimes at his stately Court,
MPERS~~83:23~~ H1211 Such Justice then, in *Persia* {*Persian* court} did remain, {reign.}
MPERS86:2 H1318 The King provok'd, sends for him to the Court,
MPERS86:37 H1353 But least {lest} some worser newes should fly to Court,
MPERS87:2 H1358 And fills the Court with tumult, and with fear.
MPERS~~91:22~~ H1534 From Court exile her unto *Babilon*:
MGREC94:25 H1663 When newes of *Alexander,* came to th' Court,
MGREC95:37 H1716 Along with him, the {greatest} Ladyes of the Court.
MGREC97:8 H1769 Besides, the Queens, and Ladies of the Court,
MGREC108:30 H2246 Besets {Beset} his Camp, or Military Court;
MGREC117:25 H2632 Now Court, and Camp, all in confusion be,
MGREC123:23 H2887 Recals *Olimpias,* the Court to grace;
MGREC126:7 H2998 She with the flow'r {chief} o'th Court to *Pidna* flyes,
DIALOG145:20 H169 {'Tis said,} My better part in Court of Parliament,
MEDDM205:12 Hp286 fro continvally, here is also the great Court of iustice erected,
MEDDM205:16 Hp286 is this Court of Judicature, that there is no appeale from it, no
MEDDM205:17 Hp286 the Court of heaven itself, for if our conscience condemn vs,
MEDDM205:20 Hp286 sure to carry a certificate from the Court of conscience that he

COURTEOUS (1) See also CURTIOUS

HUMOUR28:25 H337 They're liberal, pleasant, kinde, and courteous,

COURTEOUSLY (1)

MGREC97:18 H1779 Preserv'd their honour, us'd them courteously {bounteously},

COURTESAN See CURTEZAN

COURTESIE (8) [courtesy]
AGES39:30 H173 My wit, my bounty, and my courtesie,
MPERS71:23 H737 To hold his own, of his free courtesie;
MPERS~~74:30~~ H853 His affability, {courtesie} and milde aspect,
MPERS89:26 H1460 And courtesie to th' utmost he pretends;
MGREC99:4 H1847 But he with scorn, his courtesie rejects,
MGREC104:39 H2091 This {The} wofull King, his courtesie refuses,
MGREC121:11 H2789 His sweet demeanour, and his courtesie,
MGREC121:23 H2805 Confers {Yields} them {to} *Pithon* on, for's courtesie;
COURTESIES (1) [pl.]
SON231:5 H17 And courtesies of svndry sorts
COURTESY See COURTESIE
COURTIERS (1) [pl.]
MGREC125:36 H2986 The Courtiers wondering at her furious minde,
COURTS (1)
DIALOG147:38 H262 Then Justice shall in all thy Courts take place,
COUSEN (2)
MPERS77:28 H969 And's cousen, young *Mardonius* forsaken,
MGREC126:11 H3002 Her Cousen of *Epire* did what he might,
COVERED (3)
ELEMEN10:32 H107 *Apulia's* jacent parts were covered;
MGREC101:31 H1956 And weaknesse of a foe is covered;
MGREC104:23 H2075 Into a cart him throwes, covered with hides;
COVERTLY (1)
MGREC110:12 H2312 Then {When} covertly, the rest gets {get} o're else-where;
COVETED (1)
AGES37:34 H96 No office coveted, wherein I might
COVNT (1) [count]
MYSOUL225:23 H27 O let me covnt each hour a Day
COVNTED (1) [counted]
HOUSE236:38 H30 There lay that store I covnted best
COVNTEN^{c} (1)
MYCHILD217:26 Hp243 ye Lord would but lift vp ye light of his Covnten^{c} vpon me,
COVNTRY (3) [country]
MEDDM209:18 Hp291 hath by his prouidence so ordered, that no one Covntry hath all
MYCHILD216:8 Hp241 into this Covntry, where I fovnd a new World and new manners
SON231:3 H15 In covntry strange thou did'st provide
COVNTRYS (1) [countries] See also COUNTRYES, COUNTRYS
MEDDM209:21 Hp291 Covntrys so it is with men, there was neuer yet any one man
COW (1)
AGES42:34 H290 Oxe {thriving Cattle}, and my exuberous {new-milch-} Cow,
COWARD (3)
MASSYR67:29 H575 The coward King, whose strength lay in his walls,
MGREC95:1 H1680 And beat the coward *Persians* from the top,
MGREC107:40 H2215 But coward, durst not fight, nor could he fly,
COWARDISE (1)
HUMOUR29:30 H381 This warinesse count not for cowardise,
COWARDIZE (2)
MPERS89:10 H1444 Of this dayes cowardize, he feares the effects;
MPERS90:21 H1488 The *Asiatiques,* cowardize detects; {victoryes}

COWARDS (1) [pl.]
MGREC96:41 H1761 The cowards feeling this sharp stinging charge,
COWARDS (1) [poss.]
MPERS87:21 ~~H1374~~ *Abrocomes*, was this base cowards name,
COWSLIP (1)
SEASONS48:21 H74 The Meads with Cowslip, Hony-suckl's dight,
COYN (1) [coin] See also COYNE
MPERS77:9 H948 His men, his coyn, his honour, and his store;
COYNE (2) [coin] See also COYN
MGREC125:12 H2960 Then by intreaties, promises, and coyne,
QELIZ156:32 H59 Nor men, nor coyne she spar'd, to doe them good;
CRABBE (1) [crab]
ELEMEN10:7 H82 My Crabbe, my Scorpion, fishes, you may see,
CRABED (1) [crabbed]
SEASONS49:5 H96 Ith' first, *Sol* doth in crabed *Cancer* shine.
CRACK (2)
ELEMEN8:14 H12 The Fire, the forced Aire, in sunder crack;
DIALOG147:23 ~~H247~~ And sturdy *Tyburn* loaded till it crack,
CRAFT (6)
ELEMEN~~15:29~~ H311 The crafty {witty} Barbell, whose wit {craft} doth her commend;
AGES39:9 H152 Then let not him, which {that} hath most craft dissemble;
MPERS~~75:21~~ H880 Thy falshood, not thy {craft more then} valour did prevaile;
MPERS83:18 H1206 And by his craft, ordered the matter so,
MPERS~~89:15~~ H1449 To hinder their return by craft or force,
MPERS90:41 H1508 And hopes by craft to quit his Masters harmes;
CRAFTY (4)
ELEMEN15:29 H311 The crafty {witty} Barbell, whose wit {craft} doth her commend;
MPERS74:18 H841 Thanks for all this to's crafty Stable-groome.
MGREC115:36 H2555 He was too subtile for his crafty foe,
DIALOG~~143:8~~ H76 No crafty Tyrant now usurps the Seat,
CRAMP (2)
HUMOUR23:2 H112 The Palsie, Gout, or Cramp, or some such dolor,
AGES~~43:31~~ H326 The knotty {Cramp and} Gout doth sadly torture me,
CRANE (1)
ELEMEN19:8 H453 The Stork, the Crane, the Partrich, and the Phesant;
CRATERUS (7)
MGREC119:18 H2708 To brave *Craterus,* then, he sends with speed,
MGREC119:34 H2724 Now to *Antipater, Craterus* goes,
MGREC120:5 H2740 *Craterus,* and *Antipater* now joyn
MGREC120:7 H2742 *Craterus* doth his daughter *Phisa* {*Phila*} wed,
MGREC120:29 H2766 He, and *Craterus,* both with him now {do} joyn,
MGREC121:38 H2820 Nor could *Craterus* (whom he much did love)
MGREC121:41 H2823 And brave *Craterus* slew, amongst the rest,
CRAV'D (4) [craved]
HUMOUR20:32 H24 Only she crav'd, to have a vacant space.
MASSYR60:9 H274 promise bound, since first {which} he crav'd {firmly made},
MASSYR60:10 H275 *Medes,* and *Persians,* {when he crav'd} their assisting aide;
SIDNEY~~152:4~~ H76 The Muses aid I crav'd, they had no will
CRAVE (7)
FATHER6:10 H44 On what they are, your mild aspect I crave,
ELEMEN13:15 H216 My cold, thy (fruitfull) heat, doth crave no lesse:

HUMOUR20:13 H5 Loe! other foure step up, crave leave to shew
MASSYR58:39 H222 T'infranchise them, to grant what they could crave,
MGREC136:3 H3416 Pardon to crave, for errours, is but vaine,
SICKNES178:28 H11 Where I shall have all I can crave,
2LETTER182:2 H8 I crave this boon, this Errand by the way,

CRAVED See CRAV'D

CRAVES (3)
ELEMEN18:9 H413 The famisht, thirsty man, that craves supply:
MGREC115:40 H2559 And pardon craves, for his unwilling stay,
MGREC128:21 H3094 So therefore craves {requests} their help to take him down,

CRAVING (1)
ELEMEN14:31 H273 Ever in craving, from the other three:

CRAWL (1)
AGES46:17 H448 Mother, and sisters both; the worms, that crawl,

CREATION (1)
MEDDM200:29 Hp279 arise in far more glory, then that wch they lost at their creation,

CREATOR (3)
CONTEM169:6 H48 How full of glory then must thy Creator be?
CONTEM169:14 H55 My great Creator I would magnifie,
MED223:4 Hp250 of thy Loue. First thov art my Creator, I thy creature, thov my

CREATURE (6)
HUMOUR33:31 H545 Which life and motion to each Creature gives,
MGREC117:20 H2627 His matchlesse force no Creature could abide;
CONTEM168:37 H43 Hail Creature, full of sweetness, beauty & delight.
CONTEM173:34 H198 Man at the best a creature frail and vain,
CONTEM174:5 H205 And yet this sinfull creature, frail and vain,
MED223:4 Hp250 of thy Loue. First thov art my Creator, I thy creature, thov my

CREATURES (3) [pl.]
VANITY159:29 H1 *Of the vanity of all worldly creatures {things}.*
CONTEM169:22 H62 Shall Creatures abject, thus their voices raise?
CONTEM171:26 H128 By birth more noble then those creatures all,

CREDIT (2)
MPERS77:29 H970 His Souldiers, credit, wealth, at home had stay'd,
MGREC107:3 H2178 So heaps up gifts, his credit to redeem;

CREEP (3)
ELEMEN11:9 H129 Foolish *Caligula,* creep under's bed
AGES45:38 H428 Now stiffe and numb, can hardly creep or go.
SEASONS51:28 H204 The sap doth slily creep towards the earth,

CREEPS (2)
ELEMEN14:11 ~~H253~~ With divers moe, nay, into plants it creeps;
ELEMEN~~14:11~~ H253 Nay into herbs and plants it sometimes creeps,

CREPIDUM (1)
MGREC136:8 H3421 *Ne sutor ultra crepidum,* may write.

CRESSUS (4)
MPERS69:20 H642 Against great *Cressus,* then of *Lidia* head;
MPERS69:27 H649 Disguised *Cressus,* hop'd to scape i'th throng,
MPERS69:33 H655 *Cressus* thus known, it was great *Cyrus* doome,
MPERS~~69:38~~ H665 That *Cressus* angry, urg'd him to express,

CRESSUS (1) [poss.]
MPERS69:32 H654 Brake his long silence, cry'd, spare *Cressus* life:

CREW (5)
MPERS71:35 H749 Laughing to scorn that calvish, sottish crew.
MPERS83:6 H1194 His wicked brother, {soon} after sent {him} a crew,
MGREC104:18 H2070 Look to himselfe, and leave him to that crew;
CONTEM173:27 H192 Sets hundred notes unto thy feathered crew,
CHILDRN185:4 H30 To chat among that learned crew:
CRICKET (1)
CONTEM169:19 H59 The black clad Cricket, bear a second part,
CRIES (1)
MPERS88:24 H1417 Whom *Cyrus* spi'd, cries out, I see the man,
CRIME (6)
MASSYR~~55:11~~ H77 Adjudged to be drown'd, for what {th' crime} she'd done;
MPERS~~83:17~~ H1205 To be the Authour of the deed {crime} was done,
MGREC112:35 H2421 But *Philotas,* his unpardonable crime,
MGREC113:28 H2455 Most wickedly was slaine, without least crime,
MGREC114:29 H2499 Of *Alexander,* this th' eternall crime,
DIALOG144:11 H121 Because of Royall Stem, that was thy crime;
CRIMSON (2)
AGES36:3 H27 His Suit of Crimson, and his Scarfe of Green:
DAVID159:5 H20 Sometimes from crimson blood of gastly slaine,
CRITICKS (1) [critic's]
AUTHOR178:11 H21 In Criticks hands, beware thou dost not come;
CROAKING (1)
SEASONS47:16 H32 The croaking Frogs, whom nipping Winter kild,
CRŒSUS (1)
MASSYR67:17 H563 (Within which broiles, rich *Crœsus* was engaged,)
CROOK See CROOKE
CROOK-BACKT (1)
DIALOG143:5 ~~H73~~ No Crook-backt Tyrant, now usurps the Seat,
CROOKE (1) [crook]
HUMOUR34:19 H574 Some worthy {curious} learned *Crooke* may these reveal,
CROOKS (1) [pl.]
CONTEM172:16 H151 I markt, nor crooks, nor rubs that there did lye
CROP (7)
AGES38:11 H114 I fear'd no drought, nor wet, I had no crop,
AGES41:26 H243 Such {My} empty seed should yeeld a better crop.
AGES42:33 H289 'Twas in the crop of my manured ground:
SEASONS47:22 H38 The tender tops of budding Grasse they crop,
SEASONS50:26 H160 His fruitful crop, abundantly requites.
DIALOG146:20 H206 Because he knows not, who shall inn his crop:
MEDDM205:7 Hp285 plentifull crop may be expected in the haruest of their yeares.
CROPT (2)
DIALOG144:25 ~~H134~~ Unworthily, some backs whipt, and eares cropt;
1SIMON188:7 H8 Cropt by th' Almighties hand; yet is he good,
CROSS (1) v. See also CROSSE v.
MPERS~~79:13~~ H1035 To cross the sea such strength he found too weak,
CROSSE (2) n. [cross]
HUMOUR25:32 H221 To crosse thy wil, a challenge doth deserve.
DIALOG141:8 H7 What ayles thee hang thy head, and crosse thine armes?
CROSSE (1) v.
MEDDM197:15 Hp274 a man of weak faith and mean abilities, may vndergo a Crosse

CROSSED See CROST
CROSSES (3) [pl.]
AGES42:25 H283 Great labours, sorrows, crosses I sustain'd.
CONTEM174:9 H209 Nor all his losses, crosses and vexation,
1SIMON188:13 H14 And smile again, after our bitter crosses.
CROSSES (1) v.
SEASONS47:4 H18 Crosses the Line, and equals night and day,
CROSSIERS (1) [pl.]
DIALOG147:14 H240 Copes, Rochets, Crossiers, and such {empty} trash,
CROST (4)
AGES39:37 H180 My woful Parents longing hopes all {are} crost,
AGES45:5 H389 I've seen designes at {for} *Ree,* and *Cades* {*Rochel*} crost,
MPERS80:13 H1080 And as at Land, so he at Sea was crost,
MGREC104:10 H2062 Then with so few, how likely to be crost.
CROW (2)
SIDNEY150:16 ~~H49~~ To be saluted by a silly Crow;
SIDNEY150:18 ~~H49~~ A Crow's a Crow, and *Cæsar* is a King.
CROW'S (1) [crow is]
SIDNEY150:18 ~~H49~~ A Crow's a Crow, and *Cæsar* is a King.
CROWES (1)
SIDNEY150:17 ~~H49~~ Then let such Crowes as I, thy praises sing,
CROWN (30)
ELEMEN10:11 H86 The Crown, the Whale, the Archer, Bernice Hare,
AGES39:21 H164 Nor wait til good advice {success} our hopes do crown;
MASSYR59:1 H225 And win the Crown, which was the way to blisse,
MASSYR67:21 H567 Unworthy *Belshazzar* next weares the Crown,
MASSYR67:36 H582 Protectors of his {this} Crown, and *Babylon,*
MASSYR68:2 H588 Destruction to his Crown, to's Person end.
MASSYR68:28 H614 Who soone did terminate his Life, and Crown:
MPERS77:19 H960 He with his Crown, receive a double warre,
MPERS86:25 H1341 He hop'd, if fraud, nor force the Crown could {would} gaine;
MPERS89:14 H1448 And rob him both of Scepter, and of Crown;
MPERS92:16 ~~H1574~~ How this *Darius* did attain the Crown,
MGREC97:3 H1764 And cast away his Crown, for swifter flight;
MGREC97:41 H1802 Therefore a Crown, and great provisions {Provision} send;
MGREC99:17 H1860 (A loyall Subject to *Darius* Crown)
MGREC109:39 H2298 Did more his valour then his Crown envie;
MGREC111:37 H2382 And set his Crown on his supposed head;
MGREC117:36 H2643 Had hope themselves, to beare the Crown away;
MGREC118:29 H2678 His chief opponents who kept off the Crown, {Control'd his
MGREC128:22 H3095 Before he weare the universall Crown;
DIALOG142:6 H35 By fraud, and {or} force, usurp'd thy flowring crown,
DIALOG142:13 H42 Doe *Maud,* and *Stephen* for the Crown contend?
DIALOG143:2 H71 French *Lewis* {Jews} unjustly to the Crown to bring;
DIALOG144:7 H117 For nought, but title to a fading Crown?
DIALOG147:20 H246 But those that hurt his people and his Crown,
SIDNEY149:8 H7 Her noble *Sidney* wore the Crown of Bayes;
SIDNEY149:17 H16 Thy {His} Logick from *Euterpe* won the Crown,
SIDNEY149:28 ~~H23~~ What doe thy vertues then? Oh, honours crown!
VANITY161:4 H55 But wear his Crown unto eternitie,
FLESH177:3 H84 My Crown not Diamonds, Pearls, and gold,

2SIMON195:14 Hp271 wth grace heer and crown you wth glory heerafter. that I may

CROWN'D (1) [crowned]

MGREC126:37 H3026 With Garlands crown'd his head, bemoan'd his Fates,

CROWNE (2)

MGREC96:12 H1732 With Robes and Crowne, most glorious to behold.

MGREC109:22 H2281 Presents himselfe, {first} there with a golden Crowne,

CROWNED See CROWN'D

CROWNES (1) [crowns]

MGREC135:19 H3391 Their Crownes, their Titles, riches beares by force.

CROWNS (2) [pl.]

MGREC105:28 H2121 Their lives enjoy, their crowns, and dignity,

MGREC130:40 H3185 For to their Crowns, there's none can title make.

CROWS See CROWES

CRUCIATING (1)

CONTEM173:20 H186 Feels no sad thoughts, nor cruciating cares

CRUCIFI'D (1) [crucified]

MGREC98:19 H1821 Two thousand of the cheif he crucifi'd,

CRUDITIES (1) [pl.]

AGES38:33 H136 What crudities my cold stomach hath bred?

CRUEL (5)

HUMOUR28:5 H317 And Flegme likewise can shew, her cruel art,

MPERS71:18 H732 (But little *Marus,* {*Narus*} scap'd that cruel fate,

MPERS~~92:2~~ H1556 And in the twenty third of's cruel raign

MGREC113:37 H2464 Had his reward most cruel, and unjust.

MGREC~~125:41~~ H2991 So goes to finde this {cruel} Queen in *Macedon;*

CRUELL (8)

MPERS72:26 ~~H773~~ His cruell Master, for all service done,

MGREC93:12 H1609 The cruell, proud, *Olimpias,* was his mother,

MGREC116:29 H2595 Cruell by nature, and by custome too,

MGREC125:30 H2980 This done, the cruell Queen rests not content,

MGREC126:29 H3020 This was the end of this most cruell Queen,

MGREC130:26 H3181 By cruell father, mother, cruell son,

MGREC130:26 H3181 By cruell father, mother, cruell son,

MYCHILD218:23 Hp244 are in their Relign: together wth their lying miracles, and cruell

CRUELLY (1)

MGREC99:29 H1872 Can *Alexander* deale thus cruelly?

CRUELTIES (4) See also CRUELTYES

MPERS~~91:29~~ H1543 His match incestuous, cruelties of th' Queen,

MGREC126:6 H2997 To give her for all cruelties {her cruelty} her dues:

MGREC134:5 H3338 Horrid massacres, murders, cruelties,

DIALOG144:8 H118 'Mongst all the cruelties which I have {by great ones} done,

CRUELTY (21)

HUMOUR25:26 H215 To satisfie thy pride, and cruelty

MASSYR67:23 H569 His lust, and cruelty, {crueltyes} in books {storyes} we find,

MPERS69:15 H637 His Mothers Dream, and Grand-sires cruelty,

MPERS72:17 H765 Thy cruelty will {all} Ages still admire.

MPERS~~72:24~~ H772 His cruelty was come unto that height,

MPERS75:3 H864 That for their sakes, his cruelty he felt;

MPERS77:18 H959 As is {was} the Son, of pride, and cruelty;

MPERS79:3 ~~H1025~~ Nay, more then monstrous barb'rous cruelty!

MPERS82:21 H1168 Scorn'd *Xerxes,* hated for his cruelty,

MPERS83:8 H1196 Unto such height did grow his cruelty,
MPERS90:39 ~~H1506~~ Who of his cruelty made many tast,
MGREC94:12 H1646 For cruelty now, was his parentall sin.
MGREC101:21 H1946 Him boundlesse made, in vice, and cruelty;
MGREC103:25 H2036 In pride, and cruelty, to th' highest {high} excesse.
MGREC105:25 H2118 Of Treason, murther, and base cruelty,
MGREC108:16 H2232 But in his cruelty alike they shar'd;
MGREC112:19 H2405 'Mongst those, that of his cruelty did taste,
MGREC~~126:6~~ H2997 To give her for all cruelties {her cruelty} her dues:
MGREC126:33 ~~H3023~~ So boundlesse was her pride, and cruelty,
MGREC130:27 ~~H3181~~ Who did erect their cruelty in guilt,
DIALOG145:2 H151 Such cruelty as all reports have past.

CRUELTYES (1) [cruelties]
MASSYR~~67:23~~ H569 His lust, and cruelty, {crueltyes} in books {storyes} we find,

CRUM (1)
VERSES184:3 H7 Yet handled ill, amounts but to this crum;

CRUSH (3)
DIALOG145:22 H171 To crush the proud, and right to each man deal.
DIALOG147:10 H236 These are the dayes, the Churches foes to crush,
MEDDM200:36 Hp280 weak children as would crush them to the dust, but according

CRUSH'D (1) [crushed]
AGES42:6 H264 The proud I crush'd, th' oppressed I set free,

CRUSHT (3)
MPERS73:34 H819 So late crusht by their Princes Tyranny;
CONTEM170:34 H104 Branded with guilt, and crusht with treble woes,
MERCY188:25 H11 I stood so nigh, it crusht me down withal;

CRUST (1)
HUMOUR31:4 H437 When by thy heat, thou'st bak'd thy selfe to crust,

CRY (12)
AGES38:25 H128 Oft stubborn, peevish, sullen, pout, and cry:
SEASONS49:28 H117 Which made great *Bajazet* cry out in's woes,
SEASONS53:8 H264 *Shall at your feet for pardon cry.*
MPERS69:36 H658 He *Solon, Solon, Solon,* thrice did cry.
MPERS74:15 H838 A thousand times, God save {long live} the King, they cry,
MPERS87:5 H1361 The wife, against the mother, still doth cry
MPERS87:41 H1393 When suddenly their Scouts come in and cry,
MGREC113:4 H2431 *Philotas* after him sends out this cry,
DIALOG144:30 H138 Their silent tongues to heaven did vengeance cry,
DIALOG147:5 H231 O cry: the sword of God, and *Gideon:*
BYNIGHT220:10 H10 In vain I did not seek or cry.
HOUSE236:20 H12 And to my God my heart did cry

CRY'D (4) [cried]
MPERS69:32 H654 Brake his long silence, cry'd, spare *Cressus* life:
DIALOG144:23 H133 That cry'd, destruction to my wicked Land:
FEVER220:34 H14 Hide not thy face from me I cry'd
THEART229:3 H5 I cry'd thov seem'st to make some stay

CRYES (2) [cries] See also CRY'S, CRYS
AGES37:14 H76 With wayward cryes, I did disturbe her rest;
MPERS80:5 H1072 None cryes for quarter, nor yet seeks to run,

CRYING (2)
AGES36:38 H62 To hear the child, who crying, thus began.

DIALOG144:4 H114 From crying bloods, yet cleansed am not I,

CRY'S (1) [cries] See also CRYES, CRYS

ACK235:7 H7 Hast heard my cry's, + seen my Teares,

CRYS (2) [cries] See also CRYES, CRY'S

MASSYR68:3 H589 With quaking knees, and heart appall'd, he crys,

MEDDM202:34 Hp282 say it is enough, but like the daughters of the horsleach, crys

CRYSTAL See CHRISTALL, CHRYSTAL

CRYSTALINE See CHRISTALINE

CUMBER (1)

MEDDM206:4 Hp287 being cut down, as the dry stock, for both cumber the ground

CUMBERSOME (1)

MEDDM200:16 Hp279 cumbersome garment, she easily foresees what euents it is

CUMBRED (1) [cumbered]

PILGRIM210:29 H29 Wth cares and fears ner' cumbred be

CUP (8)

MPERS92:13 H1571 reign'd, as Chronicles expresse, {then drank of's fathers cup}

MGREC112:13 H2399 To every Guest, a cup of gold he sends,

MGREC116:5 H2565 Sons of *Antipater,* {and} bearers of his Cup,

MGREC117:9 H2616 So the same cup to his, did others fill.

MGREC125:24 H2974 A Halter, cup of Poyson, and a Sword,

MGREC127:2 H3032 Now in her age she's forc't to taste that Cup,

DIALOG145:4 H153 Nor sip I of that cup, and just 't may be,

11MAYB228:31 Hp259 loving kindnes, nor take ye cup of salvation wth Thanksgiving

CUPIDS (1) [poss.]

SIDNEY150:2 H27 Found *Cupids* Dame, had never such a Gin;

CUPS (3) [pl.]

MASSYR59:6 H230 Who revelling in Cups, sung care away,

MPERS84:3 H1231 The royall wine, in golden cups doth {did} passe,

MGREC113:41 H2468 And in his cups, his chief Companion;

CURB'D (1) [curbed]

AGES42:7 H265 The lyars curb'd but nourisht verity.

CURE (4)

PROLOG7:12 H26 A weake or wounded braine admits no cure.

ELEMEN12:34 H194 Doe cure your patients, fill your purse with pence;

DIALOG142:2 H31 What Medicine shall I seek to cure this woe,

MEDDM203:26 Hp283 that hath skill to cure it, but when he findes his diseases to

CURES (1) [pl.]

ELEMEN16:15 H338 My wholesome Bathes, together with their cures.

CURIATII (1)

MROMAN138:4 H3494 And *Curiatii,* three *Albans* provide;

CURIOUS (4)

HUMOUR28:11 H323 All to prevent, this curious care I take;

HUMOUR~~34:19~~ H574 Some worthy {curious} learned *Crooke* may these reveal,

MGREC116:22 H2588 And curious Artists evermore rewarded.

DUBART153:37 H41 And curious in-sight in Anatomy;

CURIOUSLY (1)

MASSYR55:38 H104 The walls so strong, and curiously were {was} wrought;

CURLE (1)

AGES~~40:21~~ H202 'Tis spent in curling {to curle}, frisling up {and pounce my

CURLING (1)

AGES40:21 H202 'Tis spent in curling {to curle}, frisling up {and pounce my

CURRENT (1)
ELEMEN17:3 H367 Their Cattle, Hay, and Corne, I sweep down current,
CURS'D (1) [cursed]
CONTEM171:27 H129 Yet seems by nature and by custome curs'd,
CURSE (2)
MGREC125:26 H2976 The Queen with many a curse, and bitter check,
DIALOG147:6 H232 And shall I not on those {them} with *Mero's* curse,
CURSED (2) See also CURS'D
AGES38:14 H117 Lay raked up; of all the cursed weeds,
MASSYR65:38 H503 The cursed King, by flight could no wise flee {fly}
CURST (2)
AGES43:10 ~~H305~~ Have been curst furtherers of mine intents.
SEASONS51:3 H177 Whose lively liquor oft is curst, and blest;
CURTAINS (1) [pl.]
CONTEM174:30 H227 That draws oblivions curtains over kings,
CURTEZAN (1) [courtesan]
MASSYR55:9 H75 Her Mother *Docreta,* a Curtezan;
CURTIOUS (1) [courteous]
MGREC128:33 H3106 Curtious, as noble *Ptolomy,* or more,
CURTIUS (3)
ELEMEN14:7 ~~H250~~ And *Rome,* her *Curtius,* can't forget I think;
MGREC97:9 H1770 If *Curtius* be true, in his report.
MGREC101:39 H1968 But *Quintus Curtius,* as was said before.
CUSH (1)
MASSYR53:20 H10 The boysterous Sons of *Cush, {Chus,}* Grand-child to *Ham,*
CUSTOME (3) [custom]
MGREC116:29 H2595 Cruell by nature, and by custome too,
TDUDLEY165:4 H6 By duty bound, and not by custome led
CONTEM171:27 H129 Yet seems by nature and by custome curs'd,
CUSTOMES (2) [customs]
MPERS86:30 H1346 Whose rents and customes, duly he sent in.
DIALOG145:26 H175 Old customes, new Prerogatives stood on,
CUSTOMS (1) [pl.]
MROMAN137:29 H3480 Religious Rites, and Customs instituted,
CUT (9) See also CUTT
ELEMEN17:8 H372 Thus *Albion* {*Britain* fair} (tis thought) was cut from *France,*
MPERS70:8 H679 To drain this ditch, he many sluces cut,
MPERS73:10 H797 Cut off in's wickednesse, in's strength, and prime.
MPERS76:39 H937 Which soon cut off, {inrag'd,} he with the {his} left
MPERS82:31 H1178 Cut off her lilly breasts, her nose, and ears;
MPERS82:40 H1187 Thus cut, and mangled by a hag of hell.
MGREC134:32 H3363 Next *Auletes,* who cut off *Pompey's* head:
SIDNEY150:26 H53 E're he was ripe; his thred cut *Atropos.*
MEDDM206:4 Hp287 danger of being cut down, as the dry stock, for both cumber
CUTS (7)
MPERS70:11 H682 He cuts those banks, and let the river out;
MPERS74:24 H847 By which he cuts their hopes (for future times)
MPERS74:40 H861 With his own hands cuts off his eares, and nose,
MPERS79:1 H1023 Cuts him in twain, for whom his Sire besought.
MPERS79:9 H1031 A Sea passage cuts, behind *Orthos* {*Athos*} Mount.
MGREC95:16 H1695 There {where} the Prophetick knot, he cuts in twain;

MEDDM200:21 Hp279 Christian, therfore god cuts their garments short, to keep them

CUTT (1)

FAINT222:16 H6 My life as Spiders webb's cutt off

CYNA (1)

MGREC122:21 ~~H2845~~ Her mother *Cyna* sister to *Alexander,*

CYPRUS (1)

MPERS71:20 H734 He next to *Cyprus* sends his bloudy Hoast,

CYRUS (24)

MASSYR68:27 H613 That night victorious *Cyrus* took the town,
MPERS68:34 H620 *Cyrus, Darius* (being his Vnckle,
MPERS69:1 H623 *Cyrus Cambyses,* Son of *Persia's* {Persia} King,
MPERS69:9 H631 *Cyrus, Darius* Daughter took to wife,
MPERS69:13 H635 This is of *Cyrus* the true pedigree,
MPERS69:24 H646 So over-thrown of *Cyrus,* as was just;
MPERS69:37 ~~H659~~ Upon demand, his minde to *Cyrus* broke,
MPERS~~69:37~~ H659 The Reason of those words *Cyrus* demands,
MPERS69:39 H669 With pitty *Cyrus* mov'd, knowing Kings stand,
MPERS70:4 H675 Next war, the restlesse *Cyrus* thought upon,
MPERS70:22 H693 *Cyrus* doth now the *Jewish* captives free,
MPERS70:29 H700 And sets on *Cyrus,* in a fatall houre;
MPERS73:5 H792 The Male line, of great *Cyrus* now did {had} end.
MPERS77:16 H955 Grand-childe to *Cyrus,* now sits on the throne;
MPERS85:36 H1312 Two sons she bore, the youngest *Cyrus* nam'd,
MPERS85:40 H1316 But *Cyrus* scornes, his brothers feeble wit;
MPERS86:13 H1329 *Cyrus* o'th' other side, weighs in his mind,
MPERS87:8 H1364 Which *Cyrus* heares, and so fore-slowes his pace:
MPERS87:25 H1377 *Cyrus* dispair'd, a passage there to gain;
MPERS87:37 H1389 *Cyrus* finding his campe, and no man there;
MPERS88:17 H1410 They straight adored *Cyrus* for their King,
MPERS88:24 H1417 Whom *Cyrus* spi'd, cries out, I see the man,
MPERS88:27 H1420 Down *Cyrus* fals, and yeelds to destiny;
MPERS92:10 H1568 But as 'tis thought, {most suppose} in him had {did} *Cyrus* end:

CYRUS (11) [poss.]

MPERS69:33 H655 *Cressus* thus known, it was great *Cyrus* doome,
MPERS~~72:37~~ H783 Obedience yielded as to *Cyrus* son.
MPERS74:22 H845 He two of *Cyrus* Daughters now {then} doth wed,
MPERS75:27 H884 Since *Cyrus* time, *Cambyses* did molest;
MPERS~~77:16~~ H957 Because this was, first born of *Cyrus* race.)
MPERS83:28 H1216 The best that ever sprang {sprung} of *Cyrus* race.
MPERS87:19 H1373 Their Captain hearing, but of *Cyrus* name.
MPERS92:18 ~~H1576~~ If not (as is before) of *Cyrus* race,
MPERS92:21 ~~H1579~~ And that great *Cyrus* line, yet was not run,
MPERS~~92:26~~ H1584 Some write great *Cyrus* line was not yet run,
MGREC111:34 H2379 Then visits *Cyrus* Sepulcher in's way,

D

D (1) [Dudley]
FATHER5:3 H4 Deare Sir, of late delighted with the sight, /T D on the
DAGON (1)
MASSYR55:14 H80 Sure from this fiction, *Dagon* first began,
DAIGNE (2) [deign]
PROLOG7:37 H47 If e're you daigne these lowly lines, your eyes
SIDNEY152:19 H88 For to conclude my poem two lines they daigne,
DAILY (10) See also DAYLY
HUMOUR28:33 H345 Thousand examples, you may daily see
AGES38:24 H127 And fift Commandement do daily break.
AGES38:35 H138 What breaches, knocks, and falls I daily have?
MPERS87:12 H1368 In numbers from his brother daily run.
MGREC106:22 H2156 So daily of his vertues doth he lose;
MGREC121:13 H2791 And from the other, {side} daily some did gaine.
MGREC126:18 H3009 By stealth unto *Cassander* daily fly;
MGREC134:10 H3341 By Rebells and imposters daily vext;
DIALOG143:38 H107 What injuries did daily on them lye;
CONTEM168:32 H38 Thy daily streight, and yearly oblique path,
DAINTY (1)
ELEMEN9:18 H52 Your dainty {dayly} food, I wholsome make, I warme
DAISY See DAYSEY, DAZY
DALE (1)
ELEMEN12:15 H175 But ile skip {leap} o're these Hills, not touch a Dale,
DAM (3)
CHILDRN184:24 H13 Leave not thy nest, thy Dam and Sire,
CHILDRN184:37 H26 Hath also bid her Dam adieu:
CHILDRN186:19 H86 You had a Dam that lov'd you well,
DAMAGE (1)
MGREC125:1 H2949 Which damage both to minde and body brought:
DAMASCUS (2)
MASSYR61:11 H316 *Damascus,* ancient seat of famous Kings,
MASSYR61:27 H332 Unto *Damascus* then, comes *Iudah's* King,
DAMASK (1)
QELIZ158:9 H118 *O'th' Damask Rose, sprung from the white and red,*
DAME (4)
MASSYR55:20 H86 This gallant dame, unto the *Bactrian* war;
MPERS82:24 H1171 The chaste, and beautious Dame, refuses still.
MGREC131:33 H3225 But willingly resign'd the beauteous dame:
SIDNEY150:2 H27 Found *Cupids* Dame, had never such a Gin;
DAMES (2) [pl.]
FATHER5:5 H6 Of fairer Dames, the sun near saw the face, /of the

DAVID159:13 H28 O *Israels* Dames, o're-flow your beauteous eyes,

DAMES (1) [poss.]
BIRTH180:16 H26 These O protect from step Dames injury.

DAMNIFIE (2)
MASSYR60:27 H292 The fire, those Mettals could not damnifie;
TDUDLEY166:21 H63 Where storms, nor showrs, nor ought can damnifie.

DAMNIFIED (1)
MGREC128:12 H3085 Which their late King in dust had damnified;

DAMP (1)
MEDDM196:9 Hp273 Corruptions, and y^t will damp his high thoughts

DAMS (1) [pl.]
SEASONS47:21 H37 Now {Do} jump, and play, before their feeding Dams,

DANC'D (1) [danced]
AGES37:16 H78 With weary armes, she danc'd, and *By, By,* sung,

DANE (1)
DIALOG142:8 H37 Or hath *Canutus,* that brave valiant *Dane,*

DANGER (5)
MPERS90:18 H1485 So after all {Thus finishing} their travell, danger, pain,
MGREC124:34 H2941 His Fathers danger, with his Family;
MGREC135:4 H3376 For 'twas not death, nor danger, she did dread,
MEDDM196:4 Hp272 is in danger of foundering.
MEDDM206:4 Hp287 danger of being cut down, as the dry stock, for both cumber

DANGER'S (1) [danger is]
AGES38:39 H142 At home, abroad, my danger's manifold.

DANGEROUS (3)
MGREC114:8 H2476 Upon this dangerous theam fond *Clitus* fell;
DIALOG142:3 H32 If th' wound's {wound} so dangerous I may not know?
HANNA230:10 H3 dangerous feaver.

DANGEROUSLY (1)
AGES41:30 H247 Who climbes without hold, climbes dangerously.

DANGERS (16) [pl.]
HUMOUR21:26 H54 In dangers to account himself more sure,
HUMOUR25:40 H229 Be dangers neer so high, and courage great,
AGES35:35 H21 In dangers every moment of a fall,
AGES38:18 H121 The sins, and dangers I am subject to.
AGES38:27 H130 As many was {are} my sins, so dangers too:
AGES40:34 H213 Though dangers do attend me every houre,
AGES44:6 H339 Sicknesse, dangers, and anxieties have past,
MGREC98:36 H1838 The dangers, difficulties, like to rise;
MGREC99:41 H1884 No future dangers he did ever dread.
MGREC~~109:5~~ H2263 His fights, his dangers, and the hurts he had,
MGREC120:32 H2769 To save himself from dangers eminent;
MGREC~~122:5~~ H2828 {To shew} The difficulties {dangers} *Eumenes* befell,
MEDDM207:24 Hp289 and till the expiratnon of that time, no dangers no sicknes
PILGRIM210:6 H6 his dangers past, and travailes done
SON230:28 H11 From Dangers great thou did'st him free
SON231:16 H28 Thro: want and Dangers manifold,

DANGLE (3)
ELEMEN15:32 H314 My pearles that dangle at thy darlings ears;
SEASONS51:7 H181 The Orange, Lemon, Dangle on the tree;
CONTEM169:36 H74 Fancyes the Apple, dangle on the Tree,

DANIEL (7)

MASSYR64:15	H439	Wise *Daniel,* and his fellows 'mongst the rest,
MASSYR66:27	H533	His Dreams, wise *Daniel* doth expound ful wel,
MASSYR68:15	H601	Of *Daniel* tells, who in his Grand-sires dayes,
MASSYR68:17	H603	*Daniel* in haste, is brought before the King,
MPERS70:24	H695	He with his Vnckle *Daniel* sets on high,
MGREC117:11	H2618	As *Daniel,* before had Prophesied;
MGREC133:38	H3328	The affinities and warres *Daniel* set forth,

DANIELS (1) [poss.]

MGREC99:38	H1881	The Priest shews him good *Daniels* Prophesie,

DAPH'NES (1) [poss.]

ELEMEN15:8	H290	The Pine, the Cedars, yea and *Daph'nes* tree;

DAR'D (1) [dared]

MPERS82:5	H1152	No longer dar'd, but fiercely {bravely} on-set gave,

DARE (17)

FATHER6:4	H38	I honour him, but dare not wear his wealth,
ELEMEN13:36	H237	Again, when Delvers dare in hope of gold,
ELEMEN20:8	H490	But dare not go, beyond my Element.
HUMOUR22:17	H86	She dare, {dares} not challenge if I speake amisse;
HUMOUR26:13	H243	That there are some, and best, I dare averre;
HUMOUR28:38	H350	No braggs i've us'd, t' your selves {to you} I dare appeale,
HUMOUR30:39	H431	But yet more comely far, I dare avow,
HUMOUR33:19	H533	Who is't or {that} dare, or can compare with me;
AGES39:17	H160	That dare climbe Battlements, {scale walls and forts} rear'd to
MPERS~~69:26~~	H648	Where all that doe {dare} resist, are slaughter'd down;
MPERS75:13	H874	But who dare venture such a stake for th' game;
MPERS75:35	H892	That shall, but {once} dare {to} raze those firme foundations;
MGREC106:8	H2142	To see if any dare his might oppose;
DIALOG148:18	H283	(For then what is't, but English blades dare do)
DUBART154:15	H60	Thy fame is spread as farre, I dare be bold,
JULY223:25	Hp251	manifested his Love to me, wch I dare not passe by without
28AUG226:2	Hp254	but joyfully? The Lord knowes I dare not desire that health

DARED See DAR'D

DARES (6)

HUMOUR21:33	H61	That much wil talk, but little dares she do,
HUMOUR21:37	H65	A Chamber wel, in field she dares not come;
HUMOUR~~22:17~~	H86	She dare, {dares} not challenge if I speake amisse;
MPERS89:29	H1463	The King's {King} perplext, there dares not let them stay,
MGREC131:29	H3221	Yet dares {durst} not say, he loves {lov'd} his fathers wife;
MEDDM200:2	Hp278	comes to its height by degrees, He that dares say of a lesse

DARING (2)

MPERS71:29	H743	The stormed dust o'r-whelm'd his daring bands;
MPERS80:25	H1092	But he, in daring of his forward foe,

DARINGS (1) [pl.]

ELEMEN8:18	H16	Both by their darings; Water so provoked,

DARIUS (46)

MPERS68:34	H620	*Cyrus, Darius* (being his Vnckle,
MPERS69:9	H631	*Cyrus, Darius* Daughter took to wife,
MPERS69:11	H633	*Darius* was unto *Mandana* brother,
MPERS73:12	H799	*and* Darius Hyslaspes.
MPERS74:10	H835	*Darius* lusty stallion neighed full loud;

MPERS74:19 H842 *Darius Hyslaspes.*
MPERS74:20 H843 *Darius* by election made a King
MPERS75:16 H877 Nor can *Darius* in his Monarchy,
MPERS75:24 H881 *Darius* in the second of his reign,
MPERS75:40 H897 *Darius* on the *Sythians* made a war,
MPERS76:32 H930 *Darius* multitude before them fled;
MPERS77:4 H943 *Darius* light, he {yet} heavie, home returnes,
MPERS77:15 H954 *Xerxes, Darius,* and *Attossa's* Son,
MPERS78:14 H995 Who married the sister of *Darius:*
MPERS83:16 H1204 Accus'd *Darius, Xerxes* eldest son,
MPERS~~84:12~~ H1244 His bounty did *Darius* far exceed.
MPERS91:33 H1547 *Darius Ochus.*
MPERS92:15 H1573 *Darius Codomanus.*
MPERS92:16 ~~H1574~~ How this *Darius* did attain the Crown,
MPERS~~92:16~~ H1574 *Darius* by this *Bogoas* set in throne,
MPERS92:33 H1591 That this *Darius* was last *Persian* King,
MGREC94:26 H1664 To scorn at him, *Darius* had good sport:
MGREC95:21 H1700 Then in *Darius* multitudes {multitude} beside:
MGREC95:30 H1709 And on {Then o're} he goes *Darius* {now} so to meet;
MGREC95:41 H1720 To shew, how great *Darius* plaid his part:
MGREC96:33 H1753 For sure *Darius* thought, at the first sight,
MGREC97:28 H1789 *Darius* now, more humble {less lofty} then before,
MGREC97:37 H1798 But of *Darius* King, as he should know.
MGREC98:33 H1835 *Darius* finding troubles still increase,
MGREC99:10 H1853 *Darius* offers I would not reject,
MGREC99:17 H1860 (A loyall Subject to *Darius* Crown)
MGREC100:31 H1915 About this time, *Darius* beauteous Queen,
MGREC100:37 H1921 When this sad newes (at first) *Darius* heares,
MGREC101:22 H1947 Thus to *Darius* he writes back again,
MGREC102:1 H1971 *Darius* stript of all, to *Media* came,
MGREC102:40 H2010 Which newes doth still augment *Darius* woes;
MGREC103:36 H2047 Now {The} to *Darius,* he directs his way,
MGREC104:13 H2065 Next day this treason, to *Darius* known,
MGREC104:32 H2084 *Darius* from those Traitors hands to gain;
MGREC104:37 H2089 Unto *Darius,* first he brings a Horse,
MGREC105:8 H2101 *Darius* bath'd in bloud, sends out his groanes,
MGREC105:19 H2112 Findes poore *Darius,* peirced to the heart;
MGREC105:26 H2119 If not, because *Darius* thus did pray,
MGREC108:5 H2221 Who to *Darius* Brother gives the wretch,
MGREC111:41 H2386 And *Statirah, Darius* daughter takes,
MGREC~~116:10~~ H2571 When this sad news came to *Darius* Mother,

DARIUS' (1)

MGREC129:13 H3127 But she *Darius'* daughters murthered,

DAIRY See DARY

DARK (6)

AGES44:38 H371 And then, me thought, the world {day} at noon grew dark,
AGES46:18 H449 In my dark house, such kindred I have store,
SEASONS52:2 H219 With minds more dark, then is the darkned sky;
MGREC101:30 H1955 For tumult in the dark {night} doth cause most dread,
MGREC108:32 H2248 They flew so thick they seem'd to dark the aire:
DIALOG146:36 H222 After dark Popery the day did clear,

DARKE (1) [dark]
ELEMEN14:1 H243 Because in the abysse of my darke wombe:
DARKEN (2)
SEASONS47:26 H42 Doth darken *Sols* bright face, makes us remember
CONTEM172:2 H139 Nay, they shall darken, perish, fade and dye,
DARKENED See DARKNED
DARKENESSE (1) [darkness] See also DARKNES, DARKNESSE
AGES37:5 H67 But night and darkenesse, must with shame conceal.
DARKNED (3) [darkened]
SEASONS~~47:5~~ H20 And now makes glad the darkned northern wights
SEASONS52:2 H219 With minds more dark, then is the darkned sky;
MPERS88:8 H1401 Which like a mighty cloud darkned the skye;
DARKNES (3) [darkness] See also DARKENESSE, DARKNESSE
MEDDM202:23 Hp282 darknes till he arise againe, so god doth somtime vaile his face
MYCHILD217:3 Hp242 by it: It hath been no small support to me in times of Darknes
MYCHILD217:24 Hp243 in darknes and seen no light, yet haue I desired to stay my self
DARKNESSE (3) [darkness] See also DARKENESSE, DARKNES
AGES41:7 H227 That yet my bed in darknesse is not made,
SEASONS52:1 H218 Poor wretches, that in total darknesse lye,
MEDDM202:27 Hp282 quite gone out of sight then must we needs walk in darknesse
DARKSOME (4)
AGES43:30 H325 To break the darksome prison, where it's pend;
MASSYR66:3 H509 A {Ah!} haplesse man, whose darksome contemplation,
CONTEM168:29 H36 And in the darksome womb of fruitful nature dive.
FLESH177:20 H101 For there shall be no darksome night.
DARLINGS (2) [pl.]
ELEMEN15:32 H314 My pearles that dangle at thy darlings ears;
SIDNEY152:1 ~~H75~~ Better my hap, then was his darlings fate,
DARST (1)
HUMOUR25:39 H228 For Countries good, thy life thou darst expose:
DART (3)
HUMOUR21:23 H51 Then Iron Corslet, 'gainst a sword or dart;
MPERS88:26 H1419 But {And} in his speed a Dart hit him i'th' eye,
MGREC94:17 H1651 Comming to land, his dart on shoar he throwes,
DARTING (1)
DUBART153:8 H12 Which Rayes, darting upon some richer ground,
DARTS (3) [pl.]
MGREC104:41 H2093 By throwing Darts, gives {gave} him his mortall wound,
MGREC108:31 H2247 Of Darts, and Arrowes, made so little spare,
MGREC125:19 H2967 Nor Darts, nor Arrowes now, none shoots, nor flings;
DARY (1) [dairy]
SEASONS48:19 H72 The cleanly huswives Dary, now's ith' prime,
DARYUS (1)
MPERS85:3 H1279 *Daryus Nothus.*
DASHED (1)
MASSYR67:38 H584 And with a hand, soon dashed all his pride.
DASHT (2)
AGES45:1 ~~H374~~ I saw hopes dasht, our forwardnesse was shent,
MGREC104:36 H2088 His hopes being dasht, prepares himself for flight:
DASTARDS (1) [pl.]
MPERS89:12 H1446 What dastards in the field the *Persians* are;

DATE (3)
MASSYR54:14 H41 At twenty five, ended his regal date.
QELIZ155:22 H13 Thousands bring off'rings, (though out of date)
ELIZB187:10 H18 And buds new blown, to have so short a date,
DATES (2) [pl.]
PROLOG6:21 H6 And {Or} how they all, or each, their dates have run:
MGREC135:8 H3380 Thus Kings, and Kingdoms, have their times, and dates,
DATHAN (1)
ELEMEN14:4 H246 *Korah* {*Dathan*} and all his Company well knew.
DAUGHTER (26)
HUMOUR20:16 H8 Each eldest Daughter to each Element;
SEASONS53:9 ~~H264~~ Your dutifull Daughter.
MPERS69:3 H625 She Daughter unto great *Astiages,*
MPERS69:9 H631 *Cyrus, Darius* Daughter took to wife,
MPERS82:27 H1174 Nor matching of her daughter, to his son:
MPERS91:24 H1538 And weds his Daughter for a second wife;
MPERS~~92:27~~ H1585 But from some daughter this new king was sprung
MGREC93:13 H1610 to the rich *Molossians* {*Epirus* warlike} King, was daughter.
MGREC98:41 H1843 His eldest Daughter, (him) {he} in marriage offers,
MGREC101:6 H1931 His eldest Daughter, for his Princely Bride,
MGREC111:41 H2386 And *Statirah, Darius* daughter takes,
MGREC117:30 H2637 Except by *Artabasus* daughter one;
MGREC120:7 H2742 *Craterus* doth his daughter *Phisa* {*Phila*} wed,
MGREC122:20 H2845 She daughter to his son, who had no other;
MGREC122:25 ~~H2845~~ Her Daughter she instructed in that Art,
MGREC126:31 H3022 The Daughter, Sister, Mother, Wife to Kings,
MGREC128:6 H3079 Daughter to *Phillip,* their renowned head;
MGREC131:25 H3217 Who his fair daughter *Stratonica* takes,
MGREC131:36 H3228 Two sons he left, born of King *Philips* daughter,
MGREC132:4 H3237 (Whose daughter unto wife, he'd newly {not long before} ta'n)
DIALOG141:13 H12 Ah, tell thy Daughter, she may simpathize.
DIALOG142:39 H68 Nor is it *Alcies* Son, and {nor} *Henries* Daughter,
MERCY188:17 H1-2 *To the memory of my dear Daughter in Law,*
MERCY188:34 H20 I lost a daughter dear, but thou a wife,
HANNA230:9 H1-2 Vpon my Daughter Hannah Wiggin her recouery from a
HANNA230:12 H5 To health my Daughter dear
DAUGHTERS (8) [pl.]
MPERS71:1 H713 Three Daughters, and two Sons, he left behind,
MPERS74:22 H845 He two of *Cyrus* Daughters now {then} doth wed,
MGREC95:38 H1717 His mother old, {his} beautious wife, {Queen} and daughters,
MGREC129:13 H3127 But she *Darius'* daughters murthered,
MROMAN137:14 H3465 Their Daughters by the *Romans* then were caught,
DAVID158:30 H10 Lest Daughters of the *Philistins* rejoyce,
MEDDM202:34 Hp282 say it is enough, but like the daughters of the horsleach, crys
MED223:6 Hp250 I thy child, yee shall be my Sons and Daughters saith ye Lord
DAUID (1) [david]
MEDDM204:3 Hp284 he that deliuered me, sath Dauid, from the paw of the Lion
DAUNT (1)
MPERS80:9 H1076 When as one thousand, could some Millions {a million} daunt;
DAVID (3) See also DAUID
HUMOUR24:33 H182 But *David, Judah's* most heroyick King:

MEDDM205:28 Hp286 we doe, but he that wth David, sets the lord alway in his sight
MYCHILD216:31 Hp242 haue I gone to searching, and haue said wth David Lord search

DAVIDS (2) [poss.]

MASSYR65:29 H494 Who was last King of holy *Davids* race;
DAVID158:22 H1-2 *Davids* Lamentation for *Saul,*

DAWNING (1)

CONTEM173:26 H191 The dawning morn with songs thou dost prevent,

DAY (71)

ELEMEN11:15 H135 And all therein at that great day of doome;
ELEMEN17:29 H393 And to this day, impaires her beautious face.
HUMOUR33:7 H521 As at noon day to tel, the Sun doth shine.
AGES37:3 H65 A nothing, here to day, but {and} gone to morrow.
AGES40:32 H211 Remembring not the dreadful day of Doom,
AGES42:14 H272 Was I a laborer, I wrought all day,
AGES42:28 ~~H285~~ For restlesse day and night, I'm rob'd of sleep,
AGES~~44:38~~ H371 And then, me thought, the world {day} at noon grew dark,
AGES~~45:22~~ H412 Men may more freely speak another day.
SEASONS47:4 H18 Crosses the Line, and equals night and day,
SEASONS49:32 H121 Viewing the Sun by day, the Moon by night,
SEASONS50:6 H140 Bearing the burning heat of the long day;
SEASONS50:39 H173 Now day and night are equal in each clime;
SEASONS51:38 H214 Almost at shortest is the shortned day,
SEASONS52:11 H226 I must be short, and short's, the shortned day,
SEASONS52:28 H243 The day much longer then it was before,
SEASONS52:38 H253 Which is increased by the lengthened day,
MASSYR56:10 H116 Three hundred thousand men, here day, by day;
MASSYR56:10 H116 Three hundred thousand men, here day, by day;
MASSYR56:38 H144 Which made the *Assyrians* many a day,
MASSYR~~57:23~~ H170 He many Ages liv'd after that day.
MASSYR59:7 H231 For victory obtain'd the other day;
MASSYR66:20 H526 To *Babylons* proud King, now yeelds the day.
MPERS73:28 H813 But so or no, sure tis, they won the day.
MPERS82:15 H1162 Same day, the small remainder of his Fleet,
MPERS~~84:12~~ H1248 And o're his opposites still got the day,
MGREC93:20 H1617 The very day of his nativity,
MGREC6:36 H1633 Restlesse both day and night, his heart now {then} was,
MGREC94:2 H1636 Which makes each moment seem, more then a day:
MGREC97:6 H1767 Two hundred thousand men that day were slaine,
MGREC104:9 H2061 If when he'd multitudes, the day he lost;
MGREC104:13 H2065 Next day this treason, to *Darius* known,
MGREC108:9 H2225 These not a little joy'd, this day to see,
MGREC114:13 H2483 Next day, he tore his face, for what he'd done,
MGREC121:20 H2802 Next day into the Camp comes {came} *Ptolomy,*
MGREC125:28 H2978 Praying, that fatall day might quickly haste,
MGREC126:22 H3013 Gives promise for her life, and {so} wins the day:
MGREC131:14 H3206 This day twixt these two foes {Kings} ends all the strife,
MGREC132:27 H3272 For his posterity unto this day,
MROMAN138:5 H3495 The *Romans* Conquereth, others {other} yeeld the day,
DIALOG144:20 H130 For these, were threatned the wofull day,
DIALOG146:36 H222 After dark Popery the day did clear,
DIALOG148:22 H287 For sure the day of your redemption's nigh;

SIDNEY150:22 H47 Of which, {at} this day, faire *Belgia* doth {may} boast.
VANITY160:3 H13 Its his to day, but who's his heire to morrow?
VANITY160:9 H19 They'r foul enough to day, that once was {were} fair,
CONTEM168:35 H41 Thy presence makes it day, thy absence night,
CONTEM171:32 H134 But in oblivion to the final day remain.
CONTEM174:2 H203 But day or night, within, without, vexation,
1LETTER181:20 H18 I weary grow, the tedious day so long;
2LETTER182:16 H22 That once a day, thy Spouse thou mayst imbrace;
2LETTER182:19 H25 But for one moneth I see no day (poor soul)
2LETTER182:21 H27 Which day by day long wait for thy arise,
2LETTER182:21 H27 Which day by day long wait for thy arise,
VERSES184:5 H9 My Bond remains in force unto this day;
ANNEB187:25 H15 That's here to day, perhaps gone in an hour;
1SIMON188:3 H4 *a moneth, and one day old.*
2SIMON195:15 Hp271 wth reioyceing at that great day of appearing, wch is the
MEDDM196:14 Hp273 The hireling that labours all the day comforts himself, that
MEDDM196:17 Hp273 heat and drought of the day, when he perceiues his sun apace
MEDDM200:27 Hp279 lost in the Autumn so shall it be at that great day after a long
MEDDM203:35 Hp284 aright will glorifie him that heard him in the day of his
MEDDM204:6 Hp284 same yesterday, to day and for euer, we are the same that
MEDDM204:7 Hp284 need of him, to day as well as yesterday, and so shall for euer,
MEDDM208:2 Hp289 shall fly away, and the day of eternity shall never end, seeing
PILGRIM211:2 H43 Lord make me ready for that day
MYCHILD215:23 Hp240 wth me fr my childhood to this Day.
MYCHILD217:37 Hp243 Heaven + ye Earth, the order of all things night and day,
MYSOUL224:26 H2 Boast of him all ye Day,
MYSOUL225:23 H27 O let me covnt each hour a Day
28AUG226:5 Hp254 Now I can wait, looking every day when my Sav^{r} shall call for

DAY'S (1) [day is]
2LETTER181:31 H1 *Phoebus* make haste, the day's too long, be gone,

DAYES (53) [days]
AGES40:14 H195 Dayes, {Whole} nights, with Ruffins, Roarers, Fidlers spend,
AGES~~45:2~~ H376 We joy'd in many blest and prosperous dayes.
AGES~~45:12~~ H394 Could length their dayes or once reverse their fate
SEASONS47:29 H45 Of longer dayes, and a more temperate air;
SEASONS48:36 H87 Thy dayes stil lengthen, without least decline.
MASSYR68:15 H601 Of *Daniel* tells, who in his Grand-sires dayes,
MPERS69:19 H641 He in his younger dayes an Army led,
MPERS79:16 H1042 Seven dayes and nights, his Hoast without least stay,
MPERS79:38 H1064 Two dayes and nights a fight they there maintain,
MPERS82:3 H1150 Ten dayes these Armies did each other face,
MPERS84:38 H1274 Strong poyson took, and {so} put an end to's dayes.
MPERS~~91:36~~ H1550 Two of his brothers in his Fathers dayes
MGREC100:4 H1888 For in few dayes he brought that Kingdom under.
MGREC100:11 H1895 Now {Thence} back to *Ægypt* goes, and in few dayes,
MGREC102:21 H1991 Where four and thirty dayes he now doth stay,
MGREC108:35 H2251 Upon this River banck in seventeen dayes,
MGREC109:10 H2269 When thus, ten dayes, his brain with wine he'd soak'd,
MGREC112:14 H2400 So after many dayes this {the} Banquet ends.
MGREC116:3 H2563 Poyson had put an end to's dayes 'twas thought,
MGREC118:14 H2661 Seven dayes the Corps of their great Master lyes

MGREC120:4 H2738 To end his dayes by poison, rather chose
MGREC119:12 H2702 In these tumultuous dayes, the thralled *Greeks*
MGREC131:37 H3229 Who had an end put to their dayes by slaughter.
MGREC136:9 H3423 *After some dayes of rest, my restlesse heart,*
MROMAN137:36 H3487 Accounted for some {a} god in after dayes.
DIALOG146:34 H220 To see these {those} latter dayes of hop'd for good,
DIALOG147:10 H236 These are the dayes, the Churches foes to crush,
DIALOG147:31 H255 Out of all mists, such glorious dayes will {shall} bring,
DIALOG148:27 H292 Then follows dayes of happinesse and rest,
SIDNEY149:7 H6 When *England* did injoy her Halsion dayes,
SIDNEY149:37 H24 Thy {His} wiser dayes, condemn'd thy {his} witty works,
QELIZ157:39 H107 O {Yea} happy, happy, had those dayes still been,
QELIZ158:1 H110 Full fraught with honour, riches, and with dayes:
TDUDLEY166:7 H49 As in the mean ones, of our foolish dayes,
DDUDLEY167:21 H18 *Preparing still for death, till end of dayes:*
CONTEM170:19 H91 Hath thousand thoughts to end his brothers dayes,
CONTEM171:10 H114 Our life compare we with their length of dayes
BIRTH180:5 H15 And if I see not half my dayes that's due,
CHILDRN186:2 H69 Mean while my dayes in tunes Ile spend,
ELIZB187:2 H11 Or sigh thy dayes so soon were terminate;
MEDDM203:19 Hp283 dayes of our appointed time till our chang shall come,
MEDDM207:25 Hp289 no paines nor troubles, shall put a period to our dayes, the
MEDDM207:27 Hp289 should make vs so to number our dayes as to apply our hearts
SOREFIT222:6 H25 In drawing out these wretched Dayes.
FAINT222:26 H16 O Lord, no longer bee my Dayes
JULY223:21 Hp251 I had a sore fitt of fainting wch lasted 2 or 3 dayes, but not in y^t
SAMUEL228:17 H18 And Blesse the for't even all my Dayes.
11MAYB228:27 Hp259 and sorest y^t ever I had lasting 4 dayes, and ye weather being
HANNA230:18 H11 Shee loues thee all thy Dayes.
2HUSB233:15 H48 And the Remainder of o^r Dayes
HOURS234:26 H40 Ev'n while my Dayes shall last
ACK235:20 H20 And so desire Ev'n all my Dayes.
REMB236:3 H18 But Thankfullnes even all my dayes

DAYES (1) [day's]
MPERS89:10 H1444 Of this dayes cowardize, he feares the effects;

DAYES (1) [days']
MGREC107:36 H2211 On these, together ty'd, in six dayes space,

DAYLY (4) [daily]
ELEMEN9:18 H52 Your dainty {dayly} food, I wholsome make, I warme
MYCHILD215:16 Hp240 bee dayly in y^r rembrance, (Altho: y^t is the least in my aim in
MYCHILD218:1 Hp243 Winter, Spring and Autvmne, the dayly providing for this great
HOURS233:20 H3 O Lord thou hear'st my dayly moan

DAY'S See DAYES [day is]

DAYS (1) [pl.]
MPERS83:38 H1226 Where ninescore days, are spent in banquetting,

DAYSEY (1) [daisy] See also DAZY
DUBART153:10 H14 But barren I, my Daysey here doe bring,

DAZLED (1) [dazzled]
DUBART153:4 H8 My dazled sight of late, review'd thy lines,

DAZY (1) See also DAYSEY
AGES35:30 H16 Of Dazy, Primrose, and {or} the Violet.

DAZZLED (1) See also **DAZLED**
DIALOG147:32 H256 That dazzled eyes beholding much shall wonder
DEAD (48)
ELEMEN14:34 H276 If I withhold, what art thou, dead, dry lump
ELEMEN19:17 H462 The living, scarce had power, to bury dead.
HUMOUR22:15 H84 Her teeth wil chatter, dead and wan's her face,
HUMOUR23:35 H145 Then a dead Lyon? by beasts triumpht ore.
SEASONS47:15 H31 And all that seem'd as dead, afresh do live.
SEASONS51:16 H190 Or withered stocks, {which were} all dry, and dead,
SEASONS51:33 H209 His dead old stock, again shall mount on high.
MASSYR53:36 H26 Great *Nimrod* dead, *Bellus* the next, his Son,
MASSYR54:6 H33 Alive, and dead, a god they did him make;
MASSYR54:16 H43 His father dead, *Ninus* begins his reign,
MASSYR55:4 H70 This great oppressing *Ninus* dead, and gone,
MASSYR57:2 H149 His Mother dead, *Ninias* obtains his right,
MASSYR57:11 H158 He sought no rule, til she was gone, and dead;
MASSYR61:9 H314 *Belosus* dead, *Tiglath* his warlike Son
MASSYR~~68:13~~ H599 As thus amort {dead, alive} he sits, as all {one} undone:
MASSYR68:23 H609 The guilty King, with colour pale, and dead,
MPERS72:11 H759 Hearing her harmlesse brother thus was dead,
MPERS72:36 H780 And like in feature, to the *Smerdis* dead,
MPERS73:13 H800 Childlesse *Cambyses,* on the sudden dead,
MPERS73:26 H811 And two of these great Peers, in place {Field} lay dead:
MPERS~~74:16~~ H839 Let tyranny now with {dead} *Cambyses* dye.
MPERS83:24 H1212 The eldest son, thus immaturely dead,
MPERS91:34 ~~H1548~~ Great *Artaxerxes* dead, *Ochus* succeeds,
MGREC112:17 H2403 His vertues dead, buried, and all {quite} forgot,
MGREC113:31 H2458 For *Philip* dead, and his surviving Son,
MGREC117:17 H2624 Great *Alexander* dead, his Army's left,
MGREC125:34 H2984 Digg'd up his brother dead, 'gainst natures right,
MGREC129:12 H3126 No sooner was great *Alexander* dead,
MGREC129:22 H3136 *Cassander's* dead, the Princes {do} all detest,
MGREC130:22 H3177 Except *Cassanders* wife, who yet not dead,
MGREC130:34 ~~H3181~~ Yet in the flower of's age, he must lie dead,
MGREC134:19 H3350 First *Ptolomy* being dead, his famous son,
MROMAN138:15 H3505 Nephew unto *Pomphilius* dead, and gone;
SIDNEY149:15 H14 Thy {His} Rhethorick it struck *Polimnia* dead,
SIDNEY150:27 H54 Thus man is borne to dye, and dead is he,
QELIZ157:35 H103 But she though dead, will vindicate our wrong.
QELIZ158:18 H127 Whose living vertues speak (though dead long since)
TDUDLEY165:5 H7 To celebrate the praises of the dead,
CONTEM169:27 H66 And men in being fancy those are dead,
SICKNES178:36 H19 No sooner blown, but dead and gone,
BIRTH180:12 H22 Yet love thy dead, who long lay in thine arms:
1LETTER181:15 H13 In this dead time, alas, what can I more
CHILDRN186:27 H94 And dead, yet speak, and counsel give:
MEDDM199:29 Hp278 when he is once dead, but the last mangles him in his graue
MEDDM202:13 Hp282 accounted among the dead, and no other reason can be giuen
MEDDM208:30 Hp290 it hath stayd the Course of the Sun raised the dead, cast out
TOCHILD215:3 H3 I leaue for yov when I am dead,
FAINT222:22 H12 And tho: as dead mad'st me aliue

DEADLY (7)
ELEMEN15:13 H295 His deadly mallady, I might expell.
ELEMEN19:15 H460 With divers moe, worke deadly consequence.
HUMOUR29:5 H358 That blow's most deadly, where it is intended;
MGREC115:20 H2539 The Queen *Olimpias,* bears him deadly hate,
MGREC124:39 H2946 *Olimpias, Aridæus* deadly hates,
FLESH176:5 H45 Yet deadly feud 'twixt thee and me;
FLESH176:17 H57 And count them for my deadly harms.
DEAFE (1)
MGREC103:34 H2045 But deafe to reason, (bent to have his will;)
DEAL (1)
DIALOG145:22 H171 To crush the proud, and right to each man deal.
DEALE (2) [deal]
HUMOUR26:41 H271 But thou wilt say, I deale unequally,
MGREC99:29 H1872 Can *Alexander* deale thus cruelly?
DEALES (1) [deals]
MEDDM197:32 Hp275 fit for bread, god so deales wth his servants, he grindes them
DEALING (2)
MPERS91:38 ~~H1552~~ Or dealing with the *Persian,* now no more
MYCHILD215:22 Hp240 I will observe shall bee this—I will begin wth Gods dealing
DEALINGS (1) [pl.]
MYCHILD216:20 Hp241 all my experiences of gods gratious Dealings wth me I haue
DEALS (1) [pl.] See also DEALES
MGREC102:4 H1974 Which *Alexander* deals, as suits his pleasure.
DEALT (2)
MPERS75:2 H863 Tels them, how harshly the proud King had dealt,
MYCHILD218:25 Hp244 so to bee dealt withall.
DEAR (43)
ELEMEN18:12 H416 To bid adue, to his dear Element.
SEASONS49:33 H122 *Endimions, Diana's* dear delight;
MPERS~~84:12~~ H1246 Went to *Jerusalem* his city dear,
MGREC102:34 H2004 And of good *Mordecai,* her Kinsman dear;
MGREC131:26 H3218 *Antiochus, Seleuchus* dear lov'd son,
DIALOG146:14 ~~H200~~ Pray now dear child, for sacred *Zion's* sake,
DIALOG146:28 H214 Dear mother cease complaints, and wipe your eyes,
DIALOG148:33 H298 Farewell dear mother, Parliament, {rightest cause} prevail,
SIDNEY~~150:41~~ H69 For the sad loss of her dear *Astrophel.*
SIDNEY152:2 ~~H75~~ For dear regard he had of *Sydney's* state,
SIDNEY152:15 ~~H85~~ Not because, sweet *Sydney's* fame was not dear,
TDUDLEY165:1 H1-2 *To the Memory of my dear and ever honoured Father*
DDUDLEY167:6 H1-2 *On my dear and ever honoured Mother*
FLESH176:9 H49 Whence my dear father I do love.
BIRTH179:33 H9 How soon, my Dear, death may my steps attend,
BIRTH180:14 H24 Look to my little babes my dear remains.
BIRTH180:19 H29 And kiss this paper for thy loves dear sake,
1HUSB180:22 H1 *To my Dear and loving Husband.*
3LETTER183:4 H6 A dearer Dear (far dearer Heart) then this.
3LETTER183:23 H25 Return my Dear, my joy, my only Love,
3LETTER183:31 H33 *Thy loving Love and Dearest Dear,*
VERSES183:35 H2 Most truly honoured, and as truly dear,
ELIZB186:31 H1-2 *In memory of my dear grand-child Elizabeth*

ELIZB186:34 H6 Farewel dear babe, my hearts too much content,
ANNEB187:12 H1-2 *In memory of my dear grand-child*
ANNEB187:30 H20 Farewel dear child, thou ne're shall come to me,
1SIMON188:1 H1-2 *On my dear Grand-child* Simon Bradstreet,
MERCY188:17 H1-2 *To the memory of my dear Daughter in Law,*
MERCY188:27 H13 That thou dear Son has lost both Tree and fruit:
MERCY188:34 H20 I lost a daughter dear, but thou a wife,
MERCY189:13 H34 Chear up (dear Son) thy fainting bleeding heart,
TOCHILD215:1 H1 To my dear children.
MYCHILD215:9 Hp240 My dear children.
JULY223:23 Hp251 dear husband was from home (who is my cheifest comforter on
30SEPT227:28 Hp257 Thus (dear children) haue yee seen ye many sicknesses and
RESTOR229:19 H1-2 For the restoration of my dear Husband from a burning
HANNA230:12 H5 To health my Daughter dear
2HUSB232:1 H1-2 Vpon my dear & loving husband his goeing into
2HUSB232:10 H11 My husband, my dear freind.
2HUSB233:8 H41 W^{th} Joy lend back my Dear
HOURS233:19 H1-2 In my Solitary houres in my dear husband his Absence.
HOURS234:1 H15 Tho: husband dear bee from me gone
REMB235:21 H1-3 In thankfull $Remb^{rc}$ for my dear husbands safe Arrivall.

DEARE (15)

FATHER5:3 H4 Deare Sir, of late delighted with the sight, /T D on the
ELEMEN12:10 H170 But farewell all, for deare mount *Helicon,*
MPERS80:11 H1078 This shamefull Victory cost *Xerxes* deare,
MPERS86:16 H1332 More deare to's mother, then his brother far.
MGREC105:32 H2125 To's Mother, Children deare, and Wife now gone,
MGREC112:1 H2387 Her Sister gives to his *Ephestion* deare,
MGREC125:9 H2957 In hast {haste} unto her deare *Cassander* sends,
MGREC126:25 H3016 And plead the blood of their deare Kindred {friends and
DIALOG141:6 H5 Alas, deare Mother, fairest Queen, and best,
DIALOG142:22 H51 If none of these, deare Mother, what's your woe?
DUBART152:34 H3 Great, deare, sweet *Bartas,* thou art matchlesse knowne;
DAVID159:23 H38 Distrest I am, for thee, deare *Jonathan,*
DAVID159:26 H41 So pleasant hast thou been, deare brother mine:
2SIMON195:1 Hp271 For my deare sonne
PILGRIM211:3 H44 then Come deare bridgrome Come away

DEARER (2)

3LETTER183:4 H6 A dearer Dear (far dearer Heart) then this.
3LETTER183:4 H6 A dearer Dear (far dearer Heart) then this.

DEAREST (5)

AGES40:17 H198 And dearest freinds count for mine enemies;
CONTEM174:3 H204 Troubles from foes, from friends, from dearest, near'st
1LETTER181:24 H22 The welcome house of him my dearest guest.
3LETTER183:2 H4 Her dearest Deer, might answer ear or eye;
3LETTER183:31 H33 *Thy loving Love and Dearest Dear,*

DEARTH (3)

ELEMEN13:30 H231 Then dearth prevailes, that Nature to suffice,
ELEMEN16:38 H361 So oft in my excesse, I cause a dearth:
DIALOG146:18 H204 My wealthy trading faln, my dearth of grain,

DEATH (87)

ELEMEN14:13 H255 Thus I occasion death to man and beast,

death

ELEMEN14:21	H263	And after death, whether inter'd, or burn'd;
ELEMEN18:3	H407	I aske the man condemn'd, that's near his death:
ELEMEN19:19	H464	That birds have not scap'd death, as they have flown,
ELEMEN20:4	H486	By death, or great mutations {mutation} of their States.
HUMOUR23:28	H138	Their wrathfull looks are death, their words are laws;
HUMOUR~~25:31~~	H220	That naught but blood, {death} the same may expiate.
HUMOUR30:17	H409	When death doth seize the man, your stock is lost,
AGES36:12	H36	But as he went, death waited at his heeles.
AGES37:38	H100	I gave no hand, nor vote, for death, or life:
AGES38:3	H106	My stroks did cause no death {blood}, nor wounds, nor {or}
AGES38:28	H131	For sin brings sorrow, sicknesse, death, and woe.
AGES40:35	H214	And gastly death oft threats me with her {his} power,
AGES40:41	H220	With sad affrights of death, doth menace me;
AGES46:1	H432	Shal both be broke, by wracking death so strong;
AGES46:3	H434	Sons, Nephews, leave, my death {farewell} for to deplore;
AGES46:24	H455	Triumph I shal, o're Sin, o're Death, o're Hel,
SEASONS~~46:35~~	H13	Fit to revive, the nummed earth from death.
MASSYR61:40	H345	Then by his death, releas'd, was *Israels* fears.
MASSYR66:5	H511	In mid'st of *Babel* now, til death he lyes,
MPERS72:5	~~H755~~	Complots the Princes death, in his green years,
MPERS73:2	H789	Yeelding {So yields} to death, that dreadfull Conquerer.
MPERS73:3	H790	Griefe for his brothers death, he did expresse,
MPERS~~79:13~~	H1038	The work-men put to death the bridge that made,
MPERS83:10	H1198	At last his Uncle, did his death conspire,
MPERS83:19	H1207	That the poor {Prince} innocent, to death must {did} go.
MPERS84:36	H1272	To wrong himselfe by death, he chose before:
MPERS86:5	H1321	His fathers death, did {so} put an end to's fear.
MPERS91:13	H1521	Whose courage nought but death could ever tame,
MGREC93:31	H1628	But death did terminate, those thoughts so high.
MGREC94:6	H1640	His kinsmen puts {put} to death without least {who gave no}
MGREC94:10	H1644	Now taste of death, (least they deserv't {deserv'd} in time)
MGREC95:18	H1697	Now newes, of *Memnons* death (the Kings Vice-roy)
MGREC~~100:34~~	H1918	And leaves {Whose death} her wofull Lord for to {full sadly did}
MGREC104:3	H2055	Chusing {And} rather {chose} an honorable death:
MGREC105:2	H2095	Yea, wounds the beasts (that drew him) unto death,
MGREC112:26	H2412	He death deserv'd, for this so high offence;
MGREC113:38	H2465	The next that {who} in untimely death had part,
MGREC114:10	H2478	That of *Parmenio's* death him plainly told.
MGREC114:34	H2504	Yea, and *Calisthines* to death he drew,
MGREC~~116:10~~	H2576	Till death inwrapt her in perpetual night.
MGREC~~124:10~~	H2916	By death by prison, or by banishment,
MGREC125:25	H2975	Bids chuse her death, such kindnesse she'l afford:
MGREC126:20	H3011	Expecting nothing, but of death to taste;
MGREC126:35	H3024	To Husbands death ('twas {'tis} thought) she gave consent,
MGREC126:36	H3025	The Authours death she did so much lament,
MGREC126:41	H3030	Her Husbands Wife, {wives} and Children, after's death
MGREC~~127:27~~	H3057	So *Eumenes* {(the prop)} of destiny {death} must taste.
MGREC128:1	H3074	The Mother of their King to death he'd put,
MGREC129:9	H3123	And put {So puts} to death, the mother and her son,
MGREC130:17	H3172	For straight way by command they'r put to death,
MGREC132:2	H3235	He, whom she gave his life, her death must {shall} give)

MGREC133:10 H3298 *Cassanders* Sons, soone after's death were slaine,
MGREC135:4 H3376 For 'twas not death, nor danger, she did dread,
MROMAN138:23 H3513 Then unto death unwillingly gives place.
MROMAN138:29 H3519 He after *Martius* death the Kingdome had,
SIDNEY~~150:24~~ H51 Made famous by thy fall {death}, much more's {more} the pitty;
SIDNEY150:25 H52 Ah, in his blooming prime, death pluckt this Rose,
SIDNEY150:31 H58 But yet impartiall Death {Fates} this Boone did give,
SIDNEY150:33 H60 And live it doth, in spight of death, through fame,
SIDNEY150:38 H65 In sad, sweet verse, thou didst his death deplore;
SIDNEY~~150:39~~ H67 His death present in sable to his wife.
DUBART155:3 H88 *The world rejoyc'd at's birth, at's death was sorry;*
DUBART155:7 H92 *To rescue him from death, Art had been able:*
DAVID~~159:10~~ H25 And in their deaths {death} was found no parting strife;
VANITY160:34 H44 Death and destruction, the fame hath heard,
VANITY160:41 H51 Nor death shall see, but are immortal made,
TDUDLEY165:18 H20 Who after death might make him falsly seem
TDUDLEY166:16 H58 Oft spake of death, and with a smiling chear,
TDUDLEY166:19 H61 Death as a Sickle hath him timely mown,
TDUDLEY166:33 H75 And parted more by death shal never be.
DDUDLEY167:21 H18 *Preparing still for death, till end of dayes:*
CONTEM168:28 H35 Thy heat from death and dulness doth revive:
CONTEM170:31 H101 His face like death, his heart with horror fraught,
SICKNES178:21 H4 lo here is fatal Death.
BIRTH179:33 H9 How soon, my Dear, death may my steps attend,
3LETTER183:30 H32 Let's still remain but one, till death divide.
MEDDM203:23 Hp283 malady that threatens him wth death, he will gladly entertaine
MEDDM207:33 Hp289 embleam of death, wch is their sleep (for so is death often
MEDDM207:34 Hp289 not only their death, but their graue, is liuely represented
MEDDM208:23 Hp290 but when death threatens and distresse lays hold vpon them
MYCHILD215:12 Hp240 latest, + being ignorant whether on my death bed I shall haue
MED223:18 Hp250 and let me bee no more afraid of Death, but even desire to
28AUG226:9 Hp254 & bequeath my Soul to thee and Death seem'd no terrible
THEART229:2 H4 From sicknes, death, + pain.
HANNA230:13 H6 When death did seem ev'n to approach

DEATH'S (1) [poss.]
AGES41:11 ~~H230~~ Ceas'd by the gripes of Serjeant Death's Arrests:

DEATH'S (1) [death is]
MGREC115:35 H2554 *Parmenio's* death's too fresh before his eyes;

DEATHS (1) [pl.]
DAVID159:10 H25 And in their deaths {death} was found no parting strife;

DEATHS (3) [poss.]
AGES44:15 H348 Now hath the power, Deaths Warfare, to discharge;
SICKNES179:3 H23 Then deaths arrest I shall count best,
BIRTH179:30 H6 But with deaths parting blow is sure to meet.

DEBT (3)
MPERS92:14 ~~H1572~~ Then Natures debt he paid, quite Issue-lesse.
MGREC120:37 H2774 Two years and more since, Natures debt he paid,
VERSES184:8 H12 Such is my debt, I may not say forgive,

DEBTOR (2)
HUMOUR33:17 H531 No debtor I, because 'tis {it's} paid else where;
TDUDLEY165:13 H15 Or who alive then I, a greater debtor?

DECAY (11)
MASSYR57:23 ~~H170~~ Until that potent Empire did decay.
MASSYR66:8 H514 The Towers, and Palaces, brought to decay;
MPERS81:4 H1112 He seeing {finding} all thus tend unto {to his} decay,
MGREC110:35 H2339 But doubting, wearing Time would {might} these decay,
DIALOG148:1 H266 Then High Commissions shall fall to decay,
DAVID159:1 H16 For the mighty ones did soone decay,
DAVID159:27 H42 How are the mighty falne into decay,
VANITY160:36 H46 It brings to honour, which shall not {ne're} decay,
MEDDM207:18 Hp289 that we perceiue a decay, in their greennes for were earthly
PILGRIM210:21 H21 By age and paines brought to decay
MYSOUL225:1 H5 What tho: thy outward Man decay,
DECAYES (1)
11MAYA226:22 Hp255 shall flourish while my body decayes, and ye weaknes of this
DECEAS'D (1) [deceased]
MASSYR62:2 H347 *Tiglath* deceas'd, *Salmanasser* is next,
DECEASE (2)
MGREC123:18 H2882 *Antigonus* hearing of his decease,
DIALOG141:25 H24 If I decease, dost think thou shalt survive?
DECEASED (5) See also DECEAS'D
TDUDLEY165:3 H4-5 *Who deceased,* July 31, 1653. *and of his Age,* 77.
DDUDLEY167:8 H4-5 *Who deceased* Decemb. 27. 1643. *and of her age,* 61.
ELIZB186:32 H3-4 *Bradstreet, who deceased August, 1665*
ANNEB187:14 H3-4 *Who deceased* June 20. 1669. *being three years and*
MERCY188:18 H2-4 *Mrs. Mercy Bradstreet, who deceased* Sept. 6.
DECEIT (1)
VANITY160:39 H49 And truly beautifies without deceit.
DECEITFULL (2)
MEDDM208:18 Hp290 Well doth the Apostle call riches deceitfull riches, and they
MEDDM208:19 Hp290 be compared to deceitfull friends who speak faire and promise
DECEITS (1)
MGREC123:9 H2871 'Gainst him, that all deceits could scan, and try:
DECEIV'D (2) [deceived]
MPERS89:1 H1435 But was deceiv'd; to it they make amain,
MROMAN136:27 H3441 Thus he deceiv'd his Neece, she might not know
DECEIVE (1)
HUMOUR29:41 H392 But's not thy {thine} ignorance shal thus deceive me.
DECEIVED (1) See also DECEIV'D
MYCHILD218:33 Hp244 it were possible ye very elect should bee deceived. Behold
DECEIVES (1)
ELEMEN16:22 H345 Which pitty moves, and oft deceives the wise.
DECEMB. (1) [december]
DDUDLEY167:8 H4-5 *Who deceased* Decemb. 27. 1643. *and of her age,* 61.
DECEMBER (2)
SEASONS47:27 H43 Nor-west {North-west} cold, {wind} of fierce *December.*
SEASONS52:18 H233 *December* is the {my} first, and now the Sun
DECIDE (3)
MPERS81:38 ~~H1143~~ But all their controversies to decide,
MPERS~~82:2~~ H1149 Where both their Controversies they'l decide;
DIALOG146:9 H197 But could the field alone this cause {strife} decide,

DECK (1)
DUBART154:19 H64 The Oaken garland ought to deck their browes,
DECKED (1)
CONTEM169:15 H56 That nature had, thus decked liberally:
DECKT (1)
FATHER5:4 H5 Of your four sisters, deckt {cloth'd} in black & white /four parts
DECLAR'D (1) [declared]
VANITY160:35 H45 But where, and what it is, from heaven's declar'd,
DECLARATION (1)
MGREC127:40 H3070 Sends forth his declaration from a {declarations near and}
DECLARATIONS (1)
MGREC~~127:40~~ H3070 Sends forth his declaration from a {declarations near and}
DECLARE (11)
ELEMEN8:8 ~~H6~~ For to declare, themselves they all ingage;
ELEMEN8:35 ~~H33~~ Come first ye Artists, and declare your minde.
ELEMEN~~8:35~~ H33 All sorts of Artists, here declare your mind,
HUMOUR30:16 H408 Yet time and age, shal soon declare it mine.
AGES37:7 H69 Her nine months weary burden not declare.
AGES39:5 H148 Declare some greater riches are within;
MPERS89:11 H1445 *Greeks* unto their Country-men {own Country should} declare,
MGREC106:20 H2154 To th' ignorant, her title may {will} declare.
MGREC109:30 H2289 To him doth *Alexander* thus declare,
MEDDM203:18 Hp283 that we may plainly declare that we seek a citty aboue and
MYCHILD215:18 Hp240 not studyed in this yov read to shew my skill, but to declare y^{e}
DECLARED See DECLAR'D
DECLARES (1)
MGREC128:16 H3089 For {And} he declares against his {the others} injuries;
DECLIN'D (1) [declined]
MPERS73:33 H818 The greater part, declin'd a Monarchy.
DECLINE (4)
SEASONS48:36 H87 Thy dayes stil lengthen, without least decline.
SEASONS49:10 H101 The reason why {Though he decline}, because his flames so
MEDDM196:17 Hp273 drought of the day, when he perceiues his sun apace to decline
MEDDM200:31 Hp279 their sap decline
DECLINED See DECLIN'D
DECLINEING (1)
MEDDM199:24 Hp278 that are eyes of a Republique, foretels a declineing State.
DECLINING (1)
SEASONS51:23 H199 And his declining heat is almost done.
DECREE (4)
MPERS69:34 H656 (A hard decree) to ashes he consume;
DUBART155:4 H89 *Art and Nature joyn'd, by heavens high decree,*
SICKNES179:4 H24 because it's thy decree;
1LETTER181:26 H24 Till natures sad decree shall call thee hence;
DECREED (5)
MASSYR66:32 ~~H538~~ For by the Heavens above it was decreed:
MASSYR~~66:32~~ H538 But for his pride so had the heavens decreed.
MGREC99:23 H1866 (For 'twas decreed, that Empire should be shaken)
MGREC113:23 H2450 It was decreed *Parmenio* should dye:
MGREC132:11 H3246 For blood which was decreed, that he should spill,

DECREPIT (1)
SEASONS51:27 H203 Decrepit age must also have its time;
DEDICATED (1)
SOREFIT222:1 H20 My life shall dedicated bee
DEDICATES (1)
MGREC133:32 H3322 His book of *Assurs* Monarchs dedicates,
DEED (11)
MPERS76:36 H934 Where an *Athenian* shew'd a valiant deed,
MPERS83:14 H1202 The {Then} *Artabanus* hirer of this deed,
MPERS83:17 H1205 To be the Authour of the deed {crime} was done,
MGREC108:14 H2230 Without {least} cause, given by {from} them, in deed, or word:
MGREC113:25 H2452 To doe this deed, they into *Media* send;
MGREC114:27 H2497 Of this unkingly deed, {act} doth *Seneca*
MGREC120:20 H2755 If not in word {stile}, in deed a Soveraigne.
MGREC129:8 H3122 Resolves to quit his fears by one deed done,
MGREC130:15 H3170 Her women are appointed to this deed,
SOREFIT222:2 H21 To praise in thought, in Deed, in Word.
11MAYB228:33 Hp259 testefye my thankfullnes not only in word, but in Deed, that my
DEEDS (9) [pl.]
HUMOUR24:34 H183 Whose glorious deeds in armes, the world can tel,
HUMOUR25:2 H191 Yet do abhorre, such timerarious deeds,
HUMOUR25:24 H213 Witnesse the execrable deeds thou'st done:
AGES39:40 H182 Martial deeds I love not, 'cause they're vertuous,
SEASONS50:34 H168 Yet then appears the worthy deeds he 'ath done:
MASSYR62:32 H377 Whose haughty heart is shewn in works, and deeds;
MPERS91:35 ~~H1549~~ Of whom no Record's extant of his deeds;
MPERS91:40 ~~H1554~~ Or else, perhaps the deeds of *Persian* Kings
MGREC134:4 H3337 And then {next} *Epiphanes,* whose wicked deeds,
DEEM (3) See also DEEME
MPERS84:27 H1263 Who for his wrong, he could not chuse but deem,
MPERS85:34 H1310 (For *Persian* Kings, did deem {then deem'd} themselves so
TDUDLEY165:19 H21 Such as in life, no man could justly deem.
DEEM'D (1) [deemed]
MPERS~~85:34~~ H1310 (For *Persian* Kings, did deem {then deem'd} themselves so
DEEME (1) [deem]
QELIZ155:30 H21 Which makes me deeme, my rudenesse is no wrong,
DEEMED See DEAM'D
DEEP (14)
ELEMEN16:12 ~~H335~~ Then Seas are deep, Mountains are never high.
ELEMEN~~16:12~~ H335 I soon can match them with my seas as deep.
MASSYR56:8 H114 About the wall, a ditch so deep and wide,
MASSYR57:31 H176 In deep oblivion, of acts bereft,
MASSYR65:13 H478 While *Babels* King thus deep ingaged stands;
MPERS80:4 H1071 Laid on more fiercely, their deep mortall blowes;
MPERS83:2 H1190 But for his deep complaints; and showres of tears,
MGREC~~98:9~~ H1811 With this reply, he was so sore {deep} enrag'd,
MGREC108:24 H2240 Imprinted deep in's legg, by Arrowes shot;
MGREC110:7 H2307 Within this spacious river, deep, and wide,
SIDNEY152:3 ~~H75~~ Who in his Deity, had so deep share,
CONTEM170:33 H103 When deep dispair, with wish of life hath fought,
3LETTER183:11 H13 Ev'n thus doe I, with many a deep sad groan

SON230:27 H10 The other sank low in the Deep.

DEEPE (1) [deep]

MEDDM198:5 Hp276 the still waters, if they stick in deepe mire and clay, and all his

DEEPER (1)

HUMOUR~~31:39~~ H472 With purple dye {deeper red}, to shew but {you} her disgrace.

DEEPEST (2)

MPERS89:35 H1469 And with all {the} Oathes, and deepest flattery,

MYCHILD215:11 Hp240 leaue to speak, and those espec. sink deepest wch are spoke

DEEPLY (3)

SEASONS49:20 H111 Whose fleece when purely {finely} spun, and deeply dy'd,

DUBART153:31 H35 Sits down in silence, deeply he admires:

CONTEM174:11 H211 Can make him deeply groan for that divine Translation.

DEER (2)

3LETTER182:36 H1 As loving Hind that (Hartless) wants her Deer,

3LETTER183:2 H4 Her dearest Deer, might answer ear or eye;

DEFAC'D (3) [defaced]

MASSYR56:15 H121 (Continuing, till *Xerxes* it defac'd)

MASSYR64:17 H441 The temple of rich ornaments defac'd,

MGREC~~120:36~~ H2773 Which eating time hath scarcely yet defac'd.

DEFACE (1)

AGES42:5 H263 To chear the good, and wicked to deface.

DEFACED See DEFAC'D

DEFAULT (1)

MPERS75:31 H888 Threats punishment to him, that through default

DEFECT (2)

PROLOG7:2 H17 Nor perfect beauty, where's a maine defect,

AGES41:20 H239 But more my {mine} age, the more is my defect.

DEFECTS (2) [pl.]

MPERS82:1 H1146 But that which helpt defects, and made them bold,

AUTHOR178:4 H14 I wash'd thy face, but more defects I saw,

DEFENCE (3)

AGES40:5 H186 Or stab the man, in's own defence, that's worse.

MGREC112:41 H2427 Faine would have spoke, and made his owne defence,

DIALOG146:39 H225 With (ventur'd lives) for truths defence that stand,

DEFEND (4)

HUMOUR29:29 H380 For {There} to defend my self, thy better part;

HUMOUR29:32 H383 It's no lesse glory to defend a town,

MPERS91:8 H1516 To defend, more then offend, he had {there was} need.

MGREC99:16 H1859 Where valiant *Betis,* doth defend {stoutly keeps} the town,

DEFENDANT (1)

MPERS70:13 H684 Not finding a defendant thereupon;

DEFENDED (2)

MGREC98:3 H1805 Protector of their Town; by whom defended,

MGREC99:22 H1865 But yet, this well defended town is {was} taken,

DEFENDS (1)

SEASONS48:8 H61 With wings, and beak, defends them from the gleads.

DEFENSIVE (1)

MPERS76:8 H906 He warr'd defensive, not offensive, more;

DEFIANCE (1)

SEASONS47:1 H17 And bids defiance to all tedious Winters:

DEFIE (2) [defy]
HUMOUR31:2 H435 Thy loathsome imputation I defie;
MGREC114:4 H2472 Then's Masters god-head, to defie, and wrong;
DEFILED (1)
MEDDM198:33 Hp277 it, the pure in heart shall se god, but the defiled in conscience
DEFORMED (1)
MEDDM202:10 Hp281 beauty full, and some extreamly deformed some so strong
DEFY See DEFIE
DEGENERATE (1)
MPERS80:7 H1074 O noble *Greeks,* how now, degenerate?
DEGENERATED (1)
MASSYR62:14 H359 This was that strange degenerated brood,
DEGREE (7)
ELEMEN10:1 H76 My Planets, of both Sexes, whose degree
HUMOUR21:7 H35 But she in greater, I in lesse degree;
HUMOUR21:21 H49 I make a man, a man i'th highest degree,
AGES45:9 H391 I've seen base {unworthy} men, advanc'd to great degree
MPERS69:14 H636 Whose Ancestors, were royal in degree;
MROMAN139:4 H3532 He ranks the people, into each degree,
MEDDM206:13 Hp287 some of a lesse degree, & others (and they indeed the most in
DEGREES (3)
AGES46:8 H439 From King to begger, all degrees shal finde
MEDDM200:2 Hp278 Wickednes comes to its height by degrees, He that dares say
MEDDM206:12 Hp287 degrees, euen in this life, some are Stars of the first
DEHORTS (1)
MPERS~~77:31~~ H972 The first deports, {dehorts} and layes before his eyes,
DEIECTED (1)
MEDDM199:17 Hp278 all, the most deiected
DEIFI'D (1) [deified]
MGREC112:38 H2424 By which his Majesty was deifi'd.
DEIGN See DAIGNE
DEITY (8) See also DIETY
MGREC106:40 H2174 His fained Deity, and foolish pride:
MGREC114:6 H2474 Like this, against his deity to kick:
MGREC114:22 H2492 Nor would adore him for a Deity:
MGREC115:15 H2524 The other was the greatest Deity.
MGREC118:20 H2667 Might be esteemed for a Deity;
SIDNEY152:3 ~~H75~~ Who in his Deity, had so deep share,
QELIZ155:21 H12 To say, thou wert a fleshly Deity:
CONTEM168:20 H28 No wonder, some made thee a Deity:
DEJECT (1)
FLESH175:29 H29 Which wearing time shall ne're deject.
DEJECTED See DEIECTED
DELECTABLE (1)
CONTEM167:31 H8 Rapt were my sences at this delectable view.
DELIBERATE (1)
MEDDM201:16 Hp280 a quick reception, and a deliberate cogitation argues a sound
DELICIOUS (2)
SEASONS50:30 H164 To shake his fruit, of most delicious tastes;
MGREC109:11 H2270 And with delicious meats, his Pallat choak'd,

DELIGHT (19)
AGES37:20 H82 My sillinesse did only take delight,
SEASONS49:18 H109 In the coole streames they labour with delight,
SEASONS49:33 H122 *Endimions, Diana's* dear delight;
MASSYR57:3 H150 A Prince wedded to ease, and to delight,
MPERS72:25 ~~H773~~ Having one son, in whom he did delight,
MPERS82:36 H1183 Where he had sometime gaz'd with great delight.
MGREC102:31 H2001 Here stood the Royall houses of delight,
MGREC102:36 H2006 Those beds of gold, and couches of delight,
MGREC117:8 H2615 And {But} as he took delight, much bloud to spill,
MGREC123:37 H2901 On whom ('twas thought) she set her chief delight;
CONTEM168:37 H43 Hail Creature, full of sweetness, beauty & delight.
CONTEM171:14 H118 In eating, drinking, sleeping, vain delight
CONTEM173:14 H181 Which rapt me so with wonder and delight,
CHILDRN184:35 H24 On whom I plac'd no small delight;
ANNEB187:17 H7 The Heavens have chang'd to sorrow my delight.
MEDDM207:14 Hp288 that notwthstanding we take great delight, for a season in
PILGRIM210:2 H2 Hugs wth delight his silent nest
28AUG225:30 Hp254 not afflict willingly, nor take delight in greiving ye children of
13MAY227:14 H23 To show my Duty wth delight
DELIGHTED (1)
FATHER5:3 H4 Deare Sir, of late delighted with the sight, /T D on the
DELIGHTS (3) [pl.]
SEASONS47:37 H49 All Plants, and Flowers, {set and sown} for all delights, and
MGREC112:6 H2392 Whose Sences all, were glutted with delights:
DAVID159:16 H31 And choyse delights, full of variety.
DELIUER (4) [deliver]
MEDDM204:4 Hp284 the paw of the Beare will deliuer mee from this vncircumscised
MEDDM204:5 Hp284 and he that hath deliuered mee saith paul, will deliuer me, god
30SEPT227:31 Hp257 ye like for yov if you trvst in him; And when he shall deliuer
11MAYB228:29 Hp259 his goodnes, and to hear my prayers, and to deliuer me out of
DELIUERANCES (1) [deliverances]
MEDDM204:2 Hp284 The remembrance of former deliuerances, is a great support in
DELIUERED (4) [delivered]
MEDDM196:34 Hp274 hath been deliuered vp by one traytor wthin, and that man w^{ch}
MEDDM204:3 Hp284 he that deliuered me, sath Dauid, from the paw of the Lion
MEDDM204:5 Hp284 and he that hath deliuered mee saith paul, will deliuer me, god
30SEPT227:30 Hp257 recourse to ye same God who hath heard + deliuered me,
DELIUERER (1) [deliverer]
MEDDM209:15 Hp291 to perpetuall bondage vnder them vnlesse the great deliuerer,
DELIVER (1) See also DELIUER
MGREC104:12 H2064 But to deliver him to's foes, intended.
DELIVE^{RC} (2) [deliverance]
FEVER220:21 H1 For Delive^{rc} from a feaver.
FAINT222:11 H1 Delive^{rc} from a fitt of Fainting
DELIVERANCES See DELIUERANCES
DELIVERED (1) See also DELIUERED
MGREC117:32 H2639 Was neare her time to be delivered;
DELIVERS (2)
MPERS75:11 H872 Delivers up the town, and all in it.
MGREC113:2 H2429 To his malicious foes delivers him,

DELPHOS (1)
MPERS80:38 H1105 Part of his Hoast to *Delphos* sent from thence,
DELUDE (3)
ELEMEN14:29 H271 And how your subtilty would men delude.
MROMAN137:34 H3485 So to delude the people he was bold:
MEDDM208:22 Hp290 wch miserably delude men and make them put great
DELUGE (3)
ELEMEN17:26 H390 *Ducalions* great deluge, with many moe;
MPERS92:39 H1597 One deluge came, and swept them all away;
DIALOG141:10 H9 What deluge of new woes thus over-whelme
DELVERS (1) [pl.]
ELEMEN13:36 H237 Again, when Delvers dare in hope of gold,
DEMAND (3)
MPERS69:37 ~~H659~~ Upon demand, his minde to *Cyrus* broke,
DIALOG143:25 H94 But yet, I answer not what you demand,
VERSES183:37 H4 Who can of right better demand the same?
DEMANDS (2)
MPERS~~69:37~~ H659 The Reason of those words *Cyrus* demands,
MPERS79:26 H1052 Of *Artabanus* he again demands,
DEMEAN'D (1) [demeaned]
MGREC97:15 H1776 T'ward them, demean'd himself like a Commander;
DEMEANOUR (1)
MGREC121:11 H2789 His sweet demeanour, and his courtesie,
DEMETRIUS (13)
MGREC128:29 H3102 *Demetrius* againe with *Ptolomy* did fight,
MGREC130:41 H3186 *Demetrius* is first, that so assumes, {the royal stile asum'd,}
MGREC131:2 H3192 To *Athens* then he {*Demetrius* thether} goes, is entertain'd,
MGREC131:7 H3197 *Demetrius* of *Ptolomy* doth gain;
MGREC131:18 H3210 *Demetrius* with his troops to *Athens* flies,
MGREC132:5 ~~H3238~~ The youngest by *Demetrius* kill'd in fight,
MGREC~~132:5~~ H3238 *Demetrius* is call'd in by th' youngest Son,
MGREC132:15 H3250 *Demetrius,* {thus} *Cassanders* Kingdomes gains,
MGREC~~132:20~~ H3262 *Demetrius* with so many troubles met,
MGREC133:14 H3302 His Son *Demetrius,* all *Cassanders* gaines,
MGREC133:16 H3304 *Demetrius* Son was call'd *Antigonus,*
MGREC133:17 H3305 And his againe, also {was nam'd} *Demetrius.*
MGREC133:22 H3310 *Demetrius* had *Philip* to his son,
DEMI-GODS (1) [pl.] See also DEMY GODS
HUMOUR21:28 H56 Have ye not heard of Worthies, Demi-gods?
DEMOLISH'D (1) [demolished]
ELEMEN11:2 H122 Old sacred *Zion,* I demolish'd thee;
DEMOLISHED (1)
MROMAN138:10 H3500 But now demolished, to make *Rome* great.
DEMOLISHES (1)
HUMOUR28:10 H322 At length demolishes the faberick,
DEMONISHED (1)
MASSYR60:7 H272 For he demonished that City great,
DEMOSTHENES (1)
MGREC120:4 H2735 *Demosthenes,* that sweet tongu'd oratour.
DEMY GODS (1) See also DEMI-GODS
MGREC~~115:15~~ H2534 Among the Demy Gods they might inthrone.

DEN (3)

AGES41:8 H228 And I in black oblivions den long {now} laid;

MPERS70:25 H696 And caus'd his foes in Lions den to dye.

DIALOG148:15 H280 And make his filthy den so desolate,

DENOUNC'D (1) [denounced]

MASSYR59:37 H261 When *Jonah* for their sins denounc'd such {those} woes;

DENS (1)

ELEMEN15:5 H287 The Woolves and savage Beasts, forsake their Dens.

DENY (2)

ELEMEN15:16 H298 That this is true, earth thou canst not deny;

MGREC119:8 H2698 But *Cleopatra,* this suitour did deny,

DENY'D (2) [denied]

MROMAN139:34 H3560 Though oft perswaded, I as oft deny'd,

DIALOG145:37 H186 This was deny'd, I need not say wherefore.

DEPLORE (4)

AGES40:29 H210 I want a {have no} heart {at} all this for to deplore.

AGES46:3 H434 Sons, Nephews, leave, my death {farewell} for to deplore;

DIALOG141:30 H29 And thus, alas, your state you much deplore,

SIDNEY150:38 H65 In sad, sweet verse, thou didst his death deplore;

DEPORTS (1)

MPERS77:31 H972 The first deports, {dehorts} and layes before his eyes,

DEPOS'D (2) [deposed]

AGES~~43:8~~ H304 Then Kings must be depos'd or put to flight,

DIALOG142:16 H45 Must *Edward* be depos'd, or is't the houre

DEPREST (1)

AGES39:27 H170 And by my mirth can raise the heart deprest;

DEPRIV'D (1) [deprived]

MGREC111:19 H2364 Depriv'd at once, the use of Saile, and Oare;

DEPRIVE (1)

MPERS90:5 ~~H1477~~ So to deprive them of all nourishment;

DEPRIVED See DEPRIV'D

DEPTH (3)

MPERS87:33 H1385 Six yards the {in} depth, and forty miles the length,

MPERS92:37 H1595 He fell to depth of greatest misery,

VANITY160:30 H40 The depth, and sea, hath {have} said its not in me,

DEPUTED (1)

MROMAN137:30 H3481 And Priests, and Flamines likewise he deputed;

DERCILLADAS (1)

MPERS90:26 H1493 They then *Dercilladas,* send with an Hoast,

DERIDE (4)

MASSYR67:37 H583 But he above, his doings did deride,

MGREC106:39 H2173 The ruder sort, did openly deride

MGREC112:37 H2423 He did the Oracle of *Iupiter* {*Jove*} deride,

MGREC116:37 H2603 This folly great *Augustus* did deride,

DERIDED (1)

MASSYR59:17 H241 That what *Arbaces* did, was but derided;

DERISION (1)

MPERS77:26 H967 Produced but derision, and laughter;

DERIVE (1)

HUMOUR26:15 H245 What is there living, which cannot derive

DESART (3) [desert, barren waste]
MPERS71:28 H742 But as they marched o're those desart sands,
MPERS76:3 H901 But in that Desart, 'mongst his barbarous foes,
MGREC113:39 H2466 Was one of more esteem, but lesse desart;
DESCENDED (3)
MPERS73:17 H804 Descended all, of *Achemenes* blood,
MPERS78:10 H991 To Princes of the *Persian* bloud descended,
MGREC98:4 H1806 And from whom also, lineally {he} descended:
DESCENDS (1)
CONTEM170:16 H88 On *Abels* gift the fire descends from Skies,
DESCENT (4)
HUMOUR20:15 H7 But first they wisely shew'd their high descent,
HUMOUR21:2 H30 To shew my great {high} descent, and pedigree,
MPERS69:4 H626 He in descent the seventh from *Arbaces.*
CONTEM171:3 H108 Their long descent, how nephews sons they saw,
DESCRIBE (1)
SEASONS~~48:34~~ H85 Let some describe thee better then can I.
DESERIBE (1) [describe]
MASSYR~~56:18~~ H124 This to discribe, {deseribe} in each particular,
DESERT (1) [barren waste] See also DESART
MASSYR61:29 H334 Acknowledging th' *Assyrians* high desert,
DESERT (2) [merit]
MGREC113:13 H2440 And told the world, that for desert {his guilt} he dyed.
MGREC116:27 H2593 Profusely bountifull, without desert,
ACK235:10 H10 Nor payd me after my desert
DESERTS (1) [pl., merit]
MGREC112:27 H2413 But for his Fathers great deserts, the King,
DESERV'D (3) [deserved]
MASSYR65:39 H504 His wel deserv'd, and fore-told misery;
MGREC~~94:10~~ H1644 Now taste of death, (least they deserv't {deserv'd} in time)
MGREC112:26 H2412 He death deserv'd, for this so high offence;
DESERV'T (1) [deserve it]
MGREC94:10 H1644 Now taste of death, (least they deserv't {deserv'd} in time)
DESERVE (2)
HUMOUR25:32 H221 To crosse thy wil, a challenge doth deserve.
MPERS75:15 H876 Who doth deserve a Statue made of gold;
DESERVED (3) See also DESERV'D
MASSYR55:32 ~~H98~~ And that her worth, deserved no such blame,
MASSYR58:6 H191 Kept ever close, fearing some dismal {his well deserved} fate;
MGREC115:13 H2522 To punish, where himself deserved blame:
DESERVES (1)
SEASONS48:18 H71 Whose praise deserves a page, from more then me.
DESIGNES (1) [designs]
AGES45:5 H389 I've seen designes at {for} *Ree,* and *Cades* {*Rochel*} crost,
DESIGNS (1) [pl.]
MPERS~~70:3~~ H674 Did to him still his chief designs commend.
DESIR'D (1) [desired]
HUMOUR20:26 H18 Pleading her selfe, was most of all desir'd;
DESIRE (20)
AGES36:2 H26 (As that fond age, doth most of al desire.)
AGES42:40 H296 Greater, then was the great'st, was my desire,

MASSYR58:20 H205 And the *Arabians,* to further his desire.
MPERS71:7 H723 But {Yet} to enlarge his state, had some desire;
MGREC98:39 H1841 These he may scape, and if he so desire,
MGREC103:28 H2039 He at a bold, base {proud} Strumpets, lewd desire;
MGREC129:37 H3151 Who slew the prince according to desire:
MROMAN140:2 H3565 But 'fore I could accomplish my desire,
DUBART154:9 H54 But wishes cann't accomplish my desire,
FLESH175:24 H24 What canst desire, but thou maist see
MEDDM203:12 Hp283 desire to make y^{t} his place of residence, but longs to put in at
SOREFIT222:5 H24 Nor ovght on Earth worthy Desire,
MED223:18 Hp250 and let me bee no more afraid of Death, but even desire to
28AUG226:2 Hp254 but joyfully? The Lord knowes I dare not desire that health
30SEPT227:19 Hp257 not in y^{t} sore manner somt. he hath. I desire not only willingly
30SEPT227:33 Hp257 him then before, This is the desire of y^{r} Loving mother. A. B.
11MAYB228:32 Hp259 to doe. Lord Thou y^{t} knowest All things know'st that I desire to
ACK235:20 H20 And so desire Ev'n all my Dayes.
REMB236:2 H17 What could I more desire?
HOUSE236:18 H10 Let no man know is my Desire.

DESIRED (2) See also DESIR'D
2SIMON195:6 Hp271 once desired me to leaue some thing for you in writeing that
MYCHILD217:24 Hp243 and seen no light, yet haue I desired to stay my self upon

DESIREING (1) [desiring]
MEDDM203:15 Hp283 but he must beware of desireing to make this the place of his

DESIRES (8)
MPERS91:26 ~~H1540~~ Who sooths him up, his owne desires are Lawes:
MGREC98:2 H1804 Desires to offer unto *Hercules,*
MGREC107:2 H2177 With those of worth, he still desires esteem,
MGREC119:21 H2711 (Which at this time well suited his desires)
MGREC120:21 H2758 Desires the King, to goe to *Macedon,*
DUBART153:30 H34 And {But} seeing utterance fayle his great desires,
SON231:28 H39 Particular, and how gratiovsly thov hast answered my Desires.
2HUSB232:25 H26 O Lord thov know'st my weak desires

DESIRING (2) See also DESIREING
MPERS75:4 H865 Desiring of the Prince to raise the siege,
MGREC126:26 H3017 Desiring Justice might be done for guilt;

DESIROUS (1)
MGREC127:38 H3068 *Antigonus,* desirous of the *Greeks,*

DESIST (1)
MGREC103:30 H2041 *Parmenio* wise, intreats him to desist,

DESOLATE (1)
DIALOG148:15 H280 And make his filthy den so desolate,

DESOLATION (2)
AGES45:16 H398 The desolation, of a goodly State.
MGREC134:8 ~~H3339~~ I'th' holy place, which caused desolation;

DESPAIR (2) See also DISPAIR, DISPAIRE
MGREC104:16 H2068 Sate down o'rewhelm'd, with sorrow, and despair,
MGREC112:40 H2426 Sunk in despair, without hope of releif;

DESPAIRED See DISPAIR'D

DESPERATE (2)
MPERS76:29 H927 *Athens* perceiving now their desperate state,
MGREC131:22 H3214 He sorely griev'd at this his desperate state,

DESPIGHT (3) [despite] See also DISPIGHT
PROLOG7:17 H30 For such despight they cast on female wits:
ELEMEN9:7 H41 And in despight the City keeps her owne,
MGREC128:9 H3082 And in despight of their two famous Kings,
DESPISE (4)
HUMOUR24:30 H179 Thy foolish {silly} provocations, I despise.
DIALOG148:24 H289 And him you shall adore, who now despise,
TDUDLEY166:11 H53 Such vanityes he justly did despise.
MYSOUL225:18 H22 Thy Glory I despise,
DESPITE See DESPIGHT, DISPIGHT
DESPOIL See DISPOYL
DESTINED (1)
MGREC132:10 H3245 His seed to be extirpt, was destined,
DESTINIES (1) [pl.]
AGES~~45:2~~ H380 Wailing his fate. & our own destinies.
DESTINY (7)
AGES45:12 ~~H394~~ Could once reverse, their shamefull destiny.
MASSYR59:29 H253 This his inevitable destiny;
MPERS88:27 H1420 Down *Cyrus* fals, and yeelds to destiny;
MGREC116:10 H2570 This Conquerour did yeeld to destiny;
MGREC125:20 H2968 King, and Queen, to *Amphipolis* doe fly, {seeing their destiny,}
MGREC127:27 H3057 So *Eumenes* {(the prop)} of destiny {death} must taste.
MGREC135:7 H3379 Which by the *Romans* had its destiny.
DESTITUTE (2)
MGREC100:20 H1904 And now of valour both were {are} destitute;
RESTOR230:6 H21 My Soul as destitute
DESTRESSES (1) [distresses]
MEDDM204:3 Hp284 destresses, he that deliuered me, sath Dauid, from the paw of
DESTROY (4)
MPERS82:19 H1166 Thus did the *Greeks* destroy, consume, disperce,
DIALOG147:21 H247 By force {As Duty binds,} expell, destroy, and tread them
MEDDM208:34 Hp290 the people, god sath to him Let me alone, that I may destroy
MEDDM209:8 Hp291 the Canaanites, not destroy them, but put them vnder tribute,
DESTROY'D (1) [destroyed]
DIALOG146:8 H196 Am now destroy'd, and slaughter'd by mine own,
DESTROYED (1)
MASSYR60:22 H287 Then did rebuild destroyed *Ninivie,*
DESTROYES (1) [destroys]
MPERS71:24 H738 The Temples {Their Temple} he destroyes not, for his zeal,
DESTROYS (1)
MEDDM198:28 Hp277 finger may disquiet the whole body, but an vlcer w^th^in destroys
DESTRUCTION (6)
ELEMEN19:21 H466 Men fear'd destruction epidemicall.
HUMOUR23:17 H127 But bodies wasting, and destruction.
MASSYR68:2 H588 Destruction to his Crown, to's Person end.
DIALOG143:22 H91 Destruction to a Land doth soone afford;
DIALOG144:23 H133 That cry'd, destruction to my wicked Land:
VANITY160:34 H44 Death and destruction, the fame hath heard,
DETAIN'D (1) [detained]
MPERS87:30 H1382 By reason, and by force, detain'd him still.

DETECTS (1)
MPERS90:21 H1488 The *Asiatiques,* cowardize detects; {victoryes}
DETEST (2)
MPERS81:22 H1130 But the *Athenians,* this peace detest,
MGREC129:22 H3136 *Cassander's* dead, the Princes {do} all detest,
DETESTATION (1)
MPERS79:6 H1028 Thou shame of Kings, of men the detestation,
DETESTING (1)
MGREC104:29 H2081 But some detesting, this his wicked fact,
DETRACTOR (1)
SIDNEY152:6 H77 To give to their detractor any quill.
DETRIMENT (1)
HUMOUR32:27 H501 (Although my name do suffer detriment)
DEUILS (1) [devils]
MEDDM202:9 Hp281 then men, some pious saints, some incarnate Deuils, some
DEVASTATION (1)
DIALOG146:16 H202 My plundered Townes, my houses devastation,
DEVILS See DEUILS
DEVIS'D (1) [devised]
MROMAN136:25 H3439 His Father was not *Mars,* as some devis'd,
DEVISE (1)
MPERS89:41 H1475 But *Tyssaphern* did what he could devise,
DEVISED (1) See also DEVIS'D
MPERS79:17 H1043 Was marching o're this interrupting Bay; {new devised way.}
DEVOTION (1)
MGREC123:34 H2898 Are now at the devotion of the Son,
DEVOURED (1)
MGREC135:31 H3403 Whose Iron teeth devoured every beast;
DEVOUTLY (1)
MGREC109:9 H2268 His liquors more devoutly in, for's sake.
DEW (3)
AGES43:16 ~~H308~~ Which others scatter, like the dew in *May.*
DAVID158:32 H12 O! *Gilbo* Mounts, let never pearled dew,
MEDDM201:21 Hp281 full of contrition, but it is not from any dew of grace wthin,
DEWES (1) [dews]
ELEMEN16:21 H344 Nor fruitfull dewes, nor drops {distil'd} from weeping eyes;
DEXTERITY (1)
DDUDLEY167:17 H14 *The which she ordered with dexterity.*
DFD (1) [did]
MPERS~~69:38~~ H663 His Treasures, pleasures, pomp and power dfd see,
DIABOLICAL (1)
HUMOUR25:35 H224 Nay; {No,} know 'tis pride, most diabolical.
DIABOLICALL (1)
MGREC100:9 H1893 He Diabolicall must needs remaine,
DIADEM (2)
MASSYR58:28 H211 Fear of his diadem, did force him fight:
MPERS92:11 H1569 Whose race long time had worn the Diadem,
DIADEMS (1) [pl.]
AGES38:1 H104 My quarrells, not for Diadems did rise;
DIALOGUE (1)
DIALOG141:1 H1 A dialogue between Old

DIAMETRICAL (1)
HUMOUR32:25 H499 Where opposition is diametrical:
DIAMONDS (1) [pl.]
FLESH177:3 H84 My Crown not Diamonds, Pearls, and gold,
DIANA'S (4) [poss.]
ELEMEN11:3 H123 So great *Diana's* Temple was by me.
SEASONS49:33 H122 *Endimions, Diana's* dear delight;
MGREC93:21 H1618 To th' ground was burnt, *Diana's* Temple high,
MGREC95:7 H1686 Where stood of late *Diana's,* wondrous Phane,
DICE (2)
HUMOUR21:34 H62 Unlesse to court, and claw, and {to} dice, and drink,
AGES40:24 H205 Cards, Dice, and Oaths, concomitant, I love;
DID (459) See also DFD
FATHER5:11 H12 Yet view thereof, did cause my thoughts to soare,
FATHER5:27 H28 Yours did contest, for Wealth, for Arts, for Age,
FATHER6:2 H36 Some thing {something} of all (though mean) I did intend,
FATHER6:6 H40 But if I did, I durst not send them you;
PROLOG6:27 H11 Foole, I doe grudge, the Muses did not part
PROLOG7:9 H23 By Art, he gladly found what he did seeke,
PROLOG7:26 H38 The *Greeks* did nought, but play the foole and lye.
ELEMEN8:5 H3 Fire, Aire, Earth, and Water, did all contest
ELEMEN8:10 H8 But enmity, this amity did breake:
ELEMEN8:13 H11 The quaking Earth did groan, the skie look't black,
ELEMEN8:15 H13 The sea did threat the heavens, the heavens the earth,
ELEMEN8:22 H20 The worlds confusion it did seeme to threat;
ELEMEN8:25 H23 The others enmity: {difference,} being lesse, did cease
ELEMEN~~11:1~~ H119 My raging flame did make a mournful story,
ELEMEN11:5 H125 With neighbouring Townes I did consume to dust,
ELEMEN11:24 H144 And Mother Earth, of old, men did me call,
ELEMEN12:2 H162 But chiefly, 'cause the Muses there did dwell;
ELEMEN12:25 H185 No, though the fawning dog did urge me sore
ELEMEN~~14:4~~ H247 So did that Roman, far more stout then wise,
ELEMEN15:15 H297 If not, soon ends his life, as did his voyce.
ELEMEN16:26 H349 Did they but want my Ocean, and my Flood.
ELEMEN17:11 H375 Untill straight {proud} *Gibralter,* did make them twaine,
ELEMEN18:5 H409 And all the wealth, that ever earth did give,
ELEMEN18:8 H412 If my pure Aire, thy sonnes did not sustain.
ELEMEN19:2 H447 And what those Sages, did, or {either} spake, or writ,
ELEMEN19:20 H465 Of murrain, Cattle numberlesse did fall.
ELEMEN20:5 H487 I have said lesse, then did my sisters three;
HUMOUR20:25 H17 But Sanguine did disdaine, what she requir'd,
HUMOUR20:31 H23 Cold {Mild} flegme, did not contest for highest {chiefest} place,
HUMOUR24:16 H165 Did ever sober tongue, such language speak?
HUMOUR34:28 H583 Ne're did {Nor will} I heare {yield} that Choler was the witt'est;
AGES35:33 H19 His hobby striding, did not ride, but run,
AGES36:29 H53 But wise Old-age, did with all gravity,
AGES37:10 H72 With tears into this {the} world I did arrive;
AGES37:11 H73 My mother stil did waste, as I did thrive:
AGES37:11 H73 My mother stil did waste, as I did thrive:
AGES37:14 H76 With wayward cryes, I did disturbe her rest;
AGES37:19 H81 Did act al folly, that it could expresse.

AGES37:20	H82	My sillinesse did only take delight,
AGES37:21	H83	In that which riper age did scorn, and slight:
AGES37:25	H87	That its own worth, it did not know, nor mind.
AGES37:26	H88	This little house of flesh, did spacious count:
AGES37:27	H89	Through ignorance, all troubles did surmount.
AGES37:30	H92	How to be rich, or great, I did not carke;
AGES38:1	H104	My quarrells, not for Diadems did rise;
AGES38:3	H106	My stroks did cause no death {blood}, nor wounds, nor {or}
AGES38:4	H107	My little wrath did cease {end} soon as my wars.
AGES38:5	H108	My duel was no challenge, nor did seek.
AGES38:8	H111	Nor evidence for land, {lands} did me perplex.
AGES38:12	H115	Nor yet on future things did place {set} my hope.
AGES38:31	H134	What gripes of wind, mine infancy did pain?
AGES42:8	H266	Was I a pastor, I my flock did feed:
AGES42:12	H270	If a Souldier {I}, with speed I did obey,
AGES42:19	H277	Did toile, did broile, oppress'd, did steal and lye.
AGES42:19	H277	Did toile, did broile, oppress'd, did steal and lye.
AGES42:19	H277	Did toile, did broile, oppress'd, did steal and lye.
AGES42:26	H284	The early Cock, did summon but in vaine,
AGES42:36	H292	To greater things, I never did aspire,
AGES42:41	H297	And greater stil, did {and thirst for honour,} set my heart on
AGES43:6	H301	That did oppose me, to my longed bay:
AGES44:33	H366	That but for shrubs they did themselves account;
SEASONS~~48:38~~	H89	When Spring had done, then {the} Summer must {did} begin,
SEASONS49:1	H92	As Spring did aire, blood, youth in's equipage.
SEASONS~~52:39~~	H256	Where first it did begin, in th' end its found.
MASSYR53:16	H6	Man did not {proudly} strive for Soveraignty,
MASSYR53:30	H20	By him, to Cities eminent did rise;
MASSYR53:32	H22	Whom succeeding times a god did call:
MASSYR54:5	H32	Titles divine, he to himself did take,
MASSYR54:6	H33	Alive, and dead, a god they did him make;
MASSYR54:28	H55	This Tyrant did his neighbours all oppresse,
MASSYR54:31	H58	By force, {and fraud} his tributary, he did {under Tribute} bring.
MASSYR54:32	H59	The *Median* country, he did also gain,
MASSYR54:37	H64	And all the greater *Asia* did subdue;
MASSYR54:38	H65	*Semiramis* from *Menon* he did take,
MASSYR54:39	H66	Then drown himself, did *Menon,* for her sake;
MASSYR55:22	H88	Taking a towne, such valour she did show,
MASSYR55:23	H89	That *Ninus* of her, amorous soon did grow;
MASSYR55:26	H92	She flourishing with *Ninus,* long did reigne;
MASSYR56:9	H115	That like a river, long it did abide.
MASSYR56:12	H118	But {And} that which did, all cost, and art excell,
MASSYR56:16	H122	Whose stately top, beyond {above} the clouds did rise;
MASSYR56:26	H132	Her Army of four Millions did consist,
MASSYR56:33	H139	The rest *Staurobates* in fight did slay.
MASSYR57:12	H159	What then he did, of worth, can no man tel,
MASSYR57:15	H162	'Gainst whom his trained Bands *Abram* did bring.
MASSYR57:20	~~H167~~	Each wronged Prince, or childe that did remain,
MASSYR57:23	~~H170~~	Until that potent Empire did decay.
MASSYR57:27	~~H172~~	Did then incite, them to regain their own.
MASSYR57:28	H173	What e're he was, they {or} did, or how it fel,

MASSYR57:35	H180	May feign as many acts, as he did names;
MASSYR58:3	H188	Did wear their garb, their gestures imitate,
MASSYR58:4	H189	And {in} their kind t' excel did emulate.
MASSYR~~58:8~~	H193	His master like a Strumpet chanc'd to {clad did} spy,
MASSYR58:12	H197	Who sick of his disease, he soone did finde.
MASSYR58:27	H210	And though of wars, he did abhor the sight;
MASSYR58:28	H211	Fear of his diadem, did force him fight:
MASSYR58:30	H213	*Arbaces* courage he did sore {so} abate:
MASSYR59:15	H239	The wals, and gates, their course {hast} did terminate;
MASSYR59:17	H241	That what *Arbaces* did, was but derided;
MASSYR59:22	H246	*Arbaces* marches in, the town did {he} take {takes},
MASSYR59:23	H247	For few, or none, did there {it seems} resistance make;
MASSYR59:28	H252	*Sardanapalus* did not seek to fly,
MASSYR59:38	H262	He did repent, therefore it {the threatning} was not done,
MASSYR59:41	H265	Ingeniously with each {all} did keep his word;
MASSYR60:14	H279	Who did this Monarchy begin anew.
MASSYR60:22	H287	Then did rebuild destroyed *Ninivie,*
MASSYR60:26	H291	But {For} though his Palace, did in ashes lye,
MASSYR60:32	H297	And from this heap did after Ages see,
MASSYR61:4	H309	What else he did, his Empire to advance,
MASSYR61:14	H319	And *Syria* t' obedience did subdue;
MASSYR61:16	H321	When *Resins* force his borders sore did mar.
MASSYR61:17	H322	And divers Cities, by strong hand did seize,
MASSYR62:4	H349	*Hoshea,* their last King, he did invade,
MASSYR62:7	H352	To *Ægypts* King, which did avail him nought;
MASSYR62:10	H355	And did the people, nobles, and their King
MASSYR62:13	H358	Did Justice now, by him, eradicate: [10 *years.*
MASSYR63:8	H393	And {As} *Belosus,* first, his {Soveraign} did unthrone,
MASSYR63:10	H395	After twelve years did *Essarhadon* dye,
MASSYR63:31	H418	Did neither *Homer, Hesiode, Virgil* sing;
MASSYR64:5	H429	This was that King of Kings, did what he pleas'd,
MASSYR64:21	H445	By great *Euphrates* did his Army fall,
MASSYR64:23	H447	Then into *Ægypt, Necho* did retire,
MASSYR64:31	H455	How in all Merchandise she did excell,
MASSYR66:31	H537	Which from no natural causes did proceed,
MASSYR67:8	H554	Among the Conquered Kings, that there did lye,
MASSYR67:13	H559	Prudence, and magnanimity, did lack
MASSYR67:19	H565	His Kingdome to *Belshazzar* did remain.
MASSYR67:35	H581	Did praise his gods of mettall, wood, and stone,
MASSYR67:37	H583	But he above, his doings did deride,
MASSYR67:40	H586	The fingers of his {a} hand-writing did spy.
MASSYR68:25	H611	And did one thing worthy a King (though late)
MASSYR68:28	H614	Who soone did terminate his Life, and Crown:
MASSYR68:29	H615	With him did end the race of *Baladan,*
MPERS69:2	H624	Whom Lady *Mandana* did to him bring;
MPERS69:23	H645	And the ambiguous Oracle did trust,
MPERS69:36	H658	He *Solon, Solon, Solon,* thrice did cry.
MPERS~~70:3~~	H674	Did to him still his chief designs commend.
MPERS~~70:41~~	H712	With honours great, did celebrate his fame.
MPERS71:3	~~H715~~	Some thirty years this potent Prince did reign,
MPERS71:4	~~H716~~	Unto *Cambyses* then, all did remain.

MPERS~~71:4~~ H716 But eight whilst *Babylon*, he did retain:
MPERS~~71:4~~ H719 And with an Epitaph, himself did make,
MPERS72:12 H760 His woful fate with tears did so bemoane,
MPERS72:25 ~~H773~~ Having one son, in whom he did delight,
MPERS73:3 H790 Griefe for his brothers death, he did expresse,
MPERS73:5 H792 The Male line, of great *Cyrus* now did {had} end.
MPERS73:6 H793 The Female {to} many ages did extend,
MPERS73:7 H794 A *Babylon* in *Egypt* did he make.
MPERS74:31 ~~H854~~ Did win him loyalty, and all respect;
MPERS74:32 H855 Yet notwithstanding he did all so well,
MPERS75:21 H880 Thy falshood, not thy {craft more then} valour did prevaile;
MPERS75:26 H883 The temple to re-build, for that did rest
MPERS75:27 H884 Since *Cyrus* time, *Cambyses* did molest;
MPERS75:37 H894 Built on, and prosper'd, till their walls did {house they} close;
MPERS76:4 H902 Sharp wants, not swords, his vallour did oppose;
MPERS76:9 H907 The Salvages did laugh at his distresse,
MPERS77:12 H951 Thirty six years this royall {noble} Prince did reign,
MPERS77:13 H952 Unto {Then to} his eldest {second} Son, all did remain.
MPERS77:34 H975 What infamy to's honour did accrue.
MPERS79:8 H1030 First thing, *Xerxes* {he} did worthy {of} recount,
MPERS~~79:12~~ H1034 But winds, and waves those iron bands did break;
MPERS79:24 H1050 What after did ensue, had he fore-seen,
MPERS81:1 H1109 And many thousands of these {those} men did kil;
MPERS81:24 H1132 That whilst the Sun did run his endlesse course,
MPERS82:3 H1150 Ten dayes these Armies did each other face,
MPERS82:8 H1155 The signall of their victory doth {did} rise;
MPERS82:19 H1166 Thus did the *Greeks* destroy, consume, disperce,
MPERS82:20 H1167 That Army, which did fright the Universe;
MPERS82:34 H1181 The sorrow of his heart, did close his eye:
MPERS82:39 H1186 To see those breasts, where chastity did dwel,
MPERS83:5 H1193 To *Bactria* his houshold did remove.
MPERS83:8 H1196 Unto such height did grow his cruelty,
MPERS83:10 H1198 At last his Uncle, did his death conspire,
MPERS83:11 H1199 And for that end, his Eunuch he did hire.
MPERS~~83:19~~ H1207 That the poor {Prince} innocent, to death must {did} go.
MPERS83:23 H1211 Such Justice then, in *Persia* {*Persian* court} did remain, {reign.}
MPERS~~84:3~~ H1231 The royall wine, in golden cups doth {did} passe,
MPERS84:9 H1237 What *Hester* {*Esther*} was, and did, her story reed,
MPERS~~84:12~~ H1242 Did for the Jews commission large obtain,
MPERS~~84:12~~ H1244 His bounty did *Darius* far exceed.
MPERS84:13 H1249 Unto this King *Thymistocles* did flye.
MPERS84:14 H1250 When under Ostracisme he did lye.
MPERS84:15 H1251 For such ingratitude, did *Athens* show
MPERS84:16 H1252 This valiant Knight, whom they so much did owe;
MPERS84:23 H1259 His Grand-sires old disgrace, did vex him sore,
MPERS84:25 H1261 For punishment, their breach of oath did call,
MPERS84:35 H1271 Either to wrong, did wound his heart so sore,
MPERS85:1 H1277 'Rest of his time in peace he did remain;
MPERS85:13 H1289 That for such gracelesse wretches she did groan,
MPERS85:34 H1310 (For *Persian* Kings, did deem {then deem'd} themselves so
MPERS86:5 H1321 His fathers death, did {so} put an end to's fear.

MPERS88:11 H1404 That, more then multitudes, their hearts did awe:
MPERS88:14 H1407 But long under their fears, they did not stay,
MPERS88:16 H1409 Which did such courage to the *Grecians* bring,
MPERS89:27 H1461 Such terrour on the *Persians* then did fall,
MPERS89:41 H1475 But *Tyssaphern* did what he could devise,
MPERS~~90:1~~ H1476 To {Did} stop the way in this their enterprise;
MPERS90:15 ~~H1484~~ Unto the *Spartan* Admirall did sue,
MPERS90:22 H1489 The many victories themselves did gain,
MPERS~~90:39~~ H1506 Whom the old Queen did bear a mortal hate.
MPERS91:2 H1510 height, {*Spartan* State} which now apace doth {so fast did} rise;
MPERS~~91:25~~ H1539 But long in ease and pleasure did not lye,
MPERS~~91:28~~ H1542 What troubles in his house he did sustain,
MPERS~~92:1~~ H1555 Which in rebellion sixty years did stand:
MPERS92:9 H1567 What Acts he did, time hath not now left pend,
MPERS~~92:10~~ H1568 But as 'tis thought, {most suppose} in him had {did} *Cyrus* end:
MPERS92:16 ~~H1574~~ How this *Darius* did attain the Crown,
MPERS92:35 H1593 In *Alexanders* reign who did him quell,
MPERS93:2 H1599 Of all, did scarce his winding sheet retaine.
MPERS93:4 H1601 Him, to the grave, did Traytor *Bessus* send.
MGREC93:17 H1614 His Education, much to these {those} did adde.
MGREC6:23 H1620 Whose glory to the Earth, this Prince {king} did throw,
MGREC6:31 H1628 But death did terminate, those thoughts so high.
MGREC6:33 H1630 Which honour to his son, now did befall.
MGREC94:23 H1661 He offer'd, and for good successe did pray
MGREC95:3 H1682 Who in their backs did all their wounds receive.
MGREC95:4 H1683 This Victory did *Alexander* gain;
MGREC95:6 H1685 *Sardis,* then he, and *Ephesus,* did gaine,
MGREC95:17 H1696 Which who so did {doth}, must Lord of all remain,
MGREC95:20 H1699 For in that Peer, more valour did abide;
MGREC96:24 H1744 Then such a world of Wagons did appear,
MGREC96:28 H1748 And as much good she did, as any other.
MGREC98:11 H1813 And now, as *Babels* King did once before,
MGREC~~98:13~~ H1815 But far lesse cost, and time, he doth {did} expend,
MGREC99:12 H1855 To which, brave {proud} *Alexander* did {made} reply,
MGREC99:27 H1870 Who did the like to *Hector* (of more fame)
MGREC99:41 H1884 No future dangers he did ever dread.
MGREC100:2 H1886 Where happily in's wars he did succeed;
MGREC100:8 H1892 The Son of *Jupiter* did straight him make:
MGREC100:26 H1910 Of Horse, and Foot, this {his} Army did amount;
MGREC100:34 H1918 {Whose death} her wofull Lord for to {full sadly did} lament.
MGREC101:5 H1930 And offers all he did, and Kingdoms more;
MGREC101:8 H1933 And all those Countries, which (betwixt) did lye,
MGREC102:20 H1990 This City did abundantly abound;
MGREC103:2 H2013 With open Gates, the wealthy town did stand,
MGREC103:5 H2016 None like to this in riches did abound.
MGREC103:9 H2020 Which {That} did pertain unto the *Persian* Kings.
MGREC103:14 H2025 The share of *Alexander* did amount,
MGREC~~103:35~~ H2046 Those stately streets with raging flames doth {flame did} fil.
MGREC104:28 H2080 Great recompence, in's thoughts, he did propose;
MGREC105:10 H2103 His lost felicity did greive him sore,
MGREC105:15 H2108 Wearied with his long march, did water seek,

MGREC105:26 H2119 If not, because *Darius* thus did pray,
MGREC105:31 H2124 For all that {the} Kingly Grace he did expresse,
MGREC106:3 H2137 This said, his fainting breath did fleet away,
MGREC~~106:35~~ H2169 His manners, habit, gestures, now doth {all did} fashion,
MGREC106:39 H2173 The ruder sort, did openly deride
MGREC~~107:15~~ H2190 The wealth of many Cities doth {Kindomes did} consume:
MGREC~~107:23~~ H2198 The drought, and heat, their bodies much doth {sore did}
MGREC107:26 H2201 This {Which} more mortality to them did bring,
MGREC107:27 H2202 Then did {all} their wars, against the *Persian* King.
MGREC108:40 H2256 Which did his former Army {forces} much augment,
MGREC~~109:26~~ H2285 His Presents all, with thanks he doth {did} restore;
MGREC109:39 H2298 Did more his valour then his Crown envie;
MGREC110:4 H2304 And ninety Elephants for war did bring;
MGREC110:8 H2308 Did here, and there, Isles full of trees abide;
MGREC~~110:18~~ H2322 Did *Alexander* by his answers find:
MGREC111:21 H2366 Upon those Flats they did not long abide;
MGREC111:27 H2372 That of them all, the fourth did scarce remaine.
MGREC~~111:33~~ H2378 Much time in feasts, and ryoting doth {did} wast;
MGREC112:19 H2405 'Mongst those, that of his cruelty did taste,
MGREC112:21 H2407 Accus'd, because he did not certifie
MGREC112:30 H2416 Must suffer, not for what he did, but thought:
MGREC112:37 H2423 He did the Oracle of *Iupiter* {*Jove*} deride,
MGREC113:12 H2439 At last he did: So they were justified,
MGREC113:27 H2454 Thinking {Fearing} no harme, because he none did owe {doe},
MGREC114:15 H2485 This pot companion he did more bemoan,
MGREC114:19 H2489 Who lov'd his Master more then did the rest,
MGREC114:20 H2490 As did appeare, in flattering him the least:
MGREC114:39 H2509 All this he did, who knows not to be true,
MGREC114:41 H2511 From *Macedon* his Empire did extend,
MGREC115:2 H2513 All this he did, yea, and much more, 'tis true,
MGREC~~115:15~~ H2529 Twelve thousand Talents also did intend,
MGREC~~115:15~~ H2531 What e're he did, or thought not so content,
MGREC115:22 H2541 And by her Letters did her Son incite,
MGREC116:8 H2568 That through excessive drinking he did dye.
MGREC116:10 H2570 This Conquerour did yeeld to destiny;
MGREC~~116:10~~ H2574 But pin d in grief till life did her forsake:
MGREC116:25 H2591 *Achille's* happinesse he did envy,
MGREC116:30 H2596 As oft his Acts throughout his reigne did {doth} shew:
MGREC116:35 H2601 This conquerour did oft lament ('tis sed)
MGREC116:37 H2603 This folly great *Augustus* did deride,
MGREC117:9 H2616 So the same cup to his, did others fill.
MGREC117:13 H2620 The great Horn broke, the lesse did tytannize;
MGREC117:14 H2621 What troubles, and contentions did ensue,
MGREC117:24 H2631 Did harm himself, but never reacht his foes:
MGREC~~117:29~~ H2636 Great *Alexander* has left {did leave} issue none,
MGREC118:24 H2671 The *Egyptians,* his body did enbalme;
MGREC~~118:24~~ H2672 His countenance so lively did appear,
MGREC~~118:36~~ H2685 For their security did now provide
MGREC119:8 H2698 But *Cleopatra,* this suitour did deny,
MGREC119:29 H2719 (Which did his match with *Cleopatra* mar)
MGREC119:30 H2720 For fighting still, whilst there did hope remain,

MGREC119:40	H2730	After this {which} time, the *Greeks* did never more
MGREC120:13	H2748	Yet to regain them, how he did not know,
MGREC120:36	~~H2773~~	His sumptuous monument long time did stand;
MGREC120:39	H2776	Great love did *Ptolomy* by this act gain.
MGREC121:9	H2787	Did alienate the Souldiers from his side;
MGREC121:12	H2790	Did make his owne firme to his cause remaine,
MGREC121:13	H2791	And from the other, {side} daily some did gaine.
MGREC121:14	H2792	*Perdiccas* in his pride did ill intreat
MGREC121:30	H2812	Thus *Ptolomy* rich *Ægypt* did retaine,
MGREC121:33	H2815	*Antigonus* did enter *Asia,*
MGREC121:35	H2817	But he alone now {most} faithfull did abide:
MGREC121:38	H2820	Nor could *Craterus* (whom he much did love)
MGREC122:6	H2829	His stratagems, wherein he did excel,
MGREC122:7	H2830	His policies, how he did extricate
MGREC122:41	H2862	The Army with *Antigonus* did {doth} leave,
MGREC123:11	H2873	How neatly {finely} *Eumenes* did here excell,
MGREC~~123:15~~	H2879	To *Polisperchon,* then his place he gave, {did bequeath}
MGREC123:33	H2897	Or by his favour {favours} any way did grace, {had grac'd}
MGREC~~124:3~~	H2908	For this *Antigonus* needed {did need} no spurs,
MGREC124:7	~~H2912~~	*Polisperchon,* knowing he did relye
MGREC124:20	H2927	But to the last {all in vain} he faithfull did abide;
MGREC124:38	H2945	Did make him vow her servant to be seen.
MGREC125:13	H2961	Some Forces did procure, with her to joyne.
MGREC~~125:23~~	H2973	And to the Queen, these presents she doth {did} send;
MGREC126:11	H3002	Her Cousen of *Epire* did what he might,
MGREC126:36	H3025	The Authours death she did so much lament,
MGREC127:21	H3051	*Pencestas* did betray him by a wile,
MGREC127:26	H3056	But as that to a period did haste,
MGREC128:8	H3081	Which none e're did but those of royall fame;
MGREC128:20	H3093	And Lord o'th' City {royal} *Susha* did remain.
MGREC128:26	H3099	So *Syria* to *Ptolomy* did yeeld;
MGREC128:29	H3102	*Demetrius* againe with *Ptolomy* did fight,
MGREC128:34	H3107	Who at *Gaza* did th' like to him before.
MGREC128:35	H3108	*Antigonus* did much rejoyce his son,
MGREC~~128:40~~	H3113	That each shall {should} hold what he doth {did} now possesse,
MGREC129:11	H3125	But for one act she did, just was her end,
MGREC130:27	~~H3181~~	Who did erect their cruelty in guilt,
MGREC131:16	H3208	Nor to his son did there {e're} one foot remain,
MGREC131:17	H3209	Of those dominions {vast Kindgomes} he did sometimes gain,
MGREC131:31	H3223	He wittily his fathers mind did sound,
MGREC131:32	H3224	Who did no sooner understand the same,
MGREC131:40	H3232	The eld'st enrag'd did play the vipers part,
MGREC131:41	H3233	And with his Sword did pierce his mothers {run her through
MGREC~~132:6~~	H3240	But he a Kingdome more then's friend did eye,
MGREC132:13	H3248	*Jehu* in killing *Ahabs* house did well,
MGREC132:28	H3273	Did ne'r regain one foot in *Asia.*
MGREC132:41	H3288	Whilst with these hopes, in *Greece* he did remaine,
MGREC133:3	H3291	Who for rebellion unto him did fly,
MGREC133:11	H3299	So three Successors only did remaine;
MGREC~~133:24~~	H3314	Him with his Sons in Triumph lead did he,
MGREC133:25	~~H3315~~	Did take his rule, his sons, himself and all.

MGREC~~133:25~~ H3315 Such riches too As Rome did never see:

MGREC134:17 H3348 Of *Greece,* and *Syria* thus the rule did end,

MGREC~~134:20~~ H3351 Cal'd *Philadelphus,* next sat on {did possess} the throne,

MGREC134:23 H3354 The seventy two interpreters did seek,

MGREC134:30 H3361 And next to {after} him, did false *Lathurus* reigne,

MGREC~~135:1~~ H3373 Did by his Sword his life soon after send.

MGREC135:4 H3376 For 'twas not death, nor danger, she did dread,

MGREC135:12 H3384 The *Assyrian* Monarchy long time did stand,

MGREC135:14 H3386 The *Grecian,* them did utterly subdue,

MGREC135:24 H3396 The Stone out of the Mountaine then did rise,

MGREC135:29 H3401 The third a Leopard, which four wings did rear;

MGREC135:38 H3410 And how from small beginnings it did grow,

MROMAN136:24 H3438 Whom vestall *Rhea,* into {to} th' world did bring

MROMAN136:28 H3442 The double injury, he then did doe:

MROMAN136:31 H3445 A Citty faire did *Romulus* erect:

MROMAN137:21 H3472 Some faining say, to heav'n {to the Gods} he did ascend;

MROMAN137:39 H3490 Who Martiall Discipline in use did bring;

MROMAN~~138:1~~ H3491 War with the antient *Albans* he doth {did} wage,

MROMAN138:30 H3520 A hundred Senatours he more did adde;

MROMAN138:34 H3524 Much {Some} state, and glory, {splendor} did this *Priscus* adde:

MROMAN138:35 H3525 Thirty eight yeares (this Stranger borne) did reigne,

MROMAN139:7 H3535 To eighty thousand soules then did amount:

MROMAN139:8 H3536 Forty foure yeares did *Servius Tullius* reigne,

MROMAN~~139:14~~ H3542 *Sextus* his Son, doth {did} (most unworthily)

MROMAN139:32 H3558 With many moe discouragements did speak.

MROMAN139:37 H3563 And for the same, I hours not few did spend,

DIALOG143:6 H77 Whose tearing tusks did wound, and kill, and threat:

DIALOG143:8 H75 Their hands in Kindreds blood, whom they did foyle:

DIALOG143:35 H104 For Oathes, and Blasphemies did ever eare

DIALOG143:38 H107 What injuries did daily on them lye;

DIALOG143:39 H108 What false reports, which nick-names did they take,

DIALOG144:3 H113 Did ever Land prophannesse more expresse?

DIALOG144:19 H129 That with high hand I still did perpetrate;

DIALOG144:26 ~~H135~~ Their reverent cheeks, did beare the glorious markes

DIALOG144:30 H138 Their silent tongues to heaven did vengeance cry,

DIALOG146:36 H222 After dark Popery the day did clear,

DIALOG~~147:2~~ H228 Blest be thy Counties which do {who did} aid thee still

DIALOG148:8 H273 As did thine Ancestours in *Palestine,*

SIDNEY149:7 H6 When *England* did injoy her Halsion dayes,

SIDNEY149:11 H10 *Mars* and *Minerva* did in one agree,

SIDNEY149:13 H12 *Calliope* with *Terpsechor* did sing,

SIDNEY150:12 H37 Such were prejudicate, and did not look:

SIDNEY150:29 H56 Oh, who was neare thee, but did sore repine;

SIDNEY150:31 H58 But yet impartiall Death {Fates} this Boone did give,

SIDNEY150:41 ~~H69~~ I feare thou wert a Commet, did portend

SIDNEY~~151:20~~ H70 I shew, how thou {he} fame's path didst {paths did} tread,

SIDNEY151:32 ~~H75~~ Goodwill, did make my head-long pen to run,

SIDNEY152:9 ~~H79~~ That this contempt it did the more perplex,

DUBART153:7 H11 Did thaw my frozen hearts ingratitude;

DUBART153:40 H44 Sure liberall Nature, did with Art not small,

DUBART154:40 H85 Good will, not skill, did cause me bring my mite.

QELIZ155:28	H19	Thy clemency did yerst esteeme as much
QELIZ155:36	H27	The World's the Theater where she did act;
QELIZ156:15	H42	Since first the Sun did run, his ne'r runn'd race,
QELIZ156:21	H48	Did ever wealth in *England* so {more} abound?
QELIZ156:33	H60	The rude untamed *Irish* she did quell,
QELIZ156:39	H66	Her Sea-men through all straights the world did round,
QELIZ157:3	H71	To tell of halfe she did, or she could doe;
QELIZ157:5	H73	More infamie than fame she did procure;
QELIZ158:12	H121	*On neither tree did grow such Rose before,*
DAVID158:25	H5	Illustrious *Saul,* whose beauty did excell
DAVID158:27	H7	How did the mighty fall, and falling dye?
DAVID159:1	H16	For the mighty ones did soone decay,
DAVID159:8	H23	Did *Saul* with bloodlesse Sword turne back agen:
DAVID159:19	H34	O! how in battell did the mighty fall,
VANITY160:14	H24	Yet these, the wisest man of men did find,
TDUDLEY165:36	H38	Upon the earth he did not build his nest,
TDUDLEY166:11	H53	Such vanityes he justly did despise.
TDUDLEY166:12	H54	Nor wonder 'twas, low things ne'r much did move
TDUDLEY166:17	H59	He did exult his end was drawing near,
TDUDLEY167:2	H84	*The Good him lov'd, the bad did fear,*
TDUDLEY167:4	H86	*If some rejoyc'd, more did lament.*
DDUDLEY167:15	H12	*And as they did, so they reward did find:*
DDUDLEY167:15	H12	*And as they did, so they reward did find:*
DDUDLEY167:18	H15	*The publick meetings ever did frequent,*
CONTEM172:8	H144	Where gliding streams the Rocks did overwhelm;
CONTEM172:11	H147	Now thought the rivers did the trees excel,
CONTEM172:16	H151	I markt, nor crooks, nor rubs that there did lye
FLESH175:8	H8	The other Spirit, who did rear
FLESH176:15	H55	Then when I did what thou bad'st doe.
FLESH177:12	H93	Such as no Eye did e're behold,
BIRTH180:20	H30	Who with salt tears this last Farewel did take.
1LETTER181:12	H10	His warmth such frigid colds did cause to melt.
CHILDRN184:17	H6	Nor cost, nor labour did I spare,
CHILDRN184:26	H15	My second bird did take her flight,
CHILDRN184:28	H17	*Southward* they both their course did bend,
CHILDRN184:29	H18	And Seasons twain they there did spend:
CHILDRN185:33	H59	Long did I keep you soft and warm,
CHILDRN186:20	H87	That did what could be done for young,
MERCY189:4	H25	And then her sorrows all at once did go;
MERCY189:7	H28	E're nature would, it hither did arrive,
MERCY189:8	H29	No wonder it no longer did survive.
MEDDM197:11	Hp274	had no winter the spring would not be so pleasant, if we did not
MEDDM201:8	Hp280	I haue seen an end of all Sinning, what he did say, may be
MEDDM201:9	Hp280	sayd by many, but what he did not say, cannot (truly) be
MEDDM209:7	Hp291	christians do by their lusts and corruptions as the Isralits did
PILGRIM210:32	H32	it is the bed Christ did perfume
MYCHILD217:35	Hp243	how did know but they were feigned. That there is a God my
BYNIGHT220:7	H7	I sovght him whom my Soul did Love
BYNIGHT220:10	H10	In vain I did not seek or cry.
FEVER220:26	H6	My burning flesh in sweat did boyle
FEVER220:27	H7	My aking head did break,

SOREFIT222:3 H22 Thou know'st no life I did require
RESTOR229:23 H6 When heart did faint & Spirits quail
RESTOR230:1 H16 And wth his staffe did thee support
HANNA230:13 H6 When death did seem ev'n to approach
SON231:9 H21 When royall ones y^{t} Time did dye,
2HUSB232:20 H21 Thov knowest did submitt
REMB236:1 H16 What did I ask but thov gav'st?
HOUSE236:14 H6 For sorrow neer I did not look,
HOUSE236:19 H11 I starting vp ye light did spye,
HOUSE236:20 H12 And to my God my heart did cry
HOUSE236:34 H26 My sorrowing eyes aside did cast
HOUSE236:36 H28 Where oft I sate and long did lye,
HOUSE237:12 H42 And did thy wealth on earth abide,

DIDO (1)

QELIZ157:14 H82 *Dido* first Foundresse of proud *Carthage* walls,

DID'S (1) [didst] See also DI'ST

FAINT222:20 H10 My feblee Spirit thou did's reviue

DID'ST (10) [didst] See also DI'ST

HUMOUR29:11 H364 I'le flatter for a time, as thou did'st me,
MPERS78:30 H1011 But pitty 'twas, thine ayde that {thou} here did'st lend,
AUTHOR177:31 H3 Who after birth did'st by my side remain,
RESTOR229:22 H5 Then did'st thou rid me out,
HANNA230:11 H4 Bles't bee thy Name who did'st restore
SON230:25 H8 In raging stormes did'st safely keep
SON230:26 H9 Did'st that ship bring to quiet port,
SON230:28 H11 From Dangers great thou did'st him free
SON231:3 H15 In covntry strange thou did'st provide
SON231:12 H24 Without (all fraud) did'st sett him free

DIDST (20) See also DID'S, DID'ST, DI'ST

MGREC99:33 H1876 Why didst not heap up honour, and reward?
DIALOG144:10 H120 O *Jane,* why didst thou dye in flowring prime,
DIALOG148:32 H297 But if at all, thou didst not see't before.
SIDNEY150:21 H46 What famous feats thou didst, on *Flanders* coast,
SIDNEY150:38 H65 In sad, sweet verse, thou didst his death deplore;
SIDNEY150:39 ~~H67~~ Illustrious *Stella,* thou didst thine full well,
SIDNEY151:20 H70 I shew, how thou {he} fame's path didst {paths did} tread,
DUBART154:11 H56 O *France,* in him thou didst more glory gain,
QELIZ155:26 H17 Thou never didst, nor canst thou now disdaine,
DAVID~~159:22~~ H37 In places high, full low thou dost {didst} remaine;
FEVER220:25 H5 Then didst thou rid me out.
FEVER221:7 H22 Thou hear'dst, thy rod thou didst remove
SOREFIT221:24 H10 My wasted flesh thou didst restore
SOREFIT221:25 H11 My feeble loines didst gird wth strenght
FAINT222:21 H11 My Doubting thou didst chide
RESTOR229:27 H10 Distempers thou didst chase away.
RESTOR229:28 H11 Wth strenght didst him sustain.
HOURS234:24 H38 As thou didst once my Sonne.
HOUSE237:13 H43 Didst fix thy hope on mouldring dvst,
HOUSE237:14 H44 The arm of flesh didst make thy trvst?

DIE (4)

MGREC116:33 H2599 Still fearing that his Name might hap to die,

MGREC131:34 H3226 *Cassander* now must die, his race is run,
VANITY159:35 H7 No, they like beasts, and sonnes of men shall die,
CHILDRN186:1 H68 So happy may you live and die:

DIE'S (1) [dye is]
HUMOUR27:34 H305 This scarlet die's a badge of what's within,

DIED (1) See also DY'D
MGREC132:9 H3244 Yea {And} though *Cassander* died in his bed,

DIET (1)
SEASONS52:7 H222 This time warm cloaths, ful diet, and good fires,

DIETY (1) See also DEITY
ELEMEN10:2 H77 Poor Heathen judg'd worthy a Diety:

DIFFER (1)
MEDDM206:7 Hp287 and those starres also, to differ much one from the other,

DIFFERENCE (4)
ELEMEN~~8:25~~ H23 The others enmity: {difference,} being lesse, did cease
HUMOUR33:8 H522 Next difference {that} betwixt us twain doth lye,
SEASONS~~51:19~~ H194 Nor could that temp'rate Clime such difference make,
MASSYR~~60:39~~ H304 Which makes the world of differences {difference} so ful,

DIFFERENCES (3) [pl.]
HUMOUR24:4 H153 What differences the Sex, but only heat?
MASSYR60:39 H304 Which makes the world of differences {difference} so ful,
MPERS92:30 H1588 Yet in these {such} differences, we may behold; {be bold,}

DIFFERENT (1)
MEDDM196:28 Hp273 Diuerse children, haue their different natures, some are like

DIFFICULTIES (3) [pl.]
MPERS90:2 H1477 But when through difficulties still {all} they brake,
MGREC98:36 H1838 The dangers, difficulties, like to rise;
MGREC122:5 H2828 {To shew} The difficulties {dangers} *Eumenes* befell,

DIFFLUENT (1)
HUMOUR30:4 H396 What's diffluent, I do consolidate.

DIG (1)
ELEMEN13:4 H205 Ye greedy misers who do dig for gold;

DIGEST (3)
HUMOUR20:28 H20 The second, third, or last could not digest;
HUMOUR24:2 H151 Without my boiling heat cannot digest.
SEASONS52:6 H221 And solid'st meats, our stomachs can digest;

DIGG'D (1) [digged]
MGREC125:34 H2984 Digg'd up his brother dead, 'gainst natures right,

DIGHT (2)
SEASONS48:21 H74 The Meads with Cowslip, Hony-suckl's dight,
CONTEM168:4 H14 That hath this under world so richly dight:

DIGNIFI'D (2) [dignified]
SEASONS49:21 H112 With robes thereof, Kings have been dignifi'd.
CONTEM172:9 H145 A lonely place, with pleasures dignifi'd.

DIGNIFIE (1) [dignify]
MGREC106:33 H2167 With *Persian* Robes, himselfe doth dignifie,

DIGNIFIED (1) See also DIGNIFI'D
MASSYR53:33 H23 When thus with rule he had been dignified,

DIGNITY (9)
HUMOUR27:9 H280 So wil {shall} I give the dignity to you.
MASSYR68:7 H593 And highest dignity, next to the King,

MGREC101:3 H1928 Let them on him, that {this} dignity bestow:
MGREC105:28 H2121 Their lives enjoy, their crowns, and dignity,
MGREC106:24 H2158 And not beseeming such a dignity;
SIDNEY149:30 ~~H23~~ Put with an Epithet of dignity;
SIDNEY~~150:12~~ H39 Put with an Epithite of dignity,
DAVID159:3 H18 There had his dignity so sore a soyle,
MEDDM202:5 Hp281 out of the loynes of one Adam, some set in ye highest dignity,

DIGS (1)
SEASONS47:12 H28 Now digs, then sows, his hearbs, his flowers, and roots,

DILATE (2)
HUMOUR23:20 H130 But I am weary to dilate thy shame;
HUMOUR31:41 H474 Then cause her blush, while I dilate {relate} the same.

DILIGENCE (1)
MASSYR60:28 H293 From rubbish these, with diligence he rakes,

DIM (1) See also DIMNE
PROLOG6:23 H8 My obscure Verse,{Lines} shal not so dim their worth.

DIMLY (1)
HUMOUR27:32 H303 My vertues hid, i've let you dimly see;

DIMNE (1) [dim]
MEDDM199:23 Hp278 Dimne eyes, are the concomitants of old age, and short

DIP (1)
QELIZ157:29 H97 Must dip his Pen i'th' Heliconian Well;

DIRECT (1)
MEDDM202:25 Hp282 time, yet he affords so much light as may direct our way, that

DIRECTING (1)
MYCHILD218:2 Hp243 vpon ye Earth, ye p^{r}serving + directing of All to its proper

DIRECTS (1)
MGREC103:36 H2047 Now {The} to *Darius,* he directs his way,

DIRTY (1)
SEASONS49:19 H110 Rubbing their dirty coates, till they look white.

DISABLED (1)
DISTEMP179:19 H7 Then eyes lay dry, disabled to weep more;

DIS-ALLOW (1)
SIDNEY149:33 ~~H23~~ Let then, none dis-allow of these my straines,

DISALLOW (1)
SIDNEY~~150:12~~ H42 Then let none disallow of these my straines

DISAPOINTMENT (1) [disappointment]
MEDDM206:24 Hp287 for it, shall meet with miserable disapointment, going away

DISAPPOINTED (1)
AGES~~45:4~~ H383 But saw their horrid fact soon disappointed,

DISAPPOINTMENT (1) See also DISAPOINTMENT
ANNEB187:18 H8 How oft with disappointment have I met,

DISASTER (6)
MPERS88:28 H1421 His Host in chase, knowes not of his {this} disaster,
MGREC95:25 H1704 Goes {Runs} after too {two}, and leaves all to disaster.
MGREC113:15 H2442 Look on *Parmenio,* after this disaster,
MGREC~~132:20~~ H3264 Disaster on disaster him pursue,
DIALOG146:3 H191 But now I come to speak of my disaster,

DISCERN (1)
RESTOR230:4 H19 At last thou mig'st discern

DISCERN'D (2) [discerned]
HUMOUR35:12 H608 Nor be discern'd, here's water, earth, aire, fire,
MGREC116:20 H2586 Might to the last (when sober) be discern'd.
DISCHARGE (2)
AGES44:15 H348 Now hath the power, Deaths Warfare, to discharge;
VERSES184:10 H14 Such is my bond, none can discharge but I,
DISCIPLINE (5)
MPERS88:13 H1406 And all good discipline to be neglected.
MGREC102:24 H1994 And former Discipline begins to hate;
MROMAN137:39 H3490 Who Martiall Discipline in use did bring;
DIALOG147:36 H260 And discipline erected, so I trust,
MEDDM205:3 Hp285 of discipline goe often ouer them, before they bee fit soile, to
DISCLAIM'D (1) [disclaimed]
MGREC118:3 H2650 This choyse *Perdicas,* vehemently disclaim'd,
DISCLAIMES (1)
MGREC123:30 H2894 Slights his commands, his actions he disclaimes,
DISCLOSE (1)
DIALOG141:16 H15 Or must my forced tongue these griefes disclose?
DISCLOSES (1)
SEASONS48:15 H68 All flowers before the {with his} sun-beames now discloses,
DISCONTENT (2)
MPERS91:5 H1513 They to their discontent, receiving hire,
MEDDM207:16 Hp288 of discontent or feare, or greife that lyes at the root wch in
DISCORD (2)
FATHER5:26 H27 Their discord may {doth} appear, by these harsh rimes.
MPERS91:17 H1525 But let us leave these *Greeks,* to discord bent,
DISCOURAGEMENTS (1) [pl.]
MROMAN139:32 H3558 With many moe discouragements did speak.
DISCOURSE (2)
ELEMEN~~8:8~~ H6 In placide terms they thought now to discourse,
HUMOUR20:11 H3 The former foure, now ending their Discourse,
DISCOVERED (1)
MPERS79:41 H1067 But that a Fugative discovered,
DISCRETION (2)
HUMOUR31:7 ~~H440~~ Thou wants Philosophy, and yet discretion.
HUMOUR~~31:7~~ H440 So mean thou art in art as in discretion:
DISCRIBE (1) [describe] See also DESERIBE
MASSYR56:18 H124 This to discribe, {deseribe} in each particular,
DISCRY (2)
SIDNEY150:5 H30 Yet, {But} he's a beetle head, that cann't discry
3LETTER183:6 H8 His voice to hear, or person to discry.
DISCUSSE (1)
HUMOUR33:40 H554 This point for {now} to discusse longs not to me,
DISDAIN (1) See also DISDAINE
SIDNEY152:7 H78 With high disdain, they said they gave no more,
DISDAIN'D (1) [disdained]
MGREC101:32 H1957 But he disdain'd to steale a victorie,
DISDAINE (5) [disdain]
HUMOUR20:25 H17 But Sanguine did disdaine, what she requir'd,
MGREC97:34 H1795 His {This} Letter *Alexander* doth disdaine,
MROMAN136:34 H3448 For leaping o're the Walls {wall} with some disdaine;

MROMAN137:10 H3461 But all disdaine alliance then to make,
QELIZ155:26 H17 Thou never didst, nor canst thou now disdaine,

DISDAINED (1) See also DISDAIN'D
MASSYR58:9 H194 His manly heart disdained, in the least,

DISDAINES (1) [disdains]
MGREC124:29 H2936 *Euridice* this injury disdaines,

DISEASE (2)
MASSYR58:12 H197 Who sick of his disease, he soone did finde.
MGREC131:30 H3222 When his disease the skilfull Physician found,

DISEASED (1)
MEDDM207:31 Hp289 All weak and diseased bodys, haue hourly mementos of their

DISEASES (6) [pl.]
HUMOUR28:9 H321 Her languishing diseases, though not quick,
HUMOUR32:5 H479 Unto diseases not inclin'd as ye:
AGES41:5 H225 Too many's {many} my Diseases to recite,
AGES43:26 H321 Now in a word, what my diseases be.
AGES43:35 H330 Subject to all Diseases, {distempers} that's the truth,
MEDDM203:26 Hp283 skill to cure it, but when he findes his diseases to disrest him,

DIS-FIGURES (1)
MPERS74:39 H860 His manly face dis-figures, spares no bloud,

DISGRACE (9)
HUMOUR21:16 H44 Yet many times, unto my great disgrace,
HUMOUR24:13 H162 To vent my griefe, and wipe off my disgrace.
HUMOUR~~27:19~~ H290 Nor what you've said, doth argue my disgrace,
HUMOUR31:39 H472 With purple dye {deeper red}, to shew but {you} her disgrace.
AGES43:2 ~~H297~~ To run my hull upon disgrace I fear'd,
AGES44:26 H359 Sometimes in honour, sometimes in disgrace,
MPERS75:14 H875 Then thy disgrace, thine honour's manifold,
MPERS84:23 H1259 His Grand-sires old disgrace, did vex him sore,
MGREC135:5 H3377 But some disgrace, in triumph to be led.

DISGUIS'D (1) [disguised]
MROMAN136:26 H3440 But *Æmulus,* in Armour all disguis'd.

DISGUISED (1)
MPERS69:27 H649 Disguised *Cressus,* hop'd to scape i'th throng,

DISHONOUR (3)
MGREC103:32 H2043 His names {fames} dishonour, losse unto his State.
MGREC110:17 H2317 Nor was't dishonour, at the length to yeeld;
PILGRIM210:37 H37 In weaknes and dishonour sowne

DISLIKES (1)
MGREC120:19 H2754 But this again dislikes, and {he} would remain,

DISLOYALL (2)
MPERS84:33 H1269 Nor yet disloyall to his Prince would prove,
MGREC94:28 H1666 Stiles him disloyall servant, and no better;

DISLOYALTY (3)
MPERS~~91:26~~ H1540 His sons soer vext him by disloyalty.
MGREC104:33 H2085 *Bessus* gets knowledge, his disloyalty,
MGREC105:24 H2117 And not to pardon such disloyalty,

DISMAL (1)
MASSYR58:6 H191 Kept ever close, fearing some dismal {his well deserved} fate;

DISMANTLED (1)
DIALOG144:35 H143 I saw sad *Germanie's* dismantled walls.

DISMAY'D (2) [dismayed]
MPERS79:40 H1066 And all that Army, then dismay'd, had fled,
MPERS87:7 H1363 The King dismay'd, a mighty Hoast doth raise;
DISOBED[C]. (1) [disobedience]
MYCHILD215:25 Hp240 wayes, & what I knew was sinfull as lying, disobed[c]. to parents.
DISOBEDIENT (1)
MEDDM209:12 Hp291 slauery, so it is most certain that those that are disobedient
DISOBEY (1)
MGREC115:41 H2560 He shewes his grief, he's forc'd to disobey:
DISONANT (1)
HUMOUR23:5 H115 But a good head from these are disonant;
DISPAIR (1) [despair] See also DISPAIRE
CONTEM170:33 H103 When deep dispair, with wish of life hath fought,
DISPAIR'D (1) [despaired]
MPERS87:25 H1377 *Cyrus* dispair'd, a passage there to gain;
DISPAIRE (1) [despair] See also DISPAIR
MASSYR58:31 H214 That in dispaire, he left the field and fled:
DISPATCH (1)
MGREC113:17 H2444 Was to dispatch the Father, as the Son.
DISPENSATION (1)
MEDDM202:3 Hp281 dispensation of his gifts among the sons of men, betwixt whom
DISPENSATIONS (1) [pl.]
MEDDM200:18 Hp279 god proportion his dispensations according to the stature
DISPERCE (1)
MPERS82:19 H1166 Thus did the *Greeks* destroy, consume, disperce,
DISPERS'D (1) [dispersed]
MPERS89:7 H1441 The King with his dispers'd also incampt,
DISPERSED (1)
MPERS84:40 H1276 Again dispersed, his new levyed hoast.
DISPIGHT (1) [despite] See also DESPIGHT
MGREC104:26 H2078 In more dispight, the thrawled Prince to hold.
DISPLAC'D (1) [displaced]
MGREC122:33 H2854 He plac'd, displac'd, controld, rul'd, as he list,
DISPLAY (1)
MASSYR56:39 H145 A Dove within their Ensigne to display.
DISPLAY'DST (1)
DIALOG147:35 H259 That all shall joy that thou display'dst thy banner,
DISPLAYES (1)
MPERS88:40 H1433 At last, displayes his Ensigne on a Hil,
DISPLEAS'D (2) [displeased]
MGREC115:24 H2543 His doing so, no whit displeas'd the King,
DIALOG145:38 H187 The King displeas'd, at *York* himself absents,
DISPLEASENCE (1)
MEDDM208:9 Hp290 friends, though there should be no displeasence betweene
DISPLEASURE (2)
MYCHILD216:26 Hp242 somt. on my soul in Doubts & feares of Gods displeasure, and
FEVER220:31 H11 Of thy Displeasure sore
DISPOS'D (1) [disposed]
AGES35:24 H10 Vindicative, and quarelsome dispos'd.
DISPOTION (1) [disposition]
MEDDM205:1 Hp285 land) are of so tough and morose a dispotion that the plough

DISPOYL (1) [despoil]
SEASONS50:4 H138 The Medows of their burden {riches} to dispoyl;
DISPROPORTION (1)
MEDDM202:4 Hp281 vast a disproportion that they scarcly seem made of the same
DISPROV'D (2) [disproved]
HUMOUR27:31 H302 If this {you} can't be disprov'd {disprove}, then all I hold:
MGREC115:25 H2544 Though to his Mother he disprov'd the thing;
DISPROVE (1)
HUMOUR~~27:31~~ H302 If this {you} can't be disprov'd {disprove}, then all I hold:
DISPROVED See DISPROV'D
DISPUTE (4)
HUMOUR27:2 H273 Which without all dispute, is Cholers owne;
HUMOUR32:28 H502 What's slanderous, repel; doubtful, dispute;
QELIZ156:13 H40 But can you Doctors now this point dispute,
1SIMON188:9 H10 Such was his will, but why, let's not dispute,
DISQUIET (2)
MPERS85:14 H1290 Disquiet {Revolting} Egypt, 'gainst this King rebells,
MEDDM198:28 Hp277 A sore finger may disquiet the whole body, but an vlcer wthin
DISREST (1)
MEDDM203:26 Hp283 skill to cure it, but when he findes his diseases to disrest him,
DISSECT (1)
DIALOG141:17 H16 And must my selfe dissect my tatter'd state,
DISSEMBLE (1)
AGES39:9 H152 Then let not him, which {that} hath most craft dissemble;
DISSEMBLES (1)
SEASONS52:10 H225 And melancholy, which most of all dissembles.
DISSENTION (1)
MPERS91:11 H1519 Dissention in *Greece* continued {so} long,
DISSENTIONS (1) [pl.]
MEDDM198:29 Hp277 enemy wthout may disturb a Commonwealth, but dissentions
DISSEVER'D (1) [dissevered]
MPERS79:12 ~~H1034~~ But winds, and waves, these couples soon dissever'd,
DISSOLUTE (1)
MASSYR67:25 H571 His life so base, and dissolute, invites
DISSOLVED (2)
MED223:19 Hp250 bee dissolved and bee wth thee wch is best of All.
MYSOUL225:24 H28 'Till I dissolved bee.
DI'ST (1) [didst]
SON230:24 H7 Thou di'st p^{r}serve him as he went,
DISTANCE (1)
MEDDM208:7 Hp290 other meanes to extinguish them so distance of place together
DISTASTE (1)
AGES43:33 ~~H328~~ The Quinsie, and the Feavours, oft distaste me,
DISTEMPER (3)
HUMOUR29:37 H388 'Twere but a mad, irregular distemper;
DISTEMP179:13 H1 *Vpon some distemper of body.*
30SEPT227:18 Hp257 It pleased god to viset me wth my old Distemper of weaknes
DISTEMPERS (3) [pl.]
HUMOUR28:6 H318 With cold distempers, to pain every part;
AGES~~43:35~~ H330 Subject to all Diseases, {distempers} that's the truth,
RESTOR229:27 H10 Distempers thou didst chase away.

DISTIL'D (1) [distilled] See also DISTILL'D
ELEMEN~~16:21~~ H344 Nor fruitfull dewes, nor drops {distil'd} from weeping eyes;
DISTILL (1)
SIDNEY151:11 ~~H69~~ To wait till she, her influence distill,
DISTILL'D (2) [distilled] See also DISTIL'D
HUMOUR22:40 H109 To be distill'd a drop on every line!
SEASONS49:34 H127 This Month the Roses are distill'd in Glasses,
DISTRESS'D (1) [distressed]
MASSYR61:37 H342 Who stil implor'd his love, but was distress'd,
DISTRESSE (5) [distress]
MPERS76:9 H907 The Salvages did laugh at his distresse,
MEDDM208:23 Hp290 when death threatens and distresse lays hold vpon them they
SOREFIT221:16 H2 In my distresse I sovght ye Lord
30SEPT227:32 Hp257 yov out of distresse forget not to giue him thankes, but to walk
HOUSE236:21 H13 To strenghten me in my Distresse
DISTRESSED (2) See also DISTRESS'D
MGREC99:5 H1848 And the distressed King no way {whit} respects;
QELIZ156:27 H54 She frankly help'd *Franks* (brave) distressed King,
DISTRESSES (1) [pl.] See also DESTRESSES
MEDDM203:33 Hp284 men can vse great importunity when they are in distresses and
DISTREST (3)
AGES42:31 H287 But if I rest, the more distrest my mind.
MGREC107:22 H2197 But sore {much} distrest for water, in their march,
DAVID159:23 H38 Distrest I am, for thee, deare *Jonathan,*
DISTURB (2)
FLESH175:39 H39 Disturb no more my setled heart,
MEDDM198:29 Hp277 it, so an enemy wthout may disturb a Commonwealth, but
DISTURBE (2)
HUMOUR30:19 H411 You'l say, here none shal ere disturbe my right;
AGES37:14 H76 With wayward cryes, I did disturbe her rest;
DITCH (2)
MASSYR56:8 H114 About the wall, a ditch so deep and wide,
MPERS70:8 H679 To drain this ditch, he many sluces cut,
DIUERSE (1) [diverse] See also DIVERS
MEDDM196:28 Hp273 Diuerse children, haue their different natures, some are like
DIUINE (1) [divine]
MEDDM195:21 H0 Meditations Diuine
DIURNAL (1)
CONTEM168:31 H37 Thy swift Annual, and diurnal Course,
DIVE (4)
ELEMEN13:38 H239 While they thus in my {mine} intralls seem {love} to dive;
MPERS76:15 H913 Quoth he, like Frogs, in water we must dive;
CONTEM168:29 H36 And in the darksome womb of fruitful nature dive.
CONTEM173:3 H171 Then to the colder bottome streight they dive,
DIVELS (1) [devils] See also deuils
MEDDM208:30 Hp290 stayd the Course of the Sun raised the dead, cast out divels,
DIVERS (8) [diverse] See also DIUERSE
FATHER6:1 H35 How divers natures, make one unity.
ELEMEN10:20 H95 And influence if divers of those starres,
ELEMEN14:11 ~~H253~~ With divers moe, nay, into plants it creeps;
ELEMEN16:14 H337 My divers Fountaines and their strange effect;

ELEMEN19:15 H460 With divers moe, worke deadly consequence.
MASSYR61:17 H322 And divers Cities, by strong hand did seize,
MGREC123:6 H2868 With *Eumenes* he divers Battels fought,
MGREC127:18 H3048 In divers battels, he had good successe,

DIVERSE (1) See also DIUERSE, DIVERS
MYCHILD218:11 Hp244 Diverse who haue scornd + contemd it, hath it not been

DIVIDE (4)
MPERS79:37 H1063 That pleasant *Thessaly,* from *Greece* divide;
MGREC110:9 H2309 His Army *Alexander* doth divide,
MGREC117:10 H2617 Four of his Captains, all doe now divide,
3LETTER183:30 H32 Let's still remain but one, till death divide.

DIVIDED (2)
MASSYR64:36 H460 Divided from the maine, by channel great;
MGREC97:11 H1772 Divided at the *Macedonians* pleasure.

DIVIDES (1)
MGREC126:3 H2994 His Army he divides, sends part away,

DIVIDING (1)
ELEMEN12:8 H168 Dividing great *Armenia* from the least,

DIVINE (6) See also DIUINE
PROLOG7:24 H36 So 'mongst the rest, they plac'd the Arts divine:
ELEMEN10:25 H100 Of old, when Sacrifices were divine,
HUMOUR33:26 H540 That divine Essence, {Offspring} the immortal Soul,
MASSYR54:5 H32 Titles divine, he to himself did take,
MASSYR63:36 H423 But by the Prophets, Pen-men most Divine,
CONTEM174:11 H211 Can make him deeply groan for that divine Translation.

DIVINITY (2)
SIDNEY150:11 H36 Yea, and Divinity within thy {his} Book,
DUBART153:35 H39 Thy Saint-like minde in grave Divinity,

DIVOLVED (1)
MPERS92:12 H1570 But now's divolved, to another Stem.

DO (116) See also DOE, DO'T
FATHER5:14 H15 To do their homage unto yours most {full} glad,
FATHER5:28 H29 My first do shew, their good, and then their rage,
FATHER5:29 H30 My other foures, do intermixed tell
ELEMEN9:24 H58 Ye Silver-smiths, your ure I do refine,
ELEMEN9:37 H71 And birds do sing, to see his glittering Coach.
ELEMEN~~10:21~~ H96 When in conjunction with the sun, yet {do} more,
ELEMEN10:23 H98 The Summer ripening season I do claime;
ELEMEN~~11:1~~ H120 But maugre all, that I, or foes could do
ELEMEN12:40 H200 Which guides, when Sun, nor Moon, nor Stars do shine.
ELEMEN13:4 H205 Ye greedy misers who do dig for gold;
ELEMEN13:18 H219 How the Autumnal season I do sway;
ELEMEN13:40 H241 Ye affrighted wights, appall'd how do you shake
ELEMEN~~14:10~~ H252 Some kill outright, and some do stupifye:
ELEMEN15:9 H291 Do cease to flourish in this misery.
ELEMEN15:24 H306 Fishes so numberlesse I there do hold;
ELEMEN16:2 H325 Which *Spaines Americans,* do gladly hold.
ELEMEN16:25 H348 Alas; thy ships and oares could do no good
ELEMEN~~16:41~~ H364 The Farmer, and the Plowman both {Grasier do} complain
ELEMEN18:20 H424 And so's the notes which Nightingales do frame.
HUMOUR21:33 H61 That much wil talk, but little dares she do,

HUMOUR25:2 H191 Yet do abhorre, such timerarious deeds,
HUMOUR~~26:14~~ H244 Of greatest use, if reason do not erre:
HUMOUR26:21 H251 And if vital spirits do flow from thee,
HUMOUR26:37 H267 But i'le not force retorts, nor do thee wrong,
HUMOUR26:39 H269 Challenge not all, 'cause part we do allow,
HUMOUR26:40 H270 Thou know'st I've there to do, as wel as thou;
HUMOUR27:26 H297 Of all your qualities, I do partake,
HUMOUR28:39 H351 If modesty my worth do not conceale.
HUMOUR28:41 H353 As I to you, to me, do ye the same.
HUMOUR29:2 H355 He that with two assaylents hath to do,
HUMOUR29:6 H359 Though Choler rage, and raile, i'le not do so,
HUMOUR30:4 H396 What's diffluent, I do consolidate.
HUMOUR30:35 H427 Of al the rest, thou'st nothing there to do;
HUMOUR31:26 H459 Here, there, her restlesse thoughts do ever flye;
HUMOUR31:35 H468 But I by vertue, do acquire the same.
HUMOUR32:27 H501 (Although my name do suffer detriment)
HUMOUR~~33:15~~ H529 I do as much for thee another way:
HUMOUR~~33:37~~ H551 The spirits animal, from whence doth {hence do} slide,
HUMOUR33:38 H552 The five most noble Sences, here do dwel,
HUMOUR34:39 H594 And too much talk; both which, I do {here} confesse,
HUMOUR35:1 H597 Lest we too late, this rashnesse do repent,
AGES36:33 H57 To do as he, the rest {each one} ful soon assents,
AGES37:8 H70 To shew her bearing pangs {pains}, I should do wrong,
AGES37:39 H101 I'd nought to do, 'twixt Prince, {King} and peoples strife.
AGES38:24 H127 And fift Commandement do daily break.
AGES38:30 H133 Yet griefs, in my fraile flesh, I still do find.
AGES39:8 H151 For thus to do, we on this Stage assemble,
AGES39:15 H158 Nor ignorant {And so likewise} what they in Country do;
AGES39:21 H164 Nor wait til good advice {success} our hopes do crown;
AGES39:25 H168 So affable that I do {can} suit each mind;
AGES40:22 H203 Some young {new} *Adonis* I do strive to be,
AGES40:34 H213 Though dangers do attend me every houre,
AGES41:19 H238 Now age is more, more good ye do {may} expect;
AGES42:22 H280 Such scum, as Hedges, and High-wayes do yeeld,
AGES43:21 H316 And envy gnawes, if any do surmount.
AGES45:32 H422 But do awake, {waking glad to hear} at the cocks clanging
AGES46:16 H447 Corruption, my Father, I do call,
SEASONS47:15 H31 And all that seem'd as dead, afresh do live.
SEASONS~~47:21~~ H37 Now {Do} jump, and play, before their feeding Dams,
SEASONS49:14 H105 That if you do, remove {withdtaw} her burning store,
SEASONS50:7 H141 The Forks, and Rakes do follow them amain,
SEASONS51:9 H183 And Apples now their yellow sides do show;
SEASONS51:24 H200 The fruitful trees, all withered now do stand,
SEASONS52:36 H251 The Rivers now do {'gin to} ope, and {the} Snows do {to} melt,
SEASONS52:36 H251 The Rivers now do {'gin to} ope, and {the} Snows do {to} melt,
MASSYR62:15 H360 On whom, nor threats, nor mercies could do good;
MPERS~~81:41~~ H1145 rest had} Weapons, they had none would {do little} harme;
MGREC97:40 H1801 To gain his love, the *Tyrians* do intend,
MGREC103:7 H2018 Yet to compare with this, they might not do.
MGREC103:13 H2024 Yet after all, as stories do expresse,
MGREC~~120:29~~ H2766 He, and *Craterus,* both with him now {do} joyn,

MGREC~~125:21~~ H2969 To save their lives t' *Amphipolis* do fly;
MGREC~~129:22~~ H3136 *Cassander's* dead, the Princes {do} all detest,
MGREC130:39 H3184 These Captains now, the stile of Kings do take,
MGREC131:1 H3187 To do as he, {by his Example all} the rest full soon presumes,
MROMAN140:6 H3569 No more I'le do, sith I have suffer'd wrack,
MROMAN140:7 H3570 Although my Monarchies their legs do lack:
DIALOG~~142:25~~ H54 Or, doth {do} the *Scots* play false behind your back?
DIALOG145:12 H161 Not what you feel, but what you do expect.
DIALOG~~146:25~~ H211 For my relief now use thy utmost skill {do what there lyes in
DIALOG146:32 H218 Your griefs I pity much, but should do wrong {hope to see},
DIALOG147:2 H228 Blest be thy Counties which do {who did} aid thee still
DIALOG147:4 H230 Blest be thy Preachers, who do chear thee on,
DIALOG148:18 H283 (For then what is't, but English blades dare do)
DIALOG148:20 H285 And do to *Gog,* as thou hast done to *Rome.*
SIDNEY152:22 H91 His bones do lie interr'd in stately *Pauls.*
DUBART154:35 H80 Thus *Bartas* fame shall last while starres do stand,
VANITY160:18 H28 What is it then? to do as Stoicks tell,
TDUDLEY165:40 H42 Those titles loath'd, which some too much do love
CONTEM170:15 H87 Fruits of the Earth, and Fatlings each do bring,
CONTEM171:22 H125 If winter come, and greeness then do fade,
CONTEM172:23 H157 But hundred brooks in thy cleer waves do meet,
CONTEM173:5 H173 To see what trade they great ones there do drive,
FLESH176:9 H49 Whence my dear father I do love.
FLESH176:26 H66 How I do live, thou need'st not scoff,
FLESH176:30 H70 My thoughts do yield me more content
FLESH176:36 H76 Eternal substance I do see,
2LETTER182:10 H16 Or all the grass that in the Meads do stand,
2LETTER182:32 H38 Oppressed minds, abruptest tales do tell.
3LETTER183:16 H18 Her fellow lost, nor joy nor life do wish,
VERSES183:36 H3 If worth in me, or ought I do appear,
CHILDRN184:23 H12 Till he return, or I do end,
CHILDRN185:7 H33 Striving for more then to do well,
CHILDRN185:24 H50 Some untoward boy at them do fling.
ELIZB187:5 H13 By nature Trees do rot when they are grown.
ELIZB187:6 H14 And Plumbs and Apples throughly ripe do fall,
2SIMON195:4 Hp271 their imitation Children do natureally, rather follow the failings
MEDDM195:29 Hp272 Many can speak well, but few can do well. We are better
MEDDM197:9 Hp274 they do but hope for that wch is to Come
MEDDM199:6 Hp277 do not often fall till after threat'ning.
MEDDM203:4 Hp283 for what do we obtaine of all these things, but it is wth labour
MEDDM204:29 Hp285 comfortably it will help to quiet him, but if that will not do
MEDDM205:18 Hp286 who is greater then our Conscience will do it much more, but
MEDDM209:7 Hp291 Some christians do by their lusts and corruptions as the Isralits
MEDDM209:9 Hp291 that they could do (as they thought) wth lesse hazard and more
MYCHILD218:14 Hp244 + how ye world came to bee as wee see, Do wee not know y^{e}

DOCRETA (1)
MASSYR55:9 H75 Her Mother *Docreta,* a Curtezan;

DOCTORS (1) [pl.]
QELIZ156:13 H40 But can you Doctors now this point dispute,

DOCTRIN (1)
MEDDM201:28 Hp281 not only to bid them hold fast the form of sound Doctrin, but

DOE (78) [do]

PROLOG6:26	H10	Great *Bartas* sugar'd lines doe but read o're;
PROLOG6:27	H11	Foole, I doe grudge, the Muses did not part
PROLOG6:29	H13	A *Bartas* can, doe what a *Bartas* wil,
PROLOG7:11	H25	Art can doe much, but this maxime's most sure,
PROLOG7:18	H31	If what I doe prove well, it wo'nt advance,
PROLOG7:31	H42	Men can doe best, and Women know it well;
ELEMEN8:33	H31	What I can doe, well skill'd Mechanicks may,
ELEMEN9:5	H39	Without mine ayd, alas, what can they doe?
ELEMEN11:23	H143	In wealth and use I doe surpasse you all,
ELEMEN12:34	H194	Doe cure your patients, fill your purse with pence;
ELEMEN16:29	H352	Unlesse I ease his toyle, and doe transport,
ELEMEN17:37	H401	I doe suppose, you'l yeeld without controle;
ELEMEN18:13	H417	Nay, what are words, which doe reveale the mind?
HUMOUR21:27	H55	Then timerous Hares, whom Castles doe immure?
HUMOUR22:2	H71	She'l neither say, she wil, nor wil she doe:
MASSYR60:23	H288	A costly work, which none could doe but he,
MASSYR66:21	H527	Then *Put,* and *Lud,* doe at his mercy stand,
MPERS69:26	H648	Where all that doe {dare} resist, are slaughter'd down;
MPERS70:1	H672	(His Mothers Vnckle, stories doe evince:)
MPERS70:3	~~H674~~	And with the *Lidians,* had no more to doe.
MPERS70:40	~~H711~~	Where that proud Conquerour could doe no lesse,
MPERS78:31	H1012	At *Sardis,* in *Lidia,* these all doe meet,
MPERS79:5	H1027	Is this to doe like *Xerxes,* or a Prince?
MPERS80:33	H1100	And as a friend, warns him, what e're he doe,
MPERS90:14	~~H1484~~	The King afraid what further they might doe,
MGREC97:19	H1780	Commands, no man should doe them injury,
MGREC99:2	H1845	All those rich Kingdoms large, which {that} doe abide
MGREC109:3	H2260	Those that {Such as} doe not, both they, {them} and theirs, are
MGREC109:33	H2292	His Homage unto him {to himself} as Soveraigne doe.
MGREC110:22	H2326	But so to doe, his Souldiers had no will;
MGREC113:25	H2452	To doe this deed, they into *Media* send;
MGREC~~113:27~~	H2454	Thinking {Fearing} no harme, because he none did owe {doe},
MGREC116:9	H2569	The thirty third of's age doe all agree,
MGREC117:10	H2617	Four of his Captains, all doe now divide,
MGREC120:9	H2744	Whilst they in *Macedon* doe thus agree,
MGREC~~123:13~~	H2876	But while these Chieftains doe in Asia fight,
MGREC125:20	H2968	Then {The} King, and Queen, to *Amphipolis* doe fly, {seeing
MROMAN136:28	H3442	The double injury, he then did doe:
MROMAN138:2	H3492	The strife to end, six Brothers doe ingage;
DIALOG142:13	H42	Doe *Maud,* and *Stephen* for the Crown contend?
DIALOG142:14	H43	Doe Barons rise, and side against their King?
DIALOG142:23	H52	Pray, doe not {you} feare *Spaines* bragging Armado?
DIALOG144:22	H132	The Sermons yet upon record doe stand,
SIDNEY149:28	~~H23~~	What doe thy vertues then? Oh, honours crown!
DUBART153:10	H14	But barren I, my Daysey here doe bring,
DUBART153:12	H16	If Summer, or my Autumne age, doe yeeld
DUBART154:37	H82	But lest my {mine} ignorance should doe thee wrong,
DUBART154:39	H84	Ile leave thy praise, to those shall doe thee right,
QELIZ156:28	H55	The States united now her fame doe sing;
QELIZ156:29	H56	She their Protectrix was, they well doe know,

QELIZ156:32 H59 Nor men, nor coyne she spar'd, to doe them good;
QELIZ157:3 H71 To tell of halfe she did, or she could doe;
TDUDLEY165:9 H11 To whom I ought whatever I could doe:
FLESH175:40 H40 For I have vow'd (and so will doe)
FLESH176:15 H55 Then when I did what thou bad'st doe.
FLESH176:18 H58 Thy sinfull pleasures I doe hate,
FLESH176:20 H60 Thine honours doe, nor will I love;
FLESH176:28 H68 The hidden Manna I doe eat,
3LETTER183:11 H13 Ev'n thus doe I, with many a deep sad groan
MEDDM195:24 Hp272 There is no obiect that we see. no action that we doe, no good
MEDDM205:28 Hp286 life as we doe, but he that wth David, sets the lord alway in his
MYCHILD215:17 Hp240 now doe) by y^{t} yov may gain some spirit: Advantage by my
MYCHILD216:13 Hp241 and try me & doe me Good: and it was not altogether
SOREFIT222:9 H28 O gravnt I doe it in this state,
WHAT224:7 H7 On High my heart O doe thou raise
28AUG226:6 Hp254 Lord gravnt y^{t} while I live I may doe y^{t} service I am able in this
13MAY226:27 H3 And leaues the naked Trees doe dresse
13MAY227:13 H22 I studiovs am what I shall doe
30SEPT227:31 Hp257 will doe ye like for yov if you trvst in him; And when he shall
11MAYB228:32 Hp259 ought to doe. Lord Thou y^{t} knowest All things know'st that I
2HUSB232:21 H22 It was my Duty so to doe
HOURS233:31 H14 Where I doe kneel or walk.
HOURS234:2 H16 Whom I doe loue so well
HOURS234:7 H21 And when I know not what to doe
HOURS234:35 H49 To pay the vowes wch I doe owe
HOURS234:37 H51 Vnlesse thou help w^{t} can I doe
ACK235:18 H18 Whose p^{r}sence I so much doe lack.
HOUSE237:22 H52 By him who hath Enovgh to doe.

DOG (2)
ELEMEN10:3 H78 With {There's} *Orion* arm'd, attended by his dog,
ELEMEN12:25 H185 No, though the fawning dog did urge me sore

DOING (3)
AGES40:1 H182 But doing so, might seem magnanimous.
MGREC115:24 H2543 His doing so, no whit displeas'd the King,
SICKNES179:2 H22 I doing good may be.

DOINGS (2) [pl.]
MASSYR67:37 H583 But he above, his doings did deride,
MEDDM206:27 Hp288 All the works and doings of god are wonderfull, but none more

DOLEFUL (2)
2LETTER181:36 H6 The woful accents of my doleful sound,
3LETTER183:14 H16 With thousand doleful sighs & mournfull Cooes.

DOLOR (1)
HUMOUR23:2 H112 The Palsie, Gout, or Cramp, or some such dolor,

DOLPHIN (2)
ELEMEN10:12 H87 The Hidra, Dolphin, Boys, that waters {water} bear.
ELEMEN15:28 H310 The Dolphin (loving musique) *Arions* friend.

DOMINION (1)
MASSYR58:14 H199 Both, for their King, held their dominion,

DOMINIONS (3) [pl.]
MPERS86:7 H1323 His large Dominions left, to's eldest son.
MGREC131:17 H3209 Of those dominions {vast Kindgomes} he did sometimes gain,

MGREC~~134:2~~ H3334 Whose large Dominions after was made small,

DON (1)

QELIZ156:26 H53 *Don Anthony* in's right for {there} to install;

DON'T (2)

HUMOUR26:14 ~~H244~~ More useful then the rest, don't reason erre;
2LETTER181:35 H5 (And if the whirling of thy wheels don't drown'd)

DONE (87)

ELEMEN14:24 H266 Scarce Earth had done, but th' angry waters {water} mov'd;
ELEMEN18:18 H422 Which {That} tells afar, th' exployt which he {it} hath done.
ELEMEN18:36 H440 Which may be done, by holding down my vapour.
HUMOUR24:20 H169 Ile only shew the wrongs, thou'st done to me.
HUMOUR25:24 H213 Witnesse the execrable deeds thou'st done:
HUMOUR32:15 H489 I've done, pray Sister Flegme proceed in course,
AGES36:24 H48 This {Thus} writ about: *This out, then I am done.*
AGES37:17 H79 When wretched I (ungrate) {ingrate} had done the wrong.
AGES39:1 H144 I've done unto my elders I give way.
AGES41:17 H236 What they have done, the same was done by me,
AGES41:17 H236 What they have done, the same was done by me,
AGES42:4 H262 Yea justice I have done, was I in place;
AGES42:16 H274 Thus hath mine age (in all) sometimes done wel.
AGES44:19 H352 But what I have done wel, that is my prop;
AGES45:24 H414 We old men love to tell, what's done in youth.
AGES46:14 H445 My studies, labours, readings, all are done,
SEASONS48:38 H89 When Spring had done, then {the} Summer must {did} begin,
SEASONS49:6 H97 His progresse to the North; now's fully done,
SEASONS50:34 H168 Yet then appears the worthy deeds he 'ath done:
SEASONS51:23 H199 And his declining heat is almost done.
MASSYR55:11 H77 Adjudged to be drown'd, for what {th' crime} she'd done;
MASSYR59:38 H262 He did repent, therefore it {the threatning} was not done,
MASSYR~~63:28~~ H414 This King's less fam'd for all the acts he's done,
MPERS72:26 ~~H773~~ His cruell Master, for all service done,
MPERS72:33 H777 {wisht} his short reign long, till {past before} it was done.
MPERS~~72:37~~ H782 The people ignorant of what was done,
MPERS73:25 H810 But yet, 'fore this was done, much blood was shed,
MPERS75:5 H866 This violence was done him by his Leige;
MPERS83:17 H1205 To be the Authour of the deed {crime} was done,
MPERS83:33 H1221 Which had they kept, *Greece* had more nobly done,
MPERS83:37 H1225 Which done, a sumptuous feast; makes like a King
MPERS86:32 H1348 For what was done, seemed no whit offended.
MPERS91:30 ~~H1544~~ As all the mighty ones, have done, and must:
MPERS92:8 ~~H1566~~ So fell to him, which else it had not done:
MPERS~~92:17~~ H1575 (Complotter with him in the murther done)
MGREC94:5 H1639 This done, against all {both} right, and natures laws,
MGREC101:18 H1943 Which had he done (perhaps) his fame had {he'd} kept,
MGREC105:6 H2099 This done, they with their Hoast, soon speed away,
MGREC107:12 H2187 Which done, sets fire upon those costly {goodly} spoyls
MGREC112:15 H2401 Now, *Alexanders* conquests, all are done,
MGREC113:11 H2438 For to {He might} accuse himself, as they had done;
MGREC113:16 H2443 They knew not; wherefore, best now to be done,
MGREC113:30 H2457 This is *Parmenio,* which {who} so much had done,
MGREC114:13 H2483 Next day, he tore his face, for what he'd done,

MGREC114:16 H2486 Then all the wrong to brave *Parmenio* done.
MGREC115:27 H2546 He might well dye, though he had done no wrong;
MGREC116:39 H2605 He would have found enough for {there} to be done,
MGREC120:28 H2765 Goes to *Antipater,* and tels what's done;
MGREC~~122:37~~ H2858 When to his pleasure all things they had done,
MGREC123:35 H2899 Prest to accomplish what he would have done;
MGREC125:30 H2980 This done, the cruell Queen rests not content,
MGREC126:26 H3017 Desiring Justice might be done for guilt;
MGREC129:2 H3116 This touch'd *Cassander* sore, for what he'd done,
MGREC129:8 H3122 Resolves to quit his fears by one deed done,
MGREC129:18 H3132 And for that double fact which she had done,
MGREC129:26 H3140 When this foul tragedy was past, and done,
MGREC129:30 H3144 The *Greeks* touch'd with the murther done so {of} late,
MGREC130:25 H3180 Now blood was paid with blood, for what was done
MGREC~~132:28~~ H3275 Whose obsequies with wondrous pomp was done.
MGREC133:6 H3294 Thus with these Kingly Captaines have we done,
MGREC135:36 H3408 With these three Monarchies, now have I done,
MROMAN136:37 H3451 This City built, and Sacrifices done,
DIALOG144:8 H118 'Mongst all the cruelties which I have {by great ones} done,
DIALOG145:32 H181 This done, an Act they would have passed fain,
DIALOG145:35 H184 This must be done by Gospel, not by law.
DIALOG146:2 H190 Shews all was done, I'll therefore let it go.
DIALOG146:26 H212 And recompence me {that} good, for all my ill {I've done to
DIALOG148:17 H282 This done, with brandish'd swords, to *Turky* go,
DIALOG148:20 H285 And do to *Gog,* as thou hast done to *Rome.*
SIDNEY152:10 ~~H79~~ In being done by one of their own sex;
CHILDRN186:20 H87 That did what could be done for young,
MEDDM198:22 Hp276 done, but either that or something like it, hath been both done
MEDDM198:22 Hp276 but either that or something like it, hath been both done and
MEDDM208:29 Hp290 (almost) possible to be done, it can remoue mountaines (if
PILGRIM210:6 H6 his dangers past, and travailes done
MYCHILD217:23 Hp243 not enjoyed that felicity that somt. I haue done, But when I
MYCHILD219:7 Hp245 & imperfectly done, but if yov can pick any Benefitt out of it, It
BYNIGHT220:18 H16 Who freely hath done this for me,
MED223:14 Hp250 that God who hath done so much for me, should haue so little
MED223:16 Hp250 p^{r}fectly what he hath done for me, and then shall I bee able to
WHAT224:8 H8 For what thou'st done for me.
MYSOUL225:13 H17 Then shall I know what thov hast done
SAMUEL228:19 H20 Thy Will bee done, for that is best
HANNA230:15 H8 Gravnt shee rember w^{t} thov'st done
SON231:22 H34 Tho'st done for him, + so for me.
HOURS234:22 H36 As thou before ha'st done
HOUSE237:6 H36 Nor things recovnted done of old.

DOOM (2)
AGES40:32 H211 Remembring not the dreadful day of Doom,
DIALOG148:19 H284 And lay her wast, for so's the sacred doom,

DOOM'D (1) [doomed]
HUMOUR28:20 H332 It's doom'd by an irrevocable wil:

DOOME (4)
ELEMEN11:15 H135 And all therein at that great day of doome;
MPERS69:33 H655 *Cressus* thus known, it was great *Cyrus* doome,

MPERS72:1 ~~H753~~ And contemn them, woful is his doome.
MPERS84:8 H1236 By *Memucan's* advice, this {so} was the doome.

DOOMED See DOOM'D

DOOR (2)
AUTHOR178:15 H25 Which caus'd her thus to send thee out of door.
MEDDM197:14 Hp274 A low man, can goe vpright, vnder that door, wher a taller is

DOORES (2) [doors]
MASSYR58:1 H186 That palliardizing sot, that out of doores
MEDDM202:32 Hp282 The eyes and the eares are the inlets or doores of the soule,

DORIANS (1) [pl.]
MPERS78:18 H999 *Cipriots, Dorians,* and *Cilicians,*

DOROTHY (1)
DDUDLEY167:7 H3 *Mrs. Dorothy Dudley,*

DO'S (1) [does]
HUMOUR23:39 H149 Without my lively heat, do's ought thats flat.

DO'ST (8)
HUMOUR24:18 H167 Do'st know thy selfe so well, us so amisse?
HUMOUR26:5 H235 Nextly, the spirits thou do'st wholly claime,
HUMOUR26:29 H259 Then never boast of what thou do'st receive,
HUMOUR27:11 H282 But by what right, nor do'st, nor canst thou name;
HUMOUR27:13 ~~H284~~ Thou do'st unjustly claime, her property,
HUMOUR30:33 H425 But thou most grosly do'st mistake, to thinke
HUMOUR31:5 ~~H438~~ Thou do'st assume my name, wel be it just;
HOURS234:9 H23 My weaknes thou do'st know full well,

DOST (19)
HUMOUR23:14 H124 Where paine and sore obstructions, {obstruction} thou dost
HUMOUR26:11 H241 For th' natural, thou dost not much contest,
HUMOUR27:10 H281 Again, stomachs concoction thou dost claime,
HUMOUR30:9 H401 Thirdly, {Again} thou dost confine me to the spleen,
DIALOG141:19 H18 And thou a childe, a Limbe, and dost not feele
DIALOG141:25 H24 If I decease, dost think thou shalt survive?
DIALOG141:26 H25 Or by my wasting state, dost think to thrive?
DIALOG142:29 H58 Dost feele the smart, or feare the consequence?
DIALOG146:24 H210 Or any child-like love thou dost retain,
DAVID159:22 H37 In places high, full low thou dost {didst} remaine;
CONTEM173:24 H190 Reminds not what is past, nor whats to come dost fear.
CONTEM173:26 H191 The dawning morn with songs thou dost prevent,
FLESH175:16 H16 Dost dream of things beyond the Moon
FLESH175:17 H17 And dost thou hope to dwell there soon?
FLESH175:26 H26 Dost honour like? acquire the same,
FLESH175:30 H30 For riches dost thou long full sore?
AUTHOR178:11 H21 In Criticks hands, beware thou dost not come;
2LETTER182:15 H21 Tell him, the countless steps that thou dost trace,
2LETTER182:22 H28 O how they joy when thou dost light the skyes.

DO'T (2) [do it]
FATHER6:9 H43 These ragged lines, will do't, when they appear.
SIDNEY151:39 ~~H75~~ I leave't in brief, *Apollo* do't at large.

DOTE (1)
ELEMEN12:13 H173 Sweet *Parnassus,* I dote too much on thee,

DOTH (205)
FATHER~~5:26~~ H27 Their discord may {doth} appear, by these harsh rimes.

ELEMEN9:19 H53 Your shrinking limbs, which winters cold doth harme;
ELEMEN9:34 H68 How doth his warmth refresh thy frozen backs, {back}
ELEMEN12:30 H190 Send forth your well man'd ships, where sun doth rise.
ELEMEN13:15 H216 My cold, thy (fruitfull) heat, doth crave no lesse:
ELEMEN15:18 H300 Which by my fatting Nile, doth yeeld such store;
ELEMEN15:29 H311 The crafty {witty} Barbell, whose wit {craft} doth her commend;
ELEMEN15:31 H313 Thy silence of thy beasts, doth cause the same.
ELEMEN17:20 H384 Mine Ice doth glaze *Europs* big'st Rivers o're,
ELEMEN~~18:16~~ H420 What is't? but forced Aire which must {doth} rebound,
ELEMEN18:25 H429 When burning heat, doth cause you faint, I coole,
HUMOUR21:8 H36 We both once Masculines, the world doth know,
HUMOUR25:32 H221 To crosse thy wil, a challenge doth deserve.
HUMOUR~~27:19~~ H290 Nor what you've said, doth argue my disgrace,
HUMOUR28:3 H315 The body dryes, the minde sublime doth smother,
HUMOUR29:24 H375 Nature doth teach, to sheild the head from harm,
HUMOUR30:3 H395 What is too hot, my coldnesse doth abate;
HUMOUR30:7 H399 Those {Whose} cold dry heads, {head} more subtilly doth yeild,
HUMOUR30:17 H409 When death doth seize the man, your stock is lost,
HUMOUR31:32 H465 What Sanguine is, she doth not heed, nor care.
HUMOUR32:9 H483 My sicknesse cheifly in conceit doth lye,
HUMOUR33:7 H521 As at noon day to tel, the Sun doth shine.
HUMOUR33:8 H522 Next difference {that} betwixt us twain doth lye,
HUMOUR33:9 H523 Who doth possesse the Brain, or thou, or I;
HUMOUR33:13 H527 Thy heat doth much, I candidly confesse,
HUMOUR33:29 H543 Doth doubtlesse keep its mighty residence;
HUMOUR33:33 H547 Doth shew, hence flowes {flow} the power {pow'rs} which they
HUMOUR33:34 H548 Within this high built Cittadel doth lye,
HUMOUR33:36 H550 The faculty of speech doth here abide,
HUMOUR33:37 H551 The spirits animal, from whence doth {hence do} slide,
HUMOUR33:39 H553 Of three, its hard to say, which doth excel;
AGES36:2 H26 (As that fond age, doth most of al desire.)
AGES38:40 H143 That wonder tis, my glasse till now doth hold.
AGES40:2 H183 My Lust doth hurry me, to all that's ill,
AGES40:41 H220 With sad affrights of death, doth menace me;
AGES42:29 ~~H285~~ By cankered care, who centinel doth keep.
AGES43:31 H326 The knotty {Cramp and} Gout doth sadly torture me,
AGES43:34 ~~H329~~ And the Consumption, to the bones doth wast me;
AGES45:27 H417 My {Mine} Almond-tree (gray haires) doth flourish now,
AGES45:29 H419 My grinders now are few, my sight doth faile
AGES46:12 H443 Though reading other Works, doth much refresh,
SEASONS47:8 H24 The Seeds-man now {too} doth lavish out his Grain,
SEASONS47:26 H42 Doth darken *Sols* bright face, makes us remember
SEASONS47:32 ~~H47~~ For though in's running progresse he doth take
SEASONS48:1 H54 That when the Sun (on's love) the earth doth shine,
SEASONS49:5 H96 Ith' first, *Sol* doth in crabed *Cancer* shine.
SEASONS49:9 H100 Yet doth his parching heat the {but} more augment,
SEASONS49:13 H104 Whose vehemency, at length doth grow so great,
SEASONS49:40 H133 Whose flaming breath doth melt us from afar,
SEASONS50:24 H158 He plow'd with pain, but reaping doth rejoyce;
SEASONS51:1 H175 And doth in poyzing *Libra* this month shine.
SEASONS51:28 H204 The sap doth slily creep towards the earth,

SEASONS51:30 H206 So doth Old Age stil tend unto his Grave,
SEASONS51:34 H210 *November* is my last, for time doth haste,
SEASONS52:14 H229 Cold, moist, young, flegmy Winter now doth lye
SEASONS~~52:19~~ H234 To th' Southward tropick his swift race hath {doth} run;
SEASONS52:27 H242 And North-ward his unwearied race {Course} doth run;
SEASONS52:33 H248 I care not how the Winter time doth haste;
SEASONS52:34 H249 In *Pisces* now the golden Sun doth shine,
MASSYR58:17 H202 The last, the *Medes* and *Persians* doth invite.
MASSYR58:19 H204 *Belosus* the *Chaldeans* doth require,
MASSYR61:1 H306 But circumstance, doth prove the verity;
MASSYR61:18 H323 To *Tiglath* then doth *Ahaz* send for ease.
MASSYR61:23 H328 Gladly doth *Tiglath* this advantage take,
MASSYR63:37 H424 This Prince in's magnitude doth ever shine;
MASSYR64:25 H449 A mighty Army next, he doth prepare,
MASSYR66:27 H533 His Dreams, wise *Daniel* doth expound ful wel,
MASSYR68:18 H604 Who doth not flatter, nor once cloake the thing.
MPERS70:22 H693 *Cyrus* doth now the *Jewish* captives free,
MPERS74:13 ~~H836~~ His happy wishes now doth no man spare,
MPERS74:22 H845 He two of *Cyrus* Daughters now {then} doth wed,
MPERS75:15 H876 Who doth deserve a Statue made of gold;
MPERS80:40 H1107 But mischief, Sacriledge doth ever follow;
MPERS82:8 H1155 The signall of their victory doth {did} rise;
MPERS84:3 H1231 The royall wine, in golden cups doth {did} passe,
MPERS84:30 H1266 T'*Thymistocles* he doth his {this} war commit,
MPERS85:9 H1285 Who now sole Monarch, doth of all remaine,
MPERS85:29 H1305 Re-gaines his own, and then {doth} the Rebell breaks: {break,}
MPERS87:5 H1361 The wife, against the mother, still doth cry
MPERS87:7 H1363 The King dismay'd, a mighty Hoast doth raise;
MPERS90:31 H1498 {Their King} *Agesilus* himself doth over-goe {goe};
MPERS91:2 H1510 height, {*Spartan* State} which now apace doth {so fast did} rise;
MPERS91:15 H1523 Who had (as noble *Raleigh* doth evince)
MPERS~~91:22~~ H1533 The King highly inrag'd doth hereupon
MPERS92:27 ~~H1585~~ But as before doth (well read) *Raleigh* write,
MGREC94:4 H1638 But he their mutinies, {by valour} full soon doth {he} quell.
MGREC~~95:17~~ H1696 Which who so did {doth}, must Lord of all remain,
MGREC97:26 H1787 Of which, the Government he doth commit
MGREC97:34 H1795 His {This} Letter *Alexander* doth disdaine,
MGREC97:38 H1799 Now {Next} *Alexander* unto *Tyre* doth goe,
MGREC98:13 H1815 But far lesse cost, and time, he doth {did} expend,
MGREC98:25 H1827 *Cilcia* he to *Socrates* doth give,
MGREC99:14 H1857 He now to *Gaza* goes, and there doth meet
MGREC99:16 H1859 Where valiant *Betis,* doth defend {stoutly keeps} the town,
MGREC100:12 H1896 Faire *Alexandria* from the ground doth raise;
MGREC100:21 H1905 Yet he (poore Prince) another Hoast doth muster,
MGREC101:30 H1955 For tumult in the dark {night} doth cause most dread,
MGREC102:21 H1991 Where four and thirty dayes he now doth stay,
MGREC102:40 H2010 Which newes doth still augment *Darius* woes;
MGREC103:35 H2046 Those stately streets with raging flames doth {flame did} fil.
MGREC105:38 H2131 This said, the *Greek* for water doth intreat,
MGREC106:11 H2145 Such as submits, he doth againe restore,
MGREC106:22 H2156 So daily of his vertues doth he lose;

MGREC106:25 H2159 His past sobriety doth also hate,
MGREC106:33 H2167 With *Persian* Robes, himselfe doth dignifie,
MGREC106:35 H2169 His manners, habit, gestures, now doth {all did} fashion,
MGREC107:15 H2190 The wealth of many Cities doth {Kindomes did} consume:
MGREC107:20 H2195 Now with his Army, doth he hast {post} away,
MGREC107:23 H2198 The drought, and heat, their bodies much doth {sore did}
MGREC108:26 H2242 But he their stubbornnesse full soone {in time} doth quel;
MGREC108:28 H2244 Where *Scithians* rude, his valour {army} doth oppose,
MGREC108:36 H2252 A goodly City doth compleatly raise;
MGREC108:37 H2253 Which *Alexandria* he doth also {likewise} name,
MGREC109:2 H2259 Those that submit, he doth restore {give them rule} again.
MGREC109:4 ~~H2261~~ To age, nor sex, no pitty doth expresse,
MGREC109:26 H2285 His Presents all, with thanks he doth {did} restore;
MGREC109:30 H2289 To him doth *Alexander* thus declare,
MGREC110:1 H2301 But on the banks doth {stout} *Porus* ready stand,
MGREC110:9 H2309 His Army *Alexander* doth divide,
MGREC110:27 H2331 Doth for his Camp a greater circuit take,
MGREC111:33 H2378 Much time in feasts, and ryoting doth {did} wast;
MGREC112:32 H2418 Who to the height doth aggravate each thing;
MGREC114:27 H2497 Of this unkingly deed, {act} doth *Seneca*
MGREC115:30 H2549 The King doth intimate 'twas his intent,
MGREC~~116:11~~ H2577 {This Monarchs fame} must last, whilst world shall {doth}
MGREC~~116:30~~ H2596 As oft his Acts throughout his reigne did {doth} shew:
MGREC119:17 H2707 To *Lamia,* where he shut up doth ly:
MGREC119:25 H2715 With speed his forces {Army} doth together call,
MGREC120:7 H2742 *Craterus* doth his daughter *Phisa* {*Phila*} wed,
MGREC120:34 H2771 His Masters Funerals doth celebrate;
MGREC~~121:16~~ H2795 But of his wrongs his friends doth certifie;
MGREC~~122:41~~ H2862 The Army with *Antigonus* did {doth} leave,
MGREC123:3 H2865 On which *Antigonus* his height doth raise:
MGREC123:14 H2878 Now {When} great *Antipater,* the world doth {must} leave
MGREC123:19 H2883 On most part of *Assyria* doth seize,
MGREC124:18 H2925 *Antigonus* doth all in *Asia* gaine;
MGREC125:2 H2950 She now with *Polisperchon* doth combine,
MGREC125:23 H2973 And to the Queen, these presents she doth {did} send;
MGREC~~127:28~~ H3058 *Antigonus,* all *Persia* now gains {doth gain},
MGREC127:30 H3060 Then with *Seleuchus* straight at ods doth fall,
MGREC127:31 H3061 But {And} he for aid to *Ptolomy* doth call.
MGREC~~127:41~~ H3072 *Cassanders* outrages at large doth tell,
MGREC128:40 H3113 That each shall {should} hold what he doth {did} now possesse,
MGREC129:40 H3154 *Antigonus* for all this doth not mourn,
MGREC130:2 H3157 For marriage to *Cleopatra,* doth send
MGREC130:20 H3175 The world must needs believe what he doth tell:
MGREC130:38 H3183 That hand is righteous still which doth repay:
MGREC~~131:1~~ H3189 Doth promise liberty to *Athens* State;
MGREC131:7 H3197 *Demetrius* of *Ptolomy* doth gain;
MROMAN138:1 H3491 War with the antient *Albans* he doth {did} wage,
MROMAN138:11 H3501 Thirty two years doth *Tullus* reigne, then dye,
MROMAN138:28 H3518 By wealth, and favour, doth to honour climbe;
MROMAN139:14 H3542 *Sextus* his Son, doth {did} (most unworthily)
DIALOG142:24 H53 Doth your Allye, faire *France,* conspire your wrack?

DIALOG142:25	H54	Or, doth {do} the *Scots* play false behind your back?
DIALOG142:26	H55	Doth *Holland* quit you ill, for all your love?
DIALOG143:22	H91	Destruction to a Land doth soone afford;
DIALOG148:28	H293	Whose lot doth fall to live therein is blest:
SIDNEY149:27	~~H23~~	Yet doth thy shame (with all) purchase renown,
SIDNEY150:7	H32	And doth thy {his} selfe, thy {his} worke, and {his} honour
SIDNEY150:22	H47	Of which, {at} this day, faire *Belgia* doth {may} boast.
SIDNEY150:33	H60	And live it doth, in spight of death, through fame,
SIDNEY~~150:38~~	H66	And *Phoenix Spencer* doth unto his life,
DUBART153:22	H26	And thousand times his mazed minde doth wish
DUBART154:5	H50	My full astonish'd heart doth pant to break,
QELIZ155:15	H6	Yet thy loud Herauld Fame, doth to the sky
QELIZ157:30	H98	Which I may not, my pride doth but aspire,
VANITY159:36	H8	And whilst they live, how oft doth turn their State? {fate,}
VANITY160:16	H26	And he that knows the most doth still bemoan,
VANITY160:29	H39	Who drinks thereof, the world doth naught account.
CONTEM168:13	H22	If so, all these as nought, Eternity doth scorn.
CONTEM168:25	H32	The morn doth usher thee, with smiles & blushes,
CONTEM168:28	H35	Thy heat from death and dulness doth revive:
CONTEM169:32	H71	While of their persons & their acts his mind doth treat.
CONTEM171:11	H115	Who to the tenth of theirs doth now arrive?
CONTEM174:13	H212	The Mariner that on smooth waves doth glide,
FLESH175:12	H12	Doth Contemplation feed thee so
FLESH176:38	H78	Mine Eye doth pierce the heavens, and see
FLESH176:41	H81	Nor such like trash which Earth doth hold,
FLESH177:13	H94	A Chrystal River there doth run,
FLESH177:14	H95	Which doth proceed from the Lambs Throne:
FLESH177:18	H99	For glory doth from God proceed:
SICKNES178:32	H15	Our strength doth waste, our time doth hast,
SICKNES178:32	H15	Our strength doth waste, our time doth hast,
BIRTH179:28	H4	Adversity doth still our joyes attend;
1HUSB180:28	H7	Or all the riches that the East doth hold.
3LETTER183:1	H3	Perplext, in every bush & nook doth pry,
3LETTER183:3	H5	So doth my anxious soul, which now doth miss,
3LETTER183:3	H5	So doth my anxious soul, which now doth miss,
3LETTER183:7	H9	Or as the pensive Dove doth all alone
3LETTER183:18	H20	Where she her captive husband doth espy.
MEDDM199:5	Hp277	Lightening doth vsually preceed thunder, and stormes raine,
MEDDM202:23	Hp282	darknes till he arise againe, so god doth somtime vaile his face
MEDDM202:34	Hp282	doth it euer say it is enough, but like the daughters of the
MEDDM203:21	Hp283	neuer felt, what it was to be sick or wounded, doth not much
MEDDM204:17	Hp285	god doth many times, both reward and punish for one and y^{e}
MEDDM204:22	Hp285	wch should warn him, that doth any speciall seruice for
MEDDM204:34	Hp285	land askes much more paines, then some other doth to be
MEDDM208:18	Hp290	Well doth the Apostle call riches deceitfull riches, and they
PILGRIM210:13	H13	for waters cold he doth not long
WHAT224:22	H22	That dy'd but now doth liue,
28AUG225:30	Hp254	doth not afflict willingly, nor take delight in greiving ye children
28AUG225:32	Hp254	prosperity, but he doth it for my Advantage, and y^{t} I may bee a
13MAY226:26	H2	As spring the winter doth succeed
13MAY226:31	H7	My Soul and Body doth rejoice,

DOUBLE (8)
ELEMEN12:32 H192 My rich commodities payes double rent.
ELEMEN15:37 H319 The *Roman* Purple, double *Tirian* dye.
SEASONS48:16 H69 Except the double Pinks, and matchlesse Roses.
MPERS77:19 H960 He with his Crown, receive a double warre,
MGREC129:18 H3132 And for that double fact which she had done,
MROMAN136:28 H3442 The double injury, he then did doe:
DUBART154:26 H71 Thy double portion would have served many.
2LETTER182:33 H39 Now post with double speed, mark what I say,
DOUBLING (1)
MGREC104:31 H2083 Who doubling of his march, posts on amain,
DOUBT (10)
ELEMEN15:1 H283 When I am gone, their fiercenesse none need {needs} doubt;
HUMOUR31:14 H445 If any doubt this {the} truth, whence this should come;
MASSYR54:35 H62 Against the *Bactrians* (but that I doubt)
MASSYR57:24 ~~H171~~ Again, the Country was left bare (there is no doubt)
MASSYR61:3 H308 That those two made but one, we need not doubt:
MPERS70:7 H678 That all the world they neither {need not} feare, nor doubt;
MPERS~~92:20~~ H1578 And the same sauce had served him no doubt,
MROMAN139:30 H3556 The more I mus'd, the more I was in doubt:
SIDNEY151:23 H73 For {How} to persist, my muse is more in doubt:
MED223:3 Hp250 Lord why should I doubt any more w^{n} thov hast given me such
DOUBTFUL (1)
HUMOUR32:28 H502 What's slanderous, repel; doubtful, dispute;
DOUBTING (3)
MGREC110:35 H2339 But doubting, wearing Time would {might} these decay,
2LETTER182:6 H12 My sobs, my longing hopes, my doubting fears,
FAINT222:21 H11 My Doubting thou didst chide
DOUBTLESSE (1)
HUMOUR33:29 H543 Doth doubtlesse keep its mighty residence;
DOUBTS (6) [pl.]
MPERS86:10 H1326 Yet doubts, {fears} all he injoyes, is not his own.
3LETTER183:5 H7 Still wait with doubts, & hopes, and failing eye,
MYCHILD216:26 Hp242 somt. on my soul in Doubts & feares of Gods displeasure, and
BYNIGHT220:15 H14 And banisht thence my Doubts + feares.
THEART229:10 H12 My future Doubts repell.
ACK235:8 H8 Hast known my doubts and All my feares,
DOVE (4)
MASSYR56:36 H142 The Poets feign her turn'd into a Dove,
MASSYR56:39 H145 A Dove within their Ensigne to display.
3LETTER183:7 H9 Or as the pensive Dove doth all alone
3LETTER183:24 H26 Unto thy Hinde, thy Mullet and thy Dove,
DOWN (47) adv. [downe]
ELEMEN17:3 H367 Their Cattle, Hay, and Corne, I sweep down current,
ELEMEN18:36 H440 Which may be done, by holding down my vapour.
ELEMEN19:35 H476 But some fall down, and some flye up with aire.
HUMOUR31:33 H466 Now up, now down, transported like the Aire.
MASSYR59:9 H233 Bereft of wits, were slaughtered down right.
MASSYR64:6 H430 Kild, sav'd, pull'd down, set up, or pain'd, or eas'd;
MASSYR65:1 H466 And in the channell throw {threw} each burden down;
MASSYR65:25 H490 Then from his throne, he pull'd {pluck'd} him down again:

MASSYR67:22 H568 Whose prophane acts, a sacred pen sets down.
MPERS69:26 H648 Where all that doe {dare} resist, are slaughter'd down;
MPERS69:40 H670 Now up, now {and} down, as fortune turnes her hand,
MPERS77:1 H940 Off flyes his head, down showres his frolick bloud.
MPERS79:39 H1065 Till twenty thousand *Persians* falls down slain;
MPERS88:27 H1420 Down *Cyrus* fals, and yeelds to destiny;
MPERS88:29 H1422 But treads down all, for to advance their Master;
MPERS92:17 ~~H1575~~ By favour, force, or fraud, is not set down:
MGREC97:32 H1793 But down his haughty stomach could not bring,
MGREC98:18 H1820 Whose glory, now {then} a second time's brought down;
MGREC101:2 H1927 And if they down, his Monarchy wil throw,
MGREC104:16 H2068 Sate down o'rewhelm'd, with sorrow, and despair,
MGREC107:7 H2182 Intends with speed, that Traitor down {to his end} to bring;
MGREC108:21 H2237 Down from the mountains twenty thousand came,
MGREC109:23 H2282 And {Then} eighty Tallents to his Captaines down.
MGREC111:1 H2346 Then down t' *Hidaspis* with his Fleet he went;
MGREC111:16 H2361 Hence {Then} sayling down by th' mouth of *Indus* floud,
MGREC117:12 H2619 The Leopard down, his {the} four wings 'gan to rise,
MGREC118:30 H2679 Was stiffe *Meleager,* whom he would take down {away},
MGREC124:2 H2907 To take down *Polisperchon* grown so high;
MGREC128:21 H3094 So therefore craves {requests} their help to take him down,
MGREC~~131:9~~ H3201 How some when down, straight got the upper hand
MGREC135:10 H3382 Now up, now down, now chief, and then brought under;
DIALOG142:7 H36 And {Or} by tempestuous Wars thy fields trod down?
DIALOG143:32 H101 The Gospel is trod {troden} down, and hath no right;
DIALOG144:6 H116 How many Princely heads on blocks laid down,
DIALOG147:21 H247 force {As Duty binds,} expell, destroy, and tread them down:
SIDNEY149:18 H17 More worth was thine, {his} then *Clio* could set down.
SIDNEY152:17 H86 I pensive for my fault, sat down, and then,
DUBART153:31 H35 Sits down in silence, deeply he admires:
CONTEM171:24 H127 But Man grows old, lies down, remains where once he's laid.
ELIZB187:8 H16 And time brings down what is both strong and tall.
MERCY188:25 H11 I stood so nigh, it crusht me down withal;
MEDDM195:36 Hp272 vanity and lyes must needs lye down in the Bed of sorrow.
MEDDM198:4 Hp275 then makes them lye down in green pastures and leades them
MEDDM200:7 Hp279 mustard, they wil either wipe it off, or else suck down sweet
MEDDM206:4 Hp287 danger of being cut down, as the dry stock, for both cumber
BYNIGHT220:9 H9 He bow'd his ear down from Above
28AUG226:9 Hp254 lye down & bequeath my Soul to thee and Death seem'd no

DOWN (3) n.
AGES44:16 H349 It's not my goodly house {state}, nor bed of down,
SEASONS~~50:18~~ H152 The russling tresse of *terra* for {down} to moe,
CHILDRN185:9 H35 My fifth, whose down is yet scarce gone

DOWNE (1) [down]
PILGRIM210:35 H35 A Corrupt Carcasse downe it lyes

DOWNNY (1)
MEDDM196:21 Hp273 Downny beds make drosey persons but hard lodging, keeps

DOWNWARD (1)
MEDDM207:11 Hp288 and waights that will pull us lower downward

DOWNY See DOWNNY

DOWRY (1)
MGREC99:1 H1844 And a most Princely Dowry with her proffers; {offers.}
DRAG (1)
MGREC108:3 H2219 And in this sort, they rather drag, then bring,
DRAIN (1)
MPERS70:8 H679 To drain this ditch, he many sluces cut,
DRAINES (1)
HUMOUR30:30 H422 The first it draines, o'th' last quicks appetite,
DRAKE (1)
QELIZ156:41 H68 Her *Drake* came laded home with *Spanish* gold,
DRANK (1)
MPERS92:13 H1571 reign'd, as Chronicles expresse, {then drank of's fathers cup}
DRAUGHT (2)
MPERS79:33 H1059 Was scarce enough, for each a draught to take.
CONTEM170:24 H95 The Virgin Earth, of blood her first draught drinks
DRAVE (1) See also DROVE
SIDNEY152:14 H83 And drave me from *Parnassus* in a rage,
DRAW (3)
MGREC104:4 H2056 Then still with infamy, to draw his breath.
MGREC121:34 H2816 And fain would draw *Eumenes* to their side,
MEDDM207:7 Hp288 steps to draw men to god in consideration of his bounty
DRAWES (1) [draws]
SEASONS51:32 H208 But when the Son of Righteousnesse drawes nigh,
DRAWING (2)
TDUDLEY166:17 H59 He did exult his end was drawing near,
SOREFIT222:6 H25 In drawing out these wretched Dayes.
DRAWN (3)
MGREC99:25 H1868 And by command was drawn through every street,
MGREC110:24 H2328 Could by no means be further {farther} drawn, or led:
28AUG226:3 Hp254 somt. I haue had, least my heart should bee drawn from him,
DRAWNE (1)
MGREC96:26 H1746 As if she'd drawne, whole *Sushan* at her heeles.
DRAWS (2) See also DRAWES
MGREC104:25 H2077 Then draws the Cart along, with chaines of gold;
CONTEM174:30 H227 That draws oblivions curtains over kings,
DREAD (7)
AGES43:9 ~~H305~~ Whence poyson, Pistols, and dread instruments,
AGES45:14 H396 fly their Country, through their {struck both with gilt and} dread.
MASSYR67:31 H577 To shew his little dread, but greater store,
MGREC99:41 H1884 No future dangers he did ever dread.
MGREC101:30 H1955 For tumult in the dark {night} doth cause most dread,
MGREC135:4 H3376 For 'twas not death, nor danger, she did dread,
QELIZ156:30 H57 Unto our dread Virago, what they owe:
DREADFUL (3)
AGES40:32 H211 Remembring not the dreadful day of Doom,
CONTEM170:26 H97 The wretch with gastly face and dreadful mind,
1SIMON188:8 H9 With dreadful awe before him let's be mute,
DREADFULL (7)
ELEMEN13:34 H235 Dreadfull examples, soon I might produce,
ELEMEN14:3 H245 O dreadfull Sepulcher! that this is true,
ELEMEN14:6 H250 What she hath lost by these my dreadfull {remed'less} woes.

MPERS73:2 H789 Yeelding {So yields} to death, that dreadfull Conquerer.
MGREC117:23 H2630 For ayming still amisse, his dreadfull blowes
MGREC135:30 H3402 The last more strong, and dreadfull, then the rest,
HOUSE236:16 H8 And piteovs shreiks of dreadfull voice.

DREADFULL'ST (1) [dreadfullest]
MASSYR64:2 H426 The richest, and the dreadfull'st to behold;

DREAM (3)
MPERS69:15 H637 His Mothers Dream, and Grand-sires cruelty,
FLESH175:16 H16 Dost dream of things beyond the Moon
MEDDM205:26 Hp286 to good dutys, we certainly dream of some remotnes betwixt

DREAMS (2) [pl.]
MASSYR66:27 H533 His Dreams, wise *Daniel* doth expound ful wel,
3LETTER183:26 H28 The substance gone, O me, these are but dreams.

DREGS (1) [pl.]
DIALOG145:5 H154 The bottome dregs reserved are for me.

DRESS (1)
AUTHOR178:8 H18 In better dress to trim thee was my mind,

DRESSE (1)
13MAY226:27 H3 And leaues the naked Trees doe dresse

DREST (1)
MGREC96:19 H1739 He fifteen hundred had like women drest,

DREW (5)
MPERS88:9 H1402 And black and blacker grew, as they drew nigh.
MGREC105:2 H2095 Yea, wounds the beasts (that drew him) unto death,
MGREC111:31 H2376 {And} So he at length drew neare to *Persia*;
MGREC114:34 H2504 Yea, and *Calisthines* to death he drew,
MGREC129:35 H3149 So *Polisperchon* to his Counsell drew,

DRIED See DRY'D, DRYED

DRIES See DRYES

DRINK (10)
ELEMEN14:33 H275 Which {Who} am thy drink, thy blood, thy sap, and best.
HUMOUR21:34 H62 Unlesse to court, and claw, and {to} dice, and drink,
HUMOUR25:6 H195 For drink, which of us twain, like it the best,
AGES45:34 H424 Nor sapors find, in what I drink or eat.
MPERS84:4 H1232 To drink more then he list, none bidden was:
MGREC107:25 H2200 Where most {so} immoderatly these thirsty drink;
MGREC111:8 H2353 The meat, and drink, attendants, every thing,
MGREC~~116:10~~ H2573 Nor meat, nor drink, nor comfort would she take,
CONTEM173:23 H189 Thy bed a bough, thy drink the water cleer,
MYSOUL225:7 H11 And drink at vnexhausted fovnt

DRINKING (3)
AGES40:38 H217 Sometimes by Feavers, all my moisture drinking,
MGREC116:8 H2568 That through excessive drinking he did dye.
CONTEM171:14 H118 In eating, drinking, sleeping, vain delight

DRINKS (4)
HUMOUR31:11 H444 That casts out all that man or {e're} eates, or drinks.
MPERS79:31 H1057 His Hoast, who {all} *Lissus* drinks to quench their thirst,
VANITY160:29 H39 Who drinks thereof, the world doth naught account.
CONTEM170:24 H95 The Virgin Earth, of blood her first draught drinks

DRIUE (1) [drive]
MEDDM209:13 Hp291 Command of god, and endeavour not to the vtmost to driue

DRIUEN (1) [driven
MEDDM207:8 Hp288 but haue driuen them the further from him, that they are ready
DRIVE (6) See also DRIUE
HUMOUR~~33:25~~ H539 *Galen, Hipocrates,* drives {drive} to a set.
SEASONS~~52:39~~ H254 Until by's heat he drives {drive} all cold away.
MPERS86:36 H1352 The Rovers in *Pisidia,* should drive out.
SIDNEY151:37 ~~H75~~ Fame's flaming Chariot for to drive.
SIDNEY151:41 ~~H75~~ He bad me drive, and he would hold the Sun;
CONTEM173:5 H173 To see what trade they great ones there do drive,
DRIVEN (2) See also DRIUEN
MGREC~~128:18~~ H3091 *Seleuchus* drove {driven} from government, and lands;
CONTEM170:2 H76 Who like a miscreant's driven from that place,
DRIVES (3)
HUMOUR33:25 H539 *Galen, Hipocrates,* drives {drive} to a set.
SEASONS52:39 H254 Until by's heat he drives {drive} all cold away.
MPERS85:15 H1291 Drives out his garison that therein {'mongst them} dwels.
DROOPING (2)
MEDDM198:25 Hp276 head requires a soft pillow, and a drooping heart a strong
28AUG225:28 Hp254 my drooping heart, and to manifest his Loue to me, and this is
DROOPINGS (1) [pl.]
MYCHILD217:22 Hp243 never p^{r}vail: yet haue I many Times sinkings & droopings,
DROP (1)
HUMOUR22:40 H109 To be distill'd a drop on every line!
DROPPING (1)
HOURS233:21 H4 And see'st my dropping teares.
DROPS (5) [pl.]
ELEMEN14:39 H281 Complaines to th'heaven, when {if} I withhold my drops:
ELEMEN16:21 H344 Nor fruitfull dewes, nor drops {distil'd} from weeping eyes;
2LETTER182:11 H17 The leaves in th' woods, the hail or drops of rain,
2LETTER182:14 H20 May count my sighs, and number all my drops:
MEDDM201:19 Hp280 often se stones hang wth drops not from any innate moisture,
DROPS (1) v.
SEASONS50:36 H170 Then drops his Fruits into the Eaters lap.
DROPSIE (1)
HUMOUR23:1 H111 Wil feed a Dropsie, or a Timpany,
DROPSY (1)
AGES~~43:34~~ H329 The quartan Ague, dropsy, Lunacy:
DROSEY (1) [drowsy]
MEDDM196:21 Hp273 Downny beds make drosey persons but hard lodging, keeps
DROSSE (1)
AGES41:22 ~~H239~~ And then a world of drosse among my gold.
DROUGHT (5)
AGES38:11 H114 I fear'd no drought, nor wet, I had no crop,
MGREC107:23 H2198 The drought, and heat, their bodies much doth {sore did}
DIALOG142:28 H57 Is't Drought, is't Famine, or is't Pestilence?
MEDDM196:17 Hp273 heat and drought of the day, when he perceiues his sun apace
MEDDM208:25 Hp290 empty wells in the time of drought, that those that go to finde
DROVE (1) See also DRAVE
MGREC128:18 H3091 *Seleuchus* drove {driven} from government, and lands;
DROWN (3)
MASSYR54:39 H66 Then drown himself, did *Menon,* for her sake;

MGREC103:23 H2034 Now makes this King, his vertues all to drown.
DIALOG147:27 H251 When they are gone, then drown your self in teares.
DROWN'D (3) [drowned]
ELEMEN10:14 H89 *Eridanus,* where *Phaeton* was drown'd,
MASSYR55:11 H77 Adjudged to be drown'd, for what {th' crime} she'd done;
2LETTER181:35 H5 (And if the whirling of thy wheels don't drown'd)
DROWSY (1) See also DROSEY
ELEMEN~~14:12~~ H254 In heats & colds & gripes & drowsy sleeps:
DRUDGE (1)
HUMOUR31:10 H443 The Kitchin Drudge, the cleanser of the sinks,
DRUGS (1) [pl.]
ELEMEN12:33 H193 Ye *Galenists,* my Drugs that come from thence
DRUM (2)
HUMOUR21:36 H64 She loves a Fiddle, better then a Drum,
AGES39:18 H161 The snorting Horse, the Trumpet, Drum I like,
DRUMS (2) [pl.]
ELEMEN18:15 H419 Your Drums, your Trumpets, and your Organs sound,
HUMOUR32:32 H506 I love no thundering Drums {guns}, nor bloody Wars,
DRUNK (2)
MGREC114:1 H2469 When both were drunk, *Clitus* was wont to jeere;
DIALOG143:12 H81 *France* knowes, how of {oft} my fury she hath drunk;
DRUNKE (1)
ELEMEN15:35 H317 As *Ægypts* wanton *Cleopatra* drunke.
DRUNKEN (2)
MGREC109:8 H2267 Nor had that drunken god, one that {who} would take
MGREC114:7 ~~H2475~~ Upon a time, when both had drunken well,
DRUNKENNESSE (2)
MASSYR68:21 H607 His drunkennesse, and his prophainnesse high,
DIALOG144:2 H112 For Sabbath-breaking, and for Drunkennesse,
DRY (22)
FATHER5:21 H22 These are, the hot, the cold, the moist, the dry,
FATHER5:31 H32 How hot, and dry, contend with moist, and cold,
ELEMEN13:16 H217 But how my cold, dry temper, works upon
ELEMEN14:34 H276 If I withhold, what art thou, dead, dry lump
ELEMEN15:11 H293 He knowes such sweets, lyes not in earths dry roots,
HUMOUR27:28 H299 Your hot, dry, moyst, cold, natures are {but} foure,
HUMOUR27:30 H301 As thus, if hot, then dry; if moist, then cold;
HUMOUR30:7 H399 Those {Whose} cold dry heads, {head} more subtilly doth yeild,
HUMOUR30:25 H417 And first, the firme dry bones, I justly claim:
HUMOUR35:7 H603 Her dry, dry Cholers other hand shal grasp;
HUMOUR35:7 H603 Her dry, dry Cholers other hand shal grasp;
HUMOUR35:8 H604 Two hot, two moist, two cold, two dry here be,
AGES45:26 H416 My memory is short {bad}, and braine is dry.
SEASONS51:16 H190 Or withered stocks, {which were} all dry, and dead,
SEASONS52:9 H224 Old cold, dry age, and earth, Autumne resembles,
DISTEMP179:19 H7 Then eyes lay dry, disabled to weep more;
2LETTER182:30 H36 Hath power to dry the torrent of these streams.
MEDDM199:9 Hp277 dry and sapless performances are simptoms of little spiritull
MEDDM200:25 Hp279 we se the leavlesse trees and dry stocks (at the approach of
MEDDM200:28 Hp279 when the Sun of righteoussnes shall appear those dry bones
MEDDM205:34 Hp286 among them are dry stocks so is it in the church w[ch] is gods

MEDDM206:4 Hp287 danger of being cut down, as the dry stock, for both cumber

DRY'D (1) [dried] See also DRYED

SEASONS~~49:11~~ H102 Have throughly dry'd the earth, and heat the air.

DRYED (3) [dried] See also DRY'D

SEASONS50:14 H148 The dryed earth is parched by {with} his face.
SEASONS51:6 H180 The Raisins now in clusters dryed be,
MYSOUL225:9 H13 Thy teares shall All bee dryed vp

DRYES (1) [dries]

HUMOUR28:3 H315 The body dryes, the minde sublime doth smother,

DU (1)

DUBART152:30 H1 In honour of *Du Bartas.*

DUCALIONS (1) [pl.]

ELEMEN17:26 H390 *Ducalions* great deluge, with many moe;

DUDLEY (3) See also D.

FATHER5:2 H2-3 *Thomas Dudley* Esq; *these humbly presented.*
TDUDLEY165:2 H3 *Thomas Dudley* Esq;
DDUDLEY167:7 H3 *Mrs. Dorothy Dudley,*

DUE (13)

FATHER6:7 H41 Who must reward a theife, but with his due.
ELEMEN8:9 H7 And {That} in due order each her turne should speake,
ELEMEN11:21 H141 The next in place, Earth judg'd to be her due,
ELEMEN17:36 H400 {Yet am} not through ignorance, {ignorant} first was my due,
HUMOUR27:8 H279 And let me by thy Partner, which is due.
HUMOUR27:24 H295 Shal firstly {chiefly} take her {the} place, as is her {my} due,
MGREC109:32 H2291 Unto his Kingdoms borders, and as due,
MGREC117:15 H2622 We may hereafter shew, in season due.
DIALOG145:10 H159 A sharer in your punishment's my due,
SIDNEY151:30 ~~H75~~ Which are in worth, as far short of his due,
QELIZ156:5 H32 Nor say I more then duly is her due,
BIRTH180:5 H15 And if I see not half my dayes that's due,
THEART229:5 H7 And in due time thou succour'st me

DUEL (1)

AGES38:5 H108 My duel was no challenge, nor did seek.

DUES (1) [pl.]

MGREC126:6 H2997 To give her for all cruelties {her cruelty} her dues:

DUKE (2)

AGES37:31 H93 A Baron or a Duke, ne'r made my mark.
DIALOG143:7 H74 No Duke of *York,* nor Earle of *March,* to soyle

DUL (3) [dull]

HUMOUR22:6 H75 In her dul resolution, she's {so} slow.
HUMOUR22:24 H93 {But tis} Not from our dul slow Sisters motions:
HUMOUR23:9 H119 Thy self's as dul, as is thy mother Earth.

DULL (1)

FLESH176:35 H75 Beyond thy dull Capacity;

DULLEST (1)

MPERS73:37 H822 But others thought (none of the dullest braine,)

DULNESS (1)

CONTEM168:28 H35 Thy heat from death and dulness doth revive:

DULY (2)

MPERS86:30 H1346 Whose rents and customes, duly he sent in.
QELIZ156:5 H32 Nor say I more then duly is her due,

DUMB (2)
MASSYR68:9 H595 But dumb the gazing Astrologers stand,
TDUDLEY165:25 H27 While others tell his worth, I'le not be dumb:
DUMBE (1)
MPERS69:29 H651 But as he past, his Son, who was born dumbe,
DUMPISH (1)
2LETTER182:5 H11 My dumpish thoughts, my groans, my brakish tears
DUNGHIL (1)
AGES42:37 H293 My dunghil thoughts, or hopes, could reach no higher.
DUNGHILL (1)
HOUSE237:16 H46 That dunghill mists away may flie.
DUODENUM (1)
HUMOUR31:15 H446 Show them thy passage to th' *Duodenum.*
DURANCE (1)
MGREC129:5 H3119 Whom he in durance held, now and long since,
DURATION (1)
CONTEM174:10 H210 In weight, in frequency and long duration
DURST (13)
FATHER6:6 H40 But if I did, I durst not send them you;
MPERS87:35 H1387 Yet for his brothers comming, durst not stay,
MPERS90:17 ~~H1484~~ For these incursions he durst not abide;
MGREC95:22 H1701 stead} *Arsemes* {*Arses*} was plac'd, yet {but} durst not stay;
MGREC107:40 H2215 But coward, durst not fight, nor could he fly,
MGREC117:28 H2635 Yet {But} none so hardy found as so durst say.
MGREC~~118:24~~ H2673 That for a while they durst not come so near:
MGREC122:34 H2855 And this no man durst question, or resist;
MGREC~~131:29~~ H3221 Yet dares {durst} not say, he loves {lov'd} his fathers wife;
SIDNEY151:24 ~~H73~~ Calls me ambitious fool, that durst aspire,
SIDNEY151:28 ~~H75~~ Too late my errour see, that durst presume
2LETTER182:25 H31 At thy return, if so thou could'st or durst
MED223:11 Hp250 known who or where is the man that durst in his heart haue
DUST (18) See also DVST
ELEMEN11:5 H125 With neighbouring Townes I did consume to dust,
ELEMEN14:20 H262 Remember sonnes, your mould is of my dust,
MASSYR67:2 H548 *Babels* great Monarch, now laid in the dust,
MPERS71:29 H743 The stormed dust o'r-whelm'd his daring bands;
MPERS77:24 H965 As if to dust he meant to grinde that Nation;
MPERS88:7 H1400 Was gather'd by the dust that rose from thence:
MPERS91:29 ~~H1543~~ Forty three years he rules, then turns to dust,
MPERS~~91:31~~ H1545 Forty three years he rul'd, then turn'd to dust,
MGREC128:12 H3085 Which their late King in dust had damnified;
DIALOG141:9 H8 And sit i'th dust, to sigh these sad alarms?
DIALOG146:29 H215 Shake off your dust, chear up, and now arise,
DIALOG147:37 H261 That nursing Kings, shall come and lick thy dust:
CONTEM174:33 H230 Their parts, their ports, their pomp's all laid in th' dust
FLESH176:3 H43 Untill I see thee laid in th' dust.
1SIMON188:10 H11 With humble hearts and mouths put in the dust,
MEDDM197:33 Hp275 greif and pain till they turn to dust, and then are they fine
MEDDM200:36 Hp280 weak children as would crush them to the dust, but according
FEVER221:5 H20 What tho: in dust it shall bee lay'd
DUTIES See DUTYES, DUTYS

DUTIFULL (1)
SEASONS53:9 ~~H264~~ Your dutifull Daughter.
DUTY (8)
FATHER6:12 H46 From her, that to your selfe more duty owes,
DIALOG147:21 H247 By force {As Duty binds,} expell, destroy, and tread them
TDUDLEY165:4 H6 By duty bound, and not by custome led
2SIMON195:10 Hp271 true friends much more by duty full children, I haue avoyded
MYCHILD216:34 Hp242 sin I lay vnder wch God would haue reformed, or some duty
13MAY227:14 H23 To show my Duty wth delight
SON231:24 H36 Of Duty + of Thankfullnes,
2HUSB232:21 H22 It was my Duty so to doe
DUTYES (2) [duties] See also DUTYS
MYCHILD215:28 Hp241 God. I was also troubled at ye neglect of private Dutyes tho:
11MAYA226:15 Hp255 & some ability to p^{r}form ye Dutyes I owe to him, and the work
DUTYS (2) [duties] See also DUTYES
MEDDM205:26 Hp286 quicken on to good dutys, we certainly dream of some
MEDDM205:35 Hp287 some eminent Christians, that are soe frequent in good dutys,
DVST (3) [dust]
SAMUEL228:11 H12 For mortall helpes are brittle Dvst.
HOUSE236:27 H19 That layd my goods now in ye dvst
HOUSE237:13 H43 Didst fix thy hope on mouldring dvst,
DWEL (2) [dwell]
HUMOUR33:38 H552 The five most noble Sences, here do dwel,
MPERS82:39 H1186 To see those breasts, where chastity did dwel,
DWELL (8)
ELEMEN9:41 H75 Fixed in heavenly constellations dwell,
ELEMEN12:2 H162 But chiefly, 'cause the Muses there did dwell;
MROMAN139:21 H3549 In banishment perpetuall, to dwell;
CONTEM172:12 H148 And if the sun would ever shine, there would I dwell.
FLESH175:17 H17 And dost thou hope to dwell there soon?
FLESH177:5 H86 The City where I hope to dwell,
MEDDM197:20 Hp275 temple for the spirit of god to dwell in
PILGRIM210:18 H18 and meanes in safity now to dwell.
DWELLING (1)
HOUSE236:24 H16 The flame consvme my dwelling place,
DWELLS (2)
CONTEM168:1 H11 How excellent is he that dwells on high?
MEDDM202:37 Hp282 whom all fullnes dwells
DWELS (2) [dwells]
MASSYR65:32 H497 Seven years he keeps his faith, and safe he dwels,
MPERS85:15 H1291 Drives out his garison that therein {'mongst them} dwels.
DWELT (1)
MROMAN137:17 H3468 And *Sabins,* as one people, dwelt in *Rome.*
DY'D (11) [died]
ELEMEN19:16 H461 Whereof such multitudes have dy'd and fled,
SEASONS49:20 H111 Whose fleece when purely {finely} spun, and deeply dy'd,
MASSYR56:40 H146 Forty two years she reign'd, and then she dy'd,
MPERS70:34 H705 But *Zenophon* reports, he dy'd in's bed,
MPERS85:2 H1278 And dy'd the two and fortieth of his reign.
MGREC98:20 H1822 Eight thousand by the sword now also dy'd,
MGREC120:3 H2734 Now dy'd (about the end of th' *Lamian* warre)

SIDNEY150:32 H59 Though *Sidney* dy'd, his valiant name should live;
SIDNEY152:29 H98 *That* Sidney *dy'd the quintessence {most renown'd} of men.*
DUBART155:8 H93 *But Nature vanquish'd Art, so* Bartas *dy'd,*
WHAT224:22 H22 That dy'd but now doth liue,

DYE (23) [expire]

ELEMEN15:37 H319 The *Roman* Purple, double *Tirian* dye.
MASSYR60:4 H269 Of *Ninivites,* he caused none to dye,
MASSYR63:10 H395 After twelve years did *Essarhadon* dye,
MPERS70:25 H696 And caus'd his foes in Lions den to dye.
MPERS72:6 ~~H755~~ Who for no wrong, poore innocent must dye,
MPERS74:16 H839 Let tyranny now with {dead} *Cambyses* dye.
MPERS80:6 H1073 But on their ground they dye, each Mothers Son.
MPERS82:10 H1157 And troublesome *Mardonius* now must dye:
MGREC105:29 H2122 And not by Traitors hands untimely dye.
MGREC106:6 H2140 Though gods on earth, like Sons of men shall {they} dye.
MGREC113:23 H2450 It was decreed *Parmenio* should dye:
MGREC115:11 H2520 Because he let {He suffer, his friend} *Ephestion* to dye.
MGREC115:27 H2546 He might well dye, though he had done no wrong;
MGREC116:8 H2568 That through excessive drinking he did dye.
MROMAN138:11 H3501 Thirty two years doth *Tullus* reigne, then dye,
DIALOG144:10 H120 O *Jane,* why didst thou dye in flowring prime,
SIDNEY150:27 H54 Thus man is borne to dye, and dead is he,
DAVID158:27 H7 How did the mighty fall, and falling dye?
CONTEM172:2 H139 Nay, they shall darken, perish, fade and dye,
SICKNES178:22 H5 All men must dye, and so must I
3LETTER183:17 H19 But lanches on that shore, there for to dye,
VERSES184:11 H15 Yet paying is not payd until I dye.
SON231:9 H21 When royall ones y[t] Time did dye,

DYE (5) [color] See also DIE'S

ELEMEN18:10 H414 His moveing reason is, give least I dye.
HUMOUR31:39 H472 With purple dye {deeper red}, to shew but {you} her disgrace.
MPERS84:1 H1229 His hangings, white, and green, and purple dye;
MGREC105:17 H2110 Whose wounds had made their skins of purple dye;
DAVID159:15 H30 Who cloathed you in cloath of richest dye,

DYED (8)

MASSYR53:34 H24 One hundred fourteen years, he after dyed.
MPERS73:4 H791 And more, because he dyed issulesse.
MPERS83:21 H1209 For which he dyed, and not he alone.
MGREC113:13 H2440 And told the world, that for desert {his guilt} he dyed.
MGREC118:7 H2654 And had to him, still since *Ephestion* dyed,
MGREC132:25 H3270 After three years he dyed, left what he'd won
MGREC132:29 H3276 Now {Next} dyed the brave and noble *Ptolomy,*
1SIMON188:2 H2-3 *Who dyed on* 16. Novemb. 1669. *being but*

DYES (1) [dies]

MGREC115:6 H2517 Here his cheif favourite *Ephestion* dyes,

DYING (7)

MPERS82:35 H1182 He dying to behold, that wounding sight;
MGREC~~105:13~~ H2106 Should heare, nor see, his groans, and {dying} misery:
MGREC105:21 H2114 The witnesse of his dying misery: {this horrid Tragedy;}
MGREC105:41 H2134 I've nothing left, at this my dying hour;
DIALOG144:5 H115 Martyrs, and others, dying causelesly:

DDUDLEY167:23	H20	*Then dying, left a blessed memory.*
MERCY189:6	H27	The fifth and last pledge of her dying love,

E

EACH (61)

FATHER5:30	H31	Each others faults, and where themselves excell:
PROLOG6:21	H6	And {Or} how they all, or each, their dates have run:
PROLOG7:14	H27	I am obnoxious to each carping tongue,
PROLOG7:32	H43	Preheminence in each, and all is yours,
ELEMEN8:9	H7	And {That} in due order each her turne should speake,
ELEMEN10:33	H108	And though I be a servant to each man;
ELEMEN11:18	H138	Now Sisters, pray proceed, each in her {your} course,
ELEMEN15:21	H303	To meet with want, each woefull man bethinks.
HUMOUR20:14	H6	The native qualities, that from each {them} flow,
HUMOUR20:16	H8	Each eldest Daughter to each Element;
HUMOUR20:16	H8	Each eldest Daughter to each Element;
HUMOUR20:19	H11	All having made obeysance to each Mother,
HUMOUR33:31	H545	Which life and motion to each Creature gives,
AGES36:27	H51	These being met, each in his equipage,
AGES~~36:33~~	H57	To do as he, the rest {each one} ful soon assents,
AGES36:35	H59	That each should tel, what of himselfe he knew;
AGES39:25	H168	So affable that I do {can} suit each mind;
AGES41:39	H256	For time, for place, likewise for each relation,
SEASONS48:28	H81	Each season, hath his fruit, so hath each clime.
SEASONS48:28	H81	Each season, hath his fruit, so hath each clime.
SEASONS48:29	H82	Each man his owne peculiar excellence,
SEASONS50:39	H173	Now day and night are equal in each clime;
SEASONS51:11	H185	The season's now at hand, of all, and each;
MASSYR53:17	H7	But each one thought his petty rule was high,
MASSYR56:2	H108	Each Square, was fifteen thousand paces long,
MASSYR56:18	H124	This to discribe, {deseribe} in each particular,
MASSYR56:27	H133	(Each man beleive it, as his fancy list)
MASSYR57:20	~~H167~~	Each wronged Prince, or childe that did remain,
MASSYR59:41	H265	Ingeniously with each {all} did keep his word;
MASSYR65:1	H466	And in the channell throw {threw} each burden down;
MPERS74:29	H852	Made wholsome gentle Laws, which pleas'd each mind.
MPERS79:33	H1059	Was scarce enough, for each a draught to take.
MPERS80:6	H1073	But on their ground they dye, each Mothers Son.
MPERS82:3	H1150	Ten dayes these Armies did each other face,
MPERS85:31	H1307	And so each man again possest his owne.
MPERS88:2	H1395	In this confusion, each man as he might,
MPERS89:8	H1442	With infamy upon each fore-head stampt;

MPERS89:28 H1462 They quak'd, to heare them, to each other call.
MGREC94:2 H1636 Which makes each moment seem, more then a day:
MGREC107:10 H2185 Commands forth-with, each man his fardle bring,
MGREC112:32 H2418 Who to the height doth aggravate each thing;
MGREC117:22 H2629 Each man {All men} began for {streight} to contemn his might;
MGREC117:27 H2634 Each Captain wisht this prize to beare away,
MGREC118:28 H2677 Under his name begins {began} to rule each thing.
MGREC119:1 H2691 But nothing lesse: each one himself intends.
MGREC128:40 H3113 That each shall {should} hold what he doth {did} now possesse,
MGREC130:36 ~~H3181~~ And's kingdomes rent away by each Commander:
MGREC131:11 H3203 Near *Ephesus,* each bringing all their {his} might,
MROMAN136:32 H3446 The Mistris of the World, in each respect.
MROMAN139:4 H3532 He ranks the people, into each degree,
DIALOG145:22 H171 To crush the proud, and right to each man deal.
DUBART154:27 H72 Unto each man his riches are {is} assign'd,
TDUDLEY166:32 H74 Where we with joy each others face shall see,
CONTEM170:15 H87 Fruits of the Earth, and Fatlings each do bring,
CONTEM170:27 H98 Thinks each he sees will serve him in his kind,
CONTEM172:31 H164 That for each season, have your habitation,
CONTEM173:28 H193 So each one tunes his pretty instrument,
CONTEM173:37 H201 Each storm his state, his mind, his body break,
CHILDRN186:16 H83 When each of you shall in your nest
MYSOUL225:23 H27 O let me covnt each hour a Day
13MAY226:29 H5 At Svn-shine each their joy expresse.

EAGERLY (1)
MPERS88:35 H1428 And now more eagerly their foes pursue,

EAGLE (2) See also TH'EAGLE
ELEMEN10:10 H85 The Bear, the Goate, the Raven, and the Eagle,
ELEMEN15:6 H288 The lofty Eagle and the Storke flye low,

EAGLES (3) [pl.]
DAVID159:11 H26 Swifter then swiftest Eagles, so were they,

EAGLES (2) [poss.]
FATHER5:10 H11 To mount so high, requires an Eagles quill:
SON231:15 H27 On Eagles wings him hether brovght

EAR (7)
AGES37:37 H99 Nor unto buzzing whisperors, gave ear.
MGREC126:16 H3007 Cassander will not heare {Her foe would give no Ear}, such is
2LETTER181:33 H3 But stay this once, unto my suit give ear,
3LETTER182:37 H2 Scuds through the woods and Fern with harkning ear,
3LETTER183:2 H4 Her dearest Deer, might answer ear or eye;
BYNIGHT220:9 H9 He bow'd his ear down from Above
RESTOR230:7 H22 Nor turnd his ear away from me

EARE (6) [ear]
AGES36:26 H50 And al gave eare, to what he had to say.
MGREC101:16 H1941 To this, stout *Alexander,* gives no eare,
MGREC105:12 H2105 Yea, {But} above all, that neither eare, nor eye,
MGREC113:1 H2428 The King would give no eare, but went from thence;
DIALOG143:35 H104 For Oathes, and Blasphemies did ever eare
PILGRIM211:1 H42 as eare ner' heard nor tongue ere told

EARES (8) [ears]
AGES40:15 H196 To all obscenity, my {mine} eares I bend. {lend;}

SEASONS52:30 H245 Now toes, and eares, and fingers often freeze,
MPERS69:18 H640 Are fit for such, whose eares for fables itch;
MPERS74:40 H861 With his own hands cuts off his eares, and nose,
MGREC106:41 H2175 The certainty of both comes to his eares,
DIALOG144:25 ~~H134~~ Unworthily, some backs whipt, and eares cropt;
DUBART154:22 H67 Leadst millions chained by eyes, by eares, by tongues,
MEDDM202:32 Hp282 The eyes and the eares are the inlets or doores of the soule,

EARLE (1) [earl]
DIALOG143:7 H74 No Duke of *York,* nor Earle of *March,* to soyle

EARLY (2)
AGES42:26 H284 The early Cock, did summon but in vaine,
SEASONS48:25 H78 For fruits, my season yeelds, the early Cherry,

EARNEST (1)
MGREC114:9 H2477 From jeast, to earnest, and at last so bold,

EARNESTLY (2)
BYNIGHT220:8 H8 Wth tears I sovght him earnestly
THEART229:4 H6 I sovght more earnestly

EARS (5) See also EARES
ELEMEN15:32 H314 My pearles that dangle at thy darlings ears;
MASSYR56:21 H127 All eyes that saw, or ears that hears, {hear} admires.
MPERS82:31 H1178 Cut off her lilly breasts, her nose, and ears;
MGREC130:12 H3167 *Antigonus* thus had a wolf by th' ears,
FLESH176:16 H56 Ile stop mine ears at these thy charms,

EARTH (81)
FATHER5:32 H33 How Aire, and Earth, no correspondence hold,
ELEMEN8:5 H3 Fire, Aire, Earth, and Water, did all contest
ELEMEN8:13 H11 The quaking Earth did groan, the skie look't black,
ELEMEN8:15 H13 The sea did threat the heavens, the heavens the earth,
ELEMEN8:17 H15 Fire broyled Earth, and scorched Earth it choaked,
ELEMEN8:17 H15 Fire broyled Earth, and scorched Earth it choaked,
ELEMEN9:12 H46 Subdue the earth, and fit it for your graine,
ELEMEN9:25 H59 What mingled lay with earth, I cause to shine.
ELEMEN9:33 H67 Good {Cold} sister Earth, no witnesse needs but thine;
ELEMEN11:20 H140 *Earth.*
ELEMEN11:21 H141 The next in place, Earth judg'd to be her due,
ELEMEN11:24 H144 And Mother Earth, of old, men did me call,
ELEMEN14:22 H264 As earth at first, so into earth return'd.
ELEMEN14:22 H264 As earth at first, so into earth return'd.
ELEMEN14:24 H266 Scarce Earth had done, but th' angry waters {water} mov'd;
ELEMEN15:16 H298 That this is true, earth thou canst not deny;
ELEMEN15:27 H309 Such wealth, but not such like, Earth thou mayst show.
ELEMEN16:3 H326 Earth, thou hast not more Countrys, Vales and Mounds,
ELEMEN16:37 H360 As I with showers oft time {times} refresh the earth;
ELEMEN18:1 H405 And though you love Fire, Earth, and Water wel;
ELEMEN18:5 H409 And all the wealth, that ever earth did give,
ELEMEN~~18:7~~ H411 No world {earth}, thy witching trash, were all but vain.
ELEMEN19:41 H482 That earth appeares in heaven, oh wonder great!
HUMOUR20:18 H10 Earth knew her black swarth childe, Water her faire;
HUMOUR23:9 H119 Thy self's as dul, as is thy mother Earth.
HUMOUR24:29 H178 No valour upon earth, but what thou hast.
HUMOUR35:12 H608 Nor be discern'd, here's water, earth, aire, fire,

earth

AGES35:25	H11	The last, of earth, and heavy melancholly,
AGES46:5	H436	That earth can give no consolation sound.
SEASONS~~46:35~~	H13	Fit to revive, the nummed earth from death.
SEASONS48:1	H54	That when the Sun (on's love) the earth doth shine,
SEASONS48:10	H63	Wherein the earth, is clad in rich aray:
SEASONS49:11	~~H102~~	Hath formerly much heat, the earth and aire.
SEASONS~~49:11~~	H102	Have throughly dry'd the earth, and heat the air.
SEASONS50:14	H148	The dryed earth is parched by {with} his face.
SEASONS51:28	H204	The sap doth slily creep towards the earth,
SEASONS52:9	H224	Old cold, dry age, and earth, Autumne resembles,
MASSYR64:3	H427	This was that tree, whose brances fill'd the earth,
MPERS~~71:4~~	H717	And though his conquests made the earth to groan,
MPERS76:13	H911	Possession of water, earth, and aire,
MPERS76:16	H914	Or like to Mice, under the earth must live;
MGREC93:23	H1620	Whose glory to the Earth, this Prince {king} did throw,
MGREC101:24	H1949	Two Monarchies on Earth cannot abide,
MGREC102:19	H1989	With all pleasures that on earth was {are} found,
MGREC103:4	H2015	Of all the Cities, that on Earth was found;
MGREC105:9	H2102	Invokes the heavens, and earth, to heare his moanes;
MGREC106:6	H2140	Though gods on earth, like Sons of men shall {they} dye.
MGREC~~132:20~~	H3263	As Heaven and Earth against him had been set:
MGREC135:11	H3383	The Heavens thus rule, to fill the earth {world} with wonder.
DIALOG142:27	H56	Whence is this {the} storme, from Earth, or Heaven above?
QELIZ156:4	H31	From all the Kings on earth she won the prize;
QELIZ156:16	H43	And earth had twice {once} a yeare, a new old face:
VANITY159:33	H5	On brittle earth, a consolation sound?
VANITY160:13	H23	Sure if on earth, it must be in those parts;
TDUDLEY165:36	H38	Upon the earth he did not build his nest,
TDUDLEY166:27	H69	As joy in heaven, on earth let praise resound.
CONTEM168:5	H15	More Heaven then Earth was here, no winter & no night.
CONTEM168:26	H33	The Earth reflects her glances in thy face.
CONTEM170:15	H87	Fruits of the Earth, and Fatlings each do bring,
CONTEM170:24	H95	The Virgin Earth, of blood her first draught drinks
CONTEM170:28	H99	Though none on Earth but kindred near then could he find.
CONTEM171:19	H122	And then the earth (though old) stil clad in green,
CONTEM171:34	H135	Shall I then praise the heavens, the trees, the earth
CONTEM174:24	H222	Fond fool, he takes this earth ev'n for heav'ns bower.
FLESH175:13	H13	Regardlesly to let earth goe?
FLESH175:32	H32	Earth hath more silver, pearls and gold,
FLESH175:35	H35	Earth hath enough of what you will.
FLESH176:41	H81	Nor such like trash which Earth doth hold,
FLESH177:6	H87	There's none on Earth can parallel;
1LETTER181:9	H7	I like the earth this season, mourn in black,
MEDDM202:7	Hp281	then ye earth some so wise and learned, that they seeme like
MEDDM206:16	Hp287	shine so bright while they moue on earth, how transcendently
PILGRIM210:19	H19	A pilgrim I, on earth, perplext
MYCHILD217:37	Hp243	of ye Heaven + ye Earth, the order of all things night and day,
MYCHILD218:2	Hp243	hovshold vpon ye Earth, ye p^{r}serving + directing of All to its
MYCHILD218:31	Hp244	there Faith vpon ye Earth? & I haue not known what to think,
SOREFIT221:17	H3	When novght on Earth could comfort giue
SOREFIT222:5	H24	Nor ovght on Earth worthy Desire,

JULY223:23 Hp251 was from home (who is my cheifest comforter on Earth)
13MAY226:28 H4 The earth all black is cloth'd in green
HOUSE237:12 H42 And did thy wealth on earth abide,

EARTHLY (4)

MGREC118:18 H2665 That he, who late, possest all earthly things,
CONTEM169:5 H47 As to approach it, can no earthly mould.
1LETTER181:4 H2 My joy, my Magazine of earthly store,
MEDDM207:18 Hp289 perceiue a decay, in their greennes for were earthly comforts

EARTH-QUAKS (1)

ELEMEN19:36 H477 Earth-quaks so hurtful and so fear'd of all,

EARTHS (4) [poss.]

ELEMEN15:11 H293 He knowes such sweets, lyes not in earths dry roots,
ELEMEN17:28 H392 Then wholly perish'd, earths ignoble race;
ELEMEN19:5 H450 Earths Beasts, and Waters Fish, scarce can compare.
MPERS70:15 H686 Upon earths richest spoyles his Souldiers preys;

EARTHY (1)

HUMOUR28:4 H316 And turns him to the wombe of's earthy mother,

EAS'D (3) [eased]

MASSYR64:6 H430 Kild, sav'd, pull'd down, set up, or pain'd, or eas'd;
SIDNEY152:12 H81 I to be eas'd of such a task was glad.
DISTEMP179:24 H12 He eas'd my Soul of woe, my flesh of pain,

EASE (14)

ELEMEN16:29 H352 Unlesse I ease his toyle, and doe transport,
AGES44:17 H350 That can refresh, or ease, if Conscience frown;
MASSYR57:3 H150 A Prince wedded to ease, and to delight,
MASSYR57:19 ~~H166~~ He thus voluptuous, and given to ease;
MASSYR61:18 H323 To *Tiglath* then doth *Ahaz* send for ease.
MPERS91:19 H1527 The King from forraign foes, and all {parts now well} at ease,
MPERS~~91:25~~ H1539 But long in ease and pleasure did not lye,
DIALOG141:24 H23 Which present help may ease this {my} malady.
DIALOG145:21 H170 To ease my groaning land shew {shew'd} their intent,
VANITY160:21 H31 While man is man, he shall have ease or pain.
CONTEM174:14 H213 Sings merrily, and steers his Barque with ease,
2SIMON195:8 Hp271 fit for you nor of more ease to my self then these short
BYNIGHT220:3 H4 And hath at once both ease and Rest,
FEVER220:28 H8 From side to side for ease I toyle,

EASED (1) [eas'd]

MGREC94:13 H1647 Thus eased now, of troubles, and of fears;

EASETH (1)

MASSYR67:5 H551 Easeth *Jehoiakims* captivity.

EASILY (9)

HUMOUR27:6 H277 That this is true, I easily can assent,
MGREC95:13 H1692 And easily takes old *Gordium* in his way;
MGREC98:27 H1829 For that which easily comes, as freely goes;
MGREC107:39 ~~H2214~~ He easily might have made them stay there stil;
MGREC113:7 H2434 Thy Kingly word can easily terminate;
MGREC136:15 H3429 *Yet in this Chaos, one shall easily spy,*
MEDDM196:2 Hp272 beares much saile & little or no ballast, is easily ouer set, and
MEDDM200:16 Hp279 garment, she easily foresees what euents it is like to produce,
MEDDM201:9 Hp280 easily sayd by many, but what he did not say, cannot (truly) be

EAST (6)
ELEMEN16:28 H351 Transfers his goods, from North and South and East;
MASSYR56:24 H130 An expedition to the East she made.
MASSYR62:24 H369 Whether the *Indians* of the East, or West,
MGREC106:7 H2141 Now to the East great *Alexander* goes,
QELIZ157:22 H90 *Zenobia,* potent Empresse of the East,
1HUSB180:28 H7 Or all the riches that the East doth hold.
EAST WARD (2)
MGREC110:21 H2325 East-ward, now *Alexander* would goe still,
MGREC128:28 H3101 Still gaining Countries East-ward goes he on.
EAT (4)
AGES45:34 H424 Nor sapors find, in what I drink or eat.
SEASONS50:20 H154 Which after Manchet's made, {makes} for Kings to eat;
FLESH176:28 H68 The hidden Manna I doe eat,
HOUSE237:4 H34 Nor at thy Table eat a bitt.
EATE (3)
ELEMEN13:10 H211 If ought you have to use, to wear, to eate?
MGREC135:32 H3404 And when he had no appetite to eate,
PILGRIM210:12 H12 Nor wild fruits eate, in stead of bread
EATERS (1) [poss.]
SEASONS50:36 H170 Then drops his Fruits into the Eaters lap.
EATES (1)
HUMOUR31:11 H444 That casts out all that man or {e're} eates, or drinks.
EATING (2)
MGREC~~120:36~~ H2773 Which eating time hath scarcely yet defac'd.
CONTEM171:14 H118 In eating, drinking, sleeping, vain delight
EATS See EATES
EBBE (1)
MASSYR65:14 H479 But he (alas) whose fortunes {all were} now i'th ebbe,
EBBS (1) [pl.]
ELEMEN16:17 H340 Th' uncertain cause, of certain ebbs and flowes;
EBENEZ^{R} (1) [ebenezer]
MYCHILD217:20 Hp243 knowes not, & haue sett vp my Ebenez^{r}. and haue resolved
ECBATANE (1)
MGREC~~115:15~~ H2527 Of stately *Ecbatane* who now must shew,
ECCHO (1) [echo]
DUBART154:7 H52 Vollies of praises could I eccho then,
ECCHOES (1) [echoes]
ELEMEN18:17 H421 And such are Ecchoes, and report o'th gun
ECCHOES (1) v.
MPERS74:14 H837 But {And joyfull} acclamations ecchoes in the aire; {shrill they
ECLIPSE (2)
MGREC122:4 H2827 And much eclipse his {great Acts and} glory to rehearse
13MAY227:3 H12 But if they mvst eclipse again
EDEN (2)
SEASONS51:14 H188 For then in *Eden* was not only seen
CONTEM169:34 H72 Sometimes in *Eden* fair, he seems to be,
EDG (1) [edge]
MEDDM197:4 Hp274 wthout wisedome is like a heavy axe, wthout an edg fitter to
EDICT (2)
MPERS70:23 H694 An Edict makes {made}, the Temple builded be,

MPERS75:25 H882 An Edict for the *Jews* publish'd again,
EDOM (1)
MASSYR66:14 H520 No, nor {not} when *Moab, Edom* he had got.
EDUCATION (3)
AGES39:10 H153 Mine {My} education, and my learning's {learning} such,
AGES39:36 H179 My gifts abus'd, my education lost,
MGREC93:17 H1614 His Education, much to these {those} did adde.
EDWARD (3)
DIALOG142:16 H45 Must *Edward* be depos'd, or is't the houre
DIALOG143:3 H72 No *Edward, Richard,* to lose rule, and life,
DIALOG143:13 H82 By *Edward* third, and *Henry* fifth of fame,
EDWARDS (1) [poss.]
DIALOG144:9 H119 Oh, *Edwards* Babes {youths}, and *Clarence* haplesse Son,
EFFECT (6)
ELEMEN16:14 H337 My divers Fountaines and their strange effect;
DIALOG143:27 H96 Before I tell the effect, ile shew the cause,
DIALOG145:11 H160 But all you say, amounts to this effect,
BIRTH180:4 H14 I may seem thine, who in effect am none.
1LETTER181:19 H17 O strange effect! now thou art *Southward* gone,
MYCHILD215:10 Hp240 by exper^{c}. y^{t} ye exhortat^{s}. of parents take most effect wn y^{e}
EFFECTS (2) [pl.]
MPERS89:10 H1444 Of this dayes cowardize, he feares the effects;
MEDDM201:23 Hp281 produces these sweating effects,
EFFEMINATE (1)
MGREC102:23 H1993 He, and his Souldiers, wax effeminate,
EFTSOON (1)
CONTEM173:4 H172 Eftsoon to *Neptun's* glassie Hall repair
EGIPT (1) [egypt] See also ÆGYPT
MEDDM208:24 Hp290 proue like the reeds of Egipt that peirce insteed of supporting
EGYPT (6) See also ÆGYPT, EGIPT
ELEMEN15:17 H299 I call thine *Egypt,* this to verifie;
MPERS73:7 H794 A *Babylon* in *Egypt* did he make.
MPERS85:14 H1290 Disquiet {Revolting} Egypt, 'gainst this King rebells,
MPERS~~91:40~~ H1554 Then raises forces, conquers *Egypt* land,
MGREC118:38 H2687 And *Ptolomy,* next sure of *Egypt* makes.
MGREC134:18 H3349 In *Egypt* now {next,} a little time we'l spend.
EGYPTIAN (1) See also ÆGYPTIAN
MGREC134:40 H3369 Held for a time the *Egyptian* Monarchy:
EGYPTIANS (2) [pl.] See also ÆGYPTIANS
MPERS83:35 H1223 *Greeks* and *Egyptians* both, he overthrows,
MGREC118:24 H2671 The *Egyptians,* his body did enbalme;
EGYPTS (1) [poss.] See also ÆGYPTS
MGREC133:37 H3327 Who a long warre with *Egypts* King begun.
EIGHT (7)
MASSYR61:6 H311 Forty eight years he reign'd, his race then run,
MPERS~~71:4~~ H716 But eight whilst *Babylon,* he did retain:
MPERS73:9 H796 Eight years he reign'd, a short, yet too long time,
MPERS78:6 H987 Eight hundred thousand Horse to them {these} belong;
MGREC98:20 H1822 Eight thousand by the sword now also dy'd,
MROMAN138:35 H3525 Thirty eight yeares (this Stranger borne) did reigne,
CHILDRN184:14 H3 I had eight birds hatcht in one nest,

EIGHTEEN (1)
MASSYR65:36 H501 And after eighteen months he took them all,
EIGHTH (1)
MASSYR65:33 H498 But in the eighth, against his Prince rebels;
EIGHTY (3)
MGREC97:22 H1783 Two hundred eighty *Greeks* he lost in fight,
MGREC109:23 H2282 And {Then} eighty Tallents to his Captaines down.
MROMAN139:7 H3535 To eighty thousand soules then did amount:
EITHER (10)
ELEMEN12:5 H165 On either side the country of the *Gaules,*
ELEMEN~~19:2~~ H447 And what those Sages, did, or {either} spake, or writ,
MASSYR58:29 H212 And either by his valour, or his fate,
MASSYR60:20 H285 And either by compound, or else by strength,
MPERS84:35 H1271 Either to wrong, did wound his heart so sore,
2LETTER181:34 H4 And tell my griefs in either Hemisphere:
MEDDM198:22 Hp276 done, but either that or something like it, hath been both done
MEDDM200:7 Hp279 wormwood or mustard, they wil either wipe it off, or else suck
MYCHILD216:33 Hp242 way everlasting: and seldome or never but I haue fovnd either
MYCHILD217:11 Hp242 Answers to me, either in granting ye Thing I prayed for, or else
EKRONITES (1)
MASSYR54:11 H38 This is *Belzebub,* god of *Ekronites,*
ELDER (3)
MGREC122:19 H2844 Who was *Perdicas, Philips* elder {eldest} brother,
MGREC129:28 H3142 Call'd *Hercules,* and elder then his brother,
13MAY227:11 H20 Blessd me in Youth, and elder Age
ELDERS (1) [pl.]
AGES39:1 H144 I've done unto my elders I give way.
ELDEST (11)
HUMOUR20:16 H8 Each eldest Daughter to each Element;
MPERS77:13 H952 Unto {Then to} his eldest {second} Son, all did remain.
MPERS~~77:16~~ H956 (His eldest brother put beside the place,
MPERS83:16 H1204 Accus'd *Darius, Xerxes* eldest son,
MPERS83:24 H1212 The eldest son, thus immaturely dead,
MPERS85:5 H1281 The eldest to succeed, that was his mind.
MPERS86:7 H1323 His large Dominions left, to's eldest son.
MGREC98:41 H1843 His eldest Daughter, (him) {he} in marriage offers,
MGREC101:6 H1931 His eldest Daughter, for his Princely Bride,
MGREC~~122:19~~ H2844 Who was *Perdicas, Philips* elder {eldest} brother,
MGREC~~132:20~~ H3260 Leaving *Antigonus* his eldest Son,
ELD'ST (1) [eldest]
MGREC131:40 H3232 The eld'st enrag'd did play the vipers part,
ELEAV'N (1) [eleven] See also ELEV'N, 'LEVEN
MASSYR57:32 H177 And eleav'n {many} hundred of years in silence sit,
ELECT (2)
MGREC118:10 H2657 Hoping to be elect more generally;
MYCHILD218:33 Hp244 it were possible ye very elect should bee deceived. Behold
ELECTION (2)
MPERS74:20 H843 *Darius* by election made a King
MEDDM206:28 Hp288 then his great worke of election and Reprobation, when we
ELEGIE (1)
SIDNEY149:1 H1 An Elegie upon that Honourable

ELEMENT (6)
ELEMEN8:28 ~~H26~~ Being the most impatient Element.
ELEMEN~~8:28~~ H26 The noblest and most active Element.
ELEMEN18:12 H416 To bid adue, to his dear Element.
ELEMEN18:40 H444 Me for no Element, longer to hold.
ELEMEN20:8 H490 But dare not go, beyond my Element.
HUMOUR20:16 H8 Each eldest Daughter to each Element;
ELEMENTS (3) [pl.]
ELEMEN8:4 H1-2 The *Foure Elements.*
AGES36:34 H58 Their method was, that of the Elements,
MPERS71:32 H746 But vain he found, to fight with Elements,
ELEPHANT (1)
ELEMEN15:4 H286 Hindes leave their Calves, the Elephant the Fens;
ELEPHANTS (2) [pl.]
MGREC109:20 H2279 Fifty six Elephants he brings to's hands: {hand,}
MGREC110:4 H2304 And ninety Elephants for war did bring;
ELEV'N (1) [eleven] See also ELEAV'N, 'LEVEN
MPERS76:30 H928 Arm'd all they could, which elev'n thousand make;
ELEVATE (1)
AGES~~39:29~~ H172 And elevates {elevate} my {high} thoughts above {beyond} the
ELEVATES (1)
AGES39:29 H172 And elevates {elevate} my {high} thoughts above {beyond} the
ELIZA (3)
QELIZ157:16 H84 A great *Eliza,* but compar'd with ours,
QELIZ157:41 H109 Then wonder not, *Eliza* moves not here.
QELIZ158:6 H115 *Eliza* shall rule *Albian* once again.
ELIZA'S (1) [poss.]
QELIZ155:35 H26 *Eliza's* works, wars, praise, can e're compact,
ELIZABETH (2)
QELIZ155:11 H2 Princess, Queen ELIZABETH, of
ELIZB186:31 H1-2 *In memory of my dear grand-child Elizabeth*
ELM (1)
CONTEM172:6 H142 Under the cooling shadow of a stately Elm
ELOQUENCE (2)
SIDNEY149:16 H15 Thine {His} Eloquence made *Mercury* wax red;
DUBART153:28 H32 But findes too soone his want of Eloquence,
ELSE (25)
PROLOG7:19 H32 They'l say its stolne, or else, it was by chance.
PROLOG7:22 H34 Else of our Sex, why feigned they those nine,
ELEMEN9:17 H51 Your spits, pots, jacks, what else I need not name,
ELEMEN9:39 H73 The Flye *Pyrausta* cal'd, all else expire.
ELEMEN11:32 H152 Would so passe time, I could say nothing else;
ELEMEN14:38 H280 Or else thy sun-burnt face, and gaping chapps;
HUMOUR25:19 H208 Both them and all things else, she will {would} consume.
HUMOUR33:17 H531 No debtor I, because 'tis {it's} paid else where;
MASSYR55:29 H95 Or else she sought, revenge for *Menons* fall:
MASSYR57:4 H151 Or else was his obedience very great,
MASSYR60:20 H285 And either by compound, or else by strength,
MASSYR61:4 H309 What else he did, his Empire to advance,
MASSYR62:26 H371 Or else those *Chinoes* rare, whose wealth, and Arts,
MPERS87:34 H1386 Some fifty, or else sixty foote in breadth.

MPERS91:40 ~~H1554~~ Or else, perhaps the deeds of *Persian* Kings
MPERS92:8 ~~H1566~~ So fell to him, which else it had not done:
MGREC100:7 H1891 The Pagan Priest through hire, or else mistake,
MGREC124:9 ~~H2914~~ Those absent, banished, or else he slew
MGREC132:31 H3278 Rich *Ægypt* left, and what else he had won
DIALOG145:18 H167 Which is the chief, the law, or else the King,
MEDDM200:7 Hp279 mustard, they wil either wipe it off, or else suck down sweet
MEDDM205:27 Hp286 god and vs, or else we should not so often faile in our whole
MEDDM207:17 Hp289 withers the pleasure wch else we should take in them, and well
MYCHILD215:14 Hp240 to compose some short matters, (for w^{t} else to call y^{m} I know
MYCHILD217:11 Hp242 Answers to me, either in granting ye Thing I prayed for, or else

ELSE-WHERE (1)
MGREC110:12 H2312 Then {When} covertly, the rest gets {get} o're else-where;

ELSEWHERE (2)
MASSYR60:5 H270 But suffered, with {their} goods to go elsewhere,
DIALOG142:38 H67 For they have work enough (thou knowst) elsewhere;

EMBASSADOUR (1)
MGREC130:8 H3163 With his Embassadour, her journey takes,

EMBASSADOURS (3) [pl.]
MASSYR63:15 H400 Embassadours to *Hezekiah* sent, [21 *years.*
MGREC98:34 H1836 By his Embassadours now sues for peace:
MGREC111:3 H2348 Where one hundred {Whether} Embassadours, {ninety} or

EMBASSAGE (1)
MGREC130:6 H3161 Where, by Embassage, all these Princes pray,

EMBITTER See IMBITTER

EMBLEAM (1) [emblem]
MEDDM207:33 Hp289 embleam of death, wch is their sleep (for so is death often

EMBLEM (2)
CONTEM172:26 H160 Thou Emblem true, of what I count the best,
MEDDM200:24 Hp279 The spring is a liuely emblem of the resurrection, after a long

EMBRACE See IMBRACE

EMBROILED See IMBROYL'D

EMBRYON (1)
HUMOUR26:20 H250 As plants, trees, and small Embryon know'th,

EMILLIUS (1)
MGREC133:24 H3313 {T'} *Emillius* the *Roman* Generall,

EMINENCE (1)
HUMOUR33:28 H542 Within this stately place of eminence,

EMINENT (5)
HUMOUR31:36 H469 My temperance, chastity, is eminent,
MASSYR53:30 H20 By him, to Cities eminent did rise;
MGREC120:32 H2769 To save himself from dangers eminent;
MGREC121:25 H2807 Then by more trouble to grow eminent.
MEDDM205:35 Hp286 there are some eminent Christians, that are soe frequent in

EMPEROUR (1)
SEASONS50:16 H150 *Romes* second Emperour of peaceful {lasting} fame;

EMPIRE (6)
MASSYR57:23 ~~H170~~ Until that potent Empire did decay.
MASSYR61:4 H309 What else he did, his Empire to advance,
MGREC99:23 H1866 (For 'twas decreed, that Empire should be shaken)
MGREC114:41 H2511 From *Macedon* his Empire did extend,

MGREC128:17 H3090 First, how he held the Empire in his hands,
MGREC~~133:27~~ H3317 Whose kingdomes {Empire was} were subdu'd by {to} th'

EMPLOYMENT (1)
1LETTER181:2 H0 *Publick employment.*

EMPLOYED See IMPLOYED

EMPRESSE (2)
MASSYR55:17 H83 This great renowned Empresse, issued.
QELIZ157:22 H90 *Zenobia,* potent Empresse of the East,

EMPTY (12)
AGES41:26 H243 Such {My} empty seed should yeeld a better crop.
AGES43:18 H313 Whereby my empty soule, is lur'd and caught.
SEASONS52:8 H223 Our pinched flesh, and empty panch {hungry mawes} requires:
MPERS81:3 H1111 With empty hands they to their Master go;
DIALOG~~147:14~~ H240 Copes, Rochets, Crossiers, and such {empty} trash,
DUBART153:24 H28 But seeing empty wishes nought obtaine,
MEDDM195:35 Hp272 age, and both by an empty old age, he that hath nothing to
MEDDM200:11 Hp279 these empty brests, that god is forced to hedg vp their way wth
MEDDM202:35 Hp282 giue, & wch is most strang, the more it receius the more empty
MEDDM206:25 Hp287 empty beareing the reproch of his pride and folly.
MEDDM208:25 Hp290 empty wells in the time of drought, that those that go to finde
MEDDM208:26 Hp290 them, return with their empty pitchers ashamed,

EMULATE (1)
MASSYR58:4 H189 And {in} their kind t' excel did emulate.

E'N (1)
AGES46:15 H446 And my last period now e'n almost run;

ENBALME (1)
MGREC118:24 H2671 The *Egyptians,* his body did enbalme;

ENCAMP'D (1) [encamped] See also INCAMP'D, INCAMPT
MGREC~~121:32~~ H2814 Whilst *Perdicas* thus staid {encamp'd} in *Africa,*

ENCLIN'D (1) [inclined] See also INCLIN'D
MGREC106:37 H2171 His Captains, that were vertuously enclin'd,

ENCOUNTER (2)
HUMOUR22:8 H77 Then by a quick encounter, to be slaine;
MGREC94:39 H1677 The *Persians* for encounter ready stand,

ENCOUNTERED (1)
MPERS90:32 H1499 By th' Kings Lieutenant {*Tissaphernes*} is encountered,

ENCOUNTERS (1)
MGREC110:11 H2311 *Porus* encounters them, thinking {and thinks} all's there,

ENCOURAG^{D} (1)
JULY223:28 Hp251 that I now hope for, y^{t} so they may bee encourag^{d} to trust in

ENCOURAGED See INCOURAG'D, INCOURAGED

ENCREASE (1) [increase]
MASSYR60:35 H300 Molests poor *Israel,* his wealth t' encrease.

ENCROACH (1)
MGREC123:20 H2884 And *Ptolomy,* now {next} to encroach begins,

ENCROACHED See INCROACHED

ENCROACHING See INCROACHING

ENCUMBERS See INCU¯BERS

END (56)
AGES~~38:4~~ H107 My little wrath did cease {end} soon as my wars.
AGES44:11 H344 An end of all perfection now I see.

SEASONS~~52:39~~	H256	Where first it did begin, in th' end its found.
MASSYR59:18	H242	Who there incamp'd two years, for little end,
MASSYR61:31	H336	But *Tiglath,* having gain'd his wished end,
MASSYR65:21	H486	minde, and slew him by the way; {& caus'd his life there end,}
MASSYR68:2	H588	Destruction to his Crown, to's Person end.
MASSYR68:29	H615	With him did end the race of *Baladan,*
MASSYR68:31	H617	*The end of the* Assyrian *Monarchy.*
MPERS~~69:38~~	H668	Whose happy life attains an happy end.
MPERS71:36	H750	If all his {this} heat, had been for a good {pious} end,
MPERS73:5	H792	The Male line, of great *Cyrus* now did {had} end.
MPERS83:11	H1199	And for that end, his Eunuch he did hire.
MPERS84:21	H1257	And for that end, great preparation made,
MPERS84:38	H1274	Strong poyson took, and {so} put an end to's dayes.
MPERS86:5	H1321	His fathers death, did {so} put an end to's fear.
MPERS86:39	H1355	And for that end, five hundred Horse he chose,
MPERS92:10	H1568	But as 'tis thought, {most suppose} in him had {did} *Cyrus* end:
MPERS93:3	H1600	And last; a sad catastrophe to end,
MPERS93:5	H1602	*The end of the* Persian *Monarchy.*
MGREC98:14	H1816	The former ruines, help to him now lend; {forwarded his end:}
MGREC101:35	H1964	So make {made} an end, before they {as soon as} well begun;
MGREC105:23	H2116	The just revenge of this his wofull end;
MGREC107:7	H2182	Intends with speed, that Traitor down {to his end} to bring;
MGREC115:19	H2538	And in a Tragedy there end his age.
MGREC116:3	H2563	Poyson had put an end to's dayes 'twas thought,
MGREC120:3	H2734	Now dy'd (about the end of th' *Lamian* warre)
MGREC~~120:4~~	H2738	To end his dayes by poison, rather chose
MGREC125:22	H2972	The King by extreame torments had his end,
MGREC126:29	H3020	This was the end of this most cruell Queen,
MGREC129:11	H3125	But for one act she did, just was her end,
MGREC129:41	H3155	He knows to's profit, all i'th end {this at last} will turn,
MGREC131:37	H3229	Who had an end put to their dayes by slaughter.
MGREC133:5	H3293	Yet by him had this most unworthy end.
MGREC134:17	H3348	Of *Greece,* and *Syria* thus the rule did end,
MGREC~~135:1~~	H3372	He seeing his honour lost, his Kingdome end,
MGREC~~136:8~~	H3422	*The End of the Grecian Monarchy.*
MROMAN137:16	H3467	But in the end, to finall peace they come,
MROMAN137:20	H3471	But *Romulus* then comes unto his end,
MROMAN138:2	H3492	The strife to end, six Brothers doe ingage;
MROMAN139:24	~~H3551~~	*The end of the* Roman *Monarchy,*
SIDNEY151:1	~~H69~~	Such prince as he, his race should shortly end:
TDUDLEY166:17	H59	He did exult his end was drawing near,
DDUDLEY167:21	H18	*Preparing still for death, till end of dayes:*
CONTEM170:19	H91	Hath thousand thoughts to end his brothers dayes,
BIRTH179:27	H3	All things within this fading world hath end,
CHILDRN184:23	H12	Till he return, or I do end,
CHILDRN186:3	H70	Till my weak layes with me shall end,
MEDDM201:7	Hp280	I haue seen an end of all perfection (sayd the royall prophet)
MEDDM201:8	Hp280	never sayd, I haue seen an end of all Sinning, what he did say,
MEDDM204:24	Hp285	wth Jehu's reward, wch will end in punishment
MEDDM207:5	Hp288	but most Commonly imployed for a Clean Contrary end, then
MEDDM208:2	Hp289	shall fly away, and the day of eternity shall never end, seeing

MYCHILD218:3 Hp243 End, The consideration of these things would wth amazement
JULY223:34 Hp251 my faith in Thee, 'till I shall attain ye End of my hopes, Even
30SEPT227:29 Hp257 that I haue passed thro: to ye End y^{t} if you meet wth the like

ENDEAVOUR (1) See also INDEAVOUR
MEDDM209:13 Hp291 Command of god, and endeavour not to the vtmost to driue

ENDEAVOURS (3) [pl.]
MGREC126:14 H3005 So succours, and endeavours proves but vaine:
MGREC127:14 H3044 True *Eumenes* endeavours by all skill,
MROMAN139:28 H3554 My thoughts and my endeavours thereto bent;

ENDED (4)
MASSYR54:14 H41 At twenty five, ended his regal date.
MPERS77:10 H949 And the ensuing yeare ended his life,
MPERS84:5 H1233 Queen *Vashty* also feasts, but 'fore tis ended,
HANNA230:14 H7 And life was ended near.

ENDIMIONS (1)
SEASONS49:33 H122 *Endimions, Diana's* dear delight;

ENDING (1)
HUMOUR20:11 H3 The former foure, now ending their Discourse,

ENDLESS (3)
CONTEM172:4 H141 But man was made for endless immortality.
ANNEB187:33 H23 Thou with thy Saviour art in endless bliss.
1SIMON188:15 H16 Among the blest in endless joyes remain.

ENDLESSE (3)
MPERS81:24 H1132 That whilst the Sun did run his endlesse course,
MGREC131:8 H3198 'Twould be an endlesse story to relate
SIDNEY151:22 H72 With endlesse turnes, the way I find not out,

ENDOWMENTS See INDOWMENTS

ENDS (5) [pl.]
MASSYR61:19 H324 The temple robes, so to fulfill his ends,
MGREC118:2 H2649 Their ends they might the better still attain.
MGREC118:16 H2663 So much these Princes their owne ends respected.
MGREC125:7 H2955 The better to accomplish these her ends;
MGREC125:33 H2983 That were {fell} within her reach, came to their ends;

ENDS (9) v.
ELEMEN15:15 H297 If not, soon ends his life, as did his voyce.
AGES35:36 H22 And when tis broke, then ends his life and all.
MPERS73:1 H788 Which ends before begun, the *Persian* {his home-bred} Warre,
MPERS81:21 H1129 Their infamy would last till all things ends:
MGREC112:14 H2400 So after many dayes this {the} Banquet ends.
MGREC131:14 H3206 This day twixt these two foes {Kings} ends all the strife,
MGREC135:6 H3378 Here ends at last the *Grecian* Monarchy,
MEDDM201:26 Hp281 vsed for Contrary ends, the one holds fast, the other puts
MEDDM204:23 Hp285 fixe his eye on the command, and not on his own ends, lest he

ENDURE (3) See also INDURE
HUMOUR27:37 H308 Mans life to boundlesse time might stil endure;
MGREC101:15 H1940 *Ochus* his Son a hostage shall {should} endure.
MGREC108:34 H2250 Whose {Their} nakednesse could not endure their might;

ENEMIES (3) [pl.] See also ENEMYES, ENEMYS
ELEMEN17:17 H381 That *Israels* enemies, therewith was {were} brain'd.
AGES40:17 H198 And dearest freinds count for mine enemies;
MPERS76:22 H920 His enemies scarce seen, then much lesse, slaine;

ENEMY (4)
MASSYR59:25 H249 That when the River prov'd their enemy,
MGREC99:31 H1874 Though in an enemy it should be found;
MEDDM198:29 Hp277 an enemy wthout may disturb a Commonwealth, but
MEDDM199:26 Hp278 in Scripture of three sorts of Arrows the arrow of an enemy
ENEMYES (1) [enemies] See also ENEMYS
MYCHILD218:12 Hp244 maugre all ye heathen Tyrants + all of the Enemyes who have
ENEMYS (1) [enemies] See also ENEMYES
MEDDM196:33 Hp274 That town wch thousands of enemys wthout hath not been able
ENFOLD See INFOLD
ENFRANCHISE See T'INFRANCHISE
ENFRANCHISED See INFRANCHISED
ENGAG'D (2) [engaged] See also INGAGED
MGREC98:10 H1812 To win their {the} town, his honour he engag'd;
MGREC113:19 H2446 Who was so much engag'd, to this Commander,
ENGAGE See INGAGE
ENGAGED (2) See also ENGAG'D, INGAGED
MASSYR67:17 H563 (Within which broiles, rich *Crœsus* was engaged,)
2HUSB233:17 H50 Wth an Engaged heart to sing
ENGLAND (15)
DIALOG141:2 H2 *England* and New, concerning
DIALOG141:5 H4 *New England.*
DIALOG141:14 H13 **Old England.**
DIALOG141:29 H28 *New England.*
DIALOG142:34 H63 **Old England.**
DIALOG145:6 H155 *New England.*
DIALOG145:15 H164 **Old England.**
DIALOG146:27 H213 *New England.*
SIDNEY149:7 H6 When *England* did injoy her Halsion dayes,
QELIZ156:21 H48 Did ever wealth in *England* so {more} abound?
QELIZ157:38 H106 But happy *England,* which had such a Queen,
SAMUEL228:1 H1-2 Vpon my Son Samuel his goeing for England Novem. 6. 1657.
SON230:19 H1-2 On my Sons Return out of England. July. 17. 1661.
2HUSB232:2 H3 England. Jan. 16. 1661.
ACK235:4 H3-4 husband ovt of England.
ENGLAND'S (1) [poss.]
SIDNEY152:21 H90 So *Sydney's* fame, I leave to *England's* Rolls,
ENGLANDS (1) [poss.]
DIALOG145:31 H180 All *Englands* Metropolitane that houre,
ENGLISH (3)
DIALOG142:11 H40 With *English* blood bedews thy conquered Land?
DIALOG148:18 H283 (For then what is't, but English blades dare do)
SIDNEY~~150:12~~ H43 Whilst English blood yet runs within my veins.
ENGRAVE (1)
SIDNEY150:20 H45 Engrave on Marble, in characters of Gold,
ENGRAVED See GRAV'D
ENJOY (1) See also INIOY, INJOY
MGREC105:28 H2121 Their lives enjoy, their crowns, and dignity,
ENJOYED (1) See also INJOY'D
MYCHILD217:23 Hp243 not enjoyed that felicity that somt. I haue done, But when I
ENJOYS See INJOYES

ENLARGE (1)
MPERS71:7 H723 But {Yet} to enlarge his state, had some desire;
ENLARGED (1) See also INLARG'D
MYCHILD217:13 Hp242 becavse I have fovnd my heart through his goodnes enlarged
ENLIGHTENS See INLIGHTENS
ENMITY (2)
ELEMEN8:10 H8 But enmity, this amity did breake:
ELEMEN8:25 H23 The others enmity: {difference,} being lesse, did cease
ENNOBLED See INNOBLED
ENORMITY See INORMITY
ENOUGH (22)
HUMOUR29:38 H389 Enough of that, by our Sister {sisters} heretofore,
HUMOUR32:21 H495 Enough of both, my wrongs for {now} to expresse;
AGES37:23 H85 My then ambitious thoughts, were low enough.
MASSYR57:36 H181 It is enough {may suffice}, if all be true that's past,
MPERS75:17 H878 Scarse finde enough to thank thy loyalty;
MPERS79:33 H1059 Was scarce enough, for each a draught to take.
MPERS85:35 H1311 No match was high enough, but their own blood,)
MGREC94:18 H1656 Reply'd, enough, sith only hope he kept.
MGREC96:30 H1750 Had not been spoile, and booty rich enough,
MGREC110:15 H2315 Yet work enough, here *Alexander* found,
MGREC116:39 H2605 He would have found enough for {there} to be done,
MGREC117:33 H2640 By Natures right, these had enough to claime,
DIALOG142:38 H67 For they have work enough (thou knowst) elsewhere;
SIDNEY151:25 H73 Enough for me to look, and so admire.
QELIZ156:14 H41 She's argument enough to make you mute;
VANITY160:9 H19 They'r foul enough to day, that once was {were} fair,
CONTEM172:22 H156 Nor is't enough, that thou alone may'st slide,
FLESH175:31 H31 Behold enough of precious store.
FLESH175:35 H35 Earth hath enough of what you will.
MEDDM200:34 Hp280 he knows is enough for one of twice his strength, much lesse
MEDDM202:34 Hp282 doth it euer say it is enough, but like the daughters of the
MED223:9 Hp250 enough thy maker is thy husband. Nay more, I am a member
ENOVGH (2) [enough]
HOUSE237:22 H52 By him who hath Enovgh to doe.
HOUSE237:25 H55 Ther's wealth enovgh I need no more,
ENRAG'D (2) [enraged]
MGREC98:9 H1811 With this reply, he was so sore {deep} enrag'd,
MGREC131:40 H3232 The eld'st enrag'd did play the vipers part,
ENRICHED See INRICHED, INRICHT
ENSIGNE (2)
MASSYR56:39 H145 A Dove within their Ensigne to display.
MPERS88:40 H1433 At last, displayes his Ensigne on a Hil,
ENSNARED (1) See also INSNARED
MGREC115:37 H2556 Nor by his baits could be ensnared so:
ENSUE (2) See also INSUE
MPERS79:24 H1050 What after did ensue, had he fore-seen,
MGREC117:14 H2621 What troubles, and contentions did ensue,
ENSUING (1) See also INSUING
MPERS77:10 H949 And the ensuing yeare ended his life,

ENTER (4)
HUMOUR29:15 H368 And in contentions lists, now justly enter.
MGREC121:33 H2815 *Antigonus* did enter *Asia,*
MGREC127:35 H3065 Enter {Enters} into a combination strong:
MEDDM202:33 Hp282 innumerable obiects enter, yet is not that spacious roome filled
ENTERANCE (1)
MPERS75:6 H867 This told, for enterance he stood not long,
ENTERING See ENTRING
ENTERPRETT (1) See also INTERPRET
MYCHILD218:20 Hp244 the same Christ, ye same word, They only enterprett it one
ENTERPRISE (4)
MPERS77:32 H973 His Fathers ill successe in's enterprise,
MPERS79:13 ~~H1035~~ Yet *Xerxes* in his enterprise persever'd;
MPERS79:27 H1053 How of this enterprise his thoughts now stands;
MPERS90:1 H1476 To {Did} stop the way in this their enterprise;
ENTERPRIZE (2)
MPERS86:14 H1330 What helps, {help} in's enterprize he's like to find,
MPERS86:23 H1339 If in his enterprize he should fall short,
ENTERS (7)
SEASONS46:38 H16 The tenth o'th' first *Sol* into *Aries* enters,
SEASONS48:11 H64 The sun now enters, loving *Geminie,*
MPERS70:14 H685 Enters the town, the sottish King he slayes,
MGREC109:1 H2258 He enters now {then} the *Indian* Kings among;
MGREC121:16 ~~H2795~~ Some of the Souldiers enters *Perdica's* tent,
MGREC125:14 H2962 *Olimpias* now {soon} enters *Macedon,*
MGREC~~127:35~~ H3065 Enter {Enters} into a combination strong:
ENTERTAIN'D (3) [entertained]
MGREC102:6 H1976 Is entertain'd with joy, and pompous train {showes},
MGREC131:2 H3192 To *Athens* then he {*Demetrius* thether} goes, is entertain'd,
MROMAN138:27 H3517 Is entertain'd at *Rome,* and in short time,
ENTERTAINE (1)
MEDDM203:23 Hp283 that threatens him wth death, he will gladly entertaine him,
ENTERTAINED See ENTERTAIN'D
ENTERTAINMENT (1)
MPERS84:17 H1253 Such entertainment {royal bounty} with this {his} Prince he
ENTHRONE (1) See also INTHRONE
MGREC124:28 H2935 Thinks to enthrone the Prince when riper grown;
ENTHRONED See INTHRON'D
ENTIRE (3)
HUMOUR34:16 H571 With {Which} joynt to joynt, the entire body tyes;
HUMOUR35:13 H609 But here's a {so} compact body, whole, entire:
MGREC98:40 H1842 A league of friendship make, firm, and entire;
ENTOMB See INTOMBE
ENTOMB'D (1) [entombed] See also INTOMB'D
MGREC110:40 H2344 Where he entomb'd his stately stallion.
ENTRAILS (1) See also INTRAILS, INTRALLS
MPERS82:7 H1154 Till in the entrails of their Sacrifice,
ENTREAT See INTREAT
ENTREATED (2)
MGREC121:15 ~~H2793~~ Being entreated by him scornfully,
MYCHILD216:5 Hp241 my pride and Vanity and he was entreated of me, and again

ENTREATIES See INTREATIES
ENTREATS See INTREATS
ENTRENCHED See INTRENCH'D
ENTRING (1) [entering]
MPERS75:41 H898 Entring that large and barren country far;
ENTRUSTED See INTRUSTED
ENVEIGHS (1)
MGREC112:33 H2419 Enveighs against his Father, now absent,
ENVIE (4) [envy]
MPERS74:3 H828 All envie to avoyd, this was thought on,
MPERS91:22 H1530 Their former envie, and inveterate hate;
MGREC109:39 H2298 Did more his valour then his Crown envie;
MGREC127:32 H3062 The Princes all begin now to envie
ENVIED See ENVY'D
ENVIES (1)
MPERS91:1 H1509 He knows that many towns in *Greece* envies
ENVIOUS (4)
PROLOG6:25 H9 But when my wondring eyes, and envious heart,
HUMOUR20:27 H19 Proud Melancholy, more envious then the rest,
SIDNEY150:35 H62 Where is that envious tongue, but can afford,
SICKNES179:11 H31 For ever know, thou envious foe,
ENVY (10) See also ENVIE
HUMOUR23:15 H125 Where envy, malice, thy companions lurke.
HUMOUR25:37 H226 Ile not envy thy feats, nor happinesse.
AGES37:29 H91 Freedome from Envy, and from Arrogance.
AGES42:39 H295 How was I broy'd with envy, and with hate?
AGES43:21 H316 And envy gnawes, if any do surmount.
SEASONS~~49:23~~ H114 Hath envy bred in Kings that were at strife,
SEASONS49:24 ~~H114~~ Yet hath your life, made Kings the same envy,
MGREC116:25 H2591 *Achille's* happinesse he did envy,
SIDNEY~~150:3~~ H29 And men of morose minds envy his glory:
TDUDLEY165:14 H16 Let malice bite, and envy knaw its fill,
ENVY'D (1) [envied]
QELIZ158:17 H126 Here lies the envy'd, yet unparralell'd Prince,
ENWRAPED See INWRAPT
EOLIANS (1) [pl.]
MPERS78:20 H1001 *Eolians,* and the *Helispontines;*
EPHESTION (10)
MGREC98:28 H1830 *Zidon* he on *Ephestion* bestowes:
MGREC98:31 H1833 *Ephestion* now, hath the {having chief} command o' th' Fleet,
MGREC99:15 H1858 His favourite *Ephestion,* with his fleet;
MGREC109:13 H2272 Boats to prepare, *Ephestion* first he sends,
MGREC112:1 H2387 Her Sister gives to his *Ephestion* deare,
MGREC113:40 H2467 *Clitus,* belov'd next to *Ephestion,*
MGREC115:6 H2517 Here his cheif favourite *Ephestion* dyes,
MGREC115:11 H2520 Because he let {He suffer, his friend} *Ephestion* to dye.
MGREC~~115:15~~ H2533 That by his leave his friend *Ephestion,*
MGREC118:7 H2654 And had to him, still since *Ephestion* dyed,
EPHESUS (2)
MGREC95:6 H1685 *Sardis,* then he, and *Ephesus,* did gaine,
MGREC131:11 H3203 Near *Ephesus,* each bringing all their {his} might,

EPIDEMICALL (1)
ELEMEN19:21 H466 Men fear'd destruction epidemicall.
EPIMANONDAS (1)
MPERS91:14 H1522 'Mongst these *Epimanondas* wants no fame;
EPIPHANES (2)
MGREC134:4 H3337 And then {next} *Epiphanes,* whose wicked deeds,
MGREC134:28 H3359 After *Epiphanes,* sat on the Throne
EPIRE (5)
MGREC123:25 H2889 Into *Epire,* for her great turblence;
MGREC125:6 H2954 For ayde {she} goes to *Epire,* among her friends,
MGREC125:37 H2987 Wisht in *Epire* she still had been confin'd;
MGREC126:11 H3002 Her Cousen of *Epire* did what he might,
MGREC133:20 H3308 And his son *Alexander* of *Epire,*
EPIRUS (1)
MGREC93:13 H1610 Shee to the rich *Molossians* {*Epirus* warlike} King, was
EPITAPH (6)
MPERS~~71:4~~ H719 And with an Epitaph, himself did make,
SIDNEY152:23 H92 *His Epitaph.*
DUBART155:1 H86 *His Epitaph.*
QELIZ158:7 H116 *Her Epitaph.*
TDUDLEY166:34 H76 *His Epitaph.*
DDUDLEY167:5 H1 An EPITAPH
EPITHET (1)
SIDNEY149:30 ~~H23~~ Put with an Epithet of dignity;
EPITHITE (2)
ELEMEN11:25 H145 Such was {is} my fruitfulnesse; and Epithite
SIDNEY~~150:12~~ H39 Put with an Epithite of dignity,
EPITOME (1)
HUMOUR34:21 H576 Here's my epitome of excellence,
EPITOMY (1)
MGREC123:10 H2872 In this Epitomy, too long to tell
EQUAL (1) See also EQUALL
SEASONS50:39 H173 Now day and night are equal in each clime;
EQUAL'D (1) [equaled]
MPERS~~69:38~~ H666 If ever King equal'd his happiness.
EQUALIZ'D (1) [equalized]
MASSYR55:37 H103 Admir'd of all, but equaliz'd of none.
EQUALL (1) [equal]
FATHER5:33 H34 And yet in equall tempers, how they gree,
EQUALS (1)
SEASONS47:4 H18 Crosses the Line, and equals night and day,
EQUIPAGE (2)
AGES36:27 H51 These being met, each in his equipage,
SEASONS49:1 H92 As Spring did aire, blood, youth in's equipage.
EQUITY (1)
HUMOUR26:10 H240 Yet shal with equity give thee thy part,
E'R (2) [ere] See also E'RE
DIALOG147:9 H235 If mindlesse of thy state I e'r be found.
DUBART154:25 H70 If e'r this golden gift was showr'd on any,
ERADICATE (2)
MASSYR62:13 H358 Did Justice now, by him, eradicate: [10 *years.*

ELIZB187:9 H17 But plants new set to be eradicate,

E'RE (24) [ere] See also E'R

PROLOG7:37 H47 If e're you daigne these lowly lines, your eyes
ELEMEN9:11 H45 Your shares, {Hooes} your mattocks, and what e're you see,
HUMOUR~~31:11~~ H444 That casts out all that man or {e're} eates, or drinks.
AGES37:41 H103 Where e're I went, mine innocence was shield.
AGES45:41 H431 My golden Bowl, and silver Cord, e're long,
MASSYR54:29 H56 Where e're he warr'd he had too good successe,
MASSYR57:28 H173 What e're he was, they {or} did, or how it fel,
MASSYR65:31 H496 *Iudah* {They} lost more {now} (then e're they lost) by him;
MASSYR66:22 H528 Where e're he goes, he Conquers every Land;
MPERS80:33 H1100 And as a friend, warns him, what e're he doe,
MGREC~~101:34~~ H1963 But long they stood not e're they're forc'd to run,
MGREC114:33 H2503 When e're 'tis said, he thousand thousands slew,
MGREC~~115:15~~ H2531 What e're he did, or thought not so content,
MGREC128:8 H3081 Which none e're did but those of royall fame;
MGREC~~131:16~~ H3208 Nor to his son did there {e're} one foot remain,
MGREC136:17 H3431 *What e're is found amisse, take in best {good} part,*
SIDNEY150:26 H53 E're he was ripe; his thred cut *Atropos.*
QELIZ155:35 H26 *Eliza's* works, wars, praise, can e're compact,
DAVID158:34 H14 Nor fields of offerings e're on you grow,
DAVID158:35 H15 Nor any pleasant thing e're may you show;
TDUDLEY165:34 H36 Thy love to true Religion e're shall shine,
FLESH177:12 H93 Such as no Eye did e're behold,
FLESH177:23 H104 Nor withering age shall e're come there,
MERCY189:7 H28 E're nature would, it hither did arrive,

ERE (18) See also E'R, E'RE

ELEMEN9:22 H56 And you Philosophers, if ere you made
ELEMEN11:26 H146 Which none ere gave, nor {or} you could claime of right,
HUMOUR30:19 H411 You'l say, here none shal ere disturbe my right;
AGES42:15 H273 As chearfully as ere I took my pay.
SEASONS~~49:33~~ H125 If pride within your lowly Cells ere haunt,
MASSYR56:31 H137 (They say) but twenty, ere came back agen.
MPERS~~84:12~~ H1243 With gold and silver, and what ere they need:
MPERS86:4 H1320 But in his slow approach, ere he came there;
MPERS87:1 H1357 But fame more quick, arrives ere he came {comes} there,
MGREC94:35 H1673 Ah! fond vaine man, whose pen was taught ere while,
MGREC127:34 H3064 Fearing their state {his force}, and what might hap ere long
MGREC~~132:23~~ H3268 Injoy'd what so {ere} beseem'd his Royalty,
TDUDLEY165:20 H22 Well known and lov'd, where ere he liv'd, by most
MEDDM200:3 Hp278 not a little one? will ere long say of a greater Tush god regards
PILGRIM211:1 H42 as eare ner' heard nor tongue ere told
HOUSE237:5 H35 No pleasant tale shall 'ere be told
HOUSE237:7 H37 No Candle 'ere shall shine in Thee
HOUSE237:8 H38 Nor bridegroom's voice ere heard shall bee.

ERECH (1)

MASSYR53:24 H14 *Erech, Accad,* and *Calneh* also made;

ERECT (8)

HUMOUR21:14 H42 I in his heart erect my regal throne,
MPERS73:31 H816 What forme of Government now to erect,
MGREC130:27 ~~H3181~~ Who did erect their cruelty in guilt,

MROMAN136:31 H3445 A Citty faire did *Romulus* erect:
CONTEM169:4 H46 And is thy splendid Throne erect so high?
FLESH175:28 H28 And trophyes to thy name erect
SON231:23 H35 In both o^{r} hearts erect a frame
HOUSE237:17 H47 Thou hast an house on high erect

ERECTED (3)
MGREC110:29 H2333 His Maungers he erected up so high,
DIALOG147:36 H260 And discipline erected, so I trust,
MEDDM205:12 Hp286 fro continvally, here is also the great Court of iustice erected,

ERECTS (2)
SEASONS47:11 H27 And Poles erects, for his green {young} clambering Hops;
MGREC115:8 ~~H2518~~ For him erects a stately Monument,

ERIDANUS (1)
ELEMEN10:14 H89 *Eridanus,* where *Phaeton* was drown'd,

ERRAND (2)
MGREC106:19 H2153 Then tell her errand, we had better spare
2LETTER182:2 H8 I crave this boon, this Errand by the way,

ERRATA (1)
SIDNEY152:18 H87 *Errata,* through their leave threw me my pen,

ERRE (3)
HUMOUR26:14 ~~H244~~ More useful then the rest, don't reason erre;
HUMOUR26:14 ~~H244~~ More useful then the rest, don't reason erre;
HUMOUR30:5 H397 If I be partial judg'd, or thought to erre,

ERRING (1)
PILGRIM210:11 H11 He erring pathes no more shall tread

ERE-LONG (1)
MYSOUL225:4 H8 And gloriovs made ere-long.

ERROR See ERROUR

ERRORS (2) [pl.] See also ERROURS
TDUDLEY165:32 H34 Truths friend thou wert, to errors still a foe,
AUTHOR177:35 H7 Where errors were not lessened (all may judg).

ERROUR (1)
SIDNEY151:28 ~~H75~~ Too late my errour see, that durst presume

ERROURS (1) [errors]
MGREC136:3 H3416 Pardon to crave, for errours, is but vaine,

ERST See YERST

ESCAPE See SCAPE

ESCAPED See 'SCAP'D, SCAP'D

ESCAPES See SCAPES

ESPEC (3) [especially]
MYCHILD215:11 Hp240 leaue to speak, and those espec. sink deepest wch are spoke
MYCHILD215:30 Hp241 Scriptures, espec: those places I thought most concerned my
11MAYA226:21 Hp255 pleasure espec: seing it is for my spiri^{tl}. advantage, For I hope

ESPECIALLY (1) See also ESPEC
HUMOUR29:4 H357 Especially when freindship is pretended:

ESPY (2)
MGREC105:16 H2109 So chanc'd these bloudy Horses to espy,
3LETTER183:18 H20 Where she her captive husband doth espy.

ESQ (2)
FATHER5:2 H2-3 *Thomas Dudley* Esq; *these humbly presented.*
TDUDLEY165:2 H3 *Thomas Dudley* Esq;

ESSARHADON (3)
MASSYR63:1 H386 *Essarhadon.*
MASSYR63:2 H387 His Son, weak *Essarhadon* reign'd in's place,
MASSYR63:10 H395 After twelve years did *Essarhadon* dye,
ESSAYS (1) [pl.]
MROMAN139:29 H3555 Essays I many made but still gave out,
ESSENCE (1)
HUMOUR33:26 H540 That divine Essence, {Offspring} the immortal Soul,
ESSEX (2)
DIALOG147:18 H244 Go on brave *Essex,* shew whose son thou art {with a loyal
QELIZ157:1 H69 Her *Essex* took *Cades,* their *Herculean* hold:
ESTABLISH'D (1) [established]
DIALOG147:34 H258 Thy Church and Weal, establish'd in such manner,
ESTABLISHED (1)
MASSYR65:28 H493 His Unckle, he established in's place,
ESTATE (4) See also A STATE
AGES43:38 H333 Man at his best estate is vanity.
MASSYR62:12 H357 Those that from *Ioshua's* time had been Estate {a state},
MEDDM204:27 Hp285 vpon one that is in a far better estate then himself, but let him
MYCHILD216:28 Hp242 chastened by losses in estate, and these Times (thro: his great
ESTATES (1) [pl.]
MEDDM205:37 Hp287 estates, and ther are some (and they sincere ones too) who
ESTEEM (5)
MPERS71:40 H753 And though no gods, if he esteem them some,
MPERS84:28 H1264 His Country, nor his Kindred {Friends} would {much} esteem,
MGREC107:2 H2177 With those of worth, he still desires esteem,
MGREC113:39 H2466 Was one of more esteem, but lesse desart;
MGREC114:21 H2491 In his esteem, a God he could not be,
ESTEEME (1)
QELIZ155:28 H19 Thy clemency did yerst esteeme as much
ESTEEMED (1)
MGREC118:20 H2667 Might be esteemed for a Deity;
ESTER (1)
MPERS85:11 H1287 To be by *Hester,* {fair Queen Ester} to her husband brought.
ESTHER (2)
MPERS84:9 H1237 What *Hester* {*Esther*} was, and did, her story reed,
MGREC102:33 H2003 The sumptuous Palace of Queen *Hester* {*Esther*} here,
ET^{C} (1)
MYCHILD215:26 Hp240 et^{c}. I avoided it. If at any time I was overtaken wth ye evills, it
ETC (1)
SOREFIT221:15 H1 From another sore fitt. etc.
ETERNAL (5)
AGES41:2 H222 With ugly {outward} marks of his eternal {inward loathsome}
MPERS87:20 H1374 Forsook his charge to his eternal shame:
CONTEM171:16 H120 And puts all pleasures vain unto eternal flight.
CONTEM174:8 H208 Joyes not in hope of an eternal morrow;
FLESH176:36 H76 Eternal substance I do see,
ETERNALL (4)
MGREC112:18 H2404 But vice remaines, to his eternall blot.
MGREC114:29 H2499 Of *Alexander,* this th' eternall crime,
MYCHILD218:4 Hp243 resolve me that there is an Eternall Being. But how should I

MYCHILD219:3 Hp245 Now to ye King Imortall, Eternall invisible, the only wise God,

ETERNITIE (1) [eternity]

VANITY161:4 H55 But wear his Crown unto eternitie,

ETERNITY (7)

MGREC116:34 H2600 And fame not last unto Eternity:
CONTEM168:13 H22 If so, all these as nought, Eternity doth scorn.
CHILDRN186:15 H82 But spring lasts to eternity,
ELIZB186:37 H9 Then ta'en away unto Eternity.
MEDDM208:2 Hp289 night shall fly away, and the day of eternity shall never end,
BYNIGHT220:20 H18 And Loue him to Eternity.
MYSOUL225:8 H12 Of Joy vnto Eternity.

EUBEA (1)

MPERS80:18 H1085 Inclos'd their Fleet i'th' streights {streight} of *Eubea;*

EUEN (1) [even] See also EV'N

MEDDM206:12 Hp287 degrees, euen in this life, some are Stars of the first

EUENING (1) [evening]

MEDDM196:18 Hp273 and the shadowes of his euening to be stretched out, lifts vp

EUENTS (1) [events]

MEDDM200:16 Hp279 garment, she easily foresees what euents it is like to produce,

EUER (6) [ever]

MEDDM202:34 Hp282 doth it euer say it is enough, but like the daughters of the
MEDDM202:36 Hp282 finds it self, and sees an impossibility, euer to be filled, but by
MEDDM204:6 Hp284 is the same yesterday, to day and for euer, we are the same
MEDDM204:7 Hp284 need of him, to day as well as yesterday, and so shall for euer,
MEDDM204:14 Hp284 Sin and shame euer goe together He that would be freed from
MEDDM207:29 Hp289 may be sure of an euer lasting habitation that fades not away.

EUERY (1) [every]

MEDDM204:11 Hp284 behoues euery man so to improue his talents, that when his

EUMENES (10)

MGREC121:4 H2782 Leaves *Eumenes,* the *Asian* coast to free,
MGREC121:27 H2809 That *Eumenes* got of the other three,
MGREC121:34 H2816 And fain would draw *Eumenes* to their side,
MGREC122:5 H2828 {To shew} The difficulties {dangers} *Eumenes* befell,
MGREC123:6 H2868 With *Eumenes* he divers Battels fought,
MGREC123:11 H2873 How neatly {finely} *Eumenes* did here excell,
MGREC124:19 H2926 Still labours *Eumenes* might {would} with him side,
MGREC127:14 H3044 True *Eumenes* endeavours by all skill,
MGREC127:27 H3057 So *Eumenes* {(the prop)} of destiny {death} must taste.
MGREC128:19 H3092 Had {The} valiant *Eumenes* unjustly slaine,

EUNUCH (4)

MPERS83:11 H1199 And for that end, his Eunuch he did hire.
MPERS~~92:3~~ H1557 Was by his *Eunuch* the proud *Bagoas* slain.
MPERS~~92:14~~ H1572 By the same Eunuch who first set him up.
MPERS92:25 ~~H1583~~ By one *Bagoas,* an Eunuch (as is sed.)

EUPATOR (1)

MGREC134:9 H3340 *Antiochus Eupator* was the next,

EUPHRATAN (1)

MASSYR56:22 H128 On {In} *Shinar* plain, by the *Euphratan* flood,

EUPHRATES (4)

MASSYR64:21 H445 By great *Euphrates* did his Army fall,
MGREC98:37 H1839 First, at *Euphrates,* what he's like to abide,

MGREC100:15 H1899 Unto *Euphrates* marcht, and over goes,
MGREC101:9 H1934 *Phenisian* Sea, and great *Euphrates* high,

EUPHRATES (2) [poss.]
MPERS88:4 H1397 And ranged stood, by great *Euphrates* side,
MGREC111:23 H2368 To th' coast which by *Euphrates* mouth appear'd;

EURIDICE (3)
MGREC122:12 H2837 His rule Queen *Euridice* begins to hate,
MGREC124:29 H2936 *Euridice* this injury disdaines,
MGREC125:8 H2956 *Euridice* hearing what she intends,

EUROPE (2)
MPERS77:36 H977 With certainty {conquest} of {all} *Europe* feeds his pride;
MGREC132:39 H3286 Possession he of *Europe* thinks to take,

EUROPIANS (1) [pl.]
MPERS89:16 ~~H1450~~ That so *Europians* might no more molest;

EUROPS (1) [poss.]
ELEMEN17:20 H384 Mine Ice doth glaze *Europs* big'st Rivers o're,

EUTERPE (1)
SIDNEY149:17 H16 Thy {His} Logick from *Euterpe* won the Crown,

EV'N (10) [even] See also EUEN
AGES36:23 H47 In's other hand a glasse, ev'n almost run,
AGES44:2 H335 What you have been, ev'n such have I before,
CONTEM174:24 H222 Fond fool, he takes this earth ev'n for heav'ns bower.
SICKNES178:37 H20 ev'n as a word that's speaking.
3LETTER183:11 H13 Ev'n thus doe I, with many a deep sad groan
MYSOUL225:15 H19 And praise thee shall ev'n as I ovght
HANNA230:13 H6 When death did seem ev'n to approach
HOURS234:18 H32 Ev'n for my Sav^{rs} sake
HOURS234:26 H40 Ev'n while my Dayes shall last
ACK235:20 H20 And so desire Ev'n all my Dayes.

EVAPORATES (1)
AGES39:38 H181 My wit, evaporates in meriment:

EVELTHON (1)
MPERS71:22 H736 Made *Evelthon* their King, with bended knee,

EVEN (9) See also EUEN, EV'N
HUMOUR26:3 H233 And when such thou art, even such are we.
MGREC95:15 H1694 Whose touch turn'd all to gold, yea even his meat:
MGREC100:29 H1913 Yet had some hope, that on that even {the spacious} plain,
AUTHOR178:6 H16 I stretcht thy joynts to make thee even feet,
SOREFIT221:30 H16 Even for his mercyes in his rod,
MED223:18 Hp250 and let me bee no more afraid of Death, but even desire to
JULY223:34 Hp251 faith in Thee, 'till I shall attain ye End of my hopes, Even y^e
SAMUEL228:17 H18 And Blesse the for't even all my Dayes.
REMB236:3 H18 But Thankfullnes even all my dayes

EVENING See EUENING

EVENT (2) See also EUENT
MASSYR68:12 H598 Who still expects some fearfull sad event,
MPERS69:21 H643 Who over-curious of wars event,

EVENTS See EUENTS

EVER (67) See also EUER
PROLOG7:36 H46 And ever with your prey, still catch your praise,
ELEMEN8:36 H34 What toole was ever fram'd, but by my might;

ELEMEN14:31 H273 Ever in craving, from the other three:
ELEMEN15:34 H316 Was ever gem so rich found in thy trunke?
ELEMEN18:5 H409 And all the wealth, that ever earth did give,
HUMOUR24:16 H165 Did ever sober tongue, such language speak?
HUMOUR27:15 H286 Who th' benefit o'th' whole ever intends:
HUMOUR31:26 H459 Here, there, her restlesse thoughts do ever flye;
HUMOUR32:34 H508 And {But} though the pitched field i've ever fled,
AGES42:35 H291 My fleeced Ewe {Sheep}, and ever {fruitful} farrowing Sow.
AGES45:6 H390 And poor *Palatinate* for ever lost;
MASSYR54:3 H30 But yet this blot for ever on him lyes,
MASSYR58:6 H191 Kept ever close, fearing some dismal {his well deserved} fate;
MASSYR63:37 H424 This Prince in's magnitude doth ever shine;
MPERS~~69:38~~ H666 If ever King equal'd his happiness.
MPERS80:40 H1107 But mischief, Sacriledge doth ever follow;
MPERS83:28 H1216 The best that ever sprang {sprung} of *Cyrus* race.
MPERS85:37 H1313 A hopefull Prince, whose worth {by *Xenophon*} is ever fam'd.
MPERS91:13 H1521 Whose courage nought but death could ever tame,
MGREC99:41 H1884 No future dangers he did ever dread.
MGREC116:14 H2580 Unparalel'd, for ever had remain'd;
MGREC122:27 H2846 *Pithons* commands, {as oft} She ever countermands
MGREC130:37 H3182 Thus may we hear, and fear, and ever say,
DIALOG141:11 H10 The glories of thy ever famous Realme?
DIALOG143:35 H104 For Oathes, and Blasphemies did ever eare
DIALOG144:3 H113 Did ever Land prophannesse more expresse?
DIALOG148:3 H268 So shall thy happy Nation ever flourish,
SIDNEY149:29 ~~H23~~ In all records, thy Name I ever see,
SIDNEY~~150:12~~ H38 In all Records his name I ever see
QELIZ156:12 H39 If *France* had ever hop'd for such a Queen;
QELIZ156:19 H46 Was ever people better rul'd then hers?
QELIZ156:20 H47 Was ever Land more happy, freed from stirs?
QELIZ156:21 H48 Did ever wealth in *England* so {more} abound?
QELIZ156:35 H62 Had ever Prince such Counsellors as she?
VANITY161:3 H54 Nor change of state, nor cares shall ever see,
TDUDLEY165:1 H1-2 *To the Memory of my dear and ever honoured Father*
DDUDLEY167:6 H1-2 *On my dear and ever honoured Mother*
DDUDLEY167:18 H15 *The publick meetings ever did frequent,*
CONTEM169:8 H50 Admir'd, ador'd for ever, be that Majesty.
CONTEM170:32 H102 Nor Male-factor ever felt like warr,
CONTEM172:3 H140 And when unmade, so ever shall they lye,
CONTEM172:12 H148 And if the sun would ever shine, there would I dwell.
CONTEM172:28 H162 So may we press to that vast mansion, ever blest.
FLESH177:16 H97 Which shall remain for ever pure,
SICKNES179:11 H31 For ever know, thou envious foe,
1HUSB180:23 H2 If ever two were one, then surely we.
1HUSB180:24 H3 If ever man were lov'd by wife, then thee;
1HUSB180:25 H4 If ever wife was happy in a man,
1HUSB180:34 H13 That when we live no more, we may live ever.
1LETTER181:25 H23 Where ever, ever stay, and go not thence,
1LETTER181:25 H23 Where ever, ever stay, and go not thence,
CHILDRN185:35 H61 My cares are more, and fears then ever,
ANNEB187:22 H12 Was ever stable joy yet found below?

MERCY189:12 H33 The Heavens vouchsafe she may so ever be.
MEDDM208:35 Hp291 if Moses had been able by the hand of faith, to hold the Ever
PILGRIM210:26 H26 Mine eyes no more shall ever weep
MYCHILD218:8 Hp244 If ever this God hath revealed himself it mvst bee in his word,
MYCHILD219:4 Hp245 Hon^{r}, + Glory for ever and ever,
MYCHILD219:4 Hp245 Hon^{r}, + Glory for ever and ever,
28AUG226:10 Hp254 O let me ever see Thee that Art invisible, and I shall not bee
SAMUEL228:21 H22 For ever happefy'd wth Thee.
11MAYB228:27 Hp259 and sorest y^{t} ever I had lasting 4 dayes, and ye weather being
THEART229:12 H14 For ever let me walk
SON231:20 H32 That ever I may thankfull bee
2HUSB233:14 H47 For ever vnto Thee.
HOURS234:36 H50 For ever vnto Thee.
HOUSE237:9 H39 In silence ever shalt thou lye

EVERGETE'S (1) [poss.]
MGREC134:27 H3358 *Philopater* was *Evergete's* son,

EVERGETES (2)
MGREC134:25 H3356 His son was *Evergetes* the last Prince
MGREC134:29 H3360 *Philometer:* then *Evergetes* again.

EVERLASTING (4)
MGREC110:26 H2330 Be had in everlasting memory,
ELIZB187:3 H12 Sith thou art setled in an Everlasting state.
MYCHILD216:33 Hp242 in ye way everlasting: and seldome or never but I haue fovnd
2HUSB232:7 H8 Into thy Everlasting Armes

EVERMORE (3)
MGREC116:22 H2588 And curious Artists evermore rewarded.
TDUDLEY166:15 H57 He might be cloath'd upon, for evermore.
FLESH177:22 H103 For evermore they shall be free,

EVERY (32) See also EUERY
ELEMEN11:33 H153 The rich and {the} poore, wise, foole, and every sort,
ELEMEN11:39 H159 I have not time to thinke of every part,
ELEMEN17:38 H402 I am the breath of every living soul.
ELEMEN18:28 H432 And with my selfe, I every vacuum fill.
HUMOUR22:40 H109 To be distill'd a drop on every line!
HUMOUR23:36 H146 Again, ye know, how I act every part:
HUMOUR28:6 H318 With cold distempers, to pain every part;
HUMOUR33:27 H541 Though it in all, and every part be whole:
AGES35:35 H21 In dangers every moment of a fall,
AGES40:34 H213 Though dangers do attend me every houre,
AGES44:10 H343 In every Age i've found much vanitie,
SEASONS47:19 H35 Now tune their layes, on sprays of every bush;
MASSYR66:22 H528 Where e're he goes, he Conquers every Land;
MGREC99:25 H1868 And by command was drawn through every street,
MGREC100:40 H1924 Had used her, and hers, in every thing,
MGREC106:5 H2139 Yea, {And} thus must every Son of *Adam* lye,
MGREC108:6 H2222 With wracks, and tortures, every limbe to stretch.
MGREC111:8 H2353 The meat, and drink, attendants, every thing,
MGREC112:13 H2399 To every Guest, a cup of gold he sends,
MGREC113:3 H2430 To wreak their spight, and hate, on every limbe.
MGREC118:34 H2683 To authorize his Acts in every thing.
MGREC135:31 H3403 Whose Iron teeth devoured every beast;

QELIZ155:16 H7 Thy wondrous worth proclaime, in every clime,
QELIZ155:19 H10 The sound thereof raps every humane sence;
QELIZ158:20 H129 *In every one, be her great glory famed.*
CONTEM173:22 H188 Thy cloaths ne're wear, thy meat is every where,
2LETTER182:12 H18 Or in a corn-field number every grain,
2LETTER182:13 H19 Or every mote that in the sun-shine hops,
3LETTER183:1 H3 Perplext, in every bush & nook doth pry,
3LETTER183:32 H34 *At home, abroad, and every where.*
28AUG226:5 Hp254 Now I can wait, looking every day when my Sav^{r} shall call for
SON231:4 H16 And freinds rais'd him in every place

EVIDENCE (3)
AGES38:8 H111 Nor evidence for land, {lands} did me perplex.
MEDDM205:15 Hp286 as he finds the evidence, so he absolues or condemnes, yea
FEVER220:32 H12 Nor could I read my Evidence

EVIDENT (1)
HUMOUR26:18 H248 Thine without mine, is not, 'tis evident:

EVILL (4) [evil]
AGES~~45:22~~ H410 But out of evill you may see much good.
MEDDM195:25 Hp272 inioy, no evill that we feele, or fear, but we may make some
MEDDM205:25 Hp286 allseeing eye will be a bridle to restrain from evill, and a spur,
RESTOR230:3 H18 And 'twixt ye good and evill way

EVILLS (1) [evils]
MYCHILD215:26 Hp240 I avoided it. If at any time I was overtaken wth ye evills, it was

EVILMERODACH (2)
MASSYR67:1 H547 *Evilmerodach.*
MASSYR67:12 H558 Unlike his father, *Evilmerodach,*

EVILS See EVILLS

EVINCE (3)
HUMOUR24:23 H172 But to evince the truth, by argument.
MPERS70:1 H672 (His Mothers Vnckle, stories doe evince:)
MPERS91:15 H1523 Who had (as noble *Raleigh* doth evince)

EWE (1)
AGES42:35 H291 My fleeced Ewe {Sheep}, and ever {fruitful} farrowing Sow.

EXAMPLE (1)
MGREC131:1 H3187 To do as he, {by his Example all} the rest full soon presumes,

EXAMPLES (2) [pl.]
ELEMEN13:34 H235 Dreadfull examples, soon I might produce,
HUMOUR28:33 H345 Thousand examples, you may daily see

EXCEED (1)
MPERS~~84:12~~ H1244 His bounty did *Darius* far exceed.

EXCEEDING (3)
MGREC126:10 H3001 Untill the Famine growes exceeding strong.
DAVID159:25 H40 Exceeding all the Love that's Feminine,
MEDDM202:10 Hp281 exceeding beauty full, and some extreamly deformed some so

EXCEEDS (2)
MGREC112:7 H2393 It far exceeds my meane abilities,
MGREC113:6 H2433 My foes exceeds in malice, and their hate,

EXCEL (5) See also EXCELL, T'EXCELL
HUMOUR33:39 H553 Of three, its hard to say, which doth excel;
HUMOUR35:15 H611 That Flegme was judg'd, for kindnesse to excel.
MASSYR58:4 H189 And {in} their kind t' excel did emulate.

MGREC122:6 H2829 His stratagems, wherein he did excel,
CONTEM172:11 H147 Now thought the rivers did the trees excel,

EXCELL (9) [excel] See also T'EXCELL
FATHER5:30 H31 Each others faults, and where themselves excell:
PROLOG7:29 H40 Men have precedency, and still excell,
MASSYR56:12 H118 But {And} that which did, all cost, and art excell,
MASSYR64:31 H455 How in all Merchandise she did excell,
MGREC123:11 H2873 How neatly {finely} *Eumenes* did here excell,
MGREC131:39 H3231 The mother would the youngest should {might} excell,
DAVID158:25 H5 Illustrious *Saul,* whose beauty did excell
CHILDRN185:8 H34 That nightingales he might excell.
HOURS234:4 H18 Whose comforts far excell.

EXCELLENCE (8)
HUMOUR34:21 H576 Here's my epitome of excellence,
SEASONS48:29 H82 Each man his owne peculiar excellence,
MPERS70:18 H689 This head of Kingdoms, *Caldes* excellence,
MGREC134:26 H3357 That valour shew'd, vertue or excellence.
DIALOG143:18 H87 But trust not much unto his Excellence;
QELIZ155:18 H9 So great's thy glory, and thine excellence,
QELIZ157:13 H81 And prostrate yeelded to her Excellence:
CONTEM167:34 H10 If so much excellence abide below;

EXCELLENCES (1) [pl.]
MEDDM209:22 Hp291 all excellences, let his parts naturall and acquired spirituall and

EXCELLENCIES (1) [pl.]
HUMOUR33:20 H534 My excellencies are so great, so many,

EXCELLENT (1)
CONTEM168:1 H11 How excellent is he that dwells on high?

EXCELLS (1)
MEDDM197:16 Hp274 more patiently then he that excells him, both in gifts & graces

EXCEPT (4)
HUMOUR34:14 H569 All nerves (except seven paire) to it retain;
SEASONS48:16 H69 Except the double Pinks, and matchlesse Roses.
MGREC117:30 H2637 Except by *Artabasus* daughter one;
MGREC130:22 H3177 Except *Cassanders* wife, who yet not dead,

EXCESSE (2)
ELEMEN16:38 H361 So oft in my excesse, I cause a dearth:
MGREC103:25 H2036 In pride, and cruelty, to th' highest {high} excesse.

EXCESSIVE (2)
MGREC110:23 H2327 Long with excessive travailes wearied,
MGREC116:8 H2568 That through excessive drinking he did dye.

EXCHANG (1)
MEDDM197:7 Hp274 The reason why christians are so loth to exchang this world for

EXCREMENT (2)
HUMOUR23:19 H129 The excrement, adustion of me.
HUMOUR31:1 H434 In {Is} charging me, to be thy excrement.

EXCRETION (2)
HUMOUR31:6 ~~H439~~ This transmutation is, but not excretion,
HUMOUR~~31:6~~ H439 Thou witless think'st that I am thy excretion,

EXCUSE (2)
MGREC115:38 H2557 But his excuse with humble thanks he sends,
MGREC136:1 H3414 For what is past I blush, excuse to make,

EXCUSER (1)
MEDDM205:13 Hp286 alway kept by Conscience, who is both accuser excuser witnes
EXECRABLE (3)
HUMOUR25:24 H213 Witnesse the execrable deeds thou'st done:
AGES45:3 H381 I've seen from *Rome,* an execrable thing,
MGREC104:40 H2092 Whom thus the execrable wretch abuses:
EXECRATION (1)
MPERS79:7 H1029 I Rhethorick want, to poure out execration:
EXECRATIONS (1) [pl.]
MPERS75:34 H891 And on all Kings he poures out execrations,
EXECUTE (1)
DIALOG148:12 H277 Execute toth' full {And on her pour} the vengeance threatned.
EXERCIS'D (1) [exercised]
MPERS81:37 ~~H1143~~ Where both sides exercis'd their manly feats;
EXHAUST (2)
ELEMEN15:25 H307 Shouldst thou but buy, it would exhaust thy gold.
SIDNEY149:24 H23 That this one Volumne should exhaust your store.
EXHAUSTED (3)
SEASONS50:35 H169 To feed his boughes, exhausted hath his sap,
SIDNEY152:8 H79 Since *Sydney* had exhausted all their store,
DISTEMP179:18 H6 Till nature had exhausted all her store,
EXHONORATES (1) [exonerates]
HUMOUR31:13 ~~H444~~ Til filth and thee, nature exhonorates.
EXHORTATION (1)
MEDDM205:6 Hp285 instruction and exhortation be sown, in the spring of their
EXHORTAT^{S} (1) [exhortations]
MYCHILD215:10 Hp240 I knowing by exper^{c}. y^{t} ye exhortat^{s}. of parents take most
EXILE (3)
MASSYR62:20 H365 Thus *Iacobs* Sons, in exile must remain,
MPERS~~91:22~~ H1534 From Court exile her unto *Babilon*:
DIALOG144:29 H137 Some grossely fin'd, from {house &} friends to exile went:
EXONERATES (1) See also EXHONORATES
HUMOUR~~31:15~~ H448 Till filth and thee nature exonerates:
EXPATIATE (1)
ELEMEN12:16 ~~H176~~ Nor yet expatiate, in Temple vale;
EXPECT (4)
PROLOG6:32 H15 From School-boyes tongue, no Rhethorick we expect,
HUMOUR32:16 H490 We shal expect much sound, but little force.
AGES41:19 H238 Now age is more, more good ye do {may} expect;
DIALOG145:12 H161 Not what you feel, but what you do expect.
EXPECTATION See XPECTAT^{n}
EXPECTED (4)
ELEMEN13:25 H226 Thistles and thornes, where he expected graine;
MPERS88:12 H1405 For tumult and confusion they expected,
MEDDM205:7 Hp285 plentifull crop may be expected in the haruest of their yeares.
MYCHILD216:24 Hp242 my heart out of order, but I haue expected correct^{n} for it, w^{ch}
EXPECTING (1)
MGREC126:20 H3011 Expecting nothing, but of death to taste;
EXPECTS (1)
MASSYR68:12 H598 Who still expects some fearfull sad event,

EXPEDITION (1)
MASSYR56:24 H130 An expedition to the East she made.
EXPELL (3)
ELEMEN15:13 H295 His deadly mallady, I might expell.
MROMAN139:20 H3548 The *Tarquins* they from *Rome* with speed {by force} expell,
DIALOG147:21 H247 By force {As Duty binds,} expell, destroy, and tread them
EXPENCE (1) [expense]
MPERS80:37 H1104 Yet 'fore he went, to help out his expence,
EXPEND (1)
MGREC98:13 H1815 But far lesse cost, and time, he doth {did} expend,
EXPENSE See EXPENCE
EXPER^{C} (4) [experience]
MYCHILD215:10 Hp240 I knowing by exper^{c}. y^{t} ye exhortat^{s}. of parents take most
MYCHILD215:17 Hp240 by y^{t} yov may gain some spirit: Advantage by my exper^{c}. I
30SEPT227:22 Hp257 world. I haue fovnd by Exper^{c}. I can no more liue wthout
THEART229:9 H11 And new Exper^{c} I haue gain'd
EXPERIENCE (2) See also EXPER^{C}, XPER^{C}
ANNEB187:20 H10 Experience might 'fore this have made me wise,
MEDDM203:3 Hp283 of spirit, yet our owne experience would soon haue speld it out,
EXPERIENCES (1) [pl.]
MYCHILD216:20 Hp241 Among all my experiences of gods gratious Dealings wth me I
EXPIATE (1)
HUMOUR25:31 H220 That naught but blood, {death} the same may expiate.
EXPIR'D (1) [expired]
MASSYR66:33 H539 The time expir'd, remains a Beast no more,
EXPIRATNON (1)
MEDDM207:24 Hp289 cannot passe, and till the expiratnon of that time, no dangers
EXPIRE (1)
ELEMEN9:39 H73 The Flye *Pyrausta* cal'd, all else expire.
EXPIRED See EXPIR'D
EXPLOYT (1) [exploit]
ELEMEN18:18 H422 Which {That} tells afar, th' exployt which he {it} hath done.
EXPOS'D (1) [exposed]
AUTHOR177:33 H5 Who thee abroad, expos'd to publick view,
EXPOSE (1)
HUMOUR25:39 H228 For Countries good, thy life thou darst expose:
EXPOUND (1)
MASSYR66:27 H533 His Dreams, wise *Daniel* doth expound ful wel,
EXPRESS (1)
MPERS~~69:38~~ H665 That *Cressus* angry, urg'd him to express,
EXPRESSE (18) [express]
HUMOUR32:21 H495 Enough of both, my wrongs for {now} to expresse;
HUMOUR34:4 H559 Thy perfect temperament, who can expresse?
AGES37:19 H81 Did act al folly, that it could expresse.
MPERS70:41 ~~H712~~ Then at his Herse great honours to expresse;
MPERS72:29 ~~H773~~ Who said but what, the King bad him expresse.
MPERS73:3 H790 Griefe for his brothers death, he did expresse,
MPERS76:10 H908 Their minds by Hieroglyphicks they expresse;
MPERS78:8 H989 For truth's asham'd how many to expresse;
MPERS92:13 H1571 Three years he reign'd, as Chronicles expresse, {then drank
MGREC103:13 H2024 Yet after all, as stories do expresse,

MGREC105:31 H2124 For all that {the} Kingly Grace he did expresse,
MGREC109:4 ~~H2261~~ To age, nor sex, no pitty doth expresse,
MGREC128:39 H3112 The terms of their agreement thus expresse,
MGREC130:24 H3179 Then vengeance just, against the same {them} t' expresse;
DIALOG144:3 H113 Did ever Land prophannesse more expresse?
13MAY226:29 H5 At Svn-shine each their joy expresse.
SON231:26 H38 Our vpright walking may expresse.
REMB236:8 H23 Or any way expresse.

EXPRESSED (1)
28AUG226:8 Hp254 forgett thy great Love to my soul so lately expressed, when I

EXTANT (2)
MPERS91:35 ~~H1549~~ Of whom no Record's extant of his deeds;
MGREC133:35 H3325 Which we oft wish were {was} extant as before.

EXTEND (2)
MPERS73:6 H793 The Female {to} many ages did extend,
MGREC114:41 H2511 From *Macedon* his Empire did extend,

EXTENDED (1)
MGREC105:36 H2129 And that his rule as farre extended be,

EXTENDS (1)
MGREC110:20 H2324 Restores him, and his bounds further {farther} extends;

EXTERNALL (1)
MGREC112:10 H2396 They were so wrapt with this externall glory.

EXTINCT (2)
MGREC129:39 H3153 Extinct, by this inhumane wretch *Cassander;*
MGREC132:8 H3243 And so falls out to be extinct in one,

EXTINGUISH (1)
MEDDM208:7 Hp289 vse no other meanes to extinguish them so distance of place

EXTINGUISHED (2)
MGREC130:21 H3176 Thus *Philips* house was quite extinguished,
MGREC134:12 H3343 The Royall blood was quite {nigh} extinguished.

EXTIRPT (1)
MGREC132:10 H3245 His seed to be extirpt, was destined,

EXTORTION (1)
DIALOG144:14 H124 With Usury, Extortion, and Oppression,

EXTRAUAGANTLY (1) [extravagantly]
MEDDM206:19 Hp287 Men that haue walked very extrauagantly, and at last bethink

EXTREAM (2) [extreme] See also EXTREAME
ELEMEN14:36 H278 Thy extream thirst is moistened by my love,
ELEMEN17:15 H379 My Ice and extream cold, which all men know.

EXTREAME (2) [extreme] See also EXTREAM
AGES41:28 H245 Thus out of one extreame, into another.
MGREC125:22 H2972 The King by extreame torments had his end,

EXTREAMLY (2) [extremely]
MGREC131:28 H3220 Falls so extreamly sick, all fear {fear'd} his life,
MEDDM202:10 Hp281 beauty full, and some extreamly deformed some so strong

EXTREMITY (1) See also XTREMITY
AGES45:10 H392 And worthy {better} ones, put to {suffer} extremity:

EXTRICATE (1)
MGREC122:7 H2830 His policies, how he did extricate

EXUBEROUS (1)
AGES42:34 H290 Oxe {thriving Cattle}, and my exuberous {new-milch-} Cow,

EXULT (1)
TDUDLEY166:17 H59 He did exult his end was drawing near,
EXVLTS (1) [exults]
13MAY226:32 H8 My heart exvlts & praises sings
EYE (32)
SEASONS48:12 H65 And heats us with, the glances of his eye,
MASSYR67:39 H585 The King, upon the wall casting his eye,
MPERS69:35 H657 Then on a Pike being {wood-pile} set, where all might eye,
MPERS80:34 H1101 For his retreat, to have an eye thereto:
MPERS82:34 H1181 The sorrow of his heart, did close his eye:
MPERS86:11 H1327 Still on his brother, casts a jealous eye,
MPERS88:26 H1419 But {And} in his speed a Dart hit him i'th' eye,
MGREC93:30 H1627 *Phillip,* on this great conquest had an eye;
MGREC105:12 H2105 Yea, {But} above all, that neither eare, nor eye,
MGREC105:20 H2113 Who not a little chear'd, to have some eye,
MGREC110:30 H2334 As never Horse his Provender could eye;
MGREC117:18 H2625 Like to that Giant, of his eye bereft;
MGREC119:9 H2699 For *Leonatus,* more lovely in her eye,
MGREC121:36 H2818 The others all, had kingdomes in their eye,
MGREC~~132:6~~ H3240 But he a Kingdome more then's friend did eye,
VANITY160:26 H36 There is a path, no vultures eye hath seen.
CONTEM168:7 H16 Then on a stately Oak I cast mine Eye,
CONTEM168:19 H27 Soul of this world, this Universes Eye,
CONTEM169:2 H44 Art thou so full of glory, that no Eye
CONTEM172:14 H149 While on the stealing stream I fixt mine eye,
FLESH175:6 H6 One flesh was call'd, who had her eye
FLESH176:38 H78 Mine Eye doth pierce the heavens, and see
FLESH177:12 H93 Such as no Eye did e're behold,
3LETTER183:2 H4 Her dearest Deer, might answer ear or eye;
3LETTER183:5 H7 Still wait with doubts, & hopes, and failing eye,
CHILDRN185:41 H67 O to your safety have an eye,
ELIZB186:35 H7 Farewel sweet babe, the pleasure of mine eye,
MEDDM204:23 Hp285 fixe his eye on the command, and not on his own ends, lest he
MEDDM204:26 Hp285 would be content, wth a mean condition, must not cast his eye
MEDDM205:25 Hp286 allseeing eye will be a bridle to restrain from evill, and a spur,
MEDDM206:20 Hp287 of turning to god, the first thing w[ch] they eye, is how to reform
MYSOUL225:6 H10 To Blisse vnseen by Eye,
EYES (50) [pl.]
PROLOG6:25 H9 But when my wondring eyes, and envious heart,
PROLOG7:37 H47 If e're you daigne these lowly lines, your eyes
ELEMEN16:21 H344 Nor fruitfull dewes, nor drops {distil'd} from weeping eyes;
HUMOUR22:38 H107 Out at her nose, or melteth at her eyes;
HUMOUR34:7 H562 O! good, O bad, O true, O traiterous eyes!
HUMOUR34:10 H565 Yet some may wish, oh, {O} had mine eyes ne're seene.
AGES36:15 H39 His Sword by's side, and choler in his eyes;
AGES40:39 H218 My heart lyes frying, and my {mine} eyes are sinking;
AGES41:21 ~~H239~~ But what's of worth, your eyes shal first behold,
AGES44:28 H361 Such private changes oft mine eyes have seen,
AGES44:37 H370 But ah, I saw at last those eyes to close:
AGES~~45:2~~ H379 Which fil'd our hearts with fears, with tears our eyes,
AGES46:22 H453 And I shal see, with these same very eyes,

MASSYR56:21 H127 All eyes that saw, or ears that hears, {hear} admires.
MASSYR66:2 H508 And with that woful sight his eyes close shut.
MASSYR66:6 H512 Yet as was told, ne're saw it with his eyes;
MPERS77:31 H972 The first deports, {dehorts} and layes before his eyes,
MGREC98:35 H1837 And layes before great *Alexanders* eyes,
MGREC102:13 H1983 With greedy eyes, he views this City round,
MGREC103:31 H2042 And layes before his eyes, if he persist
MGREC104:7 H2059 With sage advice, he layes {sets} before his eyes,
MGREC115:35 H2554 *Parmenio's* death's too fresh before his eyes;
DIALOG146:28 H214 Dear mother cease complaints, and wipe your eyes,
DIALOG147:32 H256 That dazzled eyes beholding much shall wonder
DIALOG148:23 H288 The scales shall fall from your long blinded eyes,
SIDNEY150:3 H28 Which makes severer eyes but scorn thy {slight that} Story,
DUBART152:35 H4 My ravisht eyes, and heart, with faltering tongue,
DUBART153:18 H22 He feeds his eyes, but understanding lacks,
DUBART153:27 H31 Of all the glorious sights his eyes have had:
DUBART154:4 H49 Mine eyes are sightlesse, and my tongue is mute;
DUBART154:22 H67 Leadst millions chained by eyes, by eares, by tongues,
DAVID159:13 H28 O *Israels* Dames, o're-flow your beauteous eyes,
VANITY160:33 H43 Its hid from eyes of men, they count it strange,
CONTEM169:12 H53 My humble Eyes to lofty Skyes I rear'd
FLESH175:33 H33 Then eyes can see, or hands can hold.
DISTEMP179:19 H7 Then eyes lay dry, disabled to weep more;
BIRTH180:17 H27 And if chance to thine eyes shall bring this verse,
1LETTER181:3 H1 My head, my heart, mine Eyes, my life, nay more,
MEDDM196:21 Hp273 beds make drosey persons but hard lodging, keeps the eyes
MEDDM198:32 Hp277 a pleasant thing to behold the light, but sore eyes are not able
MEDDM199:23 Hp278 Dimne eyes, are the concomitants of old age, and short
MEDDM199:24 Hp278 those that are eyes of a Republique, foretels a declineing
MEDDM202:32 Hp282 The eyes and the eares are the inlets or doores of the soule,
MEDDM207:35 Hp289 eyes, by beholding their bed, the morning may mind them of
MEDDM209:11 Hp291 eyes and thornes in their sides, and at last ouercame them,
PILGRIM210:26 H26 Mine eyes no more shall ever weep
BYNIGHT220:4 H5 My waking eyes were open kept
2HUSB233:1 H34 And favour in their eyes to whom
2HUSB233:11 H44 Lord let my Eyes see once Again
HOUSE236:34 H26 My sorrowing eyes aside did cast

EYNE (1)

ELEMEN19:6 H451 The Ostrich with her plumes, th'Eagle with her eyne;

EZEKIEL (1)

MASSYR64:32 H456 None but the true *Ezekiel* need to tell:

EZRA (1)

MPERS~~84:12~~ H1241 Good *Ezra* in the seventh year of his reign,

F

FABERICK (1) [fabric]
HUMOUR28:10 H322 At length demolishes the faberick,
FABIUS (1)
HUMOUR29:35 H386 Wise *Fabius* is her buckler: all accord.
FABLE (2)
MASSYR55:19 H85 Whence rose that fable, she by birds was fed.
MGREC~~132:20~~ H3265 His story seems a Fable more then true.
FABLES (1) [pl.]
MPERS69:18 H640 Are fit for such, whose eares for fables itch;
FABRIC See FRABERICK
FACE (52)
FATHER5:5 H6 Of fairer Dames, the sun near saw the face, /of the
ELEMEN13:6 H207 Will not my goodly face, your rage suffice?
ELEMEN14:38 H280 Or else thy sun-burnt face, and gaping chapps;
ELEMEN17:29 H393 And to this day, impaires her beautious face.
HUMOUR21:24 H52 What makes him face his foe, without appal?
HUMOUR22:15 H84 Her teeth wil chatter, dead and wan's her face,
HUMOUR27:19 ~~H290~~ Though cast upon my guiltlesse blushing face;
HUMOUR29:26 H377 When in Battalia my foes I face,
HUMOUR31:38 H471 Now could I stain my ruddy sisters face,
HUMOUR32:38 H512 When sister Sanguine paints my Ivory face,
AGES36:7 H31 His face as fresh, as is *Aurora* faire,
AGES38:22 H125 A serpents sting in pleasing face lay hid.
AGES41:1 H221 the loathsome {two fold} Pox, my face {me sore} be-mars,
AGES42:11 H269 And shew'd them how, in face of foes to stand.
SEASONS46:34 H10 With smiling Sun-shine face, and garments {somewhat} green,
SEASONS47:26 H42 Doth darken *Sols* bright face, makes us remember
SEASONS48:23 H76 But both rejoyce, at th'heavens clear smiling face,
SEASONS48:39 H90 With melted tauny face, and garments thinne.
SEASONS50:14 H148 The dryed earth is parched by {with} his face.
SEASONS50:22 H156 Although their Bread have not so white a face.
SEASONS~~52:37~~ H252 And some warm glances from the Sun {his face} are felt,
MASSYR55:13 H79 Her beautious face (they feign) retaining still.
MASSYR55:15 H81 Changing his {the} womans face, into a man.
MASSYR58:2 H187 Ne're shew'd his face, but revell'd with his Whores,
MPERS74:39 H860 His manly face dis-figures, spares no bloud,
MPERS82:3 H1150 Ten dayes these Armies did each other face,
MPERS82:37 H1184 To see that face, where Rose and Lilly stood,
MPERS87:16 ~~H1370~~ To look his manly brother in the face.
MGREC96:40 H1760 Let fly their Arrowes, in the *Persians* face;

MGREC114:13 H2483 Next day, he tore his face, for what he'd done,
MGREC~~115:15~~ H2528 A rueful face in this so general woe;
QELIZ156:16 H43 And earth had twice {once} a yeare, a new old face:
TDUDLEY166:32 H74 Where we with joy each others face shall see,
CONTEM168:26 H33 The Earth reflects her glances in thy face.
CONTEM170:3 H77 To get his bread with pain, and sweat of face:
CONTEM170:8 H81 The weeping Imp oft looks her in the face,
CONTEM170:26 H97 The wretch with gastly face and dreadful mind,
CONTEM170:31 H101 His face like death, his heart with horror fraught,
AUTHOR178:4 H14 I wash'd thy face, but more defects I saw,
1LETTER181:18 H16 True living Pictures of their Fathers face.
MEDDM198:3 Hp275 seuerall conditions, if he will make his face to shine vpon
MEDDM202:23 Hp282 darknes till he arise againe, so god doth somtime vaile his face
MEDDM209:1 Hp291 wrestled wth god face to face in penvel Let me go, sath that
MYCHILD217:4 Hp242 when ye Almighty hath hid his face from me, that yet I haue
FEVER220:34 H14 Hide not thy face from me I cry'd
MYSOUL225:17 H21 Base World I trample on thy face,
MYSOUL225:22 H26 Thy face when shall I see
SAMUEL228:15 H16 That I again may see his face,
SON231:6 H18 From such as 'fore nere saw his face.
2HUSB232:18 H19 Hide not thy face Away.
REMB236:9 H24 O help thy Saints y^{t} sovght thy Face

FACILITY (2)
MASSYR56:7 H113 With great facility, march safe upon't.
MPERS90:24 H1491 And now {how} their Nation with facility,

FACT (5)
AGES38:19 H122 From birth stayned, with Adams sinfull fact;
AGES~~45:4~~ H383 But saw their horrid fact soon disappointed,
MGREC104:29 H2081 But some detesting, this his wicked fact,
MGREC129:18 H3132 And for that double fact which she had done,
MROMAN139:16 H3544 She loathed so the fact, she loath'd her life,

FACTS (1) [pl.]
MPERS72:31 H775 To tell the facts, of this most bloody King.

FACULTY (5)
HUMOUR27:1 H272 There lives the irascible faculty:
HUMOUR27:12 ~~H283~~ It is her own heat, not thy faculty,
HUMOUR~~27:12~~ H283 Unless as heat, it be thy faculty,
HUMOUR33:36 H550 The faculty of speech doth here abide,
DUBART154:6 H51 Through grief it wants a faculty to speak,

FADE (4)
MGREC110:36 H2340 And so his memory might {would} fade away,
VANITY160:40 H50 Nor strength nor wisdome, nor fresh youth shall fade,
CONTEM171:22 H125 If winter come, and greeness then do fade,
CONTEM172:2 H139 Nay, they shall darken, perish, fade and dye,

FADES (1)
MEDDM207:29 Hp289 may be sure of an euer lasting habitation that fades not away.

FADING (3)
DIALOG144:7 H117 For nought, but title to a fading Crown?
BIRTH179:27 H3 All things within this fading world hath end,
ANNEB187:19 H9 When I on fading things my hopes have set?

FAIL (1) See also FAILE, FAYLE
MPERS81:20 H1128 If now in {their} need, they should thus fail {forsake} their
FAILE (5) [fail] See also FAYLE
HUMOUR22:30 H99 For when they faile, man turnes unto his clay:
AGES45:29 H419 My grinders now are few, my sight doth faile
QELIZ157:2 H70 But time would faile me, so my wit {tongue} would to,
MEDDM200:30 Hp279 this transcends the spring, that their leafe shall neuer faile nor
MEDDM205:27 Hp286 vs, or else we should not so often faile in our whole Course of
FAILED (1)
JULY223:24 Hp251 but my God who never failed me, was not absent but helped
FAILES (3) [fails]
ELEMEN12:38 H198 And Oares to row, when both my sisters failes?
MED223:13 Hp250 spirit failes in me at y[e] consideration y[r]of, and I am
2HUSB232:30 H31 Thy Goodnes never failes.
FAILING (1)
3LETTER183:5 H7 Still wait with doubts, & hopes, and failing eye,
FAILINGS (1) [pl.]
2SIMON195:4 Hp271 imitation Children do natureally, rather follow the failings then
FAILS See FAILES
FAIN (3)
MGREC121:34 H2816 And fain would draw *Eumenes* to their side,
DIALOG145:32 H181 This done, an Act they would have passed fain,
SIDNEY151:20 H70 Fain would I shew, how thou {he} fame's path didst {paths did}
FAIN'D (1) [fained]
MGREC131:3 H3193 Not like a King, but like some God they fain'd;
FAINE (3)
MGREC112:41 H2427 Faine would have spoke, and made his owne defence,
MGREC126:15 H3006 Faine would she come now to {this wretched Queen}
MGREC127:5 H3035 And *Pellas* faine to yeeld amongst the rest;
FAINED (3) See also FAIN'D
MGREC106:40 H2174 His fained Deity, and foolish pride:
MGREC118:9 H2656 But he refus'd, with fained modesty,
DIALOG142:37 H66 But forraigne Foe, nor fained friend I feare,
FAINING (1)
MROMAN137:21 H3472 Some faining say, to heav'n {to the Gods} he did ascend;
FAINT (5)
ELEMEN18:25 H429 When burning heat, doth cause you faint, I coole,
MPERS89:3 H1437 But they too faint, still to pursue their game,
MEDDM197:29 Hp275 'tis no wonder if he faint by the way.
FEVER220:29 H9 So faint I could not speak.
RESTOR229:23 H6 When heart did faint & Spirits quail
FAINTING (13)
ELEMEN16:20 H343 Which can to life, restore a fainting heart:
MGREC106:3 H2137 This said, his fainting breath did fleet away,
DIALOG141:20 H19 My weakned fainting body now to reele?
MERCY189:13 H34 Chear up (dear Son) thy fainting bleeding heart,
MEDDM203:29 Hp284 fainting,
PILGRIM210:27 H27 No fainting fits shall me assaile
FAINT222:11 H1 Delive[rc] from a fitt of Fainting
FAINT222:17 H7 Thvs fainting haue I said
JULY223:21 Hp251 I had a sore fitt of fainting w[ch] lasted 2 or 3 dayes, but not in y[t]

13MAY227:6	H15	A shadow from ye fainting heat
30SEPT227:19	Hp257	fainting, but not in y^t sore manner somt. he hath. I desire not
HOURS234:6	H20	Vphold my fainting soul
ACK235:9	H9	Thou hast releiv'd my fainting heart
FAIR (18) See also FAIRE, FAYRE		
ELEMEN~~17:8~~	H372	Thus *Albion* {*Britain* fair} (tis thought) was cut from *France,*
AGES40:7	H188	Of all at once, who not so wise, as fair,
SEASONS46:35	~~H11~~	She gently thus began, like some fair Queen;
SEASONS47:28	H44	My second month is *April,* green, and fair,
MASSYR60:33	H298	As fair a Town, as the first *Ninivie.*
MPERS73:8	H795	And built fair *Meroe,* for his sisters sake.
MPERS76:2	H900	Over fair *Ister,* at a {with labour and with} mighty charge;
MPERS84:22	H1258	Fair *Attica,* a third time to invade.
MPERS~~85:11~~	H1287	To be by *Hester,* {fair Queen Ester} to her husband brought.
MPERS86:24	H1340	She to the King, would make a fair report:
MGREC131:25	H3217	Who his fair daughter *Stratonica* takes,
MGREC134:35	H3366	Fair *Cleopatra* next, last of that race,
SIDNEY~~150:40~~	H68	*Stella* the fair, whose streams from Conduits fell
VANITY160:9	H19	They'r foul enough to day, that once was {were} fair,
CONTEM169:34	H72	Sometimes in *Eden* fair, he seems to be,
FLESH176:10	H50	Thou speak'st me fair, but hat'st me sore,
ELIZB186:36	H8	Farewel fair flower that for a space was lent,
13MAY227:10	H19	Thvs pleasant fair and good,
FAIRE (20) [fair] See also FAYRE		
ELEMEN14:5	H249	And since, faire *Italy* full sadly knowes
HUMOUR20:18	H10	Earth knew her black swarth childe, Water her faire;
HUMOUR26:36	H266	The first my self, second my sister faire,
HUMOUR29:10	H363	Faire rosie Sister, so might'st thou scape free,
AGES36:7	H31	His face as fresh, as is *Aurora* faire,
SEASONS46:37	H15	*March, April, May,* of all the rest most faire;
SEASONS49:10	H101	reason why {Though he decline}, because his flames so faire,
MASSYR67:14	H560	Faire *Ægypt* is, by his remissenesse lost;
MPERS70:21	H692	Had after {A} thousand yeares faire to be seen.
MGREC100:12	H1896	Faire *Alexandria* from the ground doth raise;
MGREC110:37	H2341	He on the faire *Hidaspis* pleasant side,
MGREC111:22	H2367	Passing faire *Indus* mouth, his course he stear'd,
MGREC117:31	H2638	And *Roxan* faire, whom late he married,
MGREC125:27	H2977	At length yeelds to the Halter, her faire neck;
MROMAN136:31	H3445	A Citty faire did *Romulus* erect:
MROMAN138:20	H3510	Faire *Ostia* he built, this Town, it stood,
DIALOG142:24	H53	Doth your Allye, faire *France,* conspire your wrack?
SIDNEY150:22	H47	Of which, {at} this day, faire *Belgia* doth {may} boast.
QELIZ158:11	H120	*This Rose is withered, once so lovely faire,*
MEDDM208:19	Hp290	to deceitfull friends who speak faire and promise much
FAIRER (1)		
FATHER5:5	H6	Of fairer Dames, the sun near saw the face, /of the
FAIREST (1)		
DIALOG141:6	H5	Alas, deare Mother, fairest Queen, and best,
FAITH (11)		
MASSYR65:32	H497	Seven years he keeps his faith, and safe he dwels,
MEDDM197:8	Hp274	because they haue more sence then faith they se what they

MEDDM197:15 Hp274 a man of weak faith and mean abilities, may vndergo a Crosse
MEDDM208:28 Hp290 It is admirable to Consider the power of faith, by wch all things
MEDDM208:35 Hp291 if Moses had been able by the hand of faith, to hold the Ever
MEDDM209:2 Hp291 not let thee go replys Jacob till thou blesse me, faith is not only
MEDDM209:3 Hp291 but it is so necessary, that wthout faith there is no salvation
MYCHILD218:31 Hp244 there Faith vpon ye Earth? & I haue not known what to think,
MYCHILD218:36 Hp244 my faith, + if I perish, I perish, But I know all ye powers of Hell
JULY223:34 Hp251 my faith in Thee, 'till I shall attain ye End of my hopes, Even
28AUG225:27 Hp254 many times my faith weak likewise, the Lord was pleased to

FAITHFULL (9)

MPERS75:1 H862 And with a faithfull fraud to' th' town he goes,
MGREC105:1 H2094 Then slew his servants, that were faithfull found;
MGREC121:35 H2817 But he alone now {most} faithfull did abide:
MGREC122:10 H2835 He was both valiant, faithfull, patient, wise.
MGREC124:20 H2927 But to the last {all in vain} he faithfull did abide;
MEDDM201:32 Hp281 the most welcom so a faithfull friend in time of adversity,
SOREFIT221:33 H19 O make it frvitfull faithfull Lord
WHAT224:21 H21 And for his sake y^{t} faithfull is
THEART229:11 H13 An hvble, faithfull life O Lord

FAITHFULLNES (1) [faithfulness]

JULY223:30 Hp251 let me neuer forgett thy Goodnes, nor question thy faithfullnes

FAITHFULLNESSE (2) [faithfulness]

MPERS72:28 ~~H773~~ And only for his fathers faithfullnesse,
MGREC103:19 H2030 But on their faithfullnesse, he never staid:

FALL (34)

ELEMEN13:28 H229 The Corne, and Hay, both fall before they'r mowne;
ELEMEN19:20 H465 Of murrain, Cattle numberlesse did fall.
ELEMEN19:35 H476 But some fall down, and some flye up with aire.
AGES35:35 H21 In dangers every moment of a fall,
AGES38:37 H140 Some times in fire, sometimes in waters {water} fall:
MASSYR55:29 H95 Or else she sought, revenge for *Menons* fall:
MASSYR61:2 H307 And times of both computed, so fall out,
MASSYR64:21 H445 By great *Euphrates* did his Army fall,
MASSYR65:37 H502 The wals so strong, that stood so long, now fall;
MASSYR68:19 H605 Re-minds him of his Grand-sires height, and fall,
MPERS84:11 H1239 Of *Hamans* fall, and *Mordica's* great rise;
MPERS86:23 H1339 If in his enterprize he should fall short,
MPERS89:27 H1461 Such terrour on the *Persians* then did fall,
MGREC~~102:38~~ H2008 Now falls {fall} into the *Macedonians* hands.
MGREC109:5 ~~H2262~~ But all fall by his sword, most mercilesse.
MGREC~~120:4~~ H2739 Then fall into the hands of mortal foes.
MGREC127:30 H3060 Then with *Seleuchus* straight at ods doth fall,
MGREC131:6 H3196 These Kings fall now afresh to {their} warres again,
DIALOG148:1 H266 Then High Commissions shall fall to decay,
DIALOG148:23 H288 The scales shall fall from your long blinded eyes,
DIALOG148:28 H293 Whose lot doth fall to live therein is blest:
SIDNEY150:24 H51 Made famous by thy fall {death}, much more's {more} the pitty;
DAVID158:27 H7 How did the mighty fall, and falling dye?
DAVID159:19 H34 O! how in battell did the mighty fall,
CONTEM171:28 H130 No sooner born, but grief and care makes fall
CHILDRN185:22 H48 They fall un'wares in Fowlers snare:

ELIZB187:6 H14 And Plumbs and Apples throughly ripe do fall,
MERCY188:24 H10 I saw the branches lopt the Tree now fall,
2SIMON195:12 Hp271 though in value they fall short of all in this kinde yet I presume
MEDDM196:7 Hp273 them vp, but spying his black feet, he soon lets fall his plumes,
MEDDM199:6 Hp277 do not often fall till after threat'ning.
MEDDM206:34 Hp288 trembling, lest they through vnbeleif fall short of a promise, it
MEDDM209:15 Hp291 last fall in to perpetuall bondage vnder them vnlesse the great
PILGRIM210:16 H16 nor stumps nor rocks cause him to fall

FALLEN See FAL'N, FALN, FALNE

FALLING (2)
AGES44:13 H346 My ruin'd house, now falling can uphold;
DAVID158:27 H7 How did the mighty fall, and falling dye?

FALLS (3) n.
AGES38:35 H138 What breaches, knocks, and falls I daily have?
DIALOG144:34 H142 Nor took I warning by my neighbours falls,
MEDDM200:17 Hp279 the best, but falls and bruises, or perhaps somewhat worse,

FALLS (7) v. See also FALS
MASSYR67:30 H576 To banquetting, and revelling now falls,
MPERS79:39 H1065 Till twenty thousand *Persians* falls down slain;
MPERS~~92:19~~ H1577 But *Bogoas* falls to's practices again,
MGREC102:38 H2008 Now falls {fall} into the *Macedonians* hands.
MGREC131:28 H3220 Falls so extreamly sick, all fear {fear'd} his life,
MGREC132:8 H3243 And so falls out to be extinct in one,
QELIZ157:7 H75 Worlds wonder for a time {while}, but yet it falls;

FAL'N (1) [fallen] See also FALN, FALNE
1SIMON188:4 H5 No sooner come, but gone, and fal'n asleep,

FALN (1) [fallen] See also FAL'N, FALNE
DIALOG146:18 H204 My wealthy trading faln, my dearth of grain,

FALNE (1) [fallen] See also FAL'N, FALN
DAVID159:27 H42 How are the mighty falne into decay,

FALS (3) v. See also FALLS
HUMOUR35:3 H599 Unlesse we 'gree all fals into confusion.
MASSYR59:12 H236 But *Salmeneus* slaine, his {the} Army fals,
MPERS88:27 H1420 Down *Cyrus* fals, and yeelds to destiny;

FALSE (11)
MPERS90:38 H1505 Of that false perjur'd wretch, this was the last {fate},
MGREC103:21 H2032 For such revolters false, what Prince will {King can} trust:
MGREC104:5 H2057 But *Bessus* false, who was his cheife Commander;
MGREC105:5 H2098 Was the false Governour of *Media)*
MGREC107:21 H2196 False *Bessus* to finde out, in *Bactria;*
MGREC134:30 H3361 And next to {after} him, did false *Lathurus* reigne,
MROMAN138:6 H3496 Yet for {in} their compact, after false they play:
DIALOG142:25 H54 Or, doth {do} the *Scots* play false behind your back?
DIALOG143:39 H108 What false reports, which nick-names did they take,
DIALOG147:19 H245 Not false to King, nor Countrey in thy heart, {to the better part;}
CONTEM170:17 H89 But no such sign on false *Cain's* offering;

FALSHOOD (1) [falsehood]
MPERS75:21 H880 Thy falshood, not thy {craft more then} valour did prevaile;

FALSLY (1) [falsely]
TDUDLEY165:18 H20 Who after death might make him falsly seem

FALTERING (1)
DUBART152:35 H4 My ravisht eyes, and heart, with faltering tongue,
FALTRING (1) [faltering]
SIDNEY151:29 ~~H75~~ To fix my faltring lines upon his tomb:
FAM'D (3) [famed]
MASSYR~~63:28~~ H414 This King's less fam'd for all the acts he's done,
MPERS85:37 H1313 A hopefull Prince, whose worth {by *Xenophon*} is ever fam'd.
MGREC133:31 H3321 To whom Ancient {the old} *Berosus* (so much fam'd)
FAME (43)
ELEMEN12:11 H171 And wonderous high *Olimpus,* of such fame,
SEASONS50:2 H136 By *Romans* celebrated to his fame.
SEASONS50:16 H150 *Romes* second Emperour of peaceful {lasting} fame;
MASSYR~~55:32~~ H98 That undeserv'd, they blur'd her name and fame
MPERS~~70:41~~ H712 With honours great, did celebrate his fame.
MPERS75:19 ~~H878~~ In that thy fame shall sound whilst men have sence;
MPERS82:18 H1165 Scarce one was left, to carry home the fame;
MPERS87:1 H1357 But fame more quick, arrives ere he came {comes} there,
MPERS91:14 H1522 'Mongst these *Epimanondas* wants no fame;
MGREC95:8 H1687 And by *Parmenio* (of renowned fame)
MGREC97:20 H1781 And this to *Alexander* is more a fame,
MGREC99:27 H1870 Who did the like to *Hector* (of more fame)
MGREC99:32 H1875 If of thy future fame thou hadst regard,
MGREC101:18 H1943 Which had he done (perhaps) his fame had {he'd} kept,
MGREC102:14 H1984 Whose fame throughout the world, was so renown'd;
MGREC110:25 H2329 Yet that his fame might to posterity,
MGREC110:38 H2342 Two Cities built, his fame {name} might there abide;
MGREC111:15 H2360 Which could not sound too oft, with too much fame;
MGREC113:35 H2462 Yet gave his Master the immortall fame;
MGREC114:31 H2501 Which vertues fame can ne're redeem by farre,
MGREC~~114:36~~ H2506 Yea, and he kild *Calisthines* by name; {of fame.}
MGREC116:11 H2577 Whose famous Acts {This Monarchs fame} must last, whilst
MGREC116:16 H2582 And so with black, be-clouded all his fame.
MGREC116:34 H2600 And fame not last unto Eternity:
MGREC127:10 H3040 Old *Thebes* he then re-built (so much of fame)
MGREC128:8 H3081 Which none e're did but those of royall fame;
DIALOG143:13 H82 By *Edward* third, and *Henry* fifth of fame,
DIALOG148:7 H272 There let thy name, thy fame, thy valour {glory} shine,
SIDNEY150:14 H49 Thy fame, and praise, is farre beyond my straine;
SIDNEY150:33 H60 And live it doth, in spight of death, through fame,
SIDNEY152:4 ~~H76~~ That those that name his fame, he needs must spare,
SIDNEY152:15 ~~H85~~ Not because, sweet *Sydney's* fame was not dear,
SIDNEY152:21 H90 So *Sydney's* fame, I leave to *England's* Rolls,
SIDNEY152:24 H93 *Here lies intomb'd in fame, under this stone,*
DUBART154:15 H60 Thy fame is spread as farre, I dare be bold,
DUBART154:35 H80 Thus *Bartas* fame shall last while starres do stand,
DUBART155:9 H94 *But Fame, out-living both, he is reviv'd.*
QELIZ155:15 H6 Yet thy loud Herauld Fame, doth to the sky
QELIZ156:28 H55 The States united now her fame doe sing;
QELIZ157:5 H73 More infamie than fame she did procure;
QELIZ158:16 H125 So blaze it fame, here's feathers for thy wings,
VANITY160:34 H44 Death and destruction, the fame hath heard,

FLESH175:27 H27 As some to their immortal fame:

FAMED (1) See also FAM'D

QELIZ158:20 H129 *In every one, be her great glory famed.*

FAMELY (1) [family]

11MAYA226:16 Hp255 of my famely.

FAME'S (2) [poss.]

SIDNEY151:20 H70 Fain would I shew, how thou {he} fame's path didst {paths did}

SIDNEY151:37 ~~H75~~ Fame's flaming Chariot for to drive.

FAMES (3) [pl.]

ELEMEN12:41 H201 Ye mighty Kings, who for your lasting fames

MASSYR57:34 H179 And such as care not, what befals their fames,

MGREC~~103:32~~ H2043 His names {fames} dishonour, losse unto his State.

FAMILY (6) See also FAMELY

AGES41:32 H249 My family to keep, but not for gaines.

MPERS83:22 H1210 But all his family was likewise slain,

MGREC121:37 H2819 But he was true to's masters family,

MGREC124:34 H2941 His Fathers danger, with his Family;

MGREC127:25 H3055 Striving t'uphold his Masters family,

DDUDLEY167:16 H13 *A true Instructer of her Family,*

FAMINE (3)

MGREC126:10 H3001 Untill the Famine growes exceeding strong.

DIALOG142:28 H57 Is't Drought, is't Famine, or is't Pestilence?

DIALOG143:21 H90 Famine, and Plague, two sisters of the Sword,

FAMINES (1) [pl.]

ELEMEN20:2 H484 Portentious signes, of Famines, Plagues and Wars.

FAMISH'D (1) [famished]

DIALOG144:36 H144 I saw her people famish'd, Nobles slain,

FAMISHT (1)

ELEMEN18:9 H413 The famisht, thirsty man, that craves supply:

FAMOUS (17)

ELEMEN10:35 H110 What famous Townes to cinders have I turn'd?

ELEMEN11:37 H157 My cities famous, rich, and populous,

ELEMEN19:26 H471 Where famous *Charles* the fift, more losse sustain'd,

MASSYR~~57:25~~ H172 When famous *Troy* was so beleaguered:

MASSYR61:11 H316 *Damascus,* ancient seat of famous Kings,

MASSYR~~63:24~~ H409 The ancient {famous} *Niniveh* by him was won;

MASSYR63:30 H417 The famous Wars {acts}, of this Heroyick King,

MGREC116:11 H2577 Whose famous Acts {This Monarchs fame} must last, whilst

MGREC125:18 H2966 The Wife, and Mother, of their famous Kings,

MGREC128:9 H3082 And in despight of their two famous Kings,

MGREC134:19 H3350 First *Ptolomy* being dead, his famous son,

MROMAN137:27 H3478 To *Janus,* he that famous Temple built,

MROMAN138:21 H3511 Close by the mouth of famous *Tyber* flood:

DIALOG141:11 H10 The glories of thy ever famous Realme?

SIDNEY150:21 H46 What famous feats thou didst, on *Flanders* coast,

SIDNEY150:24 H51 Made famous by thy fall {death}, much more's {more} the pitty;

DUBART153:17 H21 Who sees the riches of some famous Fayre;

FANCIED (1)

MGREC106:30 H2164 His fancied gods, above the firmament,

FANCIES (2) [pl.]

CONTEM173:11 H178 And thousand fancies buzzing in my brain,

FLESH176:33 H73 Nor fancies vain at which I snatch,
FANCIES v. See FANCYES
FANCY (6)
HUMOUR33:35 H549 The Reason, Fancy, and the Memory;
HUMOUR34:29 H584 Thy judgement is unsafe, thy fancy little,
MASSYR56:27 H133 (Each man beleive it, as his fancy list)
MGREC136:11 H3425 *And maugre all resolves, my fancy wrought*
CONTEM169:27 H66 And men in being fancy those are dead,
FLESH175:20 H20 Art fancy sick, or turn'd a Sot
FANCYES (2) v.
CONTEM169:36 H74 Fancyes the Apple, dangle on the Tree,
CONTEM170:30 H100 Who fancyes not his looks now at the Barr,
FANE See PHANE
FANN'D (1) [fanned]
SEASONS51:25 H201 Whose yellow saplesse leaves by winds are fann'd:
FANS (1) [pl.]
DUBART153:21 H25 The Hats, and Fans, the Plumes, and Ladies tires,
FANTASTICK (1)
QELIZ158:19 H128 If many worlds, as that fantastick framed,
FAR (24) See also FARRE
PROLOG7:21 H33 But sure the antick *Greeks* were far more milde,
ELEMEN~~14:4~~ H247 So did that Roman, far more stout then wise,
HUMOUR24:3 H152 And yet to make, my greatnesse far {still} more great:
HUMOUR30:39 H431 But yet more comely far, I dare avow,
MASSYR55:21 H87 Accompaning her husband *Menon* far,
MPERS75:41 H898 Entring that large and barren country far;
MPERS81:8 H1116 Who for his sake, he knew, would venture far,
MPERS~~84:12~~ H1244 His bounty did *Darius* far exceed.
MPERS86:16 H1332 More deare to's mother, then his brother far.
MPERS91:37 ~~H1551~~ Made Writers work at home, they sought not far?
MGREC98:13 H1815 But far lesse cost, and time, he doth {did} expend,
MGREC103:37 H2048 Who was retir'd, and gone to {as far as} *Media.*
MGREC112:7 H2393 It far exceeds my meane abilities,
MGREC119:28 H2718 The *Athenian* Army was the greater far,
SIDNEY151:30 ~~H75~~ Which are in worth, as far short of his due,
1LETTER181:10 H8 My sun is gone so far in's Zodiack,
2LETTER182:20 H26 Like those far scituate under the pole,
3LETTER183:4 H6 A dearer Dear (far dearer Heart) then this.
CHILDRN184:21 H10 To Regions far, and left me quite:
MEDDM200:29 Hp279 shall arise in far more glory, then that wch they lost at their
MEDDM203:25 Hp283 of a guilty Conscience, cares not how far he keeps from him
MEDDM204:27 Hp285 vpon one that is in a far better estate then himself, but let him
HOURS234:4 H18 Whose comforts far excell.
HOUSE236:30 H22 Far be it yt I should repine,
FARDLE (1)
MGREC107:10 H2185 Commands forth-with, each man his fardle bring,
FARE (1)
MASSYR62:23 H368 Or how they fare, rich, poor, or ill, or wel;
FAREWEL (8) [farewell] See also FARWELL
AGES46:25 H456 And in that hope, I bid you all farewel.
BIRTH180:20 H30 Who with salt tears this last Farewel did take.

CHILDRN186:28 H95 Farewel my birds, farewel adieu,
CHILDRN186:28 H95 Farewel my birds, farewel adieu,
ELIZB186:34 H6 Farewel dear babe, my hearts too much content,
ELIZB186:35 H7 Farewel sweet babe, the pleasure of mine eye,
ELIZB186:36 H8 Farewel fair flower that for a space was lent,
ANNEB187:30 H20 Farewel dear child, thou ne're shall come to me,

FAREWELL (6) See also FAREWEL, FARWELL
ELEMEN12:10 H170 But farewell all, for deare mount *Helicon,*
AGES~~46:3~~ H434 Sons, Nephews, leave, my death {farewell} for to deplore;
DIALOG148:33 H298 Farewell dear mother, Parliament, {rightest cause} prevail,
BIRTH180:2 H12 These farewell lines to recommend to thee,
HOUSE237:26 H56 Farewell my pelf, farewell my Store.
HOUSE237:26 H56 Farewell my pelf, farewell my Store.

FARMER (1)
ELEMEN16:41 H364 The Farmer, and the Plowman both {Grasier do} complain

FARRE (14) [far]
HUMOUR22:34 H103 She thinks I never shot so farre amisse;
SEASONS51:37 H213 So farre remote, his glances warm not us;
MASSYR~~57:16~~ H163 But this is farre unlike, he being Son
MPERS71:26 H740 Yea, in his pride, he ventured so farre,
MPERS76:14 H912 But wise *Gobrias* reads not half so farre:
MGREC105:36 H2129 And that his rule as farre extended be,
MGREC114:31 H2501 Which vertues fame can ne're redeem by farre,
MGREC122:32 H2851 Who vext the Queen more then the other farre;
MGREC127:40 H3070 forth his declaration from a {declarations near and} farre,
DIALOG144:21 H131 I mock'd the Preachers, put it farre away;
SIDNEY150:14 H49 Thy fame, and praise, is farre beyond my straine;
DUBART154:15 H60 Thy fame is spread as farre, I dare be bold,
VANITY160:38 H48 It yeeldeth pleasures, farre beyond conceit,
MEDDM203:10 Hp283 He that is to saile into a farre country, although the ship,

FARROWING (1)
AGES42:35 H291 My fleeced Ewe {Sheep}, and ever {fruitful} farrowing Sow.

FARTHER (2)
MGREC~~110:20~~ H2324 Restores him, and his bounds further {farther} extends;
MGREC~~110:24~~ H2328 Could by no means be further {farther} drawn, or led:

FARTHEST (4)
MPERS~~87:36~~ H1388 He surest {safest} was, when furthest {farthest} out o'th' way.
MGREC~~114:38~~ H2508 From *Hellispont,* to th' furthest {farthest} Ocean;
MGREC~~115:1~~ H2512 Unto the furthest {farthest} bounds of th' orient;
MGREC121:3 H2781 Near'st unto him, and farthest from the rest.

FARWELL (2) [farewell]
MEDDM200:13 Hp279 world before it bid them farwell
PILGRIM210:17 H17 All Cares and feares, he bids farwell

FASHION (1)
MGREC106:35 H2169 His manners, habit, gestures, now doth {all did} fashion,

FAST (6)
MASSYR65:20 H485 Fast bound, intends at {to} *Babel* he shal stay {him to send},
MPERS91:2 H1510 height, {*Spartan* State} which now apace doth {so fast did} rise;
MGREC100:3 H1887 To see how fast he gain'd, is {was} no small wonder,
DIALOG145:27 H176 Had they not held law fast, all had been gone,
MEDDM201:26 Hp281 vsed for Contrary ends, the one holds fast, the other puts

MEDDM201:28 Hp281 not only to bid them hold fast the form of sound Doctrin, but

FAT (2)

ELEMEN11:29 H149 To tell what sundry fruits my fat soyle yeelds,
DAVID159:7 H22 Nor from the fat, and spoyles, of mighty men,

FATAL (2)

CONTEM174:29 H226 O Time the fatal wrack of mortal things,
SICKNES178:21 H4 lo here is fatal Death.

FATALL (4)

MPERS70:29 H700 And sets on *Cyrus,* in a fatall houre;
MGREC125:28 H2978 Praying, that fatall day might quickly haste,
DIALOG142:18 H47 Or is {is't} the fatall jarre againe begun,
SIDNEY150:23 H50 O *Zutphon, Zutphon,* that most fatall City,

FATE (16)

AGES42:38 H294 If to be rich, or great, it was my fate;
AGES~~45:2~~ H380 Wailing his fate. & our own destinies.
AGES~~45:12~~ H394 Could length their dayes or once reverse their fate
MASSYR58:6 H191 Kept ever close, fearing some dismal {his well deserved} fate;
MASSYR58:29 H212 And either by his valour, or his fate,
MASSYR68:26 H612 Perform'd his word, to him, that told his fate;
MPERS71:18 H732 (But little *Marus,* {*Narus*} scap'd that cruel fate,
MPERS72:12 H760 His woful fate with tears did so bemoane,
MPERS~~90:38~~ H1505 Of that false perjur'd wretch, this was the last {fate},
MGREC131:9 H3199 Their severall battells, and their severall fate,
MGREC133:26 H3316 This of *Antigonus,* his seed's the fate,
SIDNEY152:1 ~~H75~~ Better my hap, then was his darlings fate,
VANITY~~159:36~~ H8 And whilst they live, how oft doth turn their State? {fate,}
CONTEM170:9 H82 Bewails his unknown hap, and fate forlorn;
ELIZB187:1 H10 Blest babe why should I once bewail thy fate,
ELIZB187:11 H19 Is by his hand alone that guides nature and fate.

FATES (5) [pl.]

ELEMEN20:3 H485 Which makes {make} the mighty Monarchs fear their Fates,
MGREC126:37 H3026 With Garlands crown'd his head, bemoan'd his Fates,
MGREC133:33 H3323 Tells of their warres, their names, their riches, fates;
MGREC135:9 H3381 Their standings, over-turnings, bounds and fates;
SIDNEY~~150:31~~ H58 But yet impartiall Death {Fates} this Boone did give,

FATHER (46)

FATHER5:1 H1 To her most Honoured Father
ELEMEN13:32 H233 The Husband knowes no Wife, nor father sons;
AGES41:35 H250 If a father {I}, then for children must provide:
AGES46:16 H447 Corruption, my Father, I do call,
MASSYR53:37 H27 Confirmes the rule his Father had begun,
MASSYR54:16 H43 His father dead, *Ninus* begins his reign,
MASSYR54:26 H53 This *Ninus* for a god, his father canoniz'd,
MASSYR~~57:17~~ H164 Unto a Father that all Countryes won
MASSYR59:36 H260 His Father was then King (as we suppose)
MASSYR61:10 H315 Next treads the {those} steps, by which his Father won.
MASSYR62:3 H348 He *Israelites,* more then his Father vext;
MASSYR~~63:28~~ H415 Then being Father to so great a Son.
MASSYR67:12 H558 Unlike his father, *Evilmerodach,*
MPERS68:35 H621 and his Father in Law) reigning
MPERS77:17 H958 The {His} Father not so full of lenity,

MPERS84:24 H1260 His father *Xerxes* losse, and shame, much more,
MPERS85:38 H1314 His father would no notice of that take;
MPERS~~91:35~~ H1549 Succeeds in th' throne his father being gone.
MPERS~~92:5~~ H1560 By him that late his father murthered.
MPERS92:22 ~~H1580~~ That *Ochus* unto *Arsames* was father,
MPERS92:24 ~~H1582~~ That son, and father, both were murthered
MGREC93:14 H1611 This Prince (his father by *Pausanias* slain)
MGREC112:33 H2419 Enveighs against his Father, now absent,
MGREC113:17 H2444 Was to dispatch the Father, as the Son.
MGREC116:6 H2566 Least {Lest} of such like, their Father chance to sup:
MGREC123:28 H2892 *Cassander* could not (like his father) see
MGREC123:32 H2896 Such as his father had advanc'd to place,
MGREC123:40 H2904 By all the Bonds 'twixt him and's father past,
MGREC124:8 ~~H2913~~ Upon those friends, his father rais'd on high,
MGREC130:26 H3181 By cruell father, mother, cruell son,
MGREC132:18 H3255 Those Countries large, his father got before,
MGREC133:4 H3292 *Seleuchus* was as {a} Father, and a friend,
MROMAN136:25 H3439 His Father was not *Mars,* as some devis'd,
TDUDLEY165:1 H1-2 *To the Memory of my dear and ever honoured Father*
TDUDLEY165:8 H10 Who was my Father, Guide, Instructor too,
TDUDLEY165:15 H17 He was my Father, and Ile praise him still.
CONTEM170:12 H85 Believing him that was, and is, Father of lyes.
FLESH176:6 H46 For from one father are we not,
FLESH176:9 H49 Whence my dear father I do love.
AUTHOR178:13 H23 If for thy Father askt, say, thou hadst none:
VERSES183:34 H1 *To her Father with some verses.*
MEDDM200:33 Hp280 A wise father will not lay a burden on a child of seven yeares
MEDDM200:35 Hp280 heauenly father (who knowes our mould) lay such afflictions
MED223:6 Hp250 father I thy child, yee shall be my Sons and Daughters saith y[e]
MED223:7 Hp250 —Christ is my Brother, I ascend vnto my father, and your
MED223:8 Hp250 father, vnto my God and your God—But least this should not

FATHERS (19) [poss.]

MASSYR64:9 H433 This Prince, the last year of his Fathers reign,
MPERS72:28 ~~H773~~ And only for his fathers faithfullnesse,
MPERS77:32 H973 His Fathers ill successe in's enterprise,
MPERS83:25 H1213 The second was inthron'd, in's fathers stead.
MPERS86:5 H1321 His fathers death, did {so} put an end to's fear.
MPERS86:9 H1325 *Mnemon* now sits {set} upon his fathers Throne,
MPERS~~91:36~~ H1550 Two of his brothers in his Fathers dayes
MPERS~~92:5~~ H1559 *Arsames* plac'd now in his fathers stead,
MPERS92:13 H1571 reign'd, as Chronicles expresse, {then drank of's fathers cup}
MGREC112:27 H2413 But for his Fathers great deserts, the King,
MGREC~~124:16~~ H2923 Firm (for his Fathers sake) to him abide.
MGREC124:34 H2941 His Fathers danger, with his Family;
MGREC131:29 H3221 Yet dares {durst} not say, he loves {lov'd} his fathers wife;
MGREC131:31 H3223 He wittily his fathers mind did sound,
MGREC132:12 H3247 Yet must his children pay for fathers ill.
TDUDLEY165:35 H37 My Fathers God, be God of me and mine.
TDUDLEY166:23 H65 And to his Fathers gathered is in peace.
CONTEM171:2 H107 Who thinks not oft upon the Fathers ages.
1LETTER181:18 H16 True living Pictures of their Fathers face.

FATHOM (1)
2LETTER182:28 H34 His little world's a fathom under water,
FATLINGS (1) [pl.]
CONTEM170:15 H87 Fruits of the Earth, and Fatlings each do bring,
FATTED (1)
AGES42:34 H290 My fatted Oxe {thriving Cattle}, and my exuberous {new-milch-
FATTING (1)
ELEMEN15:18 H300 Which by my fatting Nile, doth yeeld such store;
FATUUS (1)
ELEMEN11:10 H130 Of Meteors, *Ignis Fatuus,* and the rest,
FAULT (2)
MPERS72:23 H771 Like fault must look, for the like recompence.
SIDNEY152:17 H86 I pensive for my fault, sat down, and then,
FAULTS (4) [pl.]
FATHER5:30 H31 Each others faults, and where themselves excell:
SEASONS53:7 H263 *And all the faults which {that} you shall spy,*
MGREC136:18 H3432 *As faults proceeding from my head, not heart.*
BIRTH180:7 H17 The many faults that well you know I have,
FAVORITE (1)
MPERS~~72:25~~ H773 He spar'd nor foe, nor friend, nor favorite.
FAVOUR (15)
AGES~~45:11~~ H393 But neither favour, riches, title, State,
MPERS81:13 H1121 So should all favour to their State be shown.
MPERS84:34 H1270 To {By} whom oblig'd, by favour {bounty}, and by love;
MPERS89:20 H1454 Asking no favour, where they fear'd no bands.
MPERS92:17 ~~H1575~~ By favour, force, or fraud, is not set down:
MGREC118:8 H2655 More then to th' rest, his favour testified:
MGREC123:33 H2897 Or by his favour {favours} any way did grace, {had grac'd}
MGREC127:17 H3047 Such as nor {no} threats, nor favour could acquire;
MGREC129:4 H3118 He sees the *Greeks* now favour their young Prince,
MROMAN138:28 H3518 By wealth, and favour, doth to honour climbe;
MROMAN139:2 H3530 But by the favour, and the speciall grace
MEDDM205:14 Hp286 whom no bribes can pervert, nor flattery cause to favour but
MEDDM208:12 Hp290 good name, is as a precious oyntment, and it is a great favour
2HUSB233:1 H34 And favour in their eyes to whom
2HUSB233:7 H40 But Tokens of thy favour Give,
FAVOURITE (4)
MPERS72:24 ~~H772~~ *Praraspes,* to *Cambyses* favourite,
MGREC99:15 H1858 His favourite *Ephestion,* with his fleet;
MGREC115:6 H2517 Here his cheif favourite *Ephestion* dyes,
MGREC123:36 H2900 Besides, he was the young Queens favourite,
FAVOURS (3) [pl.]
AGES37:32 H94 Nor studious was, Kings favours how to buy,
MGREC~~123:33~~ H2897 Or by his favour {favours} any way did grace, {had grac'd}
SON231:25 H37 That all thy favours great receivd
FAWNING (1)
ELEMEN12:25 H185 No, though the fawning dog did urge me sore
FAYLE (1) [fail] See also FAILE
DUBART153:30 H34 And {But} seeing utterance fayle his great desires,
FAYRE (1) [fair]
DUBART153:17 H21 Who sees the riches of some famous Fayre;

FEAR (13) See also FEARE

ELEMEN20:3 H485 Which makes {make} the mighty Monarchs fear their Fates,
MASSYR58:28 H211 Fear of his diadem, did force him fight:
MPERS86:5 H1321 His fathers death, did {so} put an end to's fear.
MPERS87:2 H1358 And fills the Court with tumult, and with fear.
MGREC96:10 H1730 An object not so much of fear, as laughter.
MGREC102:2 H1972 Accompani'd with sorrow, fear, and shame;
MGREC130:37 H3182 Thus may we hear, and fear, and ever say,
MGREC131:28 H3220 Falls so extreamly sick, all fear {fear'd} his life,
DIALOG147:24 H248 And yee brave Nobles, chase away all fear,
TDUDLEY167:2 H84 *The Good him lov'd, the bad did fear,*
CONTEM173:24 H190 Reminds not what is past, nor whats to come dost fear.
MEDDM195:25 Hp272 no evill that we feele, or fear, but we may make some spiritull
FEVER220:30 H10 Beclouded was my Soul wth fear

FEAR'D (13) [feared] See also FEARD

FATHER6:3 H37 But fear'd you'ld judge, one *Bartas* was my friend,
ELEMEN19:21 H466 Men fear'd destruction epidemicall.
ELEMEN19:36 H477 Earth-quaks so hurtful and so fear'd of all,
AGES38:9 H112 I fear'd no stormes, nor al the windes that blows,
AGES38:11 H114 I fear'd no drought, nor wet, I had no crop,
AGES43:2 ~~H297~~ To run my hull upon disgrace I fear'd,
MASSYR64:7 H431 And this is {was} he, who when he fear'd the least,
MPERS72:32 H776 Fear'd of all, but lov'd of few, or none,
MPERS74:37 ~~H858~~ And fear'd, he now with scorn must march away:
MPERS89:20 H1454 Asking no favour, where they fear'd no bands.
MGREC~~120:4~~ H2736 Who fear'd *Antipater* would take his life
MGREC129:34 H3148 *Cassander* fear'd what might of this insue,
MGREC~~131:28~~ H3220 Falls so extreamly sick, all fear {fear'd} his life,

FEARD (1) [feared] See also FEAR'D

RESTOR229:25 H8 Thou rais'st him vp I feard to loose

FEARE (10)

HUMOUR34:33 H588 But if love be, as requisite as feare,
MPERS70:7 H678 That all the world they neither {need not} feare, nor doubt;
MPERS87:38 H1390 Rejoyced {Was} not a little {jocund} at his feare.
DIALOG142:23 H52 Pray, doe not {you} feare *Spaines* bragging Armado?
DIALOG142:29 H58 Dost feele the smart, or feare the consequence?
DIALOG142:37 H66 But forraigne Foe, nor fained friend I feare,
DIALOG143:19 H88 For wants, sure some I feele, but more I feare,
SIDNEY150:41 ~~H69~~ I feare thou wert a Commet, did portend
MEDDM206:33 Hp288 alsoe teach the children of godly parents to walk wth feare
MEDDM207:16 Hp288 of discontent or feare, or greife that lyes at the root wch in

FEARED (1) See also FEAR'D, FEARD

MPERS79:28 H1054 His answer was, both Land and Sea he feared,

FEARES (8) n. [fears]

PILGRIM210:17 H17 All Cares and feares, he bids farwell
MYCHILD216:18 Hp241 + feares brovght yov to this, I now travail in birth again of yov
MYCHILD216:26 Hp242 somt. on my soul in Doubts & feares of Gods displeasure, and
BYNIGHT220:15 H14 And banisht thence my Doubts + feares.
RESTOR229:21 H4 When feares and sorrowes me besett
SON230:21 H4 My feares to Joyes, my sighes to song
HOURS233:23 H6 My Longings and my feares.

ACK235:8	H8	Hast known my doubts and All my feares,
FEARES (3) v. [fears]		
MPERS89:10	H1444	Of this dayes cowardize, he feares the effects;
MPERS89:30	H1464	And feares as much to let them march away;
MGREC100:38	H1922	Some injury was offered, he feares;
FEARFUL (3)		
AGES45:40	H430	Now trembling, and {is all} fearful, sad, and cold;
AGES46:7	H438	To mean, to noble, fearful, or to bold:
SEASONS48:3	H56	The fearful Bird, his little house now builds,
FEARFULL (5)		
MASSYR68:12	H598	Who still expects some fearfull sad event,
MPERS87:13	H1369	The fearfull King, at last, musters his Forces;
MGREC95:24	H1703	His substitute, as fearfull as his master,
DIALOG145:8	H157	Your fearfull sinnes, great cause there's to lament,
HOUSE236:17	H9	That fearfull sovnd of fire and fire,
FEARING (8)		
MASSYR58:6	H191	Kept ever close, fearing some dismal {his well deserved} fate;
MPERS~~80:36~~	H1103	Much, {fearing} that which never was intended!
MPERS~~81:5~~	H1113	Thought it {Fearing} his best {bridge}, no longer for to {there
MPERS81:14	H1122	The *Spartans,* fearing *Athens* would agree,
MGREC~~113:27~~	H2454	Thinking {Fearing} no harme, because he none did owe {doe},
MGREC116:33	H2599	Still fearing that his Name might hap to die,
MGREC123:16	H2880	Fearing his Son *Cassander* was unstay'd,
MGREC127:34	H3064	Fearing their state {his force}, and what might hap ere long
FEARS (11) n. See also FEARES		
AGES~~45:2~~	H379	Which fil'd our hearts with fears, with tears our eyes,
MASSYR61:40	H345	Then by his death, releas'd, was *Israels* fears.
MPERS72:4	~~H755~~	He strait to rid himself of causlesse fears,
MPERS88:14	H1407	But long under their fears, they did not stay,
MGREC94:13	H1647	Thus eased now, of troubles, and of fears;
MGREC103:38	H2049	(And there with sorrows, fears, and cares surrounded)
MGREC129:8	H3122	Resolves to quit his fears by one deed done,
2LETTER182:6	H12	My sobs, my longing hopes, my doubting fears,
CHILDRN185:18	H44	Let others know what are my fears
CHILDRN185:35	H61	My cares are more, and fears then ever,
PILGRIM210:29	H29	Wth cares and fears ner' cumbred be
FEARS (5) v. See also FEARES		
MASSYR68:1	H587	Which horrid sight, he fears, must needs portend,
MPERS~~86:10~~	H1326	Yet doubts, {fears} all he injoyes, is not his own.
MGREC~~94:9~~	H1643	And many more, {all} whom he suspects {or fears} will climbe,
MGREC130:11	H3166	To let her go, or hold her still, he fears,
CONTEM173:18	H184	O merry Bird (said I) that fears no snares,
FEAST (5)		
MPERS83:37	H1225	Which done, a sumptuous feast; makes like a King
MGREC111:40	H2385	A Wedding Feast to's Nobles then he makes,
MGREC112:5	H2391	Six thousand Guests he to {unto} this feast invites,
MGREC112:12	H2398	He might this feast imagine by the same.
MGREC~~114:7~~	H2475	Both at a Feast when they had tippled well
FEASTED (1)		
MPERS70:10	H681	That night *Belshazzar* feasted all his rout,

FEASTS (6) [pl.]
MPERS89:34 H1468 Commander, as most {Commanders feasts and yet more}
MGREC109:7 H2266 Whose feasts are celebrated by this Prince;
MGREC111:33 H2378 Much time in feasts, and ryoting doth {did} wast;
FEASTS (3) v.
MPERS78:33 H1014 Feasts all this multitude, of his own charge,
MPERS84:5 H1233 Queen *Vashty* also feasts, but 'fore tis ended,
MGREC111:6 H2351 These, all he feasts in state, on beds of gold,
FEATHERED (1)
CONTEM173:27 H192 Sets hundred notes unto thy feathered crew,
FEATHERS (2) [pl.]
QELIZ158:16 H125 So blaze it fame, here's feathers for thy wings,
MEDDM196:6 Hp272 of the pea cock that prideing himself in his gay feathers
FEATS (3) [pl.]
HUMOUR25:37 H226 Ile not envy thy feats, nor happinesse.
MPERS81:37 ~~H1143~~ Where both sides exercis'd their manly feats;
SIDNEY150:21 H46 What famous feats thou didst, on *Flanders* coast,
FEATURE (1)
MPERS72:36 H780 And like in feature, to the *Smerdis* dead,
FEAVER (3) [fever] See also **FEAVOR**
FEVER220:21 H1 For Delive^{rc} from a feaver.
11MAYB228:26 Hp259 this month I had a feaver seatd vpon me wch indeed was the
HANNA230:10 H3 dangerous feaver.
FEAVERS (1) [fevers] See also **FEAVOURS**
AGES40:38 H217 Sometimes by Feavers, all my moisture drinking,
FEAVOR (1) [fever] See also **FEAVER**
HUMOUR32:7 H481 Nor Cough, nor Quinsie, nor the burning Feavor.
FEAVOURS (2) [fevers] See also **FEAVERS**
ELEMEN19:14 H459 Then Feavours, Purples, Pox, and Pestilence;
AGES43:33 ~~H328~~ The Quinsie, and the Feavours, oft distaste me,
FEBLEE (1) [feebly]
FAINT222:20 H10 My feblee Spirit thou did's reviue
FEBRUARY (1)
SEASONS52:32 H247 Moyst snowie *February* is my last,
FED (8)
AGES42:2 H260 Whose loynes {backs} I've cloth'd, and bellies I have fed;
MASSYR55:19 H85 Whence rose that fable, she by birds was fed.
MASSYR57:10 H157 It is more like, being {his lust} with pleasures fed,
MASSYR65:27 H492 And more then {seven and} thirty years in prison fed;
MGREC132:22 H3267 Within an Isle that was with pleasures fed,
DDUDLEY167:13 H10 *Whom oft she fed, and clothed with her store;*
CONTEM173:10 H177 While musing thus with contemplation fed,
CHILDRN185:32 H58 Great was my care, when I you fed,
FEDINATES (1)
MROMAN137:19 H3470 And *Fedinates* they wholly over-throw:
FEEBLE (7)
MASSYR65:18 H483 And unexpected findes the feeble Prince,
MPERS85:40 H1316 But *Cyrus* scornes, his brothers feeble wit;
MGREC118:1 H2648 That so under his feeble wit, and reign,
TDUDLEY165:27 H29 Who staid thy feeble sides when thou wast low,
AUTHOR177:30 H2 Thou ill-form'd offspring of my feeble brain,

MEDDM202:12 Hp281 and some againe so weak and feeble, that while they liue, they
SOREFIT221:25 H11 My feeble loines didst gird wth strenght

FEEBLY See FEBLEE

FEED (9)

HUMOUR23:1 H111 Wil feed a Dropsie, or a Timpany,
HUMOUR23:40 ~~H149~~ The spongy Lungs, I feed with frothy blood.
AGES41:34 H253 To bear me out i'th' world, and feed the poor,
AGES42:8 H266 Was I a pastor, I my flock did feed:
SEASONS50:35 H169 To feed his boughes, exhausted hath his sap,
FLESH175:12 H12 Doth Contemplation feed thee so
MEDDM195:35 Hp272 both by an empty old age, he that hath nothing to feed on but
MEDDM200:9 Hp279 this life, that so they might feed vpon more substantiall food,
MEDDM202:17 Hp282 haue no kernell in them, and they that feed vpon them, may

FEEDING (2)

SEASONS47:21 H37 Now {Do} jump, and play, before their feeding Dams,
CONTEM174:22 H220 Feeding on sweets, that never bit of th' sowre,

FEEDS (2)

MPERS77:36 H977 With certainty {conquest} of {all} *Europe* feeds his pride;
DUBART153:18 H22 He feeds his eyes, but understanding lacks,

FEEL (4)

ELEMEN17:30 H394 That after times, shall never feel like woe:
HUMOUR32:8 H482 I rarely feel to act his fierce indeavour.
DIALOG~~144:25~~ H134 I then believ'd not, now I feel and see,
DIALOG145:12 H161 Not what you feel, but what you do expect.

FEELE (6) [feel]

ELEMEN9:2 H36 To try your valour by, but it must feele
ELEMEN13:41 H242 If {When} once you feele me, your foundation, quake,
DIALOG141:19 H18 And thou a childe, a Limbe, and dost not feele
DIALOG142:29 H58 Dost feele the smart, or feare the consequence?
DIALOG143:19 H88 For wants, sure some I feele, but more I feare,
MEDDM195:25 Hp272 inioy, no evill that we feele, or fear, but we may make some

FEELING (2)

MGREC96:41 H1761 The cowards feeling this sharp stinging charge,
CONTEM168:34 H40 All mortals here the feeling knowledg hath.

FEELS (1)

CONTEM173:20 H186 Feels no sad thoughts, nor cruciating cares

FEEL'ST (1)

BIRTH180:11 H21 And when thou feel'st no grief, as I no harms,

FEET (12)

HUMOUR32:37 H511 That Kings have laid their Scepters at my feet,
SEASONS53:8 H264 *Shall at your feet for pardon cry.*
MPERS74:12 ~~H836~~ And after *Persian* manner, kisse his feet.
MGREC95:31 H1710 Who came with thousand thousands at his feet,
MGREC99:24 H1867 Captaine {Thus *Betis*} tane, had holes bor'd through his feet,
MGREC135:25 H3397 And smote those feet, those legs, those arms and thighs;
MGREC135:33 H3405 The residue he stamped under's feet:
DIALOG148:14 H279 And tear his flesh, and set your feet on's neck,
CONTEM169:11 H52 In pathless paths I lead my wandring feet,
AUTHOR178:6 H16 I stretcht thy joynts to make thee even feet,
MEDDM196:7 Hp272 he ruffles them vp, but spying his black feet, he soon lets fall
PILGRIM210:15 H15 No rugged stones his feet shall gaule

FEIGN (3)
MASSYR55:13 H79 Her beautious face (they feign) retaining still.
MASSYR56:36 H142 The Poets feign her turn'd into a Dove,
MASSYR57:35 H180 May feign as many acts, as he did names;
FEIGNED (3)
PROLOG7:22 H34 Else of our Sex, why feigned they those nine,
MASSYR61:32 H337 Proves unto *Ahaz* but a feigned friend;
MYCHILD217:35 Hp243 how did know but they were feigned. That there is a God my
FEILD (1) [field]
MROMAN137:15 H3466 For {Then} to recover them, a Feild was fought;
FEIRCE (1) [fierce]
QELIZ157:8 H76 Feirce *Tomris* (*Cirus* Heads-man, *Sythians* Queen)
FEL (2) [fell]
MASSYR57:28 H173 What e're he was, they {or} did, or how it fel,
MPERS91:12 H1520 Til many a Captain fel, both wise, and strong,
FELICITIES (1) [pl.]
MGREC112:8 H2394 To shadow forth these short felicities:
FELICITY (5)
MPERS92:36 H1594 How from the top of the worlds felicity;
MGREC105:10 H2103 His lost felicity did greive him sore,
MGREC114:32 H2502 Nor all felicity, of his in war;
CONTEM172:36 H169 You watry folk that know not your felicity.
MYCHILD217:23 Hp243 not enjoyed that felicity that somt. I haue done, But when I
FELL (12) See also FEL
SEASONS53:3 H259 *The first fell in so naturally,*
MPERS85:6 H1282 But he, with his next {second} brother {him} fell at strife,
MPERS92:8 ~~H1566~~ So fell to him, which else it had not done:
MPERS92:37 H1595 He fell to depth of greatest misery,
MGREC114:8 H2476 Upon this dangerous theam fond *Clitus* fell;
MGREC~~125:33~~ H2983 That were {fell} within her reach, came to their ends;
MGREC131:38 H3230 Which should succeed, at variance they fell,
MROMAN140:3 H3566 My papers fell a prey to th' raging fire.
DIALOG146:5 H193 They worded it so long, they fell to blows,
SIDNEY~~150:40~~ H68 *Stella* the fair, whose streams from Conduits fell
QELIZ156:34 H61 And {the proud} *Tiron* bound, before her picture fell.
MYCHILD216:11 Hp241 After some time I fell into a lingering sicknes like a
FELL'D (1) [felled]
SEASONS52:3 ~~H219~~ This month is timber for all uses fell'd,
FELLOW (1)
3LETTER183:16 H18 Her fellow lost, nor joy nor life do wish,
FELLOWS (1) [pl.]
MASSYR64:15 H439 Wise *Daniel,* and his fellows 'mongst the rest,
FELT (13)
ELEMEN19:22 H467 Then of my tempests, felt at Sea and Land,
SEASONS52:37 H252 And some warm glances from the Sun {his face} are felt,
MASSYR62:37 H382 Until the thundring hand of heaven he felt,
MPERS75:3 H864 That for their sakes, his cruelty he felt;
DAVID159:4 H19 As if his head ne're felt the sacred Oyle:
CONTEM170:32 H102 Nor Male-factor ever felt like warr,
CONTEM173:32 H197 Where winter's never felt by that sweet airy legion.
1LETTER181:11 H9 Whom whilst I 'joy'd, nor storms, nor frosts I felt,

CHILDRN184:18 H7 Till at the last they felt their wing.
MEDDM203:21 Hp283 He that neuer felt, what it was to be sick or wounded, doth not
MEDDM203:24 Hp283 he slighted before, so he that neuer felt the sicknes of sin,
MYCHILD216:24 Hp242 felt my heart out of order, but I haue expected correct^{n} for it,
SOREFIT221:20 H6 Thou knowest the sorrowes y^{t} I felt

FEMALE (3)
PROLOG7:17 H30 For such despight they cast on female wits:
AGES40:6 H187 Sometimes I cheat (unkind) a female Heir,
MPERS73:6 H793 The Female {to} many ages did extend,

FEMININE (1)
DAVID159:25 H40 Exceeding all the Love that's Feminine,

FEMININES (1) [pl.]
HUMOUR21:9 H37 Now Feminines (a while) for love we owe

FENCE (1)
HUMOUR21:22 H50 Be he a Souldier, I more fence his heart

FENS (1) [pl.]
ELEMEN15:4 H286 Hindes leave their Calves, the Elephant the Fens;

FERE See PHERE

FERN (1)
3LETTER182:37 H2 Scuds through the woods and Fern with harkning ear,

FERTILE (2)
HUMOUR30:8 H400 Then all the huge beasts of the fertile field.
MGREC101:10 H1935 With fertile *Ægypt,* and rich *Syria,*

FERVENT (1)
SEASONS49:15 H106 She's {Tis} for a time as fervent as before.

FERVOR (3)
SEASONS48:14 H67 Least by his fervor, we be terrifi'd,
CONTEM168:33 H39 Thy pleasing fervor, and thy scorching force,
2LETTER182:29 H35 Nought but the fervor of his ardent beams

FESTIVALLS (1) [pl.]
MPERS83:40 H1228 To be partakers in {of} these festivalls.

FESTIVITY (1)
SEASONS52:22 H237 Through Christendome, with great festivity

FETCH (3)
MASSYR64:41 H465 Fetch {Fetcht} rubbish from the opposite old town,
MROMAN138:8 H3498 And from old *Alba* fetch the wealth away;
DIALOG141:23 H22 Unlesse some Cordial thou fetch from high,

FETCHT (2)
MASSYR~~64:41~~ H465 Fetch {Fetcht} rubbish from the opposite old town,
MGREC98:16 H1818 The other by his men fetcht all by Land;

FETTERS (1) [pl.]
MPERS~~79:13~~ H1037 He fetters cast therein the same to chain.

FEUD (1)
FLESH176:5 H45 Yet deadly feud 'twixt thee and me;

FEVER See FEAVER, FEAVOR

FEVERS See FEAVERS, FEAVOURS

FEW (20)
ELEMEN10:17 H92 Out of a multitude, these few I touch,
AGES45:29 H419 My grinders now are few, my sight doth faile
MASSYR57:33 H178 Save a few names anew, *Berosus* writ.
MASSYR59:23 H247 For few, or none, did there {it seems} resistance make;

MASSYR64:24 H448 Which in few years proves the *Assyrians* hire;
MPERS72:32 H776 Fear'd of all, but lov'd of few, or none,
MPERS82:13 H1160 For pitty, let those few to *Xerxes* go,
MPERS87:24 H1376 Few might have kept it, had they but {had} a heart.
MGREC100:4 H1888 For in few dayes he brought that Kingdom under.
MGREC100:11 H1895 Now {Thence} back to *Ægypt* goes, and in few dayes,
MGREC102:12 H1982 Which in few hours was carried all away;
MGREC104:10 H2062 Then with so few, how likely to be crost.
MGREC123:4 H2866 Who in few years the rest so over-tops,
MGREC129:6 H3120 That in few years he must be forc'd or glad
MGREC135:15 H3387 And Millions were subjected unto few:
MROMAN139:37 H3563 And for the same, I hours not few did spend,
MEDDM195:29 Hp272 Many can speak well, but few can do well. We are better
MEDDM197:22 Hp275 Few men are so humble, as not to be proud of their abilitys,
MEDDM198:18 Hp276 of men, wch they all catch gre¯dily at but few perceiues
PILGRIM210:33 H33 And when a few yeares shall be gone

FICKLE (1)
HUMOUR31:25 H458 And Sanguine is more fickle many fold. {manifold,}

FICTION (1)
MASSYR55:14 H80 Sure from this fiction, *Dagon* first began,

FIDDLE (1)
HUMOUR21:36 H64 She loves a Fiddle, better then a Drum,

FIDDLERS See FIDLERS

FIDELITY (3)
MGREC106:14 H2148 For his fidelity to 's Master show'd;
MGREC121:39 H2821 From his fidelity make him once move.
MGREC127:24 H3054 Thus lost he all for his fidelity,

FIDLERS (1) [fiddlers]
AGES40:14 H195 Dayes, {Whole} nights, with Ruffins, Roarers, Fidlers spend,

FIELD (18) See also FEILD
HUMOUR21:37 H65 A Chamber wel, in field she dares not come;
HUMOUR30:8 H400 Then all the huge beasts of the fertile field.
HUMOUR32:34 H508 And {But} though the pitched field i've ever fled,
AGES37:40 H102 No Statist I: nor Marti'list i' th' field;
AGES39:24 H167 Though thus in field, at home, to all most kind,
SEASONS47:17 H33 Like Birds, now chirp, and hop about the field;
MASSYR58:31 H214 That in dispaire, he left the field and fled:
MPERS~~73:26~~ H811 And two of these great Peers, in place {Field} lay dead:
MPERS76:33 H931 At *Marathon* this bloudy field was fought,
MPERS89:12 H1446 What dastards in the field the *Persians* are;
MGREC97:24 H1785 No sooner had this Captaine {Victor} won the field,
MGREC110:18 H2318 When *Alexander* strives to win the field,
MGREC128:25 H3098 His Son at *Gaza* likewise lost the field,
DIALOG146:9 H197 But could the field alone this cause {strife} decide,
SIDNEY151:17 ~~H69~~ When such a *Hero* shoots him out o'th' field,
DUBART153:13 H17 Flowers, fruits, in garden, orchard, or in field;
CONTEM173:6 H174 Who forrage o're the spacious sea-green field,
SICKNES179:9 H29 The race is run, the field is won,

FIELDS (7) [pl.]
ELEMEN11:30 H150 In vine-yards, orchards, gardens, and corne fields,
SEASONS48:4 H57 In trees, and wals, in cities, and in fields;

SEASONS48:32 ~~H83~~ Sometime a theame that's large, proves barren fields.
SEASONS50:8 H142 Which makes the aged fields look young again,
MPERS81:36 ~~H1143~~ The *Beotian* Fields, of war, the seats,
DIALOG142:7 H36 And {Or} by tempestuous Wars thy fields trod down?
DAVID158:34 H14 Nor fields of offerings e're on you grow,

FIEND (1)
HUMOUR25:23 H212 Thou art a fury, or infernal Fiend.

FIERCE (5) See also FEIRCE
HUMOUR32:8 H482 I rarely feel to act his fierce indeavour.
AGES45:39 H429 My heart sometimes as fierce, as Lions bold,
SEASONS47:27 H43 Nor-west {North-west} cold, {wind} of fierce *December.*
MGREC96:38 H1758 Which made {To make} his over-throw more fierce, and sure.
VANITY160:27 H37 Where lions fierce, nor lions whelps hath {have} been,

FIERCELY (3)
MPERS80:4 H1071 Laid on more fiercely, their deep mortall blowes;
MPERS82:5 H1152 No longer dar'd, but fiercely {bravely} on-set gave,
MGREC108:22 H2238 And there most fiercely set upon the same;

FIERCENESSE (1)
ELEMEN15:1 H283 When I am gone, their fiercenesse none need {needs} doubt;

FIERY (4)
ELEMEN9:31 H65 A burning fiery heat we find reflect;
HUMOUR26:38 H268 Thy fiery yellow froth, is mixt among.
HUMOUR29:20 H371 Thy fiery spirit shal bear away this prize,
SEASONS50:11 H145 My next, and last, is *August,* fiery hot,

FIFT (2) [fifth]
ELEMEN19:26 H471 Where famous *Charles* the fift, more losse sustain'd,
AGES38:24 H127 And fift Commandement do daily break.

FIFTEEN (3)
MASSYR54:21 H48 On which stood fifteen hundred towers stout:
MASSYR56:2 H108 Each Square, was fifteen thousand paces long,
MGREC96:19 H1739 He fifteen hundred had like women drest,

FIFTH (5) See also FIFT
MASSYR63:3 H388 The fifth, and last, of great *Belosus* race;
MPERS71:14 H728 He wages warre, the fifth year of his reign,
DIALOG143:13 H82 By *Edward* third, and *Henry* fifth of fame,
CHILDRN185:9 H35 My fifth, whose down is yet scarce gone
MERCY189:6 H27 The fifth and last pledge of her dying love,

FIFTY (7)
ELEMEN10:24 H99 And man from thirty unto fifty frame.
MASSYR55:1 H67 Fifty two years he reign'd (as we are told)
MASSYR63:25 H410 For fifty years, or more, it had been free,
MPERS81:33 H1141 He fifty thousand joynes unto his own;
MPERS87:34 H1386 Some fifty, or else sixty foote in breadth.
MGREC100:25 H1909 Two hundred fifty thousand by account,
MGREC109:20 H2279 Fifty six Elephants he brings to's hands: {hand,}

FIGGE (1) [fig]
SEASONS51:8 H182 The Figge is {are} ripe, the Pomgranet also,

FIGHT (27)
ELEMEN9:1 H35 O {Ye} Martialist! what weapon {weapons} for your fight?
HUMOUR22:12 H81 So loving unto all, she scornes to fight.
HUMOUR29:8 H361 But sith we fight with words, we might be kind,

AGES45:36 H426 I cannot labour, nor {much less} I cannot {can} fight:
MASSYR56:33 H139 The rest *Staurobates* in fight did slay.
MASSYR58:28 H211 Fear of his diadem, did force him fight:
MPERS71:32 H746 But vain he found, to fight with Elements,
MPERS79:38 H1064 Two dayes and nights a fight they there maintain,
MPERS82:9 H1156 Which found, like *Greeks* they fight, the *Persians* fly,
MPERS88:3 H1396 Gets on his armes, arayes himselfe for fight;
MGREC95:33 H1712 He but four hundred thousand had to fight,
MGREC96:18 H1738 think {Suppos'd} he neither thought {meant} to fight nor fly,
MGREC96:34 H1754 The *Greekes* would all adore, and {but} would none fight.
MGREC97:22 H1783 Two hundred eighty *Greeks* he lost in fight,
MGREC101:34 ~~H1959~~ Both Armies meet, *Greeks* fight, the *Persians* run,
MGREC~~101:34~~ H1961 The Armyes joyn'd a while, the Persians fight,
MGREC104:6 H2058 Perswades him not to fight, with *Alexander.*
MGREC107:40 H2215 But coward, durst not fight, nor could he fly,
MGREC~~123:13~~ H2876 But while these Chieftains doe in Asia fight,
MGREC128:23 H3096 *Antigonus* {These princes} at {the} Sea soone had a fight,
MGREC128:29 H3102 *Demetrius* againe with *Ptolomy* did fight,
MGREC131:10 H3202 *Antigonus* and *Seleuchus,* now {then his} fight
MGREC132:5 ~~H3238~~ The youngest by *Demetrius* kill'd in fight,
MGREC132:20 H3257 And with his son in law, will needs go fight:
MGREC132:36 H3283 And so *Lysimachus* was slaine in fight.
MGREC134:16 H3347 Vanquish'd in fight, and took those kingdomes all,
MGREC134:41 H3370 Till great *Augustus* had with him a fight,

FIGHTING (2)
ELEMEN19:40 H481 Their joyning, fighting, forcing, and retreat;
MGREC119:30 H2720 For fighting still, whilst there did hope remain,

FIGHTS (3) [pl.]
HUMOUR33:2 H516 Country with Country, *Greece* with *Asia* fights,
MGREC~~109:5~~ H2263 His fights, his dangers, and the hurts he had,
MGREC~~131:9~~ H3200 Their fights by Sea, their victories by land,

FIGTREE (1)
ELEMEN13:27 H228 The Vine, the Olive, and the Figtree want:

FIL (1) [fill]
MGREC103:35 H2046 Those stately streets with raging flames doth {flame did} fil.

FIL'D (1) [filled] See also FILL'D, FILLD
AGES~~45:2~~ H379 Which fil'd our hearts with fears, with tears our eyes,

FILL (11) See also FIL
FATHER5:22 H23 That sinke, that swim, that fill, that upwards flye,
ELEMEN12:34 H194 Doe cure your patients, fill your purse with pence;
ELEMEN18:23 H427 Ye Mariners, tis I that fill your Sailes,
ELEMEN18:28 H432 And with my selfe, I every vacuum fill.
MGREC117:9 H2616 So the same cup to his, did others fill.
MGREC135:11 H3383 The Heavens thus rule, to fill the earth {world} with wonder.
MGREC135:39 H3411 To fill the world with terrour, and with woe:
TDUDLEY165:14 H16 Let malice bite, and envy knaw its fill,
FLESH175:34 H34 Affect's thou pleasure? take thy fill,
FLESH177:27 H108 If I of Heaven may have my fill,
MEDDM202:18 Hp282 throats, but cannot fill their bellys, they may be choaked by

FILL'D (5) [filled] See also FIL'D, FILLD
SEASONS48:20 H73 Her shelves, and Firkins fill'd for winter time.

MASSYR64:3 H427 This was that tree, whose brances fill'd the earth,
MGREC134:22 H3353 {And} With seven hundred thousand volumes fill'd,
DIALOG147:22 ~~H247~~ Let Gaoles be fill'd with th' remnant of that pack,
BYNIGHT220:12 H11 My hungry Soul fill'd wth Good,

FILLD (1) [filled] See also FIL'D, FILL'D
REMB235:30 H11 And I am filld wth shame,

FILLED (5) See also FIL'D, FILL'D, FILLD
MGREC103:27 H2038 (Filled with madnesse, and quite void of reason)
CHILDRN184:31 H20 They *Norward* steer'd with filled sayles.
MEDDM202:33 Hp282 obiects enter, yet is not that spacious roome filled neither
MEDDM202:36 Hp282 it self, and sees an impossibility, euer to be filled, but by him,
MYCHILD218:28 Hp244 new Troubles I haue had since ye world has been filled wth

FILLS (2)
MPERS87:2 H1358 And fills the Court with tumult, and with fear.
QELIZ158:10 H119 *Whose sweet perfume fills the all-filling aire,*

FILS (1) [fills]
HUMOUR26:25 H255 I am the Fountaine which thy Cisterns fils,

FILTH (2)
HUMOUR31:13 ~~H444~~ Til filth and thee, nature exhonorates.
HUMOUR~~31:15~~ H448 Till filth and thee nature exonerates:

FILTHY (2)
DIALOG148:15 H280 And make his filthy den so desolate,
MEDDM206:23 Hp287 mercy wthout mony & wthout price but bring his filthy raggs to

FINAL (1)
CONTEM171:32 H134 But in oblivion to the final day remain.

FINALL (2) [final]
MPERS82:14 H1161 To certifie this finall over-throw.
MROMAN137:16 H3467 But in the end, to finall peace they come,

FIN'D (1) [fined]
DIALOG144:29 H137 Some grossely fin'd, from {house &} friends to exile went:

FIND (31)
FATHER5:8 H9 Their paralells to find I scarcely know,
ELEMEN9:31 H65 A burning fiery heat we find reflect;
AGES38:30 H133 Yet griefs, in my fraile flesh, I still do find.
AGES42:30 H286 My weary beast, rest from his toile can find;
AGES45:34 H424 Nor sapors find, in what I drink or eat.
SEASONS48:34 ~~H85~~ In this harsh strain, I find no melody,
MASSYR67:23 H569 His lust, and cruelty, {crueltyes} in books {storyes} we find,
MPERS86:14 H1330 What helps, {help} in's enterprize he's like to find,
MPERS92:28 ~~H1586~~ And he that story reads, shall often find;
MPERS~~92:28~~ H1586 If so, or not, we cannot tell, but find
MGREC~~110:18~~ H2322 Did *Alexander* by his answers find:
MGREC119:11 H2701 That if he came, good welcome he should find:
MGREC~~122:8~~ H2833 In *Plutarchs Lives* his history many find.
MGREC131:19 H3211 Hoping {Hopes} to find succour {succours} in {his} miseries.
DIALOG143:34 H103 That Pope, had hope, to find *Rome* here againe;
SIDNEY151:22 H72 With endlesse turnes, the way I find not out,
VANITY160:4 H14 What then? content in pleasures canst thou find?
VANITY160:14 H24 Yet these, the wisest man of men did find,
VANITY160:24 H34 Where shall I climbe, sound, seek, search or find,
VANITY161:6 H57 {And all} The rest's {rest} but vanity, and vain we find.

DDUDLEY167:15	H12	*And as they did, so they reward did find:*
CONTEM170:28	H99	Though none on Earth but kindred near then could he find.
FLESH175:36	H36	Then let not goe, what thou maist find,
AUTHOR178:9	H19	But nought save home-spun Cloth, i' th' house I find.
MEDDM207:15	Hp288	find their shadow very comfortable, yet there is some worm or
TOCHILD215:4	H4	That being gone, here yov may find
MYCHILD217:28	Hp243	were it hell it self and could there find ye Love of God toward
WHAT224:15	H15	I find his Love, I know his pow'r.
MYSOUL225:19	H23	No gain I find in ovght below
HOURS233:30	H13	In secrett places, Thee I find
HOURS234:12	H26	But what from Thee I find.

FINDE (15) [find]

ELEMEN8:34	H32	The benefit all Beings, {living} by me finde;
AGES46:8	H439	From King to begger, all degrees shal finde
MASSYR58:12	H197	Who sick of his disease, he soone did finde.
MPERS71:9	H725	Then sends to finde a Law for these his sins;
MPERS71:10	H726	That Kings with Sisters match, no Law they finde,
MPERS75:17	H878	Scarse finde enough to thank thy loyalty;
MPERS92:2	~~H1556~~	That three and twenty years he reign'd, I finde,
MGREC106:18	H2152	Such country there, nor yet such people finde.
MGREC107:21	H2196	False *Bessus* to finde out, in *Bactria;*
MGREC107:33	H2208	Would by {without} some means a transportation finde;
MGREC123:27	H2891	Thinks by her Majesty much help to finde;
MGREC124:24	H2931	And act, as opportunity they finde:
MGREC125:41	H2991	So goes to finde this {cruel} Queen in *Macedon;*
MEDDM197:27	Hp275	will finde it a wearysome if not an impossible task so he that
MEDDM208:25	Hp290	wells in the time of drought, that those that go to finde water in

FINDES (8) [finds]

ELEMEN13:24	H225	He sometimes findes, maugre his toyling paine,
MASSYR65:18	H483	And unexpected findes the feeble Prince,
MGREC105:19	H2112	Findes poore *Darius,* peirced to the heart;
MGREC107:4	H2179	And for the rest new wars, and travels findes,
MGREC115:5	H2516	Findes there the want of wise *Parmenio,*
DUBART153:28	H32	But findes too soone his want of Eloquence,
MEDDM199:21	Hp278	of both, and findes nothing but vanity and vexation of spirit
MEDDM203:26	Hp283	skill to cure it, but when he findes his diseases to disrest him,

FINDING (9)

MPERS70:13	H684	Not finding a defendant thereupon;
MPERS~~81:4~~	H1112	He seeing {finding} all thus tend unto {to his} decay,
MPERS82:4	H1151	*Mardonius* finding victuals wast apace,
MPERS83:4	H1192	The grieved Prince finding nor right, nor love,
MPERS86:31	H1347	The King finding, revenues now amended;
MPERS87:37	H1389	*Cyrus* finding his campe, and no man there;
MGREC98:33	H1835	*Darius* finding troubles still increase,
MGREC101:26	H1951	The afflicted King, finding him set to jar,
MEDDM207:2	Hp288	finding out.

FINDS (7) See also FINDES

MASSYR~~57:20~~	H167	Nor can those Reasons which wise *Raleigh* finds,
MPERS82:33	H1180	Straight comes her Lord, and finds his wife thus lie,
MGREC97:5	H1766	Now finds both leggs, and Horse, to run away;
MGREC~~132:16~~	H3253	In neither finds content if he sits still:

CONTEM174:1 H202 From some of these he never finds cessation,
MEDDM202:36 Hp282 finds it self, and sees an impossibility, euer to be filled, but by
MEDDM205:15 Hp286 as he finds the evidence, so he absolues or condemnes, yea

FINE (6)
ELEMEN16:7 H330 The *Ponticke, {Aegean} Caspian,* Golden Rivers fine. {five,}
HUMOUR22:23 H92 {From} Whence flow fine spirits, and witty notions?
HUMOUR23:7 H117 Thou sayst, thy wits are stai'd, subtle and fine:
AGES40:18 H199 If any care I take, 'tis to be fine,
SEASONS48:2 H55 These might as Lace, set out her Garments fine;
MEDDM197:33 Hp275 pain till they turn to dust, and then are they fine manchet for

FINED See FIN'D

FINELY (2)
SEASONS~~49:20~~ H111 Whose fleece when purely {finely} spun, and deeply dy'd,
MGREC~~123:11~~ H2873 How neatly {finely} *Eumenes* did here excell,

FINEST (1)
MEDDM196:11 Hp273 The finest bread hath the least bran the purest hony the least

FINGER (1)
MEDDM198:28 Hp277 A sore finger may disquiet the whole body, but an vlcer wthin

FINGERS (2) [pl.]
SEASONS52:30 H245 Now toes, and eares, and fingers often freeze,
MASSYR67:40 H586 The fingers of his {a} hand-writing did spy.

FINIS (1)
VANITY161:7 H58 *FINIS.*

FINISH (2)
MGREC136:10 H3424 *To finish what {what's} begun, new thoughts impart*
MROMAN139:27 H3553 To finish what's begun, was my intent,

FINISH'D (1) [finished]
MPERS77:21 H962 The first begun, and finish'd in such hast,

FINISHED (1)
MASSYR53:28 H18 Not finished, til he his race had run;

FINISHING (1)
MPERS~~90:18~~ H1485 So after all {Thus finishing} their travell, danger, pain,

FIN-LAND (1)
SEASONS51:40 H216 Now *Green-land, Groen-land, Lap-land, Fin-land,* see

FINS (1) [pl.]
CONTEM173:8 H176 Whose armour is their scales, their spreading fins their shield.

FIR'D (1) [fired]
HUMOUR27:39 H310 So suddenly, the body all is fir'd:

FIRE (38)
ELEMEN8:5 H3 Fire, Aire, Earth, and Water, did all contest
ELEMEN8:14 H12 The Fire, the forced Aire, in sunder crack;
ELEMEN8:17 H15 Fire broyled Earth, and scorched Earth it choaked,
ELEMEN8:27 H25 That Fire should first begin, the rest consent,
ELEMEN8:29 H27 *Fire.*
ELEMEN9:28 H62 The Sun, an Orbe of Fire was held of old,
ELEMEN9:38 H72 And though nought but *Sal'manders* live in fire;
ELEMEN11:17 H137 And then, because no matter more for fire:
ELEMEN13:13 H214 Well knowest, my fuell must maintain thy fire.
ELEMEN18:1 H405 And though you love Fire, Earth, and Water wel;
ELEMEN18:34 H438 And when I'm throughly rarifi'd, turn fire.
HUMOUR20:17 H9 Choler was own'd by Fire, and Blood by Aire,

HUMOUR21:12 H40 Though under fire, we comprehend all heat,
HUMOUR25:16 H205 As with thy mother Fire, so 'tis with thee,
HUMOUR25:25 H214 Nor sparing Sex, nor age, nor fire, nor son.
HUMOUR27:4 H275 Can be imputed unto none, but Fire;
HUMOUR35:12 H608 Nor be discern'd, here's water, earth, aire, fire,
AGES35:23 H9 The third, of fire, and choler is compos'd,
AGES38:37 H140 Some times in fire, sometimes in waters {water} fall:
AGES42:41 H297 greater stil, did {and thirst for honour,} set my heart on fire.
SEASONS48:40 H91 Resembling choler, fire and middle-age;
MASSYR59:31 H255 Then on himself, and them, a fire he sets;
MASSYR60:27 H292 The fire, those Mettals could not damnifie;
MPERS91:6 H1514 With broyls, and quarrels, sets all *Greece* on fire.
MGREC96:7 H1727 The Holy fire, was borne before the Host:
MGREC96:8 H1728 (For Sun and Fire the *Persians* worship most)
MGREC103:29 H2040 Commands to set this goodly town on fire.
MGREC107:12 H2187 Which done, sets fire upon those costly {goodly} spoyls
MROMAN137:32 H3483 And vestall Maids to keep the holy fire.
MROMAN140:3 H3566 My papers fell a prey to th' raging fire.
DIALOG147:12 H238 Let's bring *Baals* vestments out, {forth} to make a fire,
DUBART154:36 H81 And whilst there's aire, or fire, or sea or land.
CONTEM170:16 H88 On *Abels* gift the fire descends from Skies,
MEDDM201:12 Hp280 Fire hath its force abated by water not by wind, and anger
MEDDM208:6 Hp289 As the brands of a fire, if once severed, will of themselues goe
MEDDM208:31 Hp290 the order of nature, quenched the violence of the fire, made
HOUSE236:17 H9 That fearfull sovnd of fire and fire,

FIRED See FIR'D

FIRES (2) [pl.]
ELEMEN9:27 H61 To match on high with the Celestiall fires.
SEASONS52:7 H222 This time warm cloaths, ful diet, and good fires,

FIRKINS (1) [pl.]
SEASONS48:20 H73 Her shelves, and Firkins fill'd for winter time.

FIRM (7) See also FIRME
AGES~~43:16~~ H308 Then thought my state firm founded sure to last,
MASSYR63:28 H413 By whom in firm obedience she's kept.
MASSYR65:3 H468 The Sea firm Land, whereon the Army past,
MPERS76:41 H939 His whetted teeth he sticks {claps} in the firm wood,
MGREC98:40 H1842 A league of friendship make, firm, and entire;
MGREC102:10 H1980 The firm foundations, {strong Foundation} and the lofty spires;
MGREC~~124:16~~ H2923 Firm (for his Fathers sake) to him abide.

FIRMAMENT (3)
MGREC101:23 H1948 The Firmament two Suns cannot contain;
MGREC106:30 H2164 His fancied gods, above the firmament,
MEDDM206:6 Hp287 We se in the firmament there is but one Sun, among a

FIRME (6) [firm]
HUMOUR30:25 H417 And first, the firme dry bones, I justly claim:
MPERS75:35 H892 That shall, but {once} dare {to} raze those firme foundations;
MGREC98:12 H1814 He leaves not, till he makes {made} the sea firme shoar;
MGREC121:12 H2790 Did make his owne firme to his cause remaine,
MGREC124:16 ~~H2923~~ Firme to *Cassander* at this time abides:
MEDDM208:32 Hp290 the water become firme footing, for peter to walk on, nay more

FIRMLY (5)

MASSYR~~60:9~~	H274	promise bound, since first {which} he crav'd {firmly made},
MPERS74:28	H851	Yet more the peoples hearts firmly to binde,
MPERS79:15	H1041	Firmly at length, {last} accomplished his wil;
MPERS80:20	H1087	In this Streight, as the other, firmly stand.
MPERS~~83:32~~	H1220	A league of amity, had sworn before. {firmly swore,}

FIRST (91)

FATHER5:28	H29	My first do shew, their good, and then their rage,
PROLOG7:8	H22	Who lisp'd at first, speake afterwards more {in future times}
ELEMEN8:27	H25	That Fire should first begin, the rest consent,
ELEMEN8:35	~~H33~~	Come first ye Artists, and declare your minde.
ELEMEN14:22	H264	As earth at first, so into earth return'd.
ELEMEN17:16	H380	Whereof the first, so ominous I rain'd,
ELEMEN17:36	H400	{Yet am} not through ignorance, {ignorant} first was my due,
HUMOUR20:15	H7	But first they wisely shew'd their high descent,
HUMOUR~~20:23~~	H15	Choler {first} hotly claim'd, right by her mother,
HUMOUR22:10	H79	She'l first advise, if't be not best to stay.
HUMOUR26:36	H266	The first my self, second my sister faire,
HUMOUR29:12	H365	But when the first offenders {offender} I have laid,
HUMOUR30:25	H417	And first, the firme dry bones, I justly claim:
HUMOUR30:30	H422	The first it draines, o'th' last quicks appetite,
HUMOUR31:23	H456	The first, my constancy, that jewel rare.
AGES35:19	H5	The first: son unto Flegme, grand-child to water,
AGES36:8	H32	When blushing first, she 'gins to red {light} the Aire.
AGES39:6	H149	But what is best i'le first present to view,
AGES41:21	~~H239~~	But what's of worth, your eyes shal first behold,
SEASONS46:38	H16	The tenth o'th' first *Sol* into *Aries* enters,
SEASONS49:5	H96	Ith' first, *Sol* doth in crabed *Cancer* shine.
SEASONS50:21	H155	The Barley, and the Rye, should first had place,
SEASONS51:12	H186	Sure at this time, Time first of all began,
SEASONS52:18	H233	*December* is the {my} first, and now the Sun
SEASONS~~52:39~~	H256	Where first it did begin, in th' end its found.
SEASONS53:3	H259	*The first fell in so naturally,*
MASSYR53:12	H2	the *Assyrian* being the first,
MASSYR53:25	H15	These were his first, all stood in *Shinar* land,
MASSYR54:4	H31	He taught the people first to Idolize;
MASSYR55:14	H80	Sure from this fiction, *Dagon* first began,
MASSYR60:9	H274	promise bound, since first {which} he crav'd {firmly made},
MASSYR60:33	H298	As fair a Town, as the first *Ninivie.*
MASSYR63:8	H393	And {As} *Belosus,* first, his {Soveraign} did unthrone,
MASSYR67:4	H550	And in the first year of his royalty,
MPERS71:8	H724	His reign with Bloud, and Incest, first begins,
MPERS71:17	H731	He seized first of life, and then of Land;
MPERS73:19	H806	And first these noble *Magi* 'gree upon,
MPERS~~77:16~~	H957	Because this was, first born of *Cyrus* race.)
MPERS77:21	H962	The first begun, and finish'd in such hast,
MPERS77:31	H972	The first deports, {dehorts} and layes before his eyes,
MPERS79:8	H1030	First thing, *Xerxes* {he} did worthy {of} recount,
MPERS79:30	H1056	But *Xerxes* resolute, to *Thrace* goes first,
MPERS82:28	H1175	But she was stil, as when it {he} first begun.
MPERS83:29	H1217	He first, war with revolting *Ægypt* made.

MPERS~~85:7~~	H1283	Stil making war, till first had lost his life:
MPERS~~85:10~~	H1286	These two lewd {first} sons, are by hystorians thought,
MPERS85:26	H1302	But they in *Asia,* must first restore
MPERS86:27	H1343	From the Lieutenant first, he takes away,
MPERS~~87:4~~	H1360	The one {last} accus'd the other, {first} for these {sad} wars:
MPERS88:15	H1408	For at first charge the *Persians* ran away.
MPERS89:23	H1457	The smiling *Greeks* reply, they first must bait,
MPERS~~92:14~~	H1572	By the same Eunuch who first set him up.
MGREC93:15	H1612	The twenty first of's age, began to reign.
MGREC96:33	H1753	For sure *Darius* thought, at the first sight,
MGREC98:37	H1839	First, at *Euphrates,* what he's like to abide,
MGREC100:37	H1921	When this sad newes (at first) *Darius* heares,
MGREC103:17	H2028	(As first at *Sushan,* and at *Babylon*)
MGREC104:37	H2089	Unto *Darius,* first he brings a Horse,
MGREC109:13	H2272	Boats to prepare, *Ephestion* first he sends,
MGREC~~109:22~~	H2281	Presents himselfe, {first} there with a golden Crowne,
MGREC110:13	H2313	But {And} whilst the first he valiantly assayl'd,
MGREC110:39	H2343	The first *Nicea,* the next *Bucephalon,*
MGREC113:8	H2435	Such torments great, as wit could first {worst} invent,
MGREC120:25	H2762	*Antigonus* of Treason first attaints,
MGREC~~121:2~~	H2780	But first 'gainst *Ptolemy* he judg'd was
MGREC128:17	H3090	First, how he held the Empire in his hands,
MGREC130:41	H3186	*Demetrius* is first, that so assumes, {the royal stile asum'd,}
MGREC133:2	H3290	The second Son of the first *Ptolomy,*
MGREC134:19	H3350	First *Ptolomy* being dead, his famous son,
MGREC134:34	H3365	For since the first, that title still they had,
MGREC135:20	H3392	The first, was likened to a head of gold,
MGREC135:28	H3400	The first a Lion, second was a Beare,
MROMAN136:23	H3437	Stout *Romulus, Romes* Founder, and first King,
MROMAN136:35	H3449	The Stones at first was cimented with bloud,
MROMAN136:36	H3450	And bloudy hath it prov'd, since first it stood:
QELIZ156:15	H42	Since first the Sun did run, his ne'r runn'd race,
QELIZ157:14	H82	*Dido* first Foundresse of proud *Carthage* walls,
VANITY160:11	H21	The first is prone to vice, the last to rage.
CONTEM170:24	H95	The Virgin Earth, of blood her first draught drinks
CONTEM171:29	H131	That state obliterate he had at first:
SICKNES178:31	H14	since first we came from womb,
2LETTER182:26	H32	Behold a Chaos blacker then the first.
CHILDRN185:1	H27	And where *Aurora* first appears,
MEDDM199:28	Hp278	first kill the body, the last the good name the two former leaue
MEDDM204:15	Hp284	must be sure to shun the company of the first.
MEDDM206:12	Hp287	euen in this life, some are Stars of the first magnitude, and
MEDDM206:20	Hp287	themselues of turning to god, the first thing wch they eye, is
MED223:4	Hp250	of thy Loue. First thov art my Creator, I thy creature, thov my
JULY223:22	Hp251	wch at first it took me, and so mvch the sorer it was to me
WHAT224:23	H23	The first and last yt liues for aye,
11MAYB228:25	Hp259	'till May I haue been by fitts very ill & weak. The first of

FIRSTLY (1)

HUMOUR27:24	H295	Shal firstly {chiefly} take her {the} place, as is her {my} due,

FISH (5)

ELEMEN19:5	H450	Earths Beasts, and Waters Fish, scarce can compare.

MASSYR55:12 H78 Transform'd into a fish, by *Venus* will,
CONTEM172:30 H163 Ye Fish which in this liquid Region 'bide,
3LETTER183:15 H17 Or as the loving Mullet, that true Fish,
MEDDM198:16 Hp276 The skillfull fisher hath his severall baits, for severall fish, but

FISHER (1)
MEDDM198:16 Hp276 The skillfull fisher hath his severall baits, for severall fish, but

FISHES (3) [pl.]
ELEMEN10:7 H82 My Crabbe, my Scorpion, fishes, you may see,
ELEMEN15:24 H306 Fishes so numberlesse I there do hold;
SEASONS~~49:33~~ H124 By purling Brooks looking how fishes swims.

FIT (1) [paroxysm] See also FITT
SICKNES178:16 H0 Upon a Fit of Sickness, *Anno,* 1632.

FIT (21) [suits] See also FITT
ELEMEN9:12 H46 Subdue the earth, and fit it for your graine,
HUMOUR34:31 H586 Again, none's fit for Kingly place but thou,
SEASONS~~46:35~~ H13 Fit to revive, the nummed earth from death.
MASSYR55:24 H90 And thought her fit, to make a Monarch's wife,
MPERS69:18 H640 Are fit for such, whose eares for fables itch;
MPERS75:10 H871 When opportunity he saw was fit,
MPERS77:38 H979 That his ambitious humour best can fit;
MPERS84:26 H1262 The {This} noble *Greek,* now fit for generall.
MPERS84:29 H1265 Provisions, {then} and season now being fit,
MPERS86:1 H1317 And takes more on him, then was judged fit.
MPERS89:32 H1466 Fit instruments t' accomplish what is ill;
MGREC93:18 H1615 By Art, and Nature both, he was made fit,
MGREC97:27 H1788 Unto *Parmenio,* of all, most fit;
MGREC100:24 H1908 Fit for to blunt the swords of *Macedon;*
QELIZ157:25 H93 Yet for our Queen is no fit parallel:
2SIMON195:8 Hp271 fit for you nor of more ease to my self then these short
MEDDM196:31 Hp274 fit their nurture according to their Nature.
MEDDM197:19 Hp275 it, and that heart wch is not continually purifieing it self is no fit
MEDDM197:32 Hp275 is not fit for bread, god so deales wth his servants, he grindes
MEDDM205:3 Hp285 goe often ouer them, before they bee fit soile, to sow the
MEDDM205:5 Hp285 nurture they are brought into a fit capacity, let the seed of good

FITLY (1)
DUBART153:16 H20 My Muse unto a Childe, I fitly may compare,

FITS (1) [suits] See also FITTS
PROLOG7:15 H28 Who sayes, my hand a needle better fits,

FITS (1) [paroxysm] See also FITTS
PILGRIM210:27 H27 No fainting fits shall me assaile

FITT (5) [fit; paroxysm]
MYCHILD215:32 Hp241 In a long fitt of sicknes wch I had on my bed I often comvned
SOREFIT221:15 H1 From another sore fitt. etc.
FAINT222:11 H1 Delive^rc^ from a fitt of Fainting
JULY223:21 Hp251 I had a sore fitt of fainting wch lasted 2 or 3 dayes, but not in y^t^
11MAYB228:24 Hp259 that I haue had no great fitt of sicknes, but this year from y^e^

FITT (6) [fit; suits]
28AUG226:1 Hp254 to make me a vessell fitt for his vse why should I not bare it

FITTER (1)
MEDDM197:4 Hp274 w^th^out wisedome is like a heavy axe, w^th^out an edg fitter to

FITTEST (4)
HUMOUR28:27 H339 For Arts, and Sciences, they are the fittest,
HUMOUR34:27 H582 Then, my head {brain} for learning is not the fittest,
MASSYR65:12 H477 Thinks this the fittest time to break his bands,
2LETTER181:32 H2 The silent night's the fittest time for moan;

FITTING (1)
HUMOUR25:38 H227 But if in fitting time, and place, on foes; {'gainst foe}

FITTS (2) [fits; paroxysm]
11MAYA226:13 Hp255 a sore sicknes and weaknes took hold of me wch hath by fitts
11MAYB228:25 Hp259 of January 'till May I haue been by fitts very ill & weak. The

FIVE (8)
ELEMEN~~16:7~~ H330 The *Ponticke, {Aegean} Caspian,* Golden Rivers fine. {five,}
HUMOUR33:38 H552 The five most noble Sences, here do dwel,
MASSYR54:14 H41 At twenty five, ended his regal date.
MPERS70:17 H688 Forty five mile {miles} this City scarce could round;
MPERS78:38 H1019 One of his five Sons there, might be releast;
MPERS86:39 H1355 And for that end, five hundred Horse he chose,
MGREC94:20 H1658 To these {which} were joyn'd, five thousand goodly horse.
MGREC101:36 H1965 Forty five thousand *Alexander* had,

FIX (2)
SIDNEY151:29 ~~H75~~ To fix my faltring lines upon his tomb:
HOUSE237:13 H43 Didst fix thy hope on mouldring dvst,

FIXE (1)
MEDDM204:23 Hp285 fixe his eye on the command, and not on his own ends, lest he

FIXED (2)
ELEMEN9:41 H75 Fixed in heavenly constellations dwell,
MEDDM205:10 Hp286 Commonwealth, his more fixed and resolued thoughts, are like

FIXT (2)
CONTEM172:14 H149 While on the stealing stream I fixt mine eye,
MEDDM206:17 Hp287 shall they be, when they are fixt in their heauenly spheres

FLAME (4)
ELEMEN9:26 H60 But let me leave these things, my flame aspires
ELEMEN~~11:1~~ H119 My raging flame did make a mournful story,
MGREC~~103:35~~ H2046 Those stately streets with raging flames doth {flame did} fil.
HOUSE236:24 H16 The flame consvme my dwelling place,

FLAMES (3) [pl.]
ELEMEN10:29 H104 The choaking flames, that from *Vesuvius* flew
SEASONS49:10 H101 reason why {Though he decline}, because his flames so faire,
MGREC103:35 H2046 Those stately streets with raging flames doth {flame did} fil.

FLAMINES (1) [pl.]
MROMAN137:30 H3481 And Priests, and Flamines likewise he deputed;

FLAMING (3)
ELEMEN20:1 H483 Sometimes strange {red} flaming swords, and blazing stars,
SEASONS49:40 H133 Whose flaming breath doth melt us from afar,
SIDNEY151:37 ~~H75~~ Fame's flaming Chariot for to drive.

FLANDERS (1)
SIDNEY150:21 H46 What famous feats thou didst, on *Flanders* coast,

FLASH (1)
DIALOG147:15 H241 And let their names consume, but let the flash

FLAT (1)
HUMOUR23:39 H149 Without my lively heat, do's ought thats flat.

FLATS (3) [pl.]
AGES43:4 H299 That over flats, and sands, and rocks I hurried,
MGREC~~111:17~~ H2362 His Gallies stuck upon the sand, {flats} and mud;
MGREC111:21 H2366 Upon those Flats they did not long abide;
FLATT'RING (1) [flattering]
FLESH176:11 H51 Thy flatt'ring shews Ile trust no more.
FLATTER (2)
HUMOUR29:11 H364 I'le flatter for a time, as thou did'st me,
MASSYR68:18 H604 Who doth not flatter, nor once cloake the thing.
FLATTERING (2) See also FLATT'RING
MPERS77:35 H976 Flattering *Mardonius* on th' other side,
MGREC114:20 H2490 As did appeare, in flattering him the least:
FLATTERY (4)
HUMOUR25:5 H194 And real complements, base flattery.
AGES37:33 H95 With costly presents, {presence} or base flattery.
MPERS89:35 H1469 And with all {the} Oathes, and deepest flattery,
MEDDM205:14 Hp286 whom no bribes can pervert, nor flattery cause to favour but
FLAW (1)
AUTHOR178:5 H15 And rubbing off a spot, still made a flaw.
FLAYD (1) [flayed]
MPERS72:20 H768 Flayd him alive, hung up his stuffed skin
FLED (12)
ELEMEN19:16 H461 Whereof such multitudes have dy'd and fled,
HUMOUR32:34 H508 And {But} though the pitched field i've ever fled,
MASSYR58:31 H214 That in dispaire, he left the field and fled:
MPERS76:32 H930 *Darius* multitude before them fled;
MPERS79:40 H1066 And all that Army, then dismay'd, had fled,
MPERS90:33 ~~H1500~~ But *Tyssaphernes* with his Army fled;
MPERS~~90:33~~ H1500 Lieftenant to the King, but soon he fled
MROMAN138:26 H3516 Who for sedition from his Country fled;
DIALOG144:38 H146 I saw (unmov'd) her Armies foil'd and fled,
CONTEM169:29 H68 And calls back moneths and years that long since fled
13MAY227:2 H11 And former clowdes seem now all fled
HOUSE237:20 H50 Stands permanent tho: this bee fled.
FLEE (1)
MASSYR65:38 H503 The cursed King, by flight could no wise flee {fly}
FLEEC'D (1) [fleeced]
SEASONS47:20 H36 The wanton frisking Kids, and soft fleec'd Lambs,
FLEECE (4)
ELEMEN15:41 H323 I lightly cast ashoare as frothy fleece.
AGES42:3 H261 With mine owne fleece, and with my houshold bread.
SEASONS47:25 H41 Yet many a fleece of Snow, and stormy showre,
SEASONS49:20 H111 Whose fleece when purely {finely} spun, and deeply dy'd,
FLEECED (1) See also FLEEC'D
AGES42:35 H291 My fleeced Ewe {Sheep}, and ever {fruitful} farrowing Sow.
FLEET (1) v.
MGREC106:3 H2137 This said, his fainting breath did fleet away,
FLEET (8) n.
MPERS78:15 H996 These {Such} his Land Forces were, then next, a Fleet
MPERS80:18 H1085 Inclos'd their Fleet i'th' streights {streight} of *Eubea;*
MPERS82:15 H1162 Same day, the small remainder of his Fleet,

MPERS87:26 H1378 So hir'd a fleet, to waft him ore the Maine,
MGREC98:31 H1833 *Ephestion* now, hath the {having chief} command o' th' Fleet,
MGREC99:15 H1858 His favourite *Ephestion,* with his fleet;
MGREC111:1 H2346 Then down t' *Hidaspis* with his Fleet he went;
DIALOG143:11 H80 *Spaines* braving Fleet a second time is sunke,

FLEETING (1)
THEART229:7 H9 Lord whilst my fleeting time shall last

FLEGME (9) [phlegm]
HUMOUR20:31 H23 Cold {Mild} flegme, did not contest for highest {chiefest} place,
HUMOUR22:11 H80 But {Now} let's give, cold, white, Sister Flegme her right.
HUMOUR22:33 H102 But Flegme her self, is now provok'd at this,
HUMOUR28:5 H317 And Flegme likewise can shew, her cruel art,
HUMOUR31:28 H461 And what Flegme is, we know, likewise {like to} her mother,
HUMOUR32:15 H489 I've done, pray Sister Flegme proceed in course,
HUMOUR32:17 H491 *Flegme.*
HUMOUR35:15 H611 That Flegme was judg'd, for kindnesse to excel.
AGES35:19 H5 The first: son unto Flegme, grand-child to water,

FLEGM'S (1) [phlegm is]
HUMOUR31:34 H467 Flegm's patient, because her nature's tame:

FLEGMY (2) [phlegmy]
ELEMEN16:33 H356 The flegmy constitution I uphold;
SEASONS52:14 H229 Cold, moist, young, flegmy Winter now doth lye

FLESH (24)
HUMOUR28:8 H320 As if she'd leave no flesh to turn to clay,
AGES37:26 H88 This little house of flesh, did spacious count:
AGES38:30 H133 Yet griefs, in my fraile flesh, I still do find.
AGES46:13 H444 Yet studying much, brings wearinesse to th' flesh;
AGES46:20 H451 And when this flesh shal rot, and be consum'd,
SEASONS52:8 H223 Our pinched flesh, and empty panch {hungry mawes} requires:
MGREC113:9 H2436 Or flesh, or {and} life, could bear, till both were spent
DIALOG146:30 H216 You are my mother, nurse, {and} I once your flesh,
DIALOG148:14 H279 And tear his flesh, and set your feet on's neck,
FLESH175:1 H1 *The Flesh and the Spirit.*
FLESH175:6 H6 One flesh was call'd, who had her eye
FLESH175:10 H10 Sister, quoth Flesh, what liv'st thou on
DISTEMP179:24 H12 He eas'd my Soul of woe, my flesh of pain,
1LETTER181:27 H25 Flesh of thy flesh, bone of thy bone,
1LETTER181:27 H25 Flesh of thy flesh, bone of thy bone,
MEDDM196:28 Hp273 children, haue their different natures, some are like flesh w[ch]
PILGRIM210:31 H31 What tho my flesh shall there consume
FEVER220:24 H4 When in my flesh no part was fovnd
FEVER220:26 H6 My burning flesh in sweat did boyle
FEVER221:4 H19 Tho: flesh consume to novght,
SOREFIT221:24 H10 My wasted flesh thou didst restore
SON231:10 H22 Thou heal'dst his flesh + cheerd his heart.
REMB235:32 H13 To Thee shall come all Flesh,
HOUSE237:14 H44 The arm of flesh didst make thy trvst?

FLESHLY (1)
QELIZ155:21 H12 To say, thou wert a fleshly Deity:

FLEW (6)
ELEMEN10:6 H81 The Horse that kill'd *Bellerophon,* then flew.

ELEMEN10:29 H104 The choaking flames, that from *Vesuvius* flew
MPERS82:30 H1177 She *Harpy*-like, upon the Lady flew:
MGREC108:32 H2248 They flew so thick they seem'd to dark the aire:
CHILDRN184:27 H16 And with her mate flew out of sight;
CHILDRN185:3 H29 One to the Academy flew

FLEXIBLE (1)
ELEMEN9:15 H49 I made it flexible unto his will.

FLIE (1) [fly] See also FLYE
HOUSE237:16 H46 That dunghill mists away may flie.

FLIES (1) See also FLYES
MGREC131:18 H3210 *Demetrius* with his troops to *Athens* flies,

FLIGHT (5) [fly]
CHILDRN184:20 H9 Chief of the Brood then took his flight,
CHILDRN184:26 H15 My second bird did take her flight,
CHILDRN185:15 H41 Or here or there, they'l take their flight,
CHILDRN185:39 H65 Oft times in grass, on trees, in flight,
CHILDRN186:10 H77 And from the top bough take my flight,

FLIGHT (14) [flee]
HUMOUR30:20 H412 You high born (from that lump) then take your flight
AGES~~43:8~~ H304 Then Kings must be depos'd or put to flight,
MASSYR65:38 H503 The cursed King, by flight could no wise flee {fly}
MGREC97:3 H1764 And cast away his Crown, for swifter flight;
MGREC101:29 H1954 To force his Camp, so put {vanquish} them all to {by} flight;
MGREC~~101:34~~ H1962 And spilt the Greeks some bloud before their flight
MGREC104:36 H2088 His hopes being dasht, prepares himself for flight:
MGREC108:33 H2249 But soone the *Grecians* {his souldiers} forc'd them to a flight,
MGREC126:12 H3003 To raise the Seige, and put her foes to flight;
MGREC128:24 H3097 {great Antigonus} *Ptolomy,* and the rest {was} put him to flight;
MGREC128:30 H3103 And comming unawares put him to flight;
MGREC135:1 H3371 At *Actium* slain, {where} his Navy {Navy's} put to flight.
CONTEM171:16 H120 And puts all pleasures vain unto eternal flight.
CONTEM173:16 H183 And wisht me wings with her a while to take my flight.

FLING (1)
CHILDRN185:24 H50 Some untoward boy at them do fling.

FLINGS (1) [pl.]
MGREC125:19 H2967 Nor Darts, nor Arrowes now, none shoots, nor flings;

FLINT (1)
ELEMEN9:3 ~~H37~~ My force? your sword, your Pike, your flint and steele,

FLITTING (1)
MEDDM205:11 Hp286 inhabitants his slight and flitting thoughts are like passengers,

FLOCK (2)
AGES42:8 H266 Was I a pastor, I my flock did feed:
SEASONS49:31 H120 But whist'leth to thy Flock in cold, and heat,

FLOCKS (1) [pl.]
SEASONS49:17 H108 To wash their {the} thick cloath'd flocks, with pipes ful glad.

FLOOD (9) See also FLOUD
ELEMEN16:26 H349 Did they but want my Ocean, and my Flood.
ELEMEN17:27 H391 But these are trifles to the Flood of *Noe.*
MASSYR54:24 H51 Upon the pleasant banks of *Tigris* flood,
MASSYR56:22 H128 On {In} *Shinar* plain, by the *Euphratan* flood,
MGREC135:17 H3389 Then came the *Romane,* like a raging flood,

MROMAN138:21 H3511 Close by the mouth of famous *Tyber* flood:
CONTEM172:18 H153 O happy Flood, quoth I, that holds thy race
FLESH175:3 H3 Close by the Banks of *Lacrim* flood
13MAY227:12 H21 My Baca made a springing flood?

FLOODS (1) [pl.]
ELEMEN17:2 H366 And with my wasting floods, and roaring torrent;

FLOUD (4) [flood]
MASSYR53:14 H4 after the Floud.
MGREC107:31 H2206 To make them rafts, to waft them or'e the floud;
MGREC109:40 H2299 Is now resolv'd to passe *Hidaspes* floud,
MGREC111:16 H2361 Hence {Then} sayling down by th' mouth of *Indus* floud,

FLOUR (1) [flower] See also FLOW'R
ANNEB187:24 H14 I knew she was but as a withering flour,

FLOURISH (6)
ELEMEN15:9 H291 Do cease to flourish in this misery.
AGES44:30 H363 I've seen a Kingdom flourish like a tree,
AGES45:27 H417 My {Mine} Almond-tree (gray haires) doth flourish now,
SEASONS47:38 H50 The Pear, the Plumbe, and Apple-tree now flourish,
DIALOG148:3 H268 So shall thy happy Nation ever flourish,
11MAYA226:22 Hp255 shall flourish while my body decayes, and y[e] weaknes of this

FLOURISHED (1)
MASSYR~~57:24~~ H171 And that *Semiramis* then flourished,

FLOURISHES (1) [pl.]
HUMOUR33:18 H532 With all your flourishes, now Sisters three,

FLOURISHING (1)
MASSYR55:26 H92 She flourishing with *Ninus*, long did reigne;

FLOURS (1) [flowers]
1SIMON188:6 H7 Three flours, two scarcely blown, the last i'th' bud,

FLOW (5)
HUMOUR20:14 H6 The native qualities, that from each {them} flow,
HUMOUR22:23 H92 {From} Whence flow fine spirits, and witty notions?
HUMOUR26:21 H251 And if vital spirits do flow from thee,
HUMOUR~~33:33~~ H547 Doth shew, hence flowes {flow} the power {pow'rs} which they
DIALOG148:25 H290 Then fulness of the Nations in shall flow,

FLOW'D (2) [flowed]
DIALOG144:17 H127 Whence flow'd the source, the sprigs, the boughs, and fruits;
DISTEMP179:17 H5 Bedrencht with tears that flow'd from mournful head.

FLOWER (3) See also FLOUR, FLOW'R
MGREC130:34 ~~H3181~~ Yet in the flower of's age, he must lie dead,
DUBART153:11 H15 A homely flower in this my latter spring:
ELIZB186:36 H8 Farewel fair flower that for a space was lent,

FLOWERING See FLOWRING

FLOWERS (7) [pl.] See also FLOURS
AGES35:31 H17 Such cold mean flowers (as these) blossome {the spring puts
SEASONS47:12 H28 Now digs, then sows, his hearbs, his flowers, and roots,
SEASONS47:37 H49 All Plants, and Flowers, {set and sown} for all delights, and
SEASONS48:15 H68 All flowers before the {with his} sun-beames now discloses,
MGREC102:7 H1977 With showers of Flowers, the streets along are strown,
DUBART153:9 H13 Had caused flowers, and fruits, soone to abound;
DUBART153:13 H17 Flowers, fruits, in garden, orchard, or in field;

FLOWES (4)
FATHER6:13 H47 Then waters, {water} in the boundlesse Ocean flowes.
ELEMEN16:17 H340 Th' uncertain cause, of certain ebbs and flowes;
HUMOUR30:31 H423 Laughter (though thou sayst malice) flowes from hence,
HUMOUR33:33 H547 Doth shew, hence flowes {flow} the power {pow'rs} which they

FLOWN (3)
PROLOG7:35 H45 And oh, ye high flown quils, that soare the skies,
ELEMEN19:19 H464 That birds have not scap'd death, as they have flown,
CHILDRN185:10 H36 Is 'mongst the shrubs and bushes flown,

FLOW'R (1) [flower] See also FLOUR
MGREC126:7 H2998 She with the flow'r {chief} o'th Court to *Pidna* flyes,

FLOWRING (3) [flowering]
DIALOG142:6 H35 By fraud, and {or} force, usurp'd thy flowring crown,
DIALOG144:10 H120 O *Jane,* why didst thou dye in flowring prime,
VANITY160:10 H20 What, Is't in flowring youth, or manly age?

FLOWS See FLOWES

FLUENT (1)
PROLOG7:7 H21 Nor can I, like that fluent sweet tongu'd *Greek*

FLUX (1)
AGES38:34 H137 Whence vomits, wormes, and flux have issued?

FLY (8) [flying] See also FLIE, FLYE
MPERS76:17 H915 Or fly like birds, in unknown wayes full quick;
MPERS86:37 H1353 But least {lest} some worser newes should fly to Court,
MGREC96:40 H1760 Let fly their Arrowes, in the *Persians* face;
MGREC104:30 H2082 To *Alexander* fly, {flyes} and told {tells} this act;
CHILDRN184:25 H14 Fly back and sing amidst this Quire.
CHILDRN186:22 H89 And 'fore she once would let you fly,
MERCY188:30 H16 But ah too soon those heavy tydings fly,
MEDDM208:2 Hp289 long night shall fly away, and the day of eternity shall never

FLY (15) [flee] See also FLYE
AGES39:23 H166 I fly to catch the Bullet that's {that} aloof;
AGES45:14 H396 And others fly their Country, through their {struck both with gilt
MASSYR59:28 H252 *Sardanapalus* did not seek to fly,
MASSYR~~65:38~~ H503 The cursed King, by flight could no wise flee {fly}
MPERS82:9 H1156 Which found, like *Greeks* they fight, the *Persians* fly,
MPERS87:27 H1379 The mazed King, was now {then} about to fly;
MPERS88:23 H1416 They {ready} were about to leave their King and fly,
MGREC96:18 H1738 think {Suppos'd} he neither thought {meant} to fight nor fly,
MGREC107:40 H2215 But coward, durst not fight, nor could he fly,
MGREC119:16 H2706 The *Athenians,* force *Antipater* to fly
MGREC125:20 H2968 King, and Queen, to *Amphipolis* doe fly, {seeing their destiny,}
MGREC~~125:21~~ H2969 To save their lives t' *Amphipolis* do fly;
MGREC126:18 H3009 By stealth unto *Cassander* daily fly;
MGREC133:3 H3291 Who for rebellion unto him did fly,
CONTEM171:8 H113 Who neither guilt, nor yet the punishment could fly.

FLYE (7) [flying] See also FLIE, FLY
FATHER5:22 H23 That sinke, that swim, that fill, that upwards flye,
ELEMEN9:39 H73 The Flye *Pyrausta* cal'd, all else expire.
ELEMEN15:6 H288 The lofty Eagle and the Storke flye low,
ELEMEN19:35 H476 But some fall down, and some flye up with aire.
HUMOUR31:26 H459 Here, there, her restlesse thoughts do ever flye;

AGES36:10 H34 He seems to flye, or swim, and not to ride.
SEASONS48:33 H84 Melodious {Sweet fragrant} Spring, with thy short pittance flye,

FLYE (2) [flee] See also FLY
MPERS84:13 H1249 Unto this King *Thymistocles* did flye.
MYSOUL225:10 H14 Thy Sorrowes all shall flye.

FLYES (3) [fly]
ELEMEN13:31 H232 The tender mother on her Infant flyes:
MPERS77:1 H940 Off flyes his head, down showres his frolick bloud.
MPERS88:38 H1431 The King unto a country Village flyes,

FLYES (3) [flee] See also FLIES
HUMOUR22:37 H106 My absence proves, it plain, her wit then flyes
MGREC~~104:30~~ H2082 To *Alexander* fly, {flyes} and told {tells} this act;
MGREC126:7 H2998 She with the flow'r {chief} o'th Court to *Pidna* flyes,

FLYING (1)
DIALOG144:1 H111 Thy flying for the Truth I made a jeast;

FLYING-FOES (1) [pl.]
MPERS76:37 H935 Pursues his flying-foes, and {then} on the strand;

FODDER (1)
SEASONS50:10 H144 To Barns, and Stacks, where it for Fodder lyes.

FOE (22)
HUMOUR21:24 H52 What makes him face his foe, without appal?
HUMOUR22:5 H74 If great perswasions, cause her meet her foe;
HUMOUR23:29 H139 Their courage, {Courage it} friend, and foe, and subject awes,
HUMOUR~~25:38~~ H227 But if in fitting time, and place, on foes; {'gainst foe}
HUMOUR29:7 H360 The tongue's no weapon to assault a foe,
AGES38:6 H109 My foe should weltering, with {in} his bowels reek.
MASSYR63:27 H412 A Vice-roy from her foe, she's glad t' accept,
MPERS~~72:25~~ H773 He spar'd nor foe, nor friend, nor favorite.
MPERS80:25 H1092 But he, in daring of his forward foe,
MGREC101:31 H1956 And weaknesse of a foe is covered;
MGREC110:19 H2323 His fortitude his Kingly {royal} foe commends;
MGREC115:36 H2555 He was too subtile for his crafty foe,
MGREC119:27 H2717 He joyn not with *Antipater,* that {their} foe.
MGREC122:2 H2825 And his beloved foe, full sore laments.
MGREC126:16 H3007 Cassander will not heare {Her foe would give no Ear}, such is
MROMAN139:13 H3541 Sate on the Throne, when he had slaine his foe;
DIALOG142:37 H66 But forraigne Foe, nor fained friend I feare,
DIALOG144:40 H148 I saw strong *Rochel* yeelding to her foe,
QELIZ156:23 H50 Ships more invincible then *Spaines,* her foe
TDUDLEY165:32 H34 Truths friend thou wert, to errors still a foe,
FLESH176:1 H41 Thee as a foe, still to pursue.
SICKNES179:11 H31 For ever know, thou envious foe,

FOES (32) [pl.]
ELEMEN10:41 H116 Which when they could not be o're come by foes
ELEMEN~~11:1~~ H120 But maugre all, that I, or foes could do
HUMOUR25:38 H227 But if in fitting time, and place, on foes; {'gainst foe}
HUMOUR29:26 H377 When in Battalia my foes I face,
AGES42:11 H269 And shew'd them how, in face of foes to stand.
AGES44:36 H369 I saw all peace at home, terror to foes,
MASSYR67:32 H578 To chear his friends, and scorn his foes the more.
MPERS70:25 H696 And caus'd his foes in Lions den to dye.

MPERS75:36 H893 They thus backt of {by} the King, in spight of foes,
MPERS76:3 H901 But in that Desart, 'mongst his barbarous foes,
MPERS80:3 H1070 They thus behemm'd with multitude of foes,
MPERS80:17 H1084 Yet thinking to out-match his foes at Sea,
MPERS87:32 H1384 For his security, against his foes.
MPERS88:35 H1428 And now more eagerly their foes pursue,
MPERS91:4 H1512 With suit, their force, {Arms} against his {their} foes be bent;
MPERS91:19 H1527 The King from forraign foes, and all {parts now well} at ease,
MGREC102:17 H1987 Though worn by time, and raz'd {rac'd} by foes full sore,
MGREC104:12 H2064 But to deliver him to's foes, intended.
MGREC113:2 H2429 To his malicious foes delivers him,
MGREC113:6 H2433 My foes exceeds in malice, and their hate,
MGREC117:24 H2631 Did harm himself, but never reacht his foes:
MGREC119:31 H2721 The valiant Chief, amidst his foes was slain,
MGREC119:35 H2725 Blockt up in *Lamia,* still by his foes;
MGREC~~120:4~~ H2739 Then fall into the hands of mortal foes.
MGREC120:41 H2778 *Perdicas* hears, his foes are now {all} combin'd,
MGREC126:12 H3003 To raise the Seige, and put her foes to flight;
MGREC131:14 H3206 This day twixt these two foes {Kings} ends all the strife,
MGREC131:23 H3215 Tries foes, since friends will not compassionate,
DIALOG147:10 H236 These are the dayes, the Churches foes to crush,
DUBART154:14 H59 Who tam'd his foes, in bloud, in skarres {warrs,} and sweat,
CONTEM170:36 H106 A City builds, that wals might him secure from foes.
CONTEM174:3 H204 Troubles from foes, from friends, from dearest, near'st

FOIL'D (2) [foiled]
MGREC124:13 H2920 the worst {beaten was} at Sea, as well as {and foil'd at} Land,
DIALOG144:38 H146 I saw (unmov'd) her Armies foil'd and fled,

FOILD (1) [foiled]
MEDDM197:1 Hp274 of Sathan without could not hurt, hath, been foild by one

FOLD (2)
HUMOUR31:25 H458 And Sanguine is more fickle many fold. {manifold,}
AGES~~41:1~~ H221 Sometimes the loathsome {two fold} Pox, my face {me sore}

FOLDS (1) [pl.]
MROMAN136:29 H3443 Where Shepheards once had Coats, and Sheep their Folds,

FOLK (2)
CONTEM172:36 H169 You watry folk that know not your felicity.
2HUSB233:3 H36 Rember Lord thy folk whom thou

FOLLIES See FOLLYES

FOLLOW (5)
SEASONS50:7 H141 The Forks, and Rakes do follow them amain,
MPERS80:40 H1107 But mischief, Sacriledge doth ever follow;
MGREC96:9 H1729 The Priests in their strange habit follow after;
CONTEM173:31 H196 Then follow thee into a better Region,
2SIMON195:4 Hp271 imitation Children do natureally, rather follow the failings then

FOLLOWED (1)
TDUDLEY166:30 H72 His pious Footsteps followed by his race,

FOLLOWES (1) [follows]
HUMOUR23:16 H126 If once thou'rt great, what followes thereupon?

FOLLOWING (1)
2SIMON195:9 Hp271 following, Such as they are I bequeath to you, Small legacys

FOLLOWS (1) See also FOLLOWES
DIALOG148:27 H292 Then follows dayes of happinesse and rest,
FOLLY (6)
HUMOUR24:19 H168 Is't ignorance, {arrogance} or folly causeth this?
HUMOUR34:25 H580 Phrensie's worse, then folly, one would more glad,
AGES35:26 H12 Solid, hating all lightnesse, and al folly.
AGES37:19 H81 Did act al folly, that it could expresse.
MGREC116:37 H2603 This folly great *Augustus* did deride,
MEDDM206:25 Hp287 empty beareing the reproch of his pride and folly.
FOLLYES (1) [follies]
MYCHILD216:2 Hp241 loose from God, vanity & ye follyes of Youth take hold of me.
FOND (5)
AGES36:2 H26 (As that fond age, doth most of al desire.)
MGREC94:35 H1673 Ah! fond vaine man, whose pen was taught ere while,
MGREC106:10 H2144 Could bound his boundlesse, fond ambition)
MGREC114:8 H2476 Upon this dangerous theam fond *Clitus* fell;
CONTEM174:24 H222 Fond fool, he takes this earth ev'n for heav'ns bower.
FOOD (5)
FATHER5:23 H24 Of these consists, our bodyes, cloathes, and food,
ELEMEN9:18 H52 Your dainty {dayly} food, I wholsome make, I warme
ELEMEN14:14 H256 When they seek food, and harme mistrust the least.
MEDDM200:9 Hp279 this life, that so they might feed vpon more substantiall food,
30SEPT227:23 Hp257 then without food. Lord wth y^{y} correction giue Instrvction and
FOOL (3)
SIDNEY151:24 ~~H73~~ Calls me ambitious fool, that durst aspire,
CONTEM174:24 H222 Fond fool, he takes this earth ev'n for heav'ns bower.
ANNEB187:28 H18 More fool then I to look on that was lent,
FOOLE (5)
PROLOG6:27 H11 Foole, I doe grudge, the Muses did not part
PROLOG7:26 H38 The *Greeks* did nought, but play the foole and lye.
ELEMEN11:33 H153 The rich and {the} poore, wise, foole, and every sort,
HUMOUR34:5 H560 He was no foole, who thought the Soul lay here {there},
HUMOUR34:26 H581 With a tame foole converse, then with a mad.
FOOLERIES (1) [pl.]
MYCHILD218:22 Hp244 somt. stuck with me, and more it would, by ye vain fooleries
FOOLES (1) [fools]
SIDNEY150:1 H26 But some infatuate fooles soone caught therein,
FOOLISH (10)
PROLOG7:3 H18 My foolish, broken, blemish'd Muse so sings;
ELEMEN11:9 H129 Foolish *Caligula,* creep under's bed
HUMOUR22:36 H105 But know'ts a foolish brain, that wanteth heat;
HUMOUR~~24:26~~ H175 Thy childish {foolish} incongruities, Ile show:
HUMOUR24:30 H179 Thy foolish {silly} provocations, I despise.
HUMOUR34:23 H578 A foolish Brain (saith {quoth} Choler) wanting heat,
MGREC106:40 H2174 His fained Deity, and foolish pride:
DIALOG143:30 H99 With foolish superstitious adoration;
SIDNEY151:36 ~~H75~~ So proudly foolish I, with *Phaeton* strive,
TDUDLEY166:7 H49 As in the mean ones, of our foolish dayes,
FOOLS See FOOLES
FOOT (9)
MASSYR54:22 H49 The walls one hundred sixty foot upright,

MASSYR56:4 H110 Three hundred sixty foot, the walls in heighth:
MPERS78:5 H986 His Foot was seventeen hundred thousand strong,
MPERS87:14 H1370 And counts nine hundred thousand foot and horses:
MGREC94:19 H1657 Thirty two thousand made up his foot force,
MGREC100:26 H1910 Of Horse, and Foot, this {his} Army did amount;
MGREC131:16 H3208 Nor to his son did there {e're} one foot remain,
MGREC132:28 H3273 Did ne'r regain one foot in *Asia.*
MEDDM198:10 Hp276 sets his foot And he that passes through the wildernes of this

FOOTE (2) [foot]
ELEMEN12:9 H169 And *Hemus,* whose steep sides, none foote upon,
MPERS87:34 H1386 Some fifty, or else sixty foote in breadth.

FOOTING (1)
MEDDM208:32 Hp290 the water become firme footing, for peter to walk on, nay more

FOOTSTEPS (2) [pl.]
TDUDLEY166:30 H72 His pious Footsteps followed by his race,
MEDDM207:1 Hp288 say how vnsearchable are his wayes and his footsteps past

FORAGE See FORRAGE

FORBID (1)
AGES38:21 H124 A perverse will, a love to what's forbid:

FORC'D (10) [forced]
ELEMEN19:30 Some have I forc'd, to gaine an unknown shoare;
HUMOUR33:10 H524 Shame forc'd thee say, the matter that was mine,
MGREC94:1 H1635 Yet for a while, in *Greece* is forc'd to stay,
MGREC99:21 H1864 That *Greece* must {was forc'd to} yeeld a fresh supply againe;
MGREC~~101:34~~ H1963 But long they stood not e're they're forc'd to run,
MGREC108:33 H2249 But soone the *Grecians* {his souldiers} forc'd them to a flight,
MGREC115:41 H2560 He shewes his grief, he's forc'd to disobey:
MGREC129:6 H3120 That in few years he must be forc'd or glad
MROMAN137:11 H3462 So *Romulus* was forc'd this course to take.
DIALOG144:39 H147 Wives forc'd, babes toss'd, her houses calcined,

FORCE (51)
ELEMEN~~8:7~~ H5 Who was of greatest use and might'est force;
ELEMEN8:20 H18 Soone made the combatants abate their force;
ELEMEN9:3 ~~H37~~ My force? your sword, your Pike, your flint and steele,
ELEMEN~~9:3~~ H37 My force? your sword, & Gun, your lance of steel
ELEMEN10:34 H109 Yet by my force, master my master can.
ELEMEN11:19 H139 As I: impart your usefulnesse, and force.
ELEMEN13:19 H220 And how I force the grey head to obey.
ELEMEN15:2 H284 The Camell hath no strength, thy Bull no force;
ELEMEN16:32 H355 I now must shew what force {ill} there in me lyes.
ELEMEN20:6 H488 But what's their worth, {wrath} or force, but more's {same's} in
HUMOUR20:12 H4 Ceasing to vaunt, their good, or threat their force.
HUMOUR26:37 H267 But i'le not force retorts, nor do thee wrong,
HUMOUR32:16 H490 We shal expect much sound, but little force.
HUMOUR35:2 H598 Such premises wil force a sad conclusion,
AGES~~45:22~~ H405 I've seen a King by force thrust from his throne,
MASSYR54:31 H58 By force, {and fraud} his tributary, he did {under Tribute} bring.
MASSYR58:28 H211 Fear of his diadem, did force him fight:
MASSYR58:41 H224 Only intreats them, {to} joyn their force with his,
MASSYR61:16 H321 When *Resins* force his borders sore did mar.
MASSYR65:16 H481 For this great King, with-drawes part of his force,

MPERS80:24 H1091 If that smal number his great force could bide;
MPERS80:29 H1096 They no way able to withstand his force,
MPERS81:25 H1133 Against the *Persians* they would use {bend} their force.
MPERS86:20 H1336 To win by force, what right could not obtain.
MPERS86:25 H1341 He hop'd, if fraud, nor force the Crown could {would} gaine;
MPERS87:30 H1382 By reason, and by force, detain'd him still.
MPERS~~89:15~~ H1449 To hinder their return by craft or force,
MPERS90:8 H1481 Nor rivers course, nor *Persians* force could stay,
MPERS91:4 H1512 With suit, their force, {Arms} against his {their} foes be bent;
MPERS92:17 ~~H1575~~ By favour, force, or fraud, is not set down:
MGREC94:19 H1657 Thirty two thousand made up his foot force,
MGREC95:29 H1708 To raise more force, for what he yet {to further his} intends.
MGREC101:29 H1954 To force his Camp, so put {vanquish} them all to {by} flight;
MGREC102:28 H1998 But needs no force, 'tis rendred to his hands;
MGREC~~109:41~~ H2300 And there {by force} his Soveraignty for to make good;
MGREC117:20 H2627 His matchlesse force no Creature could abide;
MGREC119:16 H2706 The *Athenians,* force *Antipater* to fly
MGREC125:3 H2951 To make the King by force his seat resigne;
MGREC~~127:34~~ H3064 Fearing their state {his force}, and what might hap ere long
MGREC135:19 H3391 Their Crownes, their Titles, riches beares by force.
MGREC136:14 H3428 *Will force me to a confus'd brevity;*
MROMAN139:15 H3543 *Lucretia* force, mirrour of chastety;
MROMAN~~139:20~~ H3548 The *Tarquins* they from *Rome* with speed {by force} expell,
DIALOG142:6 H35 By fraud, and {or} force, usurp'd thy flowring crown,
DIALOG147:21 H247 By force {As Duty binds,} expell, destroy, and tread them
QELIZ156:11 H38 The *Salique* Law had not in force now been,
CONTEM168:33 H39 Thy pleasing fervor, and thy scorching force,
CONTEM172:17 H152 Could hinder ought, but still augment its force:
3LETTER183:22 H24 I here, he there, alas, both kept by force:
VERSES184:5 H9 My Bond remains in force unto this day;
MEDDM201:12 Hp280 Fire hath its force abated by water not by wind, and anger

FORCED (4) See also FORC'D, FORC'T

ELEMEN8:14 H12 The Fire, the forced Aire, in sunder crack;
ELEMEN18:16 H420 What is't? but forced Aire which must {doth} rebound,
DIALOG141:16 H15 Or must my forced tongue these griefes disclose?
MEDDM200:11 Hp279 brests, that god is forced to hedg vp their way wth thornes

FORCES (12) [pl.]

MASSYR58:25 H208 These Forces mustered, and in array,
MPERS73:21 H808 Their {Then} Forces instantly they raise, and rout,
MPERS78:15 H996 These {Such} his Land Forces were, then next, a Fleet
MPERS79:18 H1044 And {Then} in *Abidus* Plaines, mustring his Forces,
MPERS85:30 H1306 Whose forces {strength} by their {*Grecians*} helpe were {was}
MPERS87:9 H1365 But as he goes, his Forces still augments,
MPERS87:13 H1369 The fearfull King, at last, musters his Forces;
MPERS~~91:40~~ H1554 Then raises forces, conquers *Egypt* land,
MGREC~~108:40~~ H2256 Which did his former Army {forces} much augment,
MGREC119:25 H2715 With speed his forces {Army} doth together call,
MGREC124:14 H2921 his opponent still got {*Cassanders* forces had the} upper hand;
MGREC125:13 H2961 Some Forces did procure, with her to joyne.

FORCING (1)

ELEMEN19:40 H481 Their joyning, fighting, forcing, and retreat;

FORC'T (2) [forced]
MPERS91:10 H1518 The Kings {on such} conditions they are forc't to take; {as King
MGREC127:2 H3032 Now in her age she's forc't to taste that Cup,
'FORE (14) [before]
ELEMEN9:9 H43 Set ope those gates, that 'fore so strong was {were} barr'd.
HUMOUR22:16 H85 And 'fore she be assaulted, quits the place,
HUMOUR33:21 H535 I am confounded, 'fore I speak of any:
MPERS71:38 H752 But he that 'fore the gods, himself preferrs,
MPERS73:25 H810 But yet, 'fore this was done, much blood was shed,
MPERS80:37 H1104 Yet 'fore he went, to help out his expence,
MPERS84:5 H1233 Queen *Vashty* also feasts, but 'fore tis ended,
MPERS~~92:5~~ H1563 But why brother 'fore his son succeeds
MGREC~~110:18~~ H2319 The kingly Captive 'fore the Victor's brought,
MROMAN140:2 H3565 But 'fore I could accomplish my desire,
CHILDRN185:36 H62 My throbs such now, as 'fore were never:
CHILDRN186:22 H89 And 'fore she once would let you fly,
ANNEB187:20 H10 Experience might 'fore this have made me wise,
SON231:6 H18 From such as 'fore nere saw his face.
FORE-HEAD (1)
MPERS89:8 H1442 With infamy upon each fore-head stampt;
FOREIGN (1) See also FORRAIGN, FORRAIGNE, FORREIGN
TDUDLEY165:21 H23 Both in his native, and in foreign coast,
FORE-NAM'D (1) [fore-named]
MPERS78:13 H994 He was the Son of the fore-nam'd *Gobrias,*
FORE-RUNNER (1)
DIALOG144:33 H141 This is fore-runner of my after clap,
FORE-SEEN (1)
MPERS79:24 H1050 What after did ensue, had he fore-seen,
FORESEES (1)
MEDDM200:16 Hp279 garment, she easily foresees what euents it is like to produce,
FORE-SLOWES (1)
MPERS87:8 H1364 Which *Cyrus* heares, and so fore-slowes his pace:
FORE-TEL (1)
MASSYR66:28 H534 And his unhappy change with grief fore-tel;
FORETELS (1)
MEDDM199:24 Hp278 that are eyes of a Republique, foretels a declineing State.
FORE-TOLD (2)
MASSYR65:39 H504 His wel deserv'd, and fore-told misery;
MPERS82:2 H1147 Was Victory, by Oracle fore-told:
FORETOLD (1)
MYCHILD218:15 Hp244 in it fullfilled wch could not haue been so long foretold by any
FORG'D (1) [forged]
ELEMEN9:14 H48 Though strong limb'd *Vulcan* forg'd it by his skill,
FORGATE (1) [forgot]
MPERS84:31 H1267 But he all injury, had soon forgate,
FORGED See FORG'D
FORGET (2)
ELEMEN14:7 ~~H250~~ And *Rome,* her *Curtius,* can't forget I think;
30SEPT227:32 Hp257 yov out of distresse forget not to giue him thankes, but to walk
FORGETT (4) [forget]
MYCHILD217:8 Hp242 at least in sight) but I haue been apt to forgett him and my Self

JULY223:30 Hp251 O Lord let me neuer forgett thy Goodnes, nor question thy
28AUG226:8 Hp254 forgett thy great Love to my soul so lately expressed, when I
SON231:27 H39 O Lord gravnt that I may never forgett thy Loving kindness in

FORGING (1)
ELEMEN18:21 H425 Ye forging Smiths, if Bellowes once were gone;

FORGIUENES (1) [forgiveness]
MEDDM206:21 Hp287 wayes rather, then to beg forgiuenes for their sinnes, nature

FORGIVE (1)
VERSES184:8 H12 Such is my debt, I may not say forgive,

FORGIVENESS See FORGIUENES

FORGOE (1)
MGREC~~127:23~~ H3053 Because he never would let go {forgoe} his trust:

FORGOT (9) See also FORGATE
HUMOUR32:22 H496 I've not forgot how bitter Choler spake,
AGES41:15 H234 Childehood and youth, forgot, sometimes I've seen,
MASSYR65:11 H476 *Jehoiakim* his Oath had clean forgot;
MASSYR67:6 H552 Poor forlorn Prince, that {who} had all state forgot,
MGREC108:18 H2234 But that they had forgot their Mother-tongue.
MGREC112:17 H2403 His vertues dead, buried, and all {quite} forgot,
MGREC115:28 H2547 His service great now's suddenly forgot,
MGREC126:34 ~~H3023~~ She oft forgot bounds of Humanity.
CONTEM174:32 H229 Their names without a Record are forgot,

FORGOTTEN (1)
TDUDLEY166:28 H70 Forgotten never be his memory,

FORKS (1) [pl.]
SEASONS50:7 H141 The Forks, and Rakes do follow them amain,

FORLORN (3)
MASSYR67:6 H552 Poor forlorn Prince, that {who} had all state forgot,
CONTEM170:9 H82 Bewails his unknown hap, and fate forlorn;
1LETTER181:13 H11 My chilled limbs now nummed lye forlorn;

FORM (5)
HUMOUR33:23 H537 The scituation, and {Its} form wil it avow,
QELIZ158:5 H114 If then new things, their old form must {forms shall} retain,
MEDDM201:28 Hp281 not only to bid them hold fast the form of sound Doctrin, but
MYCHILD216:36 Hp242 and Bonds vpon my Soul to p^{r}form his righteovs comands.
11MAYA226:15 Hp255 a respite, & some ability to p^{r}form ye Dutyes I owe to him, and

FORME (3) [form]
MASSYR56:1 H107 Quadrangle was the forme, it stood upon:
MPERS73:31 H816 What forme of Government now to erect,
MROMAN137:1 H3452 A forme of Government he next begun;

FORMED (1)
MYCHILD216:19 Hp241 Christ be formed in yov.

FORMER (14)
HUMOUR20:11 H3 The former foure, now ending their Discourse,
MPERS91:22 H1530 Their former envie, and inveterate hate;
MGREC98:14 H1816 The former ruines, help to him now lend; {forwarded his end:}
MGREC102:24 H1994 And former Discipline begins to hate;
MGREC106:23 H2157 He basenesse counts his former clemency,
MGREC107:41 H2216 Hated of all, for's former treachery,
MGREC108:40 H2256 Which did his former Army {forces} much augment,
MGREC120:2 H2733 Nor former liberty, or glory gain'd;

CHILDRN186:7 H74 But former toyes (no joyes) adieu.
MEDDM199:28 Hp278 the body, the last the good name the two former leaue a man
MEDDM200:26 Hp279 to resume their former vigor and beavty in a more ample
MEDDM204:2 Hp284 The remembrance of former deliuerances, is a great support in
MYCHILD215:20 Hp240 ye former it had been perhaps better pleasing to yov, but seing
13MAY227:2 H11 And former clowdes seem now all fled

FORMERLY (2)
SEASONS49:11 ~~H102~~ Hath formerly much heat, the earth and aire.
MGREC124:41 H2948 She gave him poyson formerly ('tis thought)

FORMS (1) [pl.]
QELIZ~~158:5~~ H114 If then new things, their old form must {forms shall} retain,

FORRAGE (1) [forage]
CONTEM173:6 H174 Who forrage o're the spacious sea-green field,

FORRAIGN (1) [foreign] See also FORRAIGNE, FORREIGN
MPERS91:19 H1527 The King from forraign foes, and all {parts now well} at ease,

FORRAIGNE (2) [foreign] See also FORRAIGN, FORREIGN
DIALOG142:37 H66 But forraigne Foe, nor fained friend I feare,
QELIZ156:22 H49 Her Victories in forraigne Coasts resound?

FORREIGN (2) [foreign] See also FORRAIGN, FORRAIGNE
DIALOG142:15 H44 And call in Forreign ayde, to help the thing?
MERCY188:28 H14 Thou then on Seas sailing to forreign Coast;

FORSAKE (3)
ELEMEN15:5 H287 The Woolves and savage Beasts, forsake their Dens.
MPERS~~81:20~~ H1128 If now in {their} need, they should thus fail {forsake} their
MGREC~~116:10~~ H2574 But pin d in grief till life did her forsake:

FORSAKEN (1)
MPERS77:28 H969 And's cousen, young *Mardonius* forsaken,

FORSAKES (1)
HUMOUR30:21 H413 Then who's mans friend, when life and all forsakes?

FORSOOK (1)
MPERS~~87:20~~ H1374 Forsook his charge to his eternal shame:

FORSOOTH (1)
HUMOUR23:33 H143 Forsooth you are to blame, he grave reply'd.

FORT (1)
CONTEM174:19 H218 Which 'gainst all adverse winds may serve for fort.

FORTH (14)
PROLOG6:22 H7 Let Poets, and Historians set these forth,
ELEMEN12:30 H190 Send forth your well man'd ships, where sun doth rise.
ELEMEN13:9 H210 My bounty calls you forth to make reports,
AGES35:31 H17 flowers (as these) blossome {the spring puts forth} betime,
AGES38:15 H118 Which sprouted forth, in my {mine} insuing age,
MGREC96:21 H1741 Their golden Ornaments so {how} to set forth,
MGREC112:8 H2394 To shadow forth these short felicities:
MGREC127:40 H3070 Sends forth his declaration from a {declarations near and}
MGREC133:38 H3328 The affinities and warres *Daniel* set forth,
DIALOG~~147:12~~ H238 Let's bring *Baals* vestments out, {forth} to make a fire,
DIALOG148:13 H278 Bring forth the beast that rul'd the world with's beck,
CONTEM169:24 H64 Whilst I as mute, can warble forth no higher layes.
CONTEM173:13 H180 And chanted forth a most melodious strain
MYCHILD215:19 Hp240 Truth, not to sett forth my self, but ye Glory of God. If I had

FORTH-WITH (2)
MPERS89:17 H1451 Forth-with {Then} he sends {that} to's Tent, they straight
MGREC107:10 H2185 Commands forth-with, each man his fardle bring,
FORTHWITH (1)
MGREC109:31 H2290 His pleasure is, that forthwith he repaire
FORTIETH (1)
MPERS85:2 H1278 And dy'd the two and fortieth of his reign.
FORTIFIED (1)
MGREC126:8 H2999 Well fortified, and on the Sea it lies;
FORTITUDE (2)
MGREC100:28 H1912 But on their fortitude he had small stay;
MGREC110:19 H2323 His fortitude his Kingly {royal} foe commends;
FORTS (3) [pl.]
ELEMEN10:36 H111 What lasting Forts my kindled wrath hath burn'd?
ELEMEN12:6 H166 Strong forts from *Spanish* and *Italian* braules,
AGES39:17 H160 climbe Battlements, {scale walls and forts} rear'd to the skies;
FORTUNATE (1)
MPERS~~80:19~~ H1086 But they as valiant by {fortunate at} Sea, as Land,
FORTUNE (3)
MPERS69:40 H670 Now up, now {and} down, as fortune turnes her hand,
MPERS74:8 H833 Praying to Fortune, for a Kingly power;
MGREC132:35 H3282 Must needs goe try their fortune, and their might,
FORTUNES (2) [pl.]
MASSYR65:14 H479 But he (alas) whose fortunes {all were} now i'th ebbe,
MGREC104:2 H2054 Thought now this once, to try his fortunes here,
FORTY (16)
MASSYR54:20 H47 Four hundred forty Furlongs, wall'd about,
MASSYR56:40 H146 Forty two years she reign'd, and then she dy'd,
MASSYR57:8 H155 But much it is, in more then forty years,
MASSYR58:21 H206 These all agree, and forty thousand make,
MASSYR61:6 H311 Forty eight years he reign'd, his race then run,
MASSYR66:39 H545 Forty four years he reign'd, which being run,
MPERS70:17 H688 Forty five mile {miles} this City scarce could round;
MPERS81:40 H1144 The *Athenians* could but forty thousand arme,
MPERS87:33 H1385 Six yards the {in} depth, and forty miles the length,
MPERS91:29 ~~H1543~~ Forty three years he rules, then turns to dust,
MPERS~~91:31~~ H1545 Forty three years he rul'd, then turn'd to dust,
MGREC97:7 H1768 And forty thousand Prisoners also tane;
MGREC101:36 H1965 Forty five thousand *Alexander* had,
MGREC103:40 H2051 Which forty thousand made; but his intent,
MROMAN137:35 H3486 Forty three yeares he rul'd with generall praise;
MROMAN139:8 H3536 Forty foure yeares did *Servius Tullius* reigne,
FORWARD (2)
MPERS80:25 H1092 But he, in daring of his forward foe,
MEDDM201:26 Hp281 for Contrary ends, the one holds fast, the other puts forward,
FORWARDED (1)
MGREC~~98:14~~ H1816 The former ruines, help to him now lend; {forwarded his end:}
FORWARDNESSE (1)
AGES45:1 ~~H374~~ I saw hopes dasht, our forwardnesse was shent,
FORWARDS (1)
MEDDM202:26 Hp282 we may go forwards to the Citty of habitation, but when he

FOUGHT (9)

MPERS70:37 ~~H708~~ Where *Alexander* fought, in hope of prize,
MPERS~~70:37~~ H708 Where some long after fought in vain for prize
MPERS76:5 H903 His Army fought with Hunger, and with Cold,
MPERS76:33 H931 At *Marathon* this bloudy field was fought,
MGREC121:40 H2822 Two battells now he fought, and had {of both} the best,
MGREC123:6 H2868 With *Eumenes* he divers Battels fought,
MGREC133:18 H3306 I must let passe those many battels fought,
MROMAN137:15 H3466 For {Then} to recover them, a Feild was fought;
CONTEM170:33 H103 When deep dispair, with wish of life hath fought,

FOUL (2)

MGREC129:26 H3140 When this foul tragedy was past, and done,
VANITY160:9 H19 They'r foul enough to day, that once was {were} fair,

FOUND (41) See also FOVND

PROLOG7:9 H23 By Art, he gladly found what he did seeke,
ELEMEN10:13 H88 Nay more then these, Rivers 'mongst stars are found,
ELEMEN12:19 H179 The Behemoth, and rare found Unicorne,
ELEMEN15:3 H285 Nor mettl's found in the couragious Horse:
ELEMEN15:34 H316 Was ever gem so rich found in thy trunke?
HUMOUR31:30 H463 With me is noble patience also found,
AGES42:32 H288 If happinesse my sordidnesse hath found,
AGES44:10 H343 In every Age i've found much vanitie,
AGES46:4 H435 In pleasures, and in labours, I have found,
SEASONS~~52:39~~ H256 Where first it did begin, in th' end its found.
MPERS70:16 H687 Here twenty yeares provision {good} he found,
MPERS70:38 H709 But in this {his} Tombe was only to be found
MPERS71:32 H746 But vain he found, to fight with Elements,
MPERS~~79:13~~ H1035 To cross the sea such strength he found too weak,
MPERS82:9 H1156 Which found, like *Greeks* they fight, the *Persians* fly,
MPERS83:13 H1201 But yet by search, he was found murthered,
MPERS84:17 H1253 entertainment {royal bounty} with this {his} Prince he found,
MPERS~~92:21~~ H1579 But that his treason timely was found out.
MGREC93:29 H1626 To save him from his might, no man was found.
MGREC99:31 H1874 Though in an enemy it should be found;
MGREC102:19 H1989 With all pleasures that on earth was {are} found,
MGREC102:29 H1999 He likewise here a world of treasure found,
MGREC103:4 H2015 Of all the Cities, that on Earth was found;
MGREC105:1 H2094 Then slew his servants, that were faithfull found;
MGREC110:15 H2315 Yet work enough, here *Alexander* found,
MGREC110:32 H2336 Which might be found, and so for {great} wonders kept:
MGREC112:24 H2410 Nothing was found {prov'd}, wherein he had offended;
MGREC116:39 H2605 He would have found enough for {there} to be done,
MGREC117:28 H2635 Yet {But} none so hardy found as so durst say.
MGREC118:25 H2674 On which, no signe of poyson could be {in his intrails} found,
MGREC131:30 H3222 When his disease the skilfull Physician found,
MGREC136:17 H3431 *What e're is found amisse, take in best {good} part,*
DIALOG142:32 H61 Such is her poverty, yet shall be found
DIALOG147:9 H235 If mindlesse of thy state I e'r be found.
DIALOG148:29 H294 No Canaanite shall then be found ith' land,
SIDNEY150:2 H27 Found *Cupids* Dame, had never such a Gin;
DAVID159:10 H25 And in their deaths {death} was found no parting strife;

VANITY159:32 H4 Where is the man can say, lo, I have found
TDUDLEY166:26 H68 His hoary head in righteousness was found:
CONTEM174:27 H225 Only above is found all with security.
ANNEB187:22 H12 Was ever stable joy yet found below?

FOUNDATION (5)
ELEMEN13:41 H242 If {When} once you feele me, your foundation, quake,
HUMOUR30:26 H418 The strong foundation of the stately frame.
MASSYR53:23 H13 The strong foundation of proud *Babel* laid,
MASSYR54:19 H46 Whose foundation was by his Grand-sire laid;
MGREC~~102:10~~ H1980 The firm foundations, {strong Foundation} and the lofty spires;

FOUNDATIONS (3) [pl.]
MPERS75:35 H892 That shall, but {once} dare {to} raze those firme foundations;
MGREC102:10 H1980 The firm foundations, {strong Foundation} and the lofty spires;
MGREC102:18 H1988 Yet old foundations shew'd, and somewhat more;

FOUNDED (2)
PROLOG6:19 H4 Of Cities founded, Common-wealths begun,
AGES~~43:16~~ H308 Then thought my state firm founded sure to last,

FOUNDER (1)
MROMAN136:23 H3437 Stout *Romulus, Romes* Founder, and first King,

FOUNDERING (1)
MEDDM196:4 Hp272 is in danger of foundering.

FOUNDERS (1) [pl.]
TDUDLEY165:26 H28 One of thy Founders, him *New-England* know,

FOUNDRESSE (1)
QELIZ157:14 H82 *Dido* first Foundresse of proud *Carthage* walls,

FOUNT (1) See also FOVNT
VANITY160:28 H38 Which leads unto that living Christall fount,

FOUNTAINE (1) [fountain]
HUMOUR26:25 H255 I am the Fountaine which thy Cisterns fils,

FOUNTAINES (2) [fountains]
ELEMEN16:4 H327 Then I have Fountaines, Rivers, Lakes and Ponds:
ELEMEN16:14 H337 My divers Fountaines and their strange effect;

FOUNTAINS (1) [pl.]
DIALOG144:16 H126 These be the bitter fountains, heads, and roots,

FOUR (26)
FATHER5:4 H5 Of your four sisters, deckt {cloth'd} in black & white /four parts
FATHER5:4 H5 Of your four sisters, deckt {cloth'd} in black & white /four parts
FATHER5:12 H13 My lowly pen, might wait upon those four,
FATHER5:13 H14 I bring my four times {and} four, now meanly clad,
FATHER5:13 H14 I bring my four times {and} four, now meanly clad,
HUMOUR25:17 H206 The best of al the four, when they agree.
HUMOUR26:2 H232 Yet such, when we al four are joyn'd in one.
AGES35:16 H1-2 {Of} The Four Ages of Man.
AGES35:17 H3 Loe now! four other acts {act} upon the stage,
SEASONS46:26 H1-2 The four Seasons of the Yeare.
SEASONS46:28 H4 Another Four i've {left} yet for to bring on,
SEASONS46:29 H5 Of four times four, the last quaternian;
SEASONS46:29 H5 Of four times four, the last quaternian;
MASSYR54:20 H47 Four hundred forty Furlongs, wall'd about,
MASSYR56:26 H132 Her Army of four Millions did consist,
MASSYR66:39 H545 Forty four years he reign'd, which being run,

MPERS78:40 H1021 The other four he freely gave away:
MPERS80:14 H1081 Four hundred stately Ships by stormes was lost,
MGREC95:5 H1684 With losse of thirty four, of his there slaine:
MGREC95:33 H1712 He but four hundred thousand had to fight,
MGREC102:21 H1991 Where four and thirty dayes he now doth stay,
MGREC117:10 H2617 Four of his Captains, all doe now divide,
MGREC117:12 H2619 The Leopard down, his {the} four wings 'gan to rise,
MGREC135:29 H3401 The third a Leopard, which four wings did rear;
CHILDRN184:15 H4 Four Cocks there were, and Hens the rest,
MERCY189:9 H30 So with her Chidren four, she's now at rest,

FOURE (11) [four]
ELEMEN8:4 H1-2 The *Foure Elements.*
HUMOUR20:9 H1 Of the foure humours in
HUMOUR20:11 H3 The former foure, now ending their Discourse,
HUMOUR20:13 H5 Loe! other foure step up, crave leave to shew
HUMOUR20:22 H14 Which of the foure should have predominance;
HUMOUR20:29 H21 She was the silencest {silentest} of all the foure,
HUMOUR27:28 H299 Your hot, dry, moyst, cold, natures are {but} foure,
MASSYR53:11 H1 The Foure Monarchies,
MPERS78:1 H982 Although he hasted, yet foure yeares was spent,
MROMAN138:22 H3512 Twenty foure yeare, {years} th' time of his royall race,
MROMAN139:8 H3536 Forty foure yeares did *Servius Tullius* reigne,

FOURES (1) [fours]
FATHER5:29 H30 My other foures, do intermixed tell

FOURSCORE (1)
MGREC112:3 H2389 He fourscore *Persian* Ladies also gave;

FOURTEEN (1)
MASSYR53:34 H24 One hundred fourteen years, he after dyed.

FOURTH (11)
MGREC103:39 H2050 Had now his fourth, and last Army compounded,
MGREC110:41 H2345 His fourth, and last supply, was hither sent,
MGREC111:27 H2372 That of them all, the fourth did scarce remaine.
MGREC120:31 H2768 Brave *Ptolomy,* to make a fourth now {then} sent,
MGREC127:37 H3067 *Lysimachus* to make a fourth combines:
MGREC~~134:3~~ H3336 {Fourth} *Seleuchus* next *Antiochus* succeeds,
MGREC135:37 H3409 But how the fourth, their Kingdoms from them won;
MGREC136:12 H3426 *This fourth to th' other three, now might be brought.*
MROMAN136:20 H3434 being the Fourth, and last,
MROMAN139:25 ~~H3551~~ *being the fourth and last.*
MEDDM204:18 Hp285 as we see in Jehu, he is rewarded wth a kingdome to the fourth

FOVND (13) [found]
MYCHILD215:29 Hp241 too often tardy y^{t} way. I also fovnd much comfort in reading y^{e}
MYCHILD216:1 Hp241 I grew vp to bee about 14. or 15. I fovnd my heart more
MYCHILD216:8 Hp241 into this Covntry, where I fovnd a new World and new manners
MYCHILD216:30 Hp242 fovnd them ye Times w^{n} ye Lord hath manifested ye most
MYCHILD216:33 Hp242 way everlasting: and seldome or never but I haue fovnd either
MYCHILD217:13 Hp242 becavse I have fovnd my heart through his goodnes enlarged
MYCHILD217:15 Hp243 I haue often been p^{r}plexed y^{t} I haue not fovnd that constant
MYCHILD218:9 Hp244 this mvst bee it or none. Haue I not fovnd y^{t} operation by it
BYNIGHT220:5 H6 And so to lye I fovnd it best.
FEVER220:24 H4 When in my flesh no part was fovnd

11MAYA226:17 Hp255 Many refreshments haue I fovnd in this my weary pilgrimage,
30SEPT227:22 Hp257 I haue fovnd by Exper^{c}. I can no more liue wthout correction
HOURS233:25 H8 Thy help my soul hath fovnd

FOVNT (1) [fount]
MYSOUL225:7 H11 And drink at vnexhausted fovnt

FOWLERS (1) [poss.]
CHILDRN185:22 H48 They fall un'wares in Fowlers snare:

FOWLES (1) [pl.]
ELEMEN19:4 H449 Next, of my Fowles such multitudes there are;

FOYL'D (1) [foiled]
CHILDRN185:27 H53 Or least by Lime-twigs they be foyl'd,

FOYLE (2) [foil]
DIALOG143:8 H75 Their hands in Kindreds blood, whom they did foyle:
SICKNES179:12 H32 the foyle belongs to thee.

FRAGRANT (2)
SEASONS~~48:33~~ H84 Melodious {Sweet fragrant} Spring, with thy short pittance flye,
SEASONS49:35 H128 Whose fragrant scent, {smel} all made-perfume surpasses;

FRAIL (6)
CONTEM173:34 H198 Man at the best a creature frail and vain,
CONTEM174:5 H205 And yet this sinfull creature, frail and vain,
FEVER221:8 H23 And spar'd by Body frail,
28AUG225:33 Hp254 by it—And if he knowes that weaknes, & a frail body is ye best
28AUG226:6 Hp254 gravnt y^{t} while I live I may doe y^{t} service I am able in this frail
2HUSB232:17 H18 Thou see'st how weak + frail I am,

FRAILE (3) [frail]
AGES36:37 H61 With heed now stood, three ages of fraile man;
AGES38:30 H133 Yet griefs, in my fraile flesh, I still do find.
PILGRIM210:28 H28 nor grinding paines, my body fraile.

FRAILTY (1)
HOURS234:38 H52 But still my frailty show?

FRAM'D (3) [framed]
ELEMEN8:36 H34 What toole was ever fram'd, but by my might;
ELEMEN9:16 H50 Ye Cooks, your kitchin implements I fram'd, {frame}
HOUSE237:18 H48 Fram'd by that mighty Architect,

FRAME (10)
ELEMEN~~9:16~~ H50 Ye Cooks, your kitchin implements I fram'd, {frame}
ELEMEN10:24 H99 And man from thirty unto fifty frame.
ELEMEN18:20 H424 And so's the notes which Nightingales do frame.
HUMOUR22:28 H97 And through the arteries sends {it} o're the frame,
HUMOUR30:26 H418 The strong foundation of the stately frame.
MGREC112:11 H2397 If an Ideall Paradise, a man should {would} frame,
MGREC136:5 H3418 To frame Apologie for some offence,
MEDDM199:13 Hp277 on his anuile into what frame he pleases
MYCHILD217:36 Hp243 soon tell me by the wondrovs workes that I see, the vast frame
SON231:23 H35 In both o^{r} hearts erect a frame

FRAMED (1) See also **FRAM'D**
QELIZ158:19 H128 If many worlds, as that fantastick framed,

FRANCE (7)
ELEMEN17:8 H372 Thus *Albion* {*Britain* fair} (tis thought) was cut from *France*,
AGES44:34 H367 Then saw I *France*, and *Holland* sav'd, *Cales* won,
DIALOG142:24 H53 Doth your Allye, faire *France*, conspire your wrack?

DIALOG143:12 H81 *France* knowes, how of {oft} my fury she hath drunk;
DUBART154:11 H56 O *France,* in him thou didst more glory gain,
DUBART155:2 H87 *Here lyes the pearle of* France, Parnassus *glory,*
QELIZ156:12 H39 If *France* had ever hop'd for such a Queen;

FRANCKLY (1)
MGREC115:9 ~~H2518~~ Twelve thousand Tallents on it franckly spent;

FRANKLY (1)
QELIZ156:27 H54 She frankly help'd *Franks* (brave) distressed King,

FRANKS (1) [pl.]
QELIZ156:27 H54 She frankly help'd *Franks* (brave) distressed King,

FRATRICIDE (1)
CONTEM170:23 H94 His brother comes, then acts his fratricide,

FRAUD (8)
MASSYR~~54:31~~ H58 By force, {and fraud} his tributary, he did {under Tribute} bring.
MASSYR57:9 H156 This fraud, in war, nor peace, at all appears;
MPERS75:1 H862 And with a faithfull fraud to' th' town he goes,
MPERS86:25 H1341 He hop'd, if fraud, nor force the Crown could {would} gaine;
MPERS92:17 ~~H1575~~ By favour, force, or fraud, is not set down:
MGREC98:6 H1808 Least he intend more fraud, then sacrifice;
DIALOG142:6 H35 By fraud, and {or} force, usurp'd thy flowring crown,
SON231:12 H24 Without (all fraud) did'st sett him free

FRAUGHT (2) [freight]
ELEMEN16:30 H353 The wealthy fraught, unto his wished Port.
ELEMEN19:28 ~~H472~~ How many rich fraught vessells, have I split?

FRAUGHT (2) [distressed]
QELIZ158:1 H110 Full fraught with honour, riches, and with dayes:
CONTEM170:31 H101 His face like death, his heart with horror fraught,

FRAUGHTS (1) [pl.]
AGES38:10 H113 I had no ships at Sea, no fraughts to loose.

FREE (17)
ELEMEN17:19 H383 That *Caucasus* high mounts, are seldom free.
HUMOUR29:10 H363 Faire rosie Sister, so might'st thou scape free,
HUMOUR32:1 H475 Nor are ye free, from this inormity,
AGES42:6 H264 The proud I crush'd, th' oppressed I set free,
MASSYR61:22 H327 From *Rezin,* and from *Pekah* set me free:
MASSYR63:13 H398 All yeelds to him, but *Ninivie* kept free,
MASSYR63:25 H410 For fifty years, or more, it had been free,
MPERS70:22 H693 *Cyrus* doth now the *Jewish* captives free,
MPERS71:23 H737 To hold his own, of his free courtesie;
MGREC107:8 H2183 Now that his Hoast from luggage might be free,
MGREC113:5 H2432 Oh, *Alexander,* thy free clemency,
MGREC121:4 H2782 Leaves *Eumenes,* the *Asian* coast to free,
MGREC129:25 H3139 And now they are, {were} free Lords, of what they had,
FLESH177:22 H103 For evermore they shall be free,
MYCHILD215:33 Hp241 made my Suplicat^{n}. to the most High who sett me free from
SON230:28 H11 From Dangers great thou did'st him free
SON231:12 H24 Without (all fraud) did'st sett him free

FREED (5)
MPERS83:15 H1203 That from suspition he might be freed,
MPERS84:10 H1238 And how her Country-men from spoile she freed.
QELIZ156:20 H47 Was ever Land more happy, freed from stirs?

MERCY189:10 H31 All freed from grief (I trust) among the blest;
MEDDM204:14 Hp284 shame euer goe together He that would be freed from the last,

FREEDOME (1) [freedom]
AGES37:29 H91 Freedome from Envy, and from Arrogance.

FREELY (8)
ELEMEN13:11 H212 But what I freely yeeld upon your sweat?
ELEMEN18:6 H410 How freely should it go, so he might live.
HUMOUR32:26 H500 To what is truth, I freely wil assent,
AGES~~45:22~~ H412 Men may more freely speak another day.
MPERS75:33 H890 Of what is freely granted by the King;
MPERS78:40 H1021 The other four he freely gave away:
MGREC98:27 H1829 For that which easily comes, as freely goes;
BYNIGHT220:18 H16 Who freely hath done this for me,

FREEZE (2)
HUMOUR22:32 H101 The nerves should I not warm, soon would they freeze.
SEASONS52:30 H245 Now toes, and eares, and fingers often freeze,

FREIGHT See FRAUGHT
FREIGHTS See FRAUGHTS

FREIND (2) [friend]
SAMUEL228:10 H11 No freind I haue like Thee to trust
2HUSB232:10 H11 My husband, my dear freind.

FREINDS (5) [friends]
HUMOUR34:41 H596 Let's now be freinds, 'tis {its} time our spight was {were} spent,
AGES40:9 H190 Until her freinds, treasure, and honour's gone.
AGES40:17 H198 And dearest freinds count for mine enemies;
SON231:4 H16 And freinds rais'd him in every place
HOURS234:14 H28 And freinds I haue also

FREINDSHIP (1) [friendship]
HUMOUR29:4 H357 Especially when freindship is pretended:

FRENCH (1)
DIALOG143:2 H71 French *Lewis* {Jews} unjustly to the Crown to bring;

FRENZY See PHRENSIE
FRENZY'S [frenzy is] See PHRENSIE'S

FREQUENCY (1)
CONTEM174:10 H210 In weight, in frequency and long duration

FREQUENT (2)
DDUDLEY167:18 H15 *The publick meetings ever did frequent,*
MEDDM205:35 Hp287 some eminent Christians, that are soe frequent in good dutys,

FRESH (11)
ELEMEN19:12 H457 As my fresh Aire preserves, all things in life;
AGES36:7 H31 His face as fresh, as is *Aurora* faire,
MASSYR58:32 H215 But with fresh hopes *Belosus* succoured.
MGREC99:21 H1864 That *Greece* must {was forc'd to} yeeld a fresh supply againe;
MGREC~~102:26~~ H1996 *Antipater,* from *Greece,* sends great {fresh} supplyes;
MGREC102:27 H1997 He then to *Sushan* goes, with his fresh {new} bands,
MGREC115:35 H2554 *Parmenio's* death's too fresh before his eyes;
MGREC124:33 H2940 He still kept fresh {lockt} within his memory,
MGREC131:27 H3219 Is for this fresh young Lady half {quite} undone,
VANITY160:40 H50 Nor strength nor wisdome, nor fresh youth shall fade,
CONTEM172:32 H165 Now salt, now fresh where you think best to glide

FRESHLY (1)

BIRTH180:10	H20	Let that live freshly in thy memory

FRIEND (19) See also FREIND

FATHER6:3	H37	But fear'd you'ld judge, one *Bartas* was my friend,
ELEMEN12:14	H174	Unlesse thou prove a better friend to me;
ELEMEN15:28	H310	The Dolphin (loving musique) *Arions* friend.
HUMOUR23:29	H139	Their courage, {Courage it} friend, and foe, and subject awes,
HUMOUR30:21	H413	Then who's mans friend, when life and all forsakes?
MASSYR59:19	H243	But in the third, the River prov'd his friend,
MASSYR61:32	H337	Proves unto *Ahaz* but a feigned friend;
MPERS~~70:2~~	H673	Gave him his life, and took him for a friend,
MPERS~~72:25~~	H773	He spar'd nor foe, nor friend, nor favorite.
MPERS80:33	H1100	And as a friend, warns him, what e're he doe,
MGREC113:24	H2451	*Polidamus,* who seem'd *Parmenio's* friend,
MGREC115:11	H2520	Because he let {He suffer, his friend} *Ephestion* to dye.
MGREC~~115:15~~	H2533	That by his leave his friend *Ephestion,*
MGREC~~132:6~~	H3240	But he a Kingdome more then's friend did eye,
MGREC133:4	H3292	*Seleuchus* was as {a} Father, and a friend,
DIALOG142:37	H66	But forraigne Foe, nor fained friend I feare,
TDUDLEY165:32	H34	Truths friend thou wert, to errors still a foe,
BIRTH179:34	H10	How soon't may be thy Lot to lose thy friend,
MEDDM201:32	Hp281	the most welcom so a faithfull friend in time of adversity,

FRIENDLY (3)

HUMOUR26:4	H234	The friendly coadjutors, stil to {of} thee.
MPERS75:38	H895	And in the sixth yeare of his friendly reign
DDUDLEY167:12	H9	*A friendly Neighbor, pitiful to poor,*

FRIENDS (21) [pl.] See also FREINDS

MASSYR59:30	H254	But all his wealth, and friends, together gets,
MASSYR67:32	H578	To chear his friends, and scorn his foes the more.
MPERS81:20	H1128	now in {their} need, they should thus fail {forsake} their friends,
MPERS~~84:28~~	H1264	His Country, nor his Kindred {Friends} would {much} esteem,
MPERS89:22	H1456	And sues for peace, that they his friends remain;
MGREC~~116:10~~	H2575	All friends she shuns, yea, banished the light,
MGREC~~121:16~~	H2795	But of his wrongs his friends doth certifie;
MGREC124:8	~~H2913~~	Upon those friends, his father rais'd on high,
MGREC~~124:10~~	H2915	Such friends away as for his Interest makes
MGREC125:6	H2954	For ayde {she} goes to *Epire,* among her friends,
MGREC125:32	H2982	His Brethern, Kinsfolk, and his chiefest friends,
MGREC~~126:25~~	H3016	the blood of their deare Kindred {friends and kindreds} spilt,
MGREC131:23	H3215	Tries foes, since friends will not compassionate,
DIALOG144:29	H137	Some grossely fin'd, from {house &} friends to exile went:
CONTEM174:3	H204	Troubles from foes, from friends, from dearest, near'st
CONTEM174:23	H221	That's full of friends, of honour and of treasure,
AUTHOR177:32	H4	Till snatcht from thence by friends, less wise then true
BIRTH179:29	H5	No tyes so strong, no friends so clear and sweet,
2SIMON195:10	Hp271	true friends much more by duty full children, I haue avoyded
MEDDM208:9	Hp290	of intimate friends, though there should be no displeasence
MEDDM208:19	Hp290	be compared to deceitfull friends who speak faire and promise

FRIENDSHIP (3) See also FREINDSHIP

MGREC98:40	H1842	A league of friendship make, firm, and entire;
MGREC120:8	H2743	Their friendship may {might} the more be strengthened:

SIDNEY150:10 H35 Justice, friendship, and kind hospitality;

FRIGHT (3)

MASSYR59:8 H232 But all {And now} surpris'd, by this unlookt for fright,
MPERS82:20 H1167 That Army, which did fright the Universe;
MGREC96:20 H1740 For so to fright the *Greekes* he judg'd was best,

FRIGID (1)

1LETTER181:12 H10 His warmth such frigid colds did cause to melt.

FRISK (1)

CONTEM173:2 H170 Look how the wantons frisk to tast the air,

FRISKING (1)

SEASONS47:20 H36 The wanton frisking Kids, and soft fleec'd Lambs,

FRISLING (1)

AGES40:21 H202 in curling {to curle}, frisling up {and pounce my new-bought}

FRO (3)

MGREC113:26 H2453 He walking in his Garden, too and fro,
DIALOG146:1 H189 The writing, printing, posting to and fro,
MEDDM205:12 Hp286 to and fro continvally, here is also the great Court of iustice

FROG (1)

MPERS76:11 H909 A Frog, a Mouse, a Bird, an Arrow sent,

FROGS (2) [pl.]

SEASONS47:16 H32 The croaking Frogs, whom nipping Winter kild,
MPERS76:15 H913 Quoth he, like Frogs, in water we must dive;

FROLICK (3)

AGES35:21 H7 The second, frolick, claimes his pedigree,
SEASONS49:16 H107 Now go those frolick swaines, the shepheard lad,
MPERS77:1 H940 Off flyes his head, down showres his frolick bloud.

FRONT (2)

MASSYR56:6 H112 Most {Some} writers say, six chariots might a front,
CONTEM171:21 H124 Nor age nor wrinkle on their front are seen;

FROST (1)

SEASONS47:24 H40 For though the Frost hath lost his binding power,

FROSTED (1)

SEASONS~~46:35~~ H11 She trim'd her locks, which late had frosted been,

FROSTS (2) [pl.]

SEASONS52:16 H231 Bound up with Frosts, and furr'd with Hails, and Snows,
1LETTER181:11 H9 Whom whilst I 'joy'd, nor storms, nor frosts I felt,

FROTH (2)

HUMOUR26:38 H268 Thy fiery yellow froth, is mixt among.
AGES39:34 H177 As vain as froth, as {or} vanity can be,

FROTHY (3)

ELEMEN15:41 H323 I lightly cast ashoare as frothy fleece.
HUMOUR23:40 ~~H149~~ The spongy Lungs, I feed with frothy blood.
MGREC94:27 H1665 Sends him a frothy, and contemptuous letter,

FROWN (1)

AGES44:17 H350 That can refresh, or ease, if Conscience frown;

FROZEN (3)

ELEMEN9:34 H68 How doth his warmth refresh thy frozen backs, {back}
SEASONS52:24 H239 Cold frozen *January* next comes in,
DUBART153:7 H11 Did thaw my frozen hearts ingratitude;

FRUIT (6)

ELEMEN16:40 H363 By adding cold to cold, no fruit proves sound;

SEASONS48:28 H81 Each season, hath his fruit, so hath each clime.
SEASONS50:30 H164 To shake his fruit, of most delicious tastes;
MPERS72:14 H762 She with her fruit was {were} both at once undone,
DIALOG~~146:32~~ H219 Out of your troubles much good fruit to be;
MERCY188:27 H13 That thou dear Son has lost both Tree and fruit:
FRUITFUL (5) See also FRUITFULL, FRVITFULL
AGES~~42:35~~ H291 My fleeced Ewe {Sheep}, and ever {fruitful} farrowing Sow.
SEASONS50:26 H160 His fruitful crop, abundantly requites.
SEASONS51:24 H200 The fruitful trees, all withered now do stand,
MPERS71:21 H735 Who landed {landing} soon upon that fruitful coast,
CONTEM168:29 H36 And in the darksome womb of fruitful nature dive.
FRUITFULL (9) [fruitful] See also FRVITFULL
ELEMEN13:15 H216 My cold, thy (fruitfull) heat, doth crave no lesse:
ELEMEN13:29 H230 And buds from fruitfull trees, before they'r {as soon as} blowne:
ELEMEN16:21 H344 Nor fruitfull dewes, nor drops {distil'd} from weeping eyes;
SEASONS47:36 H48 This is the month whose fruitfull showers produces
SEASONS48:9 H62 My next, and last, is pleasant fruitfull *May,*
MGREC100:1 H1885 From thence, to fruitfull *Ægypt* marcht with speed,
DIALOG144:37 H145 Her fruitfull land, a barren heath remain.
DAVID158:33 H13 Nor fruitfull showers your barren tops bestrew,
MEDDM205:31 Hp286 We see in orchards, some trees soe fruitfull, that the waight of
FRUITFULLNES (1) [fruitfulness]
MEDDM206:1 Hp287 attained to that fruitfullnes, altho they aime at perfection And
FRUITFULNESSE (2) [fruitfulness]
ELEMEN11:25 H145 Such was {is} my fruitfulnesse; and Epithite
ELEMEN14:27 H269 Cause of your fruitfulnesse, as you shall see:
FRUITLESSE (1)
MPERS76:20 H918 His {This} fruitlesse war, began late to repent;
FRUITS (18) [pl.]
ELEMEN11:29 H149 To tell what sundry fruits my fat soyle yeelds,
ELEMEN15:10 H292 Man wants his bread, and wine, and pleasant fruits;
AGES36:17 H41 Of Autumne {Autumns} fruits a basket on his arme.
SEASONS47:13 H29 And carefully manures his trees of fruits.
SEASONS48:25 H78 For fruits, my season yeelds, the early Cherry,
SEASONS48:27 H80 More solid fruits, require a longer time.
SEASONS50:32 H166 Hath stil ascended up in {to bear} goodly Fruits,
SEASONS50:36 H170 Then drops his Fruits into the Eaters lap.
SEASONS51:15 H189 Boughs full of leaves, or fruits, but raw, and {unripe or} green,
SEASONS51:17 H191 But trees with goodly fruits replenished;
DIALOG144:17 H127 Whence flow'd the source, the sprigs, the boughs, and fruits;
DUBART153:9 H13 Had caused flowers, and fruits, soone to abound;
DUBART153:13 H17 Flowers, fruits, in garden, orchard, or in field;
CONTEM167:29 H6 Their leaves & fruits seem'd painted, but was true
CONTEM170:15 H87 Fruits of the Earth, and Fatlings each do bring,
1LETTER181:16 H14 Then view those fruits which through thy heat I bore?
MEDDM196:30 Hp273 fruits that are best preserued wth sugar, those parents are wise
PILGRIM210:12 H12 Nor wild fruits eate, in stead of bread
FRUSTRATE (1)
MGREC119:7 H2697 That none might know, to frustrate his intent;
FRVITFULL (2) [fruitful] See also FRUITFULL
SOREFIT221:33 H19 O make it frvitfull faithfull Lord

FAINT222:27 H17 Then I may frvitfull bee.

FRY (1)

CONTEM172:34 H167 In Lakes and ponds, you leave your numerous fry,

FRY'D (1) [fried]

MGREC127:1 H3031 Some slew, some fry'd, of others, stopt the breath;

FRYING (1)

AGES40:39 H218 My heart lyes frying, and my {mine} eyes are sinking;

FUELL (1) [fuel]

ELEMEN13:13 H214 Well knowest, my fuell must maintain thy fire.

FUGATIVE (1)

MPERS79:41 H1067 But that a Fugative discovered,

FUL (8) [full]

HUMOUR24:25 H174 So ful of boasting, and prevarication.
HUMOUR24:37 H186 And how to strike ful sweet, as wel as sharpe.
AGES36:33 H57 To do as he, the rest {each one} ful soon assents,
AGES41:9 H229 Of Marrow {aches} ful my bones, of Milk {woe} my breasts
SEASONS49:17 H108 To wash their {the} thick cloath'd flocks, with pipes ful glad.
SEASONS52:7 H222 This time warm cloaths, ful diet, and good fires,
MASSYR60:39 H304 Which makes the world of differences {difference} so ful,
MASSYR66:27 H533 His Dreams, wise *Daniel* doth expound ful wel,

FULFILL (2)

MASSYR61:19 H324 The temple robes, so to fulfill his ends,
MASSYR64:40 H464 Their shoulders must their Masters minde fulfill;

FULFILL'D (1) [fulfilled] See also FULLFILLED

MASSYR59:24 H248 And now they saw fulfill'd a Prophesie;

FULL (42) See also FUL

FATHER~~5:14~~ H15 To do their homage unto yours most {full} glad,
PROLOG7:10 H24 A full requitall of his striving paine:
PROLOG7:25 H37 But this weake knot they will full soone untye,
ELEMEN14:5 H249 And since, faire *Italy* full sadly knowes
ELEMEN14:25 H267 Sister (quoth she) it had full well behov'd
SEASONS51:15 H189 Boughs full of leaves, or fruits, but raw, and {unripe or} green,
MASSYR65:6 H471 Full thirteen yeares in this strange work he spent,
MPERS74:10 H835 *Darius* lusty stallion neighed full loud;
MPERS76:17 H915 Or fly like birds, in unknown wayes full quick;
MPERS77:17 H958 The {His} Father not so full of lenity,
MPERS~~78:34~~ H1015 Then gives the King, a King-like gift, most {full} large;
MPERS88:25 H1418 And with a full career, at him he ran.
MGREC94:4 H1638 But he their mutinies, {by valour} full soon doth {he} quell.
MGREC~~100:34~~ H1918 {Whose death} her wofull Lord for to {full sadly did} lament.
MGREC102:17 H1987 Though worn by time, and raz'd {rac'd} by foes full sore,
MGREC108:26 H2242 But he their stubbornnesse full soone {in time} doth quel;
MGREC110:8 H2308 Did here, and there, Isles full of trees abide;
MGREC122:2 H2825 And his beloved foe, full sore laments.
MGREC131:1 H3187 To do as he, {by his Example all} the rest full soon presumes,
DIALOG148:9 H274 And let her spoils, full pay, with int'rest be,
DIALOG148:12 H277 Execute toth' full {And on her pour} the vengeance threatned.
SIDNEY150:39 ~~H67~~ Illustrious *Stella,* thou didst thine full well,
DUBART153:26 H30 And tells her tales; (his full heart over-glad)
DUBART154:5 H50 My full astonish'd heart doth pant to break,
QELIZ158:1 H110 Full fraught with honour, riches, and with dayes:

DAVID159:16 H31 And choyse delights, full of variety.
DAVID159:22 H37 In places high, full low thou dost {didst} remaine;
TDUDLEY166:14 H56 For which he sigh'd and pray'd & long'd full sore
CONTEM168:37 H43 Hail Creature, full of sweetness, beauty & delight.
CONTEM169:2 H44 Art thou so full of glory, that no Eye
CONTEM169:6 H48 How full of glory then must thy Creator be?
CONTEM174:23 H221 That's full of friends, of honour and of treasure,
FLESH175:30 H30 For riches dost thou long full sore?
MERCY189:15 H36 What though, thy strokes full sad & grievous be,
2SIMON195:10 Hp271 true friends much more by duty full children, I haue avoyded
MEDDM201:2 Hp280 his strong men, such as are come to a full stature in Christ,
MEDDM201:21 Hp281 sinners, seem full of contrition, but it is not from any dew of
MEDDM202:10 Hp281 exceeding beauty full, and some extreamly deformed some so
MEDDM202:11 Hp281 y[t] their bones are full of marrow & their breasts of milk,
PILGRIM210:3 H3 His wasted limbes, now lye full soft
SON231:7 H19 In sicknes when he lay full sore
HOURS234:9 H23 My weaknes thou do'st know full well,

FULLFILLED (1) See also FULFILL'D
MYCHILD218:15 Hp244 prophecyes in it fullfilled wch could not haue been so long

FULLNES (1) [fullness] See also FULLNES
MEDDM202:37 Hp282 whom all fullnes dwells

FULLY (5)
HUMOUR29:13 H366 Thy soothing girds shal fully be repaid;
SEASONS49:6 H97 His progresse to the North; now's fully done,
MASSYR58:16 H201 *Arbaces* him, fully to be repaid.
TDUDLEY166:18 H60 Now fully ripe, as shock of wheat that's grown,
SICKNES178:18 H1 Twice ten years old, not fully told

FULNESS (1) [fullness] See also FULLNES
DIALOG148:25 H290 Then fulness of the Nations in shall flow,

FUME (1)
MGREC107:14 H2189 And thus unwisely, in one raging {mading} fume,

FUNERAL (1)
MERCY188:22 H8 Ah, woe is me, to write thy Funeral Song,

FUNERALLS (1) [pl.]
MGREC127:6 H3036 The Funeralls *Cassandra* celebrates,

FUNERALS (2) [pl.]
MGREC120:34 H2771 His Masters Funerals doth celebrate;
QELIZ157:15 H83 (Who living consummates her Funerals)

FURIOUS (3)
ELEMEN~~19:32~~ H473 Again, what tempests,{furious storms} and what hericanoes
HUMOUR29:21 H372 To play such furious pranks I am too wise;
MGREC125:36 H2986 The Courtiers wondering at her furious minde,

FURLONGS (2) [pl.]
MASSYR54:20 H47 Four hundred forty Furlongs, wall'd about,
MGREC108:38 H2254 And furlongs sixty could not {but} round the same.

FURNACE (3)
MASSYR66:26 H532 Although the Furnace be seven times more hot;
MEDDM199:12 Hp277 good to cast some men into the furnace of affliction and then
30SEPT227:25 Hp257 in y[e] furnace of affliction as some haue been, but haue rather

FURNISHED (1)
HOUSE237:19 H49 W[th] glory richly furnished

FURNISHT (1)
MGREC124:5 H2910 Straight furnisht him with a sufficient aide,
FURNITURE (2)
MGREC102:37 H2007 And furniture, the richest of {in} all Lands,
MGREC111:7 H2352 His furniture most sumptuous to behold;
FURR'D (1) [furred]
SEASONS52:16 H231 Bound up with Frosts, and furr'd with Hails, and Snows,
FURROWS (1) [pl.]
MEDDM205:2 Hp285 correction must make long furrows on their back and the
FURRY See FURY
FURTHER (12)
HUMOUR25:7 H196 Ile go no further then thy nose for test.
HUMOUR27:16 H287 To meddle further, I shal be but shent,
HUMOUR31:18 H451 No further time ile spend, in confutations, {confutation}
MASSYR58:20 H205 And the *Arabians,* to further his desire.
MPERS87:10 H1366 Seven hundred *Greeks* now further {repair for} his intents:
MPERS90:14 ~~H1484~~ The King afraid what further they might doe,
MGREC95:29 H1708 To raise more force, for what he yet {to further his} intends.
MGREC110:20 H2324 Restores him, and his bounds further {farther} extends;
MGREC110:24 H2328 Could by no means be further {farther} drawn, or led:
MGREC130:10 H3165 Untill he further know his Masters will;
MROMAN139:33 H3559 All thoughts of further progress laid aside,
MEDDM207:8 Hp288 but haue driuen them the further from him, that they are ready
FURTHERERS (1) [pl.]
AGES43:10 ~~H305~~ Have been curst furtherers of mine intents.
FURTHEST (3)
MPERS87:36 H1388 He surest {safest} was, when furthest {farthest} out o'th' way.
MGREC114:38 H2508 From *Hellispont,* to th' furthest {farthest} Ocean;
MGREC115:1 H2512 Unto the furthest {farthest} bounds of th' orient;
FURY (5) [furry]
HUMOUR25:23 H212 Thou art a fury, or infernal Fiend.
HUMOUR25:41 H230 Ile praise that fury, {prowess} valour, choler, heat.
MGREC93:27 H1624 Who {That} ran in fury, {Choler} on the *Persian* Ram,
MGREC126:30 H3021 Whose fury yet unparalleld {scarcely parallel'd} hath been;
DIALOG143:12 H81 *France* knowes, how of {oft} my fury she hath drunk;
FUTURE (11)
PROLOG7:8 H22 lisp'd at first, speake afterwards more {in future times} plaine
AGES38:12 H115 Nor yet on future things did place {set} my hope.
AGES39:31 H174 Makes {Make} all to place their future hopes on me.
MPERS74:24 H847 By which he cuts their hopes (for future times)
MPERS77:40 H981 To present losse, future subversion;
MGREC97:13 H1774 Was but beginning of his future woe;
MGREC99:32 H1875 If of thy future fame thou hadst regard,
MGREC99:41 H1884 No future dangers he did ever dread.
DUBART154:34 H79 But monuments for {to} future admiration:
CONTEM170:20 H92 Upon whose blood his future good he hopes to raise.
THEART229:10 H12 My future Doubts repell.

G

GAILES (1) [gales]

2HUSB232:28	H29	And send them prosperous gailes

GAIN (26) See also GAINE

HUMOUR29:33	H384	Then by assault to gain one, not our own.
AGES41:38	H255	If not, yet wealth, {riches} Nobility can gain.
SEASONS47:9	H25	In hope, the more he casts, the more to gain;
MASSYR54:32	H59	The *Median* country, he did also gain,
MASSYR57:21	~~H168~~	Would now advantage take, their own to gain;
MASSYR64:33	H457	And for her strength, how hard she was to gain,
MASSYR65:4	H469	And took the wealthy town, but all the gain
MPERS81:27	H1135	With Rhetorick, t' gain better complement:
MPERS87:25	H1377	*Cyrus* dispair'd, a passage there to gain;
MPERS90:22	H1489	The many victories themselves did gain,
MPERS~~90:25~~	H1492	Might win {gain} the universall Monarchy;
MGREC95:4	H1683	This Victory did *Alexander* gain;
MGREC97:40	H1801	To gain his love, the *Tyrians* do intend,
MGREC104:32	H2084	*Darius* from those Traitors hands to gain;
MGREC120:39	H2776	Great love did *Ptolomy* by this act gain.
MGREC~~127:28~~	H3058	*Antigonus,* all *Persia* now gains {doth gain},
MGREC130:14	H3169	So hinders him of her, he could not gain.
MGREC131:7	H3197	*Demetrius* of *Ptolomy* doth gain;
MGREC131:17	H3209	Of those dominions {vast Kindgomes} he did sometimes gain,
DUBART154:11	H56	O *France,* in him thou didst more glory gain,
QELIZ158:13	H122	*The greater was our gain, our losse the more.*
VANITY159:38	H10	What is't in wealth, great treasures for to gain {obtain}?
CONTEM173:21	H187	To gain more good, or shun what might thee harm
SICKNES179:7	H27	O great's the gain, though got with pain,
MYCHILD215:17	Hp240	now doe) by y^{t} yov may gain some spirit: Advantage by my
MYSOUL225:19	H23	No gain I find in ovght below

GAIN'D (9) [gained]

ELEMEN19:27	H472	Then in his long hot wars, {war} which *Millain* gain'd.
MASSYR60:21	H286	*Assyria* he also gain'd at length;
MASSYR61:31	H336	But *Tiglath,* having gain'd his wished end,
MPERS~~74:31~~	H854	Much gain'd the hearts of his nobility.
MPERS85:21	H1297	Revolts, having treasure, and people gain'd:
MGREC100:3	H1887	To see how fast he gain'd, is {was} no small wonder,
MGREC101:40	H1969	At *Arbela,* this victory gain'd,
MGREC120:2	H2733	Nor former liberty, or glory gain'd;
THEART229:9	H11	And new Exper^{c} I haue gain'd

GAINE (11) [gain]

ELEMEN19:30	~~H272~~	Some have I forc'd, to gaine an unknown shoare;
AGES42:27	H285	My wakefull thoughts, up to my painefull gaine.
MPERS76:21	H919	Return'd with little honour, and lesse gaine;
MPERS86:25	H1341	He hop'd, if fraud, nor force the Crown could {would} gaine;
MGREC95:6	H1685	*Sardis,* then he, and *Ephesus,* did gaine,
MGREC107:29	H2204	How to passe {the River} over, and gaine {to} the other Land;
MGREC121:13	H2791	And from the other, {side} daily some did gaine.
MGREC124:4	H2909	Hoping still {yet} more to gaine by these new stirs;
MGREC124:18	H2925	*Antigonus* doth all in *Asia* gaine;
MGREC128:15	H3088	Now {Then} *Ptolomy* would gaine the *Greeks* likewise,
DIALOG143:33	H102	Church Offices are {were} sold, and bought, for gaine,

GAINER (1)

28AUG225:32	Hp254	but he doth it for my Advantage, and y^{t} I may bee a Gainer

GAINES (2) [gains]

AGES41:32	H249	My family to keep, but not for gaines.
MGREC133:14	H3302	His Son *Demetrius,* all *Cassanders* gaines,

GAINING (1)

MGREC128:28	H3101	Still gaining Countries East-ward goes he on.

GAINS (3) See also GAINES

MGREC127:28	H3058	*Antigonus,* all *Persia* now gains {doth gain},
MGREC132:15	H3250	*Demetrius,* {thus} *Cassanders* Kingdomes gains,
BIRTH180:13	H23	And when thy loss shall be repaid with gains

'GAINST (22) [against]

HUMOUR21:23	H51	Then Iron Corslet, 'gainst a sword or dart;
HUMOUR~~25:38~~	H227	But if in fitting time, and place, on foes; {'gainst foe}
MASSYR57:15	H162	'Gainst whom his trained Bands *Abram* did bring.
MPERS70:26	H697	Long after this, he 'gainst the *Sythians* goes,
MPERS71:15	H729	'Gainst *Ægypts* King, who there by him was slain,
MPERS74:33	H856	The *Babylonians* 'gainst their Prince rebell;
MPERS81:18	H1126	That *Xerxes* quarrel was 'gainst *Athens* State,
MPERS85:14	H1290	Disquiet {Revolting} Egypt, 'gainst this King rebells,
MGREC94:3	H1637	*Thebes,* and old {stiff} *Athens,* both 'gainst him rebell,
MGREC94:30	H1668	To lift his hand, 'gainst such a Monarchy.
MGREC108:25	H2241	And now the *Bactrians* 'gainst him {now} rebel,
MGREC120:14	H2749	For's Souldiers 'gainst those Captains would not goe;
MGREC120:30	H2767	And 'gainst *Perdicas,* all their strength combine.
MGREC121:1	H2779	('Gainst which to goe, is troubled in his minde;)
MGREC~~121:2~~	H2780	But first 'gainst *Ptolemy* he judg'd was
MGREC~~121:16~~	H2796	The souldiers 'gainst *Perdiccas* they incense,
MGREC123:9	H2871	'Gainst him, that all deceits could scan, and try:
MGREC~~125:31~~	H2981	Till {'Gainst} all that lov'd *Cassander* was nigh spent; {she was
MGREC125:34	H2984	Digg'd up his brother dead, 'gainst natures right,
MGREC129:32	H3146	Begin to mutter much 'gainst proud *Cassander,*
MGREC~~131:1~~	H3191	The better 'gainst *Cassander* to rebel.
CONTEM174:19	H218	Which 'gainst all adverse winds may serve for fort.

GAL (1) [gall]

HUMOUR30:11	H403	Let me wel make thy precincts, the gal;

GALEN (1)

HUMOUR33:25	H539	*Galen, Hipocrates,* drives {drive} to a set.

GALENISTS (1) [pl.]
ELEMEN12:33 H193 Ye *Galenists,* my Drugs that come from thence
GALES (2) See also GAILES
ELEMEN18:24 H428 And speed you to your Port, with wished gales.
CHILDRN184:30 H19 Till after blown by *Southern* gales,
GALILEE (1)
MASSYR61:34 H339 In *Galilee,* he woful havock makes;
GALL (1) See also GAL
AGES46:11 H442 Hath yet amongst that sweet, some bitter gall.
GALLANT (3)
ELEMEN15:40 H322 Thy gallant rich perfuming Amber-greece:
MASSYR55:20 H86 This gallant dame, unto the *Bactrian* war;
MGREC96:39 H1759 The *Greeks* come {came} on, and with a gallant grace,
GALLANTLY (1)
MPERS88:22 H1415 And brought his Souldiers on so gallantly,
GALLIES (7) [pl.] See also GALLYES
MASSYR64:37 H461 Of costly Ships, and Gallies, she had store,
MPERS76:35 H933 The *Persians* to their Gallies post with speed,
MPERS78:16 H997 Of two and twenty thousand Gallies meet,
MPERS78:25 H1006 Whose Gallies all the rest in neatnesse passe,
MPERS79:14 H1040 Seven thousand Gallies chain'd, by *Tyrians* skil,
MPERS80:21 H1088 And *Xerxes* mighty Gallies batter'd so,
MGREC111:17 H2362 His Gallies stuck upon the sand, {flats} and mud;
GALLY (2)
MPERS76:38 H936 He stayes a landing {lanching} Gally with his hand;
MGREC98:21 H1823 And thirteen thousand Gally slaves he made,
GALLYES (1) [gallies]
MASSYR56:28 H134 Her Camells, Chariots, Gallyes in such number,
GAME (2)
MPERS75:13 H874 But who dare venture such a stake for th' game;
MPERS89:3 H1437 But they too faint, still to pursue their game,
'GAN (2) [began]
AGES38:20 H123 From thence I 'gan to sin, as soon as act.
MGREC117:12 H2619 The Leopard down, his {the} four wings 'gan to rise,
GAOLES (1) [jails]
DIALOG147:22 ~~H247~~ Let Gaoles be fill'd with th' remnant of that pack,
GAPING (1)
ELEMEN14:38 H280 Or else thy sun-burnt face, and gaping chapps;
GARB (1)
MASSYR58:3 H188 Did wear their garb, their gestures imitate,
GARBOYLES (1) [pl.]
MGREC120:33 H2770 In midst of these, *Garboyles,* with wondrous state,
GARDEN (2)
MGREC113:26 H2453 He walking in his Garden, too and fro,
DUBART153:13 H17 Flowers, fruits, in garden, orchard, or in field;
GARDENS (2) [pl.]
ELEMEN11:30 H150 In vine-yards, orchards, gardens, and corne fields,
MASSYR56:20 H126 Her gardens, bridges, arches, mounts, and spires;
GARDNER (1)
SEASONS47:10 H26 The Gardner, now superfluous branches lops,

GARISON (1) [garrison]
MPERS85:15 H1291 Drives out his garison that therein {'mongst them} dwels.
GARLAND (3)
AGES35:29 H15 Upon his head a Garland Nature set:
AGES36:5 H29 Garland of Roses, Pinks, and Gilliflowers,
DUBART154:19 H64 The Oaken garland ought to deck their browes,
GARLANDS (1) [pl.]
MGREC126:37 H3026 With Garlands crown'd his head, bemoan'd his Fates,
GARMENT (1)
MEDDM200:16 Hp279 cumbersome garment, she easily foresees what euents it is
GARMENTS (5) [pl.]
SEASONS46:34 H10 With smiling Sun-shine face, and garments {somewhat} green,
SEASONS48:2 H55 These might as Lace, set out her Garments fine;
SEASONS48:39 H90 With melted tauny face, and garments thinne.
FLESH176:40 H80 My garments are not silk nor gold,
MEDDM200:21 Hp279 Christian, therfore god cuts their garments short, to keep them
GARRISON (1) See also GARISON
MGREC103:16 H2027 Here of his own, he sets a Garrison,
GASPE (1) [gasp]
MGREC105:3 H2096 And leaves him thus, to gaspe out his last breath.
GASTLY (4)
AGES40:35 H214 And gastly death oft threats me with her {his} power,
MASSYR66:4 H510 Was nothing, but such gastly meditation;
DAVID159:5 H20 Sometimes from crimson blood of gastly slaine,
CONTEM170:26 H97 The wretch with gastly face and dreadful mind,
GATES (7) [pl.]
ELEMEN9:9 H43 Set ope those gates, that 'fore so strong was {were} barr'd.
MASSYR56:3 H109 An hundred gates, it had, of mettall strong.
MASSYR59:15 H239 The wals, and gates, their course {hast} did terminate;
MGREC103:2 H2013 With open Gates, the wealthy town did stand,
MGREC131:21 H3213 Now shut their gates in his adversity,
FLESH177:9 H90 The Gates of Pearl, both rich and clear,
MYCHILD217:21 Hp243 y^{t} agst svch a promis, svch tasts of sweetnes ye Gates of Hell
GATH (1)
DAVID158:28 H8 In *Gath,* let not this thing {things} be spoken on,
GATHER (3)
ELEMEN~~10:18~~ H93 Your wisdom out of little gathers {gather} much,
AGES41:33 ~~H249~~ If rich, I'm urged then to gather more.
AGES~~41:36~~ H252 If rich, I'm urged then to gather more,
GATHER'D (1) [gathered]
MPERS88:7 H1400 Was gather'd by the dust that rose from thence:
GATHERED (1)
TDUDLEY166:23 H65 And to his Fathers gathered is in peace.
GATHERS (1)
ELEMEN10:18 H93 Your wisdom out of little gathers {gather} much,
GAUL (1)
HUMOUR32:23 H497 Nor how her Gaul on me she causeless brake;
GAULE (1) [gaul]
PILGRIM210:15 H15 No rugged stones his feet shall gaule
GAULES (1)
ELEMEN12:5 H165 On either side the country of the *Gaules,*

GAVE (37)

ELEMEN11:26 H146 Which none ere gave, nor {or} you could claime of right,
AGES36:26 H50 And al gave eare, to what he had to say.
AGES37:37 H99 Nor unto buzzing whisperors, gave ear.
AGES37:38 H100 I gave no hand, nor vote, for death, or life:
AGES45:18 H400 Who gave the counsel, but the Prince of hell.
MASSYR60:3 H268 To *Bactrians,* he gave their liberty,
MPERS70:2 ~~H673~~ Gave him at once, his life, and Kingdom too,
MPERS~~70:2~~ H673 Gave him his life, and took him for a friend,
MPERS72:22 H770 To whom he gave this in rememberance,
MPERS78:40 H1021 The other four he freely gave away:
MPERS82:5 H1152 No longer dar'd, but fiercely {bravely} on-set gave,
MGREC94:6 H1640 kinsmen puts {put} to death without least {who gave no} cause;
MGREC~~94:18~~ H1654 His little wealth among his Souldiers gave.
MGREC98:23 H1825 The rule of this he to *Philotas* gave,
MGREC~~102:22~~ H1992 And gives {gave} himself to banqueting, and play:
MGREC103:20 H2031 Their charge, {place} gave to his Captains (as most {was} just)
MGREC~~104:41~~ H2093 By throwing Darts, gives {gave} him his mortall wound,
MGREC112:3 H2389 He fourscore *Persian* Ladies also gave;
MGREC112:28 H2414 His Royall pardon gave, for this same thing;
MGREC113:35 H2462 Yet gave his Master the immortall fame;
MGREC118:6 H2653 Because his Master gave to him his Ring,
MGREC122:17 H2842 She knew her birthright gave her *Macedon,*
MGREC123:1 H2863 And government of *Asia* to him gave;
MGREC123:15 H2879 To *Polisperchon,* then his place he gave, {did bequeath}
MGREC123:41 H2905 And for that great gift, which he gave him last;
MGREC124:41 H2948 She gave him poyson formerly ('tis thought)
MGREC126:35 H3024 To Husbands death ('twas {'tis} thought) she gave consent,
MGREC132:2 H3235 He, whom she gave his life, her death must {shall} give)
MROMAN139:29 H3555 Essays I many made but still gave out,
SIDNEY152:7 H78 With high disdain, they said they gave no more,
DUBART153:3 H7 Gave o're the work, before begun withall:
TDUDLEY165:38 H40 High thoughts he gave no harbour in his heart,
TDUDLEY166:5 H47 Gave his in charge, that Jewel rich to prize.
CONTEM169:7 H49 Who gave this bright light luster unto thee:
SICKNES178:19 H2 Since nature gave me breath,
MYCHILD216:16 Hp241 after him gave me many more, of whom I now take ye care,
HOUSE236:26 H18 I blest his Name y^{t} gave + took,

GAVEST (1)

2HUSB233:12 H45 Him whom thov gavest me

GAV'ST (2) [gav'st]

SAMUEL228:6 H7 Thou heardst me then and gav'st him me
REMB236:1 H16 What did I ask but thov gav'st?

GAY (3)

ELEMEN9:35 H70 And trim thee gay {brave}, in green, after thy blacks?
MEDDM196:6 Hp272 of the pea cock that prideing himself in his gay feathers
MEDDM206:2 Hp287 are others that haue nothing to commend them, but only a gay

GAZA (5)

MGREC98:32 H1834 And {now} must at *Gaza, Alexander* meet;
MGREC99:14 H1857 He now to *Gaza* goes, and there doth meet
MGREC99:34 H1877 From *Gaza,* to *Jerusalem* he goes,

MGREC128:25 H3098 His Son at *Gaza* likewise lost the field,
MGREC128:34 H3107 Who at *Gaza* did th' like to him before.

GAZ'D (2) [gazed]
MPERS82:36 H1183 Where he had sometime gaz'd with great delight.
CONTEM168:15 H23 Then higher on the glistering Sun I gaz'd,

GAZING (1)
MASSYR68:9 H595 But dumb the gazing Astrologers stand,

GEDROSIA (1)
MGREC111:29 H2374 From hence he to {then unto} *Gedrosia* went,

GEM (1)
ELEMEN15:34 H316 Was ever gem so rich found in thy trunke?

GEMINIE (1)
SEASONS48:11 H64 The sun now enters, loving *Geminie,*

GEMMES (1) [gems]
ELEMEN13:5 H206 For gemmes, for silver, treasures which I hold:

GENDER (1)
HUMOUR21:11 H39 Our noble selves, in a lesse noble Gender.

GENERAL (3)
HUMOUR29:23 H374 Know, in a General its most pernicious.
MGREC~~115:15~~ H2528 A rueful face in this so general woe;
MGREC~~134:2~~ H3335 By *Scipio* the Roman General;

GENERALL (10)
MPERS78:12 H993 To *Mardonius,* Captain {made their} Generall;
MPERS84:26 H1262 The {This} noble *Greek,* now fit for generall.
MGREC93:32 H1629 The *Greeks* had chose him Captain Generall,
MGREC119:24 H2714 *Antiphilus* the *Athenian* Generall,
MGREC133:24 H3313 {T'} *Emillius* the *Roman* Generall,
MGREC134:15 H3346 Him *Lucullus,* the *Romane* Generall
MROMAN137:35 H3486 Forty three yeares he rul'd with generall praise;
MROMAN138:7 H3497 The *Romans* sore incens'd, their Generall slay,
MROMAN139:6 H3534 A generall Muster takes, which by account,
DIALOG142:1 H30 In generall terms, but will not say wherefore:

GENERALLY (2)
MGREC116:7 H2567 By others thought, and that more generally,
MGREC118:10 H2657 Hoping to be elect more generally;

GENERATION (2)
TDUDLEY166:22 H64 His Generation serv'd his labours cease;
MEDDM204:19 Hp285 generation for takeing veangence on the house of Ahab and

GENTILE (1)
DIALOG148:26 H291 And Jew and Gentile, to one worship go,

GENTLE (3)
ELEMEN~~8:23~~ H21 But {Till gentle} Aire at length, contention so abated,
MPERS74:29 H852 Made wholsome gentle Laws, which pleas'd each mind.
MROMAN137:7 H3458 And this new gentle Government abide:

GENTLY (3)
HUMOUR24:10 H159 And to your weaknesse, gently condescend.
AGES42:9 H267 And gently lead the lambes, as they had need,
SEASONS46:35 ~~H11~~ She gently thus began, like some fair Queen;

GENUINE (1)
HUMOUR27:23 H294 When 'tis untaint, pure, and most genuine

GERMANIE'S (1) [poss.]

DIALOG144:35 H143 I saw sad *Germanie's* dismantled walls.

GESTURE (1) [gesture]

MGREC~~110:18~~ H2320 In looks or gesture not abased ought,

GESTURES (2) [pl.]

MASSYR58:3 H188 Did wear their garb, their gestures imitate,

MGREC106:35 H2169 His manners, habit, gestures, now doth {all did} fashion,

GET (3)

ELEMEN18:32 H436 No place so subtilly made, but I get in.

MGREC~~110:12~~ H2312 Then {When} covertly, the rest gets {get} o're else-where;

CONTEM170:3 H77 To get his bread with pain, and sweat of face:

GETS (7)

MASSYR59:30 H254 But all his wealth, and friends, together gets,

MPERS88:3 H1396 Gets on his armes, arayes himselfe for fight;

MPERS89:36 H1470 Gets them to treat with him in privacy,

MGREC104:33 H2085 *Bessus* gets knowledge, his disloyalty,

MGREC110:12 H2312 Then {When} covertly, the rest gets {get} o're else-where;

MGREC126:2 H2993 Sea passage gets, and lands in *Thessaly;*

MROMAN~~138:38~~ H3528 Next, *Servius Tullius* sits upon {gets into} the Throne,

GETTING (2)

MEDDM195:33 Hp272 Youth is the time of getting middle age of improuing, and old

MYCHILD216:29 Hp242 haue been the times of my greatest Getting and Advantage,

GETTINGS (1) [pl.]

MEDDM209:4 Hp291 therfore wth all our seekings and gettings, let vs aboue all seek

GHASTLY See GASTLY

GHEST (1)

SEASONS~~52:23~~ H238 Now's held, a Guest, {(but ghest)} (but blest) Nativity.

GIANT (1)

MGREC117:18 H2625 Like to that Giant, of his eye bereft;

GIBRALTER (1)

ELEMEN17:11 H375 Untill straight {proud} *Gibralter,* did make them twaine,

GIDEON (1)

DIALOG147:5 H231 O cry: the sword of God, and *Gideon:*

GIFT (6)

HUMOUR31:24 H457 Choler's too rash, this golden gift to hold.

MPERS78:34 H1015 Then gives the King, a King-like gift, most {full} large;

MGREC123:41 H2905 And for that great gift, which he gave him last;

DUBART154:25 H70 If e'r this golden gift was showr'd on any,

CONTEM170:16 H88 On *Abels* gift the fire descends from Skies,

HOUSE237:24 H54 Yet by his Gift is made thine own.

GIFTS (7) [pl.] See also GUIFTS

AGES39:36 H179 My gifts abus'd, my education lost,

AGES~~45:4~~ H386 A royal one by gifts from strangers hands

MGREC107:3 H2178 So heaps up gifts, his credit to redeem;

MEDDM196:8 Hp273 so he that glorys in his gifts and adornings, should look vpon

MEDDM197:16 Hp274 more patiently then he that excells him, both in gifts & graces

MEDDM202:3 Hp281 dispensation of his gifts among the sons of men, betwixt whom

MEDDM207:4 Hp288 The gifts that god, bestows on the sons of men, are not only

GILBO (2)

DAVID158:32 H12 O! *Gilbo* Mounts, let never pearled dew,

DAVID159:14 H29 For valiant *Saul,* who on Mount *Gilbo* lyes;

GILDED (1)
CONTEM167:28 H5 Were gilded o're by his rich golden head.
GILLIFLOWERS (1) [pl.]
AGES36:5 H29 Garland of Roses, Pinks, and Gilliflowers,
GILT (3)
HUMOUR21:41 H69 She loves her sword, only because its gilt;
HUMOUR~~24:40~~ H189 Thou sayst I love my sword, because tis {it's} guilt. {gilt,}
AGES45:14 H396 fly their Country, through their {struck both with gilt and} dread.
'GIN (5) [begin]
SEASONS51:35 H211 We now of Winters sharpness 'gin to taste;
SEASONS~~52:36~~ H251 The Rivers now do {'gin to} ope, and {the} Snows do {to} melt,
MPERS91:21 H1529 The two Queens, by his means, 'gin {seem} to abate
MROMAN137:18 H3469 The *Romans* now more potent 'gin to grow,
HOUSE237:11 H41 Then streight I 'gin my heart to chide,
GIN (2) [snare]
SIDNEY150:2 H27 Found *Cupids* Dame, had never such a Gin;
SIDNEY151:15 ~~H69~~ And *Mars* himself was ta'n by *Venus* gin;
'GINS (3) [begins]
AGES36:8 H32 When blushing first, she 'gins to red {light} the Aire.
SEASONS52:21 H236 From thence he 'gins to length the shortned morn,
MGREC123:22 H2886 Now {Then} *Polisperchon* 'gins to act in's place,
GIRD (1)
SOREFIT221:25 H11 My feeble loines didst gird wth strenght
GIRDS (1) [pl.]
HUMOUR29:13 H366 Thy soothing girds shal fully be repaid;
GIUE (13) [gives]
MEDDM197:24 Hp275 receiued? Come giue an account of thy stewardship.
MEDDM202:35 Hp282 giue, & wch is most strang, the more it receius the more empty
BYNIGHT220:17 H15 What to my Sav^{r}. shall I giue?
SOREFIT221:17 H3 When novght on Earth could comfort giue
SOREFIT221:32 H18 My heart I wholly giue to Thee
FAINT222:15 H5 So shall I giue it thee.
WHAT224:24 H24 Me lasting life shall giue.
13MAY227:15 H24 All I can giue is but thine own
30SEPT227:23 Hp257 then without food. Lord wth y^{y} correction giue Instrvction and
30SEPT227:32 Hp257 yov out of distresse forget not to giue him thankes, but to walk
SAMUEL228:7 H8 Hear me again, I giue him Thee.
11MAYB228:23 Hp259 It hath pleased God to giue me a long Time of respite for these
THEART229:16 H18 For more I cannot giue
GIUEN (2) [given] See also GIV'N
MEDDM202:13 Hp282 among the dead, and no other reason can be giuen of all this
MEDDM207:6 Hp288 they were giuen for, as health wealth and honour, wch might be
GIVE (37) See also GIUE
PROLOG7:38 H48 Give wholsome {Thyme or} Parsley wreath, I aske no Bayes:
ELEMEN17:33 H397 And now give place unto our sister Aire.
ELEMEN18:5 H409 And all the wealth, that ever earth did give,
ELEMEN18:10 H414 His moveing reason is, give least I dye.
HUMOUR22:11 H80 But {Now} let's give, cold, white, Sister Flegme her right.
HUMOUR24:12 H161 Good sisters give me leave (as is my place)
HUMOUR25:13 H202 My ingenuity must give thee right.
HUMOUR26:10 H240 Yet shal with equity give thee thy part,

HUMOUR26:17 H247 If thou giv'st life, I give thee nourishment,
HUMOUR26:19 H249 But I, without thy help can give a growth,
HUMOUR27:9 H280 So wil {shall} I give the dignity to you.
AGES36:30 H54 To childish childhood, give precedency.
AGES39:1 H144 I've done unto my elders I give way.
AGES46:5 H436 That earth can give no consolation sound.
SEASONS47:14 H30 The Pleiades, their influence now give,
SEASONS51:29 H205 There rests, untill the Sun give it a birth:
MPERS92:6 H1564 I can no reason give, cause none I read;
MGREC97:33 H1794 To give his Conquerour, the stile of King;
MGREC98:25 H1827 *Cilcia* he to *Socrates* doth give,
MGREC108:17 H2233 Nor could he reason give, for this great wrong,
MGREC~~109:2~~ H2259 Those that submit, he doth restore {give them rule} again.
MGREC~~110:2~~ H2302 For to receive {To give} him, {welcome} when he comes to
MGREC113:1 H2428 The King would give no eare, but went from thence;
MGREC115:32 H2551 Of larger Provinces, the rule to give,
MGREC120:16 H2751 Was to give way, himself might be undone;
MGREC126:6 H2997 To give her for all cruelties {her cruelty} her dues:
MGREC126:16 H3007 Cassander will not heare {Her foe would give no Ear}, such is
MGREC132:2 H3235 He, whom she gave his life, her death must {shall} give)
SIDNEY150:31 H58 But yet impartiall Death {Fates} this Boone did give,
SIDNEY152:6 H77 To give to their detractor any quill.
CONTEM172:33 H166 To unknown coasts to give a visitation,
SICKNES179:1 H21 O whil'st I live, this grace me give,
1HUSB180:30 H9 Nor ought but love from thee, give recompence.
2LETTER181:33 H3 But stay this once, unto my suit give ear,
CHILDRN186:27 H94 And dead, yet speak, and counsel give:
2HUSB233:7 H40 But Tokens of thy favour Give,
HOURS234:33 H47 But give me Lord a better heart

GIVEN (9) See also GIUEN, GIV'N
AGES35:27 H13 Childhood was cloath'd in white, and given {green} to show,
MASSYR57:19 ~~H166~~ He thus voluptuous, and given to ease;
MGREC108:14 H2230 Without {least} cause, given by {from} them, in deed, or word:
MYCHILD217:18 Hp243 his holy spirit who hath oft given me his word & sett to his Seal
MED223:3 Hp250 should I doubt any more w^{n} thov hast given me such assured
JULY223:32 Hp251 Thou hast given me a pledge of y^{t} Inheritc thou hast promised
11MAYA226:14 Hp255 all this spring till this 11. May, yet hath my God given me many
HOURS234:13 H27 Tho: children thou hast given me
ACK235:15 H15 And hope thov'st given of good successe,

GIVER (1)
HUMOUR26:28 H258 If thou'rt the taker, I must be the giver:

GIVES (14)
HUMOUR30:2 H394 Then he whose brain a touch my humour gives.
HUMOUR33:31 H545 Which life and motion to each Creature gives,
MASSYR64:13 H437 His Vassal is, gives pledges for his truth,
MPERS75:30 H887 Gives sacrifices, wheat, wine, oyle, and salt,
MPERS78:34 H1015 Then gives the King, a King-like gift, most {full} large;
MGREC98:30 H1832 And therefore {So} gives this {his little} Lord-ship to another.
MGREC101:16 H1941 To this, stout *Alexander,* gives no eare,
MGREC102:22 H1992 And gives {gave} himself to banqueting, and play:
MGREC104:41 H2093 By throwing Darts, gives {gave} him his mortall wound,

MGREC108:5 H2221 Who to *Darius* Brother gives the wretch,
MGREC112:1 H2387 Her Sister gives to his *Ephestion* deare,
MGREC126:22 H3013 Gives promise for her life, and {so} wins the day:
MGREC129:36 H3150 {And} Gives *Peloponesus* unto him for {his} hire,
MROMAN138:23 H3513 Then unto death unwillingly gives place.

GIVING (1)
DUBART154:24 H69 In giving one, what would have served seven.

GIV'N (1) [given] See also GIUEN
HUMOUR25:29 H218 How often for the lye, thou'st giv'n the stab.

GIV'ST (1) [givest]
HUMOUR26:17 H247 If thou giv'st life, I give thee nourishment,

GLAD (18)
FATHER5:14 H15 To do their homage unto yours most {full} glad,
HUMOUR34:25 H580 Phrensie's worse, then folly, one would more glad,
AGES45:32 H422 But do awake, {waking glad to hear} at the cocks clanging
SEASONS47:2 ~~H17~~ And now makes glad those blinded Northern wights,
SEASONS~~47:5~~ H20 And now makes glad the darkned northern wights
SEASONS49:17 H108 To wash their {the} thick cloath'd flocks, with pipes ful glad.
MASSYR60:37 H302 Who to be rid of such a guest, was glad;
MASSYR63:27 H412 A Vice-roy from her foe, she's glad t' accept,
MPERS85:24 H1300 The King was glad, with *Sparta* to make peace,
MPERS~~91:9~~ H1517 {Their winnings} lost all, and were a peace {their glad} to
MGREC97:2 H1763 Who from his golden Coach is glad t'alight,
MGREC~~109:5~~ H2264 How to submit their necks at last they're glad.
MGREC129:6 H3120 That in few years he must be forc'd or glad
MGREC129:24 H3138 That he was {is} odious to the world, they'r glad,
DIALOG141:28 H27 Let me lament alone, while thou art glad.
SIDNEY152:12 H81 I to be eas'd of such a task was glad.
MEDDM197:14 Hp274 man, can goe vpright, vnder that door, wher a taller is glad to
SON230:22 H5 My Teares to smiles, my sad to glad

GLADLY (7)
PROLOG7:9 H23 By Art, he gladly found what he did seeke,
ELEMEN16:2 H325 Which *Spaines Americans,* do gladly hold.
ELEMEN18:4 H408 How gladly should his gold purchase his breath,
MASSYR61:23 H328 Gladly doth *Tiglath* this advantage take,
MGREC119:14 H2704 {And gladly would} Shakes {shake} off the yoke, sometimes
DIALOG146:31 H217 Your sunken bowels gladly would refresh:
MEDDM203:23 Hp283 that threatens him wth death, he will gladly entertaine him,

GLANCES (4) [pl.]
SEASONS48:12 H65 And heats us with, the glances of his eye,
SEASONS51:37 H213 So farre remote, his glances warm not us;
SEASONS52:37 H252 And some warm glances from the Sun {his face} are felt,
CONTEM168:26 H33 The Earth reflects her glances in thy face.

GLANCETH (1)
SEASONS~~47:32~~ H47 And with his warmer beams glanceth from thence

GLASS (2)
CHILDRN185:25 H51 Or whilst allur'd with bell and glass,
ANNEB187:26 H16 Like as a bubble, or the brittle glass,

GLASSE (2) [glass]
AGES36:23 H47 In's other hand a glasse, ev'n almost run,
AGES38:40 H143 That wonder tis, my glasse till now doth hold.

GLASSES (1) [pl.]
SEASONS49:34 H127 This Month the Roses are distill'd in Glasses,
GLASSIE (2) [glassy]
HUMOUR34:2 H557 Both {The} watry, glassie, and the christaline.
CONTEM173:4 H172 Eftsoon to *Neptun's* glassie Hall repair
GLAZE (1)
ELEMEN17:20 H384 Mine Ice doth glaze *Europs* big'st Rivers o're,
GLEADS (1) [pl.]
SEASONS48:8 H61 With wings, and beak, defends them from the gleads.
GLIDE (4)
CONTEM172:24 H158 So hand in hand along with thee they glide
CONTEM172:32 H165 Now salt, now fresh where you think best to glide
CONTEM174:13 H212 The Mariner that on smooth waves doth glide,
3LETTER183:29 H31 And like the Mullets in one River glide,
GLIDING (1)
CONTEM172:8 H144 Where gliding streams the Rocks did overwhelm;
GLISTERING (3)
PROLOG8:2 H50 Will make your glistering gold but more to shine.
MGREC~~96:4~~ H1724 The *Persians* clad in silk, and glitt'ring {glistering} gold;
CONTEM168:15 H23 Then higher on the glistering Sun I gaz'd,
GLISTRING (2) [glistering]
AGES39:19 H162 The glistring {glitt'ring} Sword, {the Pistol} and wel advanced
FLESH177:2 H83 More glorious then the glistring Sun;
GLITT'RING (2) [glittering]
AGES~~39:19~~ H162 The glistring {glitt'ring} Sword, {the Pistol} and wel advanced
MGREC96:4 H1724 The *Persians* clad in silk, and glitt'ring {glistering} gold;
GLITTERING (2)
ELEMEN9:37 H71 And birds do sing, to see his glittering Coach.
DUBART153:20 H24 The glittering Plate, and Jewels, he admires,
GLORIES (1) [pl.]
DIALOG141:11 H10 The glories of thy ever famous Realme?
GLORIES (1) v. See also GLORYES
MPERS79:19 H1045 He glories in his Squadrons, and his Horses;
GLORIFIE (1) [glorify]
MEDDM203:35 Hp284 conuersation aright will glorifie him that heard him in the day of
GLORIOUS (10)
HUMOUR24:34 H183 Whose glorious deeds in armes, the world can tel,
MGREC96:12 H1732 With Robes and Crowne, most glorious to behold.
DIALOG144:26 ~~H135~~ Their reverent cheeks, did beare the glorious markes
DIALOG147:31 H255 Out of all mists, such glorious dayes will {shall} bring,
DUBART153:27 H31 Of all the glorious sights his eyes have had:
QELIZ158:3 H112 No more shall rise or set such {so} glorious Sun,
CONTEM169:35 H73 Sees glorious *Adam* there made Lord of all,
FLESH177:2 H83 More glorious then the glistring Sun;
MEDDM206:15 Hp287 from that glorious sun that inlightens all in all, and if some of
PILGRIM210:36 H36 a glorious body it shall rise
GLORIOVS (1) [glorious]
MYSOUL225:4 H8 And gloriovs made ere-long.
GLORY (41) See also GLORY IS
ELEMEN~~11:1~~ H118 And stately *London,* (our great *Britain's* glory)
HUMOUR23:6 H116 But Melancholy, wouldst have this glory thine?

HUMOUR25:36 H225 If murthers be thy glory, tis no lesse.
HUMOUR26:30 H260 For of such glory I shal thee bereave;
HUMOUR29:32 H383 It's no lesse glory to defend a town,
AGES43:24 H319 I glory in my wealth, I have within.
AGES~~45:2~~ H377 I've seen a Prince, the glory of our land
MASSYR55:7 H73 And was both shame, and glory of her sex;
MPERS75:20 H879 Yet o're thy glory we must cast this vaile,
MGREC93:23 H1620 Whose glory to the Earth, this Prince {king} did throw,
MGREC98:18 H1820 Whose glory, now {then} a second time's brought down;
MGREC102:9 H1979 The glory of the Castle he admires,
MGREC102:32 H2002 Where Kings have shown their glory, wealth, and might;
MGREC109:25 H2284 He glory sought, no silver, nor yet {no} gold;
MGREC111:9 H2354 To th' utmost shew'd, the glory of a King;
MGREC112:10 H2396 They were so wrapt with this externall glory.
MGREC120:2 H2733 Nor former liberty, or glory gain'd;
MGREC122:4 H2827 And much eclipse his {great Acts and} glory to rehearse
MROMAN138:34 H3524 Much {Some} state, and glory, {splendor} did this *Priscus* adde:
DIALOG~~148:7~~ H272 There let thy name, thy fame, thy valour {glory} shine,
SIDNEY~~150:3~~ H29 And men of morose minds envy his glory:
SIDNEY150:4 ~~H29~~ And modest Maids, and Wives, blush at thy glory;
DUBART154:11 H56 O *France,* in him thou didst more glory gain,
DUBART155:2 H87 *Here lyes the pearle of* France, Parnassus *glory,*
QELIZ155:18 H9 So great's thy glory, and thine excellence,
QELIZ157:6 H74 She plac'd {built} her glory but on *Babels* walls,
QELIZ157:17 H85 How vanisheth her glory, wealth, and powers;
QELIZ157:19 H87 Instead of glory prov'd her Countries shame:
QELIZ158:20 H129 *In every one, be her great glory famed.*
CONTEM168:3 H13 Sure he is goodness, wisdome, glory, light,
CONTEM169:2 H44 Art thou so full of glory, that no Eye
CONTEM169:6 H48 How full of glory then must thy Creator be?
CONTEM169:21 H61 Seeming to glory in their little Art.
FLESH177:18 H99 For glory doth from God proceed:
2SIMON195:14 Hp271 wth grace heer and crown you wth glory heerafter. that I may
MEDDM200:29 Hp279 shall arise in far more glory, then that wch they lost at their
MYCHILD215:19 Hp240 Truth, not to sett forth my self, but ye Glory of God. If I had
MYCHILD219:4 Hp245 Hon^{r}, + Glory for ever and ever,
FEVER221:6 H21 To Glory t' shall bee brovght.
MYSOUL225:18 H22 Thy Glory I despise,
HOUSE237:19 H49 Wth glory richly furnished

GLORYING (1)
THEART228:35 H1 My thankfull heart wth glorying Tongve

GLORYS (1) [glories, v.]
MEDDM196:8 Hp273 so he that glorys in his gifts and adornings, should look vpon

GLORY'S (1) [glory is]
CONTEM168:18 H26 And softly said, what glory's like to thee?

GLOWING (1)
1LETTER181:23 H21 Within the Cancer of my glowing breast,

GLOZING (1)
AGES40:8 H189 Trusteth my loving looks, and glozing tongue,

GLUTS (1)
MEDDM196:25 Hp273 words are like hony, a little may refresh, but too much gluts the

GLUTTED (1)
MGREC112:6 H2392 Whose Sences all, were glutted with delights:
GNAW See KNAW
GNAWES (1)
AGES43:21 H316 And envy gnawes, if any do surmount.
GO (43) See also GOE
ELEMEN16:9 H332 But I should go beyond thee in thy {my} boasts,
ELEMEN18:6 H410 How freely should it go, so he might live.
ELEMEN18:11 H415 So loath he is to go, though nature's spent,
ELEMEN18:22 H426 Your red hot work, more coldly would go on.
ELEMEN20:8 H490 But dare not go, beyond my Element.
HUMOUR23:4 H114 Of greasie paunch, and palled {bloated} cheeks, go vaunt,
HUMOUR24:27 H176 So walke thee til thou'rt cold, then let thee go.
HUMOUR25:7 H196 Ile go no further then thy nose for test.
AGES38:17 H120 But yet let me relate, before I go,
AGES45:38 H428 Now stiffe and numb, can hardly creep or go.
AGES46:2 H433 I then shal go, whence I shal come no more,
SEASONS49:16 H107 Now go those frolick swaines, the shepheard lad,
SEASONS49:33 H126 Of him that was Shepherd, then King go vaunt.
SEASONS50:3 H137 Now go the Mowers to their slashing toyl,
SEASONS50:17 H151 With Sickles now, the painful {bending} Reapers go,
MASSYR55:35 H101 She for her potency, must go alone.
MASSYR60:5 H270 But suffered, with {their} goods to go elsewhere,
MPERS77:2 H941 Go *Persians,* carry home that angry peece,
MPERS81:3 H1111 With empty hands they to their Master go;
MPERS82:13 H1160 For pitty, let those few to *Xerxes* go,
MPERS83:19 H1207 That the poor {Prince} innocent, to death must {did} go.
MGREC119:22 H2712 For to *Antipater* he now might go,
MGREC127:23 H3053 Because he never would let go {forgoe} his trust:
MGREC129:19 H3133 The life of her must go, and of her son.
MGREC130:11 H3166 To let her go, or hold her still, he fears,
MGREC132:20 H3257 And with his son in law, will needs go fight:
DIALOG146:2 H190 Shews all was done, I'll therefore let it go.
DIALOG147:18 H244 Go on brave *Essex,* shew whose son thou art {with a loyal
DIALOG148:17 H282 This done, with brandish'd swords, to *Turky* go,
DIALOG148:26 H291 And Jew and Gentile, to one worship go,
VANITY160:19 H29 Nor laugh, nor weep, let things go ill or well:
SICKNES178:33 H16 and then we go to th' Tomb.
1LETTER181:25 H23 Where ever, ever stay, and go not thence,
ANNEB187:31 H21 But yet a while, and I shall go to thee;
1SIMON188:14 H15 Go pretty babe, go rest with Sisters twain
1SIMON188:14 H15 Go pretty babe, go rest with Sisters twain
MERCY189:4 H25 And then her sorrows all at once did go;
MEDDM201:4 Hp280 they go vpright vnder them, but it matters not whether the load
MEDDM202:26 Hp282 we may go forwards to the Citty of habitation, but when he
MEDDM205:19 Hp286 would haue boldnes to go to the throne of grace to be
MEDDM208:25 Hp290 wells in the time of drought, that those that go to finde water in
MEDDM209:1 Hp291 wrestled wth god face to face in penvel Let me go, sath that
MEDDM209:2 Hp291 will not let thee go replys Jacob till thou blesse me, faith is not
GOADS (1)
MEDDM201:25 Hp281 words of the wise (sath Solom) are as nailes, and as goads,

GOATE (1) [goat]
ELEMEN10:10 H85 The Bear, the Goate, the Raven, and the Eagle,
GOBRIAS (2)
MPERS76:14 H912 But wise *Gobrias* reads not half so farre:
MPERS78:13 H994 He was the Son of the fore-nam'd *Gobrias,*
GOD (100)
AGES36:18 H42 His golden god in's purse, which was his charm.
MASSYR53:32 H22 Whom succeeding times a god did call:
MASSYR54:6 H33 Alive, and dead, a god they did him make;
MASSYR54:11 H38 This is *Belzebub,* god of *Ekronites,*
MASSYR54:26 H53 This *Ninus* for a god, his father canoniz'd,
MPERS71:25 H739 But {For} he would be profest god of their Weal;
MPERS74:15 H838 A thousand times, God save {long live} the King, they cry,
MGREC100:6 H1890 For to be call'd {install'd} a god, was his intent;
MGREC109:8 H2267 Nor had that drunken god, one that {who} would take
MGREC114:21 H2491 In his esteem, a God he could not be,
MGREC117:2 H2609 A God alive him all must Idolize;
MGREC131:3 H3193 Not like a King, but like some God they fain'd;
MROMAN137:36 H3487 Accounted for some {a} god in after dayes.
DIALOG147:5 H231 O cry: the sword of God, and *Gideon:*
TDUDLEY165:35 H37 My Fathers God, be God of me and mine.
TDUDLEY165:35 H37 My Fathers God, be God of me and mine.
FLESH177:18 H99 For glory doth from God proceed:
SICKNES178:24 H7 For Adams sake, this word God spake
BIRTH180:6 H16 What nature would, God grant to yours and you;
MEDDM197:20 Hp275 temple for the spirit of god to dwell in
MEDDM197:32 Hp275 is not fit for bread, god so deales wth his servants, he grindes
MEDDM198:2 Hp275 God hath sutable comforts and supports for his children
MEDDM198:33 Hp277 it, the pure in heart shall se god, but the defiled in conscience
MEDDM199:11 Hp277 till it be throughly heat is vncapable to be wrought, so god sees
MEDDM200:3 Hp278 not a little one? will ere long say of a greater Tush god regards
MEDDM200:8 Hp279 bitter together so is it wth some Christians, let god imbitter all
MEDDM200:11 Hp279 brests, that god is forced to hedg vp their way wth thornes
MEDDM200:18 Hp279 will the alwise god proportion his dispensations according to
MEDDM200:21 Hp279 Christian, therfore god cuts their garments short, to keep them
MEDDM201:1 Hp280 he will proportion the load, as god hath his little Children so
MEDDM201:5 Hp280 more or lesse if god afford his help
MEDDM202:23 Hp282 till he arise againe, so god doth somtime vaile his face but for
MEDDM202:29 Hp282 god, and when ye morning (wch is the appointed time) is come
MEDDM204:5 Hp284 and he that hath deliuered mee saith paul, will deliuer me, god
MEDDM204:17 Hp285 god doth many times, both reward and punish for one and y^{e}
MEDDM204:20 Hp285 while (sath god) and I will avenge the blood of Jezerel vpon
MEDDM204:22 Hp285 wch should warn him, that doth any speciall seruice for god, to
MEDDM205:24 Hp286 himself alway in the awefull presence of god, the consideration
MEDDM205:27 Hp286 god and vs, or else we should not so often faile in our whole
MEDDM206:20 Hp287 themselues of turning to god, the first thing wch they eye, is
MEDDM206:27 Hp288 All the works and doings of god are wonderfull, but none more
MEDDM206:31 Hp288 Souerainty of god, who will not be tyed to time nor place, nor
MEDDM206:36 Hp288 they abide not in vnbeleif, god is able to grafte them in, the
MEDDM207:1 Hp288 god and say how vnsearchable are his wayes and his footsteps
MEDDM207:4 Hp288 The gifts that god, bestows on the sons of men, are not only

MEDDM207:7 Hp288 steps to draw men to god in consideration of his bounty
MEDDM208:14 Hp290 Commends vs to god, for by his ballance we must be weighed,
MEDDM208:34 Hp290 intercedes for the people, god sath to him Let me alone, that I
MEDDM208:36 Hp291 lasting armes of the mighty god of Jacob yea Jacob himself
MEDDM209:1 Hp291 wrestled wth god face to face in penvel Let me go, sath that
MEDDM209:13 Hp291 to the Command of god, and endeavour not to the vtmost to
MEDDM209:18 Hp291 god hath by his prouidence so ordered, that no one Covntry
MEDDM209:25 Hp291 below, as also that god will haue vs beholden one to another
TOCHILD215:7 H7 And God shall blesse yov from above.
MYCHILD215:19 Hp240 Truth, not to sett forth my self, but ye Glory of God. If I had
MYCHILD215:28 Hp241 it vnto God. I was also troubled at ye neglect of private Dutyes
MYCHILD216:2 Hp241 & sitting loose from God, vanity & ye follyes of Youth take hold
MYCHILD216:9 Hp241 my heart rose, But after I was convinced it was ye way of God,
MYCHILD216:14 Hp241 pleased God to keep me a long time wthout a child wch was a
MYCHILD216:34 Hp242 some sin I lay vnder wch God would haue reformed, or some
MYCHILD217:1 Hp242 If at any time yov are chastened of God take it as Thankfully
MYCHILD217:6 Hp242 walking after I haue been afflicted. I haue been wth God like
MYCHILD217:16 Hp243 and refreshing wch I supposed most of the servants of God
MYCHILD217:28 Hp243 were it hell it self and could there find ye Love of God toward
MYCHILD217:30 Hp243 ye Love of God, it would haue been a Hell to me for in Truth it
MYCHILD217:31 Hp243 absence and presence of God y^t makes Heaven or Hell.
MYCHILD217:34 Hp243 God, I never saw any miracles to confirm me, and those wch I
MYCHILD217:35 Hp243 know but they were feigned. That there is a God my Reason
MYCHILD218:5 Hp243 such a God as I worship in Trinity, + such a Sav^r as I rely
MYCHILD218:6 Hp244 thovsands of Times been svggested to me, yet God hath
MYCHILD218:7 Hp244 me over. I haue argved thvs wth my self, That there is a God I
MYCHILD218:8 Hp244 If ever this God hath revealed himself it mvst bee in his word,
MYCHILD218:16 Hp244 but God himself?
MYCHILD218:18 Hp244 that admitt this bee ye true God whom wee worship, and y^t bee
MYCHILD218:20 Hp244 same God, the same Christ, ye same word, They only
MYCHILD219:3 Hp245 Now to ye King Imortall, Eternall invisible, the only wise God,
FEVER221:11 H26 O praises to my mighty God
SOREFIT221:28 H14 What shall I render to my God
MED223:8 Hp250 father, vnto my God and your God—But least this should not
MED223:14 Hp250 that God who hath done so much for me, should haue so little
JULY223:24 Hp251 but my God who never failed me, was not absent but helped
JULY223:31 Hp251 for thov art my God, Thou hast said and shall not I beleiue it?
WHAT224:1 H1 What God is like to him I serve
WHAT224:13 H13 My God he is not like to y^rs
MYSOUL224:25 H1 My Soul rejoice thou in thy God
MYSOUL225:20 H24 For God hath made me wise.
28AUG225:29 Hp254 my Soul that this condition y^t I am in is ye best for me, for god
11MAYA226:14 Hp255 all this spring till this 11. May, yet hath my God given me many
11MAYA226:20 Hp255 ye will of God it should bee thus. Who am I y^t I should repine
13MAY227:8 H17 Who is a God so wondrous great.
30SEPT227:18 Hp257 It pleased god to viset me wth my old Distemper of weaknes
30SEPT227:30 Hp257 haue recourse to ye same God who hath heard + deliuered
SAMUEL228:2 H3 Thou mighty God of Sea and Land
11MAYB228:23 Hp259 It hath pleased God to giue me a long Time of respite for these
RESTOR229:30 H13 The Goodnes of Thy God,
2HUSB232:15 H16 Vphold my heart in Thee O God

HOURS233:24 H7 Thou hetherto hast been my God
HOURS234:5 H19 O stay my heart on thee my God
HOUSE236:20 H12 And to my God my heart did cry

GODDESSE (1)

MROMAN137:33 H3484 Goddesse *Ægeria* this to him told,

GOD-HEAD (2)

MGREC114:4 H2472 Then's Masters god-head, to defie, and wrong;
MGREC115:12 H2521 This act (me thinks) his god-head should ashame;

GODLY (2)

AGES44:20 H353 He that in youth is godly, wise, and sage,
MEDDM206:33 Hp288 it should alsoe teach the children of godly parents to walk wth

GODS (20) [pl.] See also DEMI-GODS, DEMY GODS

MASSYR62:35 H380 On *Hena's, {Hevahs* and on *Sepharuaim's* gods,
MASSYR67:35 H581 Did praise his gods of mettall, wood, and stone,
MPERS71:38 H752 But he that 'fore the gods, himself preferrs,
MPERS71:40 ~~H753~~ And though no gods, if he esteem them some,
MGREC96:13 H1733 And o're his head, his golden gods on high;
MGREC100:41 H1925 He prayes the immortall gods, for to {they would} reward
MGREC105:34 H2127 Praying the immortall gods, that Sea, and Land,
MGREC106:2 ~~H2136~~ Wherefore the gods requite thy kinde regard.
MGREC106:6 H2140 Though gods on earth, like Sons of men shall {they} dye.
MGREC106:30 H2164 His fancied gods, above the firmament,
MROMAN137:21 H3472 Some faining say, to heav'n {to the Gods} he did ascend;
WHAT224:10 H10 And heathen to your Gods

GODS (8) [poss.]

MEDDM196:16 Hp273 christian that hath wrought hard in gods vine yard and hath
MEDDM202:2 Hp281 There is nothing admits of more admiration, then gods various
MEDDM204:10 Hp284 wthall, the larger his accounts stands vpon gods score it
MEDDM205:34 Hp286 them are dry stocks so is it in the church wch is gods orchard,
MYCHILD215:22 Hp240 I will observe shall bee this—I will begin wth Gods dealing
MYCHILD216:20 Hp241 Among all my experiences of gods gratious Dealings wth me I
MYCHILD216:26 Hp242 somt. on my soul in Doubts & feares of Gods displeasure, and
MYCHILD217:10 Hp242 I haue had great xper^{c} of Gods hearing my prayers, and

GOE (19) [go]

ELEMEN12:17 H177 Ile here let goe, my Lions of *Numedia,*
MPERS80:1 H1068 How part, {some} might o're the Mountains goe about,
MPERS~~90:31~~ H1498 {Their King} *Agesilus* himself doth over-goe {goe};
MGREC97:38 H1799 Now {Next} *Alexander* unto *Tyre* doth goe,
MGREC110:21 H2325 East-ward, now *Alexander* would goe still,
MGREC120:14 H2749 For's Souldiers 'gainst those Captains would not goe;
MGREC120:15 H2750 To suffer them goe on, as they begun,
MGREC120:21 H2758 Desires the King, to goe to *Macedon,*
MGREC121:1 H2779 ('Gainst which to goe, is troubled in his minde;)
MGREC132:35 H3282 Must needs goe try their fortune, and their might,
FLESH175:13 H13 Regardlesly to let earth goe?
FLESH175:36 H36 Then let not goe, what thou maist find,
MEDDM197:14 Hp274 A low man, can goe vpright, vnder that door, wher a taller is
MEDDM198:6 Hp276 billows goe ouer their heads he then leads them to the Rock
MEDDM204:14 Hp284 Sin and shame euer goe together He that would be freed from
MEDDM205:3 Hp285 of discipline goe often ouer them, before they bee fit soile, to
MEDDM208:6 Hp289 brands of a fire, if once severed, will of themselues goe out

WHAT224:9 H9 Goe Worldlings to your Vanities
SAMUEL228:18 H19 If otherwise I goe to Rest

GOEING (2) [going]
SAMUEL228:1 H1-2 Vpon my Son Samuel his goeing for England Novem. 6. 1657.
2HUSB232:1 H1-2 Vpon my dear & loving husband his goeing into

GOES (36)
SEASONS47:6 H22 Now goes the Plow-man to his merry toyl,
MASSYR66:22 H528 Where e're he goes, he Conquers every Land;
MPERS70:26 H697 Long after this, he 'gainst the *Sythians* goes,
MPERS75:1 H862 And with a faithfull fraud to' th' town he goes,
MPERS79:30 H1056 But *Xerxes* resolute, to *Thrace* goes first,
MPERS82:41 H1188 With loaden heart unto the King he goes,
MPERS86:40 H1356 With posting speed {on} towards the King he goes;
MPERS87:9 H1365 But as he goes, his Forces still augments,
MGREC94:18 H1652 Then with alacrity he after goes:
MGREC95:25 H1704 Goes {Runs} after too {two}, and leaves all to disaster.
MGREC95:30 H1709 And on {Then o're} he goes *Darius* {now} so to meet;
MGREC98:27 H1829 For that which easily comes, as freely goes;
MGREC99:14 H1857 He now to *Gaza* goes, and there doth meet
MGREC99:34 H1877 From *Gaza,* to *Jerusalem* he goes,
MGREC100:11 H1895 Now {Thence} back to *Ægypt* goes, and in few dayes,
MGREC100:15 H1899 Unto *Euphrates* marcht, and over goes,
MGREC102:5 H1975 This Conquerour now {then} goes to *Babylon,*
MGREC102:27 H1997 He then to *Sushan* goes, with his fresh {new} bands,
MGREC102:39 H2009 From *Sushan,* to *Persapolis* he goes,
MGREC104:27 H2079 And thus to {t'ward} *Alexander,* on he goes,
MGREC105:18 H2111 To them he goes, and {repairs then} looking in the Cart,
MGREC106:7 H2141 Now to the East great *Alexander* goes,
MGREC108:27 H2243 From hence he to *Jaxartis* river goes,
MGREC109:6 H2265 He t' *Nisa* goes, by *Bacchus* built long since,
MGREC115:4 H2515 Now *Alexander* goes to *Media,*
MGREC119:34 H2724 Now to *Antipater, Craterus* goes,
MGREC120:28 H2765 Goes to *Antipater,* and tels what's done;
MGREC121:6 H2784 And with his Army into {unto} *Ægypt* goes,
MGREC123:39 H2903 Goes to *Antigonus,* and both implore,
MGREC124:11 H2918 *Cassander* with his Hoast to *Grecia* goes,
MGREC125:6 H2954 For ayde {she} goes to *Epire,* among her friends,
MGREC125:41 H2991 So goes to finde this {cruel} Queen in *Macedon;*
MGREC128:28 H3101 Still gaining Countries East-ward goes he on.
MGREC131:2 H3192 To *Athens* then he {*Demetrius* thether} goes, is entertain'd,
CONTEM170:18 H90 With sullen hateful looks he goes his wayes.
CONTEM170:35 H105 A Vagabond to Land of *Nod* he goes,

GOG (1)
DIALOG148:20 H285 And do to *Gog,* as thou hast done to *Rome.*

GOING (1) See also GOEING
MEDDM206:24 Hp287 for it, shall meet with miserable disapointment, going away

GOLD (41)
PROLOG8:2 H50 Will make your glistering gold but more to shine.
ELEMEN13:4 H205 Ye greedy misers who do dig for gold;
ELEMEN13:36 H237 Again, when Delvers dare in hope of gold,
ELEMEN15:25 H307 Shouldst thou but buy, it would exhaust thy gold.

ELEMEN16:1	H324	With rowling graines of purest massy gold:
ELEMEN18:4	H408	How gladly should his gold purchase his breath,
AGES41:22	~~H239~~	And then a world of drosse among my gold.
AGES43:15	~~H307~~	Then heapt up gold, and riches as the clay;
AGES44:12	H345	It's not my valour, honour, nor my gold,
MASSYR60:30	H295	He thus inricht, by this new tryed gold,
MASSYR64:1	H425	This was of Monarchies that head of gold,
MASSYR68:6	H592	With guifts of Scarlet robe, and Chaines {Chain} of gold,
MPERS75:15	H876	Who doth deserve a Statue made of gold;
MPERS78:35	H1016	Three thousand Tallents of the purest gold;
MPERS84:2	H1230	With gold and silver beds, most gorgiously.
MPERS~~84:12~~	H1243	With gold and silver, and what ere they need:
MGREC95:15	H1694	Whose touch turn'd all to gold, yea even his meat:
MGREC96:4	H1724	The *Persians* clad in silk, and glitt'ring {glistering} gold;
MGREC96:11	H1731	The King sat in a chariot made of gold,
MGREC96:29	H1749	Now least this Gold, and all this goodly stuffe,
MGREC96:32	H1752	Loaden with gold, with jewels and with Plate,
MGREC96:36	H1756	That valour was more worth than Pearls, or gold,
MGREC102:11	H1981	In this a masse {world} of gold, and treasure lay,
MGREC102:36	H2006	Those beds of gold, and couches of delight,
MGREC103:12	H2023	Statues of {some} gold, and silver numberlesse,
MGREC104:25	H2077	Then draws the Cart along, with chaines of gold;
MGREC109:25	H2284	He glory sought, no silver, nor yet {no} gold;
MGREC111:6	H2351	These, all he feasts in state, on beds of gold,
MGREC112:13	H2399	To every Guest, a cup of gold he sends,
MGREC135:20	H3392	The first, was likened to a head of gold,
MGREC135:26	H3398	Then gold, silver, brasse, iron, and all that {the} store,
SIDNEY150:20	H45	Engrave on Marble, in characters of Gold,
QELIZ156:41	H68	Her *Drake* came laded home with *Spanish* gold,
DAVID159:17	H32	On your array put ornaments of gold,
VANITY160:31	H41	With pearl and gold it shall not valued be:
CONTEM174:34	H231	Nor wit nor gold, nor buildings scape times rust;
FLESH175:32	H32	Earth hath more silver, pearls and gold,
FLESH176:40	H80	My garments are not silk nor gold,
FLESH177:3	H84	My Crown not Diamonds, Pearls, and gold,
FLESH177:11	H92	The Streets thereof transparent gold,
1HUSB180:27	H6	I prize thy love more then whole Mines of gold,

GOLDEN (15)

ELEMEN16:7	H330	The *Ponticke, {Aegean} Caspian,* Golden Rivers fine. {five,}
HUMOUR31:24	H457	Choler's too rash, this golden gift to hold.
HUMOUR35:9	H605	A golden Ring, the Posey, *Unity:*
AGES36:18	H42	His golden god in's purse, which was his charm.
AGES45:41	H431	My golden Bowl, and silver Cord, e're long,
SEASONS52:34	H249	In *Pisces* now the golden Sun doth shine,
MASSYR53:19	H9	This was the Golden Age, but after came
MPERS84:3	H1231	The royall wine, in golden cups doth {did} passe,
MGREC96:13	H1733	And o're his head, his golden gods on high;
MGREC96:21	H1741	Their golden Ornaments so {how} to set forth,
MGREC97:2	H1763	Who from his golden Coach is glad t'alight,
MGREC103:11	H2022	And taken mony, plate, and golden treasure;
MGREC109:22	H2281	Presents himselfe, {first} there with a golden Crowne,

DUBART154:25 H70 If e'r this golden gift was showr'd on any,
CONTEM167:28 H5 Were gilded o're by his rich golden head.

GOMORAHS (1) [poss.]

MASSYR57:14 H161 Who warr'd with *Sodoms,* and *Gomorahs* King,

GONE (42)

ELEMEN15:1 H283 When I am gone, their fiercenesse none need {needs} doubt;
ELEMEN18:21 H425 Ye forging Smiths, if Bellowes once were gone;
AGES37:3 H65 A nothing, here to day, but {and} gone to morrow.
AGES40:9 H190 Until her freinds, treasure, and honour's gone.
AGES40:11 H192 Until mine own be gone, my wit, and wealth;
SEASONS50:33 H167 Until his head be gray, and strength be gone,
MASSYR55:4 H70 This great oppressing *Ninus* dead, and gone,
MASSYR57:11 H158 He sought no rule, til she was gone, and dead;
MASSYR60:25 H290 And those which {that} seem'd with *Sardanapal's* gone;
MPERS86:17 H1333 His brothers little love, like to be gone,
MPERS~~91:35~~ H1549 Succeeds in th' throne his father being gone.
MGREC103:37 H2048 Who was retir'd, and gone to {as far as} *Media.*
MGREC105:32 H2125 To's Mother, Children deare, and Wife now gone,
MGREC114:14 H2484 And would have slaine himself, for *Clitus* gone,
MGREC122:29 H2848 He wearied out, at last, would needs be gone,
MGREC132:7 H3242 Thus *Philips,* and *Cassander's* race is {both} gone,
MROMAN138:15 H3505 Nephew unto *Pomphilius* dead, and gone;
DIALOG145:27 H176 Had they not held law fast, all had been gone,
DIALOG147:27 H251 When they are gone, then drown your self in teares.
SIDNEY151:4 ~~H69~~ But thou art gone, such Meteors never last,
QELIZ157:33 H101 Or had they some, but with our Queen ist gone?
CONTEM169:28 H67 It makes things gone perpetually to last,
CONTEM174:36 H233 Shall last and shine when all of these are gone.
SICKNES178:36 H19 No sooner blown, but dead and gone,
1LETTER181:10 H8 My sun is gone so far in's Zodiack,
1LETTER181:19 H17 O strange effect! now thou art *Southward* gone,
2LETTER181:31 H1 *Phoebus* make haste, the day's too long, be gone,
3LETTER183:12 H14 Bewail my turtle true, who now is gone,
3LETTER183:19 H21 Mine being gone, I lead a joyless life,
3LETTER183:26 H28 The substance gone, O me, these are but dreams.
CHILDRN185:9 H35 My fifth, whose down is yet scarce gone
CHILDRN186:26 H93 Thus gone, amongst you I may live,
ANNEB187:25 H15 That's here to day, perhaps gone in an hour;
1SIMON188:4 H5 No sooner come, but gone, and fal'n asleep,
MERCY188:20 H6 And live I still to see Relations gone,
MERCY189:1 H22 Thou being gone, she longer could not be,
MEDDM202:27 Hp282 set and be quite gone out of sight then must we needs walk in
PILGRIM210:33 H33 And when a few yeares shall be gone
TOCHILD215:4 H4 That being gone, here yov may find
MYCHILD216:31 Hp242 Then haue I gone to searching, and haue said wth David Lord
13MAY227:1 H10 My winters past my stormes are gone
HOURS234:1 H15 Tho: husband dear bee from me gone

GOOD (86)

FATHER5:24 H25 The world, the usefull, hurtfull, and the good:
FATHER5:28 H29 My first do shew, their good, and then their rage,
ELEMEN8:7 ~~H5~~ Who the most good could shew, & who most rage

ELEMEN9:33	H67	Good {Cold} sister Earth, no witnesse needs but thine;
ELEMEN16:25	H348	Alas; thy ships and oares could do no good
ELEMEN17:25	H389	That in two hundred year, it ne'r prov'd good.
HUMOUR20:12	H4	Ceasing to vaunt, their good, or threat their force.
HUMOUR23:5	H115	But a good head from these are disonant;
HUMOUR23:41	~~H149~~	They coole my heat, and so repay my good.
HUMOUR24:12	H161	Good sisters give me leave (as is my place)
HUMOUR25:4	H193	Thy rudenesse counts, good manners vanity,
HUMOUR25:39	H228	For Countries good, thy life thou darst expose:
HUMOUR34:7	H562	O! good, O bad, O true, O traiterous eyes!
HUMOUR34:40	H595	A warning good, hereafter i'le say lesse.
AGES36:14	H38	As one that cared, for a good report.
AGES36:36	H60	Both good and bad, but yet no more then's true.
AGES39:21	H164	Nor wait til good advice {success} our hopes do crown;
AGES41:19	H238	Now age is more, more good ye do {may} expect;
AGES42:5	H263	To chear the good, and wicked to deface.
AGES43:25	H320	Thus good, and bad, and what I am, you see,
AGES45:22	~~H404~~	But out of troubles, ye may see much good,
AGES~~45:22~~	H410	But out of evill you may see much good.
SEASONS50:31	H165	Like good Old Age, whose younger juycie roots,
SEASONS51:4	H178	For nought's so good, but it may be abused,
SEASONS52:7	H222	This time warm cloaths, ful diet, and good fires,
MASSYR54:29	H56	Where e're he warr'd he had too good successe,
MASSYR62:15	H360	On whom, nor threats, nor mercies could do good;
MPERS~~70:16~~	H687	Here twenty yeares provision {good} he found,
MPERS70:33	H704	Using such taunting words as she thought good.
MPERS71:36	H750	If all his {this} heat, had been for a good {pious} end,
MPERS72:37	H781	Ruling as they thought good, {best} under his head.
MPERS74:27	H850	Three strings to's bow, the least of which is good;
MPERS74:38	H859	Then brave *Zopirus,* for his Masters good,
MPERS~~79:3~~	H1025	'Twixt which his souldiers marcht in good array.
MPERS~~84:12~~	H1241	Good *Ezra* in the seventh year of his reign,
MPERS85:34	H1310	*Persian* Kings, did deem {then deem'd} themselves so good,
MPERS88:13	H1406	And all good discipline to be neglected.
MPERS91:32	~~H1546~~	He was the Master of good *Nehemie*
MPERS~~91:32~~	H1546	A King nor good, nor valiant, wise nor just
MGREC94:23	H1661	He offer'd, and for good successe did pray
MGREC94:26	H1664	To scorn at him, *Darius* had good sport:
MGREC96:28	H1748	And as much good she did, as any other.
MGREC99:38	H1881	The Priest shews him good *Daniels* Prophesie,
MGREC101:1	H1926	Great *Alexander,* for this good regard;
MGREC102:34	H2004	And of good *Mordecai,* her Kinsman dear;
MGREC105:40	H2133	Of all good things (quoth he) once in my power,
MGREC109:41	H2300	And there {by force} his Soveraignty for to make good;
MGREC119:11	H2701	That if he came, good welcome he should find:
MGREC126:32	H3023	But Royalty no good conditions brings;
MGREC127:18	H3048	In divers battels, he had good successe,
MGREC~~136:17~~	H3431	*What e're is found amisse, take in best {good} part,*
DIALOG146:26	H212	And recompence me {that} good, for all my ill {I've done to
DIALOG~~146:32~~	H219	Out of your troubles much good fruit to be;
DIALOG146:34	H220	To see these {those} latter dayes of hop'd for good,

DIALOG146:40 H226 Blest be thy Commons, who for Common good,
SIDNEY150:36 H63 Of this our noble *Scipio* some good word?
DUBART153:39 H43 Valour in War, in Peace good Husbandry.
DUBART154:40 H85 Good will, not skill, did cause me bring my mite.
QELIZ156:3 H30 Who was so good, so just, so learn'd, so wise,
QELIZ156:32 H59 Nor men, nor coyne she spar'd, to doe them good;
TDUDLEY166:40 H82 *A Prizer of good Company*
TDUDLEY167:2 H84 *The Good him lov'd, the bad did fear,*
CONTEM170:20 H92 Upon whose blood his future good he hopes to raise.
CONTEM173:21 H187 To gain more good, or shun what might thee harm
SICKNES179:2 H22 I doing good may be.
CHILDRN186:24 H91 Taught what was good, and what was ill,
1SIMON188:7 H8 Cropt by th' Almighties hand; yet is he good,
MEDDM195:24 Hp272 no obiect that we see. no action that we doe, no good that we
MEDDM199:2 Hp277 Wisedom with an inheritance is good, but wisedome without an
MEDDM199:12 Hp277 good to cast some men into the furnace of affliction and then
MEDDM199:28 Hp278 first kill the body, the last the good name the two former leaue
MEDDM203:7 Hp283 he haue good cause often to repeat that sentence, vanity of
MEDDM205:5 Hp285 nurture they are brought into a fit capacity, let the seed of good
MEDDM205:26 Hp286 quicken on to good dutys, we certainly dream of some
MEDDM205:35 Hp287 some eminent Christians, that are soe frequent in good dutys,
MEDDM206:29 Hp288 how many good parents haue had bad children, and againe
MEDDM208:4 Hp289 good conversation
MEDDM208:12 Hp290 A good name, is as a precious oyntment, and it is a great
MEDDM208:13 Hp290 to haue a good repute among good men, yet it is not that, w^{ch}
MEDDM208:13 Hp290 to haue a good repute among good men, yet it is not that, w^{ch}
MYCHILD216:13 Hp241 me & doe me Good: and it was not altogether ineffectuall. It
BYNIGHT220:12 H11 My hungry Soul fill'd wth Good,
13MAY227:10 H19 Thvs pleasant fair and good,
RESTOR230:3 H18 And 'twixt ye good and evill way
2HUSB232:32 H33 Lord gravnt thov good Successe
ACK235:15 H15 And hope thov'st given of good successe,

GOODLY (16)

ELEMEN13:6 H207 Will not my goodly face, your rage suffice?
HUMOUR23:11 H121 Yet hast thy {the} seat assign'd, a goodly part,
AGES39:4 H147 My goodly cloathing, and my beauteous skin,
AGES44:16 H349 It's not my goodly house {state}, nor bed of down,
AGES45:16 H398 The desolation, of a goodly State.
SEASONS50:32 H166 Hath stil ascended up in {to bear} goodly Fruits,
SEASONS51:17 H191 But trees with goodly fruits replenished;
MPERS79:22 H1048 But yet this goodly sight {from him} produced teares,
MGREC94:20 H1658 To these {which} were joyn'd, five thousand goodly horse.
MGREC96:3 H1723 Oh {Sure} 'twas a goodly sight, there to behold;
MGREC96:29 H1749 Now least this Gold, and all this goodly stuffe,
MGREC103:29 H2040 Commands to set this goodly town on fire.
MGREC~~107:12~~ H2187 Which done, sets fire upon those costly {goodly} spoyls
MGREC108:36 H2252 A goodly City doth compleatly raise;
MGREC111:32 H2377 Now through these goodly countries as he past,
CONTEM172:7 H143 Close sate I by a goodly Rivers side,

GOODNES (7) [goodness]

MYCHILD217:13 Hp242 becavse I have fovnd my heart through his goodnes enlarged

JULY223:30 Hp251 O Lord let me neuer forgett thy Goodnes, nor question thy
11MAYB228:29 Hp259 in his goodnes, and to hear my prayers, and to deliuer me out
THEART229:8 H10 Thy Goodnes let me Tell,
RESTOR229:30 H13 The Goodnes of Thy God,
2HUSB232:30 H31 Thy Goodnes never failes.
HOURS234:28 H42 Of all thy Goodnes past.

GOODNESS (1)
CONTEM168:3 H13 Sure he is goodness, wisdome, glory, light,

GOODS (4) [pl.]
FATHER6:5 H39 My goods are true (though poor) I love no stealth,
ELEMEN16:28 H351 Transfers his goods, from North and South and East;
MASSYR60:5 H270 But suffered, with {their} goods to go elsewhere,
HOUSE236:27 H19 That layd my goods now in ye dvst

GOODWILL (1)
SIDNEY151:32 ~~H75~~ Goodwill, did make my head-long pen to run,

GOOS-BERRY (1)
SEASONS49:36 H129 The Cherry, Goos-berry, is {are} now i'th prime,

GORDIUM (1)
MGREC95:13 H1692 And easily takes old *Gordium* in his way;

GORGEOUS (1)
AGES36:1 H25 Next, youth came up, in gorgeous attire;

GORGIOUSLY (1)
MPERS84:2 H1230 With gold and silver beds, most gorgiously.

GORGONS (1) [pl.]
MPERS88:33 H1426 Nor *Gorgons* {head} like to this, transform'd to stones.

GOSPEL (2)
DIALOG143:32 H101 The Gospel is trod {troden} down, and hath no right;
DIALOG145:35 H184 This must be done by Gospel, not by law.

GOSPELL (1)
DIALOG146:13 ~~H200~~ Religion, Gospell, here lies at the stake,

GOT (18)
ELEMEN12:37 H197 But Marriners, where got you ships and sailes?
MASSYR60:19 H284 Til *Mesopotamia* he got in's hands,
MASSYR61:7 H312 He left his new got Kingdoms to his Son.
MASSYR66:14 H520 No, nor {not} when *Moab, Edom* he had got.
MPERS~~84:12~~ H1248 And o're his opposites still got the day,
MPERS88:18 H1411 So had he been, and got the victory,
MGREC~~108:10~~ H2226 Wherein their own had {got the} soveraignity.
MGREC108:23 H2239 Repelling these two marks of honour got,
MGREC117:4 H2611 Of all those kingdomes large which he had got,
MGREC118:31 H2680 Him {And} by a wile he got within his power,
MGREC121:27 H2809 That *Eumenes* got of the other three,
MGREC124:14 H2921 And his opponent still got {*Cassanders* forces had the} upper
MGREC126:23 H3014 No sooner had he got her in his hands {hand},
MGREC~~131:9~~ H3201 How some when down, straight got the upper hand
MGREC131:35 H3227 And leaves the ill got kingdomes he had won,
MGREC132:18 H3255 Those Countries large, his father got before,
MGREC135:13 H3385 But yet the *Persian* got the upper hand;
SICKNES179:7 H27 O great's the gain, though got with pain,

GOTT (2) [got]
MYCHILD218:17 Hp244 When I haue gott over this Block y^{n} have I another pvtt in my

SON231:2 H14 That he before them gott to Land.
GOURD (1)
MEDDM207:13 Hp288 Comforts of this Life, may be compared to the gourd of Jonah,
GOUT (2)
HUMOUR23:2 H112 The Palsie, Gout, or Cramp, or some such dolor,
AGES43:31 H326 The knotty {Cramp and} Gout doth sadly torture me,
GOVERN (2)
MGREC116:40 H2606 To govern that he had already won:
MGREC118:41 H2690 These now to govern for the King pretends,
GOVERNED (1)
MPERS73:36 H821 If governed by an Aristocracy.
GOVERNMENT (10)
MASSYR66:34 H540 {But} Resumes his Government, as heretofore,
MPERS73:31 H816 What forme of Government now to erect,
MPERS78:4 H985 That the large {vast} *Persian* government surrounded;
MGREC97:26 H1787 Of which, the Government he doth commit
MGREC123:1 H2863 And government of *Asia* to him gave;
MGREC128:18 H3091 *Seleuchus* drove {driven} from government, and lands;
MGREC134:14 H3345 To take the government was called in,
MROMAN137:1 H3452 A forme of Government he next begun;
MROMAN137:7 H3458 And this new gentle Government abide:
MROMAN139:22 H3550 The Government they change, a new one bring,
GOVERNOUR (2)
MGREC102:41 H2011 In his approach, the Governour sends word,
MGREC105:5 H2098 Was the false Governour of *Media)*
GOVERNOURS (1) [pl.]
MGREC103:18 H2029 On their old Governours, titles he laid;
GRAC'D (1) [graced]
MGREC~~123:33~~ H2897 Or by his favour {favours} any way did grace, {had grac'd}
GRACE (16)
HUMOUR32:39 H513 The Monarchs bend, and sue, but for my grace;
MASSYR66:16 H522 All Vassals, at his hands, for grace must sue;
MPERS87:15 ~~H1370~~ And yet with these, had neither heart, nor grace;
MGREC96:39 H1759 The *Greeks* come {came} on, and with a gallant grace,
MGREC105:31 H2124 For all that {the} Kingly Grace he did expresse,
MGREC121:19 H2801 With stile of the Protector, would him {to} grace;
MGREC123:23 H2887 Recals *Olimpias,* the Court to grace;
MGREC123:33 H2897 Or by his favour {favours} any way did grace, {had grac'd}
MROMAN139:2 H3530 But by the favour, and the speciall grace
SICKNES179:1 H21 O whil'st I live, this grace me give,
2SIMON195:14 Hp271 wth grace heer and crown you wth glory heerafter. that I may
MEDDM196:3 Hp272 whose head hath great abilities and his heart little or no grace
MEDDM201:21 Hp281 full of contrition, but it is not from any dew of grace wthin,
MEDDM205:4 Hp285 of morality, much lesse of grace in them But when by prudent
MEDDM205:19 Hp286 boldnes to go to the throne of grace to be accepted there,
SAMUEL228:9 H10 For sure thy Grace on him is shown.
GRACED See GRAC'D
GRACELESSE (1)
MPERS85:13 H1289 That for such gracelesse wretches she did groan,
GRACES (1)
MEDDM197:16 Hp274 more patiently then he that excells him, both in gifts & graces

GRACIOUS See GRATIOUS

GRACIOUSLY See GRATIOUSLY, GRATIOVSLY

GRAFTE (1) [graft]

MEDDM206:36 Hp288 they abide not in vnbeleif, god is able to grafte them in, the

GRAIN (4)

ELEMEN17:1 H365 Of rotten sheep, lean kine, and mildew'd grain.
SEASONS47:8 H24 The Seeds-man now {too} doth lavish out his Grain,
DIALOG146:18 H204 My wealthy trading faln, my dearth of grain,
2LETTER182:12 H18 Or in a corn-field number every grain,

GRAINE (2) [grain]

ELEMEN9:12 H46 Subdue the earth, and fit it for your graine,
ELEMEN13:25 H226 Thistles and thornes, where he expected graine;

GRAINES (1) [grains]

ELEMEN16:1 H324 With rowling graines of purest massy gold:

GRANADO (1)

ELEMEN9:8 H42 But I with one Granado, or Petard,

GRAND-SIRE (4)

SEASONS~~51:19~~ H193 Great *Adam* {Our Grand-Sire} was of Paradice made King.
MASSYR54:19 H46 Whose foundation was by his Grand-sire laid;
MPERS81:29 H1137 No lesse then Grand-sire to great *Alexander.*
CONTEM169:31 H70 Then was *Methuselah*, or's grand-sire great:

GRANDAME (1)

CONTEM170:6 H79 Here sits our Grandame in retired place,

GRAND-CHILD (6)

AGES35:19 H5 The first: son unto Flegme, grand-child to water,
MASSYR53:20 H10 The boysterous Sons of *Cush, {Chus,}* Grand-child to *Ham,*
MGREC~~125:4~~ H2952 her young Nephew {grand-child} in his stead {State} t' inthrone,
ELIZB186:31 H1-2 *In memory of my dear grand-child Elizabeth*
ANNEB187:12 H1-2 *In memory of my dear grand-child*
1SIMON188:1 H1-2 *On my dear Grand-child* Simon Bradstreet,

GRANDCHILD (1)

MGREC122:18 H2843 Grandchild to him, who once sat on that throne,

GRAND-CHILDE (2)

MASSYR63:14 H399 Until his Grand-childe made her bow the knee;
MPERS77:16 H955 Grand-childe to *Cyrus,* now sits on the throne;

GRAND-SIRES (4) [poss.]

MASSYR68:15 H601 Of *Daniel* tells, who in his Grand-sires dayes,
MASSYR68:19 H605 Re-minds him of his Grand-sires height, and fall,
MPERS69:15 H637 His Mothers Dream, and Grand-sires cruelty,
MPERS84:23 H1259 His Grand-sires old disgrace, did vex him sore,

GRANICKE (1)

MGREC94:37 H1675 To th' river *Granicke, Alexander* hyes,

GRANT (7) See also GRAVNT

PROLOG7:33 H44 Yet grant some small acknowledgement of ours.
ELEMEN13:26 H227 My sap, to plants and trees, I must not grant,
HUMOUR26:23 H253 But thine the nobler, which I grant, yet mine
HUMOUR33:16 H530 And though I grant, thou art my helper here,
MASSYR58:39 H222 T'infranchise them, to grant what they could crave,
MGREC124:1 H2906 By these, and all, to grant him some supply,
BIRTH180:6 H16 What nature would, God grant to yours and you;

GRANTED (1) See also GRAVNTED, GRAUNTED

MPERS75:33 H890 Of what is freely granted by the King;

GRANTING (2)

MASSYR~~60:6~~ H271 Yet would not {granting} let them {now} to inhabite there;

MYCHILD217:11 Hp242 Answers to me, either in granting ye Thing I prayed

GRANTS (2)

MPERS75:28 H885 He like a King, now grants a Charter large,

MROMAN137:5 H3456 Great priviledges then, to all he grants,

GRANVNTED (1) [granted] See also GRAUNTED

SON231:17 H29 And thvs hath granvnted my Reqvest

GRAPES (1)

SEASONS51:2 H176 The Vintage now is ripe, the Grapes are prest,

GRASHOPPER (1) [grasshopper]

CONTEM169:18 H58 I heard the merry grashopper then sing,

GRASIER (1)

ELEMEN~~16:41~~ H364 The Farmer, and the Plowman both {Grasier do} complain

GRASP (2)

HUMOUR35:7 H603 Her dry, dry Cholers other hand shal grasp;

VANITY160:5 H15 More vain then all, that's but to grasp the wind.

GRASPT (1)

AGES41:27 H244 I then with both hands, graspt the world together,

GRASS (4)

SEASONS~~49:33~~ H123 Upon the grass resting your healthy limbs,

2LETTER182:10 H16 Or all the grass that in the Meads do stand,

CHILDRN185:39 H65 Oft times in grass, on trees, in flight,

ELIZB187:7 H15 And Corn and grass are in their season mown,

GRASSE (5)

ELEMEN14:35 H277 Thou bear'st no {nor} grasse, nor {or} plant, nor tree, nor

SEASONS47:22 H38 The tender tops of budding Grasse they crop,

SEASONS47:39 H51 And {The} Grasse growes long, the tender Lambs {hungry

SEASONS47:41 H53 Among the verduous Grasse hath Nature set,

SEASONS49:25 ~~H114~~ Though you repose on grasse under the skye.

GRASSHOPPER See GRASHOPPER

GRATIOUS (1) [gracious]

MYCHILD216:20 Hp241 Among all my experiences of gods gratious Dealings wth me I

GRATIOUSLY (1) [graciously

JULY223:25 Hp251 gratiously manifested his Love to me, wch I dare not passe by

GRATIOVSLY (1) [graciously]

SON231:28 H39 Particular, and how gratiovsly thov hast answered my Desires.

GRAUE (2) [grave; tomb]

MEDDM199:29 Hp278 when he is once dead, but the last mangles him in his graue

MEDDM207:34 Hp289 not only their death, but their graue, is liuely represented

GRAUNTED (1) [granted] See also GRAVNTED

RESTOR230:8 H23 But graunted hath my Suit.

GRAV'D (1) [engraved]

CONTEM174:35 H232 But he whose name is grav'd in the white stone

GRAV'D (1) [entombed]

MPERS71:31 H745 A second Army there {he} had almost grav'd;

GRAVE (5) [serious]

HUMOUR23:33 H143 Forsooth you are to blame, he grave reply'd.

AGES36:25 H49 His hoary haires, and grave aspect made way;

MASSYR63:33 H420 From some *Thucidides* grave History;
MGREC136:2 H3415 But humbly stand, some grave reproof to take:
DUBART153:35 H39 Thy Saint-like minde in grave Divinity,

GRAVE (8) [tomb] See also GRAUE
FATHER5:20 H21 These are of all, the life, the nurse, the grave,
FATHER6:11 H45 Accept my best, my worst vouchsafe a grave.
FATHER30:23 H415 Thus he is ours, his portion is the grave.
AGES38:36 H139 And some perhaps, I carry to my grave.
SEASONS51:30 H206 So doth Old Age stil tend unto his Grave,
MASSYR60:31 H296 Raises a Phœnix new, from grave o'th old;
MPERS93:4 H1601 Him, to the grave, did Traytor *Bessus* send.
BIRTH180:8 H18 Let be interr'd in my oblivious grave;

GRAVER (1)
AGES36:13 H37 The next came up, in a more {much} graver sort,

GRAVITY (1)
AGES36:29 H53 But wise Old-age, did with all gravity,

GRAVNT (5) [grant]
SOREFIT222:9 H28 O gravnt I doe it in this state,
28AUG226:6 Hp254 Lord gravnt y^{t} while I live I may doe y^{t} service I am able in this
HANNA230:15 H8 Gravnt shee rember w^{t} thov'st done
SON231:27 H39 O Lord gravnt that I may never forgett thy Loving kindness in
2HUSB232:32 H33 Lord gravnt thov good Successe

GRAY (3)
AGES45:27 H417 My {Mine} Almond-tree (gray haires) doth flourish now,
SEASONS50:33 H167 Until his head be gray, and strength be gone,
MEDDM199:8 Hp277 leaues argue want of sap and gray haires want of moisture so

GRAZIER See GRASIER

GREASIE (1) [greasy]
HUMOUR23:4 H114 Of greasie paunch, and palled {bloated} cheeks, go vaunt,

GREAT (197)
PROLOG6:26 H10 Great *Bartas* sugar'd lines doe but read o're;
ELEMEN8:21 H19 The rumbling, hissing, puffing was so great,
ELEMEN10:39 H114 Where's *Ninus* great wal'd Town, and *Troy* of old?
ELEMEN~~11:1~~ H118 And stately *London,* (our great *Britain's* glory)
ELEMEN11:3 H123 So great *Diana's* Temple was by me.
ELEMEN11:15 H135 And all therein at that great day of doome;
ELEMEN12:7 H167 And huge great *Taurus,* longer then the rest,
ELEMEN12:8 H168 Dividing great *Armenia* from the least,
ELEMEN~~12:22~~ H182 Out of huge {great} numbers, I might pick my choyce,
ELEMEN17:26 H390 *Ducalions* great deluge, with many moe;
ELEMEN19:41 H482 That earth appeares in heaven, oh wonder great!
ELEMEN20:4 H486 By death, or great mutations {mutation} of their States.
HUMOUR21:2 H30 To shew my great {high} descent, and pedigree,
HUMOUR21:16 H44 Yet many times, unto my great disgrace,
HUMOUR22:5 H74 If great perswasions, cause her meet her foe;
HUMOUR23:16 H126 If once thou'rt great, what followes thereupon?
HUMOUR24:3 H152 And yet to make, my greatnesse far {still} more great:
HUMOUR25:40 H229 Be dangers neer so high, and courage great,
HUMOUR33:20 H534 My excellencies are so great, so many,
HUMOUR34:24 H579 But a mad one, say I, where 'tis too great,
AGES37:30 H92 How to be rich, or great, I did not carke;

AGES37:36 H98 No malice bare, to this, or that great Peer,
AGES42:25 H283 Great labours, sorrows, crosses I sustain'd.
AGES42:38 H294 If to be rich, or great, it was my fate;
AGES44:22 H355 Great mutations, some joyful, and some sad,
AGES45:9 H391 I've seen base {unworthy} men, advanc'd to great degree
AGES45:19 ~~H401~~ I've seen a land unmoulded with great paine.
AGES46:6 H437 To great, to rich, to poore, to young, or old,
SEASONS49:13 H104 Whose vehemency, at length doth grow so great,
SEASONS49:28 H117 Which made great *Bajazet* cry out in's woes,
SEASONS49:30 H119 *Orthobulus,* nor yet *Sebastia* great,
SEASONS50:15 H149 *August,* of great *Augustus* took its name,
SEASONS51:19 H193 Great *Adam* {Our Grand-Sire} was of Paradice made King.
SEASONS~~52:5~~ H220 Beef, Brawn, and Pork, are now in great'st {great} request,
SEASONS52:22 H237 Through Christendome, with great festivity
MASSYR53:36 H26 Great *Nimrod* dead, *Bellus* the next, his Son,
MASSYR54:30 H57 *Barzanes,* the great *Armenian* King,
MASSYR55:4 H70 This great oppressing *Ninus* dead, and gone,
MASSYR55:17 H83 This great renowned Empresse, issued.
MASSYR56:7 H113 With great facility, march safe upon't.
MASSYR56:25 H131 Great King *Staurobates,* for {his Country} to invade.
MASSYR57:4 H151 Or else was his obedience very great,
MASSYR~~57:18~~ H165 So suddenly should loose so great a state,
MASSYR~~59:32~~ H256 This the last Monarch was, of {great} *Ninus* race,
MASSYR60:7 H272 For he demonished that City great,
MASSYR60:17 H282 Not so content, but aiming to be great,
MASSYR63:3 H388 The fifth, and last, of great *Belosus* race;
MASSYR~~63:28~~ H415 Then being Father to so great a Son.
MASSYR64:21 H445 By great *Euphrates* did his Army fall,
MASSYR64:36 H460 Divided from the maine, by channel great;
MASSYR65:16 H481 For this great King, with-drawes part of his force,
MASSYR66:24 H530 Which wealth, and strong ambition made so great;
MASSYR67:2 H548 *Babels* great Monarch, now laid in the dust,
MPERS69:3 H625 She Daughter unto great *Astiages,*
MPERS69:20 H642 Against great *Cressus,* then of *Lidia* head;
MPERS69:33 H655 *Cressus* thus known, it was great *Cyrus* doome,
MPERS70:41 ~~H712~~ Then at his Herse great honours to expresse;
MPERS~~70:41~~ H712 With honours great, did celebrate his fame.
MPERS71:27 H741 To spoyl the Temple of great *Jupiter;*
MPERS73:5 H792 The Male line, of great *Cyrus* now did {had} end.
MPERS73:26 H811 And two of these great Peers, in place {Field} lay dead:
MPERS78:2 H983 In great provisions, for this great intent;
MPERS78:2 H983 In great provisions, for this great intent;
MPERS79:4 H1026 For his great love, is this thy recompence?
MPERS79:20 H1046 Long viewing them, thought it great happinesse,
MPERS80:24 H1091 If that smal number his great force could bide;
MPERS81:28 ~~H1136~~ Though of this Nation borne a great Commander,
MPERS~~81:28~~ H1136 A *Macedonian* born, and great Commander,
MPERS81:29 H1137 No lesse then Grand-sire to great *Alexander.*
MPERS82:36 H1183 Where he had sometime gaz'd with great delight.
MPERS84:11 H1239 Of *Hamans* fall, and *Mordica's* great rise;
MPERS84:21 H1257 And for that end, great preparation made,

MPERS85:4 H1280 Three sons great *Artaxerxes* left behind;
MPERS86:35 H1351 Great care was his pretence, those Souldiers stout,
MPERS88:4 H1397 And ranged stood, by great *Euphrates* side,
MPERS88:6 H1399 Of whose great numbers, their intelligence,
MPERS89:25 H1459 The King great store of all provision sends,
MPERS90:29 H1496 Which rumor makes great *Artaxerxes* quake;
MPERS91:34 ~~H1548~~ Great *Artaxerxes* dead, *Ochus* succeeds,
MPERS~~91:37~~ H1551 (To his great grief) most subtilly he slayes:
MPERS92:21 ~~H1579~~ And that great *Cyrus* line, yet was not run,
MPERS~~92:26~~ H1584 Some write great *Cyrus* line was not yet run,
MGREC93:8 H1605 under *Alexander* the Great,
MGREC6:10 H1607 Great *Alexander,* was wise *Phillips* son,
MGREC6:16 H1613 Great were the guifts of nature, which he had;
MGREC6:30 H1627 *Phillip,* on this great conquest had an eye;
MGREC95:41 H1720 To shew, how great *Darius* plaid his part:
MGREC96:23 H1743 Great *Sisigambis,* she brought up the Reare;
MGREC97:41 H1802 Therefore a Crown, and great provisions {Provision} send;
MGREC98:35 H1837 And layes before great *Alexanders* eyes,
MGREC99:6 H1849 Tels him, these proffers great (in truth were none)
MGREC99:9 H1852 Was I as great, as is great *Alexander,*
MGREC99:9 H1852 Was I as great, as is great *Alexander,*
MGREC99:37 H1880 Whom with great reverence *Alexander* greets;
MGREC100:18 H1902 Great *Alexander* had been kept from Land;
MGREC100:35 H1919 Great *Alexander* mourns, as well as he,
MGREC101:1 H1926 Great *Alexander,* for this good regard;
MGREC101:9 H1934 *Phenisian* Sea, and great *Euphrates* high,
MGREC102:26 H1996 *Antipater,* from *Greece,* sends great {fresh} supplyes;
MGREC104:28 H2080 Great recompence, in's thoughts, he did propose;
MGREC106:7 H2141 Now to the East great *Alexander* goes,
MGREC108:17 H2233 Nor could he reason give, for this great wrong,
MGREC109:38 H2297 Great *Alexander* vext at this reply,
MGREC~~110:32~~ H2336 Which might be found, and so for {great} wonders kept:
MGREC112:27 H2413 But for his Fathers great deserts, the King,
MGREC113:8 H2435 Such torments great, as wit could first {worst} invent,
MGREC113:21 H2448 Nor could his Captaines bear so great regard;
MGREC115:23 H2542 This great indignity for to {he should} requite.
MGREC115:28 H2547 His service great now's suddenly forgot,
MGREC116:37 H2603 This folly great *Augustus* did deride,
MGREC117:13 H2620 The great Horn broke, the lesse did tytannize;
MGREC117:17 H2624 Great *Alexander* dead, his Army's left,
MGREC117:29 H2636 Great *Alexander* has left {did leave} issue none,
MGREC118:14 H2661 Seven dayes the Corps of their great Master lyes
MGREC119:32 H2722 'Mongst all the Captains {princes} of great *Alexander,*
MGREC~~120:20~~ H2756 (For all the princes of great *Alexander*
MGREC120:39 H2776 Great love did *Ptolomy* by this act gain.
MGREC~~121:15~~ H2793 *Python* of haughty mind, and courage great.
MGREC~~121:15~~ H2794 Who could not book so great indignity,
MGREC121:26 H2808 Now comes the newes of a great victory,
MGREC122:1 H2824 For this great {sad} strife, he pours out his complaints,
MGREC~~122:4~~ H2827 And much eclipse his {great Acts and} glory to rehearse
MGREC122:22 ~~H2845~~ Who had an Army, like a great Commander.

MGREC122:35 H2856 For all the Princes {nobles} of great {King} *Alexander*
MGREC123:14 H2878 Now {When} great *Antipater,* the world doth {must} leave
MGREC123:25 H2889 Into *Epire,* for her great turblence;
MGREC123:29 H2893 This *Polisperchons* great ability,
MGREC123:31 H2895 And to be great {chief} himselfe now bends his aymes;
MGREC123:41 H2905 And for that great gift, which he gave him last;
MGREC124:23 H2930 The great ones now begin to shew their minde,
MGREC125:11 H2959 and succour {To save the King} her, in this great {their} need;
MGREC~~128:24~~ H3097 Where {great Antigonus} *Ptolomy,* and the rest {was} put him
MGREC129:12 H3126 No sooner was great *Alexander* dead,
MGREC130:16 H3171 They for their great reward no better speed,
MGREC131:4 H3194 Most grossely base, was this {their} great adulation,
MGREC134:2 H3333 And then *Antiochus* surnam'd the great,
MGREC134:13 H3344 That {Then} *Tygranes* the great *Armenian* King,
MGREC134:41 H3370 Till great *Augustus* had with him a fight,
MROMAN137:5 H3456 Great priviledges then, to all he grants,
MROMAN137:8 H3459 Of Wives there was so great a scarsity,
MROMAN137:12 H3463 Great shewes he makes at Tilt, and Turnament,
MROMAN138:10 H3500 But now demolished, to make *Rome* great.
DIALOG144:8 H118 'Mongst all the cruelties which I have {by great ones} done,
DIALOG145:8 H157 Your fearfull sinnes, great cause there's to lament,
SIDNEY149:31 ~~H23~~ Which shewes, thy worth was great, thine honour such,
SIDNEY~~150:12~~ H40 Which shews his worth was great, his honour such,
SIDNEY150:15 ~~H49~~ Yet great *Augustus* was content (we know)
SIDNEY~~150:37~~ H64 Noble {Great} *Bartas,* this to thy praise adds more,
DUBART152:34 H3 Great, deare, sweet *Bartas,* thou art matchlesse knowne;
DUBART153:2 H6 But knowing th' taske so great, and strength but small,
DUBART153:15 H19 And prostrate off'red at great *Bartas* Herse.
DUBART153:30 H34 And {But} seeing utterance fayle his great desires,
DUBART154:13 H58 Then in Saint *Lewis,* or thy last *Henry* great,
QELIZ155:14 H5 Although great Queen, thou now in silence lye,
QELIZ157:16 H84 A great *Eliza,* but compar'd with ours,
QELIZ157:24 H92 (Whom none but great *Aurelius* could quell)
QELIZ158:4 H113 Untill the heavens great revolution:
QELIZ158:20 H129 *In every one, be her great glory famed.*
VANITY159:38 H10 What is't in wealth, great treasures for to gain {obtain}?
CONTEM169:14 H55 My great Creator I would magnifie,
CONTEM169:31 H70 Then was *Methuselah,* or's grand-sire great:
CONTEM173:5 H173 To see what trade they great ones there do drive,
CONTEM174:16 H215 And now becomes great Master of the seas;
CHILDRN185:31 H57 Great was my pain when I you bred,
CHILDRN185:32 H58 Great was my care, when I you fed,
2SIMON195:15 Hp271 wth reioyceing at that great day of appearing, wch is the
MEDDM196:3 Hp272 whose head hath great abilities and his heart little or no grace
MEDDM197:26 Hp275 will vntertake to climb vp a steep mountain wth a great burden
MEDDM198:13 Hp276 Want of prudence as well as piety hath brought men into great
MEDDM198:17 Hp276 hooke vnder all, Satan that great Angler hath his sundry baits
MEDDM200:27 Hp279 lost in the Autumn so shall it be at that great day after a long
MEDDM203:33 Hp284 men can vse great importunity when they are in distresses and
MEDDM203:34 Hp284 shew great ingratitude after their successes, but he that
MEDDM204:2 Hp284 of former deliuerances, is a great support in present

MEDDM204:9	Hp284	great receipts, call for great returnes, the more that any man is
MEDDM204:11	Hp284	man so to improue his talents, that when his great master
MEDDM205:12	Hp286	fro continvally, here is also the great Court of iustice erected,
MEDDM206:28	Hp288	then his great worke of election and Reprobation, when we
MEDDM207:14	Hp288	that notwthstanding we take great delight, for a season in
MEDDM207:16	Hp288	or feare, or greife that lyes at the root wch in great part
MEDDM207:23	Hp289	pleases our great landlord to let: All haue their bounds set ouer
MEDDM208:12	Hp290	good name, is as a precious oyntment, and it is a great favour
MEDDM208:22	Hp290	miserably delude men and make them put great Confidence in
MEDDM209:15	Hp291	to perpetuall bondage vnder them vnlesse the great deliuerer,
MYCHILD215:27	Hp240	a great Trouble, & I could not be at rest 'till by prayer I had
MYCHILD216:14	Hp241	God to keep me a long time wthout a child wch was a great
MYCHILD216:17	Hp241	brovght yov into ye world, and wth great paines, weaknes,
MYCHILD216:28	Hp242	by losses in estate, and these Times (thro: his great mercy)
MYCHILD217:10	Hp242	I haue had great xper^{c} of Gods hearing my prayers, and
MYCHILD218:1	Hp243	Winter, Spring and Autvmne, the dayly providing for this great
28AUG226:8	Hp254	forgett thy great Love to my soul so lately expressed, when I
13MAY227:8	H17	Who is a God so wondrous great.
11MAYB228:24	Hp259	I haue had no great fitt of sicknes, but this year from ye middle
SON230:28	H11	From Dangers great thou did'st him free
SON231:25	H37	That all thy favours great receivd
REMB236:5	H20	Thy mercyes Lord haue been so great

GREATER (19)

HUMOUR21:7	H35	But she in greater, I in lesse degree;
HUMOUR22:7	H76	To march her pace, to some is greater pain,
HUMOUR30:1	H393	What greater Clerke, or polititian lives?
AGES39:5	H148	Declare some greater riches are within;
AGES42:36	H292	To greater things, I never did aspire,
AGES42:40	H296	Greater, then was the great'st, was my desire,
AGES42:41	H297	And greater stil, did {and thirst for honour,} set my heart on
MASSYR54:37	H64	And all the greater *Asia* did subdue;
MASSYR67:31	H577	To shew his little dread, but greater store,
MPERS73:33	H818	The greater part, declin'd a Monarchy.
MPERS85:12	H1288	If {so} they were hers, the greater was her moan;
MGREC110:27	H2331	Doth for his Camp a greater circuit take,
MGREC119:28	H2718	The *Athenian* Army was the greater far,
MGREC121:29	H2811	With greater joy it would have been receiv'd;
QELIZ158:13	H122	*The greater was our gain, our losse the more.*
TDUDLEY165:13	H15	Or who alive then I, a greater debtor?
VERSES184:2	H6	The principle might yield a greater sum,
MEDDM200:3	Hp278	not a little one? will ere long say of a greater Tush god regards
MEDDM205:18	Hp286	who is greater then our Conscience will do it much more, but

GREATEST (11)

ELEMEN~~8:7~~	H5	Who was of greatest use and might'est force;
HUMOUR~~26:14~~	H244	Of greatest use, if reason do not erre:
HUMOUR32:2	H476	Although she beare the greatest obloquie.
MPERS75:9	H870	If he command, obey the greatest must:
MPERS92:37	H1595	He fell to depth of greatest misery,
MGREC~~95:37~~	H1716	Along with him, the {greatest} Ladyes of the Court.
MGREC115:15	H2524	The other was the greatest Deity.
FLESH176:22	H62	My greatest honour it shall be

MYCHILD216:29 Hp242 haue been the times of my greatest Getting and Advantage,
MYCHILD217:2 Hp242 Joyfully as in greatest mercyes, For if yee bee his yee shall
MYCHILD217:2 Hp242 mercyes, For if yee bee his yee shall reap the greatest

GREATNESS (1)

TDUDLEY166:9 H51 Their greatness may be judg'd by what they shew.

GREATNESSE (8) [greatness]

HUMOUR24:3 H152 And yet to make, my greatnesse far {still} more great:
HUMOUR31:8 H441 Now {But} by your leave, Ile let your greatnesse see;
AGES42:18 H276 In meannesse, greatnesse, riches, poverty;
MPERS69:41 H671 Weighing the age, and greatnesse of the Prince,
MPERS91:27 ~~H1541~~ But yet for all his greatnesse, and long reign,
MGREC106:21 H2155 As *Alexander* in his greatnesse growes,
MGREC106:29 H2163 His greatnesse now he takes, to represent,
QELIZ155:31 H22 Though I resound thy greatnesse {praises} 'mongst the throng.

GREAT'S (2) [great is]

QELIZ155:18 H9 So great's thy glory, and thine excellence,
SICKNES179:7 H27 O great's the gain, though got with pain,

GREAT'ST (3)

HUMOUR33:41 H555 I'le touch the Sight, great'st wonder of the three;
AGES42:40 H296 Greater, then was the great'st, was my desire,
SEASONS52:5 H220 Beef, Brawn, and Pork, are now in great'st {great} request,

GRECIA (4)

ELEMEN11:40 H160 Yet let me name my *Grecia,* 'tis my heart
MGREC93:26 H1623 This is the hee-goat, which from *Grecia* came,
MGREC119:38 H2728 With them and his, he into *Grecia* went,
MGREC124:11 H2918 *Cassander* with his Hoast to *Grecia* goes,

GRECIAN (7)

MPERS77:7 H946 For *Grecian* Maids ('tis said) to wait on her;
MPERS84:20 H1256 Thinking his *Grecian* wars now to advance.
MGREC93:7 H1604 {being} the *Grecian,* beginning
MGREC135:6 H3378 Here ends at last the *Grecian* Monarchy,
MGREC135:14 H3386 The *Grecian,* them did utterly subdue,
MGREC135:16 H3388 The *Grecian* longer then the *Persian* stood,
MGREC~~136:8~~ H3422 *The End of the Grecian Monarchy.*

GRECIANS (9) [pl.]

ELEMEN8:32 H30 But what I am, let learned *Grecians* say;
MPERS76:34 H932 Where *Grecians* prov'd themselves right Souldiers, stout;
MPERS77:33 H974 Against the *Sythians,* and *Grecians* too,
MPERS82:16 H1163 The *Grecians* at *Mycale* in Asia meet,
MPERS83:30 H1218 To whom the perjur'd *Grecians* lent their aide,
MPERS88:16 H1409 Which did such courage to the *Grecians* bring,
MPERS91:36 ~~H1550~~ Was it because the *Grecians* now at war,
MGREC99:18 H1861 For more repulse, the *Grecians* here abide,
MGREC108:33 H2249 But soone the *Grecians* {his souldiers} forc'd them to a flight,

GRECIANS (1) [pl., poss.]

MPERS85:30 H1306 Whose forces {strength} by their {*Grecians*} helpe were {was}

'GREE (3) [agree] See also **GREE**

HUMOUR35:3 H599 Unlesse we 'gree all fals into confusion.
MPERS73:19 H806 And first these noble *Magi* 'gree upon,

GREE (1) [agree] See also **'GREE**

FATHER5:33 H34 And yet in equall tempers, how they gree,

GREECE (23)
HUMOUR33:2 H516 Country with Country, *Greece* with *Asia* fights,
MPERS76:23 H921 He after this, intends *Greece* to invade,
MPERS77:3 H942 As the best trophe that {which} ye won in *Greece.*
MPERS77:20 H961 Th' *Ægyptians* to reduce, and *Greece* to marre;
MPERS77:30 H971 And *Greece* such wondrous triumphs ne're had made.
MPERS79:37 H1063 That pleasant *Thessaly,* from *Greece* divide;
MPERS83:33 H1221 Which had they kept, *Greece* had more nobly done,
MPERS91:1 H1509 He knows that many towns in *Greece* envies
MPERS91:6 H1514 With broyls, and quarrels, sets all *Greece* on fire.
MPERS91:11 H1519 Dissention in *Greece* continued {so} long,
MGREC93:24 H1621 His rule to *Greece,* he scorn'd should be confin'd:
MGREC94:1 H1635 Yet for a while, in *Greece* is forc'd to stay,
MGREC95:28 H1707 To *Greece* he thirty thousand talents sends;
MGREC99:21 H1864 That *Greece* must {was forc'd to} yeeld a fresh supply againe;
MGREC102:26 H1996 *Antipater,* from *Greece,* sends great {fresh} supplyes;
MGREC~~123:13~~ H2877 To *Greece* and *Macedon* lets turn our sight.
MGREC123:38 H2902 Unto these helps, in *Greece,* {at home} he seeks out more,
MGREC124:15 H2922 *Athens,* with many Townes in *Greece* besides, {beside}
MGREC124:17 H2924 Whilst hot in wars these two in *Greece* remaine,
MGREC128:10 H3083 Th' hatefull *Olinthians* to *Greece* re-brings;
MGREC132:26 H3271 In *Greece,* unto *Antigonus,* his son,
MGREC132:41 H3288 Whilst with these hopes, in *Greece* he did remaine,
MGREC134:17 H3348 Of *Greece,* and *Syria* thus the rule did end,

GRE¯DILY (1) [greedily]
MEDDM198:18 Hp276 of men, wch they all catch gre¯dily at but few perceiues

GREEDY (3)
ELEMEN13:4 H205 Ye greedy misers who do dig for gold;
MGREC102:13 H1983 With greedy eyes, he views this City round,
CHILDRN185:28 H54 Or by some greedy hawks be spoyl'd.

GREEK (5)
PROLOG7:7 H21 Nor can I, like that fluent sweet tongu'd *Greek*
MPERS84:26 H1262 The {This} noble *Greek,* now fit for generall.
MGREC105:38 H2131 This said, the *Greek* for water doth intreat,
MGREC134:24 H3355 They might translate the Bible into *Greek,*
MROMAN138:25 H3515 *Tarquin,* a *Greek,* at *Corinth* borne, and bred,

GREEKE (2) [greek]
MPERS86:34 H1350 (One *Greeke* could make ten *Persians* run away)
MGREC105:14 H2107 And thus he lay, *Polistratus* a *Greeke*

GREEKES (2) [greeks]
MGREC96:20 H1740 For so to fright the *Greekes* he judg'd was best,
MGREC96:34 H1754 The *Greekes* would all adore, and {but} would none fight.

GREEKS (36) [pl.]
PROLOG7:21 H33 But sure the antick *Greeks* were far more milde,
PROLOG7:26 H38 The *Greeks* did nought, but play the foole and lye.
PROLOG7:28 H39 Let *Greeks* be *Greeks,* and Women what they are,
PROLOG7:28 H39 Let *Greeks* be *Greeks,* and Women what they are,
MASSYR55:30 H96 Some think the *Greeks,* this slander on her cast,
MPERS80:7 H1074 O noble *Greeks,* how now, degenerate?
MPERS80:32 H1099 That *Greeks* to break his bridge shortly intends;
MPERS81:32 H1140 And of those *Greeks,* which by his skil he'd won,

MPERS81:34 H1142 The other *Greeks,* which were confederate,
MPERS82:9 H1156 Which found, like *Greeks* they fight, the *Persians* fly,
MPERS82:19 H1166 Thus did the *Greeks* destroy, consume, disperce,
MPERS83:35 H1223 *Greeks* and *Egyptians* both, he overthrows,
MPERS85:16 H1292 Joynes with the *Greeks,* and so maintains {maintain} their
MPERS87:10 H1366 Seven hundred *Greeks* now further {repair for} his intents:
MPERS88:41 H1434 Hoping with {by} that to make the *Greeks* stand stil,
MPERS89:11 H1445 If *Greeks* unto their Country-men {own Country should}
MPERS89:19 H1453 The *Greeks* with scorn reject his proud commands;
MPERS89:23 H1457 The smiling *Greeks* reply, they first must bait,
MPERS89:39 H1473 The *Greeks,* having {seeing} their valiant Captaines slaine,
MPERS90:10 H1483 There was of *Greeks,* setled a Colony,
MPERS90:20 H1487 The *Greeks* now (as the *Persian* King suspects)
MPERS90:30 H1497 The *Greeks* by this successe, incourag'd so,
MPERS91:17 H1525 But let us leave these *Greeks,* to discord bent,
MGREC93:32 H1629 The *Greeks* had chose him Captain Generall,
MGREC94:41 H1679 Those banks so steep, the *Greeks,* now {yet} scramble up
MGREC96:39 H1759 The *Greeks* come {came} on, and with a gallant grace,
MGREC97:22 H1783 Two hundred eighty *Greeks* he lost in fight,
MGREC101:34 ~~H1959~~ Both Armies meet, *Greeks* fight, the *Persians* run,
MGREC~~101:34~~ H1962 And spilt the Greeks some bloud before their flight
MGREC108:7 H2223 Here was of *Greeks,* a town in *Bactria,*
MGREC119:12 H2702 In these tumultuous dayes, the thralled *Greeks*
MGREC119:40 H2730 After this {which} time, the *Greeks* did never more
MGREC127:38 H3068 *Antigonus,* desirous of the *Greeks,*
MGREC128:15 H3088 Now {Then} *Ptolomy* would gaine the *Greeks* likewise,
MGREC129:4 H3118 He sees the *Greeks* now favour their young Prince,
MGREC129:30 H3144 The *Greeks* touch'd with the murther done so {of} late,

GREEN (16)
ELEMEN9:35 H70 And trim thee gay {brave}, in green, after thy blacks?
AGES~~35:27~~ H13 Childhood was cloath'd in white, and given {green} to show,
AGES36:3 H27 His Suit of Crimson, and his Scarfe of Green:
AGES41:16 H235 And now am grown more staid, that {who} have been green,
SEASONS46:34 H10 With smiling Sun-shine face, and garments {somewhat} green,
SEASONS47:11 H27 And Poles erects, for his green {young} clambering Hops;
SEASONS47:28 H44 My second month is *April,* green, and fair,
SEASONS51:15 H189 Boughs full of leaves, or fruits, but raw, and {unripe or} green,
MPERS72:5 ~~H755~~ Complots the Princes death, in his green years,
MPERS74:4 H829 Upon a Green to meet, by rising Sun;
MPERS84:1 H1229 His hangings, white, and green, and purple dye;
MGREC102:35 H2005 Those purple hangings, mixt with green, and white,
CONTEM167:30 H7 Of green, of red, of yellow, mixed hew,
CONTEM171:19 H122 And then the earth (though old) stil clad in green,
MEDDM198:4 Hp276 then makes them lye down in green pastures and leades them
13MAY226:28 H4 The earth all black is cloth'd in green

GREENESS (1) [greenness]
CONTEM171:22 H125 If winter come, and greeness then do fade,

GREEN-LAND (1)
SEASONS51:40 H216 Now *Green-land, Groen-land, Lap-land, Fin-land,* see

GREENNES (1) [greenness] See also GREENESS
MEDDM207:18 Hp289 we perceiue a decay, in their greennes for were earthly com

GREET (4)
MASSYR~~58:36~~ H219 And with all terms of amity, he greets, {them greet.}
MPERS74:11 H836 The Nobles all alight, {bow to} their King to greet,
MPERS78:32 H1013 Whither rich *Pithyus* comes, *Xerxes* to greet;
CONTEM172:25 H159 To *Thetis* house, where all imbrace and greet:

GREETS (3)
MASSYR58:36 H219 And with all terms of amity, he greets, {them greet.}
MGREC99:37 H1880 Whom with great reverence *Alexander* greets;
MGREC109:19 H2278 And as his Sovereign Lord, him humbly greets.

GREIF (3) [grief] See also GREIFE, GRIEFE
MGREC112:39 H2425 *Philotas* thus o're-charg'd, with wrong, and greif,
MEDDM197:33 Hp275 greif and pain till they turn to dust, and then are they fine
MYCHILD216:15 Hp241 greif to me, and cost me many prayers + tears before I obtaind

GREIFE (1) [grief] See also GREIF, GRIEFE
MEDDM207:16 Hp288 discontent or feare, or greife that lyes at the root w[ch] in great

GREIFS (1) [griefs] See also GRIEFES
AGES44:40 H373 In midst of greifs, I saw some {our} hopes revive,

GREIVE (1) [grieve]
MGREC105:10 H2103 His lost felicity did greive him sore,

GREIVING (1) [grieving]
28AUG225:30 Hp254 doth not afflict willingly, nor take delight in greiving y[e] children

GREW (7)
AGES36:32 H56 That he was young, before he grew so old.
AGES44:38 H371 And then, me thought, the world {day} at noon grew dark,
MPERS88:9 H1402 And black and blacker grew, as they drew nigh.
MPERS88:37 H1430 Their armes grew weake, through {by their} slaughters that
CONTEM168:17 H25 The more I look'd, the more I grew amaz'd,
MYCHILD215:31 Hp241 as I grew to haue more vnderstanding, so y[e] more solace I
MYCHILD216:1 Hp241 But as I grew vp to bee about 14. or 15. I fovnd my heart more

GREY (2)
ELEMEN13:19 H220 And how I force the grey head to obey.
MPERS70:35 H706 In honour, peace, and wealth, with a grey head,

GRIEF (13) See also GREIF, GREIFE, GRIEFE
MASSYR66:28 H534 And his unhappy change with grief fore-tel;
MPERS69:30 H652 With pressing grief, and sorrow, over-come,
MPERS77:11 H950 ('Tis thought) through grief and his {this} succeslesse strife.
MPERS~~91:37~~ H1551 (To his great grief) most subtilly he slayes:
MGREC97:12 H1773 Yet all this grief, this losse, this over-throw,
MGREC115:41 H2560 He shewes his grief, he's forc'd to disobey:
MGREC~~116:10~~ H2574 But pin d in grief till life did her forsake:
DIALOG142:30 H59 Your humble Childe intreats you, shew your grief,
DIALOG145:13 H162 Pray in plain termes, what is your present grief,
DUBART154:6 H51 Through grief it wants a faculty to speak,
CONTEM171:28 H130 No sooner born, but grief and care makes fall
BIRTH180:11 H21 And when thou feel'st no grief, as I no harms,
MERCY189:10 H31 All freed from grief (I trust) among the blest;

GRIEFE (3) [grief] See also GREIF, GREIFE
HUMOUR24:13 H162 To vent my griefe, and wipe off my disgrace.
MPERS73:3 H790 Griefe for his brothers death, he did expresse,
MGREC104:14 H2066 Transported sore, with griefe and passion;

GRIEFES (1) [griefs] See also GREIFS
DIALOG141:16 H15 Or must my forced tongue these griefes disclose?
GRIEFS (4) [pl.] See also GREIFS
AGES38:30 H133 Yet griefs, in my fraile flesh, I still do find.
DIALOG146:32 H218 Your griefs I pity much, but should do wrong {hope to see},
2LETTER181:34 H4 And tell my griefs in either Hemisphere:
MERCY188:33 H19 And in thy griefs still bear a second part:
GRIEV'D (3) [grieved]
MGREC106:38 H2172 Griev'd at this change of manners, and of minde:
MGREC120:11 H2746 *Perdicas* griev'd, to see the Princes bold,
MGREC131:22 H3214 He sorely griev'd at this his desperate state,
GRIEVANCE (1)
DIALOG143:26 H95 To shew the grievance of my troubled Land;
GRIEVE See GREIVE
GRIEVED (1) See also GRIEV'D
MPERS83:4 H1192 The grieved Prince finding nor right, nor love,
GRIEVING See GREIVING
GRIEVES (1)
MGREC132:17 H3254 *Seleuchus, Asia* holds, that grieves him sore,
GRIEVOUS (1)
MERCY189:15 H36 What though, thy strokes full sad & grievous be,
GRINDE (1) [grind]
MPERS77:24 H965 As if to dust he meant to grinde that Nation;
GRINDERS (1) [pl.]
AGES45:29 H419 My grinders now are few, my sight doth faile
GRINDES (1) [grinds]
MEDDM197:32 Hp275 for bread, god so deales wth his servants, he grindes them wth
GRINDING (3)
ELEMEN18:27 H431 I {help to} ripe the corne, I turne the grinding mill;
MGREC104:15 H2067 Grinding his teeth, and plucking off his haire,
PILGRIM210:28 H28 nor grinding paines, my body fraile.
GRINDS See GRINDES
GRIPES (3) [pl.]
ELEMEN~~14:12~~ H254 In heats & colds & gripes & drowsy sleeps:
AGES38:31 H134 What gripes of wind, mine infancy did pain?
AGES41:11 ~~H230~~ Ceas'd by the gripes of Serjeant Death's Arrests:
GROAN (5)
ELEMEN8:13 H11 The quaking Earth did groan, the skie look't black,
MPERS~~71:4~~ H717 And though his conquests made the earth to groan,
MPERS85:13 H1289 That for such gracelesse wretches she did groan,
CONTEM174:11 H211 Can make him deeply groan for that divine Translation.
3LETTER183:11 H13 Ev'n thus doe I, with many a deep sad groan
GROANES (2) [groans]
MGREC105:8 H2101 *Darius* bath'd in bloud, sends out his groanes,
SOREFIT221:21 H7 My plaints & Groanes were heard of Thee
GROANING (2)
SEASONS50:9 H143 The groaning Carts to bear away this prise,
DIALOG145:21 H170 To ease my groaning land shew {shew'd} their intent,
GROANS (3) [pl.] See also GROANES
MPERS88:32 H1425 Sencelesse and mute they stand, yet breath out groans,
MGREC105:13 H2106 Should heare, nor see, his groans, and {dying} misery:

2LETTER182:5 H11 My dumpish thoughts, my groans, my brakish tears

GROEN-LAND (1)

SEASONS51:40 H216 Now *Green-land, Groen-land, Lap-land, Fin-land,* see

GROSLY (1) [grossly] See also GROSSELY

HUMOUR30:33 H425 But thou most grosly do'st mistake, to thinke

GROSSE (2) [gross]

MASSYR68:22 H608 His pride, and sottish grosse Idolatry.

MPERS71:39 H753 Is more prophane, then grosse Idolaters;

GROSSELY (2) [grossly[See also GROSLY

MGREC131:4 H3194 Most grossely base, was this {their} great adulation,

DIALOG144:29 H137 Some grossely fin'd, from {house &} friends to exile went:

GROUND (9) [soil] See also GROVND

ELEMEN16:39 H362 And with aboundant wet, so coole the ground,

AGES42:33 H289 'Twas in the crop of my manured ground:

MPERS80:6 H1073 But on their ground they dye, each Mothers Son.

MGREC93:21 H1618 To th' ground was burnt, *Diana's* Temple high,

MGREC6:28 H1625 That broke {brake} his hornes, that threw him on the ground,

MGREC100:12 H1896 Faire *Alexandria* from the ground doth raise;

MGREC110:16 H2316 For to the last, stout *Porus* kept his ground.

DUBART153:8 H12 Which Rayes, darting upon some richer ground,

MEDDM206:4 Hp287 being cut down, as the dry stock, for both cumber the ground

GROUND (1) [grind] See also GROVND

MEDDM197:31 Hp275 till it haue past through the Mill and been ground to powder,

GROUND-WORK (1)

MGREC123:2 H2864 And thus *Antipater* the ground-work layes,

GROVND (1) [ground; soil]

HOURS233:27 H10 Thro: the I've kept my Grovnd.

GROVND (1) [ground; grind]

MYCHILD217:27 Hp243 grovnd me to powder it would bee but Light to me, yea oft

GROW (15)

ELEMEN18:33 H437 I grow more pure and pure, as I mount higher,

HUMOUR21:18 H46 Where if your rule once grow {prove} predominant,

AGES36:6 H30 Seemed to grow on's head (bedew'd with showers:)

SEASONS49:13 H104 Whose vehemency, at length doth grow so great,

MASSYR55:23 H89 That *Ninus* of her, amorous soon did grow;

MPERS83:8 H1196 Unto such height did grow his cruelty,

MPERS87:39 H1391 On this, he and his Souldiers carelesse grow,

MGREC121:25 H2807 Then by more trouble to grow eminent.

MGREC122:14 H2839 If once young *Alexander* grow more strong,

MGREC135:38 H3410 And how from small beginnings it did grow,

MROMAN137:18 H3469 The *Romans* now more potent 'gin to grow,

QELIZ158:12 H121 *On neither tree did grow such Rose before,*

DAVID158:34 H14 Nor fields of offerings e're on you grow,

1LETTER181:20 H18 I weary grow, the tedious day so long;

CHILDRN186:12 H79 Where old ones, instantly grow young,

GROWES (4) [grows]

SEASONS47:39 H51 And {The} Grasse growes long, the tender Lambs {hungry

SEASONS52:17 H232 And like an Infant, stil he {it} taller growes.

MGREC106:21 H2155 As *Alexander* in his greatnesse growes,

MGREC126:10 H3001 Untill the Famine growes exceeding strong.

GROWING (2)
MGREC127:33 H3063 *Antigonus,* his growing up so hye,
MROMAN138:12 H3502 Leaves {Left} *Rome,* in wealth and power, still growing high.
GROWN (11)
AGES41:16 H235 And now am grown more staid, that {who} have been green,
MPERS71:19 H733 Who grown a man, resum'd again his state)
MGREC120:24 H2761 The Acts of his Vice-royes, {Vice-Roy} now grown so high:
MGREC124:2 H2907 To take down *Polisperchon* grown so high;
MGREC124:28 H2935 Thinks to enthrone the Prince when riper grown;
MGREC128:41 H3114 Till *Alexander* unto age was grown,
DIALOG145:16 H165 Well, to the matter then, there's grown of late,
DIALOG146:4 H192 Contention's {Contention} grown 'twixt Subjects and their
TDUDLEY166:18 H60 Now fully ripe, as shock of wheat that's grown,
CHILDRN185:14 H40 Untill they'r grown, then as the rest,
ELIZB187:5 H13 By nature Trees do rot when they are grown.
GROWNE (1) [grown]
ELEMEN11:38 H158 Whose numbers now are growne innumerous;
GROWS (1) See also GROWES
CONTEM171:24 H127 But Man grows old, lies down, remains where once he's laid.
GROWTH (1)
HUMOUR26:19 H249 But I, without thy help can give a growth,
GRUDGE (1)
PROLOG6:27 H11 Foole, I doe grudge, the Muses did not part
GUARD (1)
MGREC104:20 H2072 And of {by} his Guard, and Servitors now left.
GUESSE (2) [guess]
MASSYR66:37 H543 And if by words, we may guesse at the heart,
DIALOG142:4 H33 But you perhaps would have me guesse it out,
GUEST (4) See also GVEST
SEASONS52:23 H238 Now's held, a Guest, {(but ghest)} (but blest) Nativity.
MASSYR60:37 H302 Who to be rid of such a guest, was glad;
MGREC112:13 H2399 To every Guest, a cup of gold he sends,
1LETTER181:24 H22 The welcome house of him my dearest guest.
GUESTS (1) [pl.]
MGREC112:5 H2391 Six thousand Guests he to {unto} this feast invites,
GUIDE (2)
MGREC117:19 H2626 When of his monstrous bulk it was the guide,
TDUDLEY165:8 H10 Who was my Father, Guide, Instructor too,
GUIDED (1)
SIDNEY151:33 ~~H75~~ Like unwise *Phaeton* his ill guided sonne,
GUIDES (2)
ELEMEN12:40 H200 Which guides, when Sun, nor Moon, nor Stars do shine.
ELIZB187:11 H19 Is by his hand alone that guides nature and fate.
GUIFTS (3) [gifts]
MASSYR68:6 H592 With guifts of Scarlet robe, and Chaines {Chain} of gold,
MPERS82:26 H1173 Yet words {Nor prayers}, nor guifts, could win him least
MGREC93:16 H1613 Great were the guifts of nature, which he had;
GUILEFULL (1)
ELEMEN16:16 H339 My water *Syrens,* with their guilefull lures:
GUILT (8)
HUMOUR24:40 H189 Thou sayst I love my sword, because tis {it's} guilt. {gilt,}

MGREC96:5 H1725 The stately Horses trapt, the launces guilt;
MGREC112:25 H2411 His silence, guilt was, of such consequence,
MGREC~~113:13~~ H2440 And told the world, that for desert {his guilt} he dyed.
MGREC126:26 H3017 Desiring Justice might be done for guilt;
MGREC130:27 ~~H3181~~ Who did erect their cruelty in guilt,
CONTEM170:34 H104 Branded with guilt, and crusht with treble woes,
CONTEM171:8 H113 Who neither guilt, nor yet the punishment could fly.

GUILTLESS (1)
MPERS~~82:38~~ H1185 O're-flown with torrent of her ruby {guiltless} blood.

GUILTLESSE (2)
HUMOUR27:19 ~~H290~~ Though cast upon my guiltlesse blushing face;
MROMAN139:17 H3545 And shed her guiltlesse blood, with guilty knife,

GUILTY (4)
MASSYR68:23 H609 The guilty King, with colour pale, and dead,
MROMAN139:17 H3545 And shed her guiltlesse blood, with guilty knife,
DIALOG145:9 H158 My guilty hands (in part) hold up with you,
MEDDM203:25 Hp283 the wounds of a guilty Conscience, cares not how far he keeps

GUISE (1)
DIALOG141:12 H11 What meanes this wailing tone, this mourning guise?

GUN (2)
ELEMEN~~9:3~~ H37 My force? your sword, & Gun, your lance of steel
ELEMEN18:17 H421 And such are Ecchoes, and report o'th gun

GUNS (1) [pl.]
HUMOUR~~32:32~~ H506 I love no thundering Drums {guns}, nor bloody Wars,

GVEST (1) [guest]
HOUSE237:3 H33 Vnder thy roof no gvest shall sitt,

H

HABIT (3) See also HABITE
MGREC96:9 H1729 The Priests in their strange habit follow after;
MGREC106:35 H2169 His manners, habit, gestures, now doth {all did} fashion,
MROMAN137:31 H3482 Their Augurs strange, their habit, and attire,

HABITATION (3)
CONTEM172:31 H164 That for each season, have your habitation,
MEDDM202:26 Hp282 we may go forwards to the Citty of habitation, but when he
MEDDM207:29 Hp289 may be sure of an euer lasting habitation that fades not away.

HABITATIONS (1) [pl.]
CONTEM171:31 H133 Nor habitations long their names retain,

HABITE (1) [habit]
MASSYR57:6 H153 Some write, his Mother put his habite on,

HAD (279) See also SHE'D
ELEMEN14:24 H266 Scarce Earth had done, but th' angry waters {water} mov'd;

ELEMEN14:25 H267 Sister (quoth she) it had full well behov'd
ELEMEN19:17 H462 The living, scarce had power, to bury dead.
HUMOUR20:20 H12 Had leave to speake, succeeding one the other;
HUMOUR20:24 H16 Who had precedency of all the other.
HUMOUR29:3 H356 Had need be armed wel, and active too,
HUMOUR34:10 H565 Yet some may wish, oh, {O} had mine eyes ne're seene.
AGES36:26 H50 And al gave eare, to what he had to say.
AGES37:17 H79 When wretched I (ungrate) {ingrate} had done the wrong.
AGES37:28 H90 Yet this advantage, had mine ignorance,
AGES38:7 H110 I had no Suits at law, neighbours to vex.
AGES38:10 H113 I had no ships at Sea, no fraughts to loose.
AGES38:11 H114 I fear'd no drought, nor wet, I had no crop,
AGES42:9 H267 And gently lead the lambes, as they had need,
AGES43:22 H317 I hate {not} for to be had, {held} in small {high'st} account.
AGES44:23 H356 In this short Pilgrimage I oft have had;
AGES44:39 H372 When it had lost that radiant Sun-like spark,
SEASONS46:33 H9 At present claim'd, and had priority,
SEASONS~~46:35~~ H11 She trim'd her locks, which late had frosted been,
SEASONS48:38 H89 When Spring had done, then {the} Summer must {did} begin,
SEASONS49:29 H118 Oh! happy Shepheard, which had not to lose,
SEASONS50:21 H155 The Barley, and the Rye, should first had place,
SEASONS53:2 H258 *Or better Lines you should have had;*
MASSYR53:28 H18 Not finished, til he his race had run;
MASSYR53:33 H23 When thus with rule he had been dignified,
MASSYR53:37 H27 Confirmes the rule his Father had begun,
MASSYR54:29 H56 Where e're he warr'd he had too good successe,
MASSYR56:3 H109 An hundred gates, it had, of mettall strong.
MASSYR59:33 H257 Which {That} for twelve hundred years had held that place;
MASSYR60:36 H301 A thousand tallents of *Menahem* had,
MASSYR62:12 H357 Those that from *Ioshua's* time had been Estate {a state},
MASSYR63:25 H410 For fifty years, or more, it had been free,
MASSYR64:4 H428 Under whose shadow, birds, and beasts, had birth;
MASSYR64:35 H459 Within an Island had this City seat,
MASSYR64:37 H461 Of costly Ships, and Gallies, she had store,
MASSYR64:39 H463 But the *Chaldeans* had nor ships, nor skill,
MASSYR65:11 H476 *Jehoiakim* his Oath had clean forgot;
MASSYR65:15 H480 Had all his hopes like to a Spiders web;
MASSYR66:7 H513 The Temple's burnt, the Vessels had away,
MASSYR66:14 H520 No, nor {not} when *Moab, Edom* he had got.
MASSYR66:19 H525 Who had for sixteen hundred years born sway,
MASSYR~~66:32~~ H538 But for his pride so had the heavens decreed.
MASSYR66:38 H544 This King among the righteous had a part:
MASSYR67:6 H552 Poor forlorn Prince, that {who} had all state forgot,
MASSYR67:7 H553 In seven and thirty years, had seen no jot,
MPERS69:6 H628 Who had in *Persia* the Lieutenants place.
MPERS69:8 H630 And from that time, had held it as his own;
MPERS69:28 H650 Who had no might to save himself from wrong;
MPERS69:38 ~~H660~~ And told, how *Solon* in his hight had spoke.
MPERS70:3 ~~H674~~ And with the *Lidians,* had no more to doe.
MPERS70:21 H692 Had after {A} thousand yeares faire to be seen.
MPERS71:7 H723 But {Yet} to enlarge his state, had some desire;

MPERS71:31 H745 A second Army there {he} had almost grav'd;
MPERS71:36 H750 If all his {this} heat, had been for a good {pious} end,
MPERS72:35 H779 Had set a *Smerdis* up, of the same years;
MPERS~~73:5~~ H792 The Male line, of great *Cyrus* now did {had} end.
MPERS73:23 ~~H809~~ Who little pleasure had, in his short reigne,
MPERS75:2 H863 Tels them, how harshly the proud King had dealt,
MPERS77:27 H968 Sage *Artabanus* counsell, had he taken,
MPERS77:29 H970 His Souldiers, credit, wealth, at home had stay'd,
MPERS77:30 H971 And *Greece* such wondrous triumphs ne're had made.
MPERS79:24 H1050 What after did ensue, had he fore-seen,
MPERS79:25 H1051 Of so long time, his thoughts had never been.
MPERS79:40 H1066 And all that Army, then dismay'd, had fled,
MPERS81:15 H1123 As had *Macedon, Thebes,* and *Thessalie,*
MPERS81:19 H1127 And they had helpt them, as confederate;
MPERS81:41 H1145 For other {The rest had} Weapons, they had none would {do
MPERS82:36 H1183 Where he had sometime gaz'd with great delight.
MPERS83:9 H1197 Of life, no man had least security.
MPERS83:27 H1215 Amongst the Monarchs next, this Prince had place
MPERS83:32 H1220 A league of amity, had sworn before. {firmly swore,}
MPERS83:33 H1221 Which had they kept, *Greece* had more nobly done,
MPERS83:33 H1221 Which had they kept, *Greece* had more nobly done,
MPERS84:31 H1267 But he all injury, had soon forgate,
MPERS~~85:7~~ H1283 Stil making war, till first had lost his life:
MPERS87:15 ~~H1370~~ And yet with these, had neither heart, nor grace;
MPERS87:24 H1376 Few might have kept it, had they but {had} a heart.
MPERS~~87:24~~ H1376 Few might have kept it, had they but {had} a heart.
MPERS87:29 H1381 Had not a Captain; {his Captains} sore against his will;
MPERS88:18 H1411 So had he been, and got the victory,
MPERS88:19 H1412 Had not his too much valour put him by.
MPERS90:23 H1490 The many thousand *Persians* they had slain;
MPERS91:8 H1516 To defend, more then offend, he had {there was} need.
MPERS91:15 H1523 Who had (as noble *Raleigh* doth evince)
MPERS92:7 ~~H1565~~ It may be thought, surely he had no Son,
MPERS92:8 ~~H1566~~ So fell to him, which else it had not done:
MPERS92:10 H1568 But as 'tis thought, {most suppose} in him had {did} *Cyrus* end:
MPERS92:11 H1569 Whose race long time had worn the Diadem,
MPERS~~92:20~~ H1578 And the same sauce had served him no doubt,
MPERS92:38 H1596 Whose honours, treasures, pleasures, had short stay;
MGREC93:16 H1613 Great were the guifts of nature, which he had;
MGREC6:30 H1627 *Phillip,* on this great conquest had an eye;
MGREC6:32 H1629 The *Greeks* had chose him Captain Generall,
MGREC94:26 H1664 To scorn at him, *Darius* had good sport:
MGREC95:33 H1712 He but four hundred thousand had to fight,
MGREC95:36 H1715 For this wise King, had brought to see the sport;
MGREC96:19 H1739 He fifteen hundred had like women drest,
MGREC96:30 H1750 Had not been spoile, and booty rich enough,
MGREC97:17 H1778 Conquer'd himself (now he had conquered)
MGREC97:24 H1785 No sooner had this Captaine {Victor} won the field,
MGREC98:15 H1817 Besides, {Moreover} he had a Navie at command,
MGREC98:29 H1831 He scorns to have one worse then had the other,
MGREC99:24 H1867 The Captaine {Thus *Betis*} tane, had holes bor'd through his

MGREC100:17 H1901 Had *Betis* now been there, but with his Band,
MGREC100:18 H1902 Great *Alexander* had been kept from Land;
MGREC100:28 H1912 But on their fortitude he had small stay;
MGREC100:29 H1913 Yet had some hope, that on that even {the spacious} plain,
MGREC100:32 H1916 Who had long {sore} travaile, and much sorrow seen,
MGREC100:40 H1924 Had used her, and hers, in every thing,
MGREC101:18 H1943 Which had he done (perhaps) his fame had {he'd} kept,
MGREC101:18 H1943 Which had he done (perhaps) his fame had {he'd} kept,
MGREC101:19 H1944 Nor infamy had wak'd, when he had slept;
MGREC101:19 H1944 Nor infamy had wak'd, when he had slept;
MGREC101:36 H1965 Forty five thousand *Alexander* had,
MGREC101:38 H1967 Some write, th' other had a million, some more,
MGREC103:10 H2021 For when the Souldiers, had rifled their pleasure,
MGREC103:39 H2050 Had now his fourth, and last Army compounded,
MGREC104:34 H2086 Had *Alexanders* wrath incensed high;
MGREC105:17 H2110 Whose wounds had made their skins of purple dye;
MGREC106:19 H2153 Then tell her errand, we had better spare
MGREC107:38 H2213 Had *Bessus* had but valour to his wil,
MGREC107:38 H2213 Had *Bessus* had but valour to his wil,
MGREC108:10 H2226 Wherein their own had {got the} soveraignity.
MGREC108:18 H2234 But that they had forgot their Mother-tongue.
MGREC~~109:5~~ H2263 His fights, his dangers, and the hurts he had,
MGREC109:8 H2267 Nor had that drunken god, one that {who} would take
MGREC109:15 H2274 Had to his mind, made all things now {to} accord:
MGREC110:5 H2305 Had *Alexander* such resistance seen,
MGREC110:6 H2306 On *Tygris* side, here now he had not been;
MGREC110:22 H2326 But so to doe, his Souldiers had no will;
MGREC110:26 H2330 Be had in everlasting memory,
MGREC112:24 H2410 Nothing was found {prov'd}, wherein he had offended;
MGREC112:34 H2420 And's Brethren, whom {who} for him their lives had spent;
MGREC113:11 H2438 For to {He might} accuse himself, as they had done;
MGREC113:30 H2457 This is *Parmenio,* which {who} so much had done,
MGREC113:37 H2464 Had his reward most cruel, and unjust.
MGREC113:38 H2465 The next that {who} in untimely death had part,
MGREC114:7 ~~H2475~~ Upon a time, when both had drunken well,
MGREC~~114:7~~ H2475 Both at a Feast when they had tippled well
MGREC115:17 H2536 To meet him there, t' *Antipater* had {he'd} sent,
MGREC115:26 H2545 But now, *Antipater* had liv'd thus {so} long,
MGREC115:27 H2546 He might well dye, though he had done no wrong;
MGREC116:3 H2563 Poyson had put an end to's dayes 'twas thought,
MGREC116:13 H2579 His princely qualities, had he retain'd
MGREC116:14 H2580 Unparalel'd, for ever had remain'd;
MGREC116:18 H2584 Had so instructed him in morall truth.
MGREC116:19 H2585 The principles of what he then had learn'd
MGREC116:28 H2594 For those that {such as} pleas'd him: had both wealth and
MGREC116:38 H2604 For had he had but wisdome to his pride,
MGREC116:38 H2604 For had he had but wisdome to his pride,
MGREC116:40 H2606 To govern that he had already won:
MGREC117:4 H2611 Of all those kingdomes large which he had got,
MGREC117:11 H2618 As *Daniel,* before had Prophesied;
MGREC117:33 H2640 By Natures right, these had enough to claime,

MGREC117:36 H2643 Had hope themselves, to beare the Crown away;
MGREC117:37 H2644 A Sister *Alexander* had, but she
MGREC118:7 H2654 And had to him, still since *Ephestion* dyed,
MGREC118:40 H2689 *Antipater*, had long rul'd *Macedon,*
MGREC119:4 H2694 And had a higher project in his head,
MGREC121:28 H2810 Had it but in *Perdicas* life arriv'd,
MGREC121:36 H2818 The others all, had kingdomes in their eye,
MGREC121:40 H2822 Two battells now he fought, and had {of both} the best,
MGREC122:20 H2845 She daughter to his son, who had no other;
MGREC122:22 ~~H2845~~ Who had an Army, like a great Commander.
MGREC~~122:37~~ H2858 When to his pleasure all things they had done,
MGREC123:24 H2888 *Antipater* had banisht her from thence,
MGREC123:32 H2896 Such as his father had advanc'd to place,
MGREC~~123:33~~ H2897 Or by his favour {favours} any way did grace, {had grac'd}
MGREC124:13 H2920 But had the worst {beaten was} at Sea, as well as {and foil'd
MGREC124:14 H2921 his opponent still got {*Cassanders* forces had the} upper hand;
MGREC125:17 H2965 Remembring {Calling to mind} what sometime she had been,
MGREC125:22 H2972 The King by extreame torments had his end,
MGREC125:37 H2987 Wisht in *Epire* she still had been confin'd;
MGREC126:23 H3014 No sooner had he got her in his hands {hand},
MGREC127:3 H3033 Which she had often made others to sup:
MGREC127:18 H3048 In divers battels, he had good successe,
MGREC127:20 H3050 When victor oft had {he'd} been, and so might still,
MGREC127:41 H3071 {clear} what cause they {he} had to take up {make this} warre.
MGREC128:2 H3075 His Wife, and Son, in prison close had shut;
MGREC128:5 H3078 *Thessalonica* he had newly wed,
MGREC128:7 H3080 Had built, and call'd a City by his name,
MGREC128:11 H3084 Rebellious *Thebs* he had re-edified,
MGREC128:12 H3085 Which their late King in dust had damnified;
MGREC128:19 H3092 Had {The} valiant *Eumenes* unjustly slaine,
MGREC128:23 H3096 *Antigonus* {These princes} at {the} Sea soone had a fight,
MGREC128:32 H3105 And {With} all the spoyle and booty they {he} had tane;
MGREC128:36 H3109 His lost repute with victorie had won;
MGREC129:7 H3121 To render up such kingdomes as he had
MGREC129:18 H3132 And for that double fact which she had done,
MGREC129:20 H3134 *Perdicas* had before, for his amisse,
MGREC129:25 H3139 And now they are, {were} free Lords, of what they had,
MGREC130:12 H3167 *Antigonus* thus had a wolf by th' ears,
MGREC131:35 H3227 And leaves the ill got kingdomes he had won,
MGREC131:37 H3229 Who had an end put to their dayes by slaughter.
MGREC~~132:20~~ H3263 As Heaven and Earth against him had been set:
MGREC132:31 H3278 Rich *Ægypt* left, and what else he had won
MGREC132:38 H3285 That now he had out-lived all the rest:
MGREC133:5 H3293 Yet by him had this most unworthy end.
MGREC133:22 H3310 *Demetrius* had *Philip* to his son,
MGREC~~133:23~~ H3312 *Philip* had *Perseus,* who was made a Thrale
MGREC133:41 H3331 *Seleuchus* reign'd, when he had lost his life,
MGREC134:34 H3365 For since the first, that title still they had,
MGREC134:41 H3370 Till great *Augustus* had with him a fight,
MGREC135:7 H3379 Which by the *Romans* had its destiny.
MGREC135:32 H3404 And when he had no appetite to eate,

MROMAN136:29 H3443 Where Shepheards once had Coats, and Sheep their Folds,
MROMAN138:29 H3519 He after *Martius* death the Kingdome had,
MROMAN138:33 H3523 To such rude triumphs, as young *Rome* then had,
MROMAN139:5 H3533 As wealth had made them of abilitie;
MROMAN139:13 H3541 Sate on the Throne, when he had slaine his foe;
MROMAN139:35 H3561 At length resolv'd, when many years had past,
MROMAN140:5 H3568 Which none had cause to wail, nor I to boast.
DIALOG143:34 H103 That Pope, had hope, to find *Rome* here againe;
DIALOG145:27 H176 Had they not held law fast, all had been gone,
DIALOG145:27 H176 Had they not held law fast, all had been gone,
SIDNEY149:22 H21 As if your nine-fold wit had been compacted;
SIDNEY150:2 H27 Found *Cupids* Dame, had never such a Gin;
SIDNEY152:2 ~~H75~~ For dear regard he had of *Sydney's* state,
SIDNEY152:3 ~~H75~~ Who in his Deity, had so deep share,
SIDNEY~~152:4~~ H76 The Muses aid I crav'd, they had no will
SIDNEY152:5 ~~H76~~ He promis'd much, but th' muses had no will,
SIDNEY152:8 H79 Since *Sydney* had exhausted all their store,
SIDNEY152:11 H80 They took from me, the scribling pen I had,
SIDNEY152:16 ~~H85~~ But I had blemish'd theirs, to make 't appear;
DUBART153:9 H13 Had caused flowers, and fruits, soone to abound;
DUBART153:27 H31 Of all the glorious sights his eyes have had:
DUBART154:8 H53 Had I an Angels voice, or *Barta's* pen,
DUBART155:6 H91 *And Natures Law; had it been revocable,*
DUBART155:7 H92 *To rescue him from death, Art had been able:*
QELIZ156:11 H38 The *Salique* Law had not in force now been,
QELIZ156:12 H39 If *France* had ever hop'd for such a Queen;
QELIZ156:16 H43 And earth had twice {once} a yeare, a new old face:
QELIZ156:35 H62 Had ever Prince such Counsellors as she?
QELIZ157:9 H77 Had put her Harnesse off, had she but seen
QELIZ157:9 H77 Had put her Harnesse off, had she but seen
QELIZ157:33 H101 Or had they some, but with our Queen ist gone?
QELIZ157:38 H106 But happy *England,* which had such a Queen,
QELIZ157:39 H107 O {Yea} happy, happy, had those dayes still been,
DAVID159:3 H18 There had his dignity so sore a soyle,
TDUDLEY165:37 H39 But as a Pilgrim what he had, possest.
TDUDLEY165:39 H41 Nor honours pufft him up, when he had part:
TDUDLEY166:13 H55 For he a Mansion had, prepar'd above,
CONTEM168:21 H29 Had I not better known, (alas) the same had I.
CONTEM168:21 H29 Had I not better known, (alas) the same had I.
CONTEM169:15 H56 That nature had, thus decked liberally:
CONTEM171:29 H131 That state obliterate he had at first:
CONTEM171:36 H137 Shall I wish there, or never to had birth,
CONTEM174:15 H214 As if he had command of wind and tide,
FLESH175:6 H6 One flesh was call'd, who had her eye
FLESH176:14 H54 And never had more cause of woe
DISTEMP179:18 H6 Till nature had exhausted all her store,
VERSES184:7 H11 Where nothing's to be had Kings loose their right
CHILDRN184:14 H3 I had eight birds hatcht in one nest,
CHILDRN186:19 H86 You had a Dam that lov'd you well,
MEDDM197:11 Hp274 If we had no winter the spring would not be so pleasant, if we
MEDDM198:10 Hp276 And he that passes through the wildernes of this world, had

MEDDM203:2 Hp283 Had not the wisest of men, taught vs this lesson, that all is
MEDDM206:29 Hp288 how many good parents haue had bad children, and againe
MEDDM206:30 Hp288 bad parents haue had pious children, it should make vs adore
MEDDM206:35 Hp288 may also be a support to such as haue or had wicked parents,
MEDDM208:35 Hp290 them as if Moses had been able by the hand of faith, to hold
MEDDM209:21 Hp291 so it is with men, there was neuer yet any one man that had
MYCHILD215:19 Hp240 not to sett forth my self, but ye Glory of God. If I had minded
MYCHILD215:20 Hp240 ye former it had been perhaps better pleasing to yov, but seing
MYCHILD215:27 Hp240 Trouble, & I could not be at rest 'till by prayer I had confest
MYCHILD215:32 Hp241 In a long fitt of sicknes wch I had on my bed I often comvned
MYCHILD217:4 Hp242 ye Almighty hath hid his face from me, that yet I haue had
MYCHILD217:10 Hp242 I haue had great xper^{c} of Gods hearing my prayers, and
MYCHILD218:28 Hp244 But some new Troubles I haue had since ye world has been
FEVER220:22 H2 When Sorrowes had begyrt me rovnd,
MED223:10 Hp250 he my head. Such priviledges had not ye word of Truth made
JULY223:21 Hp251 I had a sore fitt of fainting wch lasted 2 or 3 dayes, but not in y^{t}
28AUG226:3 Hp254 y^{t} somt. I haue had, least my heart should bee drawn from
11MAYA226:13 Hp255 I had a sore sicknes and weaknes took hold of me wch hath by
11MAYB228:24 Hp259 that I haue had no great fitt of sicknes, but this year from y^{e}
11MAYB228:26 Hp259 this month I had a feaver seatd vpon me wch indeed was the
11MAYB228:27 Hp259 and sorest y^{t} ever I had lasting 4 dayes, and ye weather being
REMB235:34 H15 My 'plaints haue had accesse.

HADST (5)
MGREC99:32 H1875 If of thy future fame thou hadst regard,
DUBART~~154:29~~ H74 Thou hast {hadst} thy part of all, but of the last,
AUTHOR178:13 H23 If for thy Father askt, say, thou hadst none:
2LETTER182:23 H29 O *Phoebus,* hadst thou but thus long from thine
MERCY188:29 H15 Was ignorant what riches thou hadst lost.

HAG (1)
MPERS82:40 H1187 Thus cut, and mangled by a hag of hell.

HAIL (1) [healthy, whole]
CONTEM168:37 H43 Hail Creature, full of sweetness, beauty & delight.

HAIL (1) [ice]
2LETTER182:11 H17 The leaves in th' woods, the hail or drops of rain,

HAILE (1) [hail; ice]
ELEMEN17:14 H378 I need not say much of my Haile and Snow,

HAILS (1)
SEASONS52:16 H231 Bound up with Frosts, and furr'd with Hails, and Snows,

HAIR (1)
AGES40:21 H202 curling {to curle}, frisling up {and pounce my new-bought} hair;

HAIRE (2) [hair]
SEASONS49:3 H94 With haire all wet, she puffing thus began.
MGREC104:15 H2067 Grinding his teeth, and plucking off his haire,

HAIRES (3) [pl.]
AGES36:25 H49 His hoary haires, and grave aspect made way;
AGES45:27 H417 My {Mine} Almond-tree (gray haires) doth flourish now,
MEDDM199:8 Hp277 leaues argue want of sap and gray haires want of moisture so

HALCYON See HALSION

HALF (7)
AGES44:35 H368 And *Philip,* and *Albertus,* half undone;
MASSYR56:32 H138 The River *Indus* swept them half away,

MPERS76:14 H912 But wise *Gobrias* reads not half so farre:
MPERS79:36 H1062 This 'twixt the Mountains lyes (half Acre wide)
MGREC131:27 H3219 Is for this fresh young Lady half {quite} undone,
BIRTH180:5 H15 And if I see not half my dayes that's due,
ELIZB186:33 H4-5 *being a year and half old.*

HALFE (1)
QELIZ157:3 H71 To tell of halfe she did, or she could doe;

HALICARNA'S (1) [poss.]
MPERS78:23 H1004 *Artemesia, Halicarna's* Queene,

HALL (1)
CONTEM173:4 H172 Eftsoon to *Neptun's* glassie Hall repair

HALLICARNASSUS (1)
MGREC95:10 H1689 *Hallicarnassus* and *Pisidia*

HALLIS (1)
MGREC99:3 H1846 Betwixt the *Hellespont,* and *Hallis* side;

HALSION (1) [halcyon]
SIDNEY149:7 H6 When *England* did injoy her Halsion dayes,

HALTER (2)
MGREC125:24 H2974 A Halter, cup of Poyson, and a Sword,
MGREC125:27 H2977 At length yeelds to the Halter, her faire neck;

HALTING (1)
AUTHOR177:34 H6 Made thee in raggs, halting to th' press to trudge,

HAM (1)
MASSYR53:20 H10 The boysterous Sons of *Cush, {Chus,}* Grand-child to *Ham,*

HAMANS (1) [poss.]
MPERS84:11 H1239 Of *Hamans* fall, and *Mordica's* great rise;

HAND (52)
FATHER5:17 H18 But by my humble hand thus rudely pen'd
PROLOG7:15 H28 Who sayes, my hand a needle better fits,
HUMOUR35:4 H600 Let Sanguine, Choler, with her hot hand hold,
HUMOUR35:6 H602 My cold, cold Melanchollies {melancholy} hand shal clasp,
HUMOUR35:7 H603 Her dry, dry Cholers other hand shal grasp;
AGES35:34 H20 And in his hand an hour-glasse new begun,
AGES36:23 H47 In's other hand a glasse, ev'n almost run,
AGES37:38 H100 I gave no hand, nor vote, for death, or life:
AGES43:13 H306 There set, I rid my selfe straight out of hand.
AGES45:2 H378 In prime of youth seiz'd by heavens angry hand,
SEASONS51:11 H185 The season's now at hand, of all, and each;
MASSYR58:33 H216 From *Bactaria* an Army was at hand,
MASSYR60:12 H277 Not pertinent to what we have in hand;
MASSYR61:17 H322 And divers Cities, by strong hand did seize,
MASSYR62:37 H382 Until the thundring hand of heaven he felt,
MASSYR64:19 H443 The next year he, with unresisted hand,
MASSYR67:38 H584 And with a hand, soon dashed all his pride.
MASSYR68:10 H596 Amazed at the writing, and the hand.
MPERS69:40 H670 Now up, now {and} down, as fortune turnes her hand,
MPERS71:16 H730 And all of Royal bloud that came to hand,
MPERS76:38 H936 He stayes a landing {lanching} Gally with his hand;
MPERS82:6 H1153 The other not a hand, nor sword will {would} wave,
MGREC94:30 H1668 To lift his hand, 'gainst such a Monarchy.
MGREC105:35 H2128 Might be subjected to his royall hand;

MGREC~~109:20~~ H2279 Fifty six Elephants he brings to's hands: {hand,}
MGREC117:6 H2613 For by that hand, which still revengeth bloud,
MGREC122:24 ~~H2845~~ And in a Battell slew her hand to hand;
MGREC122:24 ~~H2845~~ And in a Battell slew her hand to hand;
MGREC124:14 H2921 his opponent still got {*Cassanders* forces had the} upper hand;
MGREC~~126:23~~ H3014 No sooner had he got her in his hands {hand},
MGREC129:17 H3131 But yet at {the} last the hand of vengeance came,
MGREC130:38 H3183 That hand is righteous still which doth repay:
MGREC~~131:9~~ H3201 How some when down, straight got the upper hand
MGREC135:13 H3385 But yet the *Persian* got the upper hand;
DIALOG142:10 H39 Or is't a *Norman,* whose victorious hand
DIALOG144:19 H129 That with high hand I still did perpetrate;
SIDNEY149:10 H9 Then {As} she that sway'd the Scepter with her hand:
SIDNEY151:6 ~~H69~~ But that it is record by *Philips* hand,
SIDNEY151:34 ~~H75~~ Till taught to's cost, for his too hasty hand,
DUBART154:23 H68 Oft have I wondred at the hand of heaven,
TDUDLEY165:10 H12 Nor is't Relation near my hand shall tye;
CONTEM172:24 H158 So hand in hand along with thee they glide
CONTEM172:24 H158 So hand in hand along with thee they glide
ELIZB187:11 H19 Is by his hand alone that guides nature and fate.
ANNEB187:16 H6 With troubled heart & trembling hand I write,
1SIMON188:7 H8 Cropt by th' Almighties hand; yet is he good,
MEDDM196:19 Hp273 ioy, knowing his refreshing is at hand
MEDDM208:35 Hp290 if Moses had been able by the hand of faith, to hold the Ever
MYCHILD216:3 Hp241 About 16. The Lord layd his hand sore vpon me & smott me
SAMUEL228:3 H4 I here resigne into thy hand,
SON230:29 H12 Of pyrates who were neer at hand
2HUSB232:31 H32 Vnto thy Work he hath in hand

HANDLE (2)

HUMOUR24:36 H185 He knew {well} how, for to handle, Sword and Harpe,
MASSYR64:38 H462 And Mariners, to handle sayle, and oare;

HANDLED (1)

VERSES184:3 H7 Yet handled ill, amounts but to this crum;

HANDMAIDS (1) [pl.]

FATHER5:18 H19 They are your bounden handmaids to attend.

HANDS (28) [pl.]

AGES41:27 H244 I then with both hands, graspt the world together,
AGES~~45:4~~ H386 A royal one by gifts from strangers hands
AGES45:8 ~~H390~~ A Royall one, by almes from Subjects hands,
AGES45:35 H425 My hands and armes, once strong, have lost their might,
MASSYR58:23 ~~H207~~ By prophesie, *Belosus* strength's their hands,
MASSYR59:4 H228 Both sides their hearts, their hands, their {&} bands unite,
MASSYR60:19 H284 Til *Mesopotamia* he got in's hands,
MASSYR66:16 H522 All Vassals, at his hands, for grace must sue;
MPERS~~69:38~~ H660 Who *Solon* was? to whom he lifts his hands;
MPERS74:40 H861 With his own hands cuts off his eares, and nose,
MPERS81:3 H1111 With empty hands they to their Master go;
MGREC102:28 H1998 But needs no force, 'tis rendred to his hands;
MGREC102:38 H2008 Now falls {fall} into the *Macedonians* hands.
MGREC104:21 H2073 Straight *Bessus* comes, and with his traiterous hands,
MGREC104:32 H2084 *Darius* from those Traitors hands to gain;

MGREC105:29 H2122 And not by Traitors hands untimely dye.
MGREC109:20 H2279 Fifty six Elephants he brings to's hands: {hand,}
MGREC~~120:4~~ H2739 Then fall into the hands of mortal foes.
MGREC126:23 H3014 No sooner had he got her in his hands {hand},
MGREC128:17 H3090 First, how he held the Empire in his hands,
MGREC129:21 H3135 But from {by} their hands, who thought not once of this.
DIALOG143:8 H75 Their hands in Kindreds blood, whom they did foyle:
DIALOG145:9 H158 My guilty hands (in part) hold up with you,
DIALOG145:14 H163 Then let's join heads, and hands {& hearts} for your relief.
FLESH175:33 H33 Then eyes can see, or hands can hold.
AUTHOR178:11 H21 In Criticks hands, beware thou dost not come;
MEDDM199:31 Hp278 Sore labourers haue hard hands and old sinners haue brawnie
MEDDM200:12 Hp279 on their loynes that so they might shake hands wth the

HAND-WRITING (1)

MASSYR67:40 H586 The fingers of his {a} hand-writing did spy.

HANG (2)

DIALOG141:8 H7 What ayles thee hang thy head, and crosse thine armes?
MEDDM201:19 Hp280 We often se stones hang wth drops not from any innate

HANGINGS (2) [pl.]

MPERS84:1 H1229 His hangings, white, and green, and purple dye;
MGREC102:35 H2005 Those purple hangings, mixt with green, and white,

HANGS (2)

SEASONS48:22 H75 One hangs his head, the other stands upright:
MGREC115:10 H2519 Hangs his Phisitian, the reason why,

HANNAH (1)

HANNA230:9 H1-2 Vpon my Daughter Hannah Wiggin her recouery from a

HAP (4)

MGREC116:33 H2599 Still fearing that his Name might hap to die,
MGREC127:34 H3064 Fearing their state {his force}, and what might hap ere long
SIDNEY152:1 ~~H75~~ Better my hap, then was his darlings fate,
CONTEM170:9 H82 Bewails his unknown hap, and fate forlorn;

HAPLESS (1)

MPERS~~81:9~~ H1117 (Chief instigater of this hopelesse {hapless} War;)

HAPLESSE (3)

MASSYR66:3 H509 A {Ah!} haplesse man, whose darksome contemplation,
MPERS93:1 H1598 And in the sixt year of his haplesse reigne,
DIALOG144:9 H119 Oh, *Edwards* Babes {youths}, and *Clarence* haplesse Son,

HAPPEFY'D (1) [happefied]

SAMUEL228:21 H22 For ever happefy'd wth Thee.

HAPPILY (1)

MGREC100:2 H1886 Where happily in's wars he did succeed;

HAPPINESS (1)

MPERS~~69:38~~ H666 If ever King equal'd his happiness.
HUMOUR25:37 H226 Ile not envy thy feats, nor happinesse.
AGES42:32 H288 If happinesse my sordidnesse hath found,
MPERS79:20 H1046 Long viewing them, thought it great happinesse,
MGREC116:25 H2591 *Achille's* happinesse he did envy,
DIALOG148:27 H292 Then follows dayes of happinesse and rest,
QELIZ157:40 H108 But happinesse, lies in a higher sphere,

HAPPY (21)

SEASONS49:29 H118 Oh! happy Shepheard, which had not to lose,

MPERS~~69:38~~ H667 (Quoth he) that man for happy we commend,
MPERS~~69:38~~ H668 Whose happy life attains an happy end.
MPERS~~69:38~~ H668 Whose happy life attains an happy end.
MPERS73:35 H820 And thought the people, would more happy be,
MPERS74:13 ~~H836~~ His happy wishes now doth no man spare,
DIALOG141:7 H6 With honour, wealth, and peace, happy and blest;
DIALOG148:3 H268 So shall thy happy Nation ever flourish,
DUBART152:33 H2 Amongst the happy wits this Age hath showne,
QELIZ155:12 H3 most happy memory.
QELIZ156:2 H29 The nine {'leven} *Olimp'ades* of her happy reigne;
QELIZ156:20 H47 Was ever Land more happy, freed from stirs?
QELIZ157:38 H106 But happy *England,* which had such a Queen,
QELIZ157:39 H107 O {Yea} happy, happy, had those dayes still been,
QELIZ157:39 H107 O {Yea} happy, happy, had those dayes still been,
TDUDLEY166:24 H66 Ah happy Soul, 'mongst Saints and Angels blest,
TDUDLEY166:31 H73 At last will bring us to that happy place
CONTEM172:18 H153 O happy Flood, quoth I, that holds thy race
1HUSB180:25 H4 If ever wife was happy in a man,
CHILDRN186:1 H68 So happy may you live and die:
CHILDRN186:29 H96 I happy am, if well with you.

HARBOUR (2)
MPERS80:16 H1083 {The Harbours} to receive, {contain} the Harbour was not able;
TDUDLEY165:38 H40 High thoughts he gave no harbour in his heart,

HARBOURS (1) [pl.]
MPERS~~80:16~~ H1083 Them {The Harbours} to receive, {contain} the Harbour was

HARD (8)
HUMOUR33:39 H553 Of three, its hard to say, which doth excel;
SEASONS50:28 H162 The Prince of Plumbs, whose stone is {as} hard as Rock.
MASSYR64:33 H457 And for her strength, how hard she was to gain,
MPERS69:34 H656 (A hard decree) to ashes he consume;
DIALOG145:34 H183 Here tugg'd they hard indeed, for all men saw,
MEDDM196:16 Hp273 christian that hath wrought hard in gods vine yard and hath
MEDDM196:21 Hp273 Downny beds make drosey persons but hard lodging, keeps
MEDDM199:31 Hp278 Sore labourers haue hard hands and old sinners haue brawnie

HARDLY (2)
AGES45:38 H428 Now stiffe and numb, can hardly creep or go.
MEDDM200:6 Hp279 Some children are hardly weaned although the teat be rub'd

HARDY (1)
MGREC117:28 H2635 Yet {But} none so hardy found as so durst say.

HARE (1)
ELEMEN10:11 H86 The Crown, the Whale, the Archer, Bernice Hare,

HARES (1) [pl.]
HUMOUR21:27 H55 Then timerous Hares, whom Castles doe immure?

HARK (1)
ELEMEN12:29 H189 But hark, ye worthy Merchants who for prize

HARKEN See HEARKEN

HARKNING (1) [harkening]
3LETTER182:37 H2 Scuds through the woods and Fern with harkning ear,

HARM (5)
HUMOUR29:24 H375 Nature doth teach, to sheild the head from harm,
MGREC117:24 H2631 Did harm himself, but never reacht his foes:

CONTEM173:21 H187 To gain more good, or shun what might thee harm
CHILDRN185:19 H45 Lest this my brood some harm should catch,
CHILDRN185:34 H60 And with my wings kept off all harm,

HARME (4) [harm]
ELEMEN9:19 H53 Your shrinking limbs, which winters cold doth harme;
ELEMEN14:14 H256 When they seek food, and harme mistrust the least.
MPERS81:41 H1145 rest had} Weapons, they had none would {do little} harme;
MGREC113:27 H2454 Thinking {Fearing} no harme, because he none did owe {doe},

HARMES (3) [harms]
MPERS90:41 H1508 And hopes by craft to quit his Masters harmes;
MGREC128:14 H3087 And to requite this Traytor for those {these} harmes:
MGREC135:3 H3375 To take her life, and quit her from all harmes;

HARMLESSE (1)
MPERS72:11 H759 Hearing her harmlesse brother thus was dead,

HARMONIOUS (1)
AGES39:28 H171 Sweet Musick rapteth {raps} my {brave} harmonious Soul,

HARMONY (1)
FATHER5:25 H26 Sweet harmony they keep, yet jar oft times,

HARMS (2) See also HARMES
FLESH176:17 H57 And count them for my deadly harms.
BIRTH180:11 H21 And when thou feel'st no grief, as I no harms,

HARNESSE (1) [harness]
QELIZ157:9 H77 Had put her Harnesse off, had she but seen

HARP (1)
MASSYR66:9 H515 Where late, of Harp, and Lute, was {were} heard the noyse,

HARPE (1) [harp]
HUMOUR24:36 H185 He knew {well} how, for to handle, Sword and Harpe,

HARPY-LIKE (1)
MPERS82:30 H1177 She *Harpy*-like, upon the Lady flew:

HARROW (1)
MEDDM205:2 Hp285 must make long furrows on their back and the Harrow

HARROWED (1)
MEDDM204:35 Hp285 into tilth yet all must be ploughed and harrowed Some children

HARSH (2)
FATHER5:26 H27 Their discord may {doth} appear, by these harsh rimes.
SEASONS48:34 ~~H85~~ In this harsh strain, I find no melody,

HARSHLY (1)
MPERS75:2 H863 Tels them, how harshly the proud King had dealt,

HARTLESS (1)
3LETTER182:36 H1 As loving Hind that (Hartless) wants her Deer,

HARUEST (1) [harvest]
MEDDM205:7 Hp285 plentifull crop may be expected in the haruest of their yeares.

HARVEST (2)
AGES36:22 H46 A {An} Harvest of the best, what needs he more.
AGES41:24 H241 I then receiv'd a {an} harvest of mine owne.

HAS (6)
MPERS75:18 ~~H878~~ But yet thou has sufficient recompence,
MGREC117:29 H2636 Great *Alexander* has left {did leave} issue none,
QELIZ155:17 H8 And so has {hath} vow'd, whilst there is world, or time;
MERCY188:27 H13 That thou dear Son has lost both Tree and fruit:
MYCHILD217:7 Hp242 vntoward child, that no longer then the rod has been on my

MYCHILD218:28 Hp244 some new Troubles I haue had since ye world has been filled

HA'ST (2)

2HUSB233:4 H37 To Wildernesse ha'st brovght
HOURS234:22 H36 As thou before ha'st done

HAST (42) See also THO'ST, THOU'ST, THOV'ST

ELEMEN15:36 H318 Or hast thou any colour can come nigh;
ELEMEN16:3 H326 Earth, thou hast not more Countrys, Vales and Mounds,
ELEMEN16:10 H333 If I should shew,{name} more Seas, then thou hast Coasts.
HUMOUR22:41 H110 No, no, {Alas,} thou hast no spirits, thy company
HUMOUR23:11 H121 Yet hast thy {the} seat assign'd, a goodly part,
HUMOUR24:29 H178 No valour upon earth, but what thou hast.
HUMOUR25:27 H216 Thou oft hast broke bounds of humanity.
HUMOUR30:36 H428 But if thou hast, that malice comes {is} from you.
MASSYR~~59:15~~ H239 The wals, and gates, their course {hast} did terminate;
MASSYR61:28 H333 His humble thankfulnesse (with {in} hast) to bring,
MASSYR64:26 H450 And unto wealthy *Tyre* with {in} hast repaire.
MPERS77:21 H962 The first begun, and finish'd in such hast,
MGREC99:28 H1871 What, hast thou lost thy late magnanimity?
MGREC107:20 H2195 Now with his Army, doth he hast {post} away,
MGREC125:9 H2957 In hast {haste} unto her deare *Cassander* sends,
DIALOG148:20 H285 And do to *Gog,* as thou hast done to *Rome.*
SIDNEY151:18 ~~H69~~ Yet this preheminence thou hast above,
DUBART154:29 H74 Thou hast {hadst} thy part of all, but of the last,
DAVID159:26 H41 So pleasant hast thou been, deare brother mine:
FLESH175:18 H18 Hast treasures there laid up in store
FLESH176:12 H52 How oft thy slave, hast thou me made,
FLESH176:13 H53 When I believ'd, what thou hast said,
SICKNES178:32 H15 Our strength doth waste, our time doth hast,
MEDDM197:23 Hp275 nothing will abase them more, then this What hast thou, but
MEDDM197:23 Hp275 abase them more, then this What hast thou, but what thou hast
FEVER221:1 H16 Thov knowst my heart, and hast me try'd
MED223:3 Hp250 should I doubt any more w^{n} thov hast given me such assured
JULY223:31 Hp251 for thov art my God, Thou hast said and shall not I beleiue it?
JULY223:32 Hp251 Thou hast given me a pledge of y^{t} Inheritc thou hast promised
MYSOUL225:13 H17 Then shall I know what thov hast done
13MAY227:9 H18 O hast thou made my pilgrimage
SON231:28 H39 Particular, and how gratiovsly thov hast answered my Desires.
HOURS233:24 H7 Thou hetherto hast been my God
HOURS234:13 H27 Tho: children thou hast given me
ACK235:6 H6 And 'mongst y^{m} hast regarded Mine,
ACK235:7 H7 Hast heard my cry's, + seen my Teares,
ACK235:8 H8 Hast known my doubts and All my feares,
ACK235:9 H9 Thou hast releiv'd my fainting heart
ACK235:11 H11 Thou hast to shore him safely brovght
REMB235:33 H14 Thou hast me heard + answered,
HOUSE237:17 H47 Thou hast an house on high erect

HASTE (9)

HUMOUR29:36 H387 And if thy haste, my slownesse should not temper,
SEASONS51:34 H210 *November* is my last, for time doth haste,
SEASONS52:33 H248 I care not how the Winter time doth haste;
MASSYR57:37 H182 T' *Sardanapalus* next we wil make haste.

MASSYR68:17 H603 *Daniel* in haste, is brought before the King,
MGREC~~125:9~~ H2957 In hast {haste} unto her deare *Cassander* sends,
MGREC125:28 H2978 Praying, that fatall day might quickly haste,
MGREC127:26 H3056 But as that to a period did haste,
2LETTER181:31 H1 *Phoebus* make haste, the day's too long, be gone,

HASTED (1)
MPERS78:1 H982 Although he hasted, yet foure yeares was spent,

HASTES (1)
SEASONS50:29 H163 {Summer seems but} short, the beauteous Autumne hastes,

HASTETH (1)
SEASONS47:31 ~~H46~~ In *Taurus* Signe, yet hasteth straight from thence;

HASTY (2)
SEASONS48:26 H79 The hasty Pease, and wholesome red {cool} Strawberry,
SIDNEY151:34 ~~H75~~ Till taught to's cost, for his too hasty hand,

HAT'ST (1)
FLESH176:10 H50 Thou speak'st me fair, but hat'st me sore,

HATCHT (1)
CHILDRN184:14 H3 I had eight birds hatcht in one nest,

HATE (19)
AGES40:16 H197 All counsel hate, which tends to make me wise,
AGES42:39 H295 How was I broy'd with envy, and with hate?
AGES43:22 H317 I hate {not} for to be had, {held} in small {high'st} account.
MASSYR58:5 H190 Knowing his basenesse, and the peoples hate,
MPERS84:32 H1268 And to his Country-men {native land} could bear no hate.
MPERS~~90:39~~ H1506 Whom the old Queen did bear a mortal hate.
MPERS91:22 H1530 Their former envie, and inveterate hate;
MGREC102:24 H1994 And former Discipline begins to hate;
MGREC103:33 H2044 And just procuring of the *Persians* hate.
MGREC106:25 H2159 His past sobriety doth also hate,
MGREC113:3 H2430 To wreak their spight, and hate, on every limbe.
MGREC113:6 H2433 My foes exceeds in malice, and their hate,
MGREC115:20 H2539 The Queen *Olimpias,* bears him deadly hate,
MGREC122:12 H2837 His rule Queen *Euridice* begins to hate,
MGREC~~125:21~~ H2970 But the old Queen pursues them with her hate,
MGREC126:16 H3007 will not heare {Her foe would give no Ear}, such is his hate.
MGREC126:40 H3029 How for no cause, but her inverterate hate;
DIALOG147:17 H243 We hate *Romes* Whore, with all her trumperie.
FLESH176:18 H58 Thy sinfull pleasures I doe hate,

HATED (2)
MPERS82:21 H1168 Scorn'd *Xerxes,* hated for his cruelty,
MGREC107:41 H2216 Hated of all, for's former treachery,

HATEFUL (1)
CONTEM170:18 H90 With sullen hateful looks he goes his wayes.

HATEFULL (3)
HUMOUR23:12 H122 The sinke of all us three, the hatefull spleen;
MGREC124:31 H2938 Hatefull the Name, and House of *Alexander,*
MGREC128:10 H3083 Th' hatefull *Olinthians* to *Greece* re-brings;

HATES (1)
MGREC124:39 H2946 *Olimpias, Aridæus* deadly hates,

H^T (3) [hath]
11MAYA226:19 Hp255 is a contented thankfull h^t vnder my affliction & weaknes seing

HATH (141) See also 'ATH, HT

ELEMEN10:36 H111 What lasting Forts my kindled wrath hath burn'd?
ELEMEN14:6 H250 What she hath lost by these my dreadfull {remed'less} woes.
ELEMEN15:2 H284 The Camell hath no strength, thy Bull no force;
ELEMEN18:18 H422 Which {That} tells afar, th' exployt which he {it} hath done.
HUMOUR22:18 H87 Nor hath she wit, or heat, to blush at this.
HUMOUR26:27 H257 What hath the heart, but what's sent from the liver?
HUMOUR29:2 H355 He that with two assaylents hath to do,
HUMOUR33:1 H515 Princes hath slav'd, and Captains captived:
HUMOUR34:20 H575 But modesty hath charg'd me to conceal;
AGES35:32 H18 Before the Sun hath throughly warm'd {heat} the clime.
AGES38:33 H136 What crudities my cold stomach hath bred?
AGES39:9 H152 Then let not him, which {that} hath most craft dissemble;
AGES42:16 H274 Thus hath mine age (in all) sometimes done wel.
AGES42:32 H288 If happinesse my sordidnesse hath found,
AGES44:15 H348 Now hath the power, Deaths Warfare, to discharge;
AGES46:11 H442 Hath yet amongst that sweet, some bitter gall.
SEASONS47:24 H40 For though the Frost hath lost his binding power,
SEASONS47:41 H53 Among the verduous Grasse hath Nature set,
SEASONS48:28 H81 Each season, hath his fruit, so hath each clime.
SEASONS48:28 H81 Each season, hath his fruit, so hath each clime.
SEASONS48:30 H83 But none in all that hath preheminence.
SEASONS49:11 ~~H102~~ Hath formerly much heat, the earth and aire.
SEASONS49:12 H103 Like as an oven, that long time hath been heat.
SEASONS~~49:23~~ H114 Hath envy bred in Kings that were at strife,
SEASONS49:24 ~~H114~~ Yet hath your life, made Kings the same envy,
SEASONS49:39 H132 The Sun in {thro} Leo now hath {takes} his carrear,
SEASONS50:32 H166 Hath stil ascended up in {to bear} goodly Fruits,
SEASONS50:35 H169 To feed his boughes, exhausted hath his sap,
SEASONS52:4 ~~H219~~ When cold, the sap to th' roots hath low'st repell'd;
SEASONS52:12 H227 What Winter hath to tel, now let him say.
SEASONS52:19 H234 To th' Southward tropick his swift race hath {doth} run;
MASSYR62:27 H372 Hath bred more wonder, then beleefe in hearts;
MPERS77:37 H978 Vaine *Xerxes* thinks his counsell hath most wit,
MPERS90:37 H1504 And {Commission} hath command, to take the others head,
MPERS92:9 H1567 What Acts he did, time hath not now left pend,
MGREC98:31 H1833 *Ephestion* now, hath the {having chief} command o' th' Fleet,
MGREC~~120:36~~ H2773 Which eating time hath scarcely yet defac'd.
MGREC126:30 H3021 Whose fury yet unparalleld {scarcely parallel'd} hath been;
MGREC~~132:16~~ H3252 Though men and mony both he hath at will,
MROMAN136:36 H3450 And bloudy hath it prov'd, since first it stood:
MROMAN140:9 H3572 Hath many Ages been upon his knees.
DIALOG142:5 H34 What, hath some *Hengist,* like that *Saxon* stout,
DIALOG142:8 H37 Or hath *Canutus,* that brave valiant *Dane,*
DIALOG142:31 H60 Though Armes, nor Purse she hath, for your releif:
DIALOG143:12 H81 *France* knowes, how of {oft} my fury she hath drunk;
DIALOG143:16 H85 Though she hath bin injurious heretofore.
DIALOG143:32 H101 The Gospel is trod {troden} down, and hath no right;
DIALOG~~144:31~~ H139 heard {saw} their cause, and wrongs {hath} judg'd righteously,
DIALOG146:19 H205 The seed time's come, but Ploughman hath no hope,
DUBART152:33 H2 Amongst the happy wits this Age hath showne,

QELIZ~~155:17~~	H8	And so has {hath} vow'd, whilst there is world, or time;
QELIZ156:7	H34	She hath wip'd off th' aspersion of her Sex,
VANITY160:26	H36	There is a path, no vultures eye hath seen.
VANITY160:27	H37	Where lions fierce, nor lions whelps hath {have} been,
VANITY160:30	H40	The depth, and sea, hath {have} said its not in me,
VANITY160:34	H44	Death and destruction, the fame hath heard,
TDUDLEY166:19	H61	Death as a Sickle hath him timely mown,
TDUDLEY166:20	H62	And in celestial Barn hath hous'd him high,
CONTEM168:4	H14	That hath this under world so richly dight:
CONTEM168:11	H20	Hath hundred winters past since thou wast born?
CONTEM168:34	H40	All mortals here the feeling knowledg hath.
CONTEM169:3	H45	Hath strength, thy shining Rayes once to behold?
CONTEM170:19	H91	Hath thousand thoughts to end his brothers dayes,
CONTEM170:25	H96	But since that time she often hath been cloy'd;
CONTEM170:33	H103	When deep dispair, with wish of life hath fought,
FLESH175:23	H23	Industry hath its recompence.
FLESH175:32	H32	Earth hath more silver, pearls and gold,
FLESH175:35	H35	Earth hath enough of what you will.
BIRTH179:27	H3	All things within this fading world hath end,
2LETTER182:30	H36	Hath power to dry the torrent of these streams.
3LETTER183:10	H12	Whose loss hath made her so unfortunate:
CHILDRN184:37	H26	Hath also bid her Dam adieu:
CHILDRN185:2	H28	She now hath percht, to spend her years;
MERCY189:11	H32	She one hath left, a joy to thee and me,
MEDDM195:35	Hp272	both by an empty old age, he that hath nothing to feed on but
MEDDM196:3	Hp272	that man whose head hath great abilities and his heart little or
MEDDM196:11	Hp273	The finest bread hath the least bran the purest hony the least
MEDDM196:16	Hp273	christian that hath wrought hard in gods vine yard and hath
MEDDM196:33	Hp274	wch thousands of enemys wthout hath not been able to take
MEDDM196:34	Hp274	hath been deliuered vp by one traytor wthin, and that man w^{ch}
MEDDM197:1	Hp274	of Sathan without could not hurt, hath, been foild by one
MEDDM198:2	Hp275	God hath sutable comforts and supports for his children
MEDDM198:13	Hp276	Want of prudence as well as piety hath brought men into great
MEDDM198:16	Hp276	The skillfull fisher hath his severall baits, for severall fish, but
MEDDM198:17	Hp276	hooke vnder all, Satan that great Angler hath his sundry baits
MEDDM198:22	Hp276	but either that or something like it, hath been both done and
MEDDM201:1	Hp280	he will proportion the load, as god hath his little Children so
MEDDM201:2	Hp280	he hath his strong men, such as are come to a full stature in
MEDDM201:12	Hp280	Fire hath its force abated by water not by wind, and anger
MEDDM202:3	Hp281	his gifts among the sons of men, betwixt whom he hath put so
MEDDM203:11	Hp283	be all convenient and comfortable for him yet he hath no
MEDDM203:14	Hp283	country, and heere he hath many conueniences and comforts
MEDDM203:26	Hp283	that hath skill to cure it, but when he findes his diseases to
MEDDM204:5	Hp284	philistin and he that hath deliuered mee saith paul, will deliuer
MEDDM208:30	Hp290	it hath stayd the Course of the Sun raised the dead, cast out
MEDDM208:33	Hp290	it hath ouer come the omnipotent himself, as when Moses
MEDDM209:18	Hp291	god hath by his prouidence so ordered, that no one Covntry
MEDDM209:18	Hp291	hath by his prouidence so ordered, that no one Covntry hath
MEDDM209:24	Hp291	hath (perhaps meaner then himself) wch shews us perfection is
MYCHILD216:21	Hp241	constantly observed this y^{t} he hath never suffered me long to
MYCHILD216:22	Hp242	fr him, but by one afflict^{n} or other hath made me look home,

MYCHILD216:23	Hp242	w^{t} was amisse. So vsually thvs it hath been wth me that I haue
MYCHILD216:25	Hp242	comonly hath been vpon my own person, in sicknesse
MYCHILD216:27	Hp242	towards him. Somt. he hath smott a child wth sicknes,
MYCHILD216:30	Hp242	them ye Times w^{n} ye Lord hath manifested ye most Love to
MYCHILD217:3	Hp242	benefitt by it: It hath been no small support to me in times of
MYCHILD217:4	Hp242	when ye Almighty hath hid his face from me, that yet I haue
MYCHILD217:12	Hp242	my mind wthout it, and I haue been confident it hath been
MYCHILD217:17	Hp243	although he hath not left me altogether wthout the wittnes of
MYCHILD217:18	Hp243	his holy spirit who hath oft given me his word & sett to his Seal
MYCHILD217:32	Hp243	Many times hath Satan troubled me concerning ye verity of y^{e}
MYCHILD218:6	Hp243	this hath thovsands of Times been svggested to me, yet God
MYCHILD218:6	Hp244	thovsands of Times been svggested to me, yet God hath
MYCHILD218:8	Hp244	If ever this God hath revealed himself it mvst bee in his word,
MYCHILD218:10	Hp244	Invention can work vpon ye Soul, hath no Judgments befallen
MYCHILD218:11	Hp244	who haue scornd + contemd it, hath it not been p^{r}served
MYCHILD218:22	Hp244	This hath somt. stuck with me, and more it would, by ye vain
MYCHILD218:34	Hp244	I have told yov before. That hath stayed my heart, and I can
BYNIGHT220:3	H4	And hath at once both ease and Rest,
BYNIGHT220:18	H16	Who freely hath done this for me,
FEVER221:13	H28	Who hath redeem'd my Soul from pitt,
MED223:1	Hp250	Meditations when my Soul hath been refreshed wth the
MED223:14	Hp250	that God who hath done so much for me, should haue so little
MED223:16	Hp250	p^{r}fectly what he hath done for me, and then shall I bee able to
WHAT224:19	H19	His word he plighted hath on high
MYSOUL225:20	H24	For God hath made me wise.
28AUG225:31	Hp254	men, he hath no benefitt by my adversity, nor is he ye better
11MAYA226:13	Hp255	a sore sicknes and weaknes took hold of me wch hath by fitts
11MAYA226:14	Hp255	all this spring till this 11. May, yet hath my God given me many
30SEPT227:19	Hp257	but not in y^{t} sore manner somt. he hath. I desire not only
30SEPT227:30	Hp257	haue recourse to ye same God who hath heard + deliuered
11MAYB228:23	Hp259	It hath pleased God to giue me a long Time of respite for these
THEART229:1	H3	Who hath restor'd, redeem'd, recur'd
RESTOR230:5	H20	Praises to him who hath not left
RESTOR230:8	H23	But graunted hath my Suit.
SON230:20	H3	All praise to him who hath now turn'd
SON231:17	H29	And thvs hath granvnted my Reqvest
2HUSB232:31	H32	Vnto thy Work he hath in hand
HOURS233:25	H8	Thy help my soul hath fovnd
HOUSE237:22	H52	By him who hath Enovgh to doe.
HATING (1)		
AGES35:26	H12	Solid, hating all lightnesse, and al folly.
HATRED (1)		
HUMOUR32:24	H498	Nor wonder 'twas, for hatred there's not smal,
HATS (1) [pl.]		
DUBART153:21	H25	The Hats, and Fans, the Plumes, and Ladies tires,
HAUE (105) [have]		
2SIMON195:10	Hp271	much more by duty full children, I haue avoyded incroaching
MEDDM196:28	Hp273	Diuerse children, haue their different natures, some are like
MEDDM197:8	Hp274	is because they haue more sence then faith they se what they
MEDDM197:31	Hp275	Corne till it haue past through the Mill and been ground to
MEDDM199:16	Hp278	haue any thing to stay vpon, but take away their props and

MEDDM199:31 Hp278 Sore labourers haue hard hands and old sinners haue brawnie
MEDDM201:7 Hp280 I haue seen an end of all perfection (sayd the royall prophet)
MEDDM201:8 Hp280 never sayd, I haue seen an end of all Sinning, what he did say,
MEDDM202:17 Hp282 haue no kernell in them, and they that feed vpon them, may
MEDDM203:3 Hp283 of spirit, yet our owne experience would soon haue speld it out,
MEDDM203:7 Hp283 he haue good cause often to repeat that sentence, vanity of
MEDDM203:27 Hp284 and that he must needs perish if he haue no remedy, will
MEDDM205:19 Hp286 would haue boldnes to go to the throne of grace to be
MEDDM205:33 Hp286 and some haue nothing to shew but leaues only, and some
MEDDM205:37 Hp287 and ther are some (and they sincere ones too) who haue not
MEDDM206:2 Hp287 there are others that haue nothing to commend them, but only
MEDDM206:11 Hp287 Company of Saints, and Angels those Saintes haue their
MEDDM206:19 Hp287 Men that haue walked very extrauagantly, and at last bethink
MEDDM206:29 Hp288 how many good parents haue had bad children, and againe
MEDDM206:30 Hp288 bad parents haue had pious children, it should make vs adore
MEDDM206:35 Hp288 may also be a support to such as haue or had wicked parents,
MEDDM207:8 Hp288 but haue driuen them the further from him, that they are ready
MEDDM207:22 Hp289 sayd that all haue a lease of their liues, some longer some
MEDDM207:23 Hp289 our great landlord to let: All haue their bounds set ouer w^{ch}
MEDDM207:31 Hp289 and diseased bodys, haue hourly mementos of their mortality
MEDDM207:32 Hp289 But the soundest of men, haue likewise their nightly monitor,
MEDDM208:13 Hp290 to haue a good repute among good men, yet it is not that, w^{ch}
MEDDM209:25 Hp291 below, as also that god will haue vs beholden one to another
PILGRIM210:4 H4 That myrie steps, haue troden oft
PILGRIM210:40 H40 and of their maker haue the sight
MYCHILD215:12 Hp240 latest, + being ignorant whether on my death bed I shall haue
MYCHILD215:18 Hp240 haue not studyed in this yov read to shew my skill, but to
MYCHILD215:31 Hp241 as I grew to haue more vnderstanding, so ye more solace I
MYCHILD216:20 Hp241 all my experiences of gods gratious Dealings wth me I haue
MYCHILD216:23 Hp242 amisse. So vsually thvs it hath been wth me that I haue no
MYCHILD216:24 Hp242 felt my heart out of order, but I haue expected correct^{n} for it,
MYCHILD216:29 Hp242 haue been the times of my greatest Getting and Advantage,
MYCHILD216:29 Hp242 the times of my greatest Getting and Advantage, yea I haue
MYCHILD216:31 Hp242 Then haue I gone to searching, and haue said wth David Lord
MYCHILD216:31 Hp242 haue I gone to searching, and haue said wth David Lord search
MYCHILD216:33 Hp242 way everlasting: and seldome or never but I haue fovnd either
MYCHILD216:34 Hp242 some sin I lay vnder wch God would haue reformed, or some
MYCHILD216:35 Hp242 wch he would haue performed, and by his help I haue
MYCHILD216:35 Hp242 he would haue performed, and by his help I haue layd vowes
MYCHILD217:4 Hp242 ye Almighty hath hid his face from me, that yet I haue had
MYCHILD217:6 Hp242 circu̅spection in my walking after I haue been afflicted. I haue
MYCHILD217:6 Hp242 walking after I haue been afflicted. I haue been wth God like
MYCHILD217:8 Hp242 (or at least in sight) but I haue been apt to forgett him and my
MYCHILD217:10 Hp242 I haue had great xper^{c} of Gods hearing my prayers, and
MYCHILD217:12 Hp242 my mind wthout it, and I haue been confident it hath been
MYCHILD217:15 Hp243 I haue often been p^{r}plexed y^{t} I haue not fovnd that constant
MYCHILD217:17 Hp243 haue, although he hath not left me altogether wthout the
MYCHILD217:19 Hp243 shall bee well with me. I haue somt. tasted of y^{t} hidden Manna
MYCHILD217:20 Hp243 world knowes not, & haue sett vp my Ebenez^{r}. and haue
MYCHILD217:20 Hp243 knowes not, & haue sett vp my Ebenez^{r}. and haue resolved
MYCHILD217:22 Hp243 shall never p^{r}vail: yet haue I many Times sinkings &

MYCHILD217:23 Hp243 that felicity that somt. I haue done, But when I haue been
MYCHILD217:24 Hp243 and seen no light, yet haue I desired to stay my self upon
MYCHILD217:25 Hp243 Lord, and when I haue been in sicknes + pain, I haue thought if
MYCHILD217:27 Hp243 me to powder it would bee but Light to me, yea oft haue I
MYCHILD217:29 Hp243 would bee a Heaven And could I haue been in Heaven without
MYCHILD217:30 Hp243 ye Love of God, it would haue been a Hell to me for in Truth it
MYCHILD218:7 Hp244 me over. I haue argved thvs wth my self, That there is a God I
MYCHILD218:9 Hp244 mvst bee it or none. Haue I not fovnd y^{t} operation by it that
MYCHILD218:11 Hp244 Diverse who haue scornd + contemd it, hath it not been
MYCHILD218:15 Hp244 in it fullfilled wch could not haue been so long foretold by any
MYCHILD218:17 Hp244 When I haue gott over this Block y^{n} have I another pvtt in my
MYCHILD218:19 Hp244 yet why may not ye popish Relign. bee ye right, They haue the
MYCHILD218:28 Hp244 But some new Troubles I haue had since ye world has been
MYCHILD218:30 Hp244 Xtians haue been carryed away wth them, that somt: I haue
MYCHILD218:31 Hp244 Faith vpon ye Earth? & I haue not known what to think, But
MYCHILD218:32 Hp244 I haue reme¯bred the words of Christ that so it must bee, and
MYCHILD219:1 Hp245 against it, I know whom I haue trvsted, and whom I haue
MYCHILD219:2 Hp245 and y^{t} he is able to keep y^{t} I haue comitted to his charge.
FAINT222:17 H7 Thvs fainting haue I said
MED223:11 Hp250 known who or where is the man that durst in his heart haue
MED223:12 Hp250 p^{r}sumed to haue thought it? So wonderfull are these thoughts
MED223:14 Hp250 who hath done so much for me, should haue so little from me,
JULY223:26 Hp251 y^{t} it may bee a support to me when I shall haue occasion
28AUG226:3 Hp254 somt. I haue had, least my heart should bee drawn from him,
11MAYA226:17 Hp255 Many refreshments haue I fovnd in this my weary pilgrimage,
13MAY227:5 H14 I haue a shelter from ye storm
13MAY227:7 H16 I haue accesse vnto his Throne,
30SEPT227:22 Hp257 world. I haue fovnd by Exper^{c}. I can no more liue wthout
30SEPT227:24 Hp257 then thy stroakes shall bee welcome, I haue not been refined
30SEPT227:25 Hp257 furnace of affliction as some haue been, but haue rather been
30SEPT227:28 Hp257 Thus (dear children) haue yee seen ye many sicknesses and
30SEPT227:29 Hp257 that I haue passed thro: to ye End y^{t} if you meet wth the like
30SEPT227:30 Hp257 haue recourse to ye same God who hath heard + deliuered
SAMUEL228:10 H11 No freind I haue like Thee to trust
11MAYB228:24 Hp259 that I haue had no great fitt of sicknes, but this year from y^{e}
11MAYB228:25 Hp259 of January 'till May I haue been by fitts very ill & weak. The
THEART229:9 H11 And new Exper^{c} I haue gain'd
HOURS234:3 H17 I haue a more beloued one
HOURS234:11 H25 I in this world no comfort haue,
HOURS234:14 H28 And freinds I haue also
REMB235:34 H15 My 'plaints haue had accesse.
REMB236:5 H20 Thy mercyes Lord haue been so great

HAUEING (1) [having]
MED223:17 Hp250 as I ovght. Lord haueing this hope let me purefye my self as

HAUEST (1) [havest]
MYCHILD218:29 Hp244 Blasphemy, and Sectaries, and some who hauest been acct^{d}.

HAUGHTY (4)
MASSYR62:32 H377 Whose haughty heart is shewn in works, and deeds;
MGREC97:32 H1793 But down his haughty stomach could not bring,
MGREC~~121:15~~ H2793 *Python* of haughty mind, and courage great.
DUBART154:31 H76 Thy haughty stile, and rapted wit sublime,

HAUNT (1)

SEASONS~~49:33~~ H125 If pride within your lowly Cells ere haunt,

HAVE (155) See also HAUE, TO'VE

FATHER5:9 H10 To climbe their Climes, I have nor strength, nor skill,
FATHER5:19 H20 These same are they, of {from} whom we being have,
PROLOG6:21 H6 And {Or} how they all, or each, their dates have run:
PROLOG7:29 H40 Men have precedency, and still excell,
ELEMEN9:29 H63 Our Sages new, another tale have told:
ELEMEN10:35 H110 What famous Townes to cinders have I turn'd?
ELEMEN11:39 H159 I have not time to thinke of every part,
ELEMEN12:35 H195 Besides the use you have {of roots}, of Hearbs and Plants,
ELEMEN13:10 H211 If ought you have to use, to wear, to eate?
ELEMEN14:17 H259 whole Armies {*Cambyses* Armie} I have {was} overthrown;
ELEMEN14:18 H260 But windy sister, 'twas when you have blown.
ELEMEN14:26 H268 Among your boastings to have praised me;
ELEMEN16:4 H327 Then I have Fountaines, Rivers, Lakes and Ponds:
ELEMEN17:22 H386 All know, what {that} innundations I have made;
ELEMEN18:39 H443 Some for this cause (of late) have been so bold,
ELEMEN19:16 H461 Whereof such multitudes have dy'd and fled,
ELEMEN19:18 H463 Yea so contagious, Countries have me {we} known;
ELEMEN19:19 H464 That birds have not scap'd death, as they have flown,
ELEMEN19:28 ~~H472~~ How many rich fraught vessells, have I split?
ELEMEN19:29 ~~H472~~ Some upon sands, some upon rocks have hit.
ELEMEN19:30 ~~H472~~ Some have I forc'd, to gaine an unknown shoare;
ELEMEN20:5 H487 I have said lesse, then did my sisters three;
HUMOUR20:22 H14 Which of the foure should have predominance;
HUMOUR20:32 H24 Only she crav'd, to have a vacant space.
HUMOUR21:28 H56 Have ye not heard of Worthies, Demi-gods?
HUMOUR23:6 H116 But Melancholy, wouldst have this glory thine?
HUMOUR24:7 H156 I have been sparing, what I might have said,
HUMOUR26:7 H237 To play Philosopher, I have no list;
HUMOUR26:9 H239 For acting these, I have nor wil, nor art,
HUMOUR28:34 H346 If time I have transgrest, and been too long,
HUMOUR29:12 H365 But when the first offenders {offender} I have laid,
HUMOUR30:14 H406 If I have not more part, then al ye three:
HUMOUR30:18 H410 When you poor bankrupts prove, then have I most.
HUMOUR30:24 H416 But whilst he lives, Ile shew what part I have.
HUMOUR30:32 H424 These two in one cannot have residence.
HUMOUR32:20 H494 Though wit I want, and anger I have lesse,
HUMOUR32:35 H509 At home, the Conquerours, have conquered:
HUMOUR32:37 H511 That Kings have laid their Scepters at my feet,
AGES35:37 H23 But if he hold, til it have run its last,
AGES38:34 H137 Whence vomits, wormes, and flux have issued?
AGES38:35 H138 What breaches, knocks, and falls I daily have?
AGES~~40:29~~ H210 I want a {have no} heart {at} all this for to deplore.
AGES40:30 ~~H210~~ Thus, thus alas! I have mispent my time,
AGES41:12 H231 Thus I have said, and what i've said {been,} you see,
AGES41:16 H235 And now am grown more staid, that {who} have been green,
AGES41:17 H236 What they have done, the same was done by me,
AGES42:2 H260 Whose loynes {backs} I've cloth'd, and bellies I have fed;
AGES42:4 H262 Yea justice I have done, was I in place;

AGES43:10	~~H305~~	Have been curst furtherers of mine intents.
AGES43:20	H315	I judge, I should have room, in all mens hearts.
AGES43:24	H319	I glory in my wealth, I have within.
AGES44:2	H335	What you have been, ev'n such have I before,
AGES44:4	H337	Babes innocence, Youths wildnes I have seen,
AGES44:5	H338	And in perplexed Middle-age have bin,
AGES44:6	H339	Sicknesse, dangers, and anxieties have past,
AGES44:8	H341	I have bin young, and strong, and wise as you,
AGES44:18	H351	Nor from alliance now can I have hope,
AGES44:19	H352	But what I have done wel, that is my prop;
AGES44:23	H356	In this short Pilgrimage I oft have had;
AGES44:28	H361	Such private changes oft mine eyes have seen,
AGES45:15	H397	I've seen, and so have ye, for 'tis but late,
AGES45:35	H425	My hands and armes, once strong, have lost their might,
AGES46:4	H435	In pleasures, and in labours, I have found,
AGES46:18	H449	In my dark house, such kindred I have store,
SEASONS47:3	~~H17~~	Who for some months have seen but starry lights;
SEASONS~~47:5~~	H21	Who for some months have been but starry lights.
SEASONS47:23	H39	They joy in what they have, but more in hope,
SEASONS~~49:11~~	H102	Have throughly dry'd the earth, and heat the air.
SEASONS49:21	H112	With robes thereof, Kings have been dignifi'd.
SEASONS50:22	H156	Although their Bread have not so white a face.
SEASONS51:26	H202	Which notes, when youth, and strength, have past their prime,
SEASONS51:27	H203	Decrepit age must also have its time;
SEASONS51:31	H207	Where also he, his Winter time must have;
SEASONS53:2	H258	*Or better Lines you should have had;*
MASSYR58:40	H223	To want no priviledge, Subjects should have,
MASSYR60:12	H277	Not pertinent to what we have in hand;
MASSYR63:32	H419	Nor of his acts {Wars} have we the certainty,
MPERS72:15	H763	Who would have born a Nephew, and a Son.
MPERS74:6	H831	Of all the Peers should have precedency.
MPERS75:19	~~H878~~	In that thy fame shall sound whilst men have sence;
MPERS80:34	H1101	For his retreat, to have an eye thereto:
MPERS87:24	H1376	Few might have kept it, had they but {had} a heart.
MPERS91:30	~~H1544~~	As all the mighty ones, have done, and must:
MPERS92:29	H1587	That severall men, will have their severall mind;
MGREC98:29	H1831	He scorns to have one worse then had the other,
MGREC102:32	H2002	Where Kings have shown their glory, wealth, and might;
MGREC103:34	H2045	But deafe to reason, (bent to have his will;)
MGREC105:20	H2113	Who not a little chear'd, to have some eye,
MGREC107:39	~~H2214~~	He easily might have made them stay there stil;
MGREC~~107:39~~	H2214	With little pain there might have kept them still:
MGREC112:41	H2427	Faine would have spoke, and made his owne defence,
MGREC114:14	H2484	And would have slaine himself, for *Clitus* gone,
MGREC116:39	H2605	He would have found enough for {there} to be done,
MGREC117:26	H2633	A King they'l have, but who, none can agree:
MGREC118:11	H2658	He hold of {on} this occasion should have laid,
MGREC121:29	H2811	With greater joy it would have been receiv'd;
MGREC123:35	H2899	Prest to accomplish what he would have done;
MGREC~~125:21~~	H2971	And needs will have their lives as well as State:
MGREC133:6	H3294	Thus with these Kingly Captaines have we done,

MGREC135:8 H3380 Thus Kings, and Kingdoms, have their times, and dates,
MGREC135:36 H3408 With these three Monarchies, now have I done,
MROMAN140:6 H3569 No more I'le do, sith I have suffer'd wrack,
DIALOG141:21 H20 This Phisick-purging-potion I have taken,
DIALOG142:4 H33 But you perhaps would have me guesse it out,
DIALOG142:38 H67 For they have work enough (thou knowst) elsewhere;
DIALOG144:8 H118 'Mongst all the cruelties which I have {by great ones} done,
DIALOG145:2 H151 Such cruelty as all reports have past.
DIALOG145:32 H181 This done, an Act they would have passed fain,
DIALOG146:7 H195 I that no warres, so many yeares have known,
DIALOG146:33 ~~H219~~ To weep for that we both have pray'd for long,
DIALOG146:35 ~~H221~~ That Right may have its right, though't be with blood;
DIALOG147:1 H227 And thine {thy} infringed Lawes have boldly stood.
DIALOG147:26 H250 O mother, can you weep, and have such Peeres.
SIDNEY149:34 ~~H23~~ Which have the self-same blood yet in my veines;
SIDNEY~~152:15~~ H85 Since I the Muses thus have injured.
DUBART153:1 H5 In humble wise have vow'd their service long;
DUBART153:27 H31 Of all the glorious sights his eyes have had:
DUBART154:23 H68 Oft have I wondred at the hand of heaven,
DUBART154:24 H69 In giving one, what would have served seven.
DUBART154:26 H71 Thy double portion would have served many.
QELIZ157:12 H80 Within that Princesse to have residence,
QELIZ157:32 H100 Now say, have women worth, or have they none?
QELIZ157:34 H102 Nay Masculines, you have thus tax'd us long,
VANITY159:32 H4 Where is the man can say, lo, I have found
VANITY160:21 H31 While man is man, he shall have ease or pain.
VANITY~~160:27~~ H37 Where lions fierce, nor lions whelps hath {have} been,
VANITY~~160:30~~ H40 The depth, and sea, hath {have} said its not in me,
TDUDLEY165:29 H31 That After-comers in them might have share.
TDUDLEY166:8 H50 Which all they have, and more still set to view,
CONTEM172:31 H164 That for each season, have your habitation,
FLESH175:40 H40 For I have vow'd (and so will doe)
FLESH176:27 H67 For I have meat thou know'st not off;
FLESH177:1 H82 But Royal Robes I shall have on,
FLESH177:17 H98 Nor Sun, nor Moon, they have no need,
FLESH177:27 H108 If I of Heaven may have my fill,
SICKNES178:28 H11 Where I shall have all I can crave,
BIRTH180:7 H17 The many faults that well you know I have,
3LETTER183:20 H22 I have a loving phere, yet seem no wife:
CHILDRN184:34 H23 I have a third of colour white,
CHILDRN185:41 H67 O to your safety have an eye,
ELIZB187:10 H18 And buds new blown, to have so short a date,
ANNEB187:17 H7 The Heavens have chang'd to sorrow my delight.
ANNEB187:18 H8 How oft with disappointment have I met,
ANNEB187:19 H9 When I on fading things my hopes have set?
ANNEB187:20 H10 Experience might 'fore this have made me wise,
MERCY188:23 H9 Who might in reason yet have lived long,
MYCHILD216:17 Hp241 I have brovght yov into ye world, and wth great paines,
MYCHILD217:13 Hp242 becavse I have fovnd my heart through his goodnes enlarged
MYCHILD218:12 Hp244 maugre all ye heathen Tyrants + all of the Enemyes who have
MYCHILD218:17 Hp244 When I haue gott over this Block y^{n} have I another pvtt in my

MYCHILD218:34 Hp244 Sav^{r}. I have told yov before. That hath stayed my heart, and I

HAVING (11) See also HAUEING

HUMOUR20:19 H11 All having made obeysance to each Mother,
MASSYR55:28 H94 That having no compeer, she might rule all,
MASSYR61:31 H336 But *Tiglath,* having gain'd his wished end,
MPERS69:12 H634 Adopts her Son for his, having no other:
MPERS72:25 ~~H773~~ Having one son, in whom he did delight,
MPERS84:39 H1275 The King this noble Captaine having lost,
MPERS85:21 H1297 Revolts, having treasure, and people gain'd:
MPERS89:39 H1473 The *Greeks,* having {seeing} their valiant Captaines slaine,
MGREC~~98:31~~ H1833 *Ephestion* now, hath the {having chief} command o' th' Fleet,
MGREC117:21 H2628 But by *Ulysses,* having lost his sight,
MGREC127:16 H3046 Having Command o'th treasure he can hire,

HAVEST See HAUEST

HAVOCK (1)

MASSYR61:34 H339 In *Galilee,* he woful havock makes;

HAWKS (1)

CHILDRN185:28 H54 Or by some greedy hawks be spoyl'd.

HAY (2)

ELEMEN13:28 H229 The Corne, and Hay, both fall before they'r mowne;
ELEMEN17:3 H367 Their Cattle, Hay, and Corne, I sweep down current,

HAZARD (1)

MEDDM209:9 Hp291 could do (as they thought) wth lesse hazard and more profit,

HAZER (1)

MASSYR66:15 H521 *Kedar,* {and} *Hazer,* the *Arabians* too,

HEAD (51)

ELEMEN11:8 H128 Which made a *Cæsar,* (Romes) the worlds proud head,
ELEMEN13:19 H220 And how I force the grey head to obey.
HUMOUR23:5 H115 But a good head from these are disonant;
HUMOUR23:10 H120 Thou canst not claime, the Liver, Head nor Heart;
HUMOUR29:24 H375 Nature doth teach, to sheild the head from harm,
HUMOUR~~30:7~~ H399 Those {Whose} cold dry heads, {head} more subtilly doth yeild,
HUMOUR34:27 H582 Then, my head {brain} for learning is not the fittest,
AGES35:29 H15 Upon his head a Garland Nature set:
AGES36:6 H30 Seemed to grow on's head (bedew'd with showers:)
AGES45:13 H395 one stab'd, another {and some to} loose his head {their heads};
SEASONS48:22 H75 One hangs his head, the other stands upright:
SEASONS50:33 H167 Until his head be gray, and strength be gone,
MASSYR64:1 H425 This was of Monarchies that head of gold,
MPERS69:20 H642 Against great *Cressus,* then of *Lidia* head;
MPERS70:18 H689 This head of Kingdoms, *Caldes* excellence,
MPERS70:31 H702 And at one blow, worlds head, she headlesse makes;
MPERS70:35 H706 In honour, peace, and wealth, with a grey head,
MPERS72:37 H781 Ruling as they thought good, {best} under his head.
MPERS77:1 H940 Off flyes his head, down showres his frolick bloud.
MPERS88:30 H1423 At {But when} last his head they spy upon a Launce,
MPERS~~88:33~~ H1426 Nor *Gorgons* {head} like to this, transform'd to stones.
MPERS90:37 H1504 And {Commission} hath command, to take the others head,
MGREC96:13 H1733 And o're his head, his golden gods on high;
MGREC108:11 H2227 And now reviv'd with hopes, held up their head,
MGREC111:37 H2382 And set his Crown on his supposed head;

MGREC119:4 H2694 And had a higher project in his head,
MGREC124:36 H2943 When *Alexander* knockt his head to th' wall:
MGREC126:37 H3026 With Garlands crown'd his head, bemoan'd his Fates,
MGREC128:6 H3079 Daughter to *Phillip,* their renowned head;
MGREC134:32 H3363 Next *Auletes,* who cut off *Pompey's* head:
MGREC134:37 ~~H3367~~ Her brother by him, lost his trayterous head
MGREC135:20 H3392 The first, was likened to a head of gold,
MGREC136:18 H3432 *As faults proceeding from my head, not heart.*
DIALOG141:8 H7 What ayles thee hang thy head, and crosse thine armes?
DIALOG145:29 H178 They took high *Strafford* lower by the head,
DIALOG147:11 H237 To root out Prelates, {Popelings} head, tail, branch, and rush.
SIDNEY150:5 H30 Yet, {But} he's a beetle head, that cann't discry
DAVID158:24 H4 Alas, slaine is the head of *Israel,*
DAVID159:4 H19 As if his head ne're felt the sacred Oyle:
TDUDLEY166:26 H68 His hoary head in righteousness was found:
CONTEM167:28 H5 Were gilded o're by his rich golden head.
CONTEM173:12 H179 The sweet-tongu'd Philomel percht ore my head,
FLESH176:24 H64 And triumph shall, with laurel head,
DISTEMP179:17 H5 Bedrencht with tears that flow'd from mournful head.
1LETTER181:3 H1 My head, my heart, mine Eyes, my life, nay more,
1LETTER181:7 H5 So many steps, head from the heart to sever
MEDDM196:3 Hp272 that man whose head hath great abilities and his heart little or
MEDDM196:18 Hp273 of his euening to be stretched out, lifts vp his head wth
MEDDM198:25 Hp276 An akeing head requires a soft pillow, and a drooping heart a
FEVER220:27 H7 My aking head did break,
MED223:10 Hp250 Body he my head. Such priviledges had not ye word of Truth

HEADLESSE (1) [headless]
MPERS70:31 H702 And at one blow, worlds head, she headlesse makes;

HEAD-LONG (1)
SIDNEY151:32 ~~H75~~ Goodwill, did make my head-long pen to run,

HEAD'S (1) [head is]
HUMOUR22:35 H104 The Brain she challenges, the Head's her seat,

HEADS (11) [pl.]
HUMOUR23:26 H136 Whose Serene {profound} heads, I line with policies,
HUMOUR30:7 H399 Those {Whose} cold dry heads, {head} more subtilly doth yeild,
AGES~~45:13~~ H395 one stab'd, another {and some to} loose his head {their heads};
MASSYR65:9 H474 With peeled shoulders, and with balded heads,
MPERS70:9 H680 But till convenient time their heads kept shut;
DIALOG144:6 H116 How many Princely heads on blocks laid down,
DIALOG144:16 H126 These be the bitter fountains, heads, and roots,
DIALOG145:14 H163 Then let's join heads, and hands {& hearts} for your relief.
DIALOG148:21 H286 Oh *Abrahams* seed lift up your heads on high.
FLESH177:4 H85 But such as Angels heads infold.
MEDDM198:6 Hp276 billows goe ouer their heads he then leads them to the Rock

HEADS-MAN (1)
QELIZ157:8 H76 Feirce *Tomris* (*Cirus* Heads-man, *Sythians* Queen)

HEAL (1)
FEVER221:3 H18 O heal my Soul thov know'st I said,

HEAL'DST (1)
SON231:10 H22 Thou heal'dst his flesh + cheerd his heart.

HEALING (2)

MEDDM202:30 Hp282 of righteousnes will arise wth healing in his wings.
13MAY226:30 H6 My Svns return'd wth healing wings

HEALTH (5)

AGES40:10 H191 Sometimes I sit carousing others health,
MASSYR63:16 H401 His health congratulates with complement.
MEDDM207:6 Hp288 they were giuen for, as health wealth and honour, wch might be
28AUG226:2 Hp254 but joyfully? The Lord knowes I dare not desire that health
HANNA230:12 H5 To health my Daughter dear

HEALTHFULL (2) See also HELTHFULL

MEDDM201:15 Hp280 appetite and a through Concoction, is a signe of an healthfull
MEDDM202:11 Hp281 and healthfull y^{t} their bones are full of marrow & their breasts

HEALTHY (1)

SEASONS~~49:33~~ H123 Upon the grass resting your healthy limbs,

HEAP (2)

MASSYR60:32 H297 And from this heap did after Ages see,
MGREC99:33 H1876 Why didst not heap up honour, and reward?

HEAPES (1) [heaps]

ELEMEN13:2 H203 Was {Were} those compiled heapes of massy stones?

HEAPS (8)

ELEMEN10:38 H113 In confus'd heaps of ashes may ye see.
MPERS88:36 H1429 And heaps on heaps, such multitudes they laid,
MPERS88:36 H1429 And heaps on heaps, such multitudes they laid,
MGREC107:3 H2178 So heaps up gifts, his credit to redeem;
DIALOG146:6 H194 That thousands lay on heaps, here bleeds my woes.
DUBART154:17 H62 Their trophies were but heaps of wounded slain,
VANITY160:2 H12 He heaps up riches, and he heaps up sorrow,
VANITY160:2 H12 He heaps up riches, and he heaps up sorrow,

HEAPT (1)

AGES43:15 ~~H307~~ Then heapt up gold, and riches as the clay;

HEAR (9) See also HEARE

HUMOUR31:21 H454 Pray hear, admire, and learn instruction.
AGES36:38 H62 To hear the child, who crying, thus began.
AGES45:32 H422 awake, {waking glad to hear} at the cocks clanging {shrill}
MASSYR~~56:21~~ H127 All eyes that saw, or ears that hears, {hear} admires.
MGREC130:37 H3182 Thus may we hear, and fear, and ever say,
3LETTER183:6 H8 His voice to hear, or person to discry.
SAMUEL228:7 H8 Hear me again, I giue him Thee.
11MAYB228:29 Hp259 in his goodnes, and to hear my prayers, and to deliuer me out
HOURS234:21 H35 O hear me Lord in this Reqvest

HEARBS (2) [herbs]

ELEMEN12:35 H195 Besides the use you have {of roots}, of Hearbs and Plants,
SEASONS47:12 H28 Now digs, then sows, his hearbs, his flowers, and roots,

HEARD (16)

HUMOUR21:28 H56 Have ye not heard of Worthies, Demi-gods?
MASSYR66:9 H515 Where late, of Harp, and Lute, was {were} heard the noyse,
DIALOG144:31 H139 Who heard {saw} their cause, and wrongs {hath} judg'd
VANITY160:34 H44 Death and destruction, the fame hath heard,
TDUDLEY165:12 H14 Who heard or saw, observ'd or knew him better?
CONTEM169:10 H51 Silent alone, where none or saw, or heard,
CONTEM169:18 H58 I heard the merry grashopper then sing,

FLESH175:4 H4 I heard two sisters reason on
MEDDM203:35 Hp284 conuersation aright will glorifie him that heard him in the day of
PILGRIM211:1 H42 as eare ner' heard nor tongue ere told
SOREFIT221:21 H7 My plaints & Groanes were heard of Thee
13MAY226:33 H9 To him that heard my wailing Voice.
30SEPT227:30 Hp257 recourse to ye same God who hath heard + deliuered me,
ACK235:7 H7 Hast heard my cry's, + seen my Teares,
REMB235:33 H14 Thou hast me heard + answered,
HOUSE237:8 H38 Nor bridegroom's voice ere heard shall bee.

HEAR'DST (1)
FEVER221:7 H22 Thou hear'dst, thy rod thou didst remove

HEARDST (1)
SAMUEL228:6 H7 Thou heardst me then and gav'st him me

HEARE (10) [hear]
HUMOUR34:28 H583 Ne're did {Nor will} I heare {yield} that Choler was the witt'est;
AGES40:26 H207 And in a word, if what I am you'd heare,
SEASONS51:20 H196 *October* is my next, we heare in this,
MPERS89:28 H1462 They quak'd, to heare them, to each other call.
MGREC101:17 H1942 No, though *Parmenio* plead, he {yet} will not heare;
MGREC105:9 H2102 Invokes the heavens, and earth, to heare his moanes;
MGREC105:13 H2106 Should heare, nor see, his groans, and {dying} misery:
MGREC126:16 H3007 Cassander will not heare {Her foe would give no Ear}, such is
DIALOG143:36 H105 From *Beelzebub* himself, such language heare?
DIALOG144:18 H128 Of more then thou canst heare, or I relate,

HEARERES (1) [hearers]
MEDDM201:27 Hp281 precepts of the wise masters of assemblys to their heareres,

HEARES (2) [hears]
MPERS87:8 H1364 Which *Cyrus* heares, and so fore-slowes his pace:
MGREC100:37 H1921 When this sad newes (at first) *Darius* heares,

HEAR'ST (3) [hearest]
2HUSB232:4 H5 And hear'st the prayers of Thine
HOURS233:20 H3 O Lord thou hear'st my dayly moan
ACK235:5 H5 O Thou that hear'st ye prayers of Thine

HEAREST (1)
REMB235:31 H12 O thou yt hearest prayers Lord

HEARING (11)
MPERS72:11 H759 Hearing her harmlesse brother thus was dead,
MPERS80:35 H1102 He hearing this, his thoughts, and course home bended,
MPERS81:30 H1138 *Mardonius* proud, hearing this answer stout,
MPERS87:19 H1373 Their Captain hearing, but of *Cyrus* name.
MGREC104:1 H2053 But hearing, *Alexander* was so near;
MGREC107:6 H2181 Then {And} hearing, *Bessus* makes himselfe a King,
MGREC123:18 H2882 *Antigonus* hearing of his decease,
MGREC125:8 H2956 *Euridice* hearing what she intends,
MGREC125:39 H2989 Where hearing of this newes he speeds away,
CONTEM173:15 H182 I judg'd my hearing better then my sight,
MYCHILD217:10 Hp242 I haue had great xperc of Gods hearing my prayers, and

HEARKEN (1)
2HUSB232:5 H6 O hearken Lord vnto my suit

HEARS (5) See also HEARES
MASSYR56:21 H127 All eyes that saw, or ears that hears, {hear} admires.

MASSYR68:24 H610 There hears his *Mene,* and his *Tekel* read;
MPERS72:34 H778 At last, two of his Officers he hears,
MGREC107:1 H2176 But yet no notice takes, of what he hears;
MGREC120:41 H2778 *Perdicas* hears, his foes are now {all} combin'd,

HEARSE See HERSE

HEART (92)

PROLOG6:25 H9 But when my wondring eyes, and envious heart,
ELEMEN11:40 H160 Yet let me name my *Grecia,* 'tis my heart
ELEMEN15:14 H296 If I supply, his heart and veines rejoyce;
ELEMEN16:20 H343 Which can to life, restore a fainting heart:
HUMOUR21:14 H42 I in his heart erect my regal throne,
HUMOUR21:22 H50 Be he a Souldier, I more fence his heart
HUMOUR23:10 H120 Thou canst not claime, the Liver, Head nor Heart;
HUMOUR23:37 H147 By th' influence I send still from the heart.
HUMOUR26:27 H257 What hath the heart, but what's sent from the liver?
HUMOUR26:31 H261 But why the heart, should be usurpt by thee,
AGES39:27 H170 And by my mirth can raise the heart deprest;
AGES40:29 H210 I want a {have no} heart {at} all this for to deplore.
AGES40:39 H218 My heart lyes frying, and my {mine} eyes are sinking;
AGES~~41:9~~ H229 Marrow {aches} ful my bones, of Milk {woe} my breasts {heart},
AGES42:41 H297 And greater stil, did {and thirst for honour,} set my heart on
AGES45:39 H429 My heart sometimes as fierce, as Lions bold,
MASSYR58:9 H194 His manly heart disdained, in the least,
MASSYR61:30 H335 To whom, he ought all loyalty of heart.
MASSYR62:32 H377 Whose haughty heart is shewn in works, and deeds;
MASSYR66:37 H543 And if by words, we may guesse at the heart,
MASSYR68:3 H589 With quaking knees, and heart appall'd, he crys,
MPERS72:27 ~~H773~~ Shot through the heart of his beloved son:
MPERS77:5 H944 And for revenge his heart still restlesse burnes;
MPERS82:34 H1181 The sorrow of his heart, did close his eye:
MPERS82:41 H1188 With loaden heart unto the King he goes,
MPERS84:18 H1254 That in all {his} Loyalty his heart was bound;
MPERS84:35 H1271 Either to wrong, did wound his heart so sore,
MPERS87:15 ~~H1370~~ And yet with these, had neither heart, nor grace;
MPERS87:24 H1376 Few might have kept it, had they but {had} a heart.
MGREC93:36 H1633 Restlesse both day and night, his heart now {then} was,
MGREC~~94:18~~ H1653 And with a bount'ous heart and courage brave,
MGREC105:19 H2112 Findes poore *Darius,* peirced to the heart;
MGREC113:18 H2445 This sound advice, at heart, pleas'd *Alexander,*
MGREC~~116:10~~ H2572 She laid it more to heart, then any other,
MGREC116:28 H2594 those that {such as} pleas'd him: had both wealth and heart:
MGREC129:23 H3137 But 'twas in shew, in heart it pleas'd them best.
MGREC131:41 H3233 his Sword did pierce his mothers {run her through the} heart,
MGREC136:9 H3423 *After some dayes of rest, my restlesse heart,*
MGREC136:18 H3432 *As faults proceeding from my head, not heart.*
DIALOG145:3 H152 My {Mine} heart obdurate, stood not yet agast.
DIALOG146:23 H209 If any pity in thy heart remain,
DIALOG~~147:18~~ H244 on brave *Essex,* shew whose son thou art {with a loyal heart},
DIALOG147:19 H245 Not false to King, nor Countrey in thy heart, {to the better part;}
DUBART152:35 H4 My ravisht eyes, and heart, with faltering tongue,
DUBART153:26 H30 And tells her tales; (his full heart over-glad)

DUBART154:5 H50 My full astonish'd heart doth pant to break,
TDUDLEY165:38 H40 High thoughts he gave no harbour in his heart,
CONTEM170:31 H101 His face like death, his heart with horror fraught,
FLESH175:39 H39 Disturb no more my setled heart,
DISTEMP179:14 H2 In anguish of my heart repleat with woes,
1LETTER181:3 H1 My head, my heart, mine Eyes, my life, nay more,
1LETTER181:7 H5 So many steps, head from the heart to sever
3LETTER183:4 H6 A dearer Dear (far dearer Heart) then this.
ANNEB187:16 H6 With troubled heart & trembling hand I write,
MERCY188:26 H12 My bruised heart lies sobbing at the Root,
MERCY188:32 H18 Oh how I simpathize with thy sad heart,
MERCY189:13 H34 Chear up (dear Son) thy fainting bleeding heart,
MEDDM196:3 Hp272 whose head hath great abilities and his heart little or no grace
MEDDM197:19 Hp275 it, and that heart wch is not continually purifieing it self is no fit
MEDDM198:25 Hp276 head requires a soft pillow, and a drooping heart a strong
MEDDM198:33 Hp277 it, the pure in heart shall se god, but the defiled in conscience
MEDDM205:9 Hp286 man is called the little world so his heart may be cal'd the little
MEDDM205:23 Hp286 He that would keep a pure heart and lead a blamlesse life,
MYCHILD215:33 Hp241 heart, and made my Suplicat^{n}. to the most High who sett me
MYCHILD216:1 Hp241 grew vp to bee about 14. or 15. I fovnd my heart more carnall,
MYCHILD216:9 Hp241 wch my heart rose, But after I was convinced it was ye way of
MYCHILD216:24 Hp242 felt my heart out of order, but I haue expected correct^{n} for it,
MYCHILD217:13 Hp242 becavse I have fovnd my heart through his goodnes enlarged
MYCHILD218:34 Hp244 I have told yov before. That hath stayed my heart, and I can
FEVER221:1 H16 Thov knowst my heart, and hast me try'd
FEVER221:10 H25 My heart no more might quail.
SOREFIT221:32 H18 My heart I wholly giue to Thee
FAINT222:14 H4 My sinking heart I pray thee raise
MED223:11 Hp250 known who or where is the man that durst in his heart haue
WHAT224:7 H7 On High my heart O doe thou raise
28AUG225:28 Hp254 my drooping heart, and to manifest his Loue to me, and this is
28AUG226:3 Hp254 somt. I haue had, least my heart should bee drawn from him,
13MAY226:32 H8 My heart exvlts & praises sings
SAMUEL228:20 H21 Perswade my heart I shall him see
11MAYB228:28 Hp259 it ye more tedious, but it pleased ye Lord to support my heart
THEART228:35 H1 My thankfull heart wth glorying Tongve
RESTOR229:23 H6 When heart did faint & Spirits quail
RESTOR229:29 H12 My thankfull heart wth pen record
SON231:10 H22 Thou heal'dst his flesh + cheerd his heart.
2HUSB232:13 H14 Then let thy promis joy his heart
2HUSB232:15 H16 Vphold my heart in Thee O God
2HUSB233:17 H50 Wth an Engaged heart to sing
HOURS234:5 H19 O stay my heart on thee my God
HOURS234:33 H47 But give me Lord a better heart
ACK235:9 H9 Thou hast releiv'd my fainting heart
HOUSE236:20 H12 And to my God my heart did cry
HOUSE237:11 H41 Then streight I 'gin my heart to chide,

HEARTED (1)

MEDDM201:20 Hp281 thick ayre about them so may we sometime se, marble hearted

HEARTLESSE (1) [heartless]

MASSYR68:14 H600 In comes the Queen, to chear her heartlesse son.

HEART'S (2) [heart is]

MGREC95:19 H1698 To *Alexanders* heart's no little joy.

ANNEB187:32 H22 Mean time my throbbing heart's chear'd up with this

HEARTS (1) [heart is]

ELIZB186:34 H6 Farewel dear babe, my hearts too much content,

HEARTS (15)

AGES43:20 H315 I judge, I should have room, in all mens hearts.

AGES44:41 H374 (For 'twas our hopes then kept our hearts alive)

AGES~~45:2~~ H379 Which fil'd our hearts with fears, with tears our eyes,

MASSYR59:4 H228 Both sides their hearts, their hands, their {&} bands unite,

MASSYR59:27 H251 By this accomplishment, their hearts were shaken:

MASSYR62:27 H372 Hath bred more wonder, then beleefe in hearts;

MPERS74:28 H851 Yet more the peoples hearts firmly to binde,

MPERS~~74:31~~ H854 Much gain'd the hearts of his nobility.

MPERS88:11 H1404 That, more then multitudes, their hearts did awe:

MGREC95:27 H1706 No stroake for it he struck, their hearts so quakes.

DIALOG~~145:14~~ H163 Then let's join heads, and hands {& hearts} for your relief.

DIALOG147:3 H229 With hearts, and states, to testifie their will.

1SIMON188:10 H11 With humble hearts and mouths put in the dust,

MEDDM207:27 Hp289 should make vs so to number our dayes as to apply our hearts

SON231:23 H35 In both o^{r} hearts erect a frame

HEARTS (1) [poss.]

DUBART153:7 H11 Did thaw my frozen hearts ingratitude;

HEAT (41)

ELEMEN9:31 H65 A burning fiery heat we find reflect;

ELEMEN10:22 H97 Augment his heat, which was too hot before:

ELEMEN13:15 H216 My cold, thy (fruitfull) heat, doth crave no lesse:

ELEMEN18:25 H429 When burning heat, doth cause you faint, I coole,

HUMOUR21:12 H40 Though under fire, we comprehend all heat,

HUMOUR22:18 H87 Nor hath she wit, or heat, to blush at this.

HUMOUR22:25 H94 Nor sister Sanguine, from thy moderate heat,

HUMOUR22:27 H96 What comes from thence, my heat refines the same,

HUMOUR22:36 H105 But know'ts a foolish brain, that wanteth heat;

HUMOUR23:39 H149 Without my lively heat, do's ought thats flat.

HUMOUR23:41 ~~H149~~ They coole my heat, and so repay my good.

HUMOUR24:2 H151 Without my boiling heat cannot digest.

HUMOUR24:4 H153 What differences the Sex, but only heat?

HUMOUR25:41 H230 Ile praise that fury, {prowess} valour, choler, heat.

HUMOUR26:33 H263 The spirits through thy heat, are made perfect there,

HUMOUR27:3 H274 Besides the vehement heat, only there known,

HUMOUR27:12 ~~H283~~ It is her own heat, not thy faculty,

HUMOUR~~27:12~~ H283 Unless as heat, it be thy faculty,

HUMOUR27:38 H309 But here's {here} one thrusts her heat, where'ts not requir'd

HUMOUR31:4 H437 When by thy heat, thou'st bak'd thy selfe to crust,

HUMOUR33:13 H527 Thy heat doth much, I candidly confesse,

HUMOUR34:23 H578 A foolish Brain (saith {quoth} Choler) wanting heat,

AGES~~35:32~~ H18 Before the Sun hath throughly warm'd {heat} the clime.

SEASONS49:9 H100 Yet doth his parching heat the {but} more augment,

SEASONS49:11 ~~H102~~ Hath formerly much heat, the earth and aire.

SEASONS~~49:11~~ H102 Have throughly dry'd the earth, and heat the air.

SEASONS49:12 H103 Like as an oven, that long time hath been heat.

SEASONS49:31 H120 But whist'leth to thy Flock in cold, and heat,
SEASONS50:6 H140 Bearing the burning heat of the long day;
SEASONS51:23 H199 And his declining heat is almost done.
SEASONS52:39 H254 Until by's heat he drives {drive} all cold away.
MPERS71:36 H750 If all his {this} heat, had been for a good {pious} end,
MGREC97:23 H1784 By too much heat, not wounds (as Authors write.)
MGREC105:39 H2132 To quench his thirst, and to allay his heat;
MGREC107:23 H2198 The drought, and heat, their bodies much doth {sore did}
CONTEM168:28 H35 Thy heat from death and dulness doth revive:
1LETTER181:16 H14 Then view those fruits which through thy heat I bore?
MEDDM196:17 Hp273 heat and drought of the day, when he perceiues his sun apace
MEDDM199:11 Hp277 Iron till it be throughly heat is vncapable to be wrought, so god
PILGRIM210:7 H7 The burning sun no more shall heat
13MAY227:6 H15 A shadow from ye fainting heat

HEATH (1)

DIALOG144:37 H145 Her fruitfull land, a barren heath remain.

HEATHEN (3)

ELEMEN10:2 H77 Poor Heathen judg'd worthy a Diety:
MYCHILD218:12 Hp244 All Ages maugre all ye heathen Tyrants + all of the Enemyes
WHAT224:10 H10 And heathen to your Gods

HEATS (2)

ELEMEN~~14:12~~ H254 In heats & colds & gripes & drowsy sleeps:
SEASONS48:12 H65 And heats us with, the glances of his eye,

HEAUENLY (4) [heavenly]

MEDDM200:35 Hp280 heauenly father (who knowes our mould) lay such afflictions
MEDDM203:14 Hp283 heauenly country, and heere he hath many conueniences and
MEDDM206:17 Hp287 shall they be, when they are fixt in their heauenly spheres
MEDDM207:19 Hp289 permanent who would look for heauenly?

HEAVEN (17) See also HEAV'N, TH'HEAVEN

ELEMEN12:12 H172 That heaven it selfe was oft call'd by that name;
ELEMEN19:41 H482 That earth appeares in heaven, oh wonder great!
MASSYR62:37 H382 Until the thundring hand of heaven he felt,
MGREC~~132:20~~ H3263 As Heaven and Earth against him had been set:
DIALOG142:27 H56 Whence is this {the} storme, from Earth, or Heaven above?
DIALOG144:30 H138 Their silent tongues to heaven did vengeance cry,
DUBART154:23 H68 Oft have I wondred at the hand of heaven,
TDUDLEY166:27 H69 As joy in heaven, on earth let praise resound.
CONTEM168:5 H15 More Heaven then Earth was here, no winter & no night.
FLESH177:27 H108 If I of Heaven may have my fill,
MEDDM197:28 Hp275 thinkes to mount to heaven clog'd wth the Cares and riches of
MEDDM205:17 Hp286 the Court of heaven itself, for if our conscience condemn vs,
MYCHILD217:29 Hp243 would bee a Heaven And could I haue been in Heaven without
MYCHILD217:31 Hp243 absence and presence of God y^{t} makes Heaven or Hell.
MYCHILD217:37 Hp243 of ye Heaven + ye Earth, the order of all things night and day,
MED223:15 Hp250 is my comfort, When I come into Heaven, I shall vnderstand

HEAVENLY (3) See also HEAUENLY

ELEMEN9:41 H75 Fixed in heavenly constellations dwell,
30SEPT227:26 Hp257 wth sugar then brine, yet will he p^{r}serve me to his heavenly
2HUSB233:10 H43 Rejoice wth heavenly chear—

HEAVEN'S (1) [heaven is]

VANITY160:35 H45 But where, and what it is, from heaven's declar'd,

HEAVENS (15) [pl.]
ELEMEN8:15 H13 The sea did threat the heavens, the heavens the earth,
AGES44:24 H357 Sometimes the Heavens with plenty smil'd on me,
AGES46:19 H450 There, {Where} I shal rest, til heavens shal be no more;
MASSYR66:32 ~~H538~~ For by the Heavens above it was decreed:
MASSYR~~66:32~~ H538 But for his pride so had the heavens decreed.
MGREC105:9 H2102 Invokes the heavens, and earth, to heare his moanes;
MGREC129:16 H3130 The Heavens seem'd slow in paying her the same,
MGREC135:11 H3383 The Heavens thus rule, to fill the earth {world} with wonder.
CONTEM171:18 H121 When I behold the heavens as in their prime,
CONTEM171:34 H135 Shall I then praise the heavens, the trees, the earth
FLESH176:38 H78 Mine Eye doth pierce the heavens, and see
1HUSB180:32 H11 The heavens reward thee manifold I pray.
ANNEB187:17 H7 The Heavens have chang'd to sorrow my delight.
MERCY189:12 H33 The Heavens vouchsafe she may so ever be.

HEAVENS (3) [poss.] See also HEAV'NS, TH'HEAVENS
AGES~~45:2~~ H378 In prime of youth seiz'd by heavens angry hand,
DUBART155:4 H89 *Art and Nature joyn'd, by heavens high decree,*
QELIZ158:4 H113 Untill the heavens great revolution:

HEAVIE (1) [heavy]
MPERS77:4 H943 *Darius* light, he {yet} heavie, home returnes,

HEAV'N (1) [heaven] See also TH'HEAVEN
MROMAN137:21 H3472 Some faining say, to heav'n {to the Gods} he did ascend;

HEAV'NS (1) [heaven's] See also HEAVENS, TH'HEAVENS
CONTEM174:24 H222 Fond fool, he takes this earth ev'n for heav'ns bower.

HEAVY (5) See also HEAVIE
AGES35:25 H11 The last, of earth, and heavy melancholly,
AGES39:22 H165 I scorn the heavy Corslet, Musket-proof,
AGES40:33 H212 Nor yet that heavy reckoning for {soon} to come;
MERCY188:30 H16 But ah too soon those heavy tydings fly,
MEDDM197:4 Hp274 Authority wthout wisedome is like a heavy axe, wthout an edg

HECATOMBS (1) [pl.]
QELIZ155:24 H15 'Mongst hundred Hecatombs of roaring Verse,

HECTOR (2)
MGREC99:27 H1870 Who did the like to *Hector* (of more fame)
SIDNEY150:28 H55 Brave *Hector* by the walls of *Troy,* we see:

HE'D (11) [he had]
MPERS81:32 H1140 And of those *Greeks,* which by his skil he'd won,
MGREC~~101:18~~ H1943 Which had he done (perhaps) his fame had {he'd} kept,
MGREC104:9 H2061 If when he'd multitudes, the day he lost;
MGREC109:10 H2269 When thus, ten dayes, his brain with wine he'd soak'd,
MGREC114:13 H2483 Next day, he tore his face, for what he'd done,
MGREC~~115:17~~ H2536 To meet him there, t' *Antipater* had {he'd} sent,
MGREC~~127:20~~ H3050 When victor oft had {he'd} been, and so might still,
MGREC128:1 H3074 The Mother of their King to death he'd put,
MGREC129:2 H3116 This touch'd *Cassander* sore, for what he'd done,
MGREC132:4 H3237 (Whose daughter unto wife, he'd newly {not long before} ta'n)
MGREC132:25 H3270 After three years he dyed, left what he'd won

HEDG (1) [hedge]
MEDDM200:11 Hp279 brests, that god is forced to hedg vp their way wth thornes

HEDGES (1) [pl.]
AGES42:22 H280 Such scum, as Hedges, and High-wayes do yeeld,
HEED (2)
HUMOUR31:32 H465 What Sanguine is, she doth not heed, nor care.
AGES36:37 H61 With heed now stood, three ages of fraile man;
HEE-GOAT (1)
MGREC93:26 H1623 This is the hee-goat, which from *Grecia* came,
HEE'L (1) [he will]
MGREC~~101:34~~ H1960 By Captains twice is call'd before hee'l rise,
HEELES (2) [heels]
AGES36:12 H36 But as he went, death waited at his heeles.
MGREC96:26 H1746 As if she'd drawne, whole *Sushan* at her heeles.
HEER (2) [here] See also HEERE
2SIMON195:14 Hp271 wth grace heer and crown you wth glory heerafter. that I may
MEDDM203:17 Hp283 sees land we must therfore be heer as strangers and pilgrims,
HEERAFTER (1) [hereafter]
2SIMON195:14 Hp271 wth grace heer and crown you wth glory heerafter. that I may
HEERE (1) [here] See also HEER
MEDDM203:14 Hp283 country, and heere he hath many conueniences and comforts
HEIGHT (8) See also HEIGHTH, HIGHT
ELEMEN10:15 H90 Their magnitude and height should I recount,
MASSYR68:19 H605 Re-minds him of his Grand-sires height, and fall,
MPERS~~72:24~~ H772 His cruelty was come unto that height,
MPERS83:8 H1196 Unto such height did grow his cruelty,
MPERS91:2 H1510 The *Spartans* height, {*Spartan* State} which now apace doth
MGREC112:32 H2418 Who to the height doth aggravate each thing;
MGREC123:3 H2865 On which *Antigonus* his height doth raise:
MEDDM200:2 Hp278 Wickednes comes to its height by degrees, He that dares say
HEIGHTH (1) See also HIGHT
MASSYR56:4 H110 Three hundred sixty foot, the walls in heighth:
HEIR (2)
AGES40:6 H187 Sometimes I cheat (unkind) a female Heir,
MPERS86:15 H1331 His interest, in the Kingdome, now next heir,
HEIRE (3) [heir]
MGREC129:33 H3147 And place their hopes o'th heire of *Alexander,*
SIDNEY152:26 H95 *Heire to the Muses, the Son of* Mars *in truth,*
VANITY160:3 H13 Its his to day, but who's his heire to morrow?
HE'L (1) [he will]
CHILDRN185:12 H38 On higher boughs he'l perch at length.
HEL (1) [hell]
AGES46:24 H455 Triumph I shal, o're Sin, o're Death, o're Hel,
HELD (24)
ELEMEN9:28 H62 The Sun, an Orbe of Fire was held of old,
HUMOUR23:27 H137 They're held for Oracles, they are so wise.
AGES~~43:22~~ H317 I hate {not} for to be had, {held} in small {high'st} account.
SEASONS52:23 H238 Now's held, a Guest, {(but ghest)} (but blest) Nativity.
MASSYR53:18 H8 If of his house he held the Monarchy:
MASSYR58:14 H199 Both, for their King, held their dominion,
MASSYR59:33 H257 Which {That} for twelve hundred years had held that place;
MASSYR68:16 H602 Was held in more request, {account} then now he was,
MPERS69:8 H630 And from that time, had held it as his own;

MPERS73:30 H815 A Consultation by the {those} States was held.
MPERS85:27 H1303 All Townes, held by his Ancestors before.
MPERS86:18 H1334 Held by his mothers intercession.
MGREC108:11 H2227 And now reviv'd with hopes, held up their head,
MGREC118:39 H2688 *Seleuchus* afterward held *Babylon*;
MGREC119:3 H2693 But held command o'th' Armies {Army} which was best;
MGREC121:24 H2806 With what he held, he now was well {more} content,
MGREC128:17 H3090 First, how he held the Empire in his hands,
MGREC129:5 H3119 Whom he in durance held, now and long since,
MGREC133:28 H3318 Longer *Seleuchus* held the Royalty
MGREC134:40 H3369 Held for a time the *Egyptian* Monarchy:
MROMAN137:26 H3477 Held for his Piety, some sacred thing;
DIALOG145:27 H176 Had they not held law fast, all had been gone,
DIALOG145:30 H179 And to their *Laud* be't spoke, they held i'th' Tower,
CONTEM172:15 H150 Which to the long'd for Ocean held its course,

HELENA See HELLENA

HELICON (1)
ELEMEN12:10 H170 But farewell all, for deare mount *Helicon,*

HELICONIAN (1)
QELIZ157:29 H97 Must dip his Pen i'th' Heliconian Well;

HELISPONTINES (1) [pl.]
MPERS78:20 H1001 *Eolians,* and the *Helispontines;*

HELL (8) See also HEL
AGES42:17 H275 {again,} mine age (in all) {mine Age} been worse then hell.
AGES45:18 H400 Who gave the counsel, but the Prince of hell.
MPERS82:40 H1187 Thus cut, and mangled by a hag of hell.
MYCHILD217:21 Hp243 y^{t} agst svch a promis, svch tasts of sweetnes ye Gates of Hell
MYCHILD217:28 Hp243 thovght were it hell it self and could there find ye Love of God
MYCHILD217:30 Hp243 Love of God, it would haue been a Hell to me for in Truth it is
MYCHILD217:31 Hp243 absence and presence of God y^{t} makes Heaven or Hell.
MYCHILD218:36 Hp244 + if I perish, I perish, But I know all ye powers of Hell shall

HELLENA (1)
HUMOUR33:5 H519 Rather then loose, one beateous *Hellena;*

HELLESPONT (1) See also HELLISPONT
MGREC99:3 H1846 Betwixt the *Hellespont,* and *Hallis* side;

HELLESPONTINES See HELISPONTINES

HELLISH (2)
AGES~~45:20~~ H402 By bloudy Popish, hellish miscreants:
MPERS72:16 H764 O hellish Husband, Brother, Vnckle, Sire,

HELLISPONT (3) See also HELLESPONT
MPERS79:10 H1032 Next, o're the *Hellispont* a bridge he made,
MGREC94:16 H1650 And through the *Hellispont,* his ships make {made} way.
MGREC114:38 H2508 From *Hellispont,* to th' furthest {farthest} Ocean;

HELP (29) See also HELPE
ELEMEN9:21 H55 In chymestry, unlesse I help you Stil,
ELEMEN~~18:27~~ H431 I {help to} ripe the corne, I turne the grinding mill;
HUMOUR26:19 H249 But I, without thy help can give a growth,
HUMOUR27:14 H285 The help she needs, the loving Liver lends,.
MPERS78:24 H1005 In person {present} there, now for his help {aid} was seen;
MPERS80:37 H1104 Yet 'fore he went, to help out his expence,
MPERS~~86:14~~ H1330 What helps, {help} in's enterprize he's like to find,

MGREC98:14 H1816 The former ruines, help to him now lend; {forwarded his end:}
MGREC120:18 H2753 That by his help, the rest might low be brought:
MGREC123:27 H2891 Thinks by her Majesty much help to finde;
MGREC128:21 H3094 So therefore craves {requests} their help to take him down,
DIALOG141:24 H23 Which present help may ease this {my} malady.
DIALOG142:15 H44 And call in Forreign ayde, to help the thing?
DIALOG142:33 H62 A supplyant for your help, as she is bound.
DIALOG145:23 H172 To help the Church, and stay the Common-Weal,
DIALOG147:7 H233 That help thee not with prayers, arms, and purse,
DISTEMP179:21 H9 Who sendeth help to those in misery;
MEDDM201:5 Hp280 more or lesse if god afford his help
MEDDM204:29 Hp285 pouerty comfortably it will help to quiet him, but if that will not
MEDDM207:10 Hp288 as wings to help vs mount vpwards, they will Certainly proue
MYCHILD216:35 Hp242 wch he would haue performed, and by his help I haue layd
WHAT224:11 H11 Let them help in Adversities
THEART229:6 H8 And sent'st me help from High.
SON231:8 H20 His help & his physitian wer't
SON231:19 H31 O help me pay my Vowes O Lord
2HUSB232:14 H15 O help and bee not slack.
HOURS233:25 H8 Thy help my soul hath fovnd
HOURS234:37 H51 Vnlesse thou help w^t^ can I doe
REMB236:9 H24 O help thy Saints y^t^ sovght thy Face

HELP'D (1) [helped] See also HELPD
QELIZ156:27 H54 She frankly help'd *Franks* (brave) distressed King,

HELPD (1) [helped] See also HELP'D
MYCHILD218:7 Hp244 helpd me over. I haue argved thvs wth my self, That there is a

HELPE (3) [help]
ELEMEN11:1 H117 The Army through my helpe victorious rose;
HUMOUR25:22 H211 But when thou scorn'st to take the helpe we lend,
MPERS85:30 H1306 {strength} by their {*Grecians*} helpe were {was} overthrown,

HELPED (1) See also HELP'D, HELPD
JULY223:24 Hp251 my God who never failed me, was not absent but helped me,

HELPER (1)
HUMOUR33:16 H530 And though I grant, thou art my helper here,

HELPES (1) [helps]
SAMUEL228:11 H12 For mortall helpes are brittle Dvst.

HELPLESSE (1) [helpless]
MGREC117:3 H2610 Now like a mortall helplesse man he lies;

HELPS (2) See also HELPES
MPERS86:14 H1330 What helps, {help} in's enterprize he's like to find,
MGREC123:38 H2902 Unto these helps, in *Greece,* {at home} he seeks out more,

HELP'ST (1)
SOREFIT221:23 H9 Thov help'st and thov regard'est me.

HELPT (2)
MPERS81:19 H1127 And they had helpt them, as confederate;
MPERS82:1 H1146 But that which helpt defects, and made them bold,

HELTHFULL (1) [healthful]
MEDDM200:20 Hp279 honour, wealth, or a helthfull body, would quite ouer throw,

HEMISPHERE (1)
2LETTER181:34 H4 And tell my griefs in either Hemisphere:

HEMUS (1)
ELEMEN12:9 H169 And *Hemus,* whose steep sides, none foote upon,
HEN (1)
SEASONS48:7 H60 The clocking hen, her chipping brood now {chirping chickins}
HENA'S (1) [poss.]
MASSYR62:35 H380 On *Hena's, {Hevahs* and on *Sepharuaim's* gods,
HENAH (1)
MASSYR62:34 H379 On *Henah, Arpad,* and on *Ivdah* least {*Juahs* coast};
HENCE (10)
HUMOUR30:31 H423 Laughter (though thou sayst malice) flowes from hence,
HUMOUR33:33 H547 Doth shew, hence flowes {flow} the power {pow'rs} which they
HUMOUR~~33:37~~ H551 The spirits animal, from whence doth {hence do} slide,
HUMOUR34:15 H570 And the strong ligaments, from hence arise,
MGREC108:27 H2243 From hence he to *Jaxartis* river goes,
MGREC111:16 H2361 Hence {Then} sayling down by th' mouth of *Indus* floud,
MGREC111:29 H2374 From hence he to {then unto} *Gedrosia* went,
MGREC111:38 H2383 From hence to *Babylon,* some time there spent,
1LETTER181:26 H24 Till natures sad decree shall call thee hence;
MED223:5 Hp250 I thy servant, But hence arises not my comfort, Thou art my
HENGIST (1)
DIALOG142:5 H34 What, hath some *Hengist,* like that *Saxon* stout,
HENRIES (1) [henry's]
DIALOG142:39 H68 Nor is it *Alcies* Son, and {nor} *Henries* Daughter,
HENRY (3)
HUMOUR23:31 H141 Like our sixt *Henry,* that same worthy {virtuous} thing.
DIALOG143:13 H82 By *Edward* third, and *Henry* fifth of fame,
DUBART154:13 H58 Then in Saint *Lewis,* or thy last *Henry* great,
HENRY'S See HENRIES
HENS (1) [pl.]
CHILDRN184:15 H4 Four Cocks there were, and Hens the rest,
HERAULD (2)
MPERS89:21 H1455 The troubled King, his Herauld sends again,
QELIZ155:15 H6 Yet thy loud Herauld Fame, doth to the sky
HERBS (1) [pl.] See also HEARBS
ELEMEN~~14:11~~ H253 Nay into herbs and plants it sometimes creeps,
HERCULEAN (1)
QELIZ157:1 H69 Her *Essex* took *Cades,* their *Herculean* hold:
HERCULES (4)
MGREC98:2 H1804 Desires to offer unto *Hercules,*
MGREC98:7 H1809 Sent word, that *Hercules* his Temple stood,
MGREC129:28 H3142 Call'd *Hercules,* and elder then his brother,
SIDNEY151:14 ~~H69~~ But *Omphala,* set *Hercules* to spin,
HERE (75) See also HEER, HEERE, HERE'S
ELEMEN~~8:35~~ H33 All sorts of Artists, here declare your mind,
ELEMEN10:19 H94 Ile here let passe, my Choler cause of warres,
ELEMEN12:3 H163 I'le here skip o're my mountaines, reaching skies,
ELEMEN12:17 H177 Ile here let goe, my Lions of *Numedia,*
ELEMEN12:24 H184 But here, or there, I list now none to name;
ELEMEN12:27 H187 Whose trust, and valour I might here commend:
ELEMEN13:20 H221 I should here make a short, yet true narration,
HUMOUR~~27:38~~ H309 But here's {here} one thrusts her heat, where'ts not requir'd

HUMOUR28:23 H335 I might here shew, the noblenesse of minde,
HUMOUR30:19 H411 You'l say, here none shal ere disturbe my right;
HUMOUR31:26 H459 Here, there, her restlesse thoughts do ever flye;
HUMOUR33:16 H530 And though I grant, thou art my helper here,
HUMOUR33:30 H544 And surely the Souls {Soul} sensative here lives,
HUMOUR33:36 H550 The faculty of speech doth here abide,
HUMOUR33:38 H552 The five most noble Sences, here do dwel,
HUMOUR34:5 H560 He was no foole, who thought the Soul lay here {there},
HUMOUR34:34 H589 Then I, and thou, must make a mixture here:
HUMOUR~~34:39~~ H594 And too much talk; both which, I do {here} confesse,
HUMOUR35:8 H604 Two hot, two moist, two cold, two dry here be,
AGES37:3 H65 A nothing, here to day, but {and} gone to morrow.
MASSYR56:10 H116 Three hundred thousand men, here day, by day;
MPERS70:16 H687 Here twenty yeares provision {good} he found,
MPERS78:30 H1011 But pitty 'twas, thine ayde that {thou} here did'st lend,
MPERS87:40 H1392 And here, and there, in carts their Armes they throw,
MGREC99:18 H1861 For more repulse, the *Grecians* here abide,
MGREC101:37 H1966 But 'tis not known what slaughters here they {was} made.
MGREC102:29 H1999 He likewise here a world of treasure found,
MGREC102:31 H2001 Here stood the Royall houses of delight,
MGREC102:33 H2003 The sumptuous Palace of Queen *Hester* {*Esther*} here,
MGREC103:8 H2019 Here lay the bulk, of all those precious things;
MGREC103:16 H2027 Here of his own, he sets a Garrison,
MGREC104:2 H2054 Thought now this once, to try his fortunes here,
MGREC~~107:19~~ H2194 For {Here} to observe the rashnesse of the King.
MGREC107:28 H2203 Here *Alexander's* almost at a stand,
MGREC108:7 H2223 Here was of *Greeks,* a town in *Bactria,*
MGREC110:6 H2306 On *Tygris* side, here now he had not been;
MGREC110:8 H2308 Did here, and there, Isles full of trees abide;
MGREC110:15 H2315 Yet work enough, here *Alexander* found,
MGREC110:31 H2335 Huge Bridles made, which here, and there, he left,
MGREC111:14 H2359 A City here he built, cal'd by his name,
MGREC112:9 H2395 Spectators here, could scarce relate the story,
MGREC115:6 H2517 Here his cheif favourite *Ephestion* dyes,
MGREC123:11 H2873 How neatly {finely} *Eumenes* did here excell,
MGREC~~124:10~~ H2917 That no supply by these here might be lent,
MGREC131:15 H3207 For here *Antigonus* lost rule, and life,
MGREC135:6 H3378 Here ends at last the *Grecian* Monarchy,
DIALOG143:34 H103 That Pope, had hope, to find *Rome* here againe;
DIALOG145:34 H183 Here tugg'd they hard indeed, for all men saw,
DIALOG146:6 H194 That thousands lay on heaps, here bleeds my woes.
DIALOG146:13 ~~H200~~ Religion, Gospell, here lies at the stake,
SIDNEY152:24 H93 *Here lies intomb'd in fame, under this stone,*
DUBART153:10 H14 But barren I, my Daysey here doe bring,
DUBART155:2 H87 *Here lyes the pearle of* France, Parnassus *glory,*
QELIZ157:41 H109 Then wonder not, *Eliza* moves not here.
QELIZ158:8 H117 *Here sleeps THE Queen, this is the royall bed.*
QELIZ158:15 H124 *Here lies the pride of Queens, pattern of Kings,*
QELIZ158:17 H126 Here lies the envy'd, yet unparralell'd Prince,
VANITY160:17 H27 He knows not all, that here is to be known,
DDUDLEY167:9 H6 Here lyes,

CONTEM168:5 H15 More Heaven then Earth was here, no winter & no night.
CONTEM168:34 H40 All mortals here the feeling knowledg hath.
CONTEM170:6 H79 Here sits our Grandame in retired place,
CONTEM170:14 H86 Here *Cain* and *Abel* come to sacrifice,
SICKNES178:21 H4 lo here is fatal Death.
1LETTER181:28 H26 I here, thou there, yet both but one.
3LETTER183:22 H24 I here, he there, alas, both kept by force:
CHILDRN185:15 H41 Or here or there, they'l take their flight,
ANNEB187:25 H15 That's here to day, perhaps gone in an hour;
MEDDM205:12 Hp286 fro continvally, here is also the great Court of iustice erected,
TOCHILD215:4 H4 That being gone, here yov may find
BYNIGHT220:19 H17 I'le serve him here whilst I shall liue
FAINT222:23 H13 I here a while might 'bide.
SAMUEL228:3 H4 I here resigne into thy hand,
HOUSE236:35 H27 And here and there ye places spye
HOUSE236:37 H29 Here stood that Trunk, and there y^t chest

HEREAFTER (4) See also HEERAFTER
HUMOUR34:40 H595 A warning good, hereafter i'le say lesse.
HUMOUR35:10 H606 Nor jars, nor scoffs, let none hereafter see,
MGREC117:15 H2622 We may hereafter shew, in season due.
JULY223:27 Hp251 to read this hereafter, and to others that shall read it when I

HERE'S (11) [here is]
HUMOUR21:32 H60 Here's Sister Ruddy, worth the other two,
HUMOUR22:1 H70 Then here's our sad black Sister, worse then you,
HUMOUR22:19 H88 Here's three of you, all sees {see} now what you are,
HUMOUR27:38 H309 But here's {here} one thrusts her heat, where'ts not requir'd
HUMOUR34:21 H576 Here's my epitome of excellence,
HUMOUR35:12 H608 Nor be discern'd, here's water, earth, aire, fire,
HUMOUR35:13 H609 But here's a {so} compact body, whole, entire:
MGREC107:30 H2205 For Boats here's none, nor neare it any wood,
QELIZ158:16 H125 So blaze it fame, here's feathers for thy wings,
CONTEM174:26 H224 Here's neither honour, wealth, or safety;
2LETTER182:27 H33 Tell him here's worse then a confused matter,

HERETOFORE (6)
HUMOUR29:38 H389 Enough of that, by our Sister {sisters} heretofore,
MASSYR66:34 H540 {But} Resumes his Government, as heretofore,
MPERS91:39 ~~H1553~~ Their Acts recorded not, as heretofore
MGREC117:1 H2608 Nor can he kill, or save as heretofore,
MGREC119:41 H2731 Act any thing of worth, as heretofore,
DIALOG143:16 H85 Though she hath bin injurious heretofore.

HEREUPON (1)
MPERS~~91:22~~ H1533 The King highly inrag'd doth hereupon

HERICANOES (1) [pl.]
ELEMEN19:32 H473 Again, what tempests,{furious storms} and what hericanoes

HERO (2)
HUMOUR33:3 H517 Sixty nine Princes, all stout *Hero* Knights,
SIDNEY151:17 H69 When such a *Hero* shoots him out o'th' field,

HEROES (1) [pl.]
MGREC132:33 H3280 Of the old Heroes, now but two remaine,

HEROICK (1) [heroic]
DUBART154:18 H63 Thine the quintessence of an Heroick brain.

HEROYICK (2) [heroic]
HUMOUR24:33 H182 But *David, Judah's* most heroyick King:
MASSYR63:30 H417 The famous Wars {acts}, of this Heroyick King,
HEROYICKS (1) [heroics]
MGREC99:30 H1873 Sith valour, with Heroyicks is renown'd,
HERSE (5)
MPERS70:41 ~~H712~~ Then at his Herse great honours to expresse;
DUBART153:15 H19 And prostrate off'red at great *Bartas* Herse.
QELIZ155:25 H16 Mine bleating stands before thy royall Herse:
TDUDLEY165:7 H9 Presents my Lamentations at his Herse,
BIRTH180:18 H28 With some sad sighs honour my absent Herse;
HE'S (16) [he is]
SEASONS52:20 H235 This month he's hous'd in horned *Capricorn,*
MASSYR60:38 H303 In sacred Writ, he's known by name of *Pul,*
MASSYR63:9 H394 So he's now stil'd, the King of *Babylon;*
MASSYR~~63:28~~ H414 This King's less fam'd for all the acts he's done,
MPERS86:14 H1330 What helps, {help} in's enterprize he's like to find,
MGREC98:37 H1839 First, at *Euphrates,* what he's like to abide,
MGREC115:41 H2560 He shewes his grief, he's forc'd to disobey:
MGREC125:40 H2990 With rage, and with revenge, he's hurried on,
MGREC130:19 H3174 And now he thinks {hopes}, he's ordered all so well,
MGREC132:21 H3266 There was he {At last he's} taken and imprisoned
SIDNEY150:5 H30 Yet, {But} he's a beetle head, that cann't discry
VANITY159:37 H9 He's now a slave {captive}, that was a Prince {King} of late.
CONTEM171:24 H127 But Man grows old, lies down, remains where once he's laid.
1SIMON188:11 H12 Let's say he's merciful, as well as just,
SAMUEL228:8 H9 He's mine, but more O Lord thine own
SON230:23 H6 He's come for whom I waited long.
HESIODE (1)
MASSYR63:31 H418 Did neither *Homer, Hesiode, Virgil* sing;
HESTER (3)
MPERS84:9 H1237 What *Hester {Esther}* was, and did, her story reed,
MPERS85:11 H1287 To be by *Hester,* {fair Queen Ester} to her husband brought.
MGREC102:33 H2003 The sumptuous Palace of Queen *Hester {Esther}* here,
HETHER (1) [hither]
SON231:15 H27 On Eagles wings him hether brovght
HETHERTO (1) [hitherto]
HOURS233:24 H7 Thou hetherto hast been my God
HEVAHS (1) [poss.]
MASSYR~~62:35~~ H380 On *Hena's, {Hevahs* and on *Sepharuaim's* gods,
HEW (2) [hue]
HUMOUR30:37 H429 Again, you often touch my swarthy hew,
CONTEM167:30 H7 Of green, of red, of yellow, mixed hew,
HEZEKIAH (1)
MASSYR63:15 H400 Embassadours to *Hezekiah* sent, [21 *years.*
HID (5)
HUMOUR27:32 H303 My vertues hid, i've let you dimly see;
AGES38:22 H125 A serpents sting in pleasing face lay hid.
VANITY160:33 H43 Its hid from eyes of men, they count it strange,
MYCHILD217:4 Hp242 when ye Almighty hath hid his face from me, that yet I haue
FAINT222:25 H15 My life is hid wth Thee

HIDASPES (1) [poss.]
MGREC109:40 H2299 Is now resolv'd to passe *Hidaspes* floud,
HIDASPIS (2)
MGREC110:37 H2341 He on the faire *Hidaspis* pleasant side,
MGREC111:1 H2346 Then down t' *Hidaspis* with his Fleet he went;
HIDDEN (2)
FLESH176:28 H68 The hidden Manna I doe eat,
MYCHILD217:19 Hp243 bee well with me. I haue somt. tasted of y^t hidden Manna y^t y^e
HIDE (4) v.
MGREC105:7 H2100 To hide themselves, remote, in *Bactria;*
MGREC129:14 H3128 Both thrown into a well to hide her blot,
FEVER220:34 H14 Hide not thy face from me I cry'd
2HUSB232:18 H19 Hide not thy face Away.
HIDEOUS (1)
MGREC108:29 H2245 And with their out-cries, in a {an} hideous sort,
HIDES (2) [pl.]
MGREC104:23 H2075 Into a cart him throwes, covered with hides;
MGREC107:34 H2209 So {Then} from his carriages the Hides he takes,
HIDRA (1)
ELEMEN10:12 H87 The Hidra, Dolphin, Boys, that waters {water} bear.
HIEROGLYPHICKS (1) [pl.]
MPERS76:10 H908 Their minds by Hieroglyphicks they expresse;
HIGH (76)
FATHER5:10 H11 To mount so high, requires an Eagles quill:
PROLOG7:35 H45 And oh, ye high flown quils, that soare the skies,
ELEMEN9:27 H61 To match on high with the Celestiall fires.
ELEMEN12:11 H171 And wonderous high *Olimpus,* of such fame,
ELEMEN~~16:11~~ H334 And be thy mountains n'er so high and steep,
ELEMEN16:12 ~~H335~~ Then Seas are deep, Mountains are never high.
ELEMEN17:19 H383 That *Caucasus* high mounts, are seldom free.
HUMOUR20:15 H7 But first they wisely shew'd their high descent,
HUMOUR~~21:2~~ H30 To shew my great {high} descent, and pedigree,
HUMOUR25:30 H219 To take the wal's a sin, of such {so} high rate,
HUMOUR25:40 H229 Be dangers neer so high, and courage great,
HUMOUR30:20 H412 You high born (from that lump) then take your flight
HUMOUR30:41 H433 But that which shewes how high thy spight is bent,
HUMOUR33:34 H548 Within this high built Cittadel doth lye,
AGES~~39:29~~ H172 And elevates {elevate} my {high} thoughts above {beyond} the
AGES~~45:9~~ H391 seen base {unworthy} men, advanc'd to great degree {high},
AGES45:11 ~~H393~~ But not their Princes love, nor state so high;
SEASONS51:33 H209 His dead old stock, again shall mount on high.
MASSYR53:17 H7 But each one thought his petty rule was high,
MASSYR59:20 ~~H244~~ Which through much rain, then swelling up so high,
MASSYR61:29 H334 Acknowledging th' *Assyrians* high desert,
MASSYR~~61:38~~ H343 (This was that *Ahaz,* which so much {high} transgrest.)
MASSYR67:9 H555 Is *Judah's* King, now lifted up on high.
MASSYR68:21 H607 His drunkennesse, and his prophainnesse high,
MPERS70:24 H695 He with his Vnckle *Daniel* sets on high,
MPERS72:40 H786 Unsheathes, as he his horse mounted on high,
MPERS85:35 H1311 No match was high enough, but their own blood,)
MGREC93:21 H1618 To th' ground was burnt, *Diana's* Temple high,

MGREC6:31 H1628 But death did terminate, those thoughts so high.
MGREC6:37 H1634 His high resolves which way to bring to passe:
MGREC96:13 H1733 And o're his head, his golden gods on high;
MGREC97:31 H1792 For whom he offers him a ransome high;
MGREC99:36 H1879 Him in his Priestly Robes, high *Jaddus* meets,
MGREC101:9 H1934 *Phenisian* Sea, and great *Euphrates* high,
MGREC103:3 H2014 And all in it was at his high command;
MGREC~~103:25~~ H2036 In pride, and cruelty, to th' highest {high} excesse.
MGREC104:34 H2086 Had *Alexanders* wrath incensed high;
MGREC110:29 H2333 His Maungers he erected up so high,
MGREC112:26 H2412 He death deserv'd, for this so high offence;
MGREC~~114:11~~ H2479 Which *Alexanders* wrath incens'd so high,
MGREC120:24 H2761 The Acts of his Vice-royes, {Vice-Roy} now grown so high:
MGREC121:14 ~~H2792~~ *Pithon,* next *Perdicas,* a Captaine high,
MGREC124:2 H2907 To take down *Polisperchon* grown so high;
MGREC124:8 ~~H2913~~ Upon those friends, his father rais'd on high,
MGREC136:4 H3417 The Subject was too high, beyond my straine;
MROMAN138:12 H3502 Leaves {Left} *Rome,* in wealth and power, still growing high.
DIALOG141:23 H22 Unlesse some Cordial thou fetch from high,
DIALOG143:23 H92 They're for my punishments ordain'd on high,
DIALOG143:37 H106 What scorning of the Saints of the most high,
DIALOG144:19 H129 That with high hand I still did perpetrate;
DIALOG145:29 H178 They took high *Strafford* lower by the head,
DIALOG148:1 H266 Then High Commissions shall fall to decay,
DIALOG148:21 H286 Oh *Abrahams* seed lift up your heads on high.
SIDNEY152:7 H78 With high disdain, they said they gave no more,
DUBART153:36 H40 Thy peircing skill in high Astronomy,
DUBART155:4 H89 *Art and Nature joyn'd, by heavens high decree,*
QELIZ155:1 H10 In honour of that High and Mighty
DAVID158:26 H6 Upon thy places, mountain'ous and high,
DAVID159:22 H37 In places high, full low thou dost {didst} remaine;
VANITY159:34 H6 What is't in honour, to be set on high?
TDUDLEY165:38 H40 High thoughts he gave no harbour in his heart,
TDUDLEY166:20 H62 And in celestial Barn hath hous'd him high,
CONTEM168:1 H11 How excellent is he that dwells on high?
CONTEM169:4 H46 And is thy splendid Throne erect so high?
FLESH176:34 H74 But reach at things that are so high,
FLESH177:7 H88 The stately Walls both high and strong,
SICKNES178:25 H8 when he so high provok'd.
DISTEMP179:20 H8 And looking up unto his Throne on high,
MEDDM196:9 Hp273 Corruptions, and y^{t} will damp his high thoughts
PILGRIM210:24 H24 And soare on high among the blest.
MYCHILD215:33 Hp241 made my Suplicat^{n}. to the most High who sett me free from
WHAT224:7 H7 On High my heart O doe thou raise
WHAT224:19 H19 His word he plighted hath on high
THEART229:6 H8 And sent'st me help from High.
2HUSB232:3 H4 O thov most high who rulest All
HOUSE237:17 H47 Thou hast an house on high erect

HIGH-BORNE (1)

AGES37:24 H86 My high-borne soule, so straitly was confin'd:

HIGHER (12)
ELEMEN18:33 H437 I grow more pure and pure, as I mount higher,
HUMOUR23:24 H134 Thus {But} arms, and arts I claim, and higher things;
AGES42:37 H293 My dunghil thoughts, or hopes, could reach no higher.
AGES43:7 H302 My thirst was higher, then Nobility.
MGREC94:36 H1674 In lower termes to write {was taught} a higher stile,
MGREC119:4 H2694 And had a higher project in his head,
QELIZ157:40 H108 But happinesse, lies in a higher sphere,
CONTEM168:15 H23 Then higher on the glistering Sun I gaz'd,
CONTEM169:24 H64 Whilst I as mute, can warble forth no higher layes.
FLESH175:9 H9 Her thoughts unto a higher sphere:
CHILDRN185:12 H38 On higher boughs he'l perch at length.
MEDDM198:6 Hp276 ouer their heads he then leads them to the Rock wch is higher

HIGHEST (6) See also HIGH'ST
HUMOUR20:31 H23 Cold {Mild} flegme, did not contest for highest {chiefest} place,
HUMOUR21:21 H49 I make a man, a man i'th highest degree,
MASSYR68:7 H593 And highest dignity, next to the King,
MGREC103:25 H2036 In pride, and cruelty, to th' highest {high} excesse.
SICKNES178:27 H10 in place of highest bliss,
MEDDM202:5 Hp281 out of the loynes of one Adam, some set in ye highest dignity,

HIGHLY (1)
MPERS~~91:22~~ H1533 The King highly inrag'd doth hereupon

HIGH'ST (1) [highest]
AGES~~43:22~~ H317 I hate {not} for to be had, {held} in small {high'st} account.

HIGHT (1) [height] See also HEIGHTH
MPERS69:38 ~~H660~~ And told, how *Solon* in his hight had spoke.

HIGH-WAYES (1)
AGES42:22 H280 Such scum, as Hedges, and High-wayes do yeeld,

HIL (2) [hill]
MPERS80:41 H1108 Two mighty Rocks, brake from *Parnassus* Hil,
MPERS88:40 H1433 At last, displayes his Ensigne on a Hil,

HILL (1)
HUMOUR~~25:1~~ H190 But know, I love the blade, more then the hilt. {Hill;}

HILLS (1) [pl.]
ELEMEN12:15 H175 But ile skip {leap} o're these Hills, not touch a Dale,

HILS (1) [hills]
MPERS90:7 H1480 O're mountains, rocks, and hils, as Lions bold;

HILT (1)
HUMOUR25:1 H190 But know, I love the blade, more then the hilt. {Hill;}

HIMSELF (45)
ELEMEN~~14:4~~ H248 Bur'ing himself alive for honours prize.
HUMOUR21:26 H54 In dangers to account himself more sure,
MASSYR54:5 H32 Titles divine, he to himself did take,
MASSYR54:39 H66 Then drown himself, did *Menon,* for her sake;
MASSYR59:11 H235 And speeds himself to *Ninivie* amain;
MASSYR59:31 H255 Then on himself, and them, a fire he sets;
MASSYR62:33 H378 His Wars none better then himself can boast,
MASSYR66:1 H507 Where to the sword, all but himself was {were} put,
MPERS69:28 H650 Who had no might to save himself from wrong;
MPERS70:30 H701 There routs his Hoast, himself she prisoner takes,
MPERS~~71:4~~ H719 And with an Epitaph, himself did make,

MPERS71:38 H752 But he that 'fore the gods, himself preferrs,
MPERS72:4 ~~H755~~ He strait to rid himself of causlesse fears,
MPERS90:31 H1498 {Their King} *Agesilus* himself doth over-goe {goe};
MGREC~~94:18~~ H1655 And being ask'd what for himself was left,
MGREC97:15 H1776 T'ward them, demean'd himself like a Commander;
MGREC97:17 H1778 Conquer'd himself (now he had conquered)
MGREC102:22 H1992 And gives {gave} himself to banqueting, and play:
MGREC104:36 H2088 His hopes being dasht, prepares himself for flight:
MGREC104:38 H2090 And bids him, save himself, by speedy course:
MGREC~~109:33~~ H2292 His Homage unto him {to himself} as Soveraigne doe.
MGREC113:11 H2438 For to {He might} accuse himself, as they had done;
MGREC114:14 H2484 And would have slaine himself, for *Clitus* gone,
MGREC115:13 H2522 To punish, where himself deserved blame:
MGREC117:24 H2631 Did harm himself, but never reacht his foes:
MGREC119:1 H2691 But nothing lesse: each one himself intends.
MGREC120:16 H2751 Was to give way, himself might be undone;
MGREC120:27 H2764 This he avoyds, and ships himself, and's Son,
MGREC120:32 H2769 To save himself from dangers eminent;
MGREC122:8 H2831 Himself from out of labyrinths intricate.
MGREC~~131:1~~ H3188 *Antigonus* himself to ingratiate,
MGREC133:25 ~~H3315~~ Did take his rule, his sons, himself and all.
DIALOG143:36 H105 From *Beelzebub* himself, such language heare?
DIALOG145:38 H187 The King displeas'd, at *York* himself absents,
SIDNEY151:15 ~~H69~~ And *Mars* himself was ta'n by *Venus* gin;
MEDDM196:6 Hp272 of the pea cock that prideing himself in his gay feathers
MEDDM196:14 Hp273 The hireling that labours all the day comforts himself, that
MEDDM204:27 Hp285 one that is in a far better estate then himself, but let him look
MEDDM205:24 Hp286 himself alway in the awefull presence of god, the consideration
MEDDM208:33 Hp290 it hath ouer come the omnipotent himself, as when Moses
MEDDM208:36 Hp291 armes of the mighty god of Jacob yea Jacob himself when he
MEDDM209:24 Hp291 hath (perhaps meaner then himself) wch shews us perfection is
PILGRIM210:5 H5 Blesses himself, to think vpon
MYCHILD218:8 Hp244 If ever this God hath revealed himself it mvst bee in his word,
MYCHILD218:16 Hp244 but God himself?

HIMSELFE (12) [himself]
AGES36:35 H59 That each should tel, what of himselfe he knew;
MASSYR67:18 H564 His Army routed, and himselfe there slain,
MPERS84:36 H1272 To wrong himselfe by death, he chose before:
MPERS86:38 H1354 He meant {Prepares} himselfe to carry the report.
MPERS88:3 H1396 Gets on his armes, arayes himselfe for fight;
MGREC104:18 H2070 Look to himselfe, and leave him to that crew;
MGREC106:33 H2167 With *Persian* Robes, himselfe doth dignifie,
MGREC107:6 H2181 Then {And} hearing, *Bessus* makes himselfe a King,
MGREC109:22 H2281 Presents himselfe, {first} there with a golden Crowne,
MGREC123:31 H2895 And to be great {chief} himselfe now bends his aymes;
MGREC128:3 H3076 And how he aymes {aiming now} to make himselfe a King,
MGREC132:40 H3287 And so himselfe the only Monarch make;

HIND (1)
3LETTER182:36 H1 As loving Hind that (Hartless) wants her Deer,

HINDE (1) [hind]
3LETTER183:24 H26 Unto thy Hinde, thy Mullet and thy Dove,

HINDER (3)
MPERS87:18 H1372 To keep those streights, to hinder his intent.
MPERS~~89:15~~ H1449 To hinder their return by craft or force,
CONTEM172:17 H152 Could hinder ought, but still augment its force:
HINDERS (1)
MGREC130:14 H3169 So hinders him of her, he could not gain.
HINDES (1) [hinds]
ELEMEN15:4 H286 Hindes leave their Calves, the Elephant the Fens;
HINDRANCE (1)
MGREC117:38 H2645 Claim'd not, perhaps her Sex might hindrance be.
HINDS See HINDES
HIPOCRATES (1)
HUMOUR33:25 H539 *Galen, Hipocrates,* drives {drive} to a set.
HIR'D (1) [hired]
MPERS87:26 H1378 So hir'd a fleet, to waft him ore the Maine,
HIRE (6)
MASSYR64:24 H448 Which in few years proves the *Assyrians* hire;
MPERS83:11 H1199 And for that end, his Eunuch he did hire.
MPERS91:5 H1513 They to their discontent, receiving hire,
MGREC100:7 H1891 The Pagan Priest through hire, or else mistake,
MGREC127:16 H3046 Having Command o'th treasure he can hire,
MGREC129:36 H3150 {And} Gives *Peloponesus* unto him for {his} hire,
HIRED See HIR'D
HIRELING (1)
MEDDM196:14 Hp273 The hireling that labours all the day comforts himself, that
HIRER (1)
MPERS83:14 H1202 The {Then} *Artabanus* hirer of this deed,
HIRES (1)
MPERS70:28 H699 Which to revenge, she hires a mighty power,
HISSE (1) [hiss]
SEASONS51:21 H197 The Northern Winter blasts begin to hisse;
HISSING (1)
ELEMEN8:21 H19 The rumbling, hissing, puffing was so great,
HISTORIANS (1) [pl.] See also HYSTORIANS
PROLOG6:22 H7 Let Poets, and Historians set these forth,
HISTORY (5)
MASSYR54:2 H29 Left to the world, by any History;
MASSYR63:33 H420 From some *Thucidides* grave History;
MGREC~~122:8~~ H2833 In *Plutarchs Lives* his history many find.
QELIZ155:34 H25 No *Speeds,* nor *Chamdens* learned History;
TDUDLEY166:39 H81 *A Magazine of History,*
HIT (2)
ELEMEN19:29 ~~H472~~ Some upon sands, some upon rocks have hit.
MPERS88:26 H1419 But {And} in his speed a Dart hit him i'th' eye,
HITHER (2) See also HETHER
MGREC110:41 H2345 His fourth, and last supply, was hither sent,
MERCY189:7 H28 E're nature would, it hither did arrive,
HITHERTO See HETHERTO
HOARDS (1)
CONTEM173:19 H185 That neither toyles nor hoards up in thy barn,

HOARY (2)
AGES36:25 H49 His hoary haires, and grave aspect made way;
TDUDLEY166:26 H68 His hoary head in righteousness was found:
HOAST (16) [host]
MASSYR62:8 H353 For *Salmanasser,* with a mighty Hoast,
MPERS70:30 H701 There routs his Hoast, himself she prisoner takes,
MPERS71:20 H734 He next to *Cyprus* sends his bloudy Hoast,
MPERS74:34 H857 An Hoast he rais'd, the City to reduce,
MPERS76:7 H905 By these alone his Hoast was pinch'd so sore,
MPERS79:16 H1042 Seven dayes and nights, his Hoast without least stay,
MPERS79:31 H1057 His Hoast, who {all} *Lissus* drinks to quench their thirst,
MPERS80:38 H1105 Part of his Hoast to *Delphos* sent from thence,
MPERS84:40 H1276 Again dispersed, his new levyed hoast.
MPERS87:7 H1363 The King dismay'd, a mighty Hoast doth raise;
MPERS90:26 H1493 They then *Dercilladas,* send with an Hoast,
MGREC100:21 H1905 Yet he (poore Prince) another Hoast doth muster,
MGREC105:6 H2099 This done, they with their Hoast, soon speed away,
MGREC107:8 H2183 Now that his Hoast from luggage might be free,
MGREC124:11 H2918 *Cassander* with his Hoast to *Grecia* goes,
QELIZ156:9 H36 *Spaines* Monarch sa's not so; nor yet his Hoast,
HOBBLING See HOBLING
HOBBY (1)
AGES35:33 H19 His hobby striding, did not ride, but run,
HOBLING (1) [hobbling]
AUTHOR178:7 H17 Yet still thou run'st more hobling then is meet;
HOES See HOOES
HOLD (1) n.
QELIZ157:1 H69 Her *Essex* took *Cades,* their *Herculean* hold:
HOLD (33) v.
FATHER5:32 H33 How Aire, and Earth, no correspondence hold,
ELEMEN13:5 H206 For gemmes, for silver, treasures which I hold:
ELEMEN15:24 H306 Fishes so numberlesse I there do hold;
ELEMEN16:2 H325 Which *Spaines Americans,* do gladly hold.
ELEMEN18:40 H444 Me for no Element, longer to hold.
HUMOUR27:31 H302 If this {you} can't be disprov'd {disprove}, then all I hold:
HUMOUR31:24 H457 Choler's too rash, this golden gift to hold.
HUMOUR35:4 H600 Let Sanguine, Choler, with her hot hand hold,
AGES35:37 H23 But if he hold, til it have run its last,
AGES38:40 H143 That wonder tis, my glasse till now doth hold.
AGES41:29 H246 But yet laid hold, on vertue seemingly,
AGES41:30 H247 Who climbes without hold, climbes dangerously.
MPERS71:23 H737 To hold his own, of his free courtesie;
MPERS76:40 H938 Renews his hold; but {and} when of that bereft,
MPERS92:31 H1589 our judicious learned {learned and judicious} Knight to hold.
MGREC104:22 H2074 Lays hold on's Lord, and binding him with bands.
MGREC104:26 H2078 In more dispight, the thrawled Prince to hold.
MGREC118:11 H2658 He hold of {on} this occasion should have laid,
MGREC120:12 H2747 So many Kingdoms in their power to hold,
MGREC126:4 H2995 *Polisperchon* to hold a while in play,
MGREC126:19 H3010 *Olimpias* wills to keep it, {means to hold out} to the last,
MGREC128:40 H3113 That each shall {should} hold what he doth {did} now possesse,

MGREC130:11 H3166 To let her go, or hold her still, he fears,
DIALOG145:9 H158 My guilty hands (in part) hold up with you,
SIDNEY151:41 ~~H75~~ He bad me drive, and he would hold the Sun;
FLESH175:33 H33 Then eyes can see, or hands can hold.
FLESH176:41 H81 Nor such like trash which Earth doth hold,
1HUSB180:28 H7 Or all the riches that the East doth hold.
MEDDM201:28 Hp281 not only to bid them hold fast the form of sound Doctrin, but
MEDDM208:23 Hp290 but when death threatens and distresse lays hold vpon them
MEDDM208:35 Hp291 if Moses had been able by the hand of faith, to hold the Ever
MYCHILD216:2 Hp241 loose from God, vanity & ye follyes of Youth take hold of me.
11MAYA226:13 Hp255 a sore sicknes and weaknes took hold of me wch hath by fitts

HOLDING (1)
ELEMEN18:36 H440 Which may be done, by holding down my vapour.

HOLDS (4) n.
MROMAN136:30 H3444 Where Swaines, and rustick Peasants made {kept} their Holds.

HOLDS (3) v.
MGREC132:17 H3254 *Seleuchus, Asia* holds, that grieves him sore,
CONTEM172:18 H153 O happy Flood, quoth I, that holds thy race
MEDDM201:26 Hp281 vsed for Contrary ends, the one holds fast, the other puts

HOLES (1)
MGREC99:24 H1867 The Captaine {Thus *Betis*} tane, had holes bor'd through his

HOLINESSE (1)
DIALOG148:30 H295 And holinesse, on horses bells shall stand,

HOLLAND (3)
AGES44:34 H367 Then saw I *France,* and *Holland* sav'd, *Cales* won,
DIALOG142:26 H55 Doth *Holland* quit you ill, for all your love?
DIALOG143:17 H86 What *Holland* is, I am in some suspence,

HOLY (7)
ELEMEN10:26 H101 I of acceptance was the holy signe.
MASSYR65:29 H494 Who was last King of holy *Davids* race;
MASSYR67:33 H579 The holy vessells, thither brought long since,
MGREC96:7 H1727 The Holy fire, was borne before the Host:
MGREC134:8 ~~H3339~~ I'th' holy place, which caused desolation;
MROMAN137:32 H3483 And vestall Maids to keep the holy fire.
MYCHILD217:18 Hp243 his holy spirit who hath oft given me his word & sett to his Seal

HOMAGE (2)
FATHER5:14 H15 To do their homage unto yours most {full} glad,
MGREC109:33 H2292 His Homage unto him {to himself} as Soveraigne doe.

HOME (24)
ELEMEN12:36 H196 That with lesse cost, neare home, supplyes {supply} your
HUMOUR32:35 H509 At home, the Conquerours, have conquered:
AGES38:39 H142 At home, abroad, my danger's manifold.
AGES39:24 H167 Though thus in field, at home, to all most kind,
AGES44:36 H369 I saw all peace at home, terror to foes,
SEASONS50:23 H157 The Carter leads all home, with whistling voyce,
MASSYR65:8 H473 And though a Victor home his Army leads,
MPERS77:2 H941 Go *Persians,* carry home that angry peece,
MPERS77:4 H943 *Darius* light, he {yet} heavie, home returnes,
MPERS77:29 H970 His Souldiers, credit, wealth, at home had stay'd,
MPERS80:35 H1102 He hearing this, his thoughts, and course home bended,
MPERS82:12 H1159 Three thousand scapes, for to {only can} run home agen;

MPERS82:18 H1165 Scarce one was left, to carry home the fame;
MPERS89:40 H1474 Chose *Xenophon,* to lead them home again;
MPERS91:7 H1515 *Agesilaus* is called home with speed,
MPERS~~91:22~~ H1535 But shortly calls her home, her counsells prize,
MPERS91:37 ~~H1551~~ Made Writers work at home, they sought not far?
MGREC94:15 H1649 Leaves sage *Antipater* at home to sway,
MGREC111:10 H2355 With rich rewards, he sent them home again,
MGREC~~123:38~~ H2902 Unto these helps, in *Greece,* {at home} he seeks out more,
QELIZ156:41 H68 Her *Drake* came laded home with *Spanish* gold,
3LETTER183:32 H34 *At home, abroad, and every where.*
MYCHILD216:22 Hp242 fr him, but by one afflict^{n} or other hath made me look home,
JULY223:23 Hp251 dear husband was from home (who is my cheifest comforter on

HOME-BRED (2)
MPERS~~73:1~~ H788 Which ends before begun, the *Persian* {his home-bred} Warre,
MPERS91:20 H1528 His home-bred troubles seeketh {sought how} to appease;

HOMELY (1)
DUBART153:11 H15 A homely flower in this my latter spring:

HOMER (4)
MASSYR63:31 H418 Did neither *Homer, Hesiode, Virgil* sing;
MGREC116:23 H2589 The Illiads of *Homer* he still kept,
MGREC116:26 H2592 'Cause *Homer* kept his Acts to memory;
SIDNEY150:19 H44 O brave *Achilles,* I wish some *Homer* would

HOME-SPUN (1)
AUTHOR178:9 H19 But nought save home-spun Cloth, i' th' house I find.

HONESTIE (1) [honesty]
HUMOUR24:17 H166 Or honestie such ties, unfriendly break?

HONESTY (1)
MPERS75:22 ~~H880~~ Thy wit was more then was thine honesty,

HONEY See HONY

HONEYSUCKLE'S See HONY-SUCKL'S

HONORABLE (1) [honourable]
MGREC104:3 H2055 Chusing {And} rather {chose} an honorable death:

HON^{r} (1) [honour]
MYCHILD219:4 Hp245 Hon^{r}, + Glory for ever and ever,

HONOUR (39)
FATHER6:4 H38 I honour him, but dare not wear his wealth,
AGES41:37 H254 If Noble, then mine honour to {o} maintaine.
AGES42:41 H297 And greater stil, did {and thirst for honour,} set my heart on
AGES43:1 ~~H297~~ If honour was the point, to which I steer'd;
AGES44:12 H345 It's not my valour, honour, nor my gold,
AGES44:26 H359 Sometimes in honour, sometimes in disgrace,
MASSYR62:16 H361 Laden with honour, prisoners, and with spoyl,
MPERS70:35 H706 In honour, peace, and wealth, with a grey head,
MPERS76:21 H919 Return'd with little honour, and lesse gaine;
MPERS76:28 H926 Return'd with wondrous losse, and honour lesse:
MPERS77:9 H948 His men, his coyn, his honour, and his store;
MPERS77:34 H975 What infamy to's honour did accrue.
MPERS89:37 H1471 But violates his honour, and his word,
MGREC93:33 H1630 Which honour to his son, now did befall.
MGREC97:18 H1779 Preserv'd their honour, us'd them courteously {bounteously},
MGREC98:10 H1812 To win their {the} town, his honour he engag'd;

MGREC99:33 H1876 Why didst not heap up honour, and reward?
MGREC108:23 H2239 Repelling these two marks of honour got,
MGREC133:21 H3309 Whereby immortall honour they acquire.
MGREC~~135:1~~ H3372 He seeing his honour lost, his Kingdome end,
MROMAN138:28 H3518 By wealth, and favour, doth to honour climbe;
DIALOG141:7 H6 With honour, wealth, and peace, happy and blest;
SIDNEY149:9 H8 No lesse {As well} an Honour to our *British* Land,
SIDNEY149:31 ~~H23~~ Which shewes, thy worth was great, thine honour such,
SIDNEY150:7 H32 doth thy {his} selfe, thy {his} worke, and {his} honour wrong,
SIDNEY~~150:12~~ H40 Which shews his worth was great, his honour such,
DUBART152:30 H1 In honour of *Du Bartas.*
QELIZ155:1 H10 In honour of that High and Mighty
QELIZ158:1 H110 Full fraught with honour, riches, and with dayes:
VANITY159:34 H6 What is't in honour, to be set on high?
VANITY160:22 H32 If not in honour, beauty, age, nor treasure,
VANITY160:36 H46 It brings to honour, which shall not {ne're} decay,
CONTEM174:23 H221 That's full of friends, of honour and of treasure,
CONTEM174:26 H224 Here's neither honour, wealth, or safety;
FLESH175:26 H26 Dost honour like? acquire the same,
FLESH176:22 H62 My greatest honour it shall be
BIRTH180:18 H28 With some sad sighs honour my absent Herse;
MEDDM200:20 Hp279 honour, wealth, or a helthfull body, would quite ouer throw,
MEDDM207:6 Hp288 they were giuen for, as health wealth and honour, wch might be

HONOURABLE (2) See also HONORABLE
SIDNEY149:1 H1 An Elegie upon that Honourable
SIDNEY149:35 ~~H23~~ Who honours thee for what was honourable,

HONOUR'D (1) [honoured]
MROMAN137:3 H3454 And with the stile of *Patres* honour'd those;

HONOURED (4)
FATHER5:1 H1 To her most Honoured Father
TDUDLEY165:1 H1-2 *To the Memory of my dear and ever honoured Father*
DDUDLEY167:6 H1-2 *On my dear and ever honoured Mother*
VERSES183:35 H2 Most truly honoured, and as truly dear,

HONOURLESSE (1)
MGREC127:19 H3049 *Antigonus* came off still honourlesse,

HONOUR'S (2) [honour is]
AGES40:9 H190 Until her freinds, treasure, and honour's gone.
MPERS75:14 H875 Then thy disgrace, thine honour's manifold,

HONOURS (11) [pl.]
HUMOUR23:22 H132 Onely to raise my honours to the Skyes,
MPERS70:41 ~~H712~~ Then at his Herse great honours to expresse;
MPERS~~70:41~~ H712 With honours great, did celebrate his fame.
MPERS92:38 H1596 Whose honours, treasures, pleasures, had short stay;
MGREC106:12 H2146 And {he} makes their riches, and their honours more;
MGREC115:31 H2550 His honours, and his riches, to augment
MGREC121:18 H2800 And offers {offer} him his Honours, and his place,
QELIZ155:23 H14 Thy world of honours to accumulate,
TDUDLEY165:39 H41 Nor honours pufft him up, when he had part:
FLESH176:20 H60 Thine honours doe, nor will I love;
MEDDM208:21 Hp290 so is it wth the wealth honours and pleasures of this world

HONOURS (3) [poss.]
ELEMEN~~14:4~~ H248 Bur'ing himself alive for honours prize.
SIDNEY149:28 ~~H23~~ What doe thy vertues then? Oh, honours crown!
SIDNEY151:9 ~~H69~~ Who wert of honours band, the chief Commander.

HONOURS (1) v.
SIDNEY149:35 ~~H23~~ Who honours thee for what was honourable,

HONY (3) [honey]
SEASONS48:17 H70 Now swarmes the busie buzzing {witty,} hony Bee.
MEDDM196:11 Hp273 The finest bread hath the least bran the purest hony the least
MEDDM196:25 Hp273 Sweet words are like hony, a little may refresh, but too much

HONY-SUCKL'S (1) [honeysuckle's]
SEASONS48:21 H74 The Meads with Cowslip, Hony-suckl's dight,

HOOES (1) [hoes]
ELEMEN~~9:11~~ H45 Your shares, {Hooes} your mattocks, and what e're you see,

HOOK (1)
MEDDM198:19 Hp276 the hook till it be to late.

HOOKE (1)
MEDDM198:17 Hp276 a hooke vnder all, Satan that great Angler hath his sundry

HOP (1)
SEASONS47:17 H33 Like Birds, now chirp, and hop about the field;

HOP'D (4) [hoped]
MPERS69:27 H649 Disguised *Cressus,* hop'd to scape i'th throng,
MPERS86:25 H1341 He hop'd, if fraud, nor force the Crown could {would} gaine;
DIALOG146:34 H220 To see these {those} latter dayes of hop'd for good,
QELIZ156:12 H39 If *France* had ever hop'd for such a Queen;

HOPE (28)
ELEMEN13:36 H237 Again, when Delvers dare in hope of gold,
HUMOUR34:35 H590 Wel, to be breif, Choler I hope now's laid,
AGES38:12 H115 Nor yet on future things did place {set} my hope.
AGES41:25 H242 My reason, then bad judge, how little hope,
AGES44:18 H351 Nor from alliance now can I have hope,
AGES46:25 H456 And in that hope, I bid you all farewel.
SEASONS47:9 H25 In hope, the more he casts, the more to gain;
SEASONS47:23 H39 They joy in what they have, but more in hope,
MPERS70:37 ~~H708~~ Where *Alexander* fought, in hope of prize,
MGREC~~94:18~~ H1656 Reply'd, enough, sith only hope he kept.
MGREC100:29 H1913 Yet had some hope, that on that even {the spacious} plain,
MGREC104:8 H2060 The little hope, of profit like to rise.
MGREC112:40 H2426 Sunk in despair, without hope of releif;
MGREC117:36 H2643 Had hope themselves, to beare the Crown away;
MGREC119:30 H2720 For fighting still, whilst there did hope remain,
DIALOG143:34 H103 That Pope, had hope, to find *Rome* here againe;
DIALOG146:19 H205 The seed time's come, but Ploughman hath no hope,
DIALOG~~146:32~~ H218 Your griefs I pity much, but should do wrong {hope to see},
CONTEM174:8 H208 Joyes not in hope of an eternal morrow;
FLESH175:17 H17 And dost thou hope to dwell there soon?
FLESH177:5 H86 The City where I hope to dwell,
MEDDM197:9 Hp274 they do but hope for that wch is to Come
MED223:17 Hp250 I ovght. Lord haueing this hope let me purefye my self as thou
JULY223:28 Hp251 possesse that I now hope for, y^{t} so they may bee encourag^{d} to
11MAYA226:21 Hp255 espec: seing it is for my spiri^{tl}. advantage, For I hope my soul

ACK235:15 H15 And hope thov'st given of good successe,
HOUSE237:13 H43 Didst fix thy hope on mouldring dvst,
HOUSE237:28 H58 My hope, and Treasure lyes Above.

HOPED See HOP'D

HOPEFUL (1)
DIALOG~~147:25~~ H249 And to this blessed {hopeful} Cause closely adhere

HOPEFULL (1)
MPERS85:37 H1313 A hopefull Prince, whose worth {by *Xenophon*} is ever fam'd.

HOPELESSE (1)
MPERS81:9 H1117 (Chief instigater of this hopelesse {hapless} War;)

HOPES (26)
AGES39:21 H164 Nor wait til good advice {success} our hopes do crown;
AGES39:31 H174 Makes {Make} all to place their future hopes on me.
AGES39:37 H180 My woful Parents longing hopes all {are} crost,
AGES42:37 H293 My dunghil thoughts, or hopes, could reach no higher.
AGES44:40 H373 In midst of greifs, I saw some {our} hopes revive,
AGES44:41 H374 (For 'twas our hopes then kept our hearts alive)
AGES45:1 ~~H374~~ I saw hopes dasht, our forwardnesse was shent,
MASSYR58:32 H215 But with fresh hopes *Belosus* succoured.
MASSYR65:15 H480 Had all his hopes like to a Spiders web;
MPERS74:24 H847 By which he cuts their hopes (for future times)
MPERS90:41 H1508 And hopes by craft to quit his Masters harmes;
MGREC104:19 H2071 Who was of hopes, and comfort quite bereft;
MGREC104:36 H2088 His hopes being dasht, prepares himself for flight:
MGREC108:11 H2227 And now reviv'd with hopes, held up their head,
MGREC123:5 H2867 For universall Monarchy he hopes;
MGREC~~124:8~~ H2913 His proud opponent hopes soon to withstand.
MGREC129:33 H3147 And place their hopes o'th heire of *Alexander,*
MGREC~~130:19~~ H3174 And now he thinks {hopes}, he's ordered all so well,
MGREC~~131:19~~ H3211 Hoping {Hopes} to find succour {succours} in {his} miseries.
MGREC~~132:20~~ H3259 With these he hopes to turn the world about:
MGREC132:41 H3288 Whilst with these hopes, in *Greece* he did remaine,
CONTEM170:20 H92 Upon whose blood his future good he hopes to raise.
2LETTER182:6 H12 My sobs, my longing hopes, my doubting fears,
3LETTER183:5 H7 Still wait with doubts, & hopes, and failing eye,
ANNEB187:19 H9 When I on fading things my hopes have set?
JULY223:34 Hp251 my faith in Thee, 'till I shall attain ye End of my hopes, Even

HOPING (5)
MPERS88:41 H1434 Hoping with {by} that to make the *Greeks* stand stil,
MGREC118:10 H2657 Hoping to be elect more generally;
MGREC124:4 H2909 Hoping still {yet} more to gaine by these new stirs;
MGREC124:27 H2934 *Polisperchon* hoping for's office long,
MGREC131:19 H3211 Hoping {Hopes} to find succour {succours} in {his} miseries.

HOPS (2) [pl.]
SEASONS47:11 H27 And Poles erects, for his green {young} clambering Hops;
MEDDM199:15 Hp278 Ambitious men are like hops that neuer rest climbing soe long

HOPS (1) v.
2LETTER182:13 H19 Or every mote that in the sun-shine hops,

HORATII (1)
MROMAN138:3 H3493 Three call'd *Horatii,* on *Romans* side,

HORN (2)
MGREC117:13 H2620 The great Horn broke, the lesse did tytannize;
CONTEM168:12 H21 Or thousand since thou brakest thy shell of horn,
HORNE (1) [horn]
ELEMEN12:20 H180 Poysons sure antidote lyes in his horne.
HORNED (1)
SEASONS52:20 H235 This month he's hous'd in horned *Capricorn,*
HORNES (1) [horns]
MGREC93:28 H1625 That broke {brake} his hornes, that threw him on the ground,
HORRID (5)
AGES~~45:4~~ H383 But saw their horrid fact soon disappointed,
MASSYR68:1 H587 Which horrid sight, he fears, must needs portend,
MPERS~~92:23~~ H1581 Lost but his life for horrid treasons all.
MGREC105:21 H2114 The witnesse of his dying misery: {this horrid Tragedy;}
MGREC134:5 H3338 Horrid massacres, murders, cruelties,
HORROR (1)
CONTEM170:31 H101 His face like death, his heart with horror fraught,
HORSE (14)
ELEMEN10:6 H81 The Horse that kill'd *Bellerophon,* then flew.
ELEMEN15:3 H285 Nor mettl's found in the couragious Horse:
HUMOUR21:38 H66 She'l ride a Horse as bravely, as the best,
AGES36:9 H33 No wooden horse, but one of mettal try'd:
AGES39:18 H161 The snorting Horse, the Trumpet, Drum I like,
MPERS72:40 H786 Unsheathes, as he his horse mounted on high,
MPERS74:5 H830 And he whose Horse before the rest should neigh,
MPERS78:6 H987 Eight hundred thousand Horse to them {these} belong;
MPERS86:39 H1355 And for that end, five hundred Horse he chose,
MGREC94:20 H1658 To these {which} were joyn'd, five thousand goodly horse.
MGREC97:5 H1766 Now finds both leggs, and Horse, to run away;
MGREC100:26 H1910 Of Horse, and Foot, this {his} Army did amount;
MGREC104:37 H2089 Unto *Darius,* first he brings a Horse,
MGREC110:30 H2334 As never Horse his Provender could eye;
HORSELEACH See HORSLEACH
HORSES (8)
ELEMEN10:8 H83 The maid with ballance, wayn with horses three;
MPERS79:19 H1045 He glories in his Squadrons, and his Horses;
MPERS87:14 H1370 And counts nine hundred thousand foot and horses:
MGREC96:5 H1725 The stately Horses trapt, the launces guilt;
MGREC96:15 H1735 A number of spare horses next were led,
MGREC105:16 H2109 So chanc'd these bloudy Horses to espy,
MGREC~~115:15~~ H2525 The Mules and Horses are for sorrow shorne,
DIALOG148:30 H295 And holinesse, on horses bells shall stand,
HORSLEACH (1) [horseleach]
MEDDM202:34 Hp282 say it is enough, but like the daughters of the horsleach, crys
HOSHEA (1)
MASSYR62:4 H349 *Hoshea,* their last King, he did invade,
HOSPITALITY (1)
SIDNEY150:10 H35 Justice, friendship, and kind hospitality;
HOST (3) See also HOAST
MPERS88:1 H1394 Arme, arme, the King {with all his host} is now approaching
MPERS88:28 H1421 His Host in chase, knowes not of his {this} disaster,

MGREC96:7 H1727 The Holy fire, was borne before the Host:
HOSTAGE (1)
MGREC101:15 H1940 *Ochus* his Son a hostage shall {should} endure.
HOSTILE (1)
MGREC99:35 H1878 But in no hostile way (as I suppose)
HOSTILITY (1)
MPERS81:11 H1119 That all Hostility might {from} thence-forth cease;
HOSTILIUS (2)
MROMAN137:37 H3488 *Tullus Hostilius.*
MROMAN137:38 H3489 *Tullus Hostilius,* was third *Roman* King,
HOT (24) See also HOTT
FATHER5:21 H22 These are, the hot, the cold, the moist, the dry,
FATHER5:31 H32 How hot, and dry, contend with moist, and cold,
ELEMEN8:24 H22 That betwixt hot and cold, she arbitrated
ELEMEN10:22 H97 Augment his heat, which was too hot before:
ELEMEN14:12 ~~H254~~ In hot, and cold, and some benums with sleeps,
ELEMEN~~14:15~~ H257 Much might I say, of the *Arabian* sands; {hot *Libian* sand}
ELEMEN18:22 H426 Your red hot work, more coldly would go on.
ELEMEN18:31 H435 My moist hot nature, is so purely thinne,
ELEMEN19:27 H472 Then in his long hot wars, {war} which *Millain* gain'd.
HUMOUR27:22 H293 This hot, moist, nurtritive humour of mine,
HUMOUR27:28 H299 Your hot, dry, moyst, cold, natures are {but} foure,
HUMOUR27:30 H301 As thus, if hot, then dry; if moist, then cold;
HUMOUR30:3 H395 What is too hot, my coldnesse doth abate;
HUMOUR32:6 H480 Nor cold, nor hot, Ague, nor Plurisie;
HUMOUR35:4 H600 Let Sanguine, Choler, with her hot hand hold,
HUMOUR35:8 H604 Two hot, two moist, two cold, two dry here be,
AGES35:22 H8 From blood and aire, for hot, and moist is he.
SEASONS~~46:35~~ H12 Nor hot nor cold, she spake, but with a breath,
SEASONS49:4 H95 Bright *June, July,* and *August,* hot are mine,
SEASONS50:11 H145 My next, and last, is *August,* fiery hot,
MASSYR65:10 H475 When in the *Tyrian* wars, the {this} King was hot,
MASSYR66:26 H532 Although the Furnace be seven times more hot;
MGREC124:17 H2924 Whilst hot in wars these two in *Greece* remaine,
DUBART154:16 H61 In all the Zones, the temp'rate, hot and cold,
HOTLY (1)
HUMOUR20:23 H15 Choler {first} hotly claim'd, right by her mother,
HOT'ST (1) [hottest]
SEASONS49:38 H131 *July* my next, the hot'st in all the year,
HOTT (1) [hot]
11MAYB228:27 Hp259 y^{t} ever I had lasting 4 dayes, and ye weather being very hott
HOTTEST See HOT'ST
HOUR (4)
MGREC105:41 H2134 I've nothing left, at this my dying hour;
CONTEM167:26 H3 When *Phœbus* wanted but one hour to bed,
ANNEB187:25 H15 That's here to day, perhaps gone in an hour;
MYSOUL225:23 H27 O let me covnt each hour a Day
HOURE (6) [hour]
AGES40:34 H213 Though dangers do attend me every houre,
MPERS70:29 H700 And sets on *Cyrus,* in a fatall houre;
MPERS74:7 H832 They all attend on the appointed houre,

MGREC118:32 H2681 And {So} took his life unworthily that houre:
DIALOG142:16 H45 Must *Edward* be depos'd, or is't the houre
DIALOG145:31 H180 All *Englands* Metropolitane that houre,

HOURES (1) [hours]
HOURS233:19 H1-2 In my Solitary houres in my dear husband his Absence.

HOUR-GLASSE (1)
AGES35:34 H20 And in his hand an hour-glasse new begun,

HOURLY (1)
MEDDM207:31 Hp289 and diseased bodys, haue hourly mementos of their mortality

HOURS (4) See also HOURES
MGREC102:12 H1982 Which in few hours was carried all away;
MROMAN139:37 H3563 And for the same, I hours not few did spend,
DDUDLEY167:19 H16 *And in her Closet constant hours she spent;*
FLESH176:31 H71 Then can thy hours in pleasure spent.

HOUS'D (2) [housed]
SEASONS52:20 H235 This month he's hous'd in horned *Capricorn,*
TDUDLEY166:20 H62 And in celestial Barn hath hous'd him high,

HOUSE (26)
AGES37:26 H88 This little house of flesh, did spacious count:
AGES44:13 H346 My ruin'd house, now falling can uphold;
AGES44:16 H349 It's not my goodly house {state}, nor bed of down,
AGES46:18 H449 In my dark house, such kindred I have store,
SEASONS48:3 H56 The fearful Bird, his little house now builds,
MASSYR53:18 H8 If of his house he held the Monarchy:
MASSYR62:40 H385 And by his Sons in's Idols house was slain.
MASSYR63:7 H392 And on his Masters ruins, his house makes;
MASSYR64:18 H442 And in his Idols house the Vassal's {vessels} plac'd.
MPERS~~75:37~~ H894 Built on, and prosper'd, till their walls did {house they} close;
MPERS~~91:28~~ H1542 What troubles in his house he did sustain,
MGREC124:31 H2938 Hatefull the Name, and House of *Alexander,*
MGREC129:38 H3152 Thus was the race, and house of *Alexander*
MGREC130:21 H3176 Thus *Philips* house was quite extinguished,
MGREC132:13 H3248 *Jehu* in killing *Ahabs* house did well,
DIALOG~~144:29~~ H137 Some grossely fin'd, from {house &} friends to exile went:
CONTEM172:25 H159 To *Thetis* house, where all imbrace and greet:
AUTHOR178:9 H19 But nought save home-spun Cloth, i' th' house I find.
1LETTER181:24 H22 The welcome house of him my dearest guest.
3LETTER183:25 H27 Who neither joyes in pasture, house nor streams,
3LETTER183:28 H30 And like two Turtles roost within one house,
MEDDM197:18 Hp275 That house wch is not often swept makes the cleanly inhabitant
MEDDM204:19 Hp285 for takeing veangence on the house of Ahab and yet a little
MEDDM204:20 Hp285 god) and I will avenge the blood of Jezerel vpon the house
PILGRIM210:22 H22 and my Clay house mouldring away
HOUSE237:17 H47 Thou hast an house on high erect

HOUSED See HOUS'D
HOUSEHOLD See HOUSHOLD, HOVSHOLD
HOUSEWIVES See HUSWIVES

HOUSES (8) [pl.]
ELEMEN19:23 H468 Which neither ships nor houses could withstand.
ELEMEN19:34 H475 Where neither houses, trees, nor plants, I spare;
SEASONS47:33 ~~H47~~ Twelve houses of the oblique Zodiack,

MGREC96:25 H1745 Like severall houses moving upon wheeles:
MGREC102:31 H2001 Here stood the Royall houses of delight,
DIALOG144:39 H147 Wives forc'd, babes toss'd, her houses calcined,
DIALOG146:16 H202 My plundered Townes, my houses devastation,
MEDDM207:28 Hp289 that when wee are put out of these houses of Clay, we

HOUSHOLD (2) [household] See also HOVSHOLD
AGES42:3 H261 With mine owne fleece, and with my houshold bread.
MPERS83:5 H1193 To *Bactria* his houshold did remove.

HOVSHOLD (1) [household] See also HOUSHOLD
MYCHILD218:2 Hp243 hovshold vpon ye Earth, ye p^{r}serving + directing of All to its

HOW (116)
FATHER5:31 H32 How hot, and dry, contend with moist, and cold,
FATHER5:32 H33 How Aire, and Earth, no correspondence hold,
FATHER5:33 H34 And yet in equall tempers, how they gree,
FATHER6:1 H35 How divers natures, make one unity.
PROLOG6:21 H6 And {Or} how they all, or each, their dates have run:
ELEMEN9:34 H68 How doth his warmth refresh thy frozen backs, {back}
ELEMEN13:16 H217 But how my cold, dry temper, works upon
ELEMEN13:18 H219 How the Autumnal season I do sway;
ELEMEN13:19 H220 And how I force the grey head to obey.
ELEMEN13:23 H224 And how I oft work mans mortality.
ELEMEN13:40 H241 Ye affrighted wights, appall'd how do you shake
ELEMEN14:29 H271 And how your subtilty would men delude.
ELEMEN18:4 H408 How gladly should his gold purchase his breath,
ELEMEN18:6 H410 How freely should it go, so he might live.
ELEMEN19:28 ~~H472~~ How many rich fraught vessells, have I split?
HUMOUR23:36 H146 Again, ye know, how I act every part:
HUMOUR24:36 H185 He knew {well} how, for to handle, Sword and Harpe,
HUMOUR24:37 H186 And how to strike ful sweet, as wel as sharpe.
HUMOUR25:29 H218 How often for the lye, thou'st giv'n the stab.
HUMOUR30:41 H433 But that which shewes how high thy spight is bent,
HUMOUR32:22 H496 I've not forgot how bitter Choler spake,
HUMOUR32:23 H497 Nor how her Gaul on me she causeless brake;
AGES37:30 H92 How to be rich, or great, I did not carke;
AGES37:32 H94 Nor studious was, Kings favours how to buy,
AGES41:25 H242 My reason, then bad judge, how little hope,
AGES42:11 H269 And shew'd them how, in face of foes to stand.
AGES42:39 H295 How was I broy'd with envy, and with hate?
SEASONS~~49:33~~ H124 By purling Brooks looking how fishes swims.
SEASONS52:33 H248 I care not how the Winter time doth haste;
SEASONS53:4 H260 *I could {knew} not tell how to passe't by:*
MASSYR57:17 ~~H164~~ How he thus suddenly should be thus small?
MASSYR57:28 H173 What e're he was, they {or} did, or how it fel,
MASSYR62:23 H368 Or how they fare, rich, poor, or ill, or wel;
MASSYR64:31 H455 How in all Merchandise she did excell,
MASSYR64:33 H457 And for her strength, how hard she was to gain,
MPERS~~69:38~~ ~~H660~~ And told, how *Solon* in his hight had spoke.
MPERS~~71:4~~ H720 To shew how little Land he then should take.
MPERS75:2 H863 Tels them, how harshly the proud King had dealt,
MPERS77:22 H963 None write by whom, nor how, 'twas over-past;
MPERS78:8 H989 For truth's asham'd how many to expresse;

MPERS79:27	H1053	How of this enterprise his thoughts now stands;
MPERS80:1	H1068	How part, {some} might o're the Mountains goe about,
MPERS80:7	H1074	O noble *Greeks,* how now, degenerate?
MPERS84:10	H1238	And how her Country-men from spoile she freed.
MPERS~~90:24~~	H1491	And now {how} their Nation with facility,
MPERS~~91:20~~	H1528	His home-bred troubles seeketh {sought how} to appease;
MPERS92:16	~~H1574~~	How this *Darius* did attain the Crown,
MPERS92:36	H1594	How from the top of the worlds felicity;
MGREC95:41	H1720	To shew, how great *Darius* plaid his part:
MGREC~~96:21~~	H1741	Their golden Ornaments so {how} to set forth,
MGREC96:37	H1757	And how {that} his wealth serv'd but for baits t'allure,
MGREC99:39	H1882	How he should over-throw this Monarchy;
MGREC100:3	H1887	To see how fast he gain'd, is {was} no small wonder,
MGREC100:39	H1923	But when inform'd, how royally the King
MGREC104:10	H2062	Then with so few, how likely to be crost.
MGREC107:29	H2204	How to passe {the River} over, and gaine {to} the other Land;
MGREC~~109:5~~	H2264	How to submit their necks at last they're glad.
MGREC113:14	H2441	But how these Captaines should, or yet their Master,
MGREC120:13	H2748	Yet to regain them, how he did not know,
MGREC122:7	H2830	His policies, how he did extricate
MGREC123:11	H2873	How neatly {finely} *Eumenes* did here excell,
MGREC126:40	H3029	How for no cause, but her inverterate hate;
MGREC128:3	H3076	And how he aymes {aiming now} to make himselfe a King,
MGREC128:17	H3090	First, how he held the Empire in his hands,
MGREC~~131:9~~	H3201	How some when down, straight got the upper hand
MGREC133:7	H3295	A little now, how the Succession run:
MGREC135:37	H3409	But how the fourth, their Kingdoms from them won;
MGREC135:38	H3410	And how from small beginnings it did grow,
DIALOG143:12	H81	*France* knowes, how of {oft} my fury she hath drunk;
DIALOG143:20	H89	And for the Pestilence, who knowes how neare;
DIALOG144:6	H116	How many Princely heads on blocks laid down,
SIDNEY151:10	~~H69~~	How could that *Stella,* so confine thy will?
SIDNEY151:20	H70	would I shew, how thou {he} fame's path didst {paths did}
SIDNEY~~151:23~~	H73	For {How} to persist, my muse is more in doubt:
QELIZ157:17	H85	How vanisheth her glory, wealth, and powers;
DAVID158:27	H7	How did the mighty fall, and falling dye?
DAVID159:19	H34	O! how in battell did the mighty fall,
DAVID159:21	H36	O! lovely *Jonathan,* how wert {wast} thou slaine,
DAVID159:27	H42	How are the mighty falne into decay,
VANITY159:36	H8	And whilst they live, how oft doth turn their State? {fate,}
CONTEM168:1	H11	How excellent is he that dwells on high?
CONTEM168:9	H18	How long since thou wast in thine Infancy?
CONTEM169:6	H48	How full of glory then must thy Creator be?
CONTEM170:11	H84	And how she lost her bliss, to be more wise,
CONTEM171:3	H108	Their long descent, how nephews sons they saw,
CONTEM171:5	H110	And how their precepts to their sons were law,
CONTEM171:6	H111	How Adam sigh'd to see his Progeny,
CONTEM173:2	H170	Look how the wantons frisk to tast the air,
FLESH176:12	H52	How oft thy slave, hast thou me made,
FLESH176:26	H66	How I do live, thou need'st not scoff,
SICKNES178:34	H17	O Bubble blast, how long can'st last?

BIRTH179:33 H9 How soon, my Dear, death may my steps attend,
BIRTH179:34 H10 How soon't may be thy Lot to lose thy friend,
1LETTER181:6 H4 How stayest thou there, whilst I at *Ipswich* lye?
2LETTER182:7 H13 And if he love, how can he there abide?
2LETTER182:22 H28 O how they joy when thou dost light the skyes.
VERSES184:4 H8 My stock's so small, I know not how to pay,
ANNEB187:18 H8 How oft with disappointment have I met,
MERCY188:32 H18 Oh how I simpathize with thy sad heart,
MEDDM203:25 Hp283 of a guilty Conscience, cares not how far he keeps from him
MEDDM206:16 Hp287 bright while they moue on earth, how transcendently splendid
MEDDM206:20 Hp287 of turning to god, the first thing wch they eye, is how to reform
MEDDM206:29 Hp288 how many good parents haue had bad children, and againe
MEDDM206:29 Hp288 good parents haue had bad children, and againe how many
MEDDM207:1 Hp288 god and say how vnsearchable are his wayes and his footsteps
MEDDM207:26 Hp289 that time will come, together, wth the vncertainty, how where,
PILGRIM210:23 H23 Oh how I long to be at rest
MYCHILD217:33 Hp243 many times by Atheisme how I could know whether there was
MYCHILD217:35 Hp243 how did know but they were feigned. That there is a God my
MYCHILD218:4 Hp243 me that there is an Eternall Being. But how should I know he is
MYCHILD218:14 Hp244 Times, + how ye world came to bee as wee see, Do wee not
SOREFIT221:22 H8 And how in sweat I seem'd to melt
SON231:28 H39 Particular, and how gratiovsly thov hast answered my Desires.
2HUSB232:17 H18 Thou see'st how weak + frail I am,
REMB235:24 H5 Or how thy praises speak
REMB235:25 H6 My thankes how shall I testefye?

HUE (2) See also HEW
AGES39:7 H150 And then the worst, in a more ugly hue;
SIDNEY151:31 ~~H75~~ As *Vulcan* is, of *Venus* native hue.

HUGE (5)
ELEMEN12:7 H167 And huge great *Taurus*, longer then the rest,
ELEMEN12:22 H182 Out of huge {great} numbers, I might pick my choyce,
HUMOUR30:8 H400 Then all the huge beasts of the fertile field.
MPERS88:5 H1398 The brunt of that huge multitude to bide.
MGREC110:31 H2335 Huge Bridles made, which here, and there, he left,

HUGING (1)
MEDDM200:10 Hp279 are so childishly sottish that they are still huging and sucking

HUGS (1) [pl.]
PILGRIM210:2 H2 Hugs wth delight his silent nest

HULL (1)
AGES43:2 ~~H297~~ To run my hull upon disgrace I fear'd,

HUMANE (2)
QELIZ155:19 H10 The sound thereof raps every humane sence;
MYCHILD218:10 Hp244 humane Invention can work vpon ye Soul, hath no Judgments

HUMANITY (4)
HUMOUR25:27 H216 Thou oft hast broke bounds of humanity.
MGREC100:10 H1894 That his humanity will not retaine;
MGREC126:34 ~~H3023~~ She oft forgot bounds of Humanity.
DUBART155:5 H90 *Now shew'd what once they ought, Humanity,*

HU¯BLE (1) [humble] See also HVBLE
MYCHILD216:12 Hp241 wth a lamenesse wch correction I saw the Lord sent to hu¯ble

HUMBLE (12) See also HVBLE
FATHER5:17 H18 But by my humble hand thus rudely pen'd
HUMOUR27:21 H292 My worth in humble manner, to commend.
MASSYR61:28 H333 His humble thankfulnesse (with {in} hast) to bring,
MGREC97:28 H1789 *Darius* now, more humble {less lofty} then before,
MGREC105:30 H2123 He also sends his humble thankfulnesse,
MGREC115:38 H2557 But his excuse with humble thanks he sends,
DIALOG142:30 H59 Your humble Childe intreats you, shew your grief,
DUBART153:1 H5 In humble wise have vow'd their service long;
TDUDLEY166:2 H44 His humble mind so lov'd humility,
CONTEM169:12 H53 My humble Eyes to lofty Skyes I rear'd
1SIMON188:10 H11 With humble hearts and mouths put in the dust,
MEDDM197:22 Hp275 Few men are so humble, as not to be proud of their abilitys,
HU¯BLY (1) [humbly]
REMB236:4 H19 I hu¯bly this Require.
HUMBLY (5)
FATHER5:2 H2-3 *Thomas Dudley* Esq; *these humbly presented.*
MPERS78:37 H1018 He humbly to the King then makes request,
MGREC109:19 H2278 And as his Sovereign Lord, him humbly greets.
MGREC136:2 H3415 But humbly stand, some grave reproof to take:
DIALOG145:39 H188 They humbly beg return, shew their intents,
HUMILITY (1)
TDUDLEY166:2 H44 His humble mind so lov'd humility,
HUMOUR (3)
HUMOUR27:22 H293 This hot, moist, nurtritive humour of mine,
HUMOUR30:2 H394 Then he whose brain a touch my humour gives.
MPERS77:38 H979 That his ambitious humour best can fit;
HUMOURS (5) [pl.]
ELEMEN16:34 H357 All humours, Tumours, that {which} are bred of cold.
HUMOUR20:9 H1 Of the foure humours in
HUMOUR28:13 H325 Of all the perverse humours from mine owne,
HUMOUR34:1 H556 The optick nerve, coats, humours, all are mine,
MASSYR66:29 H535 Strange melancholly humours on him lay,
HUNDRED (40)
ELEMEN10:40 H115 *Carthage,* and hundred moe, in stories told,
ELEMEN17:25 H389 That in two hundred year, it ne'r prov'd good.
AGES~~45:19~~ H401 Three hundred thousand slaughtered innocents,
MASSYR53:34 H24 One hundred fourteen years, he after dyed.
MASSYR54:20 H47 Four hundred forty Furlongs, wall'd about,
MASSYR54:21 H48 On which stood fifteen hundred towers stout:
MASSYR54:22 H49 The walls one hundred sixty foot upright,
MASSYR56:3 H109 An hundred gates, it had, of mettall strong.
MASSYR56:4 H110 Three hundred sixty foot, the walls in heighth:
MASSYR56:10 H116 Three hundred thousand men, here day, by day;
MASSYR57:32 H177 And eleav'n {many} hundred of years in silence sit,
MASSYR59:33 H257 Which {That} for twelve hundred years had held that place;
MASSYR66:19 H525 Who had for sixteen hundred years born sway,
MPERS78:5 H986 His Foot was seventeen hundred thousand strong,
MPERS78:6 H987 Eight hundred thousand Horse to them {these} belong;
MPERS79:23 H1049 none of these should {those could} live a {an} hundred yeares:
MPERS80:14 H1081 Four hundred stately Ships by stormes was lost,

MPERS81:6 H1114 Three hundred thousand yet he left behind,
MPERS81:35 H1143 {In all} One hundred thousand, and ten thousand make.
MPERS82:11 H1158 All's lost, and of three hundred thousand men,
MPERS86:39 H1355 And for that end, five hundred Horse he chose,
MPERS87:10 H1366 Seven hundred *Greeks* now further {repair for} his intents:
MPERS87:14 H1370 And counts nine hundred thousand foot and horses:
MPERS87:17 H1371 Three hundred thousand, yet {he} to *Syria* sent;
MPERS88:20 H1413 He with six hundred, on a squadron set,
MGREC95:33 H1712 He but four hundred thousand had to fight,
MGREC96:19 H1739 He fifteen hundred had like women drest,
MGREC97:6 H1767 Two hundred thousand men that day were slaine,
MGREC97:22 H1783 Two hundred eighty *Greeks* he lost in fight,
MGREC100:25 H1909 Two hundred fifty thousand by account,
MGREC103:15 H2026 To a {an} hundred thousand Tallents by account.
MGREC108:41 H2257 And being an {one} hundred twenty thousand strong,
MGREC111:3 H2348 Where one hundred {Whether} Embassadours, {ninety} or
MGREC134:22 H3353 {And} With seven hundred thousand volumes fill'd,
MROMAN137:2 H3453 A hundred Senators he likewise chose,
MROMAN138:30 H3520 A hundred Senatours he more did adde;
QELIZ155:24 H15 'Mongst hundred Hecatombs of roaring Verse,
CONTEM168:11 H20 Hath hundred winters past since thou wast born?
CONTEM172:23 H157 But hundred brooks in thy cleer waves do meet,
CONTEM173:27 H192 Sets hundred notes unto thy feathered crew,

HUNDREDS (2) [pl.]
ELEMEN11:36 H156 Soone would they passe, not hundreds, but legions,
AGES42:1 H259 For hundreds blesse me, for my bounty sent {lent}.

HUNG (1)
MPERS72:20 H768 Flayd him alive, hung up his stuffed skin

HUNGER (4)
ELEMEN13:33 H234 But to all outrages their hunger runnes.
MPERS76:5 H903 His Army fought with Hunger, and with Cold,
MPERS90:6 H1479 But on they march, through hunger, and through cold,
MGREC111:26 H2371 By hunger, and by cold, so many slaine,

HUNGRY (5)
SEASONS~~47:39~~ H51 growes long, the tender Lambs {hungry beast} to nourish;
SEASONS~~52:8~~ H223 Our pinched flesh, and empty panch {hungry mawes} requires:
MPERS89:24 H1458 They were too hungry to capitulate;
PILGRIM210:10 H10 nor hungry wolues at him shall catch
BYNIGHT220:12 H11 My hungry Soul fill'd wth Good,

HUNTER (1)
MASSYR53:21 H11 That mighty Hunter, who in his strong toyls,

HURRICANES See HERICANOES

HURRI'D (1) [hurried]
MPERS~~89:9~~ H1443 After a while his {hurri'd} thoughts he re-collects,

HURRIED (2)
AGES43:4 H299 That over flats, and sands, and rocks I hurried,
MGREC125:40 H2990 With rage, and with revenge, he's hurried on,

HURRY (2)
AGES40:2 H183 My Lust doth hurry me, to all that's ill,
MPERS86:19 H1335 These and like motives, hurry him amain,

HURT (3)
MPERS73:27 H812 Some write that sorely hurt, they 'scap'd away;
DIALOG147:20 H246 But those that hurt his people and his Crown,
MEDDM197:1 Hp274 of Sathan without could not hurt, hath, been foild by one
HURTFUL (1)
ELEMEN19:36 H477 Earth-quaks so hurtful and so fear'd of all,
HURTFULL (1)
FATHER5:24 H25 The world, the usefull, hurtfull, and the good:
HURTS (2) [pl.]
MGREC~~109:5~~ H2263 His fights, his dangers, and the hurts he had,
DIALOG143:15 H84 My Sister *Scotland* hurts me now no more,
HUSBAND (19)
ELEMEN13:32 H233 The Husband knowes no Wife, nor father sons;
MASSYR55:21 H87 Accompaning her husband *Menon* far,
MPERS72:16 H764 O hellish Husband, Brother, Vnckle, Sire,
MPERS77:8 H947 She lost her aime; her Husband, he lost more,
MPERS85:11 H1287 To be by *Hester,* {fair Queen Ester} to her husband brought.
MGREC122:15 H2840 But that her Husband serve for supplement,
MROMAN139:18 H3546 Her Husband sore incens'd, to quit this wrong,
1HUSB180:22 H1 *To my Dear and loving Husband.*
1LETTER181:1 H0 *A Letter to her Husband, absent upon*
3LETTER183:18 H20 Where she her captive husband doth espy.
MED223:9 Hp250 enough thy maker is thy husband. Nay more, I am a member
JULY223:23 Hp251 dear husband was from home (who is my cheifest comforter on
RESTOR229:19 H1-2 For the restoration of my dear Husband from a burning
2HUSB232:1 H1-2 Vpon my dear & loving husband his goeing into
2HUSB232:10 H11 My husband, my dear freind.
HOURS233:19 H1-2 In my Solitary houres in my dear husband his Absence.
HOURS234:1 H15 Tho: husband dear bee from me gone
HOURS234:23 H37 Bring back my husband I beseech
ACK235:4 H3-4 husband ovt of England.
HUSBANDMAN (1)
MEDDM204:33 Hp285 produced wth much labour (as the husbandman well knowes)
HUSBAND-MEN (1)
ELEMEN9:10 H44 Ye Husband-men, your coulter's made by me,
HUSBANDRY (1)
DUBART153:39 H43 Valour in War, in Peace good Husbandry.
HUSBANDS (5) [poss.]
MPERS72:13 H761 That by her Husbands charge, she caught her owne;
MGREC124:40 H2947 As all her Husbands children by his Mates;
MGREC126:35 H3024 To Husbands death ('twas {'tis} thought) she gave consent,
MGREC126:41 H3030 Her Husbands Wife, {wives} and Children, after's death
REMB235:21 H1-3 In thankfull Remb^{rc} for my dear husbands safe Arrivall.
HUSHT (1)
MPERS76:25 H923 Which husht, he straight so orders his affaires;
HUSKES (1) [husks]
MEDDM202:16 Hp282 The treasures of this world may well be compared to huskes,
HUSWIVES (1) [housewives]
SEASONS48:19 H72 The cleanly huswives Dary, now's ith' prime,
HVBLE (1) [humble]
THEART229:11 H13 An hvble, faithfull life O Lord

HYÆNA (1)
ELEMEN12:21 H181 And my *Hyæna* (imitates mans voyce)
HYDRA'S (1) [pl.]
DIALOG144:15 H125 These be the *Hydra's* of my stout transgression;
HYE (1)
MGREC127:33 H3063 *Antigonus,* his growing up so hye,
HYES (1)
MGREC94:37 H1675 To th' river *Granicke, Alexander* hyes,
HYSLASPES (2)
MPERS73:12 H799 *and* Darius Hyslaspes.
MPERS74:19 H842 *Darius Hyslaspes.*
HYSTORIANS (2) [historians]
MASSYR56:29 H135 As puzzells best hystorians to remember:
MPERS85:10 H1286 These two lewd {first} sons, are by hystorians thought,

I

IACOBS (1) [jacob's]
MASSYR62:20 H365 Thus *Iacobs* Sons, in exile must remain,
ICE (3)
ELEMEN17:15 H379 My Ice and extream cold, which all men know.
ELEMEN17:20 H384 Mine Ice doth glaze *Europs* big'st Rivers o're,
HUMOUR22:14 H83 Convert from water, to conjealed Ice;
I'D (2)
HUMOUR32:18 H492 Patient I am, patient i'd need to be,
AGES37:39 H101 I'd nought to do, 'twixt Prince, {King} and peoples strife.
IDEALL (1) [ideal]
MGREC112:11 H2397 If an Ideall Paradise, a man should {would} frame,
IDLE (1)
AGES40:36 H215 Sometimes by wounds in idle combates taken,
IDOLATERS (1) [pl.]
MPERS71:39 H753 Is more prophane, then grosse Idolaters;
IDOLATRY (2)
MASSYR68:22 H608 His pride, and sottish grosse Idolatry.
DIALOG143:29 H98 Idolatry, supplanter of a Nation,
IDOLIZE (2)
MASSYR54:4 H31 He taught the people first to Idolize;
MGREC117:2 H2609 A God alive him all must Idolize;
IDOLS (2) [poss.]
MASSYR62:40 H385 And by his Sons in's Idols house was slain.
MASSYR64:18 H442 And in his Idols house the Vassal's {vessels} plac'd.
IEHOIAKIM (2) [jehoiakim]
MASSYR64:10 H434 Against *Iehoiakim* marcht with his train;

MASSYR65:30 H495 But he, as perjur'd as *Iehoiakim,*

IF (195)

FATHER6:6 H40 But if I did, I durst not send them you;
PROLOG7:18 H31 If what I doe prove well, it wo'nt advance,
PROLOG7:37 H47 If e're you daigne these lowly lines, your eyes
ELEMEN9:22 H56 And you Philosophers, if ere you made
ELEMEN10:20 H95 And influence if divers of those starres,
ELEMEN13:10 H211 If ought you have to use, to wear, to eate?
ELEMEN13:41 H242 If {When} once you feele me, your foundation, quake,
ELEMEN14:34 H276 If I withhold, what art thou, dead, dry lump
ELEMEN~~14:39~~ H281 Complaines to th'heaven, when {if} I withhold my drops:
ELEMEN15:14 H296 If I supply, his heart and veines rejoyce;
ELEMEN15:15 H297 If not, soon ends his life, as did his voyce.
ELEMEN16:10 H333 If I should shew,{name} more Seas, then thou hast Coasts.
ELEMEN18:8 H412 If my pure Aire, thy sonnes did not sustain.
ELEMEN18:21 H425 Ye forging Smiths, if Bellowes once were gone;
ELEMEN19:7 H452 The Phoenix too (if any be) are mine;
ELEMEN19:25 H470 If nought was {were} known, but that before *Algire.*
HUMOUR21:18 H46 Where if your rule once grow {prove} predominant,
HUMOUR21:20 H48 But if ye yeeld sub-servient unto me,
HUMOUR22:5 H74 If great perswasions, cause her meet her foe;
HUMOUR22:13 H82 If any threaten her, she'l in a trice,
HUMOUR22:17 H86 She dare, {dares} not challenge if I speake amisse;
HUMOUR23:16 H126 If once thou'rt great, what followes thereupon?
HUMOUR25:36 H225 If murthers be thy glory, tis no lesse.
HUMOUR25:38 H227 But if in fitting time, and place, on foes; {'gainst foe}
HUMOUR26:12 H242 For there are {is} none, thou say'st, if some, not best.
HUMOUR~~26:14~~ H244 Of greatest use, if reason do not erre:
HUMOUR26:17 H247 If thou giv'st life, I give thee nourishment,
HUMOUR26:21 H251 And if vital spirits do flow from thee,
HUMOUR26:28 H258 If thou'rt the taker, I must be the giver:
HUMOUR27:7 H278 If stil thou take along my Aliment,
HUMOUR27:30 H301 As thus, if hot, then dry; if moist, then cold;
HUMOUR27:30 H301 As thus, if hot, then dry; if moist, then cold;
HUMOUR27:31 H302 If this {you} can't be disprov'd {disprove}, then all I hold:
HUMOUR28:8 H320 As if she'd leave no flesh to turn to clay,
HUMOUR28:34 H346 If time I have transgrest, and been too long,
HUMOUR28:39 H351 If modesty my worth do not conceale.
HUMOUR29:17 ~~H368~~ If not as yet, by me, thou shalt be quell'd:
HUMOUR29:22 H373 If in a Souldier rashnesse be so precious,
HUMOUR29:34 H385 And if *Marcellus* bold, be call'd *Romes* sword,
HUMOUR29:36 H387 And if thy haste, my slownesse should not temper,
HUMOUR30:5 H397 If I be partial judg'd, or thought to erre,
HUMOUR30:14 H406 If I have not more part, then al ye three:
HUMOUR30:36 H428 But if thou hast, that malice comes {is} from you.
HUMOUR31:14 H445 If any doubt this {the} truth, whence this should come;
HUMOUR31:16 H449 If there thou'rt stopt, to th' Liver thou turn'st in,
HUMOUR34:32 H587 If Tyrants be the best, i'le it allow;
HUMOUR34:33 H588 But if love be, as requisite as feare,
AGES35:37 H23 But if he hold, til it have run its last,
AGES40:18 H199 If any care I take, 'tis to be fine,

AGES40:20	H201	If any time from company {leud Companions} I {can} spare,
AGES40:26	H207	And in a word, if what I am you'd heare,
AGES41:33	~~H249~~	If rich, I'm urged then to gather more.
AGES41:35	H250	If a father {I}, then for children must provide:
AGES41:36	H251	But if none, then for kindred near ally'd.
AGES~~41:36~~	H252	If rich, I'm urged then to gather more,
AGES41:37	H254	If Noble, then mine honour to {o} maintaine.
AGES41:38	H255	If not, yet wealth, {riches} Nobility can gain.
AGES42:12	H270	If a Souldier {I}, with speed I did obey,
AGES42:24	H282	If to Agricolture, I was ordain'd:
AGES42:31	H287	But if I rest, the more distrest my mind.
AGES42:32	H288	If happinesse my sordidnesse hath found,
AGES42:38	H294	If to be rich, or great, it was my fate;
AGES43:1	~~H297~~	If honour was the point, to which I steer'd;
AGES43:21	H316	And envy gnawes, if any do surmount.
AGES43:23	H318	If *Bias* like, I'm stript unto my skin,
AGES44:17	H350	That can refresh, or ease, if Conscience frown;
SEASONS49:14	H105	That if you do, remove {withdtaw} her burning store,
SEASONS~~49:33~~	H125	If pride within your lowly Cells ere haunt,
SEASONS~~51:19~~	H195	If scited as the most Judicious take.
MASSYR53:18	H8	If of his house he held the Monarchy:
MASSYR57:36	H181	It is enough {may suffice}, if all be true that's past,
MASSYR66:37	H543	And if by words, we may guesse at the heart,
MPERS~~69:38~~	H666	If ever King equal'd his happiness.
MPERS71:13	~~H727~~	And makes it lawful Law, if he but wil;
MPERS71:36	H750	If all his {this} heat, had been for a good {pious} end,
MPERS71:40	~~H753~~	And though no gods, if he esteem them some,
MPERS73:36	H821	If governed by an Aristocracy.
MPERS75:9	H870	If he command, obey the greatest must:
MPERS77:24	H965	As if to dust he meant to grinde that Nation;
MPERS80:24	H1091	If that smal number his great force could bide;
MPERS81:20	H1128	If now in {their} need, they should thus fail {forsake} their
MPERS85:12	H1288	If {so} they were hers, the greater was her moan;
MPERS86:23	H1339	If in his enterprize he should fall short,
MPERS86:25	H1341	He hop'd, if fraud, nor force the Crown could {would} gaine;
MPERS89:11	H1445	If *Greeks* unto their Country-men {own Country should}
MPERS92:18	~~H1576~~	If not (as is before) of *Cyrus* race,
MPERS~~92:28~~	H1586	If so, or not, we cannot tell, but find
MGREC94:11	H1645	Nor wonder is't, if he in blood begin,
MGREC96:6	H1726	As if they were, {if addrest} now all to run at {a} tilt:
MGREC~~96:6~~	H1726	As if they were, {if addrest} now all to run at {a} tilt:
MGREC96:26	H1746	As if she'd drawne, whole *Sushan* at her heeles.
MGREC97:9	H1770	If *Curtius* be true, in his report.
MGREC98:39	H1841	These he may scape, and if he so desire,
MGREC99:13	H1856	And so if I *Parmenio* were, would I.
MGREC99:32	H1875	If of thy future fame thou hadst regard,
MGREC101:2	H1927	And if they down, his Monarchy wil throw,
MGREC103:31	H2042	And layes before his eyes, if he persist
MGREC104:9	H2061	If when he'd multitudes, the day he lost;
MGREC105:26	H2119	If not, because *Darius* thus did pray,
MGREC106:8	H2142	To see if any dare his might oppose;

MGREC112:11 H2397 If an Ideall Paradise, a man should {would} frame,
MGREC115:29 H2548 Or if remembred, yet regarded not;
MGREC119:11 H2701 That if he came, good welcome he should find:
MGREC120:20 H2755 If not in word {stile}, in deed a Soveraigne.
MGREC122:14 H2839 If once young *Alexander* grow more strong,
MGREC123:17 H2881 Too young {rash} to beare that charge, if on him lay'd;
MGREC130:33 ~~H3181~~ If *Alexander* was not poysoned,
MGREC~~132:16~~ H3253 In neither finds content if he sits still:
DIALOG141:25 H24 If I decease, dost think thou shalt survive?
DIALOG142:3 H32 If th' wound's {wound} so dangerous I may not know?
DIALOG142:22 H51 If none of these, deare Mother, what's your woe?
DIALOG146:23 H209 If any pity in thy heart remain,
DIALOG147:9 H235 If mindlesse of thy state I e'r be found.
DIALOG147:28 H252 If now you weep so much, that then no more,
DIALOG148:31 H296 If this make way thereto, then sigh no more,
DIALOG148:32 H297 But if at all, thou didst not see't before.
SIDNEY149:22 H21 As if your nine-fold wit had been compacted;
SIDNEY150:40 ~~H68~~ If thine aspect was milde to *Astrophell;*
SIDNEY151:2 ~~H69~~ If such Stars as these, sad presages be,
SIDNEY151:16 ~~H69~~ Then wonder lesse, if warlike *Philip* yield,
SIDNEY~~152:14~~ H84 Then wonder not if I no better sped,
DUBART153:12 H16 If Summer, or my Autumne age, doe yeeld
DUBART154:10 H55 Pardon, if I adore, when I admire.
DUBART154:25 H70 If e'r this golden gift was showr'd on any,
QELIZ156:12 H39 If *France* had ever hop'd for such a Queen;
QELIZ156:18 H45 Come shew me such a Phoenix if you can;
QELIZ158:5 H114 If then new things, their old form must {forms shall} retain,
QELIZ158:19 H128 If many worlds, as that fantastick framed,
DAVID159:4 H19 As if his head ne're felt the sacred Oyle:
VANITY160:13 H23 Sure if on earth, it must be in those parts;
VANITY160:22 H32 If not in honour, beauty, age, nor treasure,
TDUDLEY167:4 H86 *If some rejoyc'd, more did lament.*
CONTEM167:34 H10 If so much excellence abide below;
CONTEM168:13 H22 If so, all these as nought, Eternity doth scorn.
CONTEM171:22 H125 If winter come, and greeness then do fade,
CONTEM172:12 H148 And if the sun would ever shine, there would I dwell.
CONTEM174:15 H214 As if he had command of wind and tide,
FLESH177:27 H108 If I of Heaven may have my fill,
AUTHOR178:3 H13 Thy blemishes amend, if so I could:
AUTHOR178:13 H23 If for thy Father askt, say, thou hadst none:
BIRTH180:5 H15 And if I see not half my dayes that's due,
BIRTH180:9 H19 If any worth or virtue were in me,
BIRTH180:15 H25 And if thou love thy self, or loved'st me
BIRTH180:17 H27 And if chance to thine eyes shall bring this verse,
1HUSB180:23 H2 If ever two were one, then surely we.
1HUSB180:24 H3 If ever man were lov'd by wife, then thee;
1HUSB180:25 H4 If ever wife was happy in a man,
1HUSB180:26 H5 Compare with me ye women if you can.
1LETTER181:5 H3 If two be one, as surely thou and I,
1LETTER181:8 H6 If but a neck, soon should we be together:
2LETTER181:35 H5 (And if the whirling of thy wheels don't drown'd)

2LETTER182:1 H7 If in thy swift Carrier thou canst make stay,
2LETTER182:7 H13 And if he love, how can he there abide?
2LETTER182:25 H31 At thy return, if so thou could'st or durst
VERSES183:36 H3 If worth in me, or ought I do appear,
CHILDRN185:17 H43 If birds could weep, then would my tears
CHILDRN186:29 H96 I happy am, if well with you.
ANNEB187:29 H19 As if mine own, when thus impermanent.
MEDDM197:11 Hp274 If we had no winter the spring would not be so pleasant,
MEDDM197:11 Hp274 had no winter the spring would not be so pleasant, if we did not
MEDDM197:27 Hp275 will finde it a wearysome if not an impossible task so he that
MEDDM197:29 Hp275 'tis no wonder if he faint by the way.
MEDDM198:3 Hp275 conditions, if he will make his face to shine vpon them,
MEDDM198:5 Hp276 waters, if they stick in deepe mire and clay, and all his waues
MEDDM201:5 Hp280 more or lesse if god afford his help
MEDDM203:5 Hp283 When we inioy them it is wth vanity and vexation, and if we
MEDDM203:22 Hp283 the company of the phisitian or chirurgian, but if he perceiue a
MEDDM203:27 Hp284 that he must needs perish if he haue no remedy, will
MEDDM204:28 Hp285 him that is lower then he is and if he se, that such a one
MEDDM204:29 Hp285 comfortably it will help to quiet him, but if that will not do
MEDDM205:17 Hp286 Court of heaven itself, for if our conscience condemn vs, he
MEDDM206:15 Hp287 that glorious sun that inlightens all in all, and if some of them
MEDDM206:35 Hp288 be a support to such as haue or had wicked parents, that if
MEDDM207:9 Hp288 are lords we will come no more at thee If outward blessings,
MEDDM208:6 Hp289 As the brands of a fire, if once severed, will of themselues goe
MEDDM208:8 Hp290 wth length of time (if there be no inter course) will coole the
MEDDM208:29 Hp290 possible to be done, it can remoue mountaines (if need were)
MEDDM208:35 Hp290 them as if Moses had been able by the hand of faith, to hold
MYCHILD215:19 Hp240 not to sett forth my self, but y[e] Glory of God. If I had minded
MYCHILD215:26 Hp240 et[c]. I avoided it. If at any time I was overtaken wth y[e] evills, it
MYCHILD217:1 Hp242 If at any time yov are chastened of God take it as Thankfully
MYCHILD217:2 Hp242 mercyes, For if yee bee his yee shall reap the greatest
MYCHILD217:25 Hp243 Lord, and when I haue been in sicknes + pain, I haue thought if
MYCHILD218:8 Hp244 If ever this God hath revealed himself it mvst bee in his word,
MYCHILD218:32 Hp244 reme̅bred the words of Christ that so it must bee, and that if
MYCHILD218:36 Hp244 my faith, + if I perish, I perish, But I know all y[e] powers of Hell
MYCHILD219:7 Hp245 & imperfectly done, but if yov can pick any Benefitt out of it, It
28AUG225:33 Hp254 by it— And if he knowes that weaknes, & a frail body is y[e] best
13MAY227:3 H12 But if they mvst eclipse again
30SEPT227:29 Hp257 I haue passed thro: to y[e] End y[t] if you meet wth the like yov
30SEPT227:31 Hp257 will doe y[e] like for yov if you trvst in him; And when he shall
SAMUEL228:14 H15 And if thou shalt spare me a space
SAMUEL228:18 H19 If otherwise I goe to Rest
HOURS234:15 H29 Yet if I see Thee not thro: them
HOURS235:1 H53 If thou assist me Lord I shall

IF'T (2) [if it]

HUMOUR22:10 H79 She'l first advise, if't be not best to stay.
DIALOG141:27 H26 Then weigh our case, if't be not justly sad,

IGNIS (1)

ELEMEN11:10 H130 Of Meteors, *Ignis Fatuus,* and the rest,

IGNOBLE (1)

ELEMEN17:28 H392 Then wholly perish'd, earths ignoble race;

IGNORANCE (7)
ELEMEN17:36 H400 Though {Yet am} not through ignorance, {ignorant} first was my
HUMOUR24:19 H168 Is't ignorance, {arrogance} or folly causeth this?
HUMOUR29:41 H392 But's not thy {thine} ignorance shal thus deceive me.
AGES37:27 H89 Through ignorance, all troubles did surmount.
AGES37:28 H90 Yet this advantage, had mine ignorance,
MASSYR61:5 H310 To rest content we must, in ignorance.
DUBART154:37 H82 But lest my {mine} ignorance should doe thee wrong,
IGNORANT (13)
ELEMEN~~17:36~~ H400 {Yet am} not through ignorance, {ignorant} first was my due,
HUMOUR21:19 H47 The man proves boyish, sottish, ignorant,
AGES39:15 H158 Nor ignorant {And so likewise} what they in Country do;
MPERS~~72:37~~ H782 The people ignorant of what was done,
MGREC106:20 H2154 To th' ignorant, her title may {will} declare.
DIALOG141:15 H14 Art ignorant indeed, of these my woes?
CONTEM173:35 H199 In knowledg ignorant, in strength but weak,
BIRTH180:1 H11 We both are ignorant, yet love bids me
CHILDRN185:38 H64 Of perils you are ignorant,
MERCY188:29 H15 Was ignorant what riches thou hadst lost.
MEDDM195:34 Hp272 a negligent youth is vsually attended by an ignorant middle
MEDDM202:8 Hp281 and some againe, so ignorant and sotish that they are more
MYCHILD215:12 Hp240 latest, + being ignorant whether on my death bed I shall haue
IIM (1) [jim]
MASSYR66:10 H516 Now *Zim,* and *Iim, {Jim}* lift up their shriking {scrieching}
I'LE (23) [i'll]
ELEMEN12:3 H163 I'le here skip o're my mountaines, reaching skies,
ELEMEN16:13 H336 To speake of kinds of Waters I'le {I} neglect,
HUMOUR26:37 H267 But i'le not force retorts, nor do thee wrong,
HUMOUR27:20 H291 Now through your leaves, some little time i'le spend;
HUMOUR29:6 H359 Though Choler rage, and raile, i'le not do so,
HUMOUR29:11 H364 I'le flatter for a time, as thou did'st me,
HUMOUR29:14 H367 But Choler, be thou cool'd, or chaf'd, i'le venter,
HUMOUR29:39 H390 I'le come to that which wounds me somewhat more:
HUMOUR32:31 H505 I'le leave that manly property to you;
HUMOUR33:41 H555 I'le touch the Sight, great'st wonder of the three;
HUMOUR34:32 H587 If Tyrants be the best, i'le it allow;
HUMOUR34:37 H592 To Melancholly i'le make no reply,
HUMOUR34:40 H595 A warning good, hereafter i'le say lesse.
AGES39:6 H149 But what is best i'le first present to view,
MGREC~~109:4~~ H2261 His warrs with sundry nations I'le omit,
MROMAN140:6 H3569 No more I'le do, sith I have suffer'd wrack,
TDUDLEY165:25 H27 While others tell his worth, I'le not be dumb:
VERSES184:9 H13 But as I can, I'le pay it while I live:
CHILDRN186:4 H71 In shady woods I'le sit and sing,
CHILDRN186:5 H72 And things that past, to mind I'le bring.
BYNIGHT220:19 H17 I'le serve him here whilst I shall liue
13MAY227:4 H13 I'le rvn where I was succoured.
HOURS234:8 H22 I'le on thy mercyes roll!
ILE (21) [i'll]
ELEMEN10:19 H94 Ile here let passe, my Choler cause of warres,
ELEMEN12:15 H175 But ile skip {leap} o're these Hills, not touch a Dale,

ELEMEN12:17 H177 Ile here let goe, my Lions of *Numedia,*
ELEMEN14:19 H261 Ile say no more, yet {but} this thing adde I must,
ELEMEN17:32 H396 Much might I say of wracks, but that Ile spare,
HUMOUR24:20 H169 Ile only shew the wrongs, thou'st done to me.
HUMOUR24:26 H175 Thy childish {foolish} incongruities, Ile show:
HUMOUR25:7 H196 Ile go no further then thy nose for test.
HUMOUR25:11 H200 But now Ile shew, what Souldier thou art.
HUMOUR25:37 H226 Ile not envy thy feats, nor happinesse.
HUMOUR25:41 H230 Ile praise that fury, {prowess} valour, choler, heat.
HUMOUR30:24 H416 But whilst he lives, Ile shew what part I have.
HUMOUR31:8 H441 Now {But} by your leave, Ile let your greatnesse see;
HUMOUR31:18 H451 No further time ile spend, in confutations, {confutation}
DIALOG143:27 H96 Before I tell the effect, ile shew the cause,
DUBART154:39 H84 Ile leave thy praise, to those shall doe thee right,
TDUDLEY165:15 H17 He was my Father, and Ile praise him still.
FLESH175:22 H22 Come, come, Ile shew unto thy sence,
FLESH176:11 H51 Thy flatt'ring shews Ile trust no more.
FLESH176:16 H56 Ile stop mine ears at these thy charms,
CHILDRN186:2 H69 Mean while my dayes in tunes Ile spend,

I'LL (2)

DIALOG146:2 H190 Shews all was done, I'll therefore let it go.
HOURS234:20 H34 And there content I'll take

ILL (17)

ELEMEN~~16:32~~ H355 I now must shew what force {ill} there in me lyes.
AGES40:2 H183 My Lust doth hurry me, to all that's ill,
MASSYR62:23 H368 Or how they fare, rich, poor, or ill, or wel;
MPERS76:27 H925 But as before, so now with ill successe,
MPERS77:32 H973 His Fathers ill successe in's enterprise,
MPERS89:32 H1466 Fit instruments t' accomplish what is ill;
MGREC~~121:14~~ H2792 *Perdiccas* in his pride did ill intreat
MGREC131:35 H3227 And leaves the ill got kingdomes he had won,
MGREC132:12 H3247 Yet must his children pay for fathers ill.
DIALOG142:26 H55 Doth *Holland* quit you ill, for all your love?
DIALOG146:26 H212 And recompence me {that} good, for all my ill {I've done to
SIDNEY151:33 ~~H75~~ Like unwise *Phaeton* his ill guided sonne,
VANITY160:19 H29 Nor laugh, nor weep, let things go ill or well:
CONTEM170:22 H93 There *Abel* keeps his sheep, no ill he thinks,
VERSES184:3 H7 Yet handled ill, amounts but to this crum;
CHILDRN186:24 H91 Taught what was good, and what was ill,
11MAYB228:25 Hp259 of January 'till May I haue been by fitts very ill & weak. The

ILL-FORM'D (1) [ill-formed]

AUTHOR177:30 H2 Thou ill-form'd offspring of my feeble brain,

ILLIADS (1) [pl.]

MGREC116:23 H2589 The Illiads of *Homer* he still kept,

ILLUSTRIOUS (2)

SIDNEY150:39 ~~H67~~ Illustrious *Stella,* thou didst thine full well,
DAVID158:25 H5 Illustrious *Saul,* whose beauty did excell

I'M (5)

ELEMEN18:34 H438 And when I'm throughly rarifi'd, turn fire.
AGES41:33 H252 If rich, I'm urged then to gather more.
AGES42:28 ~~H285~~ For restlesse day and night, I'm rob'd of sleep,

AGES43:23 H318 If *Bias* like, I'm stript unto my skin,
REMB235:26 H7 O Lord thov know'st I'm weak.

IMAGE (1)
MASSYR66:25 H531 His Image, *Iudahs* Captives worship not,

IMAGINE (2)
HUMOUR32:10 H484 What I imagine, that's my malady.
MGREC112:12 H2398 He might this feast imagine by the same.

IMBECILITY (1)
CONTEM169:16 H57 But Ah, and Ah, again, my imbecility!

IMBITTER (1)
MEDDM200:8 Hp279 bitter together so is it wth some Christians, let god imbitter all

IMBRACE (2)
CONTEM172:25 H159 To *Thetis* house, where all imbrace and greet:
2LETTER182:16 H22 That once a day, thy Spouse thou mayst imbrace;

IMBROYL'D (1) [embroiled]
SEASONS49:27 H116 Whilst they're imbroyl'd in Wars, and troubles ripe; {rife:}

IMITATE (2)
MASSYR58:3 H188 Did wear their garb, their gestures imitate,
MGREC99:26 H1869 To imitate *Achilles* (in his shame)

IMITATES (1)
ELEMEN12:21 H181 And my *Hyæna* (imitates mans voyce)

IMITATION (3)
ELEMEN13:21 H222 But that thy method is my {mine} imitation.
DUBART154:33 H78 Thy sacred works are not for imitation,
2SIMON195:4 Hp271 their imitation Children do natureally, rather follow the failings

IMMATURELY (1)
MPERS83:24 H1212 The eldest son, thus immaturely dead,

IMMODERATLY (1)
MGREC107:25 H2200 Where most {so} immoderatly these thirsty drink;

IMMORTAL (3)
HUMOUR33:26 H540 That divine Essence, {Offspring} the immortal Soul,
VANITY160:41 H51 Nor death shall see, but are immortal made,
FLESH175:27 H27 As some to their immortal fame:

IMMORTALITY (2)
MGREC116:32 H2598 Vain thirsting after immortality:
CONTEM172:4 H141 But man was made for endless immortality.

IMMORTALL (5)
MGREC100:41 H1925 He prayes the immortall gods, for to {they would} reward
MGREC105:34 H2127 Praying the immortall gods, that Sea, and Land,
MGREC113:35 H2462 Yet gave his Master the immortall fame;
MGREC133:21 H3309 Whereby immortall honour they acquire.
DUBART154:20 H65 Immortall bayes, all men to thee allows.

IMMOVABLE (1)
MGREC97:4 H1765 Of late, like some immovable he lay,

IMMURE (1)
HUMOUR21:27 H55 Then timerous Hares, whom Castles doe immure?

IMORTALL (1)
MYCHILD219:3 Hp245 Now to y[e] King Imortall, Eternall invisible, the only wise God,

IMP (1)
CONTEM170:8 H81 The weeping Imp oft looks her in the face,

IMPAIRES (1) [impairs]
ELEMEN17:29 H393 And to this day, impaires her beautious face.
IMPARES (1) [impairs]
MEDDM205:36 Hp287 many times, the waight thereof impares both their bodys and
IMPART (2)
ELEMEN11:19 H139 As I: impart your usefulnesse, and force.
MGREC136:10 H3424 *To finish what {what's} begun, new thoughts impart*
IMPARTIALL (1) [impartial]
SIDNEY150:31 H58 But yet impartiall Death {Fates} this Boone did give,
IMPATIENT (2)
ELEMEN8:28 ~~H26~~ Being the most impatient Element.
HUMOUR31:31 H464 Impatient Choler loveth not the sound.
IMPEACHMENT (1)
ELEMEN19:11 H456 Without impeachment, to my tale or wit.
IMPENDS (1)
MEDDM201:22 Hp281 from some black Clouds that impends them, wch produces
IMPERFECTLY (1)
MYCHILD219:7 Hp245 & imperfectly done, but if yov can pick any Benefitt out of it, It
IMPERIOSITY (1)
HUMOUR20:35 H27 They seeing her imperiosity, {impetuosity}
IMPERMANENT (1)
ANNEB187:29 H19 As if mine own, when thus impermanent.
IMPETUOSITY (1)
HUMOUR~~20:35~~ H27 They seeing her imperiosity, {impetuosity}
IMPIETY (1)
QELIZ155:20 H11 That men account it no impiety,
IMPLACABLE (1)
MPERS~~91:22~~ H1531 But the old Queen implacable in strife,
IMPLEMENTS (1) [pl.]
ELEMEN9:16 H50 Ye Cooks, your kitchin implements I fram'd, {frame}
IMPLOR'D (1) [implored]
MASSYR61:37 H342 Who stil implor'd his love, but was distress'd,
IMPLORE (2)
MGREC123:39 H2903 Goes to *Antigonus,* and both implore,
DIALOG142:20 H49 Must *Richmonds* ayd, the Nobles now implore,
IMPLORED See IMPLOR'D
IMPLOYED (1) [employed]
MEDDM207:5 Hp288 but most Commonly imployed for a Clean Contrary end, then
IMPLY (1)
MGREC115:14 H2523 Or of necessity, he must imply,
IMPORTUNITY (1)
MEDDM203:33 Hp284 men can vse great importunity when they are in distresses and
IMPOS'D (1) [imposed]
CONTEM170:4 H78 A penalty impos'd on his backsliding Race.
IMPOSES (1)
MEDDM201:3 Hp280 many times he imposes waighty burdens on their shoulders,
IMPOSSIBILITY (1)
MEDDM202:36 Hp282 it self, and sees an impossibility, euer to be filled, but by him,
IMPOSSIBLE (2)
MEDDM197:27 Hp275 will finde it a wearysome if not an impossible task so he that
REMB236:7 H22 Impossible for to recovnt

IMPOSTER (1)
MPERS73:20 H807 To thrust th' Imposter *Smerdis* out of throne,
IMPOSTERS (1) [pl.]
MGREC134:10 H3341 By Rebells and imposters daily vext;
IMPRINTED (1)
MGREC108:24 H2240 Imprinted deep in's legg, by Arrowes shot;
IMPRISONED (2)
ELEMEN19:37 H478 Imprisoned I, am the original.
MGREC132:21 H3266 There was he {At last he's} taken and imprisoned
IMPRISONING (1)
MGREC129:3 H3117 Imprisoning both the mother, and her {the} son,
IMPROUE (1)
MEDDM204:11 Hp284 behoues euery man so to improue his talents, that when his
IMPROUING (1)
MEDDM195:33 Hp272 Youth is the time of getting middle age of improuing, and old
IMPROVMENT (1)
MEDDM195:26 Hp272 of all and he that makes such improvment is wise as well as
IMPUDENCE (1)
MGREC136:6 H3419 Converts our boldnesse, into impudence.
IMPUTATION (1) See also INPUTATION
HUMOUR31:2 H435 Thy loathsome imputation I defie;
IMPUTATIONS (1) [pl.]
HUMOUR31:19 H452 I trust I've clear'd your slandrous imputations {inputation}.
IMPUTE (1)
2HUSB232:24 H25 Impute thov not to me
IMPUTED (1)
HUMOUR27:4 H275 Can be imputed unto none, but Fire;
INABILITY (1)
MGREC136:13 H3427 *Shortnesse of time, and inability,*
INCAMP'D (1) [encamped]
MASSYR59:18 H242 Who there incamp'd two years, for little end,
INCAMPT (1) [encampt]
MPERS89:7 H1441 The King with his dispers'd also incampt,
INCARNATE (1)
MEDDM202:9 Hp281 beasts then men, some pious saints, some incarnate Deuils,
INCENS'D (4) [incensed]
MPERS90:34 H1501 Which over-throw incens'd the King so sore,
MGREC~~114:11~~ H2479 Which *Alexanders* wrath incens'd so high,
MROMAN138:7 H3497 The *Romans* sore incens'd, their Generall slay,
MROMAN139:18 H3546 Her Husband sore incens'd, to quit this wrong,
INCENSE (1) n.
MGREC131:5 H3195 Who incense burnt, and offered oblation.
INCENSE (1) [insence]
MGREC~~121:16~~ H2796 The souldiers 'gainst *Perdiccas* they incense,
INCENSED (1) See also INCENS'D
MGREC104:34 H2086 Had *Alexanders* wrath incensed high;
INCEST (1)
MPERS71:8 H724 His reign with Bloud, and Incest, first begins,
INCESTUOUS (1)
MPERS~~91:29~~ H1543 His match incestuous, cruelties of th' Queen,

INCESTUOUSLY (1)

MPERS72:10 H758 His sister, whom incestuously he wed,

INCIDENT (1)

AGES43:36 H331 Though some more incident to age, or youth:

INCITE (2)

MASSYR57:27 ~~H172~~ Did then incite, them to regain their own.

MGREC115:22 H2541 And by her Letters did her Son incite,

INCIVILITY (1)

MPERS79:2 ~~H1024~~ O most inhumain incivility!

INCLIN'D (2) [inclined] See also ENCLIN'D

HUMOUR28:24 H336 Of such as to the Sanguine are inclin'd,

HUMOUR32:5 H479 Unto diseases not inclin'd as ye:

INCLOS'D (1) [inclosed]

MPERS80:18 H1085 Inclos'd their Fleet i'th' streights {streight} of *Eubea;*

INCLUDES (1)

MPERS71:12 ~~H727~~ Which Law includes all Lawes, though lawlesse stil,

INCOGNITAE (1)

QELIZ156:40 H67 *Terra incognitae* might know her {the} sound;

INCOMPATIBLE (1)

MGREC106:26 H2160 As most incompatible to his state;

INCONGRUITIES (1) [pl.]

HUMOUR24:26 H175 Thy childish {foolish} incongruities, Ile show:

INCONSTANCY (1) See also UNCONSTANCY

HUMOUR31:27 H460 Constant in nothing, but inconstancy {unconstancy},

INCONVENIENCYS (1) [inconveniencies]

MEDDM198:14 Hp276 inconveniencys, but he that is well stored wth both, seldom is

INCOURAG'D (1) [encouraged]

MPERS90:30 H1497 The *Greeks* by this successe, incourag'd so,

INCOURAGED (1) [encouraged]

MGREC99:40 H1883 By which he was so much incouraged,

INCREASE (2) See also ENCREASE

MGREC98:33 H1835 *Darius* finding troubles still increase,

CHILDRN185:11 H37 And as his wings increase in strength,

INCREASED (2)

SEASONS49:41 H134 Increased by the Star *Canicular;*

SEASONS52:38 H253 Which is increased by the lengthened day,

INCREDIBLE (1)

MASSYR56:5 H111 Almost incredible, they were in breadth.

INCREDULITY (1)

DIALOG~~144:26~~ H135 The plague of stubborn incredulity.

INCROACHED (1)

MASSYR60:18 H283 Incroached {Incroaching} stil upon the bord'ring Lands,

INCROACHING (2)

MASSYR~~60:18~~ H283 Incroached {Incroaching} stil upon the bord'ring Lands,

2SIMON195:10 Hp271 much more by duty full children, I haue avoyded incroaching

INC BERS (1) [encumbers]

SON231:11 H23 From troubles and Inc bers Thov

INCURSIONS (1) [pl.]

MPERS90:17 ~~H1484~~ For these incursions he durst not abide;

INDEAVOUR (1) [endeavour]

HUMOUR32:8 H482 I rarely feel to act his fierce indeavour.

INDEED (4)
DIALOG141:15 H14 Art ignorant indeed, of these my woes?
DIALOG145:34 H183 Here tugg'd they hard indeed, for all men saw,
MEDDM206:13 Hp287 a lesse degree, & others (and they indeed the most in number)
11MAYB228:26 Hp259 I had a feaver seatd vpon me wch indeed was the longest
INDEX (1) See also JUDEX
MPERS~~81:7~~ H1115 With his *Mardon'us,* judex {index} of his minde;
INDIAN (3)
MGREC109:1 H2258 He enters now {then} the *Indian* Kings among;
MGREC109:28 H2287 Thus all the *Indian* Kings, to him submit;
MGREC111:4 H2349 Came with submission, from the *Indian* Kings
INDIANS (2) [pl.]
MASSYR62:24 H369 Whether the *Indians* of the East, or West,
MGREC100:22 H1906 Of *Persians, Scithians, Indians,* in a cluster;
INDIGNITY (4)
HUMOUR27:25 H296 Without the least indignity to you;
MGREC115:23 H2542 This great indignity for to {he should} requite.
MGREC~~121:15~~ H2794 Who could not book so great indignity,
MGREC124:35 H2942 Nor counts {thought} he that indignity but {was} small,
INDOWMENTS (1) [endowments]
MEDDM200:19 Hp279 strength of the person he bestowes them on, larg indowments
INDURE (1) [endure]
HUMOUR25:15 H204 But useful, when a mixture can indure.
INDUS (4)
MASSYR56:32 H138 The River *Indus* swept them half away,
MGREC109:12 H2271 To th' river *Indus* next, his course he bends,
MGREC111:16 H2361 Hence {Then} sayling down by th' mouth of *Indus* floud,
MGREC111:22 H2367 Passing faire *Indus* mouth, his course he stear'd,
INDUSTRY (1)
FLESH175:23 H23 Industry hath its recompence.
INEFFECTUALL (1) [ineffectual]
MYCHILD216:13 Hp241 try me & doe me Good: and it was not altogether ineffectuall.
INEVITABLE (2)
MASSYR59:29 H253 This his inevitable destiny;
BIRTH179:32 H8 A common thing, yet oh inevitable;
INFAMIE (1)
QELIZ157:5 H73 More infamie than fame she did procure;
INFAMY (5)
MPERS77:34 H975 What infamy to's honour did accrue.
MPERS81:21 H1129 Their infamy would last till all things ends:
MPERS89:8 H1442 With infamy upon each fore-head stampt;
MGREC101:19 H1944 Nor infamy had wak'd, when he had slept;
MGREC104:4 H2056 Then still with infamy, to draw his breath.
INFANCY (5)
AGES37:18 H80 When Infancy was past, my Childishnesse,
AGES38:31 H134 What gripes of wind, mine infancy did pain?
SEASONS52:15 H230 In Swadling clouts, like new-born infancy,
MASSYR53:15 H5 When Time was young, and World in infancy,
CONTEM168:9 H18 How long since thou wast in thine Infancy?
INFANT (2)
ELEMEN13:31 H232 The tender mother on her Infant flyes:

SEASONS52:17 H232 And like an Infant, stil he {it} taller growes.

INFATUATE (1)
SIDNEY150:1 H26 But some infatuate fooles soone caught therein,

INFERNAL (1)
HUMOUR25:23 H212 Thou art a fury, or infernal Fiend.

INFIRMITY (1)
FLESH177:21 H102 From sickness and infirmity,

INFLAM'D (1) [inflamed]
MGREC103:26 H2037 Being inflam'd with wine upon a season,

INFLICTED (1)
MGREC113:10 H2437 Are {Were} now inflicted on *Parmenio's* Son,

INFLUENCE (5)
ELEMEN10:20 H95 And influence if divers of those starres,
HUMOUR22:39 H108 Oh, who would misse this influence of thine,
HUMOUR23:37 H147 By th' influence I send still from the heart.
SEASONS47:14 H30 The Pleiades, their influence now give,
SIDNEY151:11 ~~H69~~ To wait till she, her influence distill,

INFLUENCES (1) [pl.]
DUBART154:2 H47 Movelesse, stand charm'd by thy sweet influences,

INFOLD (1) [enfold]
FLESH177:4 H85 But such as Angels heads infold.

INFORM'D (1) [informed]
MGREC100:39 H1923 But when inform'd, how royally the King

INFORMATION (1)
MPERS69:22 H644 For information to *Apollo* went:

INFRANCHISED (1) [enfranchised]
MGREC108:12 H2228 From bondage, long to be infranchised;

INFRINGED (1)
DIALOG147:1 H227 And thine {thy} infringed Lawes have boldly stood.

INGAGE (3) [engage]
ELEMEN8:8 ~~H6~~ For to declare, themselves they all ingage;
MROMAN138:2 H3492 The strife to end, six Brothers doe ingage;
SIDNEY152:13 H82 For {Then} to revenge his {this} wrong, themselves ingage,

INGAGED (1) [engaged] See also ENGAG'D
MASSYR65:13 H478 While *Babels* King thus deep ingaged stands;

INGENIOUS See INGENIUS

INGENIOUSLY (1)
MASSYR59:41 H265 Ingeniously with each {all} did keep his word;

INGENIUS (1)
HUMOUR28:29 H341 {With} An ingenius working phantasie,

INGENUITY (1)
HUMOUR25:13 H202 My ingenuity must give thee right.

INGENUOUSLY (1)
ELEMEN13:14 H215 As I ingenuously (with thanks) confesse

INGRATE (1) See also UNGRATE
AGES~~37:17~~ H79 When wretched I (ungrate) {ingrate} had done the wrong.

INGRATIATE (1)
MGREC~~131:1~~ H3188 *Antigonus* himself to ingratiate,

INGRATITUDE (4)
ELEMEN14:28 H270 This your neglect, shewes your ingratitude;
MPERS84:15 H1251 For such ingratitude, did *Athens* show

DUBART153:7 H11 Did thaw my frozen hearts ingratitude;
MEDDM203:34 Hp284 shew great ingratitude after their successes, but he that
INHABIT See INHABITE
INHABITANT (1)
MEDDM197:18 Hp275 wch is not often swept makes the cleanly inhabitant soone
INHABITANTS (1) [pl.]
MEDDM205:11 Hp286 inhabitants his slight and flitting thoughts are like passengers,
INHABITE (1) [inhabit]
MASSYR60:6 H271 Yet would not {granting} let them {now} to inhabite there;
INHERITANCE (4)
MEDDM199:2 Hp277 Wisedom with an inheritance is good, but wisedome without an
MEDDM199:3 Hp277 inheritance, is better, then an inheritance wthout wisedome
MEDDM199:3 Hp277 inheritance, is better, then an inheritance wthout wisedome
2HUSB233:5 H38 Let not thine own Inheritance
INHERITC (1) [inheritance]
JULY223:32 Hp251 Thou hast given me a pledge of y^{t} Inheritc thou hast promised
INHUMAIN (1) [inhumane]
MPERS79:2 ~~H1024~~ O most inhumain incivility!
INHUMANE (1)
MGREC129:39 H3153 Extinct, by this inhumane wretch *Cassander;*
INIOY (3) [enjoy] See also INJOY
MEDDM195:25 Hp272 inioy, no evill that we feele, or fear, but we may make some
MEDDM197:8 Hp274 they haue more sence then faith they se what they inioy,
MEDDM203:5 Hp283 When we inioy them it is wth vanity and vexation, and if we
INJOY (1) [enjoy] See also INIOY
SIDNEY149:7 H6 When *England* did injoy her Halsion dayes,
INJOY'D (1) [enjoyed]
MGREC132:23 H3268 Injoy'd what so {ere} beseem'd his Royalty,
INJOYES (1) [enjoys]
MPERS86:10 H1326 Yet doubts, {fears} all he injoyes, is not his own.
INJURED (1)
SIDNEY~~152:15~~ H85 Since I the Muses thus have injured.
INJURIES (2)
MGREC128:16 H3089 For {And} he declares against his {the others} injuries;
DIALOG143:38 H107 What injuries did daily on them lye;
INJURIOUS (2)
HUMOUR32:19 H493 To bear {with} the injurious taunts of three;
DIALOG143:16 H85 Though she hath bin injurious heretofore.
INJURY (10)
HUMOUR24:21 H170 Then let my sisters, right their injury.
MPERS84:31 H1267 But he all injury, had soon forgate,
MPERS86:12 H1328 Judging all's {his} actions, tends to's injury.
MGREC97:19 H1780 Commands, no man should doe them injury,
MGREC100:38 H1922 Some injury was offered, he feares;
MGREC105:11 H2104 But this unheard of injury {treachery} much more;
MGREC107:17 H2192 The Souldiers should let passe this injury;
MGREC124:29 H2936 *Euridice* this injury disdaines,
MROMAN136:28 H3442 The double injury, he then did doe:
BIRTH180:16 H26 These O protect from step Dames injury.
INLARG'D (1) [enlarged]
MROMAN138:16 H3506 *Rome* he inlarg'd, new built againe the wall,

INLETS (2) [pl.]
MGREC111:24 H2369 Whose inlets neare unto, he winter spent,
MEDDM202:32 Hp282 The eyes and the eares are the inlets or doores of the soule,
INLIGHTENS (1)
MEDDM206:15 Hp287 from that glorious sun that inlightens all in all, and if some of
INMATES (1) [pl.]
MEDDM209:14 Hp291 all their accursed inmates, but make a league with them, they
INN (1)
DIALOG146:20 H206 Because he knows not, who shall inn his crop:
INNATE (1)
MEDDM201:19 Hp280 often se stones hang wth drops not from any innate moisture,
INNER-MAN (1)
11MAYA226:23 Hp255 man shall bee a meanes to strenghten my inner-man
INNOBLED (1)
MPERS71:2 H714 Innobled more by birth, then by their mind;
INNOCENCE (4)
FATHER6:8 H42 I shall not need my {mine} innocence to clear,
AGES37:41 H103 Where e're I went, mine innocence was shield.
AGES38:13 H116 This was mine innocence, but oh {ah!} the seeds,
AGES44:4 H337 Babes innocence, Youths wildnes I have seen,
INNOCENT (2)
MPERS72:6 ~~H755~~ Who for no wrong, poore innocent must dye,
MPERS83:19 H1207 That the poor {Prince} innocent, to death must {did} go.
INNOCENTS (2) [pl.]
AGES~~45:19~~ H401 Three hundred thousand slaughtered innocents,
MGREC130:28 ~~H3181~~ And wronging innocents whose blood they spilt,
INNUMERABLE (3)
MPERS80:15 H1082 Of Vessels small almost innumerable,
MEDDM202:33 Hp282 innumerable obiects enter, yet is not that spacious roome filled
MEDDM206:11 Hp287 innumerable Company of Saints, and Angels those Saintes
INNUMEROUS (1)
ELEMEN11:38 H158 Whose numbers now are growne innumerous;
INNUNDATIONS (1) [pl.]
ELEMEN17:22 H386 All know, what {that} innundations I have made;
INORMITY (1)
HUMOUR32:1 H475 Nor are ye free, from this inormity,
INPUTATION (1) [imputation]
HUMOUR~~31:19~~ H452 I trust I've clear'd your slandrous imputations {inputation}.
INRAG'D (2) [enraged] See also ENRAG'D
MPERS~~76:39~~ H937 Which soon cut off, {inrag'd,} he with the {his} left
MPERS~~91:22~~ H1533 The King highly inrag'd doth hereupon
INRICHED (1) [enriched]
FLESH176:37 H77 With which inriched I would be:
INRICHT (1) [enricht]
MASSYR60:30 H295 He thus inricht, by this new tryed gold,
IN-RODES (1) [inroads]
MPERS90:13 ~~H1484~~ Into *Bithynia* often in-rodes made;
INSECTS (1) [pl.]
CONTEM168:27 H34 Birds, insects, Animals with Vegative,
INSENCE (1) [incense]
MGREC102:8 H1978 And Insence burnt, the silver Altars on;

INSENSIBLE (1)
CONTEM171:20 H123 The stones and trees, insensible of time,
INSIDE (1)
SEASONS48:5 H58 The outside strong, the inside warme and neat.
IN-SIGHT (1)
DUBART153:37 H41 And curious in-sight in Anatomy;
INSINUATE (1)
AGES39:26 H169 I can insinuate into the brest,
INSNARED (1) [ensnared]
MEDDM198:14 Hp276 but he that is well stored wth both, seldom is so insnared
INSTABILITY (1)
HUMOUR34:38 H593 The worst she said, was, instability,
INSTALL (1)
QELIZ156:26 H53 *Don Anthony* in's right for {there} to install;
INSTALL'D (1) [installed]
MGREC~~100:6~~ H1890 For to be call'd {install'd} a god, was his intent;
INSTALLED (1)
MGREC129:1 H3115 Who then shall {should} be installed in the throne:
INSTANTLY (4)
MPERS73:21 H808 Their {Then} Forces instantly they raise, and rout,
MPERS81:10 H1118 He instantly to *Athens* sends for peace,
MGREC114:12 ~~H2480~~ But instantly commands him to be slaine;
CHILDRN186:12 H79 Where old ones, instantly grow young,
INSTEAD (1)
QELIZ157:19 H87 Instead of glory prov'd her Countries shame:
INSTEED (1) [instead]
MEDDM208:24 Hp290 proue like the reeds of Egipt that peirce insteed of supporting
INSTIGATER (1) [instigator]
MPERS81:9 H1117 (Chief instigater of this hopelesse {hapless} War;)
INSTITUTED (1)
MROMAN137:29 H3480 Religious Rites, and Customs instituted,
INSTRUCTED (2)
MGREC116:18 H2584 Had so instructed him in morall truth.
MGREC122:25 ~~H2845~~ Her Daughter she instructed in that Art,
INSTRUCTER (1) [instructor]
DDUDLEY167:16 H13 *A true Instructer of her Family,*
INSTRUCTION (2) See also INSTRVCTION
HUMOUR31:21 H454 Pray hear, admire, and learn instruction.
MEDDM205:6 Hp285 instruction and exhortation be sown, in the spring of their
INSTRUCTOR (1) See also INSTRUCTER
TDUDLEY165:8 H10 Who was my Father, Guide, Instructor too,
INSTRUMENT (1)
CONTEM173:28 H193 So each one tunes his pretty instrument,
INSTRUMENTS (3) [pl.]
AGES43:9 ~~H305~~ Whence poyson, Pistols, and dread instruments,
MPERS77:25 H966 Yet all his men, and instruments of slaughter,
MPERS89:32 H1466 Fit instruments t' accomplish what is ill;
INSTRVCTION (1) [instruction]
30SEPT227:23 Hp257 then without food. Lord wth y^{y} correction giue Instrvction and
INSUE (1) [ensue]
MGREC129:34 H3148 *Cassander* fear'd what might of this insue,

INSUING (1) [ensuing]
AGES38:15 H118 Which sprouted forth, in my {mine} insuing age,
INT'REST (1) [interest]
DIALOG148:9 H274 And let her spoils, full pay, with int'rest be,
INTELLECTUALL (1) [intellectual]
HUMOUR22:22 H91 Who rarifies the intellectuall parts?
INTELLIGENCE (1)
MPERS88:6 H1399 Of whose great numbers, their intelligence,
INTEND (5)
FATHER6:2 H36 Some thing {something} of all (though mean) I did intend,
AGES36:28 H52 Intend to speak, according to their age:
MGREC97:40 H1801 To gain his love, the *Tyrians* do intend,
MGREC98:6 H1808 Least he intend more fraud, then sacrifice;
MGREC~~115:15~~ H2529 Twelve thousand Talents also did intend,
INTENDED (3)
HUMOUR29:5 H358 That blow's most deadly, where it is intended;
MPERS80:36 H1103 Much, {fearing} that which never was intended!
MGREC104:12 H2064 But to deliver him to's foes, intended.
INTENDS (9)
HUMOUR27:15 H286 Who th' benefit o'th' whole ever intends:
MASSYR65:20 H485 Fast bound, intends at {to} *Babel* he shal stay {him to send},
MPERS76:23 H921 He after this, intends *Greece* to invade,
MPERS80:32 H1099 That *Greeks* to break his bridge shortly intends;
MGREC94:32 H1670 That he be tane alive, (for he intends)
MGREC95:29 H1708 To raise more force, for what he yet {to further his} intends.
MGREC107:7 H2182 Intends with speed, that Traitor down {to his end} to bring;
MGREC119:1 H2691 But nothing lesse: each one himself intends.
MGREC125:8 H2956 *Euridice* hearing what she intends,
INTENT (17)
ELEMEN20:7 H489 To adde to all I've said, was my intent,
HUMOUR24:22 H171 To pay with railings, is not mine intent,
MASSYR65:7 H472 Before he could accomplish his intent;
MASSYR68:11 H597 None answers the affrighted Kings intent.
MPERS72:9 ~~H757~~ Accomplished this wicked Kings intent;
MPERS~~72:9~~ H757 To act in secret, this his lewd intent:
MPERS76:12 H910 The King will needs interpret their intent;
MPERS78:2 H983 In great provisions, for this great intent;
MPERS87:18 H1372 To keep those streights, to hinder his intent.
MGREC100:6 H1890 For to be call'd {install'd} a god, was his intent;
MGREC103:40 H2051 Which forty thousand made; but his intent,
MGREC109:35 H2294 That to attend him there, was his intent;
MGREC115:30 H2549 The King doth intimate 'twas his intent,
MGREC119:7 H2697 That none might know, to frustrate his intent;
MGREC122:16 H2841 To warm the {his} seat, was never her intent,
MROMAN139:27 H3553 To finish what's begun, was my intent,
DIALOG145:21 H170 To ease my groaning land shew {shew'd} their intent,
INTENTS (5) [pl.]
HUMOUR28:21 H333 That my intents should meet with interruption,
AGES43:10 ~~H305~~ Have been curst furtherers of mine intents.
MPERS71:33 H747 So left his sacrilegious bold intents:
MPERS87:10 H1366 Seven hundred *Greeks* now further {repair for} his intents:

DIALOG145:39 H188 They humbly beg return, shew their intents,

INTERCEDES (1)

MEDDM208:34 Hp290 intercedes for the people, god sath to him Let me alone, that I

INTERCESSION (1)

MPERS86:18 H1334 Held by his mothers intercession.

INTER COURSE (1) [intercourse]

MEDDM208:8 Hp290 wth length of time (if there be no inter course) will coole the

INTER'D (2) [intered]

ELEMEN13:39 H240 Before they know, they are inter'd alive.
ELEMEN14:21 H263 And after death, whether inter'd, or burn'd;

INTEREST (2) See also INT'REST

MPERS86:15 H1331 His interest, in the Kingdome, now next heir,
MGREC~~124:10~~ H2915 Such friends away as for his Interest makes

INTEREST'S (1) [interest is]

2LETTER182:8 H14 My Interest's more then all the world beside.

INTERMIXED (2)

FATHER5:29 H30 My other foures, do intermixed tell
AGES35:28 H14 His spring was intermixed with some snow.

INTERPRET (2) See also ENTERPRETT

MASSYR68:8 H594 To him that could interpret clear this thing:
MPERS76:12 H910 The King will needs interpret their intent;

INTERPRETERS (1) [pl.]

MGREC134:23 H3354 The seventy two interpreters did seek,

INTERR'D (2) [interred]

SIDNEY152:22 H91 His bones do lie interr'd in stately *Pauls.*
BIRTH180:8 H18 Let be interr'd in my oblivious grave;

INTER-REGNUM (1)

MPERS73:11 H798 *The inter-Regnum between* Cambyses,

INTERRUPTING (1)

MPERS79:17 H1043 Was marching o're this interrupting Bay; {new devised way.}

INTERRUPTION (1)

HUMOUR28:21 H333 That my intents should meet with interruption,

INTESTINE (1)

DIALOG142:12 H41 Or is't intestine Wars that thus offend?

INTHRON'D (2) [enthroned]

MPERS83:25 H1213 The second was inthron'd, in's fathers stead.
MPERS~~92:5~~ H1562 Inthron'd by *Bogoas* in the room of th' other:

INTHRONE (2) [enthrone]

MGREC~~115:15~~ H2534 Among the Demy Gods they might inthrone.
MGREC125:4 H2952 her young Nephew {grand-child} in his stead {State} t' inthrone,

INTIMATE (2)

MGREC115:30 H2549 The King doth intimate 'twas his intent,
MEDDM208:9 Hp290 of intimate friends, though there should be no displeasence

INTOLLERABLE (1) [intolerable]

AGES43:28 H323 {The Strangury} Torments me with intollerable {sore} paines;

INTOMB'D (1) [entombed]

SIDNEY152:24 H93 *Here lies intomb'd in fame, under this stone,*

INTOMBE (1) [entomb]

ELEMEN14:2 H244 Your Cities and your selves I oft intombe.

INTRAILS (1) [entrails] See also INTRALLS

MGREC118:25 H2674 On which, no signe of poyson could be {in his intrails} found,

INTRALLS (1) [entrails] See also INTRAILS
ELEMEN13:38 H239 While they thus in my {mine} intralls seem {love} to dive;
INTREAT (2) [entreat]
MGREC105:38 H2131 This said, the *Greek* for water doth intreat,
MGREC~~121:14~~ H2792 *Perdiccas* in his pride did ill intreat
INTREATIES (1) [pl.]
MGREC125:12 H2960 Then by intreaties, promises, and coyne,
INTREATS (3) [entreats]
MASSYR58:41 H224 Only intreats them, {to} joyn their force with his,
MGREC103:30 H2041 *Parmenio* wise, intreats him to desist,
DIALOG142:30 H59 Your humble Childe intreats you, shew your grief,
INTRENCH'D (1) [entrenched]
AGES~~39:20~~ H163 I cannot lye in trench, {intrench'd} before a Town,
INTRICATE (1)
MGREC122:8 H2831 Himself from out of labyrinths intricate.
INTRUSTED (1) [entrusted]
MEDDM204:9 Hp284 call for great returnes, the more that any man is intrusted
INUNDATIONS See INNUNDATIONS
INVADE (5)
MASSYR56:25 H131 Great King *Staurobates,* for {his Country} to invade.
MASSYR62:4 H349 *Hoshea,* their last King, he did invade,
MASSYR67:26 H572 The Noble *Persians,* {Persian} to invade his rights.
MPERS76:23 H921 He after this, intends *Greece* to invade,
MPERS84:22 H1258 Fair *Attica,* a third time to invade.
INVADES (1)
MPERS85:22 H1298 Invades {Plunders} the Country, and much trouble {mischief}
INVASIONS (1) [pl.]
MGREC121:5 H2783 From the invasions of the other three;
INVEIGHS See ENVEIGHS
INVENT (1)
MGREC113:8 H2435 Such torments great, as wit could first {worst} invent,
INVENTION (1)
MYCHILD218:10 Hp244 humane Invention can work vpon ye Soul, hath no Judgments
INVERTERATE (1) [inveterate]
MGREC126:40 H3029 How for no cause, but her inverterate hate;
INVEST (1)
MASSYR62:19 H364 Then sent his Colonies, theirs to invest;
INVETERATE (1) See also INVERTERATE
MPERS91:22 H1530 Their former envie, and inveterate hate;
INVINCIBLE (1)
QELIZ156:23 H50 Ships more invincible then *Spaines,* her foe
INVISIBLE (3)
FLESH176:39 H79 What is Invisible to thee.
MYCHILD219:3 Hp245 Now to ye King Imortall, Eternall invisible, the only wise God,
28AUG226:10 Hp254 O let me ever see Thee that Art invisible, and I shall not bee
INVITE (1)
MASSYR58:17 H202 The last, the *Medes* and *Persians* doth invite.
INVITES (3)
MASSYR67:25 H571 His life so base, and dissolute, invites
MPERS89:34 H1468 Invites their chief Commander, as most {Commanders feasts
MGREC112:5 H2391 Six thousand Guests he to {unto} this feast invites,

INVOKES (1)
MGREC105:9 H2102 Invokes the heavens, and earth, to heare his moanes;
INWARD (2)
AGES~~41:2~~ H222 ugly {outward} marks of his eternal {inward loathsome} scars;
MYSOUL225:2 H6 Thy inward shall waxe strong,
INWRAPT (1) [enwrapt]
MGREC~~116:10~~ H2576 Till death inwrapt her in perpetual night.
IONIAN (1)
ELEMEN16:6 H329 *Ionian, Balticke,* and the vast *Atlantique;*
IONIANS (1) [pl.]
MPERS78:19 H1000 *Lycians, Carians,* and *Ionians,*
IORDAN (1) [jordan]
MASSYR61:33 H338 All *Israels* Land, {lands} beyond *Iordan,* he takes.
IOSHUA'S (1) [joshua's]
MASSYR62:12 H357 Those that from *Ioshua's* time had been Estate {a state},
IOY (1) [joy]
MEDDM196:19 Hp273 ioy, knowing his refreshing is at hand
IOYES (1) [joys] See also JOYES
PILGRIM210:41 H41 Such lasting ioyes, shall there behold
IPSWICH (1)
1LETTER181:6 H4 How stayest thou there, whilst I at *Ipswich* lye?
IRASCIBLE (1)
HUMOUR27:1 H272 There lives the irascible faculty:
IRE (2)
ELEMEN11:16 H136 Not before then, shal cease my raging ire,
ELEMEN13:12 H213 And cholerick sister, thou (for all thine ire)
IRELAND (1)
DIALOG145:1 H150 I saw poore *Ireland* bleeding out her last,
IRISH (1)
QELIZ156:33 H60 The rude untamed *Irish* she did quell,
IRKSOME (1)
AUTHOR178:1 H11 Thy Visage was so irksome in my sight;
IRON (7)
HUMOUR21:23 H51 Then Iron Corslet, 'gainst a sword or dart;
MPERS~~79:12~~ H1034 But winds, and waves those iron bands did break;
MGREC108:1 H2217 Is by his owne, now bound in Iron chaines,
MGREC135:23 H3395 And last was Iron, which breaketh all with might.
MGREC135:26 H3398 Then gold, silver, brasse, iron, and all that {the} store,
MGREC135:31 H3403 Whose Iron teeth devoured every beast;
MEDDM199:11 Hp277 Iron till it be throughly heat is vncapable to be wrought, so god
IRREGULAR (1)
HUMOUR29:37 H388 'Twere but a mad, irregular distemper;
IRREPARABLE (1)
PROLOG7:5 H20 'Cause Nature made it so irreparable.
IRRETATES (1) [irritates]
HUMOUR31:12 ~~H444~~ Thy bittering quality, stil irretates,
IRREVOCABLE (2)
HUMOUR28:20 H332 It's doom'd by an irrevocable wil:
BIRTH179:31 H7 The sentence past is most irrevocable,
IRRITATES (1) See also IRRETATES
HUMOUR~~31:15~~ H447 Thy biting quality still irritates,

IS (446) See also AFFECT'S, ALEXANDER'S, ALL'S, ANTIPATER'S, BLOW'S, BRAIN'S, BUT'S, CANNON'S, CASSANDER'S, CHOLER'S, COLD'S, CONTENTION'S, COULTER'S, CROW'S, DANGER'S, DAY'S, DEATH'S, DIE'S, FLEGM'S, GLORY'S, GREAT'S, HEAD'S, HEART'S, HEARTS, HEAVEN'S, HERE'S, HE'S, HONOUR'S, INTEREST'S, IT'S, ITS, 'ITS, KINGDOM'S, KING'S, KNOT'S, KNOW'TS, LEARNING'S, LIFE'S, MANCHET'S, MAN'S, MANY'S, MAXIME'S, METTL'S, MINE'S, MISCREANT'S, MONTH'S, MORE'S, NATURE'S, NAVY'S, NIGHT'S, NONE'S, NOTHING'S, NOUGHT'S, NOW'S, OCEAN'S, PHRENSIE'S, POMP'S, PROTECTOR'S, PUNISHMENT'S, QUARREL'S, RECORD'S, REDEMPTION'S, REST'S, REZIN'S, ROMES, ROYALTY'S, SAME'S, SARDANAPAL'S, SEASON'S, SEED'S, SELF'S, SHE'S, SHORT'S, SO'S, STOCK'S, STORY'S, STRENGTH'S, SUBJECTS, SUMMER'S, SUN'S, TEMPLE'S, THAT'S, THATS, THEN'S, THERE'S, THER'S, TIME'S, 'TIS, TIS, TONGUE'S, TOWN'S, TRUTH'S, VAINE'S, VASSAL'S, VESSELS, VICTOR'S, VICTORY'S, WALL'S, WAL'S, WAN'S, WEBB'S, WHAT'S, WHATS, WHEN'TS, WHERE'S, WHERE'TS, WHO'S, WINTER'S, WINTERS, WORLD'S, WOUND'S

PROLOG7:4 H19 And this to mend, alas, no Art is able,
PROLOG7:30 H41 It is but vaine, unjustly to wage war,
PROLOG7:32 H43 Preheminence in each, and all is yours,
ELEMEN8:30 H28 What is my worth (both ye) and all things {men} know,
ELEMEN8:31 H29 Where {In} little is, {time} I can but little show,
ELEMEN9:32 H66 And of the selfe same nature is with mine,
ELEMEN~~11:1~~ H121 That *Phaenix* from her Bed, is risen New.
ELEMEN11:11 H131 But to leave those to'th' wise, I judge is {it} best,
ELEMEN~~11:25~~ H145 Such was {is} my fruitfulnesse; and Epithite
ELEMEN12:31 H191 After three years, when men and meat is spent,
ELEMEN12:39 H199 Your Tackling, Anchor, Compasse too, is mine;
ELEMEN13:21 H222 But that thy method is my {mine} imitation.
ELEMEN14:3 H245 O dreadfull Sepulcher! that this is true,
ELEMEN14:20 H262 Remember sonnes, your mould is of my dust,
ELEMEN14:36 H278 Thy extream thirst is moistened by my love,
ELEMEN15:16 H298 That this is true, earth thou canst not deny;
ELEMEN18:10 H414 His moveing reason is, give least I dye.
ELEMEN18:11 H415 So loath he is to go, though nature's spent,
ELEMEN18:29 H433 The ruddy sweet sanguine, is like to Aire,
ELEMEN18:31 H435 My moist hot nature, is so purely thinne,
ELEMEN19:3 H448 Is more authentick then their {our} moderne wit.
ELEMEN19:13 H458 So when'ts corrupt, mortality is rife.
HUMOUR21:4 H32 It is acknowledged, from whence I came,
HUMOUR21:13 H41 Yet man for Choler, is the proper seat.
HUMOUR22:7 H76 To march her pace, to some is greater pain,
HUMOUR22:26 H95 Poor spirits the Liver breeds, which is thy seat,
HUMOUR22:33 H102 But Flegme her self, is now provok'd at this,
HUMOUR23:9 H119 Thy self's as dul, as is thy mother Earth.
HUMOUR23:34 H144 Take choler from a Prince, what is he more,
HUMOUR24:12 H161 Good sisters give me leave (as is my place)
HUMOUR24:22 H171 To pay with railings, is not mine intent,
HUMOUR24:28 H177 There is no Souldier, but thy selfe thou say'st,
HUMOUR25:10 H199 Of thy black calumnies, this is but part:
HUMOUR25:14 H203 Thy Choler is but rage, when tis most pure.
HUMOUR~~26:12~~ H242 For there are {is} none, thou say'st, if some, not best.
HUMOUR26:15 H245 What is there living, which cannot derive
HUMOUR26:18 H248 Thine without mine, is not, 'tis evident:
HUMOUR26:32 H262 I must confesse, is somewhat strange to me,

HUMOUR26:35	H265	Their wondrous mixture, is of blood, and ayre,
HUMOUR26:38	H268	Thy fiery yellow froth, is mixt among.
HUMOUR27:2	H273	Which without all dispute, is Cholers owne;
HUMOUR27:5	H276	Which is thy self, thy Mother, and thy Sire;
HUMOUR27:6	H277	That this is true, I easily can assent,
HUMOUR27:8	H279	And let me by thy Partner, which is due.
HUMOUR27:12	~~H283~~	It is her own heat, not thy faculty,
HUMOUR27:17	H288	Th' rest to our Sisters, is more pertinent.
HUMOUR27:24	H295	Shal firstly {chiefly} take her {the} place, as is her {my} due,
HUMOUR27:39	H310	So suddenly, the body all is fir'd:
HUMOUR29:4	H357	Especially when freindship is pretended:
HUMOUR29:5	H358	That blow's most deadly, where it is intended;
HUMOUR29:25	H376	The blow that's aim'd thereat is latch'd by th'arm,
HUMOUR29:31	H382	He is not truly valiant that's not wise;
HUMOUR29:35	H386	Wise *Fabius* is her buckler: all accord.
HUMOUR30:3	H395	What is too hot, my coldnesse doth abate;
HUMOUR30:15	H407	What is without, within, of theirs, or thine.
HUMOUR30:17	H409	When death doth seize the man, your stock is lost,
HUMOUR30:23	H415	Thus he is ours, his portion is the grave.
HUMOUR30:23	H415	Thus he is ours, his portion is the grave.
HUMOUR30:28	H420	Yet is a bowel cal'd wel as the rest.
HUMOUR~~30:36~~	H428	But if thou hast, that malice comes {is} from you.
HUMOUR30:38	H430	That black is black, and I am black, tis true;
HUMOUR30:40	H432	Then is thy torrid nose, or brasen brow.
HUMOUR30:41	H433	But that which shewes how high thy spight is bent,
HUMOUR~~31:1~~	H434	In {Is} charging me, to be thy excrement.
HUMOUR31:6	~~H439~~	This transmutation is, but not excretion,
HUMOUR31:25	H458	And Sanguine is more fickle many fold. {manifold,}
HUMOUR31:28	H461	And what Flegme is, we know, likewise {like to} her mother,
HUMOUR31:29	H462	Unstable is the one, so is {and} the other.
HUMOUR31:29	H462	Unstable is the one, so is {and} the other.
HUMOUR31:30	H463	With me is noble patience also found,
HUMOUR31:32	H465	What Sanguine is, she doth not heed, nor care.
HUMOUR31:36	H469	My temperance, chastity, is eminent,
HUMOUR32:25	H499	Where opposition is diametrical:
HUMOUR32:26	H500	To what is truth, I freely wil assent,
HUMOUR34:11	H566	Mine likewise is the marrow of the back,
HUMOUR34:13	H568	It is the substitute o'th royal Brain,
HUMOUR34:22	H577	For what's the Brains, is mine, by consequence;
HUMOUR34:27	H582	Then, my head {brain} for learning is not the fittest,
HUMOUR34:29	H584	Thy judgement is unsafe, thy fancy little,
HUMOUR34:30	H585	For memory, the sand is not more brittle.
AGES35:22	H8	From blood and aire, for hot, and moist is he.
AGES35:23	H9	The third, of fire, and choler is compos'd,
AGES36:7	H31	His face as fresh, as is *Aurora* faire,
AGES39:6	H149	But what is best i'le first present to view,
AGES39:32	H175	This is my best, but youth (is known) alas,
AGES39:32	H175	This is my best, but youth (is known) alas,
AGES39:33	H176	To be as wilde as is the snuffing Asse,
AGES41:7	H227	That yet my bed in darknesse is not made,
AGES41:13	H232	Child-hood and youth is {are} vaine, yea {ye} vanity.

AGES41:19 H238 Now age is more, more good ye do {may} expect;
AGES41:20 H239 But more my {mine} age, the more is my defect.
AGES43:17 H312 Sometimes vaine-glory is the only bait,
AGES43:18 H313 Whereby my empty soule, is lur'd and caught.
AGES43:38 H333 Man at his best estate is vanity.
AGES44:9 H342 But now, *Bis pueri senes,* is too true;
AGES44:19 H352 But what I have done wel, that is my prop;
AGES44:20 H353 He that in youth is godly, wise, and sage,
AGES~~45:22~~ H411 What are my thoughts, this is no time to say.
AGES45:23 H413 These are no old wives tales, but this is truth;
AGES45:26 H416 My memory is short {bad}, and braine is dry.
AGES45:26 H416 My memory is short {bad}, and braine is dry.
AGES45:30 H420 My skin is wrinkled, and my cheeks are pale.
AGES~~45:40~~ H430 Now trembling, and {is all} fearful, sad, and cold;
SEASONS47:28 H44 My second month is *April,* green, and fair,
SEASONS47:36 H48 This is the month whose fruitfull showers produces
SEASONS48:9 H62 My next, and last, is pleasant fruitfull *May,*
SEASONS48:10 H63 Wherein the earth, is clad in rich aray:
SEASONS48:35 H86 Yet above all, this priviledge is thine,
SEASONS49:7 H98 And {Then} retrograde, now is {must be} my burning Sun.
SEASONS49:8 H99 Who to his Southward tropick still is bent,
SEASONS49:36 H129 The Cherry, Goos-berry, is {are} now i'th prime,
SEASONS49:37 H130 And for all sorts of Pease this is the time.
SEASONS50:11 H145 My next, and last, is *August,* fiery hot,
SEASONS50:14 H148 The dryed earth is parched by {with} his face.
SEASONS50:28 H162 The Prince of Plumbs, whose stone is {as} hard as Rock.
SEASONS50:38 H172 Of Autumne months, *September* is the prime,
SEASONS51:2 H176 The Vintage now is ripe, the Grapes are prest,
SEASONS51:3 H177 Whose lively liquor oft is curst, and blest;
SEASONS51:8 H182 The Figge is {are} ripe, the Pomgranet also,
SEASONS51:20 H196 *October* is my next, we heare in this,
SEASONS51:23 H199 And his declining heat is almost done.
SEASONS51:34 H210 *November* is my last, for time doth haste,
SEASONS51:38 H214 Almost at shortest is the shortned day,
SEASONS52:2 H219 With minds more dark, then is the darkned sky;
SEASONS52:3 ~~H219~~ This month is timber for all uses fell'd,
SEASONS52:18 H233 *December* is the {my} first, and now the Sun
SEASONS52:32 H247 Moyst snowie *February* is my last,
SEASONS52:38 H253 Which is increased by the lengthened day,
SEASONS~~53:1~~ H257 *My Subjects bare, my Brains are {Brain is} bad,*
SEASONS53:6 H262 *Accept therefore of what is penn'd,*
MASSYR54:1 H28 Whose acts, and power, is not for certainty,
MASSYR54:7 H34 This is that *Bell,* the *Chaldees* worshipped,
MASSYR54:9 H36 This is that *Bell,{Baal}* to whom the *Israelites*
MASSYR54:11 H38 This is *Belzebub,* god of *Ekronites,*
MASSYR56:14 H120 Which is the midst, of this brave Town was plac'd,
MASSYR56:30 H136 But this is marvelous, of all those men,
MASSYR57:8 H155 But much it is, in more then forty years,
MASSYR57:10 H157 It is more like, being {his lust} with pleasures fed,
MASSYR57:13 H160 But is suppos'd to be that *Amraphel,*
MASSYR57:16 ~~H163~~ Some may object, his Parents ruling all,

MASSYR57:24 ~~H171~~ Again, the Country was left bare (there is no doubt)
MASSYR57:36 H181 It is enough {may suffice}, if all be true that's past,
MASSYR62:2 H347 *Tiglath* deceas'd, *Salmanasser* is next,
MASSYR62:32 H377 Whose haughty heart is shewn in works, and deeds;
MASSYR63:19 H404 Of whom is little said in any thing; [22 years.
MASSYR64:7 H431 And this is {was} he, who when he fear'd the least,
MASSYR64:13 H437 His Vassal is, gives pledges for his truth,
MASSYR~~65:23~~ H488 For this was {is} he, for whom none said, Alas!
MASSYR67:9 H555 Is *Judah's* King, now lifted up on high.
MASSYR67:14 H560 Faire *Ægypt* is, by his remissenesse lost;
MASSYR68:17 H603 *Daniel* in haste, is brought before the King,
MPERS69:13 H635 This is of *Cyrus* the true pedigree,
MPERS71:39 H753 Is more prophane, then grosse Idolaters;
MPERS72:1 ~~H753~~ And contemn them, woful is his doome.
MPERS~~72:7~~ H756 *Praxaspes* into *Persia* then is sent,
MPERS74:27 H850 Three strings to's bow, the least of which is good;
MPERS75:33 H890 Of what is freely granted by the King;
MPERS77:18 H959 As is {was} the Son, of pride, and cruelty;
MPERS79:4 H1026 For his great love, is this thy recompence?
MPERS79:5 H1027 Is this to doe like *Xerxes,* or a Prince?
MPERS80:8 H1075 Where is the valour, of your antient State?
MPERS80:10 H1077 Alas, it is *Leonades* you want!
MPERS85:8 H1284 Then the surviver is by *Nothus* slaine;
MPERS85:37 H1313 A hopefull Prince, whose worth {by *Xenophon*} is ever fam'd.
MPERS86:10 H1326 Yet doubts, {fears} all he injoyes, is not his own.
MPERS88:1 H1394 arme, the King {with all his host} is now approaching nigh;
MPERS89:32 H1466 Fit instruments t' accomplish what is ill;
MPERS90:32 H1499 By th' Kings Lieutenant {*Tissaphernes*} is encountered,
MPERS90:36 H1503 *Tythraustes* now {then} is placed in his stead,
MPERS91:7 H1515 *Agesilaus* is called home with speed,
MPERS91:18 H1526 And turne to *Persia,* as is pertinent;
MPERS91:31 ~~H1545~~ But this of him is worth the memory,
MPERS92:3 ~~H1557~~ The rest is but conjecture of my minde.
MPERS92:17 ~~H1575~~ By favour, force, or fraud, is not set down:
MPERS92:18 ~~H1576~~ If not (as is before) of *Cyrus* race,
MPERS92:25 ~~H1583~~ By one *Bagoas,* an Eunuch (as is sed.)
MGREC93:26 H1623 This is the hee-goat, which from *Grecia* came,
MGREC94:1 H1635 Yet for a while, in *Greece* is forc'd to stay,
MGREC97:2 H1763 Who from his golden Coach is glad t'alight,
MGREC97:20 H1781 And this to *Alexander* is more a fame,
MGREC99:9 H1852 Was I as great, as is great *Alexander,*
MGREC99:22 H1865 But yet, this well defended town is {was} taken,
MGREC99:30 H1873 Sith valour, with Heroyicks is renown'd,
MGREC100:3 H1887 To see how fast he gain'd, is {was} no small wonder,
MGREC100:19 H1903 But as the King is, so's the multitude,
MGREC101:31 H1956 And weaknesse of a foe is covered;
MGREC~~101:34~~ H1960 By Captains twice is call'd before hee'l rise,
MGREC102:6 H1976 Is entertain'd with joy, and pompous train {showes},
MGREC106:27 H2161 His temperance, is but a sordid thing,
MGREC108:1 H2217 Is by his owne, now bound in Iron chaines,
MGREC~~109:5~~ H2262 And also of the *Mallians* what is writ.

MGREC109:31 H2290 His pleasure is, that forthwith he repaire
MGREC109:40 H2299 Is now resolv'd to passe *Hidaspes* floud,
MGREC112:29 H2415 Yet is *Philotas* unto Judgement brought,
MGREC112:31 H2417 His Master is Accuser, Judge, and King,
MGREC113:30 H2457 This is *Parmenio,* which {who} so much had done,
MGREC116:12 H2578 And Conquests be talkt of, whilst there is Land;
MGREC121:1 H2779 ('Gainst which to goe, is troubled in his minde;)
MGREC121:21 H2803 And is of all received {most} joyfully;
MGREC126:13 H3004 *Cassander* is resolv'd, there to remaine,
MGREC126:16 H3007 will not heare {Her foe would give no Ear}, such is his hate.
MGREC~~129:24~~ H3138 That he was {is} odious to the world, they'r glad,
MGREC130:38 H3183 That hand is righteous still which doth repay:
MGREC130:41 H3186 *Demetrius* is first, that so assumes, {the royal stile asum'd,}
MGREC131:2 H3192 To *Athens* then he {*Demetrius* thether} goes, is entertain'd,
MGREC131:27 H3219 Is for this fresh young Lady half {quite} undone,
MGREC131:34 H3226 *Cassander* now must die, his race is run,
MGREC~~132:5~~ H3238 *Demetrius* is call'd in by th' youngest Son,
MGREC132:7 H3242 Thus *Philips,* and *Cassander's* race is {both} gone,
MGREC133:34 H3324 But this is perished with many more,
MGREC136:1 H3414 For what is past I blush, excuse to make,
MGREC136:3 H3416 Pardon to crave, for errours, is but vaine,
MGREC136:17 H3431 *What e're is found amisse, take in best {good} part,*
MROMAN137:25 H3476 *Nvma Pompilius,* is next chosen {chose they} King,
MROMAN138:27 H3517 Is entertain'd at *Rome,* and in short time,
DIALOG142:18 H47 Or is {is't} the fatall jarre againe begun,
DIALOG142:27 H56 Whence is this {the} storme, from Earth, or Heaven above?
DIALOG142:32 H61 Such is her poverty, yet shall be found
DIALOG142:33 H62 A supplyant for your help, as she is bound.
DIALOG142:39 H68 Nor is it *Alcies* Son, and {nor} *Henries* Daughter,
DIALOG143:10 H79 None knowes which is the Red, or which the White:
DIALOG143:11 H80 *Spaines* braving Fleet a second time is sunke,
DIALOG143:17 H86 What *Holland* is, I am in some suspence,
DIALOG143:32 H101 The Gospel is trod {troden} down, and hath no right;
DIALOG144:13 H123 Where is the Nation, I cann't paralize;
DIALOG144:33 H141 This is fore-runner of my after clap,
DIALOG145:13 H162 Pray in plain termes, what is your present grief,
DIALOG145:18 H167 Which is the chief, the law, or else the King,
DIALOG148:28 H293 Whose lot doth fall to live therein is blest:
SIDNEY149:25 ~~H23~~ I praise thee not for this, it is unfit,
SIDNEY150:14 H49 Thy fame, and praise, is farre beyond my straine;
SIDNEY150:18 ~~H49~~ A Crow's a Crow, and *Cæsar* is a King.
SIDNEY150:27 H54 Thus man is borne to dye, and dead is he,
SIDNEY150:27 H54 Thus man is borne to dye, and dead is he,
SIDNEY150:35 H62 Where is that envious tongue, but can afford,
SIDNEY151:6 ~~H69~~ But that it is record by *Philips* hand,
SIDNEY151:23 H73 For {How} to persist, my muse is more in doubt:
SIDNEY151:31 ~~H75~~ As *Vulcan* is, of *Venus* native hue.
SIDNEY152:28 H97 *His praise is much, this shall suffice my pen,*
DUBART154:4 H49 Mine eyes are sightlesse, and my tongue is mute;
DUBART154:15 H60 Thy fame is spread as farre, I dare be bold,
DUBART~~154:27~~ H72 Unto each man his riches are {is} assign'd,

DUBART155:9 H94 *But Fame, out-living both, he is reviv'd.*
QELIZ155:17 H8 And so has {hath} vow'd, whilst there is world, or time;
QELIZ155:30 H21 Which makes me deeme, my rudenesse is no wrong,
QELIZ156:5 H32 Nor say I more then duly is her due,
QELIZ156:6 H33 Millions will testifie that this is true;
QELIZ157:4 H72 *Semiramis* to her is but obscure,
QELIZ157:25 H93 Yet for our Queen is no fit parallel:
QELIZ157:36 H104 Let such, as say our sex is void of reason,
QELIZ158:8 H117 *Here sleeps THE Queen, this is the royall bed.*
QELIZ158:11 H120 *This Rose is withered, once so lovely faire,*
DAVID158:24 H4 Alas, slaine is the head of *Israel,*
VANITY159:32 H4 Where is the man can say, lo, I have found
VANITY160:11 H21 The first is prone to vice, the last to rage.
VANITY160:12 H22 Where is it then? in wisdome, learning, arts?
VANITY160:17 H27 He knows not all, that here is to be known,
VANITY160:18 H28 What is it then? to do as Stoicks tell,
VANITY160:21 H31 While man is man, he shall have ease or pain.
VANITY160:26 H36 There is a path, no vultures eye hath seen.
VANITY160:35 H45 But where, and what it is, from heaven's declar'd,
VANITY161:2 H53 Who is possessed of, shall reign a King.
TDUDLEY166:23 H65 And to his Fathers gathered is in peace.
TDUDLEY166:25 H67 Who after all his toyle, is now at rest:
CONTEM168:1 H11 How excellent is he that dwells on high?
CONTEM168:3 H13 Sure he is goodness, wisdome, glory, light,
CONTEM169:4 H46 And is thy splendid Throne erect so high?
CONTEM170:12 H85 Believing him that was, and is, Father of lyes.
CONTEM172:20 H155 Nor is it rocks or shoals that can obstruct thy pace.
CONTEM173:8 H176 Whose armour is their scales, their spreading fins their shield.
CONTEM173:22 H188 Thy cloaths ne're wear, thy meat is every where,
CONTEM173:24 H190 Reminds not what is past, nor whats to come dost fear.
CONTEM174:27 H225 Only above is found all with security.
CONTEM174:35 H232 But he whose name is grav'd in the white stone
FLESH176:8 H48 But my arise is from above,
FLESH176:29 H69 The word of life it is my meat.
FLESH176:39 H79 What is Invisible to thee.
FLESH177:25 H106 This City pure is not for thee,
AUTHOR178:7 H17 Yet still thou run'st more hobling then is meet;
AUTHOR178:14 H24 And for thy Mother, she alas is poor,
SICKNES178:20 H3 My race is run, my thread is spun,
SICKNES178:20 H3 My race is run, my thread is spun,
SICKNES178:21 H4 lo here is fatal Death.
SICKNES178:29 H12 no life is like to this.
SICKNES179:9 H29 The race is run, the field is won,
SICKNES179:9 H29 The race is run, the field is won,
BIRTH179:30 H6 But with deaths parting blow is sure to meet.
BIRTH179:31 H7 The sentence past is most irrevocable,
1HUSB180:29 H8 My love is such that Rivers cannot quench,
1HUSB180:31 H10 Thy love is such I can no way repay,
1LETTER181:10 H8 My sun is gone so far in's Zodiack,
3LETTER183:12 H14 Bewail my turtle true, who now is gone,
VERSES184:8 H12 Such is my debt, I may not say forgive,

VERSES184:10	H14	Such is my bond, none can discharge but I,
VERSES184:11	H15	Yet paying is not payd until I dye.
CHILDRN185:9	H35	My fifth, whose down is yet scarce gone
CHILDRN185:10	H36	Is 'mongst the shrubs and bushes flown,
CHILDRN185:16	H42	As is ordain'd, so shall they light.
CHILDRN186:9	H76	But sing, my time so near is spent.
ELIZB187:8	H16	And time brings down what is both strong and tall.
ELIZB187:11	H19	Is by his hand alone that guides nature and fate.
1SIMON188:7	H8	Cropt by th' Almighties hand; yet is he good,
MERCY188:22	H8	Ah, woe is me, to write thy Funeral Song,
MERCY189:16	H37	He knows it is the best for thee and me.
2SIMON195:15	Hp271	reioyceing at that great day of appearing, wch is the continuall
MEDDM195:24	Hp272	There is no obiect that we see. no action that we doe, no good
MEDDM195:26	Hp272	of all and he that makes such improvment is wise as well as
MEDDM195:30	Hp272	then the practique part, but he is a true Christian that is a
MEDDM195:33	Hp272	Youth is the time of getting middle age of improuing, and old
MEDDM195:34	Hp272	a negligent youth is vsually attended by an ignorant middle
MEDDM196:2	Hp272	that beares much saile & little or no ballast, is easily ouer set,
MEDDM196:4	Hp272	is in danger of foundering.
MEDDM196:6	Hp272	It is reported of the pea cock that prideing himself in his gay
MEDDM196:19	Hp273	ioy, knowing his refreshing is at hand
MEDDM197:4	Hp274	Authority wthout wisedome is like a heavy axe, wthout an edg
MEDDM197:8	Hp274	better, is because they haue more sence then faith they se
MEDDM197:9	Hp274	they do but hope for that wch is to Come
MEDDM197:14	Hp274	man, can goe vpright, vnder that door, wher a taller is glad to
MEDDM197:18	Hp275	That house wch is not often swept makes the cleanly inhabitant
MEDDM197:19	Hp275	it, and that heart wch is not continually purifieing it self is no fit
MEDDM197:32	Hp275	is not fit for bread, god so deales wth his servants, he grindes
MEDDM198:6	Hp276	ouer their heads he then leads them to the Rock wch is higher
MEDDM198:14	Hp276	but he that is well stored wth both, seldom is so insnared
MEDDM198:16	Hp276	fisher hath his severall baits, for severall fish, but there is
MEDDM198:21	Hp276	There is no new thing vnder ye Sun there is nothing that can
MEDDM198:21	Hp276	is no new thing vnder ye Sun there is nothing that can be sayd
MEDDM198:32	Hp277	It is a pleasant thing to behold the light, but sore eyes are not
MEDDM199:2	Hp277	Wisedom with an inheritance is good, but wisedome without an
MEDDM199:3	Hp277	inheritance, is better, then an inheritance wthout wisedome
MEDDM199:11	Hp277	Iron till it be throughly heat is vncapable to be wrought, so god
MEDDM199:29	Hp278	when he is once dead, but the last mangles him in his graue
MEDDM200:3	Hp278	sin, is it not a little one? will ere long say of a greater Tush god
MEDDM200:8	Hp279	bitter together so is it wth some Christians, let god imbitter all
MEDDM200:11	Hp279	brests, that god is forced to hedg vp their way wth thornes
MEDDM200:16	Hp279	garment, she easily foresees what euents it is like to produce,
MEDDM200:24	Hp279	The spring is a liuely emblem of the resurrection, after a long
MEDDM200:34	Hp280	he knows is enough for one of twice his strength, much lesse
MEDDM201:15	Hp280	appetite and a through Concoction, is a signe of an healthfull
MEDDM201:21	Hp281	full of contrition, but it is not from any dew of grace wthin,
MEDDM201:33	Hp281	is (of all other) most Comfortable
MEDDM202:2	Hp281	There is nothing admits of more admiration, then gods various
MEDDM202:6	Hp281	that Mortality is capable of, and some again so base that they
MEDDM202:14	Hp282	it pleased him, whose will is the perfect rule of righteousnesse,
MEDDM202:21	Hp282	Sometimes the sun is only shadowed by a cloud, that wee

MEDDM202:22 Hp282 although we may walk by his light, but when he is set, we are
MEDDM202:29 Hp282 when ye morning (wch is the appointed time) is come the Sun
MEDDM202:33 Hp282 obiects enter, yet is not that spacious roome filled neither
MEDDM202:34 Hp282 doth it euer say it is enough, but like the daughters of the
MEDDM202:35 Hp282 giue, & wch is most strang, the more it receius the more empty
MEDDM203:2 Hp283 not the wisest of men, taught vs this lesson, that all is vanity
MEDDM203:4 Hp283 for what do we obtaine of all these things, but it is wth labour
MEDDM203:5 Hp283 When we inioy them it is wth vanity and vexation, and if we
MEDDM203:8 Hp283 vanity of vanityes, all is vanity
MEDDM203:10 Hp283 He that is to saile into a farre country, although the ship,
MEDDM203:13 Hp283 bussines lyes, a christian is sailing through this world vnto his
MEDDM204:2 Hp284 of former deliuerances, is a great support in present
MEDDM204:6 Hp284 is the same yesterday, to day and for euer, we are the same
MEDDM204:9 Hp284 call for great returnes, the more that any man is intrusted
MEDDM204:18 Hp285 as we see in Jehu, he is rewarded wth a kingdome to the fourth
MEDDM204:27 Hp285 vpon one that is in a far better estate then himself, but let him
MEDDM204:28 Hp285 vpon him that is lower then he is and if he se, that such a one
MEDDM204:33 Hp285 Corne is produced wth much labour (as the husbandman well
MEDDM205:9 Hp286 As man is called the little world so his heart may be cal'd the
MEDDM205:12 Hp286 fro continvally, here is also the great Court of iustice erected,
MEDDM205:13 Hp286 wch is alway kept by Conscience, who is both accuser excuser
MEDDM205:16 Hp286 is this Court of Judicature, that there is no appeale from it, no
MEDDM205:18 Hp286 who is greater then our Conscience will do it much more, but
MEDDM205:32 Hp286 Burden, is the breaking of their limbes, some again, are but
MEDDM205:34 Hp286 them are dry stocks so is it in the church wch is gods orchard,
MEDDM206:6 Hp287 se in the firmament there is but one Sun, among a multitude
MEDDM206:9 Hp287 Sun, so is it in the Church both militant and triumphant, there
MEDDM206:9 Hp287 so is it in the Church both militant and triumphant, there is
MEDDM206:10 Hp287 but one Christ, who is the Sun of righteousnes, in the midest of
MEDDM206:20 Hp287 of turning to god, the first thing wch they eye, is how to reform
MEDDM206:36 Hp288 they abide not in vnbeleif, god is able to grafte them in, the
MEDDM207:15 Hp288 shadow very comfortable, yet there is some worm or other,
MEDDM207:17 Hp289 the pleasure wch else we should take in them, and well it is
MEDDM207:33 Hp289 embleam of death, wch is their sleep (for so is death often
MEDDM207:34 Hp289 their death, but their graue, is liuely represented before their
MEDDM208:12 Hp290 A good name, is as a precious oyntment, and it is a great
MEDDM208:12 Hp290 good name, is as a precious oyntment, and it is a great favour
MEDDM208:13 Hp290 to haue a good repute among good men, yet it is not that, w^{ch}
MEDDM208:21 Hp290 so is it wth the wealth honours and pleasures of this world
MEDDM208:28 Hp290 It is admirable to Consider the power of faith, by wch all things
MEDDM209:2 Hp291 not let thee go replys Jacob till thou blesse me, faith is not only
MEDDM209:3 Hp291 thus potent but it is so necessary, that wthout faith there is no
MEDDM209:3 Hp291 but it is so necessary, that wthout faith there is no salvation
MEDDM209:12 Hp291 slauery, so it is most certain that those that are disobedient
MEDDM209:20 Hp291 there may be a mutuall commerce through ye world As it is wth
MEDDM209:21 Hp291 Covntrys so it is with men, there was neuer yet any one man
MEDDM209:24 Hp291 (perhaps meaner then himself) wch shews us perfection is not
PILGRIM210:32 H32 it is the bed Christ did perfume
MYCHILD215:16 Hp240 dayly in y^{r} rembrance, (Altho: y^{t} is the least in my aim in w^{t} I
MYCHILD215:21 Hp240 last is the best, let it be best pleasing to yov.
MYCHILD217:30 Hp243 Love of God, it would haue been a Hell to me for in Truth it is

MYCHILD217:35	Hp243	know but they were feigned. That there is a God my Reason
MYCHILD218:4	Hp243	resolve me that there is an Eternall Being. But how should I
MYCHILD218:4	Hp243	me that there is an Eternall Being. But how should I know he is
MYCHILD218:7	Hp244	me over. I haue argved thvs wth my self, That there is a God I
MYCHILD218:13	Hp244	it? Is there any story but that wch showes the beginnings of
MYCHILD218:30	Hp244	haue been carryed away wth them, that somt: I haue said, Is
MYCHILD219:2	Hp245	and y^{t} he is able to keep y^{t} I haue comitted to his charge.
MYCHILD219:6	Hp245	written in mvch sicknesse and weaknes, and is very weakly
MYCHILD219:7	Hp245	imperfectly done, but if yov can pick any Benefitt out of it, It is
SOREFIT222:8	H27	O Lord for aye is my request
SOREFIT222:10	H29	And then wth thee which is the Best
FAINT222:25	H15	My life is hid wth Thee
MED223:7	Hp250	Almighty—Christ is my Brother, I ascend vnto my father, and
MED223:9	Hp250	enough thy maker is thy husband. Nay more, I am a member
MED223:11	Hp250	them known who or where is the man that durst in his heart
MED223:15	Hp250	But this is my comfort, When I come into Heaven, I shall
MED223:19	Hp250	bee dissolved and bee wth thee wch is best of All.
JULY223:23	Hp251	husband was from home (who is my cheifest comforter on
JULY223:29	Hp251	him who is the only portion of his Servants.
WHAT224:1	H1	What God is like to him I serve
WHAT224:13	H13	My God he is not like to y^{rs}
WHAT224:17	H17	He is not man y^{t} he should lye.
WHAT224:21	H21	And for his sake y^{t} faithfull is
28AUG225:28	Hp254	heart, and to manifest his Loue to me, and this is that w^{ch}
28AUG225:29	Hp254	my Soul that this condition y^{t} I am in is ye best for me, for god
28AUG225:31	Hp254	he hath no benefitt by my adversity, nor is he ye better for my
28AUG225:33	Hp254	by it— And if he knowes that weaknes, & a frail body is ye best
11MAYA226:19	Hp255	for is a contented thankfull h^{t} vnder my affliction & weaknes
11MAYA226:19	Hp255	contented thankfull h^{t} vnder my affliction & weaknes seing it is
11MAYA226:21	Hp255	pleasure espec: seing it is for my spiri^{tl}. advantage, For I hope
13MAY226:28	H4	The earth all black is cloth'd in green
13MAY227:8	H17	Who is a God so wondrous great.
13MAY227:15	H24	All I can giue is but thine own
30SEPT227:20	Hp257	thankfully to submitt to him for I trvst it is out of his abvndant
30SEPT227:21	Hp257	Love to my straying Soul wch in prosperity is too much in Love
30SEPT227:33	Hp257	him then before, This is the desire of y^{r} Loving mother. A. B.
SAMUEL228:9	H10	For sure thy Grace on him is shown.
SAMUEL228:19	H20	Thy Will bee done, for that is best
HOURS234:19	H33	In Thee Alone is more then All;
HOUSE236:18	H10	Let no man know is my Desire.
HOUSE237:23	H53	A prise so vast as is vnknown
HOUSE237:24	H54	Yet by his Gift is made thine own.
ISLAND (2)		
ELEMEN17:7	H371	And that an Island makes, which once was maine.
MASSYR64:35	H459	Within an Island had this City seat,
ISLE (1)		
MGREC132:22	H3267	Within an Isle that was with pleasures fed,
ISLES (3) [pl.]		
ELEMEN19:33	H474	Knowes {Know} Western Isles, *Christophers, Barbadoes;*
MPERS84:12	H1240	The might o'th' Prince, the tribute on {of} the Isles.
MGREC110:8	H2308	Did here, and there, Isles full of trees abide;

ISRAEL (4)
MASSYR59:35 H259 That *Amazia* was King of *Israel;*
MASSYR60:35 H300 Molests poor *Israel,* his wealth t' encrease.
MASSYR62:18 H363 {He} Plac'd *Israel* in's Land {there}, where he thought best,
DAVID158:24 H4 Alas, slaine is the head of *Israel,*
ISRAELITES (2) See also ISRALITS
MASSYR54:9 H36 This is that *Bell,{Baal}* to whom the *Israelites*
MASSYR62:3 H348 He *Israelites,* more then his Father vext;
ISRAELS (5) [poss.]
ELEMEN17:17 H381 That *Israels* enemies, therewith was {were} brain'd.
MASSYR61:33 H338 All *Israels* Land, {lands} beyond *Iordan,* he takes.
MASSYR61:40 H345 Then by his death, releas'd, was *Israels* fears.
MASSYR62:36 H381 'Twixt them and *Israels* he knew no odds. [7 *years.*
DAVID159:13 H28 O *Israels* Dames, o're-flow your beauteous eyes,
ISRALITS (1) [israelites]
MEDDM209:7 Hp291 christians do by their lusts and corruptions as the Isralits did
ISSU'D (1) [issued]
ELEMEN8:12 H10 Whence issu'd raines, and winds, lightning and thunder;
ISSUE (3)
HUMOUR34:17 H572 Some other parts there issue from the Brain,
MGREC117:29 H2636 Great *Alexander* has left {did leave} issue none,
MEDDM209:10 Hp291 but what was y^c Issue, they became a snare vnto them, .
ISSUED (2) See also ISSU'D
AGES38:34 H137 Whence vomits, wormes, and flux have issued?
MASSYR55:17 H83 This great renowned Empresse, issued.
ISSUE-LESSE (1)
MPERS92:14 ~~H1572~~ Then Natures debt he paid, quite Issue-lesse.
ISSULESSE (1) [issueless]
MPERS73:4 H791 And more, because he dyed issulesse.
IS'T (21) [is it]
ELEMEN18:16 H420 What is't? but forced Aire which must {doth} rebound,
HUMOUR23:21 H131 Nor is't my pleasure, thus to blur thy name:
HUMOUR24:19 H168 Is't ignorance, {arrogance} or folly causeth this?
HUMOUR33:19 H533 Who is't or {that} dare, or can compare with me;
MGREC94:11 H1645 Nor wonder is't, if he in blood begin,
MROMAN140:8 H3571 Nor matter is't this last, the world now sees,
DIALOG142:10 H39 Or is't a *Norman,* whose victorious hand
DIALOG142:12 H41 Or is't intestine Wars that thus offend?
DIALOG142:16 H45 Must *Edward* be depos'd, or is't the houre
DIALOG~~142:18~~ H47 Or is {is't} the fatall jarre againe begun,
DIALOG142:28 H57 Is't Drought, is't Famine, or is't Pestilence?
DIALOG142:28 H57 Is't Drought, is't Famine, or is't Pestilence?
DIALOG142:28 H57 Is't Drought, is't Famine, or is't Pestilence?
DIALOG148:18 H283 (For then what is't, but English blades dare do)
VANITY159:34 H6 What is't in honour, to be set on high?
VANITY159:38 H10 What is't in wealth, great treasures for to gain {obtain}?
VANITY160:8 H18 What is't in beauty? no, that's but a snare,
VANITY160:10 H20 What, Is't in flowring youth, or manly age?
TDUDLEY165:10 H12 Nor is't Relation near my hand shall tye;
TDUDLEY165:31 H33 Who is't can tax thee ought, but for thy zeal?
CONTEM172:22 H156 Nor is't enough, that thou alone may'st slide,

IST (2) [is it]
HUMOUR21:29 H57 'Twixt them and others, what ist makes the odds
QELIZ157:33 H101 Or had they some, but with our Queen ist gone?

ISTER (1)
MPERS76:2 H900 Over fair *Ister,* at a {with labour and with} mighty charge;

IT'S (11) [it is]
HUMOUR~~24:40~~ H189 Thou sayst I love my sword, because tis {it's} guilt. {gilt,}
HUMOUR28:20 H332 It's doom'd by an irrevocable wil:
HUMOUR29:32 H383 It's no lesse glory to defend a town,
HUMOUR~~33:17~~ H531 No debtor I, because 'tis {it's} paid else where;
AGES43:30 H325 To break the darksome prison, where it's pend;
AGES44:12 H345 It's not my valour, honour, nor my gold,
AGES44:14 H347 It's not my Learning, Rhetorick, wit so large,
AGES44:16 H349 It's not my goodly house {state}, nor bed of down,
SEASONS51:5 H179 But its a precious juyce, when wel it's used.
SICKNES179:4 H24 because it's thy decree;
FAINT222:13 H3 But ah! it's not in me

ITALIAN (1)
ELEMEN12:6 H166 Strong forts from *Spanish* and *Italian* braules,

ITALY (2)
ELEMEN14:5 H249 And since, faire *Italy* full sadly knowes
ELEMEN17:9 H373 *Cicily* from *Italy,* by th'like chance.

ITCH (1)
MPERS69:18 H640 Are fit for such, whose eares for fables itch;

ITS (15) [it is]
PROLOG7:19 H32 They'l say its stolne, or else, it was by chance.
HUMOUR21:41 H69 She loves her sword, only because its gilt;
HUMOUR23:38 H148 Its not your muscles, nerves, nor this nor that:
HUMOUR29:23 H374 Know, in a General its most pernicious.
HUMOUR33:39 H553 Of three, its hard to say, which doth excel;
HUMOUR~~34:41~~ H596 Let's now be freinds, 'tis {its} time our spight was {were} spent,
SEASONS51:5 H179 But its a precious juyce, when wel it's used.
SEASONS~~52:39~~ H256 Where first it did begin, in th' end its found.
MPERS~~73:40~~ H825 Too politicke (tis {its} like) for me to tell,
MGREC95:40 H1719 Sure its {much} beyond my time, and little Art;
DIALOG145:19 H168 One saith its he, the other no such thing.
VANITY160:3 H13 Its his to day, but who's his heire to morrow?
VANITY160:30 H40 The depth, and sea, hath {have} said its not in me,
VANITY160:33 H43 Its hid from eyes of men, they count it strange,

ITS (17) [poss]
ELEMEN8:19 H17 That roaring in it came, and with its source
HUMOUR~~33:23~~ H537 The scituation, and {Its} form wil it avow,
HUMOUR33:24 H538 Its ventricles, membranes, and wond'rous net,
HUMOUR33:29 H543 Doth doubtlesse keep its mighty residence;
AGES35:37 H23 But if he hold, til it have run its last,
AGES37:25 H87 That its own worth, it did not know, nor mind.
SEASONS~~50:1~~ H135 This month from *Julius Cæsar* took the {its} name,
SEASONS50:15 H149 *August,* of great *Augustus* took its name,
SEASONS51:27 H203 Decrepit age must also have its time;
MGREC135:7 H3379 Which by the *Romans* had its destiny.
DIALOG146:35 ~~H221~~ That Right may have its right, though't be with blood;

TDUDLEY165:14 H16 Let malice bite, and envy knaw its fill,
CONTEM172:15 H150 Which to the long'd for Ocean held its course,
CONTEM172:17 H152 Could hinder ought, but still augment its force:
FLESH175:23 H23 Industry hath its recompence.
MEDDM200:2 Hp278 Wickednes comes to its height by degrees, He that dares say .
MEDDM201:12 Hp280 Fire hath its force abated by water not by wind, and anger .
MYCHILD218:2 Hp243 .vpon ye Earth, ye p^{r}serving + directing of All to its proper

'ITS (1) [it is]
HOUSE237:21 H51 'Its purchasèd + paid for too

ITSELF (1)
MEDDM205:17 Hp286 Court of heaven itself, for if our conscience condemn vs, he

IUDA'S (1) [judah's]
MASSYR61:15 H320 *Iuda's* bad King occasioned this War,

IUDAH (1) [judah]
MASSYR65:31 H496 *Iudah* {They} lost more {now} (then e're they lost) by him;

IUDAH'S (2) [judah's] See also IUDA'S
MASSYR61:27 H332 Unto *Damascus* then, comes *Iudah's* King,
MASSYR64:11 H435 *Iudah's* poor King besieg'd, who {and} succourlesse,

IUDAHS (1) [judah's] See also IUDA'S, IUDAH'S
MASSYR66:25 H531 His Image, *Iudahs* Captives worship not,

IUPITER (1) [jupiter]
MGREC112:37 H2423 He did the Oracle of *Iupiter* {*Jove*} deride,

IUSTICE (2) [justice]
MEDDM205:12 Hp286 fro continvally, here is also the great Court of iustice erected,
MEDDM206:37 Hp288 make vs wth the Apostle to admire the iustice and mercy of

IUSTLY (1) [justly]
HOUSE236:31 H23 He might of All iustly bereft,

IVDAH (1) [judah] See also IUDAH
MASSYR62:34 H379 On *Henah, Arpad,* and on *Ivdah* least {*Juahs* coast};

I'VE (37)
ELEMEN19:24 H469 What woeful wracks I've made, may wel appear,
ELEMEN20:7 H489 To adde to all I've said, was my intent,
HUMOUR26:40 H270 Thou know'st I've there to do, as wel as thou;
HUMOUR27:32 H303 My vertues hid, i've let you dimly see;
HUMOUR28:36 H348 I've scarce wip'd off the spots, proud Choler cast,
HUMOUR28:38 H350 No braggs i've us'd, t' your selves {to you} I dare appeale,
HUMOUR28:40 H352 I've us'd no bitternesse, nor taxt your name,
HUMOUR31:19 H452 I trust I've clear'd your slandrous imputations {inputation}.
HUMOUR32:15 H489 I've done, pray Sister Flegme proceed in course,
HUMOUR32:22 H496 I've not forgot how bitter Choler spake,
HUMOUR32:29 H503 And when i've nothing left to say, be mute;
HUMOUR32:34 H508 And {But} though the pitched field i've ever fled,
AGES39:1 H144 I've done unto my elders I give way.
AGES41:12 H231 Thus I have said, and what i've said {been,} you see,
AGES41:15 H234 Childehood and youth, forgot, sometimes I've seen,
AGES42:2 H260 Whose loynes {backs} I've cloth'd, and bellies I have fed;
AGES43:11 ~~H305~~ Nor Brothers, Nephewes, Sons, nor Sires I've spar'd.
AGES44:10 H343 In every Age i've found much vanitie,
AGES44:29 H362 In various times of state i've also been.
AGES44:30 H363 I've seen a Kingdom flourish like a tree,
AGES~~45:2~~ H377 I've seen a Prince, the glory of our land

AGES45:3 H381 I've seen from *Rome,* an execrable thing,
AGES~~45:4~~ H385 I've Princes seen to live on others lands;
AGES45:5 H389 I've seen designes at {for} *Ree,* and *Cades* {*Rochel*} crost,
AGES45:7 ~~H390~~ I've seen a Prince, to live on others lands,
AGES45:9 H391 I've seen base {unworthy} men, advanc'd to great degree
AGES45:13 H395 I've seen one stab'd, another {and some to} loose his head
AGES45:15 H397 I've seen, and so have ye, for 'tis but late,
AGES45:19 ~~H401~~ I've seen a land unmoulded with great paine.
AGES45:21 ~~H403~~ I've seen it shaken, rent, and soak'd in blood,
AGES~~45:22~~ H405 I've seen a King by force thrust from his throne,
AGES~~45:22~~ H407 I've seen a state unmoulded, rent in twain,
AGES~~45:22~~ H409 I've seen it plunder'd, taxt and soak'd in bloud,
SEASONS46:28 H4 Another Four i've {left} yet for to bring on,
MGREC105:41 H2134 I've nothing left, at this my dying hour;
DIALOG~~146:26~~ H212 And recompence me {that} good, for all my ill {I've done to
HOURS233:27 H10 Thro: the I've kept my Grovnd.

IVORY (1)
HUMOUR32:38 H512 When sister Sanguine paints my Ivory face,

J

JACENT (1)
ELEMEN10:32 H107 *Apulia's* jacent parts were covered;

JACKS (1)
ELEMEN9:17 H51 Your spits, pots, jacks, what else I need not name,

JACOB (4)
MEDDM204:31 Hp285 Jacob, I am lesse then the least of thy mercys.
MEDDM208:36 Hp291 lasting armes of the mighty god of Jacob yea Jacob himself
MEDDM208:36 Hp291 armes of the mighty god of Jacob yea Jacob himself when he
MEDDM209:2 Hp291 will not let thee go replys Jacob till thou blesse me, faith is not

JACOB'S See JACOBS

JADDUS (1)
MGREC99:36 H1879 Him in his Priestly Robes, high *Jaddus* meets,

JAILS See GAOLES

JAN. (1) [january]
2HUSB232:2 H3 England. Jan. 16. 1661.

JANE (1)
DIALOG144:10 H120 O *Jane,* why didst thou dye in flowring prime,

JANUARY (2) See also JAN.
SEASONS52:24 H239 Cold frozen *January* next comes in,
11MAYB228:25 Hp259 of January 'till May I haue been by fitts very ill & weak. The

JANUS (1)
MROMAN137:27 H3478 To *Janus,* he that famous Temple built,

JAR (2)
FATHER5:25 H26 Sweet harmony they keep, yet jar oft times,
MGREC101:26 H1951 The afflicted King, finding him set to jar,
JARRE (1) [jar]
DIALOG142:18 H47 Or is {is't} the fatall jarre againe begun,
JARRES (1) [jars]
MGREC128:38 H3111 Sought for a peace, and laid aside their jarres:
JARS (2) [pl.]
HUMOUR35:10 H606 Nor jars, nor scoffs, let none hereafter see,
MPERS87:3 H1359 The young Queen, and old, at bitter jars:
JASPER (1)
FLESH177:8 H89 Are made of pretious *Jasper* stone;
JAUNDISE (1) [jaundice]
HUMOUR31:17 H450 And so {thence} with jaundise, Safferns al the skin.
JAXARTIS (1)
MGREC108:27 H2243 From hence he to *Jaxartis* river goes,
JAY (1)
ELEMEN19:9 H454 The Pye {Thrush}, the Jay {wren}, the Larke, a prey to th'
JEALOUS (2)
MPERS82:29 H1176 When jealous Queen *Amestris,* of this knew,
MPERS86:11 H1327 Still on his brother, casts a jealous eye,
JEALOUSIES (1) [pl.]
MGREC118:13 H2660 'Mongst these contentions, tumults, jealousies,
JEARS (1) [jeers]
MPERS83:3 H1191 His brothers recompence was naught but jears:
JEAST (2) [jest]
MGREC114:9 H2477 From jeast, to earnest, and at last so bold,
DIALOG144:1 H111 Thy flying for the Truth I made a jeast;
JEER'D (1) [jeered]
DIALOG143:41 H110 And thou, poore soule, wast {wert} jeer'd among the rest,
JEERE (1) [jeer]
MGREC114:1 H2469 When both were drunk, *Clitus* was wont to jeere;
JEERS See JEARS
JEHOIAKIM (1) See also IEHOIAKIM
MASSYR65:11 H476 *Jehoiakim* his Oath had clean forgot;
JEHOIAKIMS (1) [poss.]
MASSYR67:5 H551 Easeth *Jehoiakims* captivity.
JEHU (3)
MGREC132:13 H3248 *Jehu* in killing *Ahabs* house did well,
MEDDM204:18 Hp285 as we see in Jehu, he is rewarded wth a kingdome to the fourth
MEDDM204:21 Hp285 of Jehu, he was rewarded for the matter, and yet punished for
JEHU'S (1) [poss.]
MEDDM204:24 Hp285 wth Jehu's reward, wch will end in punishment
JERUSALEM (2)
MPERS~~84:12~~ H1246 Went to *Jerusalem* his city dear,
MGREC99:34 H1877 From *Gaza,* to *Jerusalem* he goes,
JESREEL (1)
MGREC132:14 H3249 Yet be aveng'd, must th' blood of *Jesreel.*
JEST (1) See also JEAST
HUMOUR21:39 H67 And break a staffe, provided't be in jest,

JESUS (3)
MEDDM209:16 Hp291 Christ Jesus come to their rescue.
MYCHILD218:35 Hp244 o my Soul to thy Rest, vpon this Rock Xt Jesus will I build
JULY223:36 Hp251 Come Lord Jesus, come quickly.

JESVS (1) [jesus]
MYSOUL225:21 H25 Come Jesvs qvickly, Blessed Lord

JEW (1)
DIALOG148:26 H291 And Jew and Gentile, to one worship go,

JEWEL (2)
HUMOUR31:23 H456 The first, my constancy, that jewel rare.
TDUDLEY166:5 H47 Gave his in charge, that Jewel rich to prize.

JEWELS (2) [pl.]
MGREC96:32 H1752 Loaden with gold, with jewels and with Plate,
DUBART153:20 H24 The glittering Plate, and Jewels, he admires,

JEWES (1) [jews]
MGREC134:6 H3339 Against {Amongst} the Jewes, we read in *Macchabees,*

JEWISH (1)
MPERS70:22 H693 *Cyrus* doth now the *Jewish* captives free,

JEWS (3) See also JEWES
MPERS75:25 H882 An Edict for the *Jews* publish'd again,
MPERS~~84:12~~ H1242 Did for the Jews commission large obtain,
DIALOG~~143:2~~ H71 French *Lewis* {Jews} unjustly to the Crown to bring;

JEZEREL (1)
MEDDM204:20 Hp285 god) and I will avenge the blood of Jezerel vpon the house

JIM (1) See also IIM
MASSYR~~66:10~~ H516 Now *Zim,* and *lim, {Jim}* lift up their shriking {scrieching}

JOCUND (1)
MPERS~~87:38~~ H1390 Rejoyced {Was} not a little {jocund} at his feare.

JOHN (1)
DIALOG143:1 H70 Nor Nobles siding, to make *John* no King

JOIN (1) See also JOYN, JOYNE
DIALOG145:14 H163 Then let's join heads, and hands {& hearts} for your relief.

JOINED (1) See also JOYN'D, JOYNED
MYCHILD216:10 Hp241 submitted to it & joined to ye chh., at Boston.

JOINS See JOYNES

JOINING See JOYNING

JOINT See JOYNT

JOINTS See JOYNTS

JONAH (2)
MASSYR59:37 H261 When *Jonah* for their sins denounc'd such {those} woes;
MEDDM207:13 Hp288 Comforts of this Life, may be compared to the gourd of Jonah,

JONATHAN (4)
DAVID158:23 H2-3 and *Jonathan,* 2 Sam. I. 19.
DAVID159:6 H21 The bow of *Jonathan* ne're turn'd in vaine,
DAVID159:21 H36 O! lovely *Jonathan,* how wert {wast} thou slaine,
DAVID159:23 H38 Distrest I am, for thee, deare *Jonathan,*

JOSHUA'S (1) [poss.]
SEASONS47:35 ~~H47~~ But only once at *Joshua's* strange command;

JOT (2)
MASSYR67:7 H553 In seven and thirty years, had seen no jot,
MGREC117:5 H2612 To his posterity remain'd no jot,

JOURNEY (2)
MGREC115:39 H2558 His age, and journey long, he now {then} pretends;
MGREC130:8 H3163 With his Embassadour, her journey takes,
JOVE (2)
MPERS71:30 H744 But scorning thus by *Jove* to be out-brav'd,
MGREC112:37 H2423 He did the Oracle of *Iupiter* {*Jove*} deride,
JOY (23) See also IOY
SEASONS47:23 H39 They joy in what they have, but more in hope,
MGREC94:22 H1660 And on *Achillis* Tombe, with wondrous joy,
MGREC95:19 H1698 To *Alexanders* heart's no little joy.
MGREC102:6 H1976 Is entertain'd with joy, and pompous train {showes},
MGREC103:1 H2012 For his receit with joy, they all accord;
MGREC121:29 H2811 With greater joy it would have been receiv'd;
MGREC132:37 H3284 'Twas no small joy, unto *Seleuchus* breast,
DIALOG147:35 H259 That all shall joy that thou display'dst thy banner,
TDUDLEY166:27 H69 As joy in heaven, on earth let praise resound.
TDUDLEY166:32 H74 Where we with joy each others face shall see,
1LETTER181:4 H2 My joy, my Magazine of earthly store,
2LETTER182:22 H28 O how they joy when thou dost light the skyes.
3LETTER183:16 H18 Her fellow lost, nor joy nor life do wish,
3LETTER183:23 H25 Return my Dear, my joy, my only Love,
CHILDRN186:23 H90 She shew'd you joy and misery;
ANNEB187:22 H12 Was ever stable joy yet found below?
MERCY189:11 H32 She one hath left, a joy to thee and me,
MYCHILD217:15 Hp243 been p^{r}plexed y^{t} I haue not fovnd that constant Joy in my
MYSOUL225:8 H12 Of Joy vnto Eternity.
13MAY226:29 H5 At Svn-shine each their joy expresse.
2HUSB232:13 H14 Then let thy promis joy his heart
2HUSB233:8 H41 Wth Joy lend back my Dear
HOURS234:16 H30 They are no Joy, but woe.
JOY'D (3) [joyed]
AGES~~45:2~~ H376 We joy'd in many blest and prosperous dayes.
MGREC108:9 H2225 These not a little joy'd, this day to see,
1LETTER181:11 H9 Whom whilst I 'joy'd, nor storms, nor frosts I felt,
JOYES (7) [joys] See also IOYES
CONTEM168:24 H31 And as a strong man, joyes to run a race,
CONTEM174:8 H208 Joyes not in hope of an eternal morrow;
BIRTH179:28 H4 Adversity doth still our joyes attend;
3LETTER183:25 H27 Who neither joyes in pasture, house nor streams,
CHILDRN186:7 H74 But former toyes (no joyes) adieu.
1SIMON188:15 H16 Among the blest in endless joyes remain.
SON230:21 H4 My feares to Joyes, my sighes to song
JOYFUL (1)
AGES44:22 H355 Great mutations, some joyful, and some sad,
JOYFULL (2) [joyful]
MPERS~~74:14~~ H837 But {And joyfull} acclamations ecchoes in the aire; {shrill they
MPERS84:19 H1255 The King not little joyfull of this chance,
JOYFULLY (4)
MPERS90:11 H1484 These {Who} after all, receiv'd them joyfully:
MGREC121:21 H2803 And is of all received {most} joyfully;
MYCHILD217:2 Hp242 Joyfully as in greatest mercyes, For if yee bee his yee shall

28AUG226:2 Hp254 willingly but joyfully? The Lord knowes I dare not desire that

JOYLESS (1)

3LETTER183:19 H21 Mine being gone, I lead a joyless life,

JOYN (5) [join] See also JOYNE

MASSYR58:41 H224 Only intreats them, {to} joyn their force with his,

MGREC119:27 H2717 He joyn not with *Antipater,* that {their} foe.

MGREC120:5 H2740 *Craterus,* and *Antipater* now joyn

MGREC120:17 H2752 With *Antipater* t' joyn, sometimes he thought,

MGREC120:29 H2766 He, and *Craterus,* both with him now {do} joyn,

JOYN'D (4) [joined] See also JOYNED

HUMOUR26:2 H232 Yet such, when we al four are joyn'd in one.

MGREC94:20 H1658 To these {which} were joyn'd, five thousand goodly horse.

MGREC~~101:34~~ H1961 The Armyes joyn'd a while, the Persians fight,

DUBART155:4 H89 *Art and Nature joyn'd, by heavens high decree,*

JOYNE (2) [join] See also JOYN

MASSYR~~57:19~~ H166 With petty Kings to joyne Confederate.

MGREC125:13 H2961 Some Forces did procure, with her to joyne.

JOYNED (1) [joined] See also JOYN'D

HUMOUR32:40 H514 My Lilly white, when joyned with her red,

JOYNES (3) [joins]

MPERS81:33 H1141 He fifty thousand joynes unto his own;

MPERS85:16 H1292 Joynes with the *Greeks,* and so maintains {maintain} their

MGREC127:36 H3066 *Seleuchus, Ptolomy, Cassander* joynes,

JOYNING (1) [joining]

ELEMEN19:40 H481 Their joyning, fighting, forcing, and retreat;

JOYNT (2) [joint]

HUMOUR34:16 H571 With {Which} joynt to joynt, the entire body tyes;

HUMOUR34:16 H571 With {Which} joynt to joynt, the entire body tyes;

JOYNTS (1) [joints]

AUTHOR178:6 H16 I stretcht thy joynts to make thee even feet,

JOYS See IOYES, JOYES

JUAHS (1) [poss.]

MASSYR62:34 H379 On *Henah, Arpad,* and on *Ivdah* least {*Juahs* coast};

JUDAH (1) See also IUDAH, IVDAH

MASSYR65:17 H482 To *Judah* marches with a speedy course,

JUDAH'S (2) [poss.] See also IUDA'S, IUDAH'S, IUDAHS

HUMOUR24:33 H182 But *David, Judah's* most heroyick King:

MASSYR67:9 H555 Is *Judah's* King, now lifted up on high.

JUDEX (1) [index]

MPERS81:7 H1115 With his *Mardon'us,* judex {index} of his minde;

JUDG (2) [judge]

AUTHOR177:35 H7 Where errors were not lessened (all may judg).

MEDDM205:14 Hp286 and Judg, whom no bribes can pervert, nor flattery cause to

JUDG'D (13) [judged]

ELEMEN10:2 H77 Poor Heathen judg'd worthy a Diety:

ELEMEN11:21 H141 The next in place, Earth judg'd to be her due,

HUMOUR30:5 H397 If I be partial judg'd, or thought to erre,

HUMOUR35:15 H611 That Flegme was judg'd, for kindnesse to excel.

MPERS~~78:28~~ H1009 For to command alone, she thought {judg'd} was best.

MPERS89:15 ~~H1449~~ That their return be stopt, he judg'd was best,

MPERS~~89:16~~ H1450 He judg'd his wisest and his safest Course.

MGREC96:20 H1740 For so to fright the *Greekes* he judg'd was best,
MGREC~~121:2~~ H2780 But first 'gainst *Ptolemy* he judg'd was
DIALOG144:31 H139 heard {saw} their cause, and wrongs {hath} judg'd righteously,
SIDNEY151:12 ~~H69~~ I rather judg'd thee of his mind that wept,
TDUDLEY166:9 H51 Their greatness may be judg'd by what they shew.
CONTEM173:15 H182 I judg'd my hearing better then my sight,

JUDGE (8) See also JUDG
FATHER6:3 H37 But fear'd you'ld judge, one *Bartas* was my friend,
ELEMEN11:11 H131 But to leave those to'th' wise, I judge is {it} best,
HUMOUR21:3 H31 Your selves would judge, but vain prolixity.
HUMOUR24:31 H180 And leave't to all, to judge where valour lyes.
AGES41:25 H242 My reason, then bad judge, how little hope,
AGES43:20 H315 I judge, I should have room, in all mens hearts.
MPERS72:19 H767 Upon a Judge, for breach of Law {taking bribes} accus'd;
MGREC112:31 H2417 His Master is Accuser, Judge, and King,

JUDGED (1) See also JUDG'D
MPERS86:1 H1317 And takes more on him, then was judged fit.

JUDGEMENT (4) See also JUDGMENT
HUMOUR32:3 H477 My prudence, judgement, now I might reveale,
HUMOUR34:29 H584 Thy judgement is unsafe, thy fancy little,
MGREC112:29 H2415 Yet is *Philotas* unto Judgement brought,
MGREC126:24 H3015 But made in Judgement her Accusers stand,

JUDGEMENTS See JUDGMENTS

JUDGES (1) [pl.]
WHAT224:14 H14 Your selves shall Judges bee;

JUDGING (2)
MPERS86:12 H1328 Judging all's {his} actions, tends to's injury.
QELIZ157:11 H79 (Judging all valour, and all Majesty)

JUDGMENT (1) [judgement]
MEDDM208:15 Hp290 Judgment we must be tryed and as he passes the sentence, so

JUDGMENTS (1) [judgements]
MYCHILD218:10 Hp244 Invention can work vpon ye Soul, hath no Judgments befallen

JUDICATURE (1)
MEDDM205:16 Hp286 is this Court of Judicature, that there is no appeale from it, no

JUDICIOUS (2)
SEASONS~~51:19~~ H195 If scited as the most Judicious take.
MPERS92:31 H1589 With our judicious learned {learned and judicious} Knight to

JUICE See JUYCE

JUICY See JUYCIE

JULIUS (2)
SEASONS50:1 H135 This month from *Julius Cæsar* took the {its} name,
MGREC134:36 H3367 Whom *Julius Cæsar* set in Royall place,

JULY (5)
SEASONS49:4 H95 Bright *June, July,* and *August,* hot are mine,
SEASONS49:38 H131 *July* my next, the hot'st in all the year,
TDUDLEY165:3 H4-5 *Who deceased,* July 31, 1653. *and of his Age,* 77.
JULY223:20 Hp251 July. 8th. 1656.
SON230:19 H1-2 On my Sons Return out of England. July. 17. 1661.

JUMP (1)
SEASONS47:21 H37 Now {Do} jump, and play, before their feeding Dams,

JUNE (4)
SEASONS49:4 H95 Bright *June, July,* and *August,* hot are mine,
CHILDRN184:13 H1-2 *In reference to her Children, 23. June, 1659.*
ANNEB187:14 H3-4 *Who deceased* June 20. 1669. *being three years and*
RESTOR229:20 H3 Ague. June 1661.

JUNIUS (1)
MROMAN139:19 H3547 With *Junius Brutus* rose, and being strong,

JUPITER (4) See also IUPITER
MPERS71:27 H741 To spoyl the Temple of great *Jupiter;*
MGREC100:5 H1889 Then to the Phane of *Jupiter,* he went,
MGREC100:8 H1892 The Son of *Jupiter* did straight him make:
MGREC~~115:15~~ H2532 His messenger to *Jupiter* he sent,

JUST (14) See also JVST
HUMOUR31:5 ~~H438~~ Thou do'st assume my name, wel be it just;
MASSYR67:3 H549 His son possesses wealth, and rule, as just;
MPERS69:24 H646 So over-thrown of *Cyrus,* as was just;
MPERS72:39 H785 But in the way, his sword just vengeance takes.
MPERS~~91:32~~ H1546 A King nor good, nor valiant, wise nor just
MGREC103:20 H2031 Their charge, {place} gave to his Captains (as most {was} just)
MGREC103:33 H2044 And just procuring of the *Persians* hate.
MGREC105:23 H2116 The just revenge of this his wofull end;
MGREC129:11 H3125 But for one act she did, just was her end,
MGREC130:24 H3179 Then vengeance just, against the same {them} t' expresse;
DIALOG145:4 H153 Nor sip I of that cup, and just 't may be,
QELIZ156:3 H30 Who was so good, so just, so learn'd, so wise,
TDUDLEY166:36 H78 *That was both pious, just and wise,*
1SIMON188:11 H12 Let's say he's merciful, as well as just,

JUSTICE (7) See also IUSTICE
AGES42:4 H262 Yea justice I have done, was I in place;
MASSYR62:13 H358 Did Justice now, by him, eradicate: [10 *years.*
MPERS83:23 H1211 Such Justice then, in *Persia* {*Persian* court} did remain, {reign.}
MGREC126:26 H3017 Desiring Justice might be done for guilt;
MGREC126:28 H3019 For Justice sake she being put to th' sword.
DIALOG147:38 H262 Then Justice shall in all thy Courts take place,
SIDNEY150:10 H35 Justice, friendship, and kind hospitality;

JUSTIFIED (1)
MGREC113:12 H2439 At last he did: So they were justified,

JUSTLY (6) See also IUSTLY
HUMOUR26:24 H254 Shal justly claime priority of thine;
HUMOUR29:15 H368 And in contentions lists, now justly enter.
HUMOUR30:25 H417 And first, the firme dry bones, I justly claim:
DIALOG141:27 H26 Then weigh our case, if't be not justly sad,
TDUDLEY165:19 H21 Such as in life, no man could justly deem.
TDUDLEY166:11 H53 Such vanityes he justly did despise.

JUYCE (1) [juice]
SEASONS51:5 H179 But its a precious juyce, when wel it's used.

JUYCIE (1) [juicy]
SEASONS50:31 H165 Like good Old Age, whose younger juycie roots,

JVST (1) [just]
HOUSE236:28 H20 Yea so it was, and so 'twas jvst.

K

KEDAR (1)
MASSYR66:15 H521 *Kedar,* {and} *Hazer,* the *Arabians* too,
KEEP (22)
FATHER5:25 H26 Sweet harmony they keep, yet jar oft times,
HUMOUR33:29 H543 Doth doubtlesse keep its mighty residence;
AGES41:32 H249 My family to keep, but not for gaines.
AGES42:29 ~~H285~~ By cankered care, who centinel doth keep.
MASSYR59:41 H265 Ingeniously with each {all} did keep his word;
MPERS75:32 H889 Shall let the work, or keep back any thing,
MPERS87:18 H1372 To keep those streights, to hinder his intent.
MGREC94:40 H1678 And think {strive} to keep his men from off the land,
MGREC126:19 H3010 *Olimpias* wills to keep it, {means to hold out} to the last,
MGREC127:15 H3045 To keep *Antigonus* from *Susha* still,
MROMAN137:32 H3483 And vestall Maids to keep the holy fire.
CHILDRN185:33 H59 Long did I keep you soft and warm,
MEDDM196:29 Hp273 nothing but salt will keep from putrefaction, some again like
MEDDM200:21 Hp279 therfore god cuts their garments short, to keep them in such
MEDDM205:23 Hp286 He that would keep a pure heart and lead a blamlesse life,
MYCHILD216:14 Hp241 pleased God to keep me a long time wthout a child wch was a
MYCHILD217:9 Hp242 I was afflicted I went astray, but now I keep thy statutes.
MYCHILD219:2 Hp245 and y^{t} he is able to keep y^{t} I haue comitted to his charge.
FEVER220:35 H15 From Burnings keep my Soul.
SON230:25 H8 In raging stormes did'st safely keep
2HUSB232:9 H10 Thy servant Lord. Keep & p^{r}serve
2HUSB232:12 H13 Nor novght could keep him back
KEEPS (10)
ELEMEN9:7 H41 And in despight the City keeps her owne,
SEASONS47:30 ~~H45~~ The Sun now keeps his posting residence
SEASONS~~47:31~~ H46 The Sun in *Taurus* keeps his residence,
SEASONS50:13 H147 This month he keeps with *Virgo* for a space,
SEASONS52:26 H241 In *Aquarias,* now keeps the loved {long wisht} Sun,
MASSYR65:32 H497 Seven years he keeps his faith, and safe he dwels,
MGREC~~99:16~~ H1859 Where valiant *Betis,* doth defend {stoutly keeps} the town,
CONTEM170:22 H93 There *Abel* keeps his sheep, no ill he thinks,
MEDDM196:21 Hp273 beds make drosey persons but hard lodging, keeps the eyes
MEDDM203:25 Hp283 of a guilty Conscience, cares not how far he keeps from him
KEPT (29)
AGES44:41 H374 (For 'twas our hopes then kept our hearts alive)
MASSYR58:6 H191 Kept ever close, fearing some dismal {his well deserved} fate;
MASSYR63:13 H398 All yeelds to him, but *Ninivie* kept free,

MASSYR63:28 H413 By whom in firm obedience she's kept.
MPERS70:9 H680 But till convenient time their heads kept shut;
MPERS78:27 H1008 {But} Hers she kept stil, seperate from the rest,
MPERS83:33 H1221 Which had they kept, *Greece* had more nobly done,
MPERS87:24 H1376 Few might have kept it, had they but {had} a heart.
MPERS90:9 H1482 But on to *Trabezond* they kept their way;
MGREC~~94:18~~ H1656 Reply'd, enough, sith only hope he kept.
MGREC100:18 H1902 Great *Alexander* had been kept from Land;
MGREC101:18 H1943 Which had he done (perhaps) his fame had {he'd} kept,
MGREC~~107:39~~ H2214 With little pain there might have kept them still:
MGREC110:16 H2316 For to the last, stout *Porus* kept his ground.
MGREC110:32 H2336 Which might be found, and so for {great} wonders kept:
MGREC116:23 H2589 The Illiads of *Homer* he still kept,
MGREC116:26 H2592 'Cause *Homer* kept his Acts to memory;
MGREC118:29 H2678 His chief opponents who kept off the Crown, {Control'd his
MGREC124:33 H2940 He still kept fresh {lockt} within his memory,
MROMAN~~136:30~~ H3444 Where Swaines, and rustick Peasants made {kept} their Holds.
MROMAN137:28 H3479 Kept shut in peace, but {set} ope when bloud was spilt;
SIDNEY151:13 ~~H69~~ To be within the bounds of one world kept,
CONTEM169:20 H60 They kept one tune, and plaid on the same string,
3LETTER183:22 H24 I here, he there, alas, both kept by force:
CHILDRN185:34 H60 And with my wings kept off all harm,
MEDDM205:13 Hp286 wch is alway kept by Conscience, who is both accuser excuser
MEDDM209:11 Hp291 thornes in their sides, and at last ouercame them, and kept
BYNIGHT220:4 H5 My waking eyes were open kept
HOURS233:27 H10 Thro: the I've kept my Grovnd.

KERNELL (1) [kernel]
MEDDM202:17 Hp282 haue no kernell in them, and they that feed vpon them, may

KICK (1)
MGREC114:6 H2474 Like this, against his deity to kick:

KIDS (1) [pl.]
SEASONS47:20 H36 The wanton frisking Kids, and soft fleec'd Lambs,

KIL (1) [kill]
MPERS81:1 H1109 And many thousands of these {those} men did kil;

KILD (3) [killed] See also KILL'D
SEASONS47:16 H32 The croaking Frogs, whom nipping Winter kild,
MASSYR64:6 H430 Kild, sav'd, pull'd down, set up, or pain'd, or eas'd;
MGREC114:36 H2506 Yea, and he kild *Calisthines* by name; {of fame.}

KILL (6) See also KIL
ELEMEN~~14:10~~ H252 Some kill outright, and some do stupifye:
MGREC114:2 H2470 *Alexander,* to rage, to kill, and sweare,
MGREC117:1 H2608 Nor can he kill, or save as heretofore,
DIALOG143:6 H77 Whose tearing tusks did wound, and kill, and threat:
CHILDRN186:25 H92 What would save life, and what would kill.
MEDDM199:28 Hp278 first kill the body, the last the good name the two former leaue

KILL'D (3) [killed] See also KILD
ELEMEN10:6 H81 The Horse that kill'd *Bellerophon,* then flew.
MGREC130:31 ~~H3181~~ Two other children by *Olympias* kill'd,
MGREC132:5 ~~H3238~~ The youngest by *Demetrius* kill'd in fight,

KILLING (1)
MGREC132:13 H3248 *Jehu* in killing *Ahabs* house did well,

KIND (7)
HUMOUR29:8 H361 But sith we fight with words, we might be kind,
AGES39:24 H167 Though thus in field, at home, to all most kind,
MASSYR58:4 H189 And {in} their kind t' excel did emulate.
SIDNEY150:10 H35 Justice, friendship, and kind hospitality;
DDUDLEY167:14 H11 *To Servants wisely aweful, but yet kind,*
CONTEM169:23 H63 And in their kind resound their makers praise:
CONTEM170:27 H98 Thinks each he sees will serve him in his kind,
KINDE (4) [kind]
HUMOUR28:25 H337 They're liberal, pleasant, kinde, and courteous,
MPERS89:34 H1468 as most {Commanders feasts and yet more} kinde;
MGREC106:2 ~~H2136~~ Wherefore the gods requite thy kinde regard.
2SIMON195:12 Hp271 though in value they fall short of all in this kinde yet I presume
KINDGOMES (1) [kingdoms] See also KINDOMES, KINGDOMES
MGREC~~131:17~~ H3209 Of those dominions {vast Kindgomes} he did sometimes gain,
KINDLED (1)
ELEMEN10:36 H111 What lasting Forts my kindled wrath hath burn'd?
KINDNES (2) [kindness]
11MAYB228:31 Hp259 loving kindnes, nor take ye cup of salvation wth Thanksgiving
HOURS234:29 H43 So both of vs thy Kindnes Lord
KINDNESS (1)
SON231:27 H39 O Lord gravnt that I may never forgett thy Loving kindness in
KINDNESSE (2) [kindness]
HUMOUR35:15 H611 That Flegme was judg'd, for kindnesse to excel.
MGREC125:25 H2975 Bids chuse her death, such kindnesse she'l afford:
KINDOMES (1) [kingdoms] See also KINDGOMES, KINGDOMES
MGREC~~107:15~~ H2190 The wealth of many Cities doth {Kindomes did} consume:
KINDRED (7)
AGES41:36 H251 But if none, then for kindred near ally'd.
AGES46:18 H449 In my dark house, such kindred I have store,
MPERS84:28 H1264 His Country, nor his Kindred {Friends} would {much} esteem,
MPERS~~91:39~~ H1553 Of brethren and of kindred to be slain.
MGREC117:7 H2614 None of his Kindred, or {nor} his Race, long stood;
MGREC126:25 H3016 the blood of their deare Kindred {friends and kindreds} spilt,
CONTEM170:28 H99 Though none on Earth but kindred near then could he find.
KINDREDS (1) [pl.]
MGREC126:25 H3016 the blood of their deare Kindred {friends and kindreds} spilt,
KINDREDS (1) [pl., poss.]
DIALOG143:8 H75 Their hands in Kindreds blood, whom they did foyle:
KINDS (2) [pl.]
ELEMEN11:31 H151 Their kinds, their tasts, their colours, and their smels,
ELEMEN16:13 H336 To speake of kinds of Waters I'le {I} neglect,
KINE (1)
ELEMEN17:1 H365 Of rotten sheep, lean kine, and mildew'd grain.
KING (193) See also TH'KING
HUMOUR23:30 H140 But one of you would make a worthy King:
HUMOUR24:33 H182 But *David, Judah's* most heroyick King:
AGES~~37:39~~ H101 I'd nought to do, 'twixt Prince, {King} and peoples strife.
AGES~~45:2~~ H375 We chang'd our queen for king under whose rayes
AGES45:4 H382 A plot to blow up Nobles, and their King;
AGES~~45:22~~ H405 I've seen a King by force thrust from his throne,

AGES46:8 H439 From King to begger, all degrees shal finde
SEASONS~~49:33~~ H126 Of him that was Shepherd, then King go vaunt.
SEASONS51:19 H193 Great *Adam* {Our Grand-Sire} was of Paradice made King.
MASSYR54:30 H57 *Barzanes,* the great *Armenian* King,
MASSYR54:33 H60 *Pharmus, {Thermus}* their King, he caused to be slain;
MASSYR54:36 H63 *Zoroaster,* their King, he likewise slew,
MASSYR56:25 H131 Great King *Staurobates,* for {his Country} to invade.
MASSYR57:14 H161 Who warr'd with *Sodoms,* and *Gomorahs* King,
MASSYR58:14 H199 Both, for their King, held their dominion,
MASSYR58:18 H203 Against their monstrous King to bring {use} their might,
MASSYR59:10 H234 The King his Brother leaves, all to sustaine,
MASSYR59:13 H237 The King pursu'd unto the City wals;
MASSYR59:35 H259 That *Amazia* was King of *Israel;*
MASSYR59:36 H260 His Father was then King (as we suppose)
MASSYR60:1 H266 Of *Babylon, Belosus* he made King,
MASSYR61:13 H318 *Resin* their valiant King, he also slew,
MASSYR61:15 H320 *Iuda's* bad King occasioned this War,
MASSYR61:20 H325 And to *Assyria's* King a Present sends.
MASSYR61:27 H332 Unto *Damascus* then, comes *Iudah's* King,
MASSYR62:4 H349 *Hoshea,* their last King, he did invade,
MASSYR62:7 H352 To *Ægypts* King, which did avail him nought;
MASSYR62:10 H355 And did the people, nobles, and their King
MASSYR63:9 H394 So he's now stil'd, the King of *Babylon;*
MASSYR63:18 H403 *Ben. Merodach,* Successor to this King,
MASSYR63:21 H406 Led King *Manasseh,* to captivity.
MASSYR63:23 H408 Brave *Nebulassar* to this King was Sonne,
MASSYR63:30 H417 The famous Wars {acts}, of this Heroyick King,
MASSYR64:5 H429 This was that King of Kings, did what he pleas'd,
MASSYR64:8 H432 Was turned {changed} from a King, unto {into} a Beast;
MASSYR64:11 H435 *Iudah's* poor King besieg'd, who {and} succourlesse,
MASSYR64:16 H440 By the victorious King to *Babel's* prest;
MASSYR65:10 H475 When in the *Tyrian* wars, the {this} King was hot,
MASSYR65:13 H478 While *Babels* King thus deep ingaged stands;
MASSYR65:16 H481 For this great King, with-drawes part of his force,
MASSYR65:29 H494 Who was last King of holy *Davids* race;
MASSYR65:38 H503 The cursed King, by flight could no wise flee {fly}
MASSYR65:40 H505 But being caught, to *Babels* wrathful King,
MASSYR66:13 H519 With all these Conquests, *Babels* King rests not,
MASSYR66:20 H526 To *Babylons* proud King, now yeelds the day.
MASSYR66:38 H544 This King among the righteous had a part:
MASSYR67:9 H555 Is *Judah's* King, now lifted up on high.
MASSYR67:29 H575 The coward King, whose strength lay in his walls,
MASSYR67:39 H585 The King, upon the wall casting his eye,
MASSYR68:7 H593 And highest dignity, next to the King,
MASSYR68:17 H603 *Daniel* in haste, is brought before the King,
MASSYR68:23 H609 The guilty King, with colour pale, and dead,
MASSYR68:25 H611 And did one thing worthy a King (though late)
MPERS69:1 H623 *Cyrus Cambyses,* Son of *Persia's* {Persia} King,
MPERS~~69:38~~ H661 Then to the King he makes this true report,
MPERS~~69:38~~ H666 If ever King equal'd his happiness.
MPERS70:14 H685 Enters the town, the sottish King he slayes,

MPERS71:11 H727 But that the *Persian* King, may act his minde;
MPERS71:15 H729 'Gainst *Ægypts* King, who there by him was slain,
MPERS71:22 H736 Made *Evelthon* their King, with bended knee,
MPERS72:29 ~~H773~~ Who said but what, the King bad him expresse.
MPERS72:31 H775 To tell the facts, of this most bloody King.
MPERS73:22 H809 This King, with {his} conspirators so stout,
MPERS74:11 H836 The Nobles all alight, {bow to} their King to greet,
MPERS74:15 H838 A thousand times, God save {long live} the King, they cry,
MPERS74:20 H843 *Darius* by election made a King
MPERS74:26 H849 And now a King, by marriage, choyce, and bloud,
MPERS75:2 H863 Tels them, how harshly the proud King had dealt,
MPERS75:28 H885 He like a King, now grants a Charter large,
MPERS75:33 H890 Of what is freely granted by the King;
MPERS75:36 H893 They thus backt of {by} the King, in spight of foes,
MPERS76:12 H910 The King will needs interpret their intent;
MPERS76:19 H917 The King, seeing his men, and victuall spent;
MPERS78:34 H1015 Then gives the King, a King-like gift, most {full} large;
MPERS78:37 H1018 He humbly to the King then makes request,
MPERS79:21 H1047 One King, so many Subjects should possesse;
MPERS82:41 H1188 With loaden heart unto the King he goes,
MPERS83:37 H1225 Which done, a sumptuous feast; makes like a King
MPERS84:13 H1249 Unto this King *Thymistocles* did flye.
MPERS84:19 H1255 The King not little joyfull of this chance,
MPERS84:39 H1275 The King this noble Captaine having lost,
MPERS85:14 H1290 Disquiet {Revolting} Egypt, 'gainst this King rebells,
MPERS85:24 H1300 The King was glad, with *Sparta* to make peace,
MPERS85:28 H1304 The King much profit reapeth, by these leagues {this league},
MPERS85:32 H1308 The {This} King, his sister, like *Cambyses,* wed;
MPERS86:2 H1318 The King provok'd, sends for him to the Court,
MPERS86:24 H1340 She to the King, would make a fair report:
MPERS86:29 H1345 Pretending still, the profit of the King,
MPERS86:31 H1347 The King finding, revenues now amended;
MPERS86:40 H1356 With posting speed {on} towards the King he goes;
MPERS87:7 H1363 The King dismay'd, a mighty Hoast doth raise;
MPERS87:13 H1369 The fearfull King, at last, musters his Forces;
MPERS87:27 H1379 The mazed King, was now {then} about to fly;
MPERS88:1 H1394 Arme, arme, the King {with all his host} is now approaching
MPERS88:17 H1410 They straight adored *Cyrus* for their King,
MPERS88:21 H1414 Of six thousand, wherein the King was yet;
MPERS88:23 H1416 They {ready} were about to leave their King and fly,
MPERS88:38 H1431 The King unto a country Village flyes,
MPERS89:2 H1436 The King upon the spur, runs back again;
MPERS89:7 H1441 The King with his dispers'd also incampt,
MPERS89:21 H1455 The troubled King, his Herauld sends again,
MPERS89:25 H1459 The King great store of all provision sends,
MPERS~~89:29~~ H1463 The King's {King} perplext, there dares not let them stay,
MPERS90:14 ~~H1484~~ The King afraid what further they might doe,
MPERS90:20 H1487 The *Greeks* now (as the *Persian* King suspects)
MPERS~~90:31~~ H1498 {Their King} *Agesilus* himself doth over-goe {goe};
MPERS~~90:33~~ H1500 Lieftenant to the King, but soon he fled
MPERS90:34 H1501 Which over-throw incens'd the King so sore,

MPERS91:10 H1518 {on such} conditions they are forc't to take; {as King will make}
MPERS91:19 H1527 The King from forraign foes, and all {parts now well} at ease,
MPERS~~91:22~~ H1533 The King highly inrag'd doth hereupon
MPERS~~91:32~~ H1546 A King nor good, nor valiant, wise nor just
MPERS~~91:38~~ H1552 And being king commands those that remain,
MPERS~~92:27~~ H1585 But from some daughter this new king was sprung
MPERS92:33 H1591 That this *Darius* was last *Persian* King,
MGREC93:13 H1610 Shee to the rich *Molossians* {*Epirus* warlike} King, was
MGREC~~6:23~~ H1620 Whose glory to the Earth, this Prince {king} did throw,
MGREC6:35 H1632 But as the King of little *Macedon.*)
MGREC94:34 H1672 That boy so mallepart, before the King.
MGREC95:36 H1715 For this wise King, had brought to see the sport;
MGREC96:11 H1731 The King sat in a chariot made of gold,
MGREC96:27 H1747 This brave Virago, to the King was mother;
MGREC97:1 H1762 Most basely run {ran}, and left their King at large,
MGREC97:21 H1782 Then that the *Persian* King he over-came;
MGREC97:33 H1794 To give his Conquerour, the stile of King;
MGREC97:36 H1797 A King he was, and that not only so,
MGREC97:37 H1798 But of *Darius* King, as he should know.
MGREC98:11 H1813 And now, as *Babels* King did once before,
MGREC99:5 H1848 And the distressed King no way {whit} respects;
MGREC100:19 H1903 But as the King is, so's the multitude,
MGREC100:39 H1923 But when inform'd, how royally the King
MGREC101:26 H1951 The afflicted King, finding him set to jar,
MGREC~~103:21~~ H2032 For such revolters false, what Prince will {King can} trust:
MGREC103:23 H2034 Now makes this King, his vertues all to drown.
MGREC104:39 H2091 This {The} wofull King, his courtesie refuses,
MGREC106:28 H2162 No ways becomming such a mighty King;
MGREC107:6 H2181 Then {And} hearing, *Bessus* makes himselfe a King,
MGREC107:11 H2186 Into the Market-place, before the King;
MGREC107:19 H2194 For {Here} to observe the rashnesse of the King.
MGREC107:27 H2202 Then did {all} their wars, against the *Persian* King.
MGREC108:4 H2220 This Malefactor vild, {vile} before the King,
MGREC109:17 H2276 And *Omphis,* King of that part of the land:
MGREC110:3 H2303 A potent Army with him, like a King,
MGREC111:9 H2354 To th' utmost shew'd, the glory of a King;
MGREC112:22 H2408 The King of treason, and conspiracy;
MGREC112:27 H2413 But for his Fathers great deserts, the King,
MGREC112:31 H2417 His Master is Accuser, Judge, and King,
MGREC113:1 H2428 The King would give no eare, but went from thence;
MGREC113:32 H2459 Who from a petty King of *Macedon,*
MGREC114:35 H2505 The mighty *Persian* King he over-came,
MGREC115:24 H2543 His doing so, no whit displeas'd the King,
MGREC115:30 H2549 The King doth intimate 'twas his intent,
MGREC115:33 H2552 And for his Counsell, ne're the King to live.
MGREC117:26 H2633 A King they'l have, but who, none can agree:
MGREC118:5 H2652 Some wished him, to take the stile of King,
MGREC118:27 H2676 *Perdicas,* seeing *Aridæus* must be King,
MGREC118:33 H2682 Using the name, and the command o'th' King
MGREC118:41 H2690 These now to govern for the King pretends,
MGREC120:21 H2758 Desires the King, to goe to *Macedon,*

MGREC122:13 H2838 Perceives {Sees} *Aridæus* must not king it long,
MGREC~~122:35~~ H2856 For all the Princes {nobles} of great {King} *Alexander*
MGREC122:38 H2859 The King, and Queen, along with him he takes. {to *Macedon*}
MGREC124:25 H2932 *Aridæus* the scorn'd, and simple King,
MGREC125:3 H2951 To make the King by force his seat resigne;
MGREC125:11 H2959 To come and succour {To save the King} her, in this great
MGREC125:20 H2968 Then {The} King, and Queen, to *Amphipolis* doe fly, {seeing
MGREC125:22 H2972 The King by extreame torments had his end,
MGREC128:1 H3074 The Mother of their King to death he'd put,
MGREC128:3 H3076 And how he aymes {aiming now} to make himselfe a King,
MGREC128:12 H3085 Which their late King in dust had damnified;
MGREC131:3 H3193 Not like a King, but like some God they fain'd;
MGREC131:36 H3228 Two sons he left, born of King *Philips* daughter,
MGREC132:16 H3251 And now as King, in *Macedon* he reigns;
MGREC133:37 H3327 Who a long warre with *Egypts* King begun.
MGREC134:13 H3344 That {Then} *Tygranes* the great *Armenian* King,
MROMAN136:23 H3437 Stout *Romulus, Romes* Founder, and first King,
MROMAN137:25 H3476 *Nvma Pompilius,* is next chosen {chose they} King,
MROMAN137:38 H3489 *Tullus Hostilius,* was third *Roman* King,
MROMAN139:11 H3539 *Roman* King. {of the Romans}
MROMAN139:23 H3551 And people sweare, ne're to accept of King.
DIALOG142:14 H43 Doe Barons rise, and side against their King?
DIALOG143:1 H70 Nor Nobles siding, to make *John* no King
DIALOG145:17 H166 'Twixt King and Peeres a question of state,
DIALOG145:18 H167 Which is the chief, the law, or else the King,
DIALOG145:38 H187 The King displeas'd, at *York* himself absents,
DIALOG147:19 H245 Not false to King, nor Countrey in thy heart, {to the better part;}
DIALOG147:30 H254 These, these, are they (I trust) with *Charles* our King,
SIDNEY149:14 H13 Of Poesie, and of Musick thou wert {he was} King;
SIDNEY150:18 ~~H49~~ A Crow's a Crow, and *Cæsar* is a King.
QELIZ156:27 H54 She frankly help'd *Franks* (brave) distressed King,
VANITY~~159:37~~ H9 He's now a slave {captive}, that was a Prince {King} of late.
VANITY161:2 H53 Who is possessed of, shall reign a King.
MYCHILD219:3 Hp245 Now to ye King Imortall, Eternall invisible, the only wise God,

KINGD: (1) [kingdom]
30SEPT227:27 Hp257 Kingd:

KINGDOM (3)
AGES44:30 H363 I've seen a Kingdom flourish like a tree,
MPERS70:2 ~~H673~~ Gave him at once, his life, and Kingdom too,
MGREC100:4 H1888 For in few dayes he brought that Kingdom under.

KINGDOME (6) [kingdom]
MASSYR67:19 H565 His Kingdome to *Belshazzar* did remain.
MPERS86:15 H1331 His interest, in the Kingdome, now next heir,
MGREC~~132:6~~ H3240 But he a Kingdome more then's friend did eye,
MGREC~~135:1~~ H3372 He seeing his honour lost, his Kingdome end,
MROMAN138:29 H3519 He after *Martius* death the Kingdome had,
MEDDM204:18 Hp285 as we see in Jehu, he is rewarded wth a kingdome to the fourth

KINGDOMES (10) [kingdoms] See also KINDGOMES, KINDOMES, TH'KINGDOMS
MPERS73:16 H803 (Who like to Kings, rul'd Kingdomes as they please,)
MGREC117:4 H2611 Of all those kingdomes large which he had got,
MGREC121:36 H2818 The others all, had kingdomes in their eye,

MGREC129:7 H3121 To render up such kingdomes as he had
MGREC130:36 ~~H3181~~ And's kingdomes rent away by each Commander:
MGREC131:35 H3227 And leaves the ill got kingdomes he had won,
MGREC132:15 H3250 *Demetrius,* {thus} *Cassanders* Kingdomes gains,
MGREC~~133:22~~ H3311 (Part of whose Kingdomes *Titus Quintius* won)
MGREC133:27 H3317 Whose kingdomes {Empire was} were subdu'd by {to} th'
MGREC134:16 H3347 Vanquish'd in fight, and took those kingdomes all,

KINGDOM'S (1) [kingdom is]
MGREC133:23 ~~H3312~~ He *Perseus,* from him the kingdom's won,

KINGDOMS (13) See also KINDGOMES, KINDOMES, KINGDOMES
MASSYR61:7 H312 He left his new got Kingdoms to his Son.
MPERS69:10 H632 And so unites two Kingdoms, without strife;
MPERS70:18 H689 This head of Kingdoms, *Caldes* excellence,
MPERS74:25 H848 That by such steps to Kingdoms often climbs {clime}.
MGREC99:2 H1845 All those rich Kingdoms large, which {that} doe abide
MGREC101:5 H1930 And offers all he did, and Kingdoms more;
MGREC101:11 H1936 And all those Kingdoms in lesse *Asia;*
MGREC114:37 H2507 All Kingdoms, Countries, Provinces, he won, {wan}
MGREC120:12 H2747 So many Kingdoms in their power to hold,
MGREC133:12 H3300 *Antigonus* his Kingdoms lost, and's life,
MGREC135:8 H3380 Thus Kings, and Kingdoms, have their times, and dates,
MGREC135:37 H3409 But how the fourth, their Kingdoms from them won;

KINGDOMS (1) [poss.]
MGREC109:32 H2291 Unto his Kingdoms borders, and as due,

KING-LIKE (1)
MPERS78:34 H1015 Then gives the King, a King-like gift, most {full} large;

KINGLY (8)
HUMOUR34:31 H586 Again, none's fit for Kingly place but thou,
MPERS74:8 H833 Praying to Fortune, for a Kingly power;
MGREC105:31 H2124 For all that {the} Kingly Grace he did expresse,
MGREC109:34 H2293 But Kingly *Porus* this brave answer sent,
MGREC~~110:18~~ H2319 The kingly Captive 'fore the Victor's brought,
MGREC110:19 H2323 His fortitude his Kingly {royal} foe commends;
MGREC113:7 H2434 Thy Kingly word can easily terminate;
MGREC133:6 H3294 Thus with these Kingly Captaines have we done,

KING'S (2) [king is]
MASSYR~~63:28~~ H414 This King's less fam'd for all the acts he's done,
MPERS89:29 H1463 The King's {King} perplext, there dares not let them stay,

KINGS (48)
PROLOG6:18 H3 To sing of Wars, of Captaines, and of Kings,
ELEMEN10:37 H112 The stately seats of mighty Kings by me:
ELEMEN11:7 H127 Which Kings, and mighty ones; amaz'd with wonder,
ELEMEN12:41 H201 Ye mighty Kings, who for your lasting fames
HUMOUR23:25 H135 The Princely quality, {qualities} befitting Kings.
HUMOUR32:37 H511 That Kings have laid their Scepters at my feet,
AGES~~43:8~~ H304 Then Kings must be depos'd or put to flight,
SEASONS49:21 H112 With robes thereof, Kings have been dignifi'd.
SEASONS~~49:23~~ H114 Hath envy bred in Kings that were at strife,
SEASONS49:24 ~~H114~~ Yet hath your life, made Kings the same envy,
SEASONS50:20 H154 Which after Manchet's made, {makes} for Kings to eat;
MASSYR~~57:19~~ H166 With petty Kings to joyne Confederate.

MASSYR61:11	H316	*Damascus,* ancient seat of famous Kings,
MASSYR64:5	H429	This was that King of Kings, did what he pleas'd,
MASSYR67:8	H554	Among the Conquered Kings, that there did lye,
MPERS71:10	H726	That Kings with Sisters match, no Law they finde,
MPERS73:16	H803	(Who like to Kings, rul'd Kingdomes as they please,)
MPERS75:34	H891	And on all Kings he poures out execrations,
MPERS79:6	H1028	Thou shame of Kings, of men the detestation,
MPERS85:34	H1310	(For *Persian* Kings, did deem {then deem'd} themselves so
MPERS89:31	H1465	But Kings ne're want such as can serve their will,
MPERS91:10	H1518	The Kings {on such} conditions they are forc't to take; {as King
MPERS91:40	~~H1554~~	Or else, perhaps the deeds of *Persian* Kings
MGREC93:11	H1608	He, to *Amintas,* Kings of *Macedon;*
MGREC98:26	H1828	For now's the time, Captains like Kings may live;
MGREC102:30	H2000	For 'twas the seat of *Persian* Kings renown'd;
MGREC102:32	H2002	Where Kings have shown their glory, wealth, and might;
MGREC103:9	H2020	Which {That} did pertain unto the *Persian* Kings.
MGREC105:27	H2120	Yet that succeeding Kings in safety may
MGREC109:1	H2258	He enters now {then} the *Indian* Kings among;
MGREC109:28	H2287	Thus all the *Indian* Kings, to him submit;
MGREC111:4	H2349	Came with submission, from the *Indian* Kings
MGREC118:17	H2664	A contemplation to astonish Kings,
MGREC125:18	H2966	The Wife, and Mother, of their famous Kings,
MGREC126:31	H3022	The Daughter, Sister, Mother, Wife to Kings,
MGREC128:9	H3082	And in despight of their two famous Kings,
MGREC130:39	H3184	These Captains now, the stile of Kings do take,
MGREC131:6	H3196	These Kings fall now afresh to {their} warres again,
MGREC~~131:14~~	H3206	This day twixt these two foes {Kings} ends all the strife,
MGREC133:19	H3307	Between those Kings, and noble *Pyrrus* stout,
MGREC133:39	H3329	And calls them there, the Kings of South, and North;
MGREC135:8	H3380	Thus Kings, and Kingdoms, have their times, and dates,
MROMAN138:9	H3499	Of *Latine* Kings this was long since the Seat,
DIALOG147:37	H261	That nursing Kings, shall come and lick thy dust:
QELIZ156:4	H31	From all the Kings on earth she won the prize;
QELIZ158:15	H124	*Here lies the pride of Queens, pattern of Kings,*
CONTEM174:30	H227	That draws oblivions curtains over kings,
VERSES184:7	H11	Where nothing's to be had Kings loose their right

KINGS (8) [poss.]

AGES37:32	H94	Nor studious was, Kings favours how to buy,
MASSYR58:34	H217	Prest for this service, by the Kings command;
MASSYR68:11	H597	None answers the affrighted Kings intent.
MPERS69:39	H669	With pitty *Cyrus* mov'd, knowing Kings stand,
MPERS72:9	~~H757~~	Accomplished this wicked Kings intent;
MPERS78:41	H1022	The Kings cals for the Youth, who being brought,
MPERS90:32	H1499	By th' Kings Lieutenant {*Tissaphernes*} is encountered,
MGREC95:18	H1697	Now newes, of *Memnons* death (the Kings Vice-roy)

KINSFOLK (1)

MGREC125:32	H2982	His Brethern, Kinsfolk, and his chiefest friends,

KINSMAN (1)

MGREC102:34	H2004	And of good *Mordecai,* her Kinsman dear;

KINSMEN (2)

MPERS73:18	H805	And kinsmen in account, to th'King they stood,

MGREC94:6 H1640 His kinsmen puts {put} to death without least {who gave no}

KISS (1)

BIRTH180:19 H29 And kiss this paper for thy loves dear sake,

KISSE (2) [kiss]

MPERS74:12 ~~H836~~ And after *Persian* manner, kisse his feet.

MYSOUL224:27 H3 Walk in his Law, and kisse his Rod

KITCHIN (2) [kitchen]

ELEMEN9:16 H50 Ye Cooks, your kitchin implements I fram'd, {frame}

HUMOUR31:10 H443 The Kitchin Drudge, the cleanser of the sinks,

KNACKS (1)

DUBART153:19 H23 To comprehend the worth of all those knacks;

KNAW (1) [gnaw]

TDUDLEY165:14 H16 Let malice bite, and envy knaw its fill,

KNEE (2)

MASSYR63:14 H399 Until his Grand-childe made her bow the knee;

MPERS71:22 H736 Made *Evelthon* their King, with bended knee,

KNEEL (1)

HOURS233:31 H14 Where I doe kneel or walk.

KNEES (2) [pl.]

MASSYR68:3 H589 With quaking knees, and heart appall'd, he crys,

MROMAN140:9 H3572 Hath many Ages been upon his knees.

KNEW (16)

ELEMEN14:4 H246 *Korah* {*Dathan*} and all his Company well knew.

HUMOUR20:18 H10 Earth knew her black swarth childe, Water her faire;

HUMOUR24:36 H185 He knew {well} how, for to handle, Sword and Harpe,

AGES36:35 H59 That each should tel, what of himselfe he knew;

SEASONS~~53:4~~ H260 *I could {knew} not tell how to passe't by:*

MASSYR62:36 H381 'Twixt them and *Israels* he knew no odds. [7 *years.*

MASSYR64:29 H453 That in her pride, she knew not which to boast,

MPERS81:8 H1116 Who for his sake, he knew, would venture far,

MPERS82:29 H1176 When jealous Queen *Amestris,* of this knew,

MGREC113:16 H2443 They knew not; wherefore, best now to be done,

MGREC122:17 H2842 She knew her birthright gave her *Macedon,*

DIALOG148:16 H281 To th' 'stonishment of all that knew his state,

TDUDLEY165:12 H14 Who heard or saw, observ'd or knew him better?

CHILDRN185:30 H56 And knew what thoughts there sadly rest,

ANNEB187:24 H14 I knew she was but as a withering flour,

MYCHILD215:25 Hp240 my wayes, & what I knew was sinfull as lying, disobed[c]. to

KNIFE (1)

MROMAN139:17 H3545 And shed her guiltlesse blood, with guilty knife,

KNIGHT (3)

MPERS84:16 H1252 This valiant Knight, whom they so much did owe;

MPERS92:31 H1589 With our judicious learned {learned and judicious} Knight to

SIDNEY149:2 H2 and renowned Knight,

KNIGHTLY (1)

HUMOUR24:39 H188 And scorn'st all Knightly sports, at turnament.

KNIGHTS (2) [pl.]

HUMOUR33:3 H517 Sixty nine Princes, all stout *Hero* Knights,

AGES39:16 H159 The brave attempts of valiant Knights I prize,

KNOCKS (2)

AGES38:35 H138 What breaches, knocks, and falls I daily have?

MGREC121:17 H2799 Knocks out his braines, to *Ptolomy* then went,

KNOCKT (1)

MGREC124:36 H2943 When *Alexander* knockt his head to th' wall:

KNOT (2)

PROLOG7:25 H37 But this weake knot they will full soone untye,
MGREC95:16 H1695 There {where} the Prophetick knot, he cuts in twain;

KNOT'S (1) [knot is]

BIRTH180:3 H13 That when that knot's unty'd that made us one,

KNOTTY (1)

AGES43:31 H326 The knotty {Cramp and} Gout doth sadly torture me,

KNOW (59)

FATHER5:8 H9 Their paralells to find I scarcely know,
PROLOG7:31 H42 Men can doe best, and Women know it well;
ELEMEN8:30 H28 What is my worth (both ye) and all things {men} know,
ELEMEN13:39 H240 Before they know, they are inter'd alive.
ELEMEN15:26 H308 There lives the oyly Whale, whom all men know,
ELEMEN17:15 H379 My Ice and extream cold, which all men know.
ELEMEN17:22 H386 All know, what {that} innundations I have made;
ELEMEN18:2 H406 Yet Aire, beyond all these ye know t'excell.
ELEMEN~~19:33~~ H474 Knowes {Know} Western Isles, *Christophers, Barbadoes;*
ELEMEN19:39 H480 As battells pitcht ith' Aire (as Countries know;)
HUMOUR21:8 H36 We both once Masculines, the world doth know,
HUMOUR23:36 H146 Again, ye know, how I act every part:
HUMOUR24:18 H167 Do'st know thy selfe so well, us so amisse?
HUMOUR25:1 H190 But know, I love the blade, more then the hilt. {Hill;}
HUMOUR25:35 H224 Nay; {No,} know 'tis pride, most diabolical.
HUMOUR29:23 H374 Know, in a General its most pernicious.
HUMOUR31:28 H461 And what Flegme is, we know, likewise {like to} her mother,
AGES37:25 H87 That its own worth, it did not know, nor mind.
AGES38:26 H129 Then nought can please, and yet I know not why.
AGES39:13 H156 Of Science, Arts, and Tongues, I know the rules,
AGES39:14 H157 The manners of the Court, I likewise {also} know,
AGES40:3 H184 I know no Law, nor reason, but my wil;
MASSYR62:28 H373 But what, or where they are, yet know we this;
MPERS73:39 H824 What arguments they us'd, I know not well,
MPERS~~91:27~~ H1541 Such as would know at large his warrs and reign,
MGREC97:37 H1798 But of *Darius* King, as he should know.
MGREC97:39 H1800 (His valour, and his victories they know)
MGREC119:7 H2697 That none might know, to frustrate his intent;
MGREC119:23 H2713 His Lady take i'th' way, and no man know.
MGREC120:13 H2748 Yet to regain them, how he did not know,
MGREC130:10 H3165 Untill he further know his Masters will;
MROMAN136:27 H3441 Thus he deceiv'd his Neece, she might not know
DIALOG142:3 H32 If th' wound's {wound} so dangerous I may not know?
SIDNEY150:15 ~~H49~~ Yet great *Augustus* was content (we know)
QELIZ156:29 H56 She their Protectrix was, they well doe know,
QELIZ156:40 H67 *Terra incognitae* might know her {the} sound;
QELIZ157:37 H105 Know 'tis a slander now, but once was treason.
TDUDLEY165:26 H28 One of thy Founders, him *New-England* know,
CONTEM168:2 H12 Whose power and beauty by his works we know.
CONTEM172:35 H168 So nature taught, and yet you know not why,

CONTEM172:36 H169 You watry folk that know not your felicity.
CONTEM174:31 H228 Their sumptuous monuments, men know them not,
SICKNES179:11 H31 For ever know, thou envious foe,
BIRTH180:7 H17 The many faults that well you know I have,
VERSES184:4 H8 My stock's so small, I know not how to pay,
CHILDRN185:18 H44 Let others know what are my fears
PILGRIM210:30 H30 Nor losses know, nor sorrowes see.
MYCHILD215:14 Hp240 to compose some short matters, (for w[t] else to call y[m] I know
MYCHILD217:33 Hp243 many times by Atheisme how I could know whether there was
MYCHILD217:35 Hp243 how did know but they were feigned. That there is a God my
MYCHILD218:4 Hp243 me that there is an Eternall Being. But how should I know he is
MYCHILD218:14 Hp244 + how y[e] world came to bee as wee see, Do wee not know y[e]
MYCHILD218:36 Hp244 + if I perish, I perish, But I know all y[e] powers of Hell shall
MYCHILD219:1 Hp245 prevail against it, I know whom I haue trvsted, and whom I
WHAT224:15 H15 I find his Love, I know his pow'r.
MYSOUL225:13 H17 Then shall I know what thov hast done
HOURS234:7 H21 And when I know not what to doe
HOURS234:9 H23 My weaknes thou do'st know full well,
HOUSE236:18 H10 Let no man know is my Desire.

KNOWES (18) [knows]

ELEMEN13:32 H233 The Husband knowes no Wife, nor father sons;
ELEMEN14:5 H249 And since, faire *Italy* full sadly knowes
ELEMEN14:30 H272 Not one of us, all knowes, that's like to thee,
ELEMEN15:11 H293 He knowes such sweets, lyes not in earths dry roots,
ELEMEN16:18 H341 Which wondring *Aristotles* wit, ne'r knowes.
ELEMEN19:33 H474 Knowes {Know} Western Isles, *Christophers, Barbadoes;*
MPERS88:28 H1421 His Host in chase, knowes not of his {this} disaster,
MPERS88:31 H1424 Who knowes the sudden change made by this chance;
DIALOG143:10 H79 None knowes which is the Red, or which the White:
DIALOG143:12 H81 *France* knowes, how of {oft} my fury she hath drunk;
DIALOG143:20 H89 And for the Pestilence, who knowes how neare;
SIDNEY149:38 H25 Who knowes the Spels that in thy {his} Rethorick lurks?
MEDDM200:35 Hp280 heauenly father (who knowes our mould) lay such afflictions
MEDDM204:33 Hp285 produced wth much labour (as the husbandman well knowes)
MYCHILD217:20 Hp243 world knowes not, & haue sett vp my Ebenez[r]. and haue
MED223:2 Hp250 Consolations w[ch] the world knowes not.
28AUG225:33 Hp254 by it— And if he knowes that weaknes, & a frail body is y[e] best
28AUG226:2 Hp254 but joyfully? The Lord knowes I dare not desire that health

KNOWEST (4) See also KNOW'ST

ELEMEN13:13 H214 Well knowest, my fuell must maintain thy fire.
SOREFIT221:20 H6 Thou knowest the sorrowes y[t] I felt
11MAYB228:32 Hp259 to doe. Lord Thou y[t] knowest All things know'st that I desire to
2HUSB232:20 H21 Thov knowest did submitt

KNOWING (8)

AGES46:10 H441 Yea knowing much, the pleasant'st {pleasants} life of all,
MASSYR58:5 H190 Knowing his basenesse, and the peoples hate,
MPERS69:39 H669 With pitty *Cyrus* mov'd, knowing Kings stand,
MPERS89:33 H1467 As *Tyssaphern,* knowing his Masters minde,
MGREC124:7 ~~H2912~~ *Polisperchon,* knowing he did relye
DUBART153:2 H6 But knowing th' taske so great, and strength but small,
MEDDM196:19 Hp273 ioy, knowing his refreshing is at hand

MYCHILD215:10 Hp240 I knowing by exper^{c}. y^{t} ye exhortat^{s}. of parents take most

KNOWLEDG (2) [knowledge]

CONTEM168:34 H40 All mortals here the feeling knowledg hath.
CONTEM173:35 H199 In knowledg ignorant, in strength but weak,

KNOWLEDGE (1)

MGREC104:33 H2085 *Bessus* gets knowledge, his disloyalty,

KNOWN (20)

ELEMEN19:18 H463 Yea so contagious, Countries have me {we} known;
ELEMEN19:25 H470 If nought was {were} known, but that before *Algire.*
HUMOUR27:3 H274 Besides the vehement heat, only there known,
AGES39:32 H175 This is my best, but youth (is known) alas,
SEASONS47:34 ~~H47~~ Yet never minute stil was known to stand,
MASSYR57:26 ~~H172~~ Which to her neighbours, when it was made known,
MASSYR60:38 H303 In sacred Writ, he's known by name of *Pul,*
MPERS69:33 H655 *Cressus* thus known, it was great *Cyrus* doome,
MPERS87:22 ~~H1374~~ Not worthy to be known, but for his shame:
MGREC101:37 H1966 But 'tis not known what slaughters here they {was} made.
MGREC104:13 H2065 Next day this treason, to *Darius* known,
DIALOG146:7 H195 I that no warres, so many yeares have known,
VANITY160:17 H27 He knows not all, that here is to be known,
TDUDLEY165:20 H22 Well known and lov'd, where ere he liv'd, by most
TDUDLEY165:22 H24 These to the world his merits could make known,
CONTEM168:21 H29 Had I not better known, (alas) the same had I.
AUTHOR178:12 H22 And take thy way where yet thou art not known,
MYCHILD218:31 Hp244 Faith vpon ye Earth? & I haue not known what to think, But
MED223:11 Hp250 them known who or where is the man that durst in his heart
ACK235:8 H8 Hast known my doubts and All my feares,

KNOWNE (3) [knowne]

HUMOUR28:14 H326 The bitter choler, most malignant knowne
MPERS83:20 H1208 But in short time, this wickednesse was knowne,
DUBART152:34 H3 Great, deare, sweet *Bartas,* thou art matchlesse knowne;

KNOWS (10) See also KNOWES

MPERS91:1 H1509 He knows that many towns in *Greece* envies
MGREC114:39 H2509 All this he did, who knows not to be true,
MGREC129:41 H3155 He knows to's profit, all i'th end {this at last} will turn,
DIALOG146:12 H200 Who knows, the worst, the best {this} may {be my} overthrow;
DIALOG146:20 H206 Because he knows not, who shall inn his crop:
VANITY160:16 H26 And he that knows the most doth still bemoan,
VANITY160:17 H27 He knows not all, that here is to be known,
DISTEMP179:15 H3 And wasting pains, which best my body knows,
MERCY189:16 H37 He knows it is the best for thee and me.
MEDDM200:34 Hp280 he knows is enough for one of twice his strength, much lesse

KNOW'ST (8)

HUMOUR24:35 H184 A rosie cheek'd {cheek} musitian, thou know'st wel.
HUMOUR26:40 H270 Thou know'st I've there to do, as wel as thou;
FLESH176:27 H67 For I have meat thou know'st not off;
FEVER221:3 H18 O heal my Soul thov know'st I said,
SOREFIT222:3 H22 Thou know'st no life I did require
11MAYB228:32 Hp259 doe. Lord Thou y^{t} knowest All things know'st that I desire to
2HUSB232:25 H26 O Lord thov know'st my weak desires
REMB235:26 H7 O Lord thov know'st I'm weak.

KNOWST (2)
DIALOG142:38 H67 For they have work enough (thou knowst) elsewhere;
FEVER221:1 H16 Thov knowst my heart, and hast me try'd
KNOW'TH (1)
HUMOUR26:20 H250 As plants, trees, and small Embryon know'th,
KNOW'TS (1) [know it is]
HUMOUR22:36 H105 But know'ts a foolish brain, that wanteth heat;
KORAH (1)
ELEMEN14:4 H246 *Korah* {*Dathan*} and all his Company well knew.

L

LAB'RINTHS (1) [labyrinths]
SIDNEY151:21 H71 But now into such Lab'rinths am I led
LABORER (1)
AGES42:14 H272 Was I a laborer, I wrought all day,
LABOUR (10)
AGES45:36 H426 I cannot labour, nor {much less} I cannot {can} fight:
SEASONS49:18 H109 In the coole streames they labour with delight,
MASSYR56:11 H117 Bestow'd their labour, and receiv'd their pay,
MPERS76:2 H900 Over fair *Ister,* at a {with labour and with} mighty charge;
VANITY160:1 H11 No, that's but labour anxious, care and pain.
CHILDRN184:17 H6 Nor cost, nor labour did I spare,
MEDDM199:19 Hp278 Much Labour wearys the body, and many thoughts oppresse
MEDDM203:4 Hp283 what do we obtaine of all these things, but it is wth labour and
MEDDM204:33 Hp285 Corne is produced wth much labour (as the husbandman well
11MAYA226:18 Hp255 of Baca many pools of water, That wch now I cheifly labour
LABOURER See LABORER
LABOURERS (1) [pl.]
MEDDM199:31 Hp278 Sore labourers haue hard hands and old sinners haue brawnie
LABOURS (7) [pl.]
AGES42:25 H283 Great labours, sorrows, crosses I sustain'd.
AGES46:4 H435 In pleasures, and in labours, I have found,
AGES46:14 H445 My studies, labours, readings, all are done,
MGREC124:12 H2919 Whom *Polisperchon* labours to oppose,
MGREC124:19 H2926 Still labours *Eumenes* might {would} with him side,
TDUDLEY166:22 H64 His Generation serv'd his labours cease;
MEDDM196:14 Hp273 The hireling that labours all the day comforts himself, that
LABYRINTHS (1) See also LAB'RINTHS
MGREC122:8 H2831 Himself from out of labyrinths intricate.
LACE (1)
SEASONS48:2 H55 These might as Lace, set out her Garments fine;
LACEDEMONS (1) [pl.]
MPERS86:33 H1349 Then next, the *Lacedemons* {*Spartans*} he takes to {into} pay;

LACK (4)
MASSYR67:13 H559 Prudence, and magnanimity, did lack
MROMAN140:7 H3570 Although my Monarchies their legs do lack:
QELIZ156:8 H35 That women wisdome lack to play the Rex;
ACK235:18 H18 Whose p^rsence I so much doe lack.
LACKS (1)
DUBART153:18 H22 He feeds his eyes, but understanding lacks,
LACKT (1)
MPERS89:5 H1439 Nor lackt they any of their number small,
LACRIM (1)
FLESH175:3 H3 Close by the Banks of *Lacrim* flood
LAD (1)
SEASONS49:16 H107 Now go those frolick swaines, the shepheard lad,
LADED (1)
QELIZ156:41 H68 Her *Drake* came laded home with *Spanish* gold,
LADEN (1)
MASSYR62:16 H361 Laden with honour, prisoners, and with spoyl,
LADIES (5) [pl.] See also LADYES
MGREC97:8 H1769 Besides, the Queens, and Ladies of the Court,
MGREC97:30 H1791 Those mournfull Ladies, from captivity,
MGREC99:11 H1854 But th'Kingdoms, and the Ladies, {Lady} soone accept;
MGREC112:3 H2389 He fourscore *Persian* Ladies also gave;
DUBART153:21 H25 The Hats, and Fans, the Plumes, and Ladies tires,
LADY (7)
MPERS69:2 H624 Whom Lady *Mandana* did to him bring;
MPERS82:30 H1177 She *Harpy*-like, upon the Lady flew:
MPERS~~91:22~~ H1536 (A Lady very wicked, but yet wise)
MGREC~~99:11~~ H1854 But th'Kingdoms, and the Ladies, {Lady} soone accept;
MGREC119:6 H2696 So, to the Lady secretly he sent,
MGREC119:23 H2713 His Lady take i'th' way, and no man know.
MGREC131:27 H3219 Is for this fresh young Lady half {quite} undone,
LADYES (1) [ladies]
MGREC95:37 H1716 Along with him, the {greatest} Ladyes of the Court.
LAID (29)
ELEMEN8:26 H24 All stormes now laid, and they in perfect peace,
ELEMEN13:3 H204 That you ambition laid, ought but my bones?
HUMOUR29:12 H365 But when the first offenders {offender} I have laid,
HUMOUR32:37 H511 That Kings have laid their Scepters at my feet,
HUMOUR34:35 H590 Wel, to be breif, Choler I hope now's laid,
AGES41:8 H228 And I in black oblivions den long {now} laid;
AGES41:29 H246 But yet laid hold, on vertue seemingly,
MASSYR53:23 H13 The strong foundation of proud *Babel* laid,
MASSYR54:19 H46 Whose foundation was by his Grand-sire laid;
MASSYR67:2 H548 *Babels* great Monarch, now laid in the dust,
MPERS~~79:2~~ H1024 Then laid his parts on both sides of the way,
MPERS79:11 H1033 Of Boats, together coupled, and there laid;
MPERS80:4 H1071 Laid on more fiercely, their deep mortall blowes;
MPERS88:36 H1429 And heaps on heaps, such multitudes they laid,
MGREC103:18 H2029 On their old Governours, titles he laid;
MGREC~~116:10~~ H2572 She laid it more to heart, then any other,
MGREC116:24 H2590 And under's pillow laid them when he slept.

MGREC118:11 H2658 He hold of {on} this occasion should have laid,
MGREC119:14 H2704 would} Shakes {shake} off the yoke, sometimes before laid on
MGREC120:38 H2775 And yet till now, at quiet was not laid.
MGREC123:12 H2874 That {And} by the selfe-same traps the other laid,
MGREC127:8 H3038 Among their Ancestors by him there {they're} laid,
MGREC128:38 H3111 Sought for a peace, and laid aside their jarres:
MROMAN139:33 H3559 All thoughts of further progress laid aside,
DIALOG144:6 H116 How many Princely heads on blocks laid down,
CONTEM171:24 H127 But Man grows old, lies down, remains where once he's laid.
CONTEM174:33 H230 Their parts, their ports, their pomp's all laid in th' dust
FLESH175:18 H18 Hast treasures there laid up in store
FLESH176:3 H43 Untill I see thee laid in th' dust.

LAKE (2)
ELEMEN16:8 H331 *Asphaltis* Lake, where nought remains alive.
MPERS79:32 H1058 And for his Cattell, all *Pissirus* Lake

LAKES (2) [pl.]
ELEMEN16:4 H327 Then I have Fountaines, Rivers, Lakes and Ponds:
CONTEM172:34 H167 In Lakes and ponds, you leave your numerous fry,

LAMB (1)
MEDDM198:35 Hp277 behold the presence of the lamb

LAMBE (1) [lamb]
MGREC135:35 H3407 All trembling stand, before that powerfull Lambe.

LAMBES (1) [lambs]
AGES42:9 H267 And gently lead the lambes, as they had need,

LAMBS (2) [pl.]
SEASONS47:20 H36 The wanton frisking Kids, and soft fleec'd Lambs,
SEASONS47:39 H51 growes long, the tender Lambs {hungry beast} to nourish;

LAMBS (1) [poss.]
FLESH177:14 H95 Which doth proceed from the Lambs Throne:

LAME (1)
AGES43:32 H327 And the restraining lame Sciatica;

LAMENESSE (1) [lameness]
MYCHILD216:12 Hp241 together wth a lamenesse wch correction I saw the Lord sent to

LAMENT (7)
MGREC100:34 H1918 {Whose death} her wofull Lord for to {full sadly did} lament.
MGREC116:35 H2601 This conquerour did oft lament ('tis sed)
MGREC126:36 H3025 The Authours death she did so much lament,
DIALOG141:28 H27 Let me lament alone, while thou art glad.
DIALOG145:8 H157 Your fearfull sinnes, great cause there's to lament,
TDUDLEY167:4 H86 *If some rejoyc'd, more did lament.*
CHILDRN186:8 H75 My age I will not once lament,

LAMENTATION (2)
MGREC127:9 H3039 And shewes of lamentation for them made.
DAVID158:22 H1-2 *Davids* Lamentation for *Saul,*

LAMENTATIONS (1) [pl.]
TDUDLEY165:7 H9 Presents my Lamentations at his Herse,

LAMENTS (1)
MGREC122:2 H2825 And his beloved foe, full sore laments.

LAMIA (2)
MGREC119:17 H2707 To *Lamia,* where he shut up doth ly:
MGREC119:35 H2725 Blockt up in *Lamia,* still by his foes;

LAMIAN (1)
MGREC120:3 H2734 Now dy'd (about the end of th' *Lamian* warre)
LANCASTRIANS (1) [pl.]
DIALOG143:4 H73 Nor no *Lancastrians,* to renew old strife;
LANCE (1) See also LAUNCE
ELEMEN~~9:3~~ H37 My force? your sword, & Gun, your lance of steel
LANCES See LAUNCES
LANCHES (1) [launches]
3LETTER183:17 H19 But lanches on that shore, there for to dye,
LANCHING (1) [launching]
MPERS~~76:38~~ H936 He stayes a landing {lanching} Gally with his hand;
LAND (55)
ELEMEN~~14:16~~ H258 Which rise like mighty {tumbling} billowes on the lands: {Land}
ELEMEN17:10 H374 And but one land was *Affrica* and *Spayne,*
ELEMEN19:22 H467 Then of my tempests, felt at Sea and Land,
AGES38:8 H111 Nor evidence for land, {lands} did me perplex.
AGES~~45:2~~ H377 I've seen a Prince, the glory of our land
AGES~~45:4~~ H384 And Land & Nobels sav'd with their anointed.
AGES45:19 ~~H401~~ I've seen a land unmoulded with great paine.
MASSYR53:25 H15 These were his first, all stood in *Shinar* land,
MASSYR61:33 H338 All *Israels* Land, {lands} beyond *lordan,* he takes.
MASSYR62:18 H363 {He} Plac'd *Israel* in's Land {there}, where he thought best,
MASSYR65:3 H468 The Sea firm Land, whereon the Army past,
MASSYR66:22 H528 Where e're he goes, he Conquers every Land;
MPERS~~71:4~~ H720 To shew how little Land he then should take.
MPERS71:17 H731 He seized first of life, and then of Land;
MPERS78:15 H996 These {Such} his Land Forces were, then next, a Fleet
MPERS79:28 H1054 His answer was, both Land and Sea he feared,
MPERS80:13 H1080 And as at Land, so he at Sea was crost,
MPERS80:19 H1086 But they as valiant by {fortunate at} Sea, as Land,
MPERS80:28 H1095 But {the} *Phocians* Land, {Country} he then wasted sore:
MPERS~~84:32~~ H1268 And to his Country-men {native land} could bear no hate.
MPERS~~91:40~~ H1554 Then raises forces, conquers *Egypt* land,
MGREC94:17 H1651 Comming to land, his dart on shoar he throwes,
MGREC94:40 H1678 And think {strive} to keep his men from off the land,
MGREC98:16 H1818 The other by his men fetcht all by Land;
MGREC100:18 H1902 Great *Alexander* had been kept from Land;
MGREC105:34 H2127 Praying the immortall gods, that Sea, and Land,
MGREC107:29 H2204 How to passe {the River} over, and gaine {to} the other Land;
MGREC109:17 H2276 And *Omphis,* King of that part of the land:
MGREC~~109:21~~ H2280 And tenders him the strength of all his lands, {land;}
MGREC110:2 H2302 to receive {To give} him, {welcome} when he comes to land;
MGREC116:12 H2578 And Conquests be talkt of, whilst there is Land;
MGREC120:35 H2772 At *Alexandria,* in *Ægypt* Land, {his tomb he plac'd}
MGREC~~124:7~~ H2912 With ships at Sea, an Army for the Land,
MGREC124:13 H2920 the worst {beaten was} at Sea, as well as {and foil'd at} Land,
MGREC~~131:9~~ H3200 Their fights by Sea, their victories by land,
DIALOG142:11 H40 With *English* blood bedews thy conquered Land?
DIALOG143:22 H91 Destruction to a Land doth soone afford;
DIALOG143:26 H95 To shew the grievance of my troubled Land;
DIALOG144:3 H113 Did ever Land prophannesse more expresse?

DIALOG144:23	H133	That cry'd, destruction to my wicked Land:
DIALOG144:37	H145	Her fruitfull land, a barren heath remain.
DIALOG145:21	H170	To ease my groaning land shew {shew'd} their intent,
DIALOG146:38	H224	Blest be the Nobles of thy Noble Land,
DIALOG148:29	H294	No Canaanite shall then be found ith' land,
SIDNEY149:9	H8	No lesse {As well} an Honour to our *British* Land,
SIDNEY151:7	~~H69~~	That such an omen once was in our land,
DUBART154:36	H81	And whilst there's aire, or fire, or sea or land.
QELIZ156:20	H47	Was ever Land more happy, freed from stirs?
CONTEM170:35	H105	A Vagabond to Land of *Nod* he goes,
MEDDM203:17	Hp283	before he sees land we must therfore be heer as strangers and
MEDDM204:34	Hp285	and some land askes much more paines, then some other doth
MEDDM205:1	Hp285	(like sowre land) are of so tough and morose a dispotion that
SAMUEL228:2	H3	Thou mighty God of Sea and Land
SON231:2	H14	That he before them gott to Land.
SON231:14	H26	To th' Land of his Nativity.
LANDED (1)		
MPERS71:21	H735	Who landed {landing} soon upon that fruitful coast,
LANDING (2)		
MPERS~~71:21~~	H735	Who landed {landing} soon upon that fruitful coast,
MPERS76:38	H936	He stayes a landing {lanching} Gally with his hand;
LANDLORD (1)		
MEDDM207:23	Hp289	pleases our great landlord to let: All haue their bounds set ouer
LANDS (11) [pl.]		
ELEMEN14:16	H258	Which rise like mighty {tumbling} billowes on the lands: {Land}
AGES~~38:8~~	H111	Nor evidence for land, {lands} did me perplex.
AGES~~45:4~~	H385	I've Princes seen to live on others lands;
AGES45:7	~~H390~~	I've seen a Prince, to live on others lands,
MASSYR58:24	~~H207~~	*Arbaces* must be master of their lands.
MASSYR60:18	H283	Incroached {Incroaching} stil upon the bord'ring Lands,
MASSYR~~61:33~~	H338	All *Israels* Land, {lands} beyond *Iordan,* he takes.
MGREC102:37	H2007	And furniture, the richest of {in} all Lands,
MGREC109:21	H2280	And tenders him the strength of all his lands, {land;}
MGREC126:2	H2993	Sea passage gets, and lands in *Thessaly;*
MGREC128:18	H3091	*Seleuchus* drove {driven} from government, and lands;
LANGUAGE (3)		
HUMOUR24:16	H165	Did ever sober tongue, such language speak?
MASSYR68:5	H591	This language strange, to read, and to unfold;
DIALOG143:36	H105	From *Beelzebub* himself, such language heare?
LANGUAGES (1) [pl.]		
CHILDRN186:18	H85	In chirping languages, oft them tell,
LANGUISHING (1)		
HUMOUR28:9	H321	Her languishing diseases, though not quick,
LANKE (1) [lank]		
MROMAN140:1	H3564	And weary lines (though lanke) I many pen'd:
LAP (3)		
SEASONS50:36	H170	Then drops his Fruits into the Eaters lap.
DIALOG144:32	H140	And will repay it sevenfold in my lap,
CONTEM170:7	H80	And in her lap, her bloody *Cain* new born,
LAP-LAND (1)		
SEASONS51:40	H216	Now *Green-land, Groen-land, Lap-land, Fin-land,* see

LARG (1) [large]
MEDDM200:19 Hp279 of the person he bestowes them on, larg indowments of
LARGE (21)
HUMOUR28:30 H342 A most volumnious large memory,
AGES44:14 H347 It's not my Learning, Rhetorick, wit so large,
SEASONS48:32 ~~H83~~ Sometime a theame that's large, proves barren fields.
MPERS75:28 H885 He like a King, now grants a Charter large,
MPERS75:41 H898 Entring that large and barren country far;
MPERS78:4 H985 That the large {vast} *Persian* government surrounded;
MPERS78:34 H1015 Then gives the King, a King-like gift, most {full} large;
MPERS~~84:12~~ H1242 Did for the Jews commission large obtain,
MPERS86:7 H1323 His large Dominions left, to's eldest son.
MPERS~~91:27~~ H1541 Such as would know at large his warrs and reign,
MGREC93:25 H1622 universe, scarce bounds {bound} his large {proud} vast minde;
MGREC97:1 H1762 Most basely run {ran}, and left their King at large,
MGREC99:2 H1845 All those rich Kingdoms large, which {that} doe abide
MGREC117:4 H2611 Of all those kingdomes large which he had got,
MGREC~~122:8~~ H2832 He that at large would satisfie his mind,
MGREC~~127:41~~ H3072 *Cassanders* outrages at large doth tell,
MGREC132:18 H3255 Those Countries large, his father got before,
MGREC~~134:2~~ H3334 Whose large Dominions after was made small,
MROMAN139:31 H3557 The subject large my mind and body weak,
SIDNEY151:39 ~~H75~~ I leave't in brief, *Apollo* do't at large.
MEDDM209:23 Hp291 be neuer so large, yet he stands in need of something w^{ch}
LARGER (3)
MGREC110:28 H2332 And for his Souldiers larger Cabins make;
MGREC115:32 H2551 Of larger Provinces, the rule to give,
MEDDM204:10 Hp284 w^{th}all, the larger his accounts stands vpon gods score it
LARKE (1)
ELEMEN19:9 H454 The Pye {Thrush}, the Jay {wren}, the Larke, a prey to th'
LAST (98) [hindmost; final]
ELEMEN17:35 H399 Content (quoth Aire) to speake the last of you,
HUMOUR20:28 H20 The second, third, or last could not digest;
HUMOUR28:12 H324 Ith' last concoction, segregation make.
HUMOUR30:30 H422 The first it draines, o'th' last quicks appetite,
AGES35:25 H11 The last, of earth, and heavy melancholly,
AGES35:37 H23 But if he hold, til it have run its last,
AGES36:19 H43 And last of al, to act upon this Stage;
AGES44:7 H340 And on this Stage am come to act my last:
AGES44:37 H370 But ah, I saw at last those eyes to close:
AGES46:15 H446 And my last period now e'n almost run;
SEASONS46:29 H5 Of four times four, the last quaternian;
SEASONS47:5 H19 Stil adds to th' last, til after pleasant *May;*
SEASONS48:9 H62 My next, and last, is pleasant fruitfull *May,*
SEASONS50:11 H145 My next, and last, is *August,* fiery hot,
SEASONS51:34 H210 *November* is my last, for time doth haste,
SEASONS52:32 H247 Moyst snowie *February* is my last,
SEASONS53:5 H261 *The last, though bad, I could not mend,*
MASSYR56:34 H140 This was last progresse of this mighty Queen,
MASSYR58:7 H192 At last {It chanc'd} *Arbaces* brave, unwarily,
MASSYR58:17 H202 The last, the *Medes* and *Persians* doth invite.

MASSYR59:32	H256	This the last Monarch was, of {great} *Ninus* race,
MASSYR62:4	H349	*Hoshea,* their last King, he did invade,
MASSYR63:3	H388	The fifth, and last, of great *Belosus* race;
MASSYR64:9	H433	This Prince, the last year of his Fathers reign,
MASSYR65:2	H467	Where after many assayes, they make {made} at last,
MASSYR65:29	H494	Who was last King of holy *Davids* race;
MPERS72:34	H778	At last, two of his Officers he hears,
MPERS77:23	H964	But for the last he made such preparation,
MPERS~~79:15~~	H1041	Firmly at length, {last} accomplished his wil;
MPERS83:10	H1198	At last his Uncle, did his death conspire,
MPERS~~87:4~~	H1360	The one {last} accus'd the other, {first} for these {sad} wars:
MPERS87:13	H1369	The fearfull King, at last, musters his Forces;
MPERS88:30	H1423	At {But when} last his head they spy upon a Launce,
MPERS88:40	H1433	At last, displayes his Ensigne on a Hil,
MPERS90:38	H1505	Of that false perjur'd wretch, this was the last {fate},
MPERS92:33	H1591	That this *Darius* was last *Persian* King,
MPERS93:3	H1600	And last; a sad catastrophe to end,
MGREC103:39	H2050	Had now his fourth, and last Army compounded,
MGREC105:3	H2096	And leaves him thus, to gaspe out his last breath.
MGREC~~109:5~~	H2264	How to submit their necks at last they're glad.
MGREC110:14	H2314	The last set on his back, and so prevail'd:
MGREC110:16	H2316	For to the last, stout *Porus* kept his ground.
MGREC110:41	H2345	His fourth, and last supply, was hither sent,
MGREC111:39	H2384	He at the last to royall *Sushan* went;
MGREC112:20	H2406	*Philotas* was not least, nor yet the last;
MGREC113:12	H2439	At last he did: So they were justified,
MGREC114:9	H2477	From jeast, to earnest, and at last so bold,
MGREC116:20	H2586	Might to the last (when sober) be discern'd.
MGREC117:39	H2646	After much tumult, they at last proclaim'd
MGREC122:29	H2848	He wearied out, at last, would needs be gone,
MGREC123:41	H2905	And for that great gift, which he gave him last;
MGREC124:20	H2927	But to the last {all in vain} he faithfull did abide;
MGREC126:19	H3010	*Olimpias* wills to keep it, {means to hold out} to the last,
MGREC128:37	H3110	At last these Princes tired out with warres,
MGREC129:17	H3131	But yet at {the} last the hand of vengeance came,
MGREC129:41	H3155	He knows to's profit, all i'th end {this at last} will turn,
MGREC130:13	H3168	Resolves at last the Princesse should be slain,
MGREC132:21	H3266	There was he {At last he's} taken and imprisoned
MGREC134:25	H3356	His son was *Evergetes* the last Prince
MGREC134:35	H3366	Fair *Cleopatra* next, last of that race,
MGREC135:6	H3378	Here ends at last the *Grecian* Monarchy,
MGREC135:23	H3395	And last was Iron, which breaketh all with might.
MGREC135:30	H3402	The last more strong, and dreadfull, then the rest,
MROMAN136:20	H3434	being the Fourth, and last,
MROMAN139:10	H3538	*Tarquinius Superbus,* the last
MROMAN139:25	~~H3551~~	*being the fourth and last.*
MROMAN139:36	H3562	To prosecute my story to the last;
MROMAN140:8	H3571	Nor matter is't this last, the world now sees,
DIALOG145:1	H150	I saw poore *Ireland* bleeding out her last,
DUBART154:13	H58	Then in Saint *Lewis,* or thy last *Henry* great,
DUBART154:29	H74	Thou hast {hadst} thy part of all, but of the last,

VANITY160:11 H21 The first is prone to vice, the last to rage.
TDUDLEY166:31 H73 At last will bring us to that happy place
BIRTH180:20 H30 Who with salt tears this last Farewel did take.
CHILDRN184:18 H7 Till at the last they felt their wing.
1SIMON188:6 H7 Three flours, two scarcely blown, the last i'th' bud,
MERCY189:6 H27 The fifth and last pledge of her dying love,
MEDDM199:28 Hp278 the body, the last the good name the two former leaue a man
MEDDM199:29 Hp278 when he is once dead, but the last mangles him in his graue
MEDDM204:14 Hp284 shame euer goe together He that would be freed from the last,
MEDDM206:19 Hp287 Men that haue walked very extrauagantly, and at last bethink
MEDDM209:11 Hp291 thornes in their sides, and at last ouercame them, and kept
MEDDM209:15 Hp291 last fall in to perpetuall bondage vnder them vnlesse the great
MYCHILD215:21 Hp240 last is the best, let it be best pleasing to yov.
WHAT224:23 H23 The first and last y^{t} liues for aye,
RESTOR230:4 H19 At last thou mig'st discern

LAST (12) v. [endure]

AGES~~43:16~~ H308 Then thought my state firm founded sure to last,
MPERS81:21 H1129 Their infamy would last till all things ends:
MGREC116:11 H2577 Whose famous Acts {This Monarchs fame} must last, whilst
MGREC116:34 H2600 And fame not last unto Eternity:
SIDNEY151:4 ~~H69~~ But thou art gone, such Meteors never last,
DUBART154:35 H80 Thus *Bartas* fame shall last while starres do stand,
CONTEM169:28 H67 It makes things gone perpetually to last,
CONTEM171:35 H136 Because their beauty and their strength last longer
CONTEM174:36 H233 Shall last and shine when all of these are gone.
SICKNES178:34 H17 O Bubble blast, how long can'st last?
THEART229:7 H9 Lord whilst my fleeting time shall last
HOURS234:26 H40 Ev'n while my Dayes shall last

LASTED (2)

JULY223:21 Hp251 I had a sore fitt of fainting wch lasted 2 or 3 dayes, but not in y^{t}
11MAYA226:14 Hp255 lasted all this spring till this 11. May, yet hath my God given

LASTING (8)

ELEMEN10:36 H111 What lasting Forts my kindled wrath hath burn'd?
ELEMEN12:41 H201 Ye mighty Kings, who for your lasting fames
SEASONS~~50:16~~ H150 *Romes* second Emperour of peaceful {lasting} fame;
MEDDM207:29 Hp289 may be sure of an euer lasting habitation that fades not away.
MEDDM208:36 Hp291 lasting armes of the mighty god of Jacob yea Jacob himself
PILGRIM210:41 H41 Such lasting ioyes, shall there behold
WHAT224:24 H24 Me lasting life shall giue.
11MAYB228:27 Hp259 and sorest y^{t} ever I had lasting 4 dayes, and ye weather being

LASTS (1)

CHILDRN186:15 H82 But spring lasts to eternity,

LATCH'D (1) [latched]

HUMOUR29:25 H376 The blow that's aim'd thereat is latch'd by th'arm,

LATE (25)

FATHER5:3 H4 Deare Sir, of late delighted with the sight, /T D on the
ELEMEN18:39 H443 Some for this cause (of late) have been so bold,
HUMOUR35:1 H597 Lest we too late, this rashnesse do repent,
AGES45:15 H397 I've seen, and so have ye, for 'tis but late,
SEASONS~~46:35~~ H11 She trim'd her locks, which late had frosted been,
MASSYR59:14 H238 But he once in, pursuers came too late,

MASSYR66:9 H515 Where late, of Harp, and Lute, was {were} heard the noyse,
MASSYR68:25 H611 And did one thing worthy a King (though late)
MPERS73:34 H819 So late crusht by their Princes Tyranny;
MPERS76:20 H918 His {This} fruitlesse war, began late to repent;
MPERS~~92:5~~ H1560 By him that late his father murthered.
MGREC95:7 H1686 Where stood of late *Diana's,* wondrous Phane,
MGREC97:4 H1765 Of late, like some immovable he lay,
MGREC99:28 H1871 What, hast thou lost thy late magnanimity?
MGREC~~106:4~~ H2138 And though a Monarch once {late}, now lyes like clay;
MGREC117:31 H2638 And *Roxan* faire, whom late he married,
MGREC118:18 H2665 That he, who late, possest all earthly things,
MGREC128:12 H3085 Which their late King in dust had damnified;
MGREC129:30 H3144 The *Greeks* touch'd with the murther done so {of} late,
MROMAN139:3 H3531 Of *Tanaquil,* late Queen, obtaines the place;
DIALOG145:16 H165 Well, to the matter then, there's grown of late,
SIDNEY151:28 ~~H75~~ Too late my errour see, that durst presume
DUBART153:4 H8 My dazled sight of late, review'd thy lines,
VANITY159:37 H9 He's now a slave {captive}, that was a Prince {King} of late.
MEDDM198:19 Hp276 the hook till it be to late.

LATELY (1)
28AUG226:8 Hp254 forgett thy great Love to my soul so lately expressed, when I

LATEST (1)
MYCHILD215:12 Hp240 latest, + being ignorant whether on my death bed I shall haue

LATHURUS (2)
MGREC134:30 H3361 And next to {after} him, did false *Lathurus* reigne,
MGREC134:31 H3362 *Alexander,* then *Lathurus* in's stead,

LATINE (1)
MROMAN138:9 H3499 Of *Latine* Kings this was long since the Seat,

LATINS (1) [pl.]
MROMAN138:31 H3521 Warres with the *Latins* he againe renewes,

LATTER (2)
DIALOG146:34 H220 To see these {those} latter dayes of hop'd for good,
DUBART153:11 H15 A homely flower in this my latter spring:

LAUD (1)
DIALOG145:30 H179 And to their *Laud* be't spoke, they held i'th' Tower,

LAUGH (2)
MPERS76:9 H907 The Salvages did laugh at his distresse,
VANITY160:19 H29 Nor laugh, nor weep, let things go ill or well:

LAUGHING (1)
MPERS71:35 H749 Laughing to scorn that calvish, sottish crew.

LAUGHT (1)
SIDNEY151:40 ~~H75~~ *Apollo* laught to patch up what's begun,

LAUGH'ST (1)
HUMOUR24:38 H187 Thou laugh'st at me, for loving merriment:

LAUGHTER (3)
HUMOUR30:31 H423 Laughter (though thou sayst malice) flowes from hence,
MPERS77:26 H967 Produced but derision, and laughter;
MGREC96:10 H1730 An object not so much of fear, as laughter.

LAUNCE (1) [lance]
MPERS88:30 H1423 At {But when} last his head they spy upon a Launce,

LAUNCES (1) [lances]

MGREC96:5 H1725 The stately Horses trapt, the launces guilt;

LAUNCHES See LANCHES

LAUNCHING See LANCHING

LAUREL (1)

FLESH176:24 H64 And triumph shall, with laurel head,

LAVISH (1)

SEASONS47:8 H24 The Seeds-man now {too} doth lavish out his Grain,

LAW (17)

AGES38:7 H110 I had no Suits at law, neighbours to vex.

AGES40:3 H184 I know no Law, nor reason, but my wil;

MPERS68:35 H621 and his Father in Law) reigning

MPERS71:9 H725 Then sends to finde a Law for these his sins;

MPERS71:10 H726 That Kings with Sisters match, no Law they finde,

MPERS71:12 ~~H727~~ Which Law includes all Lawes, though lawlesse stil,

MPERS71:13 ~~H727~~ And makes it lawful Law, if he but wil;

MPERS72:19 H767 Upon a Judge, for breach of Law {taking bribes} accus'd;

MGREC132:20 H3257 And with his son in law, will needs go fight:

DIALOG145:18 H167 Which is the chief, the law, or else the King,

DIALOG145:27 H176 Had they not held law fast, all had been gone,

DIALOG145:35 H184 This must be done by Gospel, not by law.

DUBART155:6 H91 *And Natures Law; had it been revocable,*

QELIZ156:11 H38 The *Salique* Law had not in force now been,

CONTEM171:5 H110 And how their precepts to their sons were law,

MERCY188:17 H2 *To the memory of my dear Daughter in Law,*

MYSOUL224:27 H3 Walk in his Law, and kisse his Rod

LAWES (5) [laws]

MPERS71:12 ~~H727~~ Which Law includes all Lawes, though lawlesse stil,

MPERS91:26 ~~H1540~~ Who sooths him up, his owne desires are Lawes:

MGREC114:24 H2494 Against his Soveraigne, or against his Lawes,

DIALOG143:28 H97 Which are my Sins, the breach of sacred Lawes;

DIALOG147:1 H227 And thine {thy} infringed Lawes have boldly stood.

LAWFUL (1)

MPERS71:13 ~~H727~~ And makes it lawful Law, if he but wil;

LAWFULL (1) [lawful]

MASSYR55:16 H82 But all agree, that from no lawfull bed;

LAWLESSE (1) [lawless]

MPERS71:12 ~~H727~~ Which Law includes all Lawes, though lawlesse stil,

LAWS (3) See also LAWES

HUMOUR23:28 H138 Their wrathfull looks are death, their words are laws;

MPERS74:29 H852 Made wholsome gentle Laws, which pleas'd each mind.

MGREC94:5 H1639 This done, against all {both} right, and natures laws,

LAY (34)

ELEMEN9:25 H59 What mingled lay with earth, I cause to shine.

HUMOUR34:5 H560 He was no foole, who thought the Soul lay here {there},

AGES38:14 H117 Lay raked up; of all the cursed weeds,

AGES38:22 H125 A serpents sting in pleasing face lay hid.

AGES40:4 H185 Sometimes lay wait to take a wealthy purse,

SEASONS48:13 H66 Our Winter {thicker} rayment, makes us lay aside,

MASSYR61:36 H341 And *Ahaz* open, at his mercy lay,

MASSYR66:29 H535 Strange melancholly humours on him lay,

MASSYR67:29 H575 The coward King, whose strength lay in his walls,
MPERS73:26 H811 And two of these great Peers, in place {Field} lay dead:
MPERS74:36 ~~H858~~ For twice ten months before the town he lay,
MPERS~~84:12~~ H1247 Rebuilt those walls which long in rubbish lay,
MGREC97:4 H1765 Of late, like some immovable he lay,
MGREC98:8 H1810 In the old town (which now {then} lay like a wood)
MGREC100:27 H1911 For in his multitudes his trust still lay,
MGREC102:11 H1981 In this a masse {world} of gold, and treasure lay,
MGREC103:8 H2019 Here lay the bulk, of all those precious things;
MGREC105:14 H2107 And thus he lay, *Polistratus* a *Greeke*
MGREC108:20 H2236 And in his Camp strong, and securely lay,
MGREC111:35 H2380 Who now obscure at *Passagardis* lay;
MGREC118:21 H2668 Now lay a spectacle, to testifie
MGREC125:38 H2988 In *Pelloponesus* then *Cassander* lay,
MGREC130:5 H3160 She now {then} in *Lydia* at *Sardis* lay,
DIALOG146:6 H194 That thousands lay on heaps, here bleeds my woes.
DIALOG148:19 H284 And lay her wast, for so's the sacred doom,
TDUDLEY166:1 H43 For truly his ambition lay above.
DISTEMP179:19 H7 Then eyes lay dry, disabled to weep more;
BIRTH180:12 H22 Yet love thy dead, who long lay in thine arms:
MEDDM200:12 Hp279 or lay affliction on their loynes that so they might shake hands
MEDDM200:33 Hp280 A wise father will not lay a burden on a child of seven yeares
MEDDM200:35 Hp280 heauenly father (who knowes our mould) lay such afflictions
MYCHILD216:34 Hp242 some sin I lay vnder wch God would haue reformed, or some
SON231:7 H19 In sicknes when he lay full sore
HOUSE236:38 H30 There lay that store I covnted best

LAY'D (2) [laid]
MGREC123:17 H2881 Too young {rash} to beare that charge, if on him lay'd;
FEVER221:5 H20 What tho: in dust it shall bee lay'd

LAYD (4) [laid]
MYCHILD216:3 Hp241 About 16. The Lord layd his hand sore vpon me & smott me
MYCHILD216:35 Hp242 he would haue performed, and by his help I haue layd vowes
FAINT222:19 H9 But bee in silence layd.
HOUSE236:27 H19 That layd my goods now in ye dvst

LAYES (3) n. [lays]
SEASONS47:19 H35 Now tune their layes, on sprays of every bush;
CONTEM169:24 H64 Whilst I as mute, can warble forth no higher layes.
CHILDRN186:3 H70 Till my weak layes with me shall end,

LAYES (7) v. [lays]
MASSYR67:28 H574 Layes siedge to's regall seat, proud *Babylon,*
MPERS77:31 H972 The first deports, {dehorts} and layes before his eyes,
MPERS81:31 H1139 To adde unto his numbers, layes about,
MGREC98:35 H1837 And layes before great *Alexanders* eyes,
MGREC103:31 H2042 And layes before his eyes, if he persist
MGREC104:7 H2059 With sage advice, he layes {sets} before his eyes,
MGREC123:2 H2864 And thus *Antipater* the ground-work layes,

LAYS (2) v.
MGREC104:22 H2074 Lays hold on's Lord, and binding him with bands.
MEDDM208:23 Hp290 when death threatens and distresse lays hold vpon them they

LD (1) [lord]
FAINT222:12 H2 Worthy art Thou o Ld of praise,

LEAD (9) v.

AGES42:9 H267 And gently lead the lambes, as they had need,

MPERS89:40 H1474 Chose *Xenophon,* to lead them home again;

MGREC~~133:24~~ H3314 Him with his Sons in Triumph lead did he,

TDUDLEY165:16 H18 Nor was his name, or life lead so obscure

CONTEM169:11 H52 In pathless paths I lead my wandring feet,

CONTEM172:27 H161 O could I lead my Rivolets to rest,

3LETTER183:19 H21 Mine being gone, I lead a joyless life,

MEDDM205:23 Hp286 He that would keep a pure heart and lead a blamlesse life,

MYCHILD216:32 Hp242 try me, see what wayes of wickednes are in me, and lead me

LEADER (1)

AGES42:13 H271 As readily as could my Leader say:

LEADES (1) [LEADS]

MEDDM198:4 Hp276 them lye down in green pastures and leades them besides

LEADS (6)

SEASONS48:7 H60 clocking hen, her chipping brood now {chirping chickins} leads,

SEASONS50:23 H157 The Carter leads all home, with whistling voyce,

MASSYR65:8 H473 And though a Victor home his Army leads,

MPERS91:23 H1537 Then in voluptuousnesse he leads his life,

VANITY160:28 H38 Which leads unto that living Christall fount,

MEDDM198:6 Hp276 ouer their heads he then leads them to the Rock wch is higher

LEADST (1)

DUBART154:22 H67 Leadst millions chained by eyes, by eares, by tongues,

LEAFE (1) [leaf]

MEDDM200:30 Hp279 in this transcends the spring, that their leafe shall neuer faile

LEAFLESS See LEAVLESSE

LEAFY See LEAVIE

LEAGUE (4)

MPERS83:32 H1220 A league of amity, had sworn before. {firmly swore,}

MPERS~~85:28~~ H1304 The King much profit reapeth, by these leagues {this league},

MGREC98:40 H1842 A league of friendship make, firm, and entire;

MEDDM209:14 Hp291 all their accursed inmates, but make a league with them, they

LEAGUES (1) [pl.]

MPERS85:28 H1304 The King much profit reapeth, by these leagues {this league},

LEAN (1)

ELEMEN17:1 H365 Of rotten sheep, lean kine, and mildew'd grain.

LEANING (1)

AGES36:20 H44 Leaning upon his staffe, comes {came} up old age.

LEAP (1)

ELEMEN~~12:15~~ H175 But ile skip {leap} o're these Hills, not touch a Dale,

LEAPING (1)

MROMAN136:34 H3448 For leaping o're the Walls {wall} with some disdaine;

LEARN (2)

HUMOUR31:21 H454 Pray hear, admire, and learn instruction.

RESTOR230:2 H17 That thou by both may'st learn

LEARN'D (3) [learned]

MGREC116:19 H2585 The principles of what he then had learn'd

QELIZ156:3 H30 Who was so good, so just, so learn'd, so wise,

CHILDRN184:19 H8 Mounted the Trees, and learn'd to sing;

LEARNED (10)

ELEMEN8:32 H30 But what I am, let learned *Grecians* say;

HUMOUR34:19 H574 Some worthy {curious} learned *Crooke* may these reveal,
MASSYR~~57:22~~ H169 We may with learned *Vsher* better say,
MPERS92:26 ~~H1584~~ Thus learned *Pemble,* whom we may not slight,
MPERS92:31 H1589 With our judicious learned {learned and judicious} Knight to
MGREC114:18 H2488 Was vertuous, learned wise *Calisthines,*
MGREC116:21 H2587 Learning, and learned men, he much regarded,
QELIZ155:34 H25 No *Speeds,* nor *Chamdens* learned History;
CHILDRN185:4 H30 To chat among that learned crew:
MEDDM202:7 Hp281 then ye earth some so wise and learned, that they seeme like

LEARNING (13)

ELEMEN12:1 H161 For Learning, Armes, and Arts, I love it well:
HUMOUR22:21 H90 Again, who sits, for learning, science, Arts?
HUMOUR29:40 H391 Of Learning, and of Policie, thou would'st bereave me,
HUMOUR34:27 H582 Then, my head {brain} for learning is not the fittest,
AGES~~39:10~~ H153 Mine {My} education, and my learning's {learning} such,
AGES43:19 H314 Be I of worth {wit}, of learning, or {and} of parts;
AGES44:14 H347 It's not my Learning, Rhetorick, wit so large,
MGREC116:21 H2587 Learning, and learned men, he much regarded,
SIDNEY150:9 H34 That sees not learning, valour, and morality,
SIDNEY152:27 H96 *Learning, valour, beauty {Wisdome}, all in vertuous youth:*
DUBART153:33 H37 Thy profound Learning; viewing other while
VANITY160:12 H22 Where is it then? in wisdome, learning, arts?
VANITY160:23 H33 Nor yet in learning, wisdome, youth nor pleasure,

LEARNING'S (1) [learning is]

AGES39:10 H153 Mine {My} education, and my learning's {learning} such,

LEASE (1)

MEDDM207:22 Hp289 that all haue a lease of their liues, some longer some shorter,

LEAST (35)

ELEMEN11:27 H147 Among my praises this I count not least,
ELEMEN12:8 H168 Dividing great *Armenia* from the least,
ELEMEN14:14 H256 When they seek food, and harme mistrust the least.
ELEMEN18:10 H414 His moveing reason is, give least I dye.
HUMOUR27:25 H296 Without the least indignity to you;
SEASONS48:14 H67 Least by his fervor, we be terrifi'd,
SEASONS48:36 H87 Thy dayes stil lengthen, without least decline.
MASSYR58:9 H194 His manly heart disdained, in the least,
MASSYR62:34 H379 On *Henah, Arpad,* and on *Ivdah* least {*Juahs* coast};
MASSYR64:7 H431 And this is {was} he, who when he fear'd the least,
MPERS74:27 H850 Three strings to's bow, the least of which is good;
MPERS79:16 H1042 Seven dayes and nights, his Hoast without least stay,
MPERS82:26 H1173 words {Nor prayers}, nor guifts, could win him least content:
MPERS83:9 H1197 Of life, no man had least security.
MPERS86:37 H1353 But least {lest} some worser newes should fly to Court,
MGREC94:6 H1640 kinsmen puts {put} to death without least {who gave no} cause;
MGREC94:10 H1644 Now taste of death, (least they deserv't {deserv'd} in time)
MGREC96:16 H1736 Least he should need them, in his chariots stead.
MGREC96:29 H1749 Now least this Gold, and all this goodly stuffe,
MGREC98:6 H1808 Least he intend more fraud, then sacrifice;
MGREC~~108:14~~ H2230 Without {least} cause, given by {from} them, in deed, or word:
MGREC112:20 H2406 *Philotas* was not least, nor yet the last;
MGREC113:28 H2455 Most wickedly was slaine, without least crime,

MGREC114:20 H2490 As did appeare, in flattering him the least:
MGREC116:6 H2566 Least {Lest} of such like, their Father chance to sup:
DUBART153:23 H27 Some part, at least, of that brave wealth was his;
CHILDRN185:27 H53 Or least by Lime-twigs they be foyl'd,
MEDDM196:11 Hp273 The finest bread hath the least bran the purest hony the least
MEDDM196:12 Hp273 the sincerest christian the least self loue
MEDDM204:31 Hp285 Jacob, I am lesse then the least of thy mercys.
MYCHILD215:16 Hp240 dayly in y^{r} rembrance, (Altho: y^{t} is the least in my aim in w^{t} I
MYCHILD217:8 Hp242 (or at least in sight) but I haue been apt to forgett him and my
MED223:8 Hp250 vnto my God and your God—But least this should not bee
28AUG226:3 Hp254 somt. I haue had, least my heart should bee drawn from him,

LEAUE (8) v. [leave] See also LEAV'T
2SIMON195:6 Hp271 once desired me to leaue some thing for you in writeing that
2SIMON195:11 Hp271 conceptions because I would leaue you nothing but myne
MEDDM199:28 Hp278 the body, the last the good name the two former leaue a man
MEDDM208:20 Hp290 perform nothing, and so leaue those in the lurch that most
TOCHILD215:3 H3 I leaue for yov when I am dead,
TOCHILD215:6 H6 Make vse of what I leaue in Loue
MYCHILD215:11 Hp240 speakers leaue to speak, and those espec. sink deepest wch
HOUSE236:22 H14 And not to leaue me succourlesse.

LEAUES (3) n. [leaves]
MEDDM199:8 Hp277 Yellow leaues argue want of sap and gray haires want of
MEDDM205:33 Hp286 and some haue nothing to shew but leaues only, and some
13MAY226:27 H3 And leaues the naked Trees doe dresse

LEAVE (6) n. [permission]
HUMOUR20:13 H5 Loe! other foure step up, crave leave to shew
HUMOUR20:20 H12 Had leave to speake, succeeding one the other;
HUMOUR24:12 H161 Good sisters give me leave (as is my place)
HUMOUR31:8 H441 Now {But} by your leave, Ile let your greatnesse see;
MGREC~~115:15~~ H2533 That by his leave his friend *Ephestion,*
SIDNEY152:18 H87 *Errata,* through their leave threw me my pen,

LEAVE (21) v.
ELEMEN9:26 H60 But let me leave these things, my flame aspires
ELEMEN11:11 H131 But to leave those to'th' wise, I judge is {it} best,
ELEMEN15:4 H286 Hindes leave their Calves, the Elephant the Fens;
HUMOUR25:18 H207 But let her leave the rest, and {then} I presume,
HUMOUR28:8 H320 As if she'd leave no flesh to turn to clay,
HUMOUR32:31 H505 I'le leave that manly property to you;
AGES46:3 H434 Sons, Nephews, leave, my death {farewell} for to deplore;
MPERS81:16 H1124 And leave them out, the {this} shock {now} for to sustaine,
MPERS88:23 H1416 They {ready} were about to leave their King and fly,
MPERS91:17 H1525 But let us leave these *Greeks,* to discord bent,
MPERS91:28 ~~H1542~~ He must leave all, and in the pit remain;
MGREC104:18 H2070 Look to himselfe, and leave him to that crew;
MGREC~~117:29~~ H2636 Great *Alexander* has left {did leave} issue none,
MGREC122:41 H2862 The Army with *Antigonus* did {doth} leave,
MGREC123:14 H2878 Now {When} great *Antipater,* the world doth {must} leave
MGREC125:10 H2958 To leave his Seige at *Tagra* {*Tegea*}, and with speed
MGREC127:12 H3042 But leave him building, other in their urn,
SIDNEY152:21 H90 So *Sydney's* fame, I leave to *England's* Rolls,
DUBART154:39 H84 Ile leave thy praise, to those shall doe thee right,

CONTEM172:34 H167 In Lakes and ponds, you leave your numerous fry,
CHILDRN184:24 H13 Leave not thy nest, thy Dam and Sire,

LEAVES (5) n.

HUMOUR27:20 H291 Now through your leaves, some little time i'le spend;
SEASONS51:15 H189 Boughs full of leaves, or fruits, but raw, and {unripe or} green,
SEASONS51:25 H201 Whose yellow saplesse leaves by winds are fann'd:
CONTEM167:29 H6 Their leaves & fruits seem'd painted, but was true
2LETTER182:11 H17 The leaves in th' woods, the hail or drops of rain,

LEAVES (13) v.

MASSYR58:26 H209 *Sardanapalus* leaves his Apish play.
MASSYR59:10 H234 The King his Brother leaves, all to sustaine,
MPERS82:32 H1179 And leaves her thus, besmear'd with {in} blood, and tears.
MGREC94:15 H1649 Leaves sage *Antipater* at home to sway,
MGREC95:25 H1704 Goes {Runs} after too {two}, and leaves all to disaster.
MGREC98:12 H1814 He leaves not, till he makes {made} the sea firme shoar;
MGREC100:34 H1918 And leaves {Whose death} her wofull Lord for to {full sadly did}
MGREC105:3 H2096 And leaves him thus, to gaspe out his last breath.
MGREC121:4 H2782 Leaves *Eumenes,* the *Asian* coast to free,
MGREC131:35 H3227 And leaves the ill got kingdomes he had won,
MGREC135:40 H3412 My tired braine, leaves to a {some} better pen,
MROMAN138:12 H3502 Leaves {Left} *Rome,* in wealth and power, still growing high.
SIDNEY149:36 ~~H23~~ But leaves the rest, as most unprofitable:

LEAVE'T (2) [leave it]

HUMOUR24:31 H180 And leave't to all, to judge where valour lyes.
SIDNEY151:39 ~~H75~~ I leave't in brief, *Apollo* do't at large.

LEAVIE (2) [leafy]

CONTEM168:16 H24 Whose beams was shaded by the leavie Tree,
MEDDM206:3 Hp287 and these are but leavie Christians, wch are in as much

LEAVING (2)

MASSYR56:37 H143 Leaving the world, to *Venus,* soar'd above,
MGREC~~132:20~~ H3260 Leaving *Antigonus* his eldest Son,

LEAVLESSE (1) [leafless]

MEDDM200:25 Hp279 we se the leavlesse trees and dry stocks (at the approach of

LED (14)

MASSYR54:34 H61 An army of three Millions he led out,
MASSYR63:21 H406 Led King *Manasseh,* to captivity.
MASSYR65:26 H491 Whom with his Mother, he to *Babel* led,
MASSYR66:11 H517 All now of worth, are captive led with tears,
MPERS69:19 H641 He in his younger dayes an Army led,
MPERS76:31 H929 By brave *Miltiades* (their chief) being led,
MPERS85:33 H1309 by {To which} his pride, {more} then {his} lust, thereunto led.
MGREC96:15 H1735 A number of spare horses next were led,
MGREC108:8 H2224 Whom *Xerxes* from their country led away;
MGREC110:24 H2328 Could by no means be further {farther} drawn, or led:
MGREC135:5 H3377 But some disgrace, in triumph to be led.
SIDNEY151:21 H71 But now into such Lab'rinths am I led
TDUDLEY165:4 H6 By duty bound, and not by custome led
FLESH176:25 H65 When thou my Captive shalt be led,

LEESE (1)

SEASONS52:31 H246 And Travellers sometimes their noses leese.

LEFT (1) [opposite of right]
MPERS76:39 H937 Which soon cut off, {inrag'd,} he with the {his} left
LEFT (38) v.
HUMOUR27:41 H312 Which makes the mansion, by the soul soon left;
HUMOUR32:29 H503 And when i've nothing left to say, be mute;
SEASONS~~46:28~~ H4 Another Four i've {left} yet for to bring on,
MASSYR54:2 H29 Left to the world, by any History;
MASSYR57:24 ~~H171~~ Again, the Country was left bare (there is no doubt)
MASSYR57:30 H175 For *Ninias,* and all his Race are left,
MASSYR58:31 H214 That in dispaire, he left the field and fled:
MASSYR61:7 H312 He left his new got Kingdoms to his Son.
MASSYR66:40 H546 He left his Wealth, and Conquest, to his Son.
MPERS71:1 H713 Three Daughters, and two Sons, he left behind,
MPERS71:33 H747 So left his sacrilegious bold intents:
MPERS81:6 H1114 Three hundred thousand yet he left behind,
MPERS82:18 H1165 Scarce one was left, to carry home the fame;
MPERS85:4 H1280 Three sons great *Artaxerxes* left behind;
MPERS86:7 H1323 His large Dominions left, to's eldest son.
MPERS~~92:8~~ H1566 And scarce a Nephew left that now might reign:
MPERS92:9 H1567 What Acts he did, time hath not now left pend,
MGREC~~94:18~~ H1655 And being ask'd what for himself was left,
MGREC97:1 H1762 Most basely run {ran}, and left their King at large,
MGREC102:3 H1973 At *Arbela* left, his ornaments, and treasure,
MGREC104:20 H2072 And of {by} his Guard, and Servitors now left.
MGREC105:41 H2134 I've nothing left, at this my dying hour;
MGREC110:31 H2335 Huge Bridles made, which here, and there, he left,
MGREC117:17 H2624 Great *Alexander* dead, his Army's left,
MGREC117:29 H2636 Great *Alexander* has left {did leave} issue none,
MGREC131:36 H3228 Two sons he left, born of King *Philips* daughter,
MGREC132:25 H3270 After three years he dyed, left what he'd won
MGREC132:31 H3278 Rich *Ægypt* left, and what else he had won
MROMAN~~138:12~~ H3502 Leaves {Left} *Rome,* in wealth and power, still growing high.
SIDNEY151:35 ~~H75~~ He left that charge by *Phoebus* to be man'd:
TDUDLEY166:3 H45 He left it to his race for Legacy:
DDUDLEY167:23 H20 *Then dying, left a blessed memory.*
CHILDRN184:21 H10 To Regions far, and left me quite:
MERCY189:5 H26 A Babe she left before, she soar'd above,
MERCY189:11 H32 She one hath left, a joy to thee and me,
MYCHILD217:17 Hp243 although he hath not left me altogether wthout the wittnes of
RESTOR230:5 H20 Praises to him who hath not left
HOUSE236:32 H24 But yet sufficient for us left.
LEG See LEGG
LEGACY (1)
TDUDLEY166:3 H45 He left it to his race for Legacy:
LEGACYS (1) [LEGACIES]
2SIMON195:9 Hp271 Such as they are I bequeath to you, Small legacys are accept[d]
LEGENDS (1) [pl.]
MASSYR63:35 H422 Nor his restoring from old legends took;
LEGG (1) [leg]
MGREC108:24 H2240 Imprinted deep in's legg, by Arrowes shot;

LEGGS (1) [legs]
MGREC97:5 H1766 Now finds both leggs, and Horse, to run away;
LEGION (1)
CONTEM173:32 H197 Where winter's never felt by that sweet airy legion.
LEGIONS (1) [PL.]
ELEMEN11:36 H156 Soone would they passe, not hundreds, but legions,
LEGS (3) [pl.] See also LEGGS
AGES45:37 H427 My comely legs, as nimble as the Roe,
MGREC135:25 H3397 And smote those feet, those legs, those arms and thighs;
MROMAN140:7 H3570 Although my Monarchies their legs do lack:
LEIGE (1) [liege]
MPERS75:5 H866 This violence was done him by his Leige;
LEIUTENANT (1) [lieutenant] See also LIEFTENANT
MASSYR63:5 H390 In *Babylon,* Leiutenant to this man,
LEMON (1)
SEASONS51:7 H181 The Orange, Lemon, Dangle on the tree;
LEND (5)
HUMOUR25:22 H211 But when thou scorn'st to take the helpe we lend,
AGES~~40:15~~ H196 To all obscenity, my {mine} eares I bend. {lend;}
MPERS78:30 H1011 But pitty 'twas, thine ayde that {thou} here did'st lend,
MGREC98:14 H1816 The former ruines, help to him now lend; {forwarded his end:}
2HUSB233:8 H41 Wth Joy lend back my Dear
LENDS (1)
HUMOUR27:14 H285 The help she needs, the loving Liver lends,
LENGHT (1)
SOREFIT221:27 H13 I said I shall praise thee at lenght.
LENGTH (18)
ELEMEN8:23 H21 But {Till gentle} Aire at length, contention so abated,
HUMOUR28:10 H322 At length demolishes the faberick,
HUMOUR32:13 H487 Talke I love not, reason lyes not in length.
AGES~~45:12~~ H394 Could length their dayes or once reverse their fate
SEASONS49:13 H104 Whose vehemency, at length doth grow so great,
SEASONS52:21 H236 From thence he 'gins to length the shortned morn,
MASSYR60:21 H286 *Assyria* he also gain'd at length;
MPERS79:15 H1041 Firmly at length, {last} accomplished his wil;
MPERS87:33 H1385 Six yards the {in} depth, and forty miles the length,
MGREC107:24 H2199 At length, they came to th' River *Oxus* brink,
MGREC110:17 H2317 Nor was't dishonour, at the length to yeeld;
MGREC111:31 H2376 {And} So he at length drew neare to *Persia*;
MGREC125:27 H2977 At length yeelds to the Halter, her faire neck;
MROMAN139:35 H3561 At length resolv'd, when many years had past,
CONTEM171:10 H114 Our life compare we with their length of dayes
AUTHOR178:2 H12 Yet being mine own, at length affection would
CHILDRN185:12 H38 On higher boughs he'l perch at length.
MEDDM208:8 Hp290 wth length of time (if there be no inter course) will coole the
LENGTHEN (1)
SEASONS48:36 H87 Thy dayes stil lengthen, without least decline.
LENGTHENED (1)
SEASONS52:38 H253 Which is increased by the lengthened day,
LENITY (1)
MPERS77:17 H958 The {His} Father not so full of lenity,

LENT (5)
AGES~~42:1~~ H259 For hundreds blesse me, for my bounty sent {lent}.
MPERS83:30 H1218 To whom the perjur'd *Grecians* lent their aide,
MGREC~~124:10~~ H2917 That no supply by these here might be lent,
ELIZB186:36 H8 Farewel fair flower that for a space was lent,
ANNEB187:28 H18 More fool then I to look on that was lent,
LEO (1)
SEASONS49:39 H132 The Sun in {thro} Leo now hath {takes} his carrear,
LEONADE (1)
MPERS79:35 H1061 The *Spartan* meets him, brave *Leonade,*
LEONADES (1)
MPERS80:10 H1077 Alas, it is *Leonades* you want!
LEONATUS (4)
MGREC119:9 H2699 For *Leonatus,* more lovely in her eye,
MGREC119:20 H2710 The like of *Leonatus,* he requires,
MGREC119:26 H2716 Striving {And seeks} to stop *Leonatus,* that so
MGREC119:37 H2727 And the remains of *Leonatus* takes;
LEOPARD (3)
MGREC117:12 H2619 The Leopard down, his {the} four wings 'gan to rise,
MGREC135:29 H3401 The third a Leopard, which four wings did rear;
MGREC135:34 H3406 But yet this Lion, Bear, this Leopard, Ram,
LEOPARDS (1) [pl.]
ELEMEN12:18 H178 My Panthers, and my Leopards of *Libia,*
LEPERS (1) [pl.]
MEDDM203:31 Hp284 We read of ten lepers that were Cleansed, but of one that
LESS (5)
AGES~~45:36~~ H426 I cannot labour, nor {much less} I cannot {can} fight:
MASSYR~~63:28~~ H414 This King's less fam'd for all the acts he's done,
MPERS~~85:19~~ H1295 Which from remissenesse, in *{Less} Asia* proceeds {breeds.}
MGREC~~97:28~~ H1789 *Darius* now, more humble {less lofty} then before,
AUTHOR177:32 H4 Till snatcht from thence by friends, less wise then true
LESSE (42) [less]
ELEMEN8:25 H23 The others enmity: {difference,} being lesse, did cease
ELEMEN12:36 H196 That with lesse cost, neare home, supplyes {supply} your
ELEMEN13:15 H216 My cold, thy (fruitfull) heat, doth crave no lesse:
ELEMEN20:5 H487 I have said lesse, then did my sisters three;
HUMOUR21:7 H35 But she in greater, I in lesse degree;
HUMOUR21:11 H39 Our noble selves, in a lesse noble Gender.
HUMOUR24:14 H163 Your selves may plead, your wrongs are no whit lesse,
HUMOUR25:36 H225 If murthers be thy glory, tis no lesse.
HUMOUR29:32 H383 It's no lesse glory to defend a town,
HUMOUR32:20 H494 Though wit I want, and anger I have lesse,
HUMOUR33:12 H526 Thou speakest truth, and I can speak {say} no lesse,
HUMOUR34:40 H595 A warning good, hereafter i'le say lesse.
MASSYR55:34 H100 But were her vertues, more, or lesse, or none;
MPERS70:40 ~~H711~~ Where that proud Conquerour could doe no lesse,
MPERS75:39 H896 Set up a Temple (though, a lesse) again.
MPERS76:21 H919 Return'd with little honour, and lesse gaine;
MPERS76:22 H920 His enemies scarce seen, then much lesse, slaine;
MPERS76:24 H922 But troubles in lesse *Asia* him stay'd;
MPERS76:28 H926 Return'd with wondrous losse, and honour lesse:

MPERS81:29	H1137	No lesse then Grand-sire to great *Alexander*.
MPERS86:28	H1344	Some Townes commodious in lesse *Asia*,
MGREC95:34	H1713	The rest attendants, which made up no lesse;
MGREC98:13	H1815	But far lesse cost, and time, he doth {did} expend,
MGREC100:13	H1897	Then setling all things in lesse *Asia,*
MGREC101:11	H1936	And all those Kingdoms in lesse *Asia;*
MGREC107:18	H2193	Nor wonder lesse, to Readers may it bring,
MGREC113:39	H2466	Was one of more esteem, but lesse desart;
MGREC117:13	H2620	The great Horn broke, the lesse did tytannize;
MGREC119:1	H2691	But nothing lesse: each one himself intends.
MGREC130:23	H3178	And by their means, who thought of nothing lesse
SIDNEY149:9	H8	No lesse {As well} an Honour to our *British* Land,
SIDNEY151:16	~~H69~~	Then wonder lesse, if warlike *Philip* yield,
MEDDM200:2	Hp278	comes to its height by degrees, He that dares say of a lesse
MEDDM200:34	Hp280	is enough for one of twice his strength, much lesse will our
MEDDM201:5	Hp280	more or lesse if god afford his help
MEDDM203:6	Hp283	them then they are lesse then vanity & more then vexation,
MEDDM204:31	Hp285	Jacob, I am lesse then the least of thy mercys.
MEDDM205:4	Hp285	seed of morality, much lesse of grace in them But when by
MEDDM206:13	Hp287	some of a lesse degree, & others (and they indeed the most in
MEDDM206:14	Hp287	and obscure, yet all receiue their luster (be it more or lesse)
MEDDM209:9	Hp291	that they could do (as they thought) wth lesse hazard and more
MYCHILD215:13	Hp240	opportvnity to speak to any of yov much lesse to All, thovght it
LESSENED (2)		
SEASONS52:29	H244	The cold not lessened, but augmented more.
AUTHOR177:35	H7	Where errors were not lessened (all may judg).
LESSER (1)		
MPERS86:22	H1338	By lesser {lower} steps, towards the top to climbe;
LESSON (1)		
MEDDM203:2	Hp283	Had not the wisest of men, taught vs this lesson, that all is
LEST (10)		
HUMOUR35:1	H597	Lest we too late, this rashnesse do repent,
MPERS~~86:37~~	H1353	But least {lest} some worser newes should fly to Court,
MGREC~~116:6~~	H2566	Least {Lest} of such like, their Father chance to sup:
DUBART154:37	H82	But lest my {mine} ignorance should doe thee wrong,
DAVID158:30	H10	Lest Daughters of the *Philistins* rejoyce,
DAVID158:31	H11	Lest the uncircumcis'd lift up their voyce:
CHILDRN185:19	H45	Lest this my brood some harm should catch,
MEDDM203:16	Hp283	lest he meet wth such tossings that may cause him to long for
MEDDM204:23	Hp285	eye on the command, and not on his own ends, lest he meet
MEDDM206:34	Hp288	trembling, lest they through vnbeleif fall short of a promise, it
LET (94)		
PROLOG6:22	H7	Let Poets, and Historians set these forth,
PROLOG7:28	H39	Let *Greeks* be *Greeks,* and Women what they are,
ELEMEN8:32	H30	But what I am, let learned *Grecians* say;
ELEMEN9:26	H60	But let me leave these things, my flame aspires
ELEMEN10:19	H94	Ile here let passe, my Choler cause of warres,
ELEMEN11:40	H160	Yet let me name my *Grecia,* 'tis my heart
ELEMEN12:17	H177	Ile here let goe, my Lions of *Numedia,*
ELEMEN18:41	H445	Let such suspend their thoughts, and silent be;
HUMOUR24:21	H170	Then let my sisters, right their injury.

HUMOUR24:27	H176	So walke thee til thou'rt cold, then let thee go.
HUMOUR25:18	H207	But let her leave the rest, and {then} I presume,
HUMOUR27:8	H279	And let me by thy Partner, which is due.
HUMOUR27:32	H303	My vertues hid, i've let you dimly see;
HUMOUR30:11	H403	Let me wel make thy precincts, the gal;
HUMOUR31:8	H441	Now {But} by your leave, Ile let your greatnesse see;
HUMOUR35:4	H600	Let Sanguine, Choler, with her hot hand hold,
HUMOUR35:10	H606	Nor jars, nor scoffs, let none hereafter see,
AGES38:17	H120	But yet let me relate, before I go,
AGES39:9	H152	Then let not him, which {that} hath most craft dissemble;
SEASONS~~48:34~~	H85	Let some describe thee better then can I.
SEASONS52:12	H227	What Winter hath to tel, now let him say.
MASSYR60:6	H271	Yet would not {granting} let them {now} to inhabite there;
MPERS70:11	H682	He cuts those banks, and let the river out;
MPERS74:16	H839	Let tyranny now with {dead} *Cambyses* dye.
MPERS75:32	H889	Shall let the work, or keep back any thing,
MPERS82:13	H1160	For pitty, let those few to *Xerxes* go,
MPERS89:29	H1463	The King's {King} perplext, there dares not let them stay,
MPERS89:30	H1464	And feares as much to let them march away;
MPERS91:17	H1525	But let us leave these *Greeks,* to discord bent,
MGREC96:40	H1760	Let fly their Arrowes, in the *Persians* face;
MGREC101:3	H1928	Let them on him, that {this} dignity bestow:
MGREC107:17	H2192	The Souldiers should let passe this injury;
MGREC115:11	H2520	Because he let {He suffer, his friend} *Ephestion* to dye.
MGREC122:9	H2834	For all that should be said, let this suffice,
MGREC122:30	H2849	Resign'd his place, and so let all alone;
MGREC127:23	H3053	Because he never would let go {forgoe} his trust:
MGREC130:11	H3166	To let her go, or hold her still, he fears,
MGREC133:18	H3306	I must let passe those many battels fought,
DIALOG141:28	H27	Let me lament alone, while thou art glad.
DIALOG146:2	H190	Shews all was done, I'll therefore let it go.
DIALOG147:8	H234	And for my self, let miseries abound,
DIALOG147:15	H241	And let their names consume, but let the flash
DIALOG147:15	H241	And let their names consume, but let the flash
DIALOG147:22	~~H247~~	Let Gaoles be fill'd with th' remnant of that pack,
DIALOG148:7	H272	There let thy name, thy fame, thy valour {glory} shine,
DIALOG148:9	H274	And let her spoils, full pay, with int'rest be,
DIALOG148:11	H276	Of all the woes thou canst let her be sped,
SIDNEY149:33	~~H23~~	Let then, none dis-allow of these my straines,
SIDNEY~~150:12~~	H42	Then let none disallow of these my straines
SIDNEY150:17	~~H49~~	Then let such Crowes as I, thy praises sing,
QELIZ157:36	H104	Let such, as say our sex is void of reason,
DAVID158:28	H8	In *Gath,* let not this thing {things} be spoken on,
DAVID158:32	H12	O! *Gilbo* Mounts, let never pearled dew,
VANITY160:19	H29	Nor laugh, nor weep, let things go ill or well:
TDUDLEY165:14	H16	Let malice bite, and envy knaw its fill,
TDUDLEY166:27	H69	As joy in heaven, on earth let praise resound.
FLESH175:13	H13	Regardlesly to let earth goe?
FLESH175:36	H36	Then let not goe, what thou maist find,
DISTEMP179:22	H10	He chac'd away those clouds, and let me see
BIRTH180:8	H18	Let be interr'd in my oblivious grave;

BIRTH180:10 H20 Let that live freshly in thy memory
3LETTER183:27 H29 Together at one Tree, oh let us brouze,
CHILDRN185:18 H44 Let others know what are my fears
CHILDRN186:22 H89 And 'fore she once would let you fly,
MEDDM200:8 Hp279 bitter together so is it wth some Christians, let god imbitter all
MEDDM204:27 Hp285 one that is in a far better estate then himself, but let him look
MEDDM204:30 Hp285 let him look on his owne vnworthynes and that will make him
MEDDM205:5 Hp285 nurture they are brought into a fit capacity, let the seed of good
MEDDM207:23 Hp289 pleases our great landlord to let: All haue their bounds set ouer
MEDDM208:34 Hp290 for the people, god sath to him Let me alone, that I may
MEDDM209:1 Hp291 wrestled wth god face to face in penvel Let me go, sath that
MEDDM209:2 Hp291 will not let thee go replys Jacob till thou blesse me, faith is not
MEDDM209:4 Hp291 all our seekings and gettings, let vs aboue all seek to obtain
MEDDM209:22 Hp291 all excellences, let his parts naturall and acquired spirituall and
MYCHILD215:21 Hp240 last is the best, let it be best pleasing to yov.
MED223:17 Hp250 I ovght. Lord haueing this hope let me purefye my self as thou
MED223:18 Hp250 art pure, and let me bee no more afraid of Death, but even
JULY223:30 Hp251 O Lord let me neuer forgett thy Goodnes, nor question thy
JULY223:33 Hp251 upon me. O never let Satan p^{r}vail against me, but strenghten
WHAT224:3 H3 O never let me from thee swerue
WHAT224:11 H11 Let them help in Adversities
MYSOUL225:23 H27 O let me covnt each hour a Day
28AUG226:7 Hp254 and bee in continuall xpectat^{n} of my change, and let me never
28AUG226:10 Hp254 O let me ever see Thee that Art invisible, and I shall not bee
THEART229:8 H10 Thy Goodnes let me Tell,
THEART229:12 H14 For ever let me walk
THEART229:13 H15 Let my obed^{c} testefye
RESTOR229:31 H14 Let thy obed^{c} testefye
HANNA230:17 H10 And let her Conversation say
2HUSB232:13 H14 Then let thy promis joy his heart
2HUSB233:5 H38 Let not thine own Inheritance
2HUSB233:11 H44 Lord let my Eyes see once Again
HOUSE236:18 H10 Let no man know is my Desire.
HOUSE237:27 H57 The world no longer let me Love

LETHARGIE (1) [lethargy]
AGES~~43:33~~ H328 The Astma, Megrim, Palsy, Lethargie,

LET'S (9) [let us]
HUMOUR22:11 H80 But {Now} let's give, cold, white, Sister Flegme her right.
HUMOUR34:41 H596 Let's now be freinds, 'tis {its} time our spight was {were} spent,
MGREC127:13 H3043 And {now} for a while, let's into *Asia* turn,
DIALOG145:14 H163 Then let's join heads, and hands {& hearts} for your relief.
DIALOG147:12 H238 Let's bring *Baals* vestments out, {forth} to make a fire,
3LETTER183:30 H32 Let's still remain but one, till death divide.
1SIMON188:8 H9 With dreadful awe before him let's be mute,
1SIMON188:9 H10 Such was his will, but why, let's not dispute,
1SIMON188:11 H12 Let's say he's merciful, as well as just,

LETS (2) [let us]
MGREC~~123:13~~ H2877 To *Greece* and *Macedon* lets turn our sight.
1HUSB180:33 H12 Then while we live, in love lets so persever,

LETS (1) v.
MEDDM196:7 Hp273 them vp, but spying his black feet, he soon lets fall his plumes,

LETTER (3)
MGREC94:27 H1665 Sends him a frothy, and contemptuous letter,
MGREC97:34 H1795 His {This} Letter *Alexander* doth disdaine,
1LETTER181:1 H0 *A Letter to her Husband, absent upon*
LETTERS (1) [pl.] See also LRS
MGREC115:22 H2541 And by her Letters did her Son incite,
LEUD (1) [lewd]
AGES~~40:20~~ H201 If any time from company {leud Companions} I {can} spare,
LEVEL (1)
MASSYR59:21 H245 Part of the {that stately} wal it level caus'd to lye; {was
'LEVEN (1) [eleven] See also ELEAV'N, ELEV'N
QELIZ~~156:2~~ H29 The nine {'leven} *Olimp'ades* of her happy reigne;
LEVYED (1) [levied]
MPERS84:40 H1276 Again dispersed, his new levyed hoast.
LEWD (5) See also LEUD
MPERS~~72:9~~ H757 To act in secret, this his lewd intent:
MPERS85:10 H1286 These two lewd {first} sons, are by hystorians thought,
MGREC103:28 H2039 He at a bold, base {proud} Strumpets, lewd desire;
MGREC~~130:4~~ H3159 And vile {lewd} *Cassander* too, sticks not for shame;
MGREC~~133:40~~ H3330 This *Theos* he was murthered by his {lewd} wife,
LEWIS (2)
DIALOG143:2 H71 French *Lewis* {Jews} unjustly to the Crown to bring;
DUBART154:13 H58 Then in Saint *Lewis,* or thy last *Henry* great,
LIARS See LYARS
LIBERAL (1)
HUMOUR28:25 H337 They're liberal, pleasant, kinde, and courteous,
LIBERALL (2) [liberal]
DUBART153:40 H44 Sure liberall Nature, did with Art not small,
DUBART153:41 H45 In all the Arts make thee most liberall;
LIBERALLY (1)
CONTEM169:15 H56 That nature had, thus decked liberally:
LIBERTY (6)
MASSYR60:3 H268 To *Bactrians,* he gave their liberty,
MGREC~~100:36~~ H1920 The more because not set at liberty;
MGREC119:13 H2703 Their ancient liberty, afresh now seeks,
MGREC120:2 H2733 Nor former liberty, or glory gain'd;
MGREC~~131:1~~ H3189 Doth promise liberty to *Athens* State;
MGREC132:24 H3269 Onely restrained of his liberty;
LIBIA (1) [libya]
ELEMEN12:18 H178 My Panthers, and my Leopards of *Libia,*
LIBIAN (1) [libyan]
ELEMEN14:15 H257 Much might I say, of the *Arabian* sands; {hot *Libian* sand}
LIBRA (1)
SEASONS51:1 H175 And doth in poyzing *Libra* this month shine.
LIBRARY (1)
MGREC134:21 H3352 The {At *Alexandria* a} Library at *Alexandria* built,
LIBYA See LIBIA
LIBYAN See LIBIAN
LICENCIOUSNESSE (1)
MGREC103:24 H2035 He walloweth now, {That wallowing} in all licenciousnesse,

LICENTIOUS (1)
MASSYR55:31 H97 As of {on} her life, licentious, and unchast.
LICK (1)
DIALOG147:37 H261 That nursing Kings, shall come and lick thy dust:
LIDIA (2) [lydia]
MPERS69:20 H642 Against great *Cressus,* then of *Lidia* head;
MPERS78:31 H1012 At *Sardis,* in *Lidia,* these all doe meet,
LIDIANS (1) [pl.]
MPERS70:3 ~~H674~~ And with the *Lidians,* had no more to doe.
LIE (3) [recline] See also LYE, LY
MPERS82:33 H1180 Straight comes her Lord, and finds his wife thus lie,
MGREC130:34 ~~H3181~~ Yet in the flower of's age, he must lie dead,
SIDNEY152:22 H91 His bones do lie interr'd in stately *Pauls.*
LIEFTENANT (1) [lieutenant] See also LEIUTENANT
MPERS~~90:33~~ H1500 Lieftenant to the King, but soon he fled
LIEGE See LEIGE
LIES (9)
MGREC117:3 H2610 Now like a mortall helplesse man he lies;
MGREC126:8 H2999 Well fortified, and on the Sea it lies;
DIALOG146:13 ~~H200~~ Religion, Gospell, here lies at the stake,
SIDNEY152:24 H93 *Here lies intomb'd in fame, under this stone,*
QELIZ157:40 H108 But happinesse, lies in a higher sphere,
QELIZ158:15 H124 *Here lies the pride of Queens, pattern of Kings,*
QELIZ158:17 H126 Here lies the envy'd, yet unparralell'd Prince,
CONTEM171:24 H127 But Man grows old, lies down, remains where once he's laid.
MERCY188:26 H12 My bruised heart lies sobbing at the Root,
LIEUTENANT (4) See also LEIUTENANT, LIEFTENANT
MPERS86:27 H1343 From the Lieutenant first, he takes away,
MPERS90:32 H1499 By th' Kings Lieutenant {*Tissaphernes*} is encountered,
MGREC94:31 H1669 Then to his Lieutenant, {he} in *Asia* sends,
MGREC130:9 H3164 *Antigonus'* Lieutenant stayes her still,
LIEUTENANTS (1) [poss.]
MPERS69:6 H628 Who had in *Persia* the Lieutenants place.
LIFE (89) See also LIFE'S
FATHER5:20 H21 These are of all, the life, the nurse, the grave,
ELEMEN11:13 H133 Not sparing life when I can take the same;
ELEMEN15:15 H297 If not, soon ends his life, as did his voyce.
ELEMEN16:20 H343 Which can to life, restore a fainting heart:
ELEMEN19:12 H457 As my fresh Aire preserves, all things in life;
HUMOUR25:33 H222 So spils {shed'st} that life {blood}, thou'rt bounden to preserve.
HUMOUR25:39 H228 For Countries good, thy life thou darst expose:
HUMOUR26:16 H246 His life now animal, from vegative?
HUMOUR26:17 H247 If thou giv'st life, I give thee nourishment,
HUMOUR27:37 H308 Mans life to boundlesse time might stil endure;
HUMOUR30:21 H413 Then who's mans friend, when life and all forsakes?
HUMOUR33:31 H545 Which life and motion to each Creature gives,
AGES35:36 H22 And when tis broke, then ends his life and all.
AGES37:38 H100 I gave no hand, nor vote, for death, or life:
AGES46:10 H441 Yea knowing much, the pleasant'st {pleasants} life of all,
SEASONS~~49:22~~ H113 Blest rustick Swains, your pleasant quiet life,
SEASONS49:24 ~~H114~~ Yet hath your life, made Kings the same envy,

MASSYR55:25 H91 Which was the cause, poor *Menon* lost his life,
MASSYR55:31 H97 As of {on} her life, licentious, and unchast.
MASSYR65:21 H486 minde, and slew him by the way; {& caus'd his life there end,}
MASSYR67:25 H571 His life so base, and dissolute, invites
MASSYR68:28 H614 Who soone did terminate his Life, and Crown:
MPERS69:32 H654 Brake his long silence, cry'd, spare *Cressus* life:
MPERS~~69:38~~ H668 Whose happy life attains an happy end.
MPERS70:2 ~~H673~~ Gave him at once, his life, and Kingdom too,
MPERS~~70:2~~ H673 Gave him his life, and took him for a friend,
MPERS71:17 H731 He seized first of life, and then of Land;
MPERS77:10 H949 And the ensuing yeare ended his life,
MPERS83:9 H1197 Of life, no man had least security.
MPERS85:7 ~~H1283~~ That nought appeas'd him, but his brothers life.
MPERS~~85:7~~ H1283 Stil making war, till first had lost his life:
MPERS~~91:22~~ H1532 By poyson caus'd, the young one to lose her life.
MPERS91:23 H1537 Then in voluptuousnesse he leads his life,
MPERS~~91:30~~ H1544 His life may read in *Plutarch* to be seen.
MPERS~~92:23~~ H1581 Lost but his life for horrid treasons all.
MGREC113:9 H2436 Or flesh, or {and} life, could bear, till both were spent
MGREC~~114:12~~ H2480 Nought but his life for this could satisfie;
MGREC114:26 H2496 Thus was he tortur'd, till his life was spent.
MGREC116:2 H2562 The thread of *Alexanders* life was spun;
MGREC~~116:10~~ H2574 But pin d in grief till life did her forsake:
MGREC118:32 H2681 And {So} took his life unworthily that houre:
MGREC~~120:4~~ H2736 Who fear'd *Antipater* would take his life
MGREC121:28 H2810 Had it but in *Perdicas* life arriv'd,
MGREC126:22 H3013 Gives promise for her life, and {so} wins the day:
MGREC127:22 H3052 *Antigonus,* then takes {who took} his life unjust,
MGREC129:19 H3133 The life of her must go, and of her son.
MGREC131:15 H3207 For here *Antigonus* lost rule, and life,
MGREC131:28 H3220 Falls so extreamly sick, all fear {fear'd} his life,
MGREC132:2 H3235 He, whom she gave his life, her death must {shall} give)
MGREC133:12 H3300 *Antigonus* his Kingdoms lost, and's life,
MGREC133:41 H3331 *Seleuchus* reign'd, when he had lost his life,
MGREC134:38 ~~H3367~~ For *Pompey's* life, then plac'd her in his stead,
MGREC~~135:1~~ H3373 Did by his Sword his life soon after send.
MGREC135:3 H3375 To take her life, and quit her from all harmes;
MROMAN139:16 H3544 She loathed so the fact, she loath'd her life,
DIALOG143:3 H72 No *Edward, Richard,* to lose rule, and life,
SIDNEY150:30 H57 He rescued not with life, that life of thine,
SIDNEY150:30 H57 He rescued not with life, that life of thine,
SIDNEY~~150:38~~ H66 And *Phoenix Spencer* doth unto his life,
DAVID159:9 H24 Pleasant and lovely were they both in life,
VANITY161:1 H52 This pearl of price, this tree of life, this spring,
TDUDLEY165:16 H18 Nor was his name, or life lead so obscure
TDUDLEY165:19 H21 Such as in life, no man could justly deem.
DDUDLEY167:10 H7 *A worthy Matron of unspotted life,*
CONTEM170:33 H103 When deep dispair, with wish of life hath fought,
CONTEM171:10 H114 Our life compare we with their length of dayes
FLESH176:29 H69 The word of life it is my meat.
FLESH177:15 H96 Of Life, there are the waters sure,

SICKNES178:29 H12 no life is like to this.
SICKNES178:30 H13 For what's this life, but care and strife?
1LETTER181:3 H1 My head, my heart, mine Eyes, my life, nay more,
2LETTER182:3 H9 Commend me to the man more lov'd then life,
3LETTER183:16 H18 Her fellow lost, nor joy nor life do wish,
3LETTER183:19 H21 Mine being gone, I lead a joyless life,
CHILDRN186:25 H92 What would save life, and what would kill.
MERCY188:35 H21 Who lov'd thee more (it seem'd) then her own life.
MEDDM197:28 Hp275 to mount to heaven clog'd wth the Cares and riches of this Life,
MEDDM200:9 Hp279 sweets of this life, that so they might feed vpon more
MEDDM205:23 Hp286 He that would keep a pure heart and lead a blamlesse life,
MEDDM205:28 Hp286 life as we doe, but he that wth David, sets the lord alway in his
MEDDM206:12 Hp287 degrees, euen in this life, some are Stars of the first
MEDDM207:13 Hp288 All the Comforts of this Life, may be compared to the gourd of
SOREFIT222:1 H20 My life shall dedicated bee
SOREFIT222:3 H22 Thou know'st no life I did require
FAINT222:16 H6 My life as Spiders webb's cutt off
FAINT222:25 H15 My life is hid wth Thee
WHAT224:24 H24 Me lasting life shall giue.
THEART229:11 H13 An hvble, faithfull life O Lord
HANNA230:14 H7 And life was ended near.

LIFE'S (1) [life is]
SICKNES178:26 H9 Yet live I shall, this life's but small,

LIFT (5)
MASSYR66:10 H516 Now *Zim,* and *lim, {Jim}* lift up their shriking {scriething}
MGREC94:30 H1668 To lift his hand, 'gainst such a Monarchy.
DIALOG148:21 H286 Oh *Abrahams* seed lift up your heads on high.
DAVID158:31 H11 Lest the uncircumcis'd lift up their voyce:
MYCHILD217:26 Hp243 ye Lord would but lift vp ye light of his Covnten^{c} vpon me,

LIFTED (1)
MASSYR67:9 H555 Is *Judah's* King, now lifted up on high.

LIFTS (2)
MPERS~~69:38~~ H660 Who *Solon* was? to whom he lifts his hands;
MEDDM196:18 Hp273 shadowes of his euening to be stretched out, lifts vp his head

LIGAMENTS (1) [pl.]
HUMOUR34:15 H570 And the strong ligaments, from hence arise,

LIGHT (20) [not dark]
AGES~~36:8~~ H32 When blushing first, she 'gins to red {light} the Aire.
AGES41:6 H226 That wonder 'tis I yet behold the light,
MGREC~~116:10~~ H2575 All friends she shuns, yea, banished the light,
DIALOG147:16 H242 Light Christendome, and all the world to see,
CONTEM168:3 H13 Sure he is goodness, wisdome, glory, light,
CONTEM169:7 H49 Who gave this bright light luster unto thee:
FLESH177:19 H100 No Candle there, nor yet Torch light,
AUTHOR177:38 H10 I cast thee by as one unfit for light,
2LETTER182:22 H28 O how they joy when thou dost light the skyes.
CHILDRN185:16 H42 As is ordain'd, so shall they light.
MEDDM198:32 Hp277 It is a pleasant thing to behold the light, but sore eyes are not
MEDDM202:22 Hp282 although we may walk by his light, but when he is set, we are
MEDDM202:24 Hp282 a moment that we cannot behold the light of his Countenance,
MEDDM202:25 Hp282 other time, yet he affords so much light as may direct our way,

MEDDM202:28 Hp282 and se no light, yet then must we trust in the lord and stay
MEDDM206:8 Hp287 of bignes and brightnes, yet all receiue their light from that
MYCHILD217:24 Hp243 in darknes and seen no light, yet haue I desired to stay my self
MYCHILD217:26 Hp243 ye Lord would but lift vp ye light of his Covntenc vpon me,
MYCHILD217:27 Hp243 grovnd me to powder it would bee but Light to me, yea oft
HOUSE236:19 H11 I starting vp ye light did spye,

LIGHT (1) [not heavy]
MPERS77:4 H943 *Darius* light, he {yet} heavie, home returnes,

LIGHT (1) [alight]
CHILDRN185:40 H66 Sore accidents on you may light.

LIGHTEN (1)
SEASONS51:41 H217 No Sun, to lighten their obscurity;

LIGHTENING (1) See also LIGHTNING
MEDDM199:5 Hp277 Lightening doth vsually preceed thunder, and stormes raine,

LIGHTLY (1)
ELEMEN15:41 H323 I lightly cast ashoare as frothy fleece.

LIGHTNESSE (1) [lightness]
AGES35:26 H12 Solid, hating all lightnesse, and al folly.

LIGHTNING (2) [lightening]
ELEMEN8:12 H10 Whence issu'd raines, and winds, lightning and thunder;
ELEMEN11:6 H126 What shal I say of Lightning, and of Thunder,

LIGHTS (2)
SEASONS47:3 ~~H17~~ Who for some months have seen but starry lights;
SEASONS~~47:5~~ H21 Who for some months have been but starry lights.

LIK'D (1) [liked]
DIALOG143:31 H100 And {Are} lik'd, and countenanc'd by men of might,

LIKE (3) [affection]
HUMOUR25:6 H195 For drink, which of us twain, like it the best,
AGES39:18 H161 The snorting Horse, the Trumpet, Drum I like,
FLESH176:41 H81 Nor such like trash which Earth doth hold,

LIKE (121) [similar] See also TH'LIKE
PROLOG7:7 H21 Nor can I, like that fluent sweet tongu'd *Greek*
ELEMEN8:16 H14 All looked like a Chaos, or new birth;
ELEMEN14:16 H258 Which rise like mighty {tumbling} billowes on the lands: {Land}
ELEMEN14:30 H272 Not one of us, all knowes, that's like to thee,
ELEMEN15:27 H309 Such wealth, but not such like, Earth thou mayst show.
ELEMEN17:30 H394 That after times, shall never feel like woe:
ELEMEN18:26 H430 And when I smile, your Ocean's like a Poole.
ELEMEN18:29 H433 The ruddy sweet sanguine, is like to Aire,
HUMOUR22:4 H73 And by misprisions, like to loose her wits;
HUMOUR23:31 H141 Like our sixt *Henry,* that same worthy {virtuous} thing.
HUMOUR28:26 H338 And like the Liver, all benignious;
HUMOUR~~31:28~~ H461 And what Flegme is, we know, likewise {like to} her mother,
HUMOUR31:33 H466 Now up, now down, transported like the Aire.
AGES43:16 ~~H308~~ Which others scatter, like the dew in *May.*
AGES43:23 H318 If *Bias* like, I'm stript unto my skin,
AGES44:30 H363 I've seen a Kingdom flourish like a tree,
AGES44:32 H365 And like a Cedar, others so surmount,
SEASONS46:32 H8 Sweet Spring, like man in his minority,
SEASONS46:35 ~~H11~~ She gently thus began, like some fair Queen;
SEASONS47:17 H33 Like Birds, now chirp, and hop about the field;

SEASONS49:12 H103 Like as an oven, that long time hath been heat.
SEASONS49:23 ~~H114~~ Was like that noble, brave *Archadian.*
SEASONS50:31 H165 Like good Old Age, whose younger juycie roots,
SEASONS52:15 H230 In Swadling clouts, like new-born infancy,
SEASONS52:17 H232 And like an Infant, stil he {it} taller growes.
MASSYR55:6 H72 She like a brave Virago, play'd the rex,
MASSYR56:9 H115 That like a river, long it did abide.
MASSYR57:10 H157 It is more like, being {his lust} with pleasures fed,
MASSYR58:8 H193 His master like a Strumpet chanc'd to {clad did} spy,
MASSYR65:15 H480 Had all his hopes like to a Spiders web;
MASSYR65:22 H487 Thus {Then} cast him out, like to a naked Asse,
MPERS71:6 H722 *Cambyses,* no wayes like, his noble Sire,
MPERS72:23 H771 Like fault must look, for the like recompence.
MPERS72:23 H771 Like fault must look, for the like recompence.
MPERS72:36 H780 And like in feature, to the *Smerdis* dead,
MPERS73:16 H803 (Who like to Kings, rul'd Kingdomes as they please,)
MPERS73:40 H825 Too politicke (tis {its} like) for me to tell,
MPERS75:28 H885 He like a King, now grants a Charter large,
MPERS76:15 H913 Quoth he, like Frogs, in water we must dive;
MPERS76:16 H914 Or like to Mice, under the earth must live;
MPERS76:17 H915 Or fly like birds, in unknown wayes full quick;
MPERS79:5 H1027 Is this to doe like *Xerxes,* or a Prince?
MPERS82:9 H1156 Which found, like *Greeks* they fight, the *Persians* fly,
MPERS83:37 H1225 Which done, a sumptuous feast; makes like a King
MPERS85:32 H1308 The {This} King, his sister, like *Cambyses,* wed;
MPERS86:14 H1330 What helps, {help} in's enterprize he's like to find,
MPERS86:17 H1333 His brothers little love, like to be gone,
MPERS86:19 H1335 These and like motives, hurry him amain,
MPERS88:8 H1401 Which like a mighty cloud darkned the skye;
MPERS88:33 H1426 Nor *Gorgons* {head} like to this, transform'd to stones.
MGREC96:19 H1739 He fifteen hundred had like women drest,
MGREC96:25 H1745 Like severall houses moving upon wheeles:
MGREC97:4 H1765 Of late, like some immovable he lay,
MGREC97:15 H1776 T'ward them, demean'd himself like a Commander;
MGREC98:8 H1810 In the old town (which now {then} lay like a wood)
MGREC98:26 H1828 For now's the time, Captains like Kings may live;
MGREC98:36 H1838 The dangers, difficulties, like to rise;
MGREC98:37 H1839 First, at *Euphrates,* what he's like to abide,
MGREC99:27 H1870 Who did the like to *Hector* (of more fame)
MGREC103:5 H2016 None like to this in riches did abound.
MGREC104:8 H2060 The little hope, of profit like to rise.
MGREC106:4 H2138 And though a Monarch once {late}, now lyes like clay;
MGREC106:6 H2140 Though gods on earth, like Sons of men shall {they} dye.
MGREC110:3 H2303 A potent Army with him, like a King,
MGREC114:6 H2474 Like this, against his deity to kick:
MGREC116:6 H2566 Least {Lest} of such like, their Father chance to sup:
MGREC117:3 H2610 Now like a mortall helplesse man he lies;
MGREC117:18 H2625 Like to that Giant, of his eye bereft;
MGREC119:2 H2692 *Perdicas* took no Province, like the rest,
MGREC119:20 H2710 The like of *Leonatus,* he requires,
MGREC119:33 H2723 For personage, none was like {to} this Commander:

MGREC122:22 ~~H2845~~ Who had an Army, like a great Commander.
MGREC123:28 H2892 *Cassander* could not (like his father) see
MGREC125:29 H2979 On which *Olimpias* of the like might taste.
MGREC128:34 H3107 Who at *Gaza* did th' like to him before.
MGREC131:3 H3193 Not like a King, but like some God they fain'd;
MGREC131:3 H3193 Not like a King, but like some God they fain'd;
MGREC135:17 H3389 Then came the *Romane,* like a raging flood,
MGREC135:27 H3399 Became like chaffe upon the threshing-floor;
MGREC135:41 H3413 This taske befits not women, like to men:
DIALOG142:5 H34 What, hath some *Hengist,* like that *Saxon* stout,
SIDNEY151:33 ~~H75~~ Like unwise *Phaeton* his ill guided sonne,
QELIZ158:2 H111 She set, she set, like *Titan* in his rayes,
VANITY159:35 H7 No, they like beasts, and sonnes of men shall die,
CONTEM168:18 H26 And softly said, what glory's like to thee?
CONTEM170:2 H76 Who like a miscreant's driven from that place,
CONTEM170:31 H101 His face like death, his heart with horror fraught,
CONTEM170:32 H102 Nor Male-factor ever felt like warr,
FLESH175:26 H26 Dost honour like? acquire the same,
SICKNES178:29 H12 no life is like to this.
1LETTER181:9 H7 I like the earth this season, mourn in black,
2LETTER182:20 H26 Like those far scituate under the pole,
3LETTER183:28 H30 And like two Turtles roost within one house,
3LETTER183:29 H31 And like the Mullets in one River glide,
ANNEB187:26 H16 Like as a bubble, or the brittle glass,
ANNEB187:27 H17 Or like a shadow turning as it was.
MEDDM196:25 Hp273 Sweet words are like hony, a little may refresh, but too much
MEDDM196:28 Hp273 children, haue their different natures, some are like flesh w^{ch}
MEDDM196:29 Hp273 but salt will keep from putrefaction, some again like tender
MEDDM197:4 Hp274 Authority wthout wisedome is like a heavy axe, wthout an edg
MEDDM198:22 Hp276 done, but either that or something like it, hath been both done
MEDDM199:15 Hp278 Ambitious men are like hops that neuer rest climbing soe long
MEDDM200:16 Hp279 garment, she easily foresees what euents it is like to produce,
MEDDM202:7 Hp281 earth some so wise and learned, that they seeme like Angells
MEDDM202:9 Hp281 like beasts then men, some pious saints, some incarnate
MEDDM202:34 Hp282 say it is enough, but like the daughters of the horsleach, crys
MEDDM205:1 Hp285 (like sowre land) are of so tough and morose a dispotion that
MEDDM205:10 Hp286 his more fixed and resolued thoughts, are like to
MEDDM205:11 Hp286 inhabitants his slight and flitting thoughts are like passengers,
MEDDM208:24 Hp290 like the reeds of Egipt that peirce insteed of supporting like
MYCHILD216:11 Hp241 some time I fell into a lingering sicknes like a consvmption
MYCHILD217:6 Hp242 walking after I haue been afflicted. I haue been wth God like
MYCHILD218:26 Hp244 consideration of these things and many ye like would soon turn
WHAT224:1 H1 What God is like to him I serve
WHAT224:2 H2 What Sav^{r}. like to mine?
WHAT224:13 H13 My God he is not like to y^{rs}
30SEPT227:29 Hp257 I haue passed thro: to ye End y^{t} if you meet wth the like yov
30SEPT227:31 Hp257 will doe ye like for yov if you trvst in him; And when he shall
SAMUEL228:10 H11 No freind I haue like Thee to trust

LIKED [affection] See LIK'D

LIKELY (2)

MGREC95:32 H1711 Though some there be, and that {(perhaps)} more likely, write;

MGREC104:10 H2062 Then with so few, how likely to be crost.

LIKENED (1)

MGREC135:20 H3392 The first, was likened to a head of gold,

LIKEWISE (22)

HUMOUR28:5 H317 And Flegme likewise can shew, her cruel art,
HUMOUR28:17 H329 Likewise the Whey, some use I in the veines,
HUMOUR30:27 H419 Likewise the useful spleen, though not the best,
HUMOUR31:28 H461 And what Flegme is, we know, likewise {like to} her mother,
HUMOUR34:11 H566 Mine likewise is the marrow of the back,
AGES39:14 H157 The manners of the Court, I likewise {also} know,
AGES39:15 H158 Nor ignorant {And so likewise} what they in Country do;
AGES41:39 H256 For time, for place, likewise for each relation,
MASSYR53:29 H19 *Resen, Caleh,* and *Rehoboth* likewise,
MASSYR54:12 H39 Likewise *Bal-peor,* of the *Moabites:*
MASSYR54:36 H63 *Zoroaster,* their King, he likewise slew,
MPERS71:34 H748 The Ægyptian *Apis* then he likewise slew,
MPERS83:22 H1210 But all his family was likewise slain,
MGREC102:29 H1999 He likewise here a world of treasure found,
MGREC~~108:37~~ H2253 Which *Alexandria* he doth also {likewise} name,
MGREC128:15 H3088 Now {Then} *Ptolomy* would gaine the *Greeks* likewise,
MGREC128:25 H3098 His Son at *Gaza* likewise lost the field,
MGREC130:32 ~~H3181~~ And *Cleopatra's* blood, now likewise spill'd,
MROMAN137:2 H3453 A hundred Senators he likewise chose,
MROMAN137:30 H3481 And Priests, and Flamines likewise he deputed;
MEDDM207:32 Hp289 the soundest of men, haue likewise their nightly monitor, by
28AUG225:27 Hp254 many times my faith weak likewise, the Lord was pleased to

LILLIES (1)

DIALOG143:14 H83 Her Lillies in mine Armes avouch the same.

LILLY (3)

HUMOUR32:40 H514 My Lilly white, when joyned with her red,
MPERS82:31 H1178 Cut off her lilly breasts, her nose, and ears;
MPERS82:37 H1184 To see that face, where Rose and Lilly stood,

LIMB'D (1) [limbed]

ELEMEN9:14 H48 Though strong limb'd *Vulcan* forg'd it by his skill,

LIMBE (3) [limb]

MGREC108:6 H2222 With wracks, and tortures, every limbe to stretch.
MGREC113:3 H2430 To wreak their spight, and hate, on every limbe.
DIALOG141:19 H18 And thou a childe, a Limbe, and dost not feele

LIMBED See LIMB'D

LIMBES (2) [limbs]

MEDDM205:32 Hp286 Burden, is the breaking of their limbes, some again, are but
PILGRIM210:3 H3 His wasted limbes, now lye full soft

LIMBS (5) [pl.]

ELEMEN9:19 H53 Your shrinking limbs, which winters cold doth harme;
SEASONS~~49:33~~ H123 Upon the grass resting your healthy limbs,
MGREC114:25 H2495 He on the wrack, his limbs in peeces rent,
MGREC136:16 H3430 *The vast limbs of a mighty Monarchy.*
1LETTER181:13 H11 My chilled limbs now nummed lye forlorn;

LIME-TWIGS (1) [pl.]

CHILDRN185:27 H53 Or least by Lime-twigs they be foyl'd,

LINE (7) n.
HUMOUR22:40 H109 To be distill'd a drop on every line!
SEASONS47:4 H18 Crosses the Line, and equals night and day,
SEASONS50:40 H174 The tenth {twelfth} of this, *Sol* riseth in the Line,
SEASONS52:35 H250 And North-ward stil approaches to the Line;
MPERS73:5 H792 The Male line, of great *Cyrus* now did {had} end.
MPERS92:21 ~~H1579~~ And that great *Cyrus* line, yet was not run,
MPERS~~92:26~~ H1584 Some write great *Cyrus* line was not yet run,
LINE (1) v.
HUMOUR23:26 H136 Whose Serene {profound} heads, I line with policies,
LINEALLY (1)
MGREC98:4 H1806 And from whom also, lineally {he} descended:
LINES (11) [pl.]
FATHER5:7 H8 Their worth so shines, in those rich lines you show.
FATHER6:9 H43 These ragged lines, will do't, when they appear.
PROLOG~~6:23~~ H8 My obscure Verse,{Lines} shal not so dim their worth.
PROLOG6:26 H10 Great *Bartas* sugar'd lines doe but read o're;
PROLOG7:37 H47 If e're you daigne these lowly lines, your eyes
SEASONS53:2 H258 *Or better Lines you should have had;*
MROMAN140:1 H3564 And weary lines (though lanke) I many pen'd:
SIDNEY151:29 ~~H75~~ To fix my faltring lines upon his tomb:
SIDNEY152:19 H88 For to conclude my poem two lines they daigne,
DUBART153:4 H8 My dazled sight of late, review'd thy lines,
BIRTH180:2 H12 These farewell lines to recommend to thee,
LINGERING (1)
MYCHILD216:11 Hp241 some time I fell into a lingering sicknes like a consvmption
LION (3)
MGREC135:28 H3400 The first a Lion, second was a Beare,
MGREC135:34 H3406 But yet this Lion, Bear, this Leopard, Ram,
MEDDM204:3 Hp284 he that deliuered me, sath Dauid, from the paw of the Lion
LIONS (5) [pl.]
ELEMEN12:17 H177 Ile here let goe, my Lions of *Numedia,*
AGES45:39 H429 My heart sometimes as fierce, as Lions bold,
MPERS90:7 H1480 O're mountains, rocks, and hils, as Lions bold;
DAVID159:12 H27 Stronger then Lions, ramping for their prey.
VANITY160:27 H37 Where lions fierce, nor lions whelps hath {have} been,
LIONS (2) [poss.]
MPERS70:25 H696 And caus'd his foes in Lions den to dye.
VANITY160:27 H37 Where lions fierce, nor lions whelps hath {have} been,
LIQUID (1)
CONTEM172:30 H163 Ye Fish which in this liquid Region 'bide,
LIQUOR (1)
SEASONS51:3 H177 Whose lively liquor oft is curst, and blest;
LIQUORS (1) [pl.]
MGREC109:9 H2268 His liquors more devoutly in, for's sake.
LISBONS (1) [poss.]
QELIZ156:25 H52 Her stately Troops advanc'd to *Lisbons* wall,
LISP'D (1) [lisped]
PROLOG7:8 H22 Who lisp'd at first, speake afterwards more {in future times}
LISSUS (1)
MPERS79:31 H1057 His Hoast, who {all} *Lissus* drinks to quench their thirst,

LIST (6) [desire]
ELEMEN9:30 H64 But be he what they list {will}, yet his aspect,
ELEMEN16:24 H347 Both when we list, to water we convert.
HUMOUR26:7 H237 To play Philosopher, I have no list;
MASSYR56:27 H133 (Each man beleive it, as his fancy list)
MPERS84:4 H1232 To drink more then he list, none bidden was:
MGREC122:33 H2854 He plac'd, displac'd, controld, rul'd, as he list,

LIST (2) [catalog]
ELEMEN12:24 H184 But here, or there, I list now none to name;
ELEMEN15:30 H312 With thousands moe, which now I list not name,

LISTS (1)
HUMOUR29:15 H368 And in contentions lists, now justly enter.

LITTLE (54)
ELEMEN8:31 H29 Where {In} little is, {time} I can but little show,
ELEMEN8:31 H29 Where {In} little is, {time} I can but little show,
ELEMEN10:18 H93 Your wisdom out of little gathers {gather} much,
HUMOUR21:33 H61 That much wil talk, but little dares she do,
HUMOUR27:20 H291 Now through your leaves, some little time i'le spend;
HUMOUR32:16 H490 We shal expect much sound, but little force.
HUMOUR34:29 H584 Thy judgement is unsafe, thy fancy little,
AGES37:26 H88 This little house of flesh, did spacious count:
AGES38:4 H107 My little wrath did cease {end} soon as my wars.
AGES39:2 H145 For 'tis but little, that a childe can say.
AGES41:25 H242 My reason, then bad judge, how little hope,
SEASONS48:3 H56 The fearful Bird, his little house now builds,
MASSYR59:18 H242 Who there incamp'd two years, for little end,
MASSYR63:19 H404 Of whom is little said in any thing; [22 years.
MASSYR67:31 H577 To shew his little dread, but greater store,
MPERS~~71:4~~ H720 To shew how little Land he then should take.
MPERS71:18 H732 (But little *Marus,* {*Narus*} scap'd that cruel fate,
MPERS73:23 ~~H809~~ Who little pleasure had, in his short reigne,
MPERS76:21 H919 Return'd with little honour, and lesse gaine;
MPERS~~81:41~~ H1145 rest had} Weapons, they had none would {do little} harme;
MPERS84:19 H1255 The King not little joyfull of this chance,
MPERS86:17 H1333 His brothers little love, like to be gone,
MPERS87:38 H1390 Rejoyced {Was} not a little {jocund} at his feare.
MGREC93:35 H1632 But as the King of little *Macedon.*)
MGREC~~94:18~~ H1654 His little wealth among his Souldiers gave.
MGREC95:19 H1698 To *Alexanders* heart's no little joy.
MGREC95:40 H1719 Sure its {much} beyond my time, and little Art;
MGREC~~98:30~~ H1832 And therefore {So} gives this {his little} Lord-ship to another.
MGREC102:15 H1985 And to possesse, he counts no little blisse,
MGREC104:8 H2060 The little hope, of profit like to rise.
MGREC105:20 H2113 Who not a little chear'd, to have some eye,
MGREC~~107:39~~ H2214 With little pain there might have kept them still:
MGREC108:9 H2225 These not a little joy'd, this day to see,
MGREC108:31 H2247 Of Darts, and Arrowes, made so little spare,
MGREC133:7 H3295 A little now, how the Succession run:
MGREC134:18 H3349 In *Egypt* now {next,} a little time we'l spend.
TDUDLEY165:30 H32 True Patriot of this little Commonweal,
CONTEM169:21 H61 Seeming to glory in their little Art.

CONTEM171:13	H117	Living so little while we are alive;
BIRTH180:14	H24	Look to my little babes my dear remains.
2LETTER182:28	H34	His little world's a fathom under water,
MEDDM196:2	Hp272	A ship that beares much saile & little or no ballast, is easily
MEDDM196:3	Hp272	whose head hath great abilities and his heart little or no grace
MEDDM196:25	Hp273	Sweet words are like hony, a little may refresh, but too much
MEDDM199:9	Hp277	and sapless performances are simptoms of little spiritull vigor
MEDDM200:3	Hp278	sin, is it not a little one? will ere long say of a greater Tush god
MEDDM200:15	Hp279	A prudent mother will not cloth her little childe wth a long and
MEDDM201:1	Hp280	he will proportion the load, as god hath his little Children so
MEDDM204:19	Hp285	for takeing veangence on the house of Ahab and yet a little
MEDDM205:9	Hp286	man is called the little world so his heart may be cal'd the little
MED223:14	Hp250	who hath done so much for me, should haue so little from me,
11MAYA226:24	Hp255	Yet a little while and he that shall come will come and will not
REMB235:27	H8	I ow so mvch so little can

LIUE (8) [live]

MEDDM202:12	Hp281	some againe so weak and feeble, that while they liue, they are
BYNIGHT220:19	H17	I'le serve him here whilst I shall liue
SOREFIT221:19	H5	Then Lord thou said'st vnto me Liue.
FAINT222:24	H14	Why should I liue but to thy praise
WHAT224:20	H20	And I shall liue for aye.
WHAT224:22	H22	That dy'd but now doth liue,
30SEPT227:22	Hp257	I haue fovnd by Exper^{c}. I can no more liue wthout correction
THEART229:18	H20	For of thine Almes I liue.

LIUEING (2) [living]

TOCHILD215:5	H5	What was yr liueing mothers mind.
FAINT222:18	H8	And liueing man no more shall see

LIUELY (2) [lively]

MEDDM200:24	Hp279	The spring is a liuely emblem of the resurrection, after a long
MEDDM207:34	Hp289	their death, but their graue, is liuely represented before their

LIUES (2) [lives]

2SIMON195:3	Hp271	Parents perpetuate their liues in their posterity, and their
MEDDM207:22	Hp289	sayd that all haue a lease of their liues, some longer some

LIUES (1) v. [lives]

WHAT224:23	H23	The first and last y^{t} liues for aye,

LIV'D (4) [lived]

MASSYR~~57:23~~	H170	He many Ages liv'd after that day.
MGREC115:26	H2545	But now, *Antipater* had liv'd thus {so} long,
TDUDLEY165:20	H22	Well known and lov'd, where ere he liv'd, by most
DDUDLEY167:22	H19	*Of all her Children, Children, liv'd to see,*

LIVE (31) See also LIUE

ELEMEN9:38	H72	And though nought but *Sal'manders* live in fire;
ELEMEN18:6	H410	How freely should it go, so he might live.
AGES35:38	H24	Then may he live, til {out} threescore years or past.
AGES~~45:4~~	H385	I've Princes seen to live on others lands;
AGES45:7	~~H390~~	I've seen a Prince, to live on others lands,
AGES45:20	~~H402~~	But yet may live, to see't made up again:
AGES~~45:21~~	H403	Oh may you live, and so you will I trust
AGES~~45:22~~	H408	But ye may live to see't made up again.
SEASONS47:15	H31	And all that seem'd as dead, afresh do live.
MPERS~~74:15~~	H838	A thousand times, God save {long live} the King, they cry,

HUMOUR33:30 H544 And surely the Souls {Soul} sensative here lives,
LIVING (9) See also LIUING
ELEMEN~~8:34~~ H32 The benefit all Beings, {living} by me finde;
ELEMEN17:38 H402 I am the breath of every living soul.
ELEMEN19:17 H462 The living, scarce had power, to bury dead.
HUMOUR26:15 H245 What is there living, which cannot derive
QELIZ157:15 H83 (Who living consummates her Funerals)
QELIZ158:18 H127 Whose living vertues speak (though dead long since)
VANITY160:28 H38 Which leads unto that living Christall fount,
CONTEM171:13 H117 Living so little while we are alive;
1LETTER181:18 H16 True living Pictures of their Fathers face.
LIVINGS (1) [pl.]
DIALOG144:28 H136 Some lost their livings, some in prison pent,
LIV'ST (1) [livest]
FLESH175:10 H10 Sister, quoth Flesh, what liv'st thou on
LO (2) See also LOE
VANITY159:32 H4 Where is the man can say, lo, I have found
SICKNES178:21 H4 lo here is fatal Death.
LOAD (2)
MEDDM201:1 Hp280 strength he will proportion the load, as god hath his little
MEDDM201:4 Hp280 go vpright vnder them, but it matters not whether the load be
LOADED (1)
DIALOG147:23 ~~H247~~ And sturdy *Tyburn* loaded till it crack,
LOADEN (3)
MPERS82:41 H1188 With loaden heart unto the King he goes,
MGREC96:32 H1752 Loaden with gold, with jewels and with Plate,
MEDDM205:33 Hp286 loaden, and some haue nothing to shew but leaues only, and
LOATH (2) See also LOTH
ELEMEN18:11 H415 So loath he is to go, though nature's spent,
MEDDM197:19 Hp275 loath it, and that heart wch is not continually purifieing it self is
LOATH'D (2) [loathed]
MROMAN139:16 H3544 She loathed so the fact, she loath'd her life,
TDUDLEY165:40 H42 Those titles loath'd, which some too much do love
LOATHED (1)
MROMAN139:16 H3544 She loathed so the fact, she loath'd her life,
LOATHSOME (3)
HUMOUR31:2 H435 Thy loathsome imputation I defie;
AGES41:1 H221 Sometimes the loathsome {two fold} Pox, my face {me sore}
AGES~~41:2~~ H222 ugly {outward} marks of his eternal {inward loathsome} scars;
LOCKS (1) [pl.]
SEASONS~~46:35~~ H11 She trim'd her locks, which late had frosted been,
LOCKT (1)
MGREC~~124:33~~ H2940 He still kept fresh {lockt} within his memory,
LODGING (1)
MEDDM196:21 Hp273 Downny beds make drosey persons but hard lodging, keeps
LOE (2) See also LO
HUMOUR20:13 H5 Loe! other foure step up, crave leave to shew
AGES35:17 H3 Loe now! four other acts {act} upon the stage,
LOFTY (6)
ELEMEN15:6 H288 The lofty Eagle and the Storke flye low,
MGREC~~97:28~~ H1789 *Darius* now, more humble {less lofty} then before,

MGREC98:17 H1819 space {time} he takes this lofty {took that wealthy} town,
MGREC102:10 H1980 The firm foundations, {strong Foundation} and the lofty spires;
DUBART153:32 H36 Thus weake brain'd I, reading the lofty stile,
CONTEM169:12 H53 My humble Eyes to lofty Skyes I rear'd

LOGICK (1) [logic]
SIDNEY149:17 H16 Thy {His} Logick from *Euterpe* won the Crown,

LOINES (1) [loins]
SOREFIT221:25 H11 My feeble loines didst gird wth strenght

LONDON (1)
ELEMEN~~11:1~~ H118 And stately *London,* (our great *Britain's* glory)

LONELY (1)
CONTEM172:9 H145 A lonely place, with pleasures dignifi'd.

LONG (99) [length]
ELEMEN19:27 H472 Then in his long hot wars, {war} which *Millain* gain'd.
HUMOUR28:34 H346 If time I have transgrest, and been too long,
AGES41:8 H228 And I in black oblivions den long {now} laid;
AGES45:41 H431 My golden Bowl, and silver Cord, e're long,
SEASONS47:39 H51 And {The} Grasse growes long, the tender Lambs {hungry
SEASONS49:12 H103 Like as an oven, that long time hath been heat.
SEASONS50:6 H140 Bearing the burning heat of the long day;
SEASONS~~52:26~~ H241 In *Aquarias,* now keeps the loved {long wisht} Sun,
MASSYR55:26 H92 She flourishing with *Ninus,* long did reigne;
MASSYR56:2 H108 Each Square, was fifteen thousand paces long,
MASSYR56:9 H115 That like a river, long it did abide.
MASSYR57:5 H152 To sit, thus long (obscure) wrong'd {rob'd} of his seat;
MASSYR65:37 H502 The wals so strong, that stood so long, now fall;
MASSYR67:33 H579 The holy vessells, thither brought long since,
MPERS69:32 H654 Brake his long silence, cry'd, spare *Cressus* life:
MPERS70:26 H697 Long after this, he 'gainst the *Sythians* goes,
MPERS~~70:37~~ H708 Where some long after fought in vain for prize
MPERS72:33 H777 All thought {wisht} his short reign long, till {past before} it was
MPERS73:9 H796 Eight years he reign'd, a short, yet too long time,
MPERS~~74:15~~ H838 A thousand times, God save {long live} the King, they cry,
MPERS75:6 H867 This told, for enterance he stood not long,
MPERS79:20 H1046 Long viewing them, thought it great happinesse,
MPERS79:25 H1051 Of so long time, his thoughts had never been.
MPERS83:31 H1219 Although to *Xerxes,* they not long before,
MPERS~~84:12~~ H1247 Rebuilt those walls which long in rubbish lay,
MPERS88:14 H1407 But long under their fears, they did not stay,
MPERS91:11 H1519 Dissention in *Greece* continued {so} long,
MPERS~~91:25~~ H1539 But long in ease and pleasure did not lye,
MPERS91:27 ~~H1541~~ But yet for all his greatnesse, and long reign,
MPERS~~92:7~~ H1565 His brother, as tis said, long since was slain,
MPERS92:11 H1569 Whose race long time had worn the Diadem,
MGREC93:19 H1616 T'accomplish that, which long before was writ.
MGREC100:32 H1916 Who had long {sore} travaile, and much sorrow seen,
MGREC~~101:34~~ H1963 But long they stood not e're they're forc'd to run,
MGREC105:15 H2108 Wearied with his long march, did water seek,
MGREC105:33 H2126 Which made their long restraint, seeme to be none;
MGREC108:12 H2228 From bondage, long to be infranchised;
MGREC109:6 H2265 He t' *Nisa* goes, by *Bacchus* built long since,

MGREC109:14 H2273 Who comming thither, long before his Lord;
MGREC110:23 H2327 Long with excessive travailes wearied,
MGREC110:34 H2338 Whereon his acts, and travels, long appears;
MGREC111:21 H2366 Upon those Flats they did not long abide;
MGREC112:16 H2402 And his long travells past, and over-gone;
MGREC115:26 H2545 But now, *Antipater* had liv'd thus {so} long,
MGREC115:39 H2558 His age, and journey long, he now {then} pretends;
MGREC117:7 H2614 None of his Kindred, or {nor} his Race, long stood;
MGREC118:40 H2689 *Antipater*, had long rul'd *Macedon,*
MGREC119:36 H2726 Long marches through *Cilicia* he makes,
MGREC120:36 ~~H2773~~ His sumptuous monument long time did stand;
MGREC122:13 H2838 Perceives {Sees} *Aridæus* must not king it long,
MGREC123:10 H2872 In this Epitomy, too long to tell
MGREC124:27 H2934 *Polisperchon* hoping for's office long,
MGREC126:9 H3000 There by *Cassander* she's block'd up, so long,
MGREC127:34 H3064 Fearing their state {his force}, and what might hap ere long
MGREC129:5 H3119 Whom he in durance held, now and long since,
MGREC132:4 H3237 (Whose daughter unto wife, he'd newly {not long before} ta'n)
MGREC~~132:20~~ H3261 In his long absence to rule *Macedon.*
MGREC133:37 H3327 Who a long warre with *Egypts* King begun.
MGREC135:12 H3384 The *Assyrian* Monarchy long time did stand,
MROMAN138:9 H3499 Of *Latine* Kings this was long since the Seat,
DIALOG146:5 H193 They worded it so long, they fell to blows,
DIALOG146:33 ~~H219~~ To weep for that we both have pray'd for long,
DIALOG147:40 H264 Then bribes shall cease, and suits shall not stick long,
DIALOG148:23 H288 The scales shall fall from your long blinded eyes,
DUBART153:1 H5 In humble wise have vow'd their service long;
QELIZ157:34 H102 Nay Masculines, you have thus tax'd us long,
QELIZ158:18 H127 Whose living vertues speak (though dead long since)
CONTEM168:9 H18 How long since thou wast in thine Infancy?
CONTEM169:29 H68 And calls back moneths and years that long since fled
CONTEM171:3 H108 Their long descent, how nephews sons they saw,
CONTEM171:31 H133 Nor habitations long their names retain,
CONTEM174:10 H210 In weight, in frequency and long duration
SICKNES178:34 H17 O Bubble blast, how long can'st last?
BIRTH180:12 H22 Yet love thy dead, who long lay in thine arms:
1LETTER181:20 H18 I weary grow, the tedious day so long;
2LETTER181:31 H1 *Phoebus* make haste, the day's too long, be gone,
2LETTER182:21 H27 Which day by day long wait for thy arise,
2LETTER182:23 H29 O *Phoebus,* hadst thou but thus long from thine
CHILDRN185:33 H59 Long did I keep you soft and warm,
MERCY188:23 H9 Who might in reason yet have lived long,
MEDDM199:15 Hp278 men are like hops that neuer rest climbing soe long as they
MEDDM200:3 Hp278 not a little one? will ere long say of a greater Tush god regards
MEDDM200:15 Hp279 A prudent mother will not cloth her little childe wth a long and
MEDDM200:24 Hp279 is a liuely emblem of the resurrection, after a long winter
MEDDM200:27 Hp279 lost in the Autumn so shall it be at that great day after a long
MEDDM205:2 Hp285 of correction must make long furrows on their back and the
MEDDM208:2 Hp289 long night shall fly away, and the day of eternity shall never
MYCHILD215:32 Hp241 In a long fitt of sicknes wch I had on my bed I often comvned
MYCHILD216:14 Hp241 pleased God to keep me a long time wthout a child wch was a

MYCHILD216:21 Hp241 observed this y^{t} he hath never suffered me long to sitt loose
MYCHILD218:15 Hp244 prophecyes in it fullfilled wch could not haue been so long
11MAYB228:23 Hp259 It hath pleased God to giue me a long Time of respite for these
SON230:23 H6 He's come for whom I waited long.
HOUSE236:36 H28 Where oft I sate and long did lye,

LONG (5) [yearn]
CONTEM174:18 H217 And makes him long for a more quiet port,
FLESH175:30 H30 For riches dost thou long full sore?
MEDDM203:16 Hp283 meet wth such tossings that may cause him to long for shore,
PILGRIM210:13 H13 for waters cold he doth not long
PILGRIM210:23 H23 Oh how I long to be at rest

LONG'D (3) [longed]
AGES43:8 H303 And {I} oft long'd sore, to taste on Royalty.
TDUDLEY166:14 H56 For which he sigh'd and pray'd & long'd full sore
CONTEM172:15 H150 Which to the long'd for Ocean held its course,

LONGED (1)
AGES43:6 H301 That did oppose me, to my longed bay:

LONGER (23)
ELEMEN12:7 H167 And huge great *Taurus,* longer then the rest,
ELEMEN18:40 H444 Me for no Element, longer to hold.
AGES~~43:16~~ H311 The bottom nought, and so no longer stood.
SEASONS47:29 H45 Of longer dayes, and a more temperate air;
SEASONS48:27 H80 More solid fruits, require a longer time.
SEASONS52:28 H243 The day much longer then it was before,
MASSYR58:10 H195 Longer to serve this Metamorphos'd beast;
MPERS81:5 H1113 {Fearing} his best {bridge}, no longer for to {there would} stay;
MPERS82:5 H1152 No longer dar'd, but fiercely {bravely} on-set gave,
MGREC114:11 ~~H2479~~ *Alexander* now no longer could containe,
MGREC126:21 ~~H3012~~ But he unwilling longer there to stay,
MGREC132:1 H3234 (Rather then *Philips* child must {race should} longer live
MGREC133:28 H3318 Longer *Seleuchus* held the Royalty
MGREC135:16 H3388 The *Grecian* longer then the *Persian* stood,
CONTEM171:35 H136 Because their beauty and their strength last longer
MERCY189:1 H22 Thou being gone, she longer could not be,
MERCY189:8 H29 No wonder it no longer did survive.
MEDDM207:22 Hp289 all haue a lease of their liues, some longer some shorter, as it
MYCHILD217:7 Hp242 child, that no longer then the rod has been on my back
SOREFIT222:4 H23 Longer then still thy Name to praise,
FAINT222:26 H16 O Lord, no longer bee my Dayes
HOUSE236:25 H17 And when I could no longer look
HOUSE237:27 H57 The world no longer let me Love

LONGEST (1)
11MAYB228:26 Hp259 I had a feaver seatd vpon me wch indeed was the longest

LONGIMANUS (1)
MPERS83:26 H1214 *Artaxerxes Longimanus.*

LONGING (2)
AGES39:37 H180 My woful Parents longing hopes all {are} crost,
2LETTER182:6 H12 My sobs, my longing hopes, my doubting fears,

LONGINGS (1) [pl.]
HOURS233:23 H6 My Longings and my feares.

LONGS (1) [belongs]
HUMOUR33:40 H554 This point for {now} to discusse longs not to me,
LONGS (2) [yearns]
MEDDM203:12 Hp283 make y^{t} his place of residence, but longs to put in at that port
LOOK (24)
HUMOUR21:31 H59 Nay milk-sops, at such brunts you look but blew,
HUMOUR21:40 H68 But shuns to look on wounds, and bloud that's spilt,
AGES39:35 H178 That who would see vain man, may look on me:
SEASONS49:19 H110 Rubbing their dirty coates, till they look white.
SEASONS50:8 H142 Which makes the aged fields look young again,
MPERS72:23 H771 Like fault must look, for the like recompence.
MPERS87:16 ~~H1370~~ To look his manly brother in the face.
MGREC104:18 H2070 Look to himselfe, and leave him to that crew;
MGREC113:15 H2442 Look on *Parmenio,* after this disaster,
SIDNEY150:12 H37 Such were prejudicate, and did not look:
SIDNEY151:25 ~~H73~~ Enough for me to look, and so admire.
CONTEM169:26 H65 When present times look back to Ages past,
CONTEM173:2 H170 Look how the wantons frisk to tast the air,
BIRTH180:14 H24 Look to my little babes my dear remains.
ANNEB187:28 H18 More fool then I to look on that was lent,
2SIMON195:7 Hp271 look vpon when you should see me no more, I could think of
MEDDM196:8 Hp273 he that glorys in his gifts and adornings, should look vpon his
MEDDM198:33 Hp277 look vpon it, the pure in heart shall se god, but the defiled in
MEDDM204:27 Hp285 one that is in a far better estate then himself, but let him look
MEDDM204:30 Hp285 let him look on his owne vnworthynes and that will make him
MEDDM207:19 Hp289 permanent who would look for heauenly?
MYCHILD216:22 Hp242 by one afflict^{n} or other hath made me look home, and search
HOUSE236:14 H6 For sorrow neer I did not look,
HOUSE236:25 H17 And when I could no longer look
LOOK'D (1) [looked]
CONTEM168:17 H25 The more I look'd, the more I grew amaz'd,
LOOKED (1)
ELEMEN8:16 H14 All looked like a Chaos, or new birth;
LOOKES (1) [looks]
MEDDM206:21 Hp287 rather, then to beg forgiuenes for their sinnes, nature lookes
LOOKING (4)
SEASONS~~49:33~~ H124 By purling Brooks looking how fishes swims.
MGREC105:18 H2111 To them he goes, and {repairs then} looking in the Cart,
DISTEMP179:20 H8 And looking up unto his Throne on high,
28AUG226:5 Hp254 Now I can wait, looking every day when my Sav^{r} shall call for
LOOKS (7) See also LOOKES
HUMOUR23:28 H138 Their wrathfull looks are death, their words are laws;
AGES40:8 H189 Trusteth my loving looks, and glozing tongue,
MASSYR59:2 H226 Won by his loving looks, more loving {by his} speech,
MGREC~~110:18~~ H2320 In looks or gesture not abased ought,
CONTEM170:8 H81 The weeping Imp oft looks her in the face,
CONTEM170:18 H90 With sullen hateful looks he goes his wayes.
CONTEM170:30 H100 Who fancyes not his looks now at the Barr,
LOOK'T (1) [lookt]
ELEMEN8:13 H11 The quaking Earth did groan, the skie look't black,

LOOSE (11)
HUMOUR22:4 H73 And by misprisions, like to loose her wits;
HUMOUR33:5 H519 Rather then loose, one beateous *Hellena;*
AGES38:10 H113 I had no ships at Sea, no fraughts to loose.
AGES45:13 H395 one stab'd, another {and some to} loose his head {their heads};
MASSYR~~57:18~~ H165 So suddenly should loose so great a state,
MPERS75:12 H873 To loose a nose, to win a Town's no shame,
VERSES184:7 H11 Where nothing's to be had Kings loose their right
MEDDM203:6 Hp283 loose them then they are lesse then vanity & more then
MYCHILD216:2 Hp241 & sitting loose from God, vanity & ye follyes of Youth take hold
MYCHILD216:21 Hp241 observed this y^{t} he hath never suffered me long to sitt loose
RESTOR229:25 H8 Thou rais'st him vp I feard to loose

LOPS (1)
SEASONS47:10 H26 The Gardner, now superfluous branches lops,

LOPT (1)
MERCY188:24 H10 I saw the branches lopt the Tree now fall,

LORD (65) See also LD
MASSYR59:40 H264 *Arbaces* thus, of all becomming Lord,
MPERS82:33 H1180 Straight comes her Lord, and finds his wife thus lie,
MGREC95:17 H1696 Which who so did {doth}, must Lord of all remain,
MGREC100:34 H1918 {Whose death} her wofull Lord for to {full sadly did} lament.
MGREC104:22 H2074 Lays hold on's Lord, and binding him with bands.
MGREC109:14 H2273 Who comming thither, long before his Lord;
MGREC109:19 H2278 And as his Sovereign Lord, him humbly greets.
MGREC128:20 H3093 And Lord o'th' City {royal} *Susha* did remain.
CONTEM169:35 H73 Sees glorious *Adam* there made Lord of all,
2SIMON195:13 Hp271 better pris'd by you, for the Authors sake. the lord blesse you
MEDDM202:28 Hp282 se no light, yet then must we trust in the lord and stay vpon our
MEDDM205:28 Hp286 we doe, but he that wth David, sets the lord alway in his sight
PILGRIM211:2 H43 Lord make me ready for that day
MYCHILD216:3 Hp241 16. The Lord layd his hand sore vpon me & smott me wth y^{e}
MYCHILD216:4 Hp241 When I was in my afflict^{n}. I besovght the Lord, and confessed
MYCHILD216:12 Hp241 wth a lamenesse wch correction I saw the Lord sent to hu̅ble
MYCHILD216:30 Hp242 ye Times w^{n} ye Lord hath manifested ye most Love to me.
MYCHILD216:31 Hp242 haue I gone to searching, and haue said wth David Lord search
MYCHILD217:25 Hp243 ye Lord, and when I haue been in sicknes + pain, I haue
MYCHILD217:26 Hp243 ye Lord would but lift vp ye light of his Covnten^{c} vpon me,
FEVER221:12 H27 Praise to my Lord I say,
SOREFIT221:16 H2 In my distresse I sovght ye Lord
SOREFIT221:19 H5 Then Lord thou said'st vnto me Liue.
SOREFIT221:33 H19 O make it frvitfull faithfull Lord
SOREFIT222:8 H27 O Lord for aye is my request
FAINT222:26 H16 O Lord, no longer bee my Dayes
MED223:3 Hp250 Lord why should I doubt any more w^{n} thov hast given me such
MED223:6 Hp250 I thy child, yee shall be my Sons and Daughters saith ye Lord
MED223:17 Hp250 him as I ovght. Lord haueing this hope let me purefye my self
JULY223:30 Hp251 O Lord let me neuer forgett thy Goodnes, nor question thy
JULY223:36 Hp251 Come Lord Jesus, come quickly.
MYSOUL225:21 H25 Come Jesvs qvickly, Blessed Lord
28AUG225:27 Hp254 times my faith weak likewise, the Lord was pleased to vphold
28AUG226:2 Hp254 but joyfully? The Lord knowes I dare not desire that health

28AUG226:6 Hp254 Lord gravnt y^{t} while I live I may doe y^{t} service I am able in this
30SEPT227:23 Hp257 then without food. Lord wth y^{y} correction giue Instrvction and
SAMUEL228:8 H9 He's mine, but more O Lord thine own
SAMUEL228:12 H13 P^{r}serve O Lord from stormes & wrack
11MAYB228:28 Hp259 it ye more tedious, but it pleased ye Lord to support my heart
11MAYB228:30 Hp259 But alas! I cannot render vnto ye Lord according to all his
11MAYB228:32 Hp259 doe. Lord Thou y^{t} knowest All things know'st that I desire to
THEART229:7 H9 Lord whilst my fleeting time shall last
THEART229:11 H13 An hvble, faithfull life O Lord
THEART229:15 H17 Accept O Lord my simple mite
SON231:19 H31 O help me pay my Vowes O Lord
SON231:27 H39 O Lord gravnt that I may never forgett thy Loving kindness in
2HUSB232:5 H6 O hearken Lord vnto my suit
2HUSB232:9 H10 Thy servant Lord. Keep & p^{r}serve
2HUSB232:11 H12 At thy comand O Lord he went
2HUSB232:22 H23 O Lord accept of it.
2HUSB232:25 H26 O Lord thov know'st my weak desires
2HUSB232:27 H28 Lord bee thov pilott to ye ship
2HUSB232:29 H30 In stormes and sicknes Lord p^{r}serve.
2HUSB232:32 H33 Lord gravnt thov good Successe
2HUSB233:3 H36 Rember Lord thy folk whom thou
2HUSB233:11 H44 Lord let my Eyes see once Again
HOURS233:20 H3 O Lord thou hear'st my dayly moan
HOURS234:17 H31 O shine vpon me blessed Lord
HOURS234:21 H35 O hear me Lord in this Reqvest
HOURS234:29 H43 So both of vs thy Kindnes Lord
HOURS234:33 H47 But give me Lord a better heart
HOURS235:1 H53 If thou assist me Lord I shall
REMB235:26 H7 O Lord thov know'st I'm weak.
REMB235:31 H12 O thou y^{t} hearest prayers Lord
REMB236:5 H20 Thy mercyes Lord haue been so great

LORDS (2) [pl.]
MGREC129:25 H3139 And now they are, {were} free Lords, of what they had,
MEDDM207:9 Hp288 we are lords we will come no more at thee If outward

LORD-SHIP (1)
MGREC98:30 H1832 And therefore {So} gives this {his little} Lord-ship to another.

LORDSHIP (1)
MGREC131:13 H3205 Of *Asia* the Lordship shall retain.

LOSE (5)
SEASONS49:29 H118 Oh! happy Shepheard, which had not to lose,
MPERS~~91:22~~ H1532 By poyson caus'd, the young one to lose her life.
MGREC106:22 H2156 So daily of his vertues doth he lose;
DIALOG143:3 H72 No *Edward, Richard,* to lose rule, and life,
BIRTH179:34 H10 How soon't may be thy Lot to lose thy friend,

LOSS (4)
MASSYR~~65:5~~ H470 Requited not the cost {loss}, the toyle, and pain.
SIDNEY~~150:41~~ H69 For the sad loss of her dear *Astrophel.*
BIRTH180:13 H23 And when thy loss shall be repaid with gains
3LETTER183:10 H12 Whose loss hath made her so unfortunate:

LOSSE (10) [loss]
ELEMEN19:26 H471 Where famous *Charles* the fift, more losse sustain'd,

MASSYR64:22 H446 Which was the losse of *Syria* withall;
MPERS76:28 H926 Return'd with wondrous losse, and honour lesse:
MPERS77:40 H981 To present losse, future subversion;
MPERS84:24 H1260 His father *Xerxes* losse, and shame, much more,
MGREC95:5 H1684 With losse of thirty four, of his there slaine:
MGREC97:12 H1773 Yet all this grief, this losse, this over-throw,
MGREC103:32 H2043 His names {fames} dishonour, losse unto his State.
QELIZ158:13 H122 *The greater was our gain, our losse the more.*
HOURS233:26 H9 Tho: losse and sicknes me assail'd,

LOSSES (6) [pl.]

MPERS92:34 H1592 Whose warres and losses we may better tell;
CONTEM173:36 H200 Subject to sorrows, losses, sickness, pain,
CONTEM174:9 H209 Nor all his losses, crosses and vexation,
1SIMON188:12 H13 He will return, and make up all our losses,
PILGRIM210:30 H30 Nor losses know, nor sorrowes see.
MYCHILD216:28 Hp242 chastened by losses in estate, and these Times (thro: his great

LOST (47)

ELEMEN14:6 H250 What she hath lost by these my dreadfull {remed'less} woes.
HUMOUR30:17 H409 When death doth seize the man, your stock is lost,
AGES39:36 H179 My gifts abus'd, my education lost,
AGES44:39 H372 When it had lost that radiant Sun-like spark,
AGES~~45:4~~ H388 Who lost a Prince-dome and a Monarchy.
AGES45:6 H390 And poor *Palatinate* for ever lost;
AGES45:35 H425 My hands and armes, once strong, have lost their might,
SEASONS47:24 H40 For though the Frost hath lost his binding power,
MASSYR55:25 H91 Which was the cause, poor *Menon* lost his life,
MASSYR65:31 H496 *Iudah* {They} lost more {now} (then e're they lost) by him;
MASSYR65:31 H496 *Iudah* {They} lost more {now} (then e're they lost) by him;
MASSYR66:36 H542 Contemplating those times he lost his wits;
MASSYR67:14 H560 Faire *Ægypt* is, by his remissenesse lost;
MPERS77:8 H947 She lost her aime; her Husband, he lost more,
MPERS77:8 H947 She lost her aime; her Husband, he lost more,
MPERS80:12 H1079 Amongst the rest, two brothers he lost there;
MPERS80:14 H1081 Four hundred stately Ships by stormes was lost,
MPERS82:11 H1158 All's lost, and of three hundred thousand men,
MPERS84:39 H1275 The King this noble Captaine having lost,
MPERS~~85:7~~ H1283 Stil making war, till first had lost his life:
MPERS91:9 H1517 They now {Their winnings} lost all, and were a peace {their
MPERS~~92:23~~ H1581 Lost but his life for horrid treasons all.
MGREC97:10 H1771 The Regall ornaments now {were} lost, the treasure
MGREC97:22 H1783 Two hundred eighty *Greeks* he lost in fight,
MGREC99:28 H1871 What, hast thou lost thy late magnanimity?
MGREC100:36 ~~H1920~~ For this lost Queen (though in captivity).
MGREC104:9 H2061 If when he'd multitudes, the day he lost;
MGREC105:10 H2103 His lost felicity did greive him sore,
MGREC117:21 H2628 But by *Ulysses,* having lost his sight,
MGREC127:24 H3054 Thus lost he all for his fidelity,
MGREC128:25 H3098 His Son at *Gaza* likewise lost the field,
MGREC128:36 H3109 His lost repute with victorie had won;
MGREC131:15 H3207 For here *Antigonus* lost rule, and life,
MGREC133:12 H3300 *Antigonus* his Kingdoms lost, and's life,

MGREC133:41 H3331 *Seleuchus* reign'd, when he had lost his life,
MGREC134:37 ~~H3367~~ Her brother by him, lost his trayterous head
MGREC~~135:1~~ H3372 He seeing his honour lost, his Kingdome end,
MROMAN140:4 H3567 And thus my pains (with better things) I lost,
DIALOG144:28 H136 Some lost their livings, some in prison pent,
CONTEM170:11 H84 And how she lost her bliss, to be more wise,
SICKNES179:5 H25 Bestow much cost there's nothing lost,
3LETTER183:16 H18 Her fellow lost, nor joy nor life do wish,
MERCY188:27 H13 That thou dear Son has lost both Tree and fruit:
MERCY188:29 H15 Was ignorant what riches thou hadst lost.
MERCY188:34 H20 I lost a daughter dear, but thou a wife,
MEDDM200:27 Hp279 what they lost in the Autumn so shall it be at that great day
MEDDM200:29 Hp279 arise in far more glory, then that wch they lost at their creation,

LOT (2)
DIALOG148:28 H293 Whose lot doth fall to live therein is blest:
BIRTH179:34 H10 How soon't may be thy Lot to lose thy friend,

LOTH (1) [loath]
MEDDM197:7 Hp274 The reason why christians are so loth to exchang this world for

LOUD (2)
MPERS74:10 H835 *Darius* lusty stallion neighed full loud;
QELIZ155:15 H6 Yet thy loud Herauld Fame, doth to the sky

LOUE (6) [love]
MEDDM196:12 Hp273 the sincerest christian the least self loue
TOCHILD215:6 H6 Make vse of what I leaue in Loue
BYNIGHT220:20 H18 And Loue him to Eternity.
MED223:4 Hp250 pledges of thy Loue. First thov art my Creator, I thy creature,
28AUG225:28 Hp254 my drooping heart, and to manifest his Loue to me, and this is
HOURS234:2 H16 Whom I doe loue so well

LOUES (1) [loves]
HANNA230:18 H11 Shee loues thee all thy Dayes.

LOV'D (13) [loved]
MPERS72:32 H776 Fear'd of all, but lov'd of few, or none,
MGREC114:19 H2489 Who lov'd his Master more then did the rest,
MGREC125:31 H2981 Till {'Gainst} all that lov'd *Cassander* was nigh spent; {she was
MGREC131:26 H3218 *Antiochus, Seleuchus* dear lov'd son,
MGREC~~131:29~~ H3221 Yet dares {durst} not say, he loves {lov'd} his fathers wife;
TDUDLEY165:20 H22 Well known and lov'd, where ere he liv'd, by most
TDUDLEY166:2 H44 His humble mind so lov'd humility,
TDUDLEY167:2 H84 *The Good him lov'd, the bad did fear,*
CONTEM172:10 H146 I once that lov'd the shady woods so well,
1HUSB180:24 H3 If ever man were lov'd by wife, then thee;
2LETTER182:3 H9 Commend me to the man more lov'd then life,
CHILDRN186:19 H86 You had a Dam that lov'd you well,
MERCY188:35 H21 Who lov'd thee more (it seem'd) then her own life.

LOV'DST (1)
MPERS75:23 ~~H880~~ Thou lov'dst thy Master more then verity.

LOVE (64)
FATHER6:5 H39 My goods are true (though poor) I love no stealth,
ELEMEN12:1 H161 For Learning, Armes, and Arts, I love it well:
ELEMEN~~13:38~~ H239 While they thus in my {mine} intralls seem {love} to dive;
ELEMEN14:36 H278 Thy extream thirst is moistened by my love,

ELEMEN18:1	H405	And though you love Fire, Earth, and Water wel;
HUMOUR21:9	H37	Now Feminines (a while) for love we owe
HUMOUR24:8	H157	I love no boasting, that's but childrens trade:
HUMOUR24:40	H189	Thou sayst I love my sword, because tis {it's} guilt. {gilt,}
HUMOUR25:1	H190	But know, I love the blade, more then the hilt. {Hill;}
HUMOUR32:13	H487	Talke I love not, reason lyes not in length.
HUMOUR32:32	H506	I love no thundering Drums {guns}, nor bloody Wars,
HUMOUR34:33	H588	But if love be, as requisite as feare,
AGES37:12	H74	Who yet with love, and all alacrity,
AGES38:21	H124	A perverse will, a love to what's forbid:
AGES39:40	~~H182~~	Martial deeds I love not, 'cause they're vertuous,
AGES40:24	H205	Cards, Dice, and Oaths, concomitant, I love;
AGES45:11	~~H393~~	But not their Princes love, nor state so high;
AGES45:24	H414	We old men love to tell, what's done in youth.
SEASONS48:1	H54	That when the Sun (on's love) the earth doth shine,
MASSYR61:37	H342	Who stil implor'd his love, but was distress'd,
MPERS79:4	H1026	For his great love, is this thy recompence?
MPERS83:4	H1192	The grieved Prince finding nor right, nor love,
MPERS84:34	H1270	To {By} whom oblig'd, by favour {bounty}, and by love;
MPERS86:17	H1333	His brothers little love, like to be gone,
MGREC97:40	H1801	To gain his love, the *Tyrians* do intend,
MGREC120:6	H2741	In love, and in affinity combine:
MGREC120:39	H2776	Great love did *Ptolomy* by this act gain.
MGREC121:38	H2820	Nor could *Craterus* (whom he much did love)
MGREC124:37	H2944	These, with his love, unto the amorous Queen
DIALOG142:26	H55	Doth *Holland* quit you ill, for all your love?
DIALOG146:24	H210	Or any child-like love thou dost retain,
SIDNEY149:32	~~H23~~	The love thy Country ought thee, was as much.
SIDNEY~~150:12~~	H41	The love his Country ought him, was as much.
SIDNEY151:19	~~H69~~	That thine was true, but theirs adul'rate love.
DAVID159:24	H39	Thy love was wonderfull, passing {surpassing} a man;
DAVID159:25	H40	Exceeding all the Love that's Feminine,
TDUDLEY165:34	H36	Thy love to true Religion e're shall shine,
TDUDLEY165:40	H42	Those titles loath'd, which some too much do love
FLESH176:9	H49	Whence my dear father I do love.
FLESH176:20	H60	Thine honours doe, nor will I love;
BIRTH180:1	H11	We both are ignorant, yet love bids me
BIRTH180:12	H22	Yet love thy dead, who long lay in thine arms:
BIRTH180:15	H25	And if thou love thy self, or loved'st me
1HUSB180:27	H6	I prize thy love more then whole Mines of gold,
1HUSB180:29	H8	My love is such that Rivers cannot quench,
1HUSB180:30	H9	Nor ought but love from thee, give recompence.
1HUSB180:31	H10	Thy love is such I can no way repay,
1HUSB180:33	H12	Then while we live, in love lets so persever,
2LETTER182:7	H13	And if he love, how can he there abide?
3LETTER183:9	H11	The absence of her Love, and loving Mate,
3LETTER183:23	H25	Return my Dear, my joy, my only Love,
3LETTER183:31	H33	*Thy loving Love and Dearest Dear,*
MERCY189:6	H27	The fifth and last pledge of her dying love,
MYCHILD216:30	Hp242	ye Times w^{n} ye Lord hath manifested ye most Love to me.
MYCHILD217:28	Hp243	were it hell it self and could there find ye Love of God toward

MYCHILD217:30 Hp243 ye Love of God, it would haue been a Hell to me for in Truth it
BYNIGHT220:7 H7 I sovght him whom my Soul did Love
FEVER221:9 H24 Thou shew'st to me thy tender Love,
JULY223:25 Hp251 gratiously manifested his Love to me, wch I dare not passe by
WHAT224:15 H15 I find his Love, I know his pow'r.
28AUG226:8 Hp254 forgett thy great Love to my soul so lately expressed, when I
30SEPT227:21 Hp257 Love to my straying Soul wch in prosperity is too much in Love
HOUSE237:27 H57 The world no longer let me Love

LOVED (1) See also LOV'D
SEASONS52:26 H241 In *Aquarias,* now keeps the loved {long wisht} Sun,

LOVED'ST (1) See also LOV'DST
BIRTH180:15 H25 And if thou love thy self, or loved'st me

LOVELY (4)
MGREC119:9 H2699 For *Leonatus,* more lovely in her eye,
QELIZ158:11 H120 *This Rose is withered, once so lovely faire,*
DAVID159:9 H24 Pleasant and lovely were they both in life,
DAVID159:21 H36 O! lovely *Jonathan,* how wert {wast} thou slaine,

LOVES (1) [pl.]
2LETTER182:34 H40 By all our loves conjure him not to stay.

LOVES (1) [poss.]
BIRTH180:19 H29 And kiss this paper for thy loves dear sake,

LOVES (4) v.
ELEMEN17:39 H403 Mortalls, what one of you, that loves not me,
HUMOUR21:36 H64 She loves a Fiddle, better then a Drum,
HUMOUR21:41 H69 She loves her sword, only because its gilt;
MGREC131:29 H3221 Yet dares {durst} not say, he loves {lov'd} his fathers wife;

LOVETH (2)
HUMOUR31:31 H464 Impatient Choler loveth not the sound.
AGES40:13 H194 For he that loveth Wine, wanteth no woes;

LOVING (22)
ELEMEN15:28 H310 The Dolphin (loving musique) *Arions* friend.
HUMOUR22:12 H81 So loving unto all, she scornes to fight.
HUMOUR24:38 H187 Thou laugh'st at me, for loving merriment:
HUMOUR27:14 H285 The help she needs, the loving Liver lends,
HUMOUR35:14 H610 This loving counsel pleas'd them all so wel,
AGES40:8 H189 Trusteth my loving looks, and glozing tongue,
SEASONS48:11 H64 The sun now enters, loving *Geminie,*
MASSYR59:2 H226 Won by his loving looks, more loving {by his} speech,
MASSYR59:2 H226 Won by his loving looks, more loving {by his} speech,
DDUDLEY167:11 H8 *A loving Mother and obedient wife,*
1HUSB180:22 H1 *To my Dear and loving Husband.*
2LETTER182:17 H23 And when thou canst not treat by loving mouth,
3LETTER182:36 H1 As loving Hind that (Hartless) wants her Deer,
3LETTER183:9 H11 The absence of her Love, and loving Mate,
3LETTER183:15 H17 Or as the loving Mullet, that true Fish,
3LETTER183:20 H22 I have a loving phere, yet seem no wife:
3LETTER183:31 H33 *Thy loving Love and Dearest Dear,*
CHILDRN184:36 H25 Coupled with mate loving and true,
30SEPT227:33 Hp257 him then before, This is the desire of yr Loving mother. A. B.
11MAYB228:31 Hp259 loving kindnes, nor take ye cup of salvation wth Thanksgiving
SON231:27 H39 O Lord gravnt that I may never forgett thy Loving kindness in

2HUSB232:1 H1-2 Vpon my dear & loving husband his goeing into

LOW (10)

ELEMEN15:6 H288 The lofty Eagle and the Storke flye low,
ELEMEN15:20 H302 When I run low, and not o'reflow her brinks;
AGES37:23 H85 My then ambitious thoughts, were low enough.
MGREC120:18 H2753 That by his help, the rest might low be brought:
DAVID159:22 H37 In places high, full low thou dost {didst} remaine;
TDUDLEY165:27 H29 Who staid thy feeble sides when thou wast low,
TDUDLEY166:12 H54 Nor wonder 'twas, low things ne'r much did move
MEDDM197:14 Hp274 A low man, can goe vpright, vnder that door, wher a taller is
SOREFIT221:26 H12 Yea when I was most low and poor,
SON230:27 H10 The other sank low in the Deep.

LOWER (5)

MPERS~~86:22~~ H1338 By lesser {lower} steps, towards the top to climbe;
MGREC94:36 H1674 In lower termes to write {was taught} a higher stile,
DIALOG145:29 H178 They took high *Strafford* lower by the head,
MEDDM204:28 Hp285 vpon him that is lower then he is and if he se, that such a one
MEDDM207:11 Hp288 and waights that will pull us lower downward

LOWLY (3)

FATHER5:12 H13 My lowly pen, might wait upon those four,
PROLOG7:37 H47 If e're you daigne these lowly lines, your eyes
SEASONS~~49:33~~ H125 If pride within your lowly Cells ere haunt,

LOW'ST (1)

SEASONS52:4 H219 When cold, the sap to th' roots hath low'st repell'd;

LOYAL (1)

DIALOG147:18 H244 on brave *Essex*, shew whose son thou art {with a loyal heart},

LOYALL (2)

MGREC99:17 H1860 (A loyall Subject to *Darius* Crown)
QELIZ155:27 H18 T' accept the tribute of a loyall Braine;

LOYALTY (4)

MASSYR61:30 H335 To whom, he ought all loyalty of heart.
MPERS74:31 ~~H854~~ Did win him loyalty, and all respect;
MPERS75:17 H878 Scarse finde enough to thank thy loyalty;
MPERS84:18 H1254 That in all {his} Loyalty his heart was bound;

LOYNES (3) [loins] See also LOINES

AGES42:2 H260 Whose loynes {backs} I've cloth'd, and bellies I have fed;
MEDDM200:12 Hp279 or lay affliction on their loynes that so they might shake hands
MEDDM202:5 Hp281 or sprung out of the loynes of one Adam, some set in y^{e}

LRS (1) [letters]

ACK235:3 H1-3 In thankfull acknowledgmt for ye lrs rec'd. from my

LUCRETIA (1)

MROMAN139:15 H3543 *Lucretia* force, mirrour of chastety;

LUCULLUS (1)

MGREC134:15 H3346 Him *Lucullus*, the *Romane* Generall

LUD (1)

MASSYR66:21 H527 Then *Put*, and *Lud*, doe at his mercy stand,

LUGGAGE (1)

MGREC107:8 H2183 Now that his Hoast from luggage might be free,

LUMP (4)

ELEMEN14:34 H276 If I withhold, what art thou, dead, dry lump
HUMOUR30:20 H412 You high born (from that lump) then take your flight

CONTEM174:6 H206 This lump of wretchedness, of sin and sorrow,

MEDDM202:4 Hp281 disproportion that they scarcly seem made of the same lump,

LUNA (1)

ELEMEN16:36 H359 Yet {And} *Luna* for my Regent I obey.

LUNACY (1)

AGES~~43:34~~ H329 The quartan Ague, dropsy, Lunacy:

LUNGS (2) [pl.]

HUMOUR23:40 ~~H149~~ The spongy Lungs, I feed with frothy blood.

HUMOUR28:7 H319 The Lungs, she rots, the body weares away,

LUR'D (1) [lured]

AGES43:18 H313 Whereby my empty soule, is lur'd and caught.

LURCH (1)

MEDDM208:20 Hp290 nothing, and so leaue those in the lurch that most relyed

LURES (1)

ELEMEN16:16 H339 My water *Syrens,* with their guilefull lures:

LURED See LUR'D

LURKE (1) [lurk]

HUMOUR23:15 H125 Where envy, malice, thy companions lurke.

LURKS (1)

SIDNEY149:38 H25 Who knowes the Spels that in thy {his} Rethorick lurks?

LUST (6)

ELEMEN11:4 H124 And more then bruitish *Sodome* for her lust,

AGES40:2 H183 My Lust doth hurry me, to all that's ill,

MASSYR~~57:10~~ H157 It is more like, being {his lust} with pleasures fed,

MASSYR67:23 H569 His lust, and cruelty, {crueltyes} in books {storyes} we find,

MPERS85:33 H1309 by {To which} his pride, {more} then {his} lust, thereunto led.

MEDDM197:2 Hp274 lust wthin

LUSTER (3)

CONTEM169:7 H49 Who gave this bright light luster unto thee:

MEDDM202:22 Hp282 luster, although we may walk by his light, but when he is set,

MEDDM206:14 Hp287 and obscure, yet all receiue their luster (be it more or lesse)

LUSTS (1) [pl.]

MEDDM209:7 Hp291 Some christians do by their lusts and corruptions as the Isralits

LUSTY (1)

MPERS74:10 H835 *Darius* lusty stallion neighed full loud;

LUTE (2)

MASSYR66:9 H515 Where late, of Harp, and Lute, was {were} heard the noyse,

DUBART154:3 H48 More sencelesse then the Stones to *Amphions* Lute,

LUXURIOUS (1)

MGREC106:36 H2170 After that conquer'd, and luxurious Nation;

LY (1) [lie; recline] See also LYE

MGREC119:17 H2707 To *Lamia,* where he shut up doth ly:

LYARS (1) [liars]

AGES42:7 H265 The lyars curb'd but nourisht verity.

LYCIA (1)

MGREC95:11 H1690 He for his master takes, with *Lycia,*

LYCIANS (1) [pl.]

MPERS78:19 H1000 *Lycians, Carians,* and *Ionians,*

LYDIA (1)

MGREC130:5 H3160 She now {then} in *Lydia* at *Sardis* lay,

LYE (4) [lie; falsehood]

PROLOG7:26 H38 The *Greeks* did nought, but play the foole and lye.
HUMOUR25:29 H218 How often for the lye, thou'st giv'n the stab.
AGES42:19 H277 Did toile, did broile, oppress'd, did steal and lye.
WHAT224:17 H17 He is not man y^t he should lye.

LYE (32) [lie; recline] See also LY

ELEMEN14:9 H251 Again, what veines of poyson in me lye;
HUMOUR32:9 H483 My sicknesse cheifly in conceit doth lye,
HUMOUR33:8 H522 Next difference {that} betwixt us twain doth lye,
HUMOUR33:34 H548 Within this high built Cittadel doth lye,
AGES39:20 H163 I cannot lye in trench, {intrench'd} before a Town,
SEASONS52:1 H218 Poor wretches, that in total darknesse lye,
SEASONS52:14 H229 Cold, moist, young, flegmy Winter now doth lye
MASSYR59:21 H245 Part of the {that stately} wal it level caus'd to lye; {was
MASSYR60:26 H291 But {For} though his Palace, did in ashes lye,
MASSYR67:8 H554 Among the Conquered Kings, that there did lye,
MPERS73:24 ~~H809~~ And now with his accomplyces lye slaine.
MPERS84:14 H1250 When under Ostracisme he did lye.
MPERS87:28 H1380 To th' utmost parts of *Bactr'a,* and {for a time} there lye.
MPERS~~91:25~~ H1539 But long in ease and pleasure did not lye,
MGREC96:17 H1737 But they that saw him in this state to lye;
MGREC101:8 H1933 And all those Countries, which (betwixt) did lye,
MGREC106:5 H2139 Yea, {And} thus must every Son of *Adam* lye,
DIALOG143:38 H107 What injuries did daily on them lye;
SIDNEY150:6 H31 A world of treasure, in {wealth within} that rubbish lye;
QELIZ155:14 H5 Although great Queen, thou now in silence lye,
CONTEM172:3 H140 And when unmade, so ever shall they lye,
CONTEM172:16 H151 I markt, nor crooks, nor rubs that there did lye
1LETTER181:6 H4 How stayest thou there, whilst I at *Ipswich* lye?
1LETTER181:13 H11 My chilled limbs now nummed lye forlorn;
MEDDM195:36 Hp272 vanity and lyes must needs lye down in the Bed of sorrow.
MEDDM198:4 Hp275 then makes them lye down in green pastures and leades them
PILGRIM210:3 H3 His wasted limbes, now lye full soft
BYNIGHT220:5 H6 And so to lye I fovnd it best.
28AUG226:9 Hp254 lye down & bequeath my Soul to thee and Death seem'd no
HOUSE236:36 H28 Where oft I sate and long did lye,
HOUSE237:1 H31 My pleasant things in ashes lye
HOUSE237:9 H39 In silence ever shalt thou lye

LYES (3) [lies; falsehoods]

DIALOG144:12 H122 For Bribery, Adultery, for Thefts, and Lyes,
CONTEM170:12 H85 Believing him that was, and is, Father of lyes.
MEDDM195:36 Hp272 vanity and lyes must needs lye down in the Bed of sorrow.

LYES (33) [lies; recline]

ELEMEN12:4 H164 Whether Pyrenian, or the Alpes; both lyes
ELEMEN12:20 H180 Poysons sure antidote lyes in his horne.
ELEMEN13:7 H208 But you will see what in my bowels lyes?
ELEMEN15:11 H293 He knowes such sweets, lyes not in earths dry roots,
ELEMEN16:32 H355 I now must shew what force {ill} there in me lyes.
HUMOUR24:31 H180 And leave't to all, to judge where valour lyes.
HUMOUR28:37 H349 Such venome lyes in words, though but a blast,
HUMOUR32:13 H487 Talke I love not, reason lyes not in length.

HUMOUR34:8 H563 What wonderments, within your bals there lyes?
AGES40:39 H218 My heart lyes frying, and my {mine} eyes are sinking;
SEASONS50:10 H144 To Barns, and Stacks, where it for Fodder lyes.
MASSYR54:3 H30 But yet this blot for ever on him lyes,
MASSYR66:5 H511 In mid'st of *Babel* now, til death he lyes,
MPERS70:36 H707 And in his Town of *Pasargada* {Pasargades} lyes,
MPERS~~71:4~~ H718 Now quiet lyes under one marble stone.
MPERS79:36 H1062 This 'twixt the Mountains lyes (half Acre wide)
MPERS88:39 H1432 And for a while unkingly there he lyes;
MGREC94:38 H1676 Which twixt *Phrigia,* and *Propontis* lyes.
MGREC~~101:34~~ H1959 And careless in his bed, next morne he lyes,
MGREC102:25 H1995 Whilst revelling at *Babylon,* he lyes,
MGREC106:4 H2138 And though a Monarch once {late}, now lyes like clay;
MGREC118:14 H2661 Seven dayes the Corps of their great Master lyes
DIALOG146:25 H211 For my relief now use thy utmost skill {do what there lyes in
DUBART155:2 H87 *Here lyes the pearle of* France, Parnassus *glory,*
DAVID159:14 H29 For valiant *Saul,* who on Mount *Gilbo* lyes;
TDUDLEY166:35 H77 *Within this Tomb a Patriot lyes*
DDUDLEY167:9 H6 Here lyes,
FLESH176:21 H61 For my ambition lyes above.
MEDDM203:13 Hp283 wher his bussines lyes, a christian is sailing through this world
MEDDM207:16 Hp288 or feare, or greife that lyes at the root wch in great part
PILGRIM210:35 H35 A Corrupt Carcasse downe it lyes
THEART229:14 H16 My praise lyes not in Talk.
HOUSE237:28 H58 My hope, and Treasure lyes Above.

LYING (3)

AGES38:23 H126 A lying tongue as soon as it could speak,
MYCHILD215:25 Hp240 my wayes, & what I knew was sinfull as lying, disobed^{c}. to
MYCHILD218:23 Hp244 are in their Relign: together wth their lying miracles, and cruell

LYON (3)

ELEMEN10:9 H84 The Ram, the Bull, the Lyon, and the Beagle;
ELEMEN14:40 H282 Thy Bear, thy Tyger, and thy Lyon stout,
HUMOUR23:35 H145 Then a dead Lyon? by beasts triumpht ore.

LYSIMACHUS (6)

MGREC127:37 H3067 *Lysimachus* to make a fourth combines:
MGREC130:3 H3158 *Lysimachus* and *Ptolomy,* the same,
MGREC132:3 H3236 This by *Lysimachus* soon {was} after slain,
MGREC~~132:6~~ H3239 Against *Lysimachus* who from him won.
MGREC132:34 H3281 *Seleuchus,* and *Lysimachus;* those {these} twaine
MGREC132:36 H3283 And so *Lysimachus* was slaine in fight.

M

MACCHABEES (1)
MGREC134:6 H3339 Against {Amongst} the Jewes, we read in *Macchabees,*
MACEDON (18)
MPERS81:15 H1123 As had *Macedon, Thebes,* and *Thessalie,*
MGREC93:11 H1608 He, to *Amintas,* Kings of *Macedon;*
MGREC6:35 H1632 But as the King of little *Macedon.)*
MGREC100:24 H1908 Fit for to blunt the swords of *Macedon;*
MGREC113:32 H2459 Who from a petty King of *Macedon,*
MGREC114:41 H2511 From *Macedon* his Empire did extend,
MGREC118:40 H2689 *Antipater,* had long rul'd *Macedon,*
MGREC120:9 H2744 Whilst they in *Macedon* doe thus agree,
MGREC120:21 H2758 Desires the King, to goe to *Macedon,*
MGREC122:17 H2842 She knew her birthright gave her *Macedon,*
MGREC122:37 ~~H2858~~ After a while, to *Macedon* he makes;
MGREC~~122:38~~ H2859 The King, and Queen, along with him he takes. {to *Macedon*}
MGREC~~123:13~~ H2877 To *Greece* and *Macedon* lets turn our sight.
MGREC125:14 H2962 *Olimpias* now {soon} enters *Macedon,*
MGREC125:41 H2991 So goes to finde this {cruel} Queen in *Macedon;*
MGREC127:4 H3034 Now many Townes in *Macedon* suprest,
MGREC132:16 H3251 And now as King, in *Macedon* he reigns;
MGREC~~132:20~~ H3261 In his long absence to rule *Macedon.*
MACEDONIA (1)
MGREC~~122:32~~ H2852 From *Macedonia* to Asia he came,
MACEDONIAN (2)
MPERS~~81:28~~ H1136 A *Macedonian* born, and great Commander,
MGREC95:39 H1718 It seemes to see the *Macedonians* {*Macedonian*} slaughters.
MACEDONIANS (4) [pl.]
MGREC95:39 H1718 It seemes to see the *Macedonians* {*Macedonian*} slaughters.
MGREC111:18 H2363 Which the stout *Macedonians* mazed sore
MACEDONIANS (2) [poss.]
MGREC97:11 H1772 Divided at the *Macedonians* pleasure.
MGREC102:38 H2008 Now falls {fall} into the *Macedonians* hands.
MAD (4)
HUMOUR29:37 H388 'Twere but a mad, irregular distemper;
HUMOUR34:24 H579 But a mad one, say I, where 'tis too great,
HUMOUR34:26 H581 With a tame foole converse, then with a mad.
MGREC114:3 H2471 Nothing more pleasing to mad *Clitus* tongue,
MADDS (1) [mads]
AGES41:3 H223 Sometimes the Phrensie, strangely madds my Brain,
MADE (127)
FATHER5:6 H7 (though made a pedestall for *Adams* Race) /world
PROLOG7:5 H20 'Cause Nature made it so irreparable.

PROLOG7:23 H35 And poesy made, *Calliope's* owne childe,
ELEMEN8:20 H18 Soone made the combatants abate their force;
ELEMEN9:10 H44 Ye Husband-men, your coulter's made by me,
ELEMEN9:15 H49 I made it flexible unto his will.
ELEMEN9:22 H56 And you Philosophers, if ere you made
ELEMEN11:8 H128 Which made a *Cæsar,* (Romes) the worlds proud head,
ELEMEN16:19 H342 Nor will I speake of waters made by Art,
ELEMEN17:22 H386 All know, what {that} innundations I have made;
ELEMEN18:32 H436 No place so subtilly made, but I get in.
ELEMEN19:24 H469 What woeful wracks I've made, may wel appear,
HUMOUR20:19 H11 All having made obeysance to each Mother,
HUMOUR23:3 H113 Thou wast not made for Souldier, or for Schollar;
HUMOUR23:13 H123 Of that black region, Nature made thee Queen;
HUMOUR26:33 H263 The spirits through thy heat, are made perfect there,
HUMOUR30:34 H426 The Spleen for al you three, was made a sinke,
AGES36:25 H49 His hoary haires, and grave aspect made way;
AGES37:31 H93 A Baron or a Duke, ne'r made my mark.
AGES41:7 H227 That yet my bed in darknesse is not made,
AGES45:20 ~~H402~~ But yet may live, to see't made up again:
AGES~~45:22~~ H408 But ye may live to see't made up again.
SEASONS49:24 ~~H114~~ Yet hath your life, made Kings the same envy,
SEASONS49:28 H117 Which made great *Bajazet* cry out in's woes,
SEASONS50:20 H154 Which after Manchet's made, {makes} for Kings to eat;
SEASONS51:13 H187 And in this month was made apostate man;
SEASONS51:19 H193 Great *Adam* {Our Grand-Sire} was of Paradice made King.
MASSYR53:24 H14 *Erech, Accad,* and *Calneh* also made;
MASSYR54:18 H45 And mighty *Ninivie* more mighty made,
MASSYR55:40 H106 With Towers, and Bulwarks made of costly stone
MASSYR56:24 H130 An expedition to the East she made.
MASSYR56:38 H144 Which made the *Assyrians* many a day,
MASSYR57:7 H154 Which made the people think they serv'd her Son;
MASSYR57:26 ~~H172~~ Which to her neighbours, when it was made known,
MASSYR60:1 H266 Of *Babylon, Belosus* he made King,
MASSYR~~60:9~~ H274 promise bound, since first {which} he crav'd {firmly made},
MASSYR61:3 H308 That those two made but one, we need not doubt:
MASSYR62:5 H350 And him six years his tributary made;
MASSYR62:38 H383 Which made his Army into nothing melt;
MASSYR63:14 H399 Until his Grand-childe made her bow the knee;
MASSYR~~65:2~~ H467 Where after many assayes, they make {made} at last,
MASSYR66:24 H530 Which wealth, and strong ambition made so great;
MPERS~~70:19~~ H690 For Owles, and Satyres, makes {made} a residence;
MPERS~~70:23~~ H694 An Edict makes {made}, the Temple builded be,
MPERS~~71:4~~ H717 And though his conquests made the earth to groan,
MPERS71:22 H736 Made *Evelthon* their King, with bended knee,
MPERS74:20 H843 *Darius* by election made a King
MPERS74:29 H852 Made wholsome gentle Laws, which pleas'd each mind.
MPERS75:15 H876 Who doth deserve a Statue made of gold;
MPERS75:40 H897 *Darius* on the *Sythians* made a war,
MPERS76:1 H899 A bridge he made, which serv'd for boat, and barge,
MPERS77:23 H964 But for the last he made such preparation,
MPERS77:30 H971 And *Greece* such wondrous triumphs ne're had made.

MPERS~~78:12~~ H993 To *Mardonius,* Captain {made their} Generall;
MPERS79:10 H1032 Next, o're the *Hellispont* a bridge he made,
MPERS~~79:13~~ H1038 The work-men put to death the bridge that made,
MPERS82:1 H1146 But that which helpt defects, and made them bold,
MPERS83:29 H1217 He first, war with revolting *Ægypt* made.
MPERS84:21 H1257 And for that end, great preparation made,
MPERS87:23 H1375 This place was {so} made, by nature, and by art;
MPERS88:31 H1424 Who knowes the sudden change made by this chance;
MPERS88:37 H1430 grew weake, through {by their} slaughters that they made.
MPERS90:13 ~~H1484~~ Into *Bithynia* often in-rodes made;
MPERS90:39 ~~H1506~~ Who of his cruelty made many tast,
MPERS91:37 ~~H1551~~ Made Writers work at home, they sought not far?
MGREC93:18 H1615 By Art, and Nature both, he was made fit,
MGREC~~94:16~~ H1650 And through the *Hellispont,* his ships make {made} way.
MGREC94:19 H1657 Thirty two thousand made up his foot force,
MGREC95:34 H1713 The rest attendants, which made up no lesse;
MGREC96:11 H1731 The King sat in a chariot made of gold,
MGREC96:38 H1758 Which made {To make} his over-throw more fierce, and sure.
MGREC~~98:12~~ H1814 He leaves not, till he makes {made} the sea firme shoar;
MGREC98:21 H1823 And thirteen thousand Gally slaves he made,
MGREC~~99:12~~ H1855 To which, brave {proud} *Alexander* did {made} reply,
MGREC101:21 H1946 Him boundlesse made, in vice, and cruelty;
MGREC~~101:35~~ H1964 So make {made} an end, before they {as soon as} well begun;
MGREC101:37 H1966 But 'tis not known what slaughters here they {was} made.
MGREC103:40 H2051 Which forty thousand made; but his intent,
MGREC105:17 H2110 Whose wounds had made their skins of purple dye;
MGREC105:33 H2126 Which made their long restraint, seeme to be none;
MGREC107:39 ~~H2214~~ He easily might have made them stay there stil;
MGREC108:31 H2247 Of Darts, and Arrowes, made so little spare,
MGREC109:15 H2274 Had to his mind, made all things now {to} accord:
MGREC~~109:24~~ H2283 But *Alexander,* caus'd {made} him to behold;
MGREC110:31 H2335 Huge Bridles made, which here, and there, he left,
MGREC112:41 H2427 Faine would have spoke, and made his owne defence,
MGREC118:12 H2659 For second offers {offer} there were {was} never made;
MGREC120:40 H2777 And made the Souldiers on his side remain;
MGREC122:26 ~~H2845~~ Which made her now begin to play her part;
MGREC124:6 ~~H2911~~ *Cassander* for return all speed now made:
MGREC126:24 H3015 But made in Judgement her Accusers stand,
MGREC127:3 H3033 Which she had often made others to sup:
MGREC127:9 H3039 And shewes of lamentation for them made.
MGREC~~133:23~~ H3312 *Philip* had *Perseus,* who was made a Thrale
MGREC~~134:2~~ H3334 Whose large Dominions after was made small,
MROMAN136:30 H3444 Where Swaines, and rustick Peasants made {kept} their Holds.
MROMAN138:18 H3508 A stately Bridge he over *Tyber* made,
MROMAN139:5 H3533 As wealth had made them of abilitie;
MROMAN139:29 H3555 Essays I many made but still gave out,
DIALOG144:1 H111 Thy flying for the Truth I made a jeast;
SIDNEY149:16 H15 Thine {His} Eloquence made *Mercury* wax red;
SIDNEY150:24 H51 Made famous by thy fall {death}, much more's {more} the pitty;
DAVID159:18 H33 Which made you yet more beauteous to behold.
VANITY160:41 H51 Nor death shall see, but are immortal made,

CONTEM168:20 H28 No wonder, some made thee a Deity:
CONTEM169:35 H73 Sees glorious *Adam* there made Lord of all,
CONTEM171:23 H126 A Spring returns, and they more youthfull made;
CONTEM172:4 H141 But man was made for endless immortality.
FLESH176:12 H52 How oft thy slave, hast thou me made,
FLESH177:8 H89 Are made of pretious *Jasper* stone;
AUTHOR177:34 H6 Made thee in raggs, halting to th' press to trudge,
AUTHOR178:5 H15 And rubbing off a spot, still made a flaw.
BIRTH180:3 H13 That when that knot's unty'd that made us one,
3LETTER183:10 H12 Whose loss hath made her so unfortunate:
ANNEB187:20 H10 Experience might 'fore this have made me wise,
MEDDM202:4 Hp281 disproportion that they scarcly seem made of the same lump,
MEDDM208:31 Hp290 the order of nature, quenched the violence of the fire, made
MYCHILD215:33 Hp241 heart, and made my Suplicat^{n}. to the most High who sett me
MYCHILD216:22 Hp242 him, but by one afflict^{n} or other hath made me look home,
MED223:10 Hp250 he my head. Such priviledges had not ye word of Truth made
MYSOUL225:4 H8 And gloriovs made ere-long.
MYSOUL225:20 H24 For God hath made me wise.
13MAY227:9 H18 O hast thou made my pilgrimage
13MAY227:12 H21 My Baca made a springing flood?
11MAYB228:28 Hp259 made it ye more tedious, but it pleased ye Lord to support my
HOURS233:28 H11 And thy Abode tho'st made wth me
HOUSE237:24 H54 Yet by his Gift is made thine own.

MADE-PERFUME (1)
SEASONS49:35 H128 Whose fragrant scent, {smel} all made-perfume surpasses;

MADING (1)
MGREC~~107:14~~ H2189 And thus unwisely, in one raging {mading} fume,

MADNESSE (1)
MGREC103:27 H2038 (Filled with madnesse, and quite void of reason)

MADS See MADDS

MAD'ST (1)
FAINTING222:22 H12 And tho: as dead mad'st me aliue

MAGAZEEN (1)
HUMOUR24:1 H150 Nay, th' stomach, magazeen to all the rest,

MAGAZINE (2)
TDUDLEY166:39 H81 *A Magazine of History,*
1LETTER181:4 H2 My joy, my Magazine of earthly store,

MAGI (1)
MPERS73:19 H806 And first these noble *Magi* 'gree upon,

MAGICIANS (1) [pl.]
MASSYR68:4 H590 For the Soothsayers, and Magicians wise;

MAGNANIMITY (3)
AGES~~45:4~~ H387 Admired for their magnanimity,
MASSYR67:13 H559 Prudence, and magnanimity, did lack
MGREC99:28 H1871 What, hast thou lost thy late magnanimity?

MAGNANIMOUS (1)
AGES40:1 ~~H182~~ But doing so, might seem magnanimous.

MAGNIFIE (1)
CONTEM169:14 H55 My great Creator I would magnifie,

MAGNITUDE (3)
ELEMEN10:15 H90 Their magnitude and height should I recount,

MASSYR63:37 H424 This Prince in's magnitude doth ever shine;
MEDDM206:12 Hp287 some are Stars of the first magnitude, and

MAID (2)
ELEMEN10:8 H83 The maid with ballance, wayn with horses three;
MGREC101:13 H1938 For his {the} Queen-Mother, and the royall Maid;

MAIDS (3) [pl.]
MPERS77:7 H946 For *Grecian* Maids ('tis said) to wait on her;
MROMAN137:32 H3483 And vestall Maids to keep the holy fire.
SIDNEY150:4 ~~H29~~ And modest Maids, and Wives, blush at thy glory;

MAIME (2)
ELEMEN11:12 H132 The rich I oft make poore, the strong I maime,
DIALOG142:36 H65 My beauteous Body at this present maime;

MAIN (1) n. [main sea] See also MAINE
DISTEMP179:25 H13 And brought me to the shore from troubled Main.

MAINE (2) adj.
PROLOG7:2 H17 Nor perfect beauty, where's a maine defect,
MPERS81:39 ~~H1143~~ For one maine Battell shortly, both provide;

MAINE (3) n. [main sea] See also MAIN
ELEMEN17:7 H371 And that an Island makes, which once was maine.
MASSYR64:36 H460 Divided from the maine, by channel great;
MPERS87:26 H1378 So hir'd a fleet, to waft him ore the Maine,

MAINTAIN (3)
ELEMEN13:13 H214 Well knowest, my fuell must maintain thy fire.
MPERS79:38 H1064 Two dayes and nights a fight they there maintain,
MPERS~~85:16~~ H1292 Joynes with the *Greeks,* and so maintains {maintain} their

MAINTAINE (1)
AGES41:37 H254 If Noble, then mine honour to {o} maintaine.

MAINTAINS (1)
MPERS85:16 H1292 Joynes with the *Greeks,* and so maintains {maintain} their

MAIST (2) [mayst] See also MAY'ST
FLESH175:24 H24 What canst desire, but thou maist see
FLESH175:36 H36 Then let not goe, what thou maist find,

MAJESTY (5)
MASSYR66:35 H541 In splender, and in Majesty, he sits,
MGREC112:38 H2424 By which his Majesty was deifi'd.
MGREC123:27 H2891 Thinks by her Majesty much help to finde;
QELIZ157:11 H79 (Judging all valour, and all Majesty)
CONTEM169:8 H50 Admir'd, ador'd for ever, be that Majesty.

MAKE (100)
FATHER6:1 H35 How divers natures, make one unity.
PROLOG8:2 H50 Will make your glistering gold but more to shine.
ELEMEN9:18 H52 Your dainty {dayly} food, I wholsome make, I warme
ELEMEN~~11:1~~ H119 My raging flame did make a mournful story,
ELEMEN11:12 H132 The rich I oft make poore, the strong I maime,
ELEMEN11:34 H154 Of these so common things, can make report:
ELEMEN13:9 H210 My bounty calls you forth to make reports,
ELEMEN13:20 H221 I should here make a short, yet true narration,
ELEMEN17:11 H375 Untill straight {proud} *Gibralter,* did make them twaine,
ELEMEN19:1 H446 For all Philosophers make one of me.
ELEMEN~~20:3~~ H485 Which makes {make} the mighty Monarchs fear their Fates,
HUMOUR21:21 H49 I make a man, a man i'th highest degree,

HUMOUR23:30 H140 But one of you would make a worthy King:
HUMOUR24:3 H152 And yet to make, my greatnesse far {still} more great:
HUMOUR27:27 H298 And what you singly {single} are, the whole I make.
HUMOUR28:12 H324 Ith' last concoction, segregation make.
HUMOUR30:11 H403 Let me wel make thy precincts, the gal;
HUMOUR34:34 H589 Then I, and thou, must make a mixture here:
HUMOUR34:37 H592 To Melancholly i'le make no reply,
AGES37:35 H97 Make strong my selfe, and turne aside weak right.
AGES~~39:31~~ H174 Makes {Make} all to place their future hopes on me.
AGES40:16 H197 All counsel hate, which tends to make me wise,
SEASONS~~51:19~~ H194 Nor could that temp'rate Clime such difference make,
MASSYR54:6 H33 Alive, and dead, a god they did him make;
MASSYR55:24 H90 And thought her fit, to make a Monarch's wife,
MASSYR57:37 H182 T' *Sardanapalus* next we wil make haste.
MASSYR58:21 H206 These all agree, and forty thousand make,
MASSYR59:23 H247 For few, or none, did there {it seems} resistance make;
MASSYR65:2 H467 Where after many assayes, they make {made} at last,
MPERS~~71:4~~ H719 And with an Epitaph, himself did make,
MPERS73:7 H794 A *Babylon* in *Egypt* did he make.
MPERS74:21 H844 His title to make strong omits no thing;
MPERS76:30 H928 Arm'd all they could, which elev'n thousand make;
MPERS81:35 H1143 {In all} One hundred thousand, and ten thousand make.
MPERS85:24 H1300 The King was glad, with *Sparta* to make peace,
MPERS86:24 H1340 She to the King, would make a fair report:
MPERS86:34 H1350 (One *Greeke* could make ten *Persians* run away)
MPERS88:41 H1434 Hoping with {by} that to make the *Greeks* stand stil,
MPERS89:1 H1435 But was deceiv'd; to it they make amain,
MPERS91:9 H1517 winnings} lost all, and were a peace {their glad} to make,
MPERS91:10 H1518 {on such} conditions they are forc't to take; {as King will make}
MGREC94:16 H1650 And through the *Hellispont,* his ships make {made} way.
MGREC~~96:38~~ H1758 Which made {To make} his over-throw more fierce, and sure.
MGREC98:40 H1842 A league of friendship make, firm, and entire;
MGREC100:8 H1892 The Son of *Jupiter* did straight him make:
MGREC101:35 H1964 So make {made} an end, before they {as soon as} well begun;
MGREC107:31 H2206 To make them rafts, to waft them or'e the floud;
MGREC109:41 H2300 And there {by force} his Soveraignty for to make good;
MGREC110:28 H2332 And for his Souldiers larger Cabins make;
MGREC120:31 H2768 Brave *Ptolomy,* to make a fourth now {then} sent,
MGREC121:12 H2790 Did make his owne firme to his cause remaine,
MGREC~~121:16~~ H2797 Who vow to make this captain recompence,
MGREC121:39 H2821 From his fidelity make him once move.
MGREC124:38 H2945 Did make him vow her servant to be seen.
MGREC125:3 H2951 To make the King by force his seat resigne;
MGREC127:37 H3067 *Lysimachus* to make a fourth combines:
MGREC127:39 H3069 To make *Cassander* odious to them, seeks,
MGREC~~127:41~~ H3071 {clear} what cause they {he} had to take up {make this} warre.
MGREC128:3 H3076 And how he aymes {aiming now} to make himselfe a King,
MGREC130:40 H3185 For to their Crowns, there's none can title make.
MGREC132:40 H3287 And so himselfe the only Monarch make;
MGREC136:1 H3414 For what is past I blush, excuse to make,
MROMAN137:10 H3461 But all disdaine alliance then to make,

MROMAN138:10 H3500 But now demolished, to make *Rome* great.
DIALOG143:1 H70 Nor Nobles siding, to make *John* no King
DIALOG147:12 H238 Let's bring *Baals* vestments out, {forth} to make a fire,
DIALOG148:15 H280 And make his filthy den so desolate,
DIALOG148:31 H296 If this make way thereto, then sigh no more,
SIDNEY151:32 ~~H75~~ Goodwill, did make my head-long pen to run,
SIDNEY152:16 ~~H85~~ But I had blemish'd theirs, to make 't appear;
DUBART153:41 H45 In all the Arts make thee most liberall;
QELIZ156:14 H41 She's argument enough to make you mute;
TDUDLEY165:18 H20 Who after death might make him falsly seem
TDUDLEY165:22 H24 These to the world his merits could make known,
CONTEM174:11 H211 Can make him deeply groan for that divine Translation.
AUTHOR178:6 H16 I stretcht thy joynts to make thee even feet,
SICKNES179:6 H26 to make Salvation sure,
2LETTER181:31 H1 *Phoebus* make haste, the day's too long, be gone,
2LETTER182:1 H7 If in thy swift Carrier thou canst make stay,
1SIMON188:12 H13 He will return, and make up all our losses,
MEDDM195:25 Hp272 no evill that we feele, or fear, but we may make some spiritull
MEDDM196:21 Hp273 Downny beds make drosey persons but hard lodging, keeps
MEDDM198:3 Hp275 conditions, if he will make his face to shine vpon them, he
MEDDM203:12 Hp283 desire to make y[t] his place of residence, but longs to put in at
MEDDM203:15 Hp283 must beware of desireing to make this the place of his abode,
MEDDM204:30 Hp285 look on his owne vnworthynes and that will make him say w[th]
MEDDM205:2 Hp285 of correction must make long furrows on their back and the
MEDDM206:30 Hp288 parents haue had pious children, it should make vs adore the
MEDDM206:37 Hp288 all should make vs wth the Apostle to admire the iustice and
MEDDM207:27 Hp289 should make vs so to number our dayes as to apply our hearts
MEDDM208:22 Hp290 miserably delude men and make them put great Confidence
MEDDM209:14 Hp291 all their accursed inmates, but make a league with them, they
PILGRIM211:2 H43 Lord make me ready for that day
TOCHILD215:6 H6 Make vse of what I leaue in Loue
MYCHILD215:24 Hp240 years about 6. or 7. as I take it I began to make cons[c]. of
SOREFIT221:33 H19 O make it frvitfull faithfull Lord
28AUG226:1 Hp254 to make me a vessell fitt for his vse why should I not bare it
THEART229:3 H5 I cry'd thov seem'st to make some stay
2HUSB233:2 H35 He shall make his Addresse.
HOUSE237:14 H44 The arm of flesh didst make thy trvst?

MAKER (2)

PILGRIM210:40 H40 and of their maker haue the sight
MED223:9 Hp250 enough thy maker is thy husband. Nay more, I am a member

MAKERS (1) [poss.]

CONTEM169:23 H63 And in their kind resound their makers praise:

MAKES (58)

ELEMEN17:7 H371 And that an Island makes, which once was maine.
ELEMEN20:3 H485 Which makes {make} the mighty Monarchs fear their Fates,
HUMOUR21:10 H38 Unto your Sister-hood, which makes us tender {render}
HUMOUR21:24 H52 What makes him face his foe, without appal?
HUMOUR21:29 H57 'Twixt them and others, what ist makes the odds
HUMOUR27:41 H312 Which makes the mansion, by the soul soon left;
AGES39:31 H174 Makes {Make} all to place their future hopes on me.
SEASONS47:2 ~~H17~~ And now makes glad those blinded Northern wights,

SEASONS~~47:5~~	H20	And now makes glad the darkned northern wights
SEASONS47:26	H42	Doth darken *Sols* bright face, makes us remember
SEASONS48:13	H66	Our Winter {thicker} rayment, makes us lay aside,
SEASONS50:8	H142	Which makes the aged fields look young again,
SEASONS~~50:20~~	H154	Which after Manchet's made, {makes} for Kings to eat;
MASSYR58:37	H220	Makes {With} promises, their necks for {now} to un-yoak,
MASSYR~~59:23~~	H247	few, or none, did there {it seems} resistance make; {makes:}
MASSYR60:39	H304	Which makes the world of differences {difference} so ful,
MASSYR61:26	H331	*Syria* he makes a Province of his own.
MASSYR61:34	H339	In *Galilee,* he woful havock makes;
MASSYR63:7	H392	And on his Masters ruins, his house makes;
MASSYR66:17	H523	A totall Conquest of rich *Ægypt* makes,
MPERS~~69:38~~	H661	Then to the King he makes this true report,
MPERS70:19	H690	For Owles, and Satyres, makes {made} a residence;
MPERS70:23	H694	An Edict makes {made}, the Temple builded be,
MPERS70:31	H702	And at one blow, worlds head, she headlesse makes;
MPERS71:13	~~H727~~	And makes it lawful Law, if he but wil;
MPERS72:38	H784	Toucht with this newes, to *Persia* he makes,
MPERS78:37	H1018	He humbly to the King then makes request,
MPERS83:37	H1225	Which done, a sumptuous feast; makes like a King
MPERS90:29	H1496	Which rumor makes great *Artaxerxes* quake;
MGREC94:2	H1636	Which makes each moment seem, more then a day:
MGREC98:12	H1814	He leaves not, till he makes {made} the sea firme shoar;
MGREC103:23	H2034	Now makes this King, his vertues all to drown.
MGREC106:12	H2146	And {he} makes their riches, and their honours more;
MGREC107:6	H2181	Then {And} hearing, *Bessus* makes himselfe a King,
MGREC107:35	H2210	And stuffing them with straw, he bundles makes;
MGREC111:40	H2385	A Wedding Feast to's Nobles then he makes,
MGREC118:38	H2687	And *Ptolomy,* next sure of *Egypt* makes.
MGREC119:36	H2726	Long marches through *Cilicia* he makes,
MGREC122:37	~~H2858~~	After a while, to *Macedon* he makes;
MGREC~~124:10~~	H2915	Such friends away as for his Interest makes
MGREC130:7	H3162	Choise above all, of *Ptolomy* she makes
MGREC131:24	H3216	His peace he then with old *Seleuchus* makes,
MROMAN137:12	H3463	Great shewes he makes at Tilt, and Turnament,
SIDNEY150:3	H28	Which makes severer eyes but scorn thy {slight that} Story,
SIDNEY151:26	H74	And {Which} makes me now with *Sylvester* confesse,
QELIZ155:30	H21	Which makes me deeme, my rudenesse is no wrong,
CONTEM168:35	H41	Thy presence makes it day, thy absence night,
CONTEM169:28	H67	It makes things gone perpetually to last,
CONTEM169:30	H69	It makes a man more aged in conceit,
CONTEM171:28	H130	No sooner born, but grief and care makes fall
CONTEM174:18	H217	And makes him long for a more quiet port,
CONTEM174:25	H223	But sad affliction comes & makes him see
MEDDM195:26	Hp272	aduantage of all and he that makes such improvment is wise
MEDDM196:22	Hp273	state makes a secure christian, but adversity makes
MEDDM197:18	Hp275	house wch is not often swept makes the cleanly inhabitant
MEDDM198:4	Hp275	then makes them lye down in green pastures and leades them
MYCHILD217:31	Hp243	absence and presence of God y^{t} makes Heaven or Hell.

MAKEST (1)

HUMOUR25:21	H210	A Souldier most compleat in al points makest.

MAKING (2)

MPERS~~85:7~~ H1283 Stil making war, till first had lost his life:

MGREC94:8 H1642 In seeking after {Nor making Title unto} Soveraignity:

MALADY (3) See also MALLADY

HUMOUR32:10 H484 What I imagine, that's my malady.

DIALOG141:24 H23 Which present help may ease this {my} malady.

MEDDM203:23 Hp283 malady that threatens him wth death, he will gladly entertaine

MALAPERT See MALLEPART

MALE (1)

MPERS73:5 H792 The Male line, of great *Cyrus* now did {had} end.

MALE-CONTENT (1)

HUMOUR22:3 H72 But peevish, Male-content, musing she sits,

MALE-FACTOR (1) [malefactor]

CONTEM170:32 H102 Nor Male-factor ever felt like warr,

MALEFACTOR (1)

MGREC108:4 H2220 This Malefactor vild, {vile} before the King,

MALICE (6)

HUMOUR23:15 H125 Where envy, malice, thy companions lurke.

HUMOUR30:31 H423 Laughter (though thou sayst malice) flowes from hence,

HUMOUR30:36 H428 But if thou hast, that malice comes {is} from you.

AGES37:36 H98 No malice bare, to this, or that great Peer,

MGREC113:6 H2433 My foes exceeds in malice, and their hate,

TDUDLEY165:14 H16 Let malice bite, and envy knaw its fill,

MALICIOUS (1)

MGREC113:2 H2429 To his malicious foes delivers him,

MALIGNANT (1)

HUMOUR28:14 H326 The bitter choler, most malignant knowne

MALIGNE (1)

TDUDLEY165:33 H35 Which caus'd Apostates to maligne so.

MALLADY (1) [malady]

ELEMEN15:13 H295 His deadly mallady, I might expell.

MALLEPART (1) [malapert]

MGREC94:34 H1672 That boy so mallepart, before the King.

MALLIANS (1) [pl.]

MGREC~~109:5~~ H2262 And also of the *Mallians* what is writ.

MAN (91) See also MAN's

ELEMEN9:36 H70 Both man and beast, rejoyce at his approach,

ELEMEN10:24 H99 And man from thirty unto fifty frame.

ELEMEN10:33 H108 And though I be a servant to each man;

ELEMEN11:28 H148 I am th' originall of man and beast,

ELEMEN14:13 H255 Thus I occasion death to man and beast,

ELEMEN15:10 H292 Man wants his bread, and wine, and pleasant fruits;

ELEMEN15:21 H303 To meet with want, each woefull man bethinks.

ELEMEN18:3 H407 I aske the man condemn'd, that's near his death:

ELEMEN18:9 H413 The famisht, thirsty man, that craves supply:

HUMOUR21:13 H41 Yet man for Choler, is the proper seat.

HUMOUR21:19 H47 The man proves boyish, sottish, ignorant,

HUMOUR21:21 H49 I make a man, a man i'th highest degree,

HUMOUR21:21 H49 I make a man, a man i'th highest degree,

HUMOUR22:30 H99 For when they faile, man turnes unto his clay:

HUMOUR28:1 H313 So Melancholly ceases {seizes} on a man;

HUMOUR28:22	H334	That mortal man, might turn to his corruption.
HUMOUR30:13	H405	Reduce the man to's principles, then see
HUMOUR30:17	H409	When death doth seize the man, your stock is lost,
HUMOUR31:11	H444	That casts out all that man or {e're} eates, or drinks.
AGES35:16	H1-2	{Of} The Four Ages of Man.
AGES36:37	H61	With heed now stood, three ages of fraile man;
AGES39:35	H178	That who would see vain man, may look on me:
AGES40:5	H186	Or stab the man, in's own defence, that's worse.
AGES43:38	H333	Man at his best estate is vanity.
SEASONS46:32	H8	Sweet Spring, like man in his minority,
SEASONS48:29	H82	Each man his owne peculiar excellence,
SEASONS49:22	~~H113~~	'Mongst all ye shepheards, never but one man,
SEASONS51:13	H187	And in this month was made apostate man;
MASSYR53:16	H6	Man did not {proudly} strive for Soveraignty,
MASSYR55:15	H81	Changing his {the} womans face, into a man.
MASSYR56:27	H133	(Each man beleive it, as his fancy list)
MASSYR57:12	H159	What then he did, of worth, can no man tel,
MASSYR62:22	H367	Where now those ten Tribes are, can no man tel,
MASSYR63:5	H390	In *Babylon,* Leiutenant to this man,
MASSYR66:3	H509	A {Ah!} haplesse man, whose darksome contemplation,
MPERS~~69:38~~	H667	(Quoth he) that man for happy we commend,
MPERS71:19	H733	Who grown a man, resum'd again his state)
MPERS74:13	~~H836~~	His happy wishes now doth no man spare,
MPERS83:9	H1197	Of life, no man had least security.
MPERS85:31	H1307	And so each man again possest his owne.
MPERS87:37	H1389	*Cyrus* finding his campe, and no man there;
MPERS88:2	H1395	In this confusion, each man as he might,
MPERS88:24	H1417	Whom *Cyrus* spi'd, cries out, I see the man,
MGREC93:29	H1626	To save him from his might, no man was found.
MGREC94:35	H1673	Ah! fond vaine man, whose pen was taught ere while,
MGREC97:19	H1780	Commands, no man should doe them injury,
MGREC100:16	H1900	For no man to resist {man's there} his valour showes {Army to
MGREC107:9	H2184	And no man with his burden, burdened be,
MGREC107:10	H2185	Commands forth-with, each man his fardle bring,
MGREC112:11	H2397	If an Ideall Paradise, a man should {would} frame,
MGREC117:3	H2610	Now like a mortall helplesse man he lies;
MGREC117:22	H2629	Each man {All men} began for {streight} to contemn his might;
MGREC119:23	H2713	His Lady take i'th' way, and no man know.
MGREC122:34	H2855	And this no man durst question, or resist;
DIALOG145:22	H171	To crush the proud, and right to each man deal.
SIDNEY150:27	H54	Thus man is borne to dye, and dead is he,
DUBART154:27	H72	Unto each man his riches are {is} assign'd,
QELIZ156:17	H44	Since time was time, and man unmanly man,
QELIZ156:17	H44	Since time was time, and man unmanly man,
DAVID159:24	H39	Thy love was wonderfull, passing {surpassing} a man;
VANITY159:32	H4	Where is the man can say, lo, I have found
VANITY160:14	H24	Yet these, the wisest man of men did find,
VANITY160:21	H31	While man is man, he shall have ease or pain.
VANITY160:21	H31	While man is man, he shall have ease or pain.
TDUDLEY165:19	H21	Such as in life, no man could justly deem.
CONTEM168:24	H31	And as a strong man, joyes to run a race,

CONTEM169:30 H69 It makes a man more aged in conceit,
CONTEM171:24 H127 But Man grows old, lies down, remains where once he's laid.
CONTEM172:4 H141 But man was made for endless immortality.
CONTEM173:34 H198 Man at the best a creature frail and vain,
1HUSB180:24 H3 If ever man were lov'd by wife, then thee;
1HUSB180:25 H4 If ever wife was happy in a man,
2LETTER182:3 H9 Commend me to the man more lov'd then life,
MEDDM196:3 Hp272 that man whose head hath great abilities and his heart little or
MEDDM196:34 Hp274 deliuered vp by one traytor wthin, and that man wch all the
MEDDM197:14 Hp274 A low man, can goe vpright, vnder that door, wher a taller is
MEDDM197:15 Hp274 stoop, so a man of weak faith and mean abilities, may vndergo
MEDDM199:20 Hp278 man aimes at profit by the one & content in the other, but often
MEDDM199:28 Hp278 the body, the last the good name the two former leaue a man
MEDDM204:9 Hp284 call for great returnes, the more that any man is intrusted
MEDDM204:11 Hp284 behoues euery man so to improue his talents, that when his
MEDDM205:9 Hp286 As man is called the little world so his heart may be cal'd the
MEDDM209:21 Hp291 so it is with men, there was neuer yet any one man that had
MEDDM209:23 Hp291 so large, yet he stands in need of something wch another man
FAINTING222:18 H8 And liueing man no more shall see
MED223:11 Hp250 known who or where is the man that durst in his heart haue
WHAT224:17 H17 He is not man y^{t} he should lye.
WHAT224:18 H18 Nor son of man to 'vnsay
MYSOUL225:1 H5 What tho: thy outward Man decay,
11MAYA226:23 Hp255 man shall bee a meanes to strenghten my inner-man
HOUSE236:18 H10 Let no man know is my Desire.

MANASSEH (1)
MASSYR63:21 H406 Led King *Manasseh,* to captivity.

MANCHET (1)
MEDDM197:33 Hp275 pain till they turn to dust, and then are they fine manchet for

MANCHET'S (1) [manchet is]
SEASONS50:20 H154 Which after Manchet's made, {makes} for Kings to eat;

MAN'D (2) [manned] See also MANN'D
ELEMEN12:30 H190 Send forth your well man'd ships, where sun doth rise.
SIDNEY151:35 ~~H75~~ He left that charge by *Phoebus* to be man'd:

MANDANA (2)
MPERS69:2 H624 Whom Lady *Mandana* did to him bring;
MPERS69:11 H633 *Darius* was unto *Mandana* brother,

MANGERS See MAUNGERS

MANGLED (1)
MPERS82:40 H1187 Thus cut, and mangled by a hag of hell.

MANGLES (1)
MEDDM199:29 Hp278 when he is once dead, but the last mangles him in his graue

MANHOOD (1)
HUMOUR25:34 H223 Wilt thou this valour, manhood, courage cal:

MANIFEST (1)
28AUG225:28 Hp254 my drooping heart, and to manifest his Loue to me, and this is

MANIFESTED (2)
MYCHILD216:30 Hp242 ye Times w^{n} ye Lord hath manifested ye most Love to me.
JULY223:25 Hp251 gratiously manifested his Love to me, wch I dare not passe by

MANIFOLD (5)
HUMOUR~~31:25~~ H458 And Sanguine is more fickle many fold. {manifold,}

AGES38:39 H142 At home, abroad, my danger's manifold.
MPERS75:14 H875 Then thy disgrace, thine honour's manifold,
1HUSB180:32 H11 The heavens reward thee manifold I pray.
SON231:16 H28 Thro: want and Dangers manifold,

MANLY (7)
HUMOUR32:31 H505 I'le leave that manly property to you;
AGES35:18 H4 Childhood, and Youth, the Manly, and Old-age.
MASSYR58:9 H194 His manly heart disdained, in the least,
MPERS74:39 H860 His manly face dis-figures, spares no bloud,
MPERS81:37 ~~H1143~~ Where both sides exercis'd their manly feats;
MPERS87:16 ~~H1370~~ To look his manly brother in the face.
VANITY160:10 H20 What, Is't in flowring youth, or manly age?

MANNA (2)
FLESH176:28 H68 The hidden Manna I doe eat,
MYCHILD217:19 Hp243 bee well with me. I haue somt. tasted of y^t hidden Manna y^t y^e

MANN'D (1) [manned]
MPERS78:17 H998 Mann'd by {with} *Phenisians,* and *Pamphilians,*

MANNER (8)
HUMOUR27:21 H292 My worth in humble manner, to commend.
MPERS74:12 ~~H836~~ And after *Persian* manner, kisse his feet.
MPERS80:31 H1098 In secret manner word to *Xerxes* sends,
DIALOG147:34 H258 Thy Church and Weal, establish'd in such manner,
MEDDM200:26 Hp279 their former vigor and beavty in a more ample manner then
MEDDM204:22 Hp285 manner, wch should warn him, that doth any speciall seruice
MEDDM208:3 H289 these things must be what manner of persons ought we to be,
30SEPT227:19 Hp257 fainting, but not in y^t sore manner somt. he hath. I desire not

MAN¯ERS (1) [manners]
2SIMON195:3 Hp271 perpetuate their liues in their posterity, and their man¯ers, in

MANNERS (8) [pl.]
HUMOUR25:4 H193 Thy rudenesse counts, good manners vanity,
AGES39:14 H157 The manners of the Court, I likewise {also} know,
MGREC106:35 H2169 His manners, habit, gestures, now doth {all did} fashion,
MGREC106:38 H2172 Griev'd at this change of manners, and of minde:
MROMAN139:12 H3540 *Tarquin* the proud, from manners called so,
QELIZ156:10 H37 She taught them better manners to their cost.
TDUDLEY167:1 H83 *In manners pleasant and severe*
MYCHILD216:8 Hp241 this Covntry, where I fovnd a new World and new manners at

MAN'S (1) [man is]
MGREC~~100:16~~ H1900 For no man to resist {man's there} his valour showes {Army to

MANS (6) [poss.]
ELEMEN12:21 H181 And my *Hyæna* (imitates mans voyce)
ELEMEN13:23 H224 And how I oft work mans mortality.
HUMOUR20:10 H2 Mans constitution.
HUMOUR27:37 H308 Mans life to boundlesse time might stil endure;
HUMOUR30:21 H413 Then who's mans friend, when life and all forsakes?
MGREC118:22 H2669 The wretchednesse of mans mortality.

MANSION (4)
HUMOUR27:41 H312 Which makes the mansion, by the soul soon left;
TDUDLEY166:13 H55 For he a Mansion had, prepar'd above,
CONTEM172:28 H162 So may we press to that vast mansion, ever blest.
MEDDM197:34 Hp275 his Mansion.

MANURED (1)

AGES42:33	H289	'Twas in the crop of my manured ground:

MANURES (1)

SEASONS47:13	H29	And carefully manures his trees of fruits.

MANY (76)

ELEMEN17:4	H368	Nay many times, my Ocean breaks his bounds:
ELEMEN17:26	H390	*Ducalions* great deluge, with many moe;
ELEMEN19:28	~~H472~~	How many rich fraught vessells, have I split?
HUMOUR21:16	H44	Yet many times, unto my great disgrace,
HUMOUR31:25	H458	And Sanguine is more fickle many fold. {manifold,}
HUMOUR33:20	H534	My excellencies are so great, so many,
AGES38:27	H130	As many was {are} my sins, so dangers too:
AGES~~41:5~~	H225	Too many's {many} my Diseases to recite,
AGES~~45:2~~	H376	We joy'd in many blest and prosperous dayes.
SEASONS47:25	H41	Yet many a fleece of Snow, and stormy showre,
MASSYR56:38	H144	Which made the *Assyrians* many a day,
MASSYR~~57:23~~	H170	He many Ages liv'd after that day.
MASSYR~~57:32~~	H177	And eleav'n {many} hundred of years in silence sit,
MASSYR57:35	H180	May feign as many acts, as he did names;
MASSYR65:2	H467	Where after many assayes, they make {made} at last,
MPERS70:8	H679	To drain this ditch, he many sluces cut,
MPERS73:6	H793	The Female {to} many ages did extend,
MPERS73:38	H823	But {That} better one, then many Tyrants reigne.
MPERS78:8	H989	For truth's asham'd how many to expresse;
MPERS79:21	H1047	One King, so many Subjects should possesse;
MPERS81:1	H1109	And many thousands of these {those} men did kil;
MPERS90:22	H1489	The many victories themselves did gain,
MPERS90:23	H1490	The many thousand *Persians* they had slain;
MPERS90:39	~~H1506~~	Who of his cruelty made many tast,
MPERS91:1	H1509	He knows that many towns in *Greece* envies
MPERS91:12	H1520	Til many a Captain fel, both wise, and strong,
MGREC94:9	H1643	And many more, {all} whom he suspects {or fears} will climbe,
MGREC99:20	H1863	And by these walls, so many men were slaine,
MGREC107:15	H2190	The wealth of many Cities doth {Kindomes did} consume:
MGREC111:26	H2371	By hunger, and by cold, so many slaine,
MGREC112:14	H2400	So after many dayes this {the} Banquet ends.
MGREC120:12	H2747	So many Kingdoms in their power to hold,
MGREC~~122:8~~	H2833	In *Plutarchs Lives* his history many find.
MGREC124:15	H2922	*Athens,* with many Townes in *Greece* besides, {beside}
MGREC125:26	H2976	The Queen with many a curse, and bitter check,
MGREC127:4	H3034	Now many Townes in *Macedon* suppress,
MGREC~~132:20~~	H3262	*Demetrius* with so many troubles met,
MGREC133:18	H3306	I must let passe those many battels fought,
MGREC133:34	H3324	But this is perished with many more,
MGREC134:11	H3342	So many Princes still were murthered,
MROMAN139:29	H3555	Essays I many made but still gave out,
MROMAN139:32	H3558	With many moe discouragements did speak.
MROMAN139:35	H3561	At length resolv'd, when many years had past,
MROMAN140:1	H3564	And weary lines (though lanke) I many pen'd:
MROMAN140:9	H3572	Hath many Ages been upon his knees.
DIALOG144:6	H116	How many Princely heads on blocks laid down,

DIALOG145:24 H173 So many obstacles comes {came} in their way,
DIALOG146:7 H195 I that no warres, so many yeares have known,
DUBART154:26 H71 Thy double portion would have served many.
QELIZ158:19 H128 If many worlds, as that fantastick framed,
CONTEM171:12 H116 And though thus short, we shorten many wayes,
BIRTH180:7 H17 The many faults that well you know I have,
1LETTER181:7 H5 So many steps, head from the heart to sever
3LETTER183:11 H13 Ev'n thus doe I, with many a deep sad groan
MEDDM195:29 Hp272 Many can speak well, but few can do well. We are better
MEDDM199:19 Hp278 wearys the body, and many thoughts oppresse the minde
MEDDM201:3 Hp280 and many times he imposes waighty burdens on their
MEDDM201:9 Hp280 easily sayd by many, but what he did not say, cannot (truly) be
MEDDM203:14 Hp283 country, and heere he hath many conueniences and comforts
MEDDM204:17 Hp285 god doth many times, both reward and punish for one and y^e
MEDDM205:36 Hp287 that many times, the waight thereof impares both their bodys
MEDDM206:29 Hp288 how many good parents haue had bad children, and againe
MEDDM206:29 Hp288 good parents haue had bad children, and againe how many
MEDDM207:6 Hp288 giuen for, as health wealth and honour, wch might be so many
MYCHILD216:15 Hp241 greif to me, and cost me many prayers + tears before I obtaind
MYCHILD216:16 Hp241 after him gave me many more, of whom I now take ye care,
MYCHILD217:22 Hp243 never p^{r}vail: yet haue I many Times sinkings & droopings,
MYCHILD217:32 Hp243 Many times hath Satan troubled me concerning ye verity of y^e
MYCHILD217:33 Hp243 Scriptures, many times by Atheisme how I could know whether
MYCHILD218:26 Hp244 The consideration of these things and many ye like would soon
28AUG225:27 Hp254 many times my faith weak likewise, the Lord was pleased to
11MAYA226:14 Hp255 all this spring till this 11. May, yet hath my God given me many
11MAYA226:17 Hp255 Many refreshments haue I fovnd in this my weary pilgrimage,
11MAYA226:18 Hp255 this valley of Baca many pools of water, That wch now I cheifly
30SEPT227:28 Hp257 children) haue yee seen ye many sicknesses and weaknesses
SAMUEL228:5 H6 The child I stay'd for many yeares.

MANY'S (1) [many is]
AGES41:5 H225 Too many's {many} my Diseases to recite,

MAR (2) See also MARRE
MASSYR61:16 H321 When *Resins* force his borders sore did mar.
MGREC119:29 H2719 (Which did his match with *Cleopatra* mar)

MARATHON (1)
MPERS76:33 H931 At *Marathon* this bloudy field was fought,

MARBLE (3)
MPERS~~71:4~~ H718 Now quiet lyes under one marble stone.
SIDNEY150:20 H45 Engrave on Marble, in characters of Gold,
MEDDM201:20 Hp281 thick ayre about them so may we sometime se, marble hearted

MARCELLUS (1)
HUMOUR29:34 H385 And if *Marcellus* bold, be call'd *Romes* sword,

MARCH (3) n.
SEASONS46:37 H15 *March, April, May,* of all the rest most faire;
DIALOG143:7 H74 No Duke of *York,* nor Earle of *March,* to soyle
2SIMON195:19 Hp271 March 20

MARCH (8) v.
HUMOUR22:7 H76 To march her pace, to some is greater pain,
MASSYR56:7 H113 With great facility, march safe upon't.
MPERS74:37 ~~H858~~ And fear'd, he now with scorn must march away:

MPERS89:30 H1464 And feares as much to let them march away;
MPERS90:6 H1479 But on they march, through hunger, and through cold,
MGREC104:31 H2083 Who doubling of his march, posts on amain,
MGREC105:15 H2108 Wearied with his long march, did water seek,
MGREC107:22 H2197 But sore {much} distrest for water, in their march,

MARCH'D (1) [marched]
MGREC94:21 H1659 Then on he march'd, in's way he veiw'd old *Troy;*

MARCHED (3)
MPERS71:28 H742 But as they marched o're those desart sands,
MGREC96:1 H1721 The splendor, and the pompe, he marched in,
MGREC125:15 H2963 The Queen to meet her, bravely marched {marches} on;

MARCHES (1) n.
MGREC~~125:15~~ H2963 The Queen to meet her, bravely marched {marches} on;

MARCHES (4) v.
MASSYR59:22 H246 *Arbaces* marches in, the town did {he} take {takes},
MASSYR65:17 H482 To *Judah* marches with a speedy course,
MPERS70:12 H683 And to the walls securely marches on,
MGREC119:36 H2726 Long marches through *Cilicia* he makes,

MARCHING (3)
MPERS79:17 H1043 Was marching o're this interrupting Bay; {new devised way.}
MPERS79:34 H1060 Then marching {on} to the streight *Thermopyle,*
MPERS84:37 H1273 In this sad conflict, marching on his ways,

MARCHT (7)
MASSYR61:35 H340 Through *Syria* now he marcht, none stopt his way,
MASSYR64:10 H434 Against *lehoiakim* marcht with his train;
MPERS~~79:3~~ H1025 'Twixt which his souldiers marcht in good array.
MGREC95:12 H1691 Next *Alexander* marcht, t'wards the black sea;
MGREC100:1 H1885 From thence, to fruitfull *Ægypt* marcht with speed,
MGREC100:15 H1899 Unto *Euphrates* marcht, and over goes,
MGREC111:30 H2375 And thence he marcht into *Carmania,*

MARDON'S (1) [poss.]
MPERS81:23 H1131 And thus reply'd unto *Mardon's* request;

MARDON'US (1)
MPERS81:7 H1115 With his *Mardon'us,* judex {index} of his minde;

MARDONIUS (6)
MPERS77:28 H969 And's cousen, young *Mardonius* forsaken,
MPERS77:35 H976 Flattering *Mardonius* on th' other side,
MPERS78:12 H993 To *Mardonius,* Captain {made their} Generall;
MPERS81:30 H1138 *Mardonius* proud, hearing this answer stout,
MPERS82:4 H1151 *Mardonius* finding victuals wast apace,
MPERS82:10 H1157 And troublesome *Mardonius* now must dye:

MARINER (1)
CONTEM174:13 H212 The Mariner that on smooth waves doth glide,

MARINERS (2) [pl.] See also MARRINERS
ELEMEN18:23 H427 Ye Mariners, tis I that fill your Sailes,
MASSYR64:38 H462 And Mariners, to handle sayle, and oare;

MARK (1) [name]
MGREC134:39 H3368 She with her Paramour *Mark Antony,*

MARK (2) [sign]
AGES37:31 H93 A Baron or a Duke, ne'r made my mark.
MYCHILD219:8 Hp245 the mark wch I aimed at.

MARK (1) v.
2LETTER182:33 H39 Now post with double speed, mark what I say,
MARKES (1) [marks]
DIALOG144:26 ~~H135~~ Their reverent cheeks, did beare the glorious markes
MARKET-PLACE (1)
MGREC107:11 H2186 Into the Market-place, before the King;
MARKS (2) See also MARKES
AGES41:2 H222 With ugly {outward} marks of his eternal {inward loathsome}
MGREC108:23 H2239 Repelling these two marks of honour got,
MARKT (1)
CONTEM172:16 H151 I markt, nor crooks, nor rubs that there did lye
MARRE (2) [mar]
MASSYR56:19 H125 A structure rare, I should but rudely marre,
MPERS77:20 H961 Th' *Ægyptians* to reduce, and *Greece* to marre;
MARRIAGE (3)
MPERS74:26 H849 And now a King, by marriage, choyce, and bloud,
MGREC98:41 H1843 His eldest Daughter, (him) {he} in marriage offers,
MGREC130:2 H3157 For marriage to *Cleopatra,* doth send
MARRIED (2) See also MARRYED
MPERS78:14 H995 Who married the sister of *Darius:*
MGREC117:31 H2638 And *Roxan* faire, whom late he married,
MARRINERS (1) [mariners]
ELEMEN12:37 H197 But Marriners, where got you ships and sailes?
MARROW (3)
HUMOUR34:11 H566 Mine likewise is the marrow of the back,
AGES41:9 H229 Of Marrow {aches} ful my bones, of Milk {woe} my breasts
MEDDM202:11 Hp281 y^t their bones are full of marrow & their breasts of milk,
MARRYED (1) [married]
MYCHILD216:7 Hp241 short time I changed my Condition & was marryed, and came
MARS (4) [name]
MROMAN136:25 H3439 His Father was not *Mars,* as some devis'd,
SIDNEY149:11 H10 *Mars* and *Minerva* did in one agree,
SIDNEY151:15 ~~H69~~ And *Mars* himself was ta'n by *Venus* gin;
SIDNEY152:26 H95 *Heire to the Muses, the Son of* Mars *in truth,*
MARTELL (1)
DUBART154:12 H57 Then in thy *Pippin, Martell, Charlemain.*
MARTI'LIST (1)
AGES37:40 H102 No Statist I: nor Marti'list i' th' field;
MARTIAL (1) See also MARTIALL
AGES39:40 H182 Martial deeds I love not, 'cause they're vertuous,
MARTIALIST (1)
ELEMEN9:1 H35 O {Ye} Martialist! what weapon {weapons} for your fight?
MARTIALL (1) [martial]
MROMAN137:39 H3490 Who Martiall Discipline in use did bring;
MARTIUS (3)
MROMAN138:13 H3503 *Ancus Martius.*
MROMAN138:14 H3504 Next, *Ancus Martius* sits upon the Throne,
MROMAN138:29 H3519 He after *Martius* death the Kingdome had,
MARTYRS (1) [pl.]
DIALOG144:5 H115 Martyrs, and others, dying causelesly:

MARUS (1)
MPERS71:18 H732 (But little *Marus,* {*Narus*} scap'd that cruel fate,
MARVELL (1)
MGREC107:16 H2191 But marvell 'tis, that without muteny,
MARVELOUS (1)
MASSYR56:30 H136 But this is marvelous, of all those men,
MASCULINES (2) [pl.]
HUMOUR21:8 H36 We both once Masculines, the world doth know,
QELIZ157:34 H102 Nay Masculines, you have thus tax'd us long,
MASQUES (1) [pl.]
AGES40:25 H206 To Masques, to Playes, to Taverns stil I move;
MASSACRES (1) [pl.]
MGREC134:5 H3338 Horrid massacres, murders, cruelties,
MASSE (1) [mass]
MGREC102:11 H1981 In this a masse {world} of gold, and treasure lay,
MASSY (2)
ELEMEN13:2 H203 Was {Were} those compiled heapes of massy stones?
ELEMEN16:1 H324 With rowling graines of purest massy gold:
MASTER (23)
ELEMEN10:34 H109 Yet by my force, master my master can.
ELEMEN10:34 H109 Yet by my force, master my master can.
MASSYR58:8 H193 His master like a Strumpet chanc'd to {clad did} spy,
MASSYR58:24 ~~H207~~ *Arbaces* must be master of their lands.
MPERS72:26 ~~H773~~ His cruell Master, for all service done,
MPERS75:23 ~~H880~~ Thou lov'dst thy Master more then verity.
MPERS81:3 H1111 With empty hands they to their Master go;
MPERS88:29 H1422 But treads down all, for to advance their Master;
MPERS91:32 ~~H1546~~ He was the Master of good *Nehemie*
MGREC95:11 H1690 He for his master takes, with *Lycia,*
MGREC95:24 H1703 His substitute, as fearfull as his master,
MGREC106:14 H2148 For his fidelity to 's Master show'd;
MGREC112:31 H2417 His Master is Accuser, Judge, and King,
MGREC113:14 H2441 But how these Captaines should, or yet their Master,
MGREC113:35 H2462 Yet gave his Master the immortall fame;
MGREC114:19 H2489 Who lov'd his Master more then did the rest,
MGREC118:6 H2653 Because his Master gave to him his Ring,
MGREC118:14 H2661 Seven dayes the Corps of their great Master lyes
MGREC127:29 H3059 And Master of the treasure he remains; {sole remain:}
DIALOG146:4 H192 {Contention} grown 'twixt Subjects and their Master:
CONTEM174:16 H215 And now becomes great Master of the seas;
MEDDM204:11 Hp284 man so to improue his talents, that when his great master
MED223:5 Hp250 master I thy servant, But hence arises not my comfort, Thou
MASTERS (1) [pl.]
MEDDM201:27 Hp281 should be the precepts of the wise masters of assemblys to
MASTERS (13) [poss.]
MASSYR63:7 H392 And on his Masters ruins, his house makes;
MASSYR64:40 H464 Their shoulders must their Masters minde fulfill;
MPERS74:38 H859 Then brave *Zopirus,* for his Masters good,
MPERS89:33 H1467 As *Tyssaphern,* knowing his Masters minde,
MPERS90:41 H1508 And hopes by craft to quit his Masters harmes;
MGREC111:11 H2356 Acknowledg'd for their Masters Soveraigne;

MGREC114:4 H2472 Then's Masters god-head, to defie, and wrong;
MGREC119:5 H2695 Which was his Masters sister for {secretly} to wed:
MGREC120:34 H2771 His Masters Funerals doth celebrate;
MGREC121:37 H2819 But he was true to's masters family,
MGREC127:25 H3055 Striving t'uphold his Masters family,
MGREC130:10 H3165 Untill he further know his Masters will;
DIALOG143:40 H109 Nor for their owne, but for their Masters sake;

MATCH (8)
ELEMEN9:27 H61 To match on high with the Celestiall fires.
ELEMEN~~16:12~~ H335 I soon can match them with my seas as deep.
MPERS71:10 H726 That Kings with Sisters match, no Law they finde,
MPERS85:35 H1311 No match was high enough, but their own blood,)
MPERS~~91:29~~ H1543 His match incestuous, cruelties of th' Queen,
MGREC101:7 H1932 (Nor was such match, in all the world beside)
MGREC112:2 H2388 That by this match he might be yet more neare.
MGREC119:29 H2719 (Which did his match with *Cleopatra* mar)

MATCHING (1)
MPERS82:27 H1174 Nor matching of her daughter, to his son:

MATCHLESSE (3) [matchless]
SEASONS48:16 H69 Except the double Pinks, and matchlesse Roses.
MGREC117:20 H2627 His matchlesse force no Creature could abide;
DUBART152:34 H3 Great, deare, sweet *Bartas,* thou art matchlesse knowne;

MATE (3)
3LETTER183:9 H11 The absence of her Love, and loving Mate,
CHILDRN184:27 H16 And with her mate flew out of sight;
CHILDRN184:36 H25 Coupled with mate loving and true,

MATERIALS (1) [pl.]
HUMOUR26:34 H264 But the materials none of thine, that's cleare,

MATES (1)
MGREC124:40 H2947 As all her Husbands children by his Mates;

MATRON (1)
DDUDLEY167:10 H7 *A worthy Matron of unspotted life,*

MATTER (8)
ELEMEN11:17 H137 And then, because no matter more for fire:
HUMOUR33:10 H524 Shame forc'd thee say, the matter that was mine,
SEASONS48:31 ~~H83~~ Some subject, shallow braines, much matter yeelds,
MPERS83:18 H1206 And by his craft, ordered the matter so,
MROMAN140:8 H3571 Nor matter is't this last, the world now sees,
DIALOG145:16 H165 Well, to the matter then, there's grown of late,
2LETTER182:27 H33 Tell him here's worse then a confused matter,
MEDDM204:21 Hp285 of Jehu, he was rewarded for the matter, and yet punished for

MATTERS (4) [pl.]
MASSYR60:34 H299 When this was built, and all matters in peace,
MGREC107:5 H2180 That other matters may {might} take up their minds.
MGREC~~122:32~~ H2853 That he might settle matters in the same.
MYCHILD215:14 Hp240 I was able to compose some short matters, (for w^{t} else to call

MATTERS (1) v.
MEDDM201:4 Hp280 go vpright vnder them, but it matters not whether the load be

MATTOCKS (1)
ELEMEN9:11 H45 Your shares, {Hooes} your mattocks, and what e're you see,

MAUD (1)

DIALOG142:13 H42 Doe *Maud,* and *Stephen* for the Crown contend?

MAUGRE (6)

ELEMEN~~11:1~~ H120 But maugre all, that I, or foes could do
ELEMEN13:24 H225 He sometimes findes, maugre his toyling paine,
HUMOUR28:28 H340 And maugre (Choler) stil they are the wittest,
MPERS85:17 H1293 For sixty years maugre the *Persians* might.
MGREC136:11 H3425 *And maugre all resolves, my fancy wrought*
MYCHILD218:12 Hp244 All Ages maugre all ye heathen Tyrants + all of the Enemyes

MAUL (1)

TDUDLEY166:38 H80 *To Sectaryes a whip and Maul,*

MAUNGERS (1) [mangers]

MGREC110:29 H2333 His Maungers he erected up so high,

MAWES (1) [maws]

SEASONS~~52:8~~ H223 Our pinched flesh, and empty panch {hungry mawes} requires:

MAXIME (1)

ELEMEN16:11 ~~H334~~ But note this maxime in Philosophy:

MAXIME'S (1) [maxime is]

PROLOG7:11 H25 Art can doe much, but this maxime's most sure,

MAY (9) n.

AGES43:16 ~~H308~~ Which others scatter, like the dew in *May.*
SEASONS46:37 H15 *March, April, May,* of all the rest most faire;
SEASONS47:5 H19 Stil adds to th' last, til after pleasant *May;*
SEASONS48:9 H62 My next, and last, is pleasant fruitfull *May,*
11MAYA226:12 Hp255 May—11. 1657.
11MAYA226:14 Hp255 lasted all this spring till this 11. May, yet hath my God given
13MAY226:25 H1 May. 13. 1657.
11MAYB228:22 Hp259 May. 11. 1661.
11MAYB228:25 Hp259 of January 'till May I haue been by fitts very ill & weak.

MAY (127) v.

FATHER5:26 H27 Their discord may {doth} appear, by these harsh rimes.
ELEMEN8:33 H31 What I can doe, well skill'd Mechanicks may,
ELEMEN10:7 H82 My Crabbe, my Scorpion, fishes, you may see,
ELEMEN10:38 H113 In confus'd heaps of ashes may ye see.
ELEMEN16:31 H354 These be my benefits which may suffice:
ELEMEN18:36 H440 Which may be done, by holding down my vapour.
ELEMEN19:10 H455 With thousands moe, which now I may omit;
ELEMEN19:24 H469 What woeful wracks I've made, may wel appear,
HUMOUR22:29 H98 The vitall spirits they're call'd, and wel they may,
HUMOUR24:14 H163 Your selves may plead, your wrongs are no whit lesse,
HUMOUR25:31 H220 That naught but blood, {death} the same may expiate.
HUMOUR28:33 H345 Thousand examples, you may daily see
HUMOUR~~33:14~~ H528 Yet without ostentation I may say,
HUMOUR34:10 H565 Yet some may wish, oh, {O} had mine eyes ne're seene.
HUMOUR34:19 H574 Some worthy {curious} learned *Crooke* may these reveal,
AGES35:38 H24 Then may he live, til {out} threescore years or past.
AGES39:35 H178 That who would see vain man, may look on me:
AGES~~41:19~~ H238 Now age is more, more good ye do {may} expect;
AGES43:37 H332 And to conclude, I may not tedious be,
AGES45:20 ~~H402~~ But yet may live, to see't made up again:
AGES~~45:21~~ H403 Oh may you live, and so you will I trust

AGES45:22 ~~H404~~ But out of troubles, ye may see much good,
AGES~~45:22~~ H408 But ye may live to see't made up again.
AGES~~45:22~~ H410 But out of evill you may see much good.
AGES~~45:22~~ H412 Men may more freely speak another day.
SEASONS51:4 H178 For nought's so good, but it may be abused,
MASSYR57:16 ~~H163~~ Some may object, his Parents ruling all,
MASSYR57:18 ~~H165~~ This answer may suffice, whom it wil please,
MASSYR~~57:22~~ H169 We may with learned *Vsher* better say,
MASSYR57:29 H174 We may suggest our thoughts, but cannot tel;
MASSYR57:35 H180 May feign as many acts, as he did names;
MASSYR~~57:36~~ H181 It is enough {may suffice}, if all be true that's past,
MASSYR66:37 H543 And if by words, we may guesse at the heart,
MPERS71:11 H727 But that the *Persian* King, may act his minde;
MPERS89:13 H1447 They soone may come, and {in short time might} place one in
MPERS~~91:30~~ H1544 His life may read in *Plutarch* to be seen.
MPERS92:7 ~~H1565~~ It may be thought, surely he had no Son,
MPERS92:26 ~~H1584~~ Thus learned *Pemble,* whom we may not slight,
MPERS92:30 H1588 Yet in these {such} differences, we may behold; {be bold,}
MPERS92:34 H1592 Whose warres and losses we may better tell;
MGREC98:26 H1828 For now's the time, Captains like Kings may live;
MGREC98:39 H1841 These he may scape, and if he so desire,
MGREC105:27 H2120 Yet that succeeding Kings in safety may
MGREC106:20 H2154 To th' ignorant, her title may {will} declare.
MGREC107:5 H2180 That other matters may {might} take up their minds.
MGREC107:18 H2193 Nor wonder lesse, to Readers may it bring,
MGREC117:15 H2622 We may hereafter shew, in season due.
MGREC120:8 H2743 Their friendship may {might} the more be strengthened:
MGREC130:37 H3182 Thus may we hear, and fear, and ever say,
MGREC136:8 H3421 *Ne sutor ultra crepidum,* may write.
DIALOG141:13 H12 Ah, tell thy Daughter, she may simpathize.
DIALOG141:24 H23 Which present help may ease this {my} malady.
DIALOG142:3 H32 If th' wound's {wound} so dangerous I may not know?
DIALOG145:4 H153 Nor sip I of that cup, and just 't may be,
DIALOG146:11 H199 But these may be beginnings of more woe,
DIALOG146:12 H200 Who knows, the worst, the best {this} may {be my} overthrow;
DIALOG146:35 ~~H235~~ That Right may have its right, though't be with blood;
SIDNEY~~150:22~~ H47 Of which, {at} this day, faire *Belgia* doth {may} boast.
SIDNEY151:3 ~~H69~~ I wish no more such Blazers we may see;
DUBART153:16 H20 My Muse unto a Childe, I fitly may compare,
QELIZ157:30 H98 Which I may not, my pride doth but aspire,
DAVID158:35 H15 Nor any pleasant thing e're may you show;
VANITY160:25 H35 That *summum Bonum* which may stay my mind?
TDUDLEY166:9 H51 Their greatness may be judg'd by what they shew.
CONTEM172:28 H162 So may we press to that vast mansion, ever blest.
CONTEM174:19 H218 Which 'gainst all adverse winds may serve for fort.
FLESH177:27 H108 If I of Heaven may have my fill,
AUTHOR177:35 H7 Where errors were not lessened (all may judg).
SICKNES179:2 H22 I doing good may be.
BIRTH179:33 H9 How soon, my Dear, death may my steps attend,
BIRTH179:34 H10 How soon't may be thy Lot to lose thy friend,
BIRTH180:4 H14 I may seem thine, who in effect am none.

1HUSB180:34	H13	That when we live no more, we may live ever.
1LETTER181:22	H20	I wish my Sun may never set, but burn
2LETTER182:14	H20	May count my sighs, and number all my drops:
VERSES184:1	H5	Then may your worthy self from whom it came.
VERSES184:8	H12	Such is my debt, I may not say forgive,
CHILDRN185:40	H66	Sore accidents on you may light.
CHILDRN186:1	H68	So happy may you live and die:
CHILDRN186:26	H93	Thus gone, amongst you I may live,
MERCY189:12	H33	The Heavens vouchsafe she may so ever be.
2SIMON195:14	Hp271	heer and crown you wth glory heerafter. that I may meet you
MEDDM195:25	Hp272	no evill that we feele, or fear, but we may make some spiritull
MEDDM196:25	Hp273	Sweet words are like hony, a little may refresh, but too much
MEDDM197:15	Hp274	a man of weak faith and mean abilities, may vndergo a Crosse
MEDDM198:28	Hp277	A sore finger may disquiet the whole body, but an vlcer wthin
MEDDM198:29	Hp277	it, so an enemy wthout may disturb a Commonwealth, but
MEDDM201:8	Hp280	I haue seen an end of all Sinning, what he did say, may be
MEDDM201:20	Hp280	from a thick ayre about them so may we sometime se, marble
MEDDM202:16	Hp282	The treasures of this world may well be compared to huskes,
MEDDM202:17	Hp282	in them, and they that feed vpon them, may soon Stuffe
MEDDM202:18	Hp282	but cannot fill their bellys, they may be choaked by them,
MEDDM202:22	Hp282	luster, although we may walk by his light, but when he is set,
MEDDM202:25	Hp282	other time, yet he affords so much light as may direct our way,
MEDDM202:26	Hp282	we may go forwards to the Citty of habitation, but when he
MEDDM203:16	Hp283	meet wth such tossings that may cause him to long for shore,
MEDDM203:18	Hp283	that we may plainly declare that we seek a citty aboue and
MEDDM204:12	Hp284	call him to reckoning, he may receiue his owne wth advantage
MEDDM205:7	Hp285	plentifull crop may be expected in the haruest of their yeares.
MEDDM205:9	Hp286	man is called the little world so his heart may be cal'd the little
MEDDM206:35	Hp288	may also be a support to such as haue or had wicked parents,
MEDDM207:13	Hp288	Comforts of this Life, may be compared to the gourd of Jonah,
MEDDM207:21	Hp289	men are truly sayd to be tenants at will, and it may as truly be
MEDDM207:29	Hp289	may be sure of an euer lasting habitation that fades not away.
MEDDM207:35	Hp289	eyes, by beholding their bed, the morning may mind them of
MEDDM208:18	Hp290	the Apostle call riches deceitfull riches, and they may truely
MEDDM208:34	Hp290	the people, god sath to him Let me alone, that I may destroy
MEDDM209:20	Hp291	so there may be a mutuall commerce through ye world As it is
TOCHILD215:4	H4	That being gone, here yov may find
MYCHILD215:15	Hp240	bequeath to yov, that when I am no more wth yov, yet I may
MYCHILD215:17	Hp240	doe) by y^{t} yov may gain some spirit: Advantage by my exper^{c}.
MYCHILD218:19	Hp244	yet why may not ye popish Relign. bee ye right, They haue the
FAINTING222:27	H17	Then I may frvitfull bee.
JULY223:26	Hp251	y^{t} it may bee a support to me when I shall haue occasion
JULY223:28	Hp251	that I now hope for, y^{t} so they may bee encourag^{d} to trust in
28AUG225:32	Hp254	but he doth it for my Advantage, and y^{t} I may bee a Gainer
28AUG226:6	Hp254	Lord gravnt y^{t} while I live I may doe y^{t} service I am able in this
30SEPT227:29	Hp257	passed thro: to ye End y^{t} if you meet wth the like yov may
SAMUEL228:15	H16	That I again may see his face,
11MAYB228:34	Hp259	Conversation may speak that thy vowes are vpon me.
SON231:20	H32	That ever I may thankfull bee
SON231:21	H33	And may putt him in mind of what
SON231:26	H38	Ou^{r} vpright walking may expresse.

SON231:27 H39 O Lord gravnt that I may never forgett thy Loving kindness in
2HUSB233:9 H42 That I and all thy servants may
2HUSB233:13 H46 That wee together may sing praise
HOUSE237:16 H46 That dunghill mists away may flie.

MAY'ST (2) [mayst] See also MAIST
CONTEM172:22 H156 Nor is't enough, that thou alone may'st slide,
RESTOR230:2 H17 That thou by both may'st learn

MAYST (3) See also MAIST, MAY'ST
ELEMEN15:27 H309 Such wealth, but not such like, Earth thou mayst show.
AUTHOR178:10 H20 In this array, 'mongst Vulgars mayst thou roam,
2LETTER182:16 H22 That once a day, thy Spouse thou mayst imbrace;

'MAZED (1) [amazed] See also AMAZ'D
DIALOG141:18 H17 Which 'mazed Christendome stands wondring at?

MAZED (4) See also AMAZ'D
MPERS87:27 H1379 The mazed King, was now {then} about to fly;
MGREC111:18 H2363 Which the stout *Macedonians* mazed sore
DUBART153:22 H26 And thousand times his mazed minde doth wish
CONTEM169:13 H54 To sing some Song, my mazed Muse thought meet.

MEADOWS See MEDOWS

MEADS (2) [pl.]
SEASONS48:21 H74 The Meads with Cowslip, Hony-suckl's dight,
2LETTER182:10 H16 Or all the grass that in the Meads do stand,

MEAN (10) See also MEAN TIME, MEAN WHILE
FATHER6:2 H36 Some thing {something} of all (though mean) I did intend,
PROLOG6:20 H5 For my mean Pen, are too superiour things,
HUMOUR~~31:7~~ H440 So mean thou art in art as in discretion:
AGES35:31 H17 Such cold mean flowers (as these) blossome {the spring puts
AGES37:4 H66 Whose mean beginning, blushing cann't reveale,
AGES41:31 H248 Be my condition mean, I then take paines;
AGES46:7 H438 To mean, to noble, fearful, or to bold:
TDUDLEY166:7 H49 As in the mean ones, of our foolish dayes,
MEDDM197:15 Hp274 stoop, so a man of weak faith and mean abilities, may vndergo
MEDDM204:26 Hp285 He that would be content, wth a mean condition, must not cast

MEANE (2) [mean]
PROLOG8:1 H49 This meane and unrefined stuffe {ure} of mine,
MGREC112:7 H2393 It far exceeds my meane abilities,

MEANER (1)
MEDDM209:24 Hp291 hath (perhaps meaner then himself) wch shews us perfection is

MEANES (2) [means, pl.]
MEDDM208:7 Hp289 you vse no other meanes to extinguish them so distance of
11MAYA226:23 Hp255 man shall bee a meanes to strenghten my inner-man

MEANES (2) v. [means]
DIALOG141:12 H11 What meanes this wailing tone, this mourning guise?
PILGRIM210:18 H18 and meanes in safity now to dwell.

MEANING (1)
MPERS86:3 H1319 Meaning to chastise him, in sharpest sort,

MEANLY (2)
FATHER5:13 H14 I bring my four times {and} four, now meanly clad,
MEDDM205:32 Hp286 is the breaking of their limbes, some again, are but meanly

MEANNESSE (2)
AGES42:18 H276 In meannesse, greatnesse, riches, poverty;

MGREC117:34 H2641 But meannesse of their Mothers bard the same:

MEANS (5) [pl.] See also MEANES

MASSYR56:41 H147 But by what means, we are not certifi'd.
MPERS91:21 H1529 The two Queens, by his means, 'gin {seem} to abate
MGREC107:33 H2208 Would by {without} some means a transportation finde;
MGREC110:24 H2328 Could by no means be further {farther} drawn, or led:
MGREC130:23 H3178 And by their means, who thought of nothing lesse

MEANS (2) v. See also MEANES

MGREC104:24 H2076 Who wanting means t' resist, these wrongs abides.
MGREC~~126:19~~ H3010 *Olimpias* wills to keep it, {means to hold out} to the last,

MEANT (3)

MPERS77:24 H965 As if to dust he meant to grinde that Nation;
MPERS86:38 H1354 He meant {Prepares} himselfe to carry the report.
MGREC~~96:18~~ H1738 think {Suppos'd} he neither thought {meant} to fight nor fly,

MEAN TIME (1)

ANNEB187:32 H22 Mean time my throbbing heart's chear'd up with this

MEAN WHILE (2)

VANITY160:7 H17 Mean while the conscience rage, who shall appease?
CHILDRN186:2 H69 Mean while my dayes in tunes Ile spend,

MEAT (8)

ELEMEN12:31 H191 After three years, when men and meat is spent,
AGES45:33 H423 I cannot scent, savours of pleasant meat,
MGREC95:15 H1694 Whose touch turn'd all to gold, yea even his meat:
MGREC111:8 H2353 The meat, and drink, attendants, every thing,
MGREC~~116:10,~~ H2573 Nor meat, nor drink, nor comfort would she take,
CONTEM173:22 H188 Thy cloaths ne're wear, thy meat is every where,
FLESH176:27 H67 For I have meat thou know'st not off;
FLESH176:29 H69 The word of life it is my meat.

MEATS (2) [pl.]

SEASONS52:6 H221 And solid'st meats, our stomachs can digest;
MGREC109:11 H2270 And with delicious meats, his Pallat choak'd,

MECHANICKS (1) [pl.]

ELEMEN8:33 H31 What I can doe, well skill'd Mechanicks may,

MEDDLE (2)

HUMOUR27:16 H287 To meddle further, I shal be but shent,
MGREC115:21 H2540 (Not suffering her to meddle in {with} the State)

MEDES (3) [pl.]

MASSYR58:17 H202 The last, the *Medes* and *Persians* doth invite.
MASSYR60:10 H275 Of {To} *Medes,* and *Persians,* {when he crav'd} their assisting
MASSYR67:16 H562 Wars with the *Medes,* unhappily he wag'd,

MEDIA (8)

MASSYR58:13 H198 These two rul'd *Media* and *Babylon,*
MASSYR60:8 H273 And then to {unto} *Media* transfer'd his seat.
MGREC102:1 H1971 *Darius* stript of all, to *Media* came,
MGREC103:37 H2048 Who was retir'd, and gone to {as far as} *Media.*
MGREC105:5 H2098 Was the false Governour of *Media)*
MGREC113:25 H2452 To doe this deed, they into *Media* send;
MGREC115:4 H2515 Now *Alexander* goes to *Media,*
MGREC115:16 H2535 From *Media* to *Babylon* he went,

MEDIAN (1)

MASSYR54:32 H59 The *Median* country, he did also gain,

MEDICINE (1)		
DIALOG142:2	H31	What Medicine shall I seek to cure this woe,
MEDITATION (2)		
MASSYR66:4	H510	Was nothing, but such gastly meditation;
FLESH175:11	H11	Nothing but Meditation?
MEDITATIONS (3) [pl.]		
2SIMON195:8	Hp271	you nor of more ease to my self then these short meditations
MEDDM195:21	H0	Meditations Diuine
MED223:1	Hp250	Meditations when my Soul hath been refreshed wth the
MEDLAR (1)		
SEASONS51:10	H184	Of Medlar, Quince, of Warden, {Almonds, Quinces, Wardens}
MEDOWS (1) [meadows]		
SEASONS50:4	H138	The Medows of their burden {riches} to dispoyl;
MEDUSA (1)		
ELEMEN10:5	H80	The Valiant *Perseus* who *Medusa* slew,
MEET (25)		
ELEMEN15:21	H303	To meet with want, each woefull man bethinks.
HUMOUR22:5	H74	If great perswasions, cause her meet her foe;
HUMOUR28:21	H333	That my intents should meet with interruption,
HUMOUR32:36	H510	Nay, I could tel you (what's more true then meet)
MASSYR~~58:35~~	H218	These with celerity, *Arbaces* meets {meet},
MPERS73:14	H801	The Princes meet to chuse one in his stead,
MPERS74:4	H829	Upon a Green to meet, by rising Sun;
MPERS78:16	H997	Of two and twenty thousand Gallies meet,
MPERS78:31	H1012	At *Sardis,* in *Lidia,* these all doe meet,
MPERS82:16	H1163	The *Grecians* at *Mycale* in Asia meet,
MGREC95:30	H1709	And on {Then o're} he goes *Darius* {now} so to meet;
MGREC98:32	H1834	And {now} must at *Gaza, Alexander* meet;
MGREC99:14	H1857	He now to *Gaza* goes, and there doth meet
MGREC101:34	~~H1959~~	Both Armies meet, *Greeks* fight, the *Persians* run,
MGREC115:17	H2536	To meet him there, t' *Antipater* had {he'd} sent,
MGREC125:15	H2963	The Queen to meet her, bravely marched {marches} on;
CONTEM169:13	H54	To sing some Song, my mazed Muse thought meet.
CONTEM172:23	H157	But hundred brooks in thy cleer waves do meet,
AUTHOR178:7	H17	Yet still thou run'st more hobling then is meet;
BIRTH179:30	H6	But with deaths parting blow is sure to meet.
2SIMON195:14	Hp271	heer and crown you wth glory heerafter. that I may meet you
MEDDM203:16	Hp283	lest he meet wth such tossings that may cause him to long for
MEDDM204:23	Hp285	eye on the command, and not on his own ends, lest he meet
MEDDM206:24	Hp287	barter for it, shall meet with miserable disapointment, going
30SEPT227:29	Hp257	I haue passed thro: to ye End yt if you meet wth the like yov
MEETINGS (1) [pl.]		
DDUDLEY167:18	H15	*The publick meetings ever did frequent,*
MEETS (4)		
MASSYR58:35	H218	These with celerity, *Arbaces* meets {meet},
MPERS79:35	H1061	The *Spartan* meets him, brave *Leonade,*
MGREC99:36	H1879	Him in his Priestly Robes, high *Jaddus* meets,
MGREC109:18	H2277	Through his perswasion *Alexander* meets;
MEGRIM (1)		
AGES~~43:33~~	H328	The Astma, Megrim, Palsy, Lethargie,

MELANCHOLLIES (1) [pl.]
HUMOUR35:6 H602 My cold, cold Melanchollies {melancholy} hand shal clasp,
MELANCHOLLY (5)
HUMOUR28:1 H313 So Melancholly ceases {seizes} on a man;
HUMOUR28:16 H328 The Melancholly to the Spleen to 'bide;
HUMOUR34:37 H592 To Melancholly i'le make no reply,
AGES35:25 H11 The last, of earth, and heavy melancholly,
MASSYR66:29 H535 Strange melancholly humours on him lay,
MELANCHOLY (7)
ELEMEN13:17 H218 The melancholy constitution.
HUMOUR20:27 H19 Proud Melancholy, more envious then the rest,
HUMOUR23:6 H116 But Melancholy, wouldst have this glory thine?
HUMOUR29:1 H354 *Melancholy.*
HUMOUR30:6 H398 The melancholy Snake shal it aver.
HUMOUR~~35:6~~ H602 My cold, cold Melanchollies {melancholy} hand shal clasp,
SEASONS52:10 H225 And melancholy, which most of all dissembles.
MELEAGER (1)
MGREC118:30 H2679 Was stiffe *Meleager,* whom he would take down {away},
MELODIOUS (2)
SEASONS48:33 H84 Melodious {Sweet fragrant} Spring, with thy short pittance flye,
CONTEM173:13 H180 And chanted forth a most melodious strain
MELODY (1)
SEASONS48:34 ~~H85~~ In this harsh strain, I find no melody,
MELPOMENE (1)
SIDNEY149:19 H18 *Thalia,* and *Melpomene,* say th' truth,
MELT (5)
SEASONS49:40 H133 Whose flaming breath doth melt us from afar,
SEASONS52:36 H251 The Rivers now do {'gin to} ope, and {the} Snows do {to} melt,
MASSYR62:38 H383 Which made his Army into nothing melt;
1LETTER181:12 H10 His warmth such frigid colds did cause to melt.
SOREFIT221:22 H8 And how in sweat I seem'd to melt
MELTED (1)
SEASONS48:39 H90 With melted tauny face, and garments thinne.
MELTETH (1)
HUMOUR22:38 H107 Out at her nose, or melteth at her eyes;
MEMBER (2)
HUMOUR33:22 H536 The Brain's the noblest member all allow,
MED223:9 Hp250 thy maker is thy husband. Nay more, I am a member of his
MEMBRANES (1) [pl.]
HUMOUR33:24 H538 Its ventricles, membranes, and wond'rous net,
MEMENTOS (1) [pl.]
MEDDM207:31 Hp289 and diseased bodys, haue hourly mementos of their mortality
MEMNONS (1) [poss.]
MGREC95:18 H1697 Now newes, of *Memnons* death (the Kings Vice-roy)
MEMORIES (1) [pl.]
QELIZ156:1 H28 No memories, nor volumes can containe,
MEMORY (18)
HUMOUR28:30 H342 A most volumnious large memory,
HUMOUR33:35 H549 The Reason, Fancy, and the Memory;
HUMOUR34:30 H585 For memory, the sand is not more brittle.
AGES45:26 H416 My memory is short {bad}, and braine is dry.

MPERS91:31 ~~H1545~~ But this of him is worth the memory,
MGREC110:26 H2330 Be had in everlasting memory,
MGREC110:36 H2340 And so his memory might {would} fade away,
MGREC116:26 H2592 'Cause *Homer* kept his Acts to memory;
MGREC124:33 H2940 He still kept fresh {lockt} within his memory,
QELIZ155:12 H3 most happy memory.
TDUDLEY165:1 H1-2 *To the Memory of my dear and ever honoured Father*
TDUDLEY166:28 H70 Forgotten never be his memory,
DDUDLEY167:23 H20 *Then dying, left a blessed memory.*
BIRTH180:10 H20 Let that live freshly in thy memory
ELIZB186:31 H1-2 *In memory of my dear grand-child Elizabeth*
ANNEB187:12 H1-2 *In memory of my dear grand-child*
MERCY188:17 H1-2 *To the memory of my dear Daughter in Law,*
MYSOUL225:12 H16 Nor come in memory.

MEMUCAN'S (1) [poss.]

MPERS84:8 H1236 By *Memucan's* advice, this {so} was the doome.

MEN (75)

PROLOG7:29 H40 Men have precedency, and still excell,
PROLOG7:31 H42 Men can doe best, and Women know it well;
ELEMEN~~8:30~~ H28 What is my worth (both ye) and all things {men} know,
ELEMEN9:40 H74 Yet men and beasts, {beast} Astronomers can tell,
ELEMEN11:24 H144 And Mother Earth, of old, men did me call,
ELEMEN12:31 H191 After three years, when men and meat is spent,
ELEMEN14:29 H271 And how your subtilty would men delude.
ELEMEN15:26 H308 There lives the oyly Whale, whom all men know,
ELEMEN17:15 H379 My Ice and extream cold, which all men know.
ELEMEN17:23 H387 Wherein not men, but mountaines seem'd to wade
ELEMEN19:21 H466 Men fear'd destruction epidemicall.
AGES45:9 H391 I've seen base {unworthy} men, advanc'd to great degree
AGES~~45:22~~ H412 Men may more freely speak another day.
AGES45:24 H414 We old men love to tell, what's done in youth.
MASSYR53:22 H12 Both Beasts and Men subjected to his spoyls.
MASSYR56:10 H116 Three hundred thousand men, here day, by day;
MASSYR56:30 H136 But this is marvelous, of all those men,
MASSYR57:25 ~~H172~~ Of men, and wealth, his mother carried out;
MPERS~~74:35~~ H858 But strength {men} against those walls was {were} of no use;
MPERS75:19 ~~H878~~ In that thy fame shall sound whilst men have sence;
MPERS76:19 H917 The King, seeing his men, and victuall spent;
MPERS77:9 H948 His men, his coyn, his honour, and his store;
MPERS77:25 H966 Yet all his men, and instruments of slaughter,
MPERS79:6 H1028 Thou shame of Kings, of men the detestation,
MPERS81:1 H1109 And many thousands of these {those} men did kil;
MPERS82:11 H1158 All's lost, and of three hundred thousand men,
MPERS92:29 H1587 That severall men, will have their severall mind;
MGREC94:24 H1662 To him, his mothers Ancestor (men say.)
MGREC94:40 H1678 And think {strive} to keep his men from off the land,
MGREC97:6 H1767 Two hundred thousand men that day were slaine,
MGREC98:16 H1818 The other by his men fetcht all by Land;
MGREC99:20 H1863 And by these walls, so many men were slaine,
MGREC100:23 H1907 Men but in shape, and name, of valour none,
MGREC105:37 H2130 As men, the rising, setting Sun shall see.

MGREC106:6	H2140	Though gods on earth, like Sons of men shall {they} dye.
MGREC116:21	H2587	Learning, and learned men, he much regarded,
MGREC~~117:22~~	H2629	Each man {All men} began for {streight} to contemn his might;
MGREC~~132:16~~	H3252	Though men and mony both he hath at will,
MGREC135:41	H3413	This taske befits not women, like to men:
MROMAN137:4	H3455	His City to replenish, men he wants,
DIALOG143:31	H100	And {Are} lik'd, and countenanc'd by men of might,
DIALOG145:34	H183	Here tugg'd they hard indeed, for all men saw,
DIALOG146:17	H203	My ravisht {weeping} virgins, and my young men slain,
SIDNEY~~150:3~~	H29	And men of morose minds envy his glory:
SIDNEY152:29	H98	*That* Sidney *dy'd the quintessence {most renown'd} of men.*
DUBART154:20	H65	Immortall bayes, all men to thee allows.
QELIZ155:20	H11	That men account it no impiety,
QELIZ156:32	H59	Nor men, nor coyne she spar'd, to doe them good;
DAVID159:7	H22	Nor from the fat, and spoyles, of mighty men,
VANITY159:35	H7	No, they like beasts, and sonnes of men shall die,
VANITY160:14	H24	Yet these, the wisest man of men did find,
VANITY160:33	H43	Its hid from eyes of men, they count it strange,
CONTEM169:27	H66	And men in being fancy those are dead,
CONTEM174:31	H228	Their sumptuous monuments, men know them not,
SICKNES178:22	H5	All men must dye, and so must I
MEDDM197:22	Hp275	Few men are so humble, as not to be proud of their abilitys,
MEDDM198:13	Hp276	Want of prudence as well as piety hath brought men into great
MEDDM198:18	Hp276	sundry tempers of men, w[ch] they all catch grēdily at but few
MEDDM199:12	Hp277	good to cast some men into the furnace of affliction and then
MEDDM199:15	Hp278	Ambitious men are like hops that neuer rest climbing soe long
MEDDM201:2	Hp280	he hath his strong men, such as are come to a full stature in
MEDDM202:3	Hp281	dispensation of his gifts among the sons of men, betwixt whom
MEDDM202:8	Hp281	among men, and some againe, so ignorant and sotish that they
MEDDM202:9	Hp281	like beasts then men, some pious saints, some incarnate
MEDDM203:2	Hp283	Had not the wisest of men, taught vs this lesson, that all is
MEDDM203:33	Hp284	them, men can vse great importunity when they are in
MEDDM206:19	Hp287	Men that haue walked very extrauagantly, and at last bethink
MEDDM207:4	Hp288	The gifts that god, bestows on the sons of men, are not only
MEDDM207:7	Hp288	steps to draw men to god in consideration of his bounty
MEDDM207:21	Hp289	All men are truly sayd to be tenants at will, and it may as truly
MEDDM207:32	Hp289	But the soundest of men, haue likewise their nightly monitor,
MEDDM208:13	Hp290	to haue a good repute among good men, yet it is not that, w[ch]
MEDDM208:22	Hp290	miserably delude men and make them put great Confidence
MEDDM209:21	Hp291	Covntrys so it is with men, there was neuer yet any one man
28AUG225:31	Hp254	men, he hath no benefitt by my adversity, nor is he y[e] better
MENACE (1)		
AGES40:41	H220	With sad affrights of death, doth menace me;
MENAHEM (1)		
MASSYR60:36	H301	A thousand tallents of *Menahem* had,
MEND (2)		
PROLOG7:4	H19	And this to mend, alas, no Art is able,
SEASONS53:5	H261	*The last, though bad, I could not mend,*
MENE (1)		
MASSYR68:24	H610	There hears his *Mene,* and his *Tekel* read;

MENON (4)
MASSYR54:38 H65 *Semiramis* from *Menon* he did take,
MASSYR54:39 H66 Then drown himself, did *Menon,* for her sake;
MASSYR55:21 H87 Accompaning her husband *Menon* far,
MASSYR55:25 H91 Which was the cause, poor *Menon* lost his life,
MENONS (1) [poss.]
MASSYR55:29 H95 Or else she sought, revenge for *Menons* fall:
MENS (1) [poss.]
AGES43:20 H315 I judge, I should have room, in all mens hearts.
MENTIONED (1)
MASSYR54:8 H35 Whose Preists, in Stories, oft are mentioned;
MERCHANDISE (1)
MASSYR64:31 H455 How in all Merchandise she did excell,
MERCHANT (1)
ELEMEN16:27 H350 The wary Merchant, on his weary beast
MERCHANTS (1) [pl.]
ELEMEN12:29 H189 But hark, ye worthy Merchants who for prize
MERCIES (1) [pl.] See also MERCYES, MERCYS
MASSYR62:15 H360 On whom, nor threats, nor mercies could do good;
MERCIFUL (1)
1SIMON188:11 H12 Let's say he's merciful, as well as just,
MERCILESSE (1)
MGREC109:5 ~~H2262~~ But all fall by his sword, most mercilesse.
MERCURY (2)
ELEMEN14:10 ~~H252~~ As *Stibium* and unfixt *Mercury:*
SIDNEY149:16 H15 Thine {His} Eloquence made *Mercury* wax red;
MERCY (9)
MASSYR61:36 H341 And *Ahaz* open, at his mercy lay,
MASSYR64:12 H436 Yeelds to his mercy, and the present stresse;
MASSYR66:21 H527 Then *Put,* and *Lud,* doe at his mercy stand,
MPERS89:18 H1452 And there all wait his mercy, weaponlesse;
MERCY188:18 H2-4 *Mrs. Mercy Bradstreet, who deceased* Sept. 6.
MEDDM206:23 Hp287 for mercy wthout mony & wthout price but bring his filthy raggs
MEDDM206:37 Hp288 make vs wth the Apostle to admire the iustice and mercy of
MYCHILD216:28 Hp242 by losses in estate, and these Times (thro: his great mercy)
2HUSB232:8 H9 Of mercy I commend
MERCYES (8) [mercies] See also MERCYS
MYCHILD217:2 Hp242 Joyfully as in greatest mercyes, For if yee bee his yee shall
FEVER221:2 H17 I on thy Mercyes Rowl.
SOREFIT221:30 H16 Even for his mercyes in his rod,
SON231:18 H30 That I thy Mercyes might behold.
2HUSB232:23 H24 Vnthankfullnes for mercyes past
HOURS234:8 H22 I'le on thy mercyes roll!
ACK235:19 H19 For All these mercyes I thee praise
REMB236:5 H20 Thy mercyes Lord haue been so great
MERCYS (2) [mercies] See also MERCYES
MEDDM203:32 Hp284 we are more ready to receiue mercys then we are to
MEDDM204:31 Hp285 Jacob, I am lesse then the least of thy mercys.
MERIMENT (1) [merriment]
AGES39:38 H181 My wit, evaporates in meriment:

MERIT (1)
MGREC112:36 H2422 Which no merit could obliterate, or time:
MERITS (3) [pl.]
MROMAN139:1 H3529 Ascends not up, by merits of his owne,
DUBART154:38 H83 To celebrate thy merits in my Song,
TDUDLEY165:22 H24 These to the world his merits could make known,
MERO'S (1) [poss.]
DIALOG147:6 H232 And shall I not on those {them} with *Mero's* curse,
MERODACH (5)
MASSYR63:4 H389 Brave *Merodach,* the Son of *Balladan,*
MASSYR63:11 H396 And *Merodach* assume the Monarchy.
MASSYR63:12 H397 *Merodach Baladan.*
MASSYR63:17 H402 *Ben. Merodach.*
MASSYR63:18 H403 *Ben. Merodach,* Successor to this King,
MEROE (1)
MPERS73:8 H795 And built fair *Meroe,* for his sisters sake.
MERRILY (1)
CONTEM174:14 H213 Sings merrily, and steers his Barque with ease,
MERRIMENT (1) See also MERIMENT
HUMOUR24:38 H187 Thou laugh'st at me, for loving merriment:
MERRY (3)
SEASONS47:6 H22 Now goes the Plow-man to his merry toyl,
CONTEM169:18 H58 I heard the merry grashopper then sing,
CONTEM173:18 H184 O merry Bird (said I) that fears no snares,
MESOPOTAMIA (1)
MASSYR60:19 H284 Til *Mesopotamia* he got in's hands,
MESSAGE (1)
MGREC119:10 H2700 To whom she sent a message of her mind,
MESSENGER (2)
MGREC~~115:15~~ H2532 His messenger to *Jupiter* he sent,
28AUG226:11 Hp254 vnwilling to come tho: by so rovgh a Messenger.
MET (4)
AGES36:27 H51 These being met, each in his equipage,
MGREC96:35 H1755 But when both Armies met, he might behold,
MGREC~~132:20~~ H3262 *Demetrius* with so many troubles met,
ANNEB187:18 H8 How oft with disappointment have I met,
METAL See METTAL, METTALL, METTL'S
METALS See METTALS
METAMORPHOS'D (1) [metamorphosed]
MASSYR58:10 H195 Longer to serve this Metamorphos'd beast;
METAMORPHOSIS (1)
MASSYR63:34 H421 Nor's Metamorphosis from *Ovids* Book,
METEORS (2) [pl.]
ELEMEN11:10 H130 Of Meteors, *Ignis Fatuus,* and the rest,
SIDNEY151:4 ~~H69~~ But thou art gone, such Meteors never last,
METHOD (3)
ELEMEN13:21 H222 But that thy method is my {mine} imitation.
AGES36:34 H58 Their method was, that of the Elements,
MYCHILD215:22 Hp240 The method I will observe shall bee this—I will begin wth Gods
METHUSELAH (1)
CONTEM169:31 H70 Then was *Methuselah,* or's grand-sire great:

METROPOLITANE (1)
DIALOG145:31 H180 All *Englands* Metropolitane that houre,
METTAL (1) [metal]
AGES36:9 H33 No wooden horse, but one of mettal try'd:
METTALL (2) [metal]
MASSYR56:3 H109 An hundred gates, it had, of mettall strong.
MASSYR67:35 H581 Did praise his gods of mettall, wood, and stone,
METTALS (1) [metals]
MASSYR60:27 H292 The fire, those Mettals could not damnifie;
METTL'S (1) [metal is]
ELEMEN15:3 H285 Nor mettl's found in the couragious Horse:
MICE (1)
MPERS76:16 H914 Or like to Mice, under the earth must live;
MIDAS (1)
MGREC95:14 H1693 (Of Asse-eard) *Midas,* once the regall seat,
MIDDLE (4)
AGES41:14 H233 *Middle Age.*
MEDDM195:33 Hp272 Youth is the time of getting middle age of improuing, and old
MEDDM195:34 Hp272 a negligent youth is vsually attended by an ignorant middle
11MAYB228:24 Hp259 I haue had no great fitt of sicknes, but this year from y[e] middle
MIDDLE-AGE (2)
AGES44:5 H338 And in perplexed Middle-age have bin,
SEASONS48:40 H91 Resembling choler, fire and middle-age;
MIDEST (1)
MEDDM206:10 Hp287 one Christ, who is the Sun of righteousnes, in the midest of an
MID'ST (2) [midst]
MASSYR66:5 H511 In mid'st of *Babel* now, til death he lyes,
DAVID159:20 H35 In mid'st of strength not succoured at all:
MIDST (3)
AGES44:40 H373 In midst of greifs, I saw some {our} hopes revive,
MASSYR56:14 H120 Which is the midst, of this brave Town was plac'd,
MGREC120:33 H2770 In midst of these, *Garboyles,* with wondrous state,
MIDWIFE (1)
HUMOUR23:8 H118 Tis true, when I am midwife to thy birth;
MIGHT (13) n.
ELEMEN8:36 H34 What toole was ever fram'd, but by my might;
MPERS69:28 H650 Who had no might to save himself from wrong;
MPERS84:12 H1240 The might o'th' Prince, the tribute on {of} the Isles.
MPERS85:17 H1293 For sixty years maugre the *Persians* might.
MGREC93:29 H1626 To save him from his might, no man was found.
MGREC108:34 H2250 Whose {Their} nakednesse could not endure their might;
MGREC117:22 H2629 Each man {All men} began for {streight} to contemn his might;
MGREC131:11 H3203 Near *Ephesus,* each bringing all their {his} might,
MGREC132:19 H3256 These to recover, musters all his might,
MGREC132:35 H3282 Must needs goe try their fortune, and their might,
MGREC135:23 H3395 And last was Iron, which breaketh all with might.
DIALOG143:31 H100 And {Are} lik'd, and countenanc'd by men of might,
CONTEM168:36 H42 Quaternal Seasons caused by thy might:
MIGHT (121) v.
FATHER5:12 H13 My lowly pen, might wait upon those four,
FATHER5:16 H17 Might seem of yours to claime precedency;

ELEMEN9:13	H47	That so in time it might requite your paine;
ELEMEN10:27	H102	‘Mong all my wonders which I might recount;
ELEMEN12:22	H182	Out of huge {great} numbers, I might pick my choyce,
ELEMEN12:27	H187	Whose trust, and valour I might here commend:
ELEMEN13:22	H223	Now might {must} I shew my {mine} adverse quality,
ELEMEN13:34	H235	Dreadfull examples, soon I might produce,
ELEMEN14:15	H257	Much might I say, of the *Arabian* sands; {hot *Libian* sand}
ELEMEN15:13	H295	His deadly mallady, I might expell.
ELEMEN17:32	H396	Much might I say of wracks, but that Ile spare,
ELEMEN18:6	H410	How freely should it go, so he might live.
HUMOUR24:7	H156	I have been sparing, what I might have said,
HUMOUR27:37	H308	Mans life to boundlesse time might stil endure;
HUMOUR28:22	H334	That mortal man, might turn to his corruption.
HUMOUR28:23	H335	I might here shew, the noblenesse of minde,
HUMOUR29:8	H361	But sith we fight with words, we might be kind,
HUMOUR32:3	H477	My prudence, judgement, now I might reveale,
AGES37:34	H96	No office coveted, wherein I might
AGES39:11	H154	As might my self, and others, profit much:
AGES40:1	~~H182~~	But doing so, might seem magnanimous.
AGES~~43:8~~	H305	I might possess that throne which was their right;
AGES43:14	H307	Of such as might my son, {Competitors} or his {as might in
AGES45:35	H425	My hands and armes, once strong, have lost their might,
SEASONS~~47:7~~	H23	For to {He might} unloose his Winter-locked soyl;
SEASONS48:2	H55	These might as Lace, set out her Garments fine;
MASSYR54:23	H50	So broad, three Chariots run abrest there might,
MASSYR55:28	H94	That having no compeer, she might rule all,
MASSYR56:6	H112	Most {Some} writers say, six chariots might a front,
MASSYR58:18	H203	Against their monstrous King to bring {use} their might,
MASSYR64:28	H452	As might not him, but all the world out-face;
MPERS69:35	H657	Then on a Pike being {wood-pile} set, where all might eye,
MPERS71:37	H751	*Cambyses* to the clouds, we might commend;
MPERS78:38	H1019	One of his five Sons there, might be releast;
MPERS80:1	H1068	How part, {some} might o're the Mountains goe about,
MPERS81:11	H1119	That all Hostility might {from} thence-forth cease;
MPERS83:15	H1203	That from suspition he might be freed,
MPERS85:25	H1301	So that he might, these tumults {those troubles} soon appease.
MPERS86:26	H1342	Her prevailence, a pardon might obtain.
MPERS87:24	H1376	Few might have kept it, had they but {had} a heart.
MPERS88:2	H1395	In this confusion, each man as he might,
MPERS~~89:13~~	H1447	may come, and {in short time might} place one in his Throne,
MPERS89:16	~~H1450~~	That so *Europians* might no more molest;
MPERS~~90:4~~	H1478	The Country burnt, they no relief might take.
MPERS90:14	~~H1484~~	The King afraid what further they might doe,
MPERS90:25	H1492	Might win {gain} the universall Monarchy;
MPERS~~92:8~~	H1566	And scarce a Nephew left that now might reign:
MGREC96:35	H1755	But when both Armies met, he might behold,
MGREC100:30	H1914	His numbers might the victory obtaine.
MGREC102:32	H2002	Where Kings have shown their glory, wealth, and might;
MGREC103:7	H2018	Yet to compare with this, they might not do.
MGREC105:35	H2128	Might be subjected to his royall hand;
MGREC106:8	H2142	To see if any dare his might oppose;

MGREC~~107:5~~ H2180 That other matters may {might} take up their minds.
MGREC107:8 H2183 Now that his Hoast from luggage might be free,
MGREC107:39 ~~H2214~~ He easily might have made them stay there stil;
MGREC~~107:39~~ H2214 With little pain there might have kept them still:
MGREC110:25 H2329 Yet that his fame might to posterity,
MGREC110:32 H2336 Which might be found, and so for {great} wonders kept:
MGREC~~110:35~~ H2339 But doubting, wearing Time would {might} these decay,
MGREC110:36 H2340 And so his memory might {would} fade away,
MGREC110:38 H2342 Two Cities built, his fame {name} might there abide;
MGREC112:2 H2388 That by this match he might be yet more neare.
MGREC112:12 H2398 He might this feast imagine by the same.
MGREC~~113:11~~ H2438 For to {He might} accuse himself, as they had done;
MGREC~~115:15~~ H2534 Among the Demy Gods they might inthrone.
MGREC115:18 H2537 That he might next now act upon the Stage,
MGREC115:27 H2546 He might well dye, though he had done no wrong;
MGREC116:20 H2586 Might to the last (when sober) be discern'd.
MGREC116:33 H2599 Still fearing that his Name might hap to die,
MGREC117:38 H2645 Claim'd not, perhaps her Sex might hindrance be.
MGREC118:2 H2649 Their ends they might the better still attain.
MGREC118:20 H2667 Might be esteemed for a Deity;
MGREC119:7 H2697 That none might know, to frustrate his intent;
MGREC119:22 H2712 For to *Antipater* he now might go,
MGREC~~120:8~~ H2743 Their friendship may {might} the more be strengthened:
MGREC120:16 H2751 Was to give way, himself might be undone;
MGREC120:18 H2753 That by his help, the rest might low be brought:
MGREC~~122:32~~ H2853 That he might settle matters in the same.
MGREC~~124:10~~ H2917 That no supply by these here might be lent,
MGREC124:19 H2926 Still labours *Eumenes* might {would} with him side,
MGREC125:5 H2953 That under him she might rule all alone.
MGREC125:28 H2978 Praying, that fatall day might quickly haste,
MGREC125:29 H2979 On which *Olimpias* of the like might taste.
MGREC126:11 H3002 Her Cousen of *Epire* did what he might,
MGREC126:26 H3017 Desiring Justice might be done for guilt;
MGREC127:20 H3050 When victor oft had {he'd} been, and so might still,
MGREC127:34 H3064 Fearing their state {his force}, and what might hap ere long
MGREC128:4 H3077 And that some title he might seeme to bring,
MGREC129:34 H3148 *Cassander* fear'd what might of this insue,
MGREC130:1 H3156 But that some title he might now pretend,
MGREC~~131:39~~ H3231 The mother would the youngest should {might} excell,
MGREC134:24 H3355 They might translate the Bible into *Greek,*
MGREC136:12 H3426 *This fourth to th' other three, now might be brought.*
MROMAN136:27 H3441 Thus he deceiv'd his Neece, she might not know
DIALOG146:10 H198 One battell, two or three I might abide,
QELIZ156:40 H67 *Terra incognitae* might know her {the} sound;
TDUDLEY165:17 H19 That pitty might some Trumpeters procure.
TDUDLEY165:18 H20 Who after death might make him falsly seem
TDUDLEY165:29 H31 That After-comers in them might have share.
TDUDLEY166:15 H57 He might be cloath'd upon, for evermore.
CONTEM170:36 H106 A City builds, that wals might him secure from foes.
CONTEM173:21 H187 To gain more good, or shun what might thee harm
3LETTER183:2 H4 Her dearest Deer, might answer ear or eye;

VERSES184:2 H6 The principle might yield a greater sum,
CHILDRN185:6 H32 That he might chant above the rest,
CHILDRN185:8 H34 That nightingales he might excell.
ANNEB187:20 H10 Experience might 'fore this have made me wise,
MERCY188:23 H9 Who might in reason yet have lived long,
2SIMON195:6 Hp271 me to leaue some thing for you in writeing that you might
MEDDM200:9 Hp279 this life, that so they might feed vpon more substantiall food,
MEDDM200:12 Hp279 affliction on their loynes that so they might shake hands wth
MEDDM200:22 Hp279 a trim that they might run the wayes of his Commandment
MEDDM201:29 Hp281 run that they might obtain
MEDDM207:6 Hp288 giuen for, as health wealth and honour, wch might be so many
FEVER221:10 H25 My heart no more might quail.
FAINTING222:23 H13 I here a while might 'bide.
SON231:13 H25 That wthout scandall he might come
SON231:18 H30 That I thy Mercyes might behold.
HOUSE236:31 H23 He might of All iustly bereft,

MIGHT'EST (1) [mightiest]
ELEMEN~~8:7~~ H5 Who was of greatest use and might'est force;

MIGHT'ST (1) [mightest]
HUMOUR29:10 H363 Faire rosie Sister, so might'st thou scape free,

MIGHTY (37)
ELEMEN10:37 H112 The stately seats of mighty Kings by me:
ELEMEN11:7 H127 Which Kings, and mighty ones; amaz'd with wonder,
ELEMEN12:41 H201 Ye mighty Kings, who for your lasting fames
ELEMEN14:16 H258 Which rise like mighty {tumbling} billowes on the lands: {Land}
ELEMEN17:13 H377 A mighty Country ith' *Atlanticke* Ocean.
ELEMEN20:3 H485 Which makes {make} the mighty Monarchs fear their Fates,
HUMOUR33:29 H543 Doth doubtlesse keep its mighty residence;
MASSYR53:21 H11 That mighty Hunter, who in his strong toyls,
MASSYR53:27 H17 And mighty *Ninivie,* he there begun,
MASSYR54:18 H45 And mighty *Ninivie* more mighty made,
MASSYR54:18 H45 And mighty *Ninivie* more mighty made,
MASSYR56:34 H140 This was last progresse of this mighty Queen,
MASSYR62:8 H353 For *Salmanasser,* with a mighty Hoast,
MASSYR64:25 H449 A mighty Army next, he doth prepare,
MPERS70:28 H699 Which to revenge, she hires a mighty power,
MPERS76:2 H900 Over fair *Ister,* at a {with labour and with} mighty charge;
MPERS78:36 H1017 Which mighty sum, all wondred to behold.
MPERS80:21 H1088 And *Xerxes* mighty Gallies batter'd so,
MPERS80:41 H1108 Two mighty Rocks, brake from *Parnassus* Hil,
MPERS87:7 H1363 The King dismay'd, a mighty Hoast doth raise;
MPERS87:31 H1383 Up then with speed, a mighty trench he throwes,
MPERS88:8 H1401 Which like a mighty cloud darkned the skye;
MPERS91:30 ~~H1544~~ As all the mighty ones, have done, and must:
MGREC106:28 H2162 No ways becomming such a mighty King;
MGREC114:35 H2505 The mighty *Persian* King he over-came,
MGREC~~132:20~~ H3258 A mighty Navy rig'd, an Army stout,
MGREC136:16 H3430 *The vast limbs of a mighty Monarchy.*
QELIZ155:1 H10 In honour of that High and Mighty
DAVID158:27 H7 How did the mighty fall, and falling dye?
DAVID159:1 H16 For the mighty ones did soone decay,

DAVID159:7 H22 Nor from the fat, and spoyles, of mighty men,
DAVID159:19 H34 O! how in battell did the mighty fall,
DAVID159:27 H42 How are the mighty falne into decay,
MEDDM208:36 Hp291 lasting armes of the mighty god of Jacob yea Jacob himself
FEVER221:11 H26 O praises to my mighty God
SAMUEL228:2 H3 Thou mighty God of Sea and Land
HOUSE237:18 H48 Fram'd by that mighty Architect,

MIG'ST (1) [mightest]
RESTOR230:4 H19 At last thou mig'st discern

MILD (3)
FATHER6:10 H44 On what they are, your mild aspect I crave,
HUMOUR~~20:31~~ H23 Cold {Mild} flegme, did not contest for highest {chiefest} place,
TDUDLEY166:4 H46 And oft and oft, with speeches mild and wise,

MILDE (3) [mild]
PROLOG7:21 H33 But sure the antick *Greeks* were far more milde,
MPERS74:30 H853 His affability, {courtesie} and milde aspect,
SIDNEY150:40 ~~H68~~ If thine aspect was milde to *Astrophell;*

MILDEW'D (1) [mildewed]
ELEMEN17:1 H365 Of rotten sheep, lean kine, and mildew'd grain.

MILDLY (1)
AGES36:31 H55 And to the rest, his reason mildly told;

MILE (1)
MPERS70:17 H688 Forty five mile {miles} this City scarce could round;

MILES (2) [pl.]
MPERS~~70:17~~ H688 Forty five mile {miles} this City scarce could round;
MPERS87:33 H1385 Six yards the {in} depth, and forty miles the length,

MILETUS (1)
MGREC95:9 H1688 *Miletus,* and *Pamphilia* overcame,

MILITANT (1)
MEDDM206:9 Hp287 Sun, so is it in the Church both militant and triumphant, there

MILITARY (1)
MGREC108:30 H2246 Besets {Beset} his Camp, or Military Court;

MILITIA (1)
DIALOG145:36 H185 Next the *Militia* they urged sore,

MILK (2)
AGES41:9 H229 Marrow {aches} ful my bones, of Milk {woe} my breasts {heart},
MEDDM202:11 Hp281 y^{t} their bones are full of marrow & their breasts of milk,

MILK-SOPS (1) [pl.]
HUMOUR21:31 H59 Nay milk-sops, at such brunts you look but blew,

MILL (2)
ELEMEN18:27 H431 I {help to} ripe the corne, I turne the grinding mill;
MEDDM197:31 Hp275 Corne till it haue past through the Mill and been ground to

MILLAIN (1)
ELEMEN19:27 H472 Then in his long hot wars, {war} which *Millain* gain'd.

MILLION (2)
MPERS~~80:9~~ H1076 When as one thousand, could some Millions {a million} daunt;
MGREC101:38 H1967 Some write, th' other had a million, some more,

MILLIONS (6) [pl.]
MASSYR54:34 H61 An army of three Millions he led out,
MASSYR56:26 H132 Her Army of four Millions did consist,
MPERS80:9 H1076 When as one thousand, could some Millions {a million} daunt;

MGREC135:15	H3387	And Millions were subjected unto few:
DUBART154:22	H67	Leadst millions chained by eyes, by eares, by tongues,
QELIZ156:6	H33	Millions will testifie that this is true;
MILTIADES (1)		
MPERS76:31	H929	By brave *Miltiades* (their chief) being led,
MIND (41)		
ELEMEN~~8:35~~	H33	All sorts of Artists, here declare your mind,
ELEMEN18:13	H417	Nay, what are words, which doe reveale the mind?
AGES37:25	H87	That its own worth, it did not know, nor mind.
AGES38:29	H132	And though I misse, the tossings of the mind:
AGES38:38	H141	Strangely preserv'd, yet mind it not at all.
AGES39:25	H168	So affable that I do {can} suit each mind;
AGES42:31	H287	But if I rest, the more distrest my mind.
MASSYR67:24	H570	A Royall State, rul'd by a bruitish mind.
MPERS71:2	H714	Innobled more by birth, then by their mind;
MPERS74:29	H852	Made wholsome gentle Laws, which pleas'd each mind.
MPERS~~79:13~~	H1036	Then whips the sea, and with a mind most vain
MPERS85:5	H1281	The eldest to succeed, that was his mind.
MPERS86:13	H1329	*Cyrus* o'th' other side, weighs in his mind,
MPERS92:29	H1587	That severall men, will have their severall mind;
MGREC109:15	H2274	Had to his mind, made all things now {to} accord:
MGREC~~110:18~~	H2321	But him a Prince of an undaunted mind
MGREC119:10	H2700	To whom she sent a message of her mind,
MGREC~~121:15~~	H2793	*Python* of haughty mind, and courage great.
MGREC~~122:8~~	H2832	He that at large would satisfie his mind,
MGREC125:17	H2965	Remembring {Calling to mind} what sometime she had been,
MGREC131:31	H3223	He wittily his fathers mind did sound,
MROMAN139:31	H3557	The subject large my mind and body weak,
SIDNEY151:12	~~H69~~	I rather judg'd thee of his mind that wept,
DUBART154:28	H73	Of names {Name}, of state, of body, or {and} of mind,
VANITY160:15	H25	But vanity, vexation of the mind,
VANITY160:25	H35	That *summum Bonum* which may stay my mind?
VANITY161:5	H56	This satiates the soul, this stayes the mind,
TDUDLEY165:6	H8	My mournfull mind, sore prest, in trembling verse
TDUDLEY166:2	H44	His humble mind so lov'd humility,
CONTEM169:32	H71	While of their persons & their acts his mind doth treat.
CONTEM170:26	H97	The wretch with gastly face and dreadful mind,
CONTEM173:37	H201	Each storm his state, his mind, his body break,
FLESH175:37	H37	For things unknown, only in mind.
AUTHOR178:8	H18	In better dress to trim thee was my mind,
CHILDRN186:5	H72	And things that past, to mind I'le bring.
MEDDM201:17	Hp280	mind.
MEDDM207:35	Hp289	eyes, by beholding their bed, the morning may mind them of
TOCHILD215:5	H5	What was yr liueing mothers mind.
MYCHILD217:12	Hp242	in satisfying my mind w[th]out it, and I haue been confident it
SON231:21	H33	And may putt him in mind of what
HOURS234:10	H24	Of Body and of mind
MINDE (24) [mind]		
ELEMEN8:35	~~H33~~	Come first ye Artists, and declare your minde.
HUMOUR28:3	H315	The body dryes, the minde sublime doth smother,
HUMOUR28:23	H335	I might here shew, the noblenesse of minde,

AGES46:9 H440 But vanity, vexation of the minde;
MASSYR58:11 H196 Unto *Belosus,* then he brake his minde,
MASSYR64:40 H464 Their shoulders must their Masters minde fulfill;
MASSYR65:21 H486 But chang'd his minde, and slew him by the way; {& caus'd his
MPERS69:37 ~~H659~~ Upon demand, his minde to *Cyrus* broke,
MPERS71:11 H727 But that the *Persian* King, may act his minde;
MPERS81:7 H1115 With his *Mardon'us,* judex {index} of his minde;
MPERS89:33 H1467 As *Tyssaphern,* knowing his Masters minde,
MPERS92:3 ~~H1557~~ The rest is but conjecture of my minde.
MGREC93:25 H1622 universe, scarce bounds {bound} his large {proud} vast minde;
MGREC106:17 H2151 Though some {most} of reading best, and soundest minde,
MGREC106:38 H2172 Griev'd at this change of manners, and of minde:
MGREC107:32 H2207 But he that was resolved in his minde,
MGREC121:1 H2779 ('Gainst which to goe, is troubled in his minde;)
MGREC123:26 H2890 This new Protector's of another minde,
MGREC124:23 H2930 The great ones now begin to shew their minde,
MGREC125:1 H2949 Which damage both to minde and body brought:
MGREC125:36 H2986 The Courtiers wondering at her furious minde,
DUBART153:22 H26 And thousand times his mazed minde doth wish
DUBART153:35 H39 Thy Saint-like minde in grave Divinity,
MEDDM199:19 Hp278 wearys the body, and many thoughts oppresse the minde

MINDED (1)
MYCHILD215:19 Hp240 not to sett forth my self, but ye Glory of God. If I had minded

MINDLESSE (1) [mindless]
DIALOG147:9 H235 If mindlesse of thy state I e'r be found.

MINDS (6) [pl.]
SEASONS52:2 H219 With minds more dark, then is the darkned sky;
MASSYR~~57:21~~ H168 Well satisfie the most considerate minds:
MPERS76:10 H908 Their minds by Hieroglyphicks they expresse;
MGREC107:5 H2180 That other matters may {might} take up their minds.
SIDNEY~~150:3~~ H29 And men of morose minds envy his glory:
2LETTER182:32 H38 Oppressed minds, abruptest tales do tell.

MINE See MINE'S

MINERVA (2)
SIDNEY149:11 H10 *Mars* and *Minerva* did in one agree,
QELIZ156:36 H63 Her selfe *Minerva,* caus'd them so to be;

MINE'S (1) [mine is]
ELEMEN9:6 H40 The adverse wall's not shak'd, the Mine's not blowne,

MINES (1) [pl.]
1HUSB180:27 H6 I prize thy love more then whole Mines of gold,

MINGLED (1)
ELEMEN9:25 H59 What mingled lay with earth, I cause to shine.

MINORITY (1)
SEASONS46:32 H8 Sweet Spring, like man in his minority,

MINUTE (1)
SEASONS47:34 ~~H47~~ Yet never minute stil was known to stand,

MIRACLE (1)
SIDNEY149:26 ~~H23~~ This was thy shame, O miracle of wit:

MIRACLES (2) [pl.]
MYCHILD217:34 Hp243 I never saw any miracles to confirm me, and those wch I read
MYCHILD218:23 Hp244 that are in their Relign: together wth their lying miracles, and

MIRE (1)
MEDDM198:5 Hp276 waters, if they stick in deepe mire and clay, and all his waues
MIRROUR (1)
MROMAN139:15 H3543 *Lucretia* force, mirrour of chastety;
MIRTH (1)
AGES39:27 H170 And by my mirth can raise the heart deprest;
MIRY See MYRIE
MISCHIEF (2)
MPERS80:40 H1107 But mischief, Sacriledge doth ever follow;
MPERS~~85:22~~ H1298 {Plunders} the Country, and much trouble {mischief} wrought,
MISCREANT'S (1) [miscreant is]
CONTEM170:2 H76 Who like a miscreant's driven from that place,
MISCREANTS (1) [pl.]
AGES~~45:20~~ H402 By bloudy Popish, hellish miscreants:
MISERABLE (1)
MEDDM206:24 Hp287 for it, shall meet with miserable disapointment, going away
MISERABLY (1)
MEDDM208:22 Hp290 miserably delude men and make them put great Confidence
MISERIES (2) [pl.]
MGREC131:19 H3211 Hoping {Hopes} to find succour {succours} in {his} miseries.
DIALOG147:8 H234 And for my self, let miseries abound,
MISERS (1) [pl.]
ELEMEN13:4 H205 Ye greedy misers who do dig for gold;
MISERY (9)
ELEMEN15:9 H291 Do cease to flourish in this misery.
MASSYR65:39 H504 His wel deserv'd, and fore-told misery;
MPERS69:16 H638 His preservation in his misery;
MPERS92:37 H1595 He fell to depth of greatest misery,
MGREC105:13 H2106 Should heare, nor see, his groans, and {dying} misery:
MGREC105:21 H2114 The witnesse of his dying misery: {this horrid Tragedy;}
DISTEMP179:21 H9 Who sendeth help to those in misery;
CHILDRN186:23 H90 She shew'd you joy and misery;
MERCY188:31 H17 To strike thee with amazing misery;
MISPENT (1)
AGES40:30 ~~H210~~ Thus, thus alas! I have mispent my time,
MISPRISIONS (1) [pl.]
HUMOUR22:4 H73 And by misprisions, like to loose her wits;
MISS (1)
3LETTER183:3 H5 So doth my anxious soul, which now doth miss,
MISSE (2)
HUMOUR22:39 H108 Oh, who would misse this influence of thine,
AGES38:29 H132 And though I misse, the tossings of the mind:
MISSES (1)
MEDDM199:20 Hp278 at profit by the one & content in the other, but often misses
MISSPENT See MISPENT
MISTAKE (2)
HUMOUR30:33 H425 But thou most grosly do'st mistake, to thinke
MGREC100:7 H1891 The Pagan Priest through hire, or else mistake,
MISTRIS (1) [mistress]
MROMAN136:32 H3446 The Mistris of the World, in each respect.

MISTRUST (2)
ELEMEN14:14 H256 When they seek food, and harme mistrust the least.
MGREC98:22 H1824 And thus the *Tyrians* for mistrust were paid,
MISTS (2) [pl.]
DIALOG147:31 H255 Out of all mists, such glorious dayes will {shall} bring,
HOUSE237:16 H46 That dunghill mists away may flie.
MITE (4)
DUBART154:40 H85 Good will, not skill, did cause me bring my mite.
VERSES184:6 H10 Yet for part payment take this simple mite,
13MAY227:16 H25 And at ye most a simple mite.
THEART229:15 H17 Accept O Lord my simple mite
MITRES See MYTERS
MIXED (1)
CONTEM167:30 H7 Of green, of red, of yellow, mixed hew,
MIXT (2)
HUMOUR26:38 H268 Thy fiery yellow froth, is mixt among.
MGREC102:35 H2005 Those purple hangings, mixt with green, and white,
MIXTURE (5)
HUMOUR25:15 H204 But useful, when a mixture can indure.
HUMOUR26:35 H265 Their wondrous mixture, is of blood, and ayre,
HUMOUR34:3 H558 O! mixture strange, oh {O} colour, colourlesse,
HUMOUR34:34 H589 Then I, and thou, must make a mixture here:
ANNEB187:23 H13 Or perfect bliss without mixture of woe.
MNEMON (2)
MPERS86:8 H1324 *Artaxerxes Mnemon.*
MPERS86:9 H1325 *Mnemon* now sits {set} upon his fathers Throne,
MOAB (1)
MASSYR66:14 H520 No, nor {not} when *Moab, Edom* he had got.
MOABITES (1) [pl.]
MASSYR54:12 H39 Likewise *Bal-peor,* of the *Moabites:*
MOAN (3)
MPERS85:12 H1288 If {so} they were hers, the greater was her moan;
2LETTER181:32 H2 The silent night's the fittest time for moan;
HOURS233:20 H3 O Lord thou hear'st my dayly moan
MOANES (1) [pl.]
MGREC105:9 H2102 Invokes the heavens, and earth, to heare his moanes;
MOATED (1)
MPERS70:6 H677 Now trebble wall'd, and moated so about,
MOCK'D (1) [mocked]
DIALOG144:21 H131 I mock'd the Preachers, put it farre away;
MODERATE (1)
HUMOUR22:25 H94 Nor sister Sanguine, from thy moderate heat,
MODERATELY (1)
HUMOUR27:29 H300 I moderately am all, what need I more:
MODERNE (1)
ELEMEN19:3 H448 Is more authentick then their {our} moderne wit.
MODEST (1)
SIDNEY150:4 ~~H29~~ And modest Maids, and Wives, blush at thy glory;
MODESTY (4)
HUMOUR28:39 H351 If modesty my worth do not conceale.
HUMOUR34:20 H575 But modesty hath charg'd me to conceal;

MGREC118:9 H2656 But he refus'd, with fained modesty,
MGREC121:22 H2804 Their proffers he refus'd, with modesty

MOE (8) [more]
ELEMEN10:40 H115 *Carthage,* and hundred moe, in stories told,
ELEMEN14:11 ~~H253~~ With divers moe, nay, into plants it creeps;
ELEMEN15:30 H312 With thousands moe, which now I list not name,
ELEMEN17:26 H390 *Ducalions* great deluge, with many moe;
ELEMEN19:10 H455 With thousands moe, which now I may omit;
ELEMEN19:15 H460 With divers moe, worke deadly consequence.
SEASONS50:18 H152 The russling tresse of *terra* for {down} to moe,
MROMAN139:32 H3558 With many moe discouragements did speak.

MOIST (9) See also MOYST
FATHER5:21 H22 These are, the hot, the cold, the moist, the dry,
FATHER5:31 H32 How hot, and dry, contend with moist, and cold,
ELEMEN18:31 H435 My moist hot nature, is so purely thinne,
HUMOUR27:22 H293 This hot, moist, nurtritive humour of mine,
HUMOUR27:30 H301 As thus, if hot, then dry; if moist, then cold;
HUMOUR35:8 H604 Two hot, two moist, two cold, two dry here be,
AGES35:20 H6 Unstable, supple, moist, and cold's his Naure.
AGES35:22 H8 From blood and aire, for hot, and moist is he.
SEASONS52:14 H229 Cold, moist, young, flegmy Winter now doth lye

MOISTENED (1)
ELEMEN14:36 H278 Thy extream thirst is moistened by my love,

MOISTNESSE (1)
HUMOUR35:5 H601 To take her moyst, my moistnesse {moisture} wil be bold;

MOISTURE (4)
HUMOUR~~35:5~~ H601 To take her moyst, my moistnesse {moisture} wil be bold;
AGES40:38 H217 Sometimes by Feavers, all my moisture drinking,
MEDDM199:8 Hp277 leaues argue want of sap and gray haires want of moisture so
MEDDM201:19 Hp280 se stones hang wth drops not from any innate moisture, but

MOLEST (2)
MPERS75:27 H884 Since *Cyrus* time, *Cambyses* did molest;
MPERS89:16 ~~H1450~~ That so *Europians* might no more molest;

MOLESTS (1)
MASSYR60:35 H300 Molests poor *Israel,* his wealth t' encrease.

MOLOSSIANS (1) [pl.]
MGREC93:13 H1610 Shee to the rich *Molossians* {*Epirus* warlike} King, was

MOMENT (3)
AGES35:35 H21 In dangers every moment of a fall,
MGREC94:2 H1636 Which makes each moment seem, more then a day:
MEDDM202:24 Hp282 a moment that we cannot behold the light of his Countenance,

MONARCH (8)
MASSYR59:32 H256 This the last Monarch was, of {great} *Ninus* race,
MASSYR67:2 H548 *Babels* great Monarch, now laid in the dust,
MPERS74:2 H827 That {Out} of the seven a Monarch chosen be;
MPERS85:9 H1285 Who now sole Monarch, doth of all remaine,
MGREC93:34 H1631 (For as worlds Monarch, now we speak not on,
MGREC106:4 H2138 And though a Monarch once {late}, now lyes like clay;
MGREC132:40 H3287 And so himselfe the only Monarch make;
QELIZ156:9 H36 *Spaines* Monarch sa's not so; nor yet his Hoast,

MONARCH-LIKE (1)
HUMOUR21:15 H43 Where Monarch-like I play, and sway alone.
MONARCHIES (5) [pl.]
MASSYR53:11 H1 The Foure Monarchies,
MASSYR64:1 H425 This was of Monarchies that head of gold,
MGREC101:24 H1949 Two Monarchies on Earth cannot abide,
MGREC135:36 H3408 With these three Monarchies, now have I done,
MROMAN140:7 H3570 Although my Monarchies their legs do lack:
MONARCH'S (1) [poss.] See also MONARCHS
MASSYR55:24 H90 And thought her fit, to make a Monarch's wife,
MONARCHS (4) [pl.]
ELEMEN20:3 H485 Which makes {make} the mighty Monarchs fear their Fates,
HUMOUR32:39 H513 The Monarchs bend, and sue, but for my grace;
MGREC101:25 H1950 Nor yet two Monarchs in one World reside;
MGREC133:32 H3322 His book of *Assurs* Monarchs dedicates,
MONARCHS (2) [monarch's]
MPERS83:27 H1215 Amongst the Monarchs next, this Prince had place
MGREC116:11 H2577 Whose famous Acts {This Monarchs fame} must last, whilst
MONARCHY (25)
AGES43:12 ~~H305~~ When to a Monarchy, my way they barr'd.
AGES~~45:4~~ H388 Who lost a Prince-dome and a Monarchy.
MASSYR53:18 H8 If of his house he held the Monarchy:
MASSYR60:14 H279 Who did this Monarchy begin anew.
MASSYR63:11 H396 And *Merodach* assume the Monarchy.
MASSYR68:30 H616 And now the *Persian* Monarchy began.
MASSYR68:31 H617 *The end of the* Assyrian *Monarchy.*
MPERS68:32 H618 The Second Monarchy,
MPERS73:33 H818 The greater part, declin'd a Monarchy.
MPERS75:16 H877 Nor can *Darius* in his Monarchy,
MPERS90:25 H1492 Might win {gain} the universall Monarchy;
MPERS93:5 H1602 *The end of the* Persian *Monarchy.*
MGREC93:6 H1603 The third Monarchy was
MGREC94:30 H1668 To lift his hand, 'gainst such a Monarchy.
MGREC99:19 H1862 Then in the *Persian* Monarchy beside;
MGREC99:39 H1882 How he should over-throw this Monarchy;
MGREC101:2 H1927 And if they down, his Monarchy wil throw,
MGREC123:5 H2867 For universall Monarchy he hopes;
MGREC134:40 H3369 Held for a time the *Egyptian* Monarchy:
MGREC135:6 H3378 Here ends at last the *Grecian* Monarchy,
MGREC135:12 H3384 The *Assyrian* Monarchy long time did stand,
MGREC~~136:8~~ H3422 *The End of the Grecian Monarchy.*
MGREC136:16 H3430 *The vast limbs of a mighty Monarchy.*
MROMAN136:19 H3433 The *Roman* Monarchy,
MROMAN139:24 ~~H3551~~ *The end of the* Roman *Monarchy,*
MONETH (3) [month]
SEASONS~~51:36~~ H212 This month's {moneth} the Sun {Sun's} in *Sagitarius,*
2LETTER182:19 H25 But for one moneth I see no day (poor soul)
1SIMON188:3 H4 *a moneth, and one day old.*
MONETHS (2) [months]
CONTEM169:29 H68 And calls back moneths and years that long since fled
ANNEB187:15 H5 *seven Moneths old.*

MONEY See MONY

'MONG (1) [among]

ELEMEN10:27 H102 'Mong all my wonders which I might recount;

'MONGST (20) [amongst]

PROLOG7:24 H36 So 'mongst the rest, they plac'd the Arts divine:
ELEMEN10:13 H88 Nay more then these, Rivers 'mongst stars are found,
HUMOUR20:21 H13 But 'mongst themselves they were at variance,
SEASONS49:22 ~~H113~~ 'Mongst all ye shepheards, never but one man,
MASSYR64:15 H439 Wise *Daniel,* and his fellows 'mongst the rest,
MPERS76:3 H901 But in that Desart, 'mongst his barbarous foes,
MPERS~~85:15~~ H1291 Drives out his garison that therein {'mongst them} dwels.
MPERS91:14 H1522 'Mongst these *Epimanondas* wants no fame;
MPERS92:1 ~~H1555~~ In after wars were burnt, 'mongst other things?
MPERS92:32 H1590 And this 'mongst all's no controverted thing,
MGREC112:19 H2405 'Mongst those, that of his cruelty did taste,
MGREC118:13 H2660 'Mongst these contentions, tumults, jealousies,
MGREC119:32 H2722 'Mongst all the Captains {princes} of great *Alexander,*
DIALOG144:8 H118 'Mongst all the cruelties which I have {by great ones} done,
QELIZ155:24 H15 'Mongst hundred Hecatombs of roaring Verse,
QELIZ155:31 H22 Though I resound thy greatnesse {praises} 'mongst the throng.
TDUDLEY166:24 H66 Ah happy Soul, 'mongst Saints and Angels blest,
AUTHOR178:10 H20 In this array, 'mongst Vulgars mayst thou roam,
CHILDRN185:10 H36 Is 'mongst the shrubs and bushes flown,
ACK235:6 H6 And 'mongst y^{m} hast regarded Mine,

MONITOR (1)

MEDDM207:32 Hp289 But the soundest of men, haue likewise their nightly monitor,

MONSTER (1)

AGES40:28 H209 Such wretch, such monster am I; but yet more,

MONSTROUS (3)

MASSYR58:18 H203 Against their monstrous King to bring {use} their might,
MPERS79:3 ~~H1025~~ Nay, more then monstrous barb'rous cruelty!
MGREC117:19 H2626 When of his monstrous bulk it was the guide,

MONTH (10) See also MONETH

SEASONS47:28 H44 My second month is *April,* green, and fair,
SEASONS47:36 H48 This is the month whose fruitfull showers produces
SEASONS49:34 H127 This Month the Roses are distill'd in Glasses,
SEASONS50:1 H135 This month from *Julius Cæsar* took the {its} name,
SEASONS50:13 H147 This month he keeps with *Virgo* for a space,
SEASONS51:1 H175 And doth in poyzing *Libra* this month shine.
SEASONS51:13 H187 And in this month was made apostate man;
SEASONS52:3 ~~H219~~ This month is timber for all uses fell'd,
SEASONS52:20 H235 This month he's hous'd in horned *Capricorn,*
11MAYB228:26 Hp259 this month I had a feaver seatd vpon me wch indeed was the

MONTH'S (1) [month is]

SEASONS51:36 H212 This month's {moneth} the Sun {Sun's} in *Sagitarius,*

MONTHS (7) [pl.] See also MONETHS

SEASONS46:36 H14 Three months {(quoth she)} there are allotted to my share,
SEASONS47:3 ~~H17~~ Who for some months have seen but starry lights;
SEASONS~~47:5~~ H21 Who for some months have been but starry lights.
SEASONS50:38 H172 Of Autumne months, *September* is the prime,
MASSYR65:24 H489 His Son three months he suffered to reign,

MASSYR65:36 H501 And after eighteen months he took them all,
MPERS74:36 ~~H858~~ For twice ten months before the town he lay,

MONTHS (2) [poss.]

AGES37:7 H69 Her nine months weary burden not declare.
MGREC98:17 H1819 In seven months space {time} he takes this lofty {took that

MONUMENT (4)

MGREC111:36 H2381 Upon his Monument his Robes {Robe} he spread,
MGREC115:8 ~~H2518~~ For him erects a stately Monument,
MGREC~~115:15~~ H2530 Upon a sumptuous monument to spend:
MGREC120:36 ~~H2773~~ His sumptuous monument long time did stand;

MONUMENTS (5)

ELEMEN13:1 H202 Built Cities, Monuments call'd by your names;
MPERS70:20 H691 Yet wondrous Monuments this stately Queen,
MGREC110:33 H2337 Twelve Altars, he for Monuments then rears,
DUBART154:34 H79 But monuments for {to} future admiration:
CONTEM174:31 H228 Their sumptuous monuments, men know them not,

MONY (3) [money]

MGREC103:11 H2022 And taken mony, plate, and golden treasure;
MGREC~~132:16~~ H3252 Though men and mony both he hath at will,
MEDDM206:23 Hp287 for mercy wthout mony & wthout price but bring his filthy raggs

MOON (4)

ELEMEN12:40 H200 Which guides, when Sun, nor Moon, nor Stars do shine.
SEASONS49:32 H121 Viewing the Sun by day, the Moon by night,
FLESH175:16 H16 Dost dream of things beyond the Moon
FLESH177:17 H98 Nor Sun, nor Moon, they have no need,

MORALITY (2)

SIDNEY150:9 H34 That sees not learning, valour, and morality,
MEDDM205:4 Hp285 seed of morality, much lesse of grace in them But when by

MORALL (3) [moral]

MGREC116:18 H2584 Had so instructed him in morall truth.
MEDDM195:22 H0 and morall
MEDDM209:22 Hp291 let his parts naturall and acquired spirituall and morall,

MORDECAI (1)

MGREC102:34 H2004 And of good *Mordecai,* her Kinsman dear;

MORDICA'S (1) [poss.]

MPERS84:11 H1239 Of *Hamans* fall, and *Mordica's* great rise;

MORE (305) See also MOE

FATHER6:12 H46 From her, that to your selfe more duty owes,
PROLOG7:8 H22 lisp'd at first, speake afterwards more {in future times} plaine
PROLOG7:21 H33 But sure the antick *Greeks* were far more milde,
PROLOG8:2 H50 Will make your glistering gold but more to shine.
ELEMEN10:13 H88 Nay more then these, Rivers 'mongst stars are found,
ELEMEN10:21 H96 When in conjunction with the sun, yet {do} more,
ELEMEN10:28 H103 There's none more strange then *Ætna's* sulphery mount
ELEMEN11:4 H124 And more then bruitish *Sodome* for her lust,
ELEMEN11:17 H137 And then, because no matter more for fire:
ELEMEN12:26 H186 In his behalfe to speak a word the more;
ELEMEN~~14:4~~ H247 So did that Roman, far more stout then wise,
ELEMEN14:19 H261 Ile say no more, yet {but} this thing adde I must,
ELEMEN16:3 H326 Earth, thou hast not more Countrys, Vales and Mounds,
ELEMEN16:10 H333 If I should shew,{name} more Seas, then thou hast Coasts.

ELEMEN17:21	H385	Till Sun release, their ships can saile no more.
ELEMEN17:40	H404	Aboundantly more then my sisters three?
ELEMEN18:22	H426	Your red hot work, more coldly would go on.
ELEMEN18:33	H437	I grow more pure and pure, as I mount higher,
ELEMEN19:3	H448	Is more authentick then their {our} moderne wit.
ELEMEN19:26	H471	Where famous *Charles* the fift, more losse sustain'd,
ELEMEN19:31	~~H472~~	Some overwelm'd with waves, and seen no more.
HUMOUR20:27	H19	Proud Melancholy, more envious then the rest,
HUMOUR20:30	H22	Her wisedome spake not much, but thought the more.
HUMOUR21:22	H50	Be he a Souldier, I more fence his heart
HUMOUR21:26	H54	In dangers to account himself more sure,
HUMOUR23:34	H144	Take choler from a Prince, what is he more,
HUMOUR24:3	H152	And yet to make, my greatnesse far {still} more great:
HUMOUR24:5	H154	And one thing more to close with {up} my narration.
HUMOUR24:15	H164	Your patience more then mine, I must confesse.
HUMOUR25:1	H190	But know, I love the blade, more then the hilt. {Hill;}
HUMOUR26:14	~~H244~~	More useful then the rest, don't reason erre;
HUMOUR27:17	H288	Th' rest to our Sisters, is more pertinent.
HUMOUR27:29	H300	I moderately am all, what need I more:
HUMOUR28:35	H347	Yet could not be more breif, without much wrong.
HUMOUR29:39	H390	I'le come to that which wounds me somewhat more:
HUMOUR30:7	H399	Those {Whose} cold dry heads, {head} more subtilly doth yeild,
HUMOUR30:14	H406	If I have not more part, then al ye three:
HUMOUR30:39	H431	But yet more comely far, I dare avow,
HUMOUR31:20	H453	I now speake unto al, no more to one;
HUMOUR31:25	H458	And Sanguine is more fickle many fold. {manifold,}
HUMOUR32:36	H510	Nay, I could tel you (what's more true then meet)
HUMOUR34:25	H580	Phrensie's worse, then folly, one would more glad,
HUMOUR34:30	H585	For memory, the sand is not more brittle.
AGES36:13	H37	The next came up, in a more {much} graver sort,
AGES36:22	H46	A {An} Harvest of the best, what needs he more.
AGES36:36	H60	Both good and bad, but yet no more then's true.
AGES39:7	H150	And then the worst, in a more ugly hue;
AGES40:19	H200	For sure my suit more then my vertues shine;
AGES40:28	H209	Such wretch, such monster am I; but yet more,
AGES41:16	H235	And now am grown more staid, that {who} have been green,
AGES41:19	H238	Now age is more, more good ye do {may} expect;
AGES41:19	H238	Now age is more, more good ye do {may} expect;
AGES41:20	H239	But more my {mine} age, the more is my defect.
AGES41:20	H239	But more my {mine} age, the more is my defect.
AGES41:33	~~H249~~	If rich, I'm urged then to gather more.
AGES~~41:36~~	H252	If rich, I'm urged then to gather more,
AGES42:31	H287	But if I rest, the more distrest my mind.
AGES~~43:16~~	H310	Though cemented with more the noble bloud,
AGES43:36	H331	Though some more incident to age, or youth:
AGES44:3	H336	And all you say, say I, and something {somewhat} more;
AGES~~45:22~~	H412	Men may more freely speak another day.
AGES45:31	H421	No more rejoyce, at musickes pleasant {pleasing} noyse,
AGES46:2	H433	I then shal go, whence I shal come no more,
AGES46:19	H450	There, {Where} I shal rest, til heavens shal be no more;
SEASONS47:9	H25	In hope, the more he casts, the more to gain;

SEASONS47:9 H25 In hope, the more he casts, the more to gain;
SEASONS47:23 H39 They joy in what they have, but more in hope,
SEASONS47:29 H45 Of longer dayes, and a more temperate air;
SEASONS48:18 H71 Whose praise deserves a page, from more then me.
SEASONS48:24 H77 More at her showers, which water them a space.
SEASONS48:27 H80 More solid fruits, require a longer time.
SEASONS49:9 H100 Yet doth his parching heat the {but} more augment,
SEASONS52:2 H219 With minds more dark, then is the darkned sky;
SEASONS52:29 H244 The cold not lessened, but augmented more.
MASSYR54:18 H45 And mighty *Ninivie* more mighty made,
MASSYR55:34 H100 But were her vertues, more, or lesse, or none;
MASSYR56:35 H141 Who in her Country never more was seen.
MASSYR57:8 H155 But much it is, in more then forty years,
MASSYR57:10 H157 It is more like, being {his lust} with pleasures fed,
MASSYR59:2 H226 Won by his loving looks, more loving {by his} speech,
MASSYR62:3 H348 He *Israelites,* more then his Father vext;
MASSYR62:27 H372 Hath bred more wonder, then beleefe in hearts;
MASSYR63:25 H410 For fifty years, or more, it had been free,
MASSYR65:27 H492 And more then {seven and} thirty years in prison fed;
MASSYR65:31 H496 *Iudah* {They} lost more {now} (then e're they lost) by him;
MASSYR66:26 H532 Although the Furnace be seven times more hot;
MASSYR66:33 H539 The time expir'd, remains a Beast no more,
MASSYR67:32 H578 To chear his friends, and scorn his foes the more.
MASSYR68:16 H602 Was held in more request, {account} then now he was,
MPERS70:3 ~~H674~~ And with the *Lidians,* had no more to doe.
MPERS71:2 H714 Innobled more by birth, then by their mind;
MPERS71:39 H753 Is more prophane, then grosse Idolaters;
MPERS73:4 H791 And more, because he dyed issulesse.
MPERS73:35 H820 And thought the people, would more happy be,
MPERS74:28 H851 Yet more the peoples hearts firmly to binde,
MPERS75:7 H868 For they beleev'd his nose, more then his tongue;
MPERS75:21 H880 Thy falshood, not thy {craft more then} valour did prevaile;
MPERS75:22 ~~H880~~ Thy wit was more then was thine honesty,
MPERS75:23 ~~H880~~ Thou lov'dst thy Master more then verity.
MPERS76:8 H906 He warr'd defensive, not offensive, more;
MPERS77:8 H947 She lost her aime; her Husband, he lost more,
MPERS78:22 H1003 {Which to} Three thousand (or more) {came} by best relation,
MPERS79:3 ~~H1025~~ Nay, more then monstrous barb'rous cruelty!
MPERS80:4 H1071 Laid on more fiercely, their deep mortall blowes;
MPERS80:27 H1094 Twice beaten thus by {at} Sea, he warr'd no more:
MPERS83:33 H1221 Which had they kept, *Greece* had more nobly done,
MPERS84:4 H1232 To drink more then he list, none bidden was:
MPERS84:7 H1235 And a {one} more worthy, placed in her roome,
MPERS84:24 H1260 His father *Xerxes* losse, and shame, much more,
MPERS85:33 H1309 More by {To which} his pride, {more} then {his} lust, thereunto
MPERS86:1 H1317 And takes more on him, then was judged fit.
MPERS86:16 H1332 More deare to's mother, then his brother far.
MPERS87:1 H1357 But fame more quick, arrives ere he came {comes} there,
MPERS88:11 H1404 That, more then multitudes, their hearts did awe:
MPERS88:35 H1428 And now more eagerly their foes pursue,
MPERS89:16 ~~H1450~~ That so *Europians* might no more molest;

MPERS89:34	H1468	as most {Commanders feasts and yet more} kinde;
MPERS90:35	H1502	That *Tyssapherne* must be Vice-roy no more;
MPERS90:40	H1507	*Tythraustes* trusts more to his wit then Arms,
MPERS91:8	H1516	To defend, more then offend, he had {there was} need.
MPERS91:38	~~H1552~~	Or dealing with the *Persian,* now no more
MGREC94:2	H1636	Which makes each moment seem, more then a day:
MGREC94:9	H1643	And many more, {all} whom he suspects {or fears} will climbe,
MGREC95:20	H1699	For in that Peer, more valour did abide;
MGREC95:29	H1708	To raise more force, for what he yet {to further his} intends.
MGREC95:32	H1711	Though some there be, and that {(perhaps)} more likely, write;
MGREC96:22	H1742	Would aske more time, then were {was} their bodys worth.
MGREC96:36	H1756	That valour was more worth than Pearls, or gold,
MGREC96:38	H1758	Which made {To make} his over-throw more fierce, and sure.
MGREC97:20	H1781	And this to *Alexander* is more a fame,
MGREC97:28	H1789	*Darius* now, more humble {less lofty} then before,
MGREC98:6	H1808	Least he intend more fraud, then sacrifice;
MGREC99:18	H1861	For more repulse, the *Grecians* here abide,
MGREC99:27	H1870	Who did the like to *Hector* (of more fame)
MGREC~~100:36~~	H1920	The more because not set at liberty;
MGREC101:5	H1930	And offers all he did, and Kingdoms more;
MGREC101:38	H1967	Some write, th' other had a million, some more,
MGREC102:18	H1988	Yet old foundations shew'd, and somewhat more;
MGREC104:26	H2078	In more dispight, the thrawled Prince to hold.
MGREC105:11	H2104	But this unheard of injury {treachery} much more;
MGREC106:12	H2146	And {he} makes their riches, and their honours more;
MGREC106:13	H2147	On *Artabasus* more then all bestow'd,
MGREC107:26	H2201	This {Which} more mortality to them did bring,
MGREC109:9	H2268	His liquors more devoutly in, for's sake.
MGREC109:27	H2286	And of his own, a thousand Tallents more.
MGREC109:39	H2298	Did more his valour then his Crown envie;
MGREC111:3	H2348	one hundred {Whether} Embassadours, {ninety} or more,
MGREC112:2	H2388	That by this match he might be yet more neare.
MGREC113:39	H2466	Was one of more esteem, but lesse desart;
MGREC114:3	H2471	Nothing more pleasing to mad *Clitus* tongue,
MGREC114:15	H2485	This pot companion he did more bemoan,
MGREC114:19	H2489	Who lov'd his Master more then did the rest,
MGREC115:2	H2513	All this he did, yea, and much more, 'tis true,
MGREC116:7	H2567	By others thought, and that more generally,
MGREC~~116:10~~	H2572	She laid it more to heart, then any other,
MGREC116:31	~~H2597~~	More boundles in ambition then the skie,
MGREC116:36	H2602	There was {were} no worlds, more, to be conquered:
MGREC116:41	H2607	His thoughts are perish'd he aspires no more,
MGREC118:8	H2655	More then to th' rest, his favour testified:
MGREC118:10	H2657	Hoping to be elect more generally;
MGREC119:9	H2699	For *Leonatus,* more lovely in her eye,
MGREC119:40	H2730	After this {which} time, the *Greeks* did never more
MGREC120:8	H2743	Their friendship may {might} the more be strengthened:
MGREC120:37	H2774	Two years and more since, Natures debt he paid,
MGREC~~121:24~~	H2806	With what he held, he now was well {more} content,
MGREC121:25	H2807	Then by more trouble to grow eminent.
MGREC122:14	H2839	If once young *Alexander* grow more strong,

MGREC122:32 H2851 Who vext the Queen more then the other farre;
MGREC123:38 H2902 Unto these helps, in *Greece,* {at home} he seeks out more,
MGREC124:4 H2909 Hoping still {yet} more to gaine by these new stirs;
MGREC124:26 H2933 More then he bidden was, could act no thing;
MGREC128:33 H3106 Curtious, as noble *Ptolomy,* or more,
MGREC~~132:6~~ H3240 But he a Kingdome more then's friend did eye,
MGREC~~132:20~~ H3265 His story seems a Fable more then true.
MGREC132:32 H3279 To *Philadelphus,* his more worthy Son.
MGREC133:34 H3324 But this is perished with many more,
MGREC135:30 H3402 The last more strong, and dreadfull, then the rest,
MROMAN137:18 H3469 The *Romans* now more potent 'gin to grow,
MROMAN138:17 H3507 Much stronger, and more beautifull withall;
MROMAN138:19 H3509 Of Boats, and Oares, no more they need the aide;
MROMAN138:30 H3520 A hundred Senatours he more did adde;
MROMAN139:30 H3556 The more I mus'd, the more I was in doubt:
MROMAN139:30 H3556 The more I mus'd, the more I was in doubt:
MROMAN140:6 H3569 No more I'le do, sith I have suffer'd wrack,
DIALOG143:15 H84 My Sister *Scotland* hurts me now no more,
DIALOG143:19 H88 For wants, sure some I feele, but more I feare,
DIALOG144:3 H113 Did ever Land prophannesse more expresse?
DIALOG144:18 H128 Of more then thou canst heare, or I relate,
DIALOG146:11 H199 But these may be beginnings of more woe,
DIALOG147:28 H252 If now you weep so much, that then no more,
DIALOG148:31 H296 If this make way thereto, then sigh no more,
SIDNEY149:18 H17 More worth was thine, {his} then *Clio* could set down.
SIDNEY150:13 H48 But to {The more I} say truth, {the more} thy worth I shall but
SIDNEY~~150:24~~ H51 Made famous by thy fall {death}, much more's {more} the pitty;
SIDNEY150:37 H64 Noble {Great} *Bartas,* this to thy praise adds more,
SIDNEY151:3 ~~H69~~ I wish no more such Blazers we may see;
SIDNEY151:23 H73 For {How} to persist, my muse is more in doubt:
SIDNEY152:7 H78 With high disdain, they said they gave no more,
SIDNEY152:9 ~~H79~~ That this contempt it did the more perplex,
DUBART153:5 H9 Where Art, and more then Art in Nature shines;
DUBART154:3 H48 More sencelesse then the Stones to *Amphions* Lute,
DUBART154:11 H56 O *France,* in him thou didst more glory gain,
QELIZ156:5 H32 Nor say I more then duly is her due,
QELIZ156:20 H47 Was ever Land more happy, freed from stirs?
QELIZ~~156:21~~ H48 Did ever wealth in *England* so {more} abound?
QELIZ156:23 H50 Ships more invincible then *Spaines,* her foe
QELIZ157:5 H73 More infamie than fame she did procure;
QELIZ157:27 H95 Her ashes not reviv'd more Phoenix she;
QELIZ158:3 H112 No more shall rise or set such {so} glorious Sun,
QELIZ158:13 H122 *The greater was our gain, our losse the more.*
DAVID159:18 H33 Which made you yet more beauteous to behold.
VANITY160:5 H15 More vain then all, that's but to grasp the wind.
TDUDLEY165:11 H13 For who more cause to boast his worth then I?
TDUDLEY166:8 H50 Which all they have, and more still set to view,
TDUDLEY166:10 H52 His thoughts were more sublime, his actions wise,
TDUDLEY166:33 H75 And parted more by death shal never be.
TDUDLEY167:4 H86 *If some rejoyc'd, more did lament.*
CONTEM168:5 H15 More Heaven then Earth was here, no winter & no night.

CONTEM168:10	H19	Thy strength, and stature, more thy years admire,
CONTEM168:17	H25	The more I look'd, the more I grew amaz'd,
CONTEM168:17	H25	The more I look'd, the more I grew amaz'd,
CONTEM169:30	H69	It makes a man more aged in conceit,
CONTEM170:11	H84	And how she lost her bliss, to be more wise,
CONTEM171:23	H126	A Spring returns, and they more youthfull made;
CONTEM171:26	H128	By birth more noble then those creatures all,
CONTEM173:21	H187	To gain more good, or shun what might thee harm
CONTEM174:18	H217	And makes him long for a more quiet port,
FLESH175:32	H32	Earth hath more silver, pearls and gold,
FLESH175:39	H39	Disturb no more my setled heart,
FLESH176:11	H51	Thy flatt'ring shews Ile trust no more.
FLESH176:14	H54	And never had more cause of woe
FLESH176:30	H70	My thoughts do yield me more content
FLESH177:2	H83	More glorious then the glistring Sun;
AUTHOR178:4	H14	I wash'd thy face, but more defects I saw,
AUTHOR178:7	H17	Yet still thou run'st more hobling then is meet;
DISTEMP179:19	H7	Then eyes lay dry, disabled to weep more;
1HUSB180:27	H6	I prize thy love more then whole Mines of gold,
1HUSB180:34	H13	That when we live no more, we may live ever.
1LETTER181:3	H1	My head, my heart, mine Eyes, my life, nay more,
1LETTER181:15	H13	In this dead time, alas, what can I more
2LETTER182:3	H9	Commend me to the man more lov'd then life,
2LETTER182:8	H14	My Interest's more then all the world beside.
2LETTER182:31	H37	Tell him I would say more, but cannot well,
CHILDRN185:7	H33	Striving for more then to do well,
CHILDRN185:35	H61	My cares are more, and fears then ever,
ANNEB187:28	H18	More fool then I to look on that was lent,
MERCY188:35	H21	Who lov'd thee more (it seem'd) then her own life.
2SIMON195:7	Hp271	look vpon when you should see me no more, I could think of
2SIMON195:7	Hp271	you should see me no more, I could think of nothing more
2SIMON195:8	Hp271	fit for you nor of more ease to my self then these short
2SIMON195:10	Hp271	true friends much more by duty full children, I haue avoyded
MEDDM197:8	Hp274	is because they haue more sence then faith they se what they
MEDDM197:16	Hp274	more patiently then he that excells him, both in gifts & graces
MEDDM197:23	Hp275	nothing will abase them more, then this What hast thou, but
MEDDM200:9	Hp279	this life, that so they might feed vpon more substantiall food,
MEDDM200:17	Hp279	but falls and bruises, or perhaps somewhat worse, much more
MEDDM200:26	Hp279	their former vigor and beavty in a more ample manner then
MEDDM200:29	Hp279	shall arise in far more glory, then that wch they lost at their
MEDDM201:5	Hp280	more or lesse if god afford his help
MEDDM202:2	Hp281	There is nothing admits of more admiration, then gods various
MEDDM202:8	Hp281	and some againe, so ignorant and sotish that they are more
MEDDM202:35	Hp282	& wch is most strang, the more it receius the more empty it
MEDDM203:6	Hp283	them then they are lesse then vanity & more then vexation, so
MEDDM203:32	Hp284	we are more ready to receiue mercys then we are to
MEDDM204:9	Hp284	call for great returnes, the more that any man is intrusted
MEDDM204:34	Hp285	and some land askes much more paines, then some other doth
MEDDM205:10	Hp286	Commonwealth, his more fixed and resolued thoughts, are like
MEDDM205:18	Hp286	who is greater then our Conscience will do it much more, but
MEDDM206:14	Hp287	and obscure, yet all receiue their luster (be it more or lesse)

MEDDM206:22 Hp287 more at a Compensation then at a pardon, but he that will not
MEDDM206:27 Hp288 works and doings of god are wonderfull, but none more awfull
MEDDM207:9 Hp288 are lords we will come no more at thee If outward blessings,
MEDDM208:32 Hp290 become firme footing, for peter to walk on, nay more then all
MEDDM209:9 Hp291 could do (as they thought) wth lesse hazard and more profit,
PILGRIM210:7 H7 The burning sun no more shall heat
PILGRIM210:9 H9 The bryars and thornes no more shall scrat
PILGRIM210:11 H11 He erring pathes no more shall tread
PILGRIM210:14 H14 for thirst no more shall parch his tongue
PILGRIM210:26 H26 Mine eyes no more shall ever weep
MYCHILD215:15 Hp240 bequeath to yov, that when I am no more wth yov, yet I may
MYCHILD215:31 Hp241 I grew to haue more vnderstanding, so ye more solace I took
MYCHILD216:1 Hp241 grew vp to bee about 14. or 15. I fovnd my heart more carnall,
MYCHILD216:16 Hp241 and after him gave me many more, of whom I now take y^{e}
MYCHILD217:5 Hp242 of Sweetnes and refreshment after affliction and more
MYCHILD218:22 Hp244 somt. stuck with me, and more it would, by ye vain fooleries
FEVER221:10 H25 My heart no more might quail.
FAINTING222:18 H8 And liueing man no more shall see
MED223:3 Hp250 Lord why should I doubt any more w^{n} thov hast given me such
MED223:9 Hp250 enough thy maker is thy husband. Nay more, I am a member
MED223:18 Hp250 art pure, and let me bee no more afraid of Death, but even
30SEPT227:22 Hp257 I haue fovnd by Exper^{c}. I can no more liue wthout correction
30SEPT227:32 Hp257 of distresse forget not to giue him thankes, but to walk more
SAMUEL228:8 H9 He's mine, but more O Lord thine own
11MAYB228:28 Hp259 made it ye more tedious, but it pleased ye Lord to support my
THEART229:4 H6 I sovght more earnestly
THEART229:16 H18 For more I cannot giue
HOURS234:3 H17 I haue a more beloued one
HOURS234:19 H33 In Thee Alone is more then All;
REMB236:2 H17 What could I more desire?
HOUSE237:2 H32 And them behold no more shall I.
HOUSE237:25 H55 Ther's wealth enovgh I need no more,

MORE'S (2) [more is]
ELEMEN20:6 H488 what's their worth, {wrath} or force, but more's {same's} in me.
SIDNEY150:24 H51 Made famous by thy fall {death}, much more's {more} the pitty;

MOREOVER (1)
MGREC~~98:15~~ H1817 Besides, {Moreover} he had a Navie at command,

MORN (3)
SEASONS52:21 H236 From thence he 'gins to length the shortned morn,
CONTEM168:25 H32 The morn doth usher thee, with smiles & blushes,
CONTEM173:26 H191 The dawning morn with songs thou dost prevent,

MORNE (1) [morn]
MGREC~~101:34~~ H1959 And careless in his bed, next morne he lyes,

MORNING (2)
MEDDM202:29 Hp282 when ye morning (wch is the appointed time) is come the Sun
MEDDM207:35 Hp289 eyes, by beholding their bed, the morning may mind them of

MOROSE (2)
SIDNEY~~150:3~~ H29 And men of morose minds envy his glory:
MEDDM205:1 Hp285 land) are of so tough and morose a dispotion that the plough

MORROW (3)
AGES37:3 H65 A nothing, here to day, but {and} gone to morrow.

VANITY160:3 H13 Its his to day, but who's his heire to morrow?
CONTEM174:8 H208 Joyes not in hope of an eternal morrow;

MORTAL (4) See also MORTALL

HUMOUR28:22 H334 That mortal man, might turn to his corruption.
MPERS~~90:39~~ H1506 Whom the old Queen did bear a mortal hate.
MGREC~~120:4~~ H2739 Then fall into the hands of mortal foes.
CONTEM174:29 H226 O Time the fatal wrack of mortal things,

MORTALITY (6)

ELEMEN13:23 H224 And how I oft work mans mortality.
ELEMEN19:13 H458 So when'ts corrupt, mortality is rife.
MGREC107:26 H2201 This {Which} more mortality to them did bring,
MGREC118:22 H2669 The wretchednesse of mans mortality.
MEDDM202:6 Hp281 that Mortality is capable of, and some again so base that they
MEDDM207:31 Hp289 and diseased bodys, haue hourly mementos of their mortality

MORTALL (6) [mortal]

MPERS72:41 H787 And with a mortall thrust, wounds him ith' thigh,
MPERS80:4 H1071 Laid on more fiercely, their deep mortall blowes;
MGREC104:41 H2093 By throwing Darts, gives {gave} him his mortall wound,
MGREC117:3 H2610 Now like a mortall helplesse man he lies;
PILGRIM210:34 H34 this mortall shall be cloth'd vpon
SAMUEL228:11 H12 For mortall helpes are brittle Dvst.

MORTALLS (1) [mortals]

ELEMEN17:39 H403 Mortalls, what one of you, that loves not me,

MORTALS (1)

CONTEM168:34 H40 All mortals here the feeling knowledg hath.

MOSES (2)

MEDDM208:33 Hp290 it hath ouer come the omnipotent himself, as when Moses
MEDDM208:35 Hp290 them as if Moses had been able by the hand of faith, to hold

MOST (94)

FATHER5:1 H1 To her most Honoured Father
FATHER5:14 H15 To do their homage unto yours most {full} glad,
PROLOG7:11 H25 Art can doe much, but this maxime's most sure,
ELEMEN8:7 ~~H5~~ Who the most good could shew, & who most rage
ELEMEN8:28 ~~H26~~ Being the most impatient Element.
ELEMEN~~8:28~~ H26 The noblest and most active Element.
HUMOUR20:26 H18 Pleading her selfe, was most of all desir'd;
HUMOUR24:33 H182 But *David, Judah's* most heroyick King:
HUMOUR25:14 H203 Thy Choler is but rage, when tis most pure.
HUMOUR25:21 H210 A Souldier most compleat in al points makest.
HUMOUR25:35 H224 Nay; {No,} know 'tis pride, most diabolical.
HUMOUR27:23 H294 When 'tis untaint, pure, and most genuine
HUMOUR28:14 H326 The bitter choler, most malignant knowne
HUMOUR28:30 H342 A most volumnious large memory,
HUMOUR29:5 H358 That blow's most deadly, where it is intended;
HUMOUR29:23 H374 Know, in a General its most pernicious.
HUMOUR30:18 H410 When you poor bankrupts prove, then have I most.
HUMOUR30:33 H425 But thou most grosly do'st mistake, to thinke
HUMOUR33:38 H552 The five most noble Sences, here do dwel,
AGES36:2 H26 (As that fond age, doth most of al desire.)
AGES39:9 H152 Then let not him, which {that} hath most craft dissemble;
AGES39:24 H167 Though thus in field, at home, to all most kind,

SEASONS46:37 H15 *March, April, May,* of all the rest most faire;
SEASONS50:30 H164 To shake his fruit, of most delicious tastes;
SEASONS~~51:19~~ H195 If scited as the most Judicious take.
SEASONS52:10 H225 And melancholy, which most of all dissembles.
MASSYR56:6 H112 Most {Some} writers say, six chariots might a front,
MASSYR~~57:21~~ H168 Well satisfie the most considerate minds:
MASSYR63:36 H423 But by the Prophets, Pen-men most Divine,
MASSYR64:30 H454 Whether her wealth, or yet her strength was most;
MPERS72:31 H775 To tell the facts, of this most bloody King.
MPERS77:37 H978 Vaine *Xerxes* thinks his counsell hath most wit,
MPERS78:34 H1015 Then gives the King, a King-like gift, most {full} large;
MPERS79:2 ~~H1024~~ O most inhumain incivility!
MPERS~~79:13~~ H1036 Then whips the sea, and with a mind most vain
MPERS83:7 H1195 Which {With} him, and his, most barbarously there slew,
MPERS84:2 H1230 With gold and silver beds, most gorgiously.
MPERS89:34 H1468 as most {Commanders feasts and yet more} kinde;
MPERS~~91:37~~ H1551 (To his great grief) most subtilly he slayes:
MPERS~~92:10~~ H1568 But as 'tis thought, {most suppose} in him had {did} *Cyrus* end:
MGREC96:8 H1728 (For Sun and Fire the *Persians* worship most)
MGREC96:12 H1732 With Robes and Crowne, most glorious to behold.
MGREC97:1 H1762 Most basely run {ran}, and left their King at large,
MGREC97:27 H1788 Unto *Parmenio,* of all, most fit;
MGREC99:1 H1844 And a most Princely Dowry with her proffers; {offers.}
MGREC101:30 H1955 For tumult in the dark {night} doth cause most dread,
MGREC103:20 H2031 Their charge, {place} gave to his Captains (as most {was} just)
MGREC~~106:17~~ H2151 Though some {most} of reading best, and soundest minde,
MGREC106:26 H2160 As most incompatible to his state;
MGREC107:25 H2200 Where most {so} immoderatly these thirsty drink;
MGREC108:22 H2238 And there most fiercely set upon the same;
MGREC109:5 ~~H2262~~ But all fall by his sword, most mercilesse.
MGREC111:7 H2352 His furniture most sumptuous to behold;
MGREC113:28 H2455 Most wickedly was slaine, without least crime,
MGREC113:29 H2456 (The most renowned Captaine of his time)
MGREC113:37 H2464 Had his reward most cruel, and unjust.
MGREC~~121:21~~ H2803 And is of all received {most} joyfully;
MGREC~~121:35~~ H2817 But he alone now {most} faithfull did abide:
MGREC123:19 H2883 On most part of *Assyria* doth seize,
MGREC126:29 H3020 This was the end of this most cruell Queen,
MGREC131:4 H3194 Most grossely base, was this {their} great adulation,
MGREC133:5 H3293 Yet by him had this most unworthy end.
MROMAN139:14 H3542 *Sextus* his Son, doth {did} (most unworthily)
DIALOG143:37 H106 What scorning of the Saints of the most high,
SIDNEY149:36 ~~H23~~ But leaves the rest, as most unprofitable:
SIDNEY150:23 H50 O *Zutphon, Zutphon,* that most fatall City,
SIDNEY~~152:29~~ H98 *That* Sidney *dy'd the quintessence {most renown'd} of men.*
DUBART153:41 H45 In all the Arts make thee most liberall;
QELIZ155:12 H3 most happy memory.
VANITY160:16 H26 And he that knows the most doth still bemoan,
TDUDLEY165:20 H22 Well known and lov'd, where ere he liv'd, by most
CONTEM173:13 H180 And chanted forth a most melodious strain
BIRTH179:31 H7 The sentence past is most irrevocable,

3LETTER183:8 H10 (On withered bough) most uncouthly bemoan

VERSES183:35 H2 Most truly honoured, and as truly dear,

MEDDM199:17 Hp278 all, the most deiected

MEDDM201:32 Hp281 all seasons the most welcom so a faithfull friend in time of

MEDDM201:33 Hp281 is (of all other) most Comfortable

MEDDM202:35 Hp282 giue, & wch is most strang, the more it receius the more empty

MEDDM206:13 Hp287 a lesse degree, & others (and they indeed the most in number)

MEDDM207:5 Hp288 but most Commonly imployed for a Clean Contrary end, then

MEDDM208:20 Hp290 nothing, and so leaue those in the lurch that most relyed

MEDDM209:12 Hp291 slauery, so it is most certain that those that are disobedient

MYCHILD215:10 Hp240 by exper^{c}. y^{t} ye exhortat^{s}. of parents take most effect wn y^{e}

MYCHILD215:30 Hp241 espec: those places I thought most concerned my Condition,

MYCHILD215:33 Hp241 and made my Suplicat^{n}. to the most High who sett me free

MYCHILD216:24 Hp242 heart out of order, but I haue expected correct^{n} for it, wch most

MYCHILD216:30 Hp242 ye Times w^{n} ye Lord hath manifested ye most Love to me.

MYCHILD217:16 Hp243 and refreshing wch I supposed most of the servants of God

SOREFIT221:26 H12 Yea when I was most low and poor,

SOREFIT221:31 H17 Where pitty most of all I see.

13MAY227:16 H25 And at ye most a simple mite.

2HUSB232:3 H4 O thov most high who rulest All

MOTE (1)

2LETTER182:13 H19 Or every mote that in the sun-shine hops,

MOTHER (50)

ELEMEN11:24 H144 And Mother Earth, of old, men did me call,

ELEMEN13:31 H232 The tender mother on her Infant flyes:

HUMOUR20:19 H11 All having made obeysance to each Mother,

HUMOUR20:23 H15 Choler {first} hotly claim'd, right by her mother,

HUMOUR21:6 H34 My self, and Mother, one as you shal see,

HUMOUR23:9 H119 Thy self's as dul, as is thy mother Earth.

HUMOUR25:16 H205 As with thy mother Fire, so 'tis with thee,

HUMOUR27:5 H276 Which is thy self, thy Mother, and thy Sire;

HUMOUR28:4 H316 And turns him to the wombe of's earthy mother,

HUMOUR30:22 H414 His mother (mine) him to her wombe retakes,

HUMOUR31:28 H461 And what Flegme is, we know, likewise {like to} her mother,

AGES37:11 H73 My mother stil did waste, as I did thrive:

AGES46:17 H448 Mother, and sisters both; the worms, that crawl,

MASSYR55:9 H75 Her Mother *Docreta,* a Curtezan;

MASSYR57:2 H149 His Mother dead, *Ninias* obtains his right,

MASSYR57:6 H153 Some write, his Mother put his habite on,

MASSYR57:25 ~~H172~~ Of men, and wealth, his mother carried out;

MASSYR65:26 H491 Whom with his Mother, he to *Babel* led,

MPERS86:16 H1332 More deare to's mother, then his brother far.

MPERS87:5 H1361 The wife, against the mother, still doth cry

MGREC93:12 H1609 The cruell, proud, *Olimpias,* was his mother,

MGREC95:38 H1717 His mother old, {his} beautious wife, {Queen} and daughters,

MGREC96:27 H1747 This brave Virago, to the King was mother;

MGREC105:32 H2125 To's Mother, Children deare, and Wife now gone,

MGREC115:25 H2544 Though to his Mother he disprov'd the thing;

MGREC~~116:10~~ H2571 When this sad news came to *Darius* Mother,

MGREC122:21 ~~H2845~~ Her mother *Cyna* sister to *Alexander,*

MGREC124:21 H2928 Nor could Mother, nor Sons of *Alexander,*

MGREC125:18 H2966 The Wife, and Mother, of their famous Kings,
MGREC126:31 H3022 The Daughter, Sister, Mother, Wife to Kings,
MGREC128:1 H3074 The Mother of their King to death he'd put,
MGREC129:3 H3117 Imprisoning both the mother, and her {the} son,
MGREC129:9 H3123 And put {So puts} to death, the mother and her son,
MGREC130:26 H3181 By cruell father, mother, cruell son,
MGREC131:39 H3231 The mother would the youngest should {might} excell,
DIALOG141:6 H5 Alas, deare Mother, fairest Queen, and best,
DIALOG142:22 H51 If none of these, deare Mother, what's your woe?
DIALOG145:7 H156 To all you've said, sad mother, I assent
DIALOG146:28 H214 Dear mother cease complaints, and wipe your eyes,
DIALOG146:30 H216 You are my mother, nurse, {and} I once your flesh,
DIALOG147:26 H250 O mother, can you weep, and have such Peeres.
DIALOG148:33 H298 Farewell dear mother, Parliament, {rightest cause} prevail,
DDUDLEY167:6 H1-2 *On my dear and ever honoured Mother*
DDUDLEY167:11 H8 *A loving Mother and obedient wife,*
CONTEM170:10 H83 His Mother sighs, to think of Paradise,
AUTHOR177:37 H9 My rambling brat (in print) should mother call,
AUTHOR178:14 H24 And for thy Mother, she alas is poor,
2SIMON195:18 Hp271 mother A B
MEDDM200:15 Hp279 A prudent mother will not cloth her little childe wth a long and
30SEPT227:33 Hp257 him then before, This is the desire of y[r] Loving mother. A. B.

MOTHER'S (1) [poss.]
DIALOG146:22 H208 Their wofull mother's tears unpitied.

MOTHERS (1) [pl.]
MGREC117:34 H2641 But meannesse of their Mothers bard the same:

MOTHERS (11) [mother's, poss.]
AGES37:6 H68 My mothers breeding sicknes, I will spare;
MPERS69:15 H637 His Mothers Dream, and Grand-sires cruelty,
MPERS70:1 H672 (His Mothers Vnckle, stories doe evince:)
MPERS80:6 H1073 But on their ground they dye, each Mothers Son.
MPERS86:18 H1334 Held by his mothers intercession.
MPERS86:21 H1337 And thought it best, now in his mothers time,
MPERS91:25 ~~H1539~~ His Mothers wicked counsell was the cause,
MGREC94:24 H1662 To him, his mothers Ancestor (men say.)
MGREC131:41 H3233 his Sword did pierce his mothers {run her through the} heart,
DUBART153:25 H29 At night turnes to his Mothers cot againe,
TOCHILD215:5 H5 What was yr liueing mothers mind.

MOTHER-TONGUE (1)
MGREC108:18 H2234 But that they had forgot their Mother-tongue.

MOTION (1)
HUMOUR33:31 H545 Which life and motion to each Creature gives,

MOTIONS (1) [pl.]
HUMOUR22:24 H93 {But tis} Not from our dul slow Sisters motions:

MOTIVES (1) [pl.]
MPERS86:19 H1335 These and like motives, hurry him amain,

MOUE (1) [move]
MEDDM206:16 Hp287 shine so bright while they moue on earth, how transcendently

MOULD (3)
ELEMEN14:20 H262 Remember sonnes, your mould is of my dust,
CONTEM169:5 H47 As to approach it, can no earthly mould.

MEDDM200:35 Hp280 father (who knowes our mould) lay such afflictions vpon his

MOULDRING (2)

PILGRIM210:22 H22 and my Clay house mouldring away
HOUSE237:13 H43 Didst fix thy hope on mouldring dvst,

MOUNDS (1) [pl.]

ELEMEN16:3 H326 Earth, thou hast not more Countrys, Vales and Mounds,

MOUNT (4) n.

ELEMEN10:28 H103 There's none more strange then *Ætna's* sulphery mount
ELEMEN12:10 H170 But farewell all, for deare mount *Helicon,*
MPERS79:9 H1031 A Sea passage cuts, behind *Orthos* {*Athos*} Mount.
DAVID159:14 H29 For valiant *Saul,* who on Mount *Gilbo* lyes;

MOUNT (6) v. See also MOVNT

FATHER5:10 H11 To mount so high, requires an Eagles quill:
ELEMEN18:33 H437 I grow more pure and pure, as I mount higher,
AGES~~45:22~~ H406 And an Usurper subt'ly mount thereon.
SEASONS51:33 H209 His dead old stock, again shall mount on high.
MEDDM197:28 Hp275 thinkes to mount to heaven clog'd wth the Cares and riches of
MEDDM207:10 Hp288 as wings to help vs mount vpwards, they will Certainly proue

MOUNTAIN (1)

MEDDM197:26 Hp275 will vntertake to climb vp a steep mountain wth a great burden

MOUNTAINE (1) [mountain]

MGREC135:24 H3396 The Stone out of the Mountaine then did rise,

MOUNTAINES (3) [mountains]

ELEMEN12:3 H163 I'le here skip o're my mountaines, reaching skies,
ELEMEN17:23 H387 Wherein not men, but mountaines seem'd to wade
MEDDM208:29 Hp290 possible to be done, it can remoue mountaines (if need were)

MOUNTAIN'OUS (1)

DAVID158:26 H6 Upon thy places, mountain'ous and high,

MOUNTAINS (7) [pl.] See also MOUNTAINES

ELEMEN~~16:11~~ H334 And be thy mountains n'er so high and steep,
ELEMEN16:12 ~~H335~~ Then Seas are deep, Mountains are never high.
MPERS79:36 H1062 This 'twixt the Mountains lyes (half Acre wide)
MPERS80:1 H1068 How part, {some} might o're the Mountains goe about,
MPERS90:7 H1480 O're mountains, rocks, and hils, as Lions bold;
MGREC108:21 H2237 Down from the mountains twenty thousand came,
MEDDM198:34 Hp277 rather choose to be buried vnder rocks and mountains then to

MOUNTED (2)

MPERS72:40 H786 Unsheathes, as he his horse mounted on high,
CHILDRN184:19 H8 Mounted the Trees, and learn'd to sing;

MOUNTING (1)

MPERS74:9 H834 Then mounting on their snorting coursers proud,

MOUNTS (3) [pl.]

ELEMEN17:19 H383 That *Caucasus* high mounts, are seldom free.
MASSYR56:20 H126 Her gardens, bridges, arches, mounts, and spires;
DAVID158:32 H12 O! *Gilbo* Mounts, let never pearled dew,

MOURN (2)

MGREC129:40 H3154 *Antigonus* for all this doth not mourn,
1LETTER181:9 H7 I like the earth this season, mourn in black,

MOURNFUL (3)

ELEMEN~~11:1~~ H119 My raging flame did make a mournful story,
DISTEMP179:17 H5 Bedrencht with tears that flow'd from mournful head.

CHILDRN184:22 H11 My mournful chirps I after send,

MOURNFULL (4) [mournful]

MGREC97:30 H1791 Those mournfull Ladies, from captivity,
MGREC115:7 H2518 He celebrates his mournfull obsequies;
TDUDLEY165:6 H8 My mournfull mind, sore prest, in trembling verse
3LETTER183:14 H16 With thousand doleful sighs & mournfull Cooes.

MOURNING (1)

DIALOG141:12 H11 What meanes this wailing tone, this mourning guise?

MOURNS (1)

MGREC100:35 H1919 Great *Alexander* mourns, as well as he,

MOUSE (1)

MPERS76:11 H909 A Frog, a Mouse, a Bird, an Arrow sent,

MOUTH (6)

MGREC111:16 H2361 Hence {Then} sayling down by th' mouth of *Indus* floud,
MGREC111:22 H2367 Passing faire *Indus* mouth, his course he stear'd,
MGREC111:23 H2368 To th' coast which by *Euphrates* mouth appear'd;
MROMAN138:21 H3511 Close by the mouth of famous *Tyber* flood:
2LETTER182:17 H23 And when thou canst not treat by loving mouth,
WHAT224:5 H5 My thankfull mouth shall speak thy praise

MOUTHES (1) [mouths]

DIALOG144:24 ~~H133~~ These Prophets mouthes (alas the while) was stopt,

MOUTHS (1) [pl.]

1SIMON188:10 H11 With humble hearts and mouths put in the dust,

MOV'D (4) [moved]

ELEMEN14:24 H266 Scarce Earth had done, but th' angry waters {water} mov'd;
HUMOUR29:18 H369 What mov'd thee thus to villifie my name?
MPERS~~69:38~~ H664 And viewing all, at all nought mov'd was he:
MPERS69:39 H669 With pitty *Cyrus* mov'd, knowing Kings stand,

MOVE (3) See also MOUE

AGES40:25 H206 To Masques, to Playes, to Taverns stil I move;
MGREC121:39 H2821 From his fidelity make him once move.
TDUDLEY166:12 H54 Nor wonder 'twas, low things ne'r much did move

MOVED See MOV'D

MOVEING (1) [moving]

ELEMEN18:10 H414 His moveing reason is, give least I dye.

MOVELESSE (1)

DUBART154:2 H47 Movelesse, stand charm'd by thy sweet influences,

MOVES (3)

ELEMEN16:22 H345 Which pitty moves, and oft deceives the wise.
QELIZ157:41 H109 Then wonder not, *Eliza* moves not here.
CHILDRN185:5 H31 Ambition moves still in his breast

MOVING (1) See also MOVEING

MGREC96:25 H1745 Like severall houses moving upon wheeles:

MOVNT (1) v. [mount]

MYSOUL225:5 H9 Wth Angels-wings thy Soul shall movnt

MOWERS (1) [pl.]

SEASONS50:3 H137 Now go the Mowers to their slashing toyl,

MOWN (3)

AGES41:23 H240 When my Wilde Oates, were sown, and ripe, & mown,
TDUDLEY166:19 H61 Death as a Sickle hath him timely mown,
ELIZB187:7 H15 And Corn and grass are in their season mown,

MOWNE (1)
ELEMEN13:28 H229 The Corne, and Hay, both fall before they'r mowne;
MOYST (3) [moist]
HUMOUR27:28 H299 Your hot, dry, moyst, cold, natures are {but} foure,
HUMOUR35:5 H601 To take her moyst, my moistnesse {moisture} wil be bold;
SEASONS52:32 H247 Moyst snowie *February* is my last,
MRS. (2)
DDUDLEY167:7 H3 *Mrs. Dorothy Dudley,*
MERCY188:18 H2-4 *Mrs. Mercy Bradstreet, who deceased* Sept. 6.
MUCH (109) See also MVCH
PROLOG7:11 H25 Art can doe much, but this maxime's most sure,
ELEMEN10:18 H93 Your wisdom out of little gathers {gather} much,
ELEMEN12:13 H173 Sweet *Parnassus,* I dote too much on thee,
ELEMEN14:15 H257 Much might I say, of the *Arabian* sands; {hot *Libian* sand}
ELEMEN17:14 H378 I need not say much of my Haile and Snow,
ELEMEN17:32 H396 Much might I say of wracks, but that Ile spare,
HUMOUR20:30 H22 Her wisedome spake not much, but thought the more.
HUMOUR21:33 H61 That much wil talk, but little dares she do,
HUMOUR26:11 H241 For th' natural, thou dost not much contest,
HUMOUR28:35 H347 Yet could not be more breif, without much wrong.
HUMOUR32:16 H490 We shal expect much sound, but little force.
HUMOUR33:13 H527 Thy heat doth much, I candidly confesse,
HUMOUR33:14 ~~H528~~ But yet thou art as much, I truly say,
HUMOUR~~33:15~~ H529 I do as much for thee another way:
HUMOUR34:39 H594 And too much talk; both which, I do {here} confesse,
AGES~~36:13~~ H37 The next came up, in a more {much} graver sort,
AGES39:11 H154 As might my self, and others, profit much:
AGES44:10 H343 In every Age i've found much vanitie,
AGES45:22 ~~H404~~ But out of troubles, ye may see much good,
AGES~~45:22~~ H410 But out of evill you may see much good.
AGES~~45:36~~ H426 I cannot labour, nor {much less} I cannot {can} fight:
AGES46:10 H441 Yea knowing much, the pleasant'st {pleasants} life of all,
AGES46:12 H443 Though reading other Works, doth much refresh,
AGES46:13 H444 Yet studying much, brings wearinesse to th' flesh;
SEASONS48:31 ~~H83~~ Some subject, shallow braines, much matter yeelds,
SEASONS49:11 ~~H102~~ Hath formerly much heat, the earth and aire.
SEASONS~~50:12~~ H146 For yet {For much,} the South-ward Sun abateth not;
SEASONS52:28 H243 The day much longer then it was before,
MASSYR57:8 H155 But much it is, in more then forty years,
MASSYR59:20 ~~H244~~ Which through much rain, then swelling up so high,
MASSYR61:38 H343 (This was that *Ahaz,* which so much {high} transgrest.)
MPERS73:25 H810 But yet, 'fore this was done, much blood was shed,
MPERS~~74:31~~ H854 Much gain'd the hearts of his nobility.
MPERS76:22 H920 His enemies scarce seen, then much lesse, slaine;
MPERS80:36 H1103 Much, {fearing} that which never was intended!
MPERS84:16 H1252 This valiant Knight, whom they so much did owe;
MPERS84:24 H1260 His father *Xerxes* losse, and shame, much more,
MPERS~~84:28~~ H1264 His Country, nor his Kindred {Friends} would {much} esteem,
MPERS85:22 H1298 {Plunders} the Country, and much trouble {mischief} wrought,
MPERS85:28 H1304 The King much profit reapeth, by these leagues {this league},
MPERS88:19 H1412 Had not his too much valour put him by.

MPERS89:30 H1464 And feares as much to let them march away;
MGREC93:17 H1614 His Education, much to these {those} did adde.
MGREC~~95:40~~ H1719 Sure its {much} beyond my time, and little Art;
MGREC96:10 H1730 An object not so much of fear, as laughter.
MGREC96:28 H1748 And as much good she did, as any other.
MGREC97:23 H1784 By too much heat, not wounds (as Authors write.)
MGREC99:40 H1883 By which he was so much incouraged,
MGREC100:32 H1916 Who had long {sore} travaile, and much sorrow seen,
MGREC105:11 H2104 But this unheard of injury {treachery} much more;
MGREC~~107:22~~ H2197 But sore {much} distrest for water, in their march,
MGREC107:23 H2198 The drought, and heat, their bodies much doth {sore did}
MGREC108:40 H2256 Which did his former Army {forces} much augment,
MGREC111:15 H2360 Which could not sound too oft, with too much fame;
MGREC111:33 H2378 Much time in feasts, and ryoting doth {did} wast;
MGREC113:19 H2446 Who was so much engag'd, to this Commander,
MGREC113:30 H2457 This is *Parmenio,* which {who} so much had done,
MGREC115:2 H2513 All this he did, yea, and much more, 'tis true,
MGREC116:21 H2587 Learning, and learned men, he much regarded,
MGREC117:8 H2615 And {But} as he took delight, much bloud to spill,
MGREC117:39 H2646 After much tumult, they at last proclaim'd
MGREC118:16 H2663 So much these Princes their owne ends respected.
MGREC121:38 H2820 Nor could *Craterus* (whom he much did love)
MGREC122:4 H2827 And much eclipse his {great Acts and} glory to rehearse
MGREC123:27 H2891 Thinks by her Majesty much help to finde;
MGREC126:36 H3025 The Authours death she did so much lament,
MGREC127:10 H3040 Old *Thebes* he then re-built (so much of fame)
MGREC128:35 H3108 *Antigonus* did much rejoyce his son,
MGREC129:32 H3146 Begin to mutter much 'gainst proud *Cassander,*
MGREC133:31 H3321 To whom Ancient {the old} *Berosus* (so much fam'd)
MROMAN138:17 H3507 Much stronger, and more beautifull withall;
MROMAN138:34 H3524 Much {Some} state, and glory, {splendor} did this *Priscus* adde:
DIALOG141:30 H29 And thus, alas, your state you much deplore,
DIALOG143:18 H87 But trust not much unto his Excellence;
DIALOG146:32 H218 Your griefs I pity much, but should do wrong {hope to see},
DIALOG~~146:32~~ H219 Out of your troubles much good fruit to be;
DIALOG147:28 H252 If now you weep so much, that then no more,
DIALOG147:32 H256 That dazzled eyes beholding much shall wonder
SIDNEY149:32 ~~H23~~ The love thy Country ought thee, was as much.
SIDNEY~~150:12~~ H41 The love his Country ought him, was as much.
SIDNEY150:24 H51 Made famous by thy fall {death}, much more's {more} the pitty;
SIDNEY152:5 He promis'd much, but th' muses had no will,
SIDNEY152:28 H97 *His praise is much, this shall suffice my pen,*
QELIZ155:28 H19 Thy clemency did yerst esteeme as much
TDUDLEY165:40 H42 Those titles loath'd, which some too much do love
TDUDLEY166:12 H54 Nor wonder 'twas, low things ne'r much did move
CONTEM167:34 H10 If so much excellence abide below;
SICKNES179:5 H25 Bestow much cost there's nothing lost,
ELIZB186:34 H6 Farewel dear babe, my hearts too much content,
2SIMON195:10 Hp271 true friends much more by duty full children, I haue avoyded
MEDDM196:2 Hp272 A ship that beares much saile & little or no ballast, is easily
MEDDM196:25 Hp273 words are like hony, a little may refresh, but too much gluts the

MEDDM199:19 Hp278 Much Labour wearys the body, and many thoughts oppresse
MEDDM200:17 Hp279 but falls and bruises, or perhaps somewhat worse, much more
MEDDM200:34 Hp280 is enough for one of twice his strength, much lesse will our
MEDDM202:25 Hp282 yet he affords so much light as may direct our way, that
MEDDM203:21 Hp283 neuer felt, what it was to be sick or wounded, doth not much
MEDDM204:33 Hp285 Corne is produced wth much labour (as the husbandman well
MEDDM204:34 Hp285 and some land askes much more paines, then some other doth
MEDDM205:4 Hp285 of morality, much lesse of grace in them But when by prudent
MEDDM205:18 Hp286 who is greater then our Conscience will do it much more, but
MEDDM206:3 Hp287 and these are but leavie Christians, wch are in as much
MEDDM206:7 Hp287 and those starres also, to differ much one from the other, in
MEDDM208:19 Hp290 to deceitfull friends who speak faire and promise much
MYCHILD215:13 Hp240 opportvnity to speak to any of yov much lesse to All, thovght it
MYCHILD215:29 Hp241 too often tardy y^{t} way. I also fovnd much comfort in reading y^{e}
MED223:14 Hp250 that God who hath done so much for me, should haue so little
30SEPT227:21 Hp257 to my straying Soul wch in prosperity is too much in Love wth
ACK235:18 H18 Whose p^{r}sence I so much doe lack.

MUD (1)
MGREC111:17 H2362 His Gallies stuck upon the sand, {flats} and mud;

MULES (2) [pl.]
MGREC96:31 H1751 A thousand Mules, and Camells ready wait.
MGREC~~115:15~~ H2525 The Mules and Horses are for sorrow shorne,

MULLET (2)
3LETTER183:15 H17 Or as the loving Mullet, that true Fish,
3LETTER183:24 H26 Unto thy Hinde, thy Mullet and thy Dove,

MULLETS (1) [pl.]
3LETTER183:29 H31 And like the Mullets in one River glide,

MULTITUDE (9)
ELEMEN10:17 H92 Out of a multitude, these few I touch,
HUMOUR32:14 H488 Nor multitude of words, argues our strength;
MPERS76:32 H930 *Darius* multitude before them fled;
MPERS78:33 H1014 Feasts all this multitude, of his own charge,
MPERS80:3 H1070 They thus behemm'd with multitude of foes,
MPERS88:5 H1398 The brunt of that huge multitude to bide.
MGREC~~95:21~~ H1700 Then in *Darius* multitudes {multitude} beside:
MGREC100:19 H1903 But as the King is, so's the multitude,
MEDDM206:6 Hp287 in the firmament there is but one Sun, among a multitude of

MULTITUDES (7) [pl.]
ELEMEN19:4 H449 Next, of my Fowles such multitudes there are;
ELEMEN19:16 H461 Whereof such multitudes have dy'd and fled,
MPERS88:11 H1404 That, more then multitudes, their hearts did awe:
MPERS88:36 H1429 And heaps on heaps, such multitudes they laid,
MGREC95:21 H1700 Then in *Darius* multitudes {multitude} beside:
MGREC100:27 H1911 For in his multitudes his trust still lay,
MGREC104:9 H2061 If when he'd multitudes, the day he lost;

MUNDI (1)
MROMAN136:21 H3435 beginning, *Anno Mundi,*

MURDER See MURTHER

MURTHERED See MUTHERED

MURDERS (1) [pl.] See also MURTHERS
MGREC134:5 H3338 Horrid massacres, murders, cruelties,

MURRAIN (1)
ELEMEN19:20 H465 Of murrain, Cattle numberlesse did fall.
MURTHER (3) [murder]
MPERS~~92:17~~ H1575 (Complotter with him in the murther done)
MGREC105:25 H2118 Of Treason, murther, and base cruelty,
MGREC129:30 H3144 The *Greeks* touch'd with the murther done so {of} late,
MURTHERED (6) [murdered]
MPERS83:13 H1201 But yet by search, he was found murthered,
MPERS~~92:5~~ H1560 By him that late his father murthered.
MPERS92:24 ~~H1582~~ That son, and father, both were murthered
MGREC129:13 H3127 But she *Darius'* daughters murthered,
MGREC133:40 H3330 This *Theos* he was murthered by his {lewd} wife,
MGREC134:11 H3342 So many Princes still were murthered,
MURTHERS (1) [murders]
HUMOUR25:36 H225 If murthers be thy glory, tis no lesse.
MUS'D (1) [mused]
MROMAN139:30 H3556 The more I mus'd, the more I was in doubt:
MUSCLES (1)
HUMOUR23:38 H148 Its not your muscles, nerves, nor this nor that:
MUSE (5)
PROLOG7:3 H18 My foolish, broken, blemish'd Muse so sings;
SIDNEY151:23 H73 For {How} to persist, my muse is more in doubt:
SIDNEY151:27 H75 But *Sydney's* Muse, can sing his worthinesse.
DUBART153:16 H20 My Muse unto a Childe, I fitly may compare,
CONTEM169:13 H54 To sing some Song, my mazed Muse thought meet.
MUSED See MUS'D
MUSES (6) [pl.]
PROLOG6:27 H11 Foole, I doe grudge, the Muses did not part
ELEMEN12:2 H162 But chiefly, 'cause the Muses there did dwell;
SIDNEY~~152:4~~ H76 The Muses aid I crav'd, they had no will
SIDNEY152:5 ~~H76~~ He promis'd much, but th' muses had no will,
SIDNEY~~152:15~~ H85 Since I the Muses thus have injured.
SIDNEY152:26 H95 *Heire to the Muses, the Son of* Mars *in truth,*
MUSICIAN See MUSITIAN
MUSICK (3) [music] See also MUSIQUE
AGES39:28 H171 Sweet Musick rapteth {raps} my {brave} harmonious Soul,
SIDNEY149:14 H13 Of Poesie, and of Musick thou wert {he was} King;
DUBART153:38 H42 Thy Phisick, Musick, and State policy,
MUSICKES (1) [poss.]
AGES45:31 H421 No more rejoyce, at musickes pleasant {pleasing} noyse,
MUSING (2)
HUMOUR22:3 H72 But peevish, Male-content, musing she sits,
CONTEM173:10 H177 While musing thus with contemplation fed,
MUSIQUE (1) [music] See also MUSICK
ELEMEN15:28 H310 The Dolphin (loving musique) *Arions* friend.
MUSITIAN (1) [musician]
HUMOUR24:35 H184 A rosie cheek'd {cheek} musitian, thou know'st wel.
MUSKET-PROOF (1)
AGES39:22 H165 I scorn the heavy Corslet, Musket-proof,
MUST (108) See also MVST
FATHER6:7 H41 Who must reward a theife, but with his due.

ELEMEN9:2	H36	To try your valour by, but it must feele
ELEMEN13:13	H214	Well knowest, my fuell must maintain thy fire.
ELEMEN~~13:22~~	H223	Now might {must} I shew my {mine} adverse quality,
ELEMEN13:26	H227	My sap, to plants and trees, I must not grant,
ELEMEN14:19	H261	Ile say no more, yet {but} this thing adde I must,
ELEMEN16:32	H355	I now must shew what force {ill} there in me lyes.
ELEMEN18:16	H420	What is't? but forced Aire which must {doth} rebound,
HUMOUR24:15	H164	Your patience more then mine, I must confesse.
HUMOUR25:13	H202	My ingenuity must give thee right.
HUMOUR26:28	H258	If thou'rt the taker, I must be the giver:
HUMOUR26:32	H262	I must confesse, is somewhat strange to me,
HUMOUR34:18	H573	Whose use and worth to tel, I must refrain;
HUMOUR34:34	H589	Then I, and thou, must make a mixture here:
AGES37:5	H67	But night and darkenesse, must with shame conceal.
AGES41:18	H237	As was their praise, or shame, so mine must be.
AGES41:35	H250	If a father {I}, then for children must provide:
AGES~~43:8~~	H304	Then Kings must be depos'd or put to flight,
SEASONS48:38	H89	When Spring had done, then {the} Summer must {did} begin,
SEASONS~~49:7~~	H98	And {Then} retrograde, now is {must be} my burning Sun.
SEASONS51:27	H203	Decrepit age must also have its time;
SEASONS51:31	H207	Where also he, his Winter time must have;
SEASONS52:11	H226	I must be short, and short's, the shortned day,
MASSYR55:35	H101	She for her potency, must go alone.
MASSYR58:24	~~H207~~	*Arbaces* must be master of their lands.
MASSYR60:11	H276	A while he, and his race, aside must stand,
MASSYR61:5	H310	To rest content we must, in ignorance.
MASSYR62:20	H365	Thus *Iacobs* Sons, in exile must remain,
MASSYR64:40	H464	Their shoulders must their Masters minde fulfill;
MASSYR66:16	H522	All Vassals, at his hands, for grace must sue;
MASSYR67:10	H556	But yet in *Babell,* he must still remain:
MASSYR68:1	H587	Which horrid sight, he fears, must needs portend,
MPERS72:6	~~H755~~	Who for no wrong, poore innocent must dye,
MPERS72:7	~~H756~~	*Praraspes* now must act this tragedy;
MPERS72:23	H771	Like fault must look, for the like recompence.
MPERS74:37	~~H858~~	And fear'd, he now with scorn must march away:
MPERS75:9	H870	If he command, obey the greatest must:
MPERS75:20	H879	Yet o're thy glory we must cast this vaile,
MPERS76:15	H913	Quoth he, like Frogs, in water we must dive;
MPERS76:16	H914	Or like to Mice, under the earth must live;
MPERS76:18	H916	Or *Sythian* arrows in our sides must stick.
MPERS82:10	H1157	And troublesome *Mardonius* now must dye:
MPERS83:19	H1207	That the poor {Prince} innocent, to death must {did} go.
MPERS85:26	H1302	But they in *Asia,* must first restore
MPERS89:23	H1457	The smiling *Greeks* reply, they first must bait,
MPERS90:35	H1502	That *Tyssapherne* must be Vice-roy no more;
MPERS91:28	~~H1542~~	He must leave all, and in the pit remain;
MPERS91:30	~~H1544~~	As all the mighty ones, have done, and must:
MPERS92:19	~~H1577~~	By one of these, he must obtain the place.
MGREC95:17	H1696	Which who so did {doth}, must Lord of all remain,
MGREC98:32	H1834	And {now} must at *Gaza, Alexander* meet;
MGREC99:21	H1864	That *Greece* must {was forc'd to} yeeld a fresh supply againe;

MGREC100:9 H1893 He Diabolicall must needs remaine,
MGREC106:5 H2139 Yea, {And} thus must every Son of *Adam* lye,
MGREC112:30 H2416 Must suffer, not for what he did, but thought:
MGREC115:14 H2523 Or of necessity, he must imply,
MGREC~~115:15~~ H2527 Of stately *Ecbatane* who now must shew,
MGREC116:11 H2577 Whose famous Acts {This Monarchs fame} must last, whilst
MGREC117:2 H2609 A God alive him all must Idolize;
MGREC118:27 H2676 *Perdicas,* seeing *Aridæus* must be King,
MGREC122:13 H2838 Perceives {Sees} *Aridæus* must not king it long,
MGREC~~123:14~~ H2878 Now {When} great *Antipater,* the world doth {must} leave
MGREC127:27 H3057 So *Eumenes* {(the prop)} of destiny {death} must taste.
MGREC129:6 H3120 That in few years he must be forc'd or glad
MGREC129:19 H3133 The life of her must go, and of her son.
MGREC130:20 H3175 The world must needs believe what he doth tell:
MGREC130:34 ~~H3181~~ Yet in the flower of's age, he must lie dead,
MGREC131:34 H3226 *Cassander* now must die, his race is run,
MGREC132:1 H3234 (Rather then *Philips* child must {race should} longer live
MGREC132:2 H3235 He, whom she gave his life, her death must {shall} give)
MGREC132:12 H3247 Yet must his children pay for fathers ill.
MGREC132:14 H3249 Yet be aveng'd, must th' blood of *Jesreel.*
MGREC132:35 H3282 Must needs goe try their fortune, and their might,
MGREC133:18 H3306 I must let passe those many battels fought,
MGREC134:33 H3364 To all these names we *Ptolomy* must adde,
DIALOG141:16 H15 Or must my forced tongue these griefes disclose?
DIALOG141:17 H16 And must my selfe dissect my tatter'd state,
DIALOG142:16 H45 Must *Edward* be depos'd, or is't the houre
DIALOG142:17 H46 That second *Richard* must be clapt i'th' Tower?
DIALOG142:20 H49 Must *Richmonds* ayd, the Nobles now implore,
DIALOG142:35 H64 I must confesse, some of those Sores you name,
DIALOG145:35 H184 This must be done by Gospel, not by law.
SIDNEY152:4 ~~H76~~ That those that name his fame, he needs must spare,
QELIZ157:29 H97 Must dip his Pen i'th' Heliconian Well;
QELIZ158:5 H114 If then new things, their old form must {forms shall} retain,
VANITY160:13 H23 Sure if on earth, it must be in those parts;
TDUDLEY165:24 H26 But now or never I must pay my Sum;
CONTEM169:6 H48 How full of glory then must thy Creator be?
FLESH176:2 H42 And combate with thee will and must,
SICKNES178:22 H5 All men must dye, and so must I
SICKNES178:22 H5 All men must dye, and so must I
MEDDM195:36 Hp272 vanity and lyes must needs lye down in the Bed of sorrow.
MEDDM201:12 Hp280 hath its force abated by water not by wind, and anger must be
MEDDM202:27 Hp282 quite gone out of sight then must we needs walk in darknesse
MEDDM202:28 Hp282 se no light, yet then must we trust in the lord and stay vpon our
MEDDM203:15 Hp283 but he must beware of desireing to make this the place of his
MEDDM203:17 Hp283 before he sees land we must therfore be heer as strangers and
MEDDM203:27 Hp284 and that he must needs perish if he haue no remedy, will
MEDDM204:15 Hp284 must be sure to shun the company of the first.
MEDDM204:26 Hp285 would be content, wth a mean condition, must not cast his eye
MEDDM204:35 Hp285 brought into tilth yet all must be ploughed and harrowed Some
MEDDM205:2 Hp285 of correction must make long furrows on their back and the
MEDDM205:20 Hp286 must be sure to carry a certificate from the Court of

MEDDM205:23 Hp286 would keep a pure heart and lead a blamlesse life, must set
MEDDM208:3 Hp289 these things must be what manner of persons ought we to be,
MEDDM208:14 Hp290 Commends vs to god, for by his ballance we must be weighed,
MEDDM208:15 Hp290 Judgment we must be tryed and as he passes the sentence, so
MYCHILD218:32 Hp244 I haue reme¯bred the words of Christ that so it must bee, and

MUSTARD (1)
MEDDM200:7 Hp279 wormwood or mustard, they wil either wipe it off, or else suck

MUSTER (2)
MGREC100:21 H1905 Yet he (poore Prince) another Hoast doth muster,
MROMAN139:6 H3534 A generall Muster takes, which by account,

MUSTERED (1)
MASSYR58:25 H208 These Forces mustered, and in array,

MUSTERING See MUSTRING

MUSTERS (2)
MPERS87:13 H1369 The fearfull King, at last, musters his Forces;
MGREC132:19 H3256 These to recover, musters all his might,

MUSTRING (1) [mustering]
MPERS79:18 H1044 And {Then} in *Abidus* Plaines, mustring his Forces,

MUTATION (1)
ELEMEN~~20:4~~ H486 By death, or great mutations {mutation} of their States.

MUTATIONS (2) [pl.]
ELEMEN20:4 H486 By death, or great mutations {mutation} of their States.
AGES44:22 H355 Great mutations, some joyful, and some sad,

MUTE (6)
HUMOUR32:29 H503 And when i've nothing left to say, be mute;
MPERS88:32 H1425 Sencelesse and mute they stand, yet breath out groans,
DUBART154:4 H49 Mine eyes are sightlesse, and my tongue is mute;
QELIZ156:14 H41 She's argument enough to make you mute;
CONTEM169:24 H64 Whilst I as mute, can warble forth no higher layes.
1SIMON188:8 H9 With dreadful awe before him let's be mute,

MUTENY (1) [mutiny]
MGREC107:16 H2191 But marvell 'tis, that without muteny,

MUTINIES (1)
MGREC94:4 H1638 But he their mutinies, {by valour} full soon doth {he} quell.

MUTINY See MUTENY

MUTTER (1)
MGREC129:32 H3146 Begin to mutter much 'gainst proud *Cassander,*

MUTUALL (1) [mutual]
MEDDM209:20 Hp291 so there may be a mutuall commerce through ye world As it is

MVCH (4) [much]
MYCHILD219:6 Hp245 This was written in mvch sicknesse and weaknes, and is very
JULY223:22 Hp251 first it took me, and so mvch the sorer it was to me because
28AUG225:26 Hp254 After mvch weaknes & sicknes when my spirits were worn out,
REMB235:27 H8 I ow so mvch so little can

MVST (3) [must]
MYCHILD218:8 Hp244 If ever this God hath revealed himself it mvst bee in his word,
MYCHILD218:9 Hp244 this mvst bee it or none. Haue I not fovnd y^{t} operation by it
13MAY227:3 H12 But if they mvst eclipse again

MYCALE (1)
MPERS82:16 H1163 The *Grecians* at *Mycale* in Asia meet,

MYRIE (1) [miry]
PILGRIM210:4 H4 That myrie steps, haue troden oft
MYTERS (1) [mitres]
DIALOG147:13 H239 Their Myters, Surplices, and all their tire,